The Reader's Adviser

The Reader's Adviser
A Layman's Guide to Literature
13th EDITION
Barbara A. Chernow and George A. Vallasi, Series Editors

Volume 1
The Best in American and British Fiction, Poetry, Essays, Literary Biography, Bibliography, and Reference
Edited by Fred Kaplan

Books about Books • Bibliography • Reference Books: Literature • Broad Studies and General Anthologies • British Poetry: Early to Romantic • British Poetry: Middle Period • Modern British and Irish Poetry • American Poetry: Early Period • Modern American Poetry • British Fiction: Early Period • British Fiction: Middle Period • Modern British Fiction • American Fiction: Early Period • Modern American Fiction • Commonwealth Literature • Essays and Criticism • Literary Biography and Autobiography

Volume 2
The Best in American and British Drama and World Literature in English Translation
Edited by Maurice Charney

The Drama • British Drama: Early to Eighteenth Century • Shakespeare • Modern British and Irish Drama • American Drama • World Literature • Greek Literature • Latin Literature • French Literature • Italian Literature • Spanish Literature • Portuguese Literature • German and Netherlandic Literature • Scandinavian Literature • Russian Literature • East European Literatures • Yiddish Literature • Hebrew Literature • Spanish American Literature • African Literature • Middle Eastern Literature • Literature of the Indian Subcontinent • Chinese Literature • Japanese Literature • Southeast Asian and Korean Literature

Volume 3
The Best in General Reference Literature, the Social Sciences, History, and the Arts
Edited by Paula T. Kaufman

Reference Books: General • Dictionaries • General Biography and Autobiography • The Social Sciences • Education • Ancient History • United States History • Western Hemisphere: Canada and Latin America • British History • World History • Music and Dance • Art and Architecture • The Mass Media • Folklore and Humor • Travel and Exploration

Volume 4

The Best in the Literature of Philosophy and World Religions
Edited by William L. Reese

General Philosophy • Greek and Roman Philosophy • Medieval Philosophy •
Renaissance Philosophy • Modern Philosophy • Twentieth-Century Philosophy •
Ancient Religion and Philosophy • Eastern Religion and Philosophy • Judaism •
Early Christianity • Late Christianity • Bibles • Minority Religions

Volume 5

The Best in the Literature of Science, Technology, and Medicine
Edited by Paul T. Durbin

General Science • History of Science, Technology, and Medicine • Philosophy of
Science and Pseudoscience • Mathematics • Statistics and Probability • Information
and Communication Science • Astronomy and Space Science • Earth Sciences •
Physics • Chemistry • Biology • Ecology and Environmental Science • Genetics •
Medicine and Health • Illness and Disease • Clinical Psychology and Psychiatry •
Engineering and Technology • Energy • Ethics of Science, Technology,
and Medicine • Science and Society

THE
Reader's Adviser

A Layman's Guide to Literature
13th EDITION

Volume 3

The Best in General Reference Literature, the Social Sciences, History, and the Arts

Edited by Paula T. Kaufman

Barbara A. Chernow and George A. Vallasi, Series Editors

R. R. BOWKER COMPANY
New York & London, 1986

Published by R. R. Bowker Company,
a division of Reed Publishing USA
245 West 17th Street, New York, NY 10011
Copyright © 1986 by Reed Publishing USA,
a division of Reed Holdings, Inc.

International Standard Book Numbers
0-8352-2145-8 (Volume 1)
0-8352-2146-6 (Volume 2)
0-8352-2147-4 (Volume 3)
0-8352-2148-2 (Volume 4)
0-8352-2149-0 (Volume 5)
0-8352-2315-9 (Volume 6)
International Standard Serial Number 0094-5943
Library of Congress Catalog Card Number 57-13277

The paper used in this publication meets the minimum
requirements of American National Standard for
Information Sciences—Permanence of Papers for
Printed Library Materials, ANSI Z39.48-1984.

Contents

PREFACE   xiii
CONTRIBUTING EDITORS   xix
ABBREVIATIONS   xxi
CHRONOLOGY   xxiii
INTRODUCTION   xxxi

1. Reference Books: General   1

Encyclopedias   2
General Bibliographic and Reference Tools   4
U.S. Government Publications   12
Dates and Facts   14
Yearbooks and Almanacs   15
Atlases and Gazetteers   17
    Atlases 18   *Gazetteers* 19
Quotations   19
Proverbs and Maxims   22
Writing Guides   22

2. Dictionaries   24

English-Language Dictionaries   25
British-English Dictionaries   30
Current English-Usage Dictionaries   30
Slang and Colloquial Dictionaries   31
Synonym, Antonym, and Homonym Dictionaries   33
Rhyming Dictionaries   35
Spelling Dictionaries   35
Etymological Dictionaries   36
Foreign-English Dictionaries   37
    Anglo-Saxon 37   *Arabic* 38   *Chinese* 38   *Danish* 39   *Dutch* 39
    French 39   *German* 40   *Greek* 42   *Hebrew* 42   *Hungarian* 42
    Italian 42   *Japanese* 43   *Korean* 44   *Latin* 44   *Norwegian* 44
    Polish 44   *Portuguese* 44   *Romanian* 45   *Russian* 45
    Serbo-Croatian 45   *Spanish* 45

154043

3. **General Biography and Autobiography**   **48**

On the Writing of Biography and Autobiography   49
Reference Works   50
A Selected List of Recent Biographies and Autobiographies   51
BIOGRAPHERS (Main Entries)   54
AUTOBIOGRAPHERS (Main Entries)   61
PUBLISHED PAPERS (Main Entries)   81

4. **The Social Sciences**   **98**

The Social Sciences   99
  Reference Books 99   *Methods of Social Research* 100
  Professional Aspects 101
Society of Modern America   102
Anthropology   103
  History of the Field 103   *Surveys of the Field* 103   *Methods of
  Research* 104   *Acculturation* 104   *Caste* 105   *Culture* 105
  Culture and Personality 106   *Economy* 107   *Evolution* 107
  Kinship 108   *Language* 108   *Religion* 109   *Social Structure* 109
  Societies, Modern 110   *Societies, Tribal* 110
  ANTHROPOLOGISTS AND LINGUISTS (Main Entries) 111
Economics   124
  History of the Field 124   *Surveys of the Field* 124   *Methods of
  Research* 125   *Agriculture* 126   *Capital and Human Capital* 126
  Capitalism 126   *Competition, Monopoly, Antitrust
  Legislation* 127   *The Corporation* 127   *Economic Behavior* 128
  Economic Growth 128   *Government Regulation* 129   *Income,
  Inflation, Poverty* 129   *International Economics* 130   *Labor,
  Work, Unemployment* 130   *Money and Monetary Institutions* 131
  Public Finance, Public Goods, Public Choice 132
  ECONOMISTS AND BUSINESSMEN (Main Entries) 132
Political Science   148
  History of the Field 149   *Surveys of the Field* 149   *Reference
  Books* 149   *Administration* 150   *Anarchism* 150   *Civil Liberties,
  Civil Rights* 150   *Constitutions and Federalism* 151
  Democracy 152   *Elections, Voting Behavior, Political Parties* 152
  Government 153   *Ideology and Belief* 154   *International
  Relations* 155   *Law and the Courts* 155   *Legislation, Congress* 156
  Policy Making 156   *Public Opinion* 156   *Socialism and
  Communism* 156   *Totalitarianism* 157   *War and Peace* 157
  POLITICAL SCIENTISTS AND POLITICAL THEORISTS (Main Entries) 158
Psychology   169
  History of the Field 169   *Surveys of the Field* 170   *Methods of
  Research* 170   *Reference Books* 170   *Aggression* 170   *Biological
  Bases of Behavior* 171   *Cognition* 171   *Groups* 172   *Individual
  Development* 172   *Intelligence and Artificial Intelligence* 173
  Learning and Motivation 173   *Opinions, Attitudes, and*

Beliefs 174   *Perception* 174   *Personality* 175
PSYCHOLOGISTS (Main Entries) 175

Sociology   187
History of the Field 187   *Surveys of the Field* 188   *Methods of
Research* 188   *Age and Aging* 189   *Art, Literature, Film,
Intellectuals* 189   *Collective Behavior* 190   *Communications* 190
Community 191   *Conflict and Conflict Resolution* 192
Crime 193   *Deviant Behavior* 194   *Energy, Resources, and
Environment* 194   *Ethnic Groups* 195   *Family, Marriage,
Life-Course Events* 195   *Interaction* 196   *Intergroup Relations* 196
Organizations 197   *Population* 197   *Professions* 198
Religion 198   *Science and Technology* 199   *Social Change* 200
Social Class 200   *Social Movements* 201   *Social Structure* 201
Socialization 202   *Urban Life* 202   *Utopianism and
Communes* 203   *Women* 203   *Work* 203
SOCIOLOGISTS (Main Entries) 204

5. Education   **222**
Bibliography   223
EDUCATORS (Main Entries)   229

6. Ancient History   **238**
General Works   238
Ancient Near East and Egypt   239
Greek History   239
Roman History   240
Reference Works about Antiquity   241
Sources for Ancient History   241
Documents on Ancient History   241
Archaeology   242
Coins   242
Topics in Ancient History   243
Society, Economy, and Trade 243   *Agriculture, Science,
Technology, and Material Culture* 243   *Women, the Family, and
Sex* 243   *War, Peace, and Diplomacy* 244   *Law* 244   *Philosophy,
Religion, and Intellectual History* 244
ANCIENT GREEK HISTORIANS (Main Entries)   245
ORATORS (Main Entries)   246
ANCIENT ROMAN HISTORIANS (Main Entries)   249

7. United States History   **252**
Writing of History   253
Reference Books   255
Research Guides 255   *Encyclopedias and Dictionaries* 257
Bibliographies 258   *Documentary Histories* 260

Surveys   261
Colonial Period, 1606–1762   264
Revolution and Confederation, 1763–1789   265
Early National Period, 1789–1828   268
Jacksonian Era, 1828–1860   270
Civil War and Reconstruction, 1861–1877   272
Industrialism and the Gilded Age, 1865–1896   274
Imperialism to Progressivism, 1896–1917   275
World War I to FDR, 1917–1932   276
New Deal through World War II, 1933–1945   277
Post-World War II, 1945–   280
Supplementary General Reading Lists   284
  Cultural and Intellectual History 285   *Economic History* 287
  Social History 289   *The Declaration of Independence, 1776, the*
  Constitution of the United States of America, 1787–1788, and the
  Federalist Papers, 1787–1788 294
Structure of Politics   297
Diplomacy and Foreign Relations   302
HISTORIANS—AMERICAN (Main Entries)   305

8. Western Hemisphere: Canada and Latin America   346

Canada   346
  General Surveys, Bibliographies, and Reference Works 347   *Early*
  Canada and New France 348   *The Confederation, Dominion, and*
  Modern Canada 349
Latin America   351
  General Surveys, Bibliographies, and Reference Works 352
  Pre-Columbian Peoples and Culture 353   *Discovery and*
  Conquest 355   *Colonial History* 356   *Modern Latin America:*
  General Works 357   *Modern Latin America: Individual*
  Countries 360
    Argentina 360   *Bolivia* 360   *Brazil* 361   *Chile* 361
    Colombia 361   *Costa Rica* 361   *Cuba* 361   *The Dominican*
    Republic 362   *Ecuador* 362   *El Salvador* 362   *Guatemala* 363
    Haiti 363   *Jamaica* 363   *Mexico* 363   *Nicaragua* 364
    Panama 365   *Paraguay* 365   *Peru* 365   *Puerto Rico* 365
    Trinidad 366   *Uruguay* 366   *Venezuela* 366

9. British History   367

General Reference   368
  Bibliographies 368   *Reference Books and General Histories* 369
Before the Norman Conquest, Pre-1066   371
Norman and Angevin England, 1066–1216   371
The Later Middle Ages, 1216–1485   372
The Tudors, 1485–1603   374
The Stuarts, 1603–1714   376

The Hanoverians, 1714–1837   377
The Victorian Age, 1837–1901   379
The Twentieth Century   382
Historians—British (Main Entries)   384

10. World History   **401**
Books on the Writing and Philosophy of History   401
General Reference Works   403
World History: General Works   405
War and the Problems of Peace in the Modern World   406
Europe: General   410
Europe: Separate States   413
    France 413   *Germany* 415   *Italy* 417   *Spain and Portugal* 418
    Scandinavia and the Low Countries 419   *Eastern Europe* 419
Russia and the Soviet Union   420
History of the Jews   426
The Middle East: General   432
Islam as Idea and Religion   433
The Middle East: Separate States   435
    Israel 435   *Egypt* 436   *Iran and Iraq* 437   *Saudi Arabia and the*
    Arabs 438   *Turkey* 439   *Other States, Areas, and People* 440
Africa   440
Asia: General   445
Asia: Separate States and Areas   446
    China 446   *Japan* 449   *The Indian Subcontinent* 452   *Other*
    States and Areas 454
Historians—World (Main Entries)   455

11. Music and Dance   **484**
Music   485
    History and Criticism 485   *Reference* 487   *Music*
    Appreciation 491   *Types of Music* 492
      Contemporary Music 492   *Ethnic Music* 492   *Film Music* 493
      Jazz 493   *Non-Western Music* 494   *Opera* 495
    Conductors 495   *Musical Instruments* 495   *Singers* 496
    Musicians (Main Entries) 497
Dance   518
    History and Criticism 518   *Reference* 518   *Ballet* 519   *American*
    Dance 520   *Ethnic Dance* 520   *Dance Companies* 520
    Choreographers 521
    Choreographers and Dancers (Main Entries) 521

12. Art and Architecture   **526**
Art: General Reading List   527
Art: Special Aspects   529

Art: Biography   531
Architecture: General Reading List   531
Architecture: Special Aspects   532
Architecture: Biography   533
Decorative Arts   534
ARTISTS, ARCHITECTS, DESIGNERS (Main Entries)   536

13. The Mass Media   **560**
Communications   561
     Reference Books 561   *General Works* 562
Journalism   565
     History and Criticism 565   *Journalists* 567
Broadcast Journalism   568
     History and Criticism 568   *Broadcast Journalists* 569
Radio and Television   569
     History and Criticism 569   *Radio and Television Artists* 573
Film   573
     Reference Works 574   *History and Criticism* 575   *Film Artists* 578
MASS MEDIA (Main Entries)   578

14. Folklore and Humor   **590**
General Works and Reference Titles   591
     General Works 591   *General Reference* 592
Folk Song and Dance   593
Folktale, Legend, and Myth   595
U.S. Regional and Ethnic Folklore   598
     New England 599   *The Mid-Atlantic States* 599   *The South* 600
     The Midwest 601   *The West* 602   *U.S. Indian Folklore* 603
     Afro-American Folklore 604   *Miscellaneous and Applied
     Folklore* 606
Folk and Popular Humor   609
Popular Culture   611

15. Travel and Exploration   **613**
Scholarly Reference Books   614
General Reference Works   615
The Americas: North and South   618
Europe   621
Africa, Asia, and Oceania   623
The Arctic and Antarctica   624
Individual Travels and Exploits   625
WRITERS ON TRAVEL AND EXPLORATION (Main Entries)   628

NAME INDEX   651
TITLE INDEX   693
SUBJECT INDEX   773

Preface

Over its thirteen editions, and since its first publication in 1921, chapters of *The Reader's Adviser* have been expanded and reorganized and new topics have been introduced, thus better to serve the needs of a growing and more diversified population. The first edition, entitled *The Bookman's Manual*, was based on Bessie Graham's course on book salesmanship given at the William Penn Evening High School in Philadelphia. Graham organized the book so that the chapters corresponded to the general classifications familiar to booksellers and, by providing publishers and prices in her text, she simplified book ordering for the bookseller. Since 1921, however, the book industry has experienced significant changes—comparatively few independent book dealers exist, information on titles is available from a wide variety of printed and computerized sources, and publishers are taking fewer risks by printing just enough copies of a title to meet immediate demands. At the same time that these changes were occurring, *The Reader's Adviser* was finding a broader audience; although still used by booksellers, the librarians, general readers, and high school and college students found that the topical organization of the volume with its annotated bibliographies also met their needs. For the nonspecialist who is interested in reading about a particular subject, *The Reader's Adviser* is a perfect starting point. The six-volume set provides annotated bibliographies arranged by subject, with brief biographies of authors, creative artists, and scientists worthy of special mention; in addition, it informs the reader of a book's availability, price, and purchasing source. Since the set is kept up to date by regular revisions, the volumes also serve as a reflection of the current state of the best available literature in print in the United States.

As a result of the growth of new fields of interest to the reading public and the continuing increase in the number of titles published, *The Reader's Adviser* has expanded with each succeeding edition. For this thirteenth edition, it has grown from three to six volumes. The first three volumes will appear simultaneously in 1986; the final three in 1988. The organization of the first two volumes is similar to that in the twelfth edition: Volume 1 covers mainly American and British fiction and poetry and Volume 2 covers drama, Shakespeare, and world literature in English translation. Volume 3, which covers the best in general reference literature, the social sciences, history, and the arts, has experienced the most significant changes—most chapters have been expanded, virtually new chapters have been created for the arts, and several chapters have been moved to form the nuclei of Volumes 4 and 5. Volume 4 covers the Bible, world religions, and philosophy; Volume 5 is devoted to science, technology, and medicine. Except for Volume 6, containing indexes to the entire set, each of the volumes has been edited by a specialist in the field, the whole project having been coordinated by the series editors.

Although the thirteenth edition of *The Reader's Adviser* retains the essential format and basic structure of the earlier editions, the editors and publisher have made a number of improvements designed to enhance the appearance and usefulness of the volumes. First, the design has been modified to increase readability and provide a more open look. The typeface is easier to read, biographies are printed in a larger face, and the titles in the "books about" sections following the biographies are in alphabetical order according to the authors' surnames. Finally, the authors and anonymous sagas that form the main headings in *The Reader's Adviser* are listed in alphabetical order within the chapters rather than the chronological order of previous editions. In the front matter of each volume, a Chronology of these individuals and works provides the reader with an overview of the development of a particular genre. For each chapter, the editors chose an eminent scholar or librarian with particular expertise in the subject area, so that the selection of bibliographies and main listings would reflect the best-informed judgment of a specialist in the field.

The greatest challenge was that of selection—which titles and authors to include. Since *The Reader's Adviser* is not a research tool for students and scholars, but rather a reference work designed for the nonspecialist, the editors' goal was to include those books generally available to an intelligent reader through the facilities of the library system of a moderately sized municipality. Books must be currently available in English from a publisher or distributor in the United States. Out-of-print titles are included for those major works which, because of their importance in the field, could not be excluded from the list. If a book is not presently available in English or cannot be purchased in the United States, it is considered out of print (o.p.) by the editors. In some disciplines, such as modern American poetry, publishers allow titles to go out of print quickly and the available literature was found to be surprisingly thin. The reader will also note that Volume 2 (the comparative literature volume) reveals how little of the world's non-English literature has been translated into English.

In selecting authors for main entries, contributing editors weighed a number of criteria—historical importance, current popularity as determined by the number of in-print titles, and space limitations. Particularly in American and British fiction, U.S. and world history, and the social sciences chapters, the necessity of adding new authors sometimes required eliminating authors who were previously the subjects of main entries in earlier editions of *The Reader's Adviser*. Most major authors are represented; other authors were selected as examples of particular movements or styles. The latter category is subjective; although these choices are valid, someone else's choices might have been equally valid. The constraints of space impose their own compromises.

The organization of each volume and of each chapter is designed to move the reader from the general to the specific, from reference books, books of history and criticism, and anthologies to specific authors, scientists, and creative artists. Each chapter opens with a brief introduction that provides a framework for the literature of a particular period or discipline, followed by general reading lists and then, with few exceptions, the main entries. In chapters covering more than one area of study, such as the social sciences, or more than one country, such as Southeast Asia, this pattern repeats itself for each major division. Each author selected as a main entry receives a brief biography followed by bibliographies of books by and about him or her. Wherever possible, the date of first publication follows the title of a work mentioned in the short biography or will instead appear, when available, as the first date in the "Books by..." entries below. In addition to *Books in Print, The New Columbia Encyclopedia* (1975) has served as the authority in verifying dates. The bibliographies of books by an author are mainly composed of collections of works and in-print titles of individual works in the particular genre covered by the chapter. Other titles may be mentioned in the biography, but only those works relevant to the genre under discussion appear in the bibliographies.

The bibliographic entries are so designed that the reader will be able both to locate a book in a library and to know where it is available for purchase and at what price. The editors have included the following information available or applicable for each title: author; title (translated titles or original titles are given in parentheses following the title); editor; series title; translator; authors of prefaces, introductions, and forewords; edition; number of volumes; reprint data; publisher (if more than one, publishers are listed alphabetically); date of publication; and price. The reader should be cautioned that the accuracy and completeness of information depends in large part on the information publishers supply to the *Books in Print* database and the information listed in individual publishers' catalogs.

If a date is listed directly after a title, this indicates the date of the publication of the first edition, regardless of whether that edition is still in print. For reprints, the date of the particular edition from which it was reprinted is given. If a title consists of more than one volume, and is listed with only one price, this is the price of the entire set. As book pricing changes so rapidly, some prices listed in *The Reader's Adviser* may have already changed. Although the editors considered the possibility of deleting prices from *The Reader's Adviser*, it was decided to retain them as an indication to the reader of the general price category into which an individual title falls and to assist the librarian in acquisition. Finally, the reader should be aware that not all in-print editions of a work are necessarily listed, but rather those selected by the editors because of their quality or special features.

To guide the reader through the volumes, *The Reader's Adviser* includes cross-references in three forms. The "see" reference leads the reader to the appropriate volume and chapter for information on a specific author or topic. "See also" refers the reader to additional information in another chapter or volume. Within any introductory narrative portions, the name of an author who appears as a main listing in another chapter or volume is printed in large and small capital letters. In each case, if the chapter cross-referenced is in a different volume from that being consulted, the volume number is also provided.

Each volume of *The Reader's Adviser* has three indexes—one for names, one for book titles, and one for general subjects. The Name Index includes all authors, editors, compilers, composers, directors, actors, artists, philosophers, and scientists cited in *The Reader's Adviser*. If a name appears as a main listing in the text, the name as well as the first page number of the main listing appear in boldface type. The Title Index includes book titles with two exceptions: collected works or generic titles by authors who receive main listings (e.g., *Selected Prose of T. S. Eliot*) and "books about" titles that follow the main listings and include the name of the main-entry author (e.g., *Booker T. Washington* by Louis R. Harlan). (This does not hold true in the case of Chapter 3, "Shakespeare," in Volume 2, where all works by and about him are included.) Therefore, to ensure locating all titles by and about a main-entry author, the user should look up that author in the Name Index to locate the primary listing.

In preparing the thirteenth edition of *The Reader's Adviser*, the series editors are indebted to a great many people for assistance and advice. We are especially grateful to the many people at R. R. Bowker who have worked with us; in particular, to Olga S. Weber, who provided encouragement, support, and a critical eye in reading manuscripts; to Kathy Kleibacker, for her constant faith in the project; and to Marion Sader, Julia Raymunt, Iris Topel, and Nancy Bucenec for their attention to detail and concern for quality in editing and production. We were fortunate in our choice of volume editors. Fred Kaplan, general editor of Volume 1, The Best in American and British Fiction, Poetry, Essays, Literary Biography, Bibliography, and Reference, is Professor of English at Queens College and at the Graduate Center, City University of New York; he is a distinguished Dickens and Carlyle scholar, the editor of *Dickens Studies Annual*, a member of the board of the Carlyle Papers, and is currently writing a biography of Dickens. The general editor of Volume 2, The Best in American and British Drama and World Literature in English Translation, is Maurice Charney, Distinguished Professor at Rutgers University in the department of English. His published works include *How to Read Shakespeare* and a biography of Joe Orton. Paula T. Kaufman, who served as general editor of Volume 3, The Best in General Reference Literature, the Social Sciences, History, and the Arts, is director of the academic information services group, Columbia University Libraries. Volume 4, The Best in the Literature of Philosophy and World Religions, was developed under the general editorship of William L. Reese. He is Professor of Philosophy at the State University of New York, Albany. His publications include the *Dictionary of Philosophy and Religion*. Paul T. Durbin is general editor of Volume 5, The Best in the Literature of Science, Technology, and Medicine. He is Professor of Philosophy at the University of Delaware and editor of *A Guide to the Culture of Science, Technology, and Medicine*. All made invaluable suggestions for organizing their volumes, recommended contributing editors, and reviewed each chapter for substantive content. The editors also wish to thank the following individuals for their help in the preparation of *The Reader's Adviser:* Roger Jones, Teachers College, Columbia University; and Jean R. Lutzer, New York City. Finally, a special thanks to David B. Biesel, who first brought the project to us, and to Antoinette Boone and Frank Van Orman Brown, who keyboarded all of the chapters, assisted in verifying bibliographic data, and coded material for the indexes.

In the 65 years since *The Reader's Adviser* first appeared, it has grown from a tool for booksellers to a standard reference work. In addition to bibliographic information, the introductions and biographies are enjoyable reading for someone just browsing through the volumes. *The Reader's Adviser* has a distinguished history; it is hoped that these latest volumes will continue in that tradition.

Barbara A. Chernow
George A. Vallasi

Contributing Editors

Roger S. Bagnall, ANCIENT HISTORY
Professor of Classics and History and Curator of Papyri at Columbia University, author of *Administration of the Ptolemaic Possessions Outside Egypt,* and coauthor of *Columbia Papyri Seven: Fourth Century Documents from Karanis; Greek Historical Documents: The Hellenistic Period;* and *Regnal Formulas in Byzantine Egypt*

Karen Brown, EDUCATION
Assistant Director and Head of Collection Development of The Milbank Memorial Library, Teachers College, Columbia University

Russ Chenoweth, REFERENCE BOOKS: GENERAL
Librarian in the Reference Department of the Van Pelt Library at the University of Pennsylvania

Danilo H. Figueredo, WESTERN HEMISPHERE: CANADA AND LATIN AMERICA
Librarian, Research Libraries, New York Public Library

Robert U. Goehlert, UNITED STATES HISTORY
Librarian for Economics, Political Science, and Criminal Justice at Indiana University Library, Bloomington, and editor of numerous bibliographies in political science

Charles R. Goeldner, TRAVEL AND EXPLORATION
Director of the Business Research Division of the University of Colorado, Boulder

Sandra Grilikhes, THE MASS MEDIA
Director, Annenberg School of Communications Library, University of Pennsylvania

David L. Hicks, WORLD HISTORY
Associate Professor of History at New York University

Michael A. Keller, MUSIC AND DANCE
Formerly Head of the Music Library at the University of California, Berkeley; now Associate University Librarian for Collection Development at Yale University Library

John P. McCarthy, BRITISH HISTORY
Professor of History at Fordham University and author of *Hilaire Belloc: Edwardian Radical*

Rodney Phillips, WESTERN HEMISPHERE: CANADA AND LATIN AMERICA
Librarian, Research Libraries, New York Public Library

Adolf K. Placzek, ART AND ARCHITECTURE
Librarian Emeritus of the Avery Architectural and Fine Arts Library, Professor Emeritus of Columbia University, and editor-in-chief of *Macmillan Encyclopedia of Architects*

Sally M. Roberts, DICTIONARIES
Reference Librarian at Northwestern University Library

David L. Sills, THE SOCIAL SCIENCES
Executive Associate of the Social Science Research Council and editor of the *International Encyclopedia of the Social Sciences*

Susan Steinberg, GENERAL BIOGRAPHY AND AUTOBIOGRAPHY
American and Commonwealth Studies Bibliographer, Yale University Library

Wendell Tripp, FOLKLORE AND HUMOR
Editor of *New York History*, journal of the New York State Historical Association

Abbreviations

abr.	abridged	ltd. ed.	limited edition
AHR	*American Historical Review*	MLA	Modern Language Association
Amer.	America(n)	Mod.	Modern
annot.	annotated	*N.Y. Herald Tribune*	*New York Herald Tribune*
bd.	bound		
bdg.	binding	*N.Y. Times*	*New York Times*
Bk(s).	Book(s)	o.p.	out-of-print
Class.	Classic(s)	orig.	original
coll.	collected	pap.	paperback
coll. ed.	collector's ed.	Pr.	Press
comp.	compiled, compiler	pref.	preface
corr.	corrected	pt(s).	parts
Ctr.	Center	*PW*	*Publishers Weekly*
ed.	edited, editor, edition	repr.	reprint
Eng.	English	rev. ed.	revised edition
enl. ed.	enlarged edition	*SB*	*Studies in Bibliography*
fl.	flourished	sel.	selected
fwd.	foreword	Ser.	Series
gen. ed(s).	general editor(s)	*SR*	*Saturday Review*
ill.	illustrated	Stand.	Standard
imit. lea.	imitation leather	Supp.	Supplement
intro.	introduction	*TLS*	*Times Literary Supplement*
lea.	leather		
lg.-type ed.	large-type edition	trans.	translated, translator, translation
Lib.	Library		
lib. bdg.	library binding	Univ.	University
Lit.	Literature	Vol(s).	Volume(s)
LJ	*Library Journal*		

Chronology

Main author entries appear here chronologically by year of birth. Within each chapter, main author entries are arranged alphabetically by surname.

1. Reference Books: General

2. Dictionaries

3. General Biography and Autobiography

Franklin, Benjamin. 1706–1790
Garrick, David. 1717–1779
Woolman, John. 1720–1772
Washington, George. 1732–1799
Adams, John. 1735–1826
Gibbon, Edward. 1737–1794
Jefferson, Thomas. 1743–1826
Madison, James. 1751–1836
Hamilton, Alexander. 1757–1804
Adams, John Quincy. 1767–1848
Clay, Henry. 1777–1852
Calhoun, John Caldwell. 1782–1850
Webster, Daniel. 1782–1852
Adams, Charles Francis. 1807–1886
Lincoln, Abraham. 1809–1865
Douglass, Frederick. 1817?–1895
Grant, Ulysses S. 1822–1885
Holmes, Oliver Wendell, Jr. 1841–1935
Wilson, Woodrow. 1856–1924
Hoover, Herbert. 1874–1964
Sandburg, Carl. 1878–1967
Strachey, Lytton. 1880–1932
Roosevelt, Franklin D. 1882–1945

Roosevelt, Eleanor. 1884–1962
Truman, Harry S. 1884–1972
Freeman, Douglas Southall. 1886–1953
Nicolson, Sir Harold. 1886–1968
Eisenhower, Dwight David. 1890–1969
Mao Tse-tung. 1893–1976
Khrushchev, Nikita S. 1894–1971
Macmillan, Sir Harold. 1894–
Bowen, Catherine Drinker. 1897–1973
Eden, Sir Anthony. 1897–1977
Chapman, Hester W. 1899–1976
Josephson, Matthew. 1899–1978
Stevenson, Adlai E. 1900–1965
Hammarskjold, Dag. 1905–1961
Jenkins, Elizabeth. 1907–
Johnson, Lyndon Baines. 1908–1973
Kennedy, John Fitzgerald. 1917–1963
Herold, J. Christopher. 1919–1964
Kennedy, Robert F. 1925–1968
Frank, Anne. 1929–1945

4. The Social Sciences

Plato. 427–347 B.C.
Machiavelli, Niccolò. 1469–1527

xxiii

Hobbes, Thomas. 1588–1679

Locke, John. 1632–1704

Montesquieu, Charles de Secondat. 1689–1755

Rousseau, Jean Jacques. 1712–1778

Smith, Adam. 1723–1790

Burke, Edmund. 1729–1797

Jefferson, Thomas. 1743–1826

Bentham, Jeremy. 1748–1832

Malthus, Thomas Robert. 1766–1834

Ricardo, David. 1772–1823

Senior, Nassau William. 1790–1864

Comte, Auguste. 1798–1857

Mill, John Stuart. 1806–1873

Marx, Karl. 1818–1883

Morgan, Lewis Henry. 1818–1881

Engels, Friedrich. 1820–1895

Spencer, Herbert. 1820–1903

Maine, Henry Sumner. 1822–1888

Tylor, Edward Burnett. 1832–1917

Wundt, Wilhelm. 1832–1920

Jevons, William Stanley. 1835–1882

Bryce, James. 1838–1922

Booth, Charles. 1840–1916

Menger, Carl. 1840–1921

James, William. 1842–1910

Marshall, Alfred. 1842–1924

Hall, G. Stanley. 1844–1924

Clark, John Bates. 1847–1938

Pareto, Vilfredo. 1848–1923

Pavlov, Ivan Petrovich. 1849–1936

Ebbinghaus, Hermann. 1850–1909

Wicksell, Knut. 1851–1926

Frazer, James George. 1854–1941

Tönnies, Ferdinand. 1855–1936

Freud, Sigmund. 1856–1939

Binet, Alfred. 1857–1911

Veblen, Thorstein. 1857–1929

Boas, Franz. 1858–1942

Durkheim, Emile. 1858–1917

Simmel, Georg. 1858–1918

Webb, Beatrice. 1858–1943

Webb, Sidney. 1859–1947

Commons, John R. 1862–1945

Mead, George Herbert. 1863–1931

Thomas, W. I. 1863–1947

Cooley, Charles H. 1864–1929

Park, Robert Ezra. 1864–1944

Weber, Max. 1864–1920

Fisher, Irving. 1867–1947

Merriam, Charles E. 1874–1963

Mitchell, Wesley C. 1874–1948

Kroeber, Alfred L. 1876–1960

Michels, Robert. 1876–1936

Watson, John B. 1878–1958

Radcliffe-Brown, A. R. 1881–1955

Von Mises, Ludwig. 1881–1973

Keynes, John Maynard. 1883–1946

Hull, Clark L. 1884–1952

Malinowski, Bronislaw. 1884–1942

Sapir, Edward. 1884–1939

Knight, Frank H. 1885–1972

Ogburn, William Fielding. 1886–1959

Polanyi, Karl. 1886–1964

Benedict, Ruth. 1887–1948

Bloomfield, Leonard. 1887–1949

Hansen, Alvin. 1887–1975

Sorokin, Pitirim A. 1889–1968

Lewin, Kurt. 1890–1947

Lynd, Robert S. 1892–1970

Laski, Harold J. 1893–1950

Mannheim, Karl. 1893–1947

Murray, Henry A. 1893–

Lynd, Helen Merrell. 1894–1982

Herskovits, Melville Jean. 1895–1963

Piaget, Jean. 1896–1980

Allport, Gordon W. 1897–1967

Murdock, George P. 1897–1985

Redfield, Robert. 1897–1958

Whorf, Benjamin L. 1897–1941
Myrdal, Gunnar. 1898–
Hayek, Friedrich A. von. 1899–
Klineberg, Otto. 1899–
Lippmann, Walter. 1899–1974
Dollard, John. 1900–1980
Stouffer, Samuel A. 1900–1960
Firth, Raymond. 1901–
Lazarsfeld, Paul F. 1901–1976
Mead, Margaret. 1901–1978
Erikson, Erik H. 1902–
Evans-Pritchard, E. E. 1902–1973
Lasswell, Harold D. 1902–1978
Parsons, Talcott. 1902–1979
Lorenz, Konrad. 1903–
Von Neumann, John. 1903–1957
Hicks, John R. 1904–
Skinner, B. F. 1904–
Taeuber, Conrad. 1906–
Taeuber, Irene B. 1906–1974
Tinbergen, Nikolaas. 1907–
Galbraith, John Kenneth. 1908–
Key, V. O., Jr. 1908–1963
Lévi-Strauss, Claude. 1908–
Riesman, David. 1909–
Merton, Robert K. 1910–
Friedman, Milton. 1912–
Shils, Edward. 1915–
Lewis, Oscar. 1914–1970
Mills, C. Wright. 1916–1962
Bell, Daniel. 1919–
Arrow, Kenneth J. 1921–
Goffman, Erving. 1922–1983
Geertz, Clifford. 1926–

5. **Education**
Mann, Horace. 1796–1859
Barnard, Henry. 1811–1900
Washington, Booker T.
   1856–1915
Dewey, John. 1859–1952
Montessori, Maria. 1870–1952

Kilpatrick, William Heard.
   1871–1965
Thorndike, Edward L. 1874–1949
Piaget, Jean. 1896–1980
Hutchins, Robert M. 1899–1977

6. **Ancient History**
Herodotus. c.484–425 B.C.
Thucydides. c.470–400 B.C.
Xenophon. c.434?–c.355? B.C.
Aristotle. 384–322 B.C.
Polybius. c.200–c.118 B.C.
Cicero, Marcus Tullius. 106–43 B.C.
Caesar, Julius. 100–44 B.C.
Sallust. 86–35 B.C.
Livy. c.59 B.C.–c.A.D. 17
Josephus, Flavius. 37–95
Dio Chrysostom. c.40–c.112
Plutarch. c.46–c.125
Tacitus, Cornelius. c.56–c.112/113
Pliny the Younger. c.61–c.112
Suetonius. c.69–c.140
Arrian. c.95–c.175
Ammianus Marcellinus. c.330–395
Procopius. c.500–c.565

7. **United States History**
Paine, Thomas. 1737–1809
Prescott, William Hickling.
   1796–1859
Tocqueville, Alexis de. 1805–1859
Davis, Jefferson. 1808–1889
Parkman, Francis. 1823–1893
Adams, Henry. 1838–1918
Roosevelt, Theodore. 1858–1919
Turner, Frederick Jackson.
   1861–1932
Du Bois, W. E. B. 1868–1963
Becker, Carl L. 1873–1945
Beard, Charles A. 1874–1948
Beard, Mary R. 1876–1958
Adams, James Truslow. 1878–1949
Thomas, Norman. 1884–1968

Morison, Samuel Eliot. 1887–1976
Schlesinger, Arthur M. 1888–1965
Lippmann, Walter. 1889–1974
Nevins, Allan. 1890–1971
Bemis, Samuel Flagg. 1891–1973
Agar, Herbert. 1897–1980
De Voto, Bernard. 1897–1955
Catton, Bruce. 1899–1978
Hacker, Louis M. 1899–
Millis, Walter. 1899–1968
Commager, Henry Steele. 1902–1984
Horgan, Paul. 1903–
Miller, Perry. 1905–1963
Woodward, C. Vann. 1908–
Potter, David M. 1910–1971
Boorstin, Daniel J. 1914–
Franklin, John Hope. 1915–
Handlin, Oscar. 1915–
Hofstadter, Richard. 1916–1970
Schlesinger, Arthur M., Jr. 1917–

8. Western Hemisphere: Canada and Latin America

9. British History

Bede the Venerable, Saint. 673–735
William of Malmesbury. c.1096–1143
Geoffrey of Monmouth. 1100?–1154
Paris, Matthew. 1200–1259
Fortescue, Sir John. 1394–1476
Clarendon, Edward Hyde, 1st Earl. 1609–1674
Burke, Edmund. 1729–1797
Cobbett, William. 1763–1835
Macaulay, Thomas Babington, 1st Baron. 1800–1859
Froude, James A. 1818–1894
Buckle, Henry T. 1821–1862
Freeman, Edward A. 1823–1892
Stubbs, William. 1825–1901
Bagehot, Walter. 1826–1877

Gardiner, Samuel R. 1829–1902
Acton, Lord John E. 1834–1902
Lecky, W. E. H. 1838–1903
Maitland, Frederic William. 1850–1906
Tout, Thomas Frederick. 1855–1929
Pollard, Albert Frederick. 1869–1948
Belloc, Hilaire. 1870–1953
Halevy, Elie. 1870–1937
Hammond, John L. 1872–1949
Clapham, John H. 1873–1946
Hammond, Barbara. 1873–1962
Churchill, Winston S. 1874–1965
Trevelyan, George Macaulay. 1876–1962
Powicke, Frederick Maurice. 1879–1963
Tawney, Richard H. 1880–1962
Richardson, Henry Gerald. 1884–?
Namier, Sir Lewis B. 1888–1966
Ashton, Thomas S. 1889–1968
Neale, Sir John. 1890–1975
Sayles, George Osborne. 1901–
Rowse, A. L. 1903–
Plumb, J. H. 1911–
Gash, Norman. 1912–
Hill, Christopher. 1912–
Trevor-Roper, Hugh R. 1914–
Hobsbawm, Eric J. 1917–
Stone, Lawrence. 1919–
Elton, Geoffrey R. 1921–
Thompson, Edward Palmer. 1924–

10. World History

Carlyle, Thomas. 1795–1881
Burckhardt, Jacob. 1818–1897
Mahan, Alfred Thayer. 1840–1914
Symonds, John Addington. 1840–1893
Taylor, Henry Osborn. 1856–1941
Croce, Benedetto. 1866–1952

Schevill, Ferdinand. 1868–1954
Lenin, Nikolai. 1870–1924
Gooch, G. P. 1873–1968
Stalin, Joseph. 1879–1953
Trotsky, Leon. 1879–1940
Guerard, Albert L. 1880–1959
Spengler, Oswald. 1880–1936
Latourette, Kenneth S. 1884–1968
Durant, Will. 1885–1981
Vernadsky, George. 1887–1973
Nehru, Jawaharlal. 1889–1964
Toynbee, Arnold J. 1889–1975
Kohn, Hans. 1891–1971
Brinton, C. Crane. 1898–1968
Durant, Ariel. 1898–1981
Mattingly, Garrett. 1900–1961
Braudel, Fernand. 1902–
Kennan, George F. 1904–
Aron, Raymond. 1905–
Arendt, Hannah. 1906–1975
Taylor, A. J. P. 1906–
Fairbank, John K. 1907–
Tuchman, Barbara. 1912–
Ward, Barbara. 1914–1981
McNeill, William H. 1917–
Barnett, A. Doak. 1921–

11. Music and Dance

Monteverdi, Claudio. 1567–1643
Purcell, Henry. 1659–1695
Vivaldi, Antonio. 1678–1741
Bach, Johann Sebastian.
  1685–1750
Handel, George Frideric.
  1685–1759
Haydn, Joseph. 1732–1809
Mozart, Wolfgang Amadeus.
  1756–1791
Beethoven, Ludwig van. 1770–1827
Schubert, Franz. 1797–1828
Bellini, Vincenzo. 1801–1835
Berlioz, Hector. 1803–1869

Bournonville, August. 1805–1879
Mendelssohn, Felix. 1809–1847
Chopin, Frederic. 1810–1849
Liszt, Franz. 1811–1886
Verdi, Giuseppe. 1813–1901
Wagner, Richard. 1813–1883
Bruckner, Anton. 1824–1896
Foster, Stephen. 1826–1864
Brahms, Johannes. 1833–1897
Mussorgsky, Modest. 1839–1881
Tchaikovsky, Peter Ilyich.
  1840–1893
Dvořák, Antonin. 1841–1904
Puccini, Giacomo. 1858–1924
Mahler, Gustav. 1860–1911
Debussy, Claude. 1862–1918
Strauss, Richard. 1864–1949
Joplin, Scott. 1868–1917
Diaghilev, Sergei. 1872–1929
Rachmaninoff, Serge. 1873–1943
Ives, Charles Edward. 1874–1954
Schoenberg, Arnold. 1874–1951
Ravel, Maurice. 1875–1937
Duncan, Isadora. 1878–1927
St. Denis, Ruth. 1880–1968
Bartók, Béla. 1881–1945
Pavlova, Anna. 1881–1931
Stravinsky, Igor. 1882–1971
Webern, Anton von. 1883–1945
Berg, Alban. 1885–1935
Nijinsky,Vaslav. 1890–1950
Porter, Cole. 1891–1964
Prokofiev, Serge. 1891–1953
Shawn, Ted. 1891–1972
Graham, Martha, 1894–
Hindemith, Paul. 1895–1963
Massine, Leonide. 1895–1979
Thomson, Virgil. 1896–
Gershwin, George. 1898–1937
Ellington, Edward Kennedy.
  1899–1974
Armstrong, Louis. 1900–1971

Copland, Aaron. 1900–
Ashton, Frederick. 1904–
Balanchine, George. 1904–1983
Basie, William. 1904–1984
Horowitz, Vladimir. 1904–
Tippett, Michael. 1905–
Shostakovich, Dmitri. 1906–1975
Kirstein, Lincoln. 1907–
Cage, John. 1912–
Britten, Lord Benjamin. 1913–1976
Bernstein, Leonard. 1918–
Cunningham, Merce. 1919–
Fonteyn, Dame Margot. 1919–
Parker, Charlie. 1920–1955
Xenakis, Iannis. 1922–
Callas, Maria. 1923–1977
Berio, Luciano. 1925–
Coltrane, John. 1926–1967
Davis, Miles. 1926–
Charles, Ray. 1930–
Nureyev, Rudolph. 1938–
Baryshnikov, Mikhail. 1948–

12. Art and Architecture

Leonardo da Vinci. 1452–1519
Dürer, Albrecht. 1471–1528
Michelangelo Buonarroti.
  1475–1564
Raphael. 1483–1520
Titian. c.1487–1576
Cellini, Benvenuto. 1500–1571
Bruegel the Elder, Pieter.
  c.1525–1569
Poussin, Nicolas. 1564–1665
Rubens, Peter Paul. 1577–1640
Bernini, Gianlorenzo. 1598–1680
Velazquez, Diego Rodriguez de
  Silva. 1599–1660
Rembrandt Harmensz van Rijn.
  1606–1669
Wren, Sir Christopher. 1632–1723
Watteau, Jean-Antoine. 1684–1721

Reynolds, Sir Joshua. 1723–1792
Gainsborough, Thomas. 1727–1788
Goya y Lucientes, Francisco José
  de. 1746–1828
Turner, Joseph Mallord William.
  1775–1851
Constable, John. 1776–1837
Manet, Edouard. 1832–1883
Richardson, Henry Hobson.
  1836–1886
Cézanne, Paul. 1839–1906
Monet, Claude. 1840–1926
Rodin, Auguste. 1840–1917
Renoir, Pierre Auguste. 1841–1919
Gauguin, Paul. 1848–1903
Van Gogh, Vincent. 1853–1890
Sullivan, Louis Henry. 1856–1924
Wright, Frank Lloyd. 1867–1959
Matisse, Henri. 1869–1954
Picasso, Pablo. 1881–1973
Gropius, Walter. 1883–1969
Mies van der Rohe, Ludwig.
  1886–1969
Le Corbusier. 1887–1965

13. The Mass Media

Griffith, D. W. 1875–1948
Fields, W. C. 1879–1946
Von Stroheim, Erich. 1885–1957
Chaplin, Sir Charles. 1889–1977
Cocteau, Jean. 1889–1963
Laurel, Stan. 1890–1965
The Marx Brothers—Groucho
  (Julius). 1890–1977
The Marx Brothers—Chico
  (Leonard). 1891–1961
Hardy, Oliver. 1892–1957
The Marx Brothers—Harpo
  (Arthur). 1893–1964
Von Sternberg, Joseph. 1894–1969
Ford, John. 1895–1973
Eisenstein, Sergei. 1898–1948

Bogart, Humphrey, 1899–1957
Hitchcock, Alfred. 1899–1980
Buñel, Luis. 1900–1983
Disney, Walt. 1901–1966
The Marx Brothers—Zeppo
  (Herbert). 1901–1979
Visconti, Luchino. 1906–1976
Kurosawa, Akira. 1910–
Antonioni, Michelangelo. 1912–
Welles, Orson. 1915–1985
Bergman, Ingmar. 1918–
Fellini, Federico. 1920–
Monroe, Marilyn. 1926–1962
Kubrick, Stanley. 1928–
Godard, Jean-Luc. 1930–
Truffaut, François. 1931–1984

14. Folklore and Humor

15. Travel and Exploration
Polo, Marco. 1254?–1324?
Columbus, Christopher. 1446–1506
Vespucci, Amerigo. 1451–1512
Hakluyt, Richard. 1552–1616
Cook, Captain James. 1728–1779
Clark, William. 1770–1838
Park, Mungo. 1771–1806

Lewis, Meriwether. 1774–1809
Borrow, George. 1803–1881
Kinglake, Alexander. 1809–1891
Livingstone, David. 1813–1873
Dana, Richard Henry, Jr.
  1815–1882
Burton, Sir Richard. 1821–1890
Stanley, Sir Henry Morton.
  1841–1904
Slocum, Joshua. 1844–1909
Peary, Robert E. 1856–1920
Scott, Robert Falcon. 1868–1912
Stefansson, Vilhjalmur. 1879–1962
Freuchen, Peter. 1886–1957
Byrd, Richard E. 1888–1957
Lawrence, T. E. 1888–1935
Morton, H. V. 1892–1979
Stark, Freya. 1893–
Gunther, John. 1901–1970
Lindbergh, Charles A. 1902–1974
Snow, Edward. 1902–1982
Van der Post, Laurens. 1906–
Harrer, Heinrich. 1912–
Heyerdahl, Thor. 1914–
Hillary, Sir Edmund. 1919–

Introduction

Since the publication of the twelfth edition of *The Reader's Adviser*, there has been increasing interest in and focus on a number of the subjects that are covered in this volume. The social sciences, art and architecture, the performing arts, and the mass media, in particular, have been topics of dynamic growth in the contemporary Western world. New trends and theories have emerged and a great deal of research and study has been done in these fields, resulting in an explosion of publications important to anyone interested in reading, learning, and keeping up with these topics.

This volume has been designed to reflect these changes and to be of most use to readers seeking to learn about and to locate basic materials about a wide variety of specific subjects within these broad disciplines. Each chapter is arranged to be of value to persons seeking to read about a topic for the very first time as well as to readers who wish to keep up to date about subjects in which they have some knowledge.

Also to reflect new trends, a number of substantial changes have been made to the content and organization of this volume. A chapter on art and architecture has been added and the chapter on dictionaries reinstated. The chapter on the social sciences has been expanded significantly and now includes a section on psychology, and the chapters on history have been reorganized to provide both geographical and conceptual approaches. Information on music and dance, formerly included as a section in "Lively Arts and Communications," is now a separate chapter, as is the mass media. Chapters on general reference materials, biography and autobiography, folklore and humor, and travel and exploration continue to complete the volume.

The previous edition contained chapters on Bibles and related texts, world religions, philosophy, and the sciences. These have been updated and expanded and now appear with related materials in the two new volumes 4 and 5 of *The Reader's Adviser*.

The contents of this volume have been selected and described by a group of distinguished contributors, each a noted expert in his or her field, and to whom this editor is most grateful for making her job an easy one. The presentation of each chapter represents not merely an updating of the similar section in the previous edition, but a complete rethinking of the most useful organization, selection, and description of materials deemed to be of most interest to the volume's user, the nonspecialist who is interested in reading about a particular subject and the librarian who needs to guide the library patron as well as develop the library collection.

Users of this volume should be aware that most of its subjects are dynamic, that emphases of interest in each field continue to change, and that many new and important materials are published continuously. Readers should pay careful attention to the reference book sections of each chapter, in which sources of information about newly emerging topics and publications can be found, and they should ask their librarians for additional assistance in identifying and locating items published after the appearance of this volume.

One final note: In today's fast-moving world some published materials are being issued in machine-readable forms, such as online databases, floppy disks, optical disks, CD-ROM, and so forth. Within the subjects covered here, many standard reference works, most notably periodical indexes and statistical publications, are or will soon be issued in these alternate formats. Subject experts predict that the full texts of some periodicals (especially newsletters and publications with currency-time values) and a few standard monographs will be available for general use in machine-readable forms in the very near future. It is beyond the scope of this publication to include and describe these resources. Readers interested in more information about them should consult with librarians in their local libraries.

Paula T. Kaufman

The Reader's Adviser

CHAPTER 1

Reference Books: General

Russ Chenoweth

Of shoes—and ships—and sealing-wax—
Of cabbages—and Kings—
And why the sea is boiling hot—
and whether pigs have wings.

LEWIS CARROLL, *Through the Looking Glass*

Reference books relating to particular fields, such as literature, music, art, or biography, should be sought in the early sections of the chapters on these subjects, although a few of the basic ones in special fields have been included here. Reference books of particular interest to librarians, such catalogs as the *National Union Catalog*, and foreign bibliographies are found in Chapter 2 of Volume 1.

The following selection of general reference works is intended to be representative of a large body of similar materials. These titles have been selected as much as possible on the basis of proven value or recent favorable reviews. Some are the best of their type; others are probably interchangeable with many similar titles. Many seem very expensive when compared to the prices of contemporary trade books. In some cases, these are books for libraries or organizations to purchase, rather than individuals. Their sales are small, and their high price represents not the cost of the book as an object but the cost of gathering information that the book supplies.

In the last few years, reference sources have become generally available in formats other than the printed book. Many indexes and abstracting services are now published in microform and electronically, the latter being available from computer terminals in libraries, offices, and homes. Other reference materials, such as directories and statistical publications, can be purchased on diskettes for use with personal computers, on laser disks for use in libraries, and on magnetic tape for use in large organizations. Low-cost services such as BRS/After Dark and DIALOG's Knowledge Index now make it possible for owners of home computers with communications equipment to search and retrieve bibliographic references and article abstracts from such indexes as the *Readers' Guide* and the *Index to Business Periodicals*. Beginning in 1985, all of the Wilson indexes to periodical literature will be available on "Wilsonline" for computer searching through a terminal or communicating microcomputer and telephone modem connection.

1

Cost of time online and of printing of references varies according to the indexes searched. Among the indexes included are *Applied Science and Technology Index, Art Index, Biography Index, Biological and Agricultural Index, Book Review Digest, Business Periodicals Index, Education Index, General Science Index, Humanities Index, Index to Legal Periodicals, Library Literature, Readers' Guide to Periodical Literature,* and *Social Sciences Index.*

Although many of these reference materials are available in both print and nonprint formats, some (such as current indexing of many U.S. newspapers) are not. Publication in nonprint format generally facilitates search and retrieval of data in a way not possible in the print equivalent. Only a few of the major sources have been included here. The reader should be aware that publication formats in this field are changing rapidly; librarians should be consulted for current information.

ENCYCLOPEDIAS

Although the attempt to produce an encyclopedic summary of human knowledge in a single set of volumes was abandoned after the 1911 edition of the *Encyclopaedia Britannica,* encyclopedias continue to have a useful place in homes, schools, and libraries. They can be used to answer questions and provide basic information about an unfamiliar subject. Their articles are generally written with the beginner in mind and often progress from basic facts and orientation in a topic to more advanced concepts. If articles include carefully prepared bibliographies, they can lead the reader to both the classic works in a field and the best recent treatments of a topic at the time the encyclopedia was published. A good index can make an encyclopedia particularly useful. Kenneth Kister's *Encyclopedia Buying Guide: A Consumer Guide to General Encyclopedias in Print* provides critical evaluations of 36 in-print English-language general encyclopedias, from the largest sets to one-volume works for adults and children. The *American Reference Books Annual* provides excellent evaluative reviews of new editions of general encyclopedias. The prices and edition dates listed below should be taken only as an indication.

Academic American Encyclopedia. Grolier 21 vols. rev. ed. 1982 $514.00. The *AAE* is intended for readers from junior-high school students to adults. Its stated objectives are "to provide quick access to definitive factual information . . .," to present "a readily intelligible overview of a subject that does not compel the reader to grasp intricate subtleties . . . to help [readers] visualize or recognize people, places, objects, and processes by means of maps, photographs, and drawings . . . [and] to be comprehensive, current, authoritative, objective, and easy to use." There are 28,500 articles, averaging 540 words in length, 16,616 illustrations, and 1,100 maps. In general, articles are shorter than in the other major encyclopedias.

Britannica Junior Encyclopaedia for Boys and Girls. Encyclopaedia Britannica 15 vols. 1981 $249.00. Offers brief factual information intended for elementary school students. A ready-reference index provides good access to information.

Collier's Encyclopedia. Macmillan 30 vols. 1983 ed. $599.00. A large general encyclopedia intended in particular for students, *Collier's* is somewhat smaller and more popularly written than the *Britannica* and the *Americana*. Entries tend to be broad in coverage, and the large 450,000-entry index must be relied on to find all information on a topic. Its index is the largest of the three major encyclopedias. The 1983 edition includes 25,000 articles and 17,000 illustrations, of which 1,500 are in color. There is a separate 200-page bibliography and a study guide.

The Concise Columbia Encyclopedia. Ed. by Judith Levey and Agnes Greenhall, Avon 1983 pap. $14.00; Columbia Univ. Pr. 1983 $29.95. A compact one-volume desk encyclopedia intended to provide concise up-to-date factual information. Contains approximately 15,000 brief articles in its 943 pages.

The Encyclopedia Americana. Ed. by Alan H. Smith, Grolier 30 vols. international ed. 1983 $772.00. "The *Encyclopedia Americana* is a well-balanced and clearly written authoritative work prepared by an experienced editorial staff, with an excellent index and well-designed illustrations. New editions appear every year with varied degrees of revision" (Bohdan S. Wynar, *American Reference Books Annual*). The 1983 edition of the *Americana* contains 56,000 articles supplemented by 22,000 photographs, drawings, diagrams, and maps. Science and technology are well covered. The index contains 313,000 entries.

Funk & Wagnalls New Encyclopedia. Ed. by Leon L. Bram and Robert S. Phillips, Funk & Wagnalls 29 vols. 1983 $195.00. "*Funk & Wagnalls New Encyclopedia* (*FWNE*) is intended for home use as well as for junior high school students. It is designed for the reader with little or no background in the material being researched. The majority of articles are concise, a page or less in length. For long articles containing complicated subject matter, the material is presented from the simple to the complex and from the general to the specific . . . . The *FWNE* has prepared well for its audience . . . . It is not intended to compete with encyclopedias like *Collier's* or *World Book*" (Marilyn Strong-Noronha, *American Reference Books Annual*). The *FWNE* contains 9,175 illustrations, including 317 maps. The index volume uses lay language whenever possible. A 250-page bibliography includes annotated entries for 9,000 books and other publications.

The New Book of Knowledge. Ed. by William E. Shapiro, Grolier 21 vols. 1983 $419.50. "*The New Book of Knowledge* is a relatively current, well-written encyclopedia that is responsive to the school and home needs of the elementary school-aged student . . . . The authors have made a genuine effort to make articles as interesting to read as they are informative. Of the 22,400 photographs in the set, 13,000 are in color, making the set attractive and browsable" (Janet H. Littlefield, *American Reference Books Annual*).

The New Encyclopaedia Britannica. Encyclopaedia Britannica 32 vols. 16th ed. 1985 $1,249.00. The *Britannica* is published in three parts. The *Propaedia* is a one-volume topical outline of knowledge, which is intended to serve as a guide and index to the long articles in the *Macropaedia*. The *Macropaedia* contains 681 in-depth studies of from 1,000 to 8,000 words, including annotated bibliographies and more than 8,000 illustrations. The *Micropaedia* consists of 86,000 alphabetically arranged brief articles in 12 volumes. *The Library Guide to the Encyclopaedia Britannica* (1981 $35.00) is a one-volume listing of 155,000 main entries and 235,000 index citations to the *Micropaedia* and *Macropaedia*. There have been many reviews of the *Britannica*. See in particular Kister's *Encyclopedia Buying Guide* and various volumes of *American Reference Books Annual*. Most reviewers agree that the *Britannica* is an authoritative encyclopedia that provides more information on almost all subject areas than any other general English-language encyclopedia. Its chief limitation is seen to be the lack of a standard detailed index to the main *Macropaedia* volumes.

The Random House Encyclopedia. Ed. by James Mitchell, Random rev. ed. 1983 $99.95. A one-volume encyclopedia designed for a general readership. It contains a breadth of factual information and more than 11,000 color illustrations. The arrangement is in two divisions. The Colorpedia groups related topics in seven broad categories: The Universe, The Earth, Life on Earth, Man, History and Culture, Man and Science, and Man and Machines. The 884-page Alphapedia includes 25,000 brief entries and 35 references to the Colorpedia.

The World Book Encyclopedia. World Book 22 vols. 1983 lib. bdg. $499.00. Intended for elementary, junior-high, and high-school students, its content is based in part on school curriculum analysis and classroom testing. The longer articles include such study aids as outlines, questions, a list of related articles, and suggested readings. There are many cross-references throughout and more than 29,000 illustrations, including 2,300 maps.

GENERAL BIBLIOGRAPHIC AND REFERENCE TOOLS

[SEE ALSO Chapters 2 and 3 of Volume 1.]

Abstracting and Indexing Services Directory. Ed. by John Schmittroth, Jr., Gale 1982 pap. $170.00. Describes more than 2,000 current and continuing abstracts, indexes, digests, bibliographies, and catalogs in all fields, including indexes that appear as a regular feature in journals and online bibliographic databases.

Acronyms, Initialisms, and Abbreviations Dictionary 1986–87. Ed. by Julie E. Towell and Helen E. Sheppard, Gale 3 vols. 10th ed. 1985 $170.00. Volume 1 (in two parts) is the basic volume and contains more than 300,000 entries. The emphasis is on U.S. material, but European and other acronyms are included. Volume 2, *New Acronyms, Initialisms, and Abbreviations,* and two supplements will provide approximately 15,000 additional entries. Volume 3 (in two parts), *Reverse Acronyms, Initialisms, and Abbreviations Dictionary,* leads from full name of organization, etc., to correct acronym.

American Book Publishing Record. Bowker monthly annual subscription $60.00 annual cumulative vol. $89.95. Includes nearly every book published or distributed in the United States, with full bibliographic information as cataloged by the Library of Congress. Arranged by subject under Dewey classification numbers. Separate author and title indexes.

American Library Directory. Ed. by Jaques Cattell Pr., Bowker 2 vols. 38th ed. 1985 $119.95. Geographical listing of public, academic, special, and government libraries, with address, key personnel, budget, size, and nature of collections.

American Reference Books Annual. 1970–to date. Ed. by Bohdan S. Wynar, Libraries Unlimited vol. 17 (1986) $70.00. Volume 17 provides brief evaluative reviews, typically 200–400 words in length, of more than 1,500 reference books published in the United States in 1984 and 1985. Author/subject/title index.

Arts and Humanities Citation Index. Institute for Scientific Information quarterly with annual cumulation $1,800.00. A massive computer-produced index to international journals in the arts and humanities that provides author and title word-pair indexing. Its special feature is citation indexing, which indexes current articles by the items cited in their bibliographies and thus makes it possible to follow a chain of research forward from key books and articles in a field.

Associations' Publications in Print 1984–1985. Bowker annual 3 vols. 1984 $180.00.

Lists 110,000 books, pamphlets, and serial publications available from 3,600 associations in the United States and Canada. Subject arrangement, with title, publisher/title, and association name indexes. Bibliographic and ordering information is given.

Awards, Honors, and Prizes. Ed. by Gita Siegman and Paul Wasserman, Gale 2 vols. 6th ed. 1985 vol. 1 *The United States and Canada* $145.00 vol. 2 *International and Foreign* $160.00. A 1984 supplement sells for $72.00. Describes awards, but does not list recipients.

Bibliographic Index. 1937–to date. Wilson vols. 1–4 (1937–55) ea. $85.00 vols. 5–8 (1956–58) ea. $170.00 vols. 9–19 (1969–79) ea. $100.00. Published in April and August, with a permanent bound cumulation in December sold on a service basis. A subject index to bibliographies published separately as books or articles and those appearing as parts of books or articles with 50 or more bibliographic references. More than 2,600 periodicals are regularly scanned for bibliographic material.

Biography Index. 1946–to date. Wilson vols. 1–13 (1946–85) ea. $120.00. Quarterly with an annual cumulation for $70.00. Indexes biographical material appearing in the more than 2,600 periodicals indexed by the other Wilson indexes. Books of individual or collective biography, significant biographical material in other books, and obituaries of general interest appearing in the *N.Y. Times* and other publications are included. Arranged by name of the biographee, with an index by occupation.

Book Review Digest. 1905–to date. Wilson. Published monthly, except for February and July, with annual cumulations sold on a service basis. Reprints of annual volumes for 1905–69 are available at prices ranging from $50.00 to $90.00. Includes full publishing information and price, a descriptive note, and excerpts from generally three to five reviews selected to reflect the full range of critical opinion, for more than 6,000 books a year. Limited to English-language books, published or distributed in the United States, which are reviewed in at least two (four for fiction) of the 80 journals scanned for reviews. Arrangement is by author of the books reviewed, with a title and subject index. Every fifth year, the annual volume contains a combined index for the past five years. *Book Review Digest Author/Title Index, 1905–1974* (Wilson 4 vols. 1976 $275.00) is a useful cumulation that also includes references to a few publications not indexed by *Book Review Digest.*

Book Review Index. 1965–to date. Gale. Bimonthly with quarterly and annual cumulations for an annual subscription of $160.00. All annual cumulations are permanently in print for $160.00 each. There is a master cumulation (1965–84) in ten volumes for $1,250.00. Indexes all reviews in more than 400 English-language journals. No summaries or excerpts are included. Title index.

Books in Print. 1948–to date. Bowker annual 6 vols. 1985 $199.95. Annual listings by author and title of books currently available from publishers in the United States. Each entry includes full publishing information, price, grade level, whether illustrated or not, LC card number, and ISBN. A directory of publishers' addresses is also included. The spring *Supplement* and bimonthly *Forthcoming Books* update *Books in Print. Paperbound Books in Print* is a similar Bowker publication.

Books in Series. Bowker 6 vols. 4th ed. $325.00. Access to 240,000 titles published in 25,000 popular, scholarly, and professional series. Author/title and subject indexes. Directory of publishers' addresses.

Bowker's Complete Sourcebook of Personal Computing 1985. Bowker annual 1984

$19.95. Descriptions of computers, printers, and other peripheral devices, with specifications and prices, including 3,700 software packages arranged by application and an annotated list of 3,500 books and periodicals. Directory of 5,500 computer companies.

British Books in Print. 1965–to date. Bowker annual 4 vols. $199.95. Titles currently available from British publishers, with full bibliographic and publishing information. Directory of publishers' addresses.

Canadian Books in Print: Catalogue des Livres Canadiens en Librairie. 1967–to date. Univ. of Toronto Pr. annual $57.00. Titles currently available from Canadian publishers. Arranged by author, with title and publisher indexes.

The Consumer Health Information Source Book. Ed. by Alan M. Rees and Jodith Janes, Bowker 2d ed. 1984 $39.95. Evaluates 935 publications on consumer health of interest to the layperson, with ordering information.

Consumer Sourcebook. Ed. by Paul Wasserman and Gita Siegman, Gale 2 vols. 4th ed. 1983 $170.00. Lists organizations and publications concerned with consumer protection and guidance.

Cumulative Book Index. 1898–to date. Wilson. Monthly, with quarterly and annual cumulations sold on a service basis. Permanent volumes in print, 1928–68 $120.00–$175.00, 1969–84, sold on service basis. The *CBI* is a combined author, title, and subject listing of books published in English in all countries during the time period covered by the issue or volume. Publishing information and price are given. A directory of publishers' addresses is included.

Current Index to Journals in Education. 1969–to date. C. C. M. Information Monthly issues $162.00 with semiannual cumulations in two volumes $156.00. Issues and cumulation $300. *CIJE* indexes and abstracts articles from more than 700 international education-related journals.

Dictionaries, Encyclopedias, and Other Word-Related Books. Ed. by Annie M. Brewer, Gale 3 vols. 3d ed. vol. 1 *English-Language Works* (1981) $135.00 vol. 2 *Polyglot Works* (1982) $190.00 vol. 3 *Foreign-Language Works* (1982) $190.00. Supplement 1983 $160.00. Reproductions of Library of Congress catalog cards for more than 30,000 general and highly specialized dictionaries and word books.

Directory of Directories. Ed. by James M. Ethridge, Gale 3d ed. 1985 $160.00. Describes and indexes 8,200 printed directories of all kinds. Arranged under 16 broad subject categories, with a detailed subject index. *Directory Information Service* supplements the main volume. Interedition subscription $110.00.

Directory of Special Libraries and Information Centers. 1963–to date. Ed. by Brigitte T. Darnay, Gale 3 vols. 9th ed. 1985 vol. 1 *Special Libraries and Information Centers in the United States and Canada* $320.00. vol. 2 *Geographic and Personnel Indexes* $265.00 vol. 3 *New Special Libraries.* Quarterly supplements to the annual volume $275.00. Annual subscription. Gives directory information, plus collection strengths, publications, and services to outsiders for special libraries, archives, and information centers. *Subject Directory of Special Libraries* 9th ed. vol. 1 *Business and Law* vol. 2 *Education and Information Science* vol. 3 *Health Sciences* vol. 4 *Social Sciences and Humanities* vol. 5 *Science and Technology* ea. $145.00.

Education Index. 1929–to date. Wilson. Ten issues per year, with quarterly and annual cumulations sold on a service basis. Permanent vols. in print vols. 1–8 (1929–53) ea. $65.00 vols. 9–19 (1953–69) ea. $75.00 vols. 20–33 (1969–83) sold on a service basis. Subject and author indexes to every article in 354 English-language education journals.

El-Hi Textbooks and Serials in Print, 1985. Bowker annual $60.00. Arranges more than 35,000 elementary and secondary school textbooks, reference works, and teaching aids under 22 main headings and dozens of subheadings, with author and title indexes. Entry includes bibliographic information, price, grade level, binding, and ISBN. There is a directory of publishers.

Encyclopedia of Associations. 1956–to date. Gale 3 vols. 20th ed. vol. 1 *National Organizations of the U.S.*, ed. by Katherine Gruber, 3 pts. $195.00 vol. 2 *Geographic and Executive Indexes*, 2 sections $175.00 vol. 3 *New Associations and Projects* $190.00. Covers 19,500 associations and more than 2,500 subjects. Volume 1 divides organizations into 17 subject areas and has an enhanced alphabetical and keyword index. Volume 2 lists all of the organizations in Volume 1 in state and city order and by executive. Volume 3 is a periodical supplement to Volume 1.

Encyclopedia of Associations: Regional, State, and Local Organizations. Gale 7 vols. 1985 ea. $80.00. Each volume is devoted to a region of the United States: Northeastern, Middle Atlantic, Southeastern, Great Lakes, Southwest and South Central, Western and Northwestern, and Great Plains. Covers regional, state, and local organizations in the same format as Gale's *Encyclopedia of Associations*.

Encyclopedia of Information Systems and Services. Ed. by John Schmittroth, Jr., Gale 2 vols. 6th ed. 1984 vol. 1 *United States* $200.00 vol. 2 *International* $175.00. *New Information Systems and Services.* Interedition supplement subscription $250.00. Information on nearly 25,000 organizations, services, products, and publications concerned with the contemporary information industry. Many indexes.

Encyclopedia of Philosophy. Ed. by Paul Edwards, Macmillan (Free Pr.) 8 vols. in 4 1973 $200.00

Essay and General Literature Index. 1900–to date. Wilson. Subscription to January to June issue and annual cumulation $70.00. Subscriber receives five-year cumulations at no extra cost. Five-year cumulations are permanently in print from 1900–84 at $160.00 per volume. Author and subject index to essays in published collections, emphasizing the social sciences and humanities. The 1983 annual volume indexed 3,817 essays from 302 publications.

Ethnic Information Sources of the U.S. Ed. by Paul Wasserman and Alice Kennington, Gale 2 vols. 2d ed. 1983 $150.00. Organizations and print sources of information on more than 90 identifiable ethnic groups of the United States. Omits blacks, American Indians, and Eskimos, as covered extensively in other publications.

Fiction Catalog. Wilson 10th ed. 1980 and supplements for 1981, 1982, 1983, and 1984 $70.00. An annotated selection of 5,000 new and established English-language fiction titles. Entries are arranged by author and include plot summary, bibliographic information, and latest known price. Includes English translation of major foreign-language works. Subject and title index and directory of publishers.

Forthcoming Books. Bowker bimonthly annual subscription $95.00, with *Subject Guide to Forthcoming Books* $140.00. Includes books to be published within the next five months and a cumulative index of books published since the latest annual edition of *Books in Print.* Author and title indexes.

The Foundation Directory. Ed. by Loren Renz, Foundation Ctr. 9th ed. 1983 $60.00. Gives information on more than 4,000 U.S. foundations having assets of more than one million dollars and having given more than $100,000 in grants in the year being analyzed.

Hall, James L., and Marjorie J. Brown. *Online Bibliographic Databases: A Directory and Sourcebook.* Gale 3d ed. 1983 $95.00. Directory and subject guide to 200 computer-searchable databases. Includes an overview and explanation of online searching.

Humanities Index. 1975–to date. Wilson quarterly with annual cumulation sold on a service basis. With *Social Sciences Index*, a successor to *Social Sciences and Humanities Index* (1964–74) and *International Index* (1900–64). Both are author and subject indexes to 294 English-language periodicals of a scholarly nature. Includes a separate book-review index.

IMS Directory of Publications (Ayer Directory of Publications). 1869–to date. Ayer annual $95.00. Directory of print media published in the United States, Puerto Rico, Virgin Islands, Canada, Bermuda, Panama, and the Philippines. Arranged geographically, with subject indexes.

Industrial Research Laboratories in the United States. Bowker 19th ed. 1985 $149.00. Alphabetical listing of nearly 10,000 research facilities, with address, parent organization, chief personnel, and major activities. Geographical, personnel, and subject classification indexes.

International Encyclopedia of the Social Sciences. Ed. by David L. Sills, Macmillan (Free Pr.) 17 vols. in 8 1977 $310.00. With *Biographical Supplement* published in 1979 set $340.00. Long, signed articles by recognized authorities on the concepts, principles, theories, and methods of social science disciplines. Planned to represent the state of the social sciences in the 1960s, its age must be taken into consideration. Detailed subject index.

Irregular Serials and Annuals: An International Directory. Bowker annual 11th ed. 1986 $139.95. Designed to complement *Ulrich's International Periodicals Directory* for more than 37,000 serials, annuals, yearbooks, conference proceedings, and other publications issued irregularly or less frequently than twice a year. Arrangement is under 557 broad subject classifications, with a title index. Entries give year publication began, frequency, price, language(s) of text, editor, ISSN, and Dewey decimal classification number. Separate cessations list and title, ISSN, and international organization indexes.

Magazines for Libraries. Ed. by Bill Katz and Linda Sternberg Katz, Bowker 5th ed. 1986 $95.00. Some 6,500 magazines selected and annotated by more than 137 subject experts to represent the most useful titles for school, public, and academic libraries. Broad subject arrangement.

National Newspaper Index. 1980–to date. Information Access annual subscription to the monthly full cumulations on 16mm-microfilm including motorized microfilm reader, more than $2,000.00. Subject indexing of the *N.Y. Times, Washington Post, Wall Street Monitor,* and *Los Angeles Times.* Indexing is up to date as of the previous four to six weeks. Also available online.

New Serial Titles 1950–1970. Bowker 1978 microfilm format $100.00. Supplements the *Union List of Serials* by listing serials and periodicals that began publication since 1949. Provides bibliographic data for 220,000 serials held by 800 libraries in the United States and Canada reporting to the Library of Congress. Entries include issuing body, Dewey decimal number, and place and first date of publication. Cessations and changes are listed in separate sections.

New York Times Book Review 1896–1981. Times Bks. 141 vols. including five-vol. index $9,781.00. Republication of the full text of the *N.Y. Times* reviews. The five-volume index is available from Ayer (1973 $600.00).

Nineteenth-Century Readers' Guide to Periodical Literature: 1890–1899. Wilson 2 vols. 1944 $95.00. Author and subject index to 51 American and English periodicals; includes indexing for some periodicals up to the time they were included in a later Wilson index. Includes many references to book reviews.

Official Museum Directory, United States, Canada. 1971–to date. National Register annual $77.00. Museums, botanical gardens, zoos, etc., of the United States and Canada. Geographical arrangement. Subject index.

Paperbound Books in Print. Bowker 3 vols. published biannually in April and October $85.95. Author, title, and subject index to more than 250,000 original and reprint paperback editions. Directory of publishers.

Periodical Title Abbreviations. Ed. by Leland G. Alkire, Jr., Gale 2 vols. 5th ed. vol. 1 *By Abbreviation* (1986) $150.00 vol. 2 *By Title* (1986) $150.00. Some 80,000 abbreviations and full titles.

Poole's Index to Periodical Literature. Peter Smith 17 vols. repr. $252.00 vol. 1 (1802–81) vol. 2 (1882–87) vol. 3 (1887–92) vol. 4 (1892–96) vol. 5 (1897–1902) vol. 6 (1902–06). Subject index to nineteenth-century British and U.S. periodicals.

Popular Periodical Index. 1973–to date. Popular Periodical Index biannual $25.00. Subject index to 40 popular periodicals such as *Discover, Rolling Stone, Yankee.*

Pseudonyms and Nicknames Dictionary. Ed. by Jennifer Mossman, Gale 2d. ed. rev. 1982 $200.00. Includes more than 50,000 pseudonyms used by more than 40,000 individuals. Entries give original name, birth and death dates, nationality, occupation, and sources of additional information.

Public Library Catalog. Wilson 8th ed. 1984 $140.00. "8,000 of the best currently in-print, adult, non-fiction, English-language books. Chosen by a panel of distinguished public librarians . . . the listed books encompass a broad spectrum of contemporary topics meeting the diverse reading needs of adult American library patrons" (Publisher's catalog). Arranged by Dewey decimal classification, entries include bibliographic and purchasing information, scope, and contents note. There are an author, title, subject, and analytical index and a directory of publishers' addresses. Annual supplements will be published.

Publishers Directory. Ed. by Linda S. Hubbard, Gale 2 vols. 6th ed. 1985 $240.00 interedition supplement $135.00. Directory of U.S. and Canadian publishers of books, classroom materials, databases, software, and other print and nonprint publications. Subject and geographical indexes.

Publishers' Trade List Annual. Bowker 5 vols. 1985 $124.95. *PTLA* is a collection of the catalogs and booklists of 1,800 U.S. publishers bound together alphabetically. Subject and series indexes to publishers.

Purcell, Gary R., and Gail Ann Schlachter. *Reference Sources in Library and Information Services: A Guide to the Literature.* ABC-Clio 1984 $45.00

Readers' Guide to Periodical Literature. 1900–to date. Wilson semimonthly in March, April, June, September, October, and December; monthly in January, February, May, July, August, and November, with quarterly and annual cumulations. Annual subscriptions $95.00. Vols. 1–42 available at $95.00 each. Author and subject index to articles in 186 U.S. general interest periodicals. The *Abridged Readers' Guide* indexes 68 of the most popular periodicals covered by *Readers' Guide.* Annual subscriptions $50.00.

Research Centers Directory. Ed. by Mary Michelle Watkins and James A. Ruffner, Gale 10th ed. 1985 $340.00. A guide to more than 7,500 university-related and other nonprofit research organizations established on a permanent basis in the United States and Canada. Arranged in broad categories (education, social sciences, etc.) with separate center name and parent institution name indexes and brief subject index. Entries give address, phone, chief officer, parent institution, fields of research, publications, and meetings. Periodical supplement *New Research Centers* is $200.00 for the interedition subscription.

Senior High School Library Catalog. Wilson 12th ed. 1982 $70.00. Dewey classified listing of 5,056 titles recommended for the ninth through the twelfth grades. Author, title, subject, and analytical index. Directory of publishers.

Sheehy, Eugene P. *Guide to Reference Books.* Amer. Lib. Association 9th ed. 1976 $40.00. Supplement 9th ed. 1980 pap. $15.00 2d Supplement 1982 pap. $15.00. The basic U.S. guide to nearly 15,000 reference works in all subject areas. Classified arrangement, with author, subject, and title index. Brief descriptive annotations with most entries and longer descriptions of major works.

Social Sciences Citation Index. 1972–to date. Institute for Scientific Information quarterly with annual cumulation $1,800.00. A massive computer-produced index to more than 25 international journals in the social and behavioral sciences, it provides author and title word-pair indexing. Its special feature is citation indexing, which indexes current articles by the items cited in the bibliographies and thus makes it possible to follow a chain of research forward from key books and articles in a field.

Social Sciences Index. 1975–to date. Wilson quarterly with annual cumulations sold on a service basis. With *Humanities Index,* a successor to *Social Sciences and Humanities Index* (1964–74) and *International Index* (1900–64). Both are author and subject indexes to more than 300 English-language periodicals of a scholarly nature. Includes a separate book review index.

The Software Encyclopedia 1985/86. Bowker annual 1985 $95.00. Full description information, including required memory, systems on which the programs will run, and prices for 23,000 programs. Arranged by application, with name, vendor, and system indexes. Vendor profiles on 3,000 companies.

The Standard Periodical Directory. Ed. by Patricia Hagood, Oxbridge 8th ed. 1984 $160.00. Listing of more than 66,000 U.S. and Canadian periodicals. Broad subject arrangement, with title and subject indexes. Gives publisher and address, editorial content and scope, first year of publication, and subscription rate.

Statistics Sources. Ed. by Paul Wasserman and Jacqueline O'Brien, Gale 2 vols. 9th ed. 1984 $210.00. Subject index to basic sources of statistical data, emphasizing U.S. publications of national scope.

Subject Collections: A Guide to Special Book Collections. . . . Ed. by Lee Ash, Bowker 2 vols. 6th ed. 1985 $165.00. Subject index to 20,000 special book and manuscript collections housed in academic, public, and special libraries and museums in the United States, Canada, and Puerto Rico.

Subject Guide to Books in Print 1984–1985. Bowker annual 4 vols. 1985 $142.95. "Lists over 570,000 nonfiction titles some 710,000 times under 62,000 Library of Congress Subject Headings with over 55,000 cross-references. Each entry gives full bibliographic information, ISBN, price, and binding" (Publisher's catalog).

Thinkers of the Twentieth Century. Gale 1984 $75.00. Signed essays of 1,000–3,000 words by noted experts on more than 400 major thinkers of the twentieth century, including Sigmund Freud, Albert Einstein, T. S. Eliot, etc. Extensive bibliographies include original non-English-language works.

Ulrich's International Periodicals Directory. Bowker 2 vols. 24th ed. 1985 $139.95. Lists more than 69,000 periodicals from 196 countries. Arrangement is by broad subject, with a title index. Entries include full publishing and subscription information, ISSN, indication of titles that carry advertising and book or movie reviews, and selected periodical indexes that index the title. *Ulrich's Quarterly* supplements the annual sets at $60.00 per year.

Union List of Serials in Libraries of the United States and Canada. Wilson 5 vols. 3d ed. 1965 $175.00. Lists holdings of 156,499 serial titles in 956 libraries in the United States and Canada. Continued by *New Serial Titles.*

U.S. Library of Congress, Catalog Division. *Newspapers in Microfilm: United States, 1948–1972.* Supplements 1973–77 and 1978–to date. Library of Congress. The basic volume lists 34,289 newspapers published from colonial times to the present, with holdings in major libraries.

Vertical File Index. 1932–to date. Wilson monthly (except August) annual subscription $30.00. Subject index to pamphlets, booklets, charts, posters issued by governments, universities, museums, etc., with full ordering information.

Walford, Albert J., ed. *Walford's Guide to Reference Materials.* Lib. Association 4th ed. vol. 1 *Science and Technology* (1980) $67.50 vol. 2 *Social and Historical Sciences* (1980) $67.50 vol. 3 *Generalities. Languages, the Arts, and Literature* (1985) $80.00. The British equivalent of Sheehy's *Guide to Reference Books.* Includes more European materials than Sheehy.

Washington Information Directory. Congressional Quarterly annual 1985 $39.95. Directory of more than 5,000 key persons and organizations in the public and private sectors in the Washington, D.C., area.

The Wellesley Index to Victorian Periodicals, 1824–1900. Ed. by Walter E. Houghton, Univ. of Toronto Pr. 3 vols. 1966–1978 $375.00

Wellisch, Hans H. *Indexing and Abstracting: An International Bibliography.* ABC-Clio 1980 $32.50. Bibliography of 2,383 indexing and abstracting sources published from the nineteenth century through 1976. Supplemented by *Indexing and Abstracting: An International Bibliography 1977–1981* (ABC-Clio 1984 $45.00), which adds 1,646 annotated entries.

Wiener, Philip P., ed. *Dictionary of the History of Ideas: Studies of Selected Pivotal Ideas.* Scribner 5 vols. 1973 pap. $75.00. Three hundred long, signed articles on such topics as law, faith, peace, etc., by scholars from many countries. Subject index. Brief bibliographies.

Willing's Press Guide: A Guide to the Press of the United Kingdom and the Principal Publications of Europe, Australasia, the Far East, the Middle East, and the Americas. 1874–to date. Thomas Skinner annual 110th ed. 1984 $54.25

Women Studies Abstracts. 1972–to date. Rush Publications quarterly with annual index $66.00. Topical arrangement of article abstracts with separate book-review listing. Coverage is international and includes many journals not indexed elsewhere.

Working Press of the Nation 1985. Gale 5 vols. 35th ed. 1984 $241.00 vol. 1 *Newspaper Directory* vol. 2 *Magazine Directory* vol. 3 *TV and Radio Directory* vol. 4 *Feature Writer and Photographer Directory* vol. 5 *Internal Publications.*

World Guide to Abbreviations of Organizations. Ed. by F. A. Buttress, Gale 7th ed. 1984 $115.00. Abbreviations of 42,500 companies, institutions, internal organizations, and government departments throughout the world.

World Measurement Guide. Economist Newspaper distributed by Gale 4th ed. 1980 $72.00. Tables, formulae, and other information on standards and measurements used in various countries.

Wynar, Bohdan S. *Recommended Reference Books for Small and Medium-Sized Libraries and Media Centers.* Libraries Unlimited annual 1983 ed. $27.50. The 1983 edition reviews 506 titles selected from the 1983 edition of the *American Reference Books Annual.*

Yearbook of International Organizations. Gale 3 vols. 22nd ed. 1985 $420.00. Volume 1, *Main Volume* ($168.00), is a directory of 20,000 governmental and nongovernmental organizations, giving information on structure and activities. Volume 2 is the *Geographic Volume* ($168.00). Volume 3 is the *Subject Volume* ($116.00). Classifies organizations by subject and region.

U.S. GOVERNMENT PUBLICATIONS

The U.S. government is one of the world's most prolific publishers. Besides administrative publications that are of interest to the general public, such as the *Congressional Record* and congressional committee hearings, the federal government publishes books, pamphlets, and periodicals on agriculture, science, U.S. history, world affairs, health, business and finance, consumer protection, etc. The availability of these publications is made known through a variety of price lists and catalogs and through U.S. Government Printing Office bookstores located in a number of major cities in the United States. Many academic and public libraries throughout the United States that have been designated as Depository Libraries maintain a collection of federal publications and provide access to this material to the general public. Some older libraries hold large historical collections of federal documents in their original paper form; others have supplemented their holdings by purchase of the microform reprints mentioned below. The principal catalog of U.S. government publications is the *Monthly Catalog of U.S. Government Publications*, which is described below.

American Statistics Index. 1974–to date. Congressional Information Service subscription to annual cumulation and monthly supplements sold on a service basis. All annual volumes are in print at various prices. Detailed subject, name, title, and report-number indexing of nearly all statistical publications of the U.S. government. The 1974 annual and retrospective edition attempted to cover all federally produced statistical data in print and the most significant publications since the early 1960s, including the 1970 census. The *Index* correlates to a separate Abstract section, giving content, organization, currency, and source of the publications. A complete set of the full text of the publications indexed is available on microfiche from CIS.

Ames, John G. *Comprehensive Index to the Publications of the United States Government 1881–1893*. Johnson Repr. 2 vols. repr. of 1905 ed. 1971 $140.00. An alphabetical subject list, chiefly of congressional publications. Gives author, title or brief description, and report, document, and associated bill numbers. There is a separate personal name index, including members of Congress.

Boyd, Anne M., and Rae E. Rips. *United States Government Publications*. 1949. Wilson 3d ed. rev. 1952 o.p. Detailed guide to U.S. government publications. Still useful although largely superseded by Morehead, and Schmeckebier and Eastin.

Checklist of United States Public Documents 1789–1909. Kraus 3d ed. rev. & enl. repr. of 1911 ed. Section 1 is the schedule of volumes of the *American State Papers* and of congressional publications for the period 1817–1909 in serial-set volume order. Section 2 lists departmental publications in superintendent of documents number order.

CIS Congressional Committee Hearings Index. Congressional Information Service 8 parts 1833–1969 $11,745.00. Index by title, subject, organization, personal name, and bill, report, or document number to more than 30,000 congressional hearings from 1833 to 1969, when the *CIS/Index* began publication. The hearings are available on microfiche from CIS and are also held in many large research libraries.

CIS/Index and CIS Annual. 1970–to date. Congressional Information Service subscription to monthly issues and two-volume annual cumulation sold on a service basis. Annual and four-year cumulations are in print. Since 1970, the major catalog and index of congressional publications. Attempts to catalog, abstract, and exhaustively index all publications of Congress (except the *Congressional Record* and bills). Reports, documents, hearings and testimony, and committee prints are thoroughly covered. Includes legislative histories of public laws, with references to related hearings and reports. Indexes by subject, name (author, witness, etc.), bill, report, and document number. All congressional publications covered in the *CIS/Index* are available on microfiche from CIS. Most are also available in depository and large research libraries.

CIS U.S. Serial Set Index. Congressional Information Service 36 vols. ea. $520.00. Subject and keyword index to the *American State Papers* and the U.S. serial set of congressional reports and documents. The serial set (available from CIS on microfiche for more than $160,000 but also held by many large libraries in its original form) contains more than 11 million pages of information published between 1789 and 1969 and includes most significant federal publications through the early part of the twentieth century.

Congressional Index. 1935–to date. Commerce Clearing House annual subscription to weekly loose-leaf service $524.70. Subject and sponsor indexing to all pending legislation, with brief summaries and legislative histories.

Documents Catalog. 1894–1940. U.S. Government Printing Office 25 vols. o.p. Issued biennially, and discontinued with the volume covering 1939–40. This catalog is arranged by subjects, personal authors, and government authors. Replaced for the years since 1940 by the expanded *Monthly Catalog of U.S. Government Publications.*

Goehlert, Robert U., and Fenton S. Martin. *The Presidency: A Research Guide.* ABC-Clio 1984 lib. bdg. $28.50. "A comprehensive research guide describing all of the primary and secondary resources available to students and researchers on the subject of the U.S. Presidency" (Publisher's catalog).

Index to United States Government Periodicals. 1973–to date. Infordata annual subscription $275.00. Subject index to periodicals published by U.S. government departments and agencies.

Leidy, W. Philip. *A Popular Guide to Government Publications.* Columbia Univ. Pr. 4th ed. 1976 $40.00. A selected list of publications arranged under subject headings. Each entry includes complete bibliographic information. "There's a vast bibliographical maze in Washington, and one of the few ways to solve it is to follow the thread unreeled by W. Philip Leidy" (David Glixon, *SR*).

McIlvaine, Betsy. *A Consumers', Researchers', and Students' Guide to Government Publications.* Wilson 1983 pap. $8.00. "Three sections explain: What government publications are, why they are useful, and where they can be found. How to find and use indexes that direct you to government publications. How to locate information on such topics as education, law, statistics, science, technology, history, business, and consumer affairs" (Publisher's catalog).

Monthly Catalog of U.S. Government Publications. 1895–to date. U.S. Government Printing Office annual subscription $217.00. The most comprehensive index to U.S. government publications issued by all government departments and the Congress. Author, title, title keyword, subject, series/report, and classification number indexes. The *Cumulative Subject Index to the Monthly Catalog of U.S. Government Publications, 1900–1970* is available in 15 volumes from Research Publications for $1,260.00.

Morehead, Joe. *Introduction to United States Public Documents. Lib. Science Text Ser.*

Libraries Unlimited 3d ed. 1983 lib. bdg. $28.50 pap. $19.50. General introduction to the nature and use of federal documents, including major indexing tools.

Poore, Benjamin Perley. *Poore's Descriptive Catalogue of the Government Publications of the United States, Sept. 5, 1774–March 4, 1881.* Johnson Repr. 2 vols. repr. of 1885 ed. $145.00. The first and only attempt to list completely all government publications. Entries are arranged chronologically and are annotated.

Schmeckebier, Laurence F., and Roy B. Eastin. *Government Publications and Their Use.* Brookings rev. ed. 1969 o.p. For many years the standard guide to U.S. government publications. Still useful although superseded by Morehead.

U.S. Library of Congress Serial and Government Publications Division. *Popular Names of U.S. Government Reports.* U.S. Government Printing Office 4th ed. 1984 $12.00. Index to the official names of reports generally known by a popular name, such as the "Watergate Report" or the "Kefauver Report." Subject index.

DATES AND FACTS

For quick facts and dates, the reader should consult almanacs, encyclopedias, biographical dictionaries, statistical yearbooks, and similar reference tools. The value of these works in supplying this kind of information depends on the quality of their organization and indexing. The titles listed below are a selection from the many works in all fields that are devoted to particular kinds of factual information.

American Book of Days. Ed. by Jane M. Hatch, Wilson 3d ed. 1978 $64.00. "Presents more than 700 articles that explore, day by day, our nation's history through the lives of distinguished citizens, anniversaries of great events, religious and secular holidays, and various celebrations connected with sports, commerce, and local customs. The book describes each occasion in detail, from its origin to the present day . . . ." (Publisher's catalog).

The Book of Calendars. Ed. by Frank Parise, Facts on File 1982 $29.95. Explanation and conversion tables for 40 calendars used in ancient and modern times.

The Book of Lists #3. Ed. by David Wallechinsky, Irving Wallace, and Amy Wallace, Morrow 1983 $15.95. Lists of everything, such as fungi that changed history, notable marriage proposals, winners of the Golden Fleece Award, and strange deaths.

de Ford, Miriam Allen, and Joan S. Jackson. *Who Was When? A Dictionary of Contemporaries.* Wilson 3d ed. 1976 $38.00. A chronologically arranged list of the birth and death dates of 10,000 important figures in history. Index of names, with birth and death dates.

Diggs, Ellen Irene. *Black Chronology: From 4,000 B.C. to the Abolition of the Slave Trade.* G. K. Hall 1983 lib. bdg. $39.50. "Every source is cited in the text and referenced in an extensive bibliography" (Publisher's catalog). Proper name index.

Facts on File. 1940–to date. Facts on File annual subscription to weekly loose-leaf news service $400.00. Individual yearbooks from 1941 through 1983 are available at $85.00 per vol. Summarizes current events around the world. Indexes cumulate throughout the year. Five-year indexes from 1946 to 1980 are available for $85.00 each. No sources of information are given.

The Guinness Book of World Records. 1955–to date. Ed. by David A. Boehm, Sterling rev. ed. 1981 $12.95

Holidays and Anniversaries of the World. Ed. by Laurence Urdang and Christine N.

Donohue, Gale 1985 $74.00. Holidays, anniversaries, holy days, birthdays of famous persons, significant dates in history, and special events are listed for each month and day of the year. Detailed index.

Kane, Joseph Nathan. *Facts about the Presidents*. Wilson 4th ed. 1981 $30.00. A chapter for each president includes data about their lives, families, careers, and administrations. Much comparative data.

———. *Famous First Facts*. Wilson 4th ed. 1981 $70.00. "Lists more than 9,000 inventions, discoveries, and first happenings that took place on the American continent from 1007 to the present" (Publisher's catalog). Alphabetical subject arrangement with cross-references and indexes by year, month, and day, personal names, and state and municipality.

Kurian, George Thomas. *The New Book of World Rankings*. Facts on File 1984 $29.95. Ranks more than 150 countries in more than 300 categories, including climate, defense, crime, politics, etc.

Leonard, Thomas M. *Day by Day: The 40's*. Facts on File 1977 $75.00. Major events day by day for the ten-year period. Detailed index.

Merritt, Jeffrey. *Day by Day: The 50's*. Facts on File. 1979 $75.00. Major events day by day for the ten-year period. Detailed index.

Parker, Thomas, and Douglas Nelson. *Day by Day: The 60's*. Facts on File 2 vols. 1983 $90.00. Major events day by day for the ten-year period. Detailed index.

Twentieth Century American Nicknames. Ed. by Laurence Urdang, comp. by Walter C. Kidney and George C. Kohn, Wilson 1979 $23.00. Lists 4,000 nicknames for persons, places, events, and things. Nicknames and proper names are listed in one alphabet with see references. Gives full identification and birth and death dates.

Wallechinsky, David. *The Complete Book of the Olympics*. Penguin 1984 pap. $10.95. All the records from 1896 to 1980.

Walter, Claire. *Winners: The Blue Ribbon Encyclopedia of Awards*. Facts on File rev. ed. 1982 $39.95. Winners in all fields of endeavor, emphasizing major U.S. awards with some important foreign awards. Excludes hall-of-fame lists.

YEARBOOKS AND ALMANACS

Organizations and associations frequently issue yearbooks summarizing their activities, and most of the current encyclopedias also publish yearbooks. The following is a selection of yearbooks and almanacs of general and historical use. Many others concerned with particular fields are included in appropriate chapters.

The Almanac of American Politics. 1972–to date. Ed. by Michael Barone and Grant Ujifusi, Dutton 1984 ed. $35.00 pap. $22.50. Information about senators and representatives and their districts, including major votes and ratings by interest groups.

Almanacs of the United States. Comp. by Milton Drake, Scarecrow Pr. 2 vols. 1962 o.p. This checklist of 14,300 entries includes almanacs and calendars published from 1639 on, arranged geographically by state, then chronologically by year of publication.

The American Jewish Yearbook. 1899–to date. Ed. by David Singer and Milton Himmelfarb, Jewish Publication Society annual $23.50. Published since 1899 and issued by the office of the American Jewish Committee since 1909, it contains an almanac, statistical and directory material, and special articles on contemporary issues.

The Annual Register 1984: A Record of World Events (Annual Register: A Review of Public Events at Home and Abroad). 1758–to date. Ed. by H. V. Hodson, Gale annual 1985 $90.00. "Articles written by distinguished contributors chronicle the leading events of the year concerning every country, the UN and other international organizations, social and economic trends, and major developments in all fields. Statistics, text of important documents, a chronology of events, charts and photographs add to the work's reference value" (Publisher's catalog).

Britain: An Official Handbook. 1948–to date. Prepared by the Great Britain Central Office of Information, London, British Information Services 1984 $20.50. "An excellent handbook . . . it is a factual account of the administration and national economy of the United Kingdom" (*LJ*).

Britannica Book of the Year. 1983–to date. Encyclopaedia Britannica. $21.95

Canadian Almanac and Directory 1985. 1847–to date. Ed. by Susan Bracken, Gale annual 1985 $64.00. Contains legal, commercial, statistical, governmental, ecclesiastical, educational, financial, and general information. Directory sections provide names and addresses of many organizations and companies.

Catholic Almanac 1985: An Annual. Ed. by Felician Foy and Rose M. Avato, Our Sunday Visitor 1984 $13.95

CQ Almanac. 1945–to date. Congressional Quarterly annual 1984 ed. $135.00. Topical presentation of the activities of the U.S. Congress for the year. Reorganizes and indexes the material that appears in the *CQ Weekly Report.*

Europa Yearbook. 1926–to date. Europa 2 vols. 25th ed. 1984 $210.00 vol. 1 *International Organizations and Europe including the U.S.S.R. and Turkey* vol. 2 *Africa, the Americas, Asia and Australasia.* This survey and directory provides economic and statistical data as well as details on the constitution, government, political parties, legal system, and education in each country. A directory section for each country lists major newspapers and periodicals, publishers, radio and television stations, banks, insurance companies, chambers of commerce, trade associations and unions, transport companies, learned societies, research institutes, libraries, museums, and universities. Major international organizations, their organization and purpose, are described in detail.

Facts on File Yearbooks. 1941–to date. Facts on File annual 1984 $85.00. All previous annual volumes in print at various prices. Republication in a single bound volume, with a cumulative index, of the 52 weekly issues of *Facts on File Weekly News Reference Service,* an indexed weekly news summary of 20–30 pages.

Information Please Almanac. 1947–to date. Ed. by Dan Golenpaul Associates, Simon & Schuster 1985 pap. $5.95

Middle East and North Africa: Survey and Directory of Lands of Middle East and North Africa. 1948–to date. Europa 31st ed. 1984 $120.00. Similar to *Europa Yearbook;* includes a who's who section.

The Negro Almanac: A Reference Work on the Afro-American. Ed. by Harry Ploski and James Williams, Wiley 4th ed. 1983 $79.95

The Old Farmer's Almanac. 1792–to date. Ed. by Rob Trowbridge and Judson Hale, Yankee Bks. 1984 pap. $1.75. This little publication, "established in 1792 by Robert B. Thomas," has delighted New Englanders for its 183 years of continuous publication, in the same format.

Reader's Digest Almanac and Yearbook, 1985. 1966–to date. Ed. by David C. Whitney, Random 1984 $7.50

Statesman's Yearbook: Statistical and Historical Annual of the States of the World.

1864–to date. Ed. by John Paxton, St. Martin's annual 120th ed. 1985 $37.50. Includes information on individual countries and international organizations.

United Nations, Statistical Office. *Statistical Yearbook.* 1946–to date. United Nations annual $65.00 pap. $55.00. Summary volume of the interrelated series of statistical reports published by the United Nations and its specialized agencies, which include *Demographic Yearbook, UNESCO, Statistical Yearbook,* etc.

U.S. Bureau of the Census. *Statistical Abstract of the United States.* 1878–to date. U.S. Government Printing Office annual $23.00. Standard summary of statistics on the social, political, and economic condition of the United States. Introductory texts to each major division (such as population, education, income, energy, etc.) and the source notes appearing below each statistical table serve as guides to additional sources. Detailed subject index.

Weather Almanac. Ed. by James A. Ruffner and Frank E. Bair, Gale 4th ed. 1984 $100.00. Climatic data for the United States for the period 1951–80.

Whitaker's Almanac 1986. 1869–to date. Gale 118th ed. 1985 $50.00. "Noted for its accuracy and detachment in covering the events and personalities that affect the entire world, *Whitaker's* is especially useful for its detailed reporting of current events and social, political, and economic developments in Great Britain" (Publisher's catalog).

World Almanac and Book of Facts. 1868–to date. Ed. by Hana Umlauf Lane, World Almanac 1984 pap. $12.95. Published without interruption since 1868. Strongest in its record of the United States.

World of Learning 1986. 1950–to date. Gale 36th ed. 1986 $165.00. "A comprehensive, up-to-date directory of educational, cultural, and scientific resources all over the globe" (Publisher's catalog).

The Yearbook of the United Nations. 1946–to date. International Publications vol. 35 1981 $72.00. Earlier volumes available from various publishers. Annual summary of U.N. activities throughout the world. Publication delay averages three years.

Yearbook of World Affairs. 1947–to date. Ed. by G. W. Keeton and G. Schwartzenberger, West View Pr. 1984 lib. bdg. $29.00. This annual contains information about and interpretation of world problems by eminent specialists. The Reports on World Affairs section contains reviews of books on economics, geography, institutions, law, literature, psychology, sociology, and strategy.

ATLASES AND GAZETTEERS

A great many general and special-purpose atlases are available in print. By far, the best way to judge how well any one of these meets the needs of a home, school, or office is by personal examination. (Kenneth F.) *Kister's Atlas Buying Guide: General English-Language World Atlases Available in North America* provides a 20-page guide to the process of evaluating an atlas, as well as evaluations of 105 English-language general world atlases, including references to reviews. Gerard L. Alexander's *Guide to Atlases—World, Regional, National, Thematic: An International Listing of Atlases Published since 1950* and *Guide to Atlases Supplement* list a large number of atlases of all kinds. Kenneth L. Winch's *International Maps and Atlases in Print* contains more than 8,000 detailed entries for maps and atlases available from 700 publishing firms. Ronald E. Grim's *Historical Geography of the United*

States: A Guide to Information Sources is an annotated bibliography of 688 cartographic sources, books, and articles on this topic. Historical and other special-purpose atlases are described in appropriate chapters in the *Reader's Adviser.*

Atlases

Bartholomew World Atlas. John Bartholomew rev. ed. 1982 $35.00. A medium-sized world atlas containing 112 pages of color maps. Coverage is weighted in favor of the United Kingdom.

Commercial Atlas and Marketing Guide. Rand McNally annual 115th ed. 1984 $175.00. Includes regional and state maps for the United States, including special social and economic maps. A large index-gazetteer gives estimated current population and such basic information for places as elevation and the presence of post office, railroad, and banking facilities. General social and economic statistics are given for each state.

Goode's World Atlas. Ed. by Edward B. Epenshade, Jr., Rand McNally text ed. 16th ed. 1982 $19.95 pap. $15.95. A best-selling desk-sized world atlas.

Hammond Ambassador World Atlas. Ed. by Martin A. Bacheller, Hammond new census rev. ed. 1984 $34.95. A large general atlas with 320 pages of color maps and 101,000 index entries. Of the 415 maps, 40 percent are devoted to the United States. Format is 9¾ by 12½ inches.

Hammond Medallion World Atlas. Ed. by Martin A. Bacheller, Hammond new census rev. ed. 1984 $60.00. Hammond's largest general world atlas, with 461 pages of color maps emphasizing political features and a large index with more than 100,000 entries. Format is 9¼ by 12½ inches. North America is better covered than other world regions. Separate sections on the Bible lands, world history, and the history of the United States.

Maps on File. Ed. by Lester A. Sobel, Facts on File loose leaf $145.00 annual update $35.00. An 8½-by-11-inch loose-leaf collection of more than 350 black-and-white outline maps on heavy paper, covering the world's countries and regions and special topics. The maps are intended to photocopy well, for inclusion in papers and reports.

National Geographic Atlas of the World. Ed. by Alice J. Hall, National Geographic Society 5th ed. 1981 $47.20. A large general world atlas with 200 pages of color maps emphasizing political features and an index with more than 155,000 entries. Large format of 12½ by 18½ inches.

New International Atlas. Rand McNally 1981 $100.00. A large general atlas, 11¼ by 15 inches, with 319 pages of color maps and 160,000 index entries. All world regions are evenly represented and place names are given in local languages.

New York Times Atlas of the World. Harper 2d ed. rev. 1983 $49.95. A medium-sized version of the *Times Atlas of the World,* with 147 pages of color maps and 90,000 index entries in 11-by-15-inch format.

Prentice-Hall's Great International Atlas. Prentice-Hall 1981 $69.00. A medium-sized general atlas with 159 pages of color maps and 55,000 index entries in 11½-by-14¼-inch format, it contains considerable geographical, historical, and statistical information in addition to maps.

Rand McNally Cosmopolitan World Atlas. Rand McNally new census ed. 1981 $45.00 A medium-sized general atlɔɔ with 180 pages of color maps and 82,000 index entries in 11½-by-14¾-inch format. North America receives 50 percent of the map pages.

Rand McNally Road Atlas: United States, Canada, Mexico. Rand McNally 1984 $8.95 pap. $5.95. The standard road atlas, it provides the necessary information for automobile touring.

Soviet World Atlas in English. Ed. by A. N. Baranov, Telberg Bk. 2d ed. 1967 $158.00. A large general world atlas with 250 pages of color maps and 215,000 index entries in a separately published index-gazetteer. Highly regarded by cartographic specialists.

Times Atlas of the World. Harper 2d ed. rev. 1983 $139.95. Based on the five-volume *London Times Atlas* published in the 1950s, this is one of the largest world atlases, with 244 pages of color maps and 210,000 index entries in 12¼-by-18-inch format. "Atlas critics are in general agreement that the Comprehensive Edition of the *Times Atlas* [1980] is the best in the land bar none" (Kenneth F. Kister, *Kister's Atlas Buying Guide*).

U.S. Department of the Interior, Geology Survey. *The National Atlas of the United States of America.* 1970 o.p. The major atlas of the United States, with 335 pages of color maps. Includes political, climatic, vegetation, agricultural, population, social, economic, and historical maps. The index-gazetteer gives page references and latitude and longitude.

Weather Atlas of the United States. Gale 1975 $88.00. Originally published by the U.S. Government Printing Office as *Climatic Atlas of the United States.* Contains 272 climatic maps of the United States, showing temperature, precipitation, wind, sunshine, and other climatic elements.

Gazetteers

Most atlases include indexes of place names and physical features, in some cases giving latitude and longitude and other information. A number of separately published gazetteers give more descriptive information about world places and geography.

Columbia-Lippincott Gazetteer of the World, with 1961 Supplement. Ed. by Leon E. Seltzer, Columbia Univ. Pr. 1952 $200.00. A very large gazetteer including brief information on many place names. Its age puts a limitation on its usefulness.

Forster, Klaus. *Pronouncing Dictionary of English Place Names, Including Standard Local and Archaic Variants.* Routledge & Kegan 1981 $30.00. Gives standard and local pronunciation from various published sources for more than 12,000 British places and geographical features, for example, Cholmondeley, pronounced "Chumley."

Merriam-Webster Editorial Staff. *Webster's New Geographical Dictionary.* Merriam-Webster rev. ed. 1984 $17.50

Room, Adrian. *Place-Name Changes since Nineteen Hundred: A World Gazetteer.* Scarecrow Pr. 1979 $16.00. Excludes changes resulting from administrative change and merger, where the new territory does not correspond with the old.

QUOTATIONS

Books of quotations are to be judged by their content and indexes. The four kinds of indexes are author, straight quotation, concordance, and topical. The author index is common to all. The straight quotation index gives the first word of the quotation just as it occurs in the text. A concordance indexes the principal words in the quotation. For instance, "All that glitters is not gold," in a straight quotation index, will be found under "All"; in a concordance index, it will be found under "gold" and "glitter." A topical index lists under general headings all quotations that bear on that particular subject. The quotation "All that glitters is not gold" might be found under the topic "Appearance." The purpose of a topical index is to suggest quotations on various topics. The collections listed below are among the larger and better known, although there are many others. Most overlap to some degree; none is complete, and the one quote you need will be in the last place you look.

Adler, Mortimer J., and Charles Van Doren. *The Great Treasury of Western Thought: A Compendium of Important Statements on Man and His Institutions by the Great Thinkers in Western History.* Bowker 1977 $37.50 Contains more than 8,000 quotations from Homer to Freud. Author and keyword indexes.

Allibone, Samuel A. *Prose Quotations from Socrates to Macauley.* Gale repr. of 1876 ed. 1973 $37.00

Allusions—Cultural, Literary, Biblical, and Historical: A Thematic Dictionary. Ed. by Laurence Urdang and Frederick G. Ruffner, Jr., Gale 1982 $60.00. "More than 7,000 literary, biblical, and cultural allusions and metaphors are identified in this dictionary. Entries are arranged alphabetically under 628 thematic headings. More than 1,000 biblical, literary, folklore, and other sources of allusions were consulted, with most of them being listed in the dictionary's extensive bibliography. Index" (Publisher's catalog).

Bartlett, John. *Bartlett's Familiar Quotations: Fifteenth & 125th Anniversary Edition.* Little, Brown rev. & enl. ed. 1980 $29.45. John Bartlett (1820–1905), a bookseller in Cambridge, Massachusetts, and partner of Little, Brown, compiled two famous books of reference: *A Complete Concordance to Shakespeare* (1894) and *Familiar Quotations* (1855). Bartlett lived to be 85 and brought out nine editions of his earlier book, enlarging it from 295 pages to 1,158. The present edition has 936 pages of quotations. Some quotations have been dropped, and sayings from non-Western cultures have been added as well as quotations from persons previously overlooked: Chekhov, Brandeis, Flaubert, Freud, Jung, and others. The subject-matter index, prepared with the aid of a computer, now runs to almost 600 pages.

Cohen, J. M., and M. J. Cohen. *The Penguin Dictionary of Modern Quotations.* rev. ed. 1981 pap. $5.95. Arranged by author, with keyword index.

Collison, Robert, and Mary Collison. *Dictionary of Foreign Quotations* Dodd 1982 pap. $11.95 Some 6,000 quotations in both the original language and English translation.

The Concise Oxford Dictionary of Quotations. Oxford new ed. 1981 pap. $8.95

Edelhart, Mike, and James Tinen. *America the Quotable.* Facts on File 1983 $29.95. Some 7,000 quotations about the United States, its cities, states, and landmarks. Topical and geographical arrangements.

Evans, Bergen. *Dictionary of Quotations.* Dell 1968 o.p. "[A] reference book which keeps the best from the past while utilizing choice items from the present. Thousands of familiar quotations, with the addition of many other new, contemporary, bright sayings chosen for wit as well as wisdom, and about 2,000 illuminating and amusing comments (set in italics) by the humorist and word specialist, Bergen Evans. His remarks make this book a gem and a delight for the browser. A very broad and thorough subject index [locates] and cross-indexes each quotation under each of its key words and under [general subjects]. In addition, a topical index suggests related headings under each subject. The book has more than 2,100 pages. The [more than 18,000] quotations take up 791 pages, double-column" (*PW*).

International Encyclopedia of Quotations. Doubleday rev. ed. 1978 $14.95

King, W. Francis H., comp. *Classical and Foreign Quotations: A Manual of Historical and Literary Quotations, Proverbs, and Popular Sayings*. Ungar 3d ed. repr. of 1904 $18.00. Includes 3,142 quotations with English translations and expository comments by the compiler. Author and subject indexes.

Magill, Frank N., ed. *Magill's Quotations in Context: First Series*. Salem Pr. 2 vols. 1966 $60.00. *Second Series*. 2 vols. 1966 $60.00. Familiar sayings, important passages from esteemed works, and proverbs are given in a few paragraphs of their original context with commentary. The first series has 2,020 entries, the second, 1,500.

Mencken, H. L., ed. *A New Dictionary of Quotations on Historical Principles from Ancient and Modern Sources*. Knopf 1942 $35.00. Arranged by subject in a single alphabet, this collection includes some quotations from the 1930s and a few from the 1940s, but they are mainly from the eighteenth and early nineteenth centuries. Of interest as a browsing volume, reflecting the compiler's vigorous individuality. No index.

Mottoes. Ed. by Laurence Urdang and Celia Dame Robbins, Gale 1985 $75.00. Some 9,000 mottoes of individuals, families, and institutions. Arranged by theme, with indexes by motto and person or organization.

The Oxford Dictionary of Quotations. Oxford 3d ed. 1979 $39.95. Arranged alphabetically by author and indexed by key word. Exact reference to source is given. More than 7,000 index entries.

Palmer, Alan, comp. *Quotations in History: A Dictionary of Historical Quotations— c.800 A.D. to the Present*. Barnes & Noble 1976 $22.50

Partnow, Elaine. *The Quotable Woman, 1800–1981*. Facts on File $29.95. More than 8,000 quotations on every subject from 1,500 women. Chronological arrangement; name and subject indexes.

Pater, Alan F., and Jason R. Pater, eds. *What They Said in 1981: The Yearbook of Spoken Opinion*. Monitor annual vol. 13 ($27.50). Quotations are documented with date, place, and circumstance information.

Picturesque Expressions: A Thematic Dictionary. Ed. by Walter W. Hunsinger, Gale 2d ed. 1985 $75.00. More than 7,000 picturesque expressions like "hands down" are topically arranged, with explanation, date of origin, and illustrative quotations.

Seldes, George. *The Greatest Quotations*. Citadel Pr. 1983 pap. $12.00

Slogans. Ed. by Laurence Urdang and Celia Dame Robbins, Gale 1984 $72.00. Some 6,000 slogans from the fields of advertising, politics, etc., topically arranged and giving origin and use. Index.

Stevenson, Burton Egbert. *Home Book of Quotations: Classical and Modern*. 1967. Dodd 10th ed. 1984 $39.45. Includes more than 73,000 quotations from 4,700 authors. The concordance index has more than 100,000 entries. Quotations are grouped under such subjects as love, government, religion, and law, making the index indispensable. The work is particularly strong in U.S. political quotations, campaign slogans, new coinages, and catchlines from popular songs.

Tripp, Rhoda Thomas, ed. *The International Thesaurus of Quotations*. Crowell 1970 $15.34. Topical arrangement. Author and keyword indexes.

PROVERBS AND MAXIMS

Many books of proverbs are available in print; many others no longer in print are held in library collections. A large number of these works are devoted to the proverbs of a particular people or civilization or in a particular language. Only a few of the more general English-language collections are listed in this section.

The Concise Oxford Dictionary of Proverbs. Ed. by J. A. Simpson, Oxford 1983 $16.95. Based on the *Oxford Dictionary of English Proverbs*, it includes only proverbs in common use in Great Britain today.

Fergusson, Rosalind, comp. *The Facts on File Dictionary of Proverbs.* Facts on File 1983 $21.95. Topical arrangement of 7,000 proverbs from all periods and nations. Comprehensive keyword index.

Hazlitt, William C. *English Proverbs & Proverbial Phrases.* Gale 1973 repr. of 1907 ed. o.p.

The Oxford Book of Aphorisms. Ed. by John Gross, Oxford 1983 $15.95. The entries are divided into 58 topical sections, such as nature, good and evil, and knowledge and ignorance. Author index, but no keyword index.

Whiting, Barbara J. *Early American Proverbs and Proverbial Phrases.* Harvard Univ. Pr. 1978 $30.00

Wilson, Frank P. *The Oxford Dictionary of English Proverbs.* Oxford 3d ed. 1970 $35.00

WRITING GUIDES

For works on grammar and usage, dictionaries, thesauri, and other "word" books, see Chapter 3 of Volume 1. Many books currently in print offer guidance in writing for publication.

Barzun, Jacques. *Simple and Direct: A Rhetoric for Writers.* Harper rev. ed. 1984 $15.00 pap. $6.98

The Chicago Manual of Style. Univ. of Chicago Pr. 13th ed. rev. & enl. 1982 $30.00. The standard style manual at many publishing houses and universities. Includes sections on new technology in the publishing and editing process, copyright law, manuscript preparation and script editing, and many examples of documentation (footnotes, bibliography, notes, etc.).

Crews, Frederick B. *The Random House Handbook.* Random text ed. 3d ed. 1983 $15.95. Covers grammar, usage, punctuation, documentation, and the process of composition.

Directory of Publishing Opportunities in Journals and Periodicals. Marquis 5th ed. 1981 $52.50. Information useful to contributing authors on 4,000 specialized and professional journals.

Flesch, Rudolf, and A. H. Lass. *A New Guide to Better Writing.* Warner Bks. 1982 pap. $3.50

Gibaldi, Joseph, and Walter S. Achtert. *MLA Handbook for Writers of Research Papers.* MLA text ed. 2d ed. 1984 pap. $7.50

Harbrace College Handbook. Ed. by John C. Hodges and Mary E. Whitten, Harcourt text ed. 1984 $12.95. Standard college handbook for composition.

Johnston, Donald. *Copyright Handbook.* Bowker 2d ed. 1982 $27.50. A guide to the Copyright Law of 1976 and its revisions.

Leggett, Glenn, et al. *Prentice-Hall Handbook for Writers.* Prentice-Hall 8th ed. 1982 $12.50

Literary Market Place 1986: The Directory of American Book Publishing. Bowker annual pap. $59.95. Editorial addresses, phone numbers, key personnel, publications specialties, number of titles published annually, imprints, etc., for 2,000 U.S. and Canadian publishers. Separate alphabetical "yellow pages" of 25,000 key people in book publishing.

Longyear, Marie. *The McGraw-Hill Style Manual: Concise Guide for Writers and Editors.* McGraw-Hill 1982 $24.95

Reynolds, Paul R. *The Writing and Selling of Fiction.* Morrow rev. ed. 1980 $9.95 pap. $4.95

Sears, Donald A. *Harbrace Guide to the Library and the Research Paper.* Harcourt text ed. 4th ed. 1984 pap. $6.95

Skillin, Marjorie E., and Robert M. Gay. *Words into Type.* Prentice-Hall 3d ed. 1974 $26.95. Longest of the references most favored by book editors.

Strunk, William, Jr., and E. B. White. *Elements of Style: With Index.* 1918. Macmillan text ed. 3d ed. 1979 pap. Concise guide for those who wish to use English style with simplicity and grace. "Distinguished by brevity, clarity, and prickly good sense, it is, unlike most such manuals, a book as well as a tool" (*New Yorker*).

Turabian, Kate L. *A Manual for Writers of Term Papers, Theses, and Dissertations.* Univ. of Chicago Pr. 4th ed. 1973 $14.00 pap. $4.95. Widely used by college students.

Writer's Market. B. Klein 1984 ed. $25.00

CHAPTER 2

Dictionaries

Sally M. Roberts

No dictionary of a living tongue can ever be perfect, since while it is has-
tened to publication, some words are budding, and some falling away.
—SAMUEL JOHNSON, 1755

A language is a living and dynamic entity, constantly changing to reflect the culture of those who use it. Dictionaries attempt to reflect language, its usage, grammar, pronunciation, and idiomatic expressions. They document the current use of a language and often try to offer a historical perspective, in terms of established rules and conventions, for what is current practice. Dictionaries therefore can be descriptive, reflecting the actual use; or pre-scriptive, setting out and upholding the rules for "correct" or established use. But since it is the inherent nature of language to be fluid and ever-changing, no dictionary is ever complete or entirely current.

Although the Greeks and Romans had lists of words, and there were glos-saries compiled in the Middle Ages, dictionaries are a relatively modern in-vention. Some of the dictionaries published in the seventeenth and eigh-teenth centuries have very little in the way of authority or etymology, and the definitions are very elementary by today's standards.

Dictionaries have a place in the lives of all literate people. They are con-sulted for usage, meaning, spelling, history, and sometimes because they can be interesting and entertaining reading in their own right. The numbers and kinds of dictionaries published reflect the varying needs of those who use them. A large unabridged dictionary such as *Webster's Third Interna-tional* is indispensable for a library; the many desk and pocket dictionaries in the home, or on the desks of businesspeople, students, and travelers are there to serve basic needs and the requirements of portability.

Dictionaries in English alone have been published in ever-increasing num-bers and endless variations. Certainly there is a dictionary for nearly every taste and need, and to suit every budget, for the tendency is to package books about words in a number of formats to appeal to the consumer. One cannot buy one dictionary in a lifetime and be satisfied, even if it's the *Ox-ford English Dictionary*, for updates, supplements, and new editions abound, and revisions include not only new words but new meanings and shades of meaning, combinations and idiomatic expressions, technical and scientific terms, or words borrowed from other languages. Dictionaries have become in many cases multipurpose reference books, containing a wealth of information beyond the definitions of words and how to use language. Maps, charts, gazetteers, tables of weights and measures, biographical appendixes, and illustrations are routinely included and add to the usefulness—not to mention marketability—of these volumes.

Choosing a dictionary is a personal decision that should be based on several factors. What kind of dictionary do you need for your purpose, and how comprehensive does it have to be? If you rely on it for general information, what kinds of additional material would you find most useful? Do you give a dictionary heavy use so that you need a hardbound volume, or will a paperback edition serve as well? If you are considering a foreign–English dictionary, check that it has a larger proportion of English words, since this is what is most often needed. Suit the dictionary to the use, so that you do not have to look through lists of historical use to find a simple definition, for example.

ENGLISH-LANGUAGE DICTIONARIES

The American College Dictionary. Ed. by Clarence L. Barnhart, Random 1959 o.p. A one-volume dictionary designed especially for use in schools, offices, and homes. Contains about 120,000 entries (including geographical names, foreign words and phrases, abbreviations, etc.) in one alphabetical list. The order of definitions for each entry is based on frequency of use as determined by the Thorndike-Lorge Semantic Count, with most commonly used meanings given first. Special emphasis on complete coverage of the fundamental words in each field of knowledge (chemistry, law, medicine, sociology, etc.). More than 1,700 pictures and diagrams, including 300 spot maps.

The American Heritage Desk Dictionary. Houghton Mifflin 1981 $9.95. A condensed version of the *American Heritage Dictionary*, with shorter etymologies and definitions.

The American Heritage Dictionary of the English Language. Ed. by William Morris, Houghton Mifflin 1973 thumb-indexed $9.95. "Continuously" though not greatly revised, this edition updates a standard and respected dictionary.

Barnhart, Clarence L., Sol Steinmetz, and Robert K. Barnhart, eds. *The Barnhart Dictionary of New English since 1963.* Harper 1973 $14.95. Giving meanings for common words in the order of the most commonly used sense, this covers about 5,000 words taken from books and periodicals between 1963 and 1972. Quotations show the use of the word, and sources are given.

Chambers Twentieth Century Dictionary. Ed. by A. M. MacDonald, Littlefield new ed. 1973 $7.95

The Concise Oxford Dictionary of Current English. Ed. by J. B. Sykes, Oxford 7th ed. 1982 $22.50 thumb-indexed $24.95. Based on the venerable *Oxford English Dictionary* and its supplements, the 40,000 main entries cover a number of new words and technical terms. This edition makes a distinction between American and British terms. The format is compact, the type is small, but it is a handy alternative to its parent.

Dictionary of American English on Historical Principles. Ed. by William A. Craigie and James R. Hulbert, Univ. of Chicago Pr. 2 vols. 1936–43 $300.00. This monumental work, begun in 1936, was compiled in 1943. The late Sir William Craigie directed the work. He was one of the editors of the *Oxford English Dictionary* and author of *A Dictionary of the Older Scottish Tongue.* The dictionary is modeled on the *Oxford English Dictionary* and has the like purpose of tracing each word to its entrance into the language and to its earliest users. It aims to present "those features by which the English of the American colonies and the United States is distinguished from that of England and the rest of the English-speaking world . . . including not only words or phrases which are clearly or apparently of American origin, or have greater currency here than elsewhere, but also every word denoting something which has a real connection with the development of the country and the history of its people. . . ." Neither slang nor dialect is included. This project won the Carey-Thomas Award in 1944 as the year's most distinguished example of good publishing.

A Dictionary of Americanisms on Historical Principles. Ed. by Mitford McLeod Mathews, Univ. of Chicago Pr. 3 vols. 1951 o.p. Narrower in scope than the *Dictionary of American English on Historical Principles,* this dictionary covers words and phrases that have made their first appearance in English in this country, words formerly in the language but having acquired new meanings in the United States, terms first used in this country but made up of older words, American nicknames, and slang expressions well entrenched in the language or having some historical significance.

Funk & Wagnalls Comprehensive Standard International Dictionary: Bicentennial Edition. Ferguson 1973 $49.95. This dictionary of approximately 175,000 entries "is designed to serve the practical and professional needs of all who speak or use the English language" (Foreword). Personal and geographical names are in the alphabetical list with other entries, and British, Australian, and Canadian terms, particularly, as well as some common foreign words, contribute to its international claim. Etymologies are concise. The supplementary sections are fairly standard. The editors and board are notable scholars and subject experts.

Funk & Wagnalls Standard College Dictionary. Crowell new ed. 1977 $9.95. Revision and update of the 1973 edition, in a compact and accessible format.

Funk & Wagnalls Standard Desk Dictionary. Harper 1984 pap. $8.61. At 100,000 entries it is 50,000 words smaller than the collegiate version, and its size makes it more convenient to use. Includes etymologies, excludes four-letter words, and is conservative in its preferences for usage. One of the four appendixes is a secretarial handbook.

Longman Dictionary of Contemporary English. Ed. by Paul Proctor, Longman text ed. 1979 $15.95 pap. $11.95. Anticipating their audience to be those for whom English is not the first language, the editors chose about 2,000 words as a " 'core' lexicon," which are the only prerequisite for understanding the clear and concise definitions.

Macmillan Dictionary. Ed. by William D. Halsey and others, Macmillan 1973 $5.79

The Merriam-Webster Dictionary. Pocket Bks. 1976 $1.95. Has about 57,000 entries and is based on the highly respected *Webster's Third.*

The Morrow Book of New Words: 8500 Terms Not Yet in Standard Dictionaries. Ed. by N. H. Mager and S. K. Mager, Morrow 1982 $13.50 pap. $6.25

The New Century Dictionary of the English Language. Ed. by H. G. Emery and K. G. Brewster, rev. by Catherine B. Avery, Appleton 2 vols. rev. ed. 1952 o.p. *The New Century Dictionary* is based on matter selected from the original *Century Dictionary* and entirely rewritten with the addition of new material, including new definitions and new illustrative material. The two-volume revision includes thousands of new words and new senses of words previously included, and 12,000 illustrative quotations. There are 4,000 illustrations, including color plates. Besides the dictionary of synonyms, acronyms, and discriminations, seven other supplements deal with abbreviations, foreign words and phrases, business terms, geographical, biographical, and miscellaneous place names, weights, and measures. The original *Century Dictionary and Cyclopedia*, whose editor was William Dwight Whitney, was published in 1889–91 in six volumes. The edition of 1909 was in 12 volumes, of which one was the *Cyclopedia of Names*, containing 55,000 proper names, and one the *Century Atlas*. With these supplementary volumes and its excellent pictorial illustrations, the old *Century* remains today the best example of the encyclopedic dictionary.

9,000 Words: A Supplement to Webster's Third New International Dictionary. Merriam-Webster 1983 $19.95. The latest supplement to *Webster's Third*, it is still useful as an independent tool for the 9,000 words that antedate 1960 or were never included in the *Third International*.

Oxford American Dictionary. Ed. by Eugene Ehrlich and others, Oxford 1980 $14.95. On the same pattern as *Oxford English Dictionary*, in an abridged version and strictly American, this sets the standard for American-English usage. It is abridged and does not contain etymologies, nor does it have any added sections of informational material.

The Oxford-Duden Pictorial English Dictionary. Ed. by John Pheby, Oxford 1981 $19.95. Particularly good for non-native speakers of English who are trying to identify common things in modern life.

Oxford English Dictionary: Being a Corrected Re-issue, with an Introduction, Supplement and Bibliography of a New English Dictionary on Historical Principles. Ed. by James A. H. Murray, Henry Bradley, William A. Craigie, and Charles T. Onions, Oxford 13 vols. 1933 $850.00 supplement (ed. by Robert W. Burchfield) 3 vols. 1972–82 ea. $125.00. (The supplement will be completed in four volumes.) This is a reprint of the original ten-volume work made from the same plates and printed on thinner paper. Typographic errors have been corrected and a supplementary volume added of additional material, including a list of books quoted in the principal work, which forms a bibliography of English literature. Volume 1 of the re-issue contains a historical introduction to the whole work by Sir William Craigie. The original *Oxford English Dictionary: A New English Dictionary on Historical Principles* (10 vols., published in 1898–1928) was begun in 1879 and was founded mainly on materials collected by the Philological Society as far back as 1857. The *Oxford* was planned to meet the need for a dictionary that would tell how long any word has been in the language, which of many senses of a word is the original, and when an obsolete word became obsolete. It was, therefore, designed as a supplement to all other dictionaries. It was to register all words and meanings omitted by others, and to give quotations illustrating the first and the last appearance of every word. The entire *OED* is now being computerized.

The Scribner-Bantam English Dictionary. Ed. by Edwin B. Williams and others, Scribner 1977 $8.95. Its 80,000 entries include proper names of people and places, current vocabulary and idioms, and straightforward, concise entries. It has extensive added information, of the almanac type, such as lists of colleges and tables of weights and measures.

The Second Barnhart Dictionary of New English. Ed. by Clarence L. Barnhart, Robert K. Barnhart and Sol Steinmetz, Harper 1980 $19.95. This dictionary, like its 1973 predecessor, contains newly coined words and new senses and meanings of words, many of which are not yet in most dictionaries. Some entries are encyclopedic.

The Shorter Oxford English Dictionary on Historical Principles. Ed. by William Little, Henry W. Fowler, and Jessie Coulson, rev. & ed. by Charles T. Onions, Oxford 2 vols. 3d ed. rev. & enl. 1973 $135.00 thumb-indexed $145.00. The 15,500 pages of the original work have here been compressed into 2,500 pages. This has been done largely by omitting quotations showing the use of words and using abbreviations extensively. The vocabulary of this *Shorter Oxford Dictionary* includes all words in regular literary and colloquial use with a selection of technical, archaic, and obsolete words. The selection of technical and obsolete words has been so numerous it has excluded words in current use. The *Shorter Oxford* is, like its parents, a dictionary of written rather than spoken English. There are no illustrations, no biographical entries, and few geographical ones. Lewis Gannett said: "I know of no better dictionary except the great *O.E.D.* itself" (*N.Y. Herald Tribune*).

A Supplement to the Oxford English Dictionary. Ed. by Robert W. Burchfield, Oxford 3 vols. 1972–82 ea. $125.00. *Oxford English Dictionary* continues with its supplements to make "a permanent record of the language of our time, the useful and the neutral, those that are decorous and well-informed, beside those that are controversial, tasteless or worse." Slang and offensive words or meanings are included, with many illustrative quotations. Each volume contains many new words and new meanings or status of words; the fourth and final volume is due out in 1985.

Webster's Illustrated Contemporary Dictionary. Ed. by Sidney I. Landau and others, Doubleday 1982 $12.95. Although not entirely new, this work emphasizes current vocabulary and usage. Notable is its inclusion of things Canadian, in both the word entries and the special sections.

Webster's New World Dictionary of the American Language, College Edition. Ed. by David B. Guralnik, Warner Bks. 1982 pap. $8.95. This dictionary, on which its staff of some 90 editors and consultants worked for more than ten years, was prepared "from an American point of view" and is intended primarily for American users. The one alphabet, which includes vocabulary, biographical, geographical, biblical, and classical names, abbreviations, foreign words and phrases, extensive synonyms and antonyms, contains 142,000 words. Many American slang terms, idioms and colloquialisms are included, and the definitions throughout are simple and rather informal, stressing American usage and making it unnecessary to look further to define the definitions. Recent scientific and political terms and figures such as "cortisone," "geriatrics," "cold war," "genocide," "Vishinsky," "F.M.," "flying saucer," and "napalm" are included. There are more than 1,200 illustrations.

Webster's New World Dictionary of the American Language. Ed. by David B. Guralnik, Warner Bks. 2d college ed. 1982 pap. $9.95. Updated edition of a standard favorite, comparable in many ways to the *American Heritage Dictionary*, but still censoring "vulgar" words. Includes the usual sections on colleges, weights and measures, etc. Later editions are biennial updates, adding new terms but only minor changes.

Webster's New World Quick Reference Dictionary: A New Format Printing of the "Handy Pocket Dictionary." Ed. by David B. Guralnik and others, World 1972 pap. $1.00

Webster's Ninth New Collegiate Dictionary. Merriam-Webster 9th ed. 1985 $14.95. Considered one of the best abridged dictionaries around, this edition has been extensively revised and updated, including the special sections. Sometimes faulted for a slowness to reflect change, it still includes many thousands of new terms and senses of definitions, and gives dates of first use of a sense. Of the added sections, the one of foreign words and phrases is particularly noteworthy.

Webster's Third New International Dictionary of the English Language Unabridged. Ed. by Philip Babcock Gove and others, Merriam-Webster 3d ed. 1961 $69.95. It is almost impossible in a brief space to relate the various opinions and objections expressed in the literary controversy that followed the publication of this edition. According to James Sledd, "Everyone knows that the *Third International* is an entirely new dictionary for use today. In this eighth member of a series which began in 1828, the Merriam Company has invested over $3,500,000, almost three times the cost of the 1934 *New International*, so that the statements in *Webster's Third* are backed by over a century of experience, by the evidence of more than 10,000,000 citations, and by the knowledge and skill of a large permanent staff and more than 200 special consultants. To a reviewer, these facts should be rather sobering" (*College English*).

Mario Pei wrote that "the new edition makes one startling innovation which has recommended itself to the attention of all reviewers and of the general public as well. It blurs to the point of obliteration the older distinction between standard, and substandard, colloquial, vulgar and slangy" (*SR*). This seems the basic criticism also voiced by Wilson Follett: "All of us may without brashness form summary judgments about the treatment of what belongs to all of us—the standard, staple, traditional language of general reading and speaking . . . in short, fundamental English. And it is precisely in this province that Webster III has thrust upon us a dismaying assortment of the questionable, the perverse, the unworthy, and the downright outrageous" (*Atlantic*). And in a long review, the *Library Journal* said: "Indispensable for its new (and revised old) material, deplorable for its whole-sale *abridgments*—as well as its obfuscations of the boundaries between prestige and non-prestige usages; this, regretfully, is our prefatory judgment . . . gone are the 'gazetteer,' the 'Biographical Dictionary,' 'Arbitrary Signs and Symbols,' and 'Abbreviations' ('Forms of Address' remain besides 'Abbreviations Used in This Dictionary'). . . . The deed is done, however, and to serve their users adequately most libraries will need to have both 2nd and 3rd editions." The second edition mentioned was that of 1934 compiled under the editorship of the late William Allan Neilson, a great Shakespeare scholar and president emeritus of Smith College. Most helpful to the understanding of the controversy is *Words, Words, and Words about Dictionaries* (o.p.), compiled and edited by Jack C. Gray. The first part of the book contains general discussions of words and dictionaries. "Section III reprints an editorial and three essays reacting to *Webster's Third New International Dictionary.* Sumner Ives and Mario Pei are both linguists, yet they take opposite views of the new dictionary. James Sledd's appraisal takes a middle position. The contention often pivots on the modern principles of linguistic study used in compiling the new dictionary rather than on the new dictionary itself." The documents of "the heated and bitter controversy over this work" were assembled by James Sledd and William Ebbitt in their *Dictionaries and That Dictionary* (o.p.).

Noah Webster was a Yale College graduate and first became famous as the author of Webster's *American Spelling Book* in 1783. This was a standard for 100 years, during which time 62 million copies were sold. It was because of this book that Webster became the traditional authority in spelling, while Worcester's dictionary for a long time was the authority in pronunciation.

BRITISH-ENGLISH DICTIONARIES

The American-British, British-American Dictionary with Helpful Hints to Travelers. Ed. by William Q. de Funiak, A. S. Barnes 1978 $8.95 pap. $4.95. Of a size that is not easily portable, this dictionary treats British English as a foreign language and has definitions for a number of common and not-so-common terms. Also has a large section covering tourists' concerns, such as money and transportation.

Dictionary of Contemporary American English: Contrasted with British English. Ed. by Givi Zviadadze, Humanities Pr. 1983 $27.00. An interesting volume in that it was compiled in Soviet Georgia from written sources and contains quotations for every entry from newspapers, periodicals, and books. Indicates whether a use is primarily British or American. Thesauri and index.

Fowler, Henry W., and F. G. Fowler. *The King's English*. Oxford 3d ed. 1973 pap. $2.95. This is essentially a reprint of a 1931 edition of a classic work, which emphasizes graceful and correct writing with its sections on vocabulary, syntax, punctuation, and others.

Moss, Norman. *What's the Difference? A British–American Dictionary*. Harper 1973 $8.95. A small British/American, American/British "bilingual" dictionary, with equivalent terms and/or definitions.

Schur, Norman W. *English English*. Gale 1980 $28.00. A revised version of the author's 1973 *British Self-Taught: With Comments in American*, it includes many words and phrases used in the living speech of the majority of the British, as well as a number of literary and regional uses no longer commonly encountered. In two-column dictionary format, with some cross-references, it also defines a number of the entries for meanings in both American and British English.

CURRENT ENGLISH-USAGE DICTIONARIES

Barnhart, Clarence L., Sol Steinmetz, and Robert K. Barnhart, eds. *The Barnhart Dictionary of New English since 1963*. Harper 1973 $14.95. The more than 5,000 words and phrases of modern science, technology, and culture were collected from the reading of more than half a billion running words from U.S., Canadian, and British sources—newspapers, magazines, and books published between 1963 and 1972.

Bell, James K., and Adrian Cohn. *Bell and Cohn's Handbook of Grammar, Style and Usage*. Macmillan 2d ed. 1976 text ed. pap. $3.95

Evans, Bergen, and Cornelia Evans. *A Dictionary of Contemporary American Usage*. Random 1957 o.p. The authors' premise is that no one use of language is "correct." An interesting and authoritative volume.

Follett, Wilson. *Modern American Usage: A Guide*. Ed. by Jacques Barzun, *American Century Ser*. Hill & Wang 1966 pap. $9.95; Warner 1974 pap. $2.50. "This is an unusual and a valuable . . . intensely personal book, based firmly on and edited consistently in accord with certain of Follett's basic beliefs about language" (*LJ*). Edward Weeks called the author (a distinguished editor, teacher, and essayist) "a tart and vigorous defender of the English language . . . with H. W. Fowler one of the two liveliest champions of good English usage in our time." In his introduction the author said of linguists such as those who prepared *Webster's Third New International Dictionary*: "[They] deny that there is nay such thing as correctness," but Follett argued "there is a right way to use words and construct sentences, and many wrong ways." On this basis he proceeds with his own observations and structures. He died before this book was completed, and a gifted group of editors carried on for him under Barzun's direction: Carlos Baker, F. W. Dupee, Dudley Fitts, James D. Hart, Phyllis McGinley, and Lionel Trilling.

Fowler, Henry W. *A Dictionary of Modern English Usage.* Ed. by Ernest Gowers, Oxford 2d ed. 1965 $17.95 1983 pap. $8.95. Fowler died in 1933, but in the Gowers edition his work remains the classic on English style, impeccably British, and in many of its longer entries deliciously opinionated; a volume that is not merely consulted but browsed in and read by those who love the language.

————. *Find It in Fowler: An Alphabetical Index to the Second Edition (1965) of H. W. Fowler's Modern English Usage.* Comp. by J. Arthur Greenwood, Wolfhart 1969 o.p.

Kenyon, John S., and Thomas A. Knott. *Pronouncing Dictionary of American English.* Merriam-Webster 2d ed. 1953 $9.95. Cultivated colloquial English pronunciation, using the international phonetic alphabet.

Martin, Phyllis. *Word Watcher's Handbook: A Deletionary of the Most Abused and Misused Words.* St. Martin's 1982 pap. $4.95. Includes bibliography and index.

Morris, William, and Mary Morris. *Harper Dictionary of Contemporary Usage.* Harper 1985 $19.18

Neaman, Judith, and Carole Silver. *Kind Words: A Thesaurus of Euphemisms.* Facts on File 1983 $16.95; McGraw-Hill 1984 $7.95

Nicholson, Margaret. *A Dictionary of American-English Usage.* New Amer. Lib. 1957 o.p. Starting from Fowler's *Modern English Usage,* Nicholson, who was head of the publishing department of Oxford University Press, added new words and idioms and included American variations of spelling, pronunciation, and usage that "Fowler either ignored or disdained."

Nickles, Harry. *The Dictionary of Do's and Don'ts: A Guide for Writers and Speakers.* McGraw-Hill 1974 $8.95

Partridge, Eric. *Concise Usage and Abusage: A Modern Guide to Good English.* Greenwood repr. of 1955 ed. lib. bdg. $18.75. Shortened and simplified version of *Usage and Abusage.*

————. *A Dictionary of Clichés.* Routledge & Kegan 5th ed. 1978 pap. $8.95

Shaw, Harry. *Dictionary of Problem Words and Expressions.* McGraw-Hill 1975 $21.95; Washington Square Pr. 1985 pap. $4.95

Stratton, Clarence. *Handbook of English.* Gale repr. of 1940 ed. 1975 $51.00

Suffixes and Other Word-Final Elements of English: A Compilation of More than 1500 Common and Technical Free Forms, Bound Forms, and Roots that Frequently Occur at the Ends of Words. Ed. by Laurence Urdang and others, Gale 1982 $45.00. Although the forms are listed from right to left, there is an alphabetical index for each form quoted going from left to right. Short etymologies, and general meanings, are given for each form.

Timmons, Christine, and Frank Gibney, eds. *Britannica Book of English Usage.* Doubleday 1980 $17.95

Witherspoon, Alexander M. *Common Errors in English and How to Avoid Them.* Little, Brown repr. of 1943 ed. 1976 pap. $3.95

SLANG AND COLLOQUIAL DICTIONARIES

Anderson, Dennis. *The Book of Slang.* Jonathan David 1975 $6.95

Berrey, Lester V., and Melvin Van den Bark. *The American Thesaurus of Slang: A*

Complete Reference Book of Colloquial Speech. Crowell rev. ed. 1953 o.p. More than 100,000 expressions arranged according to dominant idea, occupation, and so on; includes an alphabetical word index.

Byrne, Josefa H. *Mrs. Byrne's Dictionary of Unusual, Obscure, and Preposterous Words, Gathered from Numerous and Diverse Authoritative Sources.* Ed. by Robert Byrne, Citadel Pr. 1976 pap. $7.95. This is a very personal selection of odd or unusual words, and even the definitions do not denote every sense of a word, but it is fun to read and can be used as a supplement to an abridged dictionary.

Cowie, A. P., Ronald Mackin, and I. R. McCaig. *Oxford Dictionary of Current Idiomatic English.* Oxford 2 vols. 1975–83 ea. $15.00–$18.00. The stress here is on expressions in British English. In Volume 1, they are arranged by the verbal element, with definitions and examples of use for about 20,000 expressions with alternative forms. Volume 2 compiles those expressions where other parts of speech are the keywords in the phrases or sentences. This is a very comprehensive work, which is still easy to use.

A Dictionary of Contemporary and Colloquial Usage. Eng. Language Institute of Amer. 1972 pap. o.p. Only 32 pages, but its 2,000 entries update the classic work of Wentworth and Flexner.

A Dictionary of the Underworld, British and American. Macmillan 1961 rev. ed. o.p.

Farmer, John S., and W. E. Henley. *Slang and Its Analogues, Past and Present.* Kraus 7 vols. in 3 repr. of 1890–1904 ed. $130.00. Three centuries of slang with synonyms in English, French, German, and Italian. Entries are labeled colloquial, provincial, vulgar, etc. In these reprints the supplementary Volume 8, *Vocabula Amatoria,* of the original set has been left out. This was a translation and synthesis by Farmer of several French erotic dictionaries.

Fowler, Henry W., and F. G. Fowler. *The King's English.* Oxford 3d ed. 1985 pap. $6.95. This is essentially a reprint of a 1931 edition of a classic work, which emphasizes graceful and correct writing with its sections on vocabulary, syntax, punctuation, and other subjects.

Freeman, William. *A Concise Dictionary of English Idioms.* Writer rev. ed. 1976 pap. $5.95. A reprint of the third edition, with many obsolete expressions omitted and about 1,200 new ones added.

Grose, Francis. *A Classical Dictionary of the Vulgar Tongue.* Ed. by Eric Partridge, *Select Bibliographies Repr. Ser.* Ayer repr. of 1963 ed. $23.50. To this earliest dictionary of English slang Eric Partridge, perhaps the leading authority on slang in English (see following), "has contributed illuminating notes" and a biographical sketch of that "antiquarian Falstaff." The early compiler "would be astonished to learn that a few terms he considered vanishing vogue words—'bore' and 'twaddle,' for example—are still very much alive, just as some of us may be astonished to find that certain other terms—such as 'douse the glim' and 'elbow grease'—date to his time. An incidental asset of the book is the way it brings to sparkling life the mores, the humor and the foibles of the 18th century" (*N.Y. Times*).

Landy, Eugene E. *The Underground Dictionary.* Simon & Schuster (Touchstone Bks.) 1971 pap. $3.95. Words and phrases as recorded by a clinical psychologist.

Moss, Norman. *What's the Difference? A British–American Dictionary.* Harper 1973 $8.95. A small British/American, American/British "bilingual" dictionary, with equivalent terms and/or definitions.

Partridge, Eric. *A Dictionary of Catch Phrases.* Stein & Day 1977 $17.95 1979 pap. $11.95. A fascinating compilation of those familiar kinds of phrases everyone uses, with explanations, definitions, and background information on the evolution of the term.

————. *A Dictionary of Slang and Unconventional English.* Macmillan 8th ed. 1985 $75.00. Here is an immense body of work compressed into one volume by means of abbreviations. It deals not only with slang but with scabrous language as well.

————. *The Macmillan Dictionary of Historical Slang.* Abr. by Jacqueline Simpson, Macmillan 1974 $25.00. Apparently an abridgment of the 1961 edition of *A Dictionary of Slang and Unconventional English*, but limited as well to those terms in use before 1914.

Phythian, Brian. *Concise Dictionary of English Slang.* Writer 1976 pap. $5.95

Urdang, Laurence, ed. *Idioms and Phrases Index.* Gale 1983 3 vols. $220.00. Entries are by significant words, alphabetically arranged.

Urdang, Laurence, and Charles Hoequist, Jr., eds. *-Ologies & -Isms: A Thematic Dictionary.* Gale 1986 3rd ed. $90.00. Includes "-ist," "-ic," and "-phobia" endings as well as "-ology (-ies)" and "-isms," with definitions and historical notes.

Wentworth, Harold, and Stuart B. Flexner. *Dictionary of American Slang.* Crowell 2d ed. 1975 $16.30. Very current at the time of its publication, including a number of new pages, this slang dictionary cites the first printed references as a rough indication of the period coinage.

SYNONYM, ANTONYM, AND HOMONYM DICTIONARIES

Allen, F. Sturges. *Allen's Synonyms and Antonyms.* Ed. by T. H. Motter, Barnes & Noble pap. $4.33; Harper rev. & enl. ed. 1938 $12.50. This volume, by the general editor of the first edition of *Webster's New International Dictionary*, is arranged alphabetically, not classified in categories as *Roget's*. In the old edition the synonyms were not discriminated. In the revised edition sense discriminations have been added, as well as many new synonyms and antonyms, slang and colloquialisms, and British equivalents of American words.

Chapman, Robert L. *Roget's International Thesaurus.* Harper 4th ed. 1984 pap. $8.61. In the original format by topical arrangement, updated to include recent vocabulary in its more than 250,000 entries, with an extensive alphabetical index. Readers must consult a dictionary for finer shades of meaning, however.

Epsy, Willard R. *Thou Improper, Thou Uncommon Noun.* Potter 1978 $12.95. Divided into categories of "heavenly words" and "earthly words," this book is compiled of words derived from proper names and is fascinating to browse through. Index.

Family Word Finder. Reader's Digest 1975 $19.98. A thesaurus of 10,000 common words for home use, it clarifies meanings by using illustrative sentences, and lists synonyms in order of most common use. Includes historical information for some entries, and usage, spelling, and pronunciation notes where needed.

Fernald, James C. *Funk & Wagnalls Standard Handbook of Synonyms, Antonyms and Prepositions.* Crowell rev. ed. 1947 $13.41. More than 6,000 classified synonyms, with nearly 4,000 antonyms, together with examples of the correct use of prepositions.

Hayakawa, S. I., ed. *Funk & Wagnalls Modern Guide to Synonyms and Related Words.* Crowell 1967 $9.95. Compares and contrasts more than 6,000 synonyms. "There have been more thorough compilations, but few are as conveniently arranged or as pleasant to consult" (Glixon).

Kimball, Ruth. *Collins Gem Dictionary of Synonyms.* Collins 2d college ed. pap. $2.95. Adapted from material in *Webster's New World Dictionary of the American*

Language. Very comprehensive for a pocket-sized dictionary, it includes a number of antonyms as well as synonyms, with shades of meaning clearly differentiated.

Kloe, Donald R. *A Dictionary of Collective Onomatopoeic Sounds, Tones and Noises in English and Spanish: Including Those of Animals, Man, Nature, Machinery and Musical Instruments, together with Some That Are Not Imitative or Echoic*. Blaine Ethridge 1977 $22.50. Arranged by sounds, with a glossary and index.

Laird, Charlton. *Webster's New World Thesaurus*. New Amer. Lib. pap. $8.95; Simon & Schuster new ed. 1985 $14.95; Warner 1982 $8.95 pap. $2.95

Landau, Sidney, and Ronald Bogus, eds. *The Doubleday Roget's Thesaurus in Dictionary Form*. Doubleday 1977 $10.95. An alphabetical list, without the usual subject classifications, of about 250,000 synonyms and antonyms. Coverage is current but there are no guidelines for appropriate usage of synonymous terms.

Lewis, Norman. *The New Roget's Thesaurus of the English Language in Dictionary Form*. Putnam rev. ed. 1978 thumb-indexed $5.75 lib. ed. $6.75. Each entry refers one back to a main category, within which the terms are listed by noun form, with synonyms following, but there are no illustrations of use or distinctions for shades of meaning. Some of the synonyms given are simply inaccurate.

The Merriam-Webster Thesaurus. Pocket Bks. 1978 pap. $1.95. One of the best thesauri, based as it is on *Webster's Third New International Dictionary of the English Language Unabridged*, and in a very handy format. Besides referring the user to a more appropriate or alternative word, it provides synonyms, antonyms, related words, definitions, and illustrations of the main term, and more. It has good cross-references and refers one back to a dictionary when necessary.

Morehead, Philip D. *The New American Roget's College Thesaurus in Dictionary Form*. New Amer. Lib. (Signet Class.) rev. ed. 1985 pap. $3.50. Second edition, which has added a number of slang and colloquial expressions. The dictionary arrangement is much less useful than the original arrangement by concept, and the synonyms are often misleading here.

Newhouse, Dora. *The Encyclopedia of Homonyms, "Sound-Alikes": The Only Complete Comprehensive Collection of "Sound Alike" Words Ever Published*. Newhouse 1976 $11.50. Has a brief definition for each word, listings under variant first letter, "see" references, and lists a number of words that are not strictly homonymous.

———. *Homonyms, "Sound-Alikes": A Bilingual Reference Guide to the Most Mispronounced, Misspelled, and Confusing Words in the English Language: English-Spanish*. Newhouse 1978 $9.95. Useful mostly for those whose second language is English, this volume's 3,500 words are some of the most problematic for all English speakers. Has brief definitions, and cross-references under all spellings.

Powell, David. *Look-Alike, Sound-Alike, Not-Alike Words: An Index of Confusables*. Univ. Pr. of Amer. 1982 $20.75 pap. $9.75. The words here are in sets, arranged alphabetically, with cross-references. There are no definitions, but finding the right spelling would allow access back to any good dictionary.

Reid, Stuart. *Verb Synonyms and Related Words*. Exposition Pr. 1974 $5.00

Rodale, J. I. *The Synonym Finder*. Rodale Pr. rev. ed. 1978 $19.95. A comprehensive collection of synonyms, this revision includes more senses of meanings than the 1961 edition, and is updated with slang terms. It is alphabetically arranged and indicates the kind of use, i.e. technical or informal, but does not give examples of use.

Roget's II: The New Thesaurus. By the editors of *The American Heritage Dictionary*, Houghton Mifflin 1980 $11.95

Roget's University Thesaurus. Ed. by C. O. Sylvester Mawson, Barnes & Noble 1981 pap. $6.95. A reprint of the "classic" and well-known *Roget's Thesaurus*, and one of several revisions by Mawson, having expanded subject categories and updated vocabulary, including many technical and scientific terms. Index.

Room, Adrian. *Room's Dictionary of Confusibles*. Routledge & Kegan 1979 $16.00. Really a handbook of proper usage for easily confused terms, arranged for easy use with many cross-references, and fun to browse through for those interested in correct English use.

———. *Room's Dictionary of Distinguishables and Confusibles*. Routledge & Kegan 2 vols. 1981 $23.95. This book deals with pairs or small groups of common words that are related, such as "hare" and "rabbit," but whose differences may not be easy to distinguish. The illustrations are particularly useful here.

Sparkes, Ivan G., ed. *Dictionary of Collective Nouns and Group Terms*. Gale 2d ed. 1985 $65.00. A dictionary of terms for groups of things, dating from the medieval to modern times, and including a number of punning terms, listed alphabetically and by subject.

Webster's Collegiate Thesaurus. Merriam-Webster 1976 thumb-indexed $8.95. A new thesaurus in dictionary format, with excellent introductory material, that is perhaps easier for most people to use than the familiar, classed *Roget's Thesaurus*.

Webster's New Dictionary of Synonyms. Merriam-Webster 1984 $12.95. Particularly useful thesaurus because of its lists of related words that are carefully defined for shades of meaning, and for its quotations illustrating correct usage.

RHYMING DICTIONARIES

Baldwin, Roger, and Ruth Paris. *The Book of Similes*. Routledge & Kegan 1982 $14.95 pap. $7.95

Cahn, Sammy. *The Songwriter's Rhyming Dictionary*. Facts on File 1983 $17.95; New Amer. Lib. 1984 pap. $8.95. The main difference between this and other rhyming dictionaries is that there is a subarrangement under vowel sounds, phonetically arranged, and there is additional practical information for the songwriter.

Franklyn, Julian. *A Dictionary of Rhyming Slang*. Routledge & Kegan repr. of 1961 ed. rev. ed. 1975 pap. $8.95

Johnson, Burges, ed. *New Rhyming Dictionary and Poets' Handbook*. Harper rev. ed. 1957 $17.26

Modglin, Nel. *The Rhymer and Other Helps for Poets*. Dorrance 1977 $5.95. A dictionary of sounds, divided by up to four syllables; the second part is a guide to forms and terms in poetry.

Walker, J. *Walker's Rhyming Dictionary of the English Language: In Which the Whole Language Is Arranged According to Its Terminations*. Routledge & Kegan repr. of 1924 ed. rev. & enl. ed. 1983 $16.95. Revision and update of the standard rhyming dictionary, arranged by last syllable and with British pronunciation.

Whitfield, Jane S. *Whitfield's University Rhyming Dictionary*. Ed. by Frances Stillman, Barnes & Noble 1981 pap. $5.95; Crowell pap. $3.95

SPELLING DICTIONARIES

Deighton, Lee C. *Handbook of American English Spelling*. Van Nostrand 1973 $5.95. Guide to assist in spelling and dividing words that the average person might have difficulty with, listed under the "standard" spelling—the one most often used. Bibliography.

Emery, Donald W. *Variant Spellings in Modern American Dictionaries*. National Council of Teachers of Eng. rev. ed. 1973 pap. $5.70

Leslie, Louis A. *Twenty Thousand Words*. McGraw-Hill 7th ed. 1977 $7.50. Basic-level speller/divider, with a number of referrals to homonyms. Helpful, though incomplete, reference sections on usage and rules.

Maxwell, Christine. *The Pergamon Dictionary of Perfect Spelling*. Pergamon 2d ed. 1979 pap. $3.75. This dictionary really is not one, because it has no definitions, but it does have a handy two-column format with incorrect spellings in red. British-English spelling is emphasized.

Noory, Samuel J. *Dictionary of Pronunciation*. Cornwall Bks. 4th ed. 1981 $19.95

The Random House Speller/Divider. Ballantine 1981 pap. $2.50. Very comprehensive, it includes geographical and biographical names, and how to hyphenate, divide, spell, and pronounce them, and distinguishes between homonyms.

Webster's Instant Word Guide. Merriam-Webster 1980 $3.95. Not a dictionary with definitions, this is a tool for spelling and dividing words, although it does have some of the helpful appended sections included in most dictionaries.

Webster's New World Misspeller's Dictionary. Ed. by the editors of *Webster's New World Dictionary*, Simon & Schuster 1983 pap. $3.50. Especially useful for its referrals from usual misspellings to the correct form, and for help in usage.

ETYMOLOGICAL DICTIONARIES

Davies, Peter. *Roots: Family Histories of Familiar Words*. McGraw-Hill 1981 $24.95. For those interested in the development of the English language, this work covers a select group of words that derive from 100 Indo-European roots. The words are schematically diagrammed on the page facing the etymologies, and there is an index of words giving the root to look under.

Flexner, Stuart B. *I Hear America Talking: An Illustrated Treasury of American Words and Phrases*. Simon & Schuster (Touchstone Bks.) 1979 $8.95; Van Nostrand 1976 $18.95. American vocabulary is placed here in a historical or political context, alphabetically arranged.

Funk, Charles E. *Heavens to Betsy and Other Curious Sayings*. Harper 1955 $10.95. A very personal and speculative compilation, but fun to browse through.

——. *Hog on Ice and Other Curious Expressions*. Harper 1985 pap. $5.72

——. *Thereby Hangs a Tale: Stories of Curious Word Origins*. Harper 1950 $10.95 1985 pap. $7.64. The late lexicographer left a wonderful series of books on the origin and meaning of odd words and phrases. His son completed *Horsefeathers and Other Curious Words* after his death.

Funk, Charles E., and Charles E. Funk, Jr. *Horsefeathers and Other Curious Words*. Harper 1958 $10.95

Hendrickson, Robert. *Human Words: The Compleat Unexpurgated, Uncomputerized Human Wordbook*. Chilton 1972 $9.95. Words derived from real or mythical persons.

Klein, Ernest. *A Comprehensive Etymological Dictionary of the English Language*. Elsevier 1971 $85.00. Highly recommended for libraries. Scholarly, up-to-date research.

Morris, William, and Mary Morris. *Morris Dictionary of Word and Phrase Origins*. Harper 1977 $15.00. A more informal dictionary of etymology, covering slang terms or clichés found everywhere from general conversation to history, in alphabetical order by first word with an index by other parts of the phrases.

Onions, Charles T., ed. *The Oxford Dictionary of English Etymology.* Oxford 1966 $45.00. The most complete and most reliable etymological dictionary of the English language. The superb *Oxford English Dictionary* is also an excellent source of etymology of all English words from Chaucer to the present.

Partridge, Eric. *Origins: A Short Etymological Dictionary of Modern English.* Macmillan 1977 $45.00. Intimately cognate groups of words are arranged into single unified treatments. Thus, "can," "could," "con," "couth," "uncouth," "kith," "cunning," "keen," "ken," "kenning," "know," and "knowledge" are all treated in six numbered paragraphs under "can," to which the others are cross-referenced.

Pinkerton, Edward C. *Word for Word: A Dictionary of Etymological Cognates.* Gale 1982 $60.00; Verbatim 1982 $39.95. An etymological dictionary that groups words in families, and that is interesting and easy to understand. The index of more than 15,000 terms refers back to each numbered line, making it easy to use as well.

The Shorter Oxford English Dictionary on Historical Principles. Prepared by William Little, Henry W. Fowler, and Jessie Coulson rev. & ed. by Charles T. Onions, Oxford 2 vols. 3d ed. rev. & enl. 1973 $145.00. This revision includes updated etymologies and addenda list with new words, making it the best historical dictionary of its size. It is also a good supplement to use with the compact edition of the *Oxford English Dictionary*.

Skeat, Walter W., ed. *Concise Etymological Dictionary of the English Language.* Oxford 1911 $26.50. Skeat's dictionary gives the history of selected words of curious or disputed derivation. The Bible and Shakespeare have perpetuated many lost meanings, which Skeat alone explains. For instance, Cinderella's slipper was not originally glass but of fur. How it came to be called glass is a word story found in Skeat.

———. *An Etymological Dictionary of the English Language.* Oxford rev. ed. & enl. 1910 $69.00

Smith, Logan P. *The English Language.* Century Bookbindery repr. of 1912 ed. 1982 lib. bdg. $20.00; Folcroft repr. 1930 lib. bdg. $12.50; Telegraph Bks. repr. 1982 lib. bdg. $20.00. The author was an American who lived in England and preferred English fashions of speech. His work on English idioms explains the origin of expressions like "hoist with his own petard," "to the manor born," "sour grapes," "curry favor," etc. (See Smith's main entry in Volume 1, Chapter 16.)

FOREIGN–ENGLISH DICTIONARIES

Anglo-Saxon

Bosworth, Joseph, and Alistair Campbell, eds. *An Anglo-Saxon Dictionary.* Oxford repr. of 1898 ed. 1972 $115.00 supplement and addenda 1972 pap. $17.95

Hall, John R. *A Concise Anglo-Saxon Dictionary.* Supplement by Herbert D. Meritt, Univ. of Toronto Pr. repr. of 1960 ed. 1984 text ed. pap. $15.00. The classic lexical references for Anglo-Saxon are the "exhaustive" Bosworth and Campbell and the concise work by Clark Hall (o.p.). The latter, which is highly adequate and reliable, has been out of print for a number of years. This edition is most welcome for Meritt's 20-page supplement, which contains 1,700 new entries not in

Bosworth-Campbell—new definitions, revisions of old definitions, and definitions of compounds formerly to be deduced from their separate constituents.

Arabic

Arabic-English Dictionary of the Modern Literary Language. Comp. by Maan A. Madina, Pocket Bks. 1973 pap. $2.50. Compact dictionary that draws on several standard sources, notably Hans Wehr's *A Dictionary of Modern Written Arabic.*

A Comprehensive Persian-English Dictionary: Including the Arabic Words and Phrases to Be Met With in Persian Literature, Being Johnson and Richardson's Persian, Arabic, and English Dictionary, Revised, Enlarged, and Entirely Reconstructed. 1892. Comp. by F. Steinglass, Routledge & Kegan 1977 $42.00. "A remarkably accurate, reasonably comprehensive, and useful tool for any student or scholar of Persian" (Eugene L. Keyser, *American Reference Books Annual*).

The Concise Oxford English-Arabic Dictionary of Current Usage. Ed. by N. S. Doniach, Oxford 1982 $9.95. An abridged edition of the *Oxford English-Arabic Dictionary of Current Usage*, edited by Doniach. Includes American usage, with common phrases.

English-Arabic Vocabulary: Students' Pronouncing Dictionary. Comp. by Merrill Y. Van Wagoner, Spoken Language Services 1980 pap. $10.00. Both the English and Arabic lists that were the basis for this dictionary are from the 1940s, which is reflected in the lack of newer words and some of the obsolete meanings.

The Oxford English-Arabic Dictionary of Current Usage. Ed. by N. S. Doniach, Oxford 1972 $41.00

Shaikh, Shafi. *Handbook of English-Arabic for Professionals.* Oxford 1983 $22.50. A glossary that emphasizes technical terms in many fields, but which has little other lexical information.

Wehr, Hans. *A Dictionary of Modern Written Arabic.* Ed. by J. M. Cowan, Spoken Language Services 4th ed. rev. 1980 $115.00. "An enlarged and improved version of *Arabisches Wörterbuch für die Schriftsprache der Gegenwart* by Hans Wehr and includes the contents of the supplement *Zum Arabischen Wörterbuch für die Schriftsprache der Gegenwart* and a collection of new additional material (about 13,000 entries) by the same author."

Chinese

The Basic English-Chinese, Chinese-English Dictionary. Ed. by Peter Bergman and others, Humanities Pr. 1980 $12.00. Intended as a quick index; the simplified Chinese characters are arranged by number of strokes, the English alphabetically. Uses the Pinyin system of transliteration.

Beginners' Dictionary of Chinese-Japanese Characters: With Common Abbreviations, Variants and Numerous Compounds. Comp. by Arthur Rose-Innes, Dover 1977 pap. $6.50. A revision of the 1959 work, its 25,000 terms include new terms and modifications of characters.

Chao, Yuen R., and Lien-Sheng Yang. *Concise Dictionary of Spoken Chinese.* Harvard Univ. Pr. 1947 $20.00

Chi, Wen-Shun, and others, comps. *Chinese-English Dictionary of Contemporary Usage.* Univ. of California Pr. 1977 $20.00. The emphasis of this work's more than 20,000 terms is modern vocabulary and usage, using the Wade-Giles system of romanization with a conversion table from Pinyin.

Dobson, W. A. *A Dictionary of the Chinese Particles, with a Prolegomenon in Which the*

Problems of the Particles Are Considered and They Are Classified by Their Grammatical Functions. Univ. of Toronto Pr. 1974 $75.00. The 694 particles included are those used from the eleventh century B.C. to the sixth century A.D., although apparently many are still in use today. Their arrangement is in the National Romanization system, not Wade-Giles, although a table at the back converts them.

Lin Yutang. *Chinese-English Dictionary of Modern Usage.* McGraw-Hill 1983 $39.50. An excellent dictionary that reflects the scholarly reputation of its author. The principle on which it is based is contextual semantics, the way in which a word changes in context. Characters are listed in the regular to the simplified form and vice versa. It is also a quite handsome book.

McNaughton, William. *Reading and Writing Chinese: A Guide to the Chinese Writing System.* Tuttle 1979 $17.50. Intended primarily for students, with a number of sections on aspects of learning the language, such as tips on memorization, in addition to the actual definitions.

Montanaro, John S. *Chinese/English Phrase Book For Travellers.* Wiley 1981 pap. $8.95. A convenient, portable guide to everyday words and phrases, with a grammar section and a guide to English pronunciation.

The Pinyin Chinese-English Dictionary. Ed. by Wu Jingrong and others, Wiley 1982 pap. $15.00. Entries are given in the Pinyin romanization and the Chinese characters, which one must know to use it. Includes many modern terms and expressions.

Danish

Danish-English, English-Danish Dictionary. Ed. by L. Vinterberg, and J. Axelsen, Heinman 2 vols. 10th ed. $50.00

Dutch

Bruggencate, K. Ten. *Dutch-English, English-Dutch Dictionary.* Heinman 2 vols. $50.00

Dutch-English Dictionary. Macmillan 1979 pap. $4.95

King, P., and M. King. *Dutch-English and English-Dutch.* McKay 1974 pap. $4.95

French

Atkins, Beryl T., and others. *Collins-Robert French-English Dictionary.* Collins & World 1978 $15.95. Good, contemporary dictionary that distinguishes the various forms (American, British, Scottish, and so on) of English usage in translation and incorporates many up-to-date slang and colloquial terms in its 20,000 entries.

Brueckner's French Contextuary. Comp. and ed. by John H. Brueckner, Prentice-Hall 1975 $30.00

Cassell's Compact French-English, English-French Dictionary. Dell 1981 pap. $3.95

Dubois, Marguerite-Marie. *Modern French-English Dictionary.* With the collaboration of Charles Cestre and others, Larousse 1978 $25.00. A substantial (more than 1,500 pages) and solid dictionary of contemporary terms from various areas.

Ferrar, H., and Jean Dominique Biard, eds. *The Concise Oxford French Dictionary.* Oxford 2d ed. 1985 pap. $9.95. An extensive update of the 1934 edition, with

3,000 new terms, with an emphasis on the French for the English user, though British spelling is used.

Follett Vest-Pocket French Dictionary: French-English/English-French (American English) Comp. by Richard Switzer and Herbert S. Gochberg, Follett 1977 pap. $2.50. Hand and reasonable travel dictionary for everyday speech.

Gerber, Barbara L., and Gerald H. Storzer. *Dictionary of Modern French Idioms. Reference Lib.* Garland 2 vols. 1977 lib. bdg. $133.00

Hamlyn French Dictionary: French-English, English-French. Comp. by Laurence Urdang Associates, Larousse 1977 pap. $2.95

Hammond-Jeans Dictionary: French-English, English-French. Hammond 1981 pap. $1.95

Kirk-Greene, C. W. E. *French False Friends.* Routledge & Kegan 1981 $14.95. A helpful guide to words that mislead because of their similarity to English or their multimeanings.

Marks, Georgette A., and Charles B. Johnson. *The New English-French Dictionary of Slang and Colloquialisms.* Dutton 1975 $12.95. U.S. version of *Harrap's English-French Dictionary of Slang and Colloquialisms.* Much of it seems slanted to the British, however.

New Contemporary French/English, English/French Dictionary. Doubleday 1974 $4.95

Nutting, Teresa, and Michel Marcy. *Cortina/Grosset Basic French Dictionary: English-French/French-English.* Grosset & Dunlap 1975 o.p.

The Oxford-Duden Pictorial French-English Dictionary. Oxford 1983 $29.95. Another of the excellent Duden pictorial dictionaries, which arrange lists of things by category with line drawings to define them; particularly good with technical terms.

The Random House Basic Dictionary, French-English, English-French. Ed. by Francesco L. V. Langbaum, Ballantine 1981 pap. $1.50. Useful, quick guide for written French, of the basic vocabulary.

Rudler, Gustave, ed. *Putnam's Contemporary French Dictionary.* Putnam 1972 $2.95

U.S. Department of State. *English-French Glossary.* Government Printing Office 1976 pap. $7.70. Particularly useful for current terms in scientific and technical fields, because it was compiled from official documents and reports, and was intended for government personnel.

Webster's French & English Dictionary. Comp. by Roger J. Steiner, Castle Bks. 1980 $2.95

German

Betteridge, Harold. *Cassell's German-English, English-German Dictionary: Deutsch-Englisches, Englisch-Deutsches Wörterbuch.* Macmillan rev. ed. 1978 $13.50 thumb-indexed $14.95. This revised edition of the popular and respected Cassell's has a key to German pronunciation and phonetic transcriptions of German keywords.

Cassell's New German Dictionary (German-English and English-German). Funk & Wagnalls rev. ed. 1958 o.p. The 1940 edition was called the "bible" of the Allied Control Commission in Germany. Dr. Harold C. Betteridge undertook the thorough overhauling of the earlier work and expanded its coverage. It includes not only literary language, but also many phrases taken from other walks of life, especially the vernacular of the professions and trades, and colloquial terms. Set in roman, instead of Gothic type.

Clark, J. M., and K. E. I. Rotraud. *Putnam's Contemporary Dictionaries: English-German, Deutsch-Englisch.* Putnam 1973 $3.50. Compact, well-bound dictionary that lives up to its claim of good value and compares favorably with others of its size and type.

The English Duden: A Pictorial Dictionary with English and German Indexes. Herder Bk. Ctr. 2d ed. rev. 1960 o.p. A great number of new words and pictures have been added, particularly those of scientific and technological vintage—366 plates (8 of them in color) and 25,000 terms arranged in 15 groups comprising all manner of human activities and interests from the Stone Age to rocketry.

Farrell, R. B. *Dictionary of German Synonyms.* Cambridge Univ. Pr. 3d ed. 1977 $22.50 pap. $7.95

Hamlyn German Dictionary: German-English, English-German. Comp. by Laurence Urdang Associates, Larousse 1977 pap. $2.95

Hammond-Jeans Dictionary: German-English, English-German. Hammond 1981 pap. $1.95

Keller, Howard H. *German Root Lexicon.* Univ. Pr. of Miami 1973 $10.00. Arranged in alphabetical order by English word, this is a most useful book in choosing the correct equivalent expression in German.

———. *A German Word Family Dictionary: Together with English Equivalents.* Univ. of California Pr. 1978 $16.95. Set up like a rotated index of words, this work groups the German words in families in columns, making it very handy to use for its purpose.

Langenscheidt's Condensed Muret-Sanders German Dictionary. Langenscheidt $70.00

Langenscheidt's New College German Dictionary: German-English, English-German. Optimum Bk. Marketing 1973 $10.95 thumb-indexed $11.95. This revision gives more forms of nouns (in the German) than the earlier one, indicates irregular verbs, and has more easily understood abbreviations. The German vocabulary has also been expanded.

Messinger, Heinz. *Langenscheidt's Comprehensive English-German Dictionary.* Optimum Bk. Marketing 1972 $21.50. Of the standard type, with many new terms included, this dictionary has particularly clear print and is easy to use. Has a number of the usual appendixes of tables, abbreviations, verbs, and so on.

Messinger, Heinz, and others. *Langenscheidt's Condensed Muret-Sanders German Dictionary: German-English.* Gale 1982 $70.00. Based on the respected *New Muret-Sanders Encyclopedic German-English Dictionary*, it contains 70 percent of the same material and all the appended sections.

Moulton, Jenni H., ed. *The Random House Basic Dictionary: German-English, English-German.* Ballantine 1981 pap. $1.50. Revision of two earlier editions, it is small, portable, and solid for the basics of the language.

The Oxford-Duden Pictorial German-English Dictionary. Ed. by John Pheby, Oxford 1979 $24.95. This pictorial Duden is based on the *Duden Bildwörterbuch* and is bilingual. The 28,000 items are, as usual, arranged by subject area, and the illustrations and word lists allow users in both languages to name properly many familiar objects.

The Oxford-Harrap Standard German-English Dictionary, Volume III, L–R. Ed. by Trevor Jones, Oxford 1977 $34.00

Schoffler, Herbert. *The New Schoffler-Weis German and English Dictionary: English-German/German-English.* Updated by Erich Weis and Erwin Weis, Follett rev. & enl. ed. 1974 $9.95. A sound, comprehensive dictionary with many current terms included. A brief historical atlas is among the appended sections.

Stern, Henry R., and Richey Novak. *A Handbook of English-German Idioms and Useful Expressions.* Harcourt 1973 pap. $4.95. Really idiomatic expressions, not current slang, in a convenient presentation.

Taylor, Ronald, and Walter Gottschalk. *A German-English Dictionary of Idioms: Idiomatic and Figurative German Expressions with English Translations.* Heinman 1962 o.p.

Zotter, Josefa. *Cortina/Grosset Basic German Dictionary: English-German/German-English.* Grosset & Dunlap 1975 o.p. This revised edition of the popular and respected Cassell's has a key to German pronunciation and phonetic transcriptions of German keywords.

Greek

Hionides, Harry T. *Collins Contemporary Greek Dictionary: Greek-English, English-Greek.* Collins & World 1977 $5.95. Small dictionary that concentrates on definition but does not include indications of grammar. Pronunciation is indicated.

Liddell, H. G., and R. Scott. *Greek-English Lexicon.* Rev. by H. S. Jones and others, Oxford 2 vols. 9th ed. rev. & enl. 1968 $22.40

————. *Intermediate Greek-English Lexicon.* Oxford 1959 $30.00. Based on Liddell's *Greek-English Lexicon.*

Moulton, Harold K., ed. *The Analytical Greek Lexicon Revised.* Zondervan rev. ed. 1978 $15.95. All forms of verbs are listed alphabetically, which is repetitive but useful to the student of Greek. The definitions concentrate on New Testament meanings.

Pring, J. T., ed. *The Oxford Dictionary of Modern Greek: Greek-English, English-Greek.* Oxford 1982 $19.95. The companion volume to the earlier Greek-English dictionary, both of which are available in one volume. This work has been critically praised as a long-needed addition to the genre.

Swanson, Donald C. *Vocabulary of Modern Spoken Greek (English-Greek and Greek-English).* Ed. by Theofanis G. Stavrou, Nostos 1982 $15.00. Information on derivation, structure, and pronunciation, with sections on names, food and drink, greetings, etc.; for student-resident or tourist.

Hebrew

Ben-Yehuda, Eliezer, ed. *Dictionary and Thesaurus of the Hebrew Language.* A. S. Barnes 8 vols. $150.00. Complete international centennial edition.

Goldberg, Nathan. *The New Functional Hebrew-English, English-Hebrew Dictionary: With Illustrative Sentences and Derivative Words and Expressions.* Ktav 1958 $3.95. This basic handbook of modern Hebrew is recommended by educational agencies.

Hungarian

Orszagh, Laszlo. *Hungarian-English, English-Hungarian Concise Dictionary.* Heinman 2 vols. rev. & enl. 1976–79 $55.00; Vanous 11th ed. 1983 $30.00

Italian

Berberi, Dilaver. *Cortina/Grosset Basic Italian Dictionary: English-Italian/Italian-English.* Grosset & Dunlap 1975 o.p.

The Cambridge Italian Dictionary, Volume 2: *English-Italian.* Comp. by Barbara Reynolds and others, Cambridge Univ. Pr. 1981 $180.00. An impressive dictionary, whose main purpose is to help those who speak English to express themselves in contemporary Italian, although it does not often help in pronouncing Italian. It does translate phrases, and the extensive vocabulary includes numerous Italian equivalents for the English term. When British meaning varies from American, the British is used.

Cassell's Italian Dictionary: Italian-English, English-Italian. Macmillan 1977 $19.95 thumb-indexed $23.95

The Concise Cambridge Italian Dictionary. Comp. by Barbara Reynolds, Cambridge Univ. Pr. 1974 $49.50; Penguin 1975 pap. $9.95. Although the emphasis appears to be on British English, this concise version of the parent is useful for both the English and the Italian speaker, emphasizing current Italian use. Etymologies are omitted or shortened, but specialized uses are indicated.

Dizionario Inglése-Italiano, Italiano-Inglése. Ed. by Malcolm Skey and others, Oxford 1981 $49.95

Follett Vest-Pocket Italian Dictionary: Italian-English/English-Italian (American-English). Ed. by Vittore E. Bocchetta and Ruth E. Young, Follett 1978 pap. $2.50

Hall, Robert A., Jr., ed. *The Random House Basic Dictionary: Italian-English, English-Italian.* Ballantine 1981 pap. $1.50

Hall, Robert A., Jr., and Frances A. Hall. *2001 Italian and English Idioms: 2001 Locuzione Italiane e Inglese.* Barron text ed. 1981 pap. $9.95

Hamlyn Italian Dictionary: Italian-English, English-Italian. Comp. by Laurence Urdang Associates, Larousse 1977 pap. $2.95

Lipton, Gladys, and John Colinari. *Italian Bilingual Dictionary: A Beginner's Guide in Words and Pictures.* Barron text ed. 1980 pap. $3.95

May, Isobel. *Putnam's Contemporary Dictionaries: Italian-English, Inglese-Italiano.* Comp. by Laurence Urdang Associates, Larousse 1977 pap. $2.95

Motta, Giuseppe. *Dizionario Commerciale Inglése-Italiano, Italiano-Inglése: Economia, Legge, Finanza, Banca, Etc.* Vanni 1978 $48.00. This is included here because it "covers far more than the merely 'commercial'; it may be said to be a general utility dictionary which happens to illustrate its entries (22,000) in commercial and legal terms wherever possible."

Ragazzini, Giuseppe, and Adele Biagi. *English-Italian, Italian-English Dictionary.* Longman 1974 pap. $6.50. Based on the *English-Italian and Italian-English Dictionary* of Giuseppe Ragazzini.

Reynolds, Barbara. *The Concise Cambridge Italian Dictionary.* Cambridge Univ. Pr. 1974 $49.50; Penguin 1975 pap. $9.95. Originally begun as *An Italian Dictionary* by A. Hoare.

Japanese

All-Romanized English-Japanese Dictionary. Tuttle 1974 pap. $4.50. That there are no Japanese characters, plus the phrases and compound terms given and the pronunciation guidance, all make this a very convenient dictionary. In addition, there is a section on Japanese grammar.

Crowley, Dale P. *Manual for Reading Japanese.* Univ. of Hawaii Pr. 1972 pap. $7.50. Prepared with the assistance of Yoshiyuki Kawata and Yoko Kawata. Five hundred of the basic Kanji characters are arranged in order of frequency, and the manual's purpose is to help the user determine the correct usage and pronunciation.

Martin, Samuel. *Basic Japanese Conversation Dictionary: English-Japanese and Japanese-English.* Tuttle $3.95. Contains 6,000 of the most common English and Japanese words in Japanese characters and in standard romanization; pocket-size.

Miura, Akira. *English Loanwords in Japanese: A Selection*. Tuttle 1979 $11.50
———. *Japanese Words and Their Uses*. Tuttle 1983 $12.50. Covers 300 expressions
  that cause difficulty for the English speaker of Japanese.
The Oxford-Duden Pictorial English-Japanese Dictionary. Oxford 1983 $29.95. Al-
  though most of the things pictured are from the Western world, the Japanese
  version of the *Duden Pictorial* is as comprehensive and contemporary as the
  other works on which it is patterned.

Korean

Standard English-Korean Dictionary for Foreigners. Ed. by B. J. Jones, Hollym 1982
  pap. $7.95

Latin

Glare, P. G., ed. *Oxford Latin Dictionary*. Oxford 1982 $145.00. This is a one-volume
  edition of the nine-volume set that began coming out in 1967, and is the most
  comprehensive of the available Latin dictionaries. The same quality and care
  evident in the *Oxford English Dictionary* are present here.
Latham, R. E. *Dictionary of Medieval Latin from British Sources*. Oxford 2 fascicules
  1981–82 pap. ea. $98.00–$198.00

Norwegian

Berulfsen, B., and H. Scavenius. *McKay's Modern Norwegian-English and English-
  Norwegian Dictionary*. McKay 1953 $15.95

Polish

Bulas, Kazimierz, Francis J. Whitfield, and Lawrence L. Thomas. *The Kosciusko
  Foundation English-Polish, Polish-English Dictionary*. Kosciusko Foundation 2
  vols. repr. 1983 $20.00. "It is by far the most comprehensive, carefully compiled
  and up-to-date . . . in existence." Special features include: phonetic transcrip-
  tion of Daniel Jones for the English words, the basic words, and all the deriva-
  tives thereof, as well as essential phrase combinations with carefully chosen Polish equivalents. The American spelling is favored with cross-references from the
  British forms; alternative spellings are also connected by means of cross-references; and all colloquialisms are identified, e.g. U.S., British, Australian.
Pogonowski, Iwo. *Dictionary: Polish-English, English-Polish*. Hippocrene Bks. 2d ed.
  1983 $19.95 pap. $11.95. Intended to be practical, with phonetic descriptions of
  both the Polish and the English.

Portuguese

Ferreira, Julio A., and Armando de Morais. *Portuguese-English, English-Portuguese
  Dictionary*. Heinman 1954 $30.00
Richardson, E. L., and others. *McKay's Modern Portuguese-English and English-Portu-
  guese Dictionary*. McKay 1943 $11.95
Taylor, James L. *A Portuguese-English Dictionary*. Stanford Univ. Pr. rev. ed. 1970
  $32.50. Highly recommended for libraries, translators, and students. Contains

60,000 double-column entries with definitions followed by detailed explanations in the Webster tradition.

Romanian

Axelrad, P. *Roumanian-English Dictionary.* McKay 1942 o.p.

Russian

English-Russian Dictionary. Comp. by V. K. Muller, Dutton 14th ed. rev. 1973 $12.95. Apparently little actual revision has taken place since the seventh edition of this work.

Finegold, Leo. *Linguadex: Key-Word Index to Spoken Russian.* Linguadex 1979 pap. $15.95. This is a practical book containing about 5,000 common English expressions and their Russian equivalents, with a good keyword index.

The Pocket Oxford English-Russian Dictionary. Comp. by Nigel Rankin and Della Thompson, Oxford 1981 $9.95. An abridgment of the *Oxford Russian-English Dictionary*, it is less than half the size of the parent. The smaller format has less in the way of usage designations and illustrations of use.

The Pocket Oxford Russian-English Dictionary. Comp. by Jessie Coulson, Oxford 1975 $8.00. A compact dictionary, offering pronunciation, equivalents, and grammatical context.

Russian English Dictionary of Abbreviations and Initialisms. Wychwood Pr. 1982 $60.00

Smirnitsky, A. I. *Russian English Dictionary.* Dutton rev. ed. 1973 $24.75. A well-known dictionary, the ninth edition has 50,000 terms and is considered a reliable source for standard Russian.

U.S. War Department. *Dictionary of Spoken Russian: Russian-English, English-Russian.* Dover 1959 pap. $9.95. First published in 1945, it was prepared by linguists for the U.S. War Department training and translation programs. Phrases and sentences listed alphabetically and translated idiomatically in both Russian to English and English to Russian; includes common literary expressions, slang, and irregular verb forms.

Vitek, Alexander J. *Russian-English Idiom Dictionary.* Ed. by Harry H. Josselson, Wayne State Univ. Pr. 1973 $19.95

Wilson, E. A. *The Modern Russian Dictionary for English Speakers: English-Russian.* Pergamon 1983 $28.00. Devised for speaking Russian; emphasis is on colloquial Russian and actual equivalents for English expressions, which are given only when they actually exist.

Serbo-Croatian

An English-Serbocroatian Dictionary. Comp. by Zivajin Simic, French & European Publications text ed. 1979 pap. $14.95

Spanish

Arora, Shirley L. *Proverbial Comparisons and Related Expressions in Spanish.* Univ. of California Pr. 1977 $20.00

Bentley, Harold W. *A Dictionary of Spanish Terms in English, with Special Reference to the American Southwest.* Octagon repr. of 1932 ed. 1973 lib. bdg. $20.00

Boggs, R. S., and J. I. Dixon. *Everyday Spanish Idioms.* Regents text ed. 1978 pap. $5.95

Bomse, Marguerite D. *Practical Spanish Dictionary and Phrasebook.* Pergamon new ed. text ed. 1978 pap. $7.50

Brown, R. F. *Putnam's Contemporary Dictionaries: Spanish-English, Inglés-Español.* Putnam 1972 $2.95

Calvert, G. H. *Dictionary of the Spanish and English Languages.* Routledge & Kegan 1980 pap. $7.50. Although limited as any dictionary of this size is, it is current and has a helpful section on irregular Spanish verbs.

Cassell's Concise Spanish Dictionary (Spanish-English and English-Spanish). Macmillan 1977 $9.95. Stresses Latin American usage as well as Castilian and regional dialects of Spain.

Cassell's Spanish-English, English-Spanish Dictionary: Diccionario Español-Inglés, Inglés-Español. Comp. by Anthony Gooch and Angel García de Paredes, Macmillan 1978 $13.50 thumb-indexed $14.95. The revision has enlarged tables of verbs, and new words and colloquial terms. Perhaps not as complete as the Cuyas or Velazquez Spanish dictionaries.

Castillo, Carlos, and Otto F. Bond. *The University of Chicago Spanish Dictionary.* Univ. of Chicago Pr. 3d ed. rev. & enl. 1977 $15.95; Univ. of Chicago Pr. (Phoenix Bks.) pap. $5.95

Cuyas, Arturo. *Appleton's New Cuyas Dictionary: English-Spanish and Spanish-English.* Rev. by Lewis E. Brett and Helen S. Eaton, Appleton 5th ed. rev. 1972 $47.95 pap. $8.95. Updated version of earlier editions, with all of their attributes.

El Diccionario del Español Chicano: The Dictionary of Chicano Spanish. Comp. by Roberto A. Galvan and Richard V. Teschner, Institute of Modern Languages rev. ed. 1977 pap. $4.95. A revised edition of *El Diccionario del Español de Tejas/The Dictionary of the Spanish of Texas*, it includes words and phrases not found in the usual Spanish dictionary.

Diccionario Inglés. Ed. by Fernando de Mello Vianna and others, Houghton Mifflin 1982 pap. $7.95

García-Pelayo y Gross, Ramon, and Micheline Durand. *Diccionario Moderno Español-Inglés.* Larousse 1976 $25.00. The emphasis here is on the Anglo-Hispanic culture and vocabulary, with a definite slant on things American. Includes grammatical guidance section for both languages.

Hamlyn Spanish Dictionary: Spanish-English/English-Spanish. Comp. by Laurence Urdang Associates, Larousse 1976 pap. $2.95

Hammond Jeans Dictionary: Spanish-English/English-Spanish. Hammond 1981 pap. $1.95

Lipton, Gladys, and Olivia Muñoz. *Spanish Bilingual Dictionary: A Beginner's Guide in Words and Pictures.* Barron text ed. 1975 pap. $5.95

A New Pronouncing Dictionary of the Spanish and English Languages. Comp. by Mariano Velazquez de la Cadena, Edward Gray, and Juan L. Iribas, Appleton 1973 $7.95 thumb-indexed $8.95. The primary updating seems to be in the vocabulary, although European Spanish is favored.

Parnwell, E. C. *Oxford Picture Dictionary of American English.* Oxford 1980 pap. $6.95. English-Spanish ed.

Redfern, James. *A Glossary of Spanish Literary Composition.* Harcourt 1973 pap. $3.50

Renty, Ivan de. *El Mundo de los Negocios: Lexico Inglés-Español.* Larousse 1977 pap. $5.95

Savaiano, Eugene, and Lynn W. Winget. *2001 Modismos en Inglés: 2001 English Idioms for Spanish Speakers.* Barron 1981 pap. $3.95. This book is also published as parts 1 and 3 of *2001 Spanish and English Idioms.*

Simon and Schuster's International Dictionary: English/Spanish, Spanish/English. Ed. by Tanya de Gamez and others, Simon & Schuster 1973 $10.95 pap. $2.95

Stahl, Fred A., and Gary E. A. Scavnicky. *Reverse Dictionary of the Spanish Language.* Univ. of Illinois Pr. 1973 $10.00

Williams, Edwin B. *Webster's Williams Spanish and English Dictionary.* Castle Bks. 1980 $6.98

———. *The Williams Spanish and English Dictionary.* Scribner expanded ed. $13.50

CHAPTER 3

General Biography and Autobiography

Susan Steinberg

> It appears to me that mine is the best plan of biography that can be conceived; for my readers will, as near as may be, accompany Johnson in his progress, and, as it were, see each scene as it happened.
> —JAMES BOSWELL in Paul Kendall's *Art of Biography*

This chapter supplements and complements Chapter 17, "Literary Biography and Autobiography," of Volume 1 in *The Reader's Adviser*, and is chiefly concerned with those writers whose careers and reputations have been primarily as biographers and autobiographers. Also in this chapter will be found listings for individuals of immense importance in other fields—Benjamin Franklin and George Washington, for instance—who have written significant autobiographical works or the body of whose papers constitutes an almost autobiographical account. Because biography forms an important part of so many other subjects—literature and history most obviously, but running the gamut from the arts to sports to science— the distinction is not always an easy one to make. Life histories of great value can be found elsewhere in *The Reader's Adviser* under a number of other categories.

This chapter begins with a brief list of works on the writing of biography and relevant reference works. There follows a selected list of recent biographies and autobiographies, for the most part by authors who are not treated at length in this chapter, followed by separate sections on biographers and autobiographers. The last section discusses published papers.

Many individuals important in a number of fields had in their lifetimes little time or inclination to commit acts of autobiography, but nonetheless in their letters, diaries, and other documents have supplied a rich, if unconscious, record of their lives in their own words. Where this record took the form of memoirs or a diary—literary forms by definition requiring some conscious intent to record one's life—the writer has been considered an autobiographer and has been included in that section. Where the life history is comprised primarily of a body of papers not obviously shaped by an autobiographical intent, the writer has been discussed in the section on published papers. A few individuals—for example, Benjamin Franklin and Ulysses Grant—fit both categories.

The biographical and autobiographical impulse appears to be almost as old as the written word, and continues strong today, though the early emphasis on the improving moral content of exemplary lives has largely disappeared. Biographies take many forms other than the printed word, including the stage (*Evita*) and film (*Gandhi*).

Recent decades have seen a number of developments in the writing of biography that have brought the form far from the pious accounts of earlier periods. A more permissive atmosphere in the 1960s condoned and encouraged inclusion of much personal detail previously considered scandalous. Coupled with this has been the growth of psychohistory and psychobiography, the use of psychoanalytic techniques and insights to understand better the individual under study. More recently has come the discovery of individuals—members of minority groups and women, most obviously—formerly less focused on by biographers. At the same time there has been increased attention to and appreciation of the life histories of less famous persons. Oral history techniques, originally developed by anthropologists and folklorists, have been especially useful in recording such lives.

Presidents, secretaries of state, and other political figures and their spouses and staffs continue the well-established tradition of rushing into print with their own explanations and vindications of their careers. The flood of such works reached a high-water mark in the years immediately following Watergate, but more recent administrations have also been well represented.

ON THE WRITING OF BIOGRAPHY AND AUTOBIOGRAPHY

Altick, Richard D. *Lives and Letters: A History of Literary Biographies in England and America*. Greenwood repr. of 1965 ed. 1979 lib. bdg. $32.50

Bottrall, Margaret. *Everyman a Phoenix: Studies in Seventeenth-Century Autobiography*. *Essay Index Repr. Ser.* Ayer repr. of 1958 ed. $15.00

Bowen, Catherine D. *The Adventures of a Biographer*. Little, Brown, 1959 o.p.

———. *Biography: The Craft and the Calling*. Greenwood repr. of 1969 ed. 1978 lib. bdg. $22.50

Briscoe, Mary L. *A Bibliography of American Autobiography, 1945–1980*. Univ. of Wisconsin Pr. 1982 text ed. $30.00

Cockshut, A. O. *The Art of Autobiography in Nineteenth and Twentieth Century England*. Yale Univ. Pr. 1984 $20.00

———. *Truth to Life: The Art of Biography in the Nineteenth Century*. Harcourt 1974 $7.50

Daghlian, Philip B., ed. *Essays in Eighteenth-Century Biography*. Indiana Univ. Pr. 1968 $6.95

Edel, Leon. *Writing Lives: Principia Biographica*. Norton 1984 $15.95. A collection of essays by a master of the biographical art—its principles, problems, and noted practitioners.

Kaplan, Louis, and others, eds. *A Bibliography of American Autobiographers*. Univ. of

Wisconsin Pr. 1961 o.p. Selective list of 6,377 American autobiographies published before 1945.

Kendall, Paul M., and Stephen B. Oates. *The Art of Biography*. Ed. by Robin W. Winks, *History and Historiography Ser.* Garland 1985 lib. bdg. $20.00; Norton 1985 pap. $4.95

Matthew, William, comp. *British Autobiographies: An Annotated Bibliography of British Autobiographies Published or Written Before 1951*. Univ. of California Pr. 1984 $25.00

Pachter, Marc, ed. *Telling Lives: The Biographer's Art*. Univ. of Pennsylvania Pr. 1981 pap. $9.95. Essays by current biographers or historians practicing the art, including Leon Edel and Barbara Tuchman.

Padover, Saul K., ed. *Confessions and Self-Portraits*. *Essay Index Repr. Ser.* Ayer repr. of 1957 ed. $21.00

Pascal, Roy. *Design and Truth in Autobiography*. Ed. by Robin W. Winks, *History and Historiography Ser.* Garland 1985 lib. bdg. $20.00

REFERENCE WORKS

Biography Index. 1946–to date. Wilson quarterly. With bound annual and permanent three-year cumulations. Indexes biographical information in both books and magazines. Each issue includes useful index to occupations and professions.

Biography News. 1974–to date. Gale bimonthly. With annual clothbound volumes called *Biography Yearbook*.

Contemporary Authors: A Bio-Bibliographical Guide to Current Writers in Fiction, General Nonfiction, Poetry, Journalism, Drama, Motion Pictures, Television, and Other Fields. 1962–to date. Gale annual ea. $88.00. An up-to-date source that includes lesser-known authors. Articles are brief and followed by a list of the authors' published works.

Current Biography Yearbook 1985. Wilson annual 1985 $35.00. An annual cumulation of a valuable reference source issued monthly. Articles of medium length on people currently in the news.

Dictionary of American Biography. Scribner 17 vols. text ed. $1,100.00. Includes supplements 1–7. Known as *DAB*, this set is a guide to Americans who are no longer living, with scholarly articles noted for their balance and objectivity, signed by their authors and including bibliographies.

Dictionary of National Biography. Oxford 22 vols. 1882–1953 $998.00 supplement 1; $89.00 supplement 2; $72.00 supplement 3; $89.00 supplement 4; $89.00 supplement 5; $89.00 supplement 6. The set on which *DAB* was modeled covers British figures. Articles are signed and include bibliographies. They vary in length with the importance of the person discussed.

Notable American Women, 1607–1950: A Biographical Dictionary. Ed. by Edward T. James and Janet W. James, Harvard Univ. Pr. (Belknap Pr.) 3 vols. 1971 pap. $32.50

Notable American Women: The Modern Period. Ed. by Barbara Sicherman and others, Harvard Univ. Pr. (Belknap Pr.) 1983 pap. $12.95. One of the few reference works worth reading for its literary quality, listing women who, with the exception of the wives of U.S. presidents, achieved lasting significance in their own right.

A SELECTED LIST OF RECENT BIOGRAPHIES AND AUTOBIOGRAPHIES

Many excellent biographies appear within author entries throughout this volume and in other volumes of *The Reader's Adviser*. Most of the titles below are works of special quality and recent publication.

Alexander, Shana. *Very Much a Lady: The Untold Story of Jean Harris and Dr. Herman Tarnower*. Little, Brown 1983 $17.00. Alexander's reportorial account of the controversial murder case. While avowedly sympathetic to Harris, Alexander supplies the clearest chronology of what happened, with plausible interpretations of why. It is usefully read with Diana Trilling's more ruminative book.

Arrington, Leonard. *Brigham Young: American Moses*. Knopf 1985 $24.95. A noted Mormon historian brings both fairness and sympathy to bear in this biography of one of the Church's founders.

Baker, Leonard. *Days of Sorrow and Pain: Leo Baeck and the Berlin Jews*. Oxford 1980 pap. $9.95. Winner of the 1979 Pulitzer Prize for biography.

Baker, Russell. *Growing Up*. Congdon & Weed 1982 $15.00; New Amer. Lib. (Signet) 1984 pap. $3.95. Baker's tale of his family and the process of growing up is "touching and funny, a hopeless muddle of sadness and laughter that bears a suspicious resemblance to real life" (*N.Y. Times*). Awarded the Pulitzer Prize for biography in 1983.

Baraka, Amiri. *The Autobiography of LeRoi Jones-Amiri Baraka*. Freundlich 1984 $16.95. In an autobiography of "density and lyricism" (*N.Y. Times*), the prolific Afro-American poet, novelist, and nationalist chronicles his various metamorphoses, each symbolized by a partial or total change of names.

Bate, W. Jackson. *Samuel Johnson*. Harcourt 1977 $19.95 1979 pap. $7.95. Awarded the Pulitzer Prize for biography in 1978.

Bateson, Mary C. *With a Daughter's Eye: A Memoir of Margaret Mead and Gregory Bateson*. Ed. by Pat Golbitz, Morrow 1984 $15.95; Washington Square Pr. 1985 pap. $4.95. The author, an anthropologist herself, views her parents with affection and gentle criticism, and recounts their lives together with considerable literary skill.

Brodie, Fawn M. *Richard Nixon: The Shaping of His Character*. Harvard Univ. Pr. 1983 pap. $8.95; Norton 1981 $18.95. A controversial study of the former president using, in part, psychosocial methods of interpretation.

Buckley, William F., Jr. *Overdrive: A Personal Documentary*. Doubleday 1983 $16.95; Little, Brown 1984 pap. $8.70. Eight days in the life of the noted Conservative intended to serve as a "device for autobiographical introspection." Nora Ephron says that instead "he has written a book about money . . . a boy born to a small oil fortune grows up to be a man with . . . the secure belief that even his preference in peanut butter will be of interest to his fans. His attitude toward life is so cheerful and good-natured—and what's more, he's right about the peanut butter—that it seems almost churlish to point out that it is possible to spend too much time in a limousine."

Chesnut, Mary B. *Mary Chesnut's Civil War*. Ed. by C. Vann Woodward, Yale Univ. Pr. 1981 $40.00 pap. $14.95. Diaries of the Civil War kept by an intelligent and articulate woman whose husband was a Confederate cabinet member. Contains lengthy introduction and skilled editing by the distinguished southern historian. The book won the Pulitzer Prize.

Connell, Evan S. *Son of the Morning Star: Custer and Little Bighorn*. Harper 1985 pap.

$8.95; North Point Pr. 1984 $20.00. A bestseller that manages to be a fresh retelling of an oft-told tale.

Crankshaw, Edward. *Bismarck*. Penguin 1983 pap. $7.95; Viking 1981 $19.95. A traditional life and times that pictures Bismarck as antihero.

Dundy, Elaine. *Elvis and Gladys*. Macmillan 1985 $18.95. A humane and level-headed account of a towering figure of U.S. popular culture and his relationship with his mother, set firmly in the small-town Mississippi background that formed them both. A welcome alternative to the sensationalism of most accounts.

Erickson, Carolly. *The First Elizabeth*. Summit 1983 $19.95 1984 pap. $9.95

———. *Great Harry: The Extravagant Life of Henry VIII*. Summit 1980 $14.95 1984 pap. $9.95. A medieval historian's rich and readable portraits of the two most famous Tudors—Elizabeth I and Henry VIII.

Fraser, Antonia. *Royal Charles: Charles II and the Restoration*. Dell (Delta) 1980 pap. $8.95; Knopf 1979 $19.95. More complicated and intelligent than "The Merry Monarch" of most biographies, Charles II emerges from this biography as chiefly devoted to guaranteeing that the turmoil and tragedy of the Civil War and his father's beheading would not happen again.

Gallagher, Hugh G. *FDR's Splendid Deception*. Dodd 1985 $16.95. An absorbing account of the enormous lengths to which Franklin Roosevelt went to hide visible evidences of the ravages of polio.

Garnett, Angelica. *Deceived with Kindness: A Bloomsbury Childhood*. Harcourt 1985 $14.95. Garnett, the daughter of Vanessa Bell, the painter and pillar of the Bloomsbury Group, had an inconceivably complicated childhood that she chronicles with a mixture of baffled pain and understanding. The book includes fascinating glimpses of her aunt, Virginia Woolf, her supposed father, Clive Bell, her real father, Duncan Grant, and other Bloomsbury luminaries.

Green, Julien. *God's Fool: The Life of Francis of Assisi*. Harper 1985 $16.30. Green attempts, with considerable success, a careful portrait of the saint despite the besetting problem: "How can the truth be discovered about a man who was recognized as a saint in his own lifetime and around whom legends and stories of miracles increased yearly?" (*N.Y. Times*).

Haley, Alex. *Roots*. Doubleday 1976 $17.95. Haley's chronicle of the search for his heritage through the use of oral history and tradition, as well as imaginative reconstructions, inspired a generation of Americans to a renewed interest in their ethnic and family backgrounds.

Harlan, Louis R. *Booker T. Washington*. Oxford 2 vols. 1972–83 ea. $30.00. The second volume of Harlan's authoritative biography won him the Bancroft Prize and the Pulitzer Prize in 1984.

Hildesheimer, Wolfgang. *Mozart*. Trans. by Marion Faber, Farrar 1982 $22.50; Random (Vintage) pap. $8.95. The author, a German novelist, has produced not a systematic or chronological argument but, as he says, "a book of disagreement, a response to provocation, the attempt to cleanse and restore a fresco which has been painted over repeatedly in the course of centuries."

Iacocca, Lee, and William Novak. *Iacocca: An Autobiography*. Bantam 1984 & 1985 $19.95. The "savior of Chrysler," who has become something of a folk hero, tells his own story in the forthright and colorful way for which he is famous.

Kapuscinski, Ryszard. *The Emperor: Downfall of an Autocrat*. Trans. by William R. Brand and Katarzyna Mroczkowska Brand, Harcourt 1983 $12.95; Random (Vintage) 1984 pap. $5.95. Using interviews the author assembled an "alternatively acrid and hilarious portrait" (*Time*) of Haile Selassie, the crazed pomp and crushing poverty of Ethiopia, and how the "King of Kings, Elect of God, Lion of Judah" fell from glory.

Leakey, Mary. *Disclosing the Past: An Autobiography*. Doubleday 1984 $15.95. An account of the family whose individual and communal researches have so enriched knowledge of humankind's beginnings.

Lord, James. *Giacometti: A Biography*. Farrar 1985 $30.00. A fascinating biography of the sculptor by a man who knew him and knows the Paris in which he lived, who capably mixes keen psychological insight and perceptive gossip to portray his subject.

McFeely, William S. *Grant: A Biography*. Norton 1981 $19.95 1982 pap. $9.95. The best biography of Grant to date. McFeely's book won the Pulitzer Prize for biography in 1982.

Mack, John E. *A Prince of Our Disorder: The Life of T. E. Lawrence*. Little, Brown 1978 $15.00 pap. $7.95. An award-winning biography of the enigmatic World War I hero and man of mystery.

Malone, Dumas. *Jefferson and His Time: The Sage of Monticello*. Little, Brown 1981 $24.50 pap. $12.45. The final volume of the definitive biography of Jefferson, produced in magisterial fashion by his great biographer.

Massie, Robert K. *Peter the Great: His Life and His World*. Ballantine text ed. 1981 $10.95; Knopf 1980 $19.95. The experienced biographer of Russian czars won the Pulitzer Prize for this study of a giant of a man who brought order and a semblance of modernity to Russia.

Mellow, James R. *Invented Lives: The Marriage of F. Scott and Zelda Fitzgerald*. Ballantine 1986 pap. $4.95; Houghton Mifflin 1984 $22.50. The award-winning biographer explores the dazzle and destruction of the couple who became emblematic of the Jazz Age, and with them portrays the fever of the New York literary and theatrical world and expatriate Paris and the contemporaries from Hemingway to Dorothy Parker whose lives interwove with theirs.

Oates, Stephen B. *Let the Trumpet Sound: The Life of Martin Luther King, Jr.* Harper 1982 $22.07; New Amer. Lib. 1985 pap. $4.95

———. *With Malice Toward None: The Life of Abraham Lincoln*. Harper 1977 $15.95; New Amer. Lib. 1978 pap. $4.95. An expert biographer, Oates extends in both *Let the Trumpet Sound* and *With Malice Toward None* the study, begun in his work on John Brown, of men who shaped the struggle for black equality in the United States.

Pawel, Ernst. *The Nightmare of Reason: A Life of Franz Kafka*. Farrar $25.50; Random (Vintage) 1985 $7.95. A "corrective and amplification" of earlier biographies, this "wise and richly dimensioned" (*N.Y. Times*) book goes beyond rescuing Kafka from self-created caricature. It explores all aspects of Kafka's life and reasserts the centrality of Kafka's Austro-Hungarian and Jewish backgrounds as keys to understanding him. Pawel is wonderfully opinionated and his wit and passion in expressing his views are one of the great joys of this book.

Pym, Barbara. *A Very Private Eye: An Autobiography in Diaries and Letters*. Ed. by Hazel Holt and Hilary Pym, Dutton 1984 $19.95; Random (Vintage) 1985 pap. $6.95. A sprightly and moving autobiographical account pieced together from letters and diaries of the newly rediscovered British novelist.

Rosengarten, Theodore. *All God's Dangers: The Life of Nate Shaw*. Knopf 1974 $15.00; Random (Vintage) 1984 pap. $8.95. "The autobiography of an illiterate man" told to a skilled practitioner of the art of oral history, recounting in the rich language of a natural storyteller the life of a black sharecropper in the South in the 1930s.

Salvatore, Nick. *Eugene V. Debs: Citizen and Socialist*. Univ. of Illinois Pr. text ed.

1982 $24.95 pap. $9.95. Although successive generations have reinterpreted Debs to suit current needs, Salvatore adheres closely to the documentary record and produces a forceful and admiring narrative, and a scrupulously documented one.

Scammell, Michael. *Solzhenitsyn: A Biography.* Norton 1984 $29.95. A huge book dedicated to setting the record straight, sorting fact from myth. Scammell initially had the cooperation of his subject, although this was later withdrawn. Despite its size, the book retains its fascination throughout.

Schlesinger, Arthur M., Jr. *Robert Kennedy and His Times.* Ballantine 1985 pap. $4.95; Houghton Mifflin 1978 $19.95. Drawing on his long association with the Kennedy family, the noted historian draws a detailed, admiring, but nonetheless remarkably balanced portrait of RFK.

Silver, Eric. *Begin: The Haunted Prophet.* Random 1984 $17.45. The author manages the difficult balance of being both critical and fair to his subject, who from his beginnings as a guerrilla fighter to his appointment as prime minister of Israel was always bitterly controversial.

Silverman, Kenneth. *The Life and Times of Cotton Mather.* Columbia Univ. Pr. 1985 pap. $14.50; Harper 1984 $28.80. Too often pictured as the stereotypical Puritan, Mather emerges from this book as a complicated, passionate, and sometimes infuriating man who dominated his time by force of intellect and faith. It won the Bancroft Prize in 1985.

Steel, Ronald. *Walter Lippmann and the American Century.* Little, Brown 1980 $22.50; Random (Vintage) 1981 pap. $7.95. The Bancroft Prize in 1981 was awarded to this study of a dominant intellectual figure, whose career spanned the years from the Progressive Era to the time of John F. Kennedy.

Strousse, Jean. *Alice James: A Biography.* Houghton Mifflin 1980 $15.00 1984 pap. $7.95. A prize-winning account of the troubled and difficult life of the talented sister of William and Henry James who lived the life of an invalid in the overwhelming company of her family.

Toth, Susan A. *Blooming: A Small-Town Girlhood.* Ballantine 1985 pap. $3.50; Little, Brown 1981 $10.95; 1982 pap. $6.70. An evocative account of growing up in the Midwest in the 1950s, when there was still "a chance to grow up quietly and gradually" (*N.Y. Times*).

Troyat, Henri. *Catherine the Great.* Trans. by Joan Pinkham, Berkley 1984 pap. $3.95; Dutton 1980 $15.95

Welty, Eudora. *One Writer's Beginnings.* Harvard Univ. Pr. 1984 $10.00; Warner Bks. 1985 pap. $3.95. The major American writer, winner of the Pulitzer Prize for literature in 1973, gives us glimpses of her growing up with the ear for Mississippi voices and the eye for commonplace, but with telling detail that is so characteristic of her fiction.

Zeigler, Philip. *Mountbatten.* Harper 1986 pap. $10.95; Knopf 1985 $24.95. A perceptive biography of a great but exasperating man, the scion of a number of royal houses who forged a brilliant career in an egalitarian age, culminating in the Viceroyalty of India at the end of the British raj.

Biographers

BEMIS, SAMUEL FLAGG. 1891–1973

[SEE Chapter 7 in this volume.]

BOSWELL, JAMES. 1740–1795
[SEE Volume 1, Chapter 17.]

BOWEN, CATHERINE DRINKER. 1897–1973

Coming from a family that insisted that "music is an accomplishment, not a profession," Catherine Drinker Bowen did some free-lance writing on musical subjects and became known first for a volume of autobiographical essays for amateur music lovers entitled *Friends and Fiddlers* (1935, o.p.).

Yankee from Olympus (1944, o.p.), written with sympathy and imagination, is a study of three generations of the Holmes family in Massachusetts: Abiel, the minister, born in 1763; Oliver Wendell, the doctor and "The Autocrat of the Breakfast Table," born in 1809; and Mr. Justice Holmes, who died in 1935. In her triad on lawyers, the third, *The Lion and the Throne: The Life and Times of Sir Edward Coke*, about an early champion of civil rights, may well prove the most significant. In *Francis Bacon: The Temper of a Man* (o.p.), Bowen presented that many-sided genius "in all his complexity. The great and the near great of his age are all here in telling incidents and sharp vignettes" (*LJ*).

Bowen spent three years researching *Miracle at Philadelphia*, a study of the 55 men assembled during the hot summer of 1787 to work out the details of a constitution for the United States. "Everyone is interested in how such wonderful men came out of the Revolution. . . . These men had just shared a tremendous experience together. They were absolutely convinced of the necessity of what they were doing in Philadelphia. They began to develop a tremendous sense of responsibility, to feel that the eyes of the world were indeed on them" (*PW*). In addition to vivid portraits of the famous participants, the book catches the flavor of the endless debate on important minutiae and the terrible uncertainty about the outcome.

In the delightful series of essays *The Adventures of a Biographer*, Bowen explains why she wrote her books and tells something of the problems and adventures she encountered in the process. "An indefatigable worker, a researcher with a passion for accuracy," she writes with vivacious enthusiasm. Among her many honors are the 1958 National Book Award for Nonfiction, election to the National Institute of Arts and Letters, the Sarah Josepha Hale Award, and the Constance Lindsay Skinner Award of the Women's National Book Association.

BOOKS BY BOWEN

The Lion and the Throne: The Life and Times of Sir Edward Coke. Little, Brown 1957 pap. $9.95. The biography of the eminent English lawyer.

The Adventures of a Biographer: An Intimate Reminiscence. Little-Atlantic 1959 o.p.

Miracle at Philadelphia: The Story of the Constitutional Convention, May to September 1787. Little, Brown 1966 $12.95

Biography: The Craft and the Calling. Greenwood repr. of 1969 ed. 1978 lib. bdg. $22.50. A discussion of her views on biographical writing. "As informative and charming and elegant a bit of shoptalk as I have read" (Katherine Gauss Jackson, *Harper's*).

Family Portrait. Little-Atlantic 1970 o.p. Bowen's account of her own family, written
  with her customary vividness and sensitivity.
The Most Dangerous Man in America: Scenes from the Life of Benjamin Franklin. Little, Brown 1974 $13.95. "After a biographical sketch of Franklin's youth, essays
  written with precision and humor review his scientific experimentation, describe his efforts to pacify the Indians, and illuminate the lengthy diplomatic career that saw Franklin at his best in an increasingly unsympathetic England"
  (*Booklist*).

CECIL, LORD DAVID. 1902–

[SEE Volume 1, Chapter 17.]

CHAPMAN, HESTER W(OLFERSTAN). 1899–1976

Chapman, an Englishwoman, has a long list of distinguished novels and
biographies to her credit. However, it is her expert and entertaining studies
of Tudor-Stuart figures, major and minor, which first made her American
reputation. Of *Two Tudor Portraits* (1963, o.p.), Charles Poore said in the
N.Y. Times: "Her pages are alive with interesting detail and she recreates
the Tudor era with sharp, selective mastery."

BOOKS BY CHAPMAN

Great Villiers: A Study of George Villiers, 2nd Duke of Buckingham, 1628–1687. Rich-
  ard West repr. of 1949 ed. $25.00
Mary Second: Queen of England. Greenwood repr. of 1953 ed. 1976 lib. bdg. $19.50
Privileged Persons: Four Seventeenth-Century Studies. Reynal 1967 $6.00. Essays on
  the private lives of Sophia, Electress of Hanover; Hortense Mancini, a famous
  beauty; Louis XIII; and Thomas Bruce, Earl of Ailesbury.
The Challenge of Anne Boleyn. Putnam 1974 $7.95
Four Fine Gentlemen. Univ. of Nebraska Pr. 1978 $21.95

EDEL, (JOSEPH) LEON. 1907–

[SEE Volume 1, Chapter 17.]

FREEMAN, DOUGLAS SOUTHALL. 1886–1953

Douglas Southall Freeman is one of the greatest biographers the United
States has produced, and one of the greatest military historians as well.
Born in Richmond, Virginia, he was editor of the Richmond *News Leader*
from 1915 to 1949, when he retired to devote most of his time to writing. He
was an authority on military strategy and on military history of the Civil
War. His biographies are notable for their "almost incredibly detailed research . . . remorseless analysis of the reliability of testimony . . . steady
holding of the balances of judgment." *R. E. Lee* won the Pulitzer Prize for biography. A second Pulitzer Prize was awarded to him in 1958 for *George
Washington: A Biography.* Freeman was chosen by Princeton University and
the Jefferson Bicentennial Commission as chairman of the advisory committee for the definitive edition of *The Papers of Thomas Jefferson* (see the last
section of this chapter, "Published Papers"). "Douglas Southall Freeman
closed his useful and busy life dramatically when he died at his desk after

having written the last paragraph of the sixth volume of his biography of George Washington" (*N.Y. Times*). After Freeman's death the completion of his great work was entrusted to John Alexander Carroll, who had carried on the necessary research in the Library of Congress, and Mary Wells Ashworth, who had assisted the author at his home in Richmond. They followed "their master's style and approach so religiously that one can scarcely detect that there has been a change in authorship."

BOOKS BY FREEMAN

R. E. Lee. Scribner 4 vols. 1935 $150.00
Lee's Lieutenants. Scribner 3 vols. 1942–44 $105.00
George Washington: A Biography. Kelley 7 vols. repr. of 1957 ed. 1975 lib. bdg. ea. $27.50. Volume 7 was completed by Ashworth and Carroll.

GASKELL, MRS. ELIZABETH (CLEGHORN STEVENSON). 1810–1865
[SEE Volume 1, Chapter 11.]

HEROLD, J(EAN) CHRISTOPHER. 1919–1964

J. Christopher Herold's *Mistress to an Age* (1958) won the National Book Award in 1959 as "a witty, beautifully controlled and highly entertaining account of one of the most remarkable women in history"—Germaine de Stael (1763–1817), the militant Swiss bluestocking. His *Bonaparte in Egypt* (o.p.) deals with a phase of Napoleon's career about which little has been written in English. *The Horizon Book of the Age of Napoleon* is a panorama of a tumultuous age, 1793–1815. He edited and translated *The Mind of Napoleon*, a collection of Napoleon's written and spoken words. Born in Czechoslovakia of Austrian parents, Herold was a grandson of Artur Schnabel, the pianist. Educated at German colleges and the University of Geneva, he emigrated to the United States in 1939 and finished his studies at Columbia University. He served in World War II with Army Intelligence and later joined the editorial staff of Columbia University Press. In 1956 Herold became editor in chief of Stanford University Press while he continued his writing.

BOOKS BY HEROLD

(ed.). *The Mind of Napoleon: A Selection of His Written and Spoken Words.* Columbia Univ. Pr. 1955 pap. $12.00
Mistress to an Age: A Life of Madame de Stael. Crown 1979 pap. $2.98; Greenwood repr. of 1958 ed. 1975 lib. bdg. $25.25
The Horizon Book of the Age of Napoleon. Crown 1983 pap. $14.95; Harper 1963 $30.00. "Herold's book is essentially an attack on the view of Napoleon as a bearer of the Enlightenment. Though, according to Herold, Napoleon entered the stage of history through a door the Enlightenment opened, the part he played was a flat rebuttal of all the arguments for opening it . . . [Napoleon] exercised a reactionary influence, especially in laws affecting the family and women" (*Harper's*).

JENKINS, ELIZABETH. 1907–

Elizabeth Jenkins is best known in the United States as a biographer, although she has published a number of successful novels. Perhaps best known is *Elizabeth the Great*, a subtle and perceptive portrait of one of the most intelligent and skillful rulers in history, arguably the greatest of England's monarchs. Her account of the relationship of *Elizabeth and Leicester* (o.p.) is an equally readable sequel. Elizabeth Jenkins was educated at Newnham College, Cambridge, and received the Femina Vie Heureuse Prize for *Harriet* (1934, o.p.).

Books by Jenkins

Henry Fielding. Folcroft repr. of 1948 ed. lib. bdg. $10.00
Six Criminal Women. Biography Index Repr. Ser. Ayer repr. of 1949 ed. $18.00. Six erring Englishwomen are the subjects of these studies.
Elizabeth the Great. Putnam 1959 $8.95

JOHNSON, SAMUEL. 1709–1784

[See Volume 1, Chapter 17.]

JOSEPHSON, MATTHEW. 1899–1978

The choice of subjects for *The Robber Barons* and *The Politicos* has given Josephson a special position as the chronicler of the last half of the nineteenth century. In reviewing *Edison* the *Nation* said: " 'America's ablest biographer' as Josephson was called by John Erskine, can recreate a great technological figure just as vividly as he portrayed the robber barons, politicos and novelists of his earlier books." Josephson was elected to the National Institute of Arts and Letters in 1948.

Books by Josephson

Zola and His Time: The History of His Martial Career in Letters, with His Circle of Friends, His Remarkable Enemies, Cyclopean Labours, Public Campaigns, Trials and Ultimate Glorification. Century Bookbindery repr. of 1928 ed. 1985 lib. bdg. $50.00; Richard West repr. of 1929 ed. lib. bdg. $50.00
Jean-Jacques Rousseau. Richard West repr. of 1931 ed. $21.00
The Robber Barons, 1861–1901. 1934. Harcourt 1962 pap. $5.95. A study of such great American capitalists as Rockefeller, Morgan, Vanderbilt, Carnegie, Gould, and Frick, who flourished after the Civil War.
The Politicos. 1938. Harcourt 1963 pap. $5.95. A study of the American political leaders of the post-Civil War period.
The President Makers: The Culture of Politics in an Age of Enlightenment. 1940. Putnam (Perigee) 1979 pap. $6.95. An analysis of the political reform incited by the wealthy progressives of the time.
Victor Hugo: A Realistic Biography of the Great Romantic. Telegraph Bks. repr. of 1942 ed. 1982 lib. bdg. $45.00
Empire of the Air: Juan Trippe and the Struggle for World Airways. Lit. and History of Aviation Ser. Ayer repr. of 1944 ed. 1972 $22.00
Stendhal, or The Pursuit of Happiness. Russell repr. of 1946 ed. 1979 $14.50
Edison. McGraw-Hill 1959 pap. $7.95

Portrait of the Artist as an American. Octagon 1964 lib. bdg. $23.00. The fate of various artists in the United States.
The Money Lords. New Amer. Lib. 1972 pap. $1.95

BOOK ABOUT JOSEPHSON

Shi, David E. *Matthew Josephson: Bourgeois Bohemian.* Yale Univ. Pr. 1981 $24.00

LOCKHART, JOHN GIBSON. 1794–1854
[SEE Volume 1, Chapter 17.]

MAUROIS, ANDRE (pseud. of Émile Herzog). 1885–1967
[SEE Volume 1, Chapter 17.]

MORISON, SAMUEL ELIOT. 1887–1976
[SEE Chapter 7 in this volume.]

NEVINS, ALLAN. 1890–1971
[SEE Chapter 7 in this volume.]

PEARSON, HESKETH. 1887–1964
[SEE Volume 1, Chapter 17.]

PLUTARCH. c.46–c.125
[SEE Chapter 6 in this volume.]

QUENNELL, PETER (COURTNEY). 1905–
[SEE Volume 1, Chapter 17.]

SANDBURG, CARL. 1878–1967
When the poet Sandburg published the first two volumes of his life of Lincoln it was hailed as a subtle and deeply sympathetic study based on diligent research. The publication of the last four volumes, *Abraham Lincoln: The War Years*, brought Sandburg the 1940 Pulitzer Prize for history, as biographies of Lincoln were not then eligible for the biography award, and established the work as one of the greatest American biographies. (See also Volume 1, Chapter 9.)

BOOKS BY SANDBURG

Letters. Ed. by Herbert Mitgang, Harcourt 1968 $12.50. Some 640 letters covering 64 years.
Abraham Lincoln: The Prairie Years. Harcourt 2 vols. 1926 $80.00. Biography of Lincoln up to his inauguration.
Abe Lincoln Grows Up. Harcourt repr. of 1928 ed. 1975 pap. $3.95 repr. of 1940 ed. 1985 $14.95. Chapters from *Abraham Lincoln: The Prairie Years.*
Abraham Lincoln: The War Years. Harcourt 4 vols. 1936–39 $160.00. Story of Lincoln's life from his inauguration to his death and funeral in 1865.
Abraham Lincoln: The Prairie Years and the War Years. Harcourt 6 vols. 1926–39 $240.00 rev. ed. in 1 vol. repr. of 1954 ed. $17.95 1974 pap. $10.95

Lincoln Collector: The Story of Oliver R. Barrett's Great Private Collection. Harcourt
1949 o.p. A source book of Lincolniana and Americana with a text by Sandburg
on how the Barrett collection was amassed.
Always the Young Strangers. Harcourt 1953 $12.95

Book about Sandburg

Callahan, North. *Carl Sandburg: Lincoln of Our Literature—A Biography.* New York
Univ. Pr. 1970 $25.00

STRACHEY, (GILES) LYTTON. 1880–1932

Lytton Strachey was a pivotal member of the famed Bloomsbury Group
that included E. M. Forster (see Vol. 1), Leonard Woolf (see Vol. 1), and
Virginia Woolf (see Vol. 1), and Clive Bell. Leon Edel has described him "as
the master of human character, of brevity and lucidity, of paradox and
irony." Strachey regarded history as Gibbon did, "not as the accumulation
of facts but the relation of them." Strachey's widespread influence on other
biographers may be attributed to his tendency to emphasize what a person
was rather than what a person did, and to seize on the uneventful parts of
life as the more interesting. His masterpiece, *Queen Victoria*, is the first biography of English royalty written with complete candor and with generous
doses of irreverence and humor. The writing of biography, he felt, should be
a creative art; "in his hands it was lucid, subtle, elegant, ironic, disillusion-
ing." Michael Holroyd's detailed biography was the first frank discussion of
Strachey's homosexuality and of his often convoluted relationships with
various Bloomsbury Group members and others. Strachey was also the author of *Landmarks in French Literature* (1912).

Books by Strachey

Eminent Victorians. 1918. Harcourt repr. of 1932 ed. 1969 pap. $6.95; Peter Smith
$7.50
Queen Victoria. 1921. *Modern Class. Ser.* Harcourt 1949 $6.95 1966 pap. $5.95
Elizabeth and Essex: A Tragic History. Harcourt 1969 pap. $6.95; Telegraph Bks. repr.
of 1928 ed. lib. bdg. $30.00
Portraits in Miniature and Other Essays. Folcroft repr. of 1931 ed. 1985 lib. bdg.
$40.00
Biographical Essays. Harcourt repr. of 1949 ed. 1969 pap. $6.95

Books about Strachey

Beerbohm, Max. *Lytton Strachey.* Folcroft repr. of 1943 ed. 1976 lib. bdg. $6.00; Has-
kell 1974 lib. bdg. $40.95; Richard West repr. of 1943 ed. 1973 $10.00
Edel, Leon. *Bloomsbury: A House of Lions.* Avon 1980 pap. $2.75; Harper 1979 $14.37
Edmonds, Michael. *Lytton Strachey: A Bibliography.* Garland 1981 lib. bdg. $36.00
Holroyd, Michael. *Lytton Strachey.* Holt 1980 pap. $8.95
Kallich, Martin. *The Psychological Milieu of Lytton Strachey.* New College & Univ. Pr.
1961 o.p.

Autobiographers

CASANOVA (or Casanova de Seingalt: Giovanni Jacopo [or Giacomo] Casanova de Seingalt). 1725–1798
[SEE Volume 1, Chapter 17.]

CHESTERFIELD, (PHILIP DORMER STANHOPE), 4th Earl of. 1694–1773
[SEE Volume 1, Chapter 17.]

CHURCHILL, WINSTON S. 1874–1965 (NOBEL PRIZE 1953)
[SEE Chapter 9 in this volume.]

EDEN, SIR (ROBERT) ANTHONY, EARL OF AVON. 1897–1977
"The man who succeeded Churchill" as Prime Minister of England emerges as "one of Europe's most prescient and effective spokesmen for freedom" in his autobiographical reports on the historic times he lived through. He was Churchill's foreign secretary and succeeded him as prime minister in 1955, retiring in 1957 after the Suez debacle. As cochairman of the 1954 Geneva Conference on Far Eastern Affairs, he withstood both French and American pressure to escalate the Indochinese war.

BOOKS BY EDEN

Foreign Affairs. Kraus repr. of 1939 ed. $23.00
Freedom and Order: Selected Speeches, 1939–1946. Kraus repr. of 1948 ed. $22.00
Facing the Dictators. Houghton Mifflin 1962 o.p. The second volume of his memoirs tells the tragic story of the years 1923–38 when statesmen of Europe and the world found no way to stop the depredations of the dictators short of the war that came in 1939.
The Reckoning. Houghton Mifflin 1965 o.p. This volume of memoirs covers the war years, 1938–45, during which Eden served as Foreign Minister.

EISENHOWER, DWIGHT DAVID. 1890–1969
As Commander-in-Chief of Allied Forces in Western Europe, Eisenhower was a preeminent hero of World War II. After a brief stint as president of Columbia University, he accepted the supreme command of NATO, and the following year ran successfully against Democrat Adlai Stevenson to become the 34th president of the United States. Politically inexperienced, Eisenhower as president relied on the counsel of men of greater experience, particularly John Foster Dulles. For a period after Eisenhower's departure from office, historic interpretations of his administration were strongly negative, but more recent versions have emphasized the positive and peaceful aspects of his epoch. In any case, Eisenhower enjoyed a high level of popular and electoral support during his two terms. He died in 1969, shortly after the election of his protégé, Richard Nixon, to the presidency.

BOOKS BY EISENHOWER

The Public Papers of the Presidents of the United States: Dwight D. Eisenhower. Government Printing Office 8 vols. 1953–61 consult publisher for information
The Cumulated Indexes to the Public Papers of the President of the United States, 1953–61. Kraus 1978 $55.00
Papers. Ed. by Alfred D. Chandler, Jr., and others, Johns Hopkins Univ. Pr. 11 vols. consult publisher for information. Under the general editorship of Alfred D. Chandler, Jr., a group of Johns Hopkins historians undertook the lengthy project of publishing a letterpress edition of a selection of Eisenhower's papers. For other similar sets, see the last section in this chapter, "Published Papers."
The White House Years. Doubleday 2 vols. 1956–61 $50.00
At Ease: Stories I Tell to Friends. 1967. Eastern Acorn 1981 pap. $4.95. The president's reminiscences and anecdotes.
Crusade in Europe. Da Capo 1977 $45.00 pap. $10.95
The Eisenhower Diaries. Ed. by Robert H. Ferrell, Norton 1981 $19.95. Able editing by an important American diplomatic historian.

BOOKS ABOUT EISENHOWER

Adams, Sherman. *Firsthand Report: The Story of the Eisenhower Administration.* Greenwood repr. of 1961 ed. 1975 lib. bdg. $32.25
Ambrose, Stephen E. *Eisenhower.* Simon & Schuster 2 vols. 1983–84 ea. $24.95 pap. ea. $12.95. Probably the best researched and written of the biographical accounts so far available.
Divine, Robert A. *Eisenhower and the Cold War.* Oxford 1981 $17.50 pap. $6.95
Hughes, Emmet J. *The Ordeal of Power: A Political Memoir of the Eisenhower Years.* Atheneum text ed. 1975 pap. $5.95. The best account of the administration by one of the president's staff.

EVELYN, JOHN. 1620–1706
[SEE Volume 1, Chapter 17.]

FRANK, ANNE. 1929–1945

When Anne Frank wrote in her diary, "I hope I shall be able to confide in you completely, as I have never been able to do in anyone before. . . ," she did not realize that she would become an imperishable symbol of courage all over the Western world. This journal of a German-Jewish girl, who for two years lived in Holland in hiding from the Nazis, is one of the most moving stories of World War II. After the Nazis discovered their hiding place the members of the family were sent to concentration camps and Anne died in Bergen-Belsen in 1945. The diary, which was discovered and saved by friends, covers the years 1942 to 1944, three days before the arrival of the Nazis. "Anne, like any true writer, was at her best when, without self-consciousness or elaborate device, she poured out her personality. Such enormously difficult simplicity is the hallmark of her journal. Not even terror or the most painful constraint could deprive her of a wonderfully feminine, young, vital responsiveness. Somehow she preserved enough of the teenager's normal frivolities and irresponsibilities—enough to make her abnormal plight comprehensible. . . . She has shown us that it is possible to re-main human as long as we are alive" (*N.Y. Times*).

Books by Frank

The Works of Anne Frank. Intro. by Anne Bierstein and Alfred Kazin, Greenwood repr. of 1959 ed. 1974 lib. bdg. $32.50. An edition of the *Diary* including a group of fables, essays, and personal reminiscences not previously published.

Anne Frank: The Diary of a Young Girl. Amereon $13.95; Doubleday rev. ed. 1967 $15.95; Washington Square Pr. pap. $2.50

Anne Frank's Tales from the Secret Annex. Trans. by Ralph Manheim and Michael Mok, Doubleday 1984 $14.95

Books about Frank

Goodrich, Frances, and Albert Hackett. *Diary of Anne Frank: Drama.* Random 1956 $9.95

Levin, Meyer. *The Obsession.* Simon & Schuster 1974 $8.95

Schnabel, Ernst. *Anne Frank: A Portrait in Courage.* Harcourt 1958 $7.50. A documentation of the *Diary* that tells of Anne's normal childhood, the Amsterdam hideaway, the arrest, and the horrors of the Nazi concentration camp.

FRANKLIN, BENJAMIN. 1706–1790

A man of many careers in his long life, Franklin is best known as a statesman and founding father of the U.S. republic. He appears here as the author of his famed *Autobiography* and the producer of the contents of the monumental *Papers.* The *Autobiography* was first printed in a French translation in 1791. The four different parts of the manuscript were written at various times and places, in England, France, and Philadelphia. John Bigelow secured possession of the original manuscript discovered in France, and edited the only unmutilated and correct version of it. This was first published by Lippincott in 1867, with a second edition in 1884. The fifth edition (1905) continues the life of Franklin from the point where the *Autobiography* ends (1757) through the remaining 33 years of his life. This was compiled by means of his correspondence and other writings. The first translations of the *Autobiography* appeared in London in 1793, one published by J. Parsons, the other by G. C. and J. Robinson. William Temple Franklin, the grandson of Benjamin Franklin, who was in possession of the original manuscript, brought out his English edition of it in 1817, very much expurgated.

Franklin signed the name Richard Saunders to his shrewd maxims and proverbs in *Poor Richard's Almanack* (1732–57). (It was undoubtedly derived from and follows the pattern of the English *Poor Robin's Almanac* started in 1663.)

Books by Franklin

The Papers of Benjamin Franklin. Ed. by Leonard W. Labaree, William B. Willcox, and others, Yale Univ. Pr. 1959–84 24 vols. ea. $55.00

Writings of Benjamin Franklin. Ed. by Albert H. Smyth, *Amer. History and Americana Ser.* Haskell 10 vols. repr. of 1907 ed. 1969 lib. bdg. $350.00

Letters to the Press, 1758–1775. Ed. by Verner W. Crane, *Institute of Early Amer. History and Culture Ser.* Univ. of North Carolina Pr. 1950 $24.00

The Autobiography of Benjamin Franklin. Intro. by J. W. Bigoness, Airmont pap. $1.50; Buccaneer Bks. 1981 lib. bdg. $18.95; intro. by L. Leary, Macmillan (Collier Bks.) 1962 pap. $3.95; ed. by P. M. Zall, *Norton Critical Eds.* 1984 pap. $6.95; ed. by Kenneth Silverman, *Penguin Class. Ser.* 1986 pap. $3.50; ed. by R. Jackson Wilson, *Modern Lib. College Ed. Ser.* Random text ed. 1981 pap. $3.95; ed. by P. M. Zall, Univ. of Tennessee Pr. 1981 $29.95; ed. by Leonard W. Labaree, Yale Univ. Pr. 1964 pap. $30.00. The Yale editors used Max Farrand's 1949 text based on the original manuscript, carefully rechecking it in the process. It is likely to become the standard edition. "This is one of those rarest of historiographical achievements: a publication of the original text of a historical and literary classic in which the bookmaker's art and the historian's best technical editorial skill are combined to produce a work that is both a dependable scholar's source, a reader's delight, and a thing of beauty" (*AHR*).

Autobiography and Selected Writings. Ed. by Dixon Wecter and Larzer Ziff, *Rinehart Ed.* Holt text ed. 1949 pap. $10.95; intro. by Henry Steele Commager, Modern Lib. 1981 pap. $3.95; ed. by L. J. Lemisch, New Amer. Lib. (Signet Class.) 1961 pap. $2.75

Historical Review of the Constitution and Government of Pennsylvania, from Its Origin. Research Lib. of Colonial Americana. Ayer repr. of 1759 ed. 1972 $37.50

The Bagatelles from Passy. Eakins 1967 $15.00. Between 1905 and 1910, quite by chance, a clerk in a New York City rare book dealer's shop discovered and ordered Franklin's *Bagatelles*, lost for 100 years, when he found it listed in a French bookseller's catalog for 50 cents. What arrived from Paris was the only known copy extant, presumably one of the set of pamphlets Franklin printed for his associates at the French court. It is now part of the William Smith Mason Collection at the Yale University Library. Leslie Katz, of Eakins Press, observed: "These works take him out of the realm of the thrifty penny-pincher, and show him to be not only a rich personality and a warm human being, but a first-rate literary mind as well."

The Sayings of Poor Richard: The Prefaces, Proverbs and Poems of Benjamin Franklin. Ed. by Paul Leicester, Burt Franklin repr. of 1890 ed. 1975 $24.50

Essays on General Politics, Commerce and Political Economy. Intro. by Joseph Dorfman, Kelley repr. of 1836 ed. $35.00

An Apology for Printers. Ed. by Randolph Goodman, Acropolis 1973 pap. $3.95

BOOKS ABOUT FRANKLIN

Bowen, Catherine D. *The Most Dangerous Man in America: Scenes from the Life of Benjamin Franklin*. Little, Brown 1974 $13.95

Breitweiser, Mitchell R. *Cotton Mather and Benjamin Franklin: The Price of Representative Personality. Studies in Amer. Lit. and Culture.* Cambridge Univ. Pr. 1985 $27.95

Clark, Ronald W. *Benjamin Franklin: A Biography*. Random 1983 $22.95

Crane, Verner W. *Benjamin Franklin and a Rising People. Lib. of Amer. Biography.* Little, Brown text ed. 1962 pap. $6.95. The best short account of Franklin's life.

Fay, Bernard. *Franklin: The Apostle of Modern Times*. Richard West repr. of 1929 ed. $30.00

———. *Two Franklins: Fathers of American Democracy*. Scholarly repr. of 1933 ed. 1971 $30.00

Ford, Paul L. *Franklin Bibliography: A List of Books Written by or Relating to Benja-*

min Franklin. Burt Franklin repr. of 1889 ed. 1966 $31.50; Longwood repr. of 1889 ed. 1977 lib. bdg. $25.00. More than 1,000 entries.

Lopez, Claude-Anne, and Eugenia W. Herbert. *The Private Franklin: The Man and His Family*. Norton 1975 $11.95 1985 pap. $7.95

Newcomb, Benjamin H. *Franklin and Galloway: A Political Partnership*. Yale Univ. Pr. 1972 $30.00

Randall, Willard. *A Little Revenge: Benjamin Franklin and His Son*. Little, Brown 1984 $22.50. The story of Franklin's troubled relationship with his illegitimate son, who became a Tory at the time of the revolution.

Stourzh, Gerald. *Benjamin Franklin and American Foreign Policy*. Univ. of Chicago Pr. 2d ed. repr. of 1954 ed. pap. $3.25

Van Doren, Carl. *Benjamin Franklin: A Biography*. Greenwood repr. of 1938 ed. 1973 lib. bdg. $47.25. The definitive life; winner of the Pulitzer Prize.

GANDHI, MOHANDAS K(ARAMCHAND). 1869–1948

[SEE Volume 4.]

GARRICK, DAVID. 1717–1779

"That young man never had his equal and never will have a rival," said ALEXANDER POPE (see Vol. 1) of the brilliant actor and theater manager of eighteenth-century England. Although his family wanted him to be a lawyer, Garrick remained enchanted with the theater from childhood and abandoned his law studies when the chance came. He went to London in 1737 with SAMUEL JOHNSON (see Vol. 1) and "three halfpence in his [pocket]" and supported himself as a wine merchant there until October 1741, when he achieved his first success as Richard III at Goodman's Fields. From 1747 to 1776 he was a partner and stage manager at the Drury Lane Theatre. Garrick sought to restore SHAKESPEARE (see Vol. 2) to the stage; he cared little for the bawdiness and sentimentality of the Restoration drama. He acted brilliantly in both comedy and tragedy and made many innovations in staging technique at Drury Lane. Garrick's original works were mainly farces such as *The Lying Valet* (1741) and *Bon Ton; or, High Life Above the Stairs* (1775). He also collaborated with other playwrights and adapted many plays by Shakespeare and Jonson. Garrick is buried in the Poets' Corner of Westminster Abbey.

BOOKS BY GARRICK

The Diary of David Garrick. Ed. by R. C. Alexander, Ayer repr. of 1928 $14.00

The Journal of David Garrick Describing His Visit to France and Italy in 1763. Ed. by G. W. Stone, Jr., Kraus repr. of 1939 ed. pap. $10.00. Printed from the original manuscript in the Folger Shakespeare Library.

Pineapples of Finest Flavour; or, a Selection of Sundry Unpublished Letters of the English Roscius, David Garrick. Ed. by David M. Little, Russell repr. of 1930 ed. 1967 $8.00

BOOKS ABOUT GARRICK

Davies, Thomas. *Memoirs of the Life of David Garrick*. Ed. by Stephen Jones, Ayer 2 vols. repr. of 1808 ed. $55.00

Stein, Elizabeth P. *David Garrick: Dramatist.* Ayer repr. of 1937 ed. $24.50; Kraus repr. of 1938 ed. $29.00; Telegraph Bks. repr. of 1937 ed. 1980 lib. bdg. $40.00

Stone, George W., Jr., and George M. Kahrl. *David Garrick: A Critical Biography.* Southern Illinois Univ. Pr. 1979 $60.00

GIBBON, EDWARD. 1737–1794

Gibbon wrote no less than six autobiographies and a seventh fragmentary sketch. The first account has only to do with the history of his family; the second covers 27 years of life; the third carries the story to 35 years of age; the fourth retells the same story to 35 years of age; the fifth to 52 years; and the sixth tells his early life to 16 years old. The first editor, the Earl of Sheffield, Gibbon's literary executor, wove these separate narratives into one and greatly condensed them (1796). Later editors, Milman in 1839, John Murray in 1896, and Birkbeck Hill in 1900, have printed the manuscript verbatim with various additions to it from the *Journals* and *Letters. Gibbon's Journal to January 28, 1763. My Journal I, II and III and Ephemerides, with introductory essays by D. M. Low* (1930, o.p.) was the first complete publication of the journal, which must be distinguished from his autobiography and his memoirs. "Among the books in which men have told the story of their own lives it stands in front rank. It is a striking fact that one of the first autobiographies and the first of biographies were written in the same year. Boswell was still working at his life of Johnson when Gibbon began those memoirs from which his autobiography, in the form in which it is given to the world, was so skillfully pieced together" (G. B. Hill).

Books by Gibbon

Autobiography. Ed. by M. M. Reese, Routledge & Kegan 1970 $9.95 pap. $4.95; *World's Class. Ser.* Oxford 1907 $16.95

Memoirs of My Life. 1900. Ed. by Betty Radice, *Penguin Eng. Lib. Ser.* 1984 pap. $4.95

Private Letters of Edward Gibbon. Ed. by Rowland E. Prothero, AMS Pr. 2 vols. repr. of 1896 ed. $75.00

Miscellaneous Works. Ed. by John Sheffield AMS Pr. 5 vols. repr. of 1814 ed. ea. $48.00

The English Essays of Edward Gibbon. Ed. by Patricia B. Craddock, Oxford 1972 $59.00

Gibboniana. Garland 17 vols. 1975 ea. $52.00

Books about Gibbon

Blunden, Edmund C. *Edward Gibbon and His Age.* Arden Lib. repr. of 1935 ed. 1978 lib. bdg. $7.50; Folcroft repr. of 1935 ed. 1974 lib. bdg. $7.50

Bowersock, Glen. *Edward Gibbon & the Decline and Fall of the Roman Empire.* Harvard Univ. Pr. 1977 $14.00

De Beer, Gavin R. *Edward Gibbon and His World.* Viking 1968 o.p. "A concise, beautifully written, compassionate account of the life and work of the unhappy, fat little author of 'The Decline and Fall'" (*New Yorker*). Copious illustrations.

Jordan, David P. *Gibbon and His Roman Empire.* Univ. of Illinois Pr. 1971 $19.50. A study of Gibbon as a product of the eighteenth-century Enlightenment.

White, Lynn, Jr. *The Transformation of the Roman World: Gibbon's Problem After Two Centuries.* Univ. of California Pr. 1966 pap. $5.95

GRANT, ULYSSES S(IMPSON). 1822–1885

Grant's *Personal Memoirs* (o.p.) was written when he had retired and was ill. Ranking among the best of military autobiographies, it was published in two volumes by MARK TWAIN's (see Vol. 1) publishing firm, Charles L. Webster and Co., and after its publication quickly ran to an enormous sale, said to have been the largest nonfiction sale of U.S. publishing history.

BOOKS BY GRANT

The Papers of Ulysses S. Grant. Ed. by John Y. Simon, Southern Illinois Univ. Pr. 12 vols. 1967–84 ea. $22.50–$45.00. The definitive collection of Grant's papers, some 80 percent of which had not been previously published.
Personal Memoirs. AMS Pr. 2 vols. in 1 repr. of 1894 ed. $42.50; intro. by William McFeely, Da Capo repr. of 1894 ed. 1982 pap. $10.95; intro. by Philip Stern Van Doren, Peter Smith abr. ed. $14.50
Letters of Ulysses S. Grant to His Father and His Youngest Sister. Kraus repr. of 1912 ed. $12.00
Letters to a Friend, 1861–1880. Ed. by James G. Wilson, AMS Pr. repr. of 1897 ed. $14.25

BOOKS ABOUT GRANT

Catton, Bruce. *Grant Moves South.* Little, Brown 1960 $24.50
————. *Grant Takes Command.* Little, Brown 1969 $24.50
————. *A Stillness at Appomattox.* Doubleday 1953 $16.95; Washington Square Pr. 1970 pap. $3.95
————. *U. S. Grant and the American Military Tradition.* Amereon 1985 $15.95; *Lib. of Amer. Biography* Little, Brown text ed. 1972 pap. $6.95
Hesseltine, William B. *Ulysses S. Grant: Politician. Amer. Class. Ser.* Ungar $20.00
Lewis, Lloyd. *Captain Sam Grant.* Little, Brown 1950 $19.95. A fine presentation of Grant's early years, meticulously documented.
McFeely, William S. *Grant: A Biography.* Norton 1981 $19.95 1982 pap. $9.95. The best biography of Grant to date. This book won the Pulitzer Prize in 1982.
Miers, Earl S. *The Web of Victory: Grant at Vicksburg.* Greenwood repr. of 1955 ed. 1978 lib. bdg. $25.75; Louisiana State Univ. Pr. 1984 pap. $8.95
Smith, Gene. *Lee and Grant: A Dual Biography.* McGraw-Hill 1984 $17.50

HAMMARSKJOLD, DAG (HJALMAR AGNE CARL). 1905–1961 (NOBEL PEACE PRIZE 1961)

Primarily a political economist, Hammarskjold was Sweden's leading monetary expert and a brilliant diplomat. He was elected Secretary-General of the United Nations in 1953 by a nearly unanimous vote. He brought to this office an ideal of truly international civil service, a passion for the rule of decency and reason, and he extended the scope of the secretariat to a diplomatic and executive position of great importance. He was killed in a plane crash in 1961 while on an official mission to the strife-torn Congo.

In 1964 *Markings* (from the Swedish *vagmarken*) was posthumously published in a joint English translation by Leif Sjoberg, assistant professor of

Swedish language and literature at Columbia University, and the poet W. H. AUDEN (see Vol. 1). Hammarskjold himself had described this bestselling diary of religious and philosophical reflections "as a sort of *white book* concerning my negotiations with myself and with God." This "journal of a soul" not only startled the world, but even his friends "expressed amazement at the disclosure by the book of a profoundly religious and mystical inner life about which they had known nothing." Others felt that "his religious side, as revealed by the diary, was only one of many facets of a brilliant, complicated person."

BOOKS BY HAMMARSKJOLD

Public Papers of the Secretaries-General of the United Nations. Ed. by Andrew W. Cordier and Wilder Foote, Columbia Univ. Pr. 5 vols. 1972–75 ea. $34.00
Markings. Fwd. by W. H. Auden, Ballantine 1985 pap. $3.50; Knopf 1964 $13.95

BOOKS ABOUT HAMMARSKJOLD

Cordier, Andrew W., and Wilder Foote, eds. *The Quest for Peace: The Dag Hammarskjold Memorial Lectures.* Columbia Univ. Pr. 1964 $20.00 pap. $5.00
Lash, Joseph P. *Dag Hammarskjold: Custodian of the Brushfire Peace.* Greenwood repr. of 1961 ed. 1974 lib. bdg. $17.00. Not a definitive biography, but highly informative, by a veteran U.N. reporter.
Urquhart, Brian. *Hammarskjold.* Harper 1984 pap. $14.37. A political analysis of Hammarskjold's term as Secretary-General, with little personal detail.
Zacher, Mark W. *Dag Hammarskjold's United Nations. International Organization Ser.* Columbia Univ. Pr. 1969 $30.00. A systematic study of Hammarskjold's tactics and strategy in transforming the United Nations into a more active and effective peacekeeping body.

HARRIS, FRANK (JAMES THOMAS). 1856–1931

[SEE Volume 1, Chapter 17.]

HOLMES, OLIVER WENDELL, JR. 1841–1935

Mr. Justice Holmes, the American jurist, was born in Boston, the son of the author Oliver Wendell Holmes. He graduated from Harvard (A.B. 1861, LL.B. 1866), and served with distinction in the Union Army in the Civil War. He was professor of law at Harvard Law School, Chief Justice of the Supreme Court of Massachusetts, and Associate Justice of the U.S. Supreme Court (1902–32). In addition to letters, diaries, speeches, and judicial decisions, he was author of *The Common Law*. His dissenting opinions, *The Dissenting Opinions of Mr. Justice Holmes*, many of them "masterpieces of clear, forceful legal writing," earned him the honorific "the great dissenter."

In 1967 Mark DeWolfe Howe, Holmes's biographer and frequent editor, died suddenly, having completed only the first two volumes of a planned full-length definitive biography. Howe's long and devoted relationship with Holmes had begun in 1933 when, fresh out of law school, he went to work for the Associate Supreme Court Justice. Of this experience, he later wrote in the *N.Y. Times:* "Those young men who went to Holmes, in the example of their employer, learned that professional capacity achieves the highest fruitfulness only when it is combined with energy of character and breadth of learning."

BOOKS BY HOLMES

Collected Legal Papers. Peter Smith $11.25

Representative Opinions of Mr. Justice Holmes. Ed. by Alfred Lief; intro. by Harold J. Laski, Greenwood repr. of 1931 ed. 1972 lib. bdg. $22.50

The Holmes Reader. Ed. by Julius J. Marke, Oceana 2d ed. rev. 1964 $6.00. Life, writings, speeches, and judicial decisions.

Holmes-Laski Letters: The Correspondence of Justice Oiiver Wendell Holmes and Harold J. Laski 1916–1935. Ed. by Mark DeWolfe Howe, Atheneum 2 vols. 1963 pap. ea. $2.65

Holmes-Sheehan Correspondence: The Letters of Justice Oliver Wendell Holmes, Jr. and Canon Patrick Augustine Sheehan. Ed. by David H. Burton, Associated Faculty Pr. 1976 $8.95

Touched with Fire: Civil War Letters and Diary of Oliver Wendell Holmes, Jr. 1861– 1864. Ed. by Mark DeWolfe Howe, Da Capo repr. of 1946 ed. 1969 $24.50

The Common Law. 1881. Little, Brown rev. ed. 1923 pap. $8.70 1964 pap. $17.50

The Dissenting Opinions of Mr. Justice Holmes. 1929. Rotham 1981 $27.50

BOOKS ABOUT HOLMES

Bent, Silas. *Justice Oliver Wendell Holmes: A Biography*. AMS Pr. repr. of 1932 ed. 1969 $28.00

Howe, Mark DeWolfe. *Justice Oliver Wendell Holmes*. Harvard Univ. Pr. (Belknap Pr.) 2 vols. ea. $18.00

HOOVER, HERBERT (CLARK). 1874–1964

The first volume of the late president's *Memoirs* is an account of his early life from his birth in a Quaker family in Iowa to his adventurous life as an engineer and relief administrator in World War I to 1920, when he became secretary of commerce in the Harding cabinet. The second volume covers many public issues between 1920 and 1933 when he served eight years as secretary of commerce and four as president. The third volume is a defense of his administration, an answer to the many who talked of "Hoover's depression." The *N.Y. Times* called the series "fascinating."

BOOKS BY HOOVER

The Public Papers of the Presidents of the United States: Herbert Hoover. Government Printing Office 1975 consult publisher for information

State Papers and Other Public Writings. Ed. by W. S. Myers, Kraus 2 vols. repr. of 1934 ed. $58.00

Memoirs. Macmillan 3 vols. 1951–52 o.p.

The Challenge to Liberty. Da Capo repr. of 1934 ed. 1973 lib. bdg. $29.50

American Ideals versus the New Deal. Scholarly repr. of 1936 ed. 1971 $29.00

(and H. Gibson). *Problems of Lasting Peace*. Elliots Bks. 1943 $12.50; Kraus repr. of 1942 ed. 1969 $15.00

BOOKS ABOUT HOOVER

DeConde, Alexander. *Herbert Hoover's Latin American Policy*. Octagon 1970 lib. bdg. $17.00

Fausold, Martin L., and George T. Mazuzan, eds. *The Hoover Presidency: A Reappraisal*. State Univ. of New York Pr. 1974 $32.50

Herbert Hoover: The Postpresidential Years, 1933–64. Hoover Institution 2 vols. 1983 $75.00

Lisio, Donald J. *The President and Protest: Hoover, Conspiracy and the Bonus Riot*. Univ. of Missouri Pr. 1974 $24.00

Nash, George H. *The Life of Herbert Hoover: The Engineer, 1874–1914*. Norton 1983 $25.00

Robinson, Edgar E., and Vaughn D. Bornet. *Herbert Hoover: President of the United States*. Hoover Institution 1975 $14.95

Romasco, Albert U. *Poverty of Abundance: Hoover, the Nation, the Depression*. Oxford 1965 pap. $7.95

Smith, Gene. *Shattered Dream: Herbert Hoover and the Great Depression*. McGraw-Hill 1984 $7.95. A readable account of the coming of the depression and the largely ineffective efforts of the Hoover administration to stop its spread.

Smith, Richard N. *An Uncommon Man: The Triumph of Herbert Hoover*. Simon & Schuster 1984 $22.95

Warren, Harris G. *Herbert Hoover and the Great Depression*. Greenwood repr. of 1970 ed. 1980 lib. bdg. $32.50; *Norton Lib.* 1967 pap. $5.95

JOHNSON, LYNDON BAINES. 1908–1973

Although more than a decade has passed since Johnson's death, few definitive discussions of his life and achievements have emerged. Most analysts agree on one point—that Lyndon Johnson knew how to wield power. Assuming office after John F. Kennedy's assassination in 1963, he accomplished the seemingly impossible task of pushing Kennedy's then-stagnated New Frontier program on civil rights, poverty, and aid to education through Congress. However, his tragic involvement in Vietnam still overshadows in the public mind the civil rights and antipoverty achievements of his Great Society.

BOOKS BY JOHNSON

The Public Papers of the Presidents of the United States: Lyndon B. Johnson. Government Printing Office 1963–69 $19.00–$21.00 10 vols. some vols. o.p. consult publisher for information

The Vantage Point: Perspectives on the Presidency, 1963–69. Holt 1971 o.p. Johnson's account is "his story as he would like things to be" (*N.Y. Times Book Review*). The writing is straightforward and clear, but the president's hindsight version is a great deal more dispassionate and rational than the actual events as they occurred.

BOOKS ABOUT JOHNSON

Caro, Robert A. *The Path to Power: The Years of Lyndon Johnson*. Knopf 1982 $19.95; Random (Vintage) 1984 pap. $9.95. A huge, sometimes unwieldy narrative, but filled with relevant information.

Divine, Robert A., ed. *Exploring the Johnson Years*. Univ. of Texas Pr. text ed. 1981 $24.95

Dugger, Ronnie. *The Politician: The Life and Times of Lyndon Johnson.* Norton 1982 $18.95. An account of Johnson by a liberal Texas journalist who was a long-time opponent of the president.

Goldman, Eric F. *Tragedy of Lyndon Johnson: A Historian's Personal Interpretation.* Knopf 1969 $10.00. A personal and insightful account of the Johnson administration by a Princeton historian who worked in the administration for three years.

Harvey, James C. *Black Civil Rights during the Johnson Administration.* Univ. Pr. of Mississippi 1973 pap. $5.95

Kearns, Doris. *Lyndon Johnson and the American Dream.* Harper 1976 $14.95; New Amer. Lib. (Signet) 1977 pap. $3.95. With a large measure of cooperation from Johnson, Kearns wrote this highly personal and controversial account.

Lyndon B. Johnson: A Bibliography. Univ. of Texas Pr. 1984 $25.00. Prepared by the staff of the LBJ Library.

Miller, Merle. *Lyndon: An Oral Biography.* Ballantine 1981 pap. $9.95

Wicker, Tom. *JFK and LBJ.* Penguin (Pelican) 1969 pap. $4.95. The *New York Times's* Washington bureau chief's view of one of the absorbing political contrasts of the 1960s.

KENNAN, GEORGE F(ROST). 1904–

[SEE Chapter 10 in this volume.]

KENNEDY, JOHN FITZGERALD. 1917–1963

With the assassination of the 35th president of the United States in Dallas in 1963, the biographical flood about him, which had begun before his death, grew to a torrent. Authors and the reading public were fascinated by the personality, style, and character of this highly intelligent, rational, and witty man. Articulate and forward-looking, but with a great sense of the past, Kennedy was the only U.S. president to win a Pulitzer Prize; he won the prize for *Profiles in Courage* in 1957. The trauma of Kennedy's assassination exercised an almost equal fascination, resulting in a quantity of histories and interpretations of the circumstances surrounding his death that has only recently begun to abate.

Born in Brookline, Massachusetts, Kennedy was a Harvard graduate. He wrote *Why England Slept* (1940) while still an undergraduate. An expanded version of a pamphlet earlier published by the Anti-Defamation League has been republished as *A Nation of Immigrants* (1958).

BOOKS BY JOHN FITZGERALD KENNEDY

The Public Papers of the Presidents of the United States: John F. Kennedy. Government Printing Office 3 vols. consult publisher for information

Profiles in Courage. 1956. Fwd. by Robert F. Kennedy, Harper 1983 pap. $3.80

The Strategy of Peace. Ed. by Allan Nevins, Harper 1960 $10.00

Why England Slept. Greenwood repr. of 1961 ed. 1981 lib. bdg. $22.50

A Nation of Immigrants. Anti-Defamation League pap. $3.95; Harper rev. & enl. ed. 1964 pap. $4.95

BOOKS ABOUT JOHN FITZGERALD KENNEDY

Bishop, Jim. *A Day in the Life of President Kennedy.* 1964. Crown 1983 $6.98

———. *The Day Kennedy Was Shot.* Crowell 2d ed. 1972 $9.95; Outlet 1983 $6.98

Bradlee, Benjamin C. *Conversations with Kennedy.* Norton 1984 pap. $8.95. A memoir by a close friend and journalist, now editor of the *Washington Post.*

Greenberg, Bradley S., and Edwin B. Parker, eds. *Kennedy Assassination and the American Public: Social Communication in Crisis.* Stanford Univ. Pr. 1965 $30.00

Guth, DeLloyd J., and David R. Wrone, eds. *The Assassination of John F. Kennedy: A Comprehensive Historical and Legal Bibliography, 1963–1979.* Greenwood 1980 lib. bdg. $49.95

Halberstam, David. *The Best and the Brightest.* Fawcett 1973 pap. $3.50; Penguin 1983 pap. $9.95; Random 1972 $15.00

Kurtz, Michael L. *Crime of the Century: The Kennedy Assassination from a Historian's Perspective.* Univ. of Tennessee Pr. 1982 $24.95 pap. $12.95

Manchester, William. *The Death of a President: November 20–25, 1963.* Arbor House 1985 pap. $10.95; Harper 1967 $20.00; Penguin 1977 pap. $4.95. The originally "authorized" account whose general critical reception is summed up in the *Saturday Review*'s comment: "An infinity of detail . . . trivia and tragedy." It was finally published after a much publicized dispute between Manchester and the Kennedy family.

Martin, Ralph G. *A Hero for Our Time: An Intimate Story of the Kennedy Years.* Macmillan 1983 $19.95

Meagher, Sylvia. *Accessories after the Fact: The Warren Commission, the Authorities and the Report.* Random (Vintage) 1976 pap. $5.95

Miroff, Bruce. *Pragmatic Illusions: The Presidential Politics of John F. Kennedy.* Longman text ed. 1976 pap. $8.95

O'Donnell, Kenneth P., and Joseph McCarthy. *Johnny, We Hardly Knew Ye: Memories of John Fitzgerald Kennedy.* Little, Brown 1972 $17.50 pap. $7.70. An account by two close associates focusing on Kennedy the politician.

The Official Warren Commission Report on the Assassination of President John F. Kennedy. Analysis and commentary by Louis Nizer, afterword by Bruce Catton, Doubleday 1964 o.p.

Parmet, Herbert S. *Jack: The Struggles of John F. Kennedy.* Doubleday 1983 $14.95 pap. $12.95

Roffman, Howard. *Presumed Guilty: Lee Harvey Oswald in the Assassination of President Kennedy.* Fairleigh Dickinson Univ. Pr. 1975 $15.00

Schlesinger, Arthur M., Jr. *Thousand Days: John F. Kennedy in the White House.* Fawcett 1977 pap. $3.50; Houghton Mifflin 1965 $24.50. "A remarkable feat of scholarship and writing, set in the widest historical and intellectual frame. . . . A great President has found—perhaps he deliberately chose—a great historian" (*N.Y. Times*).

Sorensen, Theodore C. *Kennedy.* Harper 1965 $17.50. One of the best accounts by an insider, one of Kennedy's top aides and advisers during the years 1953–63.

United Press International. *Four Days: The Historical Record of the Death of President Kennedy.* Simon & Schuster 1983 $9.95

Wicker, Tom. *Kennedy Without Tears: The Man Beneath the Myth.* Fwd. by Arthur Krock, Morrow 1964 $2.95

Wofford, Harris. *Of Kennedys and Kings: Making Sense of the Sixties.* Farrar 1980 $17.50

KENNEDY, ROBERT F(RANCIS). 1925–1968

Senator Robert F. Kennedy's assassination in 1968, just after his California primary triumph in his campaign for the U.S. presidential nomination, stunned a nation already numbed by his brother's assassination in 1963 and that of Martin Luther King, Jr., earlier in 1968. Senator from New York and attorney general in his brother's administration, he had represented for many, especially black citizens of the United States, a hope for justice, unity, and peace. He left behind a manuscript, originally intended for eventual publication in *The New York Times Magazine*, which was his memoir of the Cuban missile crisis of 1962. It was offered to bidders and sold to the McCall corporation for an unprecedented $1,000,000. It first appeared in the November 1968 issue of *McCall's*, on the sixth anniversary of the missile crisis. Kennedy had earlier published a forcefully written, dramatic account of his years as counsel for the McClellan Committee investigating corruption in the Teamsters' Union.

BOOKS BY ROBERT F. KENNEDY

The Enemy Within. Greenwood repr. of 1960 ed. 1982 lib. bdg. $29.75
To Seek a Newer World. Doubleday 1967 $4.95
Thirteen Days: A Memoir of the Cuban Missile Crisis. New Amer. Lib. 1969 pap. $3.50; ed. by Richard Neustadt and Graham Allison, Norton text ed. 1971 pap. $5.95

BOOKS ABOUT ROBERT F. KENNEDY

Brown, Stuart G. *Presidency on Trial: Robert Kennedy's 1968 Campaign and Afterwards.* Univ. of Hawaii Pr. 1972 $10.00
Halberstam, David. *Unfinished Odyssey of Robert Kennedy.* Random 1969 $4.95. A moving account by an experienced journalist of Kennedy's campaign for the presidential nomination of 1968.
Navasky, Victor S. *Kennedy Justice.* Atheneum 1977 pap. $5.95. A readable, scholarly account and critique of Kennedy as attorney general.
Salinger, Pierre, ed. *Honorable Profession: A Tribute to Robert F. Kennedy.* Doubleday 1968 $125.00
Schlesinger, Arthur M., Jr. *Robert Kennedy and His Times.* Ballantine 1985 pap. $4.95; Houghton Mifflin 1978 $19.95. Allowing for Schlesinger's long-standing admiration for both Kennedy brothers, his biography is still a solid and valuable account.
Wofford, Harris. *Of Kennedys and Kings: Making Sense of the Sixties.* Farrar 1980 $17.50

KHRUSHCHEV, NIKITA S(ERGEEVICH). 1894–1971

After Khrushchev's sudden elimination as premier and first deputy of the Soviet Union in October 1964, he practically disappeared from public view. He lived for seven years in retirement until his death from natural causes, a rare enough feat in Soviet politics at that time. Preliminary biographies; studies of his rise and fall; and studies of the massive de-Stalinization campaign, which was perhaps his greatest achievement, have appeared; but current biographers and historians are greatly handicapped by the unavailability of such source materials as private letters and diaries.

Of Khrushchev's own writings, translated into English, most are now out of print including *For Victory in Peaceful Competition with Capitalism* (1960), which was his first book to be published in the United States. A partial memoir was published in the West as *Khrushchev Remembers*.

BOOKS BY KHRUSHCHEV

Khrushchev Speaks: Selected Speeches, Articles and Press Conferences, 1949–1961. Ed.
by Thomas P. Whitney, Univ. of Michigan Pr. 1963 o.p. An illuminating collection of major public statements, including Khrushchev's debate with Walter
Reuther, an interview during the U-2 crisis, and his eulogy and subsequent condemnation of Stalin.

Khrushchev Remembers. Ed. and trans. by Talbot Strobe, intro. by Edward Crankshaw, Little, Brown 1971 $15.00. Khrushchev's justification of his career, as Har-
rison Salisbury said, "on its own special terms of a formidable document. A valuable testament in the history of Russian Communism . . ." (*N.Y. Times Book Review*).

BOOKS ABOUT KHRUSHCHEV

Crankshaw, Edward. *Khrushchev: A Career.* Penguin 1971 pap. $3.95. An early assess-
ment of the Russian leader by an expert observer.

Linden, Carl A. *Khrushchev and the Soviet Leadership, 1957–1964.* Johns Hopkins
Univ. Pr. 1966 $22.50 pap. $5.95

Medvedev Roy A., and others. *Khrushchev: The Years in Power.* Columbia Univ. Pr.
1976 $21.00; Doubleday 1984 $19.95 pap. $9.95

Slusser, Robert M. *Berlin Crisis of 1961: Soviet American Relations and the Struggle
for Power in the Kremlin, June–November, 1961.* Johns Hopkins Univ. Pr. 1973
$37.00 pap. $12.95

LENIN (born VLADIMIR ILYICH ULYANOV). 1870–1924

[SEE Chapter 10 in this volume.]

MACMILLAN, SIR (MAURICE) HAROLD. 1894–

In 1963, Harold Macmillan retired from political life after seven years as
Britain's prime minister. A decade before, one London writer had commented: "He may be the last of the suave, almost courtly British statesmen." Born in London of a Scots family, Macmillan studied classics and
mathematics at Oxford; with characteristic British unflappability, as he lay
wounded in no-man's-land during World War I, he read a pocket copy of
Homer in the original Greek. Though he became a Conservative member of
Parliament in 1924, it was not until World War II that his political career
blossomed. "Under titles that changed as responsibilities grew, he was,
from January 1943, to the end of the war in Europe, *the* British
politician . . . in the Mediterranean" (*New Yorker*). In 1950 the London *Sunday Times* observed: "He has an Edwardian charm and courtesy, as well as
an Edwardian mustache. He is a political philosopher, as well as a practical
statesman." His memoirs, which he began after a cancer operation in 1963,
are marked by humor as well as insight—"I have reached the age of indiscre-
tion," he remarked on the publication of the second volume.

BOOKS BY MACMILLAN

Winds of Change, 1914–1939. Harper 1966 $20.00

The Blast of War, 1939–1945. Carroll & Graf 1983 pap. $12.95; Harper 1968 $20.00.
The second volume of memoirs, dealing with the many phases of his political

and diplomatic efforts in the Mediterranean in World War II. It is a vivid insider's account with many telling portraits of major and minor personalities.

Riding the Storm: 1956–1959. Harper 1972 $20.00

War Diaries: Politics and War in the Mediterranean, January 1943–May 1945. St. Martin's 1984 $29.95

BOOKS ABOUT MACMILLAN

Fisher, Nigel. *Harold Macmillan: A Biography.* St. Martin's 1982 $19.95

Sampson, Anthony. *Macmillan: A Study in Ambiguity.* Simon & Schuster 1967 o.p. A short, but bright and perceptive study of Macmillan's personality, a personality at once highly principled and highly political.

MAO TSE-TUNG. 1893–1976

Both a brilliant theorist and practical politician of extraordinary power, Mao Tse-tung participated in planning and carrying out the Communist Revolt against the Kuomintang in 1927. It was then that he founded the Red Army, which he led to victory over Chiang Kai-shek and the Kuomintang after World War II. In 1949 Mao assumed an official government position and in 1954 took over virtual control of all China as Chairman of the People's Republic.

A brilliant revolutionary polemicist, Mao was also a poet. His handbook on guerrilla strategy (o.p.) has become the blueprint for revolution in China, Cuba, and Vietnam.

Mao's works have been massively produced within China and many distributed abroad, with translations into 23 languages. Extraordinarily successful in bookstores around the world has been the small volume, bound in red plastic, *Mao's Quotations*—the famed "little red book." The political upheavals and changes in China since Mao's death have only slightly diminished demand for his works.

BOOKS BY MAO TSE-TUNG

Selected Works of Mao Tse-tung. China Bks. 5 vols. ea. $12.95 pap. $8.95; Pergamon 5 vols. 1978 $65.00

Selected Readings. China Bks. 1971 $9.95

Mao Tse-tung on Revolution and War. Ed. by M. Rejai, Peter Smith $15.25

Ten Poems and Lyrics by Mao Tse-tung. Trans. by Wang Hui-Ming, Univ. of Massachusetts Pr. 1975 $8.00 pap. $3.95

BOOKS ABOUT MAO TSE-TUNG

Barnett, A. Doak. *China After Mao: With Selected Documents.* Princeton Univ. Pr. 1967 $32.00 pap. $10.95

Boorman, Scott A. *Protracted Game: A Wei Ch'i Interpretation of Maoist Revolutionary Strategy.* Oxford 1969 $22.50 pap. $7.95

Cohen, Arthur A. *The Communism of Mao Tse-tung.* Univ. of Chicago Pr. 1964 pap. $2.95

Karnow, Stanley. *Mao and China: From Revolution to Revolution.* Penguin 1984 pap. $7.95; Viking 1972 $15.00

Lifton, Robert J. *Revolutionary Immortality: Mao Tse-tung and the Chinese Revolution.* Peter Smith $5.25. "An essential study of Communist China; more than

that, it is an original, intellectually exciting, gracefully written and wholly accessible essay on an aspect of human individual and mass psychology as it operates
in contemporary revolutionary circumstances around the world" (*N.Y. Times*).
Almost any book by this author-psychologist-humanist is worth reading.

Rice, Edward E. *Mao's Way.* Univ. of California Pr. 1972 pap. $4.95
Rue, John E. *Mao Tse-tung in Opposition, 1927–1935.* Stanford Univ. Pr. 1966
    $27.50. Called by the *N.Y. Times* an "extraordinarily interesting volume," Rue's
    book discusses Mao's career and Chinese Communism when Mao was but one of
    its many leaders.
Schram, Stuart R. *Mao Zedong: A Preliminary Reassessment.* St. Martin's 1983 $22.50
Schwartz, Benjamin I. *Chinese Communism and the Rise of Mao.* Harvard Univ. Pr.
    1951 $16.50 pap. $5.95. An excellent pioneer study of the Chinese Communist
    Party in the 1920s and early 1930s until Mao became its master.
Terrill, Ross. *Mao: A Biography.* Harper 1980 $18.22 pap. $8.95
Wakeman, Frederic, Jr. *History and Will: Philosophical Perspectives of Mao Tse-tung's
    Thought.* Univ. of California Pr. 1976 pap. $9.50
Wilson, Dick. *The People's Emperor: A Biography of Mao Tse-tung.* Doubleday 1980
    $17.50

MONTAGU, LADY MARY WORTLEY. 1689–1762

[SEE Volume 1, Chapter 17.]

NEHRU, JAWAHARLAL. 1889–1964

[SEE Chapter 10 in this volume.]

NEWMAN, CARDINAL JOHN HENRY. 1801–1890

[SEE Volume 4.]

NICOLSON, SIR HAROLD (GEORGE). 1886–1968

Sir Harold Nicolson was the son of Lord Carnock and the husband of the
late Victoria Sackville-West. Like Lord Carnock he spent much of his life in
the English diplomatic service. *Portrait of a Diplomatist* (1930, o.p.), his biography of his father, is really part of a trilogy of diplomatic history. In addition to a political career of mixed success, Nicolson was a well-known journalist, essayist, biographer, and diarist.

Sir Harold claimed that he had never written a *pure* biography, a life of
an individual conceived solely as a work of art. *Some People* (1927) is delightful biographical fiction, which he called the most *impure* form of biography.
He also wrote *Tennyson* (1923), *Byron* (1924), and *Swinburne* (1926) as well
as biographies of Dwight Morrow and King George V.

Diaries and Letters, skillfully edited by Sir Harold's son Nigel, a cofounder
and director of the British publishing firm, Weidenfeld and Nicolson, further established Sir Harold's standing as an autobiographer and diarist.
The three volumes, in their charming mixture of great events, gossip, and
trivia, capture the spirit and events of the 1930s through the 1950s in Britain better than most works of the period. Charles Poore said of the diaries

that they were "personal history at its best . . . [charting] one of the better current requiems for empires lost and manners gone to hell." John Mason Brown said of Nicolson's letters and his diaries, "His ferreting eye for significant detail, his sense of character and scene, his civilized mind, his alert and remembering ear, and the ease and charm of his writing place his very personal record in the forefront of English diaries."

Victoria Sackville-West was Sir Harold's wife and a noted novelist, poet, and creator of gardens. She was born at Knole, one of the great private houses of England—with 7 courts to correspond with the days of the week, 52 staircases to match the weeks of the year, and 365 rooms for every day in the year—which she described in *Knole and the Sackvilles. All Passion Spent* and *The Edwardians* were two of her most successful novels, many of which were published by the Hogarth Press of Leonard and Virginia Woolf. With Sir Harold, she created the glorious gardens at Sissinghurst Castle, their home, now owned by the National Trust.

In the more permissive spirit of the present day, several biographies of Sir Harold and Victoria Sackville-West have frankly discussed their homosexuality. The first and most controversial account of this most complicated marriage was their son Nigel's *Portrait of a Marriage.*

BOOKS BY NICOLSON

Harold Nicolson: Diaries and Letters 1930–1939. Ed. by Nigel Nicolson, Atheneum 1966 $10.00
Some People. Atheneum 1982 pap. $6.95
The Development of the English Biography. Humanities Pr. text ed. 1928 $3.50; Richard West $10.00
Tennyson: Aspects of His Life, Character and Poetry. Select Bibliographies Repr. Ser. Ayer repr. of 1923 ed. $17.25; Haskell repr. of 1925 ed. 1972 lib. bdg. $49.95; Richard West repr. of 1925 ed. $25.00; Scholarly repr. of 1925 ed. 1972 $17.25
Swinburne. 1926. Richard West repr. of 1973 $10.00; Scholarly repr. of 1928 ed. 1971 $39.00
The Poetry of Byron. Folcroft repr. of 1943 ed. lib. bdg. $9.50; Richard West repr. of 1943 ed. lib. bdg. $10.00

BOOKS ABOUT NICOLSON

Lees-Milne, James. *Harold Nicolson: A Biography.* Shoe String 1982 $25.00
Nicolson, Nigel. *Portrait of a Marriage.* Atheneum 1973 $10.00 pap. $7.95

PEPYS, SAMUEL. 1633–1703
[SEE Volume 1, Chapter 17.]

ROOSEVELT, (ANNA) ELEANOR. 1884–1962

The niece of Theodore Roosevelt and wife of a distant cousin, Franklin Delano Roosevelt, this distinguished first lady made a unique place for herself not only in the United States but in the world. Undaunted by critics, she followed her wide interests and "her tireless dedication to the cause of human welfare won her affection and honor." Her service as delegate in the General Assembly of the first United Nations from 1945 to 1953 and again in 1961 and as first chairperson of that body's Human Rights Commission was out-standing. Her travels to all parts of the globe are reflected in her writings. In recent years accounts of Eleanor Roosevelt have emphasized the difficult process by which she created an independent life of her own, while remaining part of the extraordinary partnership that was her marriage to Franklin Roosevelt.

BOOKS BY ROOSEVELT

Autobiography of Eleanor Roosevelt. Barnes & Noble pap. $6.95; G. K. Hall 1984 pap. $9.95; Harper 1961 $21.10. The first three parts are condensations of her three earlier books published by Harper, *This Is My Story* (1937), *This I Remember* (1949), and *On My Own* (1958), the first and last of which are out of print. The fourth part, *The Search for Understanding* is new material discussing her hopes for world peace.
This I Remember. Greenwood repr. of 1949 ed. 1975 lib. bdg. $45.00
You Learn by Living. Harper 1960 $15.00; Westminster 1983 pap. $9.95

BOOKS ABOUT ROOSEVELT

Asbell, Bernard, ed. *Mother and Daughter: The Letters of Eleanor and Anna Roosevelt.* Putnam 1982 o.p.
Faber, Doris. *The Life of Lorena Hickok: E. R.'s Friend.* Morrow 1980 $12.95
Hareven, Tamara. *Eleanor Roosevelt: An American Conscience.* Da Capo repr. of 1968 ed. 1975 lib. bdg. $39.50
Hoff-Wilson, Joan, and Marjorie Lightman, eds. *Without Precedent: The Life and Times of Eleanor Roosevelt.* Indiana Univ. Pr. 1984 $17.50
Lash, Joseph P. *Eleanor and Franklin: The Story of Their Relationship Based on Eleanor Roosevelt's Private Papers.* New Amer. Lib. (Signet) 1973 pap. $4.95; intro. by Franklin D. Roosevelt, Jr., fwd. by Arthur M. Schlesinger, Jr., Norton 1971 $15.95. Lash as a young man was one of the promising young people befriended by Eleanor Roosevelt, and this able account draws on that personal friendship as well as her private papers.
————. *Eleanor: The Years Alone.* Fwd. by Franklin D. Roosevelt, Jr., Norton 1972 $14.95
McClure, Ruth, ed. *Eleanor Roosevelt, an Eager Spirit: The Letters of Dorothy Dow.* Norton 1984 $16.95. By a member of Eleanor Roosevelt's staff.

ROUSSEAU, JEAN JACQUES. 1712–1778
[SEE Chapter 4 in this volume.]

SASSOON, SIEGFRIED (LORRAINE). 1886–1967
[SEE Volume 1, Chapter 17.]

SEVIGNE, MME DE. 1626–1696
[SEE Volume 2, Chapter 9.]

SITWELL, SIR OSBERT, 5th Bart. 1892–1969
[SEE Volume 1, Chapter 17.]

STALIN, JOSEPH (VISSARIONOVICH). 1879–1953

[SEE Chapter 10 in this volume.]

TRUMAN, HARRY S. 1884–1972

Truman, who became the 33rd president of the United States when Franklin Roosevelt died in 1945, was elected president in his own right in 1948, despite widespread predictions of a victory for his Republican opponent. Truman was a forthright, feisty man and these qualities emerge in the two volumes of his *Memoirs*, which give Truman's own vision and version of some of the crucial events of the modern world, including the decision to drop the atomic bomb on Japan (a subject of continuing, bitter political and historiographic controversy) and the beginning of the Cold War.

BOOKS BY TRUMAN

The Public Papers of the Presidents of the United States: Harry S Truman. Government Printing Office 8 vols. consult publisher for information

Cumulated Index to the Public Papers of the President of the United States, Harry S Truman. Kraus 1979 $55.00

Truman Speaks: On the Presidency, the Constitution, and Statecraft. Columbia Univ. Pr. 1975 $22.00 pap. $13.00; Kraus repr. of 1946 ed. $11.00

The Truman Program. Ed. by M. B. Schnapper, Greenwood repr. of 1949 ed. 1972 lib. bdg. $15.00

The Truman Administration, Its Principles and Practice. Ed. by Louis W. Koenig, Greenwood repr. of 1956 ed. 1979 lib. bdg. $27.50. An informative selection from official papers, speeches, and press conferences.

The Autobiography of Harry S Truman. Ed. by Robert H. Ferrell, Colorado Associated Univ. Pr. 1980 $10.95 pap. $5.95

Off the Record: The Private Papers of Harry S Truman. Ed. by Robert H. Ferrell, Harper 1980 $15.00

Strictly Personal and Confidential: The Letters that Harry Truman Never Mailed. Ed. by Monte M. Poen, Little, Brown 1982 $10.95 pap. $5.70

Dear Bess: The Letters from Harry to Bess Truman, 1910–1959. Ed. by Robert H. Ferrell, Norton 1982 $19.95 pap. $12.95

Letters Home. Ed. by Monte M. Poen, Putnam 1984 $16.95

BOOKS ABOUT TRUMAN

Berman, William C. *The Politics of Civil Rights in the Truman Administration*. Ohio State Univ. Pr. 1970 $8.00

Bernstein, Barton J., ed. *Politics and Policies of the Truman Administration*. New Viewpoints 1970 o.p. An admirable selection of documents is enriched by relevant and informative notes.

Daniels, Jonathan. *Man of Independence*. Amer. History and Culture in the 20th-Century Ser. Associated Faculty Pr. repr. of 1950 ed. 1971 o.p.

Donovan, Robert J. *Conflict and Crisis: The Presidency of Harry S Truman, 1945–1948*. Norton 1977 $19.95 pap. $10.95

Ferrell, Robert H. *Truman and the Modern Presidency*. Little, Brown 1983 $13.00 pap. $5.95

Hartmann, Susan. *Truman and the Eightieth Congress*. Univ. of Missouri Pr. 1971 $20.00

Haynes, Richard F. *The Awesome Power: Harry S Truman as Commander-in-Chief.* Louisiana State Univ. Pr. 1973 $30.00

Miller, Merle. *Plain Speaking: An Oral Biography of Harry S Truman.* Berkley 1984 $9.95. Based on taped interviews with Truman and others compiled in Missouri (1961–62), this work deals with Truman's life before going to Washington in 1935, as well as his national career.

Ross, Irwin. *The Loneliest Campaign: The Truman Victory of 1948.* Greenwood repr. of 1968 ed. 1977 lib. bdg. $22.50

Truman, Margaret. *Harry S Truman.* Morrow 1973 $10.95 1984 pap. $10.95; Pocket Bks. 1974 pap. $2.95

WALPOLE, HORACE, 4th Earl of Orford. 1717–1797

[SEE Volume 1, Chapter 17.]

WESLEY, JOHN. 1703–1791

[SEE Volume 4.]

WOOLF, LEONARD. 1880–1969

[SEE Volume 1, Chapter 17.]

WOOLMAN, JOHN. 1720–1772

Like William Penn's *Fruits of Solitude* and Benjamin Franklin's *Autobiography*, says Kenneth Rexroth, the journal of John Woolman is infused with the American Quaker ethic—a form of the business ethic but devoid of greed. "Even in Franklin, the main emphasis was on social responsibility, and in Penn and Woolman, the source of responsibility was found in contemplation, the highest form of prayer." Woolman was a very early Quaker opponent of slavery, which he saw as an abuse of what George Fox called "that of God in every man." He gave up his prosperous business as a merchant and spent 30 years voicing his "concern" to Friends' Meetings, some of whom—less enlightened than he—clung to their human property. Woolman traveled extensively in the 13 colonies and eventually in England. It was largely because of Woolman's simple "witness in life and person" that the Society of Friends came to renounce slavery and "became the earliest, most powerful single force in the antislavery movement" (Rexroth).

Woolman's journal, again according to Rexroth, "is the simplest possible record of his ever widening travels and his ever deepening interior life, two aspects of one reality. He came, he spoke, he conquered, solely by the power of an achieved spiritual peace, a perfectly clear personality through which that Quaker Inner Light shone unimpeded from Friend to Friend. It is this moral quality . . . that elevates Woolman's writing to the level of great prose. . . . All that Woolman needed to achieve greatness of style in language and life was perfect candor" (*SR*).

BOOKS BY WOOLMAN

Works of John Woolman. Black Heritage Lib. Collection Ser. Ayer repr. of 1885 ed. $19.75; Somerset repr. of 1774 ed. $17.00

The Journal of John Woolman. Intro. by Frederick B. Tolles, Citadel Pr. repr. of 1961 ed. 1972 pap. $5.95; Peter Smith $17.00

Journal and Major Essays. Ed. by Phillips P. Moulton, Religious Society of Friends 1971 pap. $7.95

Some Considerations on the Keeping of Negroes. Anti-Slavery Crusade in Amer. Ser. Ayer repr. of 1800 ed. 1969 $11.50

BOOKS ABOUT WOOLMAN

Moulton, Phillips P. *The Living Witness of John Woolman.* Pendle Hill 1973 $5.00

Rosenblatt, Paul. *John Woolman. Great Amer. Thinkers Ser.* Irvington 1969 lib. bdg. $16.50

Young, Mildred B. *Woolman and Blake: Prophets of Today.* Pendle Hill 1971 pap. $2.30

PUBLISHED PAPERS

The rich historical record left by many important American historical figures in the form of masses of personal papers and records has inspired a number of projects that seek to collect, edit, and publish the collected papers of such individuals. With generous support over the years from private foundations and universities, and some, although diminishing, aid from government agencies, these often huge editing projects have made available to the reading public in letterpress form nearly complete life records of some of the most influential people, so far mostly men, in American history. With the changing priorities of American society, a number of projects have begun to document the lives of such black leaders as Booker T. Washington, W. E. B. DU BOIS, AND Frederick Douglass.

Because of the large expense of the letterpress format, most projects recording the papers of important women have turned to such formats as microfilm making them available at a reasonable cost. Similarly, the records of presidents from the second half of the twentieth century on are unlikely, ever again, to be available in hardcover, due to bulk. The pattern set by Franklin Roosevelt in founding the F.D.R. library has been followed by all of his successors, making the records of their lives and administrations available to readers and researchers.

ADAMS, HENRY (BROOKS). 1838–1918

[SEE Volume 1, Chapter 17, and Volume 3, Chapter 7.]

ADAMS, JOHN. 1735–1826; ADAMS, JOHN QUINCY. 1767–1848; and ADAMS, CHARLES FRANCIS. 1807–1886

The publication of the "great archive of Adams family papers long considered the most important collection of American historical manuscripts in private hands," sponsored by the Massachusetts Historical Society, financed by Time, Inc., and edited by a distinguished staff of scholars, is a major publishing event. The papers were transferred to the Massachusetts Historical

Society in 1956 by Thomas Boylston Adams and John Quincy Adams, members of the 10th American generation. The Adamses guarded their papers well and "have always hung on to every scrap of paper that seemed to have historical value. The mammoth diary of John Quincy Adams is today regarded as one of his greatest achievements. Charles Francis Adams had a strong bent toward history and tending archives. He built the 'Stone Library' at Quincy to preserve the family papers and edited portions of them for publication. Charles Francis had four sons—John Quincy the 2nd, Charles Francis the 2nd, Henry, and Brooks Adams. The last three sons were all historians and took a keen interest in the family records, besides adding to their bulk. . . . In 1905 the three historian brothers and their nephew Charles Francis the 3rd (who later became Secretary of the Navy under Hoover) created the 'Adams Manuscript Trust' to take over ownership and care of the family papers, as well as the Old House and Library. . . . For nearly 50 years the papers—neatly bound and boxed in tempting array—reposed on shelves in a double-locked room at the Massachusetts Historical Society, where they had been placed for safekeeping. Only a few researchers were permitted to see them and then only for limited studies." Over many years the papers have been published regularly in a bewildering array of series and subseries.

BOOKS BY JOHN ADAMS

The Adams Papers. Ed. by Lyman H. Butterfield and others, Harvard Univ. Pr.:
   Series I Diaries: *Diary and Autobiography of John Adams.* 4 vols. 1961 $90.00; *The Earliest Diary of John Adams.* 1966 $10.00; *Diary of John Quincy Adams.* 2 vols. 1982 $60.00; *Diary of Charles Francis Adams.* 6 vols. 1964–74 $180.00
   Series II *Adams Family Correspondence.* 4 vols. 1963–73 $120.00
   Series III *General Correspondence and Other Papers of the Adams Family* 6 vols. 1977–83 ea. $60.00; *Statesmen: Legal Papers of John Adams.* 3 vols. 1965
   Series IV *Adams Family Portraits* (see the Oliver book under "Books about the Adams Family")
The Works of John Adams. AMS Pr. 10 vols. repr. of 1856 ed. $325.00; *Select Bibliographies Repr. Ser.* Ayer 10 vols. repr. of 1856 ed. $410.00
(and Abigail Adams). *Familiar Letters of John Adams and His Wife Abigail Adams, during the Revolution. Select Bibliographies Repr. Ser.* Ayer repr. of 1875 ed. $22.00
The Adams-Jefferson Letters: The Complete Correspondence Between Thomas Jefferson and Abigail and John Adams. Ed. by Lester J. Cappon, *Institute of Early Amer. History and Culture Ser.* Univ. of North Carolina Pr. 2 vols. 1959 $37.50
Political Writings of John Adams. Ed. by George A. Peek, Jr. Bobbs 1954 pap. $7.87
Defense of the Constitution of Government of the United States of America. Adler's 3 vols. repr. of 1797 ed. $185.00
(and Jonathan Sewall). *Novanglus, and Massachusettensis: Or, Political Essays, Published in the Years 1774 and 1775 on the Principal Points of Controversy Between Great Britain and Her Colonies.* Russell repr. of 1819 ed. 1968 o.p.
Warren-Adams Letters: Being Chiefly a Correspondence among John Adams, Samuel Adams, and James Warren. AMS Pr. 2 vols. repr. of 1917–25 ed. $85.00
The Book of Abigail and John: Selected Letters of the Adams Family, 1762–84. Ed. by Lyman Butterfield and others, Harvard Univ. Pr. 1975 $25.00 pap. $8.95

BOOKS BY JOHN QUINCY ADAMS

The Writings of John Quincy Adams. Ed. by Worthington C. Ford, Greenwood 7 vols. repr. of 1917 ed. 1968 lib. bdg. $180.00

The Diary of John Quincy Adams: 1794–1845. Ed. by Allan Nevins, *Amer. Class. Ser.* Ungar repr. of 1928 ed. 1969 $30.00

Memoirs of John Quincy Adams, Comprising Portions of His Diary from 1795 to 1848. Ed. by Charles Francis Adams, AMS Pr. 12 vols. repr. of 1887 ed. lib. bdg. $420.00; *Select Bibliographies Repr. Ser.* Ayer 12 vols. repr. $470.00

Speech of John Quincy Adams of Massachusetts, upon the Right of the People, Men and Women, to Petition. Anti-Slavery Crusade in Amer. Ser. Ayer repr. of 1838 ed. 1969 $11.50

Argument of John Quincy Adams, before the Supreme Court of the United States . . . Anti-Slavery Crusade in Amer. Ser. Ayer repr. of 1841 ed. 1969 $11.50; Greenwood repr. of 1841 ed. lib. bdg. $15.00

The Selected Writings of John and John Quincy Adams. Ed. by Adrienne Koch and William Peden, AMS Pr. repr. of 1946 ed. 1985 lib. bdg. $40.00

BOOKS ABOUT THE ADAMS FAMILY

Adams, James Truslow, *The Adams Family.* Darby repr. of 1930 ed. 1979 lib. bdg. $25.00; Greenwood repr. of 1930 ed. 1974 lib. bdg. $20.50; New Amer. Lib. (Signet) 1976 pap. $1.95

Adams, John Quincy, and Charles Francis Adams. *The Life of John Adams.* Haskell 2 vols. repr. of 1871 ed. 1969 $79.95; Scholarly 2 vols. repr. of 1871 ed. 1971 $95.00

Akers, Charles W. *Abigail Adams: An American Woman. Lib. of Amer. Biography.* Little, Brown 1980 $13.95 pap. $6.95

Bemis, Samuel Flagg. *John Quincy Adams.* Knopf 2 vols. 1949–56 $25.00

Bremer, Howard F. *John Adams, 1735–1826: Chronology, Documents, Bibliographical Aids. Presidential Chronology Ser.* Oceana 1967 $8.00

Chinard, Gilbert. *Honest John Adams.* Intro. by Douglas Adair, Peter Smith $12.00

Duberman, Martin. *Charles Francis Adams, 1807–1886.* Stanford Univ. Pr. 1961 $35.00 pap. $10.95

Morse, John T., Jr. *Charles Francis Adams, 1807–1886.* AMS Pr. repr. of 1900 ed. $22.50; Richard West $14.50

Nagel, Paul C. *Descent from Glory: Four Generations of the John Adams Family.* Galaxy Bks. Oxford 1983 $25.00 pap. $9.95. A family portrait of an authentic American dynasty, studying not only why it produced distinction among its members for so many generations but also why some members were damaged in each generation.

Oliver, Andrew. *Portraits of John Adams and Abigail Adams.* Harvard Univ. Pr. 1967 $17.50

Shaw, Peter. *The Character of John Adams.* Norton Lib. 1977 pap. $5.95

Smith, Page. *John Adams.* Greenwood 2 vols. repr. of 1962 ed. lib. bdg. $39.00

Withey, Lynne. *Dearest Friend: A Life of Abigail Adams.* Macmillan (Free Pr.) 1982 $17.95 pap. $9.95

CALHOUN, JOHN CALDWELL. 1782–1850

More than 30,000 Calhoun papers, discovered and organized in the South Caroliniana Library, form the basis of the new edition of *The Papers,* the first major compilation of his letters in more than 50 years and the first comprehensive collection of his speeches and other writings in more than a century. The "cast-iron man" who championed the rights of the minority in a democratic government, and supported states rights, served more than 40 years in the government of the state and nation. Born of Scots-Irish forebears and a native of South Carolina, he attended Yale, was a member of the South Carolina legislature and the U.S. Congress, became secretary of war, secretary of state, and vice-president of the United States.

BOOKS BY CALHOUN

Works of John C. Calhoun. Ed. by Richard K. Cralle, Russell 6 vols. repr. of 1851–56 ed. 1968 o.p.

The Papers of John C. Calhoun. Ed. by Robert L. Meriwether, W. Edwin Hemphill, and Clyde N. Wilson, Univ. of South Carolina Pr. 14 vols. 1959–81 lib. bdg. ea. $27.50–$34.95

Calhoun: Basic Documents. Ed. by John M. Anderson, Pennsylvania State Univ. Pr. $24.95

A Disquisition on Government. Peter Smith 1958 $11.25

BOOKS ABOUT CALHOUN

Capers, Gerald M. *John C. Calhoun, Opportunist: A Reappraisal.* Times Bks. repr. 1972 pap. $3.45; Univ. Pr. of Florida 1960 $8.00

Coit, Margaret L., ed. *John C. Calhoun.* Berg 1977 $17.95; *Great Lives Observed Ser.* Prentice-Hall (Spectrum Bks.) 1970 pap. $1.95

Spain, August O. *Political Theory of John C. Calhoun.* Octagon repr. of 1951 ed. 1968 lib. bdg. $20.50

Von Holst, Hermann. *John C. Calhoun.* Ed. by John T. Morse, Jr., AMS Pr. repr. of 1899 ed. $29.00

Wiltse, Charles M. *John C. Calhoun.* Russell 3 vols. 1968 o.p.

CLAY, HENRY. 1777–1852

Henry Clay, with Daniel Webster and John C. Calhoun, dominated the U.S. Senate for decades and is generally considered one of the most important men to have served in the Senate in the country's history. As speaker of the House of Representatives, as senator, as secretary of state under John Quincy Adams, and as three-time candidate for the presidency, Henry Clay of Kentucky was rarely, if ever, during his career far from the center of the stage in U.S. politics. "Clay the public man is revealed in many of his papers. So is Clay the high-living gentleman of Ashland (here are some of his liquor bills), the lawyer busy with land titles and bill collections, the horse trader, the speculator in real estate and the public-spirited citizen promoting higher education" (*N.Y. Times*).

BOOKS BY CLAY

The Papers of Henry Clay. Ed. by James F. Hopkins and Mary W. Hargreaves, Univ. Pr. of Kentucky 8 vols. 1959–84 ea. $40.00. Arrangement of documents is chronological, the location of the documents in the original is given, and useful editorial comment is supplied where necessary.

Private Correspondence of Henry Clay. Ed. by Calvin Colton, *Select Bibliographies Repr. Ser.* Ayer repr. of 1855 ed. $35.50

BOOKS ABOUT CLAY

Colton, Calvin. *The Life and Times of Henry Clay*. Intro. by Michael Hudson, *Neglected Amer. Economists Ser.* Garland 2 vols. 1975 lib. bdg. $110.00

Eaton, Clement. *Henry Clay and the Art of American Politics*. *Lib. of Amer. Biography*. Little, Brown 1962 pap. $6.95

Poge, George R. *Henry Clay and the Whig Party*. Peter Smith 1965 $10.75

Schurz, Carl. *Henry Clay*. Ed. by John T. Morse, Jr., intro. by Glyndon G. Van Deusen, *Amer. Statesmen Ser.* AMS Pr. 2 vols. repr. of 1899 ed. $70.00; Chelsea House 2 vols. repr. of 1899 ed. 1981 pap. $10.95

Van Deusen, Glyndon G. *The Life of Henry Clay*. Greenwood repr. of 1937 ed. 1979 lib. bdg. $37.50

DOUGLASS, FREDERICK. 1817?–1895

Born a slave, without ever knowing his white father, Douglass escaped from slavery in 1838. He became an agent and eloquent orator for the Massachusetts Anti-Slavery Society, lectured extensively in England and the United States, and founded his own weekly newspaper, *The North Star*, in Rochester, N.Y. (1847–64). His classic autobiography, *Narrative of the Life of Frederick Douglass*, was first published in 1845. A longer version followed in 1855 and a completed version in 1895, the year of Douglass' death. A bestseller in its own time, it has since become available in numerous editions and languages.

BOOKS BY DOUGLASS

The Frederick Douglass Papers. Ed. by John W. Blassingame, Yale Univ. Pr. 2 vols. text ed. 1982 ea. $52.00

Narrative of the Life of Frederick Douglass, an American Slave. Doubleday (Anchor) pap. $3.50; ed. by Benjamin Quarles, Harvard Univ. Pr. 1960 $10.00 pap. $3.95; pref. by W. L. Garrison, New Amer. Lib. (Signet) 1968 pap. $2.45; ed. by Houston A. Baker, Jr., *Penguin Amer. Lib. Ser.* 1982 pap. $3.95

Frederick Douglass: The Narrative and Selected Writings. Ed. by Michael Meyer, *Modern Lib. College Ed. Ser.* Random text ed. 1983 pap. $4.95

My Bondage and My Freedom. Intro. by Philip S. Foner, *Black Rediscovery Ser.* Dover repr. of 1855 ed. 1969 pap. $6.95; Peter Smith $14.50

Life and Times of Frederick Douglass. Citadel Pr. repr. of 1881 ed. 1984 $20.00 pap. $8.95; ed. by Barbara Ritchie, Crowell 1966 $7.95; Macmillan (Collier Bks.) 1962 pap. $9.95

The Life and Writings of Frederick Douglass. Ed. by Philip S. Foner, International Pubns. 5 vols. 1975 $60.00 pap. $30.00

A Black Diplomat in Haiti: The Diplomatic Correspondence of U.S. Minister Frederick Douglass from Haiti, 1889–1891. Ed. by Norma Brown, Documentary Pubns. 2 vols. 1977 lib. bdg. $44.95

BOOKS ABOUT DOUGLASS

Chesnutt, Charles W. *Frederick Douglass*. Johnson Repr. repr. of 1899 ed. 1971 $15.00

Huggins, Nathan I. *Slave and Citizen: The Life of Frederick Douglass*. *Lib. of Amer. Biography*. Little, Brown 1980 $12.95 pap. $6.95

Quarles, Benjamin. *Frederick Douglass*. Pref. by J. M. McPherson, *Studies in Amer. Negro Life* Atheneum repr. of 1948 ed. text ed. 1968 pap. $4.95

Washington, Booker T. *Frederick Douglass*. Argosy repr. of 1906 ed. 1969 $12.50;

Greenwood repr. of 1907 ed. lib. bdg. $15.75; *Studies in Black History and Culture* Haskell repr. of 1907 ed. 1969 lib. bdg. $49.95

HAMILTON, ALEXANDER. 1757–1804

The publication of the papers of Hamilton focuses attention on this interesting personality and influential founding father. "No one did more for all Americans," wrote Dorothy Bobbe in the *N.Y. Times*, "yet long-standing misconceptions about his character—his ambition, his supposed aristocratic leanings and opportunities—frequently prevent our appreciation of his extraordinary achievements." After West Indian birth and boyhood, he served in the American Revolution, rising to the rank of Lieutenant-Colonel at not much more than 20 years of age and became General Washington's chief aide. His great service to the new Constitution was made by his contributions (with Madison and Jay) to *The Federalist*. The first secretary of the treasury, his plan for the funding of the national debt and his report on manufactures gave early impetus to economic and industrial development in an economy that was still largely agricultural. Hamilton was killed in a famous duel with Aaron Burr on Weehawken Heights.

Books by Hamilton

Papers of Alexander Hamilton. Ed. by Harold C. Syrett, Columbia Univ. Pr. 26 vols. 1961–78 ea. $50.00–$60.00. Volume 27, the cumulative index, is forthcoming.
(and James Madison and John Jay). *Federalist Papers.* Intro. by Garry Willis, *Bantam Class. Ser.* 1982 pap. $2.95; ed. by Clinton Rossiter, New Amer. Lib. lib. bdg. 1961 pap. $2.95; *Modern Lib. College Ed. Ser.* Random 1964 pap. $4.95
The Alexander Hamilton Reader. Ed. by Margaret E. Hall, Oceana 1957 $15.00 pap. $2.50
Industrial and Commercial Correspondence of Alexander Hamilton Anticipating His Report on Manufactures. Ed. by Arthur H. Cole, pref. by E. F. Gay, Kelley repr. of 1928 ed. $35.00

Books about Hamilton

Bowers, Claude G. *Jefferson and Hamilton.* Scholarly repr. of 1925 ed. 1972 $69.00
Cooke, Jacob E. *Alexander Hamilton: A Biography.* Scribner 1982 $17.95
Flexner, James T. *The Young Hamilton: A Biography.* Little, Brown 1978 $17.45
Ford, Paul L. *Bibliotheca Hamiltoniana.* AMS Pr. repr. of 1886 ed. $11.50; Jenkins repr. of 1886 ed. $12.50
Goebel, Julius, Jr., and Joseph H. Smith, eds. *The Law Practice of Alexander Hamilton.* Columbia Univ. Pr. 5 vols. 1964–81 ea. $50.00–$75.00
Hecht, Marie B. *Odd Destiny: The Life of Alexander Hamilton.* Macmillan 1982 $19.95
Mitchell, Broadus. *Alexander Hamilton.* Octagon 2 vols. repr. of 1957 ed. 1981 lib. bdg. $103.50
Rossiter, Clinton. *Alexander Hamilton and the Constitution.* Harcourt $9.50
Schachner, Nathan. *Alexander Hamilton.* A. S. Barnes 1961 pap. $4.95

JEFFERSON, THOMAS. 1743–1826

Thomas Jefferson, the third president of the United States (1801–1809), was chairman of the committee that prepared the Declaration of Independence. He wrote and presented the first draft to Congress on July 2, 1776 (described in *Jefferson's Drafts of the Declaration of Independence*). He was a man of outstanding curiosity, industry, and versatility, and among other activities, the first U.S. architect of his generation. After his retirement from the presidency, he lived at Monticello, near Charlottesville, Virginia, which is still preserved as a memorial. Jefferson was fascinated by science, agriculture, literature, and music, and was instrumental in founding the University of Virginia (chartered 1819). Although a poor orator, he wrote with eloquence and ease.

BOOKS BY JEFFERSON

The Papers of Thomas Jefferson. Ed. by Julian P. Boyd and Charles T. Cullen, Princeton Univ. Pr. 60 vols. ea. $50.00. This huge storehouse of material is expected to be many years in production. One of the most monumental editing tasks ever undertaken, it is "eminently deserving the commendation not only of Americans but of the world, for free people everywhere owe more to Jefferson's fertile brain and active hand than they realize" (*Yale Review*).

Autobiography. Intro. by Dumas Malone, Putnam 1969 pap. $1.25

Complete Jefferson. Ed. by Saul K. Padover, *Select Biographies Repr. Ser.* Ayer repr. of 1943 ed. $56.00; Irvington repr. of 1943 ed. lib. bdg. $54.00

Political Writings of Thomas Jefferson. Ed. by Edward Dumbauld, Bobbs 1955 pap. $7.87

Life and Selected Writings. Modern Lib. 1944 $9.95

The Adams-Jefferson Letters: The Complete Correspondence Between Thomas Jefferson and Abigail and John Adams. Ed. by Lester J. Cappon, *Institute of Early Amer. History and Culture Ser.* Univ. of North Carolina Pr. 2 vols. 1959 $37.50

Correspondence Between Thomas Jefferson and Pierre Samuel du Pont de Nemours, 1798–1817. Burt Franklin repr. of 1931 ed. 1972 lib. bdg. $29.00; trans. by Linwood Lehmann, Da Capo repr. of 1930 ed. 1970 lib. bdg. $42.50

Notes on the State of Virginia. 1785. Ed. by Bernard Wishy and William E. Leuchtenburg, intro. by Thomas P. Abernethy, *Amer. Perspectives Ser.* Harper 1977 pap. $4.50; ed. by William Peden, *Norton Lib.* repr. of 1954 ed. 1972 pap. $8.95; intro. by Thomas P. Abernethy, Peter Smith $11.00. A description of his native state, first published in Paris.

On Democracy. Ed. by Saul K. Padover, Greenwood repr. of 1939 ed. lib. bdg. $22.50

Complete Annals of Thomas Jefferson. Ed. by Franklin R. Sawvel, Da Capo repr. of 1903 ed. 1970 lib. bdg. $37.50

The Jefferson Cyclopedia. Ed. by John P. Foley, intro. by Julian P. Boyd, Gordon 2 vols. $75.00. A comprehensive collection of Jefferson's views on government, politics, law, education, finance, art, religion, and freedom.

The Portable Thomas Jefferson. Ed. by Merrill D. Peterson, *Viking Portable Lib.* Penguin 1977 pap. $7.95. A well-chosen selection of Jefferson's writings for the general reader.

BOOKS ABOUT JEFFERSON

Becker, Carl L. *Declaration of Independence: A Study in the History of Political Ideas.* Random (Vintage) 1958 $4.95; Peter Smith $13.00

Beloff, Max. *Thomas Jefferson and American Democracy.* Ed. by A. L. Rowse, Verry 1948 $5.00

Boorstin, Daniel J. *The Lost World of Thomas Jefferson.* Beacon 1960 pap. $4.95; Peter Smith $15.25; Univ. of Chicago Pr. 1981 pap. $10.95

Bowers, Claude G. *Jefferson and Hamilton*. Scholarly repr. of 1925 ed. 1972 $69.00
Brodie, Fawn M. *Thomas Jefferson: An Intimate History*. Bantam 1975 pap. $4.95;
    Norton 1974 $24.95. Brodie investigates the ambiguities and conflicts of Jeffer-
    son's beliefs and behavior. Especially controversial are her suggestions regard-
    ing his personal relationship with one of his slaves.
Chinard, Gilbert. *Thomas Jefferson: The Apostle of Americanism*. Univ. of Michigan
    Pr. 1957 pap. $7.95
Commager, Henry Steele. *Jefferson, Nationalism and the Enlightenment*. Braziller
    1975 $7.50
Dabney, Virginius. *Mr. Jefferson's University: A History*. Univ. Pr. of Virginia 1981
    $14.95
Fleming, Thomas J. *The Man from Monticello: An Intimate Life of Thomas Jefferson*.
    Morrow 1969 $12.50
Koch, Adrienne. *Jefferson and Madison: The Great Collaboration*. Oxford 1964 pap.
    $9.95; Peter Smith $11.25
Malone, Dumas. *Jefferson and His Time: The Sage of Monticello*. Little, Brown 6 vols.
    1948–81 ea. $19.45–$24.50 pap. ea. $9.70–$12.45. The definitive biography of
    Jefferson. Volume 5 won the Pulitzer Prize in 1975.
Mayo, Bernard. *Jefferson Himself*. Univ. Pr. of Virginia repr. of 1980 pap. $7.95
McDonald, Forrest. *The Presidency of Thomas Jefferson*. Amer Presidency Ser. Univ.
    Pr. of Kansas 1976 $19.95
Miller, John C. *The Wolf by the Ears: Thomas Jefferson and Slavery*. Macmillan (Free
    Pr.) 1977 $17.95 pap. $7.95
Morgan, Edmund S. *The Meaning of Independence: John Adams, George Washington,
    Thomas Jefferson*. Norton Lib. 1978 pap. $3.95; Univ. Pr. of Virginia 1979 $8.95
Peterson, Merrill D. *Thomas Jefferson and the New Nation: A Biography*. Oxford 1970
    $39.95 pap. $15.95

LINCOLN, ABRAHAM. 1809–1865

The publication of *The Lincoln Papers* (o.p.) in 1948 opened "a veritable
treasury of source materials for the Civil War era." "Shortly after Lincoln's
death all the papers which had accumulated in his office files during the
presidency, plus many more which he had brought with him from Springfield, were removed from the White House by his son. From that time until
July 26, 1947, when the collection was first opened to the public, these papers were shrouded in secrecy" (Publisher's note). The selection includes
more than 500 vital documents from the monumental collection now in the
Library of Congress. Under the terms of the will of Robert Todd Lincoln,
who died on July 26, 1926, the collection of some 10,000 Lincoln documents, which he had given to the Library of Congress in 1921, was to remain unopened for 21 years. When the collection was opened, David C.
Mearns, then director of the library's reference department, started to work
on these invaluable papers.

The character, personality, and achievements of Lincoln continue to intrigue his country and new biographies and interpretations continue to appear regularly, including most recently the best-selling work by Gore Vidal
entitled *Lincoln: A Novel*.

BOOKS BY LINCOLN

The Collected Works of Abraham Lincoln. Ed. by Roy P. Basler, Rutgers Univ. Pr. 9 vols. 1953 $300.00

Collected Works: Supplement, 1832–65. Greenwood 1974 lib. bdg. $29.95

Famous Speeches of Abraham Lincoln. Intro. by W. H. Townsend, *Essay Index Repr. Ser.* Ayer repr. of 1935 ed. $15.00

Abraham Lincoln: His Speeches and Writings. Ed. by Roy P. Basler, pref. by Carl Sandburg, Kraus repr. of 1946 ed. 1968 $73.00

Selected Writings and Speeches. Ed. by T. Harry Williams, Hendricks House 1980 pap. $4.45

Four Speeches Hitherto Unpublished or Unknown. Intro. by E. W. Wiley, Kraus repr. of 1927 ed. $9.00

The Wisdom and Wit of Abraham Lincoln. Peter Pauper $8.95

The Lincoln-Douglas Debate of 1858. Ed. by Robert Johannsen, Oxford 1965 pap. $8.95

The Political Thought of Abraham Lincoln. Ed. by Richard N. Current, Irvington 1967 $37.50

The Collected Poetry of Abraham Lincoln. Intro. by Paul M. Angle, Southern Illinois Univ. Pr. 1971 $5.00

BOOKS ABOUT LINCOLN

Bishop, Jim. *The Day Lincoln Was Shot.* Harper 1964 pap. $3.80

Brogan, D. W. *Abraham Lincoln.* Pref. by Hugh Brogan, Biblio Dist. rev. ed. 1974 $16.00

Carpenter, Francis B. *Six Months with Lincoln in the White House.* Century House $7.00. An abridged edition of the book, which went through 16 editions, written by the writer-artist who painted "The First Reading of the Emancipation Proclamation" that hangs in the Capitol.

Catton, William, and Bruce Catton. *Two Roads to Sumter.* McGraw-Hill 1971 pap. $5.95. The "two roads" by which Lincoln and Jefferson Davis each came to the Civil War.

Current, Richard N. *Lincoln and the First Shot. Critical Periods of History Ser.* Harper text ed. 1963 pap. $7.80. A basic work by one of the foremost Lincoln scholars.

———. *The Lincoln Nobody Knows.* Greenwood repr. of 1958 ed. 1980 lib. bdg. $27.50; *Amer. Century Ser.* Hill & Wang 1963 pap. $6.95

Fehrenbacher, Don E. *Prelude to Greatness: Lincoln in the 1850's.* Stanford Univ. Pr. 1962 $17.50 pap. $6.95

Garfield, James. *Lincoln, the President: Springfield to Gettysburg.* Peter Smith 2 vols. $19.25

Handlin, Oscar, and Lilian Handlin. *Abraham Lincoln and the Union. Lib. of Amer. Biography* Little, Brown 1980 $12.95 pap. $6.95

Hay, John. *Lincoln and the Civil War in the Diaries and Letters of John Hay.* Intro. by Tyler Dennett, Greenwood repr. of 1939 ed. text ed. 1972 lib. bdg. $25.00

Herndon, William H. *Life of Lincoln.* Intro. by Henry Steele Commager, *Quality Pap. Ser.* Da Capo 1983 pap. $10.95

Hesseltine, William B. *Lincoln's Plan of Reconstruction.* Times Bks. 1972 pap. $1.95

Holzer, Harold, and Mark E. Neely, Jr. *The Lincoln Image: Abraham Lincoln and the Popular Print.* Scribner 1984 $35.00

Horgan, Paul. *Abraham Lincoln: Citizen of New Salem.* Farrar 1962 $3.75; Macmillan 1961 $2.98. Lincoln's years of self-discovery.

Nevins, Allan. *The Emergence of Lincoln*. Scribner 2 vols. o.p.

Oates, Stephen B. *Abraham Lincoln: The Man Behind the Myth*. Harper 1984 $12.45; New Amer. Lib. 1985 pap. $6.95

————. *With Malice Toward None: The Life of Abraham Lincoln*. Harper 1977 $15.95; New Amer. Lib. 1978 pap. $4.95

Sandburg, Carl. *Abraham Lincoln: The Prairie Years and the War Years*. Harcourt 6 vols. 1926–39 $240.00 rev. ed. in 1 vol. repr. of 1954 ed. $17.95 1974 pap. $10.95. (See also Sandburg's main listing in this chapter.)

Tarbell, Ida M. *The Life of Abraham Lincoln*. Richard West 2 vols. repr. of 1908 ed. 1973 set $50.00

Thomas, Benjamin P. *Abraham Lincoln: A Biography*. Knopf 1974 pap. $4.95; Modern Lib. repr. of 1965 ed. 1968 $7.95

Williams, T. Harry. *Lincoln and His Generals*. Greenwood repr. of 1952 ed. lib. bdg. $29.75

————. *Lincoln and the Radicals*. Univ. of Wisconsin Pr. 1941 pap. $11.75

MADISON, JAMES. 1751–1836

The fourth president of the United States, Virginia-born James Madison was the chief architect of the Constitution. His journals provide our principal source of knowledge about the Constitutional Convention of 1787. With Alexander Hamilton and John Jay he wrote the famous *Federalist Papers*. Madison himself was a steadfast disciple of the policies of Thomas Jefferson. When Jefferson became president, Madison served as secretary of state. Succeeding Jefferson as president, Madison faced the intricate problems in U.S. trade relations with Europe that resulted in the War of 1812. In 1817, Madison and his wife, Dolley, the famous hostess, retired from office to their home Montpellier in Orange County, Virginia. In his last years Madison served as rector of Jefferson's University of Virginia.

BOOKS BY MADISON

The Papers of James Madison. Ed. by William T. Hutchinson, Robert A. Rutland, and William M. Rachal, Univ. of Chicago Pr. 15 vols. 1962–84 ea. $22.00–$35.00

The Complete Madison: His Basic Writings. Ed. by Saul K. Padover, Kraus repr. of 1953 ed. $39.00

Notes of Debates in the Federal Convention of 1787 Reported by James Madison. Ed. by Adrienne Koch, *Norton Lib.* 1969 pap. $8.95; Ohio Univ. Pr. 1985 rev. ed. $35.00 pap. $16.95

The Virginia Report of 1799–1800, Touching the Alien and Sedition Laws. *Civil Liberties in Amer. History* Da Capo repr. of 1850 ed. 1970 lib. bdg. $35.00

Journal of the Federal Convention. Ed. by E. H. Scott, *Select Bibliographies Repr. Ser.* Ayer repr. of 1893 ed. $33.00

Calendar of the Correspondence of James Madison. *Bibliography and Reference Ser.* Burt Franklin repr of 1894 ed. 1970 $51.50

BOOKS ABOUT MADISON

Brant, Irving. *The Fourth President: The Life of James Madison*. Bobbs 1970 $12.95

Hunt, Gaillard. *Life of James Madison*. Russell repr. of 1902 ed. 1968 o.p.

Ketcham, Ralph. *James Madison: A Biography*. Macmillan 1971 o.p.

Koch, Adrienne. *Jefferson and Madison: The Great Collaboration*. Oxford 1964 pap. $9.95; Peter Smith $11.25

ROOSEVELT, THEODORE. 1858–1919
[SEE Chapter 7 in this volume.]

ROOSEVELT, FRANKLIN D(ELANO). 1882–1945

Franklin Delano Roosevelt, 32nd president of the United States, was one of the most controversial personalities of modern times, yet one of the most admired. Born to wealth and a family of distinction at Hyde Park, New York, he came to office in 1932 in the depth of the depression, having served as assistant secretary of the navy in the Wilson administration, as an unsuccessful candidate for the vice-president in 1920, and as governor of New York State. His "New Deal" policies, introducing many reforms into the social, economic, and political life of the country, have had a lasting influence on the United States, which also owes a continuing debt to his courage, confidence, and vision as leader in the days preceding and during World War II. The centenary of FDR's birth and the fortieth anniversary of World War II have seen an increase in the number of biographies of this complex and commanding figure.

BOOKS BY ROOSEVELT

Public Papers and Addresses of Franklin D. Roosevelt, 1928–1945. Ed. by Samuel I. Rosenman, Russell 13 vols. repr. of 1938 ed. 1969 o.p.

Complete Presidential Press Conferences, 1933–1945. Da Capo 12 vols. ea. $45.00 set $475.00

Rendezvous with Destiny: Addresses and Opinions of Franklin Delano Roosevelt. Ed. by J. B. Hardman, Kraus repr. of 1944 ed. 1968 $22.00

Nothing to Fear: Selected Addresses. Ed. by Ben D. Zevin, Ayer repr. of 1946 ed. $27.50

F.D.R.: His Personal Letters. Ed. by Elliott Roosevelt; fwd. by Eleanor Roosevelt, Kraus repr. of 1947–50 ed. $98.50

Franklin D. Roosevelt and Foreign Affairs. Ed. by Edgar B. Nixon, Harvard Univ. Pr. series 1, vols. 1–3 $65.00; ed. by Donald B. Schewe, Clearwater series 2, vols. 4–17 $450.00

Churchill and Roosevelt, the Complete Correspondence. Ed. by Warren F. Kimball, Princeton Univ. Pr. 3 vols. 1979 $150.00

Looking Forward. Da Capo repr. of 1933 ed. 1973 lib. bdg. $32.50

On Our Way. Da Capo repr. of 1934 ed. 1973 lib. bdg. $35.00

BOOKS ABOUT ROOSEVELT

Alsop, Joseph. *FDR: A Centenary Remembrance, 1882–1945.* Viking 1982 $25.00; Washington Square Pr. 1982 pap. $3.50

Beard, Charles A. *President Roosevelt and the Coming of the War, 1941: A Study in Appearances and Realities.* Shoe String (Archon) repr. of 1948 ed. 1968 $29.50

Burns, James M. *Roosevelt: The Lion and the Fox.* Harcourt 1956 $15.00; 1963 pap. $9.95; "If we exclude works of personal reminiscence, this book is easily the best. . . . It is thorough, scholarly, incisive in its analysis, and highly readable" (*Commonweal*).

——. *Roosevelt: The Soldier of Freedom.* Harcourt 1970 $15.00 1973 pap. $10.95. Continuing Burns's earlier volume, covering the period of World War II.

Dallek, Robert. *Franklin D. Roosevelt and American Foreign Policy, 1932–1945.* Oxford 1979 $35.00 pap. $12.95
Feingold, Henry L. *The Politics of Rescue: The Roosevelt Administration and the Holocaust, 1938–1945.* Anti-Defamation League pap. $7.95; Schocken repr. of 1976 ed. expanded and updated ed. 1980 pap. $7.95; Rutgers Univ. Pr. 1970 $30.00
Freidel, Frank. *Franklin D. Roosevelt.* Little, Brown 4 vols. 1952–73 ea. $15.00
Gallagher, Hugh G. *FDR's Splendid Deception.* Dodd 1985 $16.95
Graham, Otis L., Jr., and R. Wander Meghan, eds. *Franklin D. Roosevelt, His Life and Times: An Encyclopedia View. Presidential Encyclopedia Ser.* G. K. Hall 1985 lib. bdg. $27.50
Lash, Joseph P. *Eleanor and Franklin: The Story of Their Relationship Based on Eleanor Roosevelt's Private Papers.* New Amer. Lib. (Signet) 1973 pap. $4.95; intro. by Franklin D. Roosevelt, Jr., fwd. by Arthur M. Schlesinger, Jr., Norton 1971 $15.95
Miller, Nathan. *FDR: An Intimate History.* Doubleday 1983 $22.50
Perkins, Dexter. *The New Age of Franklin Roosevelt, 1932–1945. Chicago History of Amer. Civilization Ser.* Univ. of Chicago Pr. 1957 pap. $4.50. A balanced evaluation of the Roosevelt era from the bank failure to Hiroshima.
Roosevelt, Elliott. *As He Saw It.* Greenwood repr. of 1946 ed. 1974 lib. bdg. $15.00
Rosenman, Samuel I. *Working with Roosevelt.* Da Capo repr. of 1952 ed. 1972 lib. bdg. $55.00
Schlesinger, Arthur M., Jr. *The Age of Roosevelt.* Houghton Mifflin 3 vols. 1957–60 ea. $12.95–$19.95 pap. ea. $5.95–$7.95
Tugwell, Rexford G. *In Search of Roosevelt.* Harvard Univ. Pr. 1972 $20.00
Ward, Geoffry C. *Before the Trumpet: Young Franklin Roosevelt.* Harper 1985 $19.18. The first of two projected volumes, the book covers FDR's family background, youth, and education until the time of his marriage to Eleanor in 1905. It is the best account of his family and its influence on the bedrock self-confidence of the man.

STEVENSON, ADLAI E(WING). 1900–1965

After Adlai Stevenson's sudden death in 1965, Walter Lippmann wrote that he represented "the kind of American that Americans themselves, and the great mass of mankind, would like to think that Americans are." Democratic governor of Illinois, twice presidential candidate, and ambassador to the United Nations under Kennedy and Johnson, Stevenson was a self-styled "egghead" who was particularly admired by students and liberal intellectuals but not always by his more "realistic" fellow politicians. "He was always disposed to thought; often he gave indications of seeing another side to the question even when the Communists were involved. He was also, it was privately alleged, somewhat moral; he always worried openly about world opinion; he viewed force as a last resort; and he seemingly believed in the United Nations. Not speeches but real belief" (John Kenneth Galbraith, *N.Y. Times*). His nomination at the 1952 Democratic National Convention was one of the few genuine drafts in U.S. political history. Unlike many politicians, he wrote most of his own speeches, which were of a high order of eloquence. Unlike most politicians, he had a sense of humor.

BOOKS BY STEVENSON

Papers. Ed. by Walter Johnson and Carol Evans, Little-Atlantic 8 vols. ea. $22.50

What I Think. Greenwood repr. of 1956 ed. 1974 lib. bdg. $22.50

New America. Ed. by Seymour E. Harris, *Essay and General Lit. Index Repr. Ser.* Associated Faculty Pr. repr. of 1957 ed. 1971 $23.25

Call to Greatness. Atheneum 1962 pap. $1.25. An affirmation of democracy's will to survive and ability to cope with totalitarianism.

Looking Outward: Years of Crisis at the United Nations. Ed. by Robert L. Schiffer and Selma Schiffer, Greenwood repr. of 1963 ed. 1984 lib. bdg. $37.50; Harper 1963 $10.95. A collection of Stevenson's speeches inside and outside the United Nations.

BOOKS ABOUT STEVENSON

Brown, Stuart G. *Conscience in Politics: Adlai E. Stevenson in the 1950's.* Syracuse Univ. Pr. 1961 $16.95

Cooke, Alistair. *Six Men.* Knopf 1977 $10.95

Martin, John B. *Adlai Stevenson and the World.* Doubleday 1977 $15.00 1978 pap. $7.95

———. *Adlai Stevenson of Illinois: The Life of Adlai E. Stevenson.* Doubleday (Anchor) 1976 pap. $6.95. *Adlai Stevenson and the World* and *Adlai Stevenson of Illinois,* both by Martin, are the best biographies of Stevenson yet produced.

Rowse, Arthur E. *Slanted News: A Case Study of the Nixon and Stevenson Fund Stories.* Greenwood repr. of 1957 ed. 1973 lib. bdg. $18.75

WASHINGTON, BOOKER T(ALIAFERRO). 1856–1915

[SEE Chapter 5 in this volume.]

WASHINGTON, GEORGE. 1732–1799

Washington left many manuscript records of parts of his life, including detailed diaries, from which his many biographers have derived their raw material. Donald Jackson, Dorothy Twohig, William W. Abbot, and others are currently engaged in the lengthy project of editing and publishing a definitive edition of his papers. No figure in U.S. history, including Lincoln, has so fascinated such a large number of biographers, from John Marshall to Douglas Southall Freeman, including such mythmakers as Parson Mason L. Weems.

BOOKS BY GEORGE WASHINGTON

Writings from the Original Manuscript Sources, 1754–1799. Ed. by John C. Fitzpatrick, Greenwood 39 vols. repr. of 1931–44 ed. lib. bdg. 1968 o.p.

Diaries, 1748–1799. Ed. by John C. Fitzpatrick, Kraus 4 vols. repr. of 1925 ed. $87.00

The Journal of Major George Washington. Ed. by Thaddeus W. Tate, Jr., Univ. Pr. of Virginia 1963 $2.50

The Diary of George Washington: From 1789 to 1791: Embracing the Opening of the First Congress, His Tours through New England, Long Island and Southern States, Together with His Journal of a Tour to the Ohio, in 1753. Ed. by Benson J. Lossing, *Select Bibliographies Repr. Ser.* Ayer repr. of 1860 ed. $18.00

The Diaries of George Washington. Ed. by Donald Jackson and Dorothy Twohig, *Papers of George Washington* Univ. Pr. of Virginia 6 vols. 1979 ea. $35.00

Journal and Proceedings of the President, 1793–97. Ed. by Dorothy Twohig, *Papers of George Washington,* Univ. Pr. of Virginia 1981 $30.00

Papers of George Washington: Colonial Series. Ed. by William W. Abbot, Univ. Pr. of Virginia 4 vols. ea. $25.00. Further volumes are forthcoming.

BOOKS ABOUT GEORGE WASHINGTON

Baker, William S. *Bibliotheca Washingtoniana.* Gale repr. of 1889 ed. 1967 $35.00; Gordon $59.95. An annotated and chronological listing of 502 American and foreign titles, 1777–1889.

Bremer, Howard F., ed. *George Washington, 1732–1799: Chronology, Documents, Bibliographical Aids. Presidential Chronology Ser.* Oceana 1967 $8.00

Cunliffe, Marcus. *George Washington: Man and Monument.* New Amer. Lib. rev. ed. 1984 pap. $3.50

Davis, Burke. *George Washington and the American Revolution.* Random 1975 $15.00

Flexner, James T. *George Washington.* Little, Brown 4 vols. 1965–70 ea. $22.00

————. *Washington: The Indispensable Man.* Little, Brown 1974 $16.45 pap. $3.95. One of Washington's modern biographers emphasizes the uniqueness of Washington's role in forming the institutions and traditions of the newborn nation.

Ford, Paul L. *George Washington. Amer. Bicentennial Ser.* Associated Faculty Pr. repr. of 1896 ed. 1970 $26.00

Freeman, Douglas S. *George Washington.* Kelley 7 vols. repr. of 1957 ed. 1975 lib. bdg. ea. $27.50. Volume 7 was completed by Mary W. Ashworth and John A. Carroll. An exhaustive biography, awarded the Pulitzer Prize in 1958.

Knollenberg, Bernhard. *George Washington: The Virginia Period, 1732–1775.* Duke Univ. Pr. 1964 pap. $9.50

————. *Washington and the Revolution, a Reappraisal: Gates, Conway, and the Continental Congress.* Shoe String (Archon) repr. of 1940 ed. 1968 $18.50

Lodge, Henry C. *George Washington.* Ed. by John T. Morse, Jr. *Amer. Statesmen Ser.* AMS Pr. 2 vols. repr. of 1898 ed. $70.00; Ridgeway Bks. 2 vols. repr. of 1890 ed. $20.00

McDonald, Forrest. *The Presidency of George Washington. Norton Lib.* 1975 pap. $3.95; *Amer. Presidency Ser.* Univ. Pr. of Kansas 1974 $19.95

Morgan, Edmund S. *The Genius of George Washington.* Norton 1981 $12.95 1982 pap. $3.95; Univ. Pr. of Amer. repr. of 1980 ed. 1985 lib. bdg. $10.00

Weems, Mason L. *Life of Washington.* Ed. by Marcus Cunliffe, Harvard Univ. Pr. 1962 $14.00 pap. $5.95. This is where the cherry tree began.

Wills, Garry. *Cincinnatus: George Washington and the Enlightenment.* Doubleday 1984 $18.95

Woodward, W. E. *George Washington: The Image and the Man.* Richard West repr. of 1926 ed. 1984 $45.00

WEBSTER, DANIEL. 1782–1852

Daniel Webster was born in Franklin, New Hampshire, graduated from Dartmouth College in 1801, and was admitted to the bar four years later. In 1816 he moved to Boston where he practiced law and represented Massachusetts in the House of Representatives, vigorously championing his state's mercantile and shipping interests. Elected to the U.S. Senate in 1828, Webster became the country's best-known orator. He favored the Compromise of 1850 and helped secure its passage, for which he was reviled as a traitor by many members of his own party. Webster's reputation as an orator is based on his legal and political debates as well as the many public addresses he delivered on patriotic occasions.

BOOKS BY WEBSTER

The Papers of Daniel Webster. Ed. by Harold D. Moser and others, *Series 1, Correspondence.* Univ. Pr. of New England 7 vols. 1975–1985 ea. $45.00–$60.00; ed. by Alfred S. Konefsky and Andrew J. King, *Series 2, Legal Papers.* Univ. Pr. of New England 2 vols. 1982–83 ea. $45.00–$65.00; ed. by Kenneth Shewmaker, *Series 3, Diplomatic Papers.* Univ. Pr. of New England 1983 $70.00. A detailed, exhaustive, and authoritative editing job, covering in separate series the correspondence, legal, and diplomatic papers of Webster's many-sided career.
Letters of Daniel Webster. Ed. by C. H. Van Tyne, Greenwood repr. of 1902 ed. 1969 lib. bdg. $22.75; *Amer. Biography Ser.* Haskell repr. of 1902 ed. 1969 lib. bdg. $62.95
The Writings and Speeches of Daniel Webster. Ed. by J. W. McIntyre, AMS Pr. 18 vols. repr. of 1903 ed. ea. $22.50

BOOKS ABOUT WEBSTER

Baxter, Maurice G. *Daniel Webster and the Supreme Court.* Univ. of Massachusetts Pr. 1966 $17.50
———. *One and Inseparable: Daniel Webster and the Union.* Harvard Univ. Pr. (Belknap Pr.) 1984 $25.00
Benet, Stephen V. *The Devil and Daniel Webster and Other Stories.* Archway 1972 pap. $1.75; Pocket Bks. 1980 pap. $1.75. A frequently anthologized short story classic of American literature, capturing the formidable oratorical and debating talents of Daniel Webster, who was believed fully capable of out-arguing the Devil himself.
Current, Richard N. *Daniel Webster and the Rise of National Conservatism. Lib. of Amer. Biography* Little, Brown text ed. 1962 pap. $6.95
Dalzell, Robert F., Jr. *Daniel Webster and the Trial of American Nationalism, 1843–1852. Norton Lib.* repr. of 1973 ed. 1975 pap. $4.95
Sterling, John C. *Daniel Webster and a Small College.* Univ. Pr. of New England text ed. 1965 $12.50

WILSON, WOODROW. 1856–1924 (NOBEL PRIZE 1919)

A revival of interest in Woodrow Wilson and his brainchild, the League of Nations, followed World War II, the founding of the United Nations, and associated problems of peacemaking after that war. At the library of Princeton University, where he served as president, the project of compiling and publishing his papers has been underway for years under the editorship of Arthur S. Link. This is the first such massive work dealing with a twentieth-century U.S. statesman. Link is also the author of the definitive biography of Wilson. An earlier work by Ray S. Baker, a close friend and authorized biographer of Wilson, *Woodrow Wilson: Life & Letters*, won the 1940 Pulitzer Prize.

The first volume of *The Papers* includes a letter by Wilson the law student at the University of Virginia, who wrote: "As for myself, I suspect that one might find out almost, if not quite, as much about me from my letters as by associating with me, for I am apt to let my thoughts and feelings slip more readily from the end of my pen than from the end of my tongue."

Among his other works still in print are his study of American politics, *Congressional Government* (1885) and *Division and Reunion: 1829–1889* (1893).

BOOKS BY WILSON

The Papers of Woodrow Wilson. Ed. by Arthur S. Link and others, Princeton Univ. Pr. 46 vols. ea. $30.00–$50.00

The Public Papers of Woodrow Wilson. Ed. by W. E. Dodd, Kraus 6 vols. repr. of 1927 ed. ea. $39.00

Mere Literature and Other Essays. Essay Index Repr. Ser. Ayer repr. of 1896 ed. $18.00; Richard West repr. of 1914 ed. 1973 $9.45

The Case for the League of Nations. Ed. by Hamilton Foley, Kraus repr. of 1923 ed. 1969 $20.00

Congressional Government. Johns Hopkins Univ. Pr. 1981 pap. $7.95; Peter Smith 1958 $11.25

Division and Reunion: 1829–1889. Peter Smith $12.00

BOOKS ABOUT WILSON

Baker, Ray S. *Woodrow Wilson and the World Settlement*. Peter Smith 3 vols. 1958 $36.00

———. *Woodrow Wilson: Life & Letters*. Greenwood 8 vols. repr. of 1939 ed. 1968 lib. bdg. $222.00

Blum, John M. *Woodrow Wilson and the Politics of Morality. Lib. of Amer. Biography* Little, Brown 1962 pap. $6.95. Still the best short treatment.

Bragdon, H. W. *Woodrow Wilson: The Academic Years*. Harvard Univ. Pr. (Belknap Pr.) 1967 $32.50. An impressive study by a distinguished educator, especially interesting for its discussion of Wilson's years as president of Princeton University.

Bullitt, William, and Sigmund Freud. *Thomas Woodrow Wilson: A Psychological Study*. Avon 1967 o.p. Psychobiography as it should not be practiced. Completed in 1939 and kept in a vault until after the death of Wilson's widow, this "psychological analysis" caused a furor upon publication. A collaborative effort by Dr. Freud and the late American diplomat who resigned as adviser to Wilson in Paris in 1919, it detailed a number of severe personality problems the president was alleged to have suffered from. The book was generally criticized for its lack of objectivity and omission of much contradictory evidence.

George, Alexander L., and Juliette L. George. *Woodrow Wilson and Colonel House: A Personality Study*. Dover 1956 pap. $5.00; Peter Smith $6.75

Levin, N. Gordon., Jr. *Woodrow Wilson and World Politics: America's Response to War and Revolution*. Oxford 1968 pap. $8.95. In this Bancroft Prize-winning book Levin argues persuasively that Wilson introduced a new style and tone to U.S. diplomacy in the form of his liberal internationalism.

Link, Arthur S., ed. *Woodrow Wilson and a Revolutionary World, 1913–1921. Supplementary Volumes to the Papers of Woodrow Wilson Ser.* Univ. of North Carolina Pr. 1982 $23.00. The definitive biography, still in progress, by the editor of the

Wilson papers. Volume 2 of the set, *The New Freedom,* won the Bancroft Prize in 1958.

Mulder, John M. *Woodrow Wilson: The Years of Preparation.* Princeton Univ. Pr. 1978 $32.50

Osborn, George C. *Woodrow Wilson: The Early Years.* Louisiana State Univ. Pr. 1968 $30.00

Smith, Gene. *When the Cheering Stopped: The Last Years of Woodrow Wilson.* Intro. by Allan Nevins, Morrow 1971 pap. $7.70

Walworth, Arthur. *Woodrow Wilson.* Norton 3d ed. 1978 $19.95 1979 pap. $10.95

CHAPTER 4

The Social Sciences

David L. Sills

> One essential characteristic of all these social sciences [anthropology, economics, political science, psychology, sociology] is that they deal with the social relations between human beings, that is, with those relationships between human beings in which they interact with one another not as physical objects merely but on the basis of mutually attributed meanings.

> The social sciences, like all science, are primarily concerned for analysis, prediction, and control of behavior and values; the humanities, for their synthesis and appreciation. Each of these is a necessary function in man's adjustment to his social existence.
> —BERNARD BARBER, *Science and the Social Order*

These two statements by the Columbia University sociologist Bernard Barber highlight two important aspects of the social sciences: (1) all the social sciences study the interaction between people; and (2) the social sciences and the humanities provide complementary—not antagonistic—interpretations of human behavior. The focus on the interaction between people is obvious from an examination of the titles of the books listed in this chapter; the complementary relationship to the humanities is illustrated by the books in the Sociology section devoted to art, film, and literature and by the books in the Anthropology section devoted to language and religion generally. The humanist seeks in a work of art to understand its meaning to the artist, its "true" meaning if you will. The social scientist, on the other hand, is more interested in how a work of art reflects the society in which it was produced, or how the artist as a specialist is viewed in that society. Both approaches are complementary in that they both contribute to an understanding of artistic products.

There is no clear or authoritative statement of what scholarly fields are included in the social sciences, and there is no need for one. The five fields that Barber includes and that are included in this chapter—anthropology, economics, political science, psychology, and sociology—are widely acknowledged throughout the United States as the core disciplines. The reader should also consult the other chapters in this volume as well as in Volumes 4 and 5 for related fields and titles.

The major emphasis in this chapter is on books that describe the United States, although many books are included that describe other societies, particularly in the Anthropology section. There are three reasons for this emphasis. First, there are more social scientists in the United States than in all the other countries of the world combined, so it is reasonable that—historical works aside—there are more social science books in *Books in Print* by Americans than by any other nationality. Second, it is assumed that most users of *The Reader's Adviser* will be Americans, using a library in the United States, and primarily interested in American society. Third, the literature on American society is so extensive that there simply is not space to include books about other societies in any systematic way. The social scientific study of other countries—generally called "area studies"—is currently very active, particularly among anthropologists and political scientists, and the reader who consults a country entry in the *Subject Guide to Books in Print* will find much that is worthwhile to read.

Each disciplinary division in this chapter is headed by a short introduction to the field, and each discipline is divided into broad subject matter sections in order to guide the reader. A title may appear in more than one list, but it is annotated only when most appropriate. Cross-references to other sections and other chapters direct the reader to the author's main listing.

THE SOCIAL SCIENCES

The books listed here are devoted to the social sciences generally—or to all the social sciences—and are listed separately from the disciplinary lists. The key "Reference Books" have been annotated, so that readers will know which seem most useful for their purposes. The "Methods" books are useful in planning research in any of the social sciences; each of the disciplinary lists also contains books decribing methods of research. Books that are of particular interest to the general reader are annotated. The books listed under "Professional Aspects" are devoted to such topics as academic freedom and the ethical issues that arise in social science research.

Reference Books

Behavioral and Social Sciences Survey Committee. *The Behavioral and Social Sciences: Outlooks and Needs.* Prentice-Hall 1969 o.p. The report of a nationwide committee of scholars sponsored by the National Academy of Sciences and the Social Science Research Council.

Berelson, Bernard, and Gary A. Steiner. *Human Behavior: An Inventory of Scientific Findings.* Harcourt text ed. 1967 pap. $2.25. Most of the findings listed have not been revised; nevertheless, the reader should use this convenient but somewhat outdated book with caution.

Edwards, Paul, ed. *The Encyclopedia of Philosophy.* Macmillan (Free Pr.) 8 vols. in 4 1973 $200.00. An excellent scholarly reference. Contains hundreds of articles relevant to the social sciences as well as biographies of scores of such key figures as Aristotle, Augustine, Burke, Darwin, Durkheim, Freud, Hobbes, James, Jefferson, Locke, Machiavelli, Malthus, Marx, Mill, Pareto, Plato, Rousseau, and Weber.

Gillispie, Charles C., ed. *Dictionary of Scientific Biography: Compact Edition*. Scribner 8 vols. text ed. 1970–80 $695.00

Gould, Julius, and W. J. Kolb. *A Dictionary of the Social Sciences*. Macmillan (Free Pr.) 1964 $40.00. Useful for an introductory explanation of hundreds of concepts.

Hoselitz, Bert F., ed. *A Reader's Guide to the Social Sciences*. Macmillan (Free Pr.) rev. ed. 1972 pap. $3.95. An excellent complement to this chapter. Strong on the history of the social sciences.

Kadish, Sanford H., ed. *Encyclopedia of Crime and Justice*. Macmillan 4 vols. 1983 $300.00

Kruskal, William H., and Judith M. Tanur, eds. *International Encyclopedia of Statistics*. Macmillan (Free Pr.) 1978 $145.00

Main Trends of Research in the Social and Human Sciences. Unipub 2 pts. 1970–79 ea. $65.25–$158.00

Mitchell, G. Duncan, ed. *A New Dictionary of the Social Sciences*. Aldine text ed. 1979 $24.95

Reich, Warren T., ed. *Encyclopedia of Bioethics*. Macmillan (Free Pr.) 4 vols. 1978 $250.00 4 vols. in 2 1982 lib. bdg. $125.00

Ross, John A., ed. *International Encyclopedia of Population*. Macmillan 2 vols. 1982 lib. bdg. $125.00

Seligman, E. R. A., ed. *Encyclopaedia of the Social Sciences*. Macmillan 8 vols. 1937 o.p. Available on microfiche. Although it was prepared 50 years ago, this encyclopedia remains extremely useful, interesting, and indispensable—particularly for its 4,000 biographies of persons relevant to the social sciences. Strongest in the fields of economics and history.

Sibley, Elbridge. *Social Science Research Council: The First Fifty Years*. Social Science Research Council o.p.

Sills, David L., ed. *International Encyclopedia of the Social Sciences*. 1968. Macmillan (Free Pr.) 17 vols. in 8 1977 $310.00. With *Biographical Supplement* published in 1979 set $340.00. A scholarly summary of what was known in the social sciences in the 1960s. In addition to articles on topics, the encyclopedia contains some 600 biographies. This encyclopedia includes biographies of many of the social scientists discussed in this chapter.

Thernstrom, Stephan, Ann Orlov, and Oscar Handlin, eds. *Harvard Encyclopedia of American Ethnic Groups*. Harvard Univ. Pr. 1980 $70.00

Methods of Social Research

Bailey, Kenneth D. *Methods of Social Research*. Macmillan (Free Pr.) text ed. 1978 $17.95

Berelson, Bernard. *Content Analysis in Communications Research*. Hafner 1971 $22.95

Blalock, Hubert M. *Causal Inferences in Nonexperimental Research*. Univ. of North Carolina Pr. 1964 $16.50

———. *Theory Construction: From Verbal to Mathematical Formulations*. Prentice-Hall text ed. 1969 pap. $13.95

Brown, Robert. *Explanation in Social Science*. Beresford Bks. 1963 o.p.

Dollard, John. *Criteria for the Life History, with Analyses of Six Notable Documents. Select Bibliographies Repr. Ser.* Ayer repr. of 1935 ed. $20.00; Peter Smith $11.25

Duncan, Otis D. *Notes on Social Measurement: Historical and Cultural*. Russell Sage 1984 $14.50

Glock, Charles Y., ed. *Survey Research in the Social Sciences.* Russell Sage 1967 $10.00

Goldberger, Arthur, and Otis D. Duncan, eds. *Structural Equation Models in the Social Sciences. Quantitative Studies in Social Relations Ser.* Academic Pr. 1973 $39.50

Gorden, Raymond L. *Interviewing: Strategy, Techniques and Tactics.* Dorsey 3d ed. 1980 $25.50

Gottschalk, Louis, and others. *Use of Personal Documents in History, Anthropology, and Sociology.* Kraus repr. of 1945 ed. pap. $5.00

Guenzel, Pamela J., Tracey R. Berckmans, and Charles F. Cannell. *General Interviewing Techniques: A Self-Instructional Workbook for Telephone and Personal Interviewer Training.* Institute for Social Research 1983 $60.00

Guetzkow, Harold, ed. *Simulation in Social and Administrative Science: Overviews and Case Examples. Behavioral Science in Business Ser.* Prentice-Hall 1972 $19.95

Hopkins, Terence K., and Immanuel Wallerstein. *World-Systems Analysis: Theory and Methodology.* Sage 1982 $25.00 pap. $12.50

Nagel, Ernest. *The Structure of Science: Problems in the Logic of Scientific Explanation.* Hackett repr. of 1961 ed. 1979 lib. bdg. $35.00 text ed. pap. $13.75; Harcourt text ed. 1961 $15.95

Rattenbury, Judith, and others. *Computer Processing of Social Science Data Using OSIRIS IV.* Institute for Social Research text ed. 1984 $20.00

Riecken, Henry W., and Robert F. Boruch. *Social Experimentation: A Method for Planning and Evaluating Social Intervention.* Academic Pr. 1974 $36.00

Rossi, Peter H., and Howard E. Freeman. *Evaluation: A Systematic Approach.* Sage 2d ed. 1982 $20.00

Stone, Philip J. *The General Inquirer: A Computer Approach to Context Analysis.* MIT 1966 pap. $9.95

Tufte, Edward R. *The Visual Display of Quantitative Information.* Graphics Pr. $34.00

Webb, Eugene J. *Unobtrusive Measures: Nonreactive Research in the Social Sciences.* Rand text ed. 1966 pap. $8.95

Weber, Max. *Max Weber on Methodology of the Social Sciences.* Macmillan (Free Pr.) text ed. 1949 $16.95. Three essays first published in 1904, 1905, and 1917. (See Weber's main listing in the Sociology section.)

Woolf, Harry, ed. *Quantification: A History of the Meaning of Measurement in the Natural and Social Sciences.* Irvington repr. text ed. 1961 $34.50 pap. $14.95

Zeisel, Hans. *Say It with Figures.* Harper 6th ed. 1985 $14.50

Professional Aspects

Beauchamp, Tom L., and others, eds. *Ethical Issues in Social Science Research.* Johns Hopkins Univ. Pr. text ed. 1982 $25.00 pap. $10.95

Bower, Robert T., and Priscilla de Gasparis. *Ethics in Social Research: Protecting the Interests of Human Subjects.* Praeger 1978 $26.95

Bulmer, Martin, ed. *Social Research Ethics.* Holmes & Meier text ed. 1982 $39.50 pap. $14.50

Hofstadter, Richard, and Walter Metzger. *The Development of Academic Freedom in the United States.* Columbia Univ. Pr. 1955 o.p. Hofstadter's portion is in print under the title *Academic Freedom in the Age of the College* Columbia Univ. Pr. 1955 pap. $11.00.

Lazarsfeld, Paul, and Wagner Thielens, Jr. *The Academic Mind: Social Scientists in a Time of Crisis.* Ed. by Walter P. Metzger, Ayer repr. of 1958 ed. 1977 $35.50

SOCIETY OF MODERN AMERICA

Bell, Daniel. *The End of Ideology: On the Exhaustion of Political Ideas in the Fifties.* 1962. Macmillan (Free Pr.) text ed. 1965 pap. $3.50

Bellah, Robert N., and Steven M. Tipton. *Habits of the Heart: Individualism and Commitment in American Life.* Univ. of California Pr. 1985 $16.95

Bryce, James. *The American Commonwealth.* AMS Pr. 3 vols. repr. of 1888 ed. $150.00; Folcroft 2 vols. repr. of 1891 ed. 1978 lib. bdg. $87.00

———. *Modern Democracies.* 1921. Arden Lib. 2 vols. repr. of 1924 ed. 1983 lib. bdg. $85.00

Campbell, Angus, and others. *The Quality of American Life: Perceptions, Evaluations and Satisfactions.* Russell Sage 1976 $16.95

Douglas, Mary, and Aaron Wildavsky. *Risk and Culture: An Essay on the Selection of Technological and Environmental Dangers.* Univ. of California Pr. 1982 $17.95 1983 pap. $6.95

Fuchs, Victor R. *How We Live: An Economic Perspective on Americans from Birth to Death.* Harvard Univ. Pr. 1983 $18.50 1984 pap. $7.95

Galbraith, John Kenneth. *The Affluent Society.* Houghton Mifflin 4th ed. 1984 $18.95; New Amer. Lib. rev. ed. 1985 pap. $4.95. (See Galbraith's main listing in the Economics section.)

Harris, Marvin. *America Now: The Anthropology of a Changing Culture.* Simon & Schuster 1981 $12.95; Simon & Schuster (Touchstone Bks.) 1982 pap. $6.95

Henry, Jules. *Culture against Man.* Random (Vintage) 1965 pap. $6.95

Jackman, Mary R., and Robert W. Jackman. *Class Awareness in the United States.* Univ. of California Pr. 1983 $28.95

Karl, Barry D. *The Uneasy State: The United States from 1915 to 1945.* Univ. of Chicago Pr. 1984 lib. bdg. $22.50 1985 pap. $7.95

Lasch, Christopher. *The Culture of Narcissism: American Life in an Age of Diminishing Expectations.* Norton 1979 $14.95; Warner Bks. 1979 pap. $4.95

Lipset, Seymour Martin. *The First New Nation: The United States in Historical and Comparative Perspective.* Norton repr. 1979 pap. $6.95

Mills, C. Wright. *White Collar: The American Middle Classes.* Oxford 1951 $25.00 pap. $9.95

Murray, Charles. *Losing Ground: American Social Policy, 1950–1980.* Basic Bks. 1984 $23.95

Naisbitt, John. *Megatrends: Ten New Directions Transforming Our Lives.* Warner Bks. 6th ed. 1983 $17.00 pap. $4.50

Novak, Michael. *Freedom with Justice: Catholic Social Thought and Liberal Institutions.* Harper 1984 $17.27

Pells, Richard H. *The Liberal Mind in a Conservative Age: American Intellectuals in the 1940's and 1950's.* Harper 1985 $18.22

Riesman, David. *The Lonely Crowd: A Study of the Changing American Character.* Yale Univ. Pr. abr. ed. repr. of 1950 ed. 1973 pap. $9.95

Sayres, Sohnya, et al., eds. *The Sixties, without Apology.* Univ. of Minnesota Pr. 1984 $29.50 pap. $12.95

Shi, David E. *The Simple Life: Plain Living and High Thinking in American Culture.* Oxford 1985 $19.95

Slater, Philip. *The Pursuit of Loneliness: American Culture at the Breaking Point.* Beacon rev. ed. 1976 pap. $4.95

Steiner, Maurice, and others. *Identity and Anxiety: Survival of the Person in Mass Society.* Macmillan (Free Pr.) 1965 o.p.

Susman, Warren I. *Culture as History: The Transformation of American Society in the Twentieth Century.* Pantheon 1985 $22.95 pap. $12.95

Tocqueville, Alexis de. *Democracy in America.* 1835–40. Ed. by J. P. Mayer, trans. by George Lawrence, Doubleday (Anchor) 1969 pap. $10.95; trans. by Phillips Bradley, Random 2 vols. 1944 pap. ea. $4.95. (See Tocqueville's main listing in Chapter 7 in this volume.)

ANTHROPOLOGY

Anthropology—the study of man—is by far the most comprehensive of the social sciences in what it sets out to study. It is concerned with people anywhere in the world and throughout historical time; it is interested in such seemingly mundane matters as cooking pots and such abstract and symbolic matters as language and religion; and it studies man's physical body as well as his personality, beliefs, and culture. Traditionally, anthropologists have studied non-Western peoples, and especially preliterate peoples, but today there are applied anthropologists working on such problems as the design of seats for automobiles and urban anthropologists studying slum dwellers in large cities. What gives anthropology the degree of unity that it has is a concern for culture and how it is transmitted and a firm belief in fieldwork as a primary source of data. Some anthropologists examine the books that people write and others obtain data by means of questionnaires; but the greatly respected, ideal way for an anthropologist is through fieldwork: to live among a people, to observe what they do, and to engage them in what seems to be informal conversation, but which is in fact quite deliberate and structured.

History of the Field

Brew, J. O., ed. *One Hundred Years of Anthropology.* Harvard Univ. Pr. text ed. 1968 $22.00

Mead, Margaret, and Ruth Bunzel, eds. *The Golden Age of American Anthropology. Golden Age Ser.* Braziller 1960 o.p. (See Mead's main listing in this section.)

Stocking, George W., Jr., ed. *Functionalism Historicized: Essays on British Social Anthropology. History of Anthropology Ser.* Univ. of Wisconsin Pr. text ed. 1984 vol. 2 $19.95

Surveys of the Field

Beattie, John. *Other Cultures.* Macmillan (Free Pr.) text ed. 1968 pap. $14.95

Kroeber, Alfred L., ed. *Anthropology Today.* Univ. of Chicago Pr. 1952 o.p. A massive and useful survey of the entire field. (See Kroeber's main listing in this section.)

Leach, E. R. *Rethinking Anthropology. London School of Economics Monographs on Social Anthropology.* Longwood Pr. 1966 $34.50 pap. $16.50
Siegal, Bernard J. *Annual Review of Anthropology.* Annual Reviews 13 vols. text ed. 1972–84 ea. $20.00–$27.00
Winick, Charles. *Dictionary of Anthropology.* Greenwood repr. of 1956 ed. lib. bdg. $29.75; Little, Brown repr. of 1956 ed. 1977 pap. $5.95

Methods of Research

Barnard, Alan, and Anthony Good. *Research Practices in the Study of Kinship.* Academic Pr. 1984 $32.00
Geertz, Clifford. *Local Knowledge: Further Essays in Interpretive Anthropology.* Basic Bks. text ed. 1983 $18.50 1985 pap. $7.95. Essays by a leading contemporary anthropologist, most of them written for nonanthropologists. The author is highly critical of quantitative social sciences. (See Geertz's main listing in this section.)
Gottschalk, Louis, and others. *Use of Personal Documents in History, Anthropology, and Sociology.* Kraus repr. of 1945 ed. pap. $5.00
Jongmans, D. G., and Peter C. Gutkind. *Anthropologists in the Field.* Humanities Pr. text ed. 1967 $26.00
Lindzey, Gardner. *Projective Techniques and Cross Cultural Research. Century Psychology Ser.* Irvington repr. of 1961 ed. 1976 $29.75 text ed. pap. $12.95
Mead, Margaret. *An Anthropologist at Work.* 1959. Avon 1973 pap. $4.45
Murdock, George P., and others. *Outline of Cultural Materials.* 1938. Human Relations Area Files 5th ed. rev. 1982 pap. $15.00. (See Murdock's main listing in this section.)
Pitt, David C. *Using Historical Sources in Anthropology and Sociology. Studies in Anthropological Method* Holt text ed. 1972 pap. $5.95; Irvington repr. of 1972 ed. 1983 pap. $6.95
Radcliffe-Brown, A. R. *Method in Social Anthropology.* 1958. *Midway Repr. Ser.* Univ. of Chicago Pr. 1959 pap. $10.00. (See Radcliffe-Brown's main listing in this section.)
Spencer, Robert F. *Method and Perspective in Anthropology: Papers in Honor of Wilson D. Wallis.* Peter Smith $11.25
Spindler, George D. *Being an Anthropologist: Fieldwork in Eleven Cultures.* Holt text ed. 1970 pap. $9.95; Irvington repr. of 1970 ed. text ed. 1983 pap. $8.95

Acculturation

Firth, Raymond. *Social Change in Tikopia: Restudy of a Polynesian Community after a Generation.* Macmillan 1959 o.p. (See Firth's main listing in this section.)
Foster, George M. *Traditional Societies and Technological Change.* Harper 2d ed. text ed. 1973 pap. $15.95
Hunter, Monica. *Reaction to Conquest: Effects of Contact with Europeans on the Pondo of South Africa.* Rowman abr. ed. 1979 pap. $14.00
Linton, Ralph, ed. *Acculturation in Seven Indian Tribes.* Peter Smith $13.25
Malinowski, Bronislaw. *The Dynamics of Culture Change.* 1945. Ed. by Phyllis M. Kaberry, Greenwood repr. of 1961 ed. 1976 lib. bdg. $18.25. (See Malinowski's main listing in this section.)
Mead, Margaret. *The Changing Culture of an Indian Tribe. Columbia Univ., Contributions to Anthropology* AMS Pr. repr. of 1932 ed. $32.50

Redfield, Robert. *The Folk Culture of Yucatan.* Gordon 1976 lib. bdg. $59.95; Univ. of Chicago Pr. 1941 $25.00. (See Redfield's main listing in this section.)
———. *The Primitive World and Its Transformations.* 1953. Cornell Univ. Pr. 1957 pap. $4.95
Spicer, Edward H., ed. *Perspectives in American Indian Culture Change. Midway Repr. Ser.* Univ. of Chicago Pr. repr. of 1961 ed. 1975 o.p.
Worsley, Peter. *The Trumpet Shall Sound: A Study of Cargo Cults in Melanesia.* Schocken 1968 pap. $5.95

Caste

Bailey, Frederick G. *Caste and the Economic Frontier.* Humanities Pr. text ed. 1957 $10.50
———. *Tribe, Caste and Nation.* Humanities Pr. repr. of 1960 ed. text ed. 1971 $21.75
Dollard, John. *Caste and Class in a Southern Town.* 1937. Doubleday 1957 o.p. (See Dollard's main listing in the Psychology section.)
Leach, Edmund R. *Aspects of Caste in South India, Ceylon and North West Pakistan.* Cambridge Univ. Pr. 1971 pap. $11.95
Marriott, McKim, ed. *Village India: Studies in the Little Community.* Univ. of Chicago Pr. (Phoenix Bks.) 1969 pap. $3.45
Mayer, Adrian C. *Caste and Kinship in Central India: A Village and Its Region.* Univ. of California Pr. 1960 pap. $5.50

Culture

Bateson, Gregory. *Naven: A Survey of the Problems Suggested by a Composite Picture of the Culture of a New Guinea Tribe Drawn from Three Points of View.* 1936. Stanford Univ. Pr. 2d ed. 1958. $25.00 pap. $8.95
Benedict, Ruth. *Patterns of Culture.* 1934. Houghton Mifflin 1961 $10.95. A classic exposition of how cultures elaborate some human potentialities at the expense of others. Beautifully written. (See Benedict's main listing in this section.)
Dorson, Richard M. *American Folklore. Chicago History of Amer. Civilization Ser.* Univ. of Chicago Pr. $4.50
Dundes, Alan. *The Study of Folklore.* Prentice-Hall text ed. 1965 $22.95
Firth, Raymond, ed. *Man and Culture: An Evaluation of the Work of Bronislaw Malinowski.* Humanities Pr. 1980 $28.00; Routledge & Kegan 1957 $26.00
Geertz, Clifford. *The Interpretation of Cultures.* Basic Bks. 1973 pap. $8.95
———. *Local Knowledge: Further Essays in Interpretive Anthropology.* Basic Bks. text ed. 1983 $18.50 1985 pap. $7.95
Hallowell, A. Irving. *Culture and Experience.* Univ. of Pennsylvania Pr. repr. of 1955 ed. 1974 pap. $12.95
Harris, Marvin. *Cannibals and Kings: The Origins of Cultures.* Random 1977 $3.95
———. *Cultural Materialism: The Struggle for a Science of Culture.* Random 1979 $15.00; Random (Vintage) 1980 pap. $7.95
Huizinga, Johan. *Homo Ludens: A Study of the Play Element in Culture.* 1938. Beacon 1955 pap. $8.95; Routledge & Kegan repr. of 1949 ed. 1980 $25.00
Kluckhohn, Clyde. *Culture and Behavior: Collected Essays of Clyde Kluckhohn.* Ed. by Richard Kluckhohn, Macmillan (Free Pr.) text ed. 1965 pap. $2.45
Kroeber, Alfred L. *Configurations of Culture Growth.* Univ. of California Pr. 1944 $31.00
———. *The Nature of Culture.* Univ. of Chicago Pr. 1952 $35.00

Malinowski, Bronislaw. *A Scientific Theory of Culture and Other Essays*. Univ. of North Carolina Pr. 1944 $12.50

Redfield, Robert. *The Folk Culture of Yucatan*. Gordon 1976 lib. bdg. $59.95; Univ. of Chicago Pr. 1941 $25.00

———. *The Little Community*. 1955. Univ. of Chicago Pr. 1973 $10.00

———. *The Primitive World and Its Transformations*. 1953. Cornell Univ. Pr. 1957 pap. $4.95

Sahlins, Marshall D. *Culture and Practical Reason*. Univ. of Chicago Pr. 1977 lib. bdg. $17.50; Univ. of Chicago Pr. (Phoenix Bks.) 1978 pap. $5.95

Sahlins, Marshall D., and Elman R. Service, eds. *Evolution and Culture*. Univ. of Michigan Pr. 1960 $5.00

Sapir, Edward. *Selected Writings of Edward Sapir in Language, Culture, and Personality*. Ed. by David G. Mandelbaum, Univ. of California Pr. 1949 $37.50. (See Sapir's main listing in this section.)

Shweder, Richard A., and Robert A. Levine, eds. *Culture Theory: Essays on Mind, Self, and Emotion*. Cambridge Univ. Pr. 1984 $39.50 pap. $11.95

Steward, Julian H. *Theory of Culture Change: The Methodology of Multilinear Evolution*. Univ. of Illinois Pr. repr. of 1955 ed. 1972 pap. $7.50

Tylor, Edward Burnett. *Primitive Culture*. 1871. Gordon 2 vols. lib. bdg. $250.00; Peter Smith ea. $12.00. (See Tylor's main listing in this section.)

White, Leslie A. *The Evolution of Culture*. McGraw-Hill 1959 pap. $4.95

———. *The Science of Culture: A Study of Man and Civilization*. Farrar 1969 o.p.

Culture and Personality

Benedict, Ruth. *Patterns of Culture*. 1934. Houghton Mifflin 1961 $10.95

Deveraux, George. *Reality and Dream: Psychotherapy of a Plains Indian*. New York Univ. Pr. rev. ed. 1969 o.p.

Haring, Douglas G., ed. *Personal Character and Cultural Milieu*. Syracuse Univ. Pr. 3d ed. 1956 o.p.

Hsu, Francis L. *Rugged Individualism Reconsidered: Essays in Psychological Anthropology*. Univ. of Tennessee Pr. text ed. 1983 $34.50 pap. $14.95

Kardiner, Abram. *The Individual and His Society*. Greenwood repr. of 1939 ed. 1974 lib. bdg. $32.25

Lévi-Strauss, Claude. *Structural Anthropology*. 1938. Trans. by Monique Layton, Basic Bks. 1963 vol. 1 $14.00; Univ. of Chicago Pr. 1976 vol. 2 pap. $10.95. (See Lévi-Strauss's main listing in this section.)

Levine, Robert A., ed. *Culture, Behavior, and Personality*. Aldine 2d ed. 1982 lib. bdg. $29.95 text ed. pap. $14.95

Parsons, Talcott. *Social Structure and Personality*. Macmillan (Free Pr.) 1964 $19.95 pap. $3.45. (See Parsons's main listing in the Sociology section.)

Sapir, Edward. *Selected Writings of Edward Sapir in Language, Culture, and Personality*. Ed. by David G. Mandelbaum, Univ. of California Pr. 1949 $37.50. Essays written between 1910 and 1944 by the major founder of the study of language as a social and cultural phenomenon.

Wallace, Anthony F. C. *Culture and Personality*. Random 2d ed. text ed. 1970 pap. $7.95

Whiting, John W., and Irvin L. Child. *Child Training and Personality: A Cross Cultural Study*. Greenwood repr. of 1953 ed. 1984 lib. bdg. $39.75; Yale Univ. Pr. 1953 $22.50

Economy

Bailey, Frederick G. *Caste and the Economic Frontier.* Humanities Pr. text ed. 1957 $10.50

Cohen, Mark Nathan. *The Food Crisis in Prehistory: Overpopulation and Origins of Agriculture.* Yale Univ. Pr. 1979 $25.00 pap. $10.95

Douglas, Mary, ed. *Food in the Social Order: Studies of Food and Festivities in Three American Communities.* Russell Sage 1984 $27.50

Firth, Raymond. *Primitive Polynesian Economy.* 1939. *Norton Lib.* repr. of 1965 ed. 1975 pap. $4.95; Shoe String (Archon) 2d ed. 1965 $17.50

Goodenough, Ward H. *Property, Kin and Community on Truk.* Shoe String (Archon) rev. ed. 1978 $19.50

Herskovits, Melville J. *Economic Anthropology: A Study in Comparative Economics (The Economic Life of Primitive Peoples).* 1940. Knopf 1965 pap. $7.95. (See Herskovits's main listing in this section.)

Mauss, Marcel. *Gift: Forms and Functions of Exchange in Archaic Societies.* 1925. *Norton Lib.* 1967 pap. $5.95

Parsons, Talcott, and Neil J. Smelser. *Economy and Society: A Study in the Integration of Economic and Social Theory.* Routledge & Kegan 1984 pap. $17.95

Polanyi, Karl, and others, eds. *Trade and Market in the Early Empires: Economies in History and Theory.* Macmillan (Free Pr.) 1957 o.p. (See Polanyi's main listing in the Economics section.)

Sahlins, Marshall D. *Stone Age Economics.* Aldine text ed. 1972 $29.95 pap. $13.95

Tax, Sol. *Penny Capitalism: A Guatemalan Indian Economy.* Octagon repr. of 1953 ed. 1971 lib. bdg. $21.50

Evolution

Childe, V. Gordon. *Man Makes Himself.* Humanities Pr. text ed. 1981 $23.00; New Amer. Lib. 1983 $7.95

Clark, W. E. *The Fossil Evidence for Human Evolution: An Introduction to the Study of Paleoanthropology.* Ed. by Bernard G. Campbell, Univ. of Chicago Pr. (Phoenix Bks.) 3d ed. rev. 1979 $16.00 pap. $4.95

Dobzhansky, Theodosius. *Mankind Evolving: The Evolution of the Human Species. Silliman Memorial Lectures Ser.* Yale Univ. Pr. 1962 $33.00 1964 pap. $8.95

Gould, Stephen J. *Ontogeny and Phylogeny.* Harvard Univ. Pr. (Belknap Pr.) 1977 $25.00 1985 pap. $8.95. A brilliant discussion of evolution by a leading paleogeologist.

Huxley, Julian. *Evolution: The Main Synthesis.* Allen & Unwin 3d ed. text ed. 1974 $25.00

Lopreato, Joseph. *Human Nature and Biocultural Evolution.* Allen & Unwin text ed. 1984 $24.95

Mead, Margaret. *Continuities in Cultural Evolution.* Yale Univ. Pr. 1966 pap. o.p.

Roe, Ann, and George G. Simpson, eds. *Behavior and Evolution.* Yale Univ. Pr. 1958 o.p.

Sahlins, Marshall D., and Elman R. Service, eds. *Evolution and Culture.* Univ. of Michigan Pr. 1960 $5.00

Steward, Julian H. *Theory of Culture Change: The Methodology of Multilinear Evolution.* Univ. of Illinois Pr. repr. of 1955 ed. 1972 pap. $7.50

White, Leslie A. *The Evolution of Culture.* McGraw-Hill 1959 pap. $4.95

Kinship

Evans-Pritchard, E. E. *Kinship and Marriage among the Nuer.* Oxford 1951 $32.50

Firth, Raymond. *We, the Tikopia: A Sociological Study of Kinship in Primitive Polynesia.* 1936. Beacon 1963 pap. $6.95. A classic in the anthropological/sociological
study of kinship.

Lévi-Strauss, Claude. *The Elementary Structures of Kinship.* 1949. Ed. by Rodney
Needham, Beacon 1969 pap. $11.95

Malinowski, Bronislaw. *The Family among the Australian Aborigines: A Sociological
Study.* Intro. by J. A. Barnes, Schocken 1963 $8.00

———. *Sex and Repression in Savage Society.* 1927. *International Lib. of Psychological
Philosophy and Scientific Mathematics.* Humanities Pr. text ed. 1953 $23.00;
New Amer. Lib. 1955 pap. $3.95; Univ. of Chicago Pr. 1985 pap. $10.95. A clas-
sic; the first "modern" treatment of sexual behavior in anthropology.

Murdock, George P., ed. *Social Structure.* 1949. Macmillan (Free Pr.) text ed. 1965
pap. $12.95

Radcliffe-Brown, A. R., and C. Daryll Forde, eds. *African Systems of Kinship and Marriage.* Oxford 1950 pap. $15.95

Schneider, David M., and Kathleen Gough, eds. *Matrilineal Kinship.* Univ. of California Pr. $49.50 pap. $11.95

Young, Michael, and Peter Willmott. *Family and Kinship in East London.* Humanities Pr. text ed. 1957 $15.50; Penguin (Pelican) 1963 pap. $4.95; Peter Smith
$10.25

Language

Bloomfield, Leonard. *Language.* 1933. Holt text ed. 1963 $18.95. The first integrated
description of the field of linguistics. (See Bloomfield's main listing in this section.)

Chomsky, Noam. *The Logical Structure of Linguistic Theory.* Plenum 1975 $45.00;
Univ. of Chicago Pr. text ed. 1985 pap. $17.50

———. *Syntactic Structures.* Mouton 1978 $7.00

Goffman, Erving. *Forms of Talk. Conduct and Communications Ser.* Univ. of Pennsylvania Pr. 1981 $32.00 pap. $10.95. (See Goffman's main listing in the Sociology
section.)

Greenberg, Joseph H., et al., eds. *Universals of Human Language.* Stanford Univ. Pr.
4 vols. 1978 $142.50

Gumperz, John J., ed. *Language and Social Identity.* Cambridge Univ. Pr. 1983 $34.50
pap. $12.95

Hymes, Dell. *Pidginization and Creolization of Languages: Proceedings.* Cambridge
Univ. Pr. 1971 pap. $19.95

———, ed. *Language in Culture and Society: A Reader in Linguistics and Anthropology.*
Harper text ed. 1964 $35.95

Labov, William. *Sociolinguistic Patterns. Conduct and Communications Ser.* Univ. of
Pennsylvania Pr. 1973 $27.50 pap. $11.95

Sapir, Edward. *Selected Writings of Edward Sapir in Language, Culture, and Personality.* Ed. by David G. Mandelbaum, Univ. of California Pr. 1949 $37.50. Essays
written between 1910 and 1944 by the founder of the study of language as a social and cultural phenomenon.

Shuy, Roger, ed. *Georgetown University Round Table on Languages and Linguistics:*

Sociolinguistics—Current Trends and Prospects. Georgetown Univ. Pr. 1972 pap. $6.95

Williams, Frederick, ed. *Language and Poverty: Perspectives of a Theme.* Academic Pr. 1970 $19.00

Religion

Banton, Michael, ed. *Anthropological Approaches to the Study of Religion.* Methuen 1968 pap. $11.95

Durkheim, Emile. *The Elementary Forms of the Religious Life.* 1912. Trans. by Joseph W. Swain, intro. by Robert Nisbet, Allen & Unwin 2d ed. text ed. 1976 $21.00; trans. by Joseph W. Swain, Macmillan (Free Pr.) text ed. 1965 pap. $14.95. A classic study of religion as an expression of society.

Eliade, Mircea. *Patterns in Comparative Religion.* New Amer. Lib. pap. $9.95

Frazer, James George. *The Golden Bough.* St. Martin's 13 vols. repr. of 1890 ed. 1980 $375.00. Although flawed in many details, this monumental classic introduced the comparative method to anthropology. (See Frazer's main listing in this section.)

Geertz, Clifford. *The Religion of Java.* Univ. of Chicago Pr. (Phoenix Bks.) repr. of 1960 ed. 1976 pap. $11.00

Jules-Rosette, Bennetta, ed. *The New Religions of Africa. Modern Sociology Ser.* Ablex 1979 $27.50

Lessa, William A., and Evon Z. Vogt. *Reader in Comparative Religion: An Anthropological Approach.* Harper 4th ed. text ed. 1979 pap. $25.50

Lévi-Strauss, Claude. *The Savage Mind.* 1962. *Nature of Human Society Ser.* Univ. of Chicago Pr. 1966 $10.00; Univ. of Chicago Pr. (Phoenix Bks.) 1968 pap. $8.95

Malinowski, Bronislaw. *Magic, Science and Religion and Other Essays.* Doubleday (Anchor) 1954 pap. $2.95; Greenwood repr. of 1948 ed. 1984 lib. bdg. $35.00

Turner, Victor. *The Ritual Process: Structure and Anti Structure.* Aldine 1969 $26.95; Cornell Univ. Pr. 1977 pap. $7.95

Wallace, Anthony F. C. *Religion: An Anthropological View.* Random text ed. 1966 $17.95

Social Structure

Firth, Raymond. *Elements of Social Organization.* 1951. Greenwood 3d ed. repr. of 1961 ed. 1981 lib. bdg. $28.50

Fortes, Meyer. *Time and Social Structure and Other Essays.* Longwood Pr. 1970 $38.50

Gennep, Arnold van. *The Rites of Passage.* 1909. Trans. by Monika B. Vizedon and Gabrielle L. Caffee, Univ. of Chicago Pr. (Phoenix Bks.) 1961 pap. $3.25. This book introduced the concept of rites of passage to anthropology.

Kertzer, David L., and Jennie Keith, eds. *Age and Anthropological Theory.* Cornell Univ. Pr. 1984 $32.50 pap. $12.95

Murdock, George P. *Social Structure.* 1949. Macmillan (Free Pr.) text ed. 1965 pap. $12.95. The major theoretical work based on the famous Human Relations Area Files at Yale University.

Nadel, S. F. *The Theory of Social Structure.* Routledge & Kegan repr. of 1957 ed. 1969 $16.50

Radcliffe-Brown, A. R. *Structure and Function in Primitive Society: Essays and Addresses.* Macmillan (Free Pr.) 1952 $14.95 text ed. pap. $13.95

Young, Frank W. *Initiation Ceremonies: A Cross Cultural Study of Status Dramatization.* Bobbs pap. $3.40

Societies, Modern

Arensberg, Conrad M. *The Irish Countryman: An Anthropological Study.* Doubleday 1968 $3.95; Natural History Pr. repr. of 1937 ed. 1968 pap. $3.95; Peter Smith $11.25

Benedict, Ruth. *The Chrysanthemum and the Sword: Patterns of Japanese Culture.* 1946. New Amer. Lib. 1967 pap. $7.95. An analysis of Japanese character based on interviews with Japanese-Americans during World War II.

Davis, Allison, and others. *Deep South: A Social Anthropological Study of Caste and Class.* Univ. of Chicago Pr. 1941 o.p.

Embree, John F. *Suye Mura: A Japanese Village.* Univ. of Chicago Pr. 1939 $15.00; Univ. of Chicago Pr. (Phoenix Bks.) 1964 pap. $3.25

Fei, Hsiao Tung. *Peasant Life in China: A Field Study of Country Life in the Yangtze Valley.* AMS Pr. repr. of 1962 ed. $24.50; intro. by Bronislaw Malinowski, Routledge & Kegan 1980 $25.00

Gorer, Geoffrey, and John Rickman. *The People of Great Russia: A Psychological Study.* Norton Lib. 1962 pap. $3.25

Lowie, Robert H. *The German People: A Social Portrait to 1914.* Octagon 1972 lib. bdg. $16.50

Mead, Margaret. *And Keep Your Powder Dry: An Anthropologist Looks at America. Essay Index Repr. Ser.* Ayer repr. of 1942 ed. $18.00; Morrow 1971 pap. $7.95

Warner, W. Lloyd. *Democracy in Jonesville: A Study in Quality and Inequality.* Greenwood repr. of 1949 ed. 1976 lib. bdg. $20.00

Warner, W. Lloyd, and Paul S. Lunt. *The Social Life of a Modern Community.* Elliots Bks. text ed. 1941 $20.00; Greenwood repr. of 1941 ed. 1973 lib. bdg. $22.00. The first of the five-volume Yankee City series, a study of Newburyport, Massachusetts, that is comparable to the Lynds' study of Muncie, Indiana (Middletown), a decade earlier.

West, James. *Plainville USA.* Columbia Univ. Pr. 1945 pap. $10.00

Societies, Tribal

Driver, Harold E. *Indians of North America.* Univ. of Chicago Pr. 2d ed. rev. 1969 $25.00; Univ. of Chicago Pr. (Phoenix Bks.) pap. $15.95

Eggan, Fred. *Social Organization of the Western Pueblos.* Univ. of Chicago Pr. 1950 $12.50; Univ. of Chicago Pr. (Phoenix Bks.) 1973 pap. $2.95

Eggan, Fred, and others. *The Social Anthropology of North American Tribes.* Univ. of Chicago Pr. 1955 $15.00; Univ. of Chicago Pr. (Phoenix Bks.) text ed. 1972 $3.95

Evans-Pritchard, E. E. *The Nuer: A Description of the Modes of Livelihood and Political Institutions of a Nilotic People.* Oxford 1940 pap. $8.95

Firth, Raymond. *We, the Tikopia: A Sociological Study of Kinship in Primitive Polynesia.* 1936. Beacon 1963 pap. $6.95; pref. by Bronislaw Malinowski, Stanford Univ. Pr. abr. ed. repr. of 1936 ed. 1963 $35.00 pap. $10.95

Fortune, R. F. *The Sorcerers of Dobu: The Social Anthropology of the Dobu Islanders of the Western Pacific.* Arden Lib. repr. of 1932 ed. lib. bdg. $25.00

Kuper, Hilder. *Swazi: A South African Kingdom. Case Studies in Cultural Anthropology* Holt text ed. 1963 pap. $9.95

Leach, Edmund R. *The Political Systems of Highland Burma: A Study of Kachin Social Structure.* Longwood Pr. 1977 pap. $22.50

Lowie, Robert H. *Indians of the Plains.* Fwd. by Harry L. Shapiro, pref. by Raymond J. Demallie, Univ. of Nebraska Pr. (Bison) repr. of 1954 ed. 1982 $19.50 pap. $7.95

Malinowski, Bronislaw. *Argonauts of the Western Pacific: An Account of Native Enterprise and Adventure in the Archipelagoes of Melanesian New Guinea.* 1922. Dutton 1961 pap. $5.95; pref. by James Frazer, Waveland Pr. repr. of 1961 ed. text ed. 1984 pap. $9.95

Morgan, Lewis Henry. *The League of the Iroquois.* Intro. by William N. Fenton, Citadel Pr. repr. of 1962 ed. 1984 pap. $7.95; Peter Smith $15.25. (See Morgan's main listing in this section.)

Nadel, Siegfried. *Black Byzantium: The Kingdom of Nupe in Nigeria.* Gordon 1976 lib. bdg. $59.95; *International Institute of African Languages and Cultures Ser.* Oxford 1942 $49.00

Radcliffe-Brown, A. R. *The Andaman Islanders.* 1922. Macmillan (Free Pr.) text ed. 1964 pap. $5.95

Wissler, Clark. *The American Indian.* Peter Smith 3d ed. $11.25

BENEDICT, RUTH. 1887–1948

Ruth Benedict was an American anthropologist and poet. She had been a student of Franz Boas at Columbia University, and for many years she taught at Columbia, where she was tardily made a professor in 1948. Most of her fieldwork was with American Indians, and the two books that brought her fame—*Patterns of Culture* and *The Chrysanthemum and the Sword*—are largely about cultures that she knew only secondhand. *The Chrysanthemum and the Sword* is a brilliant reconstruction of Japanese culture on the basis of wartime interviews with Japanese people who had been living in the United States for several decades, but it has been criticized for having described nearly dead patterns of Japanese social behavior.

BOOKS BY BENEDICT

Patterns of Culture. 1934. Houghton Mifflin 1961 $10.95
Zuñi Mythology. AMS Pr. 2 vols. repr. of 1935 ed. 1969 $70.00
Race: Science and Politics. 1940. Greenwood repr. of 1950 ed. 1982 lib. bdg. $27.50
The Chrysanthemum and the Sword: Patterns of Japanese Culture. 1946. Houghton Mifflin $8.95; New Amer. Lib. 1967 pap. $7.95

BOOKS ABOUT BENEDICT

Mead, Margaret. *An Anthropologist at Work.* 1959. Avon 1973 pap. $4.45
———. *Ruth Benedict. Leaders in Modern Anthropology Ser.* Columbia Univ. Pr. 1974 $24.00 pap. $10.50
Modell, Judith. *Ruth Benedict: Patterns of a Life.* Univ. of Pennsylvania Pr. 1983 $30.00 1984 pap. $11.95. A more objective interpretation of Benedict than the biography by Margaret Mead, who was an intimate friend of Benedict.

BLOOMFIELD, LEONARD. 1887–1949

Leonard Bloomfield, an American professor of German, created the field of linguistics as a branch of science. In studying non-Western languages, he discovered the principles of language itself; his *Language* integrated the field for the first time. He was one of the founders of the Linguistic Society of America, and he wrote an article for the first issue of its journal in which he explained the need for a society for the new discipline.

BOOKS BY BLOOMFIELD

An Introduction to the Study of Language. Intro. by Joseph F. Kess, Benjamins repr. of 1914 ed. 1982 $44.00 pap. $27.00
Language. 1933. Holt text ed. 1963 $18.95; fwd. by Charles Hockett, Univ. of Chicago Pr. text ed. 1984 pap. $12.50
The Menomini Language. Elliots Bks. 1962 $49.50

BOAS, FRANZ. 1858–1942

Franz Boas, a German-born American anthropologist, became the most influential anthropologist of his time. A Columbia University professor, he created both the field of anthropology and the modern concept of culture. Both directly and through the influence of such students as Ruth Benedict, Melville J. Herskovitz, Alfred L. Kroeber, and Margaret Mead, he set the agenda for all subsequent American cultural anthropology.

BOOKS BY BOAS

The Mind of Primitive Man. 1911. Greenwood repr. of 1963 ed. rev. ed. 1983 lib. bdg. $35.00; Macmillan (Free Pr.) rev. ed. 1965 text ed. pap. $3.50
Primitive Art. Dover 1927 pap. $5.95; Peter Smith 1962 $13.50
Anthropology and Modern Life. 1928. Intro. by Ruth Bunzel, Greenwood repr. of 1962 ed. 1984 lib. bdg. $29.75
General Anthropology. Johnson Repr. repr. of 1938 ed. $17.00; Scholarly repr. of 1938 ed. 1976 $88.00

BOOKS ABOUT BOAS

Goldschmidt, Walter R. *The Anthropology of Franz Boas: Essays on the Centennial of His Birth.* Amer. Anthropological Association 1959 o.p.
Herskovits, Melville. *Franz Boas.* Kelley repr. of 1953 ed. $15.00
Stocking, George W., Jr. *A Franz Boas Reader: Shaping of American Anthropology, 1883–1911.* Basic Bks. text ed. 1973 $12.95; Univ. of Chicago Pr. 1982 pap. $11.00

EVANS-PRITCHARD, E. E. 1902–1973

E. E. Evans-Pritchard, a British anthropologist, was the leader of the field-work-based social anthropology that flourished in the United Kingdom in the years following World War II. He believed that anthropological knowledge is based on detailed ethnographic and historical research, and his studies of three African societies—the Azande, the Sanusi, and the Nuer—provided the basis for much of his theoretical work. His study of Nuer religion was the first scholarly study to present the religious beliefs of a preliterate people as having a theological significance comparable to the religious thought of more complex societies.

BOOKS BY EVANS-PRITCHARD

Witchcraft, Oracles, and Magic among the Azande. Fwd. by C. G. Seligman, Oxford 1937 $57.00; ed. by Eva Gillies, Oxford abr. ed. 1976. pap. $9.95
The Nuer: A Description of the Modes of Livelihood and Political Institutions of a Nilotic People. Oxford 1940 pap. $8.95
(and Meyer Fortes, eds.). *African Political Systems.* 1940. Oxford 1970 pap. $8.95
Social Anthropology. Cohen & West 1951 o.p.
Nuer Religion. Oxford 1956 pap. $8.95
Essays in Social Anthropology. Faber 1962 o.p.
The Azande: History and Political Institutions. Oxford 1971 $39.95

BOOKS ABOUT EVANS-PRITCHARD

Beattie, J. H., ed. *Studies in Social Anthropology: Essays in Memory of E. E. Evans-Pritchard by His Former Oxford Colleagues.* Ed. by R. G. Lienhardt, Oxford 1975 $29.95
Gluckman, Max. *Custom and Conflict in Africa.* Barnes & Noble repr. of 1956 ed. 1969 pap. $6.95
Singer, Andre, and Brian V. Street, eds. *Zande Themes: Essays Presented to Sir Edward Evans-Pritchard.* Rowman 1972 $14.50

FIRTH, RAYMOND. 1901–

Raymond Firth, a New Zealand-born English anthropologist, was Bronislaw Malinowski's successor at the London School of Economics. In 1928, he first visited the tiny island of Tikopia in the Solomons, and his monograph *We, the Tikopia* established his fame. A devoted student of Malinowski, he established no school of anthropological thought, but his productive scholarship and academic statesmanship have won him an important reputation in social anthropology.

BOOKS BY FIRTH

We, the Tikopia: A Sociological Study of Kinship in Primitive Polynesia. 1936. Beacon. 1963 pap. $6.95
Human Types. 1938. Greenwood repr. of 1975 ed. rev. ed. 1983 lib. bdg. $32.50; New Amer. Lib. pap. $1.25
Primitive Polynesian Economy. 1939. *Norton Lib.* repr. of 1965 ed. 1975 pap. $4.95; Shoe String (Archon) 2d ed. 1965 $17.50
The Work of the Gods in Tikopia. 1940. Longwood Pr. 2d ed. 1967 $48.50
Malay Fishermen: Their Peasant Economy. 1946. *Norton Lib.* 1975 pap. $4.95
Elements of Social Organization. 1951. Greenwood 3d ed. repr. of 1961 ed. 1981 lib. bdg. $28.50
(ed.). *Man and Culture: An Evaluation of the Work of Bronislaw Malinowski.* Humanities Pr. 1980 $28.00; Routledge & Kegan 1957 $26.00
Social Change in Tikopia: Restudy of a Polynesian Community after a Generation. Macmillan 1959 o.p.
Tikopia Ritual and Belief. Beacon 1967 o.p.

BOOK ABOUT FIRTH

Freedman, Maurice, ed. *Social Organization: Essays Presented to Raymond Firth*. Biblio Dist. 1967 $32.50

FRAZER, JAMES GEORGE. 1854–1941

James George Frazer was a British social anthropologist, folklorist, and classical scholar who taught for most of his life at Trinity College, Cambridge. Greatly influenced by E. B. Tylor's *Primitive Culture*, published in 1871, he wrote the massive *The Golden Bough*, a reconstruction of the whole of human thought and custom through the successive stages of.magic, religion, and science. *The Golden Bough* is regarded by many today as a much-loved but antiquated relic, but by making anthropological data and knowledge academically respectable, Frazer made modern, comparative anthropology possible.

BOOK BY FRAZER

The Golden Bough. St. Martin's 13 vols. repr. of 1890 ed. 1980 $375.00. Available in a number of abridged editions.

BOOKS ABOUT FRAZER

Besterman, Theodore. *A Bibliography of Sir James George Frazer*. Norwood repr. of 1934 ed. 1977 lib. bdg. $27.50
Dawson, Warren R., and others, eds. *The Frazer Lectures, 1922–1932. Essay Index Repr. Ser.* Ayer repr. of 1932 ed. $15.25

GEERTZ, CLIFFORD. 1926–

Clifford Geertz, an American anthropologist, is known for his studies of Islam in Indonesia and Morocco and for his studies of the peasant economy of Java. But he is also the leading exponent of an orientation in the social sciences called "interpretation." Social life, according to this view, is organized in terms of symbols whose meaning we must grasp if we are to understand that organization and formulate its principles. Interpretative explanations focus on what institutions, actions, customs, and so on, mean to the people involved. What emerges from studies of this kind are not laws of society, and certainly not statistical relationships, but rather interpretations, that is to say, understanding. Geertz taught for ten years at the University of Chicago; since 1970, he has been at the Institute for Advanced Study in Princeton, New Jersey, where he is the Harold F. Linder professor of social science.

BOOKS BY GEERTZ

The Religion of Java. Univ. of Chicago Pr. (Phoenix Bks.) repr. of 1960 ed. 1976 pap. $11.00
Islam Observed: Religious Development in Morocco and Indonesia. Univ. of Chicago Pr. (Phoenix Bks.) 1971 pap. $5.00; Yale Univ. Pr. 1968 $10.00
The Interpretation of Cultures. Basic Bks. 1973 pap. $8.95
Myth, Symbol and Culture. Norton 1974 $9.95 pap. $6.95
(and Hildred Geertz). *Kinship in Bali*. Univ. of Chicago Pr. (Phoenix Bks.) 1978 pap. $3.95

Negara: Theatre State in 19th Century Bali. Princeton Univ. Pr. 1980 $26.00 pap. $8.95
Local Knowledge: Further Essays in Interpretive Anthropology. Basic Bks. text ed. 1983
     $18.50 1985 pap. $7.95

HERSKOVITS, MELVILLE JEAN. 1895–1963

Melville Jean Herskovits, an American anthropologist who was a student
of Franz Boas at Columbia University, became a leading student of acculturation and an outstanding teacher at Northwestern University. His major
research was on African blacks and the forced relocation of their culture to
the New World. He studied religion, music, and folklore, and was particularly interested in how culture influences the arts.

BOOKS BY HERSKOVITS

The American Negro: A Study in Racial Crossing. Greenwood repr. of 1928 ed. 1985
     lib. bdg. $29.75; Indiana Univ. Pr. 1964 pap. $1.65
Life in a Haitian Valley. 1937. Octagon 1964 lib. bdg. $26.00
Acculturation: The Study of Culture Contact. 1938. Peter Smith $8.00
Dahomey: An Ancient West African Kingdom. Augustin 2 vols. 1938 o.p.
*Economic Anthropology: A Study in Comparative Economics (The Economic Life of
     Primitive Peoples).* 1940. Knopf 1965 pap. $7.95
The Myth of the Negro Past. 1941. Beacon 1958 pap. $9.95; Peter Smith $10.25
Man and His Works: The Science of Cultural Anthropology. Knopf 1948 o.p.
The Human Factor in Changing Africa. Random (Vintage) 1962 pap. $2.45

BOOK ABOUT HERSKOVITS

Simpson, George E. *Melville J. Herskovits.* Columbia Univ. Pr. 1973 $24.00 pap.
     $11.00

KROEBER, ALFRED L. 1876–1960

Alfred L. Kroeber was an American anthropologist whose life was
coterminous with the development of American anthropology. His 1902
Ph.D. from Columbia was the first ever awarded. His *Anthropology*, published in 1923, was the only textbook of its time, and it was enormously influential among students, scholars, and the general public. The 1948 edition
has the subtitle *Race, Language, Culture, Psychology, Prehistory*, indicating
the range of his interests and his contributions. His concept of "cultural configuration" was influential; his notion of culture as "superorganic" was controversial as well. Much of his research was carried out in California, and
he taught at the University of California, Berkeley, for most of his professional life.

BOOKS BY KROEBER

The Nature of Culture. Univ. of Chicago Pr. 1952 $35.00
Anthropology: Culture, Patterns, and Processes. 1923. Harcourt 1963 pap. $9.95
Handbook of the Indians of California. Dover 1976 pap. $14.95; Gannon 1976 lib.
     bdg. $22.50; Scholarly repr. of 1925 ed. 1972 $95.00
Configurations of Culture Growth. Univ. of California Pr. 1944 $31.00
(and Clyde Kluckhohn). *Culture: A Critical Review of Concepts and Definitions.* Pea-
     body Museum of Amer. Archaeology and Ethnology 1952 o.p.

BOOKS ABOUT KROEBER

Driver, Harold E. *The Contribution of A. L. Kroeber to Culture Area Theory and Practice.* Indiana Univ. Pr. 1962 o.p.

Kroeber, Theodora. *Alfred Kroeber: A Personal Configuration.* Univ. of California Pr. 1970 $15.95 pap. $4.95

Steward, Julian. *Alfred Kroeber. Leaders in Modern Anthropology Ser.* Columbia Univ. Pr. 1973 $28.00 pap. $10.50

LEVI-STRAUSS, CLAUDE. 1908–

Claude Lévi-Strauss, a French anthropologist, was the founder of structural anthropology. This theoretical position assumes that there are structural propensities in the human mind that lead unconsciously toward categorization of physical and social objects. (Hence such book titles as *The Raw and the Cooked* and such expositions of his work by others as *The Unconscious in Culture* and *Elementary Structures Reconsidered.*) The models of society that scholars create are often dualistic: status-contract (Maine): gemeinschaft-gesellschaft (Tönnies); mechanical-organic solidarity (Durkheim); folk-urban (Redfield); universalism-particularism (Parsons); and local-cosmopolitan (Merton). Lévi-Strauss's writings (some of which have been described by Clifford Geertz as "theoretical treatises set out as travelogues") have been enormously influential throughout the scholarly world. George Steiner has described him (along with Freud and Marx) as one of the major architects of the thought of our times.

BOOKS BY LÉVI-STRAUSS

The Elementary Structures of Kinship. 1949. Ed. by Rodney Needham, Beacon 1969 pap. $11.95

Tristes Tropiques. 1955. Adler's rev. ed. 1968 $24.95; Washington Square Pr. 1982 pap. $4.95

Structural Anthropology. 1958. Trans. by Monique Layton, Basic Bks. 1963 vol. 1 $14.00; Univ. of Chicago Pr. 1976 vol. 2 pap. $10.95

The Savage Mind. 1962. *Nature of Human Society Ser.* Univ. of Chicago Pr. 1966 $10.00; Univ. of Chicago Pr. (Phoenix Bks.) 1968 pap. $8.95

Totemism. 1962. Beacon 1963 pap. $6.95

The Raw and the Cooked. 1964. *Science of Mythology Ser.* Octagon repr. of 1970 ed. 1979 lib. bdg. $29.00

From Honey to Ashes. Science of Mythology Ser. Octagon. repr. of 1973 ed. 1980 lib. bdg. $34.50

The View from Afar. Trans. by Joachim Neugroschel, Basic Bks. 1985 $24.95

BOOKS ABOUT LÉVI-STRAUSS

Gardner, Howard. *The Quest for Mind: Piaget, Lévi-Strauss, and the Structuralist Movement.* Knopf 1973 $8.95; Univ. of Chicago Pr. (Phoenix Bks.) 2d ed. 1981 pap. $9.00

Hayes, E. Nelson, and Tanya Hayes, eds. *Claude Lévi-Strauss: The Anthropologist as Hero.* MIT 1970 o.p.

Korn, Francis. *Elementary Structures Reconsidered: Lévi-Strauss on Kinship.* Univ. of California Pr. 1973 $28.50

Paz, Octavio. *Claude Lévi-Strauss: An Introduction.* 1970. Dell 1974 pap. o.p.

Rossi, Ino, ed. *The Unconscious in Culture: The Structuralism of Claude Lévi-Strauss in Perspective*. Dutton 1974 pap. $6.95

Steiner, George. *Claude Lévi-Strauss*. Canadian Broadcasting Corporation 1972 o.p.

LEWIS, OSCAR. 1914–1970

Oscar Lewis, an American anthropologist, was renowned for his studies of poverty in Mexico and Puerto Rico and for his controversial concept of "the culture of poverty." After graduating from Columbia, where he studied under Ruth Benedict, Franz Boas, and Margaret Mead, his first major book was a restudy of Robert Redfield's village of Tepoztlán, *Life in a Mexican Village*, which reached a number of conclusions the opposite of those reached by Redfield. Much of the controversy over the culture of poverty disappeared when Lewis labeled it a subculture; ironically, reactionaries have used the concept to blame the poor for their poverty, while Lewis believed the poor to be victims. Many of his books are based on tape recordings of family members, a technique in which Lewis was a pioneer.

BOOKS BY LEWIS

Life in a Mexican Village: Tepoztlán Restudied. 1951. Peter Smith $20.50; Univ. of Illinois Pr. 1963 pap. $9.95

Village Life in Northern India: Studies in a Delhi Village. 1958. Random (Vintage) 1965 o.p.

Five Families: Mexican Case Studies in the Culture of Poverty. Fwd. by O. Lafarge, Basic Bks. 1959 pap. $7.50

The Children of Sánchez. 1961. Random (Vintage) 1966 pap. $5.95

Pedro Martínez: A Mexican Peasant and His Family. Random (Vintage) 1964 pap. $3.45

La Vida: A Puerto Rican Family in the Culture of Poverty—San Juan and New York. Irvington repr. of 1966 ed. text ed. 1983 $39.50 pap. $16.95

A Death in the Sánchez Family. 1969. Random (Vintage) 1970 pap. $3.95

(and Ruth M. Lewis and Susan M. Ridgon). *Living the Revolution: An Oral History of Contemporary Cuba*. Univ. of Illinois Pr. 1978 $22.50

MAINE, HENRY SUMNER. 1822–1888

Henry Sumner Maine, a lecturer on jurisprudence at Oxford and Cambridge, was the founder of anthropological jurisprudence: the study of the legal system of ancient societies. In his classic work *Ancient Law*, he contrasted early societies in which social relations are dominated by status (familylike relations) with complex societies in which social relations are dominated by contract (obligations arising from the free agreement of individuals). He also distinguished between the law of tort and the law of crime; in the former, individuals are wronged; in the latter, it is the state. His enduring contribution to the social sciences is his formulation of the concept of ideal polar types and his use of them for the comparative analysis of social phenomena.

BOOKS BY MAINE

Ancient Law: Its Connection with the Early History of Society and Its Relation to Modern Ideas. 1861. Intro. by J. H. Morgan, Biblio Dist. (Everyman's) repr. of 1917 ed. 1972 $12.95; ed. by Bernard D. Reams, Jr., *Historical Repr. in Jurisprudence and Classical Legal Lit. Ser.* Hein repr. of 1920 ed. 1983 lib. bdg. $37.50; intro. by F. Pollock, Peter Smith $13.25

Village Communities in the East and West. 1871. *Perspectives in Social Inquiry Ser.* Ayer repr. of 1974 ed. $23.00; Darby repr. of 1890 ed. 1983 lib. bdg. $50.00

Lectures on the Early History of Institutions. 1875. Associated Faculty Pr. repr. of 1914 ed. $15.00

BOOKS ABOUT MAINE

Evans, Morgan O. *Theories and Criticisms of Sir Henry Maine.* Rothman repr. of 1896 ed. 1981 lib. bdg. $18.50

Stone, Julius. *The Province and Function of Law: Law as Logic, Justice, and Social Control: A Study in Jurisprudence.* Hein repr. of 1946 ed. 2d ed. 1973 lib. bdg. $37.50

MALINOWSKI, BRONISLAW. 1884–1942

Bronislaw Malinowski, a Polish-born British anthropologist, was a major contributor to the transformation of nineteenth-century speculative anthropology into an observation-based science of man. His major interest was in the study of culture as a universal phenomenon and in the development of fieldwork techniques that would both describe one culture adequately and at the same time make systematic cross-cultural comparisons possible. He is considered the founder of the functional approach in the social sciences, which involves studying not just what a cultural trait appears to be but what it actually does for the functioning of society. Although he carried out extensive fieldwork in a number of cultures, he is most famous for his research among the Trobrianders, who live on a small island off the coast of New Guinea.

BOOKS BY MALINOWSKI

Magic, Science and Religion and Other Essays. Doubleday (Anchor) 1954 pap. $2.95; Greenwood repr. of 1948 ed. 1984 lib. bdg. $35.00. Written between the years 1916 and 1941.

Argonauts of the Western Pacific: An Account of Native Enterprise and Adventure in the Archipelagoes of Melanesian New Guinea. 1922. Dutton 1961 pap. $5.95; pref. by James Frazer, Waveland Pr. repr. of 1961 ed. text ed. 1984 pap. $9.95

Crime and Custom in Savage Society. 1926. *International Lib. of Psychological Philosophy and Scientific Mathematics* Greenwood 1984 lib. bdg. $29.95; Humanities Pr. text ed. 1970 $16.50; Little, Brown repr. of 1969 ed. 1976 pap. $3.95

Sex and Repression in Savage Society. 1927. *International Lib. of Psychological Philosophy and Scientific Mathematics* Humanities Pr. text ed. 1953 $23.00; New Amer. Lib. 1955 pap. $3.95; Univ. of Chicago Pr. 1985 pap. $10.95

Sex, Culture, and Myth. 1929. Harcourt 1962 o.p.

The Sexual Life of Savages in Northwestern Melanesia: An Ethnographic Account of Courtship, Marriage, and Family Life among the Natives of the Triobriand Islands, British New Guinea. 1929. Harcourt 1962 o.p.

Coral Gardens and Their Magic: A Study of the Methods of Tilling the Soil and of Agricultural Rites in the Triobriand Islands. 1935. Dover 1978 pap. $12.95

A Scientific Theory of Culture and Other Essays. Univ. of North Carolina Pr. 1944 $12.50

The Dynamics of Culture Change. 1945. Ed. by Phyllis M. Kaberry, Greenwood repr. of 1961 ed. 1976 lib. bdg. $18.25

BOOKS ABOUT MALINOWSKI

Firth, Raymond, ed. *Man and Culture: An Evaluation of the Work of Bronislaw Malinowski.* Humanities Pr. 1980 $28.00; Routledge & Kegan 1957 $26.00

Spiro, Melford E. *Oedipus in the Trobriands.* Univ. of Chicago Pr. 1983 lib. bdg. $26.00 text ed. pap. $8.00

MEAD, MARGARET. 1901–1978

Margaret Mead, an American anthropologist, was for most of her life the most illustrious curator at the American Museum of Natural History in New York. She was famed not only as an anthropologist, but as a public figure, a popularizer of the social sciences, a statesman of American science, and an analyst of American society. While at Columbia University she had been a student of Franz Boas, whose teaching assistant, Ruth Benedict, became one of Mead's closest colleagues and friends; after Benedict's death, Mead became her first biographer and the custodian of her field notes and papers. Mead's early research in Samoa led to her bestselling *Coming of Age in Samoa;* it also led, after her death, to a well-publicized attack on her work by the Australian anthropologist Derek Freeman. Her importance was not damaged by his book; in fact, there is probably greater awareness today of the important role she played in twentieth-century intellectual history as an advocate of tolerance, education, civil liberties, world peace, and the worldwide ecumenical movement within Christianity: she was an active and devout Episcopalian throughout her life. On January 6, 1979, she was posthumously awarded the Presidential Medal of Freedom, the nation's highest civilian honor.

BOOKS BY MEAD

Coming of Age in Samoa. 1928. Morrow 1971 pap. $6.95; Peter Smith $18.00

Sex and Temperament in Three Primitive Societies. 1935. Morrow 1963 pap. $6.95; Peter Smith $15.75

Cooperation and Competition among Primitive Peoples. 1937. Peter Smith $13.25

And Keep Your Powder Dry: An Anthropologist Looks at America. Essay Index Repr. Ser. Ayer repr. of 1942 ed. $18.00; Morrow 1971 pap. $7.95

(and Gregory Bateson). *Balinese Character: A Photographic Analysis.* 1942. New York Academy of Sciences 1962 o.p.

Male and Female: A Study of the Sexes in a Changing World. Greenwood repr. of 1949 ed. 1977 lib. bdg. $30.75; Morrow 1984 pap. $6.45

New Lives for Old: Cultural Transformation—Manus, 1928–1953. 1956. Greenwood repr. of 1975 ed. 1980 lib. bdg. $42.50; Morrow 1976 pap. $9.95

An Anthropologist at Work. 1959. Avon 1973 pap. $4.45

Continuities in Cultural Evolution. Yale Univ. Pr. 1966 pap. o.p.

Blackberry Winter: My Earlier Years. Morrow 1972 $11.95; Washington Square Pr.
    repr. 1985 pap. $5.95
Ruth Benedict. Leaders in Modern Anthropology Ser. Columbia Univ. Pr. 1974 $24.00
    pap. $10.50
Letters from the Field, 1925–1975. Ed. by Ruth N. Anshen, *World Perspectives Ser.*
    Harper 1978 $14.37 1979 pap. $4.95

BOOKS ABOUT MEAD

Bateson, Mary C. *With a Daughter's Eye: A Memoir of Margaret Mead and Gregory
    Bateson.* Ed. by Pat Golbitz, Morrow 1984 $15.95; Washington Square Pr. repr.
    1985 pap. $4.95
Freeman, Derek. *Margaret Mead and Samoa: The Making and Unmaking of an Anthro-
    pological Myth.* Harvard Univ. Pr. 1983 $20.00
Howard, Jane. *Margaret Mead: A Life.* Fawcett 1985 pap. $4.95; Simon & Schuster
    1984 $19.95
Schwartz, Theodore, ed. *Socialization as Cultural Communication.* Univ. of California
    Pr. 1976 $22.00 pap. $8.50

MORGAN, LEWIS HENRY. 1818–1881

Lewis Henry Morgan, an American lawyer, studied, lived with, and was
eventually adopted by the Iroquois Indians in New York State; this experience made him a self-taught anthropologist who went on to make substantial contributions to the field. His evolutionary theory of the family has
been largely abandoned, but his *Ancient Society* became a classic in Marxist
literature. Its account of how culture had actually evolved was the best
available in the mid-nineteenth century. Although Marx died before he was
able to write a planned book about Morgan, Engels wrote *The Origin of the
Family: Private Property and the State* in 1884 largely on the basis of
Morgan's work.

BOOKS BY MORGAN

The League of the Ho-de-no-sau-nee, or Iroquois. 1851. Ed. by Henry M. Lloyd, Burt
    Franklin 2 vols. repr. of 1904 ed. 1966 $49.50
Ancient Society. 1877. New York Labor News 1978 pap. $14.00; ed. by E. G. Leacock,
    Peter Smith $14.50; *Classics of Anthropology Ser.* Univ. of Arizona Pr. repr. of
    1877 ed. 1985 pap. $14.95
The Indian Journals, 1859–1862. Ed. by Leslie A. White, Univ. of Michigan Pr. 1959
    o.p.

BOOKS ABOUT MORGAN

Resek, Carl. *Lewis Henry Morgan: American Scholar. Midway Repr. Ser.* Univ. of Chi-
    cago Pr. repr. of 1960 ed. 1974 pap. $8.00
Stern, Bernhard J. *Lewis Henry Morgan: Social Evolutionist.* Russell repr. of 1931 ed.
    1967 $7.50

MURDOCK, GEORGE P. 1897–1985

George P. Murdock, an American anthropologist, studied both sociology
and anthropology at Yale University under Albert G. Keller, who had been
William Graham Sumner's most important student. The card file that Sum-

ner had used in preparing his famous *Folkways*, published in 1906, became Keller's, and under Murdock's guidance it ultimately became the basis for the Human Relations Area Files, a major database in the field of anthropology. Murdock's interest in cross-cultural analysis led to a number of books and to the journal *Ethnology*, which he founded in 1962. He taught at Yale until 1960 when he went to the University of Pittsburgh, from which he retired in 1973.

BOOKS BY MURDOCK

Our Primitive Contemporaries. Macmillan 1934 o.p.
(and others). *Outline of Cultural Materials*. 1938. Human Relations Area Files 5th ed. rev. 1982 pap. $15.00
(and Timothy J. O'Leary). *Ethnographic Bibliography of North America*. 1941. *Bibliographies Ser*. Human Relations Area Files 4th ed. text ed. 1975 ea. $35.00
Social Structure. 1949. Macmillan (Free Pr.) text ed. 1965 pap. $12.95
Outline of World Cultures. 1954. Human Relations Area Files 4th ed. rev. 1983 pap. $15.00
Africa: Its People and Their Culture History. McGraw-Hill 1959 o.p.
Culture and Society: Twenty-Four Essays. Univ. of Pittsburgh Pr. 1965 pap. $9.95

BOOK ABOUT MURDOCK

Goodenough, Ward H., ed. *Explorations in Cultural Anthropology: Essays in Honor of George Peter Murdock*. McGraw-Hill 1964 o.p.

RADCLIFFE-BROWN, A. R. 1881–1955

A. R. Radcliffe-Brown, an English anthropologist, by his example and his teaching helped establish social anthropology as a generalizing, theoretical discipline—both in the United Kingdom and the United States. His application of the ideas of system theory to primitive societies led to a revolution in the analysis of interpretation of social relations. He was educated in Cambridge, but he spent most of his working life abroad: in Cape Town, Sydney, Chicago, Yenching, São Paulo, and Alexandria (Egypt). At all of these universities he held teaching positions, as well as at Cambridge, Oxford, London, Birmingham, and Manchester—certainly something of a record, and a tribute to his fame. His only extended fieldwork was in the Andaman Islands (*The Andaman Islanders*) and northwestern Australia (*The Social Organization of Australian Tribes*). His genius was in applying theoretical ideas about social structure to the interpretation of the social behavior of primitive tribes.

BOOKS BY RADCLIFFE-BROWN

Structure and Function in Primitive Society: Essays and Addresses. Macmillan (Free Pr.) 1952 $14.95 text ed. pap. $13.95
The Andaman Islanders. 1922. Macmillan (Free Pr.) text ed. 1964 pap. $5.95
The Social Organization of Australian Tribes. 1931. Macmillan (Free Pr.) 1948 o.p.
Method in Social Anthropology. *Midway Repr. Ser*. Univ. of Chicago Pr. 1959 pap. $10.00

BOOKS ABOUT RADCLIFFE-BROWN

Fortes, Meyer, ed. *Social Structure: Studies Presented to A. R. Radcliffe-Brown*. Oxford
    1949 o.p.
Kuper, Leo. *The Social Anthropology of Radcliffe-Brown*. Routledge & Kegan 1977
    $22.00 pap. $10.00

REDFIELD, ROBERT. 1897–1958

Robert Redfield, an American anthropologist, carried out early in his career a study of Tepoztlán, an Aztec community near Mexico City. This led
to his first position at the Carnegie Institution in Washington, D.C. During
the next 16 years he carried out research in Yucatan and Guatemala. Based
on Henry Sumner Maine's contrast between status and contract, and on Ferdinand Tönnies's contrast between gemeinschaft and gesellschaft, he developed a set of ideas about folk culture, little communities, and Little and
Great Traditions that have been enormously influential. In 1927 he joined
the faculty of the University of Chicago, where he was dean of the social science division from 1934 to 1946.

BOOKS BY REDFIELD

Tepoztlán, a Mexican Village: A Study of Folk Life. Midway Repr. Ser. Univ. of Chicago
    Pr. repr. of 1930 ed. 1973 o.p.
(and Alfonso Villa Rojas). *Chan Kom: A Maya Village*. 1934. Univ. of Chicago Pr. 1962
    o.p.
The Folk Culture of Yucatan. Gordon 1976 lib. bdg. $59.95; Univ. of Chicago Pr. 1941
    $25.00
A Village That Chose Progress: Chan Kom Revisited. 1950. Univ. of Chicago Pr. (Phoe-
    nix Bks.) 1962 pap. $1.95
The Primitive World and Its Transformations. 1953. Cornell Univ. Pr. 1957 pap. $4.95
The Little Community. 1955. Univ. of Chicago Pr. 1973 $10.00
Peasant Society and Culture (and *The Little Community*). 1956. Univ. of Chicago Pr.
    (Phoenix Bks.) 1960 pap. $5.00

BOOK ABOUT REDFIELD

Lewis, Oscar. *Life in a Mexican Village: Tepoztlán Restudied*. Peter Smith $20.50;
    Univ. of Illinois Pr. repr. of 1951 ed. 1963 pap. $9.95

SAPIR, EDWARD. 1884–1939

Edward Sapir, an American anthropologist, was one of the founders of
both modern linguistics and the field of personality and culture. He wrote
poetry, essays, and music, as well as scholarly works. Margaret Mead noted
that "it was in the vivid, voluminous correspondence with [Edward Sapir]
that [Ruth Benedict's] own poetic interest and capacity matured." In the
field of linguistics, Sapir developed phonemic theory—the analysis of the
sounds of a language according to the pattern of their distribution—and he
analyzed some ten American Indian languages. In cultural anthropology, he
contributed to personality-and-culture studies by insisting that the true lo-
cus of culture is in the interactions of specific individuals and in the meanings that the participants abstract from these interactions.

BOOKS BY SAPIR

Language. 1921. Beekman. 2d ed. 1979 $11.95
Selected Writings of Edward Sapir in Language, Culture, and Personality. Ed. by David
   G. Mandelbaum, Univ. of California Pr. 1949 $37.50

BOOK ABOUT SAPIR

Spier, Leslie, Irving Hallowell, and Stanley Southern Newman, eds. *Language, Culture and Personality: Essays in Memory of Edward Sapir.* Greenwood 1983 lib.
   bdg. $39.75

TYLOR, EDWARD BURNETT. 1832–1917

   Edward Burnett Tylor, an English anthropologist, was a self-taught Victorian liberal who in effect became the founder of British anthropology. He is
famous for the first scientific definition of culture—"that complex whole
which includes knowledge, belief, art, morals, law, custom and any other ca-
pabilities and habits acquired by man as a member of society." He developed both the concept of cultural survival and a theory of animism, which
he believed to be religion in its minimal, most primitive, and therefore
broadest form.

BOOKS BY TYLOR

Researches into the Early History of Mankind and the Development of Civilization. Ed.
   by Paul Bohannan, Univ. of Chicago Pr. abr. ed. 1964 $15.00 pap. $2.95
Primitive Culture. 1871. Gordon 2 vols. lib. bdg. $250.00; Peter Smith ea. $12.00
Anthropology: An Introduction to the Study of Man and Civilization. 1881. Appleton
   1907 o.p.

BOOK ABOUT TYLOR

Burrow, John W. *Evolution and Society: A Study in Victorian Social Theory.* Cambridge Univ. Pr. 1966 $37.50 pap. $11.95

WHORF, BENJAMIN L. 1897–1941

   Benjamin L. Whorf, an American linguist, was throughout his life an em-
ployee of the Hartford Fire Insurance Company; linguistics was his hobby.
Nevertheless, he received a Social Science Research Council Fellowship,
and he took courses with Edward Sapir and others at Yale. According to
George L. Trager, "Whorf's monument," the Sapir-Whorf hypothesis, can be
stated as follows: "Language *is* culture, culture is stated in language; language mediates action, action is described in language." His continuing influence derives from the basic truth and value of this "trivial" assertion.

BOOK BY WHORF

Language, Thought, and Reality: Selected Writings. MIT 1956 o.p. Writings first published between 1927 and 1941.

BOOK ABOUT WHORF

Hoijer, Harry, ed. *Language in Culture: Conference on the Interrelations of Language
   and Other Aspects of Culture.* Univ. of Chicago Pr. 1958 o.p.

ECONOMICS

Economics may be said to differ from the other social sciences in two ways. First, its subject matter is comparatively narrow, confined as it is to the choices people make concerning the allocation of scarce resources. But these choices lead to profit, to capital accumulation, to employment and unemployment, and to government policies concerning all of these and more. Second, much of its data comes to it secondhand, by examining the records people keep of prices paid, the accumulation of capital, interest earned, and profits made. Some economists seek an understanding of these processes by examining the records of financial institutions in which these decisions are made or (more rarely) of the people who actually make them.

The list that follows is divided into books that report on the history of the field, on broad surveys of the field, on methods of research, and on 13 topics that economists study.

History of the Field

Blaug, Mark. *Economic Theory in Retrospect*. Cambridge Univ. Pr. 3d ed. 1983 pap. $18.95

Breit, William, and Roger L. Ransom. *The Academic Scribblers: Economists in Collision*. Dryden 2d ed. text ed. 1982 pap. $12.95

Deane, Phyllis. *The Evolution of Economic Ideas. Modern Cambridge Economics Ser*. 1978 $37.50 pap. $14.95

Dobb, Maurice. *Theories of Value and Distribution since Adam Smith*. Cambridge Univ. Pr. 1973 $47.50 pap. $17.95

Dorfman, Joseph. *The Economic Mind in American Civilization, 1606–1933*. Kelley 5 vols. 1946–59 $150.00

McConnell, John W. *Ideas of the Great Economists*. Barnes & Noble rev. ed. 1980 pap. $4.95

Schumpeter, Joseph A. *History of Economic Analysis*. Oxford 1954 $29.95

Silk, Leonard. *The Economists*. Avon 1978 pap. $3.95

Stigler, George J. *Production and Distribution Theories*. Agathon 1941 $12.00

Surveys of the Field

Ammer, Christine, and Dean Ammer. *Dictionary of Business and Economics*. Macmillan (Free Pr.) rev. & enl. ed. 1984 $29.95

Arrow, Kenneth J. *Social Choice and Individual Values*. 1963. Yale Univ. Pr. 2d ed. 1970 pap. $5.95. (See Arrow's main listing in this section.)

Becker, Gary S. *The Economic Approach to Human Behavior*. Univ. of Chicago Pr. 1977 lib. bdg. $22.00; Univ. of Chicago Pr. (Phoenix Bks.) 1978 pap. $6.95

Brown, A. A., and E. Neuberger. *Perspectives in Economics*. McGraw-Hill text ed. 1971 $19.95

Hicks, John R. *Value and Capital: An Inquiry into Some Fundamental Principles of Economic Theory*. 1939. Oxford 2d ed. 1946 $13.50. (See Hicks's main listing in this section.)

Keynes, John M. *The General Theory of Employment, Interest and Money*. 1936. Harcourt 1965 $14.50 pap. $6.95. This is one of the major classics of economics, comparable in importance to Adam Smith's *The Wealth of Nations* and Karl Marx's *Capital.* (See Keynes's main listing in this section.)

Knight, Frank H. *Risk, Uncertainty and Profit.* Kelley repr. of 1921 ed. $27.50; Univ. of Chicago Pr. 1971 pap. $12.00. (See Knight's main listing in this section.)

Koopmans, Tjalling C. *Three Essays on the State of Economic Science.* McGraw-Hill 1968 o.p.

Marshall, Alfred. *Principles of Economics.* 1890. Porcupine Pr. 8th ed. repr. of 1920 ed. pap. $16.95. (See Marshall's main listing in this section.)

McClelland, Peter D., ed. *Introductory Macroeconomics, 1981–1982: Readings on Contemporary Issues.* Cornell Univ. Pr. 8th ed. text ed. 1984 pap. $9.95

Samuelson, Paul A., and W. Nordhaus. *Economics.* McGraw-Hill 12th ed. 1985 $32.95

Smith, Adam. *An Inquiry into the Nature and Causes of the Wealth of Nations.* Ed. by Arthur H. Jenkins, Associated Faculty Pr. repr. of 1948 ed. 1969 $17.50; Kelley 2 vols. repr. of 1776 ed. 1966 lib. bdg. $150.00; Liberty Foundation 2 vols. repr. of 1976 ed. 1982 pap. $11.00; ed. by R. H. Campbell, Oxford 2 vols. 1976 $105.00; ed. by Edwin Cannan, Univ. of Chicago Pr. (Phoenix Bks.) 2 vols. in 1 1977 pap. $14.95. (See Smith's main listing in this section.)

Thurow, Lester. *Dangerous Currents: The State of Economics.* Random 1983 $16.95; Random (Vintage) 1984 pap. $5.95

Walras, Leon. *Elements of Pure Economics: Or the Theory of Social Wealth.* Trans. by William Jaffe, Kelley repr. of 1954 ed. $27.50; Orion repr. of 1954 ed. 1984 pap. $16.95. Written between 1874 and 1877.

Methods of Research

Caldwell, Bruce J. *Beyond Positivism: Economic Methodology in the Twentieth Century.* Allen & Unwin text ed. 1982 $29.50 1984 pap. $10.95

Frisch, Ragnar. *Maxima and Minima: Theory and Economic Applications.* Kluwer Academic 1966 lib. bdg. $24.00

Johnston, John. *Econometric Methods.* McGraw-Hill 2d ed. 1971 text ed. $28.95

Keynes, John M. *Scope and Method of Political Economy.* Kelley repr. of 1917 ed. 4th ed. $25.00

Knight, Frank H. *The Economic Organization.* 1933. Kelley repr. of 1935 ed. $17.50

Lansing, John B., and James N. Morgan. *Economic Survey Methods.* Institute for Social Research 1971 pap. $14.00

Latsis, Spiro J., ed. *Method and Appraisal in Economics.* Cambridge Univ. Pr. 1976 $44.50 1981 pap. $16.95

Leontief, Wasily. *Input-Output Economics.* Oxford 1966 $27.50

Machlup, Fritz. *Methodology of Economics and Other Social Sciences. Economics Theory, Econometrics and Mathematical Economic Ser.* Academic Pr. 1978 $59.00

Robbins, Lionel. *An Essay on the Nature and Significance of Economic Science.* Darby repr. of 1932 ed. 1981 lib. bdg. $40.00; St. Martin's 2d ed. 1969 $17.95

Shubik, Martin, ed. *Game Theory and Related Approaches to Social Behavior.* Krieger repr. of 1964 ed. 1975 $24.00

Von Neumann, John, and Oskar Morgenstern. *The Theory of Games and Economic Behavior.* 1944. Princeton Univ. Pr. 1980 $59.00 pap. $17.50; Wiley 3d ed. 1953 pap. $12.95. (See von Neumann's main listing in this section.)

Agriculture

Mellor, John W. *The Economics of Agricultural Development.* Cornell Univ. Pr. 1966
$39.95 pap. $11.95

Nair, Kusum. *Blossoms in the Dust: The Human Element in Indian Development. Midway Repr. Ser.* Univ. of Chicago Pr. text ed. 1979 pap. $8.00

Schultz, Theodore W. *Transforming Traditional Agriculture. World Food Supply Ser.*
Ayer repr. of 1964 ed. 1976 $21.00; Univ. of Chicago Pr. 1964 pap. $7.95

Southworth, Herman M., ed. *Agricultural Development and Economic Growth.* Ed. by
Bruce F. Johnston, Cornell Univ. Pr. 1967 $32.50

Tax, Sol. *Penny Capitalism: A Guatemalan Indian Economy.* Octagon repr. of 1953 ed.
1971 lib. bdg. $21.50

Capital and Human Capital

Becker, Gary S. *Human Capital: A Theoretical and Empirical Analysis, with Special
Reference to Education.* Columbia Univ. Pr. 2d ed. 1975 $10.00

Bohm-Bawerk, Eugen von. *Capital and Interest.* Trans. by William Smart, Kelley
repr. of 1890 ed. lib. bdg. $35.00

Haavelmo, Trygve. *A Study in the Theory of Investment. Economic Research Ser.*
Univ. of Chicago Pr. text ed. 1960 pap. $15.00

Hawtrey, R. G. *Capital and Employment.* 1937. Longman 2d ed. 1952 o.p.

Hayek, Friedrich A. von. *The Pure Theory of Capital.* 1941. *Midway Repr. Ser.* Univ. of
Chicago Pr. repr. of 1951 ed. 1975 pap. $22.00. (See Hayek's main listing in this
section.)

Machlup, Fritz. *The Production and Distribution of Knowledge in the United States.*
Princeton Univ. Pr. 1962 pap. $8.95

Marx, Karl. *Capital.* 1867–79. Ed. by Friedrich Engels. International Pubns. 3 vols.
1967 $35.00; trans. by Ben Fowkes and David Fernbach, Random (Vintage) 3
vols. 1977–82 pap. ea. $7.95–$10.95. (See Marx's main listing in this section.)

Schultz, Theodore W. *The Economic Value of Education.* Columbia Univ. Pr. 1963
$15.00

Smith, Adam. *An Inquiry into the Nature and Causes of the Wealth of Nations.* Ed. by
Arthur H. Jenkins, Associated Faculty Pr. repr. of 1948 ed. 1969 $17.50; Kelley 2
vols. repr. of 1776 ed. 1966 lib. bdg. $150.00; Liberty Foundation 2 vols. repr. of
1976 ed. 1982 pap. $11.00; ed. by R. H. Campbell, Oxford 2 vols. 1976 $105.00;
ed. by Edwin Cannan, Univ. of Chicago Pr. (Phoenix Bks.) 2 vols. in 1 1977 pap.
$14.95

Stigler, George J. *Production and Distribution Theories.* Agathon 1941 $12.00

Tobin, James. *Asset Accumulation and Economic Activity: Reflections on Contemporary Macroeconomic Theory.* Univ. of Chicago Pr. 1980 lib. bdg. $13.00 1982 pap.
$5.50

Capitalism

Burawoy, Michael, and Theda Skocpol, eds. *Marxist Inquiries: Studies of Labor, Class
and States.* Univ. of Chicago Pr. 1983 lib. bdg. $25.00 pap. $12.50

Commons, John R. *Legal Foundations of Capitalism.* Kelley repr. of 1924 ed. lib. bdg.
$25.00. (See Commons's main listing in this section.)

Friedman, Milton. *Capitalism and Freedom: With a New Preface.* 1952. Univ. of Chicago Pr. 1981 pap. $6.95. A readable introduction to the economic liberalism

(i.e., nongovernmental interference) advocated by Friedman, for many years a leading economist at the University of Chicago. (See Friedman's main listing in this section.)

Galbraith, John K. *American Capitalism: The Concept of Countervailing Power.* 1952. Houghton Mifflin pap. $3.25; Sharpe 1980 $30.00. (See Galbraith's main listing in this section.)

Gilbert, Neil. *Capitalism and the Welfare State: Dilemmas of Social Benevolence.* Yale Univ. Pr. 1983 $18.00

Goldthorpe, John H., ed. *Order and Conflict in Contemporary Capitalism: Studies in the Political Economy of West European Nations.* Oxford 1985 $34.95 pap. $15.95

Hoover, C. B. *The Economy, Liberty, and the State.* Kraus repr. of 1959 ed. $6.00

Keynes, John M. *The General Theory of Employment, Interest and Money.* 1936. Harcourt 1965 $14.50 pap. $6.95

Novak, Michael. *The Spirit of Democratic Capitalism.* Simon & Schuster 1982 $19.95

Schumpeter, Joseph A. *Capitalism, Socialism and Democracy.* Harper pap. $6.95; Peter Smith 1983 $16.75. A scholarly, comprehensive, and readable introduction to modern capitalism.

Sennett, Richard. *The Fall of Public Man: The Social Psychology of Capitalism.* Random (Vintage) 1978 pap. $4.95

Wolfe, Alan. *The Limits of Legitimacy: Contradictions of Contemporary Capitalism.* Macmillan (Free Pr.) 1977 $17.00 1980 text ed. pap. $14.95

Competition, Monopoly, Antitrust Legislation

Bork, Robert H. *The Antitrust Paradox: A Policy at War with Itself.* Basic Bks. 1980 pap. $11.95

Goldschmid, Harvey J., and others, eds. *Industrial Concentration: The New Learning.* Little, Brown 1974 pap. $11.95

Katzmann, Robert A. *Regulatory Bureaucracy: The Federal Trade Commission and Antitrust Policy. Studies in Amer. Politics and Public Policy* MIT 1979 $30.00 pap. $8.95

Leftwich, Richard H., and Ross D. Eckert. *The Price System and Resource Allocation.* Dryden 8th ed. text ed. 1982 $28.95

Robinson, Joan. *The Economics of Imperfect Competition.* St. Martin's 1969 $17.95 text ed. pap. $14.95

Stelzer, Irwin M. *Selected Antitrust Cases: Landmark Decisions.* Irwin 6th ed. 1981 pap. $17.25

Weaver, Suzanne. *Decision to Prosecute: Organization and Public Policy in the Antitrust Division.* MIT 1977 $27.50 pap. $6.95

Wilcox, Clair, and William G. Shepherd. *Public Policies toward Business: Readings and Cases.* Irwin rev. ed. 1979 pap. $17.50

The Corporation

Barnard, Chester I. *The Functions of the Executive.* 1938. Intro. by K. R. Andrews, Harvard Univ. Pr. 1968 pap. $8.95. A brilliant analysis, based not on research but rather on personal observations by the author, who for many years was president of the New Jersey Bell Telephone Company.

Berle, Adolf A., Jr., and Gardiner C. Means. *The Modern Corporation and Private Property.* Harcourt rev. ed. 1969 pap. $5.25; *Business Enterprises Repr. Ser.* Hein repr. of 1933 ed. 1982 lib. bdg. $30.00

Davis, Joseph S. *Essays in the Earlier History of American Corporations.* Russell 2 vols repr. of 1917 ed. 1965 $25.00

Drucker, Peter F. *The Concept of the Corporation.* Crowell 1972 $13.41; New Amer. Lib. 1983 pap. $3.95

Ginzberg, Eli, and George Vojta. *Beyond Human Scale: Large Corporations at Risk.* Basic Bks. 1985 $16.95

Keating, Barry P., and Maryann O. Keating. *Not-for-Profit.* Horton 1980 $12.95 pap. $8.95

Mason, Edward S., ed. *The Corporation in Modern Society.* Fwd. by A. Berle, Jr., Atheneum text ed. 1966 pap. $4.95; Harvard Univ. Pr. 1959 $17.50

Veblen, Thorstein. *The Theory of Business Enterprise.* Intro. by Joseph Dorfman, Kelley repr. of 1904 ed. $25.00; intro. by Douglas Dowd, Transaction Bks. 1978 $29.95 pap. $4.95. (See Veblen's main listing in the Sociology section.)

——. *The Theory of the Leisure Class.* Kelley repr. of 1899 ed. $35.00; intro. by Robert Lekachman, New Amer. Lib. 1954 pap. $3.95; Penguin 1979 pap. $4.95

Warner, W. Lloyd. *The Corporation in the Emergent American Society.* Harper 1962 o.p.

Wolfson, Nicholas. *The Modern Corporation: Free Markets versus Regulation.* Macmillan (Free Pr.) 1984 $25.00

Economic Behavior

Caplovitz, David. *The Poor Pay More: Consumer Practices of Low Income Families.* Intro. by E. Peterson, Macmillan (Free Pr.) repr. text ed. 1967 pap. $13.95. Based on research conducted in New York City under the auspices of the Columbia University Bureau of Applied Social Research.

Clark, Lincoln H., ed. *Consumer Behavior.* New York Univ. Pr. 2 vols. 1966 ea. $10.00

Duesenberry, James S. *Income, Saving and the Theory of Consumer Behavior.* Harvard Univ. Pr. 1949 $7.95

Henderson, Hubert. *Supply and Demand. Cambridge Economic Handbook Ser.* 1958 pap. $9.95

Hill, Martha, and others, eds. *Five Thousand Americans.* Institute for Social Research 10 vols. 1974–83 ea. $15.00–$25.00

Katona, George. *Essays on Behavioral Economics.* Institute for Social Research 1980 $10.50

——. *The Powerful Consumer: Psychological Studies of the American Economy.* Greenwood repr. of 1960 ed. 1977 lib. bdg. $24.00

——. *Psychological Analysis of Economic Behavior.* Greenwood repr. of 1951 ed. 1977 lib. bdg. $26.75

Veblen, Thorstein. *The Theory of the Leisure Class.* Kelley repr. of 1899 ed. $35.00; intro. by Robert Lekachman, New Amer. Lib. 1954 pap. $3.95; Penguin 1979 pap. $4.95

Economic Growth

Adams, Gerard F., ed. *Industrial Policies for Growth and Competitiveness: Empirical Studies. Wharton Econometric Studies* Lexington Bks. 1985 $34.00

Arndt, H. W. *The Rise and Fall of Economic Growth: A Study in Contemporary Thought.* Univ. of Chicago Pr. 1984 pap. $6.95

Daly, Herman E., ed. *Toward a Steady-State Economy.* Freeman text ed. 1973 pap. $11.95

Hicks, John R. *Capital and Growth.* Oxford 1965 $32.50 1972 pap. $9.95

Hirschman, Albert O. *The Strategy of Economic Development. Norton Lib.* repr. 1978 pap. $3.95

Kuznets, Simon. *Economic Growth of Nations: Total Output and Production Structure.* Harvard Univ. Pr. (Belknap Pr.) 1971 $22.50

———. *Six Lectures on Economic Growth.* Macmillan (Free Pr.) 1959 $22.50

Marx, Karl. *Capital.* 1867–79. Ed. by Friedrich Engels. International Pubns. 3 vols. 1967 $35.00; trans. by Ben Fowkes and David Fernbach, Random (Vintage) 3 vols. 1977–82 pap. ea. $7.95–10.95

Mellor, John W. *The New Economics of Growth: A Strategy for India and the Developing World.* Cornell Univ. Pr. 1980 pap. $9.95

Morishima, Michio. *Equilibrium, Stability, and Growth: A Multi-Sectoral Analysis.* Oxford 1964 $27.95

Olson, Mancur. *The Rise and Decline of Nations: Economic Growth, Stagflation, and Social Rigidities.* Yale Univ. Pr. 1982 $22.50 1984 pap. $8.95

Reynolds, Lloyd G. *Economic Growth in the Third World, 1850–1980.* Yale Univ. Pr. text ed. 1985 $35.00

Schmookler, Jacob. *Patents, Invention, and Economic Change: Data and Selected Essays.* Ed. by Zvi Griliches and Leonid Hurwicz, Harvard Univ. Pr. 1972 $17.50

Schumpeter, Joseph A. *The Theory of Economic Development: An Inquiry into Profits, Capital, Credit, Interest and the Business Cycle.* Trans. by Opie Redvers, intro. by John E. Elliott, *Social Science Class. Ser.* Oxford 1961 pap. $8.95; Transaction Bks. 1983 pap. $19.95

Smith, Kerry V., ed. *Scarcity and Growth Reconsidered.* Johns Hopkins Univ. Pr. text ed. 1979 $20.00 pap. $9.00

Wallerstein, Immanuel. *The Modern-World System: Capitalist Agriculture and the Origins of the European World Economy in the 16th Century.* Academic Pr. 1974 $35.00

Government Regulation

Baram, Michael S. *Alternatives to Regulation: Managing Risks to Health, Safety, and the Environment.* Lexington Bks. 1981 $27.50

Blair, Roger D., and Stephen Rubin. *Regulating the Professions: A Public Policy Symposium.* Lexington Bks. 1980 $31.00

Irland, Lloyd C. *Wilderness Economics and Policy.* Lexington Bks. 1979 $23.50

Kahn, Alfred E. *The Economics of Regulation.* Wiley 2 vols. text ed. 1970–71 ea. $35.95–$38.50

McCraw, Thomas K. *Prophets of Regulation.* Harvard Univ. Pr. 1984 $20.00

Mendeloff, John. *Regulating Safety: An Economic and Political Analysis of Occupational Safety and Health Policy.* MIT text ed. 1979 $32.50

Miller, James C., III, and Bruce Yandle, eds. *Benefit-Cost Analysis of Social Regulation: Case Studies from the Council on Wage and Price Stability.* Amer. Enterprise Institute 1979 pap. $6.25

Nyhart, J. D., and Milton M. Carrow, eds. *Law and Science in Collaboration: Resolving Regulatory Issues of Science and Technology.* Lexington Bks. 1983 $30.00

Income, Inflation, Poverty

Anderson, Martin. *Welfare: The Political Economy of Welfare Reform in the United States.* Hoover Institution 1978 $16.95

Bergson, Abram. *Welfare, Planning, and Employment: Selected Essays in Economic Theory.* MIT 1982 $32.50

Campbell, Carl. *Economic Growth, Capital Gains and Income Distribution: 1897–1956 (Doctoral Dissertation, University of California, Berkeley, 1964).* Ayer repr. of 1977 lib. bdg. $49.50

Duncan, Greg J. *Years of Poverty, Years of Plenty: The Changing Economic Fortunes of American Workers and Families.* Fwd. by Lee Rainwater, Institute for Social Research 1984 $24.00 pap. $14.00

Hall, Robert E., ed. *Inflation: Causes and Effects. National Bureau of Economic Research Project Report* Univ. of Chicago Pr. 1983 lib. bdg. $33.00 1984 pap. $10.95

Keynes, John M. *The General Theory of Employment, Interest and Money.* 1936. Harcourt 1965 $14.50 pap. $6.95

Levitan, Sar A. *Programs in Aid of the Poor.* Johns Hopkins Univ. Pr. 5th ed. text ed. 1985 $17.50 pap. $5.95

International Economics

Adams, John, ed. *The Contemporary International Economy: A Reader.* St. Martin's text ed. 1979 pap. $16.95

Bhagwati, Jagdish. *Essays in International Economic Theory.* Ed. by Robert Feenstra, MIT 2 vols. text ed. 1983 ea. $45.00

————, ed. *International Trade: Selected Readings.* MIT repr. of 1969 ed. text ed. 1981 $35.00 pap. $12.50

Corden, W. M. *Inflation, Exchange Rates, and the World Economy: Lectures on International Monetary Economics. Studies in Business and Society Ser.* Univ. of Chicago Pr. rev. ed. 1981 $15.00

Frenkel, Jacob A., ed. *Exchange Rates and International Macroeconomics. National Bureau of Economic Research Conference Ser.* Univ. of Chicago Pr. 1984 lib. bdg. $43.00

Heilbroner, Robert L. *Beyond Boom and Crash.* Norton 1979 $11.95 pap. $2.95

Kenen, Peter B. *Essays in International Economics. Princeton Ser. of Collected Essays* 1980 $33.00 pap. $11.50

————. *The International Economy.* Prentice-Hall text ed. 1985 $29.95

Lewis, W. Arthur. *Developmental Planning.* Allen & Unwin text ed. 1966 pap. $11.50

————. *The Principles of Economic Planning: A Study Prepared for the Fabian Society.* Allen & Unwin text ed. 1955 pap. $7.95

Lindblom, Charles E. *Politics and Markets: The World's Political Economic Systems.* Basic Bks. 1977 $17.50 1980 pap. $8.50

Mahler, Vincent A. *Dependency Approaches to International Political Economy: A Cross-National Study.* Columbia Univ. Pr. 1980 $25.00

Tinbergen, Jan. *Reshaping the International Order.* Dutton 1976 o.p.

Labor, Work, Unemployment

Friedman, Milton. *Unemployment versus Inflation.* Ed. by David Laidler, Transatlantic 1975 pap. $4.25

Lazarsfeld, Paul F., and others. *Marienthal: The Sociography of an Unemployed Community.* 1933. Aldine 1971 o.p. This is one of the earliest sociological studies of the meaning of unemployment to individuals and communities. (See Lazarfeld's main listing in the Sociology section.)

Martin, Donald L. *An Ownership Theory of the Trade Union: A New Approach.* Univ. of California Pr. 1981 $22.00

McNulty, Paul J. *The Origins and Development of Labor Economics.* MIT text ed. 1980 $30.00 1984 pap. $7.95

Parnes, Herbert S. *Work and Retirement: A Longitudinal Study of Men.* MIT text ed. 1981 $40.00

Phelps, Edmund S., ed. *The Microeconomic Foundations of Employment and Inflation Theory.* Norton 1973 $17.95

Reynolds, Lloyd G. *Labor Economics and Labor Relations.* Prentice-Hall 8th ed. $29.95

Rowan, Richard L. *Readings in Labor Economics and Labor Relations.* Irwin 4th ed. 1980 $17.50

Money and Monetary Institutions

Agmon, Tamir, and Richard Levich, eds. *The Future of the International Monetary System.* Lexington Bks. 1984 $30.00 pap. $15.00

Campbell, Colin, and Rosemary Campbell. *Introduction to Money and Banking.* Dryden 5th ed. text ed. 1984 $32.95

Fisher, Irving. *The Theory of Interest: As Determined by Impatience to Spend Income and Opportunity to Invest It.* Kelley repr. of 1930 ed. $27.50; Porcupine Pr. repr. of 1930 ed. $12.95. (See Fisher's main listing in this section.)

Friedman, Milton, ed. *Studies in the Quantity Theory of Money.* Univ. of Chicago Pr. 1973 pap. $4.75

Friedman, Milton, and Walter H. Heller. *Monetary versus Fiscal Policy.* Norton 1969 pap. $2.95

Friedman, Milton, and Anna J. Schwartz. *Monetary Trends in the United States and the United Kingdom: Their Relation to Income, Prices, and Interest Rates, 1867–1975.* Univ. of Chicago Pr. 1982 $55.00 pap. $22.50

George, Henry. *Progress and Poverty.* 1879. Biblio Dist. (Everyman's) 1978 $9.95; Phoenix 1979 $10.00

Hall, Robert E., ed. *Inflation: Causes and Effects.* Univ. of Chicago Pr. 1983 lib. bdg. $33.00 1984 pap. $10.95

Hickman, Bert, ed. *Econometric Models of Cyclical Behavior.* National Bureau of Economic Research 2 vols. 1972 ea. $30.00

Kidwell, David S., and Richard L. Peterson. *Financial Institutions, Markets, and Money.* Dryden 2d ed. text ed. 1984 $32.95

Malkiel, Burton G. *A Random Walk down Wall Street.* Norton rev. ed. 1973 $13.95 pap. $5.95

Moore, Henry L. *Economic Cycles: Their Law and Cause.* Kelley repr. of 1914 ed. $15.00

Pechman, Joseph A. *Who Paid the Taxes, 1966–85?* Brookings 1985 $22.95 pap. $8.95

——, ed. *Options for Tax Reform. Dialogue on Public Policy Ser.* Brookings 1984 pap. $8.00

Schumpeter, Joseph A. *Business Cycles: A Theoretical, Historical, and Statistical Analysis of the Capitalist Process.* Porcupine Pr. 2 vols. repr. of 1939 ed. 1982 lib. bdg. $67.50

Simpson, Thomas D. *Money, Banking and Economic Analysis.* Prentice-Hall 2d ed. 1981 $29.95

Weitzman, Martin L. *The Share Economy: Conquering Stagflation.* Harvard Univ. Pr. 1984 $15.00

Public Finance, Public Goods, Public Choice

Arrow, Kenneth J. *Social Choice and Individual Values.* 1963. Yale Univ. Pr. 2d ed. 1970 pap. $5.95

Buchanan, James M., and Gordon Tullock. *Calculus of Consent: Logical Foundations of Constitutional Democracy.* Univ. of Michigan Pr. 1962 pap. $9.95

Goodman, John C., and Edwin G. Dolan. *Economics of Public Policy: The Micro View.* West 3d ed. text ed. 1985 pap. $10.95

Musgrave, Richard, and Peggy Musgrave. *Public Finance in Theory and Practice.* McGraw-Hill 3d ed. text ed. 1980 $31.50

Phelps, Edmund S., ed. *Private Wants and Public Needs. Problems of Modern Economy Ser.* Norton rev. ed. 1965 pap. $4.95

Quigley, John M., and Daniel L. Rubinfeld, eds. *American Domestic Priorities.* Univ. of California Pr. 1985

Smithies, Arthur. *The Budgetary Process in the United States.* McGraw-Hill 1955 o.p.

Zysman, John. *Governments, Markets, and Growth: Financial Systems and the Politics of Industrial Change.* Cornell Univ. Pr. 1983 $29.95 1984 pap. $14.95

ARROW, KENNETH J. 1921–   (NOBEL PRIZE 1972)

Kenneth J. Arrow, an American economist, is known for his contributions to mathematical economics, for his studies of risk taking, and for his analysis of the economics of organizations. His career has been largely divided between Harvard and Stanford universities; at present, he is the Joan Kenney professor of economics and operations research at Stanford. In 1972, he was awarded the Alfred Nobel Memorial Prize in economic science.

BOOKS BY ARROW

Social Choice and Individual Values. 1963. Yale Univ. Pr. 2d ed. 1970 pap. $5.95

(and Mordecai Kurz). *Public Investment, the Rate of Return, and Optimum Fiscal Policy.* Johns Hopkins Univ. Pr. 1970 $20.00

The Limits of Organization. Norton 1974 pap. $3.95

Collected Papers of Kenneth J. Arrow. Harvard Univ. Pr. (Belknap Pr.) 2 vols. text ed. 1983 ea. $20.00–$25.00

CLARK, JOHN BATES. 1847–1938

John Bates Clark, an American economist, was one of the founders of the American Economic Association and a professor at Columbia University during the last half of his career. He is best known as the developer of the marginal productivity theory, which is based on the application of the law of diminishing returns to all factors of production—land, labor, and capital.

BOOKS BY CLARK

The Philosophy of Wealth. Kelley repr. of 1886 ed. $19.50

The Distribution of Wealth. Kelley repr. of 1899 ed. $27.50

The Control of Trusts. 1901. Kelley repr. of 1914 ed. lib. bdg. $17.50

The Problem of Monopoly: A Study of a Grave Danger and of a Natural Mode of Averting It. Macmillan 1904 o.p.

Essentials of Economic Theory as Applied to Modern Problems of Industry and Public Policy. Macmillan 1907 o.p.

BOOK ABOUT CLARK

Clark, A. H., and John M. Clark. *John Bates Clark: A Memorial.* Columbia Univ. Pr. 1938 o.p.

COMMONS, JOHN R. 1862–1945

John R. Commons, American economist, taught for most of his career at the University of Wisconsin. He became the leading scholar of American labor problems and a key figure in the institutional school of economics, which stresses the impact on human behavior of such institutions as firms and trade unions, or even such intangible institutions as slavery or a policy of laissez-faire. His two multivolume histories of labor in the United States are widely consulted today.

BOOKS BY COMMONS

The Distribution of Wealth. Intro. by Joseph Dorfman, Kelley repr. of 1893 ed. $27.50
(and others, eds.). *A Documentary History of American Industrial Society.* Intro. by John Bates Clark, Russell 10 vols. repr. of 1910–11 ed. 2d ed. 1958 $250.00
History of Labour in the United States. Kelley 4 vols. repr. of 1918–35 ed. $175.00
Institutional Economics: Its Place in Political Economy. Porcupine Pr. repr. of 1934 ed. lib. bdg. $37.50
The Economics of Collective Action. 1950. Ed. by K. H. Parsons, Macmillan 1956 o.p. Contains a bibliography of Commons's writing.

BOOKS ABOUT COMMONS

Dorfman, Joseph, and others. *Institutional Economics.* Univ. of California Pr. 1963 o.p.
Harter, Lafayette G., Jr. *John R. Commons: His Assault on Laissez-faire.* Oregon State Univ. Pr. 1962 o.p.
Somers, Gerald G., ed. *Labor, Management, and Social Policy: Essays in the John R. Commons Tradition.* Univ. of Wisconsin Pr. 1963 $27.50

ENGELS, FRIEDRICH. 1820–1895

Friedrich Engels was a German businessman and sociologist who collaborated extensively with Karl Marx and at times provided him with funds derived from his family's textile business in Manchester, England. Engels first met Marx in Paris in 1844, just before the publication of Marx's book on the English working class, and he became the coauthor with Marx of a number of important books, including *The Communist Manifesto.* After Marx's death, Engels completed the second and third volumes of Marx's *Capital.* He developed the theory of dialectical materialism; he was the cofounder of communism; but he wrote in 1886 that "Marx was a genius; we others were at best talented."

BOOKS BY ENGELS

The Condition of the Working Class in England. 1845. Intro. by Eric J. Hobsbawin, Academy Chicago repr. of 1892 ed. 1979 pap. $4.95; Beekman 1973 $14.95; Imported Pubns. 1973 $3.45; trans. by W. O. Henderson and W. H. Chaloner, Stanford Univ. Pr. 1958 $27.50 pap. $8.95

(and Karl Marx). *The German Ideology*. 1845–46. Ed. by C. J. Arthur, International
    Pubns. 1970 $6.95 pap. $2.50
(and Karl Marx). *The Communist Manifesto*. 1848. International Pubns. 1983 $3.25;
    Crofts Class. Ser. Harlan Davidson text ed. 1955 pap. $3.25; New York Labor
    News 7th ed. 1968 $1.25; pref. by Leon Trotsky, Path Pr. 1968 pap. $.95; intro.
    by A. J. P. Taylor, Penguin (Pelican) 1968 $2.25; Regnery-Gateway 1982 pap.
    $3.95; ed. by D. Ryazanoff, Russell repr. of 1930 ed. 1963 $18.00; ed. by Joseph
    Katz, trans. by Samuel Moore, intro. by F. B. Randall, Washington Square Pr.
    pap. $2.95
Socialism: Utopian and Scientific. 1880. China Bks. 1975 pap. $1.95; trans. by Ed-
    ward Aveling, Greenwood repr. of 1935 ed. 1977 lib. bdg. $15.00; intro. by
    George Novack, Path Pr. 1972 pap. $1.25
The Origin of the Family: Private Property and the State. 1884. Path Pr. 1972 pap.
    $3.45

Books about Engels

Carver, Terrell. *Marx and Engels: The Intellectual Relationship*. Indiana Univ. Pr.
    1984 $22.50
Henderson, W. O. *Life of Friedrich Engels*. Biblio Dist. 2 vols. 1974 $65.00
Ilyichov, L. F., and others. *Friedrich Engels: A Biography*. Beekman 1975 $17.95
McLellan, David. *Friedrich Engels*. Penguin 1978 pap. $3.95; ed. by Frank Kermode,
    Modern Masters Ser. Viking 1978 $9.95

FISHER, IRVING. 1867–1947

Irving Fisher was an American mathematician and economist who spent
almost his entire professional life at Yale University. He made a fortune
from a card index file system he invented; it was ultimately manufactured
by Remington Rand, of which Fisher was a director until his death. In economics, he laid the foundations for econometrics, and his book *The Nature
of Capital and Income* contains the theoretical foundations of the science of
accounting. He is said to have been the first economist to have combined
profound theory with authoritative observation.

Books by Fisher

The Nature of Capital and Income. Kelley repr. of 1906 ed. $25.00
The Purchasing Power of Money. 1911. Kelley repr. of 1922 ed. 2d ed. $27.50
*The Theory of Interest: As Determined by Impatience to Spend Income and Opportunity
    to Invest It*. Kelley repr. of 1930 ed. $27.50; Porcupine Pr. repr. of 1930 ed.
    $12.95
Booms and Depressions: Some First Principles. Adelphi 1932 o.p.

Books about Fisher

Fisher, Irving Norton. *A Bibliography of the Writings of Irving Fisher*. Yale Univ. Pr.
    1961 o.p.
———. *My Father, Irving Fisher*. Comet 1956 o.p.
Gayer, A. D., ed. *Lessons of Monetary Experience: Essays in Honor of Irving Fisher*.
    Kelley repr. of 1937 ed. $37.50
Schumpeter, Joseph A. *History of Economic Analysis*. Oxford 1954 $29.95

FRIEDMAN, MILTON. 1912–

Milton Friedman is an influential, conservative American economist. A staff member of the National Bureau of Economic Research (1937–46 and 1948–   ), he has taught at the University of Chicago since 1946. His theories, which are sometimes called monetarist or Chicago School, are at variance with the Keynesian School of economics. Unlike Keynes, Friedman believes that changes in the money supply precede changes in general economic activity. Friedman's primary belief is that the quantity of money in circulation is of prime importance. A believer in laissez-faire capitalism, he favors the abolition of such programs as welfare and social security. He is a prolific writer and has been a contributing editor to *Newsweek* magazine since 1971.

BOOKS BY FRIEDMAN

Capitalism and Freedom: With a New Preface. 1952. Univ. of Chicago Pr. 1981 pap. $6.95
Essays in Positive Economics. Univ. of Chicago Pr. 1953 $20.00 1966 pap. $8.00
Theory of the Consumption Function. National Bureau of Economic Research 1957 $18.00
(and Anna J. Schwartz). *Monetary History of the United States, 1867–1960. Business Cycles Ser.* National Bureau of Economic Research 1963 $40.00 pap. $11.95
Optimum Quantity of Money and Other Essays. Aldine 1969 $29.95
(and Wilbur J. Cohen). *Social Security: Universal or Selective.* Amer. Enterprise Institute 1972 $12.25
Studies in the Quantity Theory of Money. Univ. of Chicago Pr. 1973 pap. $4.75
Unemployment versus Inflation. Ed. by David Laidlaw, Transatlantic 1975 pap. $4.25
Price Theory. Aldine 1976 $29.95
(and Rose Friedman). *Free to Choose: A Personal Statement.* Avon 1980 $9.95 1981 pap. $3.95

GALBRAITH, JOHN KENNETH. 1908–

John Kenneth Galbraith is a Canadian-born American economist who is perhaps the most widely read economist in the world. Harshly critical of the neoclassical economics of Alfred Marshall and others, he is also critical of Keynesian economics, believing that it is not sufficient for government to manage the level of effective demand: government must manage the market itself. Galbraith stated in *American Capitalism* that the market is far from competitive, and governments and labor unions must serve as a "countervailing power." His style and wit have contributed greatly to his fame as an economist and as a television personality.

BOOKS BY GALBRAITH

American Capitalism: The Concept of Countervailing Power. 1952. Houghton Mifflin pap. $3.25; Sharpe 1980 $30.00
The Affluent Society. Houghton Mifflin 4th ed. 1984 $18.95; New Amer. Lib. rev. ed. 1985 pap. $4.95
The New Industrial State. 1967. Houghton Mifflin 3d ed. rev. 1978 $15.00 1979 pap. $6.95; New Amer. Lib. 3d ed. rev. 1979 pap. $3.95

Ambassador's Journal: A Personal Account of the Kennedy Years. Houghton Mifflin
    1969 $10.00
The Galbraith Reader. Harvard Common Pr. 1977 $12.95

BOOKS ABOUT GALBRAITH

Gambs, John S. *John Kenneth Galbraith. Twayne's World Leaders Ser.* G. K. Hall 1975
    lib. bdg. $13.50; St. Martin's 1975 pap. $4.95
Hession, Charles H. *John Kenneth Galbraith and His Critics.* New Amer. Lib. 1972
    o.p.
Sharpe, Myron E. *John Kenneth Galbraith and the Lower Economics.* Sharpe 2d ed.
    1974 $17.50

HANSEN, ALVIN. 1887–1975

Alvin Hansen was an American economist who did more to carry out the
Keynesian revolution in economics than any other, and his *A Guide to
Keynes* has been translated into at least six languages. For almost 20 years,
a Harvard seminar in fiscal policy that he chaired with John H. Williams attracted outstanding scholars and civil servants from around the country. In
addition to making many substantive contributions to economic theory, he
trained a large number of outstanding students and through his many public service activities he had an enormous influence on economists in government.

BOOKS BY HANSEN

Business-Cycle Theory: Its Development and Present Status. Hyperion Pr. repr. of 1927
    ed. 1980 $18.50
Economic Stabilization in an Unstable World. Kelley repr. of 1932 ed. $25.00
Fiscal Policy and Business Cycles. Greenwood repr. of 1941 ed. 1977 lib. bdg. $26.25
(and Harvey S. Perloff). *State and Local Finance in the National Economy.* Norton
    1944 o.p.
Monetary Theory and Fiscal Policy. Greenwood repr. of 1949 ed. 1983 lib. bdg. $29.75
Business Cycles and National Income. 1951. Norton 1964 $14.95
A Guide to Keynes. McGraw-Hill 1953 pap. $4.95
The Dollar and the International Monetary System. McGraw-Hill 1965 o.p.

HAYEK, FRIEDRICH A. VON. 1899–   (NOBEL PRIZE 1974)

Friedrich A. von Hayek, a Viennese-born economist who taught at the University of Chicago from 1950 to 1962, is a member of the so-called Chicago
School of anti-Keynesian economics. He believes that government interference in the economy leads to socialism, and his major exposition of this
theme, *The Road to Serfdom,* has been both lavishly praised and harshly
criticized. A scholar of enormous energy and with a wide range of interests,
he shared the Nobel Memorial Prize in economic science with Gunnar Myrdal in 1974.

BOOKS BY HAYEK

Monetary Theory and the Trade Cycle. 1929. Kelley repr. of 1933 ed. $17.50
Prices and Production. 1931. Kelley repr. of 1935 ed. 2d ed. enl. $17.50
(ed.). *Collectivist Economic Planning.* 1935. Kelley repr. of 1938 ed. $25.00

The Pure Theory of Capital. 1941. *Midway Repr. Ser.* Univ. of Chicago Pr. repr. of 1951 ed. 1975 pap. $22.00

The Road to Serfdom. Fwd. by J. Chamberlain, Univ. of Chicago Pr. 1944 $12.50; Univ. of Chicago Pr. (Phoenix Bks.) 1956 pap. $6.95. A classic and controversial attack on socialism generally and government interference in the economy more specifically.

The Counter-Revolution of Science. 1952. Liberty Fund 1980 $9.00 pap. $4.00

(ed.). *Capitalism and the Historians.* 1954. Univ. of Chicago Pr. (Phoenix Bks.) 1963 pap. $5.95

The Constitution of Liberty. Univ. of Chicago Pr. (Phoenix Bks.) 1960 $35.00 pap. $10.95

Law, Legislation and Liberty: Rules and Order. Univ. of Chicago Pr. 3 vols. 1973–79 ea. $16.00; Univ. of Chicago Pr. (Phoenix Bks.) pap. ea. $5.95–$7.50

BOOK ABOUT HAYEK

Machlup, Fritz, ed. *Essays on Hayek.* Intro. by Milton Friedman, New York Univ. Pr. 1976 $15.00

HICKS, JOHN R. 1904– (NOBEL PRIZE 1972)

John R. Hicks, a British economist, is one of the leading economic theorists of the twentieth century. He taught for most of his career at Oxford, where he published extensively on economic theory; the subtitle of his major book, *Value and Capital,* is *An Inquiry into Some Fundamental Principles of Economic Theory.* In 1972, he shared the Nobel Prize in economic science with Kenneth J. Arrow of Stanford University.

BOOKS BY HICKS

Value and Capital: An Inquiry into Some Fundamental Principles of Economic Theory. 1939. Oxford 2d ed. 1946 $13.50

Contribution to the Theory of the Trade Cycle. Oxford 1950 $12.95

A Revision of Demand Theory. 1956. Oxford 1959 o.p.

Capital and Growth. Oxford 1965 $32.50 1972 pap. $9.95

A Theory of Economic History. Oxford 1969 pap. $6.95

The Crisis in Keynesian Economics. Basic Bks. text ed. 1974 $12.95

BOOK ABOUT HICKS

Wolfe, J. N., ed. *Value, Capital, and Growth: Papers in Honour of Sir John Hicks.* Edinburgh Univ. Pr. 1968 o.p.

JEVONS, WILLIAM STANLEY. 1835–1882

William Stanley Jevons, one of the greatest and most original of English economists, was the founder of the so-called marginalist school, which held that "value depends upon utility." His criticism of the labor theory of value led him to make this summary:

"Cost of production determines supply;
Supply determines final degree of utility;
Final degree of utility determines value."

(Keynes commented on this with the remark "Jevons chiseled in stone while Marshall knitted in wool.") Jevons drowned in a swimming accident, leaving much of his work unfinished.

BOOKS BY JEVONS

The Coal Question. 1865. Kelley repr. of 1906 ed. 3d ed. $27.50
The Theory of Political Economy. 1871. Pref. by H. S. Jevons, Kelley repr. of 1911 ed. 4th ed. $25.00
The Principles of Science: A Treatise on Logic and Scientific Method. 1874. Intro. by Ernest Nagel, Dover 1958 o.p.

BOOK ABOUT JEVONS

Keynes, John M. *Essays in Biography.* 1933. *Norton Lib.* 1963 pap. $3.25

KEYNES, JOHN MAYNARD. 1883–1946

John Maynard Keynes, English economist, whose *The General Theory of Employment, Interest and Money* was published in 1936, is generally regarded as the most brilliant and influential economist thus far in the twentieth century. His stress on the importance to the economy of consumption (demand) greatly influenced the policies of the New Deal during the 1930s depression and stands in strong contrast to the supply-side economic policies of the Reagan administration. His *The General Theory* was the major text of the Keynesian revolution, which transformed all subsequent economic theory—whether or not an economist is a Keynesian. In it he wrote that "practical men . . . are usually the slaves of some defunct economist."

BOOKS BY KEYNES

The Economic Consequences of the Peace. 1919. Harcourt 1920 o.p.
A Treatise on Money. AMS Pr. 2 vols. repr. of 1930 ed. $75.00
The General Theory of Employment, Interest and Money. 1936. Harcourt 1965 $14.50 pap. $6.95

BOOKS ABOUT KEYNES

Bleaney, Michael. *The Rise and Fall of Keynesian Economics: An Investigation of Its Contribution to Capitalist Development.* St. Martin's 1984 $29.95
Buchanan, J. M., and others. *The Consequences of Mr. Keynes: An Analysis of the Misuse of Economic Theory for Political Profiteering, with Proposals for Constitutional Disciplines.* Transatlantic 1978 pap. $5.95
Hansen, Alvin H. *A Guide to Keynes.* McGraw-Hill 1953 pap. $4.95
Harris, Seymour E., ed. *John Maynard Keynes: Economist and Policy Maker.* Kelley repr. of 1947 ed. 1965 o.p.
Harrod, Roy F. *The Life of John Maynard Keynes.* Kelley repr. of 1952 ed. $35.00; Norton repr. of 1951 ed. 1983 pap. $10.95
Johnson, Elizabeth S., and Harry G. Johnson. *The Shadow of Keynes: Understanding Keynes, Cambridge, and Keynesian Economics.* Univ. of Chicago Pr. (Phoenix Bks.) 1979 pap. $8.95
Keynes, Milo, ed. *Essays on John Maynard Keynes.* Cambridge Univ. Pr. 1975 $44.50 1980 pap. $15.95

Lekachman, Robert. *The Age of Keynes.* McGraw-Hill repr. of 1966 ed. 1975 pap. $3.95

Patinkin, Don. *Anticipations of the General Theory and Other Essays on Keynes.* Univ. of Chicago Pr. 1982 lib. bdg. $25.00 1985 text ed. pap. $10.00

Pigou, A. C. *Keynes' General Theory: A Retrospective View.* Kelley repr. of 1959 ed. lib. bdg. $8.50

KNIGHT, FRANK H. 1885–1972

Frank H. Knight, an American economist, contributed to economic theory by clarifying the relationship among risk, uncertainty, and profit in a perfectly competitive economy. He taught at the University of Chicago for most of his career, and many of his students acquired their conservative, tough-minded view of the economic system through his books, articles, and lectures.

BOOKS BY KNIGHT

Risk, Uncertainty and Profit. Kelley repr. of 1921 ed. $27.50; Univ. of Chicago Pr. 1971 pap. $12.00

On the History and Method of Economics: Selected Essays. Univ. of Chicago Pr. (Phoenix Bks.) 1963 pap. $2.45. Essays written between the years 1928 and 1951.

Freedom and Reform. Intro. by James M. Buchanan, Liberty Fund repr. of 1947 ed. 1982 $14.00 pap. $6.50. Essays written between 1929 and 1946

The Economic Organization. 1933. Kelley repr. of 1935 ed. $17.50

MALTHUS, THOMAS ROBERT. 1766–1834

Thomas Robert Malthus, an English clergyman and economist, was moved by the publication and notoriety of a book by the anarchist and socialist William Godwin to write his own book setting forth his view that unchecked population growth constitutes an absolute barrier to societal progress. The heart of the argument of his essay on population is that the population of a country tends to grow in geometric progression (2, 4, 8, 16, and so on), while the means of subsistence grows only in arithmetic progression (2, 4, 6, 8, 10, and so on). Famine, vice, misery, and war can only be avoided if population growth is controlled by "moral constraint." Since its publication, Malthus's book has been argued over and found to have many limitations, but to this day the great debate in the population field is between the Malthusians (who think positive steps to lower birth rates are essential) and the Marxists, very broadly defined (who think that raising living standards will in itself lead to changes in values and life-style that will lower population growth).

BOOKS BY MALTHUS

First Essay on Population. 1798. Kelley repr. of 1926 ed. $27.50; Univ. of Michigan Pr. 1959 pap. $5.95

Principles of Political Economy. 1820. Kelley 2d ed. repr. of 1836 ed. $35.00

BOOKS ABOUT MALTHUS

Blaug, Mark. *Economic Theory in Retrospect*. Cambridge Univ. Pr. 3d ed. 1983 pap.
    $18.95
Dupaquier, Jacques, and Chamoux A. Fauve. *Malthus Past and Present. Population
    and Social Structure Ser*. Academic Pr. 1983 $49.00
Glass, D. V., ed. *Introduction to Malthus*. Biblio Dist. 1966 $24.00
Petersen, William. *Malthus*. Harvard Univ. Pr. text ed. 1979 $20.00
Smith, Kenneth. *The Malthusian Controversy*. Octagon repr. of 1951 ed. 1978 lib.
    bdg. $24.50

MARSHALL, ALFRED. 1842–1924

Alfred Marshall, an English economist, was a major contributor to the development of modern economic thought. His *Principles of Economics* (1890)
is one of the great classics of the social sciences, and the first 25 years of
twentieth-century economics have been called the Age of Marshall. One of
his major contributions was to the study of supply and demand. He thought
that both influence prices. In the short run, the supply is fixed, so consumer
demand influences price; in the long run, however, output can be increased
or decreased, and supply (which is based on the cost of production) is more
important. Marshall taught at Cambridge University, so he and his followers are sometimes referred to as the Cambridge school; he is also described
as a founder of the neoclassical school.

BOOKS BY MARSHALL

Principles of Economics. 1890. Porcupine Pr. 8th ed. repr. of 1920 ed. pap. $16.95
Money, Credit and Commerce. Kelley repr. of 1923 ed. $35.00

BOOKS ABOUT MARSHALL

Davenport, Herbert J. *Economics of Alfred Marshall*. Kelley repr. of 1935 ed. $37.50
Kerr, Clark. *Marshall, Marx and Modern Times*. Cambridge Univ. Pr. 1969 $14.95
Parsons, Talcott. *The Structure of Social Action*. 1937. Macmillan (Free Pr.) 2 vols.
    text ed. 1949 pap. ea. $10.95–$16.95. A brilliant analysis of the writings of Mar-
    shall, Durkheim, Weber, and Pareto.
Pigou, A. C., ed. *Memorials of Alfred Marshall*. Kelley 1925 $37.50
Wood, John C., ed. *Alfred Marshall: Critical Assessments*. Longwood Pr. 4 vols. 1982
    $495.00

MARX, KARL. 1818–1883

Karl Marx was a German economist, philosopher, sociologist, historian,
and revolutionary; today, he is both the patron saint of Soviet communism
and the ancestor of much liberal, radical, and analytical economic, social,
and political thought. As an economist, he transformed David Ricardo's labor theory of value—the doctrine that the amount of labor required for its
production is the major determinant of a commodity's price—into a demand that workers should receive the whole product of their labor. He argued, in *Capital* and elsewhere, that capitalism is headed for an inevitable
breakdown, to be followed by a Socialist revolution. His sociological notion
that men's ideas are rooted in their social and economic life led to such doc-

trines as the "false class consciousness" of many workers and to such fields as the sociology of knowledge, which asserts that knowledge itself is not a constant but is a product of the society that produces it. In 1864, he founded the International Workingmen's Association, which became the First International. In his inaugural address he used the same words with which he and his friend and supporter Friedrich Engels had ended *The Communist Manifesto* (1848) 16 years earlier: "Workers of the world, unite!"

Books by Marx

The Communist Manifesto. 1848. International Pubns. 1983 $3.25; *Crofts Class. Ser.* Harlan Davidson text ed. 1955 pap. $3.25; New York Labor News 7th ed. 1968 $1.25; pref. by Leon Trotsky, Path. Pr. 1968 pap. $.95; intro. by A. J. P. Taylor, Penguin (Pelican) 1968 $2.25; Regnery-Gateway 1982 pap. $3.95; ed. by D. Ryazanoff, Russell repr. of 1930 ed. 1963 $18.00; ed. by Joseph Katz, trans. by Samuel Moore, intro. by F. B. Randall, Washington Square Pr. pap. $2.95

A Contribution to a Critique of Political Economy. 1859. Ed. by Maurice Dobb, Beekman 1972 $14.95

Capital. 1867–79. Ed. by Friedrich Engels, International Pubns. 3 vols. 1967 $35.00; trans. by Ben Fowkes and David Fernbach, Random (Vintage) 3 vols. 1977–82 pap. ea. $7.95–10.95

Selected Writings in Sociology and Social Philosophy. Ed. by T. B. Bottomore and Maximilien Rubel, McGraw-Hill 1963 pap. $5.95

Books about Marx

Berlin, Isaiah. *Karl Marx: His Life and Environment.* Oxford 4th ed. 1978 $19.95 pap. $6.95

Harvey, David. *The Limits to Capital.* Univ. of Chicago Pr. 1982 lib. bdg. $30.00 1984 pap. $12.95

Lichtheim, George. *Marxism: An Historical and Critical Study.* Columbia Univ. Pr. repr. of 1961 ed. 1982 $26.00 pap. $12.00

Marcuse, Herbert. *Reason and Revolution: Hegel and the Rise of Social Theory.* Beacon 1960 pap. $5.95; Humanities Pr. 2d ed. repr. of 1941 ed. text ed. 1983 pap. $13.45

Wolff, Robert P. *Understanding Marx: A Reconstruction and Critique of Capital.* Ed. by Marshall Cohen, *Studies in Moral, Political, and Legal Philosophy* Princeton Univ. Pr. text ed. $25.00 pap. $7.95

MENGER, CARL. 1840–1921

Carl Menger, an Austrian economist, was the founder of what is called the Austrian school of economics. At about the same time, he, William Stanley Jevons, and Leon Walras independently set forth the principle of diminishing marginal utility: each increment of food, or income, or other product is less necessary, or possesses less utility, than the previous one. This school dominated economic thought from the 1870s to the 1930s, first replacing the classical school, represented by such persons as Adam Smith, John Stuart Mill, and Thomas Malthus, and being considerably modified by Keynesian economics after the publication in 1936 of Keynes's enormously influential *The General Theory of Employment, Interest and Money.* For most of his career, Menger was a professor at the University of Vienna.

BOOKS BY MENGER

Principles of Economics: First General Part. 1871. Trans. by James Dingwall and Bert
    F. Hoselitz, New York Univ. Pr. text ed. 1981 $25.00 pap. $10.00
Principles of Economics and Sociology. 1883. Ed. by Louis Schneider, Univ. of Illinois
    Pr. 1963 o.p.

BOOKS ABOUT MENGER

Howey, Richard S. *The Rise of the Marginal Utility School, 1870–1889.* Univ. of Kan-
    sas Pr. 1960 o.p.
Schumpeter, Joseph A. *Ten Great Economists: From Marx to Keynes.* Oxford repr. of
    1951 ed. text ed. pap. $6.95
Stigler, George J. *Production and Distribution Theories.* Agathon 1941 $12.00

MILL, JOHN STUART. 1806–1873

John Stuart Mill was an English philosopher and economist who made
many contributions to political thought as well. In his *Principles of Political
Economy* he analyzed the economics of growth and development. He was
concerned with production, population growth, distribution, and exchange.
In his law of international values, he stated that the actual terms of international trade depend on the demand for a product in a foreign country as
well as on efficient production. As a political thinker, he believed that even
a government based on the will of the people can exercise tyranny; accordingly, the restrictions placed on individuals, whether by law or by opinion,
ought to be based on some recognized principle rather than on the prefer-
ences and prejudices of some sections of the public. His ideas form the background of what is today referred to as liberal democracy.

BOOKS BY MILL

The Spirit of the Age. 1831. Intro. by Friedrich A. von Hayek, Univ. of Chicago Pr.
    1942 o.p.
Principles of Political Economy. 1848. Ed. by William J. Ashley, Kelley repr. of 1909
    ed. $37.50; ed. by William J. Ashley, Orion repr. of 1909 ed. 1983 pap. $24.95;
    ed. by J. M. Robson, intro. by V. W. Bladen, *Collected Works of John Stuart Mill
    Ser.* Univ. of Toronto Pr. 2 vols. 1965 $55.00
The Autobiography of John Stuart Mill. 1873. Columbia Univ. Pr. 1924 pap. $10.00;
    ed. by Jack Stillinger, Houghton Mifflin 1964 pap. $5.50
Essays on Politics and Culture. Ed. by Gertrude Himmelfarb, Peter Smith $13.25
Three Essays: On Liberty, Representative Government, the Subjection of Women. Intro.
    by Richard Wolheim, Oxford repr. of 1912 ed. 1975 pap. $6.95
(and Harriet T. Mill). *The Subjection of Women.* 1869. Ed. by Sue Mansfield, *Crofts
    Class. Ser.* Harlan Davidson text ed. 1980 $12.95 pap. $3.95; Merrimack 1983
    pap. $6.95

BOOKS ABOUT MILL

Eisenach, Eldon J. *Two Worlds of Liberalism: Religion and Politics in Hobbes, Locke,
    and Mill.* Univ. of Chicago Pr. 1981 lib. bdg. $20.00
Robson, John M. *The Improvement of Mankind: The Social and Political Thought of
    John Stuart Mill.* Univ. of Toronto Pr. 1968 $22.50
Schumpeter, Joseph A. *History of Economic Analysis.* Oxford 1954 $29.95

Stephen, Leslie. *The English Utilitarians: Jeremy Bentham, James Mill, John Stuart Mill.* Kelley 3 vols. repr. of 1900 ed. $67.50; Peter Smith 3 vols. in 1 $24.00

MITCHELL, WESLEY C. 1874–1948

Wesley C. Mitchell, an American economist, is known both for his extensive statistical research on the business cycle and for his role in the founding of three major institutions in New York: the New School for Social Research in 1919, the National Bureau of Economic Research in 1920, and the Social Science Research Council in 1923. He viewed the study of business cycles as a means of studying the economy as a whole, and his empirical research on it inaugurated an important new tradition in economics.

BOOKS BY MITCHELL

(ed.). *Business Cycles. National Bureau of Economic Research Ser.* Ayer repr. of 1913 ed. 1975 $37.50; Burt Franklin repr. of 1913 ed. 1970 $35.50
The Making and Using of Index Numbers. 1915. Kelley repr. of 1938 ed. $15.00
(and Arthur F. Burns). *Measuring Business Cycles.* National Bureau of Economic Research 1946 $35.00

BOOKS ABOUT MITCHELL

Burns, Arthur F., ed. *Wesley Clair Mitchell: The Economic Scientist.* National Bureau of Economic Research 1952 o.p.
Dorfman, Joseph. *The Economic Mind in American Civilization, 1606–1933.* Kelley 5 vols. 1946–59 $150.00
Hansen, Alvin H. *Business Cycles and National Income.* Norton enl. ed. 1964 $14.95

MYRDAL, GUNNAR. 1898–

[SEE the Sociology section in this chapter.]

PARETO, VILFREDO. 1848–1923

Vilfredo Pareto was an Italian economist and sociologist; his writings were greatly influenced by his expertise in mathematics and his 20 years of practice as an engineer. He made many contributions to mathematical economics, and he viewed the task of sociology to be that of dealing with those components of social action that are not handled by economics. His view of society as a system was far in advance of his time; at Harvard, it was adopted by the physiologist L. J. Henderson, who wrote a book on Pareto's sociology that influenced a generation of sociologists, including Talcott Parsons and Robert K. Merton.

BOOK BY PARETO

The Mind and Society. 1916. Ed. by Arthur Livingston, trans. by Andrew Bongiorno, AMS Pr. 4 vols. repr. of 1935 ed. $195.00

BOOKS ABOUT PARETO

Henderson, L. J. *Pareto's General Sociology.* Harvard Univ. Pr. 1935 o.p.
Homans, George C., and Charles P. Curtis, Jr. *An Introduction to Pareto: His Sociology.* Fertig repr. 1970 $27.50

Parsons, Talcott. *The Structure of Social Action*. 1937. Macmillan (Free Pr.) 2 vols. text ed. 1949 pap. ea. $10.95–$16.95. Contains a major section on Pareto.

POLANYI, KARL. 1886–1964

Karl Polanyi, an Austrian-born American economist, developed a concept he called substantive economics—a concept designed to integrate the study of economics with the study of society generally. The core of his work was the study of the role of the economy in society—the relationship between the arrangements for the production and acquisition of goods, on the one hand, and kinship, religion, and other social institutions on the other. His two principal books, *The Great Transformation* and *Trade and Market in the Early Empires*, deal with modern and ancient societies, respectively. His work has never been fully accepted by economists, but sociologists and especially anthropologists have found his ideas both exciting and useful. In the last phase of his career, he taught at Columbia University.

Books by Polanyi

The Great Transformation: The Political and Economic Origins of Our Time. 1944. Beacon 1957 pap. $9.95; Octagon 1973 lib. bdg. $21.50
(and others, eds.). *Trade and Market in the Early Empires: Economies in History and Theory*. Macmillan (Free Pr.) 1957 o.p.

RICARDO, DAVID. 1772–1823

David Ricardo, an English economist, is considered by many the greatest of the classical economists. He made a small fortune as a stockbroker, retired at age 40, purchased an estate, and devoted his life to writing. His major work is *Principles of Political Economy and Taxation*, published three years after his retirement. It contains a classic statement of the principle of comparative advantage as applied to international trade. With a lucid numerical example, he showed why it was to the mutual advantage of both countries for England to export wool to Portugal and to import wine in return, even though both products could be produced at lower cost in Portugal. The book contains much else, including a theory of rent, and for more than 50 years, English economics was said to be a comment on or an extension of Ricardian economics. Marx's starting point in his attack on capitalism was Ricardo's labor theory of value—the doctrine that the amount of labor required for its production is the major determinant of a commodity's price—which Marx transformed into a demand that workers should receive the whole product of their labor.

Books by Ricardo

Principles of Political Economy and Taxation. 1817. Biblio Dist. (Everyman's) repr. of 1911 ed. 1977 $8.95 pap. $2.95
Works and Correspondence of David Ricardo. Ed. by Piero Sraffa, Cambridge Univ. Pr. 11 vols. 1951–55 ea. $57.50. Volume 11 was edited by Maurice Dobb.

BOOKS ABOUT RICARDO

Blaug, Mark. *Ricardian Economics*. Greenwood repr. of 1958 ed. 1973 lib. bdg. $17.75

Hollander, Samuel. *The Economics of David Ricardo. Studies in Classical Political Economy Ser.* Univ. of Toronto Pr. 1979 $45.00

St. Clair, Oswald. *A Key to Ricardo*. Kelley repr. of 1957 ed. $35.00

Shoup, Carl S. *Ricardo on Taxation: An Analysis of the Chapters on Taxation in David Ricardo's Principles*. Columbia Univ. Pr. 1960 o.p.

Wood, John C., ed. *David Ricardo: Critical Assessments*. Croon Helm 4 vols. 1985 $495.00

SENIOR, NASSAU WILLIAM. 1790–1864

Nassau William Senior, a British economist, practiced law as a profession but was a prolific writer on economic theory. His best-known contribution is his abstinence theory of capital, which emerged from his attempt to find a definition of capital that would make capital coordinate with labor in explaining the influence of the real cost of goods on value. The limitation of supply, he stated, is by far the most important consideration in the determination of prices. He was thus an early exponent of what is today called supply-side economics. Throughout most of his career, he was active in public affairs; for example, he was a member of the famous Poor Law Inquiry Commission of 1833.

BOOK BY SENIOR

Outline of the Science of Political Economy. Kelley repr. of 1836 ed. $25.00

BOOKS ABOUT SENIOR

Bowley, Marian. *Nassau Senior and Classical Economics*. Octagon 1968 lib. bdg. $27.50

Levy, Samuel L. *Nassau W. Senior: The Prophet of Modern Capitalism*. R. S. Barnes 1943 $12.50

SMITH, ADAM. 1723–1790

Adam Smith, a Scottish economist, wrote just two books; the second, *An Inquiry into the Nature and Causes of the Wealth of Nations*, published in 1776, virtually created the science of economics. The greatest source of power in the economic system, of the wealth of nations, he stated, is the division of labor. In a well-known passage, he described a pin factory, pointing out the advantages of task specialization among the workers. Another source of wealth is what he called "the invisible hand" that guides the economy, unseen but nevertheless present. In another famous phrase Smith attributed our welfare to "the propensity to truck, barter, and exchange one thing for another." In this passage, Smith stressed what the sociologist Robert K. Merton nearly 200 years later was to call "the unanticipated consequences of purposive social action." Each person in a marketplace has only his or her own purposes in mind, but the net result of individual "greed" is the improved welfare of all.

BOOKS BY SMITH

The Theory of Moral Sentiments. 1759. Liberty Fund 1977 $9.95; Oxford 1976 $54.00
An Inquiry into the Nature and Causes of the Wealth of Nations. Ed. by Arthur H. Jen-
    kins, Associated Faculty Pr. repr. of 1948 ed. 1969 $17.50; Kelley 2 vols. repr. of
    1776 ed. 1966 lib. bdg. $150.00; Liberty Foundation 2 vols. repr. of 1976 ed. 1982
    pap. $11.00; ed. by R. H. Campbell, Oxford 2 vols. 1976 $105.00; ed. by Edwin
    Cannan, Univ. of Chicago Pr. (Phoenix Bks.) 2 vols. in 1 1977 pap. $14.95. A clas-
    sic book, published in the year of American independence, that virtually created
    the field of economics.

BOOKS ABOUT SMITH

Hollander, Samuel. *Economics of Adam Smith. Studies in Classical Political Economy
    Ser.* Univ. of Toronto Pr. 1973 pap. $8.50
O'Driscoll, Gerald P., Jr., ed. *Adam Smith and Modern Political Economy: Bicenten-
    nial Essays on the Wealth of Nations.* Iowa State Univ. Pr. text ed. 1979 $12.50
Rae, John. *Life of Adam Smith.* Intro. by Jacob Viner, Kelley repr. of 1895 ed. $45.00
Wood, John C., ed. *Adam Smith: Critical Assessments.* Longwood Pr. 4 vols. 1984
    $475.00

VON MISES, LUDWIG. 1881–1973

Ludwig von Mises, an Austrian-born American economist, developed and
extended the theories of the Austrian school of economics, founded by Carl
Menger. He is best known today for his analysis of socialism; he claimed
that socialism cannot possibly calculate economically, because it lacks a
price system based on the private ownership of production and an open
market. After World War II, von Mises became the intellectual leader of the
economic liberal revival in the United States; his *Socialism,* published in
1922, and his student Friedrich A. von Hayek's *The Road to Serfdom* have become the economic bibles of this revival.

BOOKS BY VON MISES

The Theory of Money and Credit. 1912. Trans. by H. E. Bason, fwd. by Murray N.
    Rothbard, intro. by Lionel Robbins, Liberty Fund repr. 1981 $12.00
Socialism. 1922. Intro. by Friedrich A. von Hayek, Liberty Fund 1981 $12.00 pap.
    $6.00
Human Action: A Treatise on Economics. 1949. Contemporary Bks. 3d ed. rev. 1966
    $37.50

BOOKS ABOUT VON MISES

Kirzner, Israel M., ed. *Method, Process, and Austrian Economics: Essays in Honor of
    Ludwig von Mises.* Lexington Bks. 1982 $29.00
Rothbard, Murray N. *Man, Economy and State: A Treatise on Economic Principles.
    Studies in Economic Theory* New York Univ. Pr. 2 vols. 2d ed. repr. of 1970 ed.
    1979 $35.00 pap. $17.50

VON NEUMANN, JOHN. 1903–1957

John von Neumann, a Hungarian-born American mathematician, was the
first major mathematician to devote most of his energies to the social sciences. In 1928, he published an article in a German journal, which he enti-

tled "On the Theory of Games of Strategy"; considerably expanded and developed, the idea underlying the paper was published in 1944 jointly with the economist Oskar Morgenstern as *The Theory of Games and Economic Behavior*. Game theory, which has had an enormous impact on all the social sciences, consists of a theory of individual choice in situations of risk. Besides analyzing games proper, it is used as a model for all situations where the participants do not control or know the probability distributions of all variables on which the outcome of their acts depends. For much of his career, von Neumann was a fellow at the Institute for Advanced Study in Princeton, New Jersey; in addition to his development of game theory, he made many contributions to the development of the computer. He was the first person to understand explicitly that a computer essentially performs logical functions; its electrical aspects are ancillary.

BOOKS BY VON NEUMANN

(and Oskar Morgenstern). *The Theory of Games and Economic Behavior*. 1944. Princeton Univ. Pr. 1980 $59.00 pap. $17.50; Wiley 3d ed. 1953 pap. $12.95
The Computer and the Brain. Yale Univ. Pr. 1958 pap. $4.95

BOOKS ABOUT VON NEUMANN

Brams, Steven J. *Superpower Games: Applying Game Theory to Superpower Conflict*. Yale Univ. Pr. text ed. 1985 $22.50 pap. $6.95
Goldstine, Herman H. *The Computer from Pascal to Von Neumann*. Princeton Univ. Pr. 1980 $36.50 pap. $8.95
Heims, Steve J. *John Von Neumann and Norbert Wiener: From Mathematics to the Technologies of Life and Death*. MIT 1980 $25.00 pap. $11.95
Rosenmuller, J. *The Theory of Games and Markets: An Introduction to Game Theory and Related Topics*. Elsevier 1981 $74.50

WEBB, SIDNEY. 1859–1947, and WEBB, BEATRICE, 1858–1943

Sidney and Beatrice Webb, English economists and social reformers, were a remarkable professional couple who deeply influenced the social thought and social institutions of Great Britain. Beatrice Webb worked as a researcher for Charles Booth on his study of the London poor; Sidney Webb was introduced by his friend Bernard Shaw into the newly formed Fabian Society, and for 50 years he held a seat on its executive committee. In 1889, Shaw and Sidney Webb contributed chapters to *Fabian Essays in Socialism*, which sold two million copies and laid the intellectual foundations of the British Labor Party and of Labor governments for the next 60 years. The Webbs were founders of the London School of Economics and Political Science, which (among others) trained thousands of Africans and Asians in the skills necessary for political independence. They believed in liberal reform, in "the inevitability of gradualness," and through their research and their membership on reform commissions of one kind or another they helped to bring Great Britain into the twentieth century.

BOOK BY SIDNEY WEBB

Facts for Socialists, from the Political Economists and Statisticians. 1887. Fabian Society 14th ed. 1938 o.p.

BOOKS BY BEATRICE WEBB

The Co-operative Movement in Great Britain. 1891. AMS Pr. repr. of 1904 ed. $24.50
My Apprenticeship. AMS Pr. repr. of 1926 ed. $27.50; intro. by N. MacKenzie, Cambridge Univ. Pr. 1980 $54.50 pap. $17.95

BOOKS BY SIDNEY AND BEATRICE WEBB

Industrial Democracy. 1897. Longman 2 vols. in 1 new ed. 1920 o.p.
The Manor and the Borough. 1980. Shoe String 2 vols. 1963 o.p.
English Poor Law History. Longman 2 vols. in 3 1927–29 o.p.

BOOKS ABOUT THE WEBBS

Cole, Margaret I., ed. *The Webbs and Their Work.* Greenwood repr. of 1949 ed. 1985 lib. bdg. $39.75
Hamilton, Mary A. *Sidney and Beatrice Webb: A Study in Contemporary Biography.* Houghton Mifflin 1933 o.p.

WICKSELL, KNUT. 1851–1926

Knut Wicksell, a Swedish economist, made important contributions to the marginalist theory of price and distribution (*Value, Capital and Rent*) and was a pioneer in monetary theory (*Interest and Prices*). He examined the question of why prices rise and fall, and he concluded that when the central bank sets too low a market rate of interest, saving is discouraged, spending increases, and prices rise. When the interest rate is too high, on the other hand, people will save more, spend less, and prices will fall. Only when the interest rate is equal to the marginal productivity of capital will prices stabilize. It took him several decades to obtain a teaching position (he taught at the Universities of Uppsala and Lund), but by the time of his death he was recognized as the founder of Swedish economics and was given a state funeral.

BOOKS BY WICKSELL

Value, Capital and Rent. 1893. Kelley repr. of 1954 ed. $17.50
Interest and Prices. 1898. Kelley repr. of 1936 ed. $17.50
Selected Papers on Economic Theory. Ed. by Erik Lindahl, Kelley repr. of 1958 ed. $22.50

BOOKS ABOUT WICKSELL

Myrdal, Gunnar. *Monetary Equilibrium.* Kelley repr. of 1939 ed. $17.50
Uhr, Carl G. *Economic Doctrines of Knut Wicksell.* Univ. of California Pr. 1960 $45.00

POLITICAL SCIENCE

Some university departments of political science are called government departments, and government is the major focus in political science, which is in part the study of legislation, legislators, administrative agencies, courts, and the executive branch. But it is also the study of voting patterns, of how people acquire political opinions, and of how people should be and are governed. Much of political science is focused on theories and descriptions of governmental institutions and on the state; much of its analytical attention is devoted to power relationships between classes, groups, and nations. In the last 25 years, political scientists have paid a great deal of attention to decision making at all levels of government: Who actually makes decisions, and what are they influenced by? Decision making is one aspect of what is called the behavorial movement within political science—a focus on what people actually do in the governmental process, rather than on what constitutions and laws say they should do.

The list of readings is divided into books that describe the history of political science as a field, broad surveys of the field, reference books, and 16 topics that political scientists have studied in some detail.

History of Field

Crick, Bernard. *The American Science of Politics: Its Origin and Conditions.* Greenwood 1982 lib. bdg. $35.00; Univ. of California Pr. 1959 $6.75

Somit, Albert, and Joseph Tanenhaus. *Development of American Political Science: From Burgess to Behavioralism.* Irvington enl. ed 1982 $27.50 text ed. pap. $12.95

Wolin, Sheldon S. *Politics and Vision: Continuity and Innovation in Western Political Thought.* Little, Brown 1960 $16.95

Surveys of the Field

Brecht, Arnold. *Political Theory: The Foundations of Twentieth Century Political Thought.* Princeton Univ. Pr. 1959 $32.50 pap. $8.95

Easton, David. *The Political System: An Inquiry into the State of Political Science.* Univ. of Chicago Pr. 2d ed. 1981 pap. $12.50

Reference Books

Greenstein, F. I., and N. W. Polsby. *The Handbook of Political Science.* Addison-Wesley 8 vols. 1975 $160.00. An extremely useful, encyclopedic survey of the entire field.

Holler, Frederick L. *The Information Sources of Political Science.* ABC-Clio 5 vols. 3d ed. text ed. 1975 $12.00

Laqueur, Walter. *Dictionary of Politics.* Macmillan (Free Pr.) rev. ed. 1974 $17.95

Paxton, John, ed. *The Statesman's Yearbook World Gazetteer.* St. Martin's 1975 $15.00

Smith, Edward C., and Arnold Zurcher. *Dictionary of American Politics.* Barnes & Noble 2d ed. 1968 $19.95 pap. $5.72

Taylor, Charles L., and others. *World Handbook of Political and Social Indicators.* Yale Univ. Pr. 2 vols. 3d ed. 1983 $26.00

Administration

Bendix, Reinhard. *Higher Civil Servants in American Society.* Greenwood repr. of 1949 ed. 1974 lib. bdg. $15.00

Crozier, Michel. *The Bureaucratic Phenomenon.* Univ. of Chicago Pr. (Phoenix Bks.) 1967 pap. $10.00

Goodnow, Frank J. *Politics and Administration: A Study in Government.* Russell repr. of 1900 ed. 1967 $16.00

LaPalombara, Joseph G., ed. *Bureaucracy and Political Development. Studies in Political Development Ser.* Princeton Univ. Pr. 1963 $36.00 pap. $11.50

Simon, Herbert A. *Administrative Behavior.* 1947. Macmillan (Free Pr.) 3d ed. 1976 $24.95 text ed. pap. $14.95

Waldo, Dwight. *The Administrative State: A Study of the Political Theory of American Public Administration.* Holmes & Meier 2d ed. text ed. 1984 $29.50 pap. $14.50; Wiley 1948 $11.95

———, ed. *Ideas and Issues in Public Administration: A Book of Readings.* Greenwood repr. of 1953 ed. lib. bdg. $22.50

Wildavsky, Aaron. *The Politics of the Budgetary Process.* Little, Brown 4th ed. text ed. 1983 pap. $9.95

Woll, Peter. *American Bureaucracy.* Norton 2d ed. 1977 pap. $6.95; Peter Smith $11.50

Anarchism

Carr, Edward H. *The Romantic Exiles: A Nineteenth-Century Portrait Gallery.* MIT 1981 pap. $8.95; Octagon repr. of 1933 ed. 1975 lib. bdg. $27.50

Hobsbawm, Eric J. *Revolutionaries.* New Amer. Lib. 1975 pap. $3.95

Kropotkin, Peter. *Mutual Aid: A Factor of Evolution.* Folcroft repr. of 1904 ed. lib. bdg. $30.00; intro. by Mann E. Kingston, Garland lib. bdg. $42.00; intro. by Paul Avrich, New York Univ. Pr. 1972 $18.50

Marsh, Margaret. *Anarchist Women: 1870–1920.* Ed. by Allen F. Davis, *Amer. Civilization Ser.* Temple Univ. Pr. 1980 $29.95

Pennock, J. Roland, ed. *Anarchism: Nomos XIX.* Ed. by John W. Chapman, New York Univ. Pr. 1978. $30.00

Proudhon, Pierre J. *What Is Property?* Fertig 1966 $20.00; Gordon $75.00. A classic statement of the philosophy of anarchism, first published in French in 1876.

Sorel, Georges. *Reflections on Violence.* AMS Pr. repr. of 1914 ed. $27.50; Peter Smith $17.25

Civil Liberties, Civil Rights

Adler, Mortimer J. *The Idea of Freedom.* Greenwood 2 vols. repr. 1973 lib. bdg. $54.00

Friedrich, Carl J., ed. *Liberty.* Lieber Atherton 1962 $15.00

Haiman, Franklyn S. *Speech and Law in a Free Society.* Univ. of Chicago Pr. 1981 lib. bdg. $30.00 pap. $14.00

Hayek, Friedrich A. von. *The Road to Serfdom.* Fwd. by J. Chamberlain, Univ. of Chicago Pr. 1944 $12.50; Univ. of Chicago Pr. (Phoenix Bks.) 1956 pap. $6.95

Hirschman, Albert O. *Exit, Voice, and Loyalty: Responses to Decline in Firms, Organizations, and States.* Harvard Univ. Pr. 1970 pap. $4.95

Laqueur, Walter, and Barry Rubin, eds. *The Human Rights Reader.* New Amer. Lib. 1979 pap. $6.95; Temple Univ. Pr. 1979 $29.95

Lazarsfeld, Paul F., and Wagner Thielens, Jr. *The Academic Mind: Social Scientists in Time of Crisis.* Ed. by Walter P. Metzger, Ayer repr. of 1958 ed. 1977 $35.50

McClosky, Herbert, and Alida Brill. *Dimensions of Tolerance: What Americans Believe about Civil Liberties.* Russell Sage 1983 $29.95

Stouffer, Samuel A. *Communism, Conformity and Civil Liberties.* 1955. Peter Smith $11.25. This and the McClosky and Brill book, published a generation apart, are both based on opinion surveys of the American people.

Constitutions and Federalism

Agresto, John. *The Supreme Court and Constitutional Democracy.* Cornell Univ. Pr. 1984 pap. $7.95

Beard, Charles A. *An Economic Interpretation of the Constitution of the United States.* 1913. Macmillan (Free Pr.) 1965 pap. $10.95. An early use of collective biography. Beard examined the lives of the framers of the Constitution and calculated how much most of them had to gain financially from the Constitution as it emerged from the convention. (See Beard's main listing in Chapter 7 in this volume.)

Bowen, Catherine Drinker. *Miracle at Philadelphia: The Story of the Constitutional Convention, May to September 1787.* Little, Brown 1966 o.p.

Brown, Robert E. *Charles Beard and the Constitution: A Critical Analysis of "An Economic Interpretation of the Constitution."* Greenwood repr. of 1956 ed. 1979 lib. bdg. $22.50; *Norton Lib.* 1965 pap. $3.25

Dahl, Robert A. *A Preface to Democratic Theory.* Univ. of Chicago Pr. (Phoenix Bks.) 1963 pap. $3.95

Dicey, Albert V. *Introduction to the Study of the Law of the Constitution.* 1885. Intro. by Roger Michener, Liberty Fund 1982 $15.00 pap. $7.00

Elazar, Daniel J. *American Federalism: A View from the States.* Harper 3d ed. 1984 pap. $11.95

Farrand, Max. *The Framing of the Constitution of the United States.* Norwood 1913 $45.00; Yale Univ. Pr. 1913 $30.00 pap. $8.95

Friedrich, Carl J. *Constitutional Government and Democracy: Theory and Practice in Europe and America (Constitutional Government and Politics: Nature and Development).* 1937. Blaisdale 4th ed. 1968 o.p.

——. *Constitutional Reason of State: The Survival of the Constitutional Order.* Univ. Pr. of New England text ed. 1957 $10.00

Friendly, Fred W., and Martha J. Elliott. *The Constitution: That Delicate Balance.* Random text ed. 1984 $17.95

Goldwin, Robert A., and William A. Schambra, eds. *How Democratic Is the Constitution?* Amer. Enterprise Institute 1980 $12.25 pap. $5.25

Grodzins, Morton. *The American System: A New View of Government in the United States.* Ed. by Daniel J. Elazar, *Political Theory Ser.* Transaction Bks. 1983 $19.95

Hamilton, Alexander, James Madison, and John Jay. *The Federalist Papers.* 1788. Intro. by Garry Wills, Bantam 1982 pap. $2.95; ed. by Benjamin F. Wright, Harvard Univ. Pr. 1961 $20.00; ed. by Clinton Rossiter, New Amer. Lib. 1961 pap. $2.95; Random 1964 pap. $4.95

Kelsen, Hans. *The General Theory of Law and State.* Trans. by Anders Wedberg, Russell repr. of 1945 ed. 1961 $25.00

McDonald, Forrest. *We the People. Midway Repr. Ser.* Univ. of Chicago Pr. 1976 pap. $14.00

Murphy, Walter F. *Congress and the Court.* Univ. of Chicago Pr. (Phoenix Bks.) 1965 pap. $3.95

Pritchett, C. Herman. *The American Constitutional System.* Ed. by Eric Munson, *Amer. Government Ser.* McGraw-Hill text ed. 1981 pap. $12.95

Reagan, Michael, and John Sanzone. *The New Federalism.* Oxford 2d ed. text ed. 1981 $5.95

Tribe, Laurence H. *Constitutional Choices.* Harvard Univ. Pr. text ed. 1985 $29.95

Democracy

Berns, Walter. *In Defense of Liberal Democracy.* Regency-Gateway 1984 pap. $9.95

Bryce, James. *Modern Democracies.* 1921. Arden Lib. 2 vols. repr. of 1924 ed. 1983 lib. bdg. $85.00 (See Bryce's main listing in this section.)

Dahl, Robert A. *A Preface to Democratic Theory.* Univ. of Chicago Pr. (Phoenix Bks.) 1963 pap. $3.95

Downs, Anthony. *An Economic Theory of Democracy.* Harper text ed. 1965 pap. $11.50

Friedrich, Carl J. *Constitutional Government and Democracy: Theory and Practice in Europe and America (Constitutional Government and Politics: Nature and Development).* 1937. Blaisdale 4th ed. 1968 o.p.

Key, V. O., Jr. *Public Opinion and American Democracy.* Knopf 1961 o.p. (See Key's main listing in this section.)

Kornhauser, William. *The Politics of Mass Society.* Macmillan (Free Pr.) text ed. 1959 $15.95

Lindsay, A. D. *The Modern Democratic State.* 1943. Oxford 1959 o.p.

Mayo, Henry B. *An Introduction to Democratic Theory.* Oxford 1960 pap. $6.95

Novak, Michael. *The Spirit of Democratic Capitalism.* Simon & Schuster 1982 $19.95

Sartori, Giovanni. *Democratic Theory.* Greenwood repr. of 1962 ed. 1973 lib. bdg. $24.75; Wayne State Univ. Pr. 1962 $10.00

Schumpeter, Joseph A. *Capitalism, Socialism and Democracy.* Harper pap. $6.95; Peter Smith 1983 $16.75

Sullivan, John L., and George E. Marcus. *Political Tolerance and American Democracy.* Univ. of Chicago Pr. 1982 lib. bdg. $27.50

Tocqueville, Alexis de. *Democracy in America.* 1835–40. Ed. by J. P. Mayer, trans. by George Lawrence, Doubleday (Anchor) 1969 pap. $10.95; trans. by Phillips Bradley, Random 2 vols. 1944 pap. ea. $4.95. A classic of political analysis; the first and still the best commentary on American democracy; by a perceptive French aristocrat.

Elections, Voting Behavior, Political Parties

Asher, Herbert B. *Presidential Elections and American Politics: Voters, Candidates and Campaigns since 1952.* Dorsey 3d ed. 1984 pap. $18.00; Irwin rev. ed. 1980 $14.95

Berelson, Bernard R. *Voting: A Study of Opinion Formation in a Presidential Campaign.* Univ. of Chicago Pr. 1954 pap. $10.00. Probably the best research on the U.S. electorate during a presidential campaign. Contains a summary of other studies and a brilliant concluding chapter on the meaning of elections for democracies.

Black, Duncan. *The Theory of Committees and Elections.* Cambridge Univ. Pr. 1958 $29.95

Buchanan, James M., and Gordon Tullock. *The Calculus of Consent: Logical Foundations of Constitutional Democracy.* Univ. of Michigan Pr. 1962 pap. $9.95

Campbell, Angus, and others. *The American Voter. Midway Repr. Ser.* Univ. of Chicago Pr. 1980 lib. bdg. $24.00

————. *Elections and the Political Order.* Wiley 1966 o.p.

Key, V. O., Jr. *Politics, Parties and Pressure Groups,* 1942. Harper 5th ed. text ed. 1964 $15.95

Kiewiet, D. Roderick. *Macroeconomics and Micropolitics: The Electoral Effects of Economic Issues.* Univ. of Chicago Pr. 1983 lib. bdg. $15.00 1984 pap. $5.00

Lazarsfeld, Paul F., and others. *The People's Choice: How the Voter Makes Up His Mind in a Presidential Campaign.* 1944. Columbia Univ. Pr. $24.00 pap. $10.00. One of the gems of American social science. A report on the 1940 presidential election in Sandusky, Ohio.

Michels, Robert. *Political Parties: A Sociological Study of the Oligarchical Tendencies of Modern Democracy.* 1911. Intro. by Seymour M. Lipset, Macmillan (Free Pr.) text ed. 1966 pap. $12.95; Peter Smith 1960 $13.25. (See Michels's main listing in the Sociology section.)

Nie, Norman H., and John R. Petrocik. *The Changing American Voter.* Harvard Univ. Pr. 1976 $22.50 pap. $10.95

Turner, Julius. *Party and Constituency: Pressures on Congress.* AMS Pr. repr. of 1951 ed. $13.50

Verba, Sidney, and Norman H. Nie. *Participation in America: Political Democracy and Social Equality.* Harper text ed. 1972 pap. $15.50

Government

Bryce, James. *Modern Democracies.* 1921. Arden Lib. 2 vols. repr. of 1924 ed. 1983 lib. bdg. $85.00

Corwin, Edward S. *The President: Office and Powers.* Ed. by Randall W. Bland, Theodore T. Hindson, and Jack W. Peltason, New York Univ. Pr. 5th ed. rev. 1984 $40.00 pap. $20.00

Dahl, Robert A. *Who Governs: Democracy and Power in an American City. Studies in Political Science* Yale Univ. Pr. 1961 $33.50 pap. $8.95

Deutsch, Karl W. *The Nerves of Government.* Macmillan (Free Pr.) 1963 $19.95

Easton, David. *A Systems Analysis of Political Life.* Univ. of Chicago Pr. (Phoenix Bks.) 1979 $8.95

Finer, Herman. *Theory and Practice of Modern Government.* Greenwood rev. ed. repr. of 1949 ed. lib. bdg. $48.75

Friedrich, Carl J. *Constitutional Government and Democracy: Theory and Practice in Europe and America (Constitutional Government and Politics: Nature and Development).* 1937. Blaisdale 4th ed. 1968 o.p.

Guterbock, Thomas M. *Machine Politics in Transition: Party and Community in Chicago. Studies in Urban Society* Univ. of Chicago Pr. 1980 lib. bdg. $25.00

Hobbes, Thomas. *Leviathan.* 1651. Biblio Dist. (Everyman's) repr. of 1914 ed. 1976 $9.95; ed. by Herbert W. Schneider, Bobbs 2 pts. 1958 pap. $9.08; ed. by Michael Oakeshott, intro. by R. Peters, Macmillan (Collier Bks.) 1962 pap. $3.95; ed. by C. B. MacPherson, *Penguin Eng. Lib. Ser.* 1982 pap. $5.95. (See Hobbes's main listing in this section.)

Lasswell, Harold D. *Politics: Who Gets What, When, and How.* 1936. Peter Smith $12.50. (See Lasswell's main listing in this section.)

Locke, John. *Two Treatises of Government.* 1690. Intro. by W. S. Carpenter, Biblio Dist. (Everyman's) repr. of 1924 ed. 1975 $12.95; ed. by Peter Laslett, Cambridge Univ. Pr. 1960 $57.50; intro. by Thomas I. Cook, *Lib. of Class. Ser.* Hafner text ed. $9.95; intro. by Peter Laslett, New Amer. Lib. pap. $4.95. (See Locke's main listing in this section.)

Lowi, Theodore J. *The Personal President: Power Invested, Promise Unfulfilled.* Cornell Univ. Pr. 1985 $19.95

Mill, John Stuart. *Considerations on Representative Government.* Ed. by Currin V. Shields, Bobbs 1958 pap. $6.25; Regnery-Gateway repr. pap. $4.95

——. *On Liberty.* 1859. Ed. by Currin V. Shields, Bobbs 1956 pap. $5.99; ed. by Elizabeth Rapaport, Hackett 1978 lib. bdg. $15.00 text ed. pap. $2.75; ed. by Alburey Castell, *Crofts Class. Ser.* Harlan Davidson text ed. 1947 pap. $3.25; ed. by David Spitz, *Norton Critical Eds.* text ed. 1975 pap. $5.95; ed. by Gertrude Himmelfarb, *Penguin Eng. Lib. Ser.* 1982 pap. $2.95

Polsby, Nelson W. *Community Power and Political Theory: A Further Look at Problems of Evidence and Inference.* Yale Univ. Pr. 2d ed. rev. text ed. 1980 $33.50 pap. $8.95

Sayre, Wallace S., and Herbert Kaufman. *Governing New York City.* Norton 1965 pap. $11.95; Russell Sage 1960 $15.00

Seymour-Ure, Colin. *The American President: Power and Communication.* St. Martin's 1982 $25.00

Tiryakian, Edward A., and Ronald Rogowski, eds. *New Nationalisms of the Developed West: Toward Explanation.* Allen & Unwin 1985 text ed. $35.00

Truman, David B. *The Governmental Process: Political Interests and Public Opinion.* Greenwood repr. of 1951 ed. 1981 lib. bdg. $45.00; Knopf 2d ed. text ed. 1951 pap. $12.95

Ideology and Belief

Almond, Gabriel A., and Sidney Verba. *The Civic Culture: Political Attitudes and Democracy in Five Nations.* Little, Brown Ser. in Comparative Politics text ed. 1965 pap. $13.95; *Center of International Studies Ser.* Princeton Univ. Pr. 1963 $32.50

——. *The Civic Culture Revisited.* Little, Brown text ed. 1980 pap. $12.95

Apter, David E., ed. *Ideology and Discontent.* Macmillan (Free Pr.) 1964 $24.95

Bell, Daniel. *The End of Ideology: On the Exhaustion of Political Ideas in the Fifties.* Macmillan (Free Pr.) text ed. 1965 pap. $3.50

Hochschild, Jennifer L. *What's Fair: America's Beliefs about Distributive Justice.* Harvard Univ. Pr. text ed. 1981 $22.50

Key, V. O., Jr. *Public Opinion and American Democracy.* Knopf 1961 o.p.

Lane, Robert E. *Political Ideology.* Macmillan (Free Pr.) text ed. 1967 pap. $3.50

Lipset, Seymour M. *The First New Nation: The United States in Historical and Comparative Perspective.* Norton 1979 pap. $6.95

——. *Political Man: The Social Bases of Politics.* Johns Hopkins Univ. Pr. repr. of 1966 ed. text ed. 1981 pap. $8.95

Mannheim, Karl. *Ideology and Utopia: An Introduction to the Sociology of Knowledge.* Harcourt 1955 pap. $4.95. Essays first published between 1929 and 1931. (See Mannheim's main listing in the Sociology section.)

International Relations

Almond, Gabriel. *The American People and Foreign Policy*. Greenwood 2d ed. repr. of 1960 ed. 1977 lib. bdg. $22.75

Aron, Raymond. *Peace and War: A Theory of International Relations*. 1962. Krieger repr. of 1966 ed. 1981 $46.50. (See Aron's main listing in Chapter 10 in this volume.)

Bishop, William W., Jr. *International Law: Cases and Materials*. Little, Brown 3d ed. 1971 $31.00

Choucri, Nazli, and Robert North. *Nations in Conflict: National Growth and International Violence*. Freeman text ed. 1975 $30.95

Clark, Grenville, and Louis Sohn. *Introduction to World Peace through World Law*. *Modern Class. of Peace Ser*. World Without War repr. of 1959 ed. 1984 pap. $4.95

Deutsch, Karl W. *Nationalism and Social Communication: An Inquiry into the Foundations of Nationality*. MIT 1953 pap. $9.95

Haas, Ernst B. *Beyond the Nation-State: Functionalism and International Organization*. Stanford Univ. Pr. 1964 $40.00 pap. $14.95

Hoffmann, Stanley, ed. *Conditions of World Order*. Simon & Schuster (Touchstone Bks.) 1970 pap. $3.95

———. *Dead Ends: American Foreign Policy in the New Cold War*. Ballinger 1983 $24.50

Riker, William H. *The Theory of Political Coalitions*. Greenwood repr. of 1962 ed. 1984 lib. bdg. $37.50

Rosenau, James N. *International Studies and the Social Sciences: Problems, Priorities and Prospects in the U.S. Sage Lib. of Social Research* 1973 $20.00 pap. $9.95

Schelling, Thomas C. *The Strategy of Conflict*. Harvard Univ. Pr. 1960 $18.50 text ed. pap. $6.95; Oxford 1963 pap. $4.50

Singer, J. D., ed. *Quantitative International Politics*. Macmillan (Free Pr.) 1968 $14.95

Law and the Courts

Ackerman, Bruce. *Reconstructing American Law*. Harvard Univ. Pr. text ed. 1984 $16.00 pap. $6.95

Ehrlich, Eugene, and Roscoe Pound. *Fundamental Principles of the Sociology of Law*. *European Sociology Ser*. Ayer repr. 1975 $46.50; *Harvard Studies in Jurisprudence* Hein 1979 lib. bdg. $32.50

Hart, Herbert L. *The Concept of Law*. Oxford text ed. 1961 pap. $8.95

Lipson, Leon, and Stanton Wheeler, eds. *Law and the Social Sciences*. Russell Sage 1985 consult publisher for information

Loh, Wallace D. *Social Research in the Judicial Process: Cases, Readings and Text*. Russell Sage 1984 $37.50

Podgorecki, Adam, and Christopher Whelan, eds. *Sociological Approaches to Law*. St. Martin's 1981 $27.50

Pound, Roscoe. *Jurisprudence*. West 5 vols. 1959 o.p.

Skolnick, Jerome H. *Justice without Trial: Law Enforcement in Democratic Society*. Wiley 2d ed. text ed. 1975 pap. $12.95

Stone, Julius. *Social Dimensions of Law and Justice*. Gaunt repr. of 1966 ed. 1971 lib. bdg. $55.00

Zeisel, Hans, and others. *Delay in Court*. Greenwood 2d ed. repr. of 1959 ed. 1978 lib. bdg. $27.75

Legislation, Congress

Goehlert, Robert, and John Sayre. *The United States Congress.* Macmillan (Free Pr.) text ed. 1981 $50.00

Martis, Kenneth C. *The Historical Atlas of United States Congressional Districts, 1789–1983.* Macmillan 1982 lib. bdg. $150.00

Mayhew, David R. *Congress: The Electoral Connection. Studies in Political Science* Yale Univ. Pr. 1974 $21.00 pap. $5.95

Robinson, James A. *Congress and Foreign Policy Making: A Study in Legislative Influence and Initiative.* Greenwood repr. of 1962 ed. 1980 lib. bdg. $32.50

Wahlke, John C., and others. *The Legislative System.* Wiley 1962 o.p.

Policy Making

Burnham, Walter D., and Martha W. Weinberg, eds. *American Politics and Public Policy. MIT Studies in Amer. Politics and Public Policy* 1978 $32.50 text ed. pap. $12.50

Ham, Christopher, and Michael J. Hill. *The Policy Process in the Modern Capitalist State.* St. Martin's 1984 $29.95

Lerner, Daniel, and Harold D. Lasswell, eds. *The Policy Sciences: Recent Developments in Scope and Method.* 1951. Stanford Univ. Pr. 1968 o.p.

MacRae, Duncan, Jr. *Policy Indicators: Links between Social Science and Public Debate. Urban and Regional Policy and Development Studies* Univ. of North Carolina Pr. $36.00

Polsby, Nelson W. *Political Innovation in America: The Politics of Policy Initiation.* Yale Univ. Pr. 1984 $22.50

Public Opinion

Bogart, Leo. *Polls and the Awareness of Public Opinion.* Transaction Bks. 1985 pap. $14.95

Dicey, Albert V. *Lectures on the Relation between Law and Public Opinion in England, during the Nineteenth Century.* 1905. AMS Pr. 2d ed. repr. of 1914 ed. $42.50

Key, V. O., Jr. *Public Opinion and American Democracy.* Knopf 1961 o.p.

Lindblom, Charles E. *The Intelligence of Democracy.* Macmillan (Free Pr.) 1965 $19.95

Lippmann, Walter. *Public Opinion.* 1922. Macmillan (Free Pr.) 1965 pap. $9.95 (See Lippmann's main listing in this section.)

Lipset, Seymour M., and William Schneider. *The Confidence Gap: Business, Labor and Government in the Public Mind. Studies of the Modern Corporation Ser.* Macmillan (Free Pr.) text ed. 1983 $19.95

Noelle-Neumann, Elisabeth. *The Spiral of Silence: Public Opinion—Our Social Skin.* Univ. of Chicago Pr. 1984 lib. bdg. $20.00

Weissberg, Robert. *Public Opinion and Popular Government.* Prentice-Hall 1976 $15.95

Socialism and Communism

Bergson, Abram. *Planning and Productivity under Soviet Socialism.* Columbia Univ. Pr. 1968 $16.00

Bottomore, Tom. *Sociology and Socialism*. St. Martin's 1984 $25.00 text ed. pap. $11.95

Cole, G. D. H. *A History of Socialist Thought*. St. Martin's 5 vols. 1953–60 o.p.

Crosland, Charles A. *The Future of Socialism*. Greenwood repr. of 1964 ed. 1977 lib. bdg. $26.75

Dallin, Alexander, ed. *Diversity in International Communism: A Documentary Record, 1961–1963*. Columbia Univ. Pr. 1963 pap. $30.00

Goodman, Elliot R. *The Soviet Design for a World State. Studies of the Russian Institute* Columbia Univ. Pr. 1960 $34.00

Schumpeter, Joseph A. *Capitalism, Socialism and Democracy*. 1942. Harper pap. $6.95; Peter Smith 1983 $16.75

Totalitarianism

Milosz, Czeslaw. *The Captive Mind*. Octagon repr. of 1953 ed. 1981 lib. bdg. $18.50; Random (Vintage) repr. of 1953 ed. 1981 pap. $4.95. A classic firsthand account of the effects of totalitarianism on intellectuals.

Mosca, Gaetano. *The Ruling Class*. 1891. Ed. by Arthur Livingston, trans. by Hannah D. Kahn, Greenwood repr. of 1939 ed. 1980 lib. bdg. $42.50; McGraw-Hill 1959 pap. $4.95

Neumann, Franz L. *Behemoth: The Structure and Practice of National Socialism, 1933–1944*. Octagon 2d ed. 1963 lib. bdg. $47.50. A wonderfully readable account of the triumph of nazism in Germany.

————. *The Democratic and the Authoritarian State: Essays in Political and Legal Theory*. Macmillan (Free Pr.) text ed. 1964 pap. $7.95

Neumann, Sigmund. *The Permanent Revolution: The Total State in a World at War. Studies in Fascism: Ideology and Practice* AMS Pr. repr. of 1942 ed. $32.00

Wittfogel, Karl A. *Oriental Despotism: A Comparative Study of Total Power*. Random (Vintage) 1981 pap. $8.95; Yale Univ. Pr. 1957 $42.00

War and Peace

Aron, Raymond. *War and Industrial Society*. Trans. by Mary Bottomore, Greenwood repr. of 1959 ed. 1980 lib. bdg. $18.75

Halperin, Morton H. *Limited War in the Nuclear Age*. Greenwood repr. of 1963 ed. 1978 lib. bdg. $22.50

Jervis, Robert. *The Illogic of American Nuclear Strategy*. Cornell Univ. Pr. 1984 $19.95

Kahn, Herman. *On Thermonuclear War*. Greenwood repr. of 1961 ed. 1978 lib. bdg. $60.50

Richardson, Lewis Fry. *Arms and Insecurity: A Mathematical Study of the Causes and Origins of War*. Ed. by Nicolas Rashevsky and Ernesto Trucco, Boxwood 1960 o.p.

————. *Statistics of Deadly Quarrels*. Ed. by Quincy Wright and C. C. Lienau, Boxwood 1960 $28.00. Richardson was a meteorologist, and these two books—first published in 1960 after his death—represent his attempt to understand war in a manner similar to how weather is understood. Antiquated, but fascinating.

Schelling, Thomas C. *The Strategy of Conflict*. Harvard Univ. Pr. 1960 $18.50 text ed. pap. $6.95; Oxford 1963 pap. $4.50

Wright, Quincy. *A Study of War*. Univ. of Chicago Pr. 1983 pap. $15.00

ACTON, LORD JOHN E. 1834–1902
[SEE Chapter 9 in this volume.]

ARISTOTLE. 384–322 B.C.
[SEE Volume 4.]

AUGUSTINE. 354–430
[SEE Volume 4.]

BENTHAM, JEREMY. 1748–1832
Jeremy Bentham, an English reformer and political philosopher, spent his life supporting countless social and political reform measures and trying as well to create a science of human behavior. He defined his goal as the objective study and measurement of passions and feelings, pleasures and pains, will and action. The principle of "the greatest happiness of the greatest number" governed all of his schemes for the improvement of society, and his advocacy of utilitarianism set a model for all subsequent reforms based on scientific principles.

BOOKS BY BENTHAM

A Fragment on Government. 1776. Ed. by F. C. Montague, Greenwood repr. of 1931 ed. 1980 lib. bdg. $24.75

An Introduction to the Principles of Morals and Legislation. 1780. Ed. by J. Lafleur, *Lib. of Class. Ser*. Hafner text ed. 1948 pap. $10.05; ed. by H. L. Hart, Longwood Pr. text ed. 1970 $75.00; ed. by H. L. Hart, Methuen 1982 $13.95

The Rationale of Judicial Evidence, Specially Applied to English Practice. 1827. Ed. by David Berkowitz and Samuel Thorne, *Classics of Eng. Legal History in the Modern Era Ser*. Garland 5 vols. 1979 lib. bdg. $303.00

The Works of Jeremy Bentham: Published under the Superintendence of His Executor, John Bowing. Scholarly repr. of 1838–43 ed. 1976 $360.00

BOOKS ABOUT BENTHAM

Hart, Herbert L. *Essays on Bentham: Studies Jurisprudence and Political Theory*. Oxford text ed. 1982 $29.95 pap. $12.95

Mack, Mary Peter. *Jeremy Bentham*. Heinemann 1962 o.p.

Rosen, Frederick. *Jeremy Bentham and Representative Democracy: A Study of the Constitutional Code*. Oxford 1983 $42.00

Rosenblum, Nancy L. *Bentham's Theory of the Modern State*. Harvard Political Studies 1978 $16.50

Steintrager, James. *Bentham*. Cornell Univ. Pr. 1977 $21.50

Stephen, Leslie. *The English Utilitarians: Jeremy Bentham, James Mill, John Stuart Mill*. Peter Smith 3 vols. in 1 $24.00

BRYCE, JAMES. 1838–1922

James Bryce, a British lawyer and writer, achieved fame primarily for his book *The American Commonwealth*. His aim was to produce the first substantial description of U.S. democracy, covering not only the constitutional structure but also state and local government, the party system, public opinion, and social institutions. Tocqueville's *Democracy in America* was in one sense his model, but Bryce deliberately avoided Tocqueville's speculative method and concentrated more on detailed description, but also on some prescription. "Law," he noted, "will never be strong or respected unless it has the sentiment of the people behind it." *The American Commonwealth* became the first textbook on U.S. government. These two books are the most illustrious to have ever been written about the United States.

BOOKS BY BRYCE

The Holy Roman Empire. 1864. AMS Pr. rev. & enl. ed. repr. of 1913 ed. $28.50; Arden Lib. repr. of 1911 ed. 1978 lib. bdg. $65.00; Foundation Class. repr. of 1866 ed. 1984 $77.85; Norwood repr. of 1911 ed. $47.50
The American Commonwealth. AMS Pr. 3 vols. repr. of 1888 ed. $150.00; Folcroft 2 vols. repr. of 1891 ed. 1978 lib. bdg. $87.00
Studies in History and Jurisprudence. Essay Index Repr. Ser. Ayer 2 vols. repr. of 1901 ed. 1968 $44.00
Modern Democracies. 1921. Arden Lib. 2 vols. repr. of 1924 ed. 1983 lib. bdg. $85.00

BOOKS ABOUT BRYCE

Brooks, Robert C., ed. *Bryce's American Commonwealth: Fiftieth Anniversary.* Macmillan 1939 o.p.
Fisher, Herbert A. *James Bryce.* Greenwood 2 vols. repr. of 1927 ed. lib. bdg. $30.50

BURKE, EDMUND. 1729–1797

Edmund Burke, British statesman and political writer, is renowned for his theory of social order, his advocacy of conservative politics, and his sustained hostility to the French Revolution. He contrasted the French Revolution with social and political change in Great Britain, where he believed the existing order is peacefully altered when it conflicts with the extension of human freedom. "All government—indeed every human benefit and enjoyment, every virtue, and every prudent act," he said in his *Second Speech on Conciliation with America*, "is founded on compromise and barter."

BOOKS BY BURKE

Edmund Burke: A Philosophical Enquiry into the Origin of Our Ideas of the Sublime and Beautiful. 1757. Ed. by James T. Boulton, Univ. of Notre Dame Pr. 1968 pap. $8.95
Burke's Politics: Selected Writings and Speeches on Reform, Revolution, and War. Ed. by Ross J. S. Hoffman and Paul Levack, Knopf 1949 o.p.
Edmund Burke: Selected Prose. 1770. Ed. by Philip Magnus, Arden Lib. repr. of 1948 ed. 1979 lib. bdg. $10.00; Norwood repr. of 1948 ed. 1977 lib. bdg. $10.00

BOOKS ABOUT BURKE

Cameron, David. *The Social Thought of Rousseau and Burke: A Comparative Study.* Univ. of Toronto Pr. 1973 $25.00

Canavan, Francis P. *The Political Reason of Edmund Burke.* Duke Univ. Pr. 1960 o.p.

Cone, Carl B. *Burke and the Nature of Politics.* Univ. of Kentucky Pr. 2 vols. 1957–64 o.p.

Fasel, George. *Edmund Burke.* Twayne's Eng. Authors Ser. G. K. Hall 1983 lib. bdg. $13.50

Graubard, Stephen R. *Burke, Disraeli, and Churchill: The Politics of Perseverance.* Harvard Univ. Pr. 1961 o.p.

HOBBES, THOMAS. 1588–1679

Thomas Hobbes, English philosopher and political theorist, established—along with but independently of DESCARTES (see Vols. 4 and 5)—early modern modes of thought in reaction to the scholasticism that characterized the seventeenth century. His writings on psychology raised the possibility (later realized) that psychology could become a natural science, but his theory of politics is his most enduring achievement. In brief, his theory states that the problem of establishing order in society requires a sovereign, to whom men owe loyalty and who in turn has duties toward his subjects. His *Leviathan* is regarded as a major contribution to the theory of the state.

BOOKS BY HOBBES

The Elements of Law: Natural and Politic. 1640. Ed. by Ferdinand Tönnies, Biblio Dist. 2d ed. rev. 1969 $35.00

De Cive or the Citizen. 1642. Ed. by Sterling P. Lamprecht, Greenwood repr. of 1949 ed. 1982 lib. bdg. $28.25

Leviathan. 1651. Biblio Dist. (Everyman's) repr. of 1914 ed. 1976 $9.95; ed. by Herbert W. Schneider, Bobbs 2 pts. 1958 pap. $9.08; ed. by Michael Oakeshott, intro. by R. Peters, Macmillan (Collier Bks.) 1962 pap. $3.95; ed. by C. B. MacPherson, *Penguin Eng. Lib. Ser.* 1981 pap. $5.95

BOOKS ABOUT HOBBES

Bowle, John. *Hobbes and His Critics: A Study in Seventeenth Century Constitutionalism.* Biblio Dist. repr. of 1951 ed. 1969 $32.50

Gauthier, David P. *Logic of Leviathan: The Moral and Political Theory of Thomas Hobbes.* Oxford 1969 $12.95

Goldsmith, M. M. *The Political Philosophy of Hobbes: The Rationale of the Sovereign State.* Columbia Univ. Pr. 1966 o.p.

Hinnant, Charles H. *Thomas Hobbes: A Reference Guide.* G. K. Hall 1980 lib. bdg. $28.50

Strauss, Leo. *Political Philosophy of Hobbes: Its Basis and Its Genesis.* Trans. by Elsa M. Sinclair, Univ. of Chicago Pr. repr. 1984 pap. $7.00

Von Leyden, W. *Hobbes and Locke: The Politics of Freedom and Obligation.* St. Martin's 1982 $25.00

JEFFERSON, THOMAS. 1743–1826

Thomas Jefferson, the third president of the United States, was the premier philosopher of American democracy. His "Summary View of the

Rights of British America," written in 1774, was one of the earliest denials of the right of the British Parliament to legislate for the American colonies. He was the principal author of the Declaration of Independence, which is based on Locke's doctrine of the rights of man; this origin of the Declaration helped transform the first great colonial revolt of modern times into the first great democratic revolution. Jefferson wrote the Virginia Statute for Religious Freedom; he wrote a Bill for the More General Diffusion of Knowledge; as the nation's first secretary of state, he made important contributions to the law of nations and ordered the first census of the U.S. population; he conceived, planned, and designed, and supervised in every detail the founding and construction of the University of Virginia; and when the British burned Washington in the War of 1812, his personal library became the Library of Congress.

BOOKS BY JEFFERSON

The Complete Jefferson. Ed. by Saul K. Padover, *Select Bibliographies Repr. Ser.* Ayer repr. of 1943 ed. $56.00
The Portable Thomas Jefferson. Ed. by Merrill D. Peterson, Viking 1975 pap. $14.95
Thomas Jefferson: Selected Writings. Ed. by Harvey C. Mansfield, Jr., *Crofts Class. Ser.* Harlan Davidson text ed. 1979 pap. $3.95
Writings. Ed. by Merrill D. Peterson, Literary Class. (Lib. of Amer.) 1984 $30.00

BOOKS ABOUT JEFFERSON

Becker, Carl L. *The Declaration of Independence: A Study in the History of Political Ideas.* Peter Smith $13.00; Random (Vintage) 1958 pap. $4.95
Boorstin, Daniel J. *The Lost World of Thomas Jefferson.* Beacon 1960 pap. $4.95; Peter Smith $15.25; Univ. of Chicago Pr. 1981 pap. $10.95
Brodie, Fawn M. *Thomas Jefferson: An Intimate History.* Bantam repr. 1975 pap. $4.95; Norton 1974 $24.95
Malone, Dumas. *Jefferson and His Time.* Little, Brown 6 vols. 1948–81 ea. $19.45–$24.45 pap. ea. $9.70–$10.95
Padover, Saul K. *Jefferson.* Arden Lib. repr. of 1942 ed. 1982 lib bdg. $50.00
Peterson, Merrill D. *The Jefferson Image in the American Mind.* Oxford 1960 $27.50
———. *Thomas Jefferson and the New Nation: A Biography.* Oxford 1970 $39.95 pap. $15.95

KEY, V. O., JR. 1908–1963

V. O. Key, Jr., an American political scientist, played a central role in the behavioral movement within American political science; that is, the study not of how the political system is supposed to function, but of how politicians, civil servants, and voters actually behave. His pioneering text, *Politics, Parties, and Pressure Groups,* discusses the interest groups that contend for power, the roles of the party system and the electorate, the use of force and violence, the uses of pecuniary sanctions, and the role of education as a form of political control. His *Southern Politics* is based on both the analysis of local election returns and interviews with politicians and observers; in subsequent books, he pioneered in the use of survey research data in the study of politics.

BOOKS BY KEY

Politics, Parties, and Pressure Groups. 1942. Harper 5th ed. text ed. 1964 $15.95
Southern Politics in State and Nation. 1949. Intro. by Alexander Heard, Univ. of Tennessee Pr. 2d ed. text ed. 1984 $29.95 pap. $14.95
A Primer of Statistics for Political Scientists. Crowell 1954 o.p.
American State Politics: An Introduction. 1956. Greenwood repr. of 1965 ed. 1983 lib. bdg. $35.00
Public Opinion and American Democracy. Knopf 1961 o.p.
The Responsible Electorate: Rationality in Presidential Voting, 1936–1960. Ed. by Milton C. Cummings, Jr., Harvard Univ. Pr. 1966 o.p.

LASKI, HAROLD J. 1893–1950

Harold J. Laski, a British political scientist and Labor Party leader, taught history at Harvard University from 1916 to 1920, when he returned to England to teach at the London School of Economics and Political Science until his death. His name and the London School became almost synonymous terms in the minds of many, particularly students from the United States and from Asia and Africa, who learned from Laski the political knowledge necessary to overthrow their British rulers. He was a prolific writer and an active Socialist politician, as well as a sensitive commentator on British and U.S. political institutions. Oddly, the letters that he exchanged during a period of 19 years with his American friend Justice Oliver Wendell Holmes, published in two volumes in 1953, are read and appreciated more widely today than any of his books.

BOOKS BY LASKI

Authority in the Modern State. Shoe String (Archon) repr. of 1919 ed. 1968 $25.00
The Foundations of Sovereignty, and Other Essays. Essay Index Repr. Ser. Ayer repr. of 1921 ed. $18.00
A Grammar of Politics. 1925. Allen & Unwin 5th ed. text ed. 1967 pap. $18.95; Elliots Bks. 1925 $47.50
Liberty in the Modern State. 1930. Kelley rev. ed. repr. of 1949 ed. $15.00
Democracy in Crisis. AMS Pr. repr. of 1933 ed. $19.25
Reflections on the Revolution of Our Time. Biblio Dist. repr. of 1943 ed. 1968 $25.00
Reflections on the Constitution: The House of Commons, the Cabinet [and] the Civil Service. 1951. Manchester Univ. Pr. 1962 o.p.
(and Oliver W. Holmes). *Holmes-Laski Letters: The Correspondence of Mr. Justice Holmes and Harold J. Laski, 1916–1935.* Ed. by Mark DeWolfe Howe, fwd. by Felix Frankfurter, Harvard Univ. Pr. 2 vols. 1953 o.p.

BOOKS ABOUT LASKI

Deane, Herbert A. *The Political Ideas of Harold J. Laski.* Shoe String (Archon) repr. of 1955 ed. 1972 $25.00
Magid, Henry M. *English Political Pluralism: The Problem of Freedom and Organization.* AMS Pr. repr. of 1941 ed. $12.45
Martin, Kingsley. *Harold Laski, 1893–1950: A Biographical Memoir.* Viking 1953 o.p.

LASSWELL, HAROLD D. 1902–1978

Harold D. Lasswell was the wunderkind of American political science. Beginning in his twenties, he attempted through his writings to develop a theory about man and society that draws on and illuminates all the social sciences. When he enrolled in the University of Chicago at age 16 he had already read widely such writers as Kant and Freud. His doctoral dissertation was published in 1927 as *Propaganda Technique in the World War,* a major work in the development of communications research. He created a phrase that set the agenda for communications research for a generation: "Who says what to whom with what effect?" After World War II, he moved to Yale Law School, where he virtually created the field of law, science, and public policy, and introduced a generation of law students to the social sciences. He believed that the creation of what he called "the policy sciences" was his greatest achievement; the book by that title that he edited with Daniel Lerner in 1951 is widely read today.

BOOKS BY LASSWELL

Psychopathology and Politics. 1930. Intro. by Fred I. Greenstein, Univ. of Chicago Pr. repr. of 1960 ed. 1977 pap. $8.50
World Politics and Personal Insecurity. 1935. Macmillan (Free Pr.) 1965 pap. o.p.
Politics: Who Gets What, When, and How. 1936. Peter Smith $10.24
The Language of Politics: Studies in Quantitative Semantics. 1949. MIT 1965 pap. $4.95
(and Daniel Lerner). *The Policy Sciences: Recent Developments in Scope and Method.* 1951. Stanford Univ. Pr. 1968 o.p.
(and Bruce M. Russett and others). *World Handbook of Political and Social Indicators.* Yale Univ. Pr. 1964 o.p.

BOOK ABOUT LASSWELL

Rogow, Arnold A., ed. *Politics, Personality and Social Science in the Twentieth Century: Essays in Honor of Harold D. Lasswell.* Univ. of Chicago Pr. 1969 $27.50

LENIN (born VLADIMIR ILYICH ULYANOV). 1870–1924

[SEE Chapter 10 in this volume.]

LIPPMANN, WALTER. 1899–1974

Walter Lippmann, an American political journalist, dominated political journalism in the United States from World War I almost until his death. In his last year at Harvard College he was an assistant to the philosopher George Santayana; he read extensively in Freud; and he was in every sense an "intellectual" journalist. His *Public Opinion* became the intellectual anchor for the study of public opinion, and it is widely read today. He came close in this book to questioning whether citizens can possibly make rational, democratic decisions. The source of the difficulty is not man's irrationality but the inherent nature of the modern system of mass communication; information must be condensed into brief slogans. These slogans become stereotypes, a concept that Lippmann brilliantly analyzed prior to its acceptance by psychologists. As a political columnist, he wrote on many topics, particularly on foreign relations, and he held a position of prestige in Washington's press corps that has never been matched. Alastair Buchan wrote in 1974 that Walter Lippmann was "the name that opened every door."

BOOKS BY LIPPMANN

A Preface to Politics. 1913. Univ. of Michigan Pr. 1962 pap. o.p.
Public Opinion. 1922. Macmillan (Free Pr.) 1965 pap. $9.95
A Preface to Morals. 1929. Macmillan 1952 o.p.
The Cold War: A Study in U.S. Foreign Policy. Harper 1947 o.p.

BOOKS ABOUT LIPPMANN

Blum, D. Steven. *Walter Lippmann: Cosmopolitanism in the Century of Total War.* Cornell Univ. Pr. 1984 $19.95
Steel, Ronald. *Walter Lippmann and the American Century.* Little, Brown 1980 $22.50; Random (Vintage) 1981 pap $7.95

LOCKE, JOHN. 1632–1704

John Locke was an English philosopher whose influence today can hardly be overestimated. From the point of view of political science, his major work is *Two Treatises of Government,* which contains a loosely presented theory of government and an analysis of the relationship of the individual to the state. He stressed that the origin of the state is a mutual contract among men, and that a sovereign people may alter the terms of this social contract to meet changing conditions. Through his doctrine of the rights of man he was one of the intellectual fathers of the American and French revolutions. His philosophy was also influential in the thought of such persons as VOLTAIRE (see Vol. 4) and GEORGE BERKELEY (see Vol. 4). His psychology—what he called "human understanding"—is reflected in nineteenth- and twentieth-century psychological theory.

BOOKS BY LOCKE

The Works of John Locke. Adler's 10 vols. repr. of 1823 ed. $524.00
Two Treatises of Government. 1690. Intro. by W. S. Carpenter, Biblio Dist. (Everyman's) repr. of 1924 ed. 1975 $12.95; ed. by Peter Laslett, Cambridge Univ. Pr. 1960 $57.50; intro. by Thomas I. Cook, *Lib. of Class. Ser.* Hafner text ed. $9.95; intro. by Peter Laslett, New Amer. Lib. pap. $4.95
An Essay Concerning Human Understanding. 1690. Biblio Dist. (Everyman's) 1976 pap. $2.95; ed. by Alexander C. Fraser, Dover 2 vols. repr. of 1894 ed. pap. ea. $8.95; ed. by A. O. Woozley, New Amer. Lib. pap. $6.95; ed. by Peter H. Nidditch, Oxford 1975 $62.00; ed. by Alexander C. Fraser, Peter Smith 2 vols. $26.50

BOOKS ABOUT LOCKE

Aaron, Richard I. *John Locke.* Oxford 3d ed. 1971 $42.00
Cranston, Maurice. *John Locke: A Biography.* Ed. by J. P. Mayer, *European Political Thought Ser.* Ayer repr. of 1957 ed. 1979 lib. bdg. $34.50

MACHIAVELLI, NICCOLO. 1469–1527

Niccolò Machiavelli was an Italian political and military theorist, civil servant, historian, playwright, and poet who lived during the Golden Age of Florence, and whose major work, *The Prince*, is dedicated to Lorenzo de Medici, the ruler of Florence. In *The Prince* Machiavelli sought to discern an order in the nature of political activity itself, not in some external cause. He examined politics in a modern, detached, and rational manner, analyzing the ways power is gained and held. He demonstrated the soundness of certain political precepts by using a kind of calculus to test them. Precisely because of the objectivity of his descriptions of the political process and of how power is obtained and held, Machiavelli is often thought of as a kind of evil adviser of princes, and Machiavellianism has come to mean a political doctrine that denies the relevance of morality in political affairs and holds that craft and deceit are justified in pursuing and maintaining political power; that is, opportunism is all. But these precepts do not describe Machiavelli as a person. He described the corrupt state of Florence, but he was not corrupt himself. He was critical of the popes and their political activities, but he was born and died a Christian. He is controversial to this day, but he is viewed by many as a forerunner of the Enlightenment and as the first modern political scientist.

Books by Machiavelli

The Art of War. 1521. Trans. by Peter Whitehorne, AMS Pr. repr. of 1560 ed. $45.00; trans. by Ellis Farneworth; intro. by N. Wood, Bobbs rev. ed. 1965 pap. $6.95.

The Prince. 1532. Ed. by Daniel Donno, *Bantam Class. Ser.* 1981 pap. $1.75; Biblio Dist. (Everyman's) repr. of 1908 ed. 1978 $9.95; ed. by James Atkinson, Bobbs 1976 pap. $13.92; trans. by Thomas G. Bergin, *Crofts Class. Ser.* Harlan Davidson text ed. 1947 pap. $3.25; New Amer. Lib. 1952 pap. $1.50; trans. by Robert M. Adams, Norton 1977 $19.95 pap. $4.95; trans. by Mark Musa, *World's Class. Pap. Ser.* Oxford 1984 pap. $2.95; trans. by George Bull, *Penguin Class. Ser.* 1961 $2.25; ed. by Mark Musa, St. Martin's 1969 pap. $9.95; trans. by Leo P. de Alvarez, Univ. of Dallas Pr. 1984 $6.95; intro. by L. G. Crocker, Washington Square Pr. pap. $1.95

The Discourses. 1532. Ed. by Bernard Crick, *Penguin Class. Ser.* 1984 pap. $4.95; trans. by Leslie J. Walker, Routledge & Kegan 2 vols. 1975 $45.00

The Portable Machiavelli. Ed. by Peter Bondanella and Mark Musa, Viking 1979 $14.95

Books about Machiavelli

Christie, Richard, and others. *Studies in Machiavellianism. Social Psychology Ser.* Academic Pr. 1970 $60.00

Mansfield, Harvey C., Jr. *Machiavelli's New Modes and Orders: A Study of the "Discourses on Livy."* Cornell Univ. Pr. 1979 $39.50

Pitkin, Hanna F. *Fortune Is a Woman: Gender and Politics in the Thought of Niccolò Machiavelli.* Univ. of California Pr. 1984 $24.95

Ridolfi, Roberto. *The Life of Niccolò Machiavelli.* 1954. Univ. of Chicago Pr. 1963 o.p.

Strauss, Leo. *Thoughts on Machiavelli.* Univ. of Chicago Pr. repr. text ed. 1984 pap. $13.00

MERRIAM, CHARLES E. 1874–1963

Charles E. Merriam, an American political scientist, spent most of his career at the University of Chicago. According to his biographer, Barry D. Karl, Merriam was determined to retain for America in the twentieth century the vision that ALEXIS DE TOCQUEVILLE had had for it in the nineteenth: that the political course of Western society was set toward more democratic government and America could lead the way. He was also dedicated to interdisciplinary research, and he was among the major founders of the Social Science Research Council in 1923. He was a member of the presidential committee that produced the monumental *Recent Social Trends in the United States* in 1933; during the Roosevelt administration, he was a member of a number of influential committees and boards; and in countless other ways he sought to combine his vision for American democracy with his commitment to scientific research.

BOOKS BY MERRIAM

The History of American Political Theories. Repr. in Government and Political Science Ser. Gordon $59.95; intro. by R. E. Merriam, Johnson Repr. repr. of 1920 ed. 1968 $22.00; Kelley repr. of 1903 ed. $35.00; Russell repr. of 1903 ed. 1968 $9.50
(and Louise Overacker). *Primary Elections: A Study of the History and Tendencies of Primary Election Legislation.* 1908. Univ. of Chicago Pr. rev. ed. 1928 o.p.
(and Harold F. Gosnell). *Non-Voting: Causes and Methods of Control.* Univ. of Chicago Pr. 1924 o.p.
Political Power: Its Composition and Incidence. McGraw-Hill 1934 o.p.

BOOKS ABOUT MERRIAM

Karl, Barry D. *Charles E. Merriam and the Study of Politics.* Univ. of Chicago Pr. 1975 $26.00
White, Leonard, ed. *The Future of Government in the United States: Essays in Honor of Charles E. Merriam.* Univ. of Chicago Pr. 1942 o.p.

MILL, JOHN STUART. 1806–1873

[SEE the Economics section in this chapter.]

MONTESQUIEU, CHARLES DE SECONDAT, BARON DE LA BREDE ET DE. 1689–1755

Charles de Secondat, Baron de la Brède et de Montesquieu, French philosopher and political theorist, is viewed variously as the most important precursor of sociology, as the father of modern historical research, and as the first modern political scientist. In *The Persian Letters*, which was an immediate publishing success, he depicted France as seen by two imaginary Persians, and thus demonstrated the possibility for objectivity that he demonstrated 27 years later in *The Spirit of the Laws*, his masterpiece. On the surface, *The Spirit* is a treatise on law, but it also describes every domain affecting human behavior and it raises questions of philosophical judgment about the merits of various kinds of legislation. It describes three types of government and their principles: virtue is the principle of republics, honor of monarchies, and fear of despotism. With these "ideal types" as starting points, he proceeded to analyze legislation and the state in great detail. He made comparison the central method of his political science and he thus directed the focus of inquiry from Europe to all societies in the world. His direct influence on the social sciences has been profound.

BOOKS BY MONTESQUIEU

The Persian Letters. 1721. Garland 2 pts. lib. bdg. ea. $61.00; trans. by George R. Healy, Irvington 1964 $27.50; trans. by C. J. Betts, *Penguin Class. Ser.* 1973 pap. $5.95
The Spirit of the Laws. 1748. Univ. of California Pr. text ed. pap. $9.95

BOOKS ABOUT MONTESQUIEU

Richter, M., ed. *The Political Theory of Montesquieu.* Cambridge Univ. Pr. 1977 $44.50 pap. $12.95
Shackleton, Robert. *Montesquieu: A Critical Biography.* Ed. by David W. Carrithers, Oxford 1961 $29.95

PLATO. 427–347 B.C.

Plato has been described as the founder of political theory and sociology and as the greatest thinker of all time. The facts of his life are disputed by scholars, and most of his books are in the form of Socratic dialogues, in which SOCRATES (see Vol. 4) is the main speaker and the superior intellect. It was the tragic death of Socrates that seems to have turned his student Plato into an author. Much of Plato's political diagnosis is concerned with the causes of political degeneration, in the Greek city-states, from hereditary kingship, the rule of one, to aristocracy, the rule of the few, to democracy, the rule of the many. In *The Republic,* democracy is shown to lead only too easily to a final stage of decay: the rule of the ruthless demagogue who makes himself the tyrant of the city. Plato's solution to this cycle—his political program—is to arrest all social change, to return to the patriarchic state. Fundamentally, many scholars believe, Plato's political philosophy is authoritarian and hostile to democratic ideas. This conclusion is hotly debated today, but all scholars agree that his influence has been immeasurable. As Karl R. Popper, a scholar critical of Plato, has asserted: "Western thought, one might say, has been either Platonic or anti-Platonic, but hardly ever non-Platonic." (See also Volume 4.)

BOOKS BY PLATO

The Laws. History of Ideas in Ancient Greece Ser. Ayer repr. of 1921 ed. 1976 $97.50; trans. by Thomas L. Pangle, Basic Bks. 1979 $26.50 pap. $11.95; *Loeb Class. Lib.* Harvard Univ. Pr. 2 vols. ea. $12.50; trans. by T. J. Saunders, *Penguin Class. Ser.* 1970 pap. $4.95
The Republic. Basic Bks. text ed. 1968 pap. $8.95; trans. by A. D. Lindsay, Biblio Dist. (Everyman's) 1980 pap. $5.95; ed. by James Adam, Cambridge Univ. Pr. 2 vols. text ed. ea. $62.50–$69.50; trans. by A. D. Lindsay, Dutton 1957 pap. $6.75; trans. by G. M. Grube, Hackett 1973 $12.50 text ed. pap. $4.95; trans. by Raymond Larson, *Crofts Class. Ser.* Harlan Davidson text ed. 1979 $14.95 pap. $6.95; *Loeb Class. Lib.* Harvard Univ. Pr. 2 vols. ea. $12.50; trans. by Benjamin Jowett,

Modern Lib. 1982 $7.95; trans. by Francis M. Cornford, Oxford 1945 pap. $4.95; trans. by H. D. Lee, *Penguin Class. Ser.* 1955 pap. $3.50; trans. by Benjamin Jowett, Random 1955 pap. $3.95

BOOKS ABOUT PLATO

Crossman, R. S. *Plato Today.* Ed. by E. B. England, Allen & Unwin 1963 pap. $3.95
Koyre, Alexandre. *Discovering Plato.* Trans. by Leonora C. Rosenfeld, Columbia Univ. Pr. 1960 pap. $2.45
Popper, Karl R. *The Open Society and Its Enemies.* Princeton Univ. Pr. 2 vols. 5th ed. rev. 1966 vol. 1 $32.00 pap. $9.95; vol. 2 $36.00 pap. $9.95
Strauss, Leo. *The Argument and the Action of Plato's Laws.* Fwd. by Joseph Cropsey, Univ. of Chicago Pr. 1983 pap. $9.00
Wilson, John F. *The Politics of Moderation: An Interpretation of Plato's "Republic."* Univ. Pr. of Amer. 1984 lib. bdg. $22.00 text ed. pap. $12.00

ROUSSEAU, JEAN JACQUES. 1712–1778

Jean Jacques Rousseau was a Swiss philosopher and political theorist who lived much of his life in France. Many reference books describe him as French, but he generally added "Citizen of Geneva" whenever he signed his name. He presented his theory of education in *Emile,* a novel, the first book to have linked the science of education to the scientific understanding of the child; Rousseau is thus regarded as the precursor if not the founder of child psychology. "The greatest good is not authority, but liberty," he wrote, and in *The Social Contract* Rousseau moved from a study of the individual to an analysis of the relationship of the individual to the state: "The art of politics consists of making each citizen extremely dependent upon the polis in order to free him from dependence upon other citizens." This doctrine of sovereignty, the absolute supremacy of the state over its members, has led many to accuse Rousseau of opening the doors to despotism, collectivism, and totalitarianism. Others say that this is the opposite of Rousseau's intent, that the surrender of rights is only apparent, and that in the end individuals retain the rights that they appear to have given up. In effect, these Rousseau supporters say, the social contract is designed to secure or to restore to individuals in the state of civilization the equivalent of the rights they enjoyed in the state of nature. Rousseau was a passionate man who lived in passionate times, and he stirs passion in those who write about him today.

BOOKS BY ROUSSEAU

Emile. 1762. Trans. by Allan Bloom, Basic Bks. 1979 pap. $10.95; Biblio Dist. (Everyman's) repr. of 1911 ed. 1972 $9.95 pap. $3.75; *Documentation Thematique* Larousse 2 vols. pap. ea. $2.95
The Social Contract. 1762. Darby repr. of 1893 ed. 1980 lib. bdg. $30.00; ed. by Charles Frankell, *Lib. of Class. Ser.* Hafner text ed. 1954 pap. $6.95; ed. by Charles M. Sheroner, New Amer. Lib. 1974 pap. $3.95; trans. by Maurice Cranston, *Penguin Class. Ser.* 1968 pap. $2.95; trans. by Kendall Willmore, Regnery-Gateway 1954 pap. $4.95
The Confessions of Jean Jacques Rousseau. Trans. by John M. Cohen, *Penguin Class. Ser.* 1953 pap. $5.95

BOOKS ABOUT ROUSSEAU

Chapman, John W. *Rousseau: Totalitarian or Liberal.* AMS Pr. 1956 $16.50

Durkheim, Emile. *Montesquieu and Rousseau: Forerunners of Sociology.* Fwd. by H. Peyre, Univ. of Michigan Pr. 1960 pap. $7.95

Masters, Roger D. *The Political Philosophy of Rousseau.* Princeton Univ. Pr. 1976 $44.00 pap. $10.95

Miller, James. *Rousseau: Dreamer of Democracy.* Yale Univ. Pr. 1984 $25.00

PSYCHOLOGY

The social sciences are all concerned with the interaction of individuals; of them all, only psychology focuses most of its attention on the individual person. Usually it is the person as he or she observes others or reacts to others or fears others, but there are some topics in physiological psychology—skin sensations and vision, for example—in which the individual is studied almost—but not quite—as if he or she did not belong to a family, a group, or a particular society. "Social psychology" focuses on the overlap between psychology and sociology; it studies the individual as a member of a social group, and groups as influenced by the individual personality traits of their members. "Physiological psychology" studies the role of various organs in the body in different psychological phenomena (the role of the brain in memory, for example). "Applied psychology" studies ways in which psychology can solve problems; one of its branches, engineering psychology, is largely focused on the man-machine relationship, and how productivity can be improved through better training and better machines. "Clinical psychology" and "counseling psychology" are concerned with the mental health or the happiness of individuals. Because many psychologists work in applied and clinical settings, there are many more psychologists in the United States than there are other social scientists. (For listings on clinical psychology and psychiatry, see Chapter 16 in Volume 5.)

History of the Field

Boring, Edwin G. *A History of Experimental Psychology.* Prentice-Hall 2d ed. 1950 $40.95

——, ed. *A History of Psychology in Autobiography.* Ed. by Gardner Lindzey, *Century Psychology Ser.* Irvington 1967 vol. 5 $34.50 text ed. pap. $18.95; Russell repr. of 1952 ed. 1968 vol. 4 $15.00

Foucault, Michel. *Madness and Civilization: A History of Insanity in the Age of Reason.* Random (Vintage) 1973 pap. $4.95

MacLeod, Robert B. *The Persistent Problems in Psychology.* Duquesne Univ. Pr. text ed. 1975 pap. $8.00

Miller, George A., and Robert Buckhout. *Psychology: The Science of Mental Life.* Harper 2d ed. text ed. 1973 $19.50

Murphy, Gardner, and Joseph K. Kovach. *Historical Introduction to Modern Psychology.* Harcourt 3d ed. text ed. 1972 $25.95

Rieber, R. W., and Kurt Salzinger, eds. *The Roots of American Psychology: Historical Influences and Implications for the Future.* New York Academy of Sciences 1977 $22.00

Smith, Samuel. *Ideas of the Great Psychologists.* Harper 1983 $15.34 pap. $6.68
Watson, Robert I. *Basic Writings in the History of Psychology.* Oxford text ed. 1979
$24.95 pap. $14.95
————. *The Great Psychologists from Aristotle to Freud.* Harper 4th ed. text ed. 1978
pap. $19.95

Surveys of the Field

Annual Review of Psychology. Annual Reviews text ed. 1974–83 vols. 25–36 ea.
$20.00–$27.00
Deutsch, Morton. *Theories in Social Psychology.* Fwd. by Edwin G. Boring, Basic Bks.
text ed. 1965 $12.95
Flanagan, Owen J., Jr. *The Science of the Mind.* MIT text ed. 1984 $25.00 pap. $12.50
Hampden-Turner, Charles. *Maps of the Mind.* Macmillan (Collier Bks.) 1982 pap.
$9.95
Kagan, Jerome, and Julius Segal. *Psychology: An Introduction.* Harcourt 5th ed. 1984
$24.95
Rosenberg, Morris, and Ralph H. Turner. *Social Psychology: Sociological Perspectives.* Basic Bks. text ed. 1981 $30.00 pap. $17.95. This text, by two sociologists,
should be compared with a text by a psychologist, such as Morton Deutsch's
Theories in Social Psychology. Both are sound texts, but the emphasis is different.

Methods of Research

Allport, Gordon W. *The Use of Personal Documents in Psychological Science.* Kraus
repr. of 1942 ed. pap. $4.50. (See Allport's main listing in this section.)
Bakan, David. *On Method: Toward a Reconstruction of Psychological Investigation. Social and Behavioral Sciences Ser.* Jossey-Bass 1967 $19.95
Bornstein, Marc H., ed. *Comparative Methods in Psychology. Crosscurrents in Contemporary Psychology Ser.* Erlbaum text ed. 1980 $29.95
Christensen, Larry B. *Experimental Methodology.* Allyn & Bacon 3d ed. text ed. 1984
$26.27
Weaver, Donald B., and others. *How to Do a Literature Search in Psychology.* Resource Pr. text ed. 1982 pap. $7.25

Reference Books

Chaplin, J. P. *Dictionary of Psychology.* Dell 3d ed. rev. 1985 pap. $5.95
Lindzey, Gardner, and Elliot Aronson, eds. *The Handbook of Social Psychology.* Erlbaum 2 vols. text ed. 1985 ea. $55.00–$65.00
Statt, David. *Dictionary of Psychology.* Harper 1982 pap. $5.29
Wolman, Benjamin B., ed. *Dictionary of Behavioral Science.* Van Nostrand 1973
$24.50

Aggression

Berkowitz, Leonard. *Aggression: A Social Psychological Analysis.* McGraw-Hill 1962
o.p.
Dollard, John, and Robert R. Sears. *Frustration and Aggression.* Greenwood repr. of
1939 ed. 1980 lib. bdg. $27.50. (See Dollard's main listing in this section.)

Lorenz, Konrad. *On Aggression.* 1963. Trans. by Marjorie K. Wilson, Harcourt 1966 $9.50 1974 pap. $7.95. (See Lorenz's main listing in this section.)

Milavsky, J. Ronald. *Television and Aggression: Results of a Panel Study. Quantitative Studies in Social Relations Ser.* Academic Pr. 1982 $34.50

Montagu, Ashley. *Man and Aggression.* Oxford 2d ed. 1973 pap. $7.95

Scott, John P. *Aggression.* Univ. of Chicago Pr. (Phoenix Bks.) 2d ed. rev. 1976 pap. $4.95

Biological Bases of Behavior

Aronson, Elliot. *The Social Animal.* Freeman 4th ed. text ed. 1984 $20.95 pap. $12.95; Viking 1972 $7.95

Caplan, David, ed. *Biological Studies of Mental Processes.* MIT 1980 $35.00 text ed. pap. $10.95

Darwin, Charles R. *The Expression of the Emotions in Man and Animals.* AMS Pr. repr. of 1897 ed. $42.50; Greenwood repr. 1955 lib. bdg. $22.50; intro. by S. J. Rachman, *Classics in Psychology and Psychiatry Ser.* Pinter repr. of 1872 ed. 1979 $20.00; Richard West repr. of 1873 ed. $35.00; intro. by Konrad Lorenz, Univ. of Chicago Pr. (Phoenix Bks.) 1965 pap. $9.00

Lorenz, Konrad. *Evolution and Modification of Behavior.* 1961. Univ. of Chicago Pr. (Phoenix Bks.) 1967 pap. $2.75

———. *King Solomon's Ring.* 1952. *Apollo Eds.* Crowell pap. $3.95; fwd. by Julian Huxley, Harper 1979 pap. $5.95; New Amer. Lib. (Signet) pap. $2.95

Nebylitsyn, V. D., and J. A. Gray, eds. *Biological Bases of Individual Behavior.* Academic Pr. 1972 $74.50

Prothro, Edwin T., and P. T. Teska. *Psychology: A Biosocial Study of Behavior.* Greenwood repr. of 1950 ed. 1972 lib. bdg. $32.50

Selye, Hans. *The Stress of My Life: A Scientist's Memoirs. McGraw-Hill Pap.* 2d ed. 1978 pap. $6.95; Van Nostrand 2d ed. text ed. 1979 $12.95

Tinbergen, Nikolaas. *The Study of Instinct.* Folcroft 1951 lib. bdg. $20.00; Oxford 1969 pap. $5.95. (See Tinbergen's main listing in this section.)

Wilson, Edward O. *Sociobiology: The New Synthesis.* Harvard Univ. Pr. 1975 $35.00. A rather controversial book by a biologist. Social scientists believe that he oversimplifies the relationship between biology and behavior.

Cognition

Anderson, J. R., and G. H. Bower. *Human Associative Memory.* Erlbaum 1980 $19.95

Bever, Thomas, and others, eds. *Talking Minds: The Study of Language in Cognitive Sciences.* MIT 1982 $19.95

Cole, Michael, and Barbara Means. *Comparative Studies of How People Think: An Introduction.* Harvard Univ. Pr. text ed. 1981 $16.50

Festinger, Leon. *A Theory of Cognitive Dissonance.* Stanford Univ. Pr. 1957 $25.00 pap. $7.95

Izard, Carroll E. *Emotions, Cognition, and Behaviour.* Cambridge Univ. Pr. 1984 $54.50

Luria, A. R. *Cognitive Development.* Harvard Univ. Pr. 1976 $15.00 pap. $4.95

Roloff, Michael E., and Charles R. Berger. *Social Cognition and Communication.* Sage 1982 $29.95 pap. $14.95

Groups

Argyle, Michael. *The Psychology of Interpersonal Behavior.* Penguin (Pelican) rev. ed. 1985 pap. $5.95

Bales, Robert F. *Interaction Process Analysis. Midway Repr. Ser.* Univ. of Chicago Pr. 1951 pap. $10.00

Bales, Robert F., and others. *Symlog: A System for the Multiple Level Observation of Groups.* Macmillan (Free Pr.) 1979 $29.95

Cartwright, Dorwin, and Alvin Zander, eds. *Group Dynamics: Research and Theory.* Harper 3d ed. text ed. 1968 $26.50

Hare, A. Paul. *Handbook of Small Group Research.* Macmillan (Free Pr.) 2d ed. 1976 $34.95

Homans, George C. *The Human Group.* Harcourt text ed. 1950 $23.95

———. *Social Behavior: Its Elementary Forms.* Harcourt rev. ed. text ed. 1974 $18.95

Mills, Theodore M. *The Sociology of Small Groups.* Prentice-Hall 2d ed. 1984 $16.95 pap. $12.95

Roethlisberger, F. J., and William J. Dickson. *Management and the Worker: An Account of a Research Program Conducted by Western Electric Co.* Harvard Business 1939 $35.00. This study, which found that experimentally changing working conditions had less impact on productivity than the mere fact of being studied and thus "paid attention to" (the so-called Hawthorne effect), had an enormous impact on the social sciences, virtually creating what is called the "human relations in industry" research tradition.

Whyte, William F. *Street Corner Society: The Social Structure of an Italian Slum.* 1943. Univ. of Chicago Pr. 3d ed. 1981 lib. bdg. $23.00 text ed. pap. $7.00

Zander, Alvin. *Groups at Work: Unresolved Issues in the Study of Organizations. Social and Behavioral Sciences Ser.* Jossey-Bass text ed. 1977 $19.95

Individual Development

Baltes, Paul B., and K. Warner Schaie, eds. *Life-Span Developmental Psychology: Personality and Socialization.* Academic Pr. 1973 $39.50

Blos, Peter. *On Adolescence: A Psychoanalytic Interpretation.* Macmillan (Free Pr.) 1962 $18.95 pap. $9.95

Bower, T. G. *Development in Infancy.* Freeman 2d ed. text ed. 1982 $27.95 pap. $13.95

Brim, Orville G., Jr., and Jerome Kagan, eds. *Constancy and Change in Human Development.* Harvard Univ. Pr. 1980 $35.00

Elder, Glen H., Jr., ed. *Life Course Dynamics: Trajectories and Transitions, 1968– 1980.* Cornell Univ. Pr. text ed. 1985 $37.50 pap. $17.95

Erikson, Erik H. *Childhood and Society.* 1950. Norton 1964 pap. $3.95. (See Erikson's main listing in this section.)

———. *Identity and the Life Cycle.* 1959. Norton 1980 $14.95 pap. $4.95

Hall, G. Stanley. *Adolescence: Its Psychology and Its Relations to Physiology, Anthropology, Sociology, Sex, Crime, Religion and Education.* Telegraph Bks. 2 vols. repr. of 1905 ed. 1981 lib. bdg. $125.00. (See Hall's main listing in this section.)

Hareven, Tamara K., ed. *Transitions: The Family and the Life Course in Historical Perspectives. Studies in Social Discontinuity Ser.* Academic Pr. 1978 $39.50

Horowitz, Francis D., ed. *Review of Child Development Research.* Univ. of Chicago Pr. 1975 vol. 4 $25.00

Kagan, Jerome, and Moss Howard. *From Birth to Maturity*. Yale Univ. Pr. text ed. 1983 $27.50 pap. $8.95

Kegan, Robert. *The Evolving Self: Problem and Process in Human Development*. Harvard Univ. Pr. text ed. 1982 $25.00 1983 pap. $7.95

Lerner, Richard M., ed. *Developmental Psychology: Historical and Philosophical Perspectives*. Erlbaum text ed. 1983 $29.95

Maccoby, Eleanor E., ed. *The Development of Sex Differences*. Stanford Univ. Pr. 1966 $27.50 pap. $8.95

Mead, Margaret. *Coming of Age in Samoa*. 1928. Morrow 1971 pap. $6.95; Peter Smith $18.00

Mussen, P. H. *Carmichael's Manual of Child Psychology*. Wiley 2 vols. 3d ed. 1970 $150.50

Piaget, Jean. *The Language and Thought of the Child*. 1923. Humanities Pr. 3d ed. text ed. 1962 $18.00; New Amer. Lib. 1955 pap. $7.95. (See Piaget's main listing in this section.)

——. *The Moral Judgment of the Child*. Macmillan (Free Pr.) 1932 $15.95 text ed. pap. $14.95

Intelligence and Artificial Intelligence

Binet, Alfred. *The Psychology of Reasoning*. 1896. Routledge & Kegan 1901 o.p. (See Binet's main listing in this section.)

Block, N. J., and Gerald Dworkin, eds. *The IQ Controversy*. Pantheon 1976 pap. $8.95

Boden, Margaret. *Artificial Intelligence and Natural Man*. Basic Bks. 1981 pap. $15.95

Cancro, Robert, ed. *Intelligence: Genetic and Environmental Influences*. Grune 1971 $49.50

Gardner, Howard. *Frames of Mind: The Theory of Multiple Intelligences*. Basic Bks. 1983 $23.50 1985 pap. $11.95

Gould, Stephen J. *The Mismeasurement of Man*. Norton 1981 $14.95 1983 pap. $5.95

Guilford, Joy P. *The Nature of Human Intelligence*. Psychology Ser. McGraw-Hill 1967 text ed. o.p.

Jensen, Arthur R. *Bias in Mental Testing*. Macmillan (Free Pr.) 1980 $29.95

Klineberg, Otto. *Race Differences*. Greenwood repr. of 1935 ed. 1974 lib. bdg. $22.50; Norwood repr. of 1935 ed. $40.00. (See Klineberg's main listing in this section.)

Loehlin, John C., and J. N. Spuhler. *Race Differences in Intelligence*. Psychology Ser. Freeman text ed. 1975 $30.95 pap. $14.95

Schank, Roger C., and Peter G. Childers. *The Cognitive Computer: On Language, Learning and Artificial Intelligence*. Addison-Wesley 1984 $17.95

Simon, Herbert A. *Sciences of the Artificial*. MIT 2d ed. text ed. 1981 $22.50 pap. $6.95

Learning and Motivation

Arnold, William J., and Monte M. Page, eds. *Nebraska Symposium on Motivation*. Univ. of Nebraska Pr. 3 vols. 1968–76 ea. $25.50–$37.50 pap. ea. $6.50–$11.95

Atkinson, John W. *An Introduction to Motivation*. Van Nostrand 2d ed. text ed. 1978 $16.95

Bandura, Albert, and R. H. Walters. *Social Learning and Personality Development*. Holt 1963 text ed. $12.95

Bower, Gordon H., and Ernest J. Hilgard. *Theories of Learning*. Prentice-Hall 5th ed. text ed. 1981 o.p.

Bruner, Jerome S. *On Knowing: Essays for the Left Hand.* Harvard Univ. Pr. (Belknap Pr.) expanded ed. 1979 $10.00 pap. $4.95

Estes, William K., ed. *Models of Learning, Memory and Choice: Selected Papers.* Praeger 1982 $33.95

Gagné, Robert M. *The Conditions of Learning.* Holt 3d ed. text ed. 1977 o.p.

McClelland, David C., and others. *The Achievement Motive. Century Psychology Ser.* Halsted Pr. 1976 $14.95; Irvington 1985 $22.50 pap. $14.95

————. *The Achieving Society. Social Relations Ser.* Halsted Pr. 1976 $17.95; Irvington 1976 $47.50

Milgram, Stanley. *Obedience to Authority: An Experimental View.* Harper 1956 $12.95 1975 pap. $6.95

Miller, Neal E., and John Dollard. *Social Learning and Imitation.* Greenwood repr. of 1962 ed. 1979 lib. bdg. $24.75

Pavlov, Ivan P. *Conditioned Reflexes: An Investigation of the Physiological Activity of the Cerebral Cortex.* Ed. by G. V. Anrep, Dover repr. of 1927 ed. text ed. pap. $6.00; ed. by G. V. Anrep, Peter Smith $14.50. (See Pavlov's main listing in this section.)

Piaget, Jean. *Play, Dreams and Imitation in Childhood.* 1946. *Norton Lib.* 1962 pap. $7.95

Skinner, B. F. *The Behavior of Organisms: Experimental Analysis.* 1938. Prentice-Hall 1966 $27.95. (See Skinner's main listing in this section.)

Spence, Kenneth W., ed. *The Psychology of Learning and Motivation: Advances in Research and Theory.* Academic Pr. 14 vols. 1967–80. ea. $49.50–$63.50

Tarde, Gabriel. *The Laws of Imitation.* Peter Smith $13.25

Watson, John B. *Behaviorism.* 1925. *Norton Lib.* repr. of 1930 ed. 1970 pap. $6.95. (See Watson's main listing in this section.)

Wilson, Edward O. *Sociobiology: The New Synthesis.* Harvard Univ. Pr. 1975 $35.00

Opinions, Attitudes, and Beliefs

[SEE ALSO Political Science, Public Opinion, in this chapter.]

Allport, Gordon W. *The Nature of Prejudice.* 1954. Anti-Defamation League repr. pap. $5.95; pref. by Thomas Pettigrew, Addison-Wesley 1979 $7.64 pap $5.95

Allport, Gordon W., and Leo Postman. *The Psychology of Rumor.* Russell repr. of 1947 ed. 1965 $20.00

Hovland, Carl I., and Harold H. Kelley. *Communication and Persuasion: Psychological Studies of Opinion Change.* Greenwood repr. of 1953 ed. 1982 lib. bdg. $32.50; Yale Univ. Pr. 1953 $19.50

Lewin, Kurt. *Resolving Social Conflicts.* Ed. by Gertrude W. Lewin, International Specialized Bk. 1978 pap. $4.50. (See Lewin's main listing in this section.)

Perception

Arnheim, Rudolf. *Art and Visual Perception: A Psychology of the Creative Eye—The New Version.* Univ. of California Pr. 2d ed. rev. & enl. 1974 $28.50 pap. $10.95

Carterette, Edward C., and Morton P. Friedman, eds. *Handbook of Perception.* Academic Pr. 10 vols. 1974–78 ea. $50.00–$60.00

Gibson, James J. *The Senses Considered as Perceptual Systems.* Greenwood repr. of 1966 ed. 1983 lib. bdg. $55.00; Houghton Mifflin text ed. 1966 $34.50; Waveland Pr. repr. of 1966 ed. text ed. 1983 pap. $15.95

Koffka, Kurt. *Principles of Gestalt Psychology.* Harcourt 1967 o.p.

Kohler, Wolfgang. *Gestalt Psychology*. 1929. Liveright 1970 pap. $5.94; New Amer. Lib. (Meridian) 1980 pap. $4.95

Marks, Lawrence E. *Sensory Processes: The New Psychophysics*. Academic Pr. 1974 $48.00

Rock, Irvin. *The Logic of Perception*. MIT text ed. 1985 pap. $10.95

Personality

Abramson, Jeffrey. *Liberation and Its Limits: The Moral and Political Thought of Freud*. Macmillan 1984 $14.95

Adorno, T. W., and others. *The Authoritarian Personality*. Fwd. by Max Horkheimer and S. H. Flowerman, *Norton Lib.* repr. of 1950 ed. 1969 pap. $9.95

Allport, Gordon W. *Personality: A Psychological Interpretation*. Holt 1937 o.p.

———. *Personality and Social Encounter: Selected Essays*. Univ. of Chicago Pr. repr. of 1960 ed. text ed. 1981 pap. $17.00

Grunbaum, Adolf. *The Foundations of Psychoanalysis: A Philosophical Critique*. Univ. of California Pr. 1984 $16.95

Hall, Calvin S. *A Primer of Freudian Psychology*. New Amer. Lib. 1979 pap. $2.50; Octagon repr. of 1954 ed. 1978 lib. bdg. $18.00

Lasswell, Harold D. *Power and Personality*. Greenwood repr. of 1948 ed. 1976 lib. bdg. $20.25

Laufer, William S., and James M. Day, eds. *Personality Theory, Moral Development, and Criminal Behavior*. Lexington Bks. 1983 $33.00

Lindzey, Gardner, and Martin Manosevitz, eds. *Theories of Personality: Primary Sources and Research*. Wiley 2d ed. text ed. 1973 pap. $29.45

Murray, H. A. *Explorations in Personality*. Wiley 1938 pap. $6.50

Rieff, Philip. *Freud: The Mind of the Moralist*. Univ. of Chicago Pr. (Phoenix Bks.) 3d ed. 1979 pap. $13.00

Shakow, David, and David Rapaport. *The Influence of Freud on American Psychology. Psychological Issues Monographs* International Univ. Pr. text ed. 1964 $22.50 pap. $17.50

ALLPORT, GORDON W. 1897–1967

Gordon W. Allport, an American psychologist, was the chief founder of the psychological study of personality. For most of his career he taught at Harvard University; he was the informal dean of American psychology during his lifetime. His research on attitudes, values, religion, and prejudice, as well as his extensive writings on what he called an "open system" of personality, are extensively quoted in the contemporary literature of psychology.

BOOKS BY ALLPORT

Personality: A Psychological Interpretation. Holt 1937 o.p.

The Use of Personal Documents in Psychological Science. Kraus repr. of 1942 ed. pap. $4.50

(and Leo Postman). *The Psychology of Rumor*. Russell repr. of 1947 ed. 1965 $20.00

The Nature of Prejudice. 1954. Anti-Defamation League repr. pap. $5.95; pref. by Thomas Pettigrew, Addison-Wesley 1979 $7.64 pap. $5.95

Personality and Social Encounter: Selected Essays. Univ. of Chicago Pr. repr. of 1960 ed. text ed. 1981 pap. $17.00

BOOKS ABOUT ALLPORT

Evans, Richard I. *Dialogue with Gordon Allport.* Praeger 1981 $31.95
——. *Gordon Allport: The Man and His Ideas.* Intro. by Thomas Pettigrew, Dutton
    1971 pap. $1.95
Lindzey, Gardner, ed. *A History of Psychology in Autobiography.* Freeman text ed.
    1980 vol. 7 $34.95 pap. $19.95; Prentice-Hall repr. text ed. 1974 vol. 6 $21.95

BINET, ALFRED. 1857–1911

Alfred Binet, a French psychologist, was a participant in the origins of scientific psychology in France. He initially worked on pathological psychology, which was the major psychological specialty in France, writing on such topics as hysteria, but in 1891 he turned to experimental psychology and established it as a subdiscipline. In 1905, at his suggestion, the Ministry of Education considered setting up special classes for mentally abnormal children. In order to determine which children could not profit from normal instruction, Binet and Theodore Simon proposed a series of 30 intelligence tests. These tests were immediately successful and assured his fame. A subsequent refinement of Binet's tests by Lewis M. Terman, the Stanford-Binet Intelligence Scale, is still in use today. Binet was one of the originators of the questionnaire method; he studied the psychology of arithmetic prodigies and chess players; and he was a pioneer in the study of small groups. But it is his applied research on intelligence for which he is best known.

BOOKS BY BINET

Alterations of Personality. 1892. Trans. by Helen G. Baldwin, Univ. Publications of
    Amer. repr. of 1896 ed. 1978 $30.00
The Psychology of Reasoning. 1896. Routledge & Kegan 1901 o.p.
On Double Consciousness. Open Court 1899 o.p.

BOOK ABOUT BINET

Wolf, Theta H. *Alfred Binet.* Univ. of Chicago Pr. 1973 $20.00

DOLLARD, JOHN. 1900–1980

John Dollard, an American psychologist, was trained in anthropology, behavior therapy, psychoanalysis, and sociology, and has been throughout his career an outspoken believer in the wholeness of knowledge. His first book, *Criteria for the Life History,* is a landmark in the study of personality and culture. His second book, *Caste and Class in a Southern Town,* is a sociological study of the system that kept children of a black-white union from legitimate descent; it contributed ultimately to the postwar changes in the legal and social status of blacks. *Frustration and Aggression* remains compulsory reading for all psychologists who study these two topics and their interrelationship. *Fear in Battle,* a study of veterans of the Abraham Lincoln Brigade in the Spanish Civil War, conducted for the military during World War II, demonstrated that all of these soldiers had been afraid; differences in behavior during combat result from more or less successful ways of learning to cope with fear.

BOOKS BY DOLLARD

Criteria for the Life History, with Analyses of Six Notable Documents. Select Bibliographies Repr. Ser. Ayer repr. of 1935 ed. $20.00; Peter Smith $11.25
Caste and Class in a Southern Town. 1937. Doubleday 1957 o.p.
(and Robert R. Sears). *Frustration and Aggression.* Greenwood repr. of 1939 ed. 1980 lib. bdg. $27.50
(and Neal E. Miller). *Social Learning and Imitation.* 1941. Greenwood repr. of 1962 ed. 1979 lib. bdg. $24.75

EBBINGHAUS, HERMANN. 1850–1909

Hermann Ebbinghaus, German psychologist, taught successively at the Universities of Berlin, Breslau, and Halle. He created two important laboratories for psychological research in his attempt to put psychology on a quantitative and experimental basis and to transform it into a natural science. He founded and edited the major German psychological journal *Zeitschrift für Psychologie,* and his book *Memory* remains the starting point for all subsequent work in this field.

BOOKS BY EBBINGHAUS

Memory: A Contribution to Experimental Psychology. 1885. Intro. by Ernest R. Hilgard, Peter Smith $6.75
Psychology: An Elementary Text Book. Ed. by Max Meyer, *Classics in Psychology Ser.* Ayer repr. of 1908 ed. $17.00

BOOKS ABOUT EBBINGHAUS

Boring, Edwin G. *A History of Experimental Psychology.* Prentice-Hall 2d ed. 1950 $40.95
Murphy, Gardner, and Joseph K. Kovach. *Historical Introduction to Modern Psychology.* Harcourt 3d ed. text ed. 1972 $25.95

ERIKSON, ERIK H. 1902–

Erik H. Erikson, a German-born American psychologist and psychoanalyst, developed theories concerning the biologically determined stages of human development as shaped by the environment, which have had an impact on clinical psychoanalysis, ethics, history, literature, child care, and the emerging interdisciplinary study of the life course. According to Erikson's life-cycle theory, first published in *Childhood and Society,* the sequence of developmental stages has always been the same for the entire human race. There are eight stages: infancy, early childhood, play age, school age, adolescence, young adulthood, mature adulthood, and old age—each of which is associated with a particular crisis (e.g., identity versus confusion in adolescence). The concept of identity crisis is now firmly embedded in psychiatric theory and crisis. Erikson has also studied the relationship between individual history and the historical period in which one lives, and his two historical-biographical studies of Luther and Gandhi are outstanding products of this inquiry.

BOOKS BY ERIKSON

Childhood and Society. 1950. Norton 1964 pap. $3.95
Young Man Luther. 1958. Norton 1962 pap. $5.95
Identity and the Life Cycle. 1959. Norton 1980 $14.95 pap. $4.95
Gandhi's Truth: On the Origins of Militant Nonviolence. 1969. *Norton Lib.* 1970 pap.
    $4.95
Toys and Reasons: Stages in the Ritualization of Experience. Norton 1977 $12.95
(and Neal E. Miller, ed.). *Themes of Work and Love in Adulthood.* Harvard Univ. Pr.
    1980 $18.50 1981 pap. $9.95

BOOKS ABOUT ERIKSON

Coles, Robert. *Erik H. Erikson: The Growth of His Work.* Little, Brown 1970 o.p.
Piers, Maria W., ed. *Play and Development: A Symposium.* Norton 1977 pap. $2.95

FREUD, SIGMUND. 1856–1939

Sigmund Freud was a Viennese neurologist who found that existing therapies were not effective for most of his patients; by talking to them, he provided a "cathartic" treatment that eventually became the field of psychoanalysis. This field is simultaneously a theory of personality, a form of treatment, and an intellectual movement that has had a profound impact on the Western world—comparable in many ways to the impact of the theories of Darwin and Marx. Freud's concepts of the unconscious; of the pervasiveness of sexuality; and of conflict, anxiety, and defense have all transformed psychology, anthropology, literature, and art, as well as the everyday behavior of millions of people.

BOOKS BY FREUD

The Standard Edition of the Complete Psychological Works of Sigmund Freud. Ed. by
    James Strachey, Norton 24 vols. 1976 $595.00
The Basic Writings of Sigmund Freud. Ed. by A. A. Brill, Modern Lib. 1938 $12.95
*Abstracts of the Standard Edition of the Complete Psychological Works of Sigmund
    Freud.* Ed. by Carrie L. Rothgeb, intro. by Bernard D. Fine, International Univ.
    Pr. text ed. 1973 $40.00 pap. $10.95
(and Joseph Breuer). *Studies on Hysteria.* Basic Bks. 1982 $17.00 pap. $6.95
Three Essays on the Theory of Sexuality. Trans. by James Strachey, Basic Bks. 1982
    $17.50 pap. $7.95

BOOKS ABOUT FREUD

Abramson, Jeffrey. *Liberation and Its Limits: The Moral and Political Thought of
    Freud.* Macmillan 1984 $14.95
Bettelheim, Bruno. *Freud and Man's Soul.* Knopf 1983 $11.95; Random (Vintage)
    1984 $3.95
Fromm, Erich. *The Greatness and Limitations of Freud's Thought.* Harper 1980
    $11.49; New Amer. Lib. 1981 pap. $2.95
Gay, Peter. *Freud, Jews and Other Germans: Masters and Victims in Modernist Culture.*
    Oxford 1978 $22.50 1979 pap. $9.95

Hale, Nathan G., Jr. *Freud and the Americans: The Origin and Foundation of the Psychoanalytic Movement in America, 1876–1918.* Oxford 1971 $27.50

Hall, Calvin S. *A Primer of Freudian Psychology.* New Amer. Lib. 1979 pap. $2.50; Octagon repr. of 1954 ed. 1978 lib. bdg. $18.00

Jahoda, Marie. *Freud and the Dilemmas of Psychology.* Univ. of Nebraska Pr. (Bison) repr. of 1977 ed. 1981 pap. $4.95

Jones, Ernest. *The Life and Work of Sigmund Freud.* Basic Bks. 3 vols. 1953–57. $75.00 The famous, and standard, biography.

Malcolm, Janet. *In the Freud Archives.* Knopf 1984 $11.95

Rieff, Philip. *Freud: The Mind of the Moralist.* Univ. of Chicago Pr. (Phoenix Bks.) 3d ed. 1979 pap. $13.00

Sears, Robert R. *Survey of Objective Studies of Psychoanalytic Concepts. Social Science Research Council Bulletin* Greenwood repr. of 1943 ed. 1979 lib. bdg. $24.75; Kraus repr. of 1943 ed. 1979 pap. $9.00

Shakow, David, and David Rapaport. *Influence of Freud on American Psychology. Psychological Issues Monographs* International Univ. Pr. text ed. 1964 $22.50 pap. $17.50

Sulloway, Frank J. *Freud, Biologist of the Mind: Beyond the Psychoanalytic Legend.* Basic Bks. 1983 pap. $13.95

HALL, G. STANLEY. 1844–1924

G. Stanley Hall, American psychologist, received a Ph.D. in psychology from Harvard University, the first person in the United States to receive this degree. He became a professor of psychology at Johns Hopkins University, where he opened the first university psychology laboratory in the United States. In 1889, he became the first president of Clark University, as well as a professor of psychology. He was one of the first Americans to teach Freud's views, and Freud's visit to the United States in 1906 was at Hall's invitation.

BOOKS BY HALL

Adolescence: Its Psychology and Its Relations to Physiology, Anthropology, Sociology, Sex, Crime, Religion and Education. 1904. Telegraph Bks. 2 vols. repr. of 1905 ed. 1981 lib. bdg. $125.00

Senescence: The Last Half of Life. Family in Amer. Ser. Ayer repr. of 1922 ed. 1972 $29.00

Life and Confessions of a Psychologist. Ed. by Walter P. Metzger, Ayer repr. of 1923 ed. lib. bdg. $48.50

BOOKS ABOUT HALL

Ross, Dorothy. *G. Stanley Hall: The Psychologist as Prophet.* Univ. of Chicago Pr. 1972 $25.00

Watson, Robert I. *The Great Psychologists from Aristotle to Freud.* Harper 4th ed. text ed. 1978 pap. $19.95

HULL, CLARK L. 1884–1952

Clark L. Hull, an American psychologist, developed a theory of learning that set the agenda for learning theory research in the decades preceding and following World War II. The first part of his career was at the University of Wisconsin, where he carried out research on the measurement and prediction of achievement; in 1928, he moved to Yale University's Institute of Human Relations, where he began to formalize his mechanistic theory of learning behavior. He believed that this work would lead to a unified theory of behavior, a goal that few now believe is possible, but his research established the pattern for logical theory construction, which has been applied in many fields.

BOOKS BY HULL

Aptitude Testing. World 1928 o.p.
(and others). *Mathematico-Deductive Theory of Rote Learning: A Study in Scientific Methodology.* Greenwood repr. of 1940 ed. lib. bdg. $19.75
Principles of Behavior: An Introduction to Behavior Theory. Appleton 1943 o.p.
A Behavior System. Greenwood repr. of 1952 ed. 1974 lib. bdg. $27.50

BOOKS ABOUT HULL

Hilgard, Ernest R., ed. *Theories of Learning and Instruction.* Univ. of Chicago Pr. 1964 lib. bdg. $6.00 pap. $4.50
Koch, Sigmund. *Modern Learning Theory: A Critical Analysis of Five Examples.* Appleton 1954 o.p.

JAMES, WILLIAM. 1842–1910

William James, an American philosopher and psychologist, was the brother of Henry James, the novelist, and a professor at Harvard University for most of his life. His *The Principles of Psychology* took 12 years to write; it is a summation of previous work in psychology and a portent of the twentieth-century psychology to come. Its chapter on the self is considered one of the classics of psychological literature.

BOOKS BY JAMES

(and George A. Miller). *The Principles of Psychology.* Dover 2 vols. repr. of 1890 ed. text ed. pap. ea. $9.95; intro. by Gerald E. Mayers and Rand B. Evans, Harvard Univ. Pr. 2 vols. text ed. 1981 $60.00 1983 pap. $17.50; Peter Smith 2 vols. $32.50
The Will to Believe. 1897. Intro. by Edward H. Madden, *Works of William James Ser.* Harvard Univ. Pr. 1979 $27.50
The Varieties of Religious Experience: A Study in Human Nature. 1902. Doubleday repr. of 1978 pap. $2.95; intro. by John E. Smith, *Works of William James Ser.* Harvard Univ. Pr. text ed. 1985 $40.00; intro. by R. Niebuhr, Macmillan (Collier Bks.) 1961 pap. $3.95; Modern Lib. repr. of 1936 ed. $6.95; New Amer. Lib. pap. $3.50; ed. by Martin Marty, *Penguin Amer. Lib. Ser.* 1982 pap. $4.95
Pragmatism: A New Name for Some Old Ways of Thinking. 1907. Ed. by Bruce Kuklick, *Philosophical Class. Ser.* Hackett 1980 lib. bdg. $15.00 text ed. pap. $3.45; ed. by Frederick Burkhardt, Harvard Univ. Pr. 1976 $22.50; ed. by Ralph B. Perry, New Amer. Lib. 1965 pap. $6.95

BOOKS ABOUT JAMES

Barzun, Jacques. *A Stroll with William James.* Harper 1983 $19.18; Univ. of Chicago Pr. 1984 pap. $10.95

Bjork, Daniel W. *The Compromised Scientist: William James in the Development of American Psychology.* Columbia Univ. Pr. 1983 $26.00 pap. $13.00

Taylor, Eugene, ed. *William James on Exceptional Mental States: The 1896 Lowell Lectures.* Scribner 1983 $19.95; Univ. of Massachusetts Pr. 1984 pap. $9.95

Wilshire, Bruce. *William James and Phenomenology: A Study of "The Principles of Psychology."* AMS Pr. repr. of 1968 ed. $24.00

KLINEBERG, OTTO. 1899–

Otto Klineberg, a Canadian-born American psychologist, was trained as a physician before he studied psychology. He was a research associate of Franz Boas and his first fieldwork was among Indian children. Moreover, he is very much an international social scientist, both substantively through his work on race and international tensions and organizationally through his long association with UNESCO. He helped organize the World Federation for Mental Health and later served as its president, and he has been an unofficial ambassador for the social sciences in many countries. But probably his most enduring research is published in *Negro Intelligence and Selective Migration,* which demonstrated through carefully controlled studies that the I.Q. scores of southern American black children improved when they moved to the North, demonstrating that environment not race is the determinant of lower I.Q. scores among black children. This research was introduced to the Supreme Court in the deliberations that led to the famous 1954 decision on school desegregation.

BOOKS BY KLINEBERG

Negro Intelligence and Selective Migration. Greenwood repr. of 1935 ed. 1975 lib. bdg. $24.75

Race Differences. Greenwood repr. of 1935 ed. 1974 lib. bdg. $22.50; Norwood repr. of 1935 ed. $40.00

Tensions Affecting International Understanding: A Survey of Research. Social Science Research Council 1950 o.p.

The Human Dimension in International Relations. Holt 1964 o.p.

BOOK ABOUT KLINEBERG

Lindzey, Gardner. *A History of Psychology in Autobiography.* Freeman text ed. 1980 vol. 7 $34.95 pap. $19.95; Prentice-Hall repr. text ed. 1974 vol. 6 $21.95

LEWIN, KURT. 1890–1947

Kurt Lewin, a German-born American psychologist, conducted research in such diverse fields as cognition, motivation, and group behavior, but he maintained a consistent theoretical position requiring an interdisciplinary approach, which he came to call "field theory." The name derives from the premise that events are determined by forces acting on them in an immediate field rather than by forces acting at a distance. Perhaps the most widely known of his concepts is that of "psychological lifespace," which refers to the totality of events or facts that determines the behavior of an individual at a given time. For example, the unconscious structures that a therapist uncovers in working with a patient are said to be active in the present, not just replicas of past realities and reactions. Lewin's work in group dynamics led to the formation of the National Training Laboratories. First held in Bethel, Maine, the summer after Lewin's death, these training sessions for leadership roles sponsored by the laboratories have become a major link between the behavioral sciences and the professions and industry.

Books by Lewin

Resolving Social Conflicts. Ed. by Gertrud W. Lewin, International Specialized Bk. 1978 pap. $4.50
A Dynamic Theory of Personality. 1935. McGraw-Hill 1955 pap. $3.95
Principles of Topological Psychology. Johnson Repr. repr. of 1936 ed. 1969 $38.00
Field Theory in Social Science. Ed. by Dorwin Cartwright, Greenwood repr. of 1951 ed. 1975 lib. bdg. $45.00; *Midway Repr. Ser.* Univ. of Chicago Pr. 1951 pap. $15.00
(and Robert Barker and Tamara Dembo). *Frustration and Aggression: An Experiment with Young Children.* Univ. of Iowa Pr. 1941 o.p.

Books about Lewin

Leeper, Robert W. *Lewin's Topological and Vector Psychology: A Digest and a Critique.* Univ. of Oregon Pr. 1943 o.p.
Schellenberg, James A. *Masters of Social Psychology: Freud, Mead, Lewin and Skinner.* Oxford 1978 $10.95 pap. $4.95

LORENZ, KONRAD. 1903–   (Nobel Prize 1973)

Konrad Lorenz, an Austrian zoologist, is listed in the Psychology section because the biological origins of social behavior are of major interest to psychologists; in recent years, anthropologists and sociologists have paid more attention to Lorenz's research. Lorenz pioneered in the direct study of animal behavior, and is the founder of modern ethology. He is known for his studies of instinctive behavior patterns and of imprinting—the process through which a young bird learns during a short, sensitive period, by the appearance of its parents, what the appearance of its future sexual companion will be. His 1963 book, *On Aggression,* was attacked by many anthropologists, psychologists, and sociologists, who maintained that Lorenz's claim that aggression is inborn means that it cannot be controlled; his supporters assert, of course, that Lorenz never stated that inborn traits could not be changed. The conflict continues, with Lorenz a key figure in the midst of this contemporary version of the nature-nurture debate.

Books by Lorenz

King Solomon's Ring. 1952. *Apollo Eds.* Crowell pap. $3.95; fwd. by Julian Huxley, Harper 1979 pap. $5.95; New Amer. Lib. (Signet) pap. $2.95
Evolution and Modification of Behavior. 1961. Univ. of Chicago Pr. (Phoenix Bks.) 1967 pap. $2.75
On Aggression. 1963. Trans. by Marjorie K. Wilson, Harcourt 1966 $9.50 1974 pap. $7.95
Behind the Mirror: A Search for a Natural History of Human Knowledge. 1973. Trans. by Ronald Taylor, Harcourt 1978 pap. $3.95

BOOK ABOUT LORENZ

Montagu, Ashley. *Man and Aggression.* Oxford 2d ed. 1973 pap. $7.95

MURRAY, HENRY A. 1893–

Henry A. Murray, an American psychologist, was a major contributor to the theory and empirical study of personality. He taught at Harvard University for most of his career. In 1943, he developed the Thematic Apperception Test (TAT), which after the Rorschach (inkblot) test is the most widely used projective test. The TAT consists of 20 cards depicting vague scenes, on the basis of which the subject is asked to construct a story. It has been used in hundreds of empirical studies of personality as well as in clinical settings for arriving at a diagnosis or an understanding of the human personality. In *Explorations in Personality*, Murray and others developed a set of 20 principal needs (e.g., achievement, affiliation, aggression, dominance), which has been widely used in teaching and research. Murray is also a scholar of Herman Melville, and he published psychological analyses of both *Moby Dick* and *Pierre*, two of Melville's most baffling novels.

BOOKS BY MURRAY

Explorations in Personality. Wiley 1938 pap. $6.50
Endeavors in Psychology: Selections from the Personology of Henry A. Murray. Ed. by Edwin S. Shneidman, Harper 1981 $35.00

BOOK ABOUT MURRAY

White, Robert W., ed. *The Study of Lives: Essays on Personality in Honor of Henry A. Murray.* Atherton 1963 o.p.

PAVLOV, IVAN PETROVICH. 1849–1936

Ivan Petrovich Pavlov, a Russian physiologist and psychologist, demonstrated, by his 62 years of active research, one model of the research career: making a major discovery by studying more and more about less and less. He first studied the neural mechanisms of blood circulation and digestion; then the mechanisms of digestion; and finally salivation. His studies of salivation led to his discovery of the conditioned reflex: a dog trained to associate feeding with the sounding of a bell would salivate when the bell was sounded even though no food was made available. The concept of the conditioned reflex (known familiarly as Pavlov's dog), and the thousands of experiments that are based on it, have had an enormous impact on experimental psychology both in the Soviet Union and the United States.

BOOKS BY PAVLOV

Lectures on Conditioned Reflexes. 1923. Intro. by Jeffrey Gray, *Classics in Psychology Ser.* St. Martin's repr. of 1927 ed. $34.50
Conditioned Reflexes: An Investigation of the Physiological Activity of the Cerebral Cortex. Ed. by G. V. Anrep, Dover repr. of 1927 ed. text ed. pap. $6.00; ed. by G. V. Anrep, Peter Smith $14.50

Books about Pavlov

Babkin, Boris P. *Pavlov: A Biography*. Univ. of Chicago Pr. (Phoenix Bks.) 1975 pap. $4.25
Gray, Jeffrey A. *Ivan Pavlov. Modern Masters Ser*. Penguin 1981 pap. $4.95; *Modern Masters Ser*. Viking 1980 $12.95

PIAGET, JEAN. 1896–1980

Jean Piaget, a Swiss psychologist, spent much of his career studying the psychological development of children, largely at his institute at the University of Geneva. The impact of this research on child psychology has been enormous, and Piaget is the starting point for those seeking to learn how children view numbers, how they think of cause-and-effect relationships, or how they make moral judgments. Put simply, Piaget described children from a perspective that no one before had seen. His last major book, *The Development of Thought*, published in 1975, took him 50 years to write; it is on the concept of equilibration, which is said by his supporters to occupy the same centrality to Piaget's system that gravity did to Newton's. According to Piaget, equilibration is the process, intrinsic to a person's intellect, that coordinates subject and object. It explains how physiological conditions and environmental experiences both contribute to development, even though they are never alone the primary cause of development. Equilibration is said to do away with the need to postulate external causes of intellectual development, just as gravity did away with the need to postulate an external cause of planetary motion. In postulating an internal cause of intellectual development, Piaget's work resembles that of the anthropologist Claude Lévi-Strauss. (See also Chapter 5 in this volume.)

Books by Piaget

The Language and Thought of the Child. 1923. Humanities Pr. 3d ed. text ed. 1962 $18.00; New Amer. Lib. 1955 pap. $7.95
The Child's Conception of the World. 1926. Humanities Pr. repr. of 1929 ed. text ed. 1960 $24.50; Little, Brown repr. of 1929 ed. 1975 pap. $6.95
The Moral Judgment of the Child. Macmillan (Free Pr.) 1932 $15.95 text ed. pap. $14.95
Play, Dreams and Imitation in Childhood. 1946. *Norton Lib*. 1962 pap. $7.95
(and Barbel Inhelder). *Psychology of the Child*. Trans. by Helen Weaver, Basic Bks. 1969 pap. $7.95
The Essential Piaget. Ed. by Howard E. Gruber and J. Jacques Voneche, Basic Bks. text ed. 1977 $35.00 1982 pap. $18.50

Books about Piaget

Decarie, Therese G. *Intelligence and Affectivity in Early Childhood: An Experimental Study of Jean Piaget's Object Concept and Object Relationships*. International Univ. Pr. text ed. 1966 $22.50
Evans, Richard I. *Jean Piaget: The Man and His Ideas*. Trans. by Eleanor Duckworth, Dutton 1973 $8.95
Furth, Hans G. *Piaget and Knowledge: Theoretical Foundations. Psychology Ser*. Pren-

tice-Hall text ed. 1968 $13.95; Univ. of Chicago Pr. (Phoenix Bks.) 2d ed. 1981
   pap. $7.50
Gardner, Howard. *The Quest for Mind: Piaget, Lévi-Strauss, and the Structuralist
   Movement.* Knopf 1973 $8.95; Univ. of Chicago Pr. (Phoenix Bks.) 2d ed. 1981
   pap. $9.00
Inhelder, Barbel, ed. *Piaget and His School: A Reader in Developmental Psychology.*
   Ed. by C. Zwingman, Springer Verlag 1976 pap. $24.00
Piattelli, Palmarini Massimo, ed. *Language and Learning: The Debate between Jean
   Piaget and Noam Chomsky.* Harvard Univ. Pr. text ed. 1984 pap. $9.95
Richmond, P. G. *An Introduction to Piaget.* Basic Bks. 1971 pap. $5.95
Schwebel, Milton, and Jane Raph. *Piaget in the Classroom.* Basic Bks. 1973 pap.
   $5.95

SKINNER, B(URRHUS) F(REDERIC). 1904–

B. F. Skinner, an American psychologist, is known for his many contributions to learning theory. His *The Behavior of Organisms* reports his experiments with the study of reflexes; ten years later, he published *Walden Two,*
a utopian novel, which describes a planned community in which positive
rather than negative reinforcers serve to maintain appropriate behavior.
The novel actually stimulated the founding of some experimental communities. In *Beyond Freedom and Dignity* (1971), Skinner attempted to show that
only a technology of behavior (an early example is the so-called Skinner box
for conditioning a human child) can save democracy from the many individual and social problems that plague it. A teacher at Harvard University
from 1948 until his retirement, Skinner is for some the model of the objective scientist, for others the epitome of the heartless empiricist unaware of
the role of subjectivity in human experience.

BOOKS BY SKINNER

Particulars of My Life. New York Univ. Pr. 1985 pap. $10.95
The Behavior of Organisms: Experimental Analysis. 1938. Prentice-Hall 1966 $27.95
Walden Two. 1949. Irvington repr. text ed. 1980 $15.00
Verbal Behavior. Prentice-Hall 1957 $31.95
(and James G. Holland). *The Analysis of Behavior: A Program for Self-Instruction.* Mc-
   Graw-Hill text ed. 1961 pap. $18.00

BOOKS ABOUT SKINNER

Carpenter, Finley. *The Skinner Primer: Behind Freedom and Dignity.* Macmillan (Free
   Pr.) 1974 $14.95 pap. $4.95
Dews, Peter B., ed. *Festschrift for B. F. Skinner.* Century Psychology Ser. Irvington
   1977 $37.00

TINBERGEN, NIKOLAAS. 1907–   (NOBEL PRIZE 1973)

Nikolaas Tinbergen, a Dutch zoologist, with the Austrian biologist Konrad Lorenz founded the field of modern ethology—the study of animals in
their natural surroundings. Tinbergen and Lorenz shared the Nobel Prize
for physiology and medicine with Karl von Frisch in 1973. Tinbergen was
convinced of the sterility of much contemporary comparative and experimental psychology, and was appalled at the far-reaching generalizations

made by psychologists on the basis of observations of a few species of caged rodents. He observed herring gulls in their natural habitat and published the first major study of their social behavior. His influential book *The Study of Instinct* had a tremendous impact on the development of ethology. It is significant that the revolution in the study of animal behavior that he brought about was based not on grand theory but on the study of a few highly specific problems: the nature of the stickleback's courtship, the stimuli causing a young herring gull to beg for food, and the reasons gulls bother to remove empty eggshells from their nests.

BOOKS BY TINBERGEN

The Study of Instinct. Folcroft 1951 lib. bdg. $20.00; Oxford 1969 pap. $5.95
The Herring Gull's World. Intro. by Konrad Lorenz, Harper 1971 pap. $3.95
Social Behavior in Animals: With Special Reference to Vertebrates. Halsted Pr. 2d ed. 1965 pap. $5.50; Methuen 1965 pap. $8.95
Curious Naturalists. Univ. of Massachusetts Pr. rev. ed. 1984 pap. $9.95
The Animal in Its World: Explorations of an Ethologist, 1932–1972. Harvard Univ. Pr. 2 vols. text ed. 1972–73 ea. $16.00–$17.50 pap. ea. $6.95

WATSON, JOHN B. 1878–1958

John B. Watson, an American psychologist, was the founder of behaviorism, an enormously influential orientation that had an impact on sociology and political science as well as psychology. His own early research was experimental, in animal psychology and in child behavior, but in 1913 he published a paper entitled "Psychology as a Behaviorist Views It." The paper enunciated the doctrine that psychology is the science of behavior. Mentalistic concepts, images, the study of consciousness, and introspection must all be abandoned, he said. They must be replaced by the objective observation of the organism's response to controlled stimuli. Watson taught at Johns Hopkins University, but a sensational divorce in 1920 forced him to leave the academic world for a business career. He did publish a semipopular book, *Behaviorism,* in 1925, which may have made him the second best known (after Freud) psychologist of his time. For many people, Watson's claims that there are no hereditary traits and that behavior consists of learned habits constituted the core of psychology. There are no pure behaviorists in the social sciences today, but Watson's work—which led, for example, to the use of rooms with one-way glass walls for studying behavior—survives in many direct and indirect ways.

BOOKS BY WATSON

Behavior: An Introduction to Comparative Psychology. Holt 1914 o.p.
Psychology from the Standpoint of a Behaviorist. Classics of Psychology and Psychiatry Ser. Pinter repr. of 1919 ed. 1983 $23.50
Behaviorism. 1925. *Norton Lib.* repr. of 1930 ed. 1970 pap. $6.95

WUNDT, WILHELM. 1832–1920

Wilhelm Wundt, a German psychologist, was the founder of experimental psychology. He was trained in medicine at Heidelberg and became a physiologist, but he soon collected data on behavior as well as structure. In 1873, he published a book of 870 pages on physiological psychology; it eventually became three volumes totaling 2,317 pages in the sixth edition of 1908–1911. These six editions were in effect the history of experimental psychology's first 40 years. From 1875 until 1910, Wundt taught at Leipzig. His laboratory research was on two topics: (1) sensation and perception; and (2) the measurement of reaction times. Remarkably, little that he did has been totally rejected, and the research he conducted created the basic character of modern experimental psychology.

BOOKS BY WUNDT

Lectures on Human and Animal Psychology. 1864–65. Macmillan 1907 o.p.
Principles of Physiological Psychology. 1873. Macmillan 1905 o.p.
Ethics: An Investigation of the Facts and Laws of the Moral Life. 1886. Macmillan 3
    vols. 1908–11 o.p.
Outlines of Psychology. Scholarly repr. of 1896 ed. $39.00

BOOK ABOUT WUNDT

Rieber, Robert W. *Wilhelm Wundt and the Making of a Scientific Psychology.* Plenum
    1980 $24.50

SOCIOLOGY

In many ways, sociology is the most basic of the social sciences, because it is the science of social behavior. In actual practice, most sociologists study the social behavior of their own society, or of other modern societies, leaving premodern societies to the anthropologists. Moreover, most sociologists study one aspect of society—whether it be the family or the group; one category of behavior in society: crime, science, education, or religion; or one social process: communication, interaction, or change.

   The reading lists start with books describing the history of the field of sociology, with books providing surveys of the field, and with books describing the major methods used by sociologists in their research. These are followed by books describing the content of sociology, divided into 27 groups.

History of the Field

Barnes, Harry Elmer, and Howard Becker. *Social Thought from Lore to Science.* Peter
    Smith 3 vols. 3d ed. ea. $15.00. A still-useful encyclopedic inventory of the history of sociology.
Bottomore, Tom. *The Frankfurt School and Critical Theory.* Methuen 1984 $11.50
    pap. $4.50. The Frankfurt (Germany) Institute for Social Research originated so-called critical theory, which stresses the subjective, political role of sociology.
Bulmer, Martin. *The Chicago School of Sociology: Institutionalization, Diversity, and
    the Rise of Sociological Research. Heritage of Sociology Ser.* Univ. of Chicago Pr.
    1985 pap. $29.00. An account of how American sociology first developed its tradition of empirical research at the sociology department of the University of Chicago.

Coser, Lewis A. *Masters of Sociological Thought: Ideas in Historical and Social Context.* Harcourt 2d ed. text ed. 1977 $24.95

Gurvich, George, and Wilbert E. Moore, eds. *Twentieth-Century Sociology. Essay Index Repr. Ser.* Ayer repr. of 1945 ed. $38.50

Madge, John H. *Origins of Scientific Sociology.* Macmillan (Free Pr.) 1962 text ed. pap. $10.95. A very readable review of the major developments in social research.

Riley, Matilda White, and Robert K. Merton, eds. *Sociological Traditions from Generation to Generation: Glimpses of the American Experience.* Ablex text ed. 1980 $22.50

Swingewood, Alan. *A Short History of Sociological Thought.* St. Martin's 1984 $27.95 pap. $12.95

Surveys of the Field

Abrams, Philip. *Historical Sociology.* Cornell Univ. Pr. text ed. 1983 $34.95 pap. $14.95; State Mutual Bk. 1981 $60.00 pap. $30.00

Annual Review of Sociology. Annual Reviews 11 vols. text ed. 1975–85 ea. $20.00–$27.00

Broom, Leonard, and Philip Selznick. *Sociology: A Text with Adapted Readings.* Harper 6th ed. rev. text ed. 1977 $19.50 1979 pap. $18.50

Cicourel, Aaron V. *Cognitive Sociology.* Macmillan (Free Pr.) text ed. 1973 pap. $9.95

Giddens, Anthony. *Central Problems in Social Theory: Action, Structure and Contradiction in Social Analysis.* Univ. of California Pr. 1979 $31.00 pap. $9.95

Short, James F., Jr., ed. *The State of Sociology: Problems and Prospects.* Sage 1981 $24.00 pap. $12.00

Theodorson, George A., and Achilles G. Theodorson. *A Modern Dictionary of Sociology.* Crowell 1969 $14.37

Zeitlin, Irving. *Rethinking Sociology: A Critique of Contemporary Theory. Sociology Ser.* Prentice-Hall 1973 $23.95

Methods of Research

Bales, Robert F. *Interaction Process Analysis. Midway Repr. Ser.* Univ. of Chicago Pr. 1951 pap. $10.00

Blalock, Hubert M. *Theory Construction: From Verbal to Mathematical Formulations.* Prentice-Hall text ed. 1969 pap. $13.95

Burt, Ronald S., and Michael J. Minor. *Applied Network Analysis: A Methodological Introduction.* Sage 1982 $27.50 pap. $12.95

Durkheim, Emile. *The Rules of Sociological Method.* 1895. Macmillan (Free Pr.) 8th ed. 1950 $12.95 text ed. pap. $13.95. (See Durkheim's main listing in this section.)

Finsterbusch, Kurt, and others, eds. *Social Impact Assessment Methods.* Sage 1983 $29.95

Jackson, David J., and Edgar F. Borgatta, eds. *Factor Analysis and Measurement in Sociological Research: A Multi Dimensional Perspective.* Sage Studies in International Sociology 1981 $28.00 pap. $14.00

Juster, F. Thomas, and Kenneth C. Land, eds. *Social Accounting Systems: Essays on the State of the Art. Studies in Population* Academic Pr. 1981 $55.00

Lazarsfeld, Paul F., and others, eds. *The Language of Social Research: A Reader in the*

Methodology of Social Research. 1955. Macmillan (Free Pr.) text ed. 1965 pap. $7.95. (See Lazarsfeld's main listing in this section.)

Merton, Robert K., and others, eds. *Qualitative and Quantitative Social Research: Papers in Honor of Paul F. Lazarsfeld.* Macmillan (Free Pr.) 1979 $23.95. (See Merton's main listing in this section.)

Sociological Methodology. Social and Behavioral Science Ser. Jossey-Bass annual 1969–84 ea. $15.95–$32.95

Taylor, James C., and David G. Bowers. *Survey of Organizations.* Institute for Social Research 1972 $16.00

Age and Aging

[SEE ALSO Psychology, Individual Development, in this chapter.]

Binstock, Robert H., and Ethel Shanas. *The Handbook of Aging and the Social Sciences.* Van Nostrand 2d ed. 1985 $65.00

Birren, James E., and K. Warner Schaie. *The Handbook of the Psychology of Aging.* Van Nostrand 1977 $36.50 pap. $18.95

Brubaker, Timothy H., ed. *Family Relationships in Later Life. Sage Focus Eds.* 1983 $25.00 pap. $12.50

Eisenstadt, Shmuel N. *From Generation to Generation: Age Groups and Social Structure.* Macmillan (Free Pr.) text ed. 1964 pap. $7.95

Elder, Glen H., Jr., ed. *Life Course Dynamics: Trajectories and Transitions, 1968–1980.* Cornell Univ. Pr. text ed. 1985 $37.50 pap. $17.95

Kertzer, D. L., and Jennie Keith, eds. *Age and Anthropological Theory.* Cornell Univ. Pr. 1984 $32.50 pap. $12.95

Ortega y Gasset, José. *The Modern Theme.* 1923. Trans. by James Cleugh, Darby repr. of 1931 ed. 1981 lib. bdg. $35.00

Riley, Matilda W., and others. *Aging and Society.* Russell Sage 3 vols. 1968–83 ea. $11.50–$20.00

——, eds. *Aging from Birth to Death: Sociotemporal Perspectives.* Westview Pr. 2 vols. 1979–82 lib. bdg. ea. $23.50–$24.50

Art, Literature, Film, Intellectuals

Ben-David, Joseph, and Terry Nicholas Clark, eds. *Culture and Its Creators: Essays in Honor of Edward Shils.* Univ. of Chicago Pr. 1977 $30.00. Includes essays by 13 leading social scientists.

Coser, Lewis A. *Men of Ideas.* Macmillan (Free Pr.) 1965 pap. $3.45

Coser, Lewis A., and others. *Books: The Culture and Commerce of Publishing.* Basic Bks. 1982 $19.00; Univ. of Chicago Pr. 1985 pap. $12.50. A brilliant sociological analysis of the book publishing industry.

Escarpit, Robert. *The Sociology of Literature.* Trans. by E. Pick, Biblio Dist. 1971 $27.50

Gardner, Howard. *Art, Mind, and Brain: A Cognitive Approach to Creativity.* Basic Bks. 1984 pap. $10.95

Hauser, Arnold. *The Social History of Art.* Random (Vintage) 4 vols. 1985 pap. ea. $6.95

Kracauer, Siegfried. *Theory of Film: The Redemption of Physical Reality.* Oxford 1960 pap. $9.95

Lowenthal, Leo. *Literature and the Image of Man. Essay Index Repr. Ser.* Ayer repr. of 1957 ed. $19.00; afterword by Helmut Dubeil, Transaction Bks. 1985 $24.95

Shils, Edward. *The Intellectual between Tradition and Modernity: The Indian Situation*. Mouton 1961 o.p. (See Shils's main listing in this section.)

———. *The Intellectuals and the Powers: And Other Essays*. Univ. of Chicago Pr. 1972 o.p.

Wolfenstein, Martha, and Nathan Leites. *Movies: A Psychological Study*. Atheneum repr. of 1950 ed. text ed. 1970 pap. $3.45

Znaniecki, Florian. *The Social Role of the Man of Knowledge*. Octagon 1965 lib. bdg. $20.00; intro. by Lewis A. Coser, Transaction Bks. text ed. 1985 pap. $19.95

Collective Behavior

Allport, Gordon W., and Leo Postman. *The Psychology of Rumor*. Russell repr. of 1947 ed. 1965 $20.00

Cantril, Hadley. *The Invasion from Mars*. Princeton Univ. Pr. 1982 $24.00 pap. $6.95. A fascinating study of public belief in an Orson Welles radio program describing an invasion of Martians.

Kornhauser, William. *The Politics of Mass Society*. Macmillan (Free Pr.) 1959 text ed. 15.95

Le Bon, Gustave. *The Crowd*. Larlin repr. of 1895 ed. 1969 $15.00 pap. $7.00; Penguin 1977 pap. $3.95

Ortega y Gasset, José. *The Revolt of the Masses*. 1932. Trans. by Anthony Kerrigan, Univ. of Notre Dame Pr. 1984 $20.00

Rose, Jerry. *Outbreaks*. Macmillan (Free Pr.) 1981 $14.95

Shibutani, Tamotsu, ed. *Human Nature and Collective Behavior: Papers in Honor of Herbert Blumer*. Transaction Bks. 1973 pap. $5.95

Smelser, Neil J. *Theory of Collective Behavior*. Macmillan (Free Pr.) text ed. 1962 $12.95 pap. $9.95

Turner, Ralph, and Lewis Killian. *Collective Behavior*. Prentice-Hall 2d ed. text ed. 1972 $26.95

Communications

Ball-Rokeach, Sandra J., and Joel W. Grube. *The Great American Values Test: Influencing Behavior and Belief through Television*. Macmillan (Free Pr.) 1983 $25.00

Berelson, Bernard, and Morris Janowitz. *Reader in Public Opinion and Mass Communication*. Macmillan (Free Pr.) text ed. 1981 pap. $13.95

Bogart, Leo. *The Age of Television: A Study of Viewing Habits and the Impact of Television on American Life*. Ungar 3d ed. o.p.

———. *The Press and Public: Who Reads What, Where, and Why in American Newspapers*. Erlbaum text ed. 1981 $24.95

Cantril, Hadley. *The Invasion from Mars*. Princeton Univ. Pr. 1982 $24.00 pap. $6.95

Compaine, Benjamin. *Understanding New Media: Trends and Issues in Electronic Distribution of Information*. Ballinger 1984 $29.95

Coser, Lewis A., and others. *Books: The Culture and Commerce of Publishing*. Univ. of Chicago Pr. 1985 pap. $12.50

DeFleur, Melvin L., and Sandra J. Ball-Rokeach. *Theories of Mass Communication*. Longman 4th ed. text ed. 1981 $22.50 pap. $16.45

Deutsch, Karl W. *Nationalism and Social Communication: An Inquiry into the Foundations of Nationality*. MIT 1953 pap. $9.95

———. *The Nerves of Government*. Macmillan (Free Pr.) 1963 $19.95

Field, Harry, and Paul F. Lazarsfeld. *The People Look at Radio.* Ayer repr. of 1946 ed. 1976 $16.00

Katz, Elihu, and Paul F. Lazarsfeld. *Personal Influence: The Part Played by People in the Flow of Mass Communications.* 1955. Macmillan (Free Pr.) text ed. 1964 pap. $11.95. A classic study of how people intervene between the mass media and the public.

Klapper, Joseph. *The Effects of Mass Communication.* Macmillan (Free Pr.) text ed. 1960 $14.95

Kracauer, Siegfried. *From Caligari to Hitler: A Psychological History of the German Film.* Princeton Univ. Pr. 1947 pap. $8.95

Lazarsfeld, Paul F. *Radio and the Printed Page: An Introduction to the Study of Radio and Its Role in the Communication of Ideas.* Ayer repr. of 1940 ed. 1971 $25.50

————. *Radio Listening in America: The People Look at Radio Again.* Ed. by Lewis A. Coser and Walter W. Powell, *Perennial Works in Sociology Ser.* Ayer repr. of 1948 ed. 1979 lib. bdg. $15.00

McLuhan, Marshall. *Understanding Media: The Extensions of Man.* McGraw-Hill 1964 pap. $4.95; New Amer. Lib. 1973 pap. $4.50

Milavsky, J. Ronald. *Television and Aggression: Results of a Panel Study. Quantitative Studies in Social Relations Ser.* Academic Pr. 1982 $34.50

Schramm, Wilbur, and Donald F. Roberts, eds. *Process and Effects of Mass Communications.* Univ. of Illinois Pr. rev. ed. 1971 $20.00

————. *Television in the Lives of Our Children.* Stanford Univ. Pr. 1961 $25.00 pap. $8.95

Shearer, Benjamin F., and Marilyn Huxford, eds. *Communications and Society: A Bibliography on Communications Technologies and Their Social Impact.* Greenwood 1983 lib. bdg. $35.00

Steiner, Gary A. *The People Look at Television.* Knopf 1963 o.p.

Tannenbaum, Percy H., ed. *The Entertainment Functions of Television.* Erlbaum text ed. 1980 $29.95

Wolfenstein, Martha, and Nathan Leites. *Movies: A Psychological Study.* Atheneum repr. of 1950 ed. text ed. 1970 pap. $3.45

Community

Agger, Robert E., and Bert Swanson. *Rulers and the Ruled.* Irvington rev. ed. repr. of 1964 ed. text ed. 1984 $24.50 pap. $9.95

Barker, Roger G., and Herbert F. Wright. *The Midwest and Its Children: The Psychological Ecology of an American Town.* Shoe String (Archon) repr. of 1955 ed. 1971 $32.50

Booth, Charles. *The Life and Labour of the People in London, 1890–1900.* 1889–91. AMS Pr. 17 vols. repr. of 1904 ed. $502.50; Kelley 5 vols. rev. ed. repr. of 1902 ed. $125.00

Coleman, James S. *Community Conflict.* Macmillan (Free Pr.) text ed. 1957 pap. $3.95

Dahl, Robert A. *Who Governs? Democracy and Power in an American City.* Yale Univ. Pr. 1961 $33.50 pap. $8.95

Erikson, Kai T. *Everything in Its Path.* Simon & Schuster (Touchstone Bks.) 1978 pap. $8.95. An account of community reaction to a dam disaster.

Gans, Herbert J. *The Levittowners: Ways of Life and Politics in a New Suburban Community.* Columbia Univ. Pr. repr. of 1967 ed. 1982 $39.00 pap. $14.50

Hawley, Amos H. *Human Ecology: A Theory of Community Structure.* Ronald Pr. 1950 o.p.

Hollingshead, August B. *Elmtown's Youth and Elmtown Revisited.* Wiley text ed. 1975 pap. $19.45

Hunter, Floyd. *Community Power Structure: A Study of Decision Makers.* Univ. of North Carolina Pr. 1953 $25.00 1969 pap. $6.95

Lewis, Oscar. *Life in a Mexican Village: Tepoztlán Restudied.* 1951. Peter Smith $20.50; Univ. of Illinois Pr. repr. of 1951 ed. 1963 pap. $9.95

Lynd, Robert S., and Helen M. Lynd. *Middletown.* 1929 Harcourt 1959 pap. $7.95. (See the Lynds' main listing in this section.)

———. *Middletown in Transition: A Study in Cultural Conflicts.* 1937. Harcourt 1963 pap. $9.95

Marriott, McKim, ed. *Village India: Studies in the Little Community.* Univ. of Chicago Pr. (Phoenix Bks.) 1969 pap. $3.45

Polsby, Nelson W. *Community Power and Political Theory: A Further Look at Problems of Evidence and Inference.* Yale Univ. Pr. 2d ed. rev. text ed. 1980 $33.50 pap. $8.95

Redfield, Robert. *The Folk Culture of Yucatan.* Gordon 1976 lib. bdg. $59.95; Univ. of Chicago Pr. 1941 $25.00

———. *Tepoztlán, a Mexican Village: A Study of Folk Life.* Midway Repr. Ser. Univ. of Chicago Pr. repr. of 1930 ed. 1973 o.p.

Seeley, John R. *Crestwood Heights: A North American Suburb.* Univ. of Toronto Pr. 1956 pap. $10.00

Suttles, Gerald D. *The Social Construction of Communities.* Studies of Urban Society Univ. of Chicago Pr. 1972 $18.00; Univ. of Chicago Pr. (Phoenix Bks.) 1973 pap. $2.95

Tönnies, Ferdinand. *Community and Society.* 1887. Trans. by Charles P. Loomis, Harper text ed. 1977 pap. $3.95. (See Tönnies's main listing in this section.)

Vidich, Arthur J., and Joseph Bensman. *Small Town in Mass Society: Class, Power, and Religion in a Rural Community.* Princeton Univ. Pr. 1968 $29.00 pap. $11.50

Whyte, William F. *Street Corner Society: The Social Structure of an Italian Slum.* 1943. Univ. of Chicago Pr. 3d ed. 1981 lib. bdg. $23.00 text ed. pap. $7.00

Wirth, Louis. *The Ghetto, the Gold Coast and the Slum.* Midway Repr. Ser. Univ. of Chicago Pr. 1982 pap. $11.00

Zorbaugh, Harvey. *The Gold Coast and the Slum: A Sociological Study of Chicago's Near Northside.* Univ. of Chicago Pr. 1983 pap. $10.00

Conflict and Conflict Resolution

Coleman, James S. *Community Conflict.* Macmillan (Free Pr.) text ed. 1957 pap. $3.95

Collins, Randall. *Conflict Sociology: Toward an Explanatory Science.* Academic Pr. 1975 $55.00

Coser, Lewis A. *The Functions of Social Conflict.* Macmillan (Free Pr.) text ed. 1964 pap. $11.95

Dahrendorf, Ralf. *Class and Class Conflict in Industrial Society.* Stanford Univ. Pr. 1959 $27.50 pap. $9.95

Deutsch, Morton. *The Resolution of Conflict: Constructive and Destructive Processes.* Yale Univ. Pr. 1973 $38.00 pap. $12.95

Gluckman, Max. *Custom and Conflict in Africa.* Barnes & Noble repr. of 1956 ed. 1969 pap. $9.95

Krauss, Ellis S., and others, eds. *Conflict in Japan.* Univ. of Hawaii Pr. text ed. 1984 $24.95 pap. $9.95

Lewin, Kurt. *Resolving Social Conflicts.* Ed. by Gertrud W. Lewin, International Specialized Bk. 1978 pap. $4.50

Powell, Walter W., and Richard Robbins, eds. *Conflict and Consensus: A Festschrift in Honor of Lewis A. Coser.* Macmillan (Free Pr.) 1984 $29.95

Raiffa, Howard. *The Art and Science of Negotiation.* Harvard Univ. Pr. (Belknap Pr.) 1985 pap. $7.95

Short, James F., Jr., and Marvin E. Wolfgang, eds. *Collective Violence.* Amer. Academy of Political and Social Science 1970 pap. $7.95

Simmel, Georg. *Conflict and the Web of Group Affiliations.* 1908. Macmillan (Free Pr.) text ed. 1955 $14.95 pap. $9.95. (See Simmel's main listing in this section.)

Crime

Beccaria, Cesare Bonesana, Marchese di. *An Essay on Crimes and Punishments.* 1764. Trans. by Henry Paolucci, Bobbs 1963 pap. $5.99

Bedau, Hugo A., ed. *Capital Punishment in the United States.* Ed. by Chester M. Pierce, AMS Pr. lib. bdg. $42.50

———. *The Death Penalty in America.* Oxford 3d ed. 1982 $19.95 pap. $10.95

Bohannan, Paul, ed. *African Homicide and Suicide.* Atheneum text ed. 1967 pap. $2.95

Clinard, Marshall B. *Black Market: A Study of White Collar Crime.* Patterson Smith repr. of 1952 ed. 1969 $17.00 pap. $7.50

Cohen, A. K. *Delinquent Boys.* Macmillan (Free Pr.) text ed. 1955 $17.00 pap. $7.95

Conwell, Chic. *The Professional Thief.* Univ. of Chicago Pr. 1937 o.p.

Cressey, Donald R. *Other People's Money: A Study in the Social Psychology of Embezzlement.* Patterson Smith repr. of 1953 ed. 1973 lib. bdg. $15.00

Gaylin, Willard. *Partial Justice: A Study of Bias in Sentencing.* Random (Vintage) pap. o.p.

Hall, Jerome. *Theft, Law and Society.* Michie 2d ed. 1952 $13.50

Healy, William. *Individual Delinquent: A Text Book of Diagnosis and Prognosis for All Concerned in Understanding Offenders.* Patterson Smith repr. of 1915 ed. 1969 $30.00

Hirschi, Travis. *Causes of Delinquency.* Univ. of California Pr. 1969 $24.95

Kadish, Sanford H., ed. *Encyclopedia of Crime and Justice.* Macmillan 4 vols. 1983 $300.00

Kornhauser, Ruth R. *Social Sources of Delinquency: An Appraisal of Analytic Models.* Univ. of Chicago Pr. 1978 lib. bdg. $22.00 1984 pap. $9.00

Kuper, Leo. *Genocide: Its Political Use in the Twentieth Century.* Yale Univ. Pr. 1982 $21.50 text ed. pap. $8.95

Sellin, Thorsten. *Culture Conflict and Crime.* Kraus repr. of 1938 ed. pap. $2.25

Silberman, Charles E. *Criminal Violence, Criminal Justice.* Random (Vintage) 1980 pap. $4.95

Stinchcombe, Arthur L. *Crime and Punishment: Changing Attitudes in America. Social and Behavioral Sciences Ser.* Jossey-Bass text ed. 1980 $25.95

Sutherland, Edwin H. *White Collar Crime.* Fwd. by Donald R. Cressey, Greenwood repr. of 1961 ed. 1983 lib. bdg. $35.00

Taft, Donald R., and R. W. England, Jr. *Criminology.* Macmillan 4th ed. text ed. 1964 o.p.

Van den Haag, Ernst, and John P. Conrad. *The Death Penalty: A Debate.* Plenum 1983
$16.95
Vold, George B. *Theoretical Criminology.* Oxford 2d ed. 1979 $19.95
Wolfgang, Marvin. *Patterns in Criminal Homicide.* Patterson Smith 1975 $20.00

Deviant Behavior

Becker, Howard S. *Outsiders: Studies in the Sociology of Deviance.* Macmillan (Free
Pr.) 1963 $14.95 pap. $8.95
———, ed. *The Other Side: Perspectives on Deviance.* Macmillan (Free Pr.) 1967 pap.
$8.95
Conrad, Peter, and Joseph W. Schneider. *Deviance and Medicalization: From Badness
to Sickness.* Mosby text ed. 1980 pap. $15.95
Douglas, Jack D., ed. *Observations of Deviance: Deviant Situations, Styles, and Ways
of Life.* Random 1970 text ed. pap. $6.95; Univ. Pr. of Amer. repr. of 1970 ed. text
ed. 1981 pap. $13.25
Durkheim, Emile. *Suicide.* 1897. Macmillan (Free Pr.) 1951 $24.95 text ed. pap.
$9.95. A sociological classic.
Gibbons, Don C., and John F. Jones. *The Study of Deviance: Perspectives and Prob-
lems.* Prentice-Hall 1975 text ed. pap. $19.95
Goffman, Erving. *Behavior in Public Places: Notes on Social Organization of Gather-
ings.* Greenwood repr. of 1963 ed. 1980 lib. bdg. $24.75; Macmillan (Free Pr.)
1963 $17.00 pap. $9.95. (See Goffman's main listing in this section.)
———. *Stigma: Notes on the Management of Spoiled Identity.* Prentice-Hall (Spectrum
Bks.) 1963 pap. $4.95
Grove, Walter R. *The Labelling of Deviance: Evaluating a Perspective.* Sage 1980 pap.
$14.95

Energy, Resources, and Environment

Brito, Dagobert, and Adele E. Wick, eds. *Strategies for Managing Nuclear Prolifera-
tion: Economic and Political Issues.* Lexington Bks. 1983 $33.00
Brown, Lester R. *State of the World.* Norton 1985 $18.95 pap. $8.95; Worldwatch
1984 $15.95 pap. $8.95
Cole, H. S. D., and K. L. Pavitt, eds. *Models of Doom: A Critique of The Limits to
Growth.* Universe 1973 $10.00 pap. $5.00. Should be read in conjunction with
Meadows and others, listed below, of which it is a detailed criticism.
Erikson, Kai T. *Everything in Its Path.* Simon & Schuster (Touchstone Bks.) 1978
pap. $8.95
Klausner, Samuel Z. *On Man in His Environment: Social Scientific Foundations for
Research and Policy. Social and Behavioral Sciences Ser.* Jossey-Bass 1971 $25.95
Levine, Adeline G. *Love Canal: Science, Politics, and People.* Intro. by Rose K.
Goldsen, Lexington Bks. 1982 $25.00 pap. $14.00
Meadows, Donella H., and others. *The Limits to Growth: A Report for the Club of
Rome's Project on the Predicament of Mankind.* Universe 2d ed. 1974 $10.00 pap.
$5.00
Passmore, John. *Man's Responsibility for Nature: Ecological Problems and Western Tra-
ditions.* Scribner text ed. 1974 pap. $10.95
Schnaiberg, Allan. *The Environment: From Surplus to Scarcity.* Oxford text ed. 1980
pap. $14.95

Sills, David L., C. P. Wolf, and Vivien B. Shelanski, eds. *Accident at Three Mile Island: The Human Dimensions.* Westview Pr. 1981 pap. $12.50

Weinberg, Alvin M., ed. *Economic and Environmental Impacts of a U.S. Nuclear Moratorium, 1985–2010.* MIT 1979 $30.00

Ethnic Groups

Bean, Frank D., and W. Parker Frisbie, eds. *Demography of Racial and Ethnic Groups. Studies in Population* Academic Pr. 1978 $42.00

Deloria, Vine, Jr., and Clifford Lyttle. *The Nations Within: The Past and Future of American Indian Sovereignty.* Pantheon 1984 pap. $10.95

Farley, Reynolds. *Blacks and Whites.* (See under Sociology, Intergroup Relations, in this chapter.)

Glazer, Nathan, and Daniel P. Moynihan, eds. *Ethnicity: Theory and Experience.* Harvard Univ. Pr. 1975 $25.00 pap. $8.95

Lincoln, Charles E. *The Black Muslims in America.* Beacon rev. ed. 1973 $12.50 pap. $4.95; fwd. by Gordon W. Allport, Greenwood repr. of 1973 ed. 1982 lib. bdg. $29.75

Moynihan, Daniel P., and Nathan Glazer. *Beyond the Melting Pot: The Negroes, Puerto Ricans, Jews, Italians, and Irish of New York City.* MIT 2d ed. rev. 1970 pap. $9.95

Portes, Alejandro, and Robert L. Bach. *Latin Journey: Cuban and Mexican Immigrants in the United States.* Univ. of California Pr. text ed. 1984 $45.00 pap. $11.95

Snipp, C. Matthew. *Native Americans.* Russell Sage 1986 in progress

Steinberg, Stephen. *The Ethnic Myth: Race, Ethnicity and Class in America.* Atheneum 1981 $14.95; Beacon 1982 pap. $9.95

Sutherland, Anne. *Gypsies: The Hidden Americans.* Macmillan (Free Pr.) repr. of 1975 $16.95

Thernstrom, Stephan, Ann Orlov, and Oscar Handlin, eds. *The Harvard Encyclopedia of American Ethnic Groups.* Harvard Univ. Pr. 1980 $70.00. An extremely useful summary of what is known about hundreds of ethnic groups in the United States.

Family, Marriage, Life-Course Events

Aries, Philippe. *Centuries of Childhood: A Social History of Family Life.* Random (Vintage) 1965 pap. $6.95

Becker, Gary S. *A Treatise on the Family.* Harvard Univ. Pr. text ed. 1985 pap. $7.95

Burgess, Ernest W., and others. *The Family: From Traditional to Companionship.* 1945. Van Nostrand 4th ed. 1971 $12.95

Cherlin, Andrew. *Marriage, Divorce, Remarriage.* Harvard Univ. Pr. 1981 $14.00 1983 pap. $4.95

D'Antonio, William V., and Joan Aldous, eds. *Families and Religions: Conflict and Change in Modern Society.* Sage 1983 $25.00

Feifel, Herman, ed. *The Meaning of Death.* McGraw-Hill 1959 pap. $4.95

Fulton, Robert J., and Robert Bendiksen. *Death and Identity.* Charles rev. ed. text ed. 1978 o.p.

Glaser, Barney G., and Anselm L. Strauss. *Awareness of Dying.* Aldine 1965 lib. bdg. $26.95

Goode, William J. *The Family.* Prentice-Hall 2d ed. 1982 $15.95 pap. $11.95

————. *World Revolution and Family Patterns*. Macmillan (Free Pr.) 1970 text ed. pap. $12.95

Henderson, Ronald W., ed. *Parent-Child Interaction: Theory, Research and Prospects. Educational Psychology Ser.* Academic Pr. 1981 $39.50

Henslin, James M., ed. *Marriage and Family in a Changing Society*. Macmillan (Free Pr.) 2d ed. text ed. 1985 pap. $14.95

Lasswell, Marcia, and Thomas E. Lasswell. *Marriage and the Family*. Heath text ed. 1982 $23.95

Parsons, Talcott. *Family, Socialization and Interaction Process*. Macmillan (Free Pr.) 1955 o.p. (See Parsons's main listing in this section.)

Weitzman, Lenore J. *The Divorce Revolution: The Unexpected Social and Economic Consequences for Women and Children in America*. Macmillan (Free Pr.) 1985 $19.95

Winch, Robert F., and Louis W. Goodman, eds. *Selected Studies in Marriage and the Family*. Holt 4th ed. text ed. 1974 pap. $10.95

Interaction

Barber, Bernard. *The Logic and Limits of Trust*. Rutgers Univ. Pr. 1983 $27.50 pap. $9.95

Blau, Peter M. *Exchange and Power in Social Life*. Transaction Bks. text ed. 1985 pap. $14.95; Wiley 1964 $38.45

Blumer, Herbert. *Symbolic Interactionism: Perspective and Method*. Prentice-Hall text ed. 1969 $21.95

Fischer, Claude S. *To Dwell among Friends: Personal Networks in Town and City*. Univ. of Chicago Pr. (Phoenix Bks.) 1982 lib. bdg. $35.00 pap. $12.00

Mead, George H. *Mind, Self, and Society: From the Standpoint of a Social Behaviorist*. 1934. Ed. by Charles W. Morris, Univ. of Chicago Pr. 1967 lib. bdg. $30.00; Univ. of Chicago Pr. (Phoenix Bks.) pap. $7.00

Intergroup Relations

Allport, Gordon W. *The Nature of Prejudice*. 1954. Pref. by Thomas Pettigrew, Addison-Wesley 1979 $7.64 pap. $5.95; Anti-Defamation League repr. pap. $5.95

Apostle, Richard A., and Marijean Suelzle. *The Anatomy of Racial Attitudes*. Univ. of California Pr. 1983 $30.00

Campbell, Angus. *White Attitudes toward Black People*. Institute for Social Research 1971 $12.00 pap. $8.00

Clark, Kenneth B. *Dark Ghetto: Dilemmas of Social Power*. Harper 1965 $10.00

Coleman, James S. *Equality of Educational Opportunity*. Ed. by Lewis A. Coser and Walter W. Powell, *Perennial Works in Sociology Ser.* Ayer 2 vols. repr. of 1966 ed. 1979 lib. bdg. $76.00

Eisenstadt, Shmuel N. *The Absorption of Immigrants*. Greenwood repr. of 1954 ed. 1975 lib. bdg. $15.75

Farley, Reynolds. *Blacks and Whites: Narrowing the Gap? Social Trends in the United States Ser.* Harvard Univ. Pr. text ed. 1984 $19.50

Freyre, Gilberto. *The Masters and the Slaves*. Knopf 1964 $17.50

Myrdal, Gunnar. *An American Dilemma*. 1944. Harper 1962 $25.00. A monumental study of blacks in American life, conducted by an eminent Swedish economist. (See Myrdal's main listing in this section.)

Pettigrew, Thomas F. *The Sociology of Race Relations: Reflection and Reform.* Macmillan (Free Pr.) text ed. 1980 pap. $15.95
Pettigrew, Thomas F., and others. *Prejudice. Dimensions in Ethnicity Ser.* Harvard Univ. Pr. text ed. 1982 pap. $4.95
Quinley, Harold E., and Charles Y. Glock. *Anti-Semitism in America.* Anti-Defamation League repr. $12.95; Macmillan (Free Pr.) 1979 $11.95; Transaction Bks. 1983 pap. $12.95
Selznick, Gertude J., and Stephen Steinberg. *The Tenacity of Prejudice: Anti-Semitism in Contemporary America.* Greenwood repr. of 1969 ed. 1979 lib. bdg. $24.75

Organizations

Barnard, Chester I. *The Functions of the Executive.* Intro. by K. R. Andrews, Harvard Univ. Pr. 1968 pap. $8.95
Blau, Peter M. *The Dynamics of Bureaucracy.* Univ. of Chicago Pr. (Phoenix Bks.) 2d ed. rev. text ed. 1973 $6.95
Cyert, Richard M., and J. G. March. *A Behavioral Theory of the Firm.* Prentice-Hall 1963 $30.95
Festinger, Leon, and others. *When Prophecy Fails: A Social and Psychological Study of a Modern Group That Predicted the Destruction of the World.* Harper pap. $6.95
Glaser, William A., and David L. Sills, eds. *The Government of Associations.* Bedminster Pr. 1966 o.p.
Goffman, Erving. *Asylums: Essays on the Social Situation of Mental Patients and Other Inmates.* Aldine 1961 $22.95; Doubleday (Anchor) pap. $6.95
March, James G., ed. *Handbook of Organizations.* Rand McNally 1965 o.p.
March, James G., and Herbert A. Simon. *Organizations.* Wiley 1958 $30.45
Merton, Robert K., and others, eds. *A Reader in Bureaucracy.* Macmillan (Free Pr.) 1965 text ed. pap. $17.95
Selznick, Philip. *TVA and the Grass Roots: A Study of Politics and Organization.* Univ. of California Pr. 1980 $25.50 1984 pap. $8.95
Sills, David L. *The Volunteers: Means and Ends in a National Organization.* Ed. by Harriet Zuckerman and Robert K. Merton, *Dissertations on Sociology Ser.* Ayer repr. of 1957 ed. 1980 lib. bdg. $28.50
Sills, David L., C. P. Wolf, and Vivien B. Shelanski, eds. *Accident at Three Mile Island: The Human Dimensions.* Westview Pr. 1981 pap. $12.50
Simon, Herbert A. *Administrative Behavior.* Macmillan (Free Pr.) 3d ed. 1976 $24.95 text ed. pap. $14.95
Smith, Constance, and Anne Freedman. *Voluntary Associations: Perspectives on the Literature.* Harvard Univ. Pr. 1972 pap. $14.00
Weber, Max. *The Theory of Social and Economic Organization.* 1922. Trans. by Talcott Parsons, Macmillan (Free Pr.) 1947 $17.95 text ed. pap. $14.95. (See Weber's main listing in this sectio

Population

Bean, Frank D., and W. Parker Frisbie, eds. *The Demography of Racial and Ethnic Groups. Studies in Population* Academic Pr. 1978 $42.00
Bogue, Donald J. *The Population of the United States: Historical Trends and Future Projections.* Macmillan (Free Pr.) 1984 $70.00

Graunt, John. *Natural and Political Observations Made upon the Bills of Mortality.* 1622. *European Sociology Ser.* Ayer repr. 1975 $13.00

Petersen, William, and Renée Petersen. *Dictionary of Demography.* Greenwood 2 vols. 1985 lib. bdg. $125.00

Ross, John A., ed. *International Encyclopedia of Population.* Macmillan 2 vols. 1982 lib. bdg. $125.00. A useful and authoritative general reference.

Westoff, Charles F. *Family Growth in Metropolitan America. Office of Population Research Ser.* Princeton Univ. Pr. 1961 $42.00

Whelpton, Pascal K. *Social and Psychological Factors Affecting Fertility.* Milbank Memorial Fund 5 vols. 1943–58 o.p.

Willigan, Dennis J., and K. L. Lynch. *Sources and Methods of Historical Demography. Studies in Social Discontinuity* Academic Pr. 1982 $39.50 pap. $18.00

Professions

Ben-David, Joseph. *The Scientist's Role in Society: A Comparative Study with a New Introduction.* Univ. of Chicago Pr. 1984 $20.00 text ed. pap. $8.95

Blau, Judith R. *Architects and Firms: A Sociological Perspective on Architectural Practices.* MIT text ed. 1984 $19.95

Coser, Lewis A. *Men of Ideas.* Macmillan (Free Pr.) 1965 pap. $3.45

Heinz, John P., and Edward O. Laumann. *Chicago Lawyers: The Social Structure of the Bar.* Amer. Bar Foundation $32.50; Russell Sage 1983 $32.50

Hirsch, Walter. *Scientists in American Society.* Peter Smith $7.00

Huntington, Samuel P. *The Soldier and the State: The Theory and Politics of Civil-Military Relations.* Harvard Univ. Pr. (Belknap Pr.) 1957 $25.00 1981 pap. $8.95

Janowitz, Morris. *The Professional Soldier: A Social and Political Portrait.* Macmillan (Free Pr.) 1960 $12.95 pap. $11.95

Kornhauser, William. *Scientists in Industry: Conflict and Accommodation.* Fwd. by Arthur M. Ross, Greenwood repr. of 1962 ed. 1982 lib. bdg. $32.50

Lazarsfeld, Paul F., and Wagner Thielens, Jr. *The Academic Mind: Social Scientists in Time of Crisis.* Ed. by Walter P. Metzger, Ayer repr. of 1958 ed. 1977 $35.50

Lorber, Judith. *Women Physicians: Careers, Status and Power.* Methuen 1985 $22.00 pap. $9.95

Merton, Robert K., and Patricia Kendall, eds. *The Student-Physician: Introductory Studies in the Sociology of Medical Education.* Harvard Univ. Pr. 1957 o.p.

Starr, Paul. *The Social Transformation of American Medicine.* Basic Bks. 1983 $24.95 1984 pap. $11.95

Wilensky, Harold L. *Intellectuals in Labor Unions.* Macmillan (Free Pr.) 1956 o.p.

Wilson, Logan. *The Academic Man.* Octagon 1964 lib. bdg. $18.50

Znaniecki, Florian. *The Social Role of the Man of Knowledge.* 1940. Octagon 1965 lib. bdg. $20.00; intro. by Lewis A. Coser, Transaction Bks. text ed. 1985 pap. $19.95. A pioneering work.

Religion

Arjomand, Said A., ed. *From Nationalism to Revolutionary Islam: Essays on Social Movements in the Contemporary Near and Middle East.* State Univ. of New York Pr. 1984 $39.50 pap. $15.95

Bellah, Robert N. *Tokugawa Religion: The Values of Pre-Industrial Japan.* Beacon repr. of 1957 ed. 1970 pap. $4.95; Macmillan (Free Pr.) pap. $9.95

Caplow, Theodore, and others. *All Faithful People: Change and Continuity in*

Middletown's Religion. Univ. of Minnesota Pr. 1983 $19.50. Based on a restudy of the Lynds' classic study of Middletown (Muncie, Indiana).

Geertz, Clifford. *The Religion of Java.* Univ. of Chicago Pr. (Phoenix Bks.) repr. of 1960 ed. 1976 pap. $11.00

Gollin, Gillian. *Moravians in Two Worlds.* Columbia Univ. Pr. 1967 o.p.

Hammond, Phillip E., ed. *The Sacred in a Secular Age.* Univ. of California Pr. 1985 $32.50 pap. $9.95

Herberg, Will. *Protestant, Catholic, Jew: An Essay in American Religious Sociology.* Univ. of Chicago Pr. repr. of 1955 ed. 1983 pap. $11.00

Jules-Rosette, Bennetta, ed. *The New Religions of Africa. Modern Sociology Ser.* Ablex 1979 $27.50

Niebuhr, H. Richard. *The Social Sources of Denominationalism.* 1929. Peter Smith 1984 $16.00

Troeltsch, Ernst, and H. Richard Niebuhr. *The Social Teaching of the Christian Churches.* 1912. Univ. of Chicago Pr. 2 vols. repr. of 1931 ed. 1981 pap. $17.00

Weber, Max. *Ancient Judaism.* 1917–19. Macmillan (Free Pr.) text ed. 1967 pap. $13.95

———. *The Protestant Ethic and the Spirit of Capitalism.* 1904–05. Intro. by Anthony Giddens, *Counterpoint Pap. Ser.* Allen & Unwin pap. $6.95; Peter Smith 1984 $15.50; Scribner rev. ed. repr. of 1930 ed. 1977 pap. $8.95

———. *The Religion of China.* 1915. Macmillan (Free Pr.) text ed. 1968 $14.95

———. *The Religion of India.* 1916–17. Macmillan (Free Pr.) 1967 o.p.

———. *The Sociology of Religion.* 1922. Trans. by Ephraim Fischoff, Beacon 1964 pap. $9.95

Wolf, Arthur P., ed. *Religion and Ritual in Chinese Society. Studies in Chinese Society* Stanford Univ. Pr. 1974 $27.50

Science and Technology

Barber, Bernard. *Science and the Social Order.* Fwd. by Robert K. Merton, Greenwood repr. of 1952 ed. 1978 lib. bdg. $32.50

Barber, Bernard, and others. *Research on Human Subjects: Problems of Social Control in Medical Experimentation.* Russell Sage 1973 $10.50; Transaction Bks. text ed. 1979 pap. $4.95

Ben-David, Joseph. *The Scientist's Role in Society: A Comparative Study with a New Introduction.* Univ. of Chicago Pr. 1984 $20.00 text ed. pap. $8.95

Cole, Jonathan R., and Stephen Cole. *Social Stratification in Science.* Univ. of Chicago Pr. 1973 $20.00 pap. $10.00

Crane, Diana. *Invisible Colleges: Diffusion of Knowledge in Scientific Communities.* Univ. of Chicago Pr. 1972 $10.50

Ellul, Jacques. *Technological Society.* Intro. by Robert K. Merton, Knopf 1964 $12.50; Random (Vintage) 1967 pap. $4.95

Fischhoff, Baruch. *Acceptable Risk.* Cambridge Univ. Pr. 1981 $21.25 1984 pap. $8.95

Gieryn, Thomas, ed. *Science and Social Structure: A Festschrift for Robert K. Merton.* New York Academy of Sciences 1980 $17.00. Essays on the sociology of science in honor of the leading scholar in the field.

Kuhn, Thomas S. *The Structure of Scientific Revolutions. Foundations of the Unity of Science Ser.* Univ. of Chicago Pr. (Phoenix Bks.) 2d ed. 1970 $17.50 pap. $5.95. A book that transformed how science as an institution is studied.

Mannheim, Karl. *Essays on the Sociology of Knowledge.* Ed. by Paul Kecskemeti, Oxford 2d ed. 1952 o.p. Essays by the founder of the sociology of science, first published between 1923 and 1929. (See Mannheim's main listing in this section.)

Merton, Robert K. *The Sociology of Science: Theoretical and Empirical Investigations.* Southern Illinois Univ. Pr. 1979 pap. $4.95; ed. by Norman W. Storer, Univ. of Chicago Pr. 1973 $30.00; Univ. of Chicago Pr. (Phoenix Bks.) 1979 pap. $11.00

Merton, Robert K., and Jerry Gaston, eds. *The Sociology of Science in Europe.* 1975. *Perspectives in Sociology* Southern Illinois Univ. Pr. 1977 $22.95

Nelkin, Dorothy. *Controversy: Politics of Technical Decisions. Focus Eds.* Sage 1979 $24.00 pap. $12.00

———. *Science as Intellectual Property: Who Controls Scientific Research.* Macmillan text ed. 1983 $15.95 text ed. pap. $7.95

Perrow, Charles. *Normal Accidents: Living with High Risk Technologies.* Basic Bks. 1984 $21.95

Price, Derek J. de Solla. *Big Science, Little Science.* Columbia Univ. Pr. 1986 $35.00 pap. $14.95

Shils, Edward. *The Intellectuals and the Powers: And Other Essays.* Univ. of Chicago Pr. 1972 o.p.

Spiegel-Rosing, Ina, and Derek J. de Solla Price, eds. *Science, Technology and Society: A Cross Disciplinary Perspective.* Sage 1977 $37.50

Winner, Langdon. *Autonomous Technology: Technics out of Control as a Theme in Political Thought.* MIT 1977 pap. $8.95

Zuckerman, Harriet. *Scientific Elites: Nobel Laureates in the United States.* Macmillan (Free Pr.) 1977 $14.95 text ed. pap. $7.95

Social Change

Chirot, Daniel. *Social Change in the Twentieth Century.* Harcourt text ed. 1977 pap. $15.95

Juster, F. Thomas, and Kenneth C. Land, eds. *Social Accounting Systems: Essays on the State of the Art. Studies in Population* Academic Pr. 1981 $55.00

Lerner, Daniel. *The Passing of Traditional Society.* Macmillan (Free Pr.) 1964 pap. $2.45

Ogborn, William F. *Social Change: With Respect to Culture and Original Nature.* 1922. Peter Smith repr. of 1950 ed. 1964 $8.00. (See Ogborn's main listing in this section.)

Rogers, Everett M. *The Diffusion of Innovations.* Macmillan (Free Pr.) 3d ed. text ed. 1982 $18.95

Sheldon, Eleanor B., and Wilbert E. Moore, eds. *Indicators of Social Change: Concepts and Measurements.* Russell Sage 1968 $17.95

Sorokin, Pitirim. *Social and Cultural Dynamics: A Study of Changes in Major Systems of Art, Truth, Ethics, and Social Relationships.* Transaction Bks. 1981 pap. $19.95

Tilly, Charles. *Big Structures, Large Processes, Huge Comparisons.* Russell Sage 1985 $14.50

Social Class

Dohrenwend, Bruce P., and Barbara S. Dohrenwend. *Social Status and Psychological Disorder: A Casual Inquiry. Personality Processes Ser.* Wiley 1969 o.p.

Duncan, Otis Dudley, and others. *Socioeconomic Background and Achievement. Studies in Population* Academic Pr. 1972 $39.50

Featherman, David L., and Robert M. Hauser. *Opportunity and Change. Studies in Population* Academic Pr. 1978 $30.00

Jencks, Christopher. *Inequality: A Reassessment of the Effect of Family and Schooling in America*. Harper 1973 pap. $5.95

Kohn, Melvin L., and Carmi Schooler. *Work and Personality: An Inquiry into the Impact of Social Stratification*. Ablex text ed. 1983 $42.50 pap. $22.50

Lipset, Seymour M., and Reinhard Bendix. *Social Mobility in Industrial Society: A Study of Political Sociology*. Univ. of California Pr. 1959 pap. $1.95

Sewell, William H., and Robert M. Hauser, eds. *Schooling and Achievement in American Society. Studies in Population* Academic Pr. 1976 $47.50

Verba, Sidney, and Gary Orren. *Equality in America: The View from the Top*. Harvard Univ. Pr. text ed. 1985 $25.00

Social Movements

D'Emilio, John. *Sexual Politics, Sexual Communities: The Making of a Homosexual Minority in the United States, 1940–1970*. Univ. of Chicago Pr. 1983 $20.00 1984 pap. $7.95

Freeman, Jo, ed. *Social Movements of the Sixties and Seventies*. Longman text ed. 1982 pap. $17.95

Mauss, Armand L. *Social Problems as Social Movements*. Harper 1975 $13.50

Piven, Frances F., and Richard A. Cloward. *Poor People's Movements: Why They Succeed, How They Fail*. Random (Vintage) 1979 pap. $5.95

Skocpol, Theda. *States and Social Revolutions*. Cambridge Univ. Pr. 1979 pap. $11.95

Smelser, Neil J. *Theory of Collective Behavior*. Macmillan (Free Pr.) text ed. 1962 $12.95 pap. $9.95

Zald, Mayer N., and John D. McCarthy. *The Dynamic of Social Movements: Resource Mobilization, Social Control, and Tactics*. Little, Brown text ed. 1979 $18.95

Social Structure

Blau, Peter M. *Inequality and Heterogeneity: A Primitive Theory of Social Structure*. Macmillan (Free Pr.) 1977 $19.95

———, ed. *Approaches to the Study of Social Structure*. Macmillan (Free Pr.) 1975 $19.95

Burt, Ronald. *Toward a Structural Theory of Action: Network Models of Social Structure, Perception and Action. Quantitative Studies in Social Relations Ser.* Academic Pr. 1982 $37.50

Coser, Lewis A., ed. *The Idea of Social Structure: Papers in Honor of Robert K. Merton*. Harcourt text ed. 1975 $24.95

Giddens, Anthony. *The Constitution of Society: Outline of the Theory of Structuration*. Univ. of California Pr. 1984 $35.00

Lienhardt, Samuel. *Social Networks: A Developing Paradigm*. Academic Pr. 1977 $35.00

Merton, Robert K. *Social Theory and Social Structure*. 1949. Macmillan (Free Pr.) text ed. 1968 $24.95

———. *Sociological Ambivalence and Other Essays*. Macmillan (Free Pr.) 1976 $13.95

Parsons, Talcott. *The Social System*. 1951. Macmillan (Free Pr.) text ed. 1964 pap. $18.95

———. *The Structure of Social Action*. 1937. Macmillan (Free Pr.) 1949 $18.00 2 vols. text ed. pap. ea. $10.95–$16.95

Socialization

Brim, Orville G., Jr. *Socialization after Childhood: Two Essays.* Wiley text ed. 1966 pap. $16.50

Denzin, Norman K. *Childhood Socialization: Studies in the Development of Language, Social Behavior, and Identity. Social and Behavioral Science Ser.* Jossey-Bass text ed. 1978 $21.95

Goslin, David A. *Handbook of Socialization Theory and Research.* Houghton Mifflin 1969 $55.00

Hess, Beth B., and Elizabeth W. Markson. *Aging and Old Age: An Introduction to Social Gerontology.* Macmillan text ed. 1980 o.p.

Hyman, Herbert H. *Political Socialization: A Study in the Psychology of Political Behavior.* Macmillan (Free Pr.) 1969 pap. $1.95

Rose, Peter I., ed. *Socialization and the Life Cycle.* St. Martin's text ed. 1979 pap. $11.95

Rosow, Irving. *Socialization to Old Age.* Univ. of California Pr. 1975 pap. $3.65

Urban Life

Bradbury, Katherine L., and Kenneth A. Small. *Urban Decline and the Future of American Cities.* Brookings 1982 $29.95 pap. $11.95

Duncan, Otis D., and Albert J. Reiss, Jr. *Social Characteristics of Urban and Rural Communities.* Russell repr. of 1956 ed. 1976 $25.00

Gans, Herbert J. *The Urban Villagers.* Macmillan (Free Pr.) 2d ed. text ed. 1982 pap. $8.95

Gorham, William, and Nathan Glazer, eds. *The Urban Predicament.* Urban Institute Pr. 1976 $19.95 pap. $9.95

Gottman, Jean. *Megalopolis: The Urbanized Northeastern Seaboard of the United States.* Kraus repr. 1961 $12.00; MIT 1964 pap. $5.95

Jacobs, Jane. *Cities and the Wealth of Nations: Principles of Economic Life.* Random (Vintage) 1985 $4.95

Laska, Shirley, and Daphne Spain. *Back to the City: The Making of a Movement. Pergamon Policy Studies* 1980 $50.00 pap. $9.95

Lofland, L. *A World of Strangers: Order and Action in Urban Public Space.* Basic Bks. 1973 $9.50; Waveland Pr. repr. of 1973 ed. text ed. 1985 pap. $8.95

Masotti, Louis H., and Jeffrey K. Hadden, eds. *The Urbanization of the Suburbs.* Sage 1973 o.p.

Mumford, Lewis. *The City in History: Its Origins, Its Transformations and Its Prospects.* Harcourt 1968 pap. $9.95

———. *The Culture of Cities.* Greenwood repr. of 1970 ed. 1981 lib. bdg. $45.00; Harcourt repr. of 1938 ed. 1970 pap. $9.95

Park, Robert E. *City.* Intro. by Morris Janowitz, *Heritage of Sociology Ser.* Univ. of Chicago Pr. repr. of 1967 ed. 1984 pap. $10.00

Schoenberg, Sandra Perlman, and Patricia Rosenbaum. *Neighborhoods That Work: Sources for Viability in the Inner City.* Rutgers Univ. Pr. 1980 $16.00

Sennett, Richard. *Uses of Disorder: Personal Identity and City Life.* Knopf 1970 $6.95

Sjoberg, Gideon. *Preindustrial City: Past and Present.* Macmillan (Free Pr.) text ed. 1965 pap. $9.95

Solomon, Arthur P., ed. *The Prospective City: Economic, Population, Energy, and Environmental Developments Shaping Our Cities and Suburbs.* MIT text ed. 1979 $37.50 pap. $10.95

Stein, Maurice R. *The Eclipse of Community: An Interpretation of American Studies.* Princeton Univ. Pr. 1971 pap. $11.95
Timberlake, Michael. *Urbanization in the World Economy. Studies in Social Disconti-nuity* Academic Pr. 1985 pap. $46.50
Weber, Max. *The City.* 1921. Macmillan (Free Pr.) 1958 $14.95 text ed. pap. $11.95

Utopianism and Communes

Berger, Bennett. *Survival of a Counterculture: Ideological Work and Everyday Life among Rural Communards.* Univ. of California Pr. 1981 $15.95 1985 pap. $7.95
Bestor, Arthur. *Backwoods Utopia.* Univ. of Pennsylvania Pr. 1971 o.p.
Erasmus, Charles J. *In Search of the Common Good: Utopian Experiments Past and Future.* Macmillan (Free Pr.) 1977 $22.95 1985 pap. $12.95
Kanter, Rosabeth M. *Commitment and Community: Communes and Utopias in Socio-logical Perspective.* Harvard Univ. Pr. 1972 $20.00 pap. $6.95
Moore, Sally F., and Barbara G. Myerhoff, eds. *Symbol and Politics in Communal Ide-ology: Cases and Questions. Symbol, Myth and Ritual Ser.* Cornell Univ. Pr. 1975 pap. $8.95
Zablocki, Benjamin. *Alienation and Charisma: A Study of Contemporary American Communes.* Macmillan (Free Pr.) 1980 $27.95

Women

Bernard, Jessie. *The Female World.* Macmillan (Free Pr.) 1981 $27.50 1982 pap. $11.95
Cole, Jonathan R. *Fair Science: Women in the Scientific Community.* Macmillan (Free Pr.) 1979 $24.95
Klein, Ethel. *Gender Politics.* Harvard Univ. Pr. text ed. 1984 $16.50
Mill, John Stuart, and Harriet T. Mill. *The Subjection of Women and Enfranchise-ment of Women.* 1869. Ed. by Sue Mansfield, *Crofts Class. Ser.* Harlan Davidson text ed. 1980 $12.95 pap. $3.95; Merrimack 1983 pap. $6.95
Rosaldo, Michelle Zimbaliste, and Louise Lamphere, eds. *Women, Culture, and Soci-ety.* Stanford Univ. Pr. 1974 $27.50 pap. $8.95
Rosenberg, Rosalind. *Beyond Separate Spheres: Intellectual Roots of Modern Femi-nism.* Yale Univ. Pr. $30.00 pap. $9.95
Rossi, Alice S., ed. *Gender and the Life Course.* Aldine text ed. 1985 $34.95 pap. $14.95
Rothschild, Joan, ed. *Machina Ex Dea: Feminist Perspectives on Technology.* Perga-mon 1983 $27.50 pap. $10.95
Treiman, Donald J., and H. I. Hartmann, eds. *Women, Work and Wages.* Academic Pr. 1981 pap. $9.95

Work

Blau, Peter M., and Otis D. Duncan. *The American Occupational Structure.* Mac-millan (Free Pr.) repr. of 1967 ed. text ed. 1978 pap. $14.95
French, John R. P., Jr., and others. *Career Change in Midlife: Stress, Social Support and Adjustment.* Institute for Social Research text ed. 1983 pap. $15.00
Jackall, Robert, and Henry M. Levin, eds. *Worker Cooperatives in America.* Univ. of California Pr. 1985 $24.95

Kohn, Melvin L., and Carmi Schooler. *Work and Personality: An Inquiry into the Impact of Social Stratification.* Ablex text ed. 1983 $42.50 pap. $22.50
Nelkin, Dorothy, and Michael S. Brown. *Workers at Risk: Voices from the Workplace.* Univ. of Chicago Pr. 1984 $20.00
Parsons, Talcott, and Neil J. Smelser. *Economy and Society.* Routledge & Kegan 1984 pap. $17.95
Roethlisberger, F. J., and William J. Dickson. *Management and the Worker: An Account of a Research Program Conducted by Western Electric Co.* Harvard Business 1939 $35.00
Smith, Ralph E., ed. *The Subtle Revolution: Women at Work.* Urban Institute Pr. 1979 $18.95 pap. $8.95
Thomas, William I., and Florian Znaniecki. *The Polish Peasant in Europe and America.* 1918–20. Octagon 2 vols. 1971 lib. bdg. $144.00

BELL, DANIEL. 1919–

Daniel Bell, an American sociologist, was the labor editor of *Fortune* magazine before he joined the Columbia University faculty in 1952 (he has been at Harvard since 1969), and he has maintained an interest in socialism, capitalism, and the meaning of work ever since. In *The Coming of Post-Industrial Society* he analyzed the role of information in such societies as the United States and Western Europe, which he believes are postindustrial in the sense that the manufacture of industrial products is less important than the production of knowledge and the management of information.

BOOKS BY BELL

Work and Its Discontents. Beacon 1956 o.p.
The End of Ideology: On the Exhaustion of Political Ideas in the Fifties. 1962. Macmillan (Free Pr.) text ed. 1965 pap. $3.50
(ed.). *Toward the Year 2000.* Beacon repr. of 1968 ed. 1969 pap. $3.95
The Coming of Post-Industrial Society. Basic Bks. 1976 o.p.
The Cultural Contradictions of Capitalism. Basic Bks. 1976 pap. $8.95
The Winding Passage: Essays and Sociological Journeys, 1960–1980. Abt Bks. 1980 $25.00; Basic Bks. 1981 pap. $8.00; Univ. Pr. of Amer. 1984 lib. bdg. $32.50

BOOTH, CHARLES. 1840–1916

Charles Booth was a British social reformer and social scientist who was also a wealthy shipowner and industrialist. His monumental 17-volume classic, *The Life and Labour of the People in London, 1890–1900,* based on an enormous amount of statistical and descriptive data, revealed—to cite just one finding that has a modern ring—that 30 percent of the people of London were "below the line of poverty." He was a methodological and sociological precursor of Robert Ezra Park and the Chicago School of urban studies, and all subsequent community studies owe something to his work.

BOOK BY BOOTH

The Life and Labour of the People in London, 1890–1900. 1889–91. AMS Pr. 17 vols. repr. of 1904 ed. $502.50; Kelley 5 vols. rev. ed. repr. of 1902 ed. $125.00

BOOK ABOUT BOOTH

Simey, Thomas S., and Margaret B. Simey. *Charles Booth, Social Scientist.* Greenwood repr. of 1960 ed. 1980 lib. bdg. $27.50

COMTE, AUGUSTE. 1798–1857

Auguste Comte was a French philosopher and moralist who, in 1838, first used the term "sociology." Although his influence is universally acknowledged, his many books are not widely read today. What lives is the name of a core social science discipline and Comte's insight that sociology as a science would develop within the framework of a general reorientation of human thought, a reorientation that characterizes modern industrial society.

BOOKS BY COMTE

System of Positive Polity. 1851–54. Longman 4 vols. 1875–77 o.p.
The Positive Philosophy. 1853. Trans. by Harriet Martineau, AMS Pr. repr. of 1955 ed. $38.50

BOOKS ABOUT COMTE

Aron, Raymond. *Main Currents in Sociological Thought.* Doubleday (Anchor) 2 vols. 1968–70 pap. ea. $5.95
Marvin, Francis S. *Comte: The Founder of Sociology.* Russell repr. of 1936 ed. 1965 $7.50

COOLEY, CHARLES H. 1864–1929

Charles H. Cooley, an American sociologist, was born in Ann Arbor, Michigan, where he spent most of his life. He did little empirical research, but his writings on the individual and the group, and particularly on how the sense of self develops through social interaction (the "looking-glass" self, he called it), have had an enormous influence on all subsequent social psychology. He was an early (1897) critic of Sir Francis Galton's notions about the biological inheritance of genius.

BOOKS BY COOLEY

Sociological Theory and Social Research. Intro. by Roger C. Angell, Kelley repr. of 1930 ed. $29.50. Papers written between 1894 and 1929.
Human Nature and the Social Order. 1902. Intro. by Philip Rieff, *Social Science Class. Ser.* Transaction Bks. 1983 $19.95
Social Organization: A Study of the Larger Mind. 1909. Intro. by Philip Rieff, *Social Science Class. Ser.* Transaction Bks. 1983 pap. $19.95
Social Process. 1918. Intro. by R. C. Hinkle, *Perspectives in Sociology* Southern Illinois Univ. Pr. 1966 $10.00 pap. $3.45

BOOK ABOUT COOLEY

Jandy, Edward C. *Charles Horton Cooley: His Life and His Social Theory.* Octagon repr. of 1942 ed. 1969 lib. bdg. $19.00

DURKHEIM, EMILE. 1858–1917

Emile Durkheim, French sociologist, is—with Max Weber—one of the two principal founders of modern sociology. (Although they were near-contemporaries, they seem not to have known of each other.) He became a professor of sociology at the Sorbonne, where he founded and edited the very important journal *L'année sociologique*. He is renowned for the breadth of his scholarship; for his studies of primitive religion; for creating the concept of *anomie* (normlessness); for his study of the division of labor; and for his insistence that sociologists must use sociological (e.g., rates of behavior) rather than psychological data. His *Suicide* is a major sociological classic, one that is still read today, not so much for its data, which are limited and out-of-date, but for the brilliance of his analysis of suicide rates and other data that had been initially obtained for administrative rather than scientific purposes.

BOOKS BY DURKHEIM

The Division of Labor in Society. 1893. Trans. by W. D. Hall, Macmillan (Free Pr.) text ed. 1985 $9.95
The Rules of Sociological Method. 1895. Macmillan (Free Pr.) 8th ed. 1950 $12.95 text ed. pap. $13.95
Suicide. 1897. Macmillan (Free Pr.) 1951 $24.95 text ed. pap. $9.95
Primitive Classification. 1903. Trans. by Rodney Needham, Univ. of Chicago Pr. 1967 pap. $3.95
The Elementary Forms of the Religious Life. 1912. Trans. by Joseph W. Swain, intro. by Robert Nisbet, Allen & Unwin 2d ed. text ed. 1976 $21.00; trans. by Joseph W. Swain, Macmillan (Free Pr.) text ed. 1965 pap. $14.95
Durkheim and the Law. St. Martin's 1983 $29.95

BOOKS ABOUT DURKHEIM

Alpert, Harry. *Emile Durkheim and His Sociology.* Russell repr. of 1939 ed. 1961 $12.00
Lukes, Steven. *Emile Durkheim: His Life and Work—A Historical and Critical Study.* Harper 1973 $20.00; Penguin 1977 pap. $4.95; Stanford Univ. Pr. 1985 $42.50 pap. $14.95
Parsons, Talcott. *The Structure of Social Action.* 1937. Macmillan (Free Pr.) 2 vols. text ed. 1949 pap. ea. $10.95–$16.95. Includes a major section on Durkheim.
Wolff, Kurt H., ed. *Emile Durkheim, 1858–1917: A Collection of Essays, with Translations and a Bibliography.* Ayer repr. 1979 lib. bdg. $38.00

GOFFMAN, ERVING. 1922–1983

Erving Goffman, an American sociologist, is known for his distinctive method of research and writing. His subject matter was social interaction, and he studied it by observing it himself—no questionnaires, no research assistants, no experiments. The title of his first book, *The Presentation of Self in Everyday Life,* became one of the themes of all of his subsequent research. He also observed and wrote about the social environment in which people live, as in his *Total Institutions* (o.p.). He taught his version of sociology at the University of Pennsylvania; he died during the year in which he served as president of the American Sociological Association.

BOOKS BY GOFFMAN

The Presentation of Self in Everyday Life. Doubleday (Anchor) 1959 pap. $4.95; Overlook Pr. repr. of 1959 ed. 1973 $22.50

Asylums: Essays on the Social Situation of Mental Patients and Other Inmates. Aldine 1961 $22.95; Doubleday (Anchor) pap. $6.95

Encounters: Two Studies in the Sociology of Interaction. Bobbs 1961 pap. $7.20

Forms of Talk. Conduct and Communications Ser. Univ. of Pennsylvania Pr. 1981 $32.00 pap. $10.95

Interaction Ritual: Essays in Face-to-Face Behavior. Pantheon 1982 pap. $4.95

Stigma: Notes on the Management of Spoiled Identity. Prentice-Hall (Spectrum Bks.) 1963 pap. $4.95

Frame Analysis: An Essay on the Organization of Experience. Harper 1974 pap. $7.95; Harvard Univ. Pr. 1974 $25.00

Gender Advertisements. Harper 1979 pap. $9.57; Harvard Univ. Pr. 1979 $15.00

LAZARSFELD, PAUL F. 1901–1976

Paul F. Lazarsfeld was a Viennese-born American mathematician, psychologist, and sociologist who immigrated to the United States in 1933. In Vienna, he had established an applied social research center, which became a model for others in the United States; the most famous product of the Vienna center is *Marienthal*, a pioneering study of unemployment in an Austrian village. In the United States, Lazarsfeld became director of a Rockefeller Foundation-supported study of the impact of radio; through this study, communications research was established as a field of social science inquiry. In 1937, Lazarsfeld founded a research center, which became the Bureau of Applied Social Research at Columbia University; he taught at Columbia from 1940 until 1969. His research areas included mass communications, voting, latent structure analysis, mathematical models, the history of quantitative research, and the analysis of survey data; his major goal was to find intellectual convergences: between the social sciences and the humanities, between concept formation and index construction, and between quantitative and qualitative research. His enthusiasm and his originality had an enormous impact on his colleagues and hundreds of his students; an annual evening lecture and reception at Columbia University provided an opportunity for them to share both vivid memories and current experiences.

BOOKS BY LAZARSFELD

(and others). *Marienthal: The Sociography of an Unemployed Community*. 1933. Aldine 1971 o.p.

(and Frank N. Stanton, eds.). *Radio Research, 1941*. Essential 1941 o.p.

(and others). *The People's Choice: How the Voter Makes Up His Mind in a Presidential Campaign*. 1944. Columbia Univ. Pr. $24.00 pap. $10.00

(and others, eds.). *Continuities in the Language of Social Research*. Macmillan (Free Pr.) 1972 $22.50

(and others). *Voting: A Study of Opinion Formation in a Presidential Campaign*. Univ. of Chicago Pr. 1954 o.p.

(and others, eds.). *The Language of Social Research: A Reader in the Methodology of Social Research.* 1955. Macmillan (Free Pr.) text ed. 1965 pap. $7.95

(and Elihu Katz). *Personal Influence: The Part Played by People in the Flow of Mass Communications.* 1955. Macmillan (Free Pr.) text ed. 1964 pap. $11.95

(and Wagner Thielens, Jr.). *The Academic Mind: Social Scientists in a Time of Crisis.* Ed. by Walter P. Metzger, Ayer repr. of 1958 ed. 1977 $35.50

Qualitative Analysis: Historical and Critical Essays. Allyn & Bacon text ed. 1972 pap. $14.95

The Varied Sociology of Paul F. Lazarsfeld. Ed. by Patricia L. Kendall, intro. by James S. Coleman, Columbia Univ. Pr. 1982 $40.50 pap. $20.00

BOOK ABOUT LAZARSFELD

Merton, Robert K., and others, eds. *Qualitative and Quantitative Social Research: Papers in Honor of Paul F. Lazarsfeld.* Macmillan (Free Pr.) 1979 $23.95

LYND, ROBERT S. 1892–1970, and LYND, HELEN MERRELL. 1894–1982

Robert S. Lynd and Helen Merrell Lynd, American sociologists, became renowned for their pioneering studies of the small city of Muncie, Indiana, which they called Middletown. Not since Tocqueville's *Democracy in America* (1835–1840) has there been such a careful analysis of daily life in an American community. The research in Middletown won Robert Lynd a professorship at Columbia University and Helen Lynd one at Sarah Lawrence College. In the 1970s, Middletown was restudied by a team of sociologists led by Theodore Caplow.

BOOK BY ROBERT S. LYND

Knowledge for What? The Place of Social Science in American Culture. 1939. Princeton Univ. Pr. 1969 o.p.

BOOKS BY ROBERT S. LYND AND HELEN MERRELL LYND

Middletown. 1929. Harcourt 1959 pap. $7.95

Middletown in Transition: A Study in Cultural Conflicts. 1937. Harcourt 1963 pap. $9.95

BOOKS ABOUT ROBERT S. LYND AND HELEN MERRELL LYND

Caplow, Theodore, and others. *All Faithful People: Change and Continuity in Middletown's Religion.* Univ. of Minnesota Pr. 1983 $19.50

———. *Middletown Families: Fifty Years of Change and Continuity.* Univ. of Minnesota Pr. 1982 $18.95

MANNHEIM, KARL. 1893–1947

Karl Mannheim, a Hungarian-born German sociologist, taught at the Universities of Heidelberg and Frankfort until 1933, when the coming of the National Socialists to power forced him to find refuge at the University of London. His major fields of inquiry were the sociology of knowledge and the sociology of intellectual life. His masterpiece *Ideology and Utopia* asserts that there are two types of knowledge: true knowledge based on science, and knowledge based on social class. Ideas are of two types: "utopian" ideas support underprivileged groups, while "ideologies" support privileged groups. His pioneering work in the sociology of knowledge has had relatively little direct influence on contemporary research, but his bringing the concept of ideology to the attention of sociologists has been of consequential importance.

BOOKS BY MANNHEIM

Essays on Sociology and Social Psychology. Oxford 1953 $12.75. Essays first published between 1922 and 1940.

Essays on the Sociology of Knowledge. Ed. by Paul Kecskemeti, Oxford 2d ed. 1952 o.p. Essays first published between 1923 and 1929.

Ideology and Utopia: An Introduction to the Sociology of Knowledge. Harcourt 1955 pap. $4.95. Essays first published between 1929 and 1931.

BOOKS ABOUT MANNHEIM

Loader, Colin. *The Intellectual Development of Karl Mannheim.* Cambridge Univ. Pr. 1985 $34.50

Merton, Robert K. *Social Theory and Social Structure.* 1949. Macmillan (Free Pr.) text ed. 1968 $24.95. See the essay "Karl Mannheim and the Sociology of Knowledge."

MEAD, GEORGE HERBERT. 1863–1931

George Herbert Mead, an American social psychologist, taught at the University of Chicago for his entire career. The task he set for himself was to explain how man learns to think in abstractions, becomes self-conscious, and behaves purposefully and morally. He contended that these attributes rest on language and are acquired and maintained through group life. Social psychology, for Mead, was the study of regularities in individual behavior that result from participation in groups. He was something of a cult figure during and after his lifetime; he published no books, and his posthumous books were reconstructed from his notes and from the notes of students. He was a man far ahead of his time, and many of the concepts he developed at the turn of the century are widely accepted today: the selective nature of perception, cognition through linguistic symbols, role playing, decision processes, reference groups, and socialization through participation in group activities.

BOOKS BY MEAD

Mind, Self, and Society: From the Standpoint of a Social Behaviorist. 1934. Ed. by Charles W. Morris, Univ. of Chicago Pr. 1967 lib. bdg. $30.00; Univ. of Chicago Pr. (Phoenix Bks.) pap. $7.00

Selected Writings: George Herbert Mead. 1964. Ed by Andrew J. Reck, Univ. of Chicago Pr. 1981 $30.00 pap. $10.95

George Herbert Mead on Social Psychology. Ed. by Anselm Strauss, *Heritage of Sociology Ser.* Univ. of Chicago Pr. 1964 $22.50; Univ. of Chicago Pr. (Phoenix Bks.) 1964 pap. $4.95

BOOKS ABOUT MEAD

Miller, David L. *George Herbert Mead: Self, Language, and the World.* Univ. of Chicago
    Pr. (Phoenix Bks.) 1980 pap. $7.95; Univ. of Texas Pr. 1973 $14.50
Schellenberg, James A. *Masters of Social Psychology: Freud, Mead, Lewin and Skin-
    ner.* Oxford 1978 $10.95 pap. $4.95

MERTON, ROBERT K. 1910–

Robert K. Merton, an American sociologist, has had a major impact on almost all branches of sociology and on contemporary intellectual life as well.
Three of his interests are the study of social structure, structural-functional
analysis, and the sociology of science. Many of his concepts have become
central to sociological research today. "The unanticipated consequences of
purposive social action" calls attention to the difference between the intent
and the consequences of social behavior. "The self-fulfilling prophecy" explains, for example, how the beliefs of others about individuals or groups
lead these individuals or groups to act as the others had prophesized. The
"Matthew effect" points out that in science, recognition tends to accrue to
those who already have it, a phenomenon that may both penalize individuals and frustrate the diffusion of new ideas; "Obliteration by incorporation"
is a pattern of success in science and scholarship in which a person's work
becomes so widely accepted that his or her identity is often not mentioned.
Merton has taught at Columbia University since 1941; he is the leader of an
active tradition of empirical research in the sociology of science and scientists; and he is frequently referred to as "the dean of American sociology."

BOOKS BY MERTON

Science, Technology and Society in Seventeenth Century England. 1938. Fertig 1970
    $35.00; Humanities Pr. text ed. 1978 pap. $7.45
Social Theory and Social Structure. 1949. Macmillan (Free Pr.) text ed. 1968 $24.95
(and Paul F. Lazarsfeld, eds.). *Continuities in Social Research: Studies in the Scope
    and Method of the American Soldier.* 1950. *Perspectives in Social Inquiry Ser.* Ayer
    repr. 1974 $16.00
(and others, eds.). *Reader in Bureaucracy.* 1952. Macmillan (Free Pr.) text ed. 1965
    pap. $17.95
(and Patricia Kendall, eds.). *The Student-Physician: Introductory Studies in the Sociol-
    ogy of Medical Education.* Harvard Univ. Pr. 1957 o.p.
(and others, eds.). *Sociology Today: Problems and Prospects.* Basic Bks. 1959 o.p.
On the Shoulders of Giants: A Shandean Postscript. 1965. Afterword by Denis
    Donoghue, Harcourt 1985 $14.95. A brilliant history of the idea that scientists
    can see farther than their predecessors because they stand "on the shoulders of
    giants."
The Sociology of Science: Theoretical and Empirical Investigations. Southern Illinois
    Univ. Pr. 1979 pap. $4.95; ed. by Norman W. Storer, Univ. of Chicago Pr. 1973
    $30.00; Univ. of Chicago Pr. (Phoenix Bks.) 1979 pap. $11.00
(and Jerry Gaston, eds.). *The Sociology of Science in Europe.* 1975. *Perspectives in Soci-
    ology* Southern Illinois Univ. Pr. 1977 $22.95
(and others, eds.). *Toward a Metric of Science: The Advent of Science Indicators.* Wiley
    1978 o.p.

BOOKS ABOUT MERTON

Coser, Lewis A., ed. *The Idea of Social Structure: Papers in Honor of Robert K. Merton.*
Harcourt text ed. 1975 $24.95

Gieryn, Thomas, ed. *Science and Social Structure: A Festschrift for Robert K. Merton.*
New York Academy of Sciences 1980 $17.00

Sztompka, Piotr. *Robert K. Merton's Social Theory.* St. Martin's in progress

MICHELS, ROBERT. 1876–1936

Robert Michels was a German sociologist who spent the last ten years of his life in Italy. In the English-speaking world, he is most famous for his book *Political Parties*, in which he formulated the problem of the oligarchic tendencies of organizations. "He who says organization," he asserted, "says oligarchy." But political parties, he believed, are less oligarchic than single-purpose organizations concerned with specific reforms or with technical problems. An important study of the International Typographical Union, *Union Democracy* by Seymour M. Lipset, Martin A. Trow, and James S. Coleman (1956), has been said by some scholars to challenge many of Michels's findings about organizations. Rather, by printing out the essential characteristics of a democratic trade union, this book confirms Michels's thesis. Michels also wrote about democracy, socialism, revolution, class conflict, trade unionism, mass society, nationalism, imperialism, and intellectuals, and he made intensive studies of the politics of the working class.

BOOKS BY MICHELS

Political Parties: A Sociological Study of the Oligarchical Tendencies of Modern Democracy. 1911. Intro. by Seymour M. Lipset, Macmillan (Free Pr.) text ed. 1966 pap.
$12.95; Peter Smith 1960 $13.25

First Lectures in Political Sociology. Trans. by Alfred de Grazia, *Perspectives in Social Inquiry Ser.* Ayer repr. 1974 $13.00

BOOK ABOUT MICHELS

Coser, Lewis A. *Masters of Sociological Thought: Ideas in Historical and Social Context.* Harcourt 2d ed. text ed. 1977 $24.95

MILLS, C. WRIGHT. 1916–1962

C. Wright Mills, an American sociologist, was one of the most controversial figures in recent decades in the social sciences. He considered himself a rebel against both the academic establishment and American society in general, and he rarely tried to separate his radical ideas from his teaching and writing. Irving Louis Horowitz summarized much of Mills in the subtitle of his biography of him: *An American Utopian.* Mills's most traditionally sociological study is *The Puerto Rican Journey;* his most direct attack on his colleagues in sociology is *The Sociological Imagination* (which he found left much to be desired); and his most ideological sociological book is *The Power Elite,* an attempt to explain the overall power structure of the United States. Mills thought that the dominant "value-free" methodology of American sociology was an ideological mask, hiding values that he did not share.

According to his younger colleague Immanuel Wallerstein, Mills was essentially a utopian reformer who thought that knowledge properly used could bring about a better society.

BOOKS BY MILLS

The New Men of Power. Kelley repr. of 1948 ed. $29.50
(and others.). *The Puerto Rican Journey: New York's Newest Migrants.* Fwd. by Francesco Cordasco, Russell repr. of 1950 ed. 1967 $13.50
White Collar: The American Middle Classes. Oxford 1951 $25.00 pap. $9.95
The Power Elite. Oxford 1956 $27.50 pap. $8.95
The Sociological Imagination. Oxford 1959 $19.95 1967 pap. $6.95
Power, Politics, and People. Ed. by Irving Louis Horowitz, Oxford 1963 $27.50 pap. $11.95

BOOKS ABOUT MILLS

Aptheker, Herbert. *The World of C. Wright Mills.* Kraus repr. of 1960 ed. 1976 $10.00
Horowitz, Irving Louis. *C. Wright Mills: An American Utopian.* Macmillan (Free Pr.) 1983 $19.95 1985 pap. $10.95
————, ed. *The New Sociology: Essays in Social Science and Social Theory in Honor of C. Wright Mills.* Oxford 1964 $19.95 pap. $11.95

MYRDAL, GUNNAR. 1898–   (NOBEL PRIZE 1973)

Gunnar Myrdal, a Swedish economist, gained fame in American sociology for writing one book, *An American Dilemma*, the report of a large-scale Carnegie Corporation-supported study of the status of blacks in American life. (He was awarded the Nobel Peace Prize in 1973; his wife, Alva, a sociologist, received it in 1982.) Myrdal was selected by Carnegie to direct the study of American blacks because he was from "a non-imperialist country with no background of discrimination of one race against another." He arrived in the United States in September 1938 and soon acquired as collaborators of one kind or another nearly all the luminaries of American social science: from Franz Boas to W. I. Thomas to Margaret Mead. The massive report and a large number of complementary books cannot of course be easily summarized; the title refers to Myrdal's conclusion that the black problem does not concern blacks; rather, the problem is how to guide the individual American in reconciling his Christian principles with his behavior and attitudes in his dealings with blacks. The study remains a classic of large-scale, organized research; the extent to which it contributed to the postwar changes in the status of blacks in American society is difficult to determine.

BOOKS BY MYRDAL

An American Dilemma. 1944. Harper 1962 $25.00
Beyond the Welfare State: Economic Planning and Its International Implications. Greenwood repr. of 1960 ed. 1982 lib. bdg. $35.00
Asian Drama: An Inquiry into the Poverty of Nations. Kraus 3 vols. 1968 $30.00; Pantheon 3 vols. 1968 pap. $10.00; Random (Vintage) 1972 pap. $4.95
Against the Stream: Critical Essays on Economics. 1973. Random 1974 o.p.

BOOK ABOUT MYRDAL

Bohrn, Harald. *Gunnar Myrdal.* Garland 1983 lib. bdg. $30.00

OGBURN, WILLIAM FIELDING. 1886–1959

William Fielding Ogburn, an American sociologist, was a professor at the University of Chicago for most of his career. His research into social change, and in the quantitative measurement of social change, lives today in the field of social indicators. Ogburn also created the concept of culture lag to describe how one facet of culture gets out of phase with the others. The most common illustration is that technology develops while the necessary social institutions to control technology lag behind. In the 1920s, Ogburn was appointed by President Hoover chairman of a presidential commission to study social change; its massive report, *Recent Social Trends in the United States,* was published in 1933. It is said that when President-elect Franklin D. Roosevelt took a cruise on Vincent Astor's yacht prior to his inauguration, the page proofs of this book were his major serious reading. Ogburn's many students, particularly Otis Dudley Duncan and Albert J. Reiss, Jr., carry on and extend his interest in the quantitative study of social and cultural change.

BOOKS BY OGBURN

Social Change: With Respect to Culture and Original Nature. 1922. Peter Smith repr. of 1950 ed. 1964 $8.00

Recent Social Trends in the United States. Fwd. by Herbert Hoover, Ayer 2 vols. repr. of 1933 ed. 1979 lib. bdg. $111.00; Greenwood 2 vols. repr. of 1933 ed. lib. bdg. $80.00. Although the President's Research Committee on Social Trends is listed as the author of this book, Ogburn was in fact the editor.

William F. Ogburn on Culture and Social Change: Selected Papers. Ed. by Otis Dudley Duncan, *History of Sociology Ser.* Univ. of Chicago Pr. (Phoenix Bks.) 1964 pap. $2.95

PARK, ROBERT EZRA. 1864–1944

Robert Ezra Park, an American sociologist, was a leading figure in the so-called Chicago School of sociology. The department of sociology at the University of Chicago trained a large number of sociologists in the 1920s and 1930s; it emphasized the study of crime and of urban neighborhoods. Park coauthored with Ernest W. Burgess the most influential text in sociology of the time. With his student R. D. McKenzie he adapted the concepts of animal ecology to the study of the city: invasion, succession, dominance, and so on. They coined the term "human ecology" and published a number of now-famous maps of Chicago showing by means of concentric circles the morphology of the city's growth.

BOOK BY PARK

Collected Papers of Robert Ezra Park. Ed. by Everett C. Hughes and others, Macmillan (Free Pr.) 3 vols. 1950–55 o.p.

PARSONS, TALCOTT. 1902–1979

Talcott Parsons, an American sociologist, introduced Max Weber to American sociology and became himself the leading theorist of American sociology in the postwar year. His 1937 book *The Structure of Social Action* is a detailed comparison of Alfred Marshall, Emile Durkheim, Max Weber, and Vilfredo Pareto. Parsons concluded that these four scholars, coming from contrasting backgrounds and from four different countries, converged, without their knowing of the others, on a common theoretical and methodological position that he called "the voluntaristic theory of action." Subsequently, Parsons worked closely with the anthropologists Clyde Kluckhohn, Elton Mayo, and W. Lloyd Warner, and the psychologists Gordon W. Allport and Henry A. Murray, to define social, cultural, and personality systems as the three main interpenetrative types of action organization. He is widely known for his use of four pattern variables for characterizing social relationships: affectivity versus neutrality, diffuseness versus specificity, particularism versus universalism, and ascription versus achievement.

BOOKS BY PARSONS

The Structure of Social Action. 1937. Macmillan (Free Pr.) 1949 $18.00 2 vols. text ed. pap. ea. $10.95–$16.95
Essays in Sociological Theory. 1949. Macmillan (Free Pr.) rev. ed. text ed. 1964 pap. $14.95
The Social System. 1951. Macmillan (Free Pr.) text ed. 1964 pap. $18.95
Family, Socialization, and Interaction Process. Macmillan (Free Pr.) 1955 o.p.
Sociological Theory and Modern Society. Macmillan (Free Pr.) 1967 $28.50
The Evolution of Societies. Ed. by Jackson Toby, Prentice-Hall text ed. 1977 pap. $17.95

BOOKS ABOUT PARSONS

Black, Max, ed. *The Social Theories of Talcott Parsons: A Critical Examination.* Southern Illinois Univ. Pr. repr. of 1961 ed. 1976 pap. $8.95
Bourricaud, François. *The Sociology of Talcott Parsons.* Trans. by Arthur Goldhammer, Univ. of Chicago Pr. 1981 lib. bdg. $20.00
Hamilton, Peter, ed. *Talcott Parsons. Key Sociologists Ser.* Methuen 1983 $11.50 pap. $4.95
Loubser, Jan J., and others, eds. *Explorations in General Theory in Social Science: Essays in Honor of Talcott Parsons.* Macmillan 1976 (Free Pr.) $85.00

RIESMAN, DAVID. 1909–

David Riesman, an American sociologist, was trained as a lawyer, but became interested in the study of contemporary American society. His book *The Lonely Crowd* became an instant bestseller, as readers saw in it insightful descriptions of themselves and their neighbors. He has subsequently written extensively on American higher education. Within the field of sociology, he is known as the major exponent of qualitative analysis—of learning about the whole through careful and detailed interviews with individuals. He is currently Henry Ford II emeritus professor of sociology at Harvard University.

BOOKS BY RIESMAN

Individualism Reconsidered. Macmillan (Free Pr.) 1954 o.p.

(and Christopher Jencks). *The Academic Revolution.* Univ. of Chicago Pr. (Phoenix Bks.) 1977 pap. $7.95

The Lonely Crowd: A Study of the Changing American Character. Yale Univ. Pr. abr. ed. repr. of 1950 ed. 1973 pap. $9.95

Abundance for What? And Other Essays. Doubleday 1965 o.p.

SHILS, EDWARD. 1915–

Edward Shils, an American sociologist, is a professor at both the University of Chicago and King's College, Cambridge. The editors of a festschrift prepared in his honor note that he has been a pioneer in clearing up the logical confusion over the concept of ideology, and in exploring the role of intellectuals in contemporary life; that his work on the institutionalization of sociology as an academic discipline has been fundamental to all discussions of these questions; that his interpretation of "charisma" and his own concepts of "center" and "periphery" have been indispensable in the analysis of political and cultural leadership and societal cohesion; that his criticism and revision of the term "mass society" have been crucial to a balanced treatment of literature in the modern world; and that he introduced into sociology the concept of "scientific community," now central to the sociology of science. He is the founding editor of *Minerva*, a major journal in the field of higher education and the sociology of knowledge generally.

BOOKS BY SHILS

The Calling of Sociology: And Other Essays on the Pursuit of Learning. Univ. of Chicago Pr. 1980 lib. bdg. $27.50

Center and Periphery: Essays in Macro Sociology. Univ. of Chicago Pr. 1975 vol. 2 $32.50

The Intellectuals and the Powers: And Other Essays. Univ. of Chicago Pr. 1972 o.p.

Tradition. Univ. of Chicago Pr. 1981 lib. bdg. $25.00 pap. $10.95

BOOK ABOUT SHILS

Ben-David, Joseph, and Terry N. Clark. *Culture and Its Creators: Essays in Honor of Edward Shils.* Univ. of Chicago Pr. 1977 $30.00

SIMMEL, GEORG. 1858–1918

Georg Simmel, a German sociologist, was a brilliant scholar who wrote about many aspects of human existence but never developed a systematic theory. He lectured at Berlin for many years, never being given a permanent position because of his Jewish origins, his nonprofessorial brilliance, and what some took to be his destructive intellectual attitude. He is remembered in the United States for a number of insightful essays on such topics as the social role of the stranger and the nature of group affiliation; his book on conflict formed the basis of Lewis A. Coser's *The Functions of Social Conflict*, one of the classics of American sociology.

BOOKS BY SIMMEL

Conflict and the Web of Group Affiliations. 1908. Macmillan (Free Pr.) text ed. 1955
    $14.95 pap. $9.95
The Sociology of Georg Simmel. 1950. Trans. by Kurt H. Wolff, Macmillan (Free Pr.)
    1964 pap. $9.95
Georg Simmel: On Women, Sexuality, and Love. Trans. by Guy Oakes, Yale Univ. Pr.
    1984 $20.00

BOOKS ABOUT SIMMEL

Coser, Lewis A. *The Functions of Social Conflict.* Macmillan (Free Pr.) text ed. 1964
    pap. $11.95
Frisby, David. *Georg Simmel.* Methuen 1984 $11.95 pap. $4.95
Spykman, Nicholas J. *Social Theory of Georg Simmel.* Russell repr. of 1925 ed. 1964
    $8.50
Wolff, Kurt H., ed. *Georg Simmel, 1858–1918: A Collection of Essays, with Transla-
    tions and a Bibliography.* Ohio State Univ. Pr. 1959 $7.50

SOROKIN, PITIRIM A. 1889–1968

   Pitirim A. Sorokin, a Russian-born American sociologist, wrote extensively on such subjects as the sociology of knowledge, the sociology of art,
political sociology, social stratification, and methodology. A scholar of enormous learning, he attempted to analyze the processes of social organization,
disorganization, and reorganization—all within a panoramic view of history that stressed periodic fluctuation as the heart of social change. He
came to the United States in 1922 after he was banned from the Soviet
Union because of his opposition to the Bolshevik regime; during the revolution of 1917, he had been a member of the Constituent Assembly, the private secretary of Prime Minister Kerensky, and the editor of a newspaper.
In the United States, he taught first for six years at the University of Minnesota and then for most of his career at Harvard University. His *Social and
Cultural Dynamics* contains his sociological interpretation of history; his
Fads and Foibles in Modern Sociology and Related Sciences is a comprehensive methodological critique of the quantification and formalization of sociocultural phenomena that he belie,ed characterized sociology in the
United States.

BOOKS BY SOROKIN

Social and Cultural Dynamics. 1937–41. Bedminster Pr. 4 vols. 1962 o.p.
Fads and Foibles in Modern Sociology and Related Sciences. Greenwood repr. of 1956
    ed. 1976 lib. bdg. $26.75
A Long Journey: The Autobiography of Pitirim A. Sorokin. New College & Univ. Pr.
    1963 $13.95

BOOKS ABOUT SOROKIN

Cowell, Frank R. *History, Civilization and Culture: An Introduction to the Historical
    and Social Philosophy of Pitirim A. Sorokin.* Hyperion Pr. repr. of 1950 ed. 1979
    $24.75

Tiryakian, Edward A., ed. *Sociocultural Theory, Values, and Sociocultural Change: Essays in Honor of Pitirim A. Sorokin*. Macmillan (Free Pr.) 1963 o.p.

SPENCER, HERBERT. 1820–1903

Herbert Spencer, an English philosopher-scientist was—with the anthropologists Edward Burnett Tylor and Lewis Henry Morgan—one of the three great cultural evolutionists of the nineteenth century. He was a contemporary of Charles Darwin, and he rejected special creation and espoused organic evolution at about the same time. He did not, however, discover—as did Darwin—that the mechanism for evolution is natural selection. He was immensely popular as a writer in England, and his *The Study of Sociology* became the first sociology textbook ever used in the United States. With the recent revival of interest in evolution, Spencer may receive more attention than he has for half a century.

BOOKS BY SPENCER

The Principles of Psychology. 1855. Longwood Pr. 2 vols. repr. of 1881 ed. 1977 lib. bdg. $70.00
The Study of Sociology. 1873. Intro. by Talcott Parsons, Univ. of Michigan Pr. 1961 pap. $3.25
The Evolution of Society: Selections from Herbert Spencer's "Principles of Sociology." Ed. by Robert L. Carniero, *Midway Repr. Ser.* Univ. of Chicago Pr. repr. of 1967 ed. 1974 pap. $10.50
An Autobiography. 1904. Watts 1926 o.p.

BOOKS ABOUT SPENCER

Rumney, Jay. *Herbert Spencer's Sociology: A Study in the History of Social Theory*. Atherton 1966 o.p.
Wiltshire, David. *The Social and Political Thought of Herbert Spencer*. Oxford Historical Monographs 1978 $29.95

STOUFFER, SAMUEL A. 1900–1960

Samuel A. Stouffer, an American sociologist, was a principal founder of large-scale social research. In 1937, he was asked by the Social Science Research Council to commission a series of research volumes on the depression. He commissioned 13 volumes and saw them all through to publication that same year. In 1940, when Gunnar Myrdal had to return to Stockholm, he completed the research for *An American Dilemma* (1944) and did much of the writing as well. During World War II, he directed a large staff of social scientists, which carried out research for the army, research that was ultimately published in four volumes, including the two volumes of *The American Soldier*. And in 1955 he conducted a major, nationwide study of American attitudes toward civil liberties. He was a master analyst of survey data, and he created the concept of "relative deprivation"—which explains why some soldiers, such as infantrymen, who have poor chances of promotion, did not feel as deprived as far as promotions are concerned as did soldiers in the air force, which had a high promotion rate. His analysis techniques and his writings provide models on which all the best in contemporary survey research is based.

BOOKS BY STOUFFER

(and others). *The American Soldier.* Military Affairs/Aerospace Historian 2 vols. text ed. 1949 ea. $30.00
Measurement and Prediction. 1950. Peter Smith 1966 $16.50
Communism, Conformity and Civil Liberties. 1955. Peter Smith $11.25
Social Research to Test Ideas: Selected Writings. Macmillan (Free Pr.) 1962 o.p.

BOOK ABOUT STOUFFER

Merton, Robert K., and Paul F. Lazarsfeld, eds. *Continuities in Social Research: Studies in the Scope and Method of the American Soldier.* 1950. *Perspectives in Social Inquiry Ser.* Ayer repr. of 1974 ed. $16.00

TAEUBER, CONRAD. 1906–   , and IRENE B. TAEUBER, 1906–1974

Irene B. Taeuber and Conrad Taeuber were leading figures in American demography for nearly 50 years. For most of her life, Irene Taeuber worked physically at the Library of Congress in Washington, D.C., but she was in fact a staff member of the Office of Population Research, Princeton University. Her major interest was in the demography of East Asia, and her masterpiece *The Population of Japan* has been widely acclaimed as the best volume on the demography of one country every produced. Conrad Taeuber was one of the able professionals attracted to Washington in the early days of the Roosevelt administration; he served in the Department of Agriculture from 1935 to 1946, at the United Nations from 1946 to 1951, and at the Bureau of the Census from 1951 to 1973, where he was associate director and the major architect of the 1960 and 1970 censuses. With his wife, he wrote synthetic volumes on each of these two censuses, *The Changing Population of the United States* and *People of the United States in the Twentieth Century.* Together, their work went far toward establishing demography as a scientific discipline and as a source of information crucial to modern government.

BOOKS BY CONRAD TAEUBER AND IRENE B. TAEUBER

The Changing Population of the United States. Wiley 1958 o.p.
The People of the United States in the Twentieth Century. Government Printing Office 1971 o.p.

BOOK BY IRENE TAEUBER

The Population of Japan. Princeton Univ. Pr. 1958 o.p.

THOMAS, W. I. 1863–1947

W. I. Thomas, an American sociologist, published a number of important books on a variety of subjects, but he probably would not have become famous had he not written *The Polish Peasant in Europe and America.* Coauthored with Florian Znaniecki, a Polish sociologist who helped him interpret Polish culture, this massive two-volume work became a classic example of how personal documents such as letters and diaries can be combined with interviews to study social change. Ten years after its publication, in a journal article, Thomas used the phrase "If men define situations as real they are real in their consequences"—a phrase extensively quoted to this day in order to stress the importance of perception over reality in the lives of men and women.

BOOKS BY THOMAS

(and Florian Znaniecki). *The Polish Peasant in Europe and America*. 1918–20. Octagon 2 vols. 1971 lib. bdg. $144.00

The Unadjusted Girl, with Cases and Standpoints for Behavior Analysis. Gannon 1967 lib. bdg. $15.00; fwd. by W. Dummer, Patterson Smith repr. of 1923 ed. 1969 $12.00

Social Behavior and Personality: Contributions of W. I. Thomas to Theory and Social Research. Ed. by Edmund H. Volkart, fwd. by Donald Young, Greenwood repr. of 1951 ed. 1981 lib. bdg. $35.00

W. I. Thomas on Social Organization and Social Personality. Ed. by Morris Janowitz, Heritage of Sociology Ser. Univ. of Chicago Pr. (Phoenix Bks.) 1966 pap. $3.95

TOCQUEVILLE, ALEXIS DE. 1805–1859

[SEE Chapter 7 in this volume.]

TÖNNIES, FERDINAND. 1855–1936

Ferdinand Tönnies, a German sociologist, was a major figure in Germany at the turn of the century. He, Georg Simmel, Werner Sombart, and Max Weber founded the German Sociological Society, and Tönnies was president from 1909 until 1933, when he was dismissed from all his positions by the Nazis. His fame rests largely on his first book, *Gemeinschaft und Gesellschaft*, published in 1887, which went through seven editions in German and was published in English in 1957 as *Community and Society*. Social clubs and religious sects, for example, result from mutual sympathy, habit, or common belief; these involve gemeinschaft-like social relationships. Business and political organizations, on the other hand, are intended by their members to be means to specific ends; these involve gesellschaft-like relationships. This typology is closely related to others: status-contract (Henry Sumner Maine); rural-urban; organic-mechanical solidarity (Emile Durkheim); folk-urban (Robert Redfield); and particularism-universalism (Talcott Parsons).

BOOK BY TÖNNIES

Community and Society. 1887. Trans. by Charles P. Loomis, Harper text ed. 1977 pap. $3.95

VEBLEN, THORSTEIN. 1857–1929

Thorstein Veblen, an American economist and sociologist, was an unorthodox teacher who had a troubled domestic life. Accordingly, he never held an academic position for long. For a few years in the early 1920s he was one of the "big four" on the faculty of the New School for Social Research; the others were JOHN DEWEY, James Harvey Robertson, and Wesley C. Mitchell. In

1926 he retired to a cabin in California where he died in obscurity and poverty three years later. He published a remarkable series of books, all critical of the major institutions of American society; it was said of him that he was the last man who knew everything. His fame today rests largely on *The Theory of the Leisure Class*, an analysis of the latent functions of "conspicuous consumption" and "conspicuous waste" as symbols of upper-class status and as competitive methods of enhancing individual prestige.

BOOKS BY VEBLEN

The Theory of the Leisure Class. Kelley repr. of 1899 ed. $35.00; intro. by Robert Lekachman, New Amer. Lib. 1954 pap. $3.95; Penguin 1979 pap. $4.95
The Higher Learning in America. Kelley repr. of 1918 ed. $25.00
The Engineers and the Price System. 1919. Kelley repr. of 1921 ed. $19.50; intro. by Daniel Bell, *Social Science Class. Ser.* Transaction Bks. 1983 pap. $12.95
The Portable Veblen. Ed. by Max Lerner, *Viking Portable Lib.* Penguin 1958 pap. $4.95

BOOKS ABOUT VEBLEN

Dorfman, Joseph. *Thorstein Veblen and His America.* Kelley repr. of 1934 ed. $37.50
Duffus, Robert L. *The Innocents at Cedro: A Memoir of Thorstein Veblen and Some Others.* Kelley repr. of 1944 ed. lib. bdg. $22.50
Riesman, David. *Thorstein Veblen: A Critical Interpretation.* Continuum repr. of 1960 ed. 1975 pap. $4.95

WEBER, MAX. 1864–1920

Max Weber, a German political economist, legal historian, and sociologist, has had an impact on the social sciences that is difficult to overestimate. According to a widely held view, he was the founder of the modern way of conceptualizing society and thus the modern social sciences. His major interest was in the process of rationalization, which characterizes Western civilization—what he called the "demystification of the world." This led him to examine the three types of domination or authority that characterize hierarchical relationships: charismatic, traditional, and legal. It also led him to the study of bureaucracy and all of the world's major religions; and it led him to examine capitalism, which he viewed as a product of the Protestant ethic. With his contemporary the French sociologist Emile Durkheim—they seem not to have known each other's work—he created modern sociology.

BOOKS BY WEBER

The Protestant Ethic and the Spirit of Capitalism. 1904–05. Intro. by Anthony Giddens, *Counterpoint Pap. Ser.* Allen & Unwin pap. $6.95; Peter Smith 1984 $15.50; Scribner rev. ed. repr. of 1930 ed. 1977 pap. $8.95
The Religion of China. 1915. Macmillan (Free Pr.) text ed. 1968 $14.95
The Religion of India. 1916–17. Macmillan (Free Pr.) 1967 o.p.
Ancient Judaism. 1917–19. Macmillan (Free Pr.) text ed. 1967 pap. $13.95
The Sociology of Religion. 1922. Trans. by Ephraim Fischoff, Beacon 1964 pap. $9.95
The Theory of Social and Economic Organization. 1922. Trans. by Talcott Parsons, Macmillan (Free Pr.) 1947 $17.95 text ed. pap. $14.95

From Max Weber: Essays in Sociology. Trans. by Hans H. Gerth and C. Wright Mills, Oxford 1946 pap. $9.95

Max Weber on Methodology of the Social Sciences. Macmillan (Free Pr.) text ed. 1949 $16.95. Three essays first published in 1904, 1905, and 1917.

BOOKS ABOUT WEBER

Bendix, Reinhard. *Max Weber: An Intellectual Portrait.* Univ. of California Pr. 1978 $40.00 pap. $9.95

Giddens, Anthony. *Capitalism and Modern Social Theory: An Analysis of the Writings of Marx, Durkheim and Max Weber.* Cambridge Univ. Pr. 1971 $44.50 pap. $12.95

Mitzman, Arthur. *The Iron Cage: An Historical Interpretation of Max Weber.* Intro. by Lewis A. Coser, Transaction Bks. 1984 pap. $12.95

Parsons, Talcott. *The Structure of Social Action.* 1937. Macmillan (Free Pr.) 2 vols. text ed. 1949 pap. ea. $10.95–$16.95

Weber, Marianne. *Max Weber: A Biography.* Ed. and trans. by Harry Zohn, Wiley 1975 $34.95

Wrong, Dennis, ed. *Max Weber.* Prentice-Hall (Spectrum Bks.) 1970 pap. $2.45

CHAPTER 5

Education

Karen Brown

> I believe that all education proceeds by the participation of the individual in the social consciousness of the race.
> —John Dewey, *Dewey on Education*

> Education is the acquisition of the art of the utilization of knowledge.
> —Alfred North Whitehead, *The Aims of Education and Other Essays*

As an integral part of our society, education touches everyone—students, teachers, parents, taxpayers, legislators, and researchers. The history of education in the United States reflects a history of public participation and debate. The importance of equal educational opportunities and the Jeffersonian ideal that only an informed, educated person can preserve the principles of freedom are strongly held. But as Lawrence A. Cremin points out in *Traditions of American Education*, "The institutions of American education are human institutions." Everyone has a stake in the aims and outcomes of the educational system, and as a result, the literature of the field abounds. Of particular note is the range of disciplines and interests represented in the literature. It is not only teachers and educational researchers who write. A quick review shows that journalists, historians, parents, politicians, philosophers, and scientists also join in the dialogue. Recurrent themes emerge: How can learning best be fostered? What are the goals of schools? Who is best qualified to teach? What should be taught and when? The search for answers to these questions has often led to educational reforms and even to how we define education. In the summary of his book, Cremin urges that "individual institutions and individual variables are important, to be sure, but it is the ways in which they pattern themselves and relate to one another that give them their educational significance, and the ways in which their outcomes confirm, complement, or contradict one another that determine their educational effects."

The literature of education written in the last decade continues to raise these questions and seek new answers. What makes the questions different is the expanded concept of education. Education is no longer confined to traditional institutions, such as schools and universities. Parents are being encouraged to develop the intellectual abilities of their infants at home, and middle-aged and older adults are returning to the classroom (or in many cases, the classroom is brought to them). The public school system continues to educate the masses of children, but private and religious schools have increasingly emerged as an alternative, and some would argue that this has occurred to fill a gap in quality not being maintained by the public schools.

As in past years there is continued concern about quality education for ethnic minority groups, but the notion of equal educational opportunities has broadened to include individuals with learning disabilities and children who do not speak English as their first language. And questions are being asked about the content of education. What is the role of liberal arts, sciences, and basic skills in preparing students for the future needs of society (and the world), and are present educational institutions best equipped for this responsibility? In the works mentioned below there are examples of corporations and businesses turning away from colleges and universities for the continued education of their employees.

Finally, and perhaps most significantly, teachers and schools are finding themselves immersed in issues of accountability. Recent public pressure and, in some cases, court decisions are having a profound impact on education. The results of changes initiated to improve the quality and value of education have not been fully assessed and will continue to be discussed and debated.

The literature of education invites the reader to join in the discussion. The capacity for learning is closely tied to both an individual's growth and a society's potential. The complexities of contemporary society are demanding participation in educational endeavors by people of all ages and vocations. It is this changing perspective that has given recent educational literature its richness and diversity.

BIBLIOGRAPHY

Adams, Anthony, and Esnor Jones. *Teaching Humanities in the Microelectronic Age.* Taylor & Francis 1983 pap. $13.00. This is not a how-to manual, but rather a collection of essays that explores the issues surrounding the introduction and use of computers in the language arts curriculum.

Adler, Mortimer J. *The Paideia Proposal: An Educational Manifesto.* Macmillan 1984 $7.95 pap. $3.95. ". . . Adler sounds confident that those most concerned about public schooling will heed his appeal: parents alarmed over declining educational standards, school boards disheartened by the middle-class flight to private and parochial schools, and teachers genuinely committed to academic excellence. . . . If the Paideia proposal provokes the sort of serious-minded consideration it deserves, . . . this slim little missive might contribute immeasurably to the larger on-going debate about the future of American public education" (Christopher Lucas, *Educational Studies*).

Altbach, Philip G., ed. *Comparative Higher Education Abroad: Bibliography and Analysis.* Interbk. 1976 pap. $5.50; Praeger text ed. 1976 $19.95; Wilson 1979 $31.00. Includes an essay that surveys the historical, political, and international comparative nature of higher education.

Apps, Jerold W. *Problems in Continuing Education.* McGraw-Hill 1979 $19.95. An overview of the goals of continuing adult education as reflected through a study of human nature, the context and content of continuing education, and teaching/learning principles.

Aslanian, Carol B., and Henry M. Brickell. *Americans in Transition: Life Changes as Reasons for Adult Learning.* College Board 1980 $6.50. Summary report based on interviews with 2,000 U.S. adults on what type of life transitions trigger learning. Excellent background reading.

Avrich, Paul. *The Modern School Movement: Anarchism and Education in the United States.* Princeton Univ. Pr. 1980 $40.00 pap. $14.50. "Avrich's immensely engaging book . . . brings back to life the marvelously rich and vivid personalities associated with the education experiment . . . [of] the Modern School Movement" (Alan Ryan, *TLS*).

Barth, Roland S. *Run School Run.* Harvard Univ. Pr. text ed. 1980 $20.00. Written by an elementary school principal, who relates his experiences in encouraging pluralistic education in the schools.

Bennis, Warren. *The Leaning Ivory Tower. Higher Education Ser.* Jossey-Bass 1974 $18.95

Bergevin, Paul. *A Philosophy of Adult Education.* Winston Pr. (Seabury) repr. 1970 pap. $4.95

Bloom, Benjamin S. *All Our Children Learning: A Primer for Parents, Teachers, and Other Educators.* McGraw-Hill 1980 $17.95 1982 pap. $6.95. ". . . a fine book which should be read by everyone interested in understanding more about how children learn and how we should teach them" (B. M. Caldwell, *Harvard Educational Review*).

Bowen, James. *A History of Western Education.* St. Martin's 3 vols. 1972–81 ea. $27.50–$35.00. "Bowen's three-volume work supersedes all previous histories of Western education" (*Choice*).

Boyer, Ernest L. *High School: A Report of the Carnegie Foundation for the Advancement of Teaching.* Harper 1983 $14.42. "This book is an important contribution to the coming educational policy debate of the 1980's; beyond that, it is a powerful and well-articulated vision of what secondary education can be" (*Choice*).

Brodinsky, Ben. *Defining the Basics of American Education.* Phi Delta Kappa 1977 pap. $.75. A concise summary of a meeting of national educators concerned with basic skills in the school curriculum.

Bruner, Jerome S. *The Relevance of Education. Norton Lib.* 1971 $5.95 pap. $4.95

Cahn, Steven M. *Education and the Democratic Ideal.* Nelson-Hall 1979 $19.95 pap. $9.95. "The intention of the author is to present a coherent, thorough, and sound philosophy of higher education. He effectively achieves this. . . . Although the examples are drawn from higher education, the message is applicable to any education level" (J. J. Groark, *LJ*).

Calvin, Allen, ed. *Perspectives on Education.* Addison-Wesley text ed. 1977 pap. $10.95. A collection of 17 original articles focusing on contemporary issues in education.

Churgin, Jonah R. *The New Woman and the Old Academe: Sexism and Higher Education.* Libra 1979 $7.95. "In three parts, Churgin deals successfully with the problems women face in society today, the particular manifestations of these problems on the college campus, and the beneficial effects of affirmative action for both men and women" (*Choice*).

Commager, Henry S. *The Commonwealth of Learning.* Harper 1968 o.p.

Cremin, Lawrence A. *American Education: The Colonial Experience, 1607–1783.* Harper o.p.

———. *American Education: The National Experience, 1783–1876.* Harper 1980 $29.95 1982 pap. $11.06. With the volume above, the first two of a planned three-volume comprehensive history.

———. *Traditions of American Education.* Basic Bks. 1979 $9.95. In this series of published lectures, the complexity of the U.S. educational system is put in a historical framework.

Dewey, John. (See Dewey's main listing in this chapter.)

Duke, Daniel L. *Teaching: The Imperiled Profession.* State Univ. of New York 1983 $34.50 pap. $8.95. Examines not only contemporary issues, but also the rewards and frustrations of the teaching profession.

Education Index. 1929–to date. Wilson annual ea. $65.00. A comprehensive index to more than 250 educational periodicals.

Eisner, Elliot W. *The Educational Imagination: On the Design and Education of School Programs.* Macmillan 2d ed. text ed. 1985. "This seminal work in curriculum theory effectively challenges most of the conventional wisdom of current educational thinking" (*Choice*).

Finn, Chester E., Jr., and others, eds. *Against Mediocrity: The Humanities in America's High Schools.* Fwd. by William J. Bennett, Holmes & Meier text ed. 1984 $29.50 pap. $11.50

Freire, Paulo. *Pedagogy of the Oppressed.* Intro. by R. Schaull, trans. by Myro B. Ramos, Continuum 1970 pap. $9.95. A radical theory of education that evolved from the author's work with illiterate adults in Third World countries.

Fuller, R. Buckminster. *R. Buckminster Fuller on Education.* Ed. by Peter H. Wagschal and Robert D. Kahn, Univ. of Massachusetts Pr. 1979 pap. $8.50. A collection of essays by an ardent critic of American education. He argues for increased and more innovative uses of technology as an educational medium.

Gardner, John W. *Excellence: Can We Be Equal and Excellent Too?* Norton rev. ed. 1984 $12.95. Revision of Gardner's 1961 work that examines the social contexts that promote or stifle excellence and the role of schools in this process.

Garibaldi, Antoine, ed. *Black Colleges and Universities: Challenges for the Future.* Praeger 1984 $29.95. Fifteen papers addressing the current and future roles for black colleges.

Garms, Walter I., James W. Guthrie, and L. C. Pierce. *School Finance: The Economics and Politics of Public Education.* Prentice-Hall text ed. 1978 $27.95. "Stimulating and controversial, . . . the book is worth thoughtful reading by concerned laymen in spite of a few technical chapters" (*LJ*).

Giametti, A. Bartlett. *The University and the Public Interest.* Atheneum 1981 $12.95. The president of Yale University explores "such topics as private universities, the federal government, language, athletics, power and politics, and teachers. Although each is a self-contained piece, the refreshing writing style, vocabulary, and relationship to the theme tie them into an intellectually stimulating volume" (*Choice*).

Goodlad, John I. *What Schools Are For.* Foundation Monograph Ser. Phi Delta Kappa 1979 pap. $5.50. "An exceptionally readable and potentially helpful book. . . . [It] is a book in praise of the American dream of a common school, but, instead of calling us to quick action, Goodlad speaks of the need for thoughtful dialogue" (N. V. Overly, *Phi Delta Kappan*).

Grambs, Jean D. *Schools, Scholars and Society.* Prentice-Hall rev. ed. 1978 pap. $18.95. "The major emphasis of her book . . . centers on the discussion of elementary, secondary, and post-secondary educational organizations as cultural systems. . . . She devotes attention to the problems of racism and sexism in the community as well as the school" (R. G. Salem, *Contemporary Sociology*).

Greene, Maxine. *Landscapes of Learning*. Teachers College Pr. text ed. 1978 pap. $13.95. The author's essays delve into emancipatory education, social issues as they affect pedagogy, artistic-aesthetic concerns, and the predicaments of women.

Grosjean, François. *Life with Two Languages: An Introduction to Bilingualism*. Harvard Univ. Pr. text ed. 1982 $22.50 1984 pap. $9.95

Hawkridge, David G. *New Information Technology in Education*. Johns Hopkins Univ. Pr. 1983 $20.00. Interesting and informative reading that surveys the new information technologies, how they are being used for learning (preschool through adult education), the social, economic, and educational problems that arise with their use, and forecasts for the future.

Hoffman, Nancy, ed. *Woman's "True" Profession: Voices from the History of Teaching*. Feminist Pr. 1981 $17.95 pap. $8.95. Excerpts from autobiographies, letters, diaries, oral histories, and other primary sources provide insights into the experiences and personal lives of classroom teachers between 1830 and 1920.

Hofstadter, Richard, and Wilson Smith. *American Higher Education: A Documentary History*. Univ. of Chicago Pr. 2 vols. 1968 lib. bdg. $35.00; Univ. of Chicago Pr. (Phoenix Bks.) pap. ea. $3.95–$4.50

Holt, John. *How Children Learn*. Delacorte rev. ed. 1983 $14.95; Dell rev. ed. 1983 pap. $5.95. Expands on Holt's earlier work to include preschool children. Concludes that education at its best avoids intruding on children's natural desire to learn.

Houle, Cyril O. *Patterns of Learning: New Perspectives on Life Span Education*. *Higher Education Ser*. Jossey-Bass text ed. 1984 $16.95. Successfully highlights an eclectic group of individuals (sixteenth-century Frenchman Michel de Montaigne, Henry David Thoreau, Billy Graham, to name a few) and educational methods (for example, travel and oratory) to show the complex nature of education as a lifelong activity.

Hurn, Christopher J. *The Limits and Possibilities of Schooling: An Introduction to the Sociology of Education*. Allyn & Bacon text ed. 1978 $29.29. "Few (if any) secondary materials of this quality exist which include discussion of recent radical thinking about schools" (D. W. Alwin, *Contemporary Sociology*).

Illich, Ivan. *Deschooling Society*. *World Perspective Ser*. Harper 1983 pap. $4.76

Jacoby, Susan. *Inside Soviet Schools*. Hill & Wang 1974 $8.95; Schocken 1975 pap. $4.95

Jencks, Christopher, and David Riesman. *The Academic Revolution*. Fwd. by Martin Trow, Univ. of Chicago Pr. (Phoenix Bks.) 1977 pap. $7.95. "A whopping sociological and historical analysis of American higher education" (*New York*).

Kerr, Clark. *The Uses of the University*. Harvard Univ. Pr. 3d ed. text ed. 1982 pap. $7.95. The author reviews his original, widely read work to assess the changing nature and role of higher education.

Kilpatrick, William Heard. (See Kilpatrick's main listing in this chapter.)

Knowles, Malcolm M. *Self-Directed Learning: A Guide for Learners and Teachers*. Cambridge Bk. 1975 pap. $7.67. A classic work that establishes a rationale for self-directed learning experiences and then provides a framework for implementing the ideas.

Kohl, Herbert. *Basic Skills: A Guide for Parents and Teachers on the Subjects Most Vital to Education*. Bantam 1984 pap. $3.95

————. *Basic Skills: A Plan for Your Child, A Program for All Children*. Little, Brown 1982 $12.95. Defines five basic skills (language ability, problem solving, scientific understanding, use of the imagination, and an understanding of group process) and proposes a program for implementing them in public education.

————. *Thirty-Six Children*. New Amer. Lib. (Signet) 1973 pap. $2.95

Lightfoot, Sara L. *The Good High School: Portraits of Character and Culture*. Basic Bks. 1983 $19.95 1985 pap. $9.95. Descriptions of two inner-city high schools, two upper middle-class high schools, and two elite preparatory schools based on interviews and observations. All schools are judged excellent, but each succeeds in different ways.

Madaus, George F., Peter W. Airasian, and Thomas Kellaghan. *School Effectiveness: A Reassessment of the Evidence*. McGraw-Hill text ed. 1980 $18.50. Discusses the concepts and issues that emerged following the 1960s' federally based educational reform efforts.

McCarthy, Martha M. *Public School Law: Teachers' and Students' Rights*. Fwd. by Alexander Kern, Allyn & Bacon 1981 $29.95. A well-organized and relatively nontechnical account of the legal foundations of American public education.

Morris, Robert C. *Reading, Writing and Reconstruction: The Education of Freedmen in the South, 1861–1870*. Univ. of Chicago Pr. 1982 lib. bdg. $25.00. A comprehensive history of the contributions of religious and secular organizations and the government toward schooling of the freedmen.

Nachtigal, Paul M., ed. *Rural Education: In Search of a Better Way*. Education Ser. Westview Pr. 1982 lib. bdg. $32.00 text ed. pap. $13.00. "The editor . . . led a team of observers in on-site visits of 13 different [rural education] programs. . . . The results are reported by the observers in a case-study format written in a free-flowing journalistic . . . [that is] easy to read" (*Choice*).

Nasaw, David. *Schooled to Order: A Social History of Public Schooling in the United States*. Oxford 1979 $22.50 pap. $8.95. "Carefully researched, well written, and evenhanded, Nasaw's book is an important addition to the debate over the evolution of public education in the United States" (E. Beauchamp, *LJ*).

Nathan, Joe. *Free to Teach: Achieving Equity and Excellence in Schools*. Intro. by Herbert Kohl, Pilgrim Pr. 1983 $14.95; Winston Pr. 1984 pap. $7.95. An assistant principal describes his own experiences and presents ideas for educational program innovation and policy reforms.

Neill, A. S. *Summerhill: A Radical Approach to Child Rearing*. Pocket Bks. 1977 pap. $8.95

Ogbu, John U. *Minority Education and Caste: The American System in Cross-Cultural Perspective*. Academic Pr. 1978 o.p. The author, an anthropologist born in Nigeria, argues that lower school performance of blacks is tied to the myths and stereotypes perpetuated by the U.S. system of racial stratification.

O'Neil, Robert M. *Classrooms in the Crossfire: The Rights and Interests of Students, Parents, Teachers, Administrators, Librarians and the Community*. Indiana Univ. Pr. 1981 $17.50. A balanced, clear analysis of the current increase in attacks on the public school curriculum, textbooks, and libraries.

Ortiz, Flora I. *Career Patterns in Education: Women, Men and Minorities in Public School Administration*. Holt 1981 $19.95; Bergin & Garvey 1982 $24.95. Using the public school as a framework, this study explores the interaction of organizations and the individuals in them.

Papert, Seymour. *Mindstorms: Children, Computers, and Powerful Ideas*. Basic Bks. 1982 $15.95 pap. $6.95. "Papert worked with Piaget for five years on how children become thinkers, and then he worked at MIT on how to make machines

that think. Using this background, he has examined the current use of computers in the classrooms. . . . *Mindstorms* should prove stimulating for parents and
educators alike" (Sarah Berman, *Science Bks. & Films*).

Parsons, Talcott, and Gerald Platt. *The American University.* Harvard Univ. Pr. text
ed. 1973 $27.50. "Not only is its senior author America's most influential sociolo-
gist, but the volume provides one of the very few efforts to place the university
in its societal context" (*Choice*).

Passmore, John. *The Philosophy of Teaching.* Harvard Univ. Pr. text ed. 1980 $27.50.
"There is nothing he discusses which he does not illuminate" (Kenneth Minogue,
TLS).

Perkinson, Henry J. *Since Socrates: Studies in the History of Western Educational
Thought.* Longman text ed. 1980 pap. $14.95. A historical survey of significant
trends in educational philosophy and thought.

Piaget, Jean. (See Piaget's main listing in this chapter and in Chapter 4.)

Postman, Neil. *Teaching as a Conserving Activity.* Dell (Delta) 1980 pap. $9.95. Post-
man proposes an idea-centered educational program—one that includes the
study of history, standard English, and the philosophies of science and religion.

Pusey, Nathan M. *American Higher Education, 1945–1970: A Personal Report.* Harvard Univ. Pr. 1978 $15.00. The president of Harvard University presents a read-
able account of the quantitative and qualitative changes in higher education
from the postwar boom to the 1970s reevaluation.

Ravitch, Diane. *The Schools We Deserve: Reflections on the Educational Crisis of Our
Time.* Basic Bks. 1985 $19.95

———. *The Troubled Crusade: American Education, 1945–1980.* Basic Bks. 1983
$19.95 1985 pap. $8.95. A well-documented survey that takes into account the
numerous political, racial, and cultural issues influencing schools during the
post-World War II period.

Reutter, Edmund E., Jr. *The Supreme Court's Impact on Public Education.* Phi Delta
Kappa 1982 $9.00 pap. $7.00. "Up to date and comprehensive, the book summarizes the decisions of the Supreme Court that directly affect or have had substantial effect on public education policies and procedures. . . . Reutter's writing [is
to be admired] for its precision and its freedom from legal and education argot"
(Robert E. Phay, *Phi Delta Kappan*).

Roedell, Wendy C., Nancy E. Jackson, and Halbert B. Robinson. *Gifted Young Children.* Ed. by Abraham J. Tannenbaum, *Perspectives on Gifted and Talented Education Ser.* Teachers College Pr. text ed. 1980 pap. $7.95. "This information would
be useful to parents of precocious preschoolers, to directors of early childhood
education programs, and to school districts interested in providing appropriate
differentiated education to gifted students throughout their school careers"
(M. C. Rhodes, *Phi Delta Kappan*).

Sewall, Gilbert T. *Necessary Lessons: Decline and Renewal in American Schools.* Macmillan (Free Pr.) 1983 $16.75. "*Newsweek*'s education editor critically evaluates
the current state of America's schooling, beset as it is with academic and attitu-
dinal problems" (Shirley L. Hopkinson, *LJ*).

Simon, John B. *To Become Somebody: Growing Up against the Grain of Society.* Fwd.
by Robert Coles, Houghton Mifflin 1982 $12.95. "Simon draws on his own fam-
ily history, personal values, and lifework for this well-written account of a com-
munity-based educational program that tried to build better lives and greater
understanding out of the chaotic and oppressive background of the inner city
ghetto" (Corrine Muldoon, *LJ*).

Sizler, Theodore R. *Horace's Compromise: The Dilemma of the American High School.*

Houghton Mifflin 1984 $16.95. Cosponsored by the National Association of Secondary School Principals and the Commission on Educational Issues of the National Association of Independent Schools, this report on teachers, students, and the subjects they study emerges from interviews and observations at 15 high schools across the country.

Strike, Kenneth A., and Kieran Egan, eds. *Ethics and Educational Policy. International Lib. of the Philosophy of Education* Routledge & Kegan 1978 $18.50. This collection of well-written, insightful essays addresses the aims of education from elementary school to higher education.

Taylor, John F. A. *The Public Commission of the University: The Role of the Community of Scholars in an Industrial, Urban, and Corporate Society.* New York Univ. Pr. 1981 $29.50. "A provocative study . . .Taylor's well-penned volume represents a timely and valuable contribution to the literature regarding the commission of American universities" (D. Weller, *Educational Studies*).

Thorndike, Edward L. (See Thorndike's main listing in this chapter.)

Tyack, David B. *The One Best System: A History of American Urban Education.* Harvard Univ. Pr. text ed. 1974 $20.00 pap. $7.95 "This excellent analysis by one of the new revisionist historians of education, concentrates on the decision-making processes and organization of urban public schools during the last fifteen years" (*LJ*).

U.S. National Commission on Excellence in Education. *Nation at Risk: The Imperative for Educational Reform.* Government Printing Office 1983 pap. $4.50. This committee report, which has stirred considerable debate, defines problems and solutions in American educational curricula, standards, basic skills, teacher preparation and the teaching profession, educational leadership, and fiscal support.

Washington, Booker T. (See Washington's main listing in this chapter.)

Williams, Frederick, and Victoria Williams. *Microcomputers in Elementary Education: Perspectives on Implementation.* Wadsworth text ed. 1984 $21.75. Based upon on-site investigations of 12 elementary schools and the issues surrounding their implementation of computers and how they are being used.

BARNARD, HENRY. 1811–1900

As the first U.S. commissioner of education (1867–70), Barnard was influential in shaping the future direction of the U.S. Office of Education. He initiated numerous reforms and promoted the importance of education (not just schools) through federally sponsored experimentation, research, and scholarship, and the collection and dissemination of educational statistics and information.

Barnard's emphasis on a need to create common school districts throughout the United States was based on his strong belief in public education and the notion that schools should foster moral education and temper social unrest. In addition to his books, which cover a wide range of educational issues and concerns, Barnard was the founder and editor of a widely read journal, *The American Journal of Education* (1855–82).

BOOKS BY BARNARD

Reformatory Education: Papers on Preventive, Correctional and Reformatory Institutions and Agencies in Different Countries. Folcroft repr. 1978 lib. bdg. $20.00; Richard West repr. of 1857 ed. 1980 lib. bdg. $32.50

Henry Barnard on Education. Ed. by John S. Brubacher, Russell repr. of 1931 ed. 1965 $8.50

BOOKS ABOUT BARNARD

Downs, Robert B. *Henry Barnard. World Leaders Ser.* G. K. Hall (Twayne) 1977 $13.50

Lannie, Vincent P. *Henry Barnard: American Educator.* Teachers College Pr. text ed. 1974 $10.00 pap. $5.00

Neuman, A. R. *Dr. Barnard as I Knew Him. Educational Ser.* Norwood repr. of 1914 ed. $8.50

Thursfield, Richard E. *Henry Barnard's American Journal of Education.* AMS Pr. repr. of 1945 ed. $28.50

DEWEY, JOHN. 1859–1952

John Dewey is known as the foremost authority on progressive education in the United States. In 1899, he published his revolutionary book *The School and Society,* "which is considered," says BERTRAND RUSSELL (see Vol. 4), "the most influential of all his writings." "Progressive" schools, embodying his concept of learning while experiencing—or becoming involved in the process of knowledge, as opposed to mere book learning and rote reproduction of the words of the teacher—burgeoned in this country in the 1920s. Taking field trips, making model cities and villages, using dramatization, and freer classrooms with movable furniture are just a few of the elements in which Dewey's view of education as personal inquiry is pursued in education today.

Logic: The Theory of Inquiry, published when he was nearly 80, is Dewey's major philosophical work. He made his field the whole of human experience—including politics and psychology—following eagerly wherever the spirit of inquiry might lead him. Dewey accepted American democracy completely and believed that democracy is a primary ethical value.

He taught at the Universities of Michigan and Minnesota before becoming the chairperson of the philosophy and education department at the University of Chicago (1894–1904). While at Chicago, he initiated reform movements in educational theory and methods, testing many of them in the university's high school. In 1904, Dewey became professor of philosophy at Columbia University, where he remained until his retirement in 1930.

Dewey was also active in a number of other areas, including the founding of the New School for Social Research and the organization of New York City's first teachers' union. He was recognized as honorary vice-president of the New York State Liberal Party.

BOOKS BY DEWEY

The Early Works of John Dewey, 1882–1898. Ed. by Jo Ann Boydston, Southern Illinois Univ. Pr. 5 vols. 1967–72 ea. $17.50–$19.95 pap. ea. $6.95–$7.95

The Middle Works of John Dewey, 1899–1924. Ed. by Jo Ann Boydston, Southern Illinois Univ. Pr. 15 vols. 1976–1983 ea. $19.95–$25.00

The Later Works of John Dewey, 1925–1953. Southern Illinois Univ. Pr. 5 vols. 1981–84 ea. $22.50–$30.00

Experience and Nature. Dover repr. of 1929 ed. pap. $6.95; Open Court rev. ed. 1925 $29.95 pap. $6.95; Peter Smith $14.50

Moral Principles in Education. Pref. by Sidney Hook, Southern Illinois Univ. Pr. repr. of 1909 ed. 1975 pap. $3.45

Democracy and Education: An Introduction to the Philosophy of Education. Darby repr. of 1932 ed. 1982 lib. bdg. $30.00; Macmillan (Free Pr.) 1966 pap. $10.95

How We Think: A Restatement of the Relation of Reflective Thinking to the Educative Process. Heath text ed. 1933 $16.95

A Common Faith. Yale Univ. Pr. 1934 pap. $3.95

Human Nature and Conduct. Modern Lib. 1935 $5.95

Logic: The Theory of Inquiry. Irvington repr. of 1938 ed. 1982 $39.50

Education Today. Ed. by Joseph Ratner, Greenwood repr. of 1940 ed. lib. bdg. $65.00

Philosophy and Civilization. Peter Smith $10.25

The Child and the Curriculum (and *The School and Society*). Univ. of Chicago Pr. (Phoenix Bks.) 2d ed. 1956 $10.00 pap. $4.95

The School and Society. Intro. by Joe R. Burnett, Southern Illinois Univ. Pr. 1980 pap. $5.95

Experience and Education. Macmillan (Collier Bks.) 1963 pap. $3.95; Peter Smith 1983 $12.50

BOOKS ABOUT DEWEY

Bernstein, Richard J. *John Dewey.* Ridgeview repr. of 1966 ed. 1981 lib. bdg. $24.00 text ed. pap. $8.50

Geiger, George R. *John Dewey in Perspective.* Greenwood repr. of 1958 ed. 1974 lib. bdg. $22.50

Gouinlock, James. *John Dewey's Philosophy of Value.* Humanities Pr. text ed. 1972 $15.00

Hook, Sidney. *John Dewey: An Intellectual Portrait.* Greenwood repr. of 1939 ed. lib. bdg. $19.75

Nathanson, Jerome. *John Dewey: The Reconstruction of the Democratic Life.* Ungar 1967 pap. $3.95

Roth, Robert J. *John Dewey and Self-Realization.* Greenwood repr. of 1963 ed. 1978 lib. bdg. $25.00

Williams, Robert B. *John Dewey: Recollections.* Univ. Pr. of Amer. 1982 lib. bdg. $25.25 text ed. pap. $12.25

Zeltner, Philip M. *John Dewey's Aesthetic Philosophy.* Humanities Pr. text ed. 1975 pap. $17.75

HUTCHINS, ROBERT M. 1899–1977

Hutchins wrote widely about education and is best known for his support of liberal education, which he believed "prepares the young for anything that may happen; it has value under any circumstances. . . . It gets them ready for a lifetime of learning. It connects man with man. It introduces all men to the dialogue about the common good of their own country and of the world community. It frees their mind of prejudice. It lays the basis of practical wisdom." He felt that the increasing complexities of civilization did not justify any modification in this approach. "The more technological the Society," he says in *The Learning Society* (1968), "the less *ad hoc* education can be. The reason is that the more technological the society is, the more rapidly it will change and the less valuable *ad hoc* education will become. It now seems safe to say that the best practical education is the best theoretical one."

After serving as dean of Yale Law School in 1929, Hutchins became (at age 29) president, and in 1949 chancellor of the University of Chicago, remaining there until 1951. During this period, he and Mortimer Adler introduced the Great Books program into the Chicago curriculum. They believed that the best education is achieved through reading and understanding the great minds of the past. Later he became associate director of the Ford Foundation and president of the Fund for the Republic—the latter in the face of the oppressive climate for free expression brought about by McCarthyism. But he saw that the Fund's projects included studies of the federal loyalty-security program, of political blacklisting in the entertainment industries, and of the nature of communism in the United States. Hutchins survived, along with the freedoms he had helped to preserve. He retired as the chief executive officer of the Center for the Study of Democratic Institutions in Santa Barbara, California, a "community of scholars" under the aegis of the Ford Foundation.

BOOKS BY HUTCHINS

The Higher Learning in America. AMS Pr. repr. of 1936 ed. $14.00; Greenwood repr. of 1962 ed. 1979 lib. bdg. $19.75; Yale Univ. Pr. 1962 pap. $5.95
No Friendly Voice. Greenwood repr. of 1936 ed. lib. bdg. $15.00
Saint Thomas and the World State. Marquette Univ. Pr. 1949 $7.95
The Conflict in Education in a Democratic Society. Greenwood repr. of 1953 ed. 1972 lib. bdg. $15.00
The University of Utopia. Univ. of Chicago Pr. 1964 pap. $4.00

BOOK ABOUT HUTCHINS

Cohen, Arthur A., ed. *Humanistic Education and Western Civilization: Essays for Robert M. Hutchins. Essay Index Repr. Ser.* Ayer repr. of 1964 ed. $15.00

KILPATRICK, WILLIAM HEARD. 1871–1965

William Heard Kilpatrick's friendship with John Dewey strongly influenced his work as a teacher-educator and particularly his numerous works in the area of educational philosophy. Kilpatrick promoted the principles of progressive education when discussing the need for curriculum reform in U.S. schools. As an alternative to the teaching of traditional and, what he saw as, disjointed subjects, he originated the project method of education.

Kilpatrick earned A.B. and A.M. degrees from Mercer University, where he taught mathematics and served as the university's acting president from 1903 to 1938. He completed his doctorate at Columbia University. From 1909 to 1938, Kilpatrick taught at Teachers College. He also helped found Bennington College in Vermont.

BOOKS BY KILPATRICK

Dutch Schools of New Netherland and Colonial New York. Ayer repr. of 1912 ed. 1969
    $16.00
Montessori System Examined. Ayer repr. of 1914 ed. 1971 $8.00
Education for a Changing Civilization. Ayer repr. of 1926 ed. 1972 $10.00
Foundations of Method: Informed Talks on Teaching. Ayer repr. of 1925 ed. 1972
    $19.00
(and William Van Til). *Intercultural Attitudes in the Making: Parents, Youth Leaders
    and Teachers at Work.* Ayer repr. of 1947 ed. $19.00

BOOK ABOUT KILPATRICK

*Bertrand Russell, A. S. Neill, Homer Lane, W. H. Kilpatrick: Four Progressive Educa-
    tors.* Macmillan 1968 o.p.

MANN, HORACE. 1796–1859

Horace Mann is often thought of as the founder of U.S. public education
because of his pioneering educational leadership. Assisted by a number of
public figures, Mann, as a member of the Massachusetts legislature, promoted the lyceum movement, which resulted in a series of key legislative
acts that are often considered the basis for the public educational system.
Mann founded the first state normal schools in the United States and advocated free public education for both boys and girls. The spread of common
schools led to a need for teachers, and Mann was instrumental in helping to
organize teacher education institutions and improved teacher training.

Mann later served as first secretary of the Massachusetts State Board of
Education and remained in the position for 12 years. He later became the
first president of Antioch College.

BOOKS BY MANN

Letters of Horace Walpole, Earl of Oxford, to Sir Horace Mann. Arden Lib. 2 vols. repr.
    of 1843 ed. 1979 lib. bdg. $75.00
Slavery: Letters and Speeches. Black Heritage Lib. Collection Ser. Ayer repr. of 1851 ed.
    1969 $24.50; Burt Franklin repr. of 1851 ed. 1969 $23.95; Greenwood repr. of
    1851 ed. $25.00
Lectures on Education. Ayer repr. of 1855 ed. 1969 $17.00

BOOKS ABOUT MANN

Hinsdale, Burke A. *Horace Mann and the Common School Revival in the United States.*
    Somerset repr. of 1898 ed. $29.00
Morgan, Joy E. *Horace Mann: His Ideas and Ideals. Educational Ser.* Norwood repr.
    of 1936 ed. $10.00

MONTESSORI, MARIA. 1870–1952

Since the early 1900s, the name of Maria Montessori, the Italian educator
who was the first woman doctor granted a degree in Italy, is often heard in
the field of childhood education. Dissatisfied with the educational methods
of her time, she developed her own theories in systematic fashion. The Montessori Method, as it became known, allows each child to develop at his or

her own pace through the manipulation of materials. This and others of her concepts have had considerable influence on modern education.

She first worked with retarded children, then classified as "untrainable," most of whom she succeeded in teaching to read and write. She established a number of Houses of Children in Italy devoted to providing new opportunities for underprivileged children. Recent U.S. efforts in this direction have led to a strong revival of interest in her work.

BOOKS BY MONTESSORI

Collected Works. Gordon $500.00

The Montessori Method: The Education of Children from Three to Six. Educational Ser. Intro. by M. Mayer, Bentley 1964 $7.50; Norwood repr. of 1912 ed. $25.00; intro. by J. M. Hunt, Schocken rev. ed. 1964 pap. $7.95

Pedagogical Anthropology. 1913. Foundation Class. 3 vols. repr. 1984 $37.15

Dr. Montessori's Own Handbook. 1914. Amer. Institute of Psychology 1984 $49.95; Bentley 1964 $5.95; intro. by N. M. Rambusch, Schocken 1965 pap. $4.95

The Advanced Montessori Method. 1917–18. Bentley 2 vols. 1964 ea. $10.00–$12.00

The Secret of Childhood: A Book for All Parents and Teachers. 1936. Trans. by Barbara B. Carter, Apt Bks. repr. of 1978 ed. text ed. 1983 $17.95; Ballantine 1982 pap. $2.95

The Absorbent Mind. Trans. by Claude A. Claremont, Dell 1984 pap. $4.95; Holt 1967 $6.95

The Child in the Family. Avon 1970 pap. $3.95

The Discovery of the Child. Ballantine 1980 pap. $2.75

BOOKS ABOUT MONTESSORI

Blessington, John P. *Let My Children Work.* Doubleday (Anchor) 1975 pap. $2.95

Kramer, Rita. *Maria Montessori: A Biography.* Fwd. by Anna Freud, Univ. of Chicago Pr. 1983 pap. $12.50

Lillard, Paula P. *Montessori: A Modern Approach.* Schocken 1973 pap. $4.95

Packard, Rosa C. *The Hidden Hinge.* Packard 1977 $5.95

PIAGET, JEAN. 1896–1980

Jean Piaget's research and writings about the developmental psychology of children have had profound impact on the field of education, particularly on early childhood and elementary educational programs and methods of instruction. Through extensive and systematic observations of children, he worked on the identification of distinct stages of intellectual development (sensorimotor, preoperational, concrete operational, and formal operational).

Piaget was a Swiss scientist, who published his first paper (one dealing with albino sparrows) at age ten. He completed a doctorate in natural science at the University of Neuchâtel, Switzerland, in 1918. In addition to teaching at a number of Swiss and French universities, Piaget codirected the institute of J. J. Rousseau in Geneva (1933–80) and helped found the International Center on Genetic Epistemology in 1954. He also contributed to the fields of zoology, philosophy, religion, sociology, and mathematics. (See also Chapter 4 in this volume.)

BOOKS BY PIAGET

Judgment and Reasoning in the Child. Humanities Pr. repr. of 1928 ed. text ed. 1962
     $16.00; Littlefield repr. of 1966 ed. 1976 pap. $3.95
The Child's Conception of the World. Humanities Pr. repr. of 1929 ed. text ed. 1960
     $24.50; Littlefield repr. of 1929 ed. 1975 pap. $6.95
The Child's Conception of Physical Causality. Humanities Pr. repr. of 1930 ed. text ed.
     1966 $18.25; Littlefield repr. 1972 pap. $3.95
Language and Thought of the Child. Humanities Pr. 3d ed. text ed. 1962 $18.00
Play, Dreams and Imitation in Childhood. Norton Lib. 1962 pap. $7.95
The Child's Conception of Number. Norton Lib. 1965 pap. $5.95
The Origins of Intelligence in Children. Trans. by Margaret Cook, International Univ.
     Pr. text ed. 1966 $37.50 pap. $7.95
The Psychology of Intelligence. Littlefield repr. of 1966 ed. 1976 pap. $4.95; Routledge
     & Kegan repr. of 1950 ed. 1971 $16.95
Genetic Epistemology. Trans. by Eleanor Duckworth, Columbia Univ. Pr. 1970
     $16.00; *Norton Lib.* 1971 pap. $4.95
*Biology and Knowledge: An Essay on the Relations between Organic Regulations and
     Cognitive Processes.* Trans. by Beatrix Walsh, Univ. of Chicago Pr. 1971 $19.00;
     Univ. of Chicago Pr. (Phoenix Bks.) 1974 pap. $5.45
The Child and Reality: Problems of Genetic Psychology. Trans. by Arnold Rosin,
     Beekman text ed. 1973 $8.95; Penguin 1976 pap. $3.95
Adaptation and Intelligence: Organic Selection and Phenocopy. Trans. by Steward
     Eames, fwd. by Terence A. Brown, Univ. of Chicago Pr. 1980 $11.00 1982 pap.
     $5.95

BOOKS ABOUT PIAGET

Almy, Millie, and others. *Young Children's Thinking: Studies of Some Aspects of Pia-
     get's Theory.* Teachers College Pr. 1966 pap. $5.75
Elkind, David. *Child Development and Education: A Piagetian Perspective.* Oxford text
     ed. 1976 pap. $8.95
Forman, George E., and David S. Kuschner. *The Child's Construction of Knowledge:
     Piaget for Teaching Children.* National Association for the Education of Young
     Children 1983 pap. $6.00
Furth, Hans G., and Harry Wachs. *Thinking Goes to School: Piaget's Theory in Prac-
     tice with Additional Thoughts.* Oxford text ed. 1975 pap. $7.95
Modgil, Sohan, and Celia Modgil. *Jean Piaget: Consensus and Controversy.* Praeger
     1982 $39.50

SKINNER, B(URRHUS) F(REDERIC). 1904–

[SEE Chapter 4 in this volume.]

THORNDIKE, EDWARD L. 1874–1949

Educational psychologist and author of the intelligence test bearing his
name, Thorndike is also known for his work in educational statistics. He
studied under WILLIAM JAMES (see Chapter 4 in this volume and Volume 4)
at Harvard and carried out experiments on animal intelligence with some
chickens he kept in the basement of James's house—his landlady having refused to let him keep them in his room! Thorndike's first papers were on
"The Psychology of Fishes" and "The Mental Life of Monkeys." When he re-

ceived his doctorate from Columbia in 1898, the statistical treatment of test results in psychology was experimental. He became an instructor in genetic psychology at Teachers College in 1899. He believed that "everything that exists exists in quantity" and could be measured as a key to scientific progress in education. He devised scales for measuring excellence in reading, English composition, handwriting, and drawing, as well as intelligence tests for various grade levels. The former dean of Teachers College, James E. Russell, said of him: "His service to pedagogical procedure has revolutionized educational administration." Thorndike's "Law of Effect," which had its origin in his early tests on animals, was strengthened by his later experiments on human learning. He concluded that the important factors in learning are repetition and reward. His techniques of animal experimentation and his methods of psychological measurement were important advances in U.S. psychology before World War I, and he is often thought of as the founder of modern educational psychology.

Books by Thorndike

Education. Educational Ser. Norwood repr. of 1912 ed. $15.00

Educational Psychology. Ayer repr. of 1913 ed. $44.00; Greenwood 3 vols. repr. of 1913–14 ed. lib. bdg. $56.25

Human Learning. Johnson Repr. repr. of 1931 ed. $15.00; MIT pap. $6.95; Norwood repr. of 1931 ed. lib. bdg. $27.50; Richard West repr. of 1931 ed. lib. bdg. $50.00

Fundamentals of Learning. AMS Pr. repr. of 1932 ed. $28.50

The Psychology of Wants, Interests and Attitudes. Psychology Ser. Johnson Repr. repr. of 1935 ed. $28.00

Man and His Works. Essay and General Lit. Index Repr. Ser. Associated Faculty Pr. repr. of 1943 ed. 1969 $20.50

Selected Writings from a Connectionist's Psychology. Greenwood repr. of 1949 ed. lib. bdg. $22.50

Notes on Child Study. Classics in Child Development Ser. Ayer repr. 1975 $19.00

Book about Thorndike

Joncich, Geraldine. *The Sane Positivist: A Biography of Edward L. Thorndike.* Wesleyan Univ. Pr. 1968 $32.50

WASHINGTON, BOOKER T(ALIAFERRO). 1856–1915

Booker T. Washington was born into slavery, but he became a leading educator of blacks. After graduating from and teaching at Hampton Normal and Industrial Institute, he was chosen to found the coeducational Tuskegee Normal and Industrial Institute in Alabama.

Between 1880 and 1915, Washington expanded Tuskegee from two buildings to a higher educational institution of more than 100 buildings, a faculty of 200, and an enrollment exceeding 1,500 students by 1915. He held strong beliefs about the dignity of manual work and the importance of character building, and he promoted these principles in his speeches and writing. Highly respected both as an educator and as a spokesperson for blacks, he was granted honorary degrees from Harvard and Dartmouth.

BOOKS BY WASHINGTON

The Booker T. Washington Papers. Ed. by Louis R. Harlan and others. Univ. of Illinois Pr. 13 vols. 1972–84 ea. $20.00–$32.50

Up from Slavery. Corner House repr. of 1900 ed. 1971 $16.95; Dell 1965 pap. $.95

The Negro in the South: His Economic Progress in Relation to His Moral and Religious Development. AMS Pr. repr. of 1907 ed. $10.00; intro. by Herbert Aptheker, Citadel Pr. 1970 $6.50 pap. $2.45; Metro Bks. repr. of 1907 ed. 1972 lib. bdg. $12.50

BOOKS ABOUT WASHINGTON

Harlan, Louis R. *Booker T. Washington: The Making of a Black Leader, 1856–1901.* Oxford 1972 $30.00 pap. $10.95

———. *Booker T. Washington: The Wizard of Tuskegee, 1901–1915.* Oxford 1983 $30.00 pap. $7.95

Hawkins, Hugh. *Booker T. Washington and His Critics. Problems in Amer. Civilization* Heath 2d ed. text ed. 1974 pap. $5.95

Meier, August. *Negro Thought in America, 1880–1915: Racial Ideologies in the Age of Booker T. Washington.* Univ. of Michigan Pr. 1963 pap. $10.95

CHAPTER 6

Ancient History

Roger S. Bagnall

> For myself, my duty is to report all that is said, but I am not obliged to believe it all alike—a remark for which may be understood to apply to my whole History.
>
> —HERODOTUS 7.152

The study of ancient history, like that of any time distant from our own, involves a perpetual contest between the sense of the familiar and the sense of the alien. The ancient Greeks and Romans created much of our whole way of thinking, about good and evil, war and peace, and almost every other matter affecting human beings. At a more pedestrian level, they ate and drank, earned livings, raised families, died—in short, shared the basic experiences of daily life with people of all times. Historians have brought both sorts of familiarity to life in many of the works listed below. And yet the ancients are also distant and strange to moderns brought up in an industrial society. Their economy was primitive, technology more so; only free citizen men had full rights (and produced almost all the literature that transmits the ancient experience to us); slavery was standard; pagan religion involved a relationship to the world that we find difficult to enter into sympathetically. Recapturing this strangeness, too, is part of the ancient historian's task.

GENERAL WORKS

Bengtson, Hermann. *Introduction to Ancient History.* Trans. by R. I. Frank and F. D. Gilliard, Univ. of California Pr. 1976 $29.50. Translation of a standard German introductory manual for students. Very substantial bibliography about the ancient historians and ancient history.

Bickerman, Elias J., and Morton Smith. *The Ancient History of Western Civilization.* Harper text ed. 1976 $16.95. A brief survey from prehistory to late antiquity; very readable.

The Cambridge Ancient History. Ed. by I. E. Edwards and others, Cambridge Univ. Pr. rev. ed. 12 vols. 1970–81 pap. ea. $19.50–$39.50. A massive and detailed reference work, with chapters by authorities on different periods and subjects. As such, *The Cambridge Ancient History* is hardly unified, and the quality of the sections varies greatly. It is, however, the only work of its scope in English, and it contains extensive bibliographies. Beginning with the earliest times, it treats the ancient Near East and Egypt in great detail. Vols. 1 and 2 cover prehistory and the ancient Near East; vols. 3–12 cover Greece and Rome.

Finley, Moses I. *Politics in the Ancient World*. Cambridge Univ. Pr. 1983 $27.50 pap. $9.95

Harvey, Paul. *The Oxford Companion to Classical Literature*. Clarendon 1937; Oxford Univ. Pr. repr. 1984 pap. $8.95

Ste-Croix, G. E. M. de. *The Class Struggle in the Ancient Greek World: From the Archaic Age to the Arab Conquest*. Cornell Univ. Pr. 1982 $54.50

Snowden, Frank M., Jr. *Before Color Prejudice: The Ancient View of Blacks*. Harvard Univ. Pr. text ed. 1983 $17.50

————. *Blacks in Antiquity: Ethiopians in the Greco-Roman Experience*. Harvard Univ. Pr. (Belknap Pr.) 1970 pap. $8.95

Starr, Chester G. *A History of the Ancient World*. Oxford 3d ed. 1983 $35.00. A well-balanced treatment from the Paleolithic Period to the end of antiquity, in some detail.

Trump, D. H. *The Prehistory of the Mediterranean*. Yale Univ. Pr. 1980 $32.00 1981 pap. $7.95

ANCIENT NEAR EAST AND EGYPT

Aldred, Cyril. *The Egyptians. Ancient Peoples and Places Ser.* Thames & Hudson 2d ed. rev. & enl. 1984 $19.95

Edwards, I. E. *The Pyramids of Egypt*. Penguin (Pelican) 1975 pap. $4.95

Emery, Walter B. *Archaic Egypt*. Penguin 1961 o.p.

Erman, Adolf, ed. *The Ancient Egyptians: A Source Book of Their Writings*. Peter Smith $13.25

Frankfort, Henri, and others. *Before Philosophy*. Penguin 1949 o.p.

Gardiner, Alan H. *Egypt of the Pharoahs: An Introduction*. Oxford 1966 pap. $11.95

Gurney, O. R. *The Hittites*. Penguin 1954 o.p.

Hallo, William W., and William Kelly Simpson. *The Ancient Near East: A History*. Harper text ed. 1971 pap. $14.95

James, T. G. H., ed. *Excavating in Egypt: The Egypt Exploration Society, 1882–1982*. Univ. of Chicago Pr. 1984 pap. $12.95

Lichtheim, Miriam. *Ancient Egyptian Literature*. Univ. of California Pr. 3 vols. vol. 1 (1973) pap. $8.95 vol. 2 (1976) pap. $7.95 vol. 3 (1980) $20.00 pap. $4.95

Mallowan, M. E. L. *Early Mesopotamia and Iran*. McGraw-Hill 1965 o.p.

Mellaart, James. *Catal Huyuk: A Neolithic Town in Anatolia*. McGraw-Hill 1967 o.p.

GREEK HISTORY

Andrewes, Antony. *The Greeks. Norton Lib.* 1978 pap. $7.95

Davies, J. K. *Democracy and Classical Greece. Fontana History of the Ancient World Ser.* Humanities Pr. text ed. 1978 $22.75; Stanford Univ. Pr. 1978 pap. $7.95

Ehrenberg, Victor. *From Solon to Socrates: Greek History and Civilization during the 6th–5th Centuries B.C.* Methuen 2d ed. 1973 pap. $14.95

————. *The Greek State*. Methuen 2d ed. 1974 pap. $12.95

Fine, John V. A. *The Ancient Greeks: A Critical History*. Harvard Univ. Pr. (Belknap Pr.) text ed. 1983 $35.00. The most recent example of its genre; mainly political narrative.

Finley, M. I. *The Ancient Greeks: An Introduction to Their Life and Thought.* Penguin
     1977 pap. $5.95
——. *The World of Odysseus.* Penguin (Pelican) rev. ed. repr. of 1978 ed. 1979 pap.
     $4.95; Viking rev. ed. 1978 $13.95
Fitzhardinge, L. F. *The Spartans. Ancient Peoples and Places Ser.* Thames & Hudson
     1980 $16.95 1985 pap. $10.95
Godolphin, Frances R. B., ed. *The Greek Historians.* Random 2 vols. 1942 o.p. Com-
     plete translations, with introduction and notes, of Herodotus, Thucydides, Xeno-
     phon, and Arrian.
Greek Political Oratory. Trans. by A. N. W. Saunders, *Penguin Class. Ser.* 1978 pap.
     $5.95
Jeffery, Lillian H. *Archaic Greece: The City-States c.700–500 B.C.* St. Martin's 1976
     $29.95
Jones, A. H. *The Greek City from Alexander to Justinian.* Oxford 1979 text ed. pap.
     $19.95
Meiggs, Russell. *The Athenian Empire.* Oxford 1979 pap. $26.00
Murray, Oswyn. *Early Greece. Fontana History of the Ancient World Ser.* Humanities
     Pr. text ed. 1980 $32.50; Stanford Univ. Pr. 1980 pap. $8.95
Rostovtzeff, Mikhail. *The Social and Economic History of the Hellenistic World.* Ox-
     ford 3 vols. 1941 $109.00. A detailed but readable account with very extensive
     annotation and considerable illustration.
Saunders, A. N. W., trans. *Greek Political Oratory. Penguin Class. Ser.* 1978 pap. $5.95
Snodgrass, Anthony M. *Archaic Greece: The Age of Experiment.* Univ. of California Pr.
     1981 pap. $7.95
Vermeule, Emily T. *Aspects of Death in Early Greek Art and Poetry.* Univ. of California
     Pr. 1979 $38.50 pap. $7.95
——. *Greece in the Bronze Age.* Univ. of Chicago Pr. 1964 $27.50 pap. $15.00
Walbank, F. W. *The Hellenist World. Fontana History of the Ancient World Ser.* Hu-
     manities Pr. text ed. 1981 $35.00. The best survey in English of political, social,
     and cultural developments from Alexander to the Roman conquest of the Helle-
     nistic East.
Webster, T. B. L. *Athenian Culture and Society.* Univ. of California Pr. 1973 o.p.

ROMAN HISTORY

Bowersock, G. W. *Julian the Apostate.* Harvard Univ. Pr. 1978 $12.50 pap. $5.95
Brown, Peter. *The World of Late Antiquity: 150–750. History of European Civilization
     Lib.* Harcourt text ed. 1971 pap. $7.95. A brilliant evocation of the transforma-
     tion of the Roman Empire into Byzantium and the Western Middle Ages.
Gibbon, Edward. *The Decline and Fall of the Roman Empire.* Ed. by John B. Bury,
     AMS Pr. 7 vols. repr. of 1914 ed. $300.00; Biblio Dist. (Everyman's) 6 vols. repr.
     of 1910 ed. 1978 ea. $9.95
Kaegi, Walter E. *Byzantium and the Decline of Rome.* Princeton Univ. Pr. 1968 o.p.
Laistner, M. M. W. *The Greater Roman Historians.* Univ. of California Pr. 1947 $21.00
Lewis, Naphtali. *Life in Egypt under Roman Rule.* Oxford 1983 $29.95
Millar, Fergus. *The Emperor in the Roman World. Aspects of Greek and Roman Life
     Ser.* Cornell Univ. Pr. 1977 $49.50
——, ed. *The Roman Empire and Its Neighbors.* Holmes & Meier 2d ed. 1981 $39.50
Rostovtzeff, Mikhail. *The Social and Economic History of the Roman Empire.* Ed. by
     P. M. Fraser, Oxford 2 vols. 2d ed. 1957 $115.00

Scullard, H. H. *From the Gracchi to Nero: A History of Rome from 133 B.C. to A.D. 68.* Methuen 5th ed. 1983 $33.00 pap. $14.95

Syme, Ronald. *The Roman Revolution. Oxford Pap. Ser.* 1939 pap. $10.95. The decisive work about Augustus and his times, a highly critical account of power politics in the late Republic. Fundamental for all subsequent discussions.

Wells, Colin. *The Roman Empire. Fontana History of the Ancient World Ser.* Humanities Pr. text ed. 1981 $23.75; Stanford Univ. Pr. 1984 $35.00 pap. $9.95

REFERENCE WORKS ABOUT ANTIQUITY

Bowder, Diana, ed. *Who Was Who in the Roman World.* Cornell Univ. Pr. 1980 $32.50; Washington Square Pr. 1984 pap. $8.95

Hammond, N. G. L., and H. H. Scullard, eds. *Oxford Classical Dictionary.* Oxford 2d ed. 1970 $45.00

Kenney, E. J., ed. *Latin Literature.* Vol. 2 in *The Cambridge History of Classical Literature.* Ed. by W. V. Clausen, Cambridge Univ. Pr. 5 pts. 1982–83 pap. ea. $12.95

Stillwell, Richard, ed. *The Princeton Encyclopedia of Classical Sites.* Princeton Univ. Pr. 1976 $175.00

SOURCES FOR ANCIENT HISTORY

Crawford, Michael, ed. *Ancient Greece and Rome. Sources of History Ser.* Cambridge Univ. Pr. 1984 $37.50 pap. $13.95. Contributions on literature, epigraphy, archaeology, and numismatics. Shows how the ancient historian uses evidence to write history.

Reynolds, L. D., and N. G. Wilson. *Scribes and Scholars: A Guide to the Transmission of Greek and Latin Literature.* Oxford 2d ed. text ed. 1974 pap. $10.95. An introduction to the history of texts, which helps the reader understand how the works of the ancient historians are preserved and what sorts of problems may be encountered in their texts.

DOCUMENTS ON ANCIENT HISTORY

Much of what historians know about antiquity comes not from ancient literary works but from inscriptions, papyri, coins, and other documentary sources. The books listed below give an introduction to what documents there are and what one can learn from them, along with substantial selections of translated documents.

Austin, Michel M. *The Hellenistic World from Alexander to the Roman Conquest: A Selection of Ancient Sources in Translation.* Cambridge Univ. Pr. 1981 $65.00 pap. $19.95

Bagnall, Roger, and Peter Derow. *Greek Historical Documents: The Hellenistic Period.* Scholars Pr. text ed. 1981 pap. $13.50

Crawford, Michael, and David Whitehead. *Archaic and Classical Greece: A Selection of Ancient Sources in Translation.* Cambridge Univ. Pr. 1983 $69.50 pap. $19.95

Fornara, Charles W., and E. Badian, eds. *Translated Documents of Greece and Rome:*

Archaic Times to the End of the Peloponnesian War. Trans. by Charles W. Fornara, Johns Hopkins Univ. Pr. 1977 vol. 1 $14.50 pap. $3.95

Lewis, Naphtali. *Greek Historical Documents.* Samuel-Stevens 2 vols. 1971–74 o.p.

Lewis, Naphtali, and Reinhold Meyer, eds. *Roman Civilization.* Harper 2 vols. pap. ea. $7.50–$8.50. The most extensive collection of translated sources, inscriptions, papyri, and literary works.

Turner, E. G. *Greek Papyri: An Introduction.* Oxford repr. of 1968 ed. text ed. 1981 pap. $18.95. The best introduction in English to the papyri and their contents, both literary and documentary. The author's account of his craft is both lovingly detailed and lively.

Wickersham, John, and Gerald Verbrugghe. *Greek Historical Documents: The Fourth Century B.C.* Samuel-Stevens 1973 o.p. Mostly translations of Greek inscriptions.

ARCHAEOLOGY

The excavation of ancient sites—cities, farms, fortresses, graves, sanctuaries, and the like—has deepened the understanding of antiquity enormously during the last century. The books listed here are only a small selection of those that take the results of archaeology and put them into the service of history.

Biers, William R. *The Archaeology of Greece: An Introduction.* Cornell Univ. Pr. 1981 $42.50 pap. $17.95

Boardman, John. *The Greeks Overseas: Their Early Colonies and Trade.* Thames & Hudson rev. ed. 1982 pap. $12.95

MacDonald, William L. *The Architecture of the Roman Empire.* Yale Univ. Pr. 2d ed. text ed. 1982 $40.00 pap. $12.95

MacKendrick, Paul. *The Greek Stones Speak: The Story of Archaeology in Greek Lands.* Norton 2d ed. 1982 $24.95 1983 pap. $9.95

———. *The Mute Stones Speak: The Story of Archaeology in Italy.* Norton 2d ed. 1983 $25.50 pap. $9.95

———. *Romans on the Rhine: Archaeology in Germany.* Funk and Wagnalls 1970 o.p.

McKay, Alexander G. *Houses, Villas and Palaces in the Roman World.* Cornell Univ. Pr. 1975 o.p.

Pallottino, Massimo. *The Etruscans.* Trans. by J. Cremona, Indiana Univ. Pr. rev. ed. 1975 $12.50; Penguin (Pelican) repr. of 1975 ed. text ed. 1978 pap. $7.95

Richardson, Emeline. *The Etruscans: Their Art and Civilization.* Univ. of Chicago Pr. (Phoenix Bks.) 1976 pap. $9.50. A broad survey based on the artistic and archaeological remains. Numerous plates.

Sear, Frank. *Roman Architecture.* Cornell Univ. Pr. 1983 $32.50 pap. $14.95

COINS

Kent, J. P. *Roman Coins.* Abrams 1978 $60.00

Kraay, Colin. *Archaic and Classical Greek Coins. Lib. of Numismatics* Univ. of California Pr. 1977 $74.50

TOPICS IN ANCIENT HISTORY

Society, Economy, and Trade

Austin, Michel M., and Pierre Vidal-Naquet. *Economic and Social History of Ancient Greece: An Introduction.* Univ. of California Pr. 1978 $39.75 pap. $8.95. Ancient sources (mostly literary) in translation with extensive annotation and commentary.

Carcopino, Jerome. *Daily Life in Ancient Rome: The People and the City at the Height of the Empire.* Trans. by E. O. Lorimer, ed. by Harry T. Rowell, Yale Univ. Pr. 1960 pap. $7.95

Finley, Moses I. *The Ancient Economy.* Univ. of California Pr. 1973 $24.00 pap. $7.95. A highly readable and argumentative account emphasizing the primitive characteristics of the ancient economy and the centrality of agriculture.

Frank, Tenney, ed. *An Economic Survey of Ancient Rome.* Octagon 6 vols. 1972 lib. bdg. $172.50. A massive compilation, arranged by region, of evidence about the economic life of the Roman Empire. Particularly noteworthy are the numerous translated documents and the lists of economic data.

Hands, A. R. *Charities and Social Aid in Greece and Rome.* Cornell Univ. Pr. 1968 o. p.

Harris, H. A. *Sport in Greece and Rome.* Ed. by H. H. Scullard, *Aspects of Greek and Roman Life Ser.* Cornell Univ. Pr. 1972 $19.50

Lewis, Naphtali. *Life in Egypt under Roman Rule.* Oxford 1983 $29.95

MacMullen, Ramsay. *Enemies of the Roman Order: Treason, Unrest, and Alienation in the Empire.* Harvard Univ. Pr. text ed. 1966 $22.50

———. *Roman Social Relations, 50 B.C. to A.D. 284.* Yale Univ. Pr. 1974 $15.00 1981 pap. $7.95

Meeks, Wayne A. *The First Urban Christians: The Social World of the Apostle Paul.* Yale Univ. Pr. 1982 $19.95 1984 pap. $8.95. An analysis of the Pauline letters in terms of our knowledge of contemporary society.

Agriculture, Science, Technology, and Material Culture

Burford, Alison. *Craftsmen in Greek and Roman Society.* Cornell Univ. Pr. 1972 o.p.

Casson, Lionel. *Ships and Seamanship in the Ancient World.* Princeton Univ. Pr. 1971 $49.50

Phillips, E. D. *Greek Medicine.* Cornell Univ. Pr. 1973 o.p.

Scarborough, John. *Roman Medicine.* Ed. by H. H. Scullard, *Aspects of Greek and Roman Life Ser.* Cornell Univ. Pr. 1970 $29.50

White, K. D. *Greek and Roman Technology. Aspects of Greek and Roman Life Ser.* Cornell Univ. Pr. 1983 $39.50

———. *Roman Farming.* Ed. by H. H. Scullard, *Aspects of Greek and Roman Life Ser.* Cornell Univ. Pr. 1970 $34.50

———, trans. *Country Life in Classical Times.* Beekman text ed. 1980 $21.00; Cornell Univ. Pr. 1977 $22.50

Women, the Family, and Sex

Cameron, Averil, and Amelie Kuhrt. *Images of Women in Antiquity.* Wayne State Univ. Pr. 1983 $25.00 pap. $14.95

Dover, K. J. *Greek Homosexuality.* Harvard Univ. Pr. 1978 $22.50; Random (Vintage) 1980 pap. $5.95

Hallett, Judith P. *Fathers and Daughters in Roman Society.* Princeton Univ. Pr. 1984
$40.00 pap. $12.50
Lacey, W. K. *The Family in Classical Greece. Aspects of Greek and Roman Life Ser.* Cornell Univ. Pr. 1984 pap. $10.95
Lefkowitz, Mary R., and Maureen B. Fant, eds. *Women's Life in Greece and Rome.*
Johns Hopkins Univ. Pr. rev. ed. text ed. 1982 pap. $8.95. A collection of ancient
sources in translation.
Pomeroy, Sarah B. *Goddesses, Whores, Wives and Slaves: Women in Classical Antiquity.* Schocken 1976 pap. $7.95

War, Peace, and Diplomacy

Adcock, Frank E. *Diplomacy in Ancient Greece.* Cornell Univ. Pr. 1975 o.p.
———. *The Greek and Macedonian Art of War.* Univ. of California Pr. 1974 pap. $3.50
Harris, William V. *War and Imperialism in Republican Rome, 327–70 B.C.* Oxford
1979 $42.00
Luttwak, Edward N. *The Grand Strategy of the Roman Empire: From the First Century
A.D. to the Third.* Johns Hopkins Univ. Pr. 1977 pap. $6.95
Watson, G. R. *The Roman Soldier. Aspects of Greek and Roman Life Ser.* Cornell Univ.
Pr. 1969 $27.50

Law

Berger, Adolf. *Encyclopedic Dictionary of Roman Law.* Amer. Philosophical Society
1953 o.p.
Buckland, W. W. *Roman Law and Common Law: A Comparison in Outline.* Rev. by
F. H. Lawson, Cambridge Univ. Pr. 2d ed. 1952 o.p.
Buckland, W. W., and Arnold D. McNair. *A Text-Book of Roman Law from Augustus
to Justinian.* Rev. by Peter Stein, Cambridge Univ. Pr. 4th ed. o.p. The standard
English textbook, with great detail and full citation of the ancient texts.
Cohen, Edward E. *Ancient Athenian Maritime Courts.* Princeton Univ. Pr. 1973 o.p.
Crook, J. A. *Law and Life of Rome: 90 B.C. to A.D. 212.* Cornell Univ. Pr. 1984 pap.
$10.95
Daube, David. *Roman Law.* Columbia Univ. Pr. 1969 $15.00. A set of public lectures,
distinguished for sharp observation, unusual perspectives, and great wit.
Frier, Bruce W. *Landlords and Tenants in Imperial Rome.* Princeton Univ. Pr. 1980
$25.00
Jolowicz, H. F., and Barry Nicholas. *Historical Introduction to the Study of Roman
Law.* Cambridge Univ. Pr. 3d ed. 1972 $87.50
MacDowell, Douglas M. *The Law in Classical Athens. Aspects of Greek and Roman Life
Ser.* Cornell Univ. Pr. 1978 $32.50
Nicholas, Barry. *Introduction to Roman Law. Clarendon Law Ser.* Oxford 1962 $14.95

Philosophy, Religion, and Intellectual History

Brown, Peter. *Augustine of Hippo: A Biography.* Univ. of California Pr. 1967 pap.
$7.95. A classic study of Augustine's life, thought, and environment.
Ferguson, John. *The Religions of the Roman Empire. Aspects of Greek and Roman Life
Ser.* Cornell Univ. Pr. 1970 $27.50 1985 text ed. pap. $8.95
MacMullen, Ramsay. *Paganism in the Roman Empire.* Yale Univ. Pr. 1981 $30.00 text
ed. pap. $7.95. A sympathetic attempt to understand paganism in its own terms.

Marrou, H. I. *History of Education in Antiquity.* Univ. of Wiconsin Pr. text ed. 1982 pap. $10.95

ANCIENT GREEK HISTORIANS

HERODOTUS. c.484–425 B.C.

The "father of history," Herodotus wrote of the relations between East and West down to 478 B.C., with most of the narrative centered on the Persian invasions of Greece. His histories are divided into nine books, named after the nine muses. He was the first writer to handle historical materials critically. The Rawlinson translation has long been considered the standard version.

BOOKS BY HERODOTUS

Histories. Trans. by Aubrey de Selincourt, *Penguin Class. Ser.* 1954 pap. $5.95
The Persian Wars. Trans. by George R. Rawlinson, Random 1964 $3.95. The *Histories* with a different title.

BOOKS ABOUT HERODOTUS

Evans, J. A. *Herodotus. Twayne's World Authors Ser.* G. K. Hall 1982 lib. bdg. $16.95. For the general reader.
Immerwahr, Henry R. *Form and Thought in Herodotus.* Scholars Pr. 1981 pap. $22.50. An original scholarly treatment.
Lang, Mabel. *Herodotean Narrative and Discourse.* Harvard Univ. Pr. text ed. 1984 $20.00

THUCYDIDES. c.470–400 B.C.

As the founder of political history, Thucydides wrote about the fall of Athens. As the first military historian, he wrote about the Peloponnesian War, in which he fought as a commander of Athenian troops in Thrace. His account of the war covers the years 431–411 B.C., with the remainder of the war described by Xenophon. His writing is astringent and analytic, yet full of powerful rhetorical pieces.

BOOK BY THUCYDIDES

The Peloponnesian War. Trans. by Richard Crawley, Modern Lib. new ed. 1981 pap. $4.95; trans. by Rex Warner, Penguin 1954 pap. $5.95; trans. by Terry Wick, *Modern Lib. College Ed. Ser.* Random text ed. 1982 pap. $4.95

BOOKS ABOUT THUCYDIDES

Connor, W. Robert. *Thucydides.* Princeton Univ. Pr. 1984 $30.00
Finley, John H., Jr. *Three Essays on Thucydides.* Ed. by Terry Wick, *Loeb Class. Monographs Ser.* Harvard Univ. Pr. 1967 $15.00
Pouncey, Peter. *The Necessities of War: A Study of Thucydides' Pessimism.* Columbia Univ. Pr. 1980 $25.00
Rawlings, Hunter R., III. *The Structure of Thucydides' History.* Princeton Univ. Pr. 1981 $25.00

XENOPHON. c.434?–c.355? B.C.

Xenophon left a considerable output of historical writing and essays. These include *The Hellenica*, a continuation of Thucydides's history down to 362 B.C., *The Anabasis*, the story of the expedition of Cyrus the Younger and 10,000 Greek mercenaries in revolt against his brother, Artaxerxes, and *Memorabilia*, an anecdotal account about Socrates.

BOOKS BY XENOPHON

Complete Works. Loeb Class. Lib. Harvard Univ. Pr. 7 vols. ea. $12.95
A History of My Times. Trans. by Rex Warner, *Penguin Class. Ser.* 1979 pap. $6.95
The Persian Expedition. Trans. by Rex Warner, Penguin 1949 o.p.

BOOK ABOUT XENOPHON

Anderson, J. K. *Xenophon. Class. Life and Letters Ser.* Biblio Distr. 1979 $40.50 pap. $12.50

ORATORS

Much of our evidence about Athenian politics and economic life in the fourth century comes from speeches by such orators as Demosthenes, Lysias, and Isocrates.

ARISTOTLE. 384–322 B.C.

Aristotle's lifetime bridges the world of the classical city and that of the Hellenistic monarchies. Among his interests, the philosopher and scientist Aristotle included political science. Although only one treatise on the constitutions of individual Greek states produced by Aristotle and his school survives, it is a source of great importance for Athenian history and Greek political institutions. (See also Volume 4.)

BOOKS BY ARISTOTLE

Aristotle's Constitution of Athens. Trans. and ed. by Kurt von Fritz and Ernst Kapp, *Lib. of Class. Ser.* Hafner text ed. 1966 pap. $9.95
The Politics. Trans. by Ernest Barker, Oxford 1946 pap. $8.95; trans. by Trevor J. Saunders, *Penguin Class. Ser.* 1982 pap. $3.95

BOOK ABOUT ARISTOTLE

Jaeger, Werner. *Aristotle.* Oxford 2d ed. 1948 o.p.

ARRIAN (FLAVIUS ARRIANUS). c.95–c.175

Arrian came from a wealthy Greek family of Asia Minor. He had a military and official career under Hadrian and retired to literary pursuits. He wrote several geographical and historical works in the style of Xenophon. His account of Alexander the Great is generally considered the best surviving ancient narrative.

BOOKS BY ARRIAN

The Anabasis of Alexander and the Indica. Trans. by P. A. Brunt and E. Iliff Robson, *Loeb Class. Lib.* Harvard Univ. Pr. 2 vols. 1976 ea. $12.00
The Campaigns of Alexander. Trans. by Aubrey de Selincourt, rev. by J. R. Hamilton, *Penguin Class. Ser.* 1976 pap. $5.95

BOOK ABOUT ARRIAN

Stadter, Philip A. *Arrian of Nicomedia.* Univ. of North Carolina Pr. 1980 $22.50

DIO CHRYSOSTOM. c.40–c.112

Dio was an orator and philosophical writer from a wealthy Greek family of Asia Minor. His speeches present a great deal of information about the society of his times.

BOOK BY DIO

Discourses. Trans. by J. W. Cohoon and H. L. Crosby, *Loeb Class. Lib.* Harvard Univ. Pr. 5 vols. ea. $12.50

BOOK ABOUT DIO

Jones, C. P. *The Roman World of Dio Chrysostom. Loeb Class. Monographs Ser.* Harvard Univ. Pr. 1978 $15.00. An evocation of the social and intellectual milieu of a leading Greek orator of the Roman Empire.

JOSEPHUS, FLAVIUS. 37–95

A member of a wealthy priestly family in Judea, Josephus was a Jew who wrote both in Greek and Hebrew. At one point, he was the governor of Galilee. He played an active and controversial role in anti-Roman activity, eventually becoming a supporter of Rome, where he lived and wrote his surviving works. His writings are neither remarkably fine representatives of classical culture nor the product of deep learning in Jewish literature and history, but they tell the reader a great deal not known from other sources.

BOOKS BY JOSEPHUS

Works. Trans. by H. Thackeray and others, ed. by E. H. Warmington, *Loeb Class. Lib.* Harvard Univ. Pr. 9 vols. ea. $12.50
The Jewish War. Trans. by G. A. Williamson, ed. by E. Mary Smallwood, *Penguin Class. Ser.* 1984 pap. $6.95

BOOK ABOUT JOSEPHUS

Rajak, Tessa. *Josephus: The Historian and His Society.* Ed. by E. H. Warmington, Fortress Pr. 1984 $24.95

PLUTARCH. c.46–c.125

Plutarch was a member of a well-to-do Greek family, a priest at Delphi, and an exceptionally well read man. His *Parallel Lives of Greeks and Romans* number 38 was originally written to inspire emulation in youth; its chief value today is historical. Besides the *Parallel Lives*, he wrote numerous essays (the "Moralia"), which have been published as part of the Loeb Classical Library. His culture is that of the Greek upper class in the earlier Roman Empire (from before 50 to after 120).

BOOKS BY PLUTARCH

Plutarch's Lives. Trans. by John Dryden, Modern Lib. 1967 $10.95; *Loeb Class. Lib.* Harvard Univ. Pr. 11 vols. ea. $12.50
The Rise and Fall of Athens: Nine Greek Lives. Trans. by Ian Scott-Kilvert, *Penguin Class. Ser.* 1975 pap. $4.95
The Age of Alexander: Nine Greek Lives. Trans. by Ian Scott-Kilvert, *Penguin Class. Ser.* 1973 pap. $4.95
The Fall of the Roman Republic: Six Roman Lives. Trans. by Rex Warner, *Penguin Class. Ser.* 1974 pap. $4.95
The Makers of Rome. Trans. by Ian Scott-Kilvert, *Penguin Class. Ser.* 1965 pap. $4.95

BOOKS ABOUT PLUTARCH

Russell, D. A. *Plutarch.* Ed. by John S. White, *Class. Life and Letters Ser.* Biblio Dist. 1979 $34.00 pap. $12.00
Stadter, Philip A. *Plutarch's Historical Methods: An Analysis of the Mulierum Virtues.* *Loeb Class. Lib.* Harvard Univ. Pr. 1965 $12.50

POLYBIUS. c.200–c.118 B.C.

Polybius was a well-educated Greek politician who witnessed, participated in, and wrote of the rise and triumph of the Roman Empire. As a result of years spent as a hostage in Rome, he came to admire that empire and its institutions, and became friendly with many eminent Roman statesmen. Of the 40 books contained in his *Histories*, only the first five have survived intact, with portions of the others in excerpts.

BOOKS BY POLYBIUS

Histories. Trans. by W. R. Paton, *Loeb Class. Lib.* Harvard Univ. Pr. 6 vols. 1922–27 ea. $12.50
The Rise of the Roman Empire. Trans. by Ian Scott-Kilvert, Penguin 1980 pap. $8.95

BOOK ABOUT POLYBIUS

Walbank, F. W. *A Historical Commentary on Polybius.* Ed by E. Badian, Oxford 3 vols. text ed. 1957–79 ea. $62.00–$89.00

PROCOPIUS. c.500–c.565

Procopius was born in Caesarea in Palestine, had a distinguished military and official career under Justinian (and Justinian's great general Belisarius), and wrote two very different histories of his times: one official and military, the other unofficial, anecdotal, and scurrilous.

BOOK BY PROCOPIUS

Works. Trans. by H. B. Ewing, *Loeb Class. Lib.* Harvard Univ. Pr. 7 vols. ea. $12.50

ANCIENT ROMAN HISTORIANS

AMMIANUS MARCELLINUS. c.330–395

Ammianus was a Greek-speaking native of Antioch in Syria who had a military career of some substance. His history, in Latin, originally covered the period 96–378, continuing Tacitus's *Histories*. Only the last part, from 353 on, survives, and is the best source available for its period. Ammianus is the greatest Roman historian of the later empire.

BOOK BY AMMIANUS

Roman History. Trans. by J. C. Rolfe, *Loeb Class. Lib.* Harvard Univ. Pr. 3 vols. ea.
$12.50

BOOK ABOUT AMMIANUS

Syme, Ronald. *Ammianus and the Historia Augusta*. Oxford 1968 $34.50

CAESAR, JULIUS (GAIUS JULIUS CAESAR). 100–44 B.C.

Besides having a remarkable career as a general and politician, Julius Caesar wrote an account of his campaigns that is a model of Latin style and clear narration.

BOOKS BY CAESAR

The Civil War. Trans. by Jane F. Mitchell, *Penguin Class. Ser.* 1976 pap. $4.95
The Conquest of Gaul. Trans. by S. A. Handford, rev. by Jane F. Gardner, *Penguin Class. Ser.* 1983 pap. $4.95

BOOK ABOUT CAESAR

Adcock, F. E. *Caesar as Man of Letters*. 1956. Shoe String 1969 o.p.

CICERO, MARCUS TULLIUS. 106–43 B.C.

Although not a historian, Cicero, the orator and politician, left a large legacy of works crucial to an understanding of the later Roman Republic. (See also Volume 2.)

BOOKS BY CICERO

Letters to Atticus. Trans. by D. R. Shackleton Bailey, *Penguin Class. Ser.* 1978 pap.
$5.75
The Murder Trials. Trans. by Michael Grant, *Penguin Class. Ser.* 1975 pap. $4.75
Selected Political Speeches. Trans. by Michael Grant, *Penguin Class. Ser.* 1977 pap.
$4.95
Selected Works. Trans. by Michael Grant, *Penguin Class. Ser.* 1960 pap. $4.95. Includes political and legal speeches, as well as some philosophical writings.

HISTORIA AUGUSTA

The *Augustan History* is an assemblage of lives of the emperors, camouflaged as the work of several authors but in reality (it seems) the work of a single writer toward the end of the fourth century. Much of its material is not reliable, even fictional. The selection below comes from the earlier and more factual lives.

Lives of the Later Caesars. Trans. by Anthony Birley, ed. by A. N. Sherwin-White, *Penguin Class. Ser.* 1976 pap. $4.95

LIVY. c.59 B.C.–c.A.D.17

Although little is known about Livy's life, this Paduan's work covers a vast sweep of Rome's history from its origins to Livy's own time. Of the 142 books that formed his history, only 35 are extant. As the court historian, Livy emphasized the moral lessons to be learned from Roman history.

BOOKS BY LIVY

The Early History of Rome. Trans. by Aubrey de Selincourt, rev. by Robert Ogilvie, *Penguin Class. Ser.* 1960 pap. $4.95. Contains Books 1–5.
Rome and Italy. Trans. by Betty Radice, *Penguin Class. Ser.* 1982 pap. $5.95. Contains Books 6–10.
The War with Hannibal. Trans. by Aubrey de Selincourt, *Penguin Class. Ser.* 1965 pap. $6.95. Contains Books 21–30.
Rome and the Mediterranean. Trans. by Henry Bettenson, *Penguin Class. Ser.* 1976 pap. $6.95. Contains Books 31–45.

PLINY THE YOUNGER. c.61–c.112

Pliny's letters are a major source of information about the personal, financial, and political life of a wealthy Roman of the upper class in the early Roman Empire. (See also Volume 2.)

BOOK BY PLINY

The Letters. Trans. by Betty Radice, *Penguin Class. Ser.* $4.95

SALLUST. 86–35 B.C.

Sallust was a Roman senator who supported Caesar and finally retired to literary pursuits, in which he distinguished himself more for style than for substance.

BOOK BY SALLUST

The Jugurthine War (and *The Conspiracy of Catiline*). Trans. by S. A. Handford, *Penguin Class. Ser.* 1964 pap. $3.95

BOOK ABOUT SALLUST

Syme, Ronald. *Sallust*. Univ. of California Pr. 1964 $38.50

SUETONIUS. c.69–c.140

Although Suetonius held a variety of official positions under emperors of the late first and early second centuries, he achieved no distinction in such pursuits. His literary achievement is represented now mainly by his lives of the emperors, which are distinguished more for encyclopedic compilation of detail than for critical historical inquiry. Their racy character has, however, given them durable popularity. (See also Volume 2.)

BOOK BY SUETONIUS

The Twelve Caesars. Trans. by Robert Graves, *Penguin Class. Ser.* 1957 pap. $3.95

BOOK ABOUT SUETONIUS

Wallace-Hadrill, Andrew. *Suetonius: The Scholar and His Caesars.* Yale Univ. Pr. 1984 $22.50

TACITUS, CORNELIUS. c.56–c.112/113

Tacitus was a Roman senator, but his reputation comes from his historical works, which cover the first century of the empire. He wrote, in a distinctive laconic style, an indictment of the principate and the behavior of the senatorial aristocracy under imperial rule.

BOOKS BY TACITUS

The Agricola and the Germania. Trans. by Hugh Mattingly, *Penguin Class. Ser.* 1971 pap. $3.95

The Annals of Imperial Rome. Trans. by Michael Grant, *Penguin Class. Ser.* 1956 pap. $4.95

The Histories. Trans. by Kenneth Wellesley, *Penguin Class. Ser.* 1976 pap. $4.95

BOOK ABOUT TACITUS

Syme, Ronald. *Tacitus.* Oxford 2 vols. 1980 $76.00

CHAPTER 7

United States History

Robert U. Goehlert

> History is a tangled skein that one may take up at any point, and break
> when one has unravelled enough; but complexity precedes evolution.
> —HENRY ADAMS, *The Education of Henry Adams*

In the last few decades revisionist historians have been preoccupied with
a vast reinterpretation of America's past as it has been presented in the
standard texts. These new readings of U.S. history, often based on the
same old evidence, range from Daniel Boorstin's "cheerful vision of the
American past" to savage attacks on Franklin Roosevelt's New Deal and a
devastating reassessment of Jacksonian democracy. At the moment, another dominant concern among these revisionist scholars appears to be a
reevaluation of our revolutionary heritage and its impact on the greater
Western society.

Other American historians have, meanwhile, addressed themselves to
problems to which there are quantitative answers. The computer revolution
that engulfed the social sciences in the 1950s has now infiltrated the ranks
of historians. Recent computer-assisted works have included studies of community structure, immigration, slavery, geographical mobility, and the process of urbanization. A body of numerical data, drawn from both printed
and manuscript sources, has been gathered and programmed to provide
striking reinterpretation of many aspects of our social and political history.
Included in this section are several recent works that are based, at least in
part, on data quantification and statistical evidence.

Another recent trend has been the reemergence of social and cultural history, including oral histories and psychohistorical approaches. There is a
special emphasis in this chapter on examples of these kinds of works. As
there has been a growing literature focusing on social phenomena rather
than specific historical events, the materials selected for this chapter reflect
the new directions that historical research is taking.

Organizationally, this chapter is designed to provide an introduction to
U.S. historical research according to generally accepted historical periods,
beginning with the Colonial Period (1606–1762), and ending with the post-
World War II era (1945–to date). This arrangement allows one to get a
sense of the ebb and flow of U.S. history as well as to approach the study
from a more structured perspective.

In addition to the works cited in this chapter, special mention should be made of two important indexes, which can be used for further research. *Writings on American History* and *America: History and Life* are two indispensable reference tools. Likewise, the *Journal of American History* and the *American Historical Review* are two major research journals, which should be consulted not only for their articles but for their extensive book-review and notes sections. Between the two journals, one can quite easily keep up with new publications in the field of American history.

It should be noted that the works shown in the main entries for each author generally represent that individual's historical writings, not necessarily all of his or her work. For additional information regarding the writings and philosophy of U.S. historians, one should consult *American Historians, 1607–1865* and *Twentieth-Century American Historians*, both edited by Clyde N. Wilson.

The many new editions of the public and personal papers of our great leaders and thinkers furnish the best source material of our historical heritage. These are discussed in Chapter 3 in this volume. The reader should also consult Chapter 1 in this volume for additional information on reference books.

WRITING OF HISTORY

American Foreign Relations: A Historiographical Review. Contributions in American History Ser. Greenwood 1981 $35.00. Analyzes past historiographical trends and methodologies in American diplomatic history. A good introduction to the discipline of diplomatic history.

Bailey, Thomas A. *The American Spirit: American History as Seen by Contemporaries.* Heath 2 vols. 5th ed. 1984 pap. ea. $12.95

Benson, Lee. *Turner and Beard: American Historical Writing Reconsidered.* Greenwood repr. of 1960 ed. 1980 lib. bdg. $22.50

Billias, George A., and Gerald N. Grob. *American History: Retrospect and Prospect.* Macmillan (Free Press) 1971 pap. $8.95

Brugger, Robert J. *Our Selves/Our Past: Psychological Approaches to American History.* Johns Hopkins Univ. Pr. text ed. 1981 pap. $9.95. This collection was compiled to reflect the wide range of research done in the new field of psychohistory.

Fogel, Robert W., and G. R. Elton. *Which Road to the Past? Two Views of History.* Yale Univ. Pr. 1983 $14.95 1984 pap. $6.95. A dialogue comparing two main schools of historical inquiry—the traditional and the scientific.

Gardner, James B., and George R. Adams, eds. *Ordinary People and Everyday Life: Perspectives on the New Social History.* Amer. Association for State and Local History text ed. 1983 $17.95. This anthology is a good example of the growing trend in contemporary historiography, as well as local and regional history.

Gay, Peter. *A Loss of Mastery: Puritan Historians in Colonial America.* Univ. of California Pr. 1966 $23.50. Includes analyses of William Bradford, Cotton Mather, and Jonathan Edwards.

Higham, John. *Writing American History: Essays on Modern Scholarship.* Peter Smith 1972 $7.00. "Writing beautifully and incisively, Higham outlines the growth of American historiography, analyzes some of its methodological and philosophical problems, and suggests ways of overcoming confining limitations. He urges historians to move beyond the so-called consensus approach and be more evaluative" (*Choice*).

Hofstadter, Richard. *The Progressive Historians: Turner, Beard, Parrington.* Univ. of Chicago Pr. 1979 pap. $7.95. (See Hofstadter's main listing in this chapter.)

Kammen, Michael, ed. *The Past before Us: Contemporary Historical Writing in the United States.* Cornell Univ. Pr. 1982 pap. $12.95. This collection investigates the trends and directions that current research on American history is taking. It includes essays on new trends, the growth of social history, and quantification.

Malone, Michael P., ed. *Historians and the American West.* Univ. of Nebraska Pr. 1983 $24.95. A survey of the history of scholarly research on the West, these historiographical essays are excellent.

Miller, David H., and Jerome O. Steffen, eds. *The Frontier: Comparative Studies.* Univ. of Oklahoma Pr. 1977 $17.95. This collection of 13 essays is a good example of the variety of approaches. It includes essays by archaeologists, demographers, anthropologists, geographers, sociologists, and historians.

Parrington, Vernon L. *Main Currents in American Thought.* 1927. Harcourt 3 vols. 1955 pap. ea. $6.95. Awarded the Pulitzer Prize for history in 1928.

Robertson, James Oliver. *American Myth, American Reality.* Amer. Century Ser. Hill & Wang 1980 $16.95 pap. $7.95. Through the use of numerous examples and illustrative stories, the author attempts to show how myths have obscured historical realities.

Steffen, Jerome O., ed. *The American West: New Perspectives, New Dimensions.* Univ. of Oklahoma Pr. 1979 $17.95 1981 pap. $7.95. This set of essays suggests new methodologies for studying the West, including the need for new research on the environment, demography, and behavior.

———. *Comparative Frontiers: A Proposal for Studying the American West.* Univ. of Oklahoma Pr. 1980 $14.95. Examines the major approaches and methodologies that have been used to study the frontier.

Turner, Frederick Jackson. *The Frontier in American History.* Fwd. by Ray A. Billington, Krieger repr. of 1920 ed. 1976 $16.50. (See Turner's main listing in this chapter.)

Vecsey, Christopher T., and Robert W. Venables, eds. *American Indian Environments: Ecological Issues in Native American History.* Syracuse Univ. Pr. text ed. 1980 pap. $9.95. This collection covers such topics as the environment, natural resources, and cultural relationships to the land.

Vitzthum, Richard C. *The American Compromise: Theme and Method in the Histories of Bancroft, Parkman, and Adams.* Univ. of Oklahoma Pr. 1974 $17.95 pap. $7.95

Wish, Harvey. *The American Historian: A Social-Intellectual History of the Writing of the American Past.* Greenwood repr. of 1960 ed. $45.00. An evaluation of the men who have recorded the story of our history from colonial times to the present.

Woodward, C. Vann, ed. *The Comparative Approach to American History.* Basic Bks. 1968 pap. $8.95. The Sterling Professor of American History at Yale University edited "this collection of 24 essays by eminent American historians who test the uniqueness of American history by comparing it with the histories of other countries in similar stages of development. Contributors include Seymour Martin Lipset, John Higham, Richard Hofstadter, George E. Mowry, Ernest R. May, and David M. Potter.... Intended for the serious student, the book is highly recommended for college and large public libraries" (*LJ*). (See Woodward's main listing in this chapter.)

Zenderland, Leila, ed. *Recycling the Past: Popular Uses of American History.* Univ. of

Pennsylvania Pr. 1978 pap. $8.95. Examines how various opinion leaders have used events from the past to create myths that affect current views.

REFERENCE BOOKS

While there is a wealth of reference material on American history, this section includes only a representative overview of the kinds of materials one can use. Because of the number of reference books available, the following lists include a few titles that cover all the chronological and supplementary lists. This section has been subdivided into four categories: Research Guides, Encyclopedias and Dictionaries, Bibliographies, and Documentary Histories. The U.S. Government Printing Office publishes the *Public Papers of the Presidents of the United States* and can provide a small catalog of this series. For additional titles of interest, see Chapter 1.

Research Guides

Biographical Directory of the American Congress, 1774–1971. U.S. Government Printing Office 1971 $11.75. Short, concise, objective sketches of all congressmen and congresswomen during those years; a section on the officers of the executive branch and cabinets from Washington to Eisenhower; and a chronological listing by state of congressmen and congresswomen from the First to the Eighty-sixth Congress.

Biographical Directory of the United States Executive Branch, 1774–1977. Ed. by Robert Sobel, Greenwood 2d ed. rev. 1977 $45.00. Patterned on the preceding publication, it includes brief sketches of the presidents, heads of state, and cabinet officers during those dates.

Cappon, Lester J. *Atlas of Early American History: The Revolutionary Era, 1760–1790.* Princeton Univ. Pr. 1975 $200.00. This well-designed atlas is the most complete work of its kind.

Carrington, Henry B. *Maps and Charts of the American Revolution.* Ayer repr. of 1877 ed. 1974 $35.00. "This book is living history. It will bring to life the excitement and drama—as well as the deep significance of those battles where men fought and died to wrest their nation out of the British Empire" (Publisher's note).

Congressional Quarterly, Inc. *Guide to Congress.* Congressional Quarterly 3d ed. 1982 $100.00. The most authoritative source for finding out how Congress works.

———. *Guide to the U.S. Supreme Court.* Congressional Quarterly 1979 $95.00. The most encyclopedic guide to the court, it includes not only informative narratives on the origins, history, and development of the court, but is full of figures and dates.

———. *Guide to U.S. Elections.* Congressional Quarterly 2d ed. 1985 $100.00. Without doubt, the most detailed and reliable volume of U.S. election statistics.

DeGregorio, William A. *The Complete Book of U.S. Presidents.* Dembner Bks. 1984 $22.50. This fact book provides a wealth of information about the lives and careers of the presidents.

Ebony Editors. *The Ebony Handbook (The Negro Handbook).* Johnson Publishing 1974 $20.00

Ebony Pictorial History of Black America. Ed. by Lerone Bennett, Jr., Johnson Publishing 4 vols. 1971 set $38.90. "A complete illustrated history of black people in America—more than 1,000 pictures" (Publisher's note).

Franklin, John Hope, and August Meier, eds. *Black Leaders of the Twentieth Century.* Univ. of Illinois Pr. 1982 $19.95 1983 pap. $7.95. Includes essays on Booker T. Washington, Martin Luther King, Jr., and Malcolm X. (See Franklin's main listing in this chapter.)

Friedel, Frank, and Richard Showman, eds. *Harvard Guide to American History.* 1954. Harvard Univ. Pr. 2 vols. rev. ed. $60.00 text ed. 2 vols. in 1 pap. $15.00. A comprehensive guide to American history. Approximately one-third of the entries are new. Includes practical suggestions on research, writing, and publication.

Friedman, Leon, and Fred L. Israel, eds. *The Justices of the United States Supreme Court, 1789–1978.* Chelsea House 5 vols 1980 pap. set $75.00. Gives a profile of each justice, including major decisions and contributions to the Court.

Goehlert, Robert U. *Congress and Law-Making: Researching the Legislative Process.* ABC-Clio text ed. 1979 pap. $13.50. This concise guide is a useful introduction to congressional publications and the tools used to research the legislative process. It also discusses secondary source material on Congress.

Goehlert, Robert U., and Fenton S. Martin. *The Presidency: A Research Guide.* ABC-Clio 1984 $28.50. An extensive guide to primary and secondary sources used in studying the presidency.

Graff, Henry F., ed. *The Presidents: A Reference History.* Scribner 1984 lib. bdg. $65.00. Analytical biographies and short bibliographical essays on each of the presidents from Washington to Carter.

A Guide to the Study of the United States of America: Representative Books Reflecting the Development of American Life and Thought, Supplement, 1956–1965. Lib. of Congress 1976 $18.00

Gustafson, Milton O., ed. *The National Archives and Foreign Relations Research.* Ohio Univ. Pr. 1974 $17.50

Hacker, Andrew, ed. *U.S.: A Statistical Portrait of the American People.* Viking 1983 $25.00. While this is a statistical compendium, the narrative and figures provide a unique picture of the United States in numbers.

Hotten, John Campden, ed. *The Original Lists of Persons of Quality: Emigrants, Religious Exiles, Political Rebels, Serving Men Sold for a Term of Years, Apprentices . . . and Others Who Went from Great Britain to the American Plantations, 1600–1700.* Genealogical Publishing repr. of 1874 ed. 1983 $20.00. More than 11,000 names are listed and the authority for the lists is clearly stated.

Jackson, Kenneth T. *Atlas of American History.* Scribner rev. ed. 1978 lib. bdg. $50.00. The best general historical atlas for U.S. history.

Kane, Joseph N. *Facts about the Presidents.* Wilson 4th ed. 1981 $30.00. This compendium of factual data is a useful source for statistical information.

Leidy, W. Philip. *A Popular Guide to Government Publications.* Columbia Univ. Pr. 4th ed. 1976 $40.00. Bibliographical data for a selected list of government publications.

Long, E. B., and Barbara Long. *The Civil War Day by Day: An Almanac, 1861–1865.* Doubleday 1971 $19.95

Merritt, Jeffrey D. *Day by Day: The 50s.* Facts on File 1979 $75.00. A useful chronology of the 1950s that pinpoints dates and is enjoyable to browse through.

Morehead, Joe. *Introduction to United States Public Documents. Lib. Science Text Ser.* Libraries Unlimited 3d ed. 1983 lib. bdg. $28.50 pap. $19.50. The best introduction to the use of U.S. government documents, it describes the distribution of documents and the tools needed for accessing information.

Notable Names in American History. Gale 3d ed. 1979 $120.00. This concise biographical dictionary is a good tool for finding basic information about the most important figures in American history.

Peirce, Neal R., and Jerry Hagstrom. *The Book of America: Inside 50 States Today.* Norton 1983 $25.00; Warner Bks. 1984 pap. $14.95. Encyclopedic in nature, this massive work details the political, social, and economic aspects of major cities and regions of states. Containing numerous maps, the volume is both colorful and lively reading.

Poulton, Helen, and Marguerite S. Howland. *The Historian's Handbook: A Descriptive Guide to Reference Works.* Univ. of Oklahoma Pr. 1972 pap. $10.95

Raimo, John, ed. *Biographical Directory of American Colonial and Revolutionary Governors, 1607–1789.* Meckler 1980 $75.00. Brief sketches and bibliographical information on all governors up to 1789.

Sabin, Joseph, and others, eds. 1869–92 1928–36. *Dictionary of Books Relating to America from Its Discovery to the Present Time.* Scarecrow Pr. 29 vols. in 2 miniprint vols. 1966 $190.00

Schlesinger, Arthur M., Jr., ed. *The Almanac of American History.* Putnam 1984 $24.95 pap. $10.95. An excellent source. (See Schlesinger's main listing in this chapter.)

Sloan, Irving J. *The Blacks in America, 1492–1977: A Chronology and Fact Book.* Oceana 4th ed. rev. 1977 lib. bdg. $8.50

Statistical Abstract of the United States. 1878–to date. U.S. Government Printing Office annual $23.00. This outstanding compendium is a boon to librarians who have to answer a large volume of public inquiries for factual data. Both government and private data sources are reviewed and evaluated annually.

U.S. Congress. *The Congressional Directory.* 1809–to date. U.S. Government Printing Office annual $6.00

U.S. Government Manual. 1935–to date. National Archives & Records Service annual $12.00. This indispensable tool lists and describes the functions of all departments of the federal government, their divisions, bureaus, commissions, and services. Revised annually.

Urdang, Laurence, ed. *The Timetables of American History.* Simon & Schuster (Touchstone Bks.) 1983 pap. $13.95. A straightforward chronology of American historical events.

Whitnah, Donald R., ed. *Government Agencies.* Greenwood 1983 lib. bdg. $49.95. Encyclopedic in nature, this volume provides historical sketches of the origin and organization of all the major departments and agencies of the federal government.

Who's Who in American Politics. Ed. by Jaques Cattell Pr., Bowker 10th ed. 1985 $125.00

Encyclopedias and Dictionaries

Boatner, Mark M., III, *The Civil War Dictionary.* McKay 1959 $25.00. Includes illustrations, maps, and diagrams.

————. *Encyclopedia of the American Revolution.* McKay 1980 $9.98. A concise and informative fact book, providing information about individuals, events, and places.

Carruth, Gordon, and others, eds. *The Encyclopedia of American Facts and Dates.*

Crowell 7th ed. rev. 1979 $14.95. The most comprehensive chronology of U.S. history, providing factual information about lesser-known events.

Concise Dictionary of American History. Scribner 1983 $65.00. The best single-volume dictionary of a general nature relating to U.S. history.

DeConde, Alexander. *Encyclopedia of American Foreign Policy: Studies of the Principal Movements and Ideas.* Scribner 3 vols. 1978 $180.00. Includes both factual information and conceptual and theoretical essays.

Findling, John E. *Dictionary of American Diplomatic History.* Greenwood 1980 lib. bdg. $45.00. An excellent starting place for basic information about events, individuals, and terminology.

Hochman, Stanley. *Yesterday and Today: A Dictionary of Recent American History.* McGraw-Hill 1979 $37.95. A popular and readable general encyclopedia.

Martin, Michael, and Leonard Gelber. *Dictionary of American History.* Littlefield rev. ed. 1981 pap. $9.95; ed. by Leo Lieberman, Rowman rev. & enl. ed. 1978 $15.00. Intended to be more popular than a scholarly historical dictionary, it is more lively and interesting than most dictionaries.

Morris, Richard B., and others, eds. *Encyclopedia of American History.* Harper 6th ed. 1982 $22.50. The most up-to-date encyclopedia intended for a general audience.

Neely, Mark E., Jr., *The Abraham Lincoln Encyclopedia.* Da Capo 1984 pap. $17.50. A gold mine of information and facts about Lincoln.

Plano, Jack C., and Milton Greenberg, eds. *The American Political Dictionary.* Holt 6th ed. 1982 $18.95 pap. $14.95. Clear and precise definitions for U.S. political terms and jargon.

Porter, Glenn, ed. *Encyclopedia of American Economic History: Studies of the Principal Movements and Ideas.* Scribner 3 vols. 1980 lib. bdg. $180.00. Covers all aspects of the U.S. economic experience. The first volume contains an excellent historiography of U.S. economic history.

Roller, David C., and Robert Twyman, eds. *The Encyclopedia of Southern History.* Louisiana State Univ. Pr. 1979 $90.00. In-depth essays on the institutions and customs especially peculiar to the South.

Sperber, Hans, and Travis Trittschuh. *American Political Terms: An Historical Dictionary.* Wayne State Univ. Pr. 1962 $17.95. Defines approximately 1,000 words and phrases, with information on usage.

Bibliographies

The American Presidency: A Historical Bibliography. ABC-Clio 1984 $60.00. The most up-to-date and comprehensive bibliography on the presidency.

Beers, Henry P. *Bibliographies in American History, 1942–1978: Guide to Materials for Research.* Research Publications 2 vols. 1982 $245.00. This bibliography of bibliographies covers all aspects of historical information. A gold mine of resources.

Blanco, Richard L. *The War of the American Revolution: A Selected Annotated Bibliography of Published Sources.* Garland 1983 lib. bdg. $49.00. An excellent guide to the major writings and additional sources for further study.

Burke, Robert E., and Richard Lowitt, comps. *The New Era and the New Deal, 1920–1940. Goldentree Bibliographies in Amer. History Ser.* Harlan Davidson 1981 text ed. $24.95 pap. $19.95. Though there are numerous bibliographies covering this period, this one provides the best overall coverage to the economics, politics, and social development of the era.

Burns, Richard Dean, ed. *Guide to American Foreign Relations since 1700*. ABC-Clio text ed. 1982 $135.00. The best and most-comprehensive bibliography and historiography on U.S. foreign policy and diplomacy.

Cassara, Ernest, ed. *History of the United States of America: A Guide to Information Sources*. Gale 1977 $55.00. This volume attempts to cover all aspects of U.S. history. Given the size of the task, this is a useful place to start one's research.

Church, Elihu Dwight. *Catalog of Books Relating to the Discovery and Early History of North and South America*. 1907. Comp. by G. W. Cole, Peter Smith 5 vols. $120.00

Cronon, E. David, and Theodore D. Rosenof, comps. *The Second World War and the Atomic Age, 1940–1973. Goldentree Bibliographies in Amer. History Ser.* Harlan Davidson 1975 pap. $13.95. One of the few bibliographies that covers post-World War II history. An excellent source of current historical research.

Donald, David, comp. *The Nation in Crisis, 1861–1877. Goldentree Bibliographies in Amer. History Ser.* Harlan Davidson 1969 pap. $6.95. Although relatively short given the volume of literature written about the Civil War and Reconstruction, this is an excellent introductory bibliography.

Dornbusch, Charles E., comp. *Military Bibliography of the Civil War*. 1961–72. NYPL 3 vols. vol. 1 (1983) $25.00 vol. 2 (1975) $20.00 vol. 3 (1982) $20.00

Evans, Charles. *American Bibliography*. 1903–34. Peter Smith 14 vols. vols. 1–12 $135.00 vol. 13 $20.00 vol. 14 $20.00; Scarecrow Pr. 13 vols. in 1 miniprint vol. 1967 $42.00. Volume 14 is an index by R. P. Bristol.

Ferguson, E. James, comp. *Confederation, Constitution, and Early National Period, 1781–1815. Goldentree Bibliographies in Amer. History Ser.* Harlan Davidson 1975 pap. $12.95. Especially useful for finding materials relating to the economics and politics of the post-Constitution period.

Gephart, Ronald M. *Revolutionary America, 1763–1789: A Bibliography*. Lib. of Congress 2 vols. 1984 $38.00. The most up-to-date bibliography of prerevolutionary America, including political, economic, and social histories.

Goehlert, Robert U., and John R. Sayre. *The United States Congress: A Bibliography*. Macmillan (Free Press) 1981 $50.00. This comprehensive bibliography covers the origins, history, and workings of Congress. It includes citations to both scholarly and popular material.

Grim, Ronald E., ed. *Historical Geography of the United States and Canada: A Guide to Information Sources*. Gale 1982 $55.00. Introduces the literature of historical geography, including exploration as well as the more specialized works in the discipline.

Hall, Kermit L. *A Comprehensive Bibliography of American Constitutional and Legal History, 1896–1979*. Kraus 5 vols. 1984 $575.00. This huge bibliography includes more than 18,000 citations on American constitutional history, and is the most comprehensive reference source on the topic.

Hutchinson, William K., ed. *American Economic History: A Guide to Information Sources. Economic Information Guide Ser.* Gale 1980 $55.00. Arranged by broad categories, including banking, industry, trade, and the role of the government.

Leary, William M., and Arthur S. Link, eds. *The Progressive Era and the Great War, 1896–1920. Goldentree Bibliographies in Amer. History Ser.* Harlan Davidson 2d ed. 1978 $24.95 pap. $23.95. A basic bibliography arranged by topic and period. Includes numerous biographical citations.

Maurer, David J., ed. *U.S. Politics and Elections: A Guide to Information Sources. Amer. Government and History Information Guide Ser.* Gale 1978 $55.00. Citations to biographical material on important political figures as well as major events.

McCarrick, Earlean M. *U.S. Constitution: A Guide to Information Sources. Amer. Government and History Information Guide Ser.* Gale 1980 $55.00. A good bibliography on the Constitution, providing citations by topic and for all amendments.

Miller, Elizabeth W., and Mary Fisher, comps. *The Negro in America: A Bibliography.* Harvard Univ. Pr. rev. ed. 1970 $22.50 pap. $7.95. "Compiled for the American Academy of Arts and Sciences, this selective, scholarly bibliography will be a welcome addition to the reference collections of both public and college libraries. Some older works are noted, but the main concentration is on titles appearing in the years 1954 to 1965. Topically arranged. Many references are accompanied by brief, descriptive annotations. Author index" (*LJ*).

Mitterling, Philip I. *U.S. Cultural History: A Guide to Information Sources. Amer. Government and History Information Guide Ser.* Gale 1980 $55.00. An excellent bibliography for cultural history that includes popular culture as well as the fine arts.

Nevins, Allan, and others, eds. *Civil War Books: A Critical Bibliography.* Louisiana State Univ. Pr. 2 vols. 1967–68. (See Nevins's main listing in this chapter.)

Shaw, Ralph, and Richard H. Shoemaker, comps. *American Bibliography, 1801–1819.* Scarecrow Pr. 22 vols. 1958–65 $290.00. Taken together, the contributors are distinguished observers of the American religious scene. The bibliography is invaluable for those who wish to investigate the historical implications.

Shy, John, comp. *The American Revolution. Goldentree Bibliographies in Amer. History Ser.* Harlan Davidson 1972 pap. $6.95. This short work is still very useful.

Smith, Dwight L., ed. *Afro-American History: A Bibliography.* ABC-Clio 1981 $98.50

Tingley, Donald F. *Social History of the United States: A Guide to Information Sources. Amer. Government and History Information Guide Ser.* Gale 1979 $55.00. A good introduction to the enormous increase in the literature of the social sciences in the last 25 years.

Documentary Histories

Adler, Mortimer J., and Charles Van Doren, eds. *The Annals of America.* Encyclopaedia Britannica 23 vols. 1976 $429.00. Twenty-one volumes, chronologically arranged, of original source materials from specific periods in American history from 1493 to 1973. The two-volume *Conspectus* provides a topical index to the great issues in U.S. history and a bibliography of recommended reading and additional source material.

Aptheker, Herbert. *A Documentary History of the Negro People in the United States.* Citadel Pr. 1973 $17.50 3 vols. 1962–74 pap. ea. $9.95. "Still an important source book" (*Choice*).

———. *Nat Turner's Slave Rebellion: The Environment, the Event, the Effects. AMS Historical Ser.* Humanities Pr. 1966 text ed. $10.45. Includes the full text of the "confessions" of Nat Turner made in prison in 1831.

Bailyn, Bernard, and N. Garrett, eds. *Pamphlets of the American Revolution, 1750–1776.* Harvard Univ. Pr. 1965 $30.00

Boller, Paul F., and Ronald Story. *A More Perfect Union: Documents in U.S. History.* Houghton Mifflin 2 vols. text ed. 1984 pap. ea. $12.95. An extensive collection of primary source documents from colonial times to the present.

Boorstin, Daniel J., ed. *An American Primer.* Univ. of Chicago Pr. 2 vols. 1969 $25.00. Eighty-three chronologically arranged documents, statements, essays, etc., beginning with the Mayflower Compact of 1620 to President Johnson's Address on Voting Rights of 1965. (See Boorstin's main listing in this chapter.)

Commager, Henry Steele, ed. *Documents of American History*. 1934. Prentice-Hall (Appleton) 2 vols. 9th ed. 1974 pap. ea. $19.95. (See Commager's main listing in this chapter.)

Hofstadter, Richard, and Michael Wallace, eds. *American Violence: A Documentary History*. Random (Vintage) 1971 pap. $4.95. This book is "a collection of well-chosen, brief, primary accounts of incidents [which give] a good cumulative sense of the extent and variety of the nation's social violence" (*AHR*).

Johnson, Donald B., comp. *National Party Platforms, 1840–1976*. Univ. of Illinois Pr. 2 vols. 6th ed. rev. 1978 $42.50

Miller, Perry, and Thomas H. Johnson, eds. *The Puritans: A Sourcebook of Their Writings*. 1938. Harper 2 vols. pap. vol. 1 $8.50 vol. 2 $8.95

Morris, Richard B. *Basic Documents in American History*. Krieger 1980 pap. $5.95. A short compendium of the major documents.

Peckham, Howard Henry. *Historical Americana: Books from Which Our Early History Is Written*. Univ. of Michigan Pr. 1980 pap. $5.95. A fascinating study of the major publications of the colonial and early national periods.

Scott, Donald M., and Bernard Wishy, eds. *America's Families: A Documentary History*. Harper 1982 pap. $12.45. Includes documents, letters, and excerpts from monographs on such topics as marriage, childrearing, and courtship.

Washburn, Wilcomb E., comp. *The American Indian and the United States: A Documentary History*. Greenwood 4 vols. 1973 $195.00. "These four volumes of primary source material have been compiled to show how the relationship between the American Indian and the U.S. Government evolved" (*Booklist*).

———. *The Indian in America*. New Amer. Nation Ser. Harper 1975 $19.18 pap. $5.25. "The Director of the Office of American Studies at the Smithsonian Institution systematically ties together the history of North American Indian culture into three periods: first, the early years of confrontation with Europeans during which Indians maintained an equal footing with white men; second, the period between the end of the colonial era and the second half of the nineteenth century, in which Indian equality was corroded; and third, the years that followed the organization of reservations" (*Booklist*).

SURVEYS

Among the various histories of the United States, the bookseller will perhaps be more interested in shorter surveys than in the varied representation of special periods and aspects that the librarian will need. There are many such histories. Most are school or college texts. Some, however, are written for general readers, or at least with their preference for literary style in view.

Adams, James Truslow, ed. *Album of American History*. Scribner 3 vols. rev. ed. 1969 $225.00. Pictorial account from colonial times to the present. (See Adams's main listing in this chapter.)

Bailyn, Bernard, and others. *The Great Republic: A History of the American People*. Heath text ed. 1981 $25.95 2 vols. pap. ea. $17.95; Little, Brown 1977 $27.50. One of the best general surveys. Very readable and entertaining.

Blum, John M., and others. *The National Experience: A History of the United States.* Harcourt 2 vols. in 1 text ed. 5th ed. 1981 ea. $16.95

Boorstin, Daniel J. *The Americans.* Random 3 vols. 1958–73 ea. $20.00 set $60.00. "Totally delightful . . . a profoundly arresting contribution to American history" (*SR*). The story of how Europeans became Americans. Volume 1 won a Bancroft Prize and Volume 2 the 1965 Parkman Prize. (See Boorstin's main listing in this chapter.)

Brock, William R. *The United States, 1789–1890. Sources of History Ser.* Cornell Univ. Pr. 1975 $27.50. "Brock [an eminent British scholar] has essayed an introductory survey of the sources that are basic to an understanding of American history in the years 1789–1890" (*LJ*).

Burns, James MacGregor. *The Vineyard of Liberty.* Vol. 1 in *The American Experiment.* Knopf 1982 $22.95. Written as a general history, this superb survey covers the years between the ratification of the Constitution and the Emancipation Proclamation.

Carroll, Peter N., and David W. Noble. *The Free and the Unfree: A New History of the United States.* Penguin 1977 pap. $7.95. This history employs a different approach by looking at the Europeanization of America and the fate of minority groups.

Cooke, Alistair. *Alistair Cooke's America.* Knopf 1973 $30.00 1977 pap. $11.95. "A panoramic book, traveling fast and high, and the view it gives of our land and the people below is exhilarating" (*Atlantic*).

Current, Richard N., and T. Harry Williams. *American History: A Survey.* Knopf 2 vols. text ed. 6th ed. 1983 pap. ea. $17.50. Well-written and straightforward narrative useful to the scholar and layperson alike.

Davidson, Marshall B. *The Drawing of America: Eyewitnesses to History.* Abrams 1983 $49.50. Although this volume includes more than 300 illustrations, it is designed to be a visual history of the United States through its images of the past and future.

Garraty, John A. *A Short History of the American Nation.* Harper text ed. 3d. ed. 1981 pap. $19.95. Contrary to the notion that a good historical survey needs to be lengthy, this concise history reflects a careful and judicious treatment of the United States.

Garraty, John A., and the editors of American Heritage. *The American Nation.* Intro. by Roger Butterfield, Harper 2 vols. text ed. 5th ed. 1982 $29.95 2 vols. pap. ea. $19.95

Goode, Kenneth G. *From Africa to the United States and Then: A Concise Afro-American History.* Scott, Foresman 2d ed. 1976 pap. $7.95

Grob, Gerald N., and George A. Billias. *Interpretations of American History.* Macmillan (Free Press) 2 vols. 3d ed. 1978 pap. vol. 1 $8.95 vol. 2 $7.95. An excellent survey of U.S. historiography, including all the major schools of thought and methodologies.

Johnson, Thomas H., ed. *The Oxford Companion to American History.* Oxford 1966 $39.95. "An incredibly good job . . . as comprehensive and authoritative in substance as one could possibly hope from so wide-ranging but highly condensed a work" (Lyman H. Butterfield).

Link, Arthur S., and William B. Catton. *American Epoch: A History of the United States since the 1890's.* Knopf 3 vols. 4th ed. 1967 ea. $14.00. An excellent text on modern U.S. history from the Gilded Age to the present.

Lukacs, John. *Outgrowing Democracy: A History of the United States in the Twentieth Century.* Doubleday 1984 $19.95. This volume is actually not a history, but a collection of theoretical and provocative essays about the past and future of American democracy.

Merk, Frederick. *History of the Westward Movement*. Knopf 1978 $20.00. An excellent survey of the West from pre-Columbian times to the present. A solid and standard history.

Miller, William, and Daniel Aaron. *The United States: A History of a Republic*. Prentice-Hall 2d ed. 1985 pap. $19.95. Written for college undergraduates, this text has sold more than 110,000 copies since publication and is used in major colleges and universities. The authors have woven into the political narrative the significant developments in economic and cultural matters to provide a synthesis of American history for this generation. Bibliographies and maps are valuable additions.

Morison, Samuel Eliot. *The Oxford History of the American People*. New Amer. Lib. 3 vols. pap. ea. $3.95–$4.50; Oxford 1965 $39.95 text ed. $19.95. A general history from prehistoric times to the assassination of President Kennedy. A "quick reference book for young people, and a really delightful book to read" (*LJ*). (See Morison's main listing in this chapter.)

Morison, Samuel Eliot, Henry Steele Commager, and William E. Leuchtenburg. *The Growth of the American Republic*. Oxford 2 vols. 7th ed. 1980 ea. $18.95. Incorporating the material of the original 1930 single-volume edition, this new edition carries events up to the 1970s. Each volume has a bibliography and index. *The Christian Science Monitor* wrote of the 5th edition: "It constitutes the standard by which other inclusive American histories are to be judged."

Nevins, Allan, and Henry Steele Commager. *A Short History of the United States*. Knopf 6th ed. 1976 $22.95. (See Nevins's main listing in this chapter.)

Patterson, James T. *America in the Twentieth Century: A History*. Harcourt 2d ed. 1983 pap. $18.95. This well-known historian has written a clear and vivid history of modern America, giving special emphasis to political developments.

Quint, Howard H., and others. *Main Problems in American History*. Dorsey 4th ed. 1978 $17.50. Attempts to provide a framework for U.S. history by looking at the interpretations of major events.

Rhodes, James Ford. *History of the United States from the Compromise of 1850 to the McKinley-Bryan Campaign of 1896*. 1893–1919. Associated Faculty Pr. 8 vols. $225.00; ed. by Allan Nevins, Univ. of Chicago Pr. abr. ed. 1966 pap. $3.95

Savage, Henry. *Discovering America, 1700–1875*. New Amer. Nation Ser. Harper 1979 $21.10. Records not only the exploration of North America, but the landscape, flora, and fauna that the explorers encountered.

Thernstrom, Stephan. *A History of the American People*. Harcourt 2 vols. text ed. 1984 pap. ea. $15.95. An excellent introductory survey of U.S. history, discussing all the significant economic, political, social, and intellectual developments.

Tindall, George B. *America: A Narrative History*. Norton 2 vols. in 1 text ed. 1984 $18.95 2 vols. pap. ea. $9.95. Written for the general reader, this broad survey more than adequately covers all the controversies and major events in American history.

Williams, George W. *The History of the Negro Race in America from 1619 to 1880*. Amer. Negro: His History and Lit. Ser. Ayer 2 vols. repr. of 1883 ed. 1968 $43.00. "A monument in American historiography" (C. Vann Woodward, *SR*).

Zinn, Howard. *A People's History of the United States*. Harper 1981 $8.17. The author has attempted to write a history of the United States from the point of view of those who were exploited. As a result, this is a unique and strikingly different style of historical writing.

COLONIAL PERIOD, 1606–1762

Breen, T. H. *Puritans and Adventurers: Changes and Persistence in Early America.* Oxford 1980 $22.50 pap. $8.95. This collection of seven essays on colonial Massachusetts and Virginia examines the significant differences between the two kinds of societies that were developing simultaneously.

Bridenbaugh, Carl. *Cities in Revolt: Urban Life in America, 1743–1776.* Oxford 1971 pap. $9.95

Bushman, Richard L. *King and People in Provincial Massachusetts.* Univ. of North Carolina Pr. 1985 $25.00. This is the newest and most comprehensive study of prerevolutionary Massachusetts. While on the one hand it is a highly detailed history of colonial Massachusetts, it is also a landmark volume in the field of colonial history.

Fitzhugh, William. *William Fitzhugh and His Chesapeake World, 1676–1701.* Ed. by Richard Beale Davis, Univ. Pr. of Virginia 1963 $20.00. Fitzhugh (1651–1701), lawyer, successful colonist, and prosperous planter-resident on the Potomac, wrote the 212 letters (May 15, 1679 to April 26, 1699) that cover a great variety of commercial, professional, and personal subjects. His descendants were to play an important part during the founding of the Republic and later. Carefully edited with an excellent introduction, this will be the definitive edition barring the discovery of many new letters.

Gura, Philip F. *A Glimpse of Sion's Glory: Puritan Radicalism in New England, 1620–1660.* Wesleyan Univ. Pr. 1984 $25.95. The difference between this study and earlier research on Puritanism is that this work stresses the pluralistic and dynamic aspects of radicalism. This work is an interesting analysis of the various religious radicals, including the Separatists, Quakers, and Anabaptists.

Hall, David D., and David Grayson Allen, eds. *Seventeenth-Century New England.* Colonial Society of Massachusetts 1984 $30.00. The contributions to this collection of conference proceedings reflect some of the very best essays on colonial history. The volume includes a wide-ranging assortment of topics, including diet, popular culture, magic, and the daily life of the fishermen.

Hall, David D., John M. Murrin, and Thad W. Tate, eds. *Saints and Revolutionaries: Essays on Early American History.* Norton 1984 $27.50. Reflects a renewed scholarly interest and analysis of colonial history.

Kolodny, Annette. *The Land before Her: Fantasy and Experience of American Frontiers, 1630–1860.* Univ. of North Carolina Pr. 1984 $28.00 pap. $9.95. This work is a rich and detailed study of women's writings about the frontier, including travel diaries and novels. It is an interesting study that contrasts with the popular conception of a male-oriented picture of the frontier.

Main, Jackson Turner. *Society and Economy in Colonial Connecticut.* Princeton Univ. Pr. text ed. 1985 $34.00. This study of the social and economic development of Connecticut relies heavily on detailed statistical data. The main focus is an analysis of the wealth, position, and standard of living of workers and professionals.

Nobles, Gregory H. *Divisions throughout the Whole: Politics and Society in Hampshire County, Massachusetts, 1740–1775.* Cambridge Univ. Pr. 1983 $29.95. Using extensive source material, Nobles argues that the prerevolutionary opposition to the Crown was considerably less than most theorists contend. Instead, the author depicts the political and religious conflicts as related to social and class differences.

Rice, Kym S. *Early American Taverns: Entertainment of Friends and Strangers.*

Fraunces Tavern Museum 1983 $16.95 pap. $12.95. This amply and beautifully illustrated volume provides a lively history of colonial taverns, both urban and rural, throughout all the colonies. The book covers such aspects as the food, innkeepers, drink, and entertainment.

Rutman, Darrett B., and Anita H. Rutman. *A Place in Time: Middlesex County Virginia, 1650–1750.* Norton 1984 $19.95. This highly detailed study of colonial Virginia focuses on the personal and community aspects of social history. The book is especially good in providing engaging analyses of the economic and political life of the community.

Stick, David. *Roanoke Island: The Beginning of English America.* Univ. of North Carolina Pr. 1983 $14.95 pap. $5.95. This volume, a popular account of the English attempts at settlement in America, is a readable volume and an excellent addition to general early American history.

Van Dusen, Albert E., ed. *Adventures for Another World: Jonathan Trumble's Commonplace Book.* Connecticut Historical Society 1983 pap. $5.95. Unlike a true diary, the commonplace book is a repository of random observations, thoughts, and notes. This is an excellent volume, which gives the flavor and feeling of eighteenth-century New England.

Vaughan, Alden T. *New England Frontier: Indians and Puritans, 1620–1675.* Norton rev. ed. pap. $7.95

Webb, Stephen. *1676: The End of American Independence.* Knopf 1984 $25.00. This controversial study argues that English governance was virtually ended 100 years prior to independence. Despite the controversial thesis of the book, it is still a useful survey of colonial-Anglo relations.

Yazawa, Melvin. *From Colonies to Commonwealth: Familial Ideology and the Beginnings of the American Republic.* Johns Hopkins Univ. Pr. 1985 $28.50. This study analyzes both colonial and postrevolutionary family relations and authority structures. The book examines the role of education and politics in changing family allegiance to the nation.

REVOLUTION AND CONFEDERATION, 1763–1789

Alden, John R. *The American Revolution, 1775–1783. New Amer. Nation Ser.* Harper 1954 $21.10 pap. $7.95

Bailyn, Bernard. *The Ideological Origins of the American Revolution.* Harvard Univ. Pr. 1967 $18.50 pap. $6.95. Awarded the Pulitzer Prize in history and a Bancroft Prize in 1968.

———. *The Ordeal of Thomas Hutchinson.* Harvard Univ. Pr. 1974 $25.00; Harvard Univ. Pr. (Belknap Pr.) pap. $8.95. "A sympathetic picture of the much vilified Loyalist governor of Massachusetts at the time of the American Revolution" (*Booklist*).

Bailyn, Bernard, and John B. Hench, eds. *The Press and the American Revolution.* New England Univ. Pr. text ed. 1981 $24.95 pap. $9.95. Examines the communication of news and information during the American Revolution.

Bennett, Lerone, Jr. *Before the Mayflower: A History of Black America.* Johnson Publishing 1982 $19.95; Penguin rev. ed. 1984 pap. $6.95. "Panoramic history of Negro Life in America which dispels some popular notions and accepted myths" (James E. Wright, *LJ*).

Berkin, Carol. *Jonathan Sewall: Odyssey of an American Loyalist.* Columbia Univ. Pr. 1974 $20.00. "An excellent history of Sewall's involvement in the struggle for power in Massachusetts between 1761 and 1775" (*LJ*).

Bonomi, Patricia U., ed. *Party and Political Opposition in Revolutionary America.* Sleepy Hollow Pr. text ed. 1980 $17.50. A useful collection because it is intended to question traditional views about party politics and tactics.

Bowler, R. Arthur. *Logistics and the Failure of the British Army in America, 1775–1783.* Princeton Univ. Pr. 1975 $30.00

Bridenbaugh, Carl. *The Spirit of '76: The Growth of American Patriotism before Independence.* Oxford 1975 $16.95 pap. $5.95

Cohen, Lester H. *The Revolutionary Histories: Contemporary Narratives of the American Revolution.* Cornell Univ. Pr. 1980 $24.95. This historiography of research on the revolutionary era is an important contribution to the intellectual history of the period.

Dann, John C., ed. *The Revolution Remembered: Eyewitness Accounts of the War for Independence. Clements Lib. Bicentennial Studies* Univ. of Chicago Pr. 1980 $20.00. Based on the pension records of revolutionary war soldiers, this volume provides an oral history from the reminiscences of the militia.

Dinkin, Robert J. *Voting in Revolutionary America: A Study of Elections in the Original Thirteen States, 1776–1789. Contributions in Amer. History Ser.* Greenwood lib. bdg. $27.50. Helps clarify the origins and evolution of the U.S. electoral system.

Fowler, William M., Jr., and Wallace Coyle, eds. *The American Revolution: Changing Perspectives.* Northeastern Univ. Pr. 1979 $20.95. This engaging set of essays explores the lesser-known groups in the Revolution, including American Indians and blacks.

Gelb, Norman. *Less Than Glory.* Putnam 1984 $15.95. This popular history depicts everything that went wrong, failed, or was corrupt. While the picture is not appealing, it provides a side of the Revolution not often written about.

Hoffman, Ronald, and Peter J. Albert. *Arms and Independence: The Military Character of the American Revolution.* Univ. Pr. of Virginia text ed. 1984 $20.00. Examines the relationship between military affairs and society as well as the concept of warfare.

Kammen, Michael G. *A Rope of Sand: The Colonial Agents, British Politics, and the American Revolution.* Cornell Univ. Pr. 1968 $27.50

———. *A Season of Youth: The American Revolution and the Historical Imagination.* Knopf 1978 $15.00; Oxford 1980 pap. $8.95. Examines how writers, poets, novelists, and playwrights have tried to use the Revolution as a symbol in American culture.

Knollenberg, Bernhard. *The Growth of the American Revolution, 1766–1775.* Macmillan (Free Pr.) 1975 $19.95. "A detailed inventory of the elements that led to the Revolution" (*LJ*).

MacLeod, Duncan J. *Slavery, Race and the American Revolution.* Cambridge Univ. Pr. 1975 pap. $11.95

Maier, Pauline. *The Old Revolutionaries: Political Lives in the Age of Samuel Adams.* Knopf 1980 $15.00; Random (Vintage) pap. $7.95. Focuses on several political leaders who formed the older revolutionary elite.

Martin, James Kirby. *In the Course of Human Events: An Interpretive Exploration of the American Revolution.* Harlan Davidson text ed. 1979 $24.95 pap. $14.95. The intent of this volume is to digest and summarize recent research and historiography.

Middlekauff, Robert. *The Glorious Cause: The American Revolution, 1763–1789.* Vol. 2 in *History of the United States.* Oxford 1982 $30.00. Written for a general audience, this is a superior history.

Mitchell, Broadus. *The Price of Independence: A Realistic View of the American Revolution.* Oxford 1974 $25.00. "This is a highly readable collection of nineteen essays [portraying] the non-heroic and ugly reality, the follies without the grandeur of 1776" (*TLS*).

Morris, Richard B. *The American Revolution Reconsidered.* Greenwood repr. of 1967 lib. bdg. $24.50

———. *The Peacemakers: The Great Powers and American Independence.* Northeastern Univ. Pr. repr. of 1965 ed. 1983 $24.95 pap. $9.95. "The making of the peace that ended the American Revolution and gave independence to the United States was the most crucial engagement and most notable victory in American diplomatic history. This brilliant book, winner of the 1965 Bancroft Prize, is the first full account of how America's 'undisciplined marines,' Benjamin Franklin, John Adams, and John Jay, outmaneuvered the Great Powers to win that victory" (*History Book Club Review*).

Muenchhausen, Friedrich von. *At General Howe's Side, 1776–1778. Revolutionary War Bicentennial Ser.* Trans. by Ernst Kipping, Freneau Pr. 1974 lib. bdg. $15.95. "Captain von Muenchhausen's diary . . . helps to fill a gap in our knowledge of the Howe campaign. . . . On matters that came under his direct observation, he was perceptive, honest, and lively. His diary is very useful in giving us a day-by-day account of routine at headquarters, the social life of the British high command and European attitudes toward America and its soldiers" (*Choice*).

Neuenschwander, John A. *The Middle Colonies and the Coming of the American Revolution.* Associated Faculty Pr. (National Univ. Publications) 1974 $25.00

Onuf, Peter S. *The Origins of the Federal Republic: Jurisdictional Controversies in the United States, 1775–1787.* Univ. of Pennsylvania Pr. 1983 $30.00 pap. $12.95. Because of the importance of the state system to the American political system, the book provides a useful history of the early jurisdictional disputes.

Palmer, David R. *The Way of the Fox: American Strategy in the War for America, 1775–1783. Contributions to Military History* Greenwood 1974 lib. bdg. $27.50. This study "investigates in logical sequence . . . General Washington's strategic conduct of the war" (Publisher's note).

Peckham, Howard H. *The Toll of Independence: Engagements and Battle Casualties of the American Revolution.* Univ. of Chicago Pr. 1974 $17.00

Quarles, Benjamin. *The Negro in the American Revolution. Norton Lib.* 1973 pap. $6.95; Univ. of North Carolina Pr. 1961 $20.00. In addition to ten thoroughly documented chapters, there is a precise bibliography, denoting even primary sources, such as manuscripts and unpublished dissertations.

Rakove, Jack N. *The Beginnings of National Politics: An Interpretive History of the Continental Congress. Pap. Repr. Ser.* Johns Hopkins Univ. Pr. text ed. 1982 pap. $8.95; Knopf 1979 $15.95. A complete history of the formation and operation of the Continental Congresses.

Reuter, Frank T. *Trials and Triumphs: George Washington's Foreign Policy.* Texas Christian Univ. Pr. 1983 $19.50. Written for the general reader, this book is a good example of how scholarly analysis can be written dramatically and understandably.

Rezneck, Samuel. *Unrecognized Patriots: The Jews in the American Revolution.* Greenwood 1975 lib. bdg. $29.95

Rice, Howard C., and Anne S. Broun, eds. *The American Campaigns of Rochambeau's Army, 1780–1783: The Journals of Clermont-Crevecoeur, Verger, and Berthier.* Princeton Univ. Pr. 2 vols. 1972 $165.00

Schlesinger, Arthur M. *The Birth of the Nation: A Portrait of the American People on the Eve of Independence.* Intro. by Arthur M. Schlesinger, Jr., Houghton Mifflin 1981 pap. $6.95. (See Schlesinger's main listing in this chapter.)

Smith, Page. *A New Age Now Begins: A People's History of the American Revolution.* McGraw-Hill 2 vols. 1976 $24.95. Comprising the first part of a multivolume history, these initial volumes give a complete historical overview of the founding of the nation.

Van Doren, Carl C. *The Secret History of the American Revolution.* Kelley repr. of 1941 ed. 1973 $27.50

Wood, Gordon S. *The Creation of the American Republic, 1776–1787.* Norton Lib. 1972 pap. $9.95; Univ. of North Carolina Pr. 1969 $35.00. "One of the half dozen most important books ever written about the American Revolution" (*N.Y. Times*).

Young, Alfred F. *The American Revolution: Explorations in the History of American Radicalism.* Northern Illinois Univ. Pr. 1975 $15.00 pap. $8.50

EARLY NATIONAL PERIOD, 1789–1828

Bartlett, Irving H. *Daniel Webster.* Norton 1981 pap. $6.95. The best biography to date on Webster, focusing on his role as a national politician.

Bridenbaugh, Carl. *Early Americans.* Oxford 1981 $22.50. A truly fascinating anthology on little-known individuals and events.

Brown, Roger H. *The Republic in Peril, 1812.* 1964. *Norton Lib.* 1971 pap. $5.95. "A major revision of thinking about the War of 1812" (*LJ*).

Cochran, Thomas C. *Frontiers of Change: Early Industrialism in America.* Oxford 1891 $17.50 pap. $7.95. Covering the time from the Revolution to the Civil War, the author examines how industrialization shaped the distinctive character of American society.

Davidson, Basil. *Black Mother: The African Slave Trade.* Little, Brown rev. ed. 1981 $16.95 pap. $7.95. Examination of the African beginnings of the American slave trade.

Davis, David Brion. *The Problem of Slavery in an Age of Revolution, 1770–1823.* Cornell Univ. Pr. 1975 $34.50 pap. $9.95. Davis "explores the international impact and social significance of anti-slavery thought in a critical era" (Publisher's note).

Eaton, Clement. *The Growth of Southern Civilization, 1790–1860.* Harper 1961 $17.26. This extensive and thorough study of the pre-Civil War South is fascinating reading and important as a background for an understanding of some of the conditions and problems in the southern regions today.

——. *History of the Southern Confederacy.* Macmillan (Free Press) text ed. 1965 pap. $12.95

Formisano, Ronald P. *The Transformation of Political Culture: Massachusetts Parties, 1790s–1840s.* Oxford 1983 $35.00. While this volume concentrates on Massachusetts, it is an important work on early political parties in the United States.

Goodman, Paul. *The Federalists vs. the Jeffersonian Republicans.* Krieger text ed. 1977 pap. $5.95

Heale, Michael J. *The Presidential Quest: Candidates and Images in American Political Culture, 1787–1852.* Longman text ed. 1982 pap. $11.95. Concentrating predominantly on Jacksonian America, this work demonstrates how presidential elections were a key factor in the two-party competition.

Hoffer, Peter C. *Revolution and Regeneration: Life Cycle and the Historical Vision of the Generation of 1776.* Univ. of Georgia Pr. 1983 $15.00 text ed. pap. $8.00. An important contribution to the genre of psychohistory, it examines how the generation of revolutionaries changed and matured as its members became adults.

Hoffman, Daniel N. *Governmental Secrecy and the Founding Fathers: A Study in Constitutional Controls. Contributions in Legal Studies* Greenwood 1981 lib. bdg. $35.00. Investigates how government secrecy began and proposes several reforms.

Hofstadter, Richard. *The Age of Reform: From Bryan to F. D. R.* Knopf 1955 $12.95. Winner of the Pulitzer Prize in history in 1955. (See Hofstadter's main listing in this chapter.)

———. *Anti-Intellectualism in American Life.* Knopf 1963 $13.95; Random (Vintage) 1966 pap. $5.95. This is "chiefly a history of movements in this country which, from the first broadsides against Jefferson through the preachings of Billy Sunday to the conformist training in our high schools today, have used the stereotype of the intellectual to knock down opponents" (*N.Y. Times*).

Hyneman, Charles S., and Donald S. Lutz. *American Political Writing during the Founding Era, 1760–1805.* Liberty Pr. 2 vols. 1983 $28.50 pap. $13.50. The best collection of political writings from the founding period. The editors have written enlightening introductions for each of the essays.

Lewis, Jan. *The Pursuit of Happiness: Family and Values in Jefferson's Virginia.* Cambridge Univ. Pr. 1983 $24.95. An interesting account of the role that the Virginia gentry played in public life, including politics, commerce, and religion, between 1750 and 1830.

Matthews, Richard K. *The Radical Politics of Thomas Jefferson: A Revisionist View.* Univ. Pr. of Kansas 1984 $22.50. Examines the philosophy of Jefferson, arguing that his thought was very revolutionary.

Miller, John C. *The Federalist Era, 1789–1801. New Amer. Nation Ser.* Harper 1960 $19.18 pap. $.95

Morgan, Edmund S. *The Genius of George Washington.* Norton 1981 $12.95 1982 pap. $2.95. Contends that Washington was a master of understanding and using power, both militarily and politically.

Rutland, Robert A. *James Madison and the Search for Nationhood.* Lib. of Congress 1981 $18.00. Incorporating letters, paintings, and other illustrations along with a concise narrative on Jefferson's life, this book is a wonderful introduction for the general reader.

Smith, Page. *The Rise of Industrial America: A People's History of the Years 1879–1901.* McGraw-Hill 1984 $29.95. This massive narrative history of the last two decades of the nineteenth century emphasizes developments in the social, cultural, and intellectual spheres.

———. *The Shaping of America: A People's History of the Young Republic.* McGraw-Hill 1980 $20.00. Covering the period from 1783 to 1824, this popular history provides a balanced blend of social, political, and cultural aspects of U.S. history.

Stites, Frances N. *John Marshall: Defender of the Constitution.* Ed. by Oscar Handlin, *Lib. of Amer. Biography* Little, Brown 1981 $11.95 text ed. pap. $5.95. An excellent introduction to Marshall's life and times designed for the general reader.

Stuart, Reginald C. *War and American Thought: From the Revolution to the Monroe Doctrine.* Kent State Univ. Pr. 1982 $19.50. Explores how the debate over the proper role of diplomacy and military force in a democracy has shaped U.S. foreign policy thinking.

Walters, Ronald G. *American Reformers, 1815–1860. Amer. Century Ser.* Hill & Wang 1978 $8.95 pap. $6.25. While most of the research on reform movements has fo-

cused on postbellum America, this is an excellent introduction to a wide variety
of earlier reform movements, including pacifism, utopianism, and temperance.

Wills, Garry. *Cincinnatus: George Washington and the Enlightenment*. Doubleday
1984 $18.95. This unique and stimulating biography focuses on the iconography
of Washington, that is, the citizen-soldier-hero.

JACKSONIAN ERA, 1828–1860

Berlin, Ira. *Slaves without Masters: The Free Negro in the Antebellum South*. Oxford
1981 pap. $9.95; Pantheon 1975 $15.00. "Berlin poses new questions and offers
revised analyses of the status, ideas and way of life of the free Negroes of the
Antebellum South. At the same time, the study explores race relations as enunciated by whites in the differing Southern states" (*Booklist*).

Blassingame, John W. *The Slave Community: Plantation Life in the Antebellum South*.
Oxford 2d ed. rev. & enl. 1979 $22.50 text ed. pap. $8.95. "Using a variety of
sources, including the memoirs of former slaves, the author examines the ways
that blacks became enslaved, their processes of acculturation in the American
South, and their . . . ties to their African heritage. He shows how the slave was
able to control parts of his own life while often wearing the mask of submissive-
ness" (Publisher's note).

Channing, Steven A. *Crisis of Fear: Secession in South Carolina*. Norton Lib. 1974
pap. $6.95. "A study of the months preceding [the] state's secession from the
Union in December 1860 . . . it was fear of emancipation, or of black men not enslaved, that brought on secession" (*LJ*).

Craven, Avery O. *The Coming of the Civil War*. Univ. of Chicago Pr. 2d ed. 1966 pap.
$4.50

Curry, Leonard P. *The Free Black in Urban America, 1800–1850: The Shadow of the
Dream*. Univ. of Chicago Pr. 1981 lib. bdg. $27.50. Focuses on the plight of free
blacks, who while not slaves still struggled against poverty and abuse.

De Voto, Bernard. *Across the Wide Missouri*. AMS Pr. repr. of 1947 ed. $94.50; Crown
1981 $8.98; Houghton Mifflin 1964 pap. $10.95; Univ. of Nebraska Pr. 1983 pap.
$12.95 (See De Voto's main listing in this chapter.)

Donald, David. *Charles Sumner and the Coming of the Civil War*. Univ. of Chicago Pr.
1981 pap. $12.50. Awarded the Pulitzer Prize in biography in 1961.

Fehrenbacher, Don E. *The Dred Scott Case: Its Significance in American Law and Politics*. Oxford 1978 $39.95. A new and fresh interpretation of the famous Supreme
Court case that preceded the Civil War.

Feldberg, Michael. *The Turbulent Era: Riot and Disorder in Jacksonian America*. Oxford text ed. 1980 pap. $5.95. Analyzes why urban unrest was so widespread. A
useful work on the history of riots in the United States.

Finkelman, Paul. *An Imperfect Union: Slavery, Federalism, and Comity*. Studies in Legal History Univ. of North Carolina Pr. 1981 $25.00 pap. $8.95. Examines the legal culture that shaped Reconstruction politics.

Freehling, Alison G. *Drift Toward Dissolution: The Virginia Slavery Debate of 1831–
1832*. Louisiana State Univ. Pr. text ed. 1982 $32.50. This study of the slavery de-
bate shows that the issue was much broader in nature, including geographical,
class, and demographic concerns.

Friedman, Lawrence J. *Gregarious Saints: Self and Community in American Abolition-
ism, 1830–1870*. Cambridge Univ. Pr. 1982 $42.50 pap. $12.95. A social-psycho-

logical history of the abolitionists that focuses more on the emotional and personal motives of the leaders.

Fry, Gladys-Marie. *Night Riders in Black Folk History.* Univ. of Tennessee Pr. 1975 pap. $7.95. "The night riders referred to are slave owners and their descendants who used various techniques to keep blacks in their quarters at night (and thus unable to get together to plan insurrections). . . . A patrol system was instituted whereby slaves would receive severe beatings if found away from home without a pass" (*LJ*).

Goetzmann, William H. *Exploration and Empire: The Explorer and the Scientist in the Winning of the American West.* Norton Lib. 1978 pap. $11.95

Holliday, J. S. *The World Rushed In: The California Gold Rush Experience.* Simon & Schuster 1981 $16.95. Captures some of the fever of the gold rush by combining historical research and primary documents, letters, and diaries.

Jackson, Donald Dale. *Gold Dust.* Knopf 1980 $13.95; Univ. of Nebraska Pr. (Bison) 1982 pap. $8.95. While not scholarly, this popular account of the gold rush is very detailed and comprehensive.

Kaufman, Allen. *Capitalism, Slavery, and Republican Values: Antebellum Political Economists, 1819–1848.* Univ. of Texas Pr. text ed. 1982 $25.00. A Marxist critique of antebellum economists; the author attempts to make a case for the ideological dimension of American economic thought.

Kraut, Alan M., ed. *Crusaders and Compromisers: Essays on the Relationship of the Antislavery Struggle to the Antebellum Party System. Contributions in Amer. History Ser.* Greenwood 1983 lib. bdg. $35.00. An anthology that focuses on how the abolitionists struggled in the political arena. The introduction includes a useful historiography of research on abolitionism.

Kushima, John J., and Stephen E. Maizlish. *Essays on American Antebellum Politics, 1840–1860.* Texas A & M Univ. Pr. 1982 $19.50. A good collection by the new political historians. While the volume has no theme, it presents a different kind of historical methodology.

Mullin, Gerald. *Flight and Rebellion: Slave Resistance in Eighteenth-Century Virginia.* Oxford 1972 $7.95. "Two features distinguish this from many similar studies: slavery is examined as a condition modified by time and circumstance rather than as a constant relationship to be morally condemned or practically excused; a further . . . attempt is made to assess the cultural and psychological effects of bondage upon the slaves" (*TLS*).

Oakes, James. *The Ruling Race: A History of American Slaveholders.* Knopf 1982 $16.95; Random (Vintage) 1983 pap. $7.95. This study of the typical slaveholder contends that most were democratic rather than authoritarian.

Oates, Stephen B. *The Fires of Jubilee: Nat Turner's Fierce Rebellion.* New Amer. Lib. 1983 pap. $3.95

———. *To Purge This Land with Blood: A Biography of John Brown.* Univ. of Massachusetts Pr. 2d ed. 1984 lib. bdg. $25.00 pap. $12.95. "Based on contemporary letters, diaries, journals, newspapers, published reports, and recollections of eyewitnesses [this is an account] of Brown's career before he went to Kansas—a period of misfortune, frustration, and personal anguish which deeply influenced his character and later actions" (Publisher's note).

Perry, Lewis, and Michael Fellman, eds. *Antislavery Reconsidered: New Perspectives on the Abolitionists.* Louisiana State Univ. Pr. 1979 $32.50 pap. $8.95. These historiographical essays seek to provide a better understanding of the era as it was, and how current events may now color the past.

Porter, Kenneth Wiggins. *The Negro on the American Frontier.* Ayer repr. of 1971 ed.

$15.00. A compilation of research done during a 40-year period by the foremost authority on the subject.

Pred, Allan R. *Urban Growth and City-Systems in the United States, 1840-1860. Studies in Urban History* Harvard Univ. Pr. text ed. 1980 $28.00. Containing a mass of statistics, this study substantiates the idea that big cities grew faster than smaller ones.

Remini, Robert Vincent. *Andrew Jackson and the Course of American Freedom, 1822-1832.* Harper 1981 $22.07. This study of Jackson's first administration by an eminent historian argues that Jackson was one of the first presidents to be a strong political reformer.

————. *The Revolutionary Age of Andrew Jackson.* Avon 1977 pap. $1.50; Harper 1976 $12.89. Well-written and captivating history of Jackson and American society between 1828 and 1837.

Saum, Lewis O. *The Popular Mood of Pre-Civil War America. Contributions in Amer. Studies* Greenwood 1980 lib. bdg. $29.95. The author puts forth the thesis that the popular mood before the Civil War was not one of optimism, but more of despair. A good picture of prewar public opinion.

Smith, Page. *The Nation Comes of Age: A People's History of the Ante-Bellum Years.* McGraw-Hill 1981 $24.95. Covering the period from 1825 to 1861, this historical survey focuses on the new forces that shaped modern America, such as the economic system and the rise of the arts.

Stampp, Kenneth M. *The Peculiar Institution.* Knopf 1956 $15.50. A very important discussion of slavery.

Unruh, John D. *The Plains Across: The Overland Emigrants and the Trans-Mississippi West, 1840-1860.* Univ. of Illinois Pr. 1979 $27.50 1981 pap. $7.95. The definitive study of the westward movement. In addition to covering every topic, the book provides descriptions of daily life on the westward trails.

CIVIL WAR AND RECONSTRUCTION, 1861–1877

Bogue, Allan G. *The Earnest Men: Republicans of the Civil War Senate.* Cornell Univ. Pr. 1981 $34.95. This analysis of the radicalism of the Civil War Senate breaks new ground by depicting the differences and distinctiveness of leading senators.

Bremner, Robert H. *The Public Good: Philanthropy and Welfare in the Civil War Era.* Knopf 1980 $15.00. Documents the shift in philanthropic and reform movements from the notion of prevention to amelioration.

Chesnut, Mary Boykin Miller. *Mary Chesnut's Civil War.* Ed. by C. Vann Woodward, Yale Univ. Pr. 1981 $40.00 pap. $14.95. This diary by the wife of a prominent plantation owner is a lively and historically important document.

Collins, Bruce. *The Origins of America's Civil War.* Holmes & Meier text ed. 1981 $24.50 pap. $13.50. Describes the events between 1844 and 1861 that led to the Civil War.

Cook, Darian. *The Armies of the Streets: The New York City Draft Riots of 1863.* Univ. Pr. of Kentucky 1974 $28.00. "A vivid, exciting, hour-by-hour account of the bloody violence" (*LJ*).

Cox, LaWanda. *Lincoln and Black Freedom: A Study in Presidential Leadership.* Univ. of South Carolina Pr. 1981 $17.95. The thesis is that while Lincoln was ahead of his time, his leadership was not enough to overcome all the obstacles to complete emancipation.

Cox, LaWanda, and John H. Cox, eds. *Reconstruction: The Negro and the New South. Documentary History of the U.S. Ser.* Univ. of South Carolina Pr. 1973 $19.95

Douglass, Frederick. *My Bondage and My Freedom.* Ayer repr. of 1855 ed. 1968 $34.00; *Black Rediscovery Ser.* Dover 1969 pap. $6.95; *Ebony Class. Ser.* Johnson Publishing $7.95. "The classic fugitive slave narrative and one of the classics of American autobiography" (C. Vann Woodward, *SR*).

Foner, Eric. *Nothing but Freedom: Emancipation and Its Legacy.* Louisiana State Univ. Pr. 1983 $14.95 1984 pap. $5.95. Attempts to demonstrate how emancipated blacks, unlike former slaves in other countries, were able to use political resources to start their economic emancipation.

————. *Politics and Ideology in the Age of the Civil War.* Oxford 1980 $19.95 pap. $7.95. Emphasizes the role of racial attitudes and ideological issues.

Foote, Shelby. *The Civil War: A Narrative.* Random 3 vols. 1958–74 ea. $40.00 set $90.00. A "recapitulation of both sides of the Civil War which weaves together political issues, military strategy, and the personalities of contemporaries" (*Booklist*).

Frassanito, William A. *Gettysburg: A Journey in Time.* Scribner 1976 pap. $12.95. "In this unique combination of history and photography, Frassanito has collected all available photographs of Gettysburg which were taken just after that decisive battle was over. . . . [His aim] is to recreate the battle on a day-to-day basis using the photographs as illustrations enabling the reader to visualize the scene" (*LJ*).

Freidel, Frank B., ed. *Union Pamphlets of the Civil War, 1861–1865.* Harvard Univ. Pr. 2 vols. 1967 $60.00

Futch, Ovid L. *History of Andersonville Prison.* Univ. Pr. of Florida 1968 pap. $4.50. "The purpose of this study is to determine what happened at Andersonville, to examine the conditions which resulted in high mortality among the prisoners and to consider the question of responsibility for those conditions" (Preface).

Hattaway, Herman, and Archer Jones. *How the North Won: A Military History of the Civil War.* Univ. of Illinois Pr. 1983 $24.95. Emphasizes the logistical and strategic planning behind the battlefield encounters. An important study of military leadership during the Civil War.

Holzer, Harold, and others. *The Lincoln Image: Abraham Lincoln and the Popular Print.* Scribner 1984 $35.00. Combines a lively narrative with more than 100 prints of Lincoln to demonstrate how his image evolved.

Litwack, Leon F. *Been in the Storm So Long: The Aftermath of Slavery.* Knopf 1979 $20.00; Random (Vintage) 1980 pap. $7.95. The intent of this book is to relate the emotional and personal meaning of emancipation to blacks at the time.

McPherson, James M. *The Negro's Civil War: How American Negroes Felt and Acted during the War for the Union.* Univ. of Illinois Pr. 1982 pap. $8.95

————. *Ordeal by Fire: The Civil War and Reconstruction.* Knopf 1982 $29.95. Concentrates on the social, economic, and political changes that resulted from the war and changed dramatically the future of American society.

McWhiney, Grady, and Perry D. Jamieson. *Attack and Die: Civil War Military Tactics and the Southern Heritage.* Univ. of Alabama Pr. 1982 $17.95. Examines the strategy and tactics used by the commanders, especially those of the Confederacy, and argues that in light of technological changes, they were a failure.

Myers, Robert Manson, ed. *The Children of Pride: A True Story of Georgia and the Civil War.* Yale Univ. Pr. 1972 $25.00. "This is a collection of more than 1,000 letters written by the members of a large and prominent Georgia family in the years

1854–68" (Publisher's note). This work won the Fletcher Pratt Award for 1972 for the best nonfiction book on the Civil War.

Oates, Stephen B. *Abraham Lincoln: The Man behind the Myth.* Harper 1984 $12.45. The author tries to reveal the real Lincoln by discrediting many of the myths and misconceptions about the man. A superb biography.

Paludan, Philip Shaw. *Victims: A True Story of the Civil War.* Univ. of Tennessee Pr. 1981 $11.95. A case study of 13 Union soldiers who were suspected of guerrilla activities and who were massacred. A human story of war atrocities.

Parish, Peter J. *The American Civil War.* Holmes & Meier text ed. 1975 $39.50 pap. $24.50. "A judicious blend of social, political and military history covering every conceivable facet of the struggle" (*LJ*).

Powell, Lawrence N. *New Masters: Northern Planters during the Civil War and Reconstruction.* Yale Univ. Pr. 1980 $26.50 pap. $8.95. Examines a neglected aspect of social history—the Yankee planters who settled in the South after the Civil War. An important contribution to the study of social classes during Reconstruction.

Quarles, Benjamin. *The Negro in the Civil War.* Little, Brown 1969 pap. $5.95

Randall, James G., and David Donald. *The Civil War and Reconstruction.* Heath text ed. 2d ed. rev. 1969 $21.95; Little, Brown 2d ed. rev. 1973 $20.00

Rawley, James A. *Turning Points of the Civil War.* Univ. of Nebraska Press (Bison) 1974 pap. $5.50

Roland, Charles P. *The Confederacy.* Univ. of Chicago Pr. 1960 $12.00 pap. $7.00

Rose, Willie Lee. *Rehearsal for Reconstruction.* 1964. Oxford 1976 pap. $10.95. Winner of the 1965 Francis Parkman Award.

———. *Slavery and Freedom.* Ed. by William Freehling, Oxford 1982 $19.95 pap. $7.95. Stresses the changing nature of slavery and argues that slavery needs to be understood in light of the specific time and environment.

Smith, Page. *Trial by Fire: A People's History of the Civil War and Reconstruction.* Mc-Graw-Hill 1982 $29.95. Written for the general reader, this is a truly narrative history of the Civil War, conveying the drama and excitement of the era.

Strozier, Charles B. *Lincoln's Quest for Union: Public and Private Meanings.* Basic Bks. 1982 $17.50. This popular psychohistory of Lincoln is different from most biographies of the man in that it attempts to explain the human complexities of his life.

Thomas, Emory M. *The Confederate Nation, 1861–1865.* New Amer. Nation Ser. Harper 1979 $16.30 pap. $6.95. Attempts to explain the Confederacy as a part of southern nationalism.

Tucker, Glenn. *High Tide at Gettysburg.* 1958. Morningside rev. ed. 1974 $15.00 pap. $8.95

Wiley, Bell I. *Confederate Women. Contributions in Amer. History Ser.* Greenwood 1975 lib. bdg. $25.00 text ed. pap. $5.95

INDUSTRIALISM AND THE GILDED AGE, 1865–1896

Berwanger, Eugene H. *The West and Reconstruction.* Univ. of Illinois Pr. 1981 $18.95. While most studies of Reconstruction concentrate on the North and the South, this work examines a neglected area of research—the role of the West in postbellum development.

Bettman, Otto L. *The Good Old Days—They Were Terrible.* Random 1974 pap. $5.95. This book "presents some of the realistic and less pleasant aspects of the human conditions in the U.S. from the Civil War through the early 1900's" (*LJ*).

Brown, Dee. *Bury My Heart at Wounded Knee: An Indian History of the American West.* Holt 1971 $16.95; Washington Square Pr. 1984 pap. $4.95. Brown "has tried to describe the settlement of the West as the Indians saw it. The story is inevitably disjointed, sometimes hopelessly confusing despite the author's inclusion of brief chapter headings explaining what the U.S. government was really up to, and always no picture to be proud of" (*Atlantic*).

————. *Hear That Lonesome Whistle Blow: Railroads in the West*. Holt 1977 $13.95. A popular history of the building of the transcontinental railroads, especially the Union Pacific and the Central Pacific.

Dick, Everett. *The Sod-House Frontier, 1854–1890*. Univ. of Nebraska Pr. (Bison) 1979 pap. $12.95

————. *Vanguards of the Frontier: A Social History of the Northern Plains and Rocky Mountains from the Fur Traders to the Sod Busters*. Univ. of Nebraska Pr. (Bison) 1965 pap. $9.95. This book "seeks to discover the [pioneers'] manner of living, their dress, food, ways of enjoying themselves, methods of labor, and their mode of life in general" (Preface).

Jeffrey, Julie Roy. *Frontier Women: The Trans-Mississippi West, 1840–1880*. Ed. by Eric Foner, *Amer. Century Ser.* Hill & Wang 1979 pap. $7.25. Written for a general audience, this is a lively history of women's experiences during the westward migration.

Jensen, Richard. *The Winning of the Midwest: Social and Political Conflict, 1888–1896*. Univ. of Chicago Pr. 1971 $12.50. "An appreciation of McKinley's political genius is a major theme of Richard Jensen's superb study of Midwestern electoral politics in the 1890's" (*AHR*).

La Feber, Walter. *The New Empire: An Interpretation of American Expansion, 1860–1898*. Cornell Univ. Pr. 1963 pap. $9.95

Leckie, William H. *The Buffalo Soldiers: A Narrative of the Negro Cavalry in the West*. Univ. of Oklahoma Pr. 1967 pap. $8.95. "Well written and thoroughly documented" (*LJ*).

Nelson, William E. *The Roots of American Bureaucracy, 1830–1900*. Harvard Univ. Pr. text ed. 1982 $22.50. Traces the growth and development of the U.S. bureaucracy, seeing it as an outgrowth of pluralism.

Reps, John W. *The Forgotten Frontier: Urban Planning in the American West before 1890*. Univ. of Missouri Pr. text ed. 1982 $25.00 pap. $12.95. Examines the history of city planning in the West, pointing out how extensive the planning movement was in the United States.

Tariello, Frank. *The Reconstruction of American Political Ideology, 1865–1917*. Univ. Pr. of Virginia 1982 $20.00. Charts the change in U.S. political ideology that emphasized the belief in natural rights and limited government.

Teaford, Jon C. *The Unheralded Triumph: City Government in America, 1870–1900*. Johns Hopkins Univ. Pr. text ed. 1984 $28.50 pap. $14.95. The author argues convincingly that U.S. city governments have by and large been very successful in solving economic and social problems prior to the turn of the century.

Wyman, Mark. *Hard Rock Epic: Western Miners and the Industrial Revolution, 1860–1910*. Univ. of California Pr. 1979 $18.95. Discusses the struggle of western miners for wages, safety, and the right to organize as well as with changing technology.

IMPERIALISM TO PROGRESSIVISM, 1896–1917

Blum, John Morton. *The Progressive Presidents: Roosevelt, Wilson, Roosevelt, Johnson*. Norton 1982 pap. $6.95. Depicts how four presidents established strong administrations and concludes with a recommendation for a concept of progressive presidents.

Crunden, Robert M. *Ministers of Reform: The Progressives' Achievement in American Civilization, 1889–1920.* Basic Bks. 1982 $17.95. Focuses on what motivated individuals and turned them into opinion makers.

Dobson, John M. *America's Ascent: The United States Becomes a Great Power, 1880–1914.* Northern Illinois Univ. Pr. 1978 $17.50 pap. $6.00

Feinman, Ronald L. *Twilight of Progressivism: The Western Republican Senators and the New Deal.* Johns Hopkins Univ. Pr. text ed. 1981 $22.50. Investigates the impact of the western progressive Republicans on U.S. politics during the New Deal.

Juergens, George. *News from the White House: The Presidential-Press Relationship in the Progressive Era.* Univ. of Chicago Pr. 1982 lib. bdg. $25.00. Carefully researched and written, this work analyzes how three presidents—Theodore Roosevelt, William Howard Taft, and Woodrow Wilson—managed their relationships with the press.

Link, Arthur S., ed. *Woodrow Wilson and a Revolutionary World, 1913–1921.* Univ. of North Carolina Pr. 1982 $23.00. Includes seven essays on a variety of topics all relating to Wilson's role in international affairs.

Link, Arthur S., and Richard L. McCormick. *Progressivism.* Amer. History Ser. Harlan Davidson text ed. 1983 pap. $6.95. A concise and straightforward overview of the Progressive Era. The merit of this volume is that it is a readable synopsis of the rich literature on the era.

McClymer, John F. *War and Warfare: Social Engineering in America, 1890–1925.* Contributions in Amer. History Greenwood 1980 lib. bdg. $27.50. Describes the rise and growth of social experts in the United States and evaluates their influence and impact on society.

McCullough, David. *The Path between the Seas: The Creation of the Panama Canal, 1870–1914.* Simon & Schuster (Touchstone Bks.) 1978 pap. $12.95. While essentially a history of the building of the canal, this book encompasses much more, including U.S. foreign policy in Latin America and domestic affairs as well.

O'Toole, G. J. A. *The Spanish War: An American Epic, 1898.* Norton 1984 $19.95. This popular history covers both the events leading up to the war and the war itself. Gives an excellent description of the battlefield events.

Pearlman, Michael. *To Make Democracy Safe for America: Patricians and Preparedness in the Progressive Era.* Univ. of Illinois Pr. 1984 $19.95. Covering the period from the Spanish-American War to World War II, this volume analyzes the concept of preparedness in U.S. foreign affairs. The book focuses on a number of dominant personalities during the period.

Urofsky, Melvin I. *Louis D. Brandeis and the Progressive Tradition.* Ed. by Oscar Handlin, Little, Brown text ed. 1980 pap. $5.95. A general introduction to the judicial career of Brandeis and his times intended for the general reader.

Wagenknecht, Edward. *American Profile, 1900–1909.* Univ. of Massachusetts Pr. 1982 $22.50 pap. $12.00. A charming overview of the first decade of the century, including chapters on art, popular entertainment, music, books, and personalities.

West, Rebecca. *1900.* Viking 1982 $19.95. A personal assessment of the turn of the century by a well-known author; includes more than 100 illustrations.

WORLD WAR I TO FDR, 1917–1932

Carter, Paul A. *Another Part of the Twenties.* Columbia Univ. Pr. 1977 $20.00 pap. $10.00. Attempts to look at the neglected side of the 1920s, showing how it was not the "roaring" era that it has been portrayed as in most histories.

Dallek, Robert. *Franklin D. Roosevelt and American Foreign Policy, 1932–1945.* Oxford 1979 $35.00 pap. $10.95. An excellent overview of the events and domestic forces that shaped FDR's foreign policy.

Fass, Paula S. *The Damned and the Beautiful: American Youth in the 1920's.* Oxford 1977 $35.00 pap. $9.95. Looks at the college youth of the decade, including social and political interests as well as life style.

Foster, Mark S. *From Streetcar to Superhighway: American City Planners and Urban Transportation, 1900–1940.* Technology and Urban Growth Ser. Temple Univ. Pr. 1981 $34.95. This historical study of transportation and the planners who designed the new transit systems of the twentieth century covers a new aspect of U.S. history.

Hawley, Ellis Wayne. *The Great War and the Search for a Modern Order: A History of the American People and Their Institutions, 1917–1933.* Twentieth-Century U.S. History Ser. St. Martin's text ed. 1979 pap. $10.95. Contends that the period covered was a time of modernization and the drive to organize and structure the economy and society.

Karl, Barry D. *The Uneasy State: The United States from 1915–1945.* Univ. of Chicago Pr. 1984 lib. bdg. $22.50. Writing on both a popular and scholarly level, the author gives a synthesis of the reform era, especially the growing industrial and bureaucratic state.

Kennedy, David M. *Over Here: The First World War and American Society.* Oxford 1980 $27.50 pap. $8.95. Focusing on the events and trends taking place at home during the First World War, the author recounts the changes and experiences that had an impact on shaping twentieth-century American society.

Levin, N. Gordon, Jr. *Woodrow Wilson and World Politics: America's Response to War and Revolution.* Oxford 1968 pap. $8.95

Mowry, George E., and Blaine A. Brownell. *The Urban Nation, 1920–1980.* Hill & Wang rev. ed. 1981 $12.50 pap. $5.95. This lively survey of urbanization contains excellent chapters on the social and cultural changes that accompany the growth of cities.

Murphy, Paul L. *World War I and the Origin of Civil Liberties in the United States.* Essays in Amer. History Norton 1980 pap. $4.95. Argues that civil rights as a public policy concern stems from the domestic problems surrounding World War I.

Nash, George H. *The Life of Herbert Hoover: The Engineer, 1874–1914.* Norton 1983 $25.00. Covers Hoover's life as a businessman and engineer. The best work on his early life.

Perrett, Geoffrey. *America in the Twenties: A History.* Simon & Schuster 1982 $20.95; Simon & Schuster (Touchstone Bks.) 1983 pap. $9.95. A comprehensive history of the 1920s, covering a variety of topics from politics and economics to sports, sex, literature, and the arts.

NEW DEAL THROUGH WORLD WAR II, 1933–1945

Alsop, Joseph. *FDR, 1882–1945: A Centenary Remembrance.* Viking 1982 $25.00; Washington Square Pr. 1982 pap. $3.50. This collection of photographs and commentary is an excellent visual history of FDR that provides a good understanding of what the New Deal meant at the time.

Banks, Ann, ed. *First-Person America.* Knopf 1980 $13.95; Random (Vintage) 1981 pap. $5.95. Taken from interviews conducted by the Federal Writers' Project between 1938 and 1942, this oral history recreates a description of the early U.S. experience that is enjoyable to read.

Blum, John Morton. *V Was for Victory: Politics and American Culture during World War II*. Harcourt 1976 pap. $7.95. Because of the attention given to the war itself, little research has been done on domestic history during World War II. This book fills that void.

Brinkley, Alan. *Voice of Protest: Huey Long, Father Coughlin, and the Great Depression*. Knopf 1982 $18.50; Random (Vintage) 1983 pap. $6.95. This analysis of two controversial figures puts forth the thesis that their appearance was due to a strong populist ideology embedded in society.

Campbell, D'Ann. *Women at War with America: Private Lives in a Patriotic Era*. Harvard Univ. Pr. text ed. 1984 $20.00. A history of the role of women during World War II, the book uses a number of interesting primary sources.

Cole, Wayne S. *Roosevelt and the Isolationists, 1932–1945*. Univ. of Nebraska Pr. 1983 $26.50. The definitive study of the isolationists of 1930 and the break between them and FDR at the beginning of World War II.

Costello, John. *The Pacific War*. Rawson 1981 $23.95. While this is basically an overview of the war in the Pacific, the analysis includes a great deal of information regarding the U.S. presence in the Pacific during the nineteenth century.

Dawson, Nelson Lloyd. *Louis D. Brandeis, Felix Frankfurter, and the New Deal*. Shoe String (Archon) 1980 $19.50. Excellent study of two of the most important Supreme Court justices. Analyzes their impact on the New Deal.

Gaddis, John L. *The United States and the Origins of the Cold War, 1941–1947*. Contemporary Amer. History Ser. Columbia Univ. Pr. 1972 $32.50 pap. $11.00. Winner of the Bancroft Prize for 1972.

Harris, Mark Jonathan, and others. *The Homefront: America during World War II*. Putnam 1984 $17.95. Based on the experiences of 37 ordinary people, this is an oral history of how the home front changed the lives of individuals.

Honey, Maureen. *Creating Rosie the Riveter: Class, Gender, and Propaganda during World War II*. Univ. of Massachusetts Pr. 1984 lib. bdg. $20.00. This combination of cultural history and women's studies examines the shifting image of women from the war years to the 1950s.

Jaffe, Philip J. *The Rise and Fall of American Communism*. Horizon Pr. 1975 pap. $5.95. "The career of Earl Browder, who led the Communist Party, U.S.A. from 1930 until 1945 when he was purged on Moscow's orders" (*LJ*).

Kanawada, Leo V. *Franklin D. Roosevelt's Diplomacy and American Catholics, Italians, and Jews*. Ed. by Robert Berkhofer, *Studies in Amer. History and Culture* UMI Research 1982 $39.95. A fascinating combination of diplomatic and ethnic history, the author demonstrates that ethnic groups played an important role in shaping foreign policy.

Kee, Robert. *1939: In the Shadow of War*. Little, Brown 1984 $19.45. Using materials from newspapers, photographs, cartoons, advertisements, and headlines, the author gives a colorful recreation of a single year as people lived it.

Klehr, Harvey. *The Heyday of American Communism: The Depression Decade*. Basic Bks. 1984 $26.50. The standard history of the Communist party and its influence in the United States during the 1930s.

Leuchtenburg, William E. *Franklin D. Roosevelt and the New Deal, 1932–1940. New Amer. Nation Ser.* Harper 1963 $17.26. Winner of the Bancroft Prize.

Louchheim, Katie, ed. *The Making of the New Deal: The Insiders Speak*. Harvard Univ. Pr. 1983 $20.00 pap. $7.95. A compendium of 24 recollections by individuals who participated in the making of the New Deal. The reminiscences are enjoyable and fascinating.

Lowitt, Richard. *The New Deal and the West. West in the 20th-Century Ser.* Indiana Univ. Pr. 1984 $25.00. A good survey of the impact the New Deal had on the West. Highlights federal involvement in developing and conserving the resources of the West.

Manchester, William R. *American Caesar: Douglas MacArthur, 1880–1964.* Dell 1982 pap. $4.50; Little, Brown 1978 $19.95. This lengthy biography is well written and focuses more on MacArthur the man than the soldier.

McElvaine, Robert S., ed. *Down and Out in the Great Depression: Letters from the "Forgotten Man."* Univ. of North Carolina Pr. 1983 $23.00 pap. $8.95. Provides a look at how the Depression affected the lives of ordinary citizens.

Mee, Charles L., Jr., *Meeting at Potsdam.* Evans 1982 $10.95 pap. $7.95. Here, "in this close and lively look at the three Potsdam participants, Charles Mee, the former editor of *Horizon* now turned popular historian, gives nobody credit for good intentions . . . . [His] postrevisionist thesis is that all 'three men rescued discord from the threatened outbreak of peace' " (*Time*).

Miller, Nathan. *FDR: An Intimate History.* Doubleday 1983 $22.50; New Amer. Lib. 1984 pap. $10.95. This journalistic biography is comprehensive in scope and an excellent introduction for the layperson.

Neal, Steve. *Dark Horse: A Biography of Wendell Willkie.* Doubleday 1984 $17.95. A lively political biography of an important Republican leader by a journalist.

Offner, Arnold. *The Origins of the Second World War: American Foreign Policy and World Politics, 1919–1941.* Holt text ed. 1975 pap. $15.95. "A cogent, detailed, well-organized survey" (*LJ*).

Petrocik, John R. *Party Coalitions: Realignment and the Decline of the New Deal Party System.* Univ. of Chicago Pr. 1981 lib. bdg. $10.00. Analyzes the changes that have taken place in the party system in U.S. politics. The author identifies turnout as the major factor affecting electoral behavior.

Porter, David L. *Congress and the Waning of the New Deal.* Associated Faculty Pr. 1980 $17.95. This study of Congress between 1938 and 1940 examines a neglected period in congressional studies. The author contends that this was a period when Congress began to assert itself.

Prange, Gordon W. *At Dawn We Slept: The Untold Story of Pearl Harbor.* McGraw-Hill 1981 $22.95; Penguin 1982 pap. $10.95. Rich in both scholarly detail and anecdotal material, this massive volume is the definitive account of Pearl Harbor. Both lively and factual, this book provides extensive information about personalities and events.

———. *Miracle at Midway.* Ed. by D. M. Goldstein and K. V. Dillon, McGraw-Hill 1982 $19.95; Penguin 1983 pap. $8.95. This superb volume gives a brilliant account of the U.S. victory at Midway. While the volume is detailed and important academically, it is easy to read.

Romasco, Albert U. *The Politics of Recovery: Roosevelt's New Deal.* Oxford 1983 $19.95. The aim of this work is to recount how FDR dealt with economic crisis. An excellent combination of political and economic history.

Spector, Ronald. *Eagle against the Sun: The American War with Japan. Macmillan Wars of the U.S. Ser.* Macmillan (Free Pr.) 1984 $24.95. The best one-volume history of the war in the Pacific, it covers both U.S. and Japanese planning and strategy.

Stott, William. *Documentary Expression and Thirties America.* Oxford 1973 pap. $8.95

Terkel, Studs. *"The Good War": An Oral History of World War Two*. Pantheon 1984 $19.95. Another oral history by a real master of the genre. A truly wonderful book that seeks to capture U.S. memories of the war.

———. *Hard Times: An Oral History of the Great Depression*. Pantheon 1970 $16.95; Washington Square Pr. 1978 pap. $5.95. "While there have been a number of recent accounts of the Depression published, these unusual and intriguing interviews deserve their own separate place in the essential historiography of the era" (*Choice*).

Toland, John. *Infamy: Pearl Harbor and Its Aftermath*. Doubleday 1982 $17.95. This popular revisionist history contends that FDR needed a Japanese attack and did not work to prevent it.

Ware, Susan. *Beyond Suffrage: Women in the New Deal*. Harvard Univ. Pr. text ed. 1981 $18.50. Looking beyond suffrage, the author explores how women began to actively participate in the administration of government.

Weigley, Russell F. *Eisenhower's Lieutenants: The Campaign of France and Germany, 1944–1945*. Indiana Univ. Pr. 1981 $22.50. More than a study of the military leadership, it encompasses the entire military strategy in Western Europe.

Weiss, Nancy J. *Farewell to the Party of Lincoln: Black Politics in the Age of FDR*. Princeton Univ. Pr. 1983 $32.50 pap. $12.50. The central thesis is the change of black political allegiance from the Republican to the Democratic party due to the new economic and social concerns.

POST–WORLD WAR II, 1945–

Abernathy, M. Glenn, and others. *The Carter Years: The President and Policy Making*. St. Martin's 1984 $22.50. These essays cover the major themes, accomplishments, and failings of the Carter administration.

Ambrose, Stephen E. *Eisenhower*. Simon & Schuster 2 vols. 1984 vol. 1 $19.95 vol. 2 $24.95. The definitive biography, covering his boyhood to his years as general in World War II.

Aron, Raymond. *The Imperial Republic: The United States and the World, 1945–1973*. Trans. by Frank Jellinek, Univ. Pr. of America 1982 lib. bdg. $29.00 text ed. pap. $14.00. "The book is not easy to read and understand because of its complex analyses and the difficulties of translation, but it is nevertheless of fundamental importance providing as it does relief from the bankrupt scholarly confrontation among American experts. Aron's analysis of the international economy is perhaps the most useful part of the book" (*Choice*).

Berman, Larry. *Planning a Tragedy: The Americanization of the War in Vietnam*. Norton 1983 pap. $16.95. Attempts to delineate how major policy decisions were made and with hindsight to show how intelligence information was inadequate.

Bernard, Richard M., and Bradley R. Rice. *Sunbelt Cities: Politics and Growth since World War II*. Univ. of Texas Pr. text ed. 1983 $25.00 pap. $9.95. A multidisciplinary analysis of the politics, planning, economics, and urban history of the new sunbelt metropolitan center.

Bernstein, Carl, and Bob Woodward. *All the President's Men*. Warner Bks. 1976 pap. $4.50. "The *Washington Post* reporters whose investigative journalism first revealed the Watergate scandal tell the way it happened from first suspicions . . . to the final moments when they were able to put the pieces of the puzzle together and write the series that won the *Post* a Pulitzer Prize" (Publisher's note).

Bornet, Vaughn Davis. *The Presidency of Lyndon B. Johnson*. Amer. Presidency Ser.

Univ. Pr. of Kansas 1984 $25.00 pap. $14.95. A solid and basic biography of LBJ the president that is quite readable and useful for the general reader.

Branyan, Robert L., and Lawrence H. Larsen, eds. *The Eisenhower Administration, 1953–1961: A Documentary History.* Greenwood 2 vols. 1971 lib. bdg. $95.00

Bremner, Robert H., and Gary W. Reichard, eds. *Reshaping America: Society and Institutions, 1945–1960. Studies in Recent Amer. History* Ohio State Univ. Pr. 1982 $22.50. Focuses on a wide-ranging number of themes, including feminism, rural America, children and the state, and other more contemporary trends and institutions.

Burch, Philip H. *The New Deal to the Carter Administration. Elites in Amer. History* Holmes & Meier text ed. 1980 $38.50 pap. $22.50. The study of elites in modern political history examines the rise and fall of political leaders and appointees.

Capps, Walter H. *The Unfinished War: Vietnam and the American Conscience.* Beacon 1983 pap. $6.68. In addition to recounting the course of the war, this book continues to discuss the impact of the war on life in the United States up to the present.

Caro, Robert A. *The Years of Lyndon Johnson: The Path to Power.* Random (Vintage) 1984 pap. $9.95. The massive and critical biography of LBJ covers his personal and political life up to his years in Congress.

Carroll, Peter N. *It Seemed Like Nothing Happened: The Tragedy and Promise of America in the 1970s.* Holt 1982 $19.95 1984 pap. $9.95. A superb social and political history of the decade, whose constant theme is the conflict between traditional values and the new alternative ideas.

Davis, Lynn E. *The Cold War Begins: Soviet-American Conflict over Eastern Europe.* Princeton Univ. Pr. 1974 $38.50. "In a dispute over who started the Cold War, Davis offers a thorough and scholarly argument in favor of acquitting the U.S." (*LJ*).

Divine, Robert A. *Eisenhower and the Cold War.* Oxford 1981 $17.50 pap. $4.95. In contrast to earlier research on Eisenhower, this work sets out to prove that in the area of foreign affairs Eisenhower was not a "do-nothing" president.

Dobbs, Charles M. *The Unwanted Symbol: American Foreign Policy, the Cold War and Korea, 1945–1950.* Kent State Univ. Pr. 1981 $20.00. Concentrates on the early years of the Cold War and investigates how Korea became the symbol of anti-communism.

Donovan, Robert J. *Conflict and Crisis: The Presidency of Harry S. Truman, 1945–1948.* Norton 1977 $19.95 pap. $10.95. Being a journalist, the author has written a clear and informative narrative of Truman's first term.

———. *Nemesis: Truman and Johnson in the Coils of War in Asia.* St. Martin's 1984 $14.95. Compares U.S. involvement in Korea and Vietnam by analyzing the leadership of Truman and Johnson.

———. *Tumultuous Years: The Presidency of Harry S. Truman, 1949–1953.* Norton 1982 $19.95 pap. $9.95. The most comprehensive study of Truman's second term, being both critical and favorable in its analysis of his policies.

Dugger, Ronnie. *The Politician: The Life and Times of Lyndon Johnson: The Drive for Power—From the Frontier to Master of the Senate.* Norton 1982 $18.95. An interpretive rendering rather than a straightforward biography.

Ewald, William Bragg. *Eisenhower the President: Crucial Days, 1951–1960.* Prentice–Hall 1981 $12.95. Written by an assistant to Eisenhower during the preparation of his memoirs. The author discusses aspects of the president's character and workings of the White House.

Ferrell, Robert H. *Harry S. Truman and the Modern American Presidency. Lib. of Amer. Biography* Little, Brown 1983 $13.00 text ed. pap. $5.95. A brief biography of Truman's political career and times that is a good introduction to his presidency.

Foley, Michael. *The New Senate: Liberal Influence on a Conservative Institution, 1959–1972.* Yale Univ. Pr. 1980 $26.50. The thesis is that the Senate is no longer the conservative body it traditionally was, but rather a more activist body.

Gilbert, James. *Another Chance: Postwar America, 1945–1968.* Ed. by R. Jackson Wilson, Knopf text ed. pap. $8.00; fwd. by R. Wilson, Temple Univ. Pr. 1981 $29.95. While covering mainly political and historical events, this study also includes a lively commentary on film, television, music, and other developments in U.S. culture.

Gosnell, Harold Foote. *Truman's Crises: A Political Biography of Harry S. Truman. Contributions in Political Science* Greenwood 1980 lib. bdg. $35.00. Emphasizes Truman's role in foreign affairs. A very detailed and comprehensive biography.

Greenstein, Fred I. *The Hidden-Hand Presidency: Eisenhower as Leader.* Basic Bks. 1982 $16.95; 1984 pap. $8.95. Portrays Eisenhower as an activist president and as the model of a more modern president.

Hart, Jeffrey. *When the Going Was Good! American Life in the Fifties.* Crown (Arlington House) 1982 $15.95. A vivid history of the social, cultural, political, and economic trends of the 1950s, which the author depicts as a more engaging period than usually portrayed.

Heller, Francis H., ed. *The Truman White House: The Administration of the Presidency, 1945–1953.* Univ. Pr. of Kansas 1980 $22.50. An interesting oral history of the Truman administration drawn from the materials of former cabinet members, staffers, and other members of the executive office.

Herring, George C. *America's Longest War: The United States and Vietnam, 1950–1975.* Random text ed. pap. $10.50. A basic survey of U.S. involvement in Vietnam.

Hodgson, Godfrey. *America in Our Time: From World War II to Nixon—What Happened and Why.* Random 1978 pap. $6.95. The author, a journalist, has written an enticing history. The material on the 1960s is especially informative.

Holsti, Ole R., and James N. Rosenau. *American Leadership in World Affairs: Vietnam and the Breakdown of Consensus.* Allen & Unwin text ed. 1984 $28.50 pap. $9.95. Focuses on the role of the United States in global policy and strategies.

Janowitz, Morris. *The Last Half-Century: Societal Change and Politics in America.* Univ. of Chicago Pr. (Phoenix Bks.) 1979 pap. $15.00. A general survey of political history during the last 50 years that is an especially useful overview of U.S. political developments.

Jezer, Marty. *The Dark Ages: Life in the United States, 1945–1960.* South End Pr. 1982 $20.00 pap. $8.00. A popular survey of the 15 years following World War II that focuses on the political and social events that led to the changes and unrest of the 1960s.

Johnpoll, Bernard K., and Lillian Johnpoll. *The Impossible Dream: The Rise and Demise of the American Left. Contributions in Political Science* Greenwood 1981 lib. bdg. $29.95. A comprehensive survey of U.S. radical leaders since the beginning of the nineteenth century, the authors make a compelling case for the argument that the leaders were more successful in initiating reforms than in actually reshaping society.

Kattenburg, Paul M. *The Vietnam Trauma in American Foreign Policy, 1945–75.* Transaction Bks. 1981 pap. $9.95. As a foreign service officer for 20 years, the author draws on his own experience, as well as primary and secondary material, to explain how the United States became involved in Vietnam.

Kearns, Doris. *Lyndon Johnson and the American Dream*. New Amer. Lib. 1977 pap. $3.95. Written for a general audience, this psychohistorical biography analyzes the character, personal ambitions, and dreams of Lyndon Johnson.

Kissinger, Henry. *White House Years*. Little, Brown 1979 $24.95. This memoir provides a superb insight into the processes of foreign policymaking and the politics inside the White House.

Lee, R. Alton. *Dwight D. Eisenhower: Soldier and Statesman*. Nelson-Hall text ed. 1981 $22.95 pap. $11.95. A concise biography of Eisenhower's military and political career.

Levering, Ralph B. *The Cold War, 1945–1972*. Amer. History Ser. Harlan Davidson text ed. 1983 pap. $7.95. A concise and scholarly history. The author does an excellent job of showing the interaction between domestic and foreign affairs.

Levitan, Sar A. *Still a Dream: The Changing Status of Blacks since 1960*. Harvard Univ. Pr. 1975 $22.50 pap. $8.95. "An abundance of statistical data [intended] to demonstrate that in several key areas—such as income, health, and education—American blacks have made significant socioeconomic advances since the early 1960's" (*LJ*).

Maclear, Michael. *The Ten Thousand Day War: Vietnam, 1945–1975*. Avon 1982 pap. $8.95. This informative and popular history of the war makes excellent use of interviews and secondary sources.

Manchester, William R. *The Glory and the Dream: A Narrative History of America, 1932–1972*. Little, Brown 1974 $24.95. "A 40 year era of vivid change is minutely unraveled beginning with the F.D.R. administration during the Depression through World War II, the Truman/McCarthy era, and the years of turmoil from Kennedy and Johnson to Nixon" (*Booklist*).

Martin, Ralph G. *A Hero for Our Time: An Intimate Story of the Kennedy Years*. Macmillan 1983 $19.95; Random 1984 pap. $4.95. Focuses on the personal life of the man and is quite revealing. Lively and easy to read.

Matusow, Allen J. *The Unraveling of America: A History of Liberalism in the 1960s*. New Amer. Nation Ser. Harper 1984 $22.07. Argues that the liberal policies were not successful but caused even more problems.

Messer, Robert L. *The End of an Alliance: James F. Byrnes, Roosevelt, Truman, and the Origins of the Cold War*. Univ. of North Carolina Pr. 1982 $19.95. Looks at the personal and political relations between two presidents and the secretary of state.

Miller, Merle. *Lyndon: An Oral Biography*. Ballantine 1981 pap. $9.95. A fascinating look at LBJ's personal life.

Morris, Charles R. *Times of Passion: America, 1960–1980*. Harper 1984 $17.50. This popular history examines the changes that took place during this period and concludes that despite the turmoil little has changed.

Oates, Stephen B. *Let the Trumpet Sound: The Life of Martin Luther King, Jr.* Harper 1982 $19.18; New Amer. Lib. 1983 pap. $9.95

O'Neill, William L. *Coming Apart: An Informal History of America in the 1960's*. Times Bks. 1972 pap. $8.95. "Coming Apart is that rare thing—a work of true perspective on the contemporary scene" (Publisher's note).

Parmet, Herbert S. *Jack: The Struggles of John F. Kennedy*. Doubleday 1983 $14.95 pap. $12.95. An excellent biography from Kennedy's early years to his presidential nomination. The author used extensive interviews and oral history.

Prussen, Ronald W. *John Foster Dulles: The Road to Power*. Macmillan (Free Press) 1982 $19.95. An objective biography of one of America's most important and influential statesmen. Covers his career up to his appointment as secretary of state.

Rowe, Frank. *The Enemy among Us: A Story of Witch-Hunting in the McCarthy Era.* Cougar Bks. 1980 pap. $5.95. Written by a California professor who was a victim of the oath test, this is a compelling history of the anticommunist years and the fate of academic freedom.

Schlesinger, Arthur M., Jr. *Robert Kennedy and His Times.* Houghton Mifflin 1978 $19.95; Random (Vintage) 1985 pap. $4.95. A very personal and readable account of RFK's life in politics and the major trends in U.S. politics during the 1950s and 1960s.

Shafer, Byron E. *Quiet Revolution: The Struggle for the Democratic Party and the Shaping of Post-Reform Politics.* Russell Sage 1983 $29.95. Details the enormous changes and reforms that the Democratic party underwent between 1968 and 1972. An excellent insight into party politics.

Smith, Curt. *Long Time Gone: The Years of Turmoil Remembered.* Icarus Pr. 1982 $15.95. Combining information from the author's interviews and personal perspective, this is a lively review of the turbulent years from 1960 to 1973.

Stiegel, Frederick F. *Troubled Journey: From Pearl Harbor to Ronald Reagan. Amer. Century Ser.* Hill & Wang 1984 $17.50 pap. $7.25. Examines the growing power of the United States in global affairs in the context of social and domestic tensions.

Stikoff, Harvard. *The Struggle for Black Equality, 1954–1980.* Ed. by Eric Foner, *Amer. Century Ser.* Hill & Wang 1981 pap. $6.95. This history of the civil rights movement concentrates on the developments and changes since the Supreme Court's decision on segregation in public education.

Viorst, Milton. *Fire in the Streets: America in the 1960s.* Simon & Schuster (Touchstone Bks.) 1981 pap. $11.95. Focuses on the social unrest and movements of the decade. Includes many excellent character studies.

White, Theodore H. *America in Search of Itself: The Making of the President 1956– 1980.* Warner Bks. 1983 pap. $8.95. A popular history of presidential campaigns and elections by a well-known journalist and commentator.

———. *Breach of Faith: The Fall of Richard Nixon.* Dell 1975 pap. $2.25. White "retells the whole story of the President's fall, even dealing with his character as a rootless outsider who bitterly resented social slights offered him by men like Eisenhower and Rockefeller" (*Time*).

Woodward, Bob, and Carl Bernstein. *The Final Days.* Avon 1976 pap. $4.95. A chronology of the last 100 days of the Nixon administration, covering the story of his decision to resign.

Zaroulis, Nancy, and Gerald Sullivan. *Who Spoke Up? American Protest against the War in Vietnam, 1963–1975.* Doubleday 1984 $18.95. Recreates the public protest that emerged in opposition to the war. Extremely lively and stimulating.

SUPPLEMENTARY GENERAL READING LISTS

These lists of books do not necessarily fit into the previous chronological lists. Many aspects of American life are covered in other chapters. The following three sections—Cultural and Intellectual History, Economic History, and Social History—are more specialized in nature, covering a wide variety of topics, such as the arts, philosophy, popular culture, urban and rural history, black and women's history, demography, and education. The books listed in these sections demonstrate the breadth of historical research as well as the growing amount of literature on these topics. Generally, they are not only serious historical monography, but fascinating reading as well.

Cultural and Intellectual History

Alexander, Charles C. *Here the Country Lies: Nationalism and the Arts in Twentieth-Century America.* Indiana Univ. Pr. 1980 $32.50. Traces the influence and impact that nationalism has had on art.

Anderson, Jervis. *This Was Harlem: A Cultural Portrait, 1900–1950.* Farrar 1982 $17.95 pap. $10.95. Emphasizes the energy and creativity of the community instead of the problems of a ghetto.

Badger, Reid. *The Great American Fair: The World's Columbian Exposition and American Culture.* Nelson-Hall 1979 $32.95. Treats the 1893 exposition as a reflection of U.S. culture and institutions during the late nineteenth century.

Barth, Gunther. *City People: The Culture of the Modern City in Nineteenth-Century America.* Oxford 1980 $27.50 pap. $7.95. This interesting social and cultural history of U.S. cities attempts to explain why people moved to the cities and what the allure of the cities was.

Ceplair, Larry, and Steven Englung. *The Inquisition in Hollywood: Politics in the Film Community, 1930–1960.* Univ. of California Pr. 1983 pap. $9.95. An interesting case study of the relationship between the arts and government.

Clecak, Peter. *America's Quest for the Ideal Self: Dissent and Fulfillment in the 60s and 70s.* Oxford 1983 $27.50. This unique social history examines the American search for personal fulfillment, concluding that the search was largely successful.

Curti, Merle. *Human Nature in American Thought: A History.* Univ. of Wisconsin Pr. 1980 $32.50. Examines almost 400 years of political thought, pointing out the significant concept of human nature peculiar to American philosophy.

Dary, David. *Cowboy Culture: A Saga of Five Centuries.* Avon 1982 pap. $7.95; Knopf 1981 $18.50. Intended for the general reader, this is a comprehensive history of the cowboy, including his origins and life-style.

Davis, Allen F. *American Heroine: The Life and Legend of Jane Addams.* 1975. Peter Smith 1983 $13.25. "An impressively researched and splendidly written new biography . . . a major contribution both to urban and to intellectual history" (*TLS*).

DeBenedetti, Charles. *The Peace Reform in American History.* Indiana Univ. Pr. 1980 $18.50 1984 pap. $7.95. A clear and coherent history of the longest and most organized reform movement in U.S. history.

Diggins, John P. *The Lost Soul of American Politics: Virtue, Self-Interest, and the Foundations of Liberalism.* Basic Bks. 1984 $23.95. Essentially a history of U.S. political thought during the first 100 years of the Republic.

Erenberg, Lewis A. *Steppin' Out: New York Nightlife and the Transformation of American Culture, 1890–1930. Contributions in Amer. Studies* Greenwood 1981 $29.95; Univ. of Chicago Pr. 1984 pap. $9.95. Traces the origins and development of the mass consumer culture of the twentieth century. Looks at a variety of recreational activities, such as amusement parks, jazz, baseball, and other forms of commercial entertainment.

Flower, Elizabeth, and Murray G. Murphey. *A History of Philosophy in America.* Hackett 2 vols. 1977 ea. $17.50. The most up-to-date, clearly written synthesis of the history of American philosophy. Appropriate for the general reader.

Hall, Peter Dobkin. *The Organization of American Culture, 1700–1900.* New York

Univ. Pr. 1984 pap. $12.50. Attempts to examine the rise of an American national culture.

Higham, John, and Paul K. Conkin, eds. *New Directions in American Intellectual History*. Johns Hopkins Univ. Pr. 1980 $15.00 pap. $5.95. Examination of the discipline of intellectual history, including its methodology, foundations, and framework.

Johnson, John W. *American Legal Culture, 1908–1940. Contributions to Legal Studies*. Greenwood 1981 lib. bdg. $25.00. A good introduction to the development of U.S. legal culture in the first half of the twentieth century.

Kaledin, Eugenia. *The Education of Mrs. Henry Adams. Amer. Civilization Ser*. Temple Univ. Pr. 1982 $29.95. This biography of Clover Adams is a long overdue study of the wife of historian Henry Adams and a useful companion to her husband's classic autobiography, *The Education of Henry Adams*.

Kelley, Robert L. *The Cultural Pattern in American Politics: The First Century*. Knopf 1979 $15.00; Univ. Pr. of America text ed. 1981 pap. $11.75. Analyzes the impact of religion and ethnicity on U.S. politics.

Kerber, Linda K. *Women of the Republic: Intellect and Ideology in Revolutionary America*. Univ. of North Carolina Pr. 1980 $22.50 pap. $8.95. An important contribution to U.S. women's history, it examines the role and status of women in the formative postrevolutionary period.

Larson, Gary O. *The Reluctant Patron: The United States Government and the Arts, 1943–1965*. Univ. of Pennsylvania Pr. 1983 $30.00 pap. $12.95. An important history of the relationship between the arts and the federal government showing how the present relationship was initiated.

Lewis, David. *When Harlem Was in Vogue*. Knopf 1981 $22.50. A first-rate intellectual and social history of Harlem from 1905 to 1935 that captures the spirit and energy of the community.

Pells, Richard H. *The Liberal Mind in a Conservative Age: American Intellectuals in the 1940s and 1950s*. Harper 1984 $18.22. Analyzes the rise of anticommunism during the Cold War and the new critics of the problems that developed along the postindustrial society in the United States.

Perry, Lewis. *Intellectual Life in America: A History*. Watts 1984 $19.95. A well-written and easy to understand survey of U.S. intellectual history from colonial times to the present. An excellent and concise introduction to a difficult subject.

Rose, Anne C. *Transcendentalism as a Social Movement, 1830–1850*. Yale Univ. Pr. 1981 $26.00. This well-researched analysis of antebellum intellectual and social history examines the role and responsibilities of thinkers in national affairs.

Savage, William W. *The Cowboy Hero: His Image in American History and Culture*. Univ. of Oklahoma Pr. 1979 $14.95. A contemporary analysis of how the image of the cowboy has been portrayed in books, movies, television, radio, and other forms of communication.

Schiller, Dan. *Objectivity and the News: The Public and the Rise of Commercial Journalism*. Univ. of Pennsylvania Pr. 1981 $22.50

Shi, David E. *The Simple Life: Plain Living and High Thinking in American Culture*. Oxford 1985 $19.95. A cultural history of America's search for luxury and the development of social life-styles.

Skotheim, Robert Allen. *American Intellectual Histories and Historians*. Greenwood repr. of 1966 ed. 1978 lib. bdg. $26.00. Although this historiographical survey "ignores a great deal of what most people would think is American intellectual history [it] was worth writing and is worth reading. Even when he is dealing with an author now rightly almost totally unknown . . . he has a good deal of interest to say" (*TLS*). Discusses such historians as Charles A. Beard, Carl Becker, Merle Curti, Ralph Gabriel, Perry Miller, Samuel Eliot Morison, Vernon L. Parrington, and James Harvey Robinson.

Thorpe, William. *The Mind of the Negro: An Intellectual History of Afro-Americans*. Greenwood repr. of 1961 ed. $55.00

Trachtenberg, Alan. *The Incorporation of America: Culture and Society in the Gilded Age. Amer. Century Ser.* Hill & Wang 1982 $12.95 pap. $6.95. Analyzing the three decades after the Civil War, the author shows how the notion of incorporation changed both the industrial and cultural systems of the United States.

Udelson, Joseph H. *The Great Television Race: A History of the American Television Industry, 1925–1941*. Univ. of Alabama Pr. 1982 $18.95. A serious historical treatment of the development and influence of television in the United States.

Economic History

Becker, Robert A. *Revolution, Reform, and the Politics of American Taxation, 1763–1783*. Louisiana State Univ. Pr. 1980 $27.50. A highly specialized and detailed history of the politics and economics of internal colonial taxation.

Bonnifield, Paul. *The Dust Bowl: Men, Dirt, and Depression*. Univ. of New Mexico Pr. 1979 $14.95. Beyond being a study of the impact of the New Deal on farms, this book also discusses the consequences of the New Deal and the complexities in general of agricultural planning.

Collier, Peter, and David Horowitz. *The Rockefellers: An American Dynasty*. New Amer. Lib. 1977 pap. $4.95. A good example of family history based on extensive interviews and family records.

Conkin, Paul K. *Prophets of Prosperity: America's First Political Economists*. Indiana Univ. Pr. 1980 $25.00. Essentially a reader's guide to 20 U.S. economists between 1800 and 1850.

Corn, Joseph J. *The Winged Gospel: America's Romance with Aviation, 1900–1950*. Oxford 1983 $17.95

Crouch, Tom D. *A Dream of Wings: Americans and the Airplane, 1875–1905*. Norton 1981 $15.95. A lively and entertaining history that covers a neglected aspect of U.S. history.

Fogel, Robert W., and Stanley L. Engerman. *Time on the Cross: The Economics of American Negro Slavery*. Little, Brown 2 vols. text ed. 1974 pap. vol. 1 $9.95 vol. 2 $8.95. This is "the first full-scale treatment of American Negro slavery grounded in the quantitative method" (*TLS*).

Fox, Richard Wightman, and T. J. Jackson Lears, eds. *The Culture of Consumption: Critical Essays in American History, 1880–1980*. Pantheon 1983 $20.00 pap. $9.95. Attempts to identify the meaning of the term modern consumer culture and its usefulness in interpreting U.S. society.

Frazier, E. Franklin. *Black Bourgeoisie: The Rise of a New Middle Class in the United States*. Macmillan (Collier Bks.) 1962 pap. $3.95; Macmillan (Free Press) 1965 pap. $11.95. "Analysis of the life of the upper middle-class American Negro, by an outstanding Negro sociologist" (James E. Wright, *LJ*).

———. *The Negro Family in the United States*. Univ. of Chicago Pr. abr. rev. ed. 1966 pap. $8.00

Genovese, Eugene D. *The Political Economy of Slavery: Studies in the Economy and Society of the Slave South*. Random (Vintage) 1967 pap. $4.95

———. *Roll, Jordan, Roll: The World the Slaves Made*. Random (Vintage) 1976 pap.

$10.95. "A Marxist account of slaves and their masters in the Old South" (Publisher's note).

Harris, William H. *The Harder We Run: Black Workers since the Civil War.* Oxford text ed. 1982 pap. $5.95. A basic introduction to the history of black workers in the United States.

Hurt, R. Douglas. *The Dust Bowl: An Agricultural and Social History.* Nelson-Hall text ed. 1981 $21.95 pap. $10.95. Using newspaper and journal accounts, the author has reconstructed an entertaining history of an important aspect of U.S. history.

Jacoway, Elizabeth, and David R. Colburn, eds. *Southern Businessmen and Desegregation.* Louisiana State Univ. Pr. text ed. 1982 $27.50. This collection deals with how civic and business leaders in various southern cities handled integration. Using oral histories and primary sources, this is a good elite study.

Kessler-Harris, Alice. *Out to Work: A History of Wage-Earning Women in the United States.* Oxford 1982 $19.95 pap. $8.95. A detailed survey of the role of women in the labor force from colonial times to the present. Discusses how the employment of women affected their lives and family.

Matthaei, Julie A. *An Economic History of Women in America: Women's Work, the Sexual Division of Labor, and the Development of Capitalism.* Schocken 1983 $29.50 pap. $11.95. A Marxist study of the economic history of women in the United States.

McCoy, Drew R. *The Elusive Republic: Political Economy in Jeffersonian America.* Univ. of North Carolina Pr. 1980 $21.50; Norton 1983 pap. $5.95. Argues that the Jeffersonian Americans did not eagerly turn to industrialization, but sought to perpetuate an ideal of Republican agrarianism.

Patterson, James T. *America's Struggle against Poverty, 1900–1980.* Harvard Univ. Pr. 1981 $17.50 pap. $6.95. An interesting account of government involvement in alleviating poverty. An important work on American reform and the rise of the welfare state.

Perkins, Edwin J. *The Economy of Colonial America.* Columbia Univ. Pr. 1980 $24.00 pap. $9.00. Basic survey of the colonial economy that aptly summarizes trends, patterns, and major problems.

Prude, Jonathan. *The Coming of Industrial Order: Town and Factory Life in Rural Massachusetts, 1810–1860.* Cambridge Univ. Pr. 1983 $34.50. A study of industrialization as a process rather than as an event. Analysis of nonunionized workers is an important contribution to the literature.

Ransom, Roger L., and Richard Sutch. *One Kind of Freedom: The Economic Consequences of Emancipation.* Cambridge Univ. Pr. 1977 $47.50 pap. $14.95. Examines why the South did not participate in the economic post-Civil War boom and argues that it was the failure of southern institutions.

Rosenberg, Emily S. *Spreading the American Dream: American Economic and Cultural Expansion, 1890–1945.* Ed. by Eric Foner, *Amer. Century Ser.* Hill & Wang 1982 $12.95 pap. $6.95. Written for a popular audience. The author reviews the U.S. drive to export its technological and consumer-oriented society.

Stone, Alan. *Regulation and Its Alternatives.* Congressional Quarterly 1982 pap. $10.25. A detailed study of the regulatory agencies and their impact on the government and society.

Strasser, Susan. *Never Done: A History of American Housework.* Pantheon 1982 $22.50 pap. $11.95. Examines the role of women in light of changing technology and social trends. An enriching account of daily life.

Thernstrom, Stephan. *The Other Bostonians: Poverty and Progress in the American*

Metropolis, 1880–1970. Studies in Urban History. Harvard Univ. Pr. 1973 text ed. $20.00 pap. $7.95. "This volume is a valuable contribution to what is known as quantitative history. Thernstrom uses modern statistical methods in studying the movement of a significant urban population" (*Choice*). This book was awarded a Bancroft Prize in American history in 1974.

Thomas, Gordon, and Max Morgan-Witts. *The Day the Bubble Burst: A Social History of the Wall Street Crash of 1929.* Penguin 1980 pap. $6.95. This lively account of the stock market crash uses a combination of interviews, eyewitness accounts, memoirs, and oral histories.

Wallace, Anthony. *The Growth of an American Village in the Early Industrial Revolution.* Knopf 1978 $17.50; Random text ed. 1966 $17.95. Using perspectives of cultural anthropology, this is a fascinating study of the transformation of Pennsylvania textile towns in the early 1800s.

Wertheimer, Barbara Mayer. *We Were There: The Story of Working Women in America.* Pantheon 1977 pap. $8.95. A general survey of U.S. working women over the past 200 years. Particularly useful for understanding women's struggle to unionize.

Yellowitz, Irwin. *Industrialization and the American Labor Movement, 1850–1900.* Associated Faculty Pr. 1976 $18.50. Focuses on how the unions sought to cope with the impact of early technological changes and advances.

Social History

The American Indian Reader: A History. Indian Historian Pr. 1972 $4.00

Archdeacon, Thomas J. *Becoming American: An Ethnic History.* Macmillan (Free Press) 1983 $17.95. The standard history of immigration and ethnicity in the United States, including racial and religious aspects of migration.

Banner, Lois W. *Women in Modern America: A Brief History.* Harcourt 1974 pap. $11.95. "The book will be useful to the general reader and as a supplement to college courses in U.S. history which often underemphasize women's roles and activities" (*Choice*).

Barbrook, Alec, and Christine Bolt. *Power and Protest in American Life.* St. Martin's 1980 $29.00. Instead of examining the better-known reform movements, this work studies the newer and little-known protest groups.

Bartlett, Richard. *The New Country: A Social History of the American Frontier, 1776–1890.* Oxford 1976 pap. $10.95

Bell, Daniel. *The Coming of Post-Industrial Society: A Venture in Social Forecasting.* Basic Bks. 1976 pap. $9.95

Berry, Mary F., and John W. Blassingame. *Long Memory: The Black Experience in America.* Oxford 1982 $29.95 pap. $12.95. What makes this history of the black experience in the United States different is its thematic approach, covering such topics as the family and education.

Billington, Ray Allen. *America's Frontier Heritage.* Univ. of New Mexico Pr. 1974 $10.95

——. *Westward Expansion: History of the American Frontier.* Macmillan 5th ed. 1982

Bontemps, Arna. *One Hundred Years of Negro Freedom.* Greenwood repr. of 1961 ed. 1980 $24.50

Bordley, James, III, and A. McGehee Harvey. *Two Centuries of American Medicine, 1776–1976.* Saunders text ed. 1976 $42.00. A descriptive history that gives special emphasis to the period since 1946.

Bullock, Henry Allen. *A History of Negro Education in the South: From 1619 to the Present*. Harvard Univ. Pr. 1967 $22.50. Awarded a Bancroft Prize in 1968.

Catlin, George. *Letters and Notes on the Manners, Customs and Conditions of the North American Indian*. 1844. Dover 2 vols. 1973 pap. ea. $6.95. "Catlin's 'letters'—traveler's accounts sent to Eastern newspapers—are vividly descriptive as his famous portraits of Western chiefs" (*LJ*).

Cott, Nancy F., and Elizabeth H. Pleck, eds. *A Heritage of Her Own: Toward a New Social History of American Women*. Simon & Schuster (Touchstone Bks.) 1980 pap. $11.95. A collection of essays designed to display the wide-ranging research done on women's studies in all disciplines.

Cranz, Galen. *The Politics of Park Design: A History of Urban Parks in America*. MIT 1982 $29.95. A well-written and organized presentation of the political and historical development of parks from 1850 to the present.

Cremin, Lawrence A. *American Education: The National Experience, 1783–1876*. Harper 1980 $29.95 1982 pap. $11.06. Recounts the effort to make education popular and specifically American in content.

Debo, Angie. *A History of the Indians of the United States*. Civilization of Amer. Indians Ser. Univ. of Oklahoma Pr. 1970 $21.95 1984 pap. $12.95. "An outstanding student of American Indian history has here synthesized her almost 50 years' research" (*Choice*).

Degler, Carl N. *At Odds: Women and the Family in America from the Revolution to the Present*. Oxford 1980 $29.95 pap. $9.95. A comprehensive social history of U.S. women during the last 200 years that includes chapters on marriage, suffrage, childrearing, and participation in the labor force.

Delany, Martin R. *The Condition, Elevation, Emigration, and Destiny of the Colored People of the United States*. Amer. Negro: His History and Lit Ser. Ayer repr. of 1852 ed. 1968 $10.00

Deloria, Vine, Jr. *Custer Died for Your Sins: An Indian Manifesto*. Avon 1970 pap. $3.50. An informative and angry catalog of abuses . . . [the author] is perceptive in his analysis of the differences between Indian problems and those of blacks and other minority groups and his commentary on Indian affairs is enlightening" (*LJ*).

Dick, Everett. *The Lure of the Land: A Social History of the Public Lands from the Articles of Confederation to the New Deal*. Univ. of Nebraska Pr. 1970 $27.95. "A specialist on the history of the West, Dick has written a social history of the public lands from the formation of the public domain in 1776 to 1935 when F.D.R. withdrew all lands from private entry" (*Choice*).

Driver, Harold E. *Indians of North America*. 1961. Univ. of Chicago Pr. 2d ed. rev. 1969 $25.00 pap. $14.95

Durham, Philip, and Everett L. Jones. *Negro Cowboys*. Univ. of Nebraska Pr. (Bison) 1983 pap. $7.95. "Among the cowboys who rode the ranges from Texas to Montana . . . were more than 5,000 Negroes. This startling fact was uncovered by Univ. of California professor Philip Durham and Everett L. Jones, who plowed through 300 memoirs and histories in search of references to Negro cowboys" (*Time*).

Edmunds, David, ed. *American Indian Leaders: Studies in Diversity*. Univ. of Nebraska Pr. (Bison) 1980 $19.50 pap. $5.95. This collection of 12 biographies demonstrates the richness and variety of leadership roles American Indians have pursued in U.S. history.

Epstein, Barbara Leslie. *The Politics of Domesticity: Women, Evangelism and Temperance*. Wesleyan Univ. Pr. 1981 $19.50. Argues that the development of class and sex differences in institutions and cultural patterns has resulted in significantly different values for women.

Fitzgerald, Frances. *America Revised: History Schoolbooks in the Twentieth Century.* Atlantic Monthly Pr. 1979 $11.95; Random (Vintage) 1980 pap. $3.95. An intellectual history and report about what textbooks have failed to explain or ignored and how they have served to manipulate public opinion.

Fox, Stephen R. *John Muir and His Legacy: The American Conservation Movement.* Little, Brown 1981 $19.95. While this is essentially a biography of the first preservationist, it is also a history of the U.S. conservation movement since 1890.

Frady, Marshall. *Southerners: A Journalist's Odyssey.* New Amer. Lib. 1980 pap. $6.95. This anthology contains a variety of essays on southern history over the last 50 years and numerous essays on prominent political personalities.

Fraser, Walter J., Jr., and Winfred B. Moore, Jr., eds. *From the Old South to the New: Essays on the Transitional South. Contributions in Amer. History Ser.* Greenwood 1981 $35.00. Reflects the two schools of thought that emphasize either continuity or change in the history of the South.

Furlong, William Rea, and Byron McCandless. *So Proudly We Hail: The History of the United States Flag.* Ed. by Harold D. Langley, Smithsonian 1981 $25.00 pap. $12.50. The definitive and comprehensive history of the flag, including its textile, design, and role.

Garrison, William Lloyd. *Thoughts on African Colonization. Amer. Negro: His History and Lit. Ser.* Ayer repr. of 1832 ed. 1968 $4.00. Written by the outstanding white abolitionist of the nineteenth century.

Gordon, Michael, ed. *The American Family in Social-Historical Perspective.* St. Martin's text ed. 3d ed. 1983 $19.95 pap. $13.95

Grob, Gerald N. *Mental Illness and American Society, 1875–1940.* Princeton Univ. Pr. 1983 $25.00. Concentrating on the evolution of the psychiatric profession and history of American mental hospitals, this work is an interesting social history.

Hagan, William T. *American Indians.* Ed. by Daniel J. Boorstin, *History of Civilization Ser.* Univ. of Chicago Pr. rev. ed. 1979 lib. bdg. $15.00 pap. $5.95. In brief but vivid form, the author presents the story of a clash between two cultures—the American Indian nations and the rising United States—and shows that the conflict with the newcomers and the resulting defeat of the Indians were inevitable.

Harding, Vincent. *The Other American Revolution. Afro-Amer. Culture and Society Monographs* Center for Afro-Amer. Studies 1981 $14.50 pap. $8.50. Traces the course of the black struggle in the United States from its African roots to the civil rights marches.

———. *There Is a River: The Black Struggle for Freedom in America.* Harcourt 1981 $19.95; Random (Vintage) 1983 pap. $6.95. Written by a leading black intellectual historian, this work provides a more personal view of the history of black radicalism in the United States.

Hareven, Tamara K., and Maris Vinovskis, eds. *Family and Population in Nineteenth-Century America. Quantitative Studies in History Ser.* Princeton Univ. Pr. 1978 $33.00 pap. $11.50

Herskovits, Melville J. *The Myth of the Negro Past.* Beacon 1958 pap. $9.95. "Anthropological study of the American Negro, from African origins to his position in contemporary society" (James E. Wright, *LJ*).

Hook, J. N. *Family Names: How Our Surnames Came to America.* Macmillan 1982 $16.95 1983 pap. $7.95. This enjoyable book gives a history of surnames, including information relating to immigration and the story of names.

Howe, Irving. *World of Our Fathers.* Bantam 1981 pap. $3.95; Simon & Schuster

1983 pap. $12.95. Though being a study of the East European Jewish migration to the United States, this work is important for anyone interested in ethnic and social history.

Johnson, Daniel M., and Rex R. Campbell. *Black Migration in America: A Social Demographic History. Social and Economic Demography Ser.* Duke Univ. Pr. 1981 $18.50 pap. $9.75. A history of black migration from the beginning of slavery to the civil rights movement of the twentieth century. A useful short guide to the themes of black American history.

Jordan, Teresa. *Cowgirls: Women of the American West.* Doubleday (Anchor) 1982 $19.95. Based on interviews, diaries, newspaper stories, poetry, and songs, this is an enjoyable study of the women who were the counterparts to the cowboys.

Jordan, Winthrop D. *The White Man's Burden: Historical Origins of Racism in the United States.* Oxford 1974 $8.95 pap. $6.95. An abridgment of his *White Over Black.*

————. *White Over Black: American Attitudes toward the Negro, 1550–1812.* Norton Lib. 1977 pap. $10.95; Univ. of North Carolina Pr. 1968 $32.50. "A major effort to distinguish and analyze the sources of American responses" (*Choice*).

Katzman, David M., and William H. Tuttle, Jr., eds. *Plain Folk: The Life Stories of Undistinguished Americans.* Univ. of Illinois Pr. 1982 $18.95 pap. $6.95

Kehoe, Alice B. *North American Indians: A Comprehensive Account.* Prentice-Hall text ed. 1981 pap. $10.95. Covering pre-Columbian civilizations to the present, this massive survey is an excellent history and analysis of Indians in the United States.

Kerber, Linda K., and Jane D. Mathews, eds. *Women's America: Refocusing the Past.* Oxford 1982 $25.00 pap. $13.95. As a compilation of historical essays and primary sources and documents, this long anthology provides an excellent collection of materials on the entire history of U.S. women.

Kett, Joseph F. *Rites of Passage: Adolescence in America, 1790 to the Present.* Basic Bks. 1979 pap. $8.95. Explores how economic and class factors have changed the status and role of youth in society.

Kolodny, Annette. *The Land before Her: Fantasy and Experience of the American Frontiers, 1630–1860.* Univ. of North Carolina Pr. 1984 $28.00 pap. $9.95. A rich and very thorough analysis of women's writing about the frontier that provides new information about the images created by women that form our present notion of the West.

Kraut, Alan M. *The Huddled Masses: The Immigrant in American Society, 1880–1921. Amer. History Ser.* Harlan Davidson text ed. 1982 pap. $8.95. An excellent history of the immigrant experience, relating how, where, and why millions of immigrants came to the United States.

Lender, Mark E., and James Kirby Martin. *Drinking in America: A History.* Macmillan (Free Pr.) 1982 $19.95. A fascinating history of drinking in the United States from colonial times to the present that attempts to relate drinking to a number of social and reform movements.

Lerner, Gerda, ed. *The Female Experience: An American Documentary.* Cobbs text ed. 1977 pap. $14.47. An important collection of documentary material from colonial times to the present.

Lingeman, Richard. *Small Town America: A Narrative History, 1620 to the Present.* Houghton Mifflin 1981 pap. $8.95. Analyzing a neglected aspect of U.S. history, the author presents a rich and absorbing history.

Luchetti, Cathy, and Carol Olwell. *Women of the West.* Antelope Island Pr. 1982

$25.00 pap. $17.00. Extensively illustrated, this volume describes the experiences of women in the West during the nineteenth century.

Magdol, Edward, and John L. Wakelyn, eds. *The Southern Common People: Studies in Nineteenth-Century Social History. Contributions in Amer. History Ser.* Greenwood text ed. 1982 pap. $9.95. This collection of 18 essays covers the social history of the South, including both the ante- and postbellum periods.

Martin, Paul S., and others. *Indians before Columbus: Twenty Thousand Years of North American History Revealed by Archaeology.* Univ. of Chicago Pr. 1947 $27.50; Univ. of Chicago Pr. (Phoenix Bks.) 1975 pap. $6.95

Meltzer, Milton. *In Their Own Words: A History of the American Negro.* Apollo 3 vols. 1967 pap. ea. $1.65

Mintz, Sidney W., ed. *Slavery, Colonialism, and Racism.* Norton text ed. 1975 $10.95 1974 pap. $3.95. "Each of the 11 essays in this broad-ranging and important collection surveys a major aspect of the black experience in Africa and the Americas" (*LJ*).

Morgan, H. Wayne. *Drugs in America: A Social History, 1800–1980.* Syracuse Univ. Pr. 1981 pap. $9.95. An important contribution to the growing literature of social history, delineating the role of drugs in U.S. society.

Mrozek, Donald J. *Sport and American Mentality, 1880–1910.* Univ. of Tennessee Pr. text ed. 1983 $24.95 pap. $12.95. A good example of the growing number of serious books in the genre of sports history, this is a social history of how Americans approach leisure time.

Namias, June. *First Generation: Oral Histories of Twentieth-Century American Immigrants.* Beacon 1978 pap. $6.95. A collection of 31 interviews with individuals who came to America between 1900 and 1975.

National Geographic Society. *The World of the American Indian.* National Geographic Society 1974 $9.95

Nugent, Walter. *Structures of American Social History.* Indiana Univ. Pr. 1981 $12.95. Focuses on the demographic forces in U.S. history rather than on the economic and political aspects. One of the best demographic studies on U.S. history.

Prucha, Francis P. *The Great Father: The United States Government and the American Indians.* Univ. of Nebraska Pr. 2 vols. 1984 $60.00. The definitive and comprehensive study of the relations between the U.S. government and the American Indians.

Ravitch, Diane. *The Troubled Crusade: American Education, 1945–1980.* Basic Bks. 1983 $19.95. Chronicles the various reform movements and problems that face the educational system.

Rothman, Ellen K. *Hands and Hearts: A History of Courtship in America.* Basic Bks. 1984 $19.95. A scholarly history of courtship from 1770 to 1920. Overall, the author depicts a surprising continuity through the years.

Shaw, Nate. *All God's Dangers: The Life of Nate Shaw.* 1974. Ed. by Theodore Rosengarten, Avon 1975 pap. $3.95; Knopf 1974 $15.00; Random (Vintage) 1984 pap. $8.95. An oral autobiography of an 85-year-old black tenant farmer, recorded during four years of taping by the editor.

Simon, Kate. *Fifth Avenue: A Very Special History.* Harcourt 1979 $12.95 pap. $4.95. Approaches U.S. social history by looking at the families and buildings that make up Fifth Avenue.

Sowell, Thomas. *Ethnic America: A History.* Basic Bks. 1983 pap. $9.50. Argues that ethnic groups need to be understood not as minorities, but in terms of age, heritage, geography, and other social factors.

Starr, Paul. *The Social Transformation of American Medicine.* Basic Bks. 1982 $24.95

1984 pap. $11.95. Analyzes two historical trends—the rise of the American medical profession and the change of medicine into a twentieth-century industry.

Steiner, Stanley. *The New Indians.* Harper 1968 $14.37. This study "attempts to present the thoughts and attitudes of the Indian toward his past" (*LJ*).

Walker, Samuel. *Popular Justice: A History of American Criminal Justice.* Oxford text ed. 1980 $19.95 pap. $9.95. A pioneering analysis because criminal justice is a fairly new endeavor for historians. A clear and well-written survey.

Weinberg, Meyer. *A Chance to Learn: The History of Race and Education in the United States.* Cambridge Univ. Pr. 1977 $47.50 pap. $11.95. The most comprehensive history of U.S. education.

Wells, Robert V. *Revolutions in Americans' Lives: A Demographic Perspective on the History of Americans, Their Families and Their Society. Contributions in Family Studies* Greenwood 1982 lib. bdg. $29.95. Shows how demographic changes affected individuals, families, and society as a whole.

Western Writers of America. *The Women Who Made the West.* Ed. by Nellie Snyder Yost, Doubleday 1980 $11.95. An anthology of 18 vignettes on a variety of frontier women, including a hotel owner, journalist, rancher, and doctor.

Wissler, Clark. *Indians of the United States: Four Centuries of Their History and Culture.* 1946. Ed. by Lucy W. Cluckhohn, Doubleday rev. ed. 1966 pap. $4.95

Wright, Richard. *Black Boy: A Record of Childhood and Youth.* Harper repr. of 1945 ed. 1969 $16.30 pap. $3.37. "Honest, shocking autobiography of one of America's most able writers" (James E. Wright, *LJ*).

———. *Native Son.* Harper repr. of 1940 ed. 1969 $14.37

———. *Twelve Million Black Voices: A Folk History of the Negro in the U.S. Amer. Negro: His History and Lit. Ser.* Ayer repr. of 1941 ed. 1969 $17.00

The Declaration of Independence, 1776, the Constitution of the United States of America, 1787–1788, and the Federalist Papers, 1787–1788

The full and formal Declaration of Independence, adopted July 4, 1776, by representatives of the 13 North American colonies, announced the separation of the colonies from Great Britain and the birth of the United States. The Constitution of the United States, embodying the fundamental principles on which the U.S. Republic is conducted, was drawn up at the Federal Constitutional Convention at Philadelphia in 1787, was signed on September 17, 1787, and was ratified by the required number of states (nine) by June 21, 1788.

The widely read "Federalist Papers," a series of 85 political essays, was initiated by Alexander Hamilton with the intention of persuading New York to approve the federal Constitution. He wrote 51 of the essays and of his two collaborators, James Madison wrote 14 and John Jay 5. The authorship of 15 is in dispute (between Hamilton and Madison). The essays "have been acclaimed from the time of their appearance to the present day with praise for their cogency of argument, exposition of American political philosophy, and literary quality" (*Columbia Encyclopedia*).

Adams, Willi Paul. *The First American Constitutions: Republican Ideology and the Making of the State Constitutions in the Revolutionary Era.* Trans. by Rita Kimber and Robert Kimber, Univ. of North Carolina Pr. 1980 $29.50. Extends the research on constitutional history by examining how the state constitutions evolved and the emergence of various popular ideas.

Agresto, John. *The Supreme Court and Constitutional Democracy.* Cornell Univ. Pr.

1984 $25.00 pap. $7.95. Concentrates on the role of the Court in the entire political system, not just as a judicial body.

Barber, Sotirios A. *On What the Constitution Means.* Johns Hopkins Univ. Pr. 1983 $17.50. Attempts to explain and discuss the meaning of the Constitution in simple and general terms.

Beard, Charles. *An Economic Interpretation of the Constitution of the United States.* 1913. Macmillan (Free Pr.) 1965 $12.95. One of the classic interpretations of the Constitution. (See Beard's main listing in this chapter.)

Becker, Carl L. *The Declaration of Independence: A Study in the History of Political Ideas.* 1922. Random (Vintage) 1958 pap. $3.95. The definitive study. (See Becker's main listing in this chapter.)

Corwin, Edward S. *Edward S. Corwin's Constitution and What It Means Today.* Ed. by Harold W. Chase and Craig R. Ducat, Princeton Univ. Pr. 14th ed. rev. 1979 pap. $14.50. The standard analysis of the Constitution by one of America's foremost constitutional scholars.

Crosskey, W. W., and William Jeffrey, Jr. *Politics and Constitution in the History of the United States.* Univ. of Chicago Pr. 3 vols. 1981 lib. bdg. $115.00. This massive study of the significance and impact of the Constitution in U.S. politics is both stimulating and thought provoking.

Dietze, Gottfried. *The Federalist: A Classic on Federalism and Free Government.* Greenwood repr. of 1960 ed. lib. bdg. $22.25; Johns Hopkins Univ. Pr. 1960 pap. $7.95

Documentary History of the Constitution of the United States of America, 1786–1870: Derived from Records, Manuscripts, and Rolls Deposited in the Bureau of Rolls and Library of the Department of State. Johnson Repr. 5 vols. repr. of 1894 ed. 1966 $320.00

Dumbauld, Edward. *The Declaration of Independence and What It Means Today.* Univ. of Oklahoma Pr. repr. of 1950 ed. 1968 $10.95

Fairfield, Roy P., ed. *The Federalist Papers.* Johns Hopkins Univ. Pr. 2d ed. 1981 pap. $6.95

Farrand, Max, ed. *The Records of the Federal Convention of 1787.* 1911. Yale Univ. Pr. 4 vols. 1966 vols. 1–2 ea. $40.00 vol. 3 $45.00 vol. 4 $45.00. "Nothing official was published about the Convention which framed the Constitution until at least 30 years after its occurrence.... The documents are reprinted exactly from the originals and are presented in chronological sequence. The work presents statements of proceedings in the Convention rather than theoretical interpretations of clauses" (*PW*).

Fisher, Louis. *The Constitution between Friends: Congress, the President and the Law.* St. Martin's text ed. 1978 pap. $9.95. Focuses on the relationship between Congress and the president in the making and interpretation of legislation.

Garraty, John A., ed. *Quarrels That Have Shaped the Constitution.* Harper 1964 pap. $4.95. Sixteen major Supreme Court decisions presented in a most interesting manner by a group of "distinguished and competent" authors (*LJ*). Civil rights cases loom large in it.

Hamilton, Alexander, James Madison, and John Jay. *The Federalist.* Ed. by Jacob E. Cooke, Wesleyan Univ. Pr. 1961 $35.00 1982 pap. $14.95. Vital for scholarly reference and recommended for all academic and large public libraries, this is "the first accurate edition ... to reconstruct the definitive text from the newspapers, from subsequent editions and from the authors' revisions. All versions have been collated and annotated, and the whole indexed completely with cross references. The disputed authorship of some numbers among the papers is discussed in a lengthy introductory essay" (*LJ*).

Havard, William C., and Joseph L. Bernd, eds. *Two Hundred Years of the Republic in*

Retrospect. Univ. Pr. of Virginia repr. 1976 $13.95. A wide-ranging collection of essays on constitutional history.

Jensen, Merrill. *The Making of the American Constitution.* Krieger 1979 pap. $5.95. This narrative history is easy to read and comprehend.

Kelly, Alfred H., and Winfred A. Harbison. *The American Constitution.* Norton 6th ed. 1983 $19.95

Latham, Earl, ed. *The Declaration of Independence and the Constitution. Problems in Amer. Civilization* Heath 3d ed. 1976 pap. $6.95

Lundberg, Ferdinand. *Cracks in the Constitution.* Lyle Stuart 1980 $15.00. Argues that in order to counteract the growing power of the state, the national government should be decentralized.

Lynd, Staughton. *Class Conflict, Slavery, and the United States Constitution: Ten Essays.* Greenwood repr. of 1967 ed. 1980 lib. bdg. $32.50. "Staughton Lynd seeks to contribute to a new kind of history. He writes: 'The new (perhaps New Left) American history emphasizes economic causes while avoiding the caricature that limits "the economic factor" to conscious pursuit of pecuniary advantage. It insists on a comparative approach to the revolutions of 1776–1783 and 1861–1865, without denying that American history has a variety of "exceptional features." ' For the most part, this is a collection of essays which have appeared in scholarly journals. [Professor Lynd] contends that C. A. Beard's version of the nature of strife in this constitutional period requires revision. Rather than a conflict between capitalists and farmers, Mr. Lynd argues, the conflict was between commercial and non-commercial interests" (*LJ*).

Main, Jackson Turner. *The Antifederalists: Critics of the Constitution, 1781–1788.* Norton Lib. 1974 pap. $7.95. "First-rate scholarship" (*LJ*).

McDonald, Forrest. *We the People: The Economic Origins of the Constitution. Midway Repr. Ser.* Univ. of Chicago Pr. 1976 pap. $14.00

Mitchell, Broadus, and Louise Mitchell. *A Biography of the Constitution of the United States: Its Origin, Formation, Adoption, Interpretation.* Oxford 2d ed. 1975 pap. $25.00. Includes the document itself; the personalities and legal struggles are analyzed.

Murphy, Bruce A. *The Brandeis/Frankfurter Connection: The Secret Political Activities of Two Supreme Court Justices.* Doubleday 1983 pap. $12.95; Oxford 1982 $22.50. This dual biography provides new insights into the personal and political relationship between two of the most important Supreme Court justices.

Padover, Saul K., and Jacob W. Landynski. *The Living U.S. Constitution.* New Amer. Lib. 2d ed. rev. 1983 pap. $4.95. A well-written commentary on the evolution of the Constitution.

Pritchett, C. Herman. *Constitutional Law of the Federal System.* Prentice-Hall 1984 pap. $17.95. Goes beyond an analysis of the Constitution proper to detail the entire fabric of constitutional law in the United States.

Rutland, Robert Allen. *The Birth of the Bill of Rights, 1776–1791.* Northeastern Univ. Pr. rev. ed. 1983 $24.95. text ed. pap. $9.95

———. *The Ordeal of the Constitution: The Antifederalists and the Ratification Struggle of 1787–1788.* Northeastern Univ. Pr. text ed. 1983 $24.95 pap. $9.95. "This is a valuable examination of the struggle for ratification of the Constitution of the United States especially with regard to those who opposed it. [Important are] its research of original sources and the casting of new light and shadows on this formative period" (*LJ*).

Schwartz, Bernard. *Roots of the Bill of Rights: An Illustrated Sourcebook of American Freedom.* Chelsea House 5 vols. 1981 pap. $64.95. Scholarly and enjoyable.

Shapiro, Martin, ed. *The Constitution of the United States and Related Documents.* Harlan Davidson text ed. 1966 pap. $3.25

Smith, Edward C., ed. *The Constitution of the United States: With Case Summaries.* Barnes & Noble 11th ed. 1979 pap. $3.95

Smith, Page. *The Constitution: A Documentary and Narrative History.* Morrow 1978 $19.95 pap. $7.95. An excellent introduction.

Storing, Herbert J., and Murray Dry, eds. *The Complete Anti-Federalist.* Univ. of Chicago Pr. 7 vols. 1982 $175.00. A massive collection of the writings of the Antifederalists.

Swindler, William F. *Sources and Documents of U.S. Constitutions.* Oceana 3 vols. 1983 ea. $50.00. Includes not only information and documents pertaining to the federal Constitution, but the constitutions of all 50 states.

Wills, Garry. *Explaining America: The Federalist.* Doubleday 1980 $14.95; Penguin 1982 pap. $5.95. A controversial interpretation of *The Federalist*, arguing that virtue was the most important concept put forth.

———. *Inventing America: Jefferson's Declaration of Independence.* Doubleday 1978 $12.95; Random (Vintage) 1979 pap. $6.95. A provocative interpretation of Jefferson's philosophy and the Declaration of Independence. Argues that his ideas were not based on John Locke, but on the Scottish moral philosophers.

STRUCTURE OF POLITICS

Public interest in the workings of the federal government is at an all time high, perhaps because people now seek with such great urgency answers to the questions: "How did we get where we are now?" and "Where do we go from here?" Several hundred titles have been carefully considered in order to provide a balanced list of books, both scholarly and popular, on the current topics. While there are materials on a wide-ranging number of topics, this section does focus on the three primary branches of the federal government—the Congress, the presidency, and the Supreme Court and judiciary. Also included are selected titles on political parties and elections. In short, the focus is on providing a selection of books that adequately introduces the national political system. Many U.S. presidents and statesmen are main entries in Chapter 3. The U.S. Government Printing Office is an excellent source of material, and senators, congressmen, and congresswomen will usually send verbatim records of congressional hearings free on request. For additional titles of interest, see Chapter 1.

Abraham, Henry J. *The Judiciary: The Supreme Court in the Governmental Process.* Allyn & Bacon 6th ed. 1983 pap. $13.30. One of the best introductory texts.

Alexander, Herbert E. *Financing Politics: Money, Elections, and Political Reform.* Congressional Quarterly 3d ed. 1984 pap. $9.95. The central theme is to explore to what extent money influences political campaigns and elections.

Asher, Herbert. *Presidential Elections and American Politics: Voters, Candidates and Campaigns since 1952.* Dorsey 3d ed. 1984 pap. $15.95. Analyzes presidential elections from the point of view of both the voter and the candidates who are trying to win their support.

Bailey, Thomas A. *Presidential Saints and Sinners.* Macmillan (Free Press) 1981 $17.95

———. *The Pugnacious Presidents: White House Warriors on Parade.* Macmillan (Free

Press) 1980 $19.95. A novel history of the presidency, looking at the militant aspects of each president. Enjoyable and informative.

Bailyn, Bernard. *The Origins of American Politics*. Random (Vintage) 1970 pap. $4.95. Three essays, given in 1965 as the Charles Colver Lectures at Brown University.

Barnes, Catherine A. *Men of the Supreme Court: Profiles of the Justices*. Facts on File 1978 lib. bdg. $22.50. Biographies of 26 justices who served on the Court between 1945 and 1976.

Berger, Raoul. *Executive Privilege: A Constitutional Myth. Studies in Legal History* Harvard Univ. Pr. 1974 $22.50. Seeks to disprove "the Nixon administration's view that the propriety of the use of executive privilege is a question solely for the President" (*Christian Science Monitor*).

————. *Impeachment: The Constitutional Problems. Studies in Legal History* Harvard Univ. Pr. 1973 $18.50 pap. $7.95

Bickel, Alexander M. *The Supreme Court and the Idea of Progress*. Yale Univ. Pr. 1978 $20.00 pap. $7.95. Although other branches of the government receive more attention, the thesis is that the Court plays a key role in shaping the political environment.

Boller, Paul F. *Presidential Anecdotes*. Oxford 1981 $17.95; Penguin 1982 pap. $6.95. Enjoyable compendium that is delightful to read and informative at the same time.

————. *Presidential Campaigns*. Oxford 1984 $16.95. Intended for the general reader, the volume provides concise and factual accounts of each election campaign.

Broder, David. *Changing of the Guard: Power and Leadership in America*. Penguin 1981 pap. $7.95. Written by a well-known national commentator on politics, this book looks at the nature of political leadership at the national level.

Buckley, William F., Jr. *Up from Liberalism*. Stein & Day 1984 $16.95. An attack on liberalism by the publisher of the *National Review*.

Bunzel, John H. *Anti-Politics in America: Reflections on the Anti-Political Temper and Its Distortions of the Democratic Process*. Greenwood repr. of 1967 ed. 1979 lib. bdg. $24.75

Burnham, Walter Dean. *The Current Crisis in American Politics*. Oxford 1982 $29.95 pap. $10.95. Written by an eminent political scientist, this general interpretive essay is a good introduction to contemporary political issues.

Cigler, Allan J., and Burdell A. Loomis, eds. *Interest Group Politics*. Congressional Quarterly 1983 pap. $11.95. An in-depth look at what interest groups are, how they develop, and their role in politics.

Clubb, Jerome M., and others, eds. *Analyzing Electoral History: A Guide to the Study of American Voter Behavior*. Sage Focus Eds. 1981 $28.00 pap. $14.00. Attempts to present the methodology and findings that have formed the quantitative analysis of voting behavior.

Congressional Quarterly, Inc. *How Congress Works*. Congressional Quarterly 1983 pap. $9.75

Congressional Quarterly, Inc. *Origins and Development of Congress*. Congressional Quarterly 2d ed. 1982 pap. $9.50

Congressional Quarterly, Inc. *Powers of Congress*. Congressional Quarterly 2d ed. 1982 pap. $9.50. A readable survey that discusses the power of the purse, foreign affairs, commerce, investigations, confirmations, and other powers of Congress.

Congressional Quarterly, Inc. *The Supreme Court: Justice and the Law*. Congressional Quarterly 3d ed. 1983 pap. $9.75. A concise reference guide to the development of the court—its major decisions and most influential justices.

Congressional Quarterly, Inc. *The Washington Lobby.* Congressional Quarterly 4th ed. 1982 pap. $9.75

Corwin, Edward S. *The President: Office and Powers.* Ed. by Randall W. Bland and others, New York Univ. Pr. 5th ed. 1984 $40.00 pap. $20.00. One of the best general texts on the presidency, focusing on its institutional powers and responsibilities.

Edwards, George C. *Presidential Influence in Congress.* W. H. Freeman text ed. 1980 $21.95 pap. $11.95. Examines the role of the president as chief legislator and as a party leader.

Edwards, George C., and Stephen J. Wayne, eds. *Studying the Presidency.* Univ. of Tennessee Pr. text ed. 1983 $19.95 pap. $9.95. Discusses the major approaches and methodologies used in researching the presidency.

Fenno, Richard F. *Home Style: House Members in Their Districts.* Little, Brown text ed. 1978 pap. $10.95. This award-winning book looks at the life and work of congressmen and congresswomen in their districts. An entertaining and informative look at how they work and relate to their constituents.

Goldenberg, Edie, and Michael Traugott. *Campaigning for Congress.* Congressional Quarterly 1984 pap. $9.95. Examines all aspects of campaigns, including their development, the distribution of resources, communications with the public, and their impact on the electoral process.

Goldman, Ralph M. *Search for Consensus: The Story of the Democratic Party.* Temple Univ. Pr. 1979 $34.95. Covers intraparty struggles, the rise and fall of leaders, and its grass-roots organization.

Graber, Doris A. *Mass Media and American Politics.* Congressional Quarterly 2d ed. 1984 pap. $8.95. Analyzes the impact of the media on campaigning, public policy, voting, and politics in general.

Green, Mark J. *The Other Government: The Unseen Power of Washington Lawyers.* Norton Lib. new ed. 1978 $3.45. "In this book, Mark Green, a very literate lawyer and, in the past, an exceptionally valuable man on the Washington scene, examines two of the major firms of lawyer-lobbyists—Covington and Burling, and another somewhat more recent arrival on the scene, Wilmer, Cutler, and Pickering" (*N.Y. Times Bk. Review*).

Green, Mark J., and Michael Waldman. *Who Runs Congress?* Dell 4th ed. 1984 pap. $3.95. Intended for the general reader, this is an extremely lively and critical look at how Congress works.

Hargrove, Erwin C. *The Power of the Modern Presidency.* Temple Univ. Pr. 1975 $24.95. "Full-scale judgment of the contemporary presidency as it stands in the light of mid-twentieth century developments" (*Booklist*).

Hargrove, Erwin C., and Michael Nelson. *Presidents, Politics, and Policy.* Johns Hopkins Univ. Pr. text ed. 1984 $25.00. Emphasizes the role of the presidency in domestic policymaking and legislation.

Hess, Stephen. *The Presidential Campaign: The Leadership Selection Process after Watergate.* Brookings rev. ed. 1978 pap. $5.95. The author "presents a concise, fairly comprehensive account of the role of the campaign in the Presidential selection process" (*LJ*).

Hinckley, Barbara. *Stability and Change in Congress.* Harper 3d ed. 1983 pap. $13.50. Examines the changes and reforms that have altered and shaped Congress since World War II.

Hofstadter, Richard. *The American Political Tradition: And the Men Who Made It.* Knopf 2d ed. 1973 $15.50. Biographical studies of the principal formers of American political thought. (See Hofstadter's main listing in this chapter.)

Horowitz, David. *The Fate of Midas and Other Essays.* Ramparts Pr. 1973 $7.95 pap.
    $4.95
Jackson, John E. *Constituencies and Leaders in Congress: Their Effects on Senate Vot-
    ing Behavior.* Harvard Univ. Pr. text ed. 1974 $15.00. "A sophisticated statistical
    model of the important influences upon individual U.S. Senators' voting" (*LJ*).
Jeffreys-Jones, Rhodri, and Bruce Collins, eds. *The Growth of Federal Power in Ameri-
    can History.* Columbia Univ. Pr. 1983 $16.00; Northern Illinois Univ. Pr. 1983
    $22.50. This collection of essays mainly by British historians examines whether
    the growth in federal power was a constant feature of the U.S. tradition or a
    more recent departure from the past.
Jones, Charles O. *United States Congress: People, Place and Policy.* Dorsey 1982
    $21.95. Focuses on both the institutional and outside activities of members of
    Congress.
Keefe, William J. *Congress and the American People.* Prentice-Hall 2d ed. 1984 pap.
    $12.95. A general text.
Kennedy, John F. *Profiles in Courage.* 1956. Harper 1983 pap. $2.95. The late presi-
    dent's study of U.S. statesmen who risked their political lives for a principle.
Ketcham, Ralph P. *Presidents above Party: The First American Presidency, 1789–1829.*
    Univ. of North Carolina Pr. 1984 $24.95. This thought-provoking work argues
    that the early presidents sought to create a political system in which the chief
    executive was above party politics.
Koenig, Louis W. *The Chief Executive.* Harcourt text ed. 4th ed. 1981 pap. $13.95.
    One of the standard overviews.
Ladd, Everett C., Jr. *Where Have All the Voters Gone? The Fracturing of America's Po-
    litical Parties.* Norton text ed. 2d ed. 1982 pap. $4.95. Explores the relationship
    between the party system and party identification and voting.
Leuchtenburg, William E. *In the Shadow of FDR: From Harry Truman to Ronald Rea-
    gan.* Cornell Univ. Pr. 1983 $19.95. This original and absorbing study traces the
    influence FDR has had on the eight presidents who followed him. This unique
    historiographical work is an important contribution to modern political history.
Lurie, Leonard. *Party Politics: Why We Have Poor Presidents.* Stein & Day 1980
    $12.95 1982 pap. $8.95. Because of the decline of presidential leadership and the
    problems inherent in party politics, the author argues that the party system
    should be replaced with a no-party system.
McCarthy, Mary. *The Mask of State: Watergate Portraits.* Harcourt 1975 pap. $2.65.
    McCarthy provides "descriptions of the chief Watergate characters, based upon
    her immediate personal reactions as the hearings unfolded" (*LJ*).
McCormick, Richard P. *The Presidential Game: The Origins of American Presidential
    Politics.* Oxford 1982 $22.50. Analyzes the presidential selection process, depict-
    ing the evolution of the convention and electoral system.
McKay, Robert B. *Reapportionment: The Law and Politics of Equal Representation.*
    Fwd. by August Heckscher, Kraus repr. of 1965 ed. $8.00
Morgenthau, Hans J. *The Purpose of American Politics.* Univ. Pr. of America 1983
    pap. $13.25. Instead of looking at the institutions of U.S. politics, this work
    takes a more theoretical approach to politics in general.
Nelson, Michael, ed. *The Presidency and the Political System.* Congressional Quarterly
    1984 pap. $13.95. Designed to analyze the office in the context of contemporary
    constitutional and political issues.
Oleszek, Walter J. *Congressional Procedures and the Policy Process. Politics and Public
    Policy Ser.* Congressional Quarterly text ed. 2d ed. 1984 pap. $10.25. Describes

the rules, procedures, and organization of both houses of Congress and includes an easy-to-understand presentation of the budgetary process.

Pessen, Edward. *The Log Cabin Myth: The Social Backgrounds of the Presidents.* Yale Univ. Pr. 1984 $16.95. Attempts to destroy the myth that presidents have risen from humble origins. An important study of elites.

Petersen, Svend. *A Statistical History of the American Presidential Elections: With Supplementary Tables Covering 1968 to 1980.* Intro. by Louis Filler, Greenwood repr. of 1963 ed. 1981 lib. bdg. $23.50. "Like most statistical histories, these columnar tabulations are dry as dust until actually needed; then they become invaluable. Nowhere else in a single source can one find the answer to practically any question on Presidential elections. . . . Convenient, indispensable aid for political leaders, journalists, students, historians—and all libraries" (*LJ*).

Pfeffer, Leo. *This Honorable Court: A History of the United States Supreme Court.* Octagon repr. of 1965 ed. 1978 lib. bdg. $29.00. An ideological history of the Court as a group exerting liberal or conservative influence, as the pendulum swung.

Pious, Richard M. *The American Presidency.* Basic Bks. 1979 $19.50 pap. $9.95. A well-balanced narrative of all the dimensions of a president, including the roles of legislator, diplomat, and opinion leader.

Polsby, Nelson W., and Aaron Wildavsky, eds. *Presidential Elections: Strategies of American Electoral Politics.* Scribner 6th ed. 1984 $15.95. Includes chapters on every aspect of presidential elections, including financing to voting behavior.

Price, David E. *Bringing Back the Parties.* Congressional Quarterly 1984 pap. $11.95. Examines the historical and current status of the two-party system and its role in the future.

Redford, Emmette S., and Marlan Blissett. *Organizing the Executive Branch: The Johnson Presidency.* Univ. of Chicago Pr. 1981 lib. bdg. $21.00. Examines how organizational change and management style are related to the power and policy outcomes of decision making.

Ripley, Randall B. *Congress: Process and Policy.* Norton text ed. 3d ed. 1983 $18.95. Covers both the role of Congress in the context of the entire political system and the internal workings of that body.

Rossiter, Clinton L. *Conservatism in America: The Thankless Persuasion.* Greenwood repr. of 1962 ed. 2d ed. rev. 1981 lib. bdg. $27.50; Harvard Univ. Pr. 1982 pap. $7.95

Rubin, Richard L. *Press, Party, and Presidency.* Norton text ed. 1981 pap. $6.95 1982 $18.95. Probing study.

Schlesinger, Arthur M., Jr., gen. ed. *History of U.S. Political Parties.* Chelsea House 4 vols. 1981 pap. $75.00. (See Schlesinger's main listing in this chapter.)

Schwartz, Bernard. *Super Chief: Earl Warren and His Supreme Court: A Judicial Biography.* New York Univ. Pr. 1983 $29.95 1984 pap. $14.95. The definitive biography of one of the most famous chief justices.

Silbey, Joel H., Allan G. Bogue, and William J. Flanigan. *The History of American Electoral Behavior. Quantitative Studies in History* Princeton Univ. Pr. text ed. 1978 $41.00 pap. $14.50. Intended to show how quantitative research has affected and changed the study of U.S. electoral history.

Sindler, Allan P. *American Politics and Public Policy: Seven Case Studies.* Congressional Quarterly 1982 pap. $9.95. Discusses the formation of public policy covering all the major institutions of U.S. politics.

Smith, Steven S., and Christopher J. Deering. *Committees in Congress.* Congressional

Quarterly 1984 pap. $9.95. Provides a thorough understanding of the role of committees, their operations and crucial place in the legislative process.

Sorensen, Theodore C. *Watchmen in the Night: Presidential Accountability after Watergate.* MIT 1975 $22.00 pap. $5.95. "Sorensen's solution [to the problem of presidential power] is to preserve a constitutionally strong Presidency while urging Congress, the courts, and the people to hold the President more accountable" (*LJ*).

Vaughan, Robert G. *The Spoiled System: A Call for Civil Service Reform.* Ctr. Responsive Law 1975 $12.95. This book "presents 53 detailed remedies on such issues as discipline, appeals, and equal employment" (*LJ*).

Vogler, David. *The Politics of Congress.* Allyn & Bacon 4th ed. 1983 pap. $13.95. Discusses representation, parties, committees, and the role of rules and norms in Congress.

Wasby, Stephen L. *The Supreme Court in the Federal Judicial System.* Holt 2d ed. 1984 pap. $14.95. A basic text that explains the role of the Supreme Court and the various federal courts.

Wayne, Stephen J. *The Road to the White House: The Politics of Presidential Elections.* St. Martin's 2d ed. 1984 $13.95 text ed. pap. $8.95. While this is an analysis of elections, the book also extensively covers the primary and convention systems as well as campaigning.

Woodward, Bob, and Scott Armstrong. *The Brethren.* Avon 1980 pap. $3.50. Written in a journalistic style, this is a critical look inside the Burger Court.

Woodward, C. Vann, comp. *Responses of the Presidents to Charges of Misconduct.* Delacorte 1974 o.p. "At the request of the Impeachment Inquiry Staff of the House Committee on the Judiciary, Woodward and 14 other historians prepared this 'factual account without evaluation' for the staff's use in studying grounds for impeachment of Richard Nixon" (*Booklist*). (See Woodward's main listing in this chapter.)

DIPLOMACY AND FOREIGN RELATIONS

A good series is the *American Foreign Policy Library*, coedited by Crane Brinton and Lincoln Gordon. The question of the Cold War has been treated in general here as has the Vietnam War. Books on the foreign policy of specific historical eras can be found in the previous chronological listings. For the most part, this section includes material of a more general nature, i.e., overviews of foreign affairs and military histories.

Abrahamson, James L. *America Arms for a New Century: The Making of a Great Military Power.* Macmillan (Free Press) 1981 $19.95. A probing study of the military's efforts between 1880 and 1920 to build a modern and progressive military establishment.

Ambrose, Stephen E. *Rise to Globalism: 1938–1970.* Penguin 3d ed. 1983 pap. $5.95

Bailey, Thomas A. *The Art of Diplomacy: The American Experience.* Irvington 1968 $26.50 pap. $11.95

———. *A Diplomatic History of the American People.* Prentice-Hall 10th ed. 1980 $31.95. A classic in its field.

Barnet, Richard J. *Intervention and Revolution: The United States in the Third World.* New Amer. Lib. 1969 pap. $6.95. "A founder and co-director of the Institute for Policy Studies has written a calm, dispassionate book, perceptive and truthful, that quietly demolishes the basis of most American foreign policy since the war" (*Nation*).

————. *The Roots of War: The Men and Institutions behind U.S. Foreign Policy.* Penguin 1973 pap. $6.95

Brown, Seyom. *The Crisis of Power: An Interpretation of United States Foreign Policy during the Kissinger Years.* Columbia Univ. Pr. 1979 $16.00. Covering the Nixon and Ford administrations, this book looks at the policies and impact Kissinger had on American foreign policy.

Clarkfield, Gerard H., and William M. Wiecek. *Nuclear America: Military and Civilian Nuclear Power in the United States, 1940–1980.* Harper 1984 $19.95. An important contribution to a contemporary issue.

Clough, Ralph N. *East Asia and U.S. Security.* Brookings 1975 pap. $8.95. "Former diplomat Clough systematically and perceptively analyzes current U.S. interests and argues for a continuation of detente with Mainland China and Russia" (*LJ*).

Combs, Jerald A. *American Diplomatic History: Two Centuries of Changing Interpretations.* Univ. of California Pr. 1982 $37.50. This bibliographic essay examines the significant foreign policy decisions that have influenced the writing of diplomatic history.

Crabb, Cecil V., Jr. *The Doctrines of American Foreign Policy: Their Meaning, Role, and Future.* Louisiana State Univ. Pr. $35.00 pap. $14.95. A careful analysis of the origin of U.S. foreign policy, assessing the successes and failures.

Crabb, Cecil V., Jr., and Pat M. Holt. *Invitation to Struggle: Congress, the President and Foreign Policy. Politics and Public Policy Ser.* Congressional Quarterly 2d ed. 1984 pap. $8.75. Looks at who formulates and implements foreign policy. Uses several case studies to highlight the roles of the various participants.

Dallek, Robert. *The American Style of Foreign Policy: Cultural Politics and Foreign Affairs.* Knopf 1983 $16.95. Based on the premise that domestic concerns play a major part in determining foreign policy.

De Conde, Alexander. *A History of American Foreign Policy.* Scribner 2 vols. 3d ed. 1978 pap. ea. $15.95. Intelligent and fair, this readable survey deals with U.S. diplomatic history from the Monroe Doctrine to Yalta.

De Novo, John A. *American Interests and Policies in the Middle East, 1900–1939.* Univ. of Minnesota Pr. 1963 $19.50

Divine, Robert A. *American Foreign Policy: A Documentary History.* New Amer. Lib. 1950 $3.95

————. *Second Chance: The Triumph of Internationalism in America during World War II.* Atheneum 1967 pap. $3.45. "A first-rate history of the international organization movement and its effect upon American foreign policy before and during World War II" (*LJ*).

Dulles, Foster R. *American Policy toward Communist China, 1949–1969.* Harlan Davidson 1972 pap. $12.95. "Written in masterful prose Dulles' book should command the attention of scholars and laymen alike" (*Choice*).

Gaddis, John L. *Strategies of Containment: A Critical Appraisal of Postwar American National Security Policy.* Oxford 1982 $29.95 pap. $10.95

Gardner, Lloyd C. *A Convenant with Power: America and World Order from Wilson to Reagan.* Oxford 1984 $22.95. A general survey.

Halberstam, David. *The Best and the Brightest.* Fawcett 1973 pap. $3.50; Penguin 1983 pap. $9.95; Random 1972 $15.00. "This is a study of the decision-making process that got us into the Vietnam War and kept us there, a study of the nature of political power that concentrates on the men who made the critical decisions, the assumptions they brought to their various jobs, and the society that produced these assumptions" (*Newsweek*).

Halle, Louis J. *The Cold War as History.* Harper 1971 pap. $8.50. "The book is founded, diffidently but firmly, on the balance of power as the inescapable law of life, inside nations and among them" (*Nation*).

————. *Dream and Reality: Aspects of American Foreign Policy.* Greenwood repr. of 1959 ed. 1973 $17.50

Hassler, Warren W., Jr. *With Shield and Sword: American Military Affairs, Colonial Times to the Present.* Iowa State Univ. Pr. text ed. 1982 $29.50. A comprehensive survey of the role of the military forces and leaders in U.S. history.

Karsten, Peter, ed. *The Military in America: From the Colonial Era to the Present.* Macmillan (Free Press) text ed. 1980 pap. $14.95. A compendium of materials drawn from books, articles, documents, and other sources focusing on the relationship between the military and society. Intended to demonstrate how military history has changed during the last century and a half.

Kegley, Charles W., Jr., and Eugene R. Wittkopf. *American Foreign Policy: Patterns and Process.* St. Martin's 2d ed. 1982 $19.95 text ed. pap. $15.95. A text on U.S. foreign policy decision making, providing an overview of the entire process.

Kennan, George F. *The Cloud of Danger: Current Realities of American Foreign Policy.* Atlantic Monthly Pr. 1977 $10.95. An extended interpretive essay on the direction of U.S. foreign affairs by a prominent critic of foreign policy.

Kissinger, Henry A. *American Foreign Policy.* Norton 3d ed. 1977 pap. $9.95. An insightful view of U.S. foreign policy by a former secretary of state that is especially interesting for its analysis of nuclear policy.

Kutler, Stanley I. *The American Inquisition: Justice and Injustice in the Cold War.* Amer. Century Ser. Hill & Wang 1982 $16.50 pap. $6.95. This readable series of essays approaches the subject of law in the Cold War by relating the encounters between persecutors and victims in the courts and bureaucracy. An original and fresh approach to the period.

Leckie, Robert. *The Wars of America.* Intro. by Richard B. Morris, Harper rev. ed. 1981 $29.95. "A splendidly dramatic and fascinating panoramic narrative, and probably as good a popular access to the wars of America and the men who led them and fought them, all in a single volume" (*N.Y. Times*).

Leonard, Thomas C. *Above the Battles: War-Making in America from Appomattox to Versailles.* Oxford 1978 $19.95. Attempts to show how soldiers, industrialists, and politicians sought to glorify war instead of presenting it as it really is.

Lomperis, Timothy J. *The War Everyone Lost—and Won: America's Intervention in Viet Nam's Twin Struggles.* Louisiana State Univ. Pr. text ed. 1984 $22.50. Contends that the key struggle was over the notion of national legitimacy between the Communists and the South Vietnamese government.

May, Ernest R. *Imperial Democracy: The Emergence of America as a Great Power.* Harper 1973 pap. $6.95. "This careful study by Professor May of Harvard traces the interplay of diplomacy, politics and jingoism that powered our imperial adventure . . . it is a masterful synthesis of diplomatic and political history which will serve scholars and informed general readers as the definitive story. . . . Highly recommended for all but small libraries" (*LJ*).

Millett, Allan R. *Semper Fidelis: The History of the United States Marine Corps.* Macmillan Wars of the U.S. Ser. Macmillan (Free Press) 1980 $29.95 1980 pap. $13.95. An institutional history that focuses on the corps as a complex organization.

Millett, Allan, R., and Peter Maslowski. *For the Common Defense: A Military History* of the United States. Macmillan (Free Press) 1984 $24.95. A straightforward and informative history of the military.

Morgenthau, Hans J. *Politics among Nations: The Struggle for Power and Peace.* Knopf text ed. 6th rev. 1985 $25.00

Parker, Thomas. *America's Foreign Policy, 1945–1976: Its Creators and Critics.* Facts on File 1980 $22.50. This biographical dictionary contains extensive articles on the individuals—both official and unofficial—who shaped U.S. foreign policy between 1945 and 1976.

Salisbury, Harrison E., ed. *Vietnam Reconsidered: Lessons from War.* Harper 1984 pap. $16.83 pap. $6.68. Intended to reexamine the whole Vietnam experience. Includes contributions from policymakers, soldiers, historians, journalists, and some Vietnamese.

Schulzinger, Robert D. *American Diplomacy in the Twentieth Century.* Oxford 1984 $22.50 pap. $12.95. A straightforward survey of U.S. diplomacy since 1898 that is a good introduction for the general reader.

Simpson, Smith. *Resources and Needs of American Diplomacy.* Ed. by Thorsten Sellin, Amer. Academy of Political and Social Science 1968 $15.00 pap. $9.95

Stein, Arthur A. *The Nation at War.* Johns Hopkins Univ. Pr. text ed. 1981 $14.00. Although written primarily for foreign policymakers, this short volume analyzes U.S. wars from their point of view of their costs and benefits. A provocative and stimulating work.

Stoessinger, John G. *Crusaders and Pragmatists: Movers of Modern American Foreign Policy.* Norton text ed. 1979 $19.95 pap. $4.95. This study of decision makers in U.S. foreign policy classifies them as either idealists or politicians who were realists.

Troy, Thomas F. *Donovan and the CIA: A History of the Establishment of the Central Intelligence Agency.* Univ. Publications of Amer. 1981 lib. bdg. $29.50. This massive institutional history gives a comprehensive account of the origins and growth of the CIA.

Tucker, Robert W. *The Radical Left and American Foreign Policy. Studies in International Affairs* Johns Hopkins Univ. Pr. 1971 pap. $3.95. Probably the best critique of the revisionist school.

Widenor, William C. *Henry Cabot Lodge and the Search for an American Foreign Policy.* Univ. of California Pr. 1980 $25.50 1983 pap. $8.95. The best biography of Lodge to date. Gives a complete picture of Lodge, including both his intellectual and political sides.

Williams, T. Harry. *A History of American Wars from 1745 to 1918.* Knopf 1981 $20.00. Informative and popular history that provides a complete overview through World War I.

Williams, William Appleman. *American-Russian Relations, 1781–1947.* Octagon 1971 lib. bdg. $27.50

———. *The Tragedy of American Diplomacy.* Dell (Delta Bks.) 2d ed. rev. 1972 pap. $7.95

Yergin, Daniel. *Shattered Peace: The Origins of the Cold War and the National Security State.* Houghton Mifflin text ed. 1977 $15.00 pap. $12.95. Based on recent government documents and sources, this is a vivid history of the Cold War and the major personalities involved.

ADAMS, HENRY (BROOKS). 1838–1918

Henry Adams was the grandson of John Quincy Adams, the sixth president of the United States. Adams's history was disappointing to historians, as they had looked to him to explain his ancestor's change from Federalism to Republicanism. Instead, he confined himself mainly to the political and constitutional history of two presidential administrations. His history is a brilliant one, illuminating politics and politicians, issues and struggles. (See also Chapter 17 in Volume 1.)

BOOKS BY HENRY ADAMS

The United States in 1800. Cornell Univ. Pr. 1855 pap. $4.95. Reprint of the first six chapters of the *History of the United States.*

John Randolph of Roanoke. AMS Pr. repr. of 1882 ed. $27.00; ed. by John T. Morse, Jr., *Amer. Statesman Ser.* Peter Smith $10.25

Democracy: An American Novel. Crown 1982 pap. $4.95; New Amer. Lib. 1983 pap. $3.50; Scholarly repr. of 1883 ed. 1976 $36.00

History of the United States during the Administrations of Jefferson and Madison. 1889–91. Gordon 9 vols. 1980 $995.00; ed. by Ernest Samuels, Univ. of Chicago Pr. abr. ed. 1979 pap. $14.00

Historical Essays. Adler's repr. of 1891 ed. $39.50

Tahiti: Memoirs of Arii Taimai. Ed. by Robert E. Spiller, Parnassus repr. of 1901 ed. 1968 $20.00; Scholars' Facsimiles repr. of 1901 ed. 1976 $35.00

Mont-Saint-Michel and Chartres. 1904. Larkin 1982 $25.00

(ed.). *Documents Relating to New England Federalism, 1800–1815.* Burt Franklin repr. of 1905 ed. 1964 $24.50

The Education of Henry Adams. 1906. Ed. by Ernest Samuels, Houghton Mifflin (Riv. Eds.) 1973 pap. $7.95

The Life of George Cabot Lodge. Scholars' Facsimiles repr. of 1911 ed. 1978 $30.00

Degradation of the Democratic Dogma. 1919. Intro. by Brooks Adams, Peter Smith $11.00

Letters to a Niece and Prayer to the Virgin of Chartres. Ed. by Mabel La Farge, Scholarly repr. of 1920 ed. 1970 $17.00

A Catalogue of the Books of John Quincy Adams Deposited in the Boston Athenaeum. Boston Athenaeum 1938 $25.00

Formative Years. Ed. by Herbert Agar, Greenwood 2 vols. repr. of 1947 ed. 1974 lib. bdg. $43.50

The Great Secession Winter of 1860–61 and Thirteen Other Essays. Ed. by George Hochfield, A. S. Barnes 1962 o.p.

Esther. Ed. by Robert E. Spiller, Scholars' Facsimiles repr. 1976 $39.00

Novels, Mont-Saint-Michel, the Education. Ed. by Ernest Samuels and Jayne N. Samuels, Lib. of Amer. 1983 $27.50

The Letters of Henry Adams. Ed. by J. C. Levenson and Ernest Samuels, Harvard Univ. Pr. 3 vols. text ed. 1983 $110.00

BOOKS ABOUT HENRY ADAMS

Adams, James Truslow. *Henry Adams.* Scholarly repr. of 1933 ed. 1970 $10.50

Auchincloss, Louis. *Henry Adams.* Pamphlets on Amer. Writers Ser. Univ. of Minnesota Pr. 1971 pap. $1.25

Baym, M. I. *French Education of Henry Adams.* Kraus repr. of 1951 ed. $22.00

Blackmur, R. P., ed. *Henry Adams.* Harcourt 1980 $19.95

Chalfant, Edward. *His First Life, 1838–1862.* Vol. 1 in *Both Sides of the Ocean: A Biography of Henry Adams.* Shoe String (Archon) 1982 $32.50

Conder, John. *Formula of His Own: Henry Adams' Literary Experiment.* Univ. of Chicago Pr. 1970 $8.50

Contosta, David R. *Henry Adams and the American Experiment. Lib. of Amer. Biography* Little, Brown 1980 $10.95 pap. $5.95

Harbert, Earl N. *Critical Essays on Henry Adams. Critical Essays on Amer. Lit. Ser.* G. K. Hall (Twayne) 1981 $26.00

Hume, Robert A. *Runaway Star: An Appreciation of Henry Adams.* Greenwood repr. of 1951 ed. 1973 $15.00

Jordy, William H. *Henry Adams: Scientific Historian.* 1952. Shoe String 1970 $19.50

Kaledin, Eugenia. *The Education of Mrs. Henry Adams. Amer. Civilization Ser.* Temple Univ. Pr. 1982 $29.95

Kaplan, Harold. *Power and Order: Henry Adams and the Naturalist Tradition in American Fiction.* Univ. of Chicago Pr. 1981 lib. bdg. $15.00

Levenson, J. C. *The Mind and the Art of Henry Adams.* Stanford Univ. Pr. 1957 $30.00

Lyon, Melvin. *Symbol and Idea in Henry Adams.* Univ. of Nebraska Pr. 1970 $23.95

Mane, Robert. *Henry Adams on the Road to Chartres.* Harvard Univ. Pr. 1971 $18.50

Nagel, Paul C. *Descent from Glory: Four Generations of the John Adams Family.* Oxford 1983 pap. $8.95

Rowe, John C. *Henry Adams and Henry James: The Emergence of a Modern Consciousness.* Cornell Univ. Pr. 1976 $24.50

Samuels, Ernest. *Henry Adams.* Harvard Univ. Pr. 3 vols. vol. 1 (1948) $20.00 vol. 2 (1958) $25.00 vol. 3 (1964) $32.50. Volume 2 won the Bancroft Prize in 1959 as well as the Francis Parkman Prize of the Society of American Historians. "[This is] one of the great biographical achievements of our time . . . a joy to every intelligent reader" (Edward Wagenknecht, *Chicago Tribune*).

Shepherd, Jack. *The Adams Chronicles (1750–1900): Four Generations of Greatness.* Little, Brown 1976 $17.50

Stevenson, Elizabeth. *Henry Adams: A Biography.* Octagon 1977 lib. bdg. $31.50

Tehan, Arline B. *Henry Adams in Love: The Pursuit of Elizabeth Sherman Cameron.* Universe 1983 $20.00

ADAMS, JAMES TRUSLOW. 1878–1949

James Truslow Adams was not a member of the famous Adams family, on which he was the greatest authority. He was descended from Francis Adams, who came to Maryland in 1658 and later settled in Virginia. His first volume, *The Founding of New England* (1921), won the Pulitzer Prize in history, although its frank appraisal of the founders became controversial. *The Epic of America* (1931) is a compressed account of the American people from the early days of the Spanish explorers, an excellent single-volume history. Adams edited *The Dictionary of American History* (o.p.), *The Atlas of American History* (o.p.), and the *Album of American History*.

BOOKS BY JAMES TRUSLOW ADAMS

The Founding of New England. 1921. Little, Brown o.p.

Revolutionary New England. 1923. Little, Brown 1963 o.p.

The History of New England. 1923. Scholarly 1971 o.p.

Revolutionary New England, 1691–1776. Cooper Square Pr. repr. of 1923 ed. $27.50; Telegraph Bks. 1981 lib. bdg. $30.00

New England in the Republic. 1926. Scholarly $39.00

Provincial Society: 1690–1763. 1927. Ed. by Arthur M. Schlesinger and Dixon R. Fox, Macmillan o.p.
Our Business Civilization: Some Aspects of Our American Culture. AMS Pr. repr. of 1929 ed. $17.50
The Adams Family. Darby repr. of 1930 ed. lib. bdg. $25.00; Greenwood repr. of 1930 ed. 1974 lib. bdg. $20.50
The Epic of America. Greenwood repr. of 1931 ed. 1980 $32.50
Henry Adams. Scholarly repr. of 1933 ed. 1970 $10.50
Death in the Dark. Folcroft repr. of 1941 ed. 1977 lib. bdg. $20.00
The American: The Making of a New Man. AMS Pr. repr. of 1943 ed. $21.00
Album of American History. 1944–48. Scribner 3 vols. rev. ed. 1969 $225.00
Frontiers of American Culture: A Study of Adult Education in a Democracy. AMS Pr. repr. of 1944 ed. $20.00

AGAR, HERBERT (SEBASTIAN). 1897–1980

For many years editor of the Louisville *Courier-Journal,* Agar called himself a "creative conservative." His "harsh dissection of the American Presidency," *The People's Choice* (1933), won the Pulitzer Prize in history. He was a founder in 1941 and the first president of Freedom House, an organization for the promotion of peace and international cooperation. *The Saving Remnant: An Account of Jewish Survival* (1960) reflected his deep concern with the Nazi aggression.

BOOKS BY AGAR

The People's Choice. Berg repr. of 1933 ed. 1968 lib. bdg. $15.95
Who Owns America? A New Declaration of Independence. Essay Index Repr. Ser. 1936. Univ. Pr. of America text ed. 1983 pap. $13.50
The Price of Union. Houghton Mifflin 1950 o.p.
The Price of Power: America since 1945. History of Amer. Civilization Ser. Univ. of Chicago Pr. 1957 pap. $4.95
The Perils of Democracy. Background Ser. Dufour 1965 $7.95

BEARD, CHARLES A(USTIN). 1874–1948, and
MARY R. BEARD. 1876–1958

Charles A. Beard, a political scientist whose histories were always written from the economic point of view, was an authority on U.S. government and politics. *The Rise of American Civilization* (o.p.) treats politics, economics, war, imperialism, literature, art, music, religion, the sciences, the press, and woman's relation to social development. He described his collaboration with his wife on this book as "division of argument." Mary R. Beard wrote *Women as a Force in History, On Understanding Women,* and *The Force of Women in Japanese History.* The Beards' books are scholarly, well written, often witty, at times somewhat ponderous. Their *Basic History* is, the *New Yorker* commented, "perhaps, all in all, the best one-volume history that has ever been written about the United States."

BOOKS BY CHARLES A. BEARD

Introduction to English Historians. Research and Source Works Ser. Burt Franklin repr. of 1906 ed. 1968 $18.50

American City Government: A Survey of Newer Tendencies. Rise of Urban Amer. Ayer repr. of 1912 ed. 1970 $26.50

Contemporary American History, 1877–1913. Amer. History and Culture in the 19th-Century Ser. Associated Faculty Pr. repr. of 1914 ed. 1971 $29.50

An Economic Interpretation of the Constitution of the United States. 1913. Macmillan (Free Press) 1965 pap. $12.95

The Supreme Court and the Constitution. 1926. Ed. by A. F. Westin, Peter Smith o.p.

Industrial Revolution. Greenwood repr. of 1927 ed. $15.00

(ed.). *Whither Mankind. Essay Index Repr. Ser.* Ayer repr. of 1928 ed. $24.50; Greenwood repr. of 1934 ed. $18.50

(ed.). *America Faces the Future. Essay Index Repr. Ser.* Ayer repr. of 1932 ed. $25.50

(ed.). *Century of Progress. Essay Index Repr. Ser.* Ayer repr. of 1932 ed. $27.50

(and George H. Smith). *The Future Comes: A Study of the New Deal.* Greenwood repr. of 1933 ed. 1972 lib. bdg. $15.00

The Idea of National Interest: An Analytical Study in American Foreign Policy. Greenwood repr. of 1934 ed. 1977 lib. bdg. $39.25

The Nature of the Social Sciences: In Relation to Objectives of Instruction. Perspectives in Social Inquiry Ser. Ayer repr. of 1934 ed. 1974 $15.00

The Open Door at Home: A Trial Philosophy of National Interest. Greenwood repr. of 1934 ed. 1972 lib. bdg. $15.00

Devil Theory of War: An Inquiry into the Nature of History and the Possibility of Keeping out of War. Greenwood repr. of 1936 ed. 1968 lib. bdg. $15.00

The Republic: Conversations on Fundamentals. Greenwood repr. of 1943 ed. 1980 $32.50

Economic Basis of Politics. Essay Index Repr. Ser. Ayer 3d ed. rev. repr. of 1945 ed. $14.00

American Foreign Policy in the Making, 1932–1940: A Study in Responsibilities. Shoe String (Archon) repr. of 1946 ed. 1968 $27.50

President Roosevelt and the Coming of the War, 1941: A Study in Appearances and Realities. 1948. Shoe String 1968 o.p.

Written History as an Act of Faith. Texas Western Pr. 1960 pap. $3.00

BOOKS BY MARY R. BEARD

Short History of the American Labor Movement. Greenwood repr. of 1925 ed. 1968 o.p.

(ed.). *America through Women's Eyes.* Greenwood repr. of 1933 ed. 1968 o.p.

BOOKS BY CHARLES A. BEARD AND MARY R. BEARD

America in Midpassage. 1939. *Rise of Amer. Civilization Ser.* Peter Smith 1966 $12.50

The American Spirit: A Study of the Idea of Civilization in the United States. 1942. Macmillan (Collier Bks.) o.p.

The Beards' New Basic History of the United States. 1944. Doubleday rev. ed. 1960 o.p. "New" was added to the title of the revised edition by William Beard.

BOOKS ABOUT CHARLES A. BEARD

Benson, Lee. *Turner and Beard: American Historical Writing Reconsidered.* Greenwood repr. of 1960 ed. 1980 $22.50

Borning, Bernard C. *The Political and Social Thought of Charles A. Beard.* Greenwood repr. of 1962 ed. 1984 $45.00

Brown, Robert E. *Charles Beard and the Constitution: A Critical Analysis of "An Economic Interpretation of the Constitution."* Greenwood repr. of 1956 ed. 1979 $22.50. "It is difficult, if not impossible, to refute the specific points made by the author of this painstaking and admirable study. On the other hand, many readers will undoubtedly have some reservations concerning Brown's sweeping indictment" (*Political Science Quarterly*).

Hofstadter, Richard. *The Progressive Historians: Turner, Beard, Parrington.* Univ. of Chicago Pr. 1979 pap. $7.95

Kennedy, Thomas C. *Charles A. Beard and the American Foreign Policy.* Univ. Pr. of Florida 1975 $9.50

Nore, Ellen. *Charles A. Beard: An Intellectual Biography.* Southern Illinois Univ. Pr. 1983 $24.95

Skotheim, Robert Allen. *American Intellectual Histories and Historians.* Greenwood repr. of 1966 ed. 1978 $26.00

Strout, Cushing. *The Pragmatic Revolt in American History: Carl Becker and Charles Beard.* Greenwood repr. of 1966 ed. 1980 $22.50

BECKER, CARL L. 1873–1945

Few U.S. historians have written as well as Becker, Cornell's famous professor of modern European history. *The Heavenly City of the Eighteenth-Century Philosophers* has become a classic, as has *The Heavenly City Revisited.* In *Detachment and the Writing of History,* Snyder has gathered Becker's little gems on historical writing, education, and democracy from hitherto inaccessible sources. Freedom and democracy were Becker's themes as a leading historian and distinguished historical essayist.

BOOKS BY BECKER

Detachment and the Writing of History: Essays and Letters of Carl L. Becker. Ed. by Phil L. Snyder, Greenwood repr. of 1958 ed. 1972 $15.00

What Is the Good of History? Selected Letters, 1900–1945. Ed. by Michael Kammen, Cornell Univ. Pr. 1973 o.p.

A History of Political Parties in the Province of New York, 1760–1776. 1908. Univ. of Wisconsin Pr. 1960 pap. $7.95

The Beginnings of the American People. 1915. Cornell Univ. Pr. 1960 o.p.

The Eve of the Revolution: A Chronicle of the Breach with England. Yale Chronicles of Amer. U.S. Publishers Association $8.95

The Declaration of Independence: A Study in the History of Political Ideas. 1922. Random (Vintage) 1958 pap. $3.95

The Spirit of '76 and Other Essays. 1927. Irvington lib. bdg. $20.00

The Heavenly City of the Eighteenth-Century Philosophers. Storrs Lecture Ser. Yale Univ. Pr. 1932 pap. $5.95

How New Will the Better World Be? A Discussion of Post-War Reconstruction. Essay Index Repr. Ser. Ayer repr. of 1944 ed. $20.00

Freedom and Responsibility in the American Way of Life. Greenwood repr. of 1945 ed. 1980 $22.50

Progress and Power. AMS Pr. repr. of 1949 ed. $21.50

Safeguarding Civil Liberty Today. Peter Smith 1949 $10.25

Everyman His Own Historian. Quadrangle 1966 o.p.

BOOKS ABOUT BECKER

Rockwood, Raymond O., ed. *Carl Becker's Heavenly City Revisited.* Shoe String (Archon) repr. of 1958 ed. 1968 $17.50

Skotheim, Robert Allen. *American Intellectual Histories and Historians.* Greenwood
  repr. of 1966 ed. 1978 $26.00
Smith, Charlotte C. *Carl Becker: On History and the Climate of Opinion.* Southern Illinois Univ. Pr. 1973 pap. $2.65
Strout, Cushing. *The Pragmatic Revolt in American History: Carl Becker and Charles
  Beard.* Greenwood repr. of 1966 ed. 1980 $22.50
Wilkins, Charlotte W. *Carl Becker: A Biographical Study of American Intellectual History.* MIT 1961 pap. $4.95. "Professor Wilkins' book must be regarded as the de-
  finitive work on Becker, as a personality and as a historian by virtue of both ade-
  quate coverage and admirable discretion and wisdom in appraisal. It is difficult
  to discern how anything of vital significance could be added or any of the cogent
  generalizations about Becker and his work successfully cancelled" (*The Annals*).

BEMIS, SAMUEL FLAGG. 1891–1973

An outstanding authority on the history of U.S. foreign policy, Bemis was
Sterling Professor of Diplomatic History and Inter-American Relations at
Yale University for nearly 30 years. He was a two-time winner of the Pulit-
zer Prize in history for *Pinckney's Treaty* and for *John Quincy Adams.* He
served as advisory editor on the series *The American Secretaries of State and
Their Diplomacy.*

Born in Worcester, Massachusetts, Bemis received his Ph.D. from Harvard University. He had served as president of the American Historical Association.

BOOKS BY BEMIS

Jay's Treaty: A Study in Commerce and Diplomacy. 1923. Greenwood repr. of 1962 ed.
  1975 lib. bdg. $29.50. The first international treaty (with Great Britain, 1794) of
  Washington's presidency.
Pinckney's Treaty: America's Advantage from Europe's Distress, 1783–1800. 1926.
  Greenwood repr. of 1960 ed. 1973 $20.50
(ed.). *The American Secretaries of State and Their Diplomacy, 1776–1925.* 1927. Cooper Square Pr. 10 vols. in 5 repr. of 1928 ed. $175.00
*The Hussey-Cumberland Mission and American Independence: An Essay in the Diplo-
  macy of the American Revolution.* 1931. Peter Smith $10.25
The Diplomacy of the American Revolution. 1935. Greenwood repr. of 1957 ed. 1983
  $37.50
(and Grace Gardner Griffin). *Guide to the Diplomatic History of the United States,
  1775–1921.* 1935. Peter Smith 1959 o.p.
The Latin American Policy of the United States: An Historical Interpretation. 1943. Norton 1967 o.p.
John Quincy Adams. Greenwood repr. of 1949–56 ed. 1980–81 vol. 1 $49.50 vol. 2
  $55.00. With the second volume, "Bemis . . . completes his superb biography
  of America's sixth President. . . . The second volume opens with Adams' election in 1824. It portrays the stormy years of his administration, sees him go
  down to defeat before Andrew Jackson, and then describes his extraordinary
  post-Presidential career in the House of Representatives. The result is a noble
  picture of one of the noblest of Americans" (Arthur M. Schlesinger, Jr., *N.Y.
  Times*).
American Foreign Policy and the Blessings of Liberty, and Other Essays. Greenwood
  repr. of 1962 ed. 1975 $24.50

BOORSTIN, DANIEL J. 1914–

Boorstin is the author of more than a dozen scholarly works that have received numerous awards. In 1959 he received Columbia University's Bancroft Prize for *The Americans: The Colonial Experience*, the first volume of his trilogy, *The Americans*. In 1966 he received the Francis Parkman Award for Volume 2, *The Americans: The National Experience*, and in 1974 he received the Pulitzer Prize for the third volume, *The Americans: The Democratic Experience*. He has served as Professor of American History at the University of Paris, Cambridge University, and the University of Chicago. In 1969 he left the University of Chicago to assume the position of director of the National Museum of History and Technology of the Smithsonian Institution. In 1973 he became the senior historian of the Smithsonian. In November 1975 he resigned this position to become Librarian of Congress.

BOOKS BY BOORSTIN

The Mysterious Science of the Law. 1941 1958. Peter Smith $10.25

The Lost World of Thomas Jefferson. 1948. Beacon 1960 pap. $2.95; Peter Smith $13.75; Univ. of Chicago Pr. 1981 pap. $9.95

The Genius of American Politics. Univ. of Chicago Pr. 1953 $10.50; Univ. of Chicago Pr. (Phoenix Bks.) pap. $3.95

The Americans. Random 3 vols. 1958–73. ea. $20.00 set $60.00; Random (Vintage) 1958–74 vol. 1 $6.95 vol. 2 $7.95 vol 3 $8.95. "An excellent socio-history of the American community.... Highly organized, with a wealth of material never previously drawn from primary sources" (*LJ*). In Volume 2, Boorstin cites the dominance of our society by wealth and technology as the origin of illusions and delusions from which the United States must free itself to meet the future successfully. Volume 3 is concerned with the democratization of the national character during the past 100 years and the growth of technology.

America and the Image of Europe: Reflections on American Thought. 1960. Peter Smith $10.25

Image: A Guide to Pseudo-Events in America (Image of What Happened to the American Dream). 1962. Atheneum text ed. pap. 1971 $4.95; Peter Smith 1984 $13.75. "An effective phrase-coiner, Dr. Boorstin develops his theme of pseudo-events by compiling an inventory of commercialized folly" (*AHR*).

(ed.). *The American Primer.* New Amer. Lib. pap. $4.95; Univ. of Chicago Pr. 2 vols. 1969 $25.00

Sociology of the Absurd. Simon & Schuster 1970 o.p.

Decline of Radicalism: Reflections on America Today. Random (Vintage) 1969 $5.95

(ed.). *American Civilization: A Portrait from the Twentieth Century.* McGraw-Hill 1972 o.p.

(ed.). *Technology and Society.* Ayer 53 vols. repr. 1972 $1,502.00

Portraits from the Americans: The Democratic Experience. Random 1975 pap. $6.95

(and others). *We Americans. Story of Man Lib.* National Geographic Society 1975 $16.95

The Exploring Spirit: America and the World, Then and Now. Random 1976 $6.95

The Discoverers. Random 1983 $25.00; Random (Vintage) pap. $9.95

CATTON, (CHARLES) BRUCE. 1899–1978

Bruce Catton, "a journalist, turned historian," made the Civil War his own special bailiwick and proved himself a master in combining readability with marshaling an amazing number of facts. He was a founding editor of the *American Heritage* magazine from 1954 to 1959 and continued to serve as senior editor. His *A Stillness at Appomattox* won the National Book Award and the Pulitzer Prize in history in 1954. The *Centennial History* has been called "the finest type of popular yet factual historical writing" (*LJ*). In 1968 he was appointed an honorary consultant in American history by the Library of Congress for a three-year term. He received honorary degrees from some 20 universities.

BOOKS BY CATTON

War Lords of Washington. Greenwood repr. of 1948 ed. lib. bdg. $22.25

Mister Lincoln's Army. 1951. Doubleday 1960 $12.95

The Glory Road: The Bloody Route from Fredericksburg to Gettysburg. 1952. Doubleday 1962 $12.95

A Stillness at Appomattox. Doubleday 1953 $16.95; Washington Square Pr. 1970 pap. $3.95

U.S. Grant and the American Military Tradition. 1954 *Lib. of Amer. Biography* Little, Brown text ed. 1972 pap. $5.95. Grant as man, soldier, and president.

Banners at Shenandoah. Queens House repr. of 1955 ed. 1976 $15.95

This Hallowed Ground. Doubleday 1956 $13.95; Washington Square Pr. 1969 pap. $3.95. The story of the Union side of the Civil War.

(ed.). *American Heritage Book of Great Historic Places.* Simon & Schuster 1957 o.p.

America Goes to War: The Civil War and Its Meaning to Americans Today. 1958. Wesleyan Univ. Pr. pap. 1971 $8.95

(ed.). *American Heritage Book of the Revolution.* Simon & Schuster 1958 o.p.

(ed.). *American Heritage Picture History of the Civil War.* Doubleday 1960 $24.95

Grant Moves South. Little, Brown 1960 $19.95. Volume 2 in a three-volume biography of Grant begun by the late historian Lloyd Lewis. The first volume is entitled *Captain Sam Grant.*

The Army of the Potomac: A Trilogy. Doubleday 3 vols. 1962 $14.95

(and William B. Catton). *Two Roads to Sumter.* 1963. McGraw-Hill 1971 pap. $5.95

(and others). *Grant, Lee, Lincoln and the Radicals: Essays on Civil War Leadership.* Ed. by Grady McWhiney, Northwestern Univ. Pr. 1964 o.p.

Grant Takes Command. Little, Brown 1969 $18.95. Volume 3 in the biography goes to the end of the war.

Never Call Retreat. Centennial History of the Civil War Ser. Washington Square Pr. 1969 pap. $3.95

The Civil War. McGraw-Hill 1971 pap. $6.95

Coming Fury. Centennial History of the Civil War Ser. Washington Square Pr. 1972 pap. $3.95

Waiting for the Morning Train: An American Boyhood. Doubleday 1972 $12.95. Autobiographical.

Michigan. States and the Nation Ser. Norton 1976 $14.95 pap. $1.95

(and William B. Catton). *The Bold and Magnificent Dream: America's Founding Years, 1492–1815. Basic History of the U.S.* Doubleday 1978 $6.50

Confederates. Berkley Publishing 1984 pap. $3.95

Gettysburg: The Final Fury. Berkley Publishing 1984 pap. $6.95; Doubleday 1974
    $17.95
Reflections on the Civil War. Ed. by John Leekley, Berkley Publishing 1984 pap.
    $3.95; Doubleday 1981 $17.95

COMMAGER, HENRY STEELE. 1902–1984

Commager, who taught American history at Columbia University from
1938 to 1956, is now teaching at Amherst College. His writings are popular
with both scholars and the general reader, but his specialty is in the field of
early American documents. He is said to consider his *Documents of American History* (1934) one of his most significant contributions.

Among his other works are *Theodore Parker: Yankee Crusader* (1936) and
The Commonwealth of Learning (1968, o.p.), in which he proposes major reforms in the university structure, asking that it abandon its passive role in
favor of showing revolutionary new directions to the society of which it is a
part. On the study of history, he wrote *The Nature and Study of History*
(1965, o.p.).

Books by Commager

(ed.). *Documents of American History.* 1934. Prentice-Hall 9th ed. 1974 $17.50 text
    ed. 2 vols. pap. ea. $19.95
Theodore Parker: Yankee Crusader. 1936. Peter Smith $10.25
(with Allan Nevins). *The Heritage of America.* 1939. Little, Brown 2d ed. rev. 1949
    o.p.
(with Allan Nevins). *Pocket History of the United States.* 1942. Washington Square Pr.
    2d ed. rev. 1982 pap. $4.95
Majority Rule and Minority Rights. 1943. Peter Smith $10.25
(with Allan Nevins). *A Short History of the United States.* 1945. Knopf 6th ed. 1976
    $22.95
*The American Mind: An Interpretation of American Thought and Character since the
    1880's.* Yale Univ. Pr. 1950 $35.00 pap. $9.95
(ed.). *The Blue and the Gray: The Story of the Civil War as Told by Participants.* 1950.
    New Amer. Lib. 2 vols. 1973 pap. ea. $3.95
(and others). *Civil Liberties Under Attack: Publications of the William J. Cooper Foun-
    dation, Swarthmore College. Essay Index Repr. Ser.* Ayer repr. of 1951 ed. $17.00
Freedom, Loyalty, Dissent. Oxford 1954 $14.95
(ed.). *The Photographic History of the Civil War.* A. S. Barnes 5 vols. 1957 o.p.
(and Richard B. Morris). *The Spirit of '76: The Story of the American Revolution as
    Told by Participants.* 1958. Harper 1967 o.p.
Immigration and American History: Essays in Honor of Theodore C. Blegen. Univ. of
    Minnesota Pr. 1961 $8.95
Noah Webster's American Spelling Book. Teachers College Pr. text ed. 1963 $9.50 pap.
    $5.00
(ed.). *Fifty Basic Civil War Documents.* 1965. Krieger repr. 1982 pap. $5.95
Freedom and Order: A Commentary on the American Political Scene. Braziller 1966
    $6.50
Lester Ward and the Welfare State. Irvington 1967 $29.00
(ed.). *The Struggle for Racial Equality: A Documentary Record.* 1967. Peter Smith o.p.
    A selection of writings dealing with the civil rights struggle from Reconstruc-
    tion to Stokely Carmichael.

Commonwealth of Learning. Harper 1968 o.p.

Britain through American Eyes. McGraw-Hill 1974 o.p.

The Defeat of America: Presidential Power and the National Character. Simon & Schuster 1975 o.p.

Jefferson, Nationalism, and the Enlightenment. Braziller 1975 $7.50

(and Raymond H. Muessig). *The Study and Teaching of History.* Merrill text ed. 2d ed. 1980 pap. $7.95

The Empire of Reason: How Europe Imagined and America Realized the Enlightenment. Oxford 1982 pap. $9.95; Peter Smith 1984 $16.50

The Era of Reform Eighteen Thirty to Eighteen Sixty. Krieger 1982 pap. $5.95

DAVIS, JEFFERSON. 1808–1889

Chosen by the provisional congress as president of the Confederate States of America in 1861, Davis's policies aroused serious opposition within the Confederacy. As the fortunes of war turned against the South, criticism of Davis increased in intensity. He was indicted for treason in May 1866. Released on bond, he spent the last years of his life in retirement at his estate, Beauvoir, on the Gulf of Mexico in Mississippi. There he wrote *The Rise and Fall of the Confederate Government.*

Hudson Strode's three-volume *Jefferson Davis* is valuable for its scholarly presentation of hitherto unpublished material.

BOOKS BY DAVIS

Papers of Jefferson Davis. Louisiana State Univ. Pr. 1971–to date. 4 vols. vols. 1, 2, and 4 ea. $37.50 vol. 3 $40.00. Volume 1 was edited by Haskell M. Monroe, Jr., and James T. McIntosh. McIntosh edited Volumes 2 and 3, and Linda L. Cris edited Volume 4.

Jefferson Davis, Constitutionalist: His Letters, Papers and Speeches. Ed. by Dunbar Rowland, AMS Pr. 10 vols. repr. of 1923 ed. ea. $42.50 set $425.00

The Calendar of the Jefferson Davis Postwar Manuscripts in the Louisiana Historical Association Collection. Burt Franklin repr. of 1943 ed. 1970 $29.50

The Rise and Fall of the Confederate Government. 1878–81. A. S. Barnes $75.00; Peter Smith abr. ed. $12.75

BOOKS ABOUT DAVIS

Arsenault, Raymond. *The Wild Ass of the Ozarks: Jeff Davis and the Social Bases of Southern Politics.* Temple Univ. Pr. 1983 $34.95

Catton, Bruce, and William B. Catton. *Two Roads to Sumter.* 1963. McGraw-Hill 1971 pap. $5.95

Davis, Varina. *Jefferson Davis, Ex-President of the Confederate States of America: A Memoir by His Wife. Select Bibliographies Repr. Ser.* Ayer 2 vols. repr. of 1890 ed. $95.00

Eaton, Clement. *Jefferson Davis.* Macmillan (Free Press) text ed. 1979 pap. $12.95

———. *Jefferson Davis: The Sphinx of the Confederacy.* Macmillan (Free Press) 1977 $21.95

Eckenrode, Hamilton J. *Jefferson Davis: President of the South. Select Bibliographies Repr. Ser.* Ayer repr. of 1923 ed. $23.50

Escott, Paul D. *After Secession: Jefferson Davis and the Failure of Confederate Nationalism.* Louisiana State Univ. Pr. 1978 $25.00

Everett, Frank E. *Brierfield: Plantation Home of Jefferson Davis.* Univ. Pr. of Mississippi repr. of 1971 ed. 1979 $3.95

Gibson, Ronald. *Jefferson Davis and the Confederacy: Chronology-Documents-Biblio-
graphical Aids. Presidential Chronology Ser.* Oceana 1977 $15.00

Govan, Gilbert E., and James W. Livingood. *A Different Valor: The Story of General Joseph E. Johnson, C.S.A.* Greenwood repr. of 1956 ed. 1973 lib. bdg. $24.75

Hamilton, Holman. *The Three Kentucky Presidents: Lincoln, Taylor, Davis. Bicentennial Bookshelf Ser.* Univ. Pr. of Kentucky 1978 $6.95

Patrick, Rembert W. *Jefferson Davis and His Cabinet.* AMS Pr. repr. of 1944 ed.
$43.50

Pollard, Edward A. *Life of Jefferson Davis, with a Secret History of the Southern Confederacy, Gathered behind the Scenes in Richmond. Select Bibliographies Repr. Ser.*
Ayer repr. of 1869 ed. $33.00

Ross, Ishbel. *First Lady of the South: The Life of Mrs. Jefferson Davis.* Greenwood
repr. of 1958 ed. 1973 lib. bdg. $27.75

Strode, Hudson. *Jefferson Davis.* Harcourt 3 vols. 1955–64 o.p. "The magnificent
documentation of all three volumes, the spirited style, and the careful and candid judgments . . . make this trilogy a landmark in the writing of American biography" (*Washington Star*).

Tate, A. *Jefferson Davis: His Rise and Fall.* Kraus repr. of 1929 ed. $17.00

Wiley, Bell I. *Road to Appomattox.* Atheneum text ed. 1968 pap. $5.95

DE VOTO, BERNARD (AUGUSTINE). 1897–1955

A Harvard graduate and impassioned student and teacher of American
history and literature, De Voto held faculty positions at Northwestern and
at Harvard. He was also the second editor of the *Saturday Review of Literature* and conducted The Editor's Easy Chair column in *Harper's* magazine
for many years. For *Across the Wide Missouri* he visited the western trails
first blazed by Lewis and Clark. Henry Steele Commager called *The Course
of Empire*, covering the exploration of the United States to the year 1805,
"the largest of the books, largest in conception and in scope, largest, too, in
spirit. It is . . . the best book that has been written about the West since
Webb's 'Great Plains' and it is the best written book about the West since
Parkman."

Books by De Voto

Forays and Rebuttals. Essay Index Repr. Ser. Ayer repr. of 1936 ed. $27.50

Mark Twain at Work. AMS Pr. repr. of 1942 ed. $38.50

Minority Report. Essay Index Repr. Ser. Ayer repr. of 1940 ed. $21.00

The Year of Decision: 1846. 1943. Houghton Mifflin 1950 o.p. " 'A monumental narrative,' based on contemporary diaries and other records, of a single but vastly significant year in the history of the American West. His scholarship is sound and
thorough, his style vigorous and dramatic" (*Twentieth-Century Authors*).

Literary Fallacy. Essay Index Repr. Ser. Associated Faculty Pr. repr. of 1944 ed. 1969
$21.00

Across the Wide Missouri. AMS Pr. repr. of 1947 ed. $94.50; Crown 1981 $8.98;
Houghton Mifflin 1964 pap. $10.95. Struthers Burt found that De Voto here ex-
pressed "a passion as strong as Chinook wind—as just and as lucid as the moun-
tain-clearness of the original American idea" (*Twentieth-Century Authors*).

Hour. Greenwood rep. of 1951 ed. lib. bdg. $15.00

The Course of Empire. 1952. Univ. of Nebraska Pr. 1983 pap. $12.95
(ed.). *The Journals of Lewis and Clark.* Houghton Mifflin 1953 $22.50
Easy Chair. Essay Index Repr. Ser. Ayer repr. of 1955 ed. $20.00
Mark Twain's America. Greenwood repr. of 1967 ed. 1978 lib. bdg. $25.75
The Portable Mark Twain. Viking 1983 $18.75

BOOKS ABOUT DE VOTO

Bowen, Catherine Drinker, Edith Mirrielees, Arthur M. Schlesinger, Jr., and Wallace Stegner. *Four Portraits and One Subject: Bernard De Voto.* Houghton Mifflin 1963 o.p. Includes a bibliography prepared by Julius P. Barclay with the collaboration of Elaine Helmer Parnie.

Forsythe, Robert S. *Bernard De Voto: A New Force in American Letters.* Folcroft repr. of 1928 ed. 1974 lib. bdg. $7.50

Mattingly, Garrett. *Bernard De Voto.* Richard West repr. of 1938 ed. 1977 $17.50

Sawey, Orlan. *Bernard De Voto. Twayne's U.S. Authors Ser.* Irvington 1969 lib. bdg. $11.95

Stegner, Wallace. *The Uneasy Chair: Biography of Bernard De Voto.* Doubleday 1974 o.p.

DU BOIS, W(ILLIAM) E(DWARD) B(URGHARDT). 1868–1963

This man of towering intellect was born in Great Barrington, Massachusetts, five years after the Emancipation Proclamation was signed. He earned a B.A. from both Harvard and Fisk universities, an M.A. and Ph.D. from Harvard, and studied at the University of Berlin. He taught briefly at Wilberforce University before he became professor of history and economics at Atlanta University (1896–1910). There, to prove the fallacy of theories that raised racial barriers to intelligence, he wrote *The Souls of Black Folk.* In 1905, Du Bois became a major figure in the Niagara Movement, a crusading effort to end discrimination. This weak organization collapsed, but it prepared the way for the founding (in which Du Bois played a major role) of the National Association for the Advancement of Colored People. He became its director of publicity and research as well as editor of *The Crisis,* its official organ.

He returned to Atlanta University and tried to implement a plan to make the Negro Land Grant Colleges centers of black power. Atlanta approved of his idea, but later retracted its support. When Du Bois tried to return to the NAACP, it too rejected him.

In 1961 President Kwame Nkrumah invited Du Bois, then well over age 90, to Ghana as director of an *Encyclopedia Africana* project (Du Bois had organized the first Pan African Congress, which met in Paris in 1919). He died in Ghana after becoming a citizen of that country—and at age 93, a member of the Communist party.

BOOKS BY DU BOIS

Correspondence. Ed. by Herbert Aptheker, Univ. of Mass. Pr. 3 vols. 1973 ea. $27.50
Papers of W. E. B. Du Bois. Ed. by Robert M. McDonnell, Microfilming Corp. 1981 $15.00

W. E. B. Du Bois Speaks. Ed. by Philip Foner, Path Pr. 2 vols. 1970 $44.00 pap.
  $15.90 pap. $24.00 ea. $7.95
Negro in Business. AMS Pr. repr. of 1899 ed. $12.50
The Philadelphia Negro: A Social Study. 1899 Kraus 1973 $22.00
Black North in 1901: A Social Study. Amer. Negro: His History and Lit. Ser. Ayer repr.
  of 1901 ed. 1970 $7.00
The Negro Artisan. Atlanta Univ. Publications Ser. Kraus repr. of 1902 ed. pap. $8.00
The Souls of Black Folk. 1903. Dodd 1979 $8.95; New Amer. Lib. 1969 pap. $2.95
Some Notes on Negro Crime Particularly in Georgia. Atlanta Univ. Publications Ser.
  Kraus repr. of 1904 ed. pap. $6.00
A Select Bibliography of the Negro American. Atlanta Univ. Publications Ser. Kraus
  repr. of 1905 ed. pap. $6.00
Economic Co-operation among Negro Families. Atlanta Univ. Publications Ser. Kraus
  repr. of 1907 ed. pap. $9.00
(ed.). *Negro American Family.* Greenwood repr. of 1908 ed. lib. bdg. $19.75
Efforts for Social Betterment among Negro Americans. Atlanta Univ. Publications Ser.
  Kraus repr. of 1909 ed. $8.00
John Brown. Kraus repr. of 1909 ed. $18.00
(ed.). *The College-Bred Negro American. Atlanta Univ. Publications Ser.* Kraus repr. of
  1910 ed. pap. $6.00
(ed.). *The Common School and the Negro American. Atlanta Univ. Publications Ser.*
  Kraus repr. of 1911 ed. pap. $8.00
Quest of the Silver Fleece: A Novel. Greenwood repr. of 1911 ed. lib. bdg. $25.00
Morals and Manners among Negro Americans. Atlanta Univ. Publications Ser. Kraus
  repr. of 1914 ed. pap. $8.00
The Negro. Kraus repr. of 1915 ed. 1975 $14.00
The Gift of Black Folk. AMS Pr. repr. of 1924 ed. $15.00; Kraus 1975 $17.00
Dark Princess: A Romance. Kraus repr. of 1928 ed. 1975 $15.00
Black Folk Then and Now: An Essay in the History and Sociology of the Negro Race.
  Kraus repr. of 1930 ed. 1975 $18.00
Black Reconstruction in America, 1860–1880. 1935. Atheneum 1969 pap. $8.95
The Dusk of Dawn: An Essay toward an Autobiography of a Race Concept. 1940. Kraus
  1975 $17.00; Transaction Bks. 1982 pap. $19.95
The Suppression of the African Slave Trade. 1940. Louisiana State Univ. Pr. 1970 pap.
  $7.95. Du Bois' doctoral thesis, described by *Current Biography* as "the standard
  work on the subject."
Color and Democracy: Colonies and Peace. Kraus repr. of 1945 ed. 1975 $8.00
In Battle for Peace: The Story of My 83rd Birthday. Kraus repr. of 1952 ed. 1976
  $11.00
*The World and Africa: An Inquiry into the Part Which Africa Has Played in World His-
  tory.* 1955. Kraus repr. of 1965 ed. $17.00
Education of Black Peoples, 1906–1960: Ten Critiques. Ed. by Herbert Aptheker,
  Univ. of Massachusetts Pr. 1973 $12.00; Monthly Review 1975 pap. $4.50
*Autobiography: A Soliloquy on Viewing My Life from the Last Decade of Its First Cen-
  tury.* Ed. by Herbert Aptheker, International Publishing 1968 $15.00 pap. $4.75;
  Kraus 1976 $17.00
Prayers for Dark People. Ed. by Herbert Aptheker, Univ. of Massachusetts Pr. 1980
  $12.00 pap. $5.95
W. E. B. Du Bois on Sociology and the Black Community. Ed. by Dan S. Green and Ed-
  win D. Driver, Univ. of Chicago Pr. (Phoenix Bks.) 1980 pap. $5.50

BOOKS ABOUT DU BOIS

Aptheker, Herbert. *Annotated Bibliography of the Published Writings of W. E. B. Du Bois.* Kraus 1973 $54.00

Broderick, Francis L. *W. E. B. Du Bois: Negro Leader in a Time of Crisis.* Stanford Univ. Pr. 1959 $20.00. "Applying an easy style and a gift for trenchant analysis to a thorough knowledge of his material Broderick has produced a highly readable and scholarly intellectual biography" *(AHR).* "Broderick has effectively unravelled the complex facets of his subject's fascinating career" *(The Annals).*

De Marco, Joseph P. *The Social Thought of W. E. B. Du Bois.* Univ. Pr. of America text ed. 1983 $23.50 pap. $11.50

Du Bois, Shirley G. *His Day Is Marching On: Memoirs of W. E. B. Du Bois.* Okpaku 1971 $10.00 pap. $5.95

———. *Pictorial History of W. E. B. Du Bois.* Johnson Publishing $14.95

Hawkins, Hugh. *Booker T. Washington and His Critics. Problems in Amer. Civilization* Heath text ed. 2d ed. 1974 pap. $5.95

Moore, Jack B. *W. E. B. Du Bois. Twayne's U.S. Authors Ser.* G. K. Hall 1981 lib. bdg. $12.50

Partington, Paul G. *W. E. B. Du Bois: A Bibliography of His Published Writings.* Partington 2 vols. rev. ed. 1979–84 vol. 1 $15.00 vol. 2 $5.00

Rudwick, Elliot M. *W. E. B. Du Bois: Propagandist of the Negro Protest. Studies in Amer. Negro Life.* Atheneum text ed. 1968 pap. $6.95

Sterne, Emma G. *His Was the Voice: The Life of W. E. B. Du Bois.* Ed. by Carolyn Trager, Macmillan 1971 $9.95

Tuttle, William M., Jr., ed. *W. E. B. Du Bois. Great Lives Observed Ser.* Prentice-Hall 1974 o.p.

FAIRBANK, JOHN K(ING). 1907–

[SEE Chapter 10 in this volume.]

FRANKLIN, JOHN HOPE. 1915–

Born in Oklahoma, Franklin has had a distinguished career as teacher, scholar, and historian of the black experience in the United States. Son of a lawyer who practiced before the U.S. Supreme Court, he was a Phi Beta Kappa graduate of Fisk University and took his Ph.D. at Harvard University in 1941. "He owes his international recognition to his books on American history, including *From Slavery to Freedom* (1947) and *The Militant South* (1956). He is also known for his work in the classrooms of Fisk University, Howard University, Brooklyn College, Cambridge University, and other schools, and for his services in professional, civic, and governmental organizations" *(Current Biography).* Of *From Slavery to Freedom,* his comprehensive history, the *N.Y. Herald Tribune* wrote: "Dr. Franklin's book is a mature, balanced, scholarly account of the American Negro from his African beginnings to his participation in the late war. . . . A rich, absorbing book, with a clarity of design which all readers will appreciate." The *Saturday Review* said: "Throughout, the documentation and the bibliography add to the usefulness of the book to students. . . . 'From Slavery to Freedom' has before it a path of constructive public serviceableness; it will be a long while until another book in this field supersedes it." Within a short time, it was recognized as one of the most important surveys to have appeared of the history of the black race in this country; it became a basic textbook in the subject and has been twice revised.

He has been active in many learned and professional societies, edited many volumes, especially on the Civil War, and served on the editorial boards of the *Journal of American History* and the *Journal of Negro History*. He is a founding member of the Black Academy of Arts and Letters and has served on the U.S. Commission for UNESCO.

BOOKS BY FRANKLIN

The Free Negro in North Carolina, 1790–1860. 1943. *Norton Lib.* 1971 pap. $2.25

From Slavery to Freedom: A History of American Negroes. 1947. Knopf text ed. 5th ed. 1980 pap. $14.00

The Militant South, 1800–1961. 1956. Harvard Univ. Pr. rev. ed. 1970 $20.00. "Franklin's study is in many ways a pioneer work. His sources are original, his work is thorough and his book makes a fresh and significant contribution to the understanding of the mind of the South" (C. Vann Woodward, *N.Y. Times*). "Franklin has assembled an unrivalled body of data on the diverse manifestations of the fighting spirit in the South, and has presented it in a book which enables the reader better to understand a whole range of behavior from the valor of Pickett's charge to the infamy of the Emmett Till murder" (David M. Potter, *Yale Review*).

Reconstruction after the Civil War. History of Amer. Civilization Ser. Univ. of Chicago Pr. 1961 $16.00 pap. $7.00. An important study. "A great deal of careful research has gone into the book and the conclusions are set down logically and forcefully. An excellent bibliography adds much to its value" *(LJ).*

The Emancipation Proclamation. Doubleday 1963 o.p. "A work of scholarship that is lucid and attractive to the general reader. With self-restraint and detachment, [Franklin] has more or less successfully abstracted and told the story of the Emancipation Proclamation. There are enough misconceptions about that single great document to justify his attempt to separate its genesis and its content from its indispensable predecessor, the abolitionist movement, from the Civil War itself, and from the bitter aftermath" *(Commonweal).*

(ed.). *Three Negro Classics.* Avon 1965 pap. $3.95

(and Isidore Starr, eds.). *The Negro in Twentieth Century America: A Reader on the Struggle for Civil Rights* Random (Vintage) 1967 o.p.

Narrative of a Journey to the Shores of the Polar Sea, in the Years 1819–1822. Greenwood repr. of 1823 ed. 1968 lib. bdg. $40.25

(ed.). *Color and Race.* Houghton Mifflin 1969 o.p.

Illustrated History of Black Americans. Time-Life 1970 $7.95

Narrative of a Second Expedition to the Shores of the Polar Sea. Tuttle repr. 1971 $35.00

Racial Equality in America. Univ. of Chicago Pr. 1976 $7.95

A Southern Odyssey—Travelers in the Antebellum North. Louisiana State Univ. Pr. 1976 $25.00 pap. $6.95

(and August Meier). *Black Leaders of the Twentieth Century.* Univ. of Illinois Pr. 1982 $19.95 1983 pap. $7.95

George Washington Williams: The Massachusetts Years. Univ. Pr. of Virginia 1983 pap. $3.50

HACKER, LOUIS M(ORTON). 1899–

A leading authority on the development of American capitalism, Hacker has said, "I write economic history, never losing sight, however, of the close links between politics and economic development." Born in New York, the son of Austrian immigrants, he graduated after considerable hardship from Columbia University and became a free-lance historical writer. He taught at Columbia (1935–67), where he was dean of the School of General Studies (1949–58). Hacker feels "that our civilization is in process of transformation; it is becoming more and more collectivized, with the authority of the central state increasingly powerful. This is the leading question of our time: how to permit collectivization to continue and at the same time hold in check the growth of a state bureaucracy. In America, I feel that it can and will be done: so that the long-term outlook, as I see it, is not dark" *(Twentieth-Century Authors)*.

BOOKS BY HACKER

(and Benjamin B. Kendrick). *The United States since 1865*. 1932. Irving Publishing 4th ed. 1949 $49.50

A Short History of the New Deal. Greenwood repr. of 1934 ed. 1977 lib. bdg. $12.75

The Triumph of American Capitalism. 1940. Columbia Univ. Pr. 1947 o.p.

The Shaping of the American Tradition. Columbia Univ. Pr. 1947 $60.00

American Capitalism: Its Promises and Achievements. 1957. Krieger text ed. repr. 1979 pap. $5.95

(ed.). *Major Documents in American Economic History*. Van Nostrand 2 vols. 1961 o.p.

The World of Andrew Carnegie, 1865–1901. Lippincott 1968 o.p.

Course of American Economic Growth and Development. Wiley 1970 o.p.

(and Mark D. Hirsch). *Proshauer: His Life and Times*. Univ. of Alabama Pr. 1978 $16.25

HANDLIN, OSCAR. 1915–

Handlin, the director of the Center for the Study of the History of Liberty at Harvard University until 1966, won the Pulitzer Prize in 1952 for *The Uprooted*, his study of immigrants in the eastern cities of America. The son of immigrant parents, he made his special field the social history of immigrant groups who came to the United States in the nineteenth century from central and southern Europe. In *The Americans*, as in others of his books, he dispensed with footnotes, bibliography, and identification of quotations in favor of "unobtrusive" learning. He edited *Children of the Uprooted*, which includes excerpts from various authors on the subject of the "marginality" of immigrants. On the subject of education, he wrote *The American University as an Instrument of Republican Culture* (1970, o.p.) and *John Dewey's Challenge to Education: Historical Perspectives on the Cultural Context* (1959). With his wife, Mary Handlin, he edited *The Popular Sources of Political Authority: Documents on the Massachusetts Constitution of 1780* (1966). Handlin taught at Harvard for many years where he was Charles Warren Professor of History. He was also responsible for a book review column for the *Atlantic*.

Books by Handlin

The Uprooted. 1951. Atlantic Monthly Pr. 2d ed. enl. 1973 $9.95 pap. $6.95
The American People in the Twentieth Century. 1954. Harvard Univ. Pr. 1966 o.p.
Adventures in Freedom. 1954. *Amer. History and Culture in the 20th-Century Ser.* Kennikat 1971 o.p.
Chance or Destiny: Turning Points in American History. Greenwood repr. of 1955 ed. 1977 lib. bdg. $19.00
Race and Nationality in American Life. Atlantic Monthly Pr. 1957 o.p.
Al Smith and His America. Lib. of Amer. Biography Atlantic Monthly Pr. 1958 o.p.
Boston's Immigrants: A Study of Acculturation. Harvard Univ. Pr. (Belknap Pr.) rev. & enl. ed. 1959 $25.00 pap. $8.95
(ed.). *Immigration as a Factor in American History.* Prentice-Hall (Spectrum Bks.) 1959 o.p.
John Dewey's Challenge to Education: Historical Perspectives on the Cultural Context. Greenwood repr. of 1959 ed. 1972 $15.00
Newcomers: Negroes and Puerto Ricans in a Changing Metropolis. Harvard Univ. Pr. 1959 $12.50
(and Mary Handlin). *The Dimensions of Liberty.* Atheneum 1966 text ed. pap. $1.75; Harvard Univ. Pr. (Belknap Pr.) 1961 $14.00
The Americans: A New History of the People of the United States. Atlantic Monthly Pr. 1963 o.p. A study of the influence of immigration on people of the United States from Leif Ericson to 1962.
Fire-Bell in the Night: The Crisis in Civil Rights. Atlantic Monthly Pr. 1964 o.p.
A Continuing Task. Random 1965 o.p.
(ed.). *Children of the Uprooted.* Braziller 1966 o.p. "In three brief explanatory essays, the editor gives a quick account of types of migration to America and the changing American scene into which the migrants came. He also explains the concept of 'marginality'. . . . Recommended" *(LJ).*
(and John Burchard, eds.). *The Historian and the City.* MIT 1966 pap. $6.95
(and Mary Handlin, eds.). *Popular Sources of Political Authority: Documents on the Massachusetts Constitution of 1780.* Harvard Univ. Pr. (Belknap Press) 1966 $40.00
The History of the United States. Holt 2 vols. 1967–68 o.p.
America: A History. Holt 1968 o.p.
(ed.). *American Immigration Collection, Series 1.* Ayer 42 vols. repr. 1969 $1,493.00
(and Mary Handlin). *Commonwealth: A Study of the Role of Government in the American Economy, Massachusetts, 1774–1861.* Harvard Univ. Pr. (Belknap Pr.) 1969 $20.00
(ed.). *This Was America: True Accounts of People and Places, Manners and Customs, as Recorded by European Travelers to the Western Shore in the 18th, 19th and 20th Centuries.* Harvard Univ. Pr. 1969 $35.00
(and Mary Handlin). *Facing Life: Youth and the Family in American History.* Atlantic Monthly Pr. 1971 pap. $5.95
A Pictorial History of Immigration. Crown 1972 o.p.
Truth in History. Harvard Univ. Pr. (Belknap Pr.) 1979 $25.00 pap. $9.95
(and Lilian Handlin). *Abraham Lincoln and the Union. Lib. of Amer. Biography.* Little, Brown 1980 $12.95 pap. $5.95
(and Lilian Handlin). *A Restless People: Americans in Rebellion, 1770–1787.* Doubleday (Anchor) 1982 $14.95

BOOK ABOUT HANDLIN

Bushman, Richard L. *Uprooted Americans: Essays to Honor Oscar Handlin.* Little, Brown 1979 $15.00

HOFSTADTER, RICHARD. 1916–1970

The DeWitt Clinton Professor of History at Columbia University, Richard Hofstadter was the author of several important volumes on American social history that have cast valuable light on the intellectual and political heritage of the United States. He received the Pulitzer Prize in history in 1955 for *The Age of Reform.* Written in brisk and lucid prose, "it illuminates the whole landscape of American social history and allows its readers to see the intellectuals and the anti-intellectuals as they really exist. . . . His range of experience has been wide, his perception is acute" (Harold Taylor). He won the Pulitzer Prize again in 1964 for general nonfiction, the Ralph Waldo Emerson Award of Phi Beta Kappa, and the Sidney Hillman Prize Award, all for *Anti-Intellectualism in American Life.* He was also a visiting professor at Cambridge University.

BOOKS BY HOFSTADTER

The American Political Tradition. 1948. Knopf new ed. 1973 $15.00; Random (Vintage) pap. $3.95

(and C. De Witt Hardy). *Development and Scope of Higher Education in the United States.* Columbia Univ. Pr. 1952 $27.50

Social Darwinism in American Thought. Beacon 1954 pap. $7.95

The Age of Reform: From Bryan to F. D. R. Knopf 1955 $12.95

(and others). *The United States: The History of a Republic.* 1957. Prentice-Hall 3d ed. 1972 o.p.

(and others). *The American Republic.* 1959. Prentice-Hall 2 vols. 2d ed. 1970 o.p.

Anti-Intellectualism in American Life. Knopf 1963 $13.95; Random (Vintage) pap. $5.95

(ed.). *The Progressive Movement, 1900–1915.* Prentice-Hall (Spectrum Bks.) 1964 o.p.

(and others). *The Structure of American History.* 1964. Prentice-Hall 2d ed. 1973 o.p.

The Paranoid Style in American Politics and Other Essays. 1965. Univ. of Chicago Pr. (Phoenix Bks.) 1979 pap. $7.95

The Progressive Historians: Turner, Beard, Parrington. 1968. Univ. of Chicago Pr. 1979 pap. $7.95. Hofstadter "treats Frederick Jackson Turner, Charles A. Beard and Vernon L. Parrington as exemplars of Progressive historiography. These men, Hofstadter asserts, gave Americans the pivotal ideas of the first half of the twentieth century. . . . Turner, Beard and Parrington were influential insofar as they located and rode the crests of current waves of thought and thus met the expressed needs of the politically oriented intellectuals of the time" (Oscar Handlin, *N.Y. Times*).

(and Seymour M. Lipset, eds.). *Sociology and History: Methods.* Basic Bks. 1968 o.p.

(ed.). *Ten Major Issues in American Politics.* Oxford 1968 o.p.

The Idea of a Party System: The Rise of Legitimate Opposition in the United States, 1780–1840. Univ. of California Pr. 1969 $23.50 pap. $3.95

America at 1750: A Social History. Knopf 1971 $12.95; Random (Vintage) 1973 pap. $4.95

(and Michael Wallace, eds.). *American Violence: A Documentary History.* Random
(Vintage) 1971 pap. $4.95
Great Issues in American History. Random 2 vols. pap. vol. 1 $5.95 vol. 2 $7.95

HORGAN, PAUL. 1903–

Paul Horgan's *Great River* received both the Pulitzer Prize and the Bancroft Prize in 1955. It is not only a history of the Rio Grande River, but a saga of New Mexico and Texas from ancient to modern times. Horgan was director of the Center for Advanced Studies in the Liberal Arts, Sciences and Professions at Wesleyan University from 1962 to 1967. In 1969, he became one of the judges of the Book-of-the-Month Club.

BOOKS BY HORGAN

Far from Cibola. Ayer repr. of 1936 ed. $12.00; Univ. of New Mexico Pr. 1974 pap.
$6.95
Great River: The Rio Grande in North American History. 1954. Texas Monthly Pr. rev.
ed. 1984 $24.95 pap. $14.95. The history of the Southwest and its four civilizations—the aboriginal Indians, the Spanish, the Mexicans, and the Anglo-Americans.
The Saintmaker's Christmas Eve. Gannon repr. of 1955 ed. 1978 $15.00
Centuries of Santa Fe. 1956. Gannon 1976 $20.00 pap. $9.95
Abraham Lincoln: Citizen of New Salem. Macmillan 1961 $2.98
Mountain Standard Time. Farrar 1962 $7.95
Conquistadors in North American History. 1963. Texas Western Pr. 1982 pap. $12.00
Peter Hurd: A Portrait Sketch from Life. Univ. of Texas Pr. 1965 pap. $8.95
Songs after Lincoln. Farrar 1965 $4.95
Memories of the Future. Farrar 1966 $4.95
Everything to Live For. Farrar 1968 $8.95
Whitewater. Farrar 1970 $6.95
Approaches to Writing. Farrar 1973 $10.00 pap. $3.25
The Thin Mountain Air. Farrar 1977 $10.00
Josiah Gregg and His Vision of the Early West. Farrar 1979 $8.95
Lamy of Sante-Fe: His Life and Times. Farrar 1980 $25.00 pap. $12.95
Mexico Bay. Farrar 1982 $12.95
Of America East and West: Selections from the Writings of Paul Horgan. Farrar 1984
$25.00

LIPPMANN, WALTER. 1889–1974

"As widely respected by those who differ with his views as by those who agree with them," Lippmann was considered one of the great spokesmen for liberal democracy and the outstanding American political philosopher of this century. Born in New York City, he earned his Harvard B.A. in three years, assisting GEORGE SANTAYANA (see Vol. 4) in his fourth year while he studied philosophy in the graduate school. He was associate editor of the *New Republic* in its early days, but left to become assistant secretary of war at the outbreak of World War I. Later he helped to prepare data for the Versailles peace conference. He served as editor of the New York *World*, and his newspaper column, "Today and Tomorrow," was widely read for many years. His television interviews offered an opportunity for many to listen to his opinions and advice on domestic and world affairs. He received the Pulitzer Prize for international reporting (1962), the Presidential Medal of Freedom (1964), a special citation with the Peabody Award to CBS News (1965), and the gold medal for essays and criticism from the National Institute of Arts and Letters (1965). When, at 77, he gave up his regular newspaper column, he explained, "More and more I have come to wish to get rid of the necessity of knowing, day in and day out, what the blood pressure is at the White House and who said what and who saw whom and who is listened to and who is not listened to." He continued to write longer articles on a more relaxed basis.

BOOKS BY LIPPMANN

The Essential Lippmann: A Political Philosophy for Liberal Democracy. Ed. by Clinton Rossiter and James Lare, Harvard Univ. Pr. 1982 pap. $8.95. A selection of Lippmann's writings published during more than half a century issued on the fiftieth anniversary of *Preface to Politics.*
Early Writings. Liveright 1970 o.p.
Preface to Politics. 1913. Univ. of Michigan Pr. 1962 o.p.
Public Opinion. 1922. Macmillan (Free Press) 1965 o.p.
The Good Society. 1937 1943. Peter Smith o.p.
An Inquiry into the Principles of the Good Society. Greenwood repr. of 1943 ed. 1973 lib. bdg. $29.75
U.S. Foreign Policy: Shield of the Republic. Johnson Repr. of 1943 ed. 1971 $28.00
The Public Philosophy. Little, Brown 1955 o.p.; New Amer. Lib. o.p.
The Communist World and Ours. Atlantic Monthly Pr. 1955 o.p. A report on his Moscow interview with Khrushchev.
Drift and Mastery: An Attempt to Diagnose the Current Unrest. Greenwood repr. of 1961 ed. 1978 lib. bdg. $20.50
Men of Destiny. Americana Lib. Ser. Univ. of Washington Pr. 1970 pap. $6.95
The Cold War. Harper 1972 o.p.
Public Persons. Ed. by Gilbert A. Harrison, Liveright 1976 $7.95

BOOKS ABOUT LIPPMANN

Adams, Larry L. *Walter Lippmann. World Leaders Ser.* G. K. Hall 1977 $13.50
Blum, D. Steven. *Walter Lippmann: Cosmopolitan in the Century of Total War.* Cornell Univ. Pr. 1984 $19.95
Cary, Francine Curro. *The Influence of War on Walter Lippmann, 1914–1944.* Wisconsin State Historical Society 1967 o.p.
Dam, Hari N. *The Intellectual Odyssey of Walter Lippmann.* Gordon 1973 $69.95
Forcey, Charles. *Crossroads of Liberalism: Croly, Weyl, Lippmann and the Progressive Era, 1900–1925.* Oxford 1961 o.p.
Luskin, John. *Lippmann, Liberty and the Press.* Univ. of Alabama Pr. 1972 $15.00
Schapsmeier, Edward, and Frederick Schapsmeier. *Walter Lippmann, Philosopher-Journalist.* Public Affairs Pr. 1969 $9.00
Steel, Ronald. *Walter Lippmann and the American Century.* Atlantic Monthly Pr. 1980 $22.50; Random (Vintage) 1981 pap. $7.95
Syed, Anwar H. *Walter Lippmann's Philosophy of International Politics.* Univ. of Pennsylvania Pr. 1963 o.p.

Weingast, David E. *Walter Lippmann: A Study in Personal Journalism.* Greenwood
    repr. of 1949 ed. lib. bdg. $15.00
Wellborn, Charles. *Twentieth-Century Pilgrimage: Walter Lippmann and the Public Phi-
    losophy.* Louisiana State Univ. Pr. 1969 $17.50
Wright, Benjamin F. *Five Public Philosophies of Walter Lippmann.* Univ. of Texas Pr.
    1973 o.p.

MILLER, PERRY (GILBERT EDDY). 1905–1963

"While the late Perry Miller was generally recognized as one of the country's most distinguished intellectual historians, his considerable achievements as an urbane and witty writer were sometimes overshadowed by the
originality of his ideas" *(PW).* Born and educated in Chicago, Miller taught
at Harvard University for more than 30 years until his death. Working with
such source materials as diaries and letters, he studied the literature and
history of New England in the colonial era and that of the early Republic.
His books, and especially his most popular work, *The New England Mind,*
should dispel once and for all any impression that the life of American Puritans was dreary. "He respected the Puritans as thinkers, and he regarded
them more highly than he did their successors who moderated their teach-
ings" (Granville Hicks, *SR*).

A professor of American literature, Miller wrote critical essays and compiled anthologies of early American poetry and prose. *Nature's Nation* is "a
collection of essays and lectures that Miller wrote in the later years of his
life. The first six or seven are by-products of his studies of Puritanism, and
they show how his mind worked. As he comes down to the nineteenth century his tone grows sharper, and there is a ruthless analysis of the shortcom-
ings of Theodore Parker. He sees the weaknesses of EMERSON [see Vol. 1],
too, especially the vestiges of Boston Unitarian snobbishness. . . . Yet in
the end he does Emerson justice. He also writes about Thoreau and Melville, and there are two brilliant essays that have not appeared before in
book form—'An American Language' and 'Romance and the Novel.' . . .
The final essay is amusingly and pointedly entitled 'Sinners in the Hands of
a Benevolent God' " (Hicks).

BOOKS BY MILLER

Jonathan Edwards. Amer. Men of Letters Ser. Greenwood repr. of 1949 ed. 1973 lib.
    bdg. $28.75
Society and Literature in America. 1949. Folcroft lib. bdg. $8.50
(ed.). *Transcendentalists: An Anthology.* Harvard Univ. Pr. 1950 pap. $9.95
The New England Mind. 1953–54. Harvard Univ. Pr. (Belknap Pr.) 2 vols. 1983 pap.
    ea. $8.95
(ed.). *American Thought: The Civil War to World War I.* Holt 1954 o.p.
(and others). *Religion and Freedom of Thought.* Essay Index Repr. Ser. Ayer repr. of
    1954 ed. $10.00
(ed.). *American Puritans: Their Prose and Poetry.* 1956. Columbia Univ. Pr. 1982 pap.
    $11.00
The Raven and the Whale: The War of Worlds and Wits in the Era of Poe and Melville.
    Greenwood repr. of 1956 ed. 1973 lib. bdg. $35.00

Errand into the Wilderness. Harvard Univ. Pr. 1956 $14.00; Harvard Univ. Pr. (Belknap Pr.) pap. $5.95. Essays, mostly on American (Protestant) religion. "For a certain type of specialized reader this book can be endlessly stimulating. Mr. Miller is a man of learning who writes, if not for scholars alone, then for readers who combine a passion for ideas with tireless precision of thought. To such an audience, he must rank among the most delightful and rewarding of intellectual historians" (Robert Peel, *Christian Science Monitor*).

(ed.). *American Transcendentalists: Their Prose and Poetry.* 1957. Johns Hopkins Univ. Pr. 1981 pap. $6.95

(ed.). *Major Writers of America.* Harcourt text ed. 1962 $19.95

(and T. H. Johnson, eds.). *The Puritans: A Sourcebook of Their Writings.* Harper 2 vols. 1963 vol. 1 $8.50 vol. 2 $8.95; Peter Smith $36.00

The Life of the Mind in America: From the Revolution to the Civil War. 1966. Harcourt 1970 pap. $7.95. "The Enlightenment ideal was that of perfect adaptation of individual to society and society to nature. . . . No more hollow human ideal . . . has ever been conceived; and . . . Perry Miller's discovery that the Enlightenment Sublime was the source of the absurd and disturbing (and oddly touching) American falsity is a great intellectual achievement" (Morse Peckham, *SR*). Unfortunately, Miller died before he could complete this work, which was planned for several volumes.

Nature's Nation. Harvard Univ. Pr. (Belknap Pr.) 1967 $18.50

(and Alan Heimart, eds.). *The Great Awakening: Documents Illustrating the Crisis and Its Consequences.* Bobbs 1967 pap. $14.47

(ed.). *The Legal Mind in America: From Independence to the Civil War.* Cornell Univ. Pr. 1970 o.p.

MILLIS, WALTER. 1899–1968

For 30 years an editorial writer on the *N.Y. Herald Tribune,* Millis, whose last years were occupied with the Fund for the Republic, spent most of his adult life examining the genesis and breeding of war in the United States and elsewhere. His *Arms and Men* was reviewed in the *N.Y. Times* as "a book for the years . . . a distinguished job of writing made so by Millis' skill as a narrator, his powers as a penetrative analyst and his ingrained habit of viewing skeptically any idea so long popular that it is accepted as truth." *The Abolition of War* produced under the auspices of the Center for the Study of Democratic Institutions, is a "clear-sighted, penetrating, cogent, passionately worded but rational and hopeful document." Of *An End of Arms* (1965, o.p.), Hans J. Morgenthau said, "By presenting his views in so able a manner, he has contributed to bringing about the world that reason requires." In *This Is Pearl! The United States and Japan, 1941* (1947), Millis blames the U.S. commanders in Hawaii for the bombing of Pearl Harbor.

Son of a professional soldier and himself an officer in World War I, Millis became an isolationist until World War II. As the *N.Y. Times* wrote in his obituary, "One of the nation's foremost thinkers in the field of arms control, he was a leading proponent of the view that nuclear weapons make general warfare unthinkable as an instrument of national policy, and many of his late writings were on this theme."

BOOKS BY MILLIS

The Martial Spirit. Ed. by Richard H. Kohn, *Amer. Military Experience Ser*. Ayer repr.
    of 1931 ed. 1979 $34.50
The Road to War: America, 1914–1917. 1935. Howard Fertig 1970 o.p.
This Is Pearl! The United States and Japan, 1941. Greenwood repr. of 1947 ed. lib.
    bdg. $29.75
Arms and Men: A Study in American Military History. 1956. Rutgers Univ. Pr. 1981
    pap. $9.95
Arms and the State: Civil-Military Elements in National Policy. *Twentieth-Century
    Fund Ser*. Kraus repr. of 1958 ed. $6.00
(and C. J. Murray, eds.). *Foreign Policy and the Free Society*. Oceana 1958 $7.50
(and others). *A World without War*. Washington Square Pr. 1961 o.p.
(and James Real). *The Abolition of War*. Macmillan 1963 pap. $1.95
(ed.). *American Military Thought*. Bobbs 1966 o.p.

MORISON, SAMUEL ELIOT. 1887–1976

Among our foremost historians, Admiral Morison wrote with authority
and an engaging grace of style. The seaman's and the scholar's expert knowledge are perfectly blended in his books, for which he usually studied the geographical setting firsthand. He prepared for writing *Admiral of the Ocean
Sea* by four times "following the routes of Columbus' voyages in small sailing vessels comparable in size and rig to those used by Columbus." This
magnificent biography was awarded the 1943 Pulitzer Prize. *Christopher Columbus, Mariner* is a rewriting of *Admiral of the Ocean Sea* in a straight narrative, leaving out lengthy notes and less significant details. Again in 1960
his *John Paul Jones* won the Pulitzer Prize for biography. Appointed historian of naval operations by the navy in 1942, he wrote its 15-volume *History*
for World War II, one of the most ambitious government-sponsored historical studies ever undertaken. It received the first Balzan Foundation Award
in 1963. His great *Oxford History of the United States, 1783–1917* (o.p.) was
written for English college students.

He wrote a number of biographies, including those of Harrison Gray Otis,
an ancestor of Morison's, and Matthew C. Perry, which Bruce Catton called
"a remarkably fine book. . . . Morison presents to us a Perry who was salty,
vigorous and highly interesting."

Many of his books describe life in early Massachusetts. Between 1930 and
1936, Harvard University Press published his four volumes on the history of
that university. *One Boy's Boston, 1887–1901* is a delightful book of reminiscences of his boyhood days in a world rich in material and intellectual gifts.

BOOKS BY MORISON

(ed.). *Sources and Documents Illustrating the American Revolution, 1764–1788, and
    the Formation of the Federal Constitution*. 1923. Oxford 2d ed. 1965 pap. $9.95
The Oxford History of the American People. 1927. New Amer. Lib. 3 vols. pap. ea.
    $4.50–$4.95; Oxford 1965 $39.95 text ed. $19.95
(ed.). *Winthrop Papers: Prepared for the Massachusetts Historical Society*. 1929–31.
    Russell repr. 2 vols. 1968 Vol. 1 $15.00 Vol. 2 $12.50

Builders of the Bay Colony. AMS Pr. repr. of 1930 ed. $26.45; Northeastern Univ. Pr. 2d ed. 1982 $24.95

(and Henry Steele Commager and William E. Leuchtenburg). *The Growth of the American Republic.* 1930. Oxford 2 vols. seventh edition 1980 text edition each $18.95

Founding of Harvard College. Harvard Univ. Pr. 1935 $25.00

Harvard College in the Seventeenth Century. Harvard Univ. Pr. 2 vols. 1936 $40.00

Three Centuries of Harvard, 1636–1936. Harvard Univ. Pr. (Belknap Press) 1936 $25.00

Portuguese Voyagers to America in the Fifteenth Century. 1940. Octagon 1965 $15.00

Admiral of the Ocean Sea: A Life of Christopher Columbus. Atlantic Monthly Pr. 1942 $24.95; Northeastern Univ. Pr. 1983 pap. $10.95

History of the United States Naval Operations in World War II, 1939–1945. Little, Brown 15 vols. 1947–62 ea. $24.50 set $367.50

The Ropemakers of Plymouth: A History of the Plymouth Cordage Company, 1824–1849. Companies and Men: Business Enterprise in Amer. Ser. Ayer repr. of 1950 ed. 1976 $21.00

John Paul Jones: A Sailor's Biography. AMS Pr. repr. of 1952 ed. $12.95; Northeastern Univ. Pr. 1984 pap. $9.95

Christopher Columbus, Mariner. Atlantic Monthly Pr. 1955 $8.95; National Amer. Lib. 1983 pap. $5.95

Freedom in Contemporary Society. Essay Index Repr. Ser. Ayer repr. of 1956 ed. $14.00

Strategy and Compromise. Little, Brown 1958 o.p. Concise survey of American-British World War II strategy.

The Intellectual Life of Colonial New England. Cornell Univ. Pr. 1960 pap. $9.95; Greenwood repr. of 1956 ed. 1980 lib. bdg. $24.75

The Story of Mt. Desert Island, Maine. Atlantic Monthly Pr. 1960 $7.95

One Boy's Boston: 1887–1901. Northeastern Univ. Pr. repr. of 1962 ed. 1983 $10.00

The Two-Ocean War: A Short History of the United States Navy in the Second World War. Atlantic Monthly Pr. 1963 $19.95. A one-volume condensation of his 15-volume history, concentrating on major battles and campaigns.

Vistas of History. Knopf 1964 o.p. A selection of previously published papers, including "The Experiences and Principles of an Historian"—"a lucid *curriculum vitae* of an intellect" (*LJ*).

(and others). *Dissent in Three American Wars.* Harvard Univ. Pr. 1970 $9.00 pap. $2.95

European Discovery of America: The Northern Voyages. Oxford 1971 $19.95

Samuel De Champlain: Father of New France. Atlantic Monthly Pr. 1972 o.p.

European Discovery of America: The Southern Voyages. Oxford 1974 $29.95. "This sweeping narrative recaptures in sparkling prose the adventures of Columbus, Magellan, Drake, and other explorers of their time" (*Booklist*).

Sailor Historian. Ed. by Emily Morison Beck. Houghton Mifflin 1977 $15.00

The Great Explorers: The European Discovery of America Oxford 1978 $25.00

The Maritime History of Massachusetts: 1783–1860. Northeastern Univ. Pr. text ed. 1979 $24.95 pap. $9.95

BOOK ABOUT MORISON

Skotheim, Robert Allen. *American Intellectual Histories and Historians.* 1960. Princeton Univ. Pr. 1978 $26.00

NEVINS, ALLAN. 1890–1971

With some 40 books written or edited and two Pulitzer Prizes to his credit, Nevins was a senior associate at the Huntington Library in California, having become emeritus professor of history at Columbia University in 1958 after more than 25 years on its faculty. Nevins had done editorial work on the *Nation* and several New York newspapers before beginning his teaching career at Cornell University in 1927. His biography of Grover Cleveland won the 1932 Pulitzer Prize and five years later his biography of Hamilton Fish was similarly honored.

BOOKS BY NEVINS

Evening Post: A Century of Journalism. Russell repr. of 1922 ed. 1968 $16.00

(ed.). *American Social History as Recorded by British Travellers.* Kelley repr. of 1923 ed. 1969 $27.50

The American States during and after the Revolution, 1775–1798. 1924. Kelley repr. $37.50

(ed.). *Diary of Philip Hone, 1828–1851. Rise of Urban Amer.* Ayer repr. of 1927 ed. 1970 $52.00

Emergence of Modern America, 1865–1978. Scholarly repr. of 1927 ed. 1971 $49.00

Fremont: Pathmarker of the West. 1928 1939. Ungar 2 vols. $40.00

American Press Opinion: Washington to Coolidge. 1928. Associated Faculty Pr. 2 vols. 1969 $45.00

(ed.). *Letters of Grover Cleveland, 1850–1908. Amer. Public Figures Ser.* Da Capo repr. of 1933 ed. 1970 $75.00

History of the Bank of New York and Trust Company, 1784–1934. Companies and Men: Business Enterprise in Amer. Ser. Ayer repr. of 1934 ed. 1976 $24.50

John D. Rockefeller: The Heroic Age of American Enterprise. Kraus 2 vols. repr. of 1940 ed. 1976 $87.00

(and Henry Steele Commager). *A Pocket History of the United States.* 1942. Washington Square Pr. 2d ed. rev. 1982 pap. $4.95

(and Frank Weitenkampf). *A Century of Political Cartoons.* Octagon repr. of 1944 ed. lib. bdg. $20.00

The Ordeal of the Union. Scribner 8 vols. 1947–71 ea. $25.00

America through British Eyes. 1948. Peter Smith o.p.

(and John A. Kraut, eds.). *The Greater City: New York, 1898 to 1948.* Greenwood repr. of 1948 ed. 1981 lib. bdg. $35.00

The United States in a Chaotic World. 1950. U.S. Publishers Association $8.95

(and Milton H. Thomas, eds.). *The Diary of George Templeton Strong, 1835–1875.* Octagon 4 vols. repr. of 1952 ed. 1974 $138.00

The State Universities and Democracy. Greenwood repr. of 1962 ed. 1977 lib. bdg. $15.00

The Place of Franklin D. Roosevelt in History. Humanities Pr. 1965 o.p.

James Truslow Adams: Historian of the American Dream. Univ. of Illinois Pr. 1968 $22.95

(and Frank E. Hill). *Ford. Companies and Men: Business Enterprise in Amer. Ser.* Ayer repr. 3 vols 1976 $140.00

PAINE, THOMAS. 1737–1809

Paine was born in England, the son of a Quaker corset maker. In 1774 he emigrated to America with letters of introduction from BENJAMIN FRANKLIN, whom he had met in London. He soon became involved in clashes between England and the American colonies, and in early 1776 his famous pamphlet *Common Sense* was published, which exerted a powerful influence in the revolutionary struggle. He returned to England in 1787, and while there wrote *The Rights of Man*, a reply to EDMUND BURKE's critical *Reflections on the French Revolution*. Paine's sharp criticism of the British government caused his exile to France, where he became involved in French politics, which later led to his imprisonment there (1793–94). His deistic treatise *The Age of Reason, Being an Investigation of True and Fabulous Theology* created a furor both abroad and in America, and his critical *Letter to Washington* (1796) brought further resentment against him in the United States. He returned to New York in 1802 where he died impoverished and embittered seven years later.

BOOKS BY PAINE

The Writings of Thomas Paine: The Standard Edition. Ed. by Moncure D. Conway, AMS Pr. repr. of 1896 ed. 4 vols. ea. $24.50 set $98.00
Common Sense. 1776. Penguin 1982 pap. $2.95
Common Sense and Other Political Writings. Ed. by Nelson F. Adkins, Bobbs 1953 pap. $7.87
Common Sense, the Rights of Man, and Other Essential Writings. New Amer. Lib. 1984 pap. $4.95
The Rights of Man. 1791 and 1792. Biblio Dist. repr. of 1915 ed. 1979 $12.95; Citadel Pr. 1976 pap. $3.95; Penguin 1984 pap. $2.95
The Age of Reason. 1794 and 1795. Ed. by Alburey Castell, pt. 1, 2d ed. Bobbs 1957 pap. $4.24; Citadel Pr. 1976 pap. $3.95; Prometheus Bks. 1985 pap. $9.95

BOOKS ABOUT PAINE

Clark, Harry H. *Thomas Paine.* Arden Lib. 1980 $35.00
Conway, Moncure D. *The Life of Thomas Paine.* 1892. Folcroft 1973 $37.50; Norwood Edns. 1909 $37.50
Foner, Eric. *Tom Paine and the American Revolution.* Oxford Univ Pr. 1976 $22.50 pap. $8.95
Hawke, David Freeman. *Paine.* Harper 1974 o.p.

PARKMAN, FRANCIS. 1823–1893

Parkman made seven trips to Europe to search French and English archives to verify the data on which he based his remarkable histories. He chose for his general subject the rise and decline of France's power in North America. KENNETH REXROTH (see Vol. 1) wrote of *France and England in North America*, "Parkman's history is the story of our heroic age, and, like the *Iliad*, it is the story of the war between two basic types of personality. It is from this archetypal struggle that it derives its epic power. As Parkman works his history out in detail, the personal conflicts of its actors give it the intricacy and ambiguity of a psychological novel. That this struggle is echoed in the spiritual conflict of the author gives the book an intimacy and depth beyond that of factual history" (*SR*). Of the same book Edmund Wilson said, "The clarity, the momentum and color of the first volumes of Parkman's narrative are among the most brilliant achievements of the writing of history as an art." (Wilson's section on Parkman in *O Canada* is rewarding indeed.)

The *Journals*, rediscovered after almost 40 years, were started while Parkman was a Harvard University undergraduate, determined even then to write the histories in spite of poor health and eyesight. The early journals include precise and dramatic descriptions of summer trips from 1841 to 1846 in the wilds of New England, New York State, Canada, the Northwest, and Europe. Most interesting are his notes for *The Oregon Trail*, which he dictated, after a breakdown in health, to a cousin.

Books by Parkman

Works. AMS Pr. 20 vols. ea. $38.50 set $770.00

Letters. Ed. by Wilbur R. Jacobs, Univ. of Oklahoma Pr. 2 vols. 1960 o.p. More than 400 letters that tell a romantic story of the Old West.

Journals. Ed. by Mason Wade, Kraus 2 vols. in 1 1947 o.p.

The Parkman Reader. Ed. by Samuel Eliot Morison, Little, Brown 1955 o.p. From the nine-volume *France and England in North America*, Morison has chosen complete sections that have the greatest interest for readers and that together give a coherent account of early North American colonial history.

Seven Years War: A Narrative Taken from "Montcalm and Wolfe," "The Conspiracy of Pontiac" and "A Half Century of Conflict." Ed. by John H. McCallum, Harper 1968 o.p.

The Oregon Trail: Sketches of Prairie and Rocky Mountain Life. 1849. Airmont 1964 pap. $1.50; New Amer. Lib. 1950 pap. $2.25

The Conspiracy of Pontiac. 1851. Macmillan (Collier Bks.) o.p.

France and England in North America. 1865–92. ed. by David Levin, Literary Class. 2 vols. 1958 ea. $30.00; Ungar 9 vols. $180.00. "The best way to lay a foundation for the understanding of Canada is to read Francis Parkman's great history.... An unrivalled work, fascinating as well as informative" (Edmund Wilson, *O Canada*).

Pioneers of France in the New World. Corner House repr. of 1865 ed. 1970 $18.50

Montcalm and Wolfe. 1884. Peter Smith $16.00

La Salle and the Discovery of the Great West. Corner House repr. of 1889 ed. 1968 $18.50

The Jesuits in North America. Corner House repr. of 1895 ed. 1970 $18.50

Books about Parkman

Doughty, Howard. *Francis Parkman.* Harvard Univ. Pr. text ed. 1983 $9.95

Farnham, Charles H. *The Life of Francis Parkman.* Greenwood repr. of 1901 ed. lib. bdg. $17.50; *Amer. Biography Ser.* Haskell $54.95; Scholarly repr. of 1901 ed. 1970 $19.00

Gale, Robert L. *Francis Parkman.* Twayne 1973 o.p.

Parkman Club, Milwaukee. *Parkman Club Papers*. AMS Pr. 2 vols. repr. of 1897 ed. $35.00

Pease, Otis A. *Parkman's History: The Historian as Literary Critic*. Shoe String (Archon) repr. of 1953 ed. 1968 $12.50

Schramm, Wilbur J. *Francis Parkman: Representative Selections, with Introduction, Bibliography and Notes*. Arden Lib. repr. of 1938 ed. 1982 lib. bdg. $30.00

Sedgwick, Henry D. *Francis Parkman*. Richard West repr. of 1904 ed. 1973 $25.00

Wade, Mason. *Francis Parkman: Heroic Historian*. Shoe String (Archon) repr. of 1942 ed. 1972 $25.00

POTTER, DAVID M(ORRIS). 1910–1971

Potter was described in the *N.Y. Times* in 1968 by Martin Duberman of Princeton University as a man who "may be the greatest living historian of the United States. With the additional evidence of this collection of his essays [*The South and the Sectional Conflict*] I'm glad for the chance to say that in print, not least because Potter is little known outside the historical profession, in part because he has written only a few volumes . . . and in part because he has always shied away from self-advertisement."

Potter graduated from Emory University in 1932 and took his Ph.D. at Yale University in 1940. He was Harmsworth Professor at Oxford University (1947–48) and Commonwealth Fund Lecturer at London University (1963). He lectured widely and taught at a number of universities in the United States, particularly Yale University (from 1942 to 1961), leaving his Coe Professorship to go to Stanford University.

BOOKS BY POTTER

Lincoln and His Party in the Secession Crisis. AMS Pr. repr. of 1942 ed. $27.00. "Whether or not the Civil War might have been avoided is a question which Dr. Potter refrains from answering. It is a question constantly posed by his material, and the author's declaration of opinion might have strengthened his book and resolved some of his estimates. But the material is excellently presented, and Dr. Potter's position as the sworn enemy of hindsight lends a freshness and illumination to the treatment" (*Nation*).

People of Plenty: Economic Abundance and the American Character. Univ. of Chicago Pr. 1954 $15.00; Univ. of Chicago Pr. (Phoenix Bks.) pap. $5.95. " 'What then is the American, this new man?' For generations this ever fascinating question asked by Crevecoeur in 1782, has been repeated the world over. Just how, we ask, does American behavior differ from that of other peoples, and why do we act the way we do? David M. Potter, Coe Professor of American History and Chairman of American Studies at Yale University, has summarized much of the unceasing debate in a brief, important book which lifts the whole problem to a new level of analysis and understanding" (*Yale Review*).

(and Curtis Grant). *Eight Issues in American History: Views and Counterviews*. Scott, Foresman 1966 o.p.

The South and the Sectional Conflict. Louisiana State Univ. Pr. 1968 $27.50 text ed. pap. $8.95

The South and the Concurrent Majority. Ed. by Don E. Fehrenbacher and Carl N. Degler, Louisiana State Univ. Pr. 1972 $6.95

Division and the Stresses of Reunion, 1845–1876. Scott, Foresman 1973 pap. $9.95

History and American Society: The Essays of David Potter. Ed. by Don E. Fehren-
bacher, Oxford 1973 $22.50
Freedom and Its Limitations in American Life. Ed. by Don E. Fehrenbacher, Stanford
Univ. Pr. 1976 $10.00 pap. $3.95
Impending Crisis, 1848–1861. Ed. by Don E. Fehrenbacher, *New Amer. Nation Ser.*
Harper 1976 $19.18 pap. $9.95

PRESCOTT, WILLIAM HICKLING. 1796–1859

This great American historian, a native of Massachusetts and a Harvard
University graduate, injured his eye in youth and gave up his legal training.
With his sight partially restored, he became interested in the writing of history and produced his historical classics in the constant struggle against
blindness. All his books are marked by careful research, great narrative
power, and impartiality.

BOOKS BY PRESCOTT

Works. Ed. by Wilfred H. Munroe and others, AMS Pr. 22 vols. repr. of 1904 ed. ea.
$37.50 set $825.00
Papers. Ed. by C. Harvey Gardiner, Univ. of Illinois Pr. 1964 o.p. "This book, consisting of items from 34 institutional and private holders of Prescott manuscripts,
has been assembled with admirable diligence. And the manuscripts have been
edited with an even, common-sensical hand. Somehow, though, the Prescott to
be found here is not the revered historian at all but a New England dilettante
who collected Spanish-language documents and engaged in endless crabbed ex-
changes over the publication of his books" (*N.Y. Times*).
Correspondence, 1833–1847. Ed. by Roger Wolcott, Da Capo repr. of 1925 ed. $49.50
Literary Memoranda. Ed. by C. Harvey Gardiner, Univ. of Oklahoma Pr. 2 vols. 1961
$29.50. These memoranda cover most of the historian's adult life, from 1823 to
1858.
Biography and Critical Miscellanies. Arden Lib. repr. of 1875 ed. 1978 $40.00
History of the Reign of Ferdinand and Isabella the Catholic. 1838. Ed. by C. Harvey
Gardiner, Heritage o.p.
History of the Conquest of Mexico. 1843. Ed. by C. Harvey Gardiner, Univ. of Chicago
Pr. 1966 $25.00 pap. $12.00
History of the Conquest of Peru. 1847. Dutton (Everyman's) 1953 o.p.
History of the Conquest of Mexico (and *The Conquest of Peru*). Ed. by Roger Howell, Ir-
vington $22.50

BOOKS ABOUT PRESCOTT

Carter, Jimmy. *Letters to Hon. William Prescott.* Gordon 1977 $59.95
Charvat, William, and Michael Kraus. *William Hickling Prescott: Representative Selec-
tions, with Introduction, Bibliography and Notes.* Darby repr. of 1943 ed. 1983
$50.00; Norwood $35.00
Cline, Howard F., and others, eds. *William Hickling Prescott: A Memorial.* Duke Univ.
Pr. 1959 o.p.
Gardiner, C. Harvey. *Prescott and His Publishers.* Southern Illinois Univ. Pr. 1959
$5.95. "Gardiner has given us in very readable fashion and on the basis of re-
search in a wide range of sources a book that adds much insight into one of our
greatest historians" (*AHR*).
——. *William Hickling Prescott: A Biography.* Univ. of Texas Pr. 1970 $20.00

Peck, Harry T. *William Hickling Prescott: American Historian.* AMS Pr. repr. of 1905
    ed. 1970 $5.00; Greenwood repr. of 1905 ed. lib. bdg. $15.00; Associated Faculty
    Pr. repr. of 1905 ed. $15.00
Ticknor, George. *Life of William Hickling Prescott.* Richard West repr. of 1864 ed.
    $30.00

ROOSEVELT, THEODORE. 1858–1919 (NOBEL PEACE PRIZE 1906)

In 1963 the two homes of Theodore Roosevelt, the Manhattan brownstone
on East Twentieth Street where he was born, and Sagamore Hill, his Oyster
Bay, Long Island, country house, were given to the nation by the Theodore
Roosevelt Association, with $500,000 to maintain the shrines. It was at
Sagamore Hill that Roosevelt accepted the nomination for the governorship
of New York, the vice-presidency, and finally the presidency of the United
States, and it was there that he died. Through his efforts the peace conference that ended the Russo-Japanese War met at Portsmouth, New Hamp-
shire, for which Roosevelt won the Nobel Peace Prize.

One of the important scholarly projects is the publication of the remarkable collection of 10,000 Theodore Roosevelt letters, an undertaking "which
will do more to restore Theodore Roosevelt to his rightful place in the gallery of American statesmen than anything else, and one which illuminates a
whole epoch of our history" (Henry Steele Commager, *N.Y. Herald Tribune*).
Roosevelt's *Letters to His Children* is endearing and reveals the tender side of
the Rough Rider and the fun-loving disposition of a devoted father.

In 1967 an immense bronze and stone memorial to Roosevelt was un-
veiled on a wild island in the Potomac River, a setting that would have
pleased that hearty outdoorsman. President Lyndon B. Johnson spoke at the
ceremonies, calling Roosevelt a "giant" of American history and recalled his
words, "Woe to the country where a generation arises which . . . shrinks
from doing the rough work of the world."

BOOKS BY ROOSEVELT

Writings. Ed. by William H. Harbaugh, Irvington text ed. 1967 $24.50
Presidential Addresses and State Papers. Intro. by Albert Shaw, Kraus 4 vols. repr. of
    1905 ed. 1968 $68.00
Addresses and Presidential Messages, 1902–1904. Intro. by Henry Cabot Lodge, Kraus
    repr. $22.00
*The Roosevelt Policy: Speeches, Letters and State Papers, Relating to Corporate Wealth
    and Closely Allied Topics.* Ed. by William Griffith, Kraus 3 vols. in 1 repr. of 1919
    ed. $51.00
Letters. Ed. by Elting E. Morison and John M. Blum, Harvard Univ. Pr. 8 vols. 1951–
    54 vols. 1–2, 5–6 o.p. vols. 3–4 set $65.00 vols. 7–8 set $60.00
Letters to His Children. Ed. by Joseph B. Bishop, Norwood repr. of 1919 ed. $20.00
*Selections from the Correspondence of Theodore Roosevelt and Henry Cabot Lodge,
    1884–1918.* Amer. Public Figures Ser. Da Capo 2 vols. repr. of 1925 ed. 1971 lib.
    bdg. $125.00
*The Naval War of 1812; or The History of the United States Navy during the Last War
    with Great Britain.* Scholarly repr. of 1882 ed. 1971 $59.00
Hunting Trips of a Ranchman: Sketches of Sport on the Northern Cattle Plains. Irving-
    ton repr. of 1885 ed. $34.50

Gouverneur Morris. AMS Pr. repr. of 1888 ed. $22.00; Scholarly repr. of 1888 ed. 1971 $14.00

Ranch Life and the Hunting Trail. 1888. Univ. of Nebraska Pr. (Bison) 1983 $19.95 pap. $8.95

The Winning of the West. Ed. by Harvey Wish, Peter Smith 4 vols. repr. of 1889–96 ed. $11.00; Somerset Pub. $125.00

American Ideals and Other Essays, Social and Political. AMS Pr. repr. of 1897 ed. $17.00; Scholarly repr. of 1897 ed. $16.00

Rough Riders. Corner House repr. of 1899 ed. 1971 $17.50

Thomas Hart Benton. Ed. by John T. Morse, *Amer. Statesmen Ser.* AMS Pr. repr. of 1899 ed. $32.00

The Wilderness Hunter: An Account of the Big Game of the United States and Its Chase with Horse, Hound and Rifle. Irvington repr. of 1900 ed. $29.50

Strenuous Life: Essays and Addresses. Scholarly repr. of 1902 ed. $17.00

Maxims. Irvington repr. of 1903 ed. $14.00

Outdoor Pastimes of an American Hunter. *Amer. Environmental Studies* Ayer repr. of 1905 ed. $29.00

The New Nationalism. Peter Smith repr. of 1910 ed. $10.25

Recognizable Ideals. Essay Index Repr. Ser. Ayer repr. of 1911 ed. $17.00

Autobiography. Da Capo repr. of 1913 ed. 1985 pap. $12.95

History as Literature and Other Essays. Associated Faculty Pr. repr. of 1913 ed. $24.00

BOOKS ABOUT ROOSEVELT

Bailey, Thomas A. *Roosevelt and the Japanese-American Crisis.* Peter Smith 1964 o.p.

Barron, Gloria J. *Leadership in Crisis.* Associated Faculty Pr. 1973 $14.95

Beale, Howard K. *Theodore Roosevelt and the Rise of America to World Power.* 1956. Johns Hopkins Univ. Pr. 1984 pap. $10.95. Excellent scholarship.

Beers, Henry A. *Four Americans.* Essay Index Repr. Ser. Ayer repr. of 1919 ed. $13.50

Black, G. J., ed. *Theodore Roosevelt, 1858–1919: Chronology, Documents, Bibliographic Aids.* Presidential Chronology Ser. Oceana 1969 $8.00

Blum, John M. *Republican Roosevelt.* 1954. Harvard Univ. Pr. 2d ed. 1962 $10.00 pap. $4.95.

Burton, David H. *Theodore Roosevelt.* World Leaders Ser. G. K. Hall (Twayne) 1973 lib. bdg. $12.50

———. *Theodore Roosevelt and His English Correspondents: A Special Relationship of Friends.* Transaction Ser. Amer. Philosophical Society 1973 pap. $1.00

Butt, Archibald W. *Taft and Roosevelt.* Amer. History and Culture in the 20th-Century Ser. Associated Faculty Pr. 1971 $65.00

Cadenheard, I. E. *Theodore Roosevelt: the Paradox of Progressivism.* Ed. by Kenneth Colegrove, *Shapers of History Ser.* Barron 1974 pap. $3.95

Charnwood, Lord. *Theodore Roosevelt.* Folcroft repr. of 1923 ed. lib. bdg. $20.00

Chessman, G. Wallace. *Theodore Roosevelt and the Politics of Power.* Little, Brown 1969 o.p. "Perhaps wisely, the author has shunned Roosevelt as a 'colorful' character, huntsman, Rough Rider and all that, and set his direct, unadorned prose to the task of showing him in political action" (*PW*).

Cooper, John Milton. *The Warrior and the Priest: Woodrow Wilson and Theodore Roosevelt.* Harvard Univ. Pr. (Belknap Pr.) 1983 $20.00

Dennett, Tyler. *Theodore Roosevelt and the Russo-Japanese War.* Peter Smith 1958 $10.75

Dyer, Thomas G. *Theodore Roosevelt and the Idea of Race.* Louisiana State Univ. Pr. 1980 $17.50

Esthus, Raymond A. *Theodore Roosevelt and Japan.* Univ. of Washington Pr. 1967 o.p. "A clear and straightforward narrative of a complicated and important period of American diplomatic history" (*LJ*).

——. *Theodore Roosevelt and the International Rivalries. Amer. Diplomatic History Ser.* Regina Bks. text ed. repr. of 1970 ed. 1982 $16.95

Gable, John A. *The Bull Moose Years: Theodore Roosevelt and the Progressive Party.* Associated Faculty Pr. 1978 $25.50

Gardner, Joseph L. *Departing Glory: Theodore Roosevelt as Ex-President.* Scribner 1973 o.p.

Gibson, William M. *Theodore Roosevelt among the Humorists: W. D. Howells, Mark Twain, and Mr. Dooley.* Univ. of Tennessee Pr. 1980 $8.95

Gosnell, Harold F. *Boss Platt and His New York Machine: A Study of the Political Leadership of Thomas C. Platt, Theodore Roosevelt, and Others.* Scholarly repr. of 1924 ed. 1971 $49.00

Grantham, Dewey, ed. *Theodore Roosevelt.* Prentice-Hall 1971 o.p.

Hagedorn, Hermann. *The Roosevelt Family of Sagamore Hill.* Macmillan 1954 o.p. A graceful and refreshing account of the domestic felicity of Roosevelt.

Harvard University Library: Theodore Roosevelt Collection, Dictionary Catalogue and Shelflist. Harvard Univ. Pr. 5 vols. 1970 $250.00

Howland, Harold. *Theodore Roosevelt and His Times.* Elliots Bks. text ed. 1921 $8.50

Hurwitz, Howard L. *Theodore Roosevelt and Labor in New York State, 1880–1900. Columbia Univ. Studies in the Social Sciences* AMS Pr. repr. of 1943 ed. $18.00

Jones, V. C. *Roosevelt's Rough Riders.* Doubleday 1971 o.p.

Keller, Morton, ed. *Theodore Roosevelt: A Profile. World Profiles Ser.* Hill & Wang o.p. Selections from William Allen White, John M. Blum, Stuart Sherman, H. L. Mencken, Hamilton Basso, John Chamberlain, Louis Filler, Dixon Wector, Richard Hofstadter, and Howard K. Beale.

Marks, Frederick W., III. *Velvet on Iron: The Diplomacy of Theodore Roosevelt.* Univ. of Nebraska Pr. (Bison) 1982 $18.95 pap. $5.95

McCullough, David G. *Mornings on Horseback.* G. K. Hall 1981 $19.95; Simon & Schuster (Touchstone Bks.) 1982 pap. $9.95

McKee, Delber. *Chinese Exclusion versus the Open Door Policy, 1900–1906: Clashes over China Policy in the Roosevelt Era.* Wayne State Univ. Pr. 1977 $17.95

Merriam, Charles E. *Four American Party Leaders: Henry Ward Beecher Foundation Letters, Amherst College. Essay Index Repr. Ser.* Ayer 1926 $11.50

Morris, Edmund. *The Rise of Theodore Roosevelt.* Ballantine 1980 pap. $8.95

Mowry, George E. *The Era of Theodore Roosevelt and the Birth of Modern America, 1900–1912.* 1958. *New Amer. Nation Ser.* Harper 1963 pap. $6.95

——. *Theodore Roosevelt and the Progressive Movement.* 1946. Hill & Wang 1960 o.p. "A scholarly, critical and original" work containing valuable material on U.S. political development.

Murphy, Eloise C. *Theodore Roosevelt's Night Ride to the Presidency.* Adirondack Museum 1977 pap. $2.50

Musso, Louis, III. *Theodore Roosevelt: Soldier, Statesman and President.* Ed. by Sigurd C. Rahmas. *Outstanding Personalities Ser.* SamHar Pr. 1982 $3.25 pap. $1.95

Neu, Charles E. *An Uncertain Friendship: Theodore Roosevelt and Japan, 1906–1909.* Harvard Univ. Pr. 1967 $18.50. "Neu omits any extensive treatment of the Russo-Japanese War of 1904–05 and tends to place much more emphasis upon the domestic background of Roosevelt's foreign policy. Roosevelt emerges from the pages of this book as a shrewd politician as well as a diplomat. Recommended" (*Choice*).

Norton, Aloysius A. *Theodore Roosevelt. Twayne's U.S. Authors Ser.* G. K. Hall 1980
     $12.50
O'Gara, Gordon C. *Theodore Roosevelt and the Rise of the Modern Navy.* Greenwood
     repr. of 1943 ed. lib. bdg. $15.00
Pringle, H. F. *Theodore Roosevelt.* 1931. Harvest Bks. 1956 pap. $8.95. This biography
     won the Pulitzer Prize in 1932.
Riis, Jacob A. *Theodore Roosevelt: The Citizen.* AMS Pr. repr. of 1904 ed. $17.50;
     Scholarly repr. of 1904 ed. 1970 $17.00
Roosevelt, Kermit. *Memories of My Father.* Foundation Class repr. of 1920 ed. $54.85
Schoch, Henry A. *Theodore Roosevelt: The Story behind the Scenery.* Ed. by Gweneth
     R. DenDooven, KC Publications 1974 $8.95 pap. $3.75
Trami, Eugene P. *The Treaty of Portsmouth: An Adventure in American Diplomacy.*
     Univ. Pr. of Kentucky 1969 $19.00

SCHLESINGER, ARTHUR M(EIER). 1888–1965

Called the "leading interpreter of America's past," Arthur Schlesinger, Sr.,
was born in Xenia, Ohio, and graduated from Ohio State University. He
taught at Harvard University for many years and went on many "professional pilgrimages to worldwide houses of learning." His volume of essays
New Viewpoints in American History was far-reaching in its influence; it
marked the turning point in methods of research. He once said, "In my writing and teaching I have done all I could to disseminate the idea that history
should be as inclusive as life itself."

He was, of course, the father of a distinguished living historian, Arthur
Schlesinger, Jr. In 1965 Radcliffe College renamed its Women's Archives
the Arthur and Elizabeth Schlesinger Library on the History of Women
in America because of Schlesinger's work as the first historian to emphasize the American woman's contribution to history and to honor his
wife's work in this field.

BOOKS BY ARTHUR SCHLESINGER

New Viewpoints in American History. Greenwood repr. of 1922 ed. 1977 lib. bdg.
     $19.25
Learning How to Behave: A Historical Study of American Etiquette Books. Cooper
     Square Pr. repr. of 1946 ed. 1968 $20.00
Paths to the Present. AMS Pr. repr. of 1949 ed. 1963 $29.95
(and Dixon R. Fox, eds.). *History of American Life Series.* Macmillan 12 vols. 1950 o.p.
Colonial Merchants and the American Revolution, 1763–1776. Atheneum 1968 o.p.;
     Ungar 1957 o.p.
Prelude to Independence: The Newspaper War on Britain, 1764–1776. Greenwood repr.
     of 1958 ed. 1979 $27.50; Northeastern Univ. Pr. 1980 pap. $9.95
In Retrospect: The History of a Historian. Harcourt 1963 o.p. "A rewarding autobio-
     graphical memoir—an engaging causerie, not a reverie" (Charles Poore, *N.Y.
     Times*).
The Critical Period in American Religion, 1875–1900. Fortress Pr. 1967 o.p.
The Birth of the Nation: A Portrait of the American People on the Eve of Independence.
     1968. Houghton Mifflin 1981 pap. $6.95. "A masterly summation of a distin-
     guished historian's lifelong study of American national character. It comments
     wisely and lucidly not only on the traits which helped shape American indepen-

dence, but also on the enduring characteristics of the American people" (Oscar Handlin).

Nothing Stands Still: Essays by Arthur M. Schlesinger. Harvard Univ. Pr. (Belknap Pr.) 1969 $14.00

The New Deal in Action. Folcroft repr. 1977 $15.00

SCHLESINGER, ARTHUR M(EIER), JR. 1917–

The Age of Jackson, which won the Pulitzer Prize in 1946, established Arthur Schlesinger, Jr., as one of the most challenging of U.S. historians. After graduating summa cum laude from Harvard University in 1938, he returned as a junior fellow that year and collected the material for his book on Jackson. He was awarded a Guggenheim Fellowship to complete his study of the New Deal and received a grant from the American Academy of Arts and Letters for distinguished writing. In 1947, he was appointed an associate professor of history at Harvard, where his father had been professor of history. The younger Schlesinger has become the chronicler of the Roosevelt era and was closely associated with the Kennedy administration, having served as special assistant to the president until his death. In 1964 he returned briefly to Harvard. With Morton White, he edited *Paths of American Thought,* which the *Library Journal* called "the first full-scale effort to synthesize American intellectual history since Parrington's landmark of the 1920's." He was a vigorous critic of the Vietnam War. In 1967, Schlesinger received the gold medal for his total literary achievement from the National Institute of Arts and Letters.

BOOKS BY ARTHUR SCHLESINGER, JR.

The Age of Jackson. Little, Brown 1945 $15.95 1963 pap. $7.70

Vital Center. Houghton Mifflin 1949 o.p.

The Age of Roosevelt. Houghton Mifflin 3 vols.. 1957–60 vol. 1 $12.95 pap. $5.95 vols 2–3 o.p.

The Politics of Hope. Houghton Mifflin 1963 o.p. A compilation taken from essays, articles, speeches, and reviews during a 13-year period.

(and Morton M. White, eds.). *Paths of American Thought.* Houghton Mifflin 1963 o.p.

A Thousand Days: John F. Kennedy in the White House. Fawcett repr. of 1965 ed. 1977 pap. $3.50. Winner of the 1966 National Book Award for history and biography and the Pulitzer Prize for biography. "A remarkable feat of scholarship and writing, set in the widest historical and intellectual frame—and all the more astounding for having been written in something less than 18 months. . . . The chronicle is fresh, vivid and informative, but what the historian has done is to recreate the historical, political and personal context in which the events take place. . . . He has a sure grasp of the party rivalries, factional quarrels, intellectual and policy differences and quirks of personality in which issues and policies were entangled. . . . This is Arthur Schlesinger's best book. A great President has found—perhaps he deliberately chose—a great historian" (James McGregor Burns, *N.Y. Times*).

The Bitter Heritage: Vietnam and American Democracy, 1941–1966. 1966. Fawcett rev. ed. 1972 o.p.

(and Alfred De Grazia). *Congress and the Presidency: Their Role in Modern Times.* Amer. Enterprise Institute 1967 $14.25

American as Reformer. Harvard Univ. Pr. 2d ed. 1968 $7.95

The Crisis of Confidence: Ideas, Power and Violence in America. Houghton Mifflin 1969 o.p. "Whether discussing the role and responsibilities of intellectuals, the anarchist impulse in undergraduate extremism or the prospects for politics in the years ahead, Schlesinger is sensitive to the 'crisis of self-confidence' which this country is undergoing and fully aware of the current rash of despair about our political system. But he gives no quarter to those who would reject the process of reason. . . . To no one's surprise, Professor Schlesinger again shows himself to be as much a man of politics as he is a historian" (John H. Bunzel, *SR*).

(and F. L. Israel). *The History of American Presidential Elections.* Chelsea House 10 vols. repr. of 1971 ed. 1981 $300.00

The Coming to Power: Critical Presidential Elections in American History. Chelsea House repr. of 1972 ed. 1981 pap. $10.00

The Imperial Presidency. Houghton Mifflin 1973 o.p. "A survey of nearly 200 years of conflict . . . arising from the Constitution's establishment of an inherently unstable division of powers" (*Newsweek*).

(ed.). *A History of U.S. Political Parties.* Chelsea House 4 vols. repr. of 1973 ed. pap. $75.00

(and Eugene P. Moehring, eds.). *America To-Day: Observations and Reflections.* Ayer repr. 1974 $19.00

(ed.). *Foreign Travelers in America, 1810–1935.* Ayer 39 vols. 1974 $1,088.00

Robert Kennedy and His Times. Houghton Mifflin 1978 $19.95

(ed.). *American Statesmen.* Chelsea House 24 vols. 1982 pap. $172.90

(ed.). *Dynamics of World Power: A Documentary History of U.S. Foreign Policy, 1945–73.* Chelsea House 10 vols. 1983 pap. $80.00

(ed.). *The Almanac of American History.* Putnam 1984 $24.95

THOMAS, NORMAN (MATTOON). 1884–1968

Norman Thomas stands out as the Great Dissenter of our Age, representing as he did, even at 84, half-blind and crippled with arthritis, the reformer whom young people had flocked to hear at 83, the indomitable idealist and fighter for his ideals to the end, charming and humorous always but uncompromising as to his goals. After his death, the many organizations and causes he supported (civil liberties, help to the underprivileged—particularly the victims of the ghetto—the ending of the Vietnam War, nuclear arms control) were still sending out the letters signed by him which he had composed in the nursing home where he died. There, too, he had with characteristic energy conferred regularly nearly to the last minute with the editor of his final book, *The Choices.*

Born of a family of clergymen, Thomas studied at Union Theological Seminary and himself became a Presbyterian clergyman but decided, after a period working as a minister in East Harlem, that the Socialist party was the only means by which he could try to do something about the poverty and degradation he found there. He became a crusader for socialism, its strongest and most compelling voice, and ran six times for president on the Socialist ticket as well as for many other offices—which he never won—and never, indeed, expected to win.

In his later years, Thomas was no longer a politician, but a fighter for civilized values whenever he saw them jeopardized or betrayed. At his death, President Lyndon B. Johnson said, "With the passing of Norman Thomas,

America loses one of its most eloquent speakers, finest writers and most creative thinkers. Mr. Thomas was once asked what he considered to be his greatest achievements. With characteristic modesty he replied, 'To live to be my age and feel that one has kept the faith, or tried to . . . to be able to sleep at night with reasonable satisfaction.' Norman Thomas kept the faith. He was a humane and courageous man who lived to see many of the causes he championed become the law of the land."

BOOKS BY THOMAS

Is Conscience a Crime? (The Conscientious Objector in America). 1927. Oyez 1972 $19.95

The Choice before Us: Mankind at the Crossroads. AMS Pr. repr. of 1934 ed. 1970 $17.50

Socialist's Faith. Associated Faculty Pr. repr. of 1951 ed. $23.00

The Test of Freedom. Greenwood repr. of 1954 ed. 1974 lib. bdg. $15.00

The Prerequisites for Peace. Greenwood repr. of 1959 ed. 1978 $19.75

Great Dissenters. Norton 1961 o.p.

Socialism Re-examined. Greenwood repr. of 1963 ed. 1984 lib. bdg. $37.50

The Choices. McKay 1969 o.p.

BOOKS ABOUT THOMAS

Durham, James C. *Norman M. Thomas.* Twayne 1974 o.p.

Gorham, Charles. *Leader at Large: The Long and Fighting Life of Norman Thomas.* Farrar 1970 o.p.

Johnpoll, Bernard. *Pacifist's Progress: Norman Thomas and the Decline of American Socialism.* Garland 1974 $42.00

Seidler, Murray B. *Norman Thomas: Respectable Rebel.* Syracuse Univ. Pr. 2d ed. 1967 $10.95

Steward, Bright. *Mister Socialism: Norman Thomas, His Life and Times.* Lyle Stuart 1974 $7.95

TOCQUEVILLE, ALEXIS (CHARLES HENRI MAURICE CLEREL) DE. 1805–1859

The French writer Alexis de Tocqueville is best known in this country for his *Democracy in America.* In 1831 he was sent on a mission to the United States to study American penitentiaries. The results of his findings, written in collaboration with Gustave de Beaumont de la Bonnière, were published in 1833 under the title *Du Système Penitentiaire aux Etats-Unis et de son Application en France.* It was this journey that inspired his more famous work, written soon after. He became French minister of foreign affairs in 1849.

BOOKS BY TOCQUEVILLE

(and Gustave de Beaumont). *On the Penitentiary System in the United States.* 1833. Trans. by Francis Lieber, Patterson Smith o.p.; Southern Illinois Univ. Pr. 1964 o.p. "This is a fascinating book from the point of view of social history; much is here that could have relevance to our so-called modern methods" (*LJ*).

Democracy in America. 1835–40. Ed. by J. P. Mayer, trans. by George Lawrence; Doubleday (Anchor) 1969 pap. $10.95; trans. by Phillips Bradley, Random 2 vols. 1944 ea. $4.95. The Lawrence translation is excellent.

Old Regime and the French Revolution. 1856. Ed. by J. P. Mayer and A. P. Kerr, Dou-
bleday 1955 pap. $5.50
The Recollections of Alexis de Tocqueville. 1893 Ed. by J. P. Mayer, trans. by Alexan-
der de Mattos; Greenwood repr. of 1896 ed. 1979 $20.50
The European Revolution and Correspondence with Gobineau. Trans. and ed. by John
Luckacs, Greenwood repr. of 1959 ed. 1975 $22.75
Alexis de Tocqueville on Democracy, Revolution and Society. Ed. by John Stone and
Stephen Mennell, *Heritage of Sociology Ser.* Univ. of Chicago Pr. 1980 $27.50
Tocqueville's America: The Great Quotations. Ohio Univ. Pr. 1983 pap. $5.95

BOOKS ABOUT TOCQUEVILLE

Adams, Herbert B. *Jared Sparks and Alexis de Tocqueville.* AMS Pr. repr. of 1898 ed.
$11.50; Johnson Repr. 1898 ed. pap. $9.00
Bryce, James B. *Predictions of Hamilton and De Tocqueville.* AMS Pr. repr. of 1887 ed.
$11.50; Johnson Repr. 1887 ed. 1973 pap. $9.00
Drescher, Seymour. *Dilemmas of Democracy: Tocqueville and Modernization.* Univ. of
Pittsburgh Pr. 1968 $19.95
——. *Tocqueville and England.* Harvard Univ. Pr. 1964 $16.50.
Gargan, Edward T. *De Tocqueville.* Hillary House 1965 o.p. "Gargan has given us a
brief study that should be useful to undergraduates who are unfamiliar with the
main outlines of Tocqueville's work. . . . Gargan somewhat modifies the fashion-
able view that Tocqueville was simply a pessimist whose prophecies concerning
the development of democracy were delivered in tones of utter despair. There is
a good bibliography, including editions and translations of Tocqueville's works,
and a list of 20 critical studies in four languages" (*Choice*).
Goldstein, Doris. *Trial of Faith: Religion and Politics in Tocqueville's Thought.*
Elsevier 1975 $21.00
Herr, Richard. *Tocqueville and the Old Regime.* Princeton Univ. Pr. 1962 o.p. Insightful interpretation.
Lerner, Max. *Tocqueville and America.* Harper 1969 o.p.
Mayer, J. P. *Alexis de Tocqueville: A Biographical Study in Political Science.* 1940. Pe-
ter Smith 1960 $10.25
Pierson, George W. *Tocqueville in America.* 1959. Peter Smith 1960 $12.00
Poggi, Gianfranco. *Images of Society: Essays on the Sociological Theories of Tocque-
ville, Marx and Durkheim.* Stanford Univ. Pr. 1972 $22.50
Reeves, Richard. *American Journey: Travelling with Tocqueville in Search of Democ-
racy in America.* Simon & Schuster 1982 $15.95
Schleifer, James T. *The Making of Tocqueville's "Democracy in America."* Univ. of
North Carolina Pr. 1980 $26.00
Zeitlin, Irving M. *Liberty, Equality and Revolution in Alexis de Tocqueville.* Little,
Brown 1971 o.p.
Zetterbaum, Marvin. *Tocqueville and the Problem of Democracy.* Stanford Univ. Pr.
1967 $15.00

TURNER, FREDERICK JACKSON. 1861–1932

Born in Wisconsin, Turner graduated from the University of Wisconsin,
where he later taught, and received his Ph.D. from Johns Hopkins University. His estimate of the importance of the frontier struggles in the development of the American character and consciousness was unique in his day.
He once described U.S. history as "a series of social evolutions recurring in

differing geographic basins across a raw continent." He was professor of history at Harvard University from 1910 to 1924. Oscar Handlin wrote of him, "Turner himself best explained his role: 'My work really grew out of preliminary training in Medieval history, where I learned to recognize the reactions between a people in the gristle, and their environment, and saw the interplay of economic, social and geographic factors in the politics, institutions, ideals and life of a nation and its relations with its neighbors.' He did not set his students to work on the frontier of the West in any narrow sense. He asked the best of them to deal with the interplay he recognized, demanding of them also a commitment to precise methods; and did much to vitalize American historiography in the Progressive era" (*N.Y. Times*).

The Significance of Sections in American History won him a posthumous Pulitzer Prize.

BOOKS BY TURNER

Early Writings. Ayer repr. of 1938 ed. $19.00

America's Great Frontiers and Section: Unpublished Essays. 1965. Ed. by Wilbur R. Jacobs, Peter Smith o.p.

The Historical World of Frederick Jackson Turner with Selections from His Correspondence. Ed. by Wilbur R. Jacobs, Yale Univ. Pr. 1968 o.p.

Frederick Jackson Turner's Legacy: Unpublished Writings in American History. Ed. by Wilbur R. Jacobs, Univ. of Nebraska Pr. 1965 $17.95

The Character and Influence of the Indian Trade in Wisconsin. 1891. AMS Pr. repr. of 1891 ed. $11.50

(ed.). *Correspondence of the French Ministers to the United States, 1791–1797.* Da Capo repr. of 1904 ed. $115.00

The Significance of the Frontier in American History. 1894. Ed. by Harold P. Simonson, Ungar pap. $2.95. Essays delivered at the 1893 meeting of the American Historical Association.

The Rise of the New West, 1819–1829. 1906. Macmillan (Collier Bks.) 1962 o.p.

Europe, 1789–1920. Norwood repr. of 1920 ed. $15.00

The Frontier in American History. Krieger repr. of 1920 ed. 1976 $16.50

The Significance of Sections in American History. 1932 Peter Smith o.p.

The United States, 1830–1850. 1935. Peter Smith $12.00

Beyond Geography: The Western Spirit against the Wilderness. Rutgers Univ. Pr. 1983 pap. $10.95; Viking 1980 $16.95

BOOKS ABOUT TURNER

Alexander, Fred. *Moving Frontiers.* Associated Faculty Pr. repr. of 1947 ed. 1969 $13.50

Benson, Lee. *Turner and Beard: American Historical Writing Reconsidered.* Greenwood repr. 1980 $22.50.

Billington, Ray Allen. *Frederick Jackson Turner: Historian, Scholar, Teacher.* Oxford 1973 $35.00. "This is the rich harvest of decades of fruitful study devoted to the thought and writings of Turner. It is not another analysis of the frontier and sectional hypotheses but rather a full account of the intellectual and professional life of this most eminent historian" (*Choice*).

————. *Genesis of the Frontier Thesis: A Study in Historical Creativity.* Huntington Lib. 1971 $12.50

————, ed. *Frontier Thesis: Valid Interpretation of American History. Amer. Problems Studies Ser.* Krieger 1977 pap. $5.95

Carpenter, Ronald H. *The Eloquence of Frederick Jackson Turner.* Huntington Lib. 1983 $20.00

Fox, Dixon R., ed. *Sources of Culture in the Middle West.* Russell repr. of 1934 ed. 1964 $7.95

Gaunt, William. *Turner.* Merrimack 1983 $17.95

Hofstadter, Richard. *The Progressive Historians: Turner, Beard, Parrington.* Univ. of Chicago Pr. 1979 pap. $7.95. "The sympathetic portrayal of the Progressive intellectual as underdog does not diminish from the objective, indeed clinical, quality of Hofstadter's criticism, which is as full on the failings of his subjects as on their achievements. His discussion is incisive and lucid, written with grace and wit, unflaggingly interesting" (Oscar Handlin, *N.Y. Times*).

Jacobs, Wilbur R., and others. *Turner, Bolton, and Webb: Three Historians of the American Frontier.* Univ. of Washington Pr. 1979 pap. $5.95

Taylor, George R., ed. *Turner Thesis Concerning the Role of the Frontier in American History. Problems in Amer. Civilization* Heath 3d ed. 1972 pap. $5.95

WOODWARD, C(OMER) VANN. 1908–

C. Vann Woodward, the distinguished historian of the South, is Sterling Professor of History at Yale University. Born in Arkansas, he graduated from Emory University in 1930 and received his Ph.D. from the University of North Carolina in 1937.

His modest volume (the second revised edition is only 205 pages) *The Strange Career of Jim Crow* has become an American classic. William Styron has called it "one of the most valuable works we have in the entire literature of the American racial dilemma," and the late Ralph McGill wrote of the new edition, "A revised edition of 'The Strange Career of Jim Crow' by C. Vann Woodward to include events of the past decade and to relate them to the past out of which they came is an outstanding service to those wishing to understand the South, the nation, and the traumatic experiences in our slums and in the South. Mr. Vann Woodward is not merely a great American historian, but is without peer in his knowledge of, and ability to write about, things Southern." *The Burden of Southern History* became a second classic, and it too has recently appeared in revision.

Professor Woodward has taught and lectured widely, principally—before his Yale tenure—at Johns Hopkins University, from 1946 to 1961. He was Harmsworth Professor at Oxford University (1954–55), and has won the award of the American Council of Learned Societies, the National Institute of Arts and Letters Award, and the Bancroft Prize for his historical writing. With the recent intensification of interest in Afro-American history and the southern past, he has been much in demand for articles on the subject and has contributed to many periodicals as well as to the Sunday magazine section of the *N.Y. Times*.

BOOKS BY WOODWARD

The Origins of the New South, 1877–1913. 1951. *History of the South Ser.* Louisiana State Univ. Pr. 1972 $27.50 text ed. pap. $7.95. "Beyond all question this is the most valuable book that has been written about the South in these years. Because of its freshness of view and its critical scholarship in a period long neglected, it is the most useful volume of 'A History of the South' that has appeared. Although the awkward dates assigned to the volume prevented a clearly defined synthesis, the book clearly established the author's primacy among the scholars of the 'New South' (a term which he righteously deplores)" (W. B. Hesseltine, *AHR*).

Reunion and Reaction: The Compromise of 1877 and the End of Reconstruction. 1951. Little, Brown rev. ed. 1966 pap. $2.45. "Dr. Woodward has tracked down masses of hitherto unknown yet important material, but from it he has articulated a fresh, vital thing, full-bodied, incisive, revealing. At long last we know all the unsavory details of an episode which—even in the incomplete form that we knew in the past—already smelled to high heaven" (*The Annals*).

The Strange Career of Jim Crow. 1955 Oxford 3d ed. rev. 1974 pap. $5.95. This is an "up-to-date" edition of one of the most valuable books in the entire canon of race relations in the United States. It was Mr. Woodward who in 1955 reminded a forgetful South that segregation of the Negro was not at all an inviolate tenet of the Southern way of life, that for many years after the Civil War Negroes mixed freely with whites in the South, and that the most rigorous opponents of separation of the races by Jim Crow laws were the leaders of Southern society themselves" (*New Yorker*).

The Burden of Southern History. 1960. Louisiana State Univ. Pr. 2d ed., rev. & enl. 1968 $20.00 pap. $7.95. "It is in the magnificent flowering of the Southern literary renascence, of course, that Dr. Woodward finds the most perfect expression of the Southern ethic: its haunting sense of guilt, its sense of place, as opposed to the rootlessness of typically American writers like Hemingway and their characters; and most of all, its overwhelming consciousness of the past in the present, as Allen Tate has expressed it, Dr. Woodward overstates his case, somewhat, when he excludes New England authors, generally, from this traditionalism. . . . Stimulating and thoughtful book" (*SR*).

(ed.). *The Comparative Approach to American History.* Basic Bks. 1968 pap. $8.95. "Until recently, American historians have been accused of parochialism in their approach, of neglecting the comparative method and dwelling on the *in*comparable in our history. In this collection of 24 essays, top-flight historians display their virtuosity in applying the comparative method. They compare the American and French revolutions; the Enlightenment here and in Europe; the differences in slavery in North and South America; the failure of Marxist socialists with the labor movement in the U.S. compared to their success in other countries. From the Colonial period to the Cold War, they find comparisons everywhere. Most of the essays were originally lectures heard over the Voice of America; their foreign-audience slant will give new perspectives to historians and lay readers alike" (*PW*).

American Counterpoint: Slavery and Race in the North-South Dialogue. Oxford 1971 pap. $7.95

(ed.). *The American South.* Ayer 7 vols. 1973 $108.00

(ed.). *Mary Chesnut's Civil War.* Yale Univ. Pr. 1981 $40.00 pap. $14.95

Tom Watson: Agrarian Rebel. Univ. Pr. of Virginia repr. 1982 $15.00

CHAPTER 8

Western Hemisphere:
Canada and Latin America

Rodney Phillips and Danilo H. Figueredo

Not life, liberty and the pursuit of happiness, but peace, order and good government are what the national government of Canada guarantees. Under these it is assumed life, liberty and happiness may be achieved, but each according to his taste. For a society of allegiance admits of a diversity the society of compact does not, and one of the blessings of the Canadian way of life is that there is no Canadian way of life, much less two, but a unity under the crown admitting a thousand diversities.
> —W. L. MORTON, quoted in Charles Taylor's *Radical Tories*

These huge countreys of the Indies, having no common links of affinitie, lawe, language or religion, and being of themselves able to maintain themselves without forreine commerce, are not so simple, as not to knowe their owne strength, and to finde, that they doe rather possesse Spaniardes, than that they are possessed by them.
> —LAURENCE KEYMIS, as quoted in V. S. Naipaul, *The Loss of El Dorado*

For what lands can men take more pride in than in our long-suffering American Republics, raised up from among the silent Indian masses by the bleeding arms of a hundred apostles, to the sounds of battle between the book and the processional candle? Never in history have such advanced and united nations been forged in so short a time from such disorganized elements.
> —JOSÉ MARTÍ, in a letter of July 27, 1881, printed in *Our America*

CANADA

Atop the North American continent lies a giant who has spent nearly two centuries rising from her torn roots to take her place in the pantheon of world powers. Canada, the second largest country in the world, a nation that is both European and American, has often been overshadowed by the presence of its long-term ally, the United States. A nation rich in resources, Canada has played a quiet role in international politics, participating in two world wars, yet staying away from conflicts and confrontations with other countries. The bilingual issue—both in language and culture—has kept it occupied, and the vast resources have always made Canadians look inward for growth and expansion.

But as modern Canada struggles to maintain its identity and not become like its neighbor to the south, its voice, through colorful politicians, talented writers, and naturalists fervently fighting to conserve the beauty of the land, is heard more and more in the world's arena. And the one thing Canada wants, as the writers listed below tell so eloquently, is to shape its own destiny.

General Surveys, Bibliographies, and Reference Works

Brebner, John Bartlet. *Canada: A Modern History. History of the Modern World Ser.* Univ. of Michigan Pr. rev. & enl. ed. 1970 $10.00. A good, solid, very readable text and overview.

Callwood, June. *Portrait of Canada.* Doubleday 1981 $14.95. An entertaining chronology of Canadian history written for the general reader by a well-known journalist. A good introduction.

Canadian Almanac and Directory. Gale annual 1985 $64.00. This is the one hundred thirty-eighth edition of a popular reference work that provides information on libraries, government agencies, organizations, etc. Arranged by topic and similar in format to the *United States Government Manual.*

Halpenny, Frances, and others, eds. *Dictionary of Canadian Biography.* Univ. of Toronto Pr. 11 vols. 1966–82 ea. $45.00. An outstanding reference work with superior biographical articles including bibliographies. Each volume in the series covers a particular period and is introduced by excellent survey articles.

Lanctot, Gustave. *A History of Canada: From the Treaty of Utrecht to the Treaty of Paris, 1713–1963.* Trans. by Margaret Cameron, Harvard Univ. Pr. vol. 3 1965 $20.00. A solid, well-written, well-researched history of Canada by the eminent French-Canadian scholar.

MacGregor, James C. *A History of Alberta.* Univ. of Washington Pr. 1981 $15.95. An acceptable general survey of the province of Alberta, center of Canada's oil industry and heart of the Canadian Rockies.

McNaught, Kenneth. *Pelican History of Canada.* Penguin rev. ed. 1975 pap. $5.95. A history of Canada written for the general reader. Comprehensive, fast reading. A good introduction to the subject.

Morton, W. L., and Donald G. Creighton, eds. *The Canadian Centenary Series.* Oxford 15 vols. 1963–85 consult publisher for individual volumes and prices. Traces the history of Canada from the discovery to the twentieth century. The volumes, each by an eminent scholar, are well researched and present a descriptive and accurate picture of different historical epochs. Representative volumes include Tryggvi Oleson's *Early Voyages and Northern Approaches, 100–1632;* William J. Eccles's *Canada under Louis XIV, 1663–1700;* Donald G. Creighton's *The Forked Road: Canada, 1839–1857;* and Fernand Ouellet's *Lower Canada, 1791–1840.* An excellent set; a standard history of Canada.

A Reader's Guide to Canadian History. Ed. by D. A. Muise, Univ. of Toronto Pr. no. 1 1982 pap. $8.95; ed. by J. L. Granatstein and Paul Stevens, Univ. of Toronto Pr. no. 2 1982 pap. $9.95. Annotated bibliography that lists important titles in the field. Arranged by sections, each treating a specific historical or geographical area, such as "The Atlantic Provinces," "Urban History," and "Canada during the French Regime," with materials selected by eminent scholars. A valuable reference work.

Smith, Dwight L. *The History of Canada: An Annotated Bibliography.* ABC-Clio 1983

$55.00. A good annotated bibliography that includes many titles on North American Indians not listed elsewhere.

Story, Norah. *The Oxford Companion to Canadian History and Literature.* Oxford 1967 $35.00. Alphabetically arranged, this reference volume attempts to provide in a single source biographical and historical information on Canada. Entries are short and give good summaries of important events.

Woodcock, George. *The Canadians.* Harvard Univ. Pr. 1980 $22.50. A general survey, with plentiful illustrations, by the prolific historian. The work stresses the diversity and individuality of the people of Canada.

Early Canada and New France

Costain, Thomas B. *White and the Gold.* Doubleday $5.95. An entertaining popular history of Canada from the discovery to the middle of the seventeenth century. Although somewhat overwritten, this history offers much valuable information, particularly on the early years of New France.

Eccles, William J. *The Canadian Frontier, 1534–1821. Histories of the Amer. Frontier Ser.* Univ. of New Mexico Pr. rev. ed. 1983 pap. $10.95. A revisionist history of New France, focusing on trade as a motivating force in Canada's development, and devoting much attention to the role of the Indian and the merchant in the building of early Canada.

Kenton, Edna, ed. *Jesuit Relations and Allied Documents: Travels and Explorations of the Jesuit Missionaries in North America (1610–1791).* Intro. by Reuben Gold Thwaites, Boni 1925 o.p. Primary source material for the historian, the famous *Jesuit Relations* was originally translated into English and published in 73 volumes from 1896 to 1901. This volume is a judicious selection for the general reader, containing reports of Jesuit life, travel, exploration, and adventure sent from North America to superiors at Quebec or in France. Covers from the first Acadian Mission in 1611 to the surrender of the Jesuit estates in 1789.

Knox, John. *The Siege of Quebec and the Campaigns in North America, 1757–1860.* Pendragon 1980 pap. $6.95. Edited version of the classic eyewitness account of the war between Great Britain and France that resulted in the loss of the French Empire in North America. An important chronicle filled with revealing descriptions of contemporary society and exciting accounts of military engagements.

Parkman, Francis. *France and England in North America.* Ed. by David Levin, Literary Class. 2 vols. 1983 $30.00; ed. by Allan Nevins, *Amer. Class. Ser.* Ungar 9 vols. $180.00. The great nineteenth-century American historian's magnum opus on the early history of Canada, particularly focusing on the British-French conflict. Although somewhat prejudiced and inaccurate, Parkman's work is a masterpiece of literature, compelling in its narrative and style.

Ray, Arthur J., and Donald Freeman. *Give Us Good Measure: An Economic Analysis of Relations between the Indians and the Hudson's Bay Company before 1763.* Univ. of Toronto Pr. 1978 $25.00 pap. $7.50. An examination of the Indian-European nexus of the fur trade, stressing quantitative data and economic analysis. An important, if rather difficult, specialized study.

Repplier, Agnes. *Mere Marie of the Ursulines: A Study in Adventure.* Arden Lib. repr. of 1931 ed. 1979 lib. bdg. $15.00. A somewhat romanticized biography of Marie de l'Incarnation, who first established the Ursuline Order in Canada and worked tirelessly to establish the city of Quebec for more than 30 years in seventeenth-century Canada. Her letters, selected and translated in 1967 as *Word from New France,* are now unfortunately out of print.

The Confederation, Dominion, and Modern Canada

Arnopoulos, Sheila M., and Dominique Clift. *The English Fact in Quebec.* McGill-Queens Univ. Pr. 1984 $30.00 pap. $9.95. An important sociological analysis of the English-speaking community that makes Quebec home. The authors, political journalists, examine the problems that arise when two cultures, the French and the English, clash.

Berton, Pierre. *Flames across the Border: The Canadian-American Tragedy.* Little, Brown 1982 $19.95. An entertaining military narrative of the U.S. invasion of Canada during the final two years of the War of 1812. The author captures the excitement of combat and the lives of the common men involved in the conflict.

———. *The Invasion of Canada: 1812–1813.* Little, Brown 1980 $17.50. An account of the U.S. effort to invade and annex Canada. The author focuses on the role the Indians played in the war. Anecdotal and readable.

Bothwell, Robert, and John English. *Canada since 1945: Power, Politics, and Provincialism.* Univ. of Toronto Pr. 1981 pap. $14.95. A journalistic account of contemporary Canadian politics, economy, and culture. The authors advocate a more centralized government and decry the individualist tendencies of the provinces. A lucid, stimulating, and politically biased book.

Brody, Hugh. *Maps and Dreams. Pantheon Village Ser.* 1982 $16.00 pap. $7.95. A perceptive personal account by a young anthropologist of the clash between British Columbia's Beaver Indians, one of the last surviving hunting societies, and the culture of the pipeline builders.

Carroll, John E. *Environmental Diplomacy: An Examination and a Perspective of Canadian-U.S. Transboundary Environmental Relations.* Univ. of Michigan Pr. 1983 $22.50. A scholarly, readable overview of the environmental dispute between the United States and Canada, highlighting the opposing points of view.

Coleman, William D. *The Independence Movement in Quebec, 1945–1980. Studies in the Structures of Power* Univ. of Toronto Pr. 1984 $30.00 pap. $12.95. A very detailed, specialized study of the Separatist movement in Quebec, stressing economic and political factors.

Elliot, Jean. *Two Nations, Two Cultures: Ethnic Groups in Canada.* Prentice-Hall 1979 $14.50 1983 pap. $13.95. A strong collection of 31 essays by a variety of writers and scholars (most members of ethnic groups) concentrating on three topics: native peoples, the French Canadians, and other ethnic groups—Italians, Jews, Ukrainians, and Chinese.

Frye, Northrop. *Divisions on a Ground: Essays on Canadian Culture.* Ed. by James Polk, Univ. of Toronto Pr. 1982 $19.95. Insightful essays by a major thinker who is regarded as one of the best critics of Canadian literature and art. His observations reveal much about Canadian history, politics, and civilization.

Getty, Ian A., and Antoine S. Lussier, eds. *As Long as the Sun Shines and Water Flows: A Reader in Canadian Native Studies.* International Specialized Bk. 1983 $29.95 pap. $12.50. A collection of essays on various aspects of Canadian Indian history, particularly oriented toward political analyses and public policy studies. Contains a good bibliographic essay and suggestions for further reading.

Griffin, Anne. *Quebec: The Challenge of Independence.* Intro. by Andrew M. Greeley, Fairleigh Dickinson Univ. Pr. 1983 $27.50. Based on personal interviews, this is an excellent psychological and social study of the independence movement in Quebec.

Hoagland, Edward. *Notes from the Century Before: A Journal from British Columbia.* North Point Pr. repr. of 1969 ed. 1982 pap. $10.00. The author's diary of a trip through British Columbia's northern wilderness in 1966. A sensitive, unstructured volume; an elegy to the quickly disappearing Canadian wilderness.

Holmes, John W. *Life with Uncle: The Canadian-American Relationship*. Univ. of Toronto Pr. 1981 pap. $7.95. Humorous, sarcastic, serious insightful lectures by a distinguished scholar examining the uncomfortable friendship of the two giants of the North American continent and emphasizing the traits that make Canada so different from the United States.

——. *The Shaping of Peace: Canada and the Search for World Order, 1943–57*. Univ. of Toronto Pr. 2 vols. 1979–82 ea. $30.00–$40.00. A scholarly history of Canada's role in world politics and its participation in the United Nations and the creation of NATO.

Jacobs, Jane. *The Question of Separation: Quebec and the Struggle over Sovereignty*. Random 1980 $8.95 1981 pap. $3.95. A quiet, thoughtful, almost meditative book exploring the French-Canadian case for separatism. The author argues in a restrained manner for separation and the superiority of small and varied political and cultural structure over a large and centralized government.

Jenness, Diamond. *People of the Twilight*. Univ. of Chicago Pr. (Phoenix Bks.) 1959 pap. $3.25. An intelligently written account of the author's two-year stay with the Eskimos of the Canadian Arctic. A plea for the Eskimos' threatened way of life.

Johnston, Hugh. *The Voyage of the Komagata Maru: The Sikh Challenge to Canada's Colour Bar*. Oxford 1979 $14.95. Shortly before World War I, 150 Indian Sikhs boarded the steamer *Komagata Maru* bound for Canada unaware the British government had no intention of allowing them to set foot on Canadian soil. What began as a dream for a better life for the Sikhs ended in tragedy. A dispassionate telling of a sorry event in Canadian history.

McKillop, A. B. *A Disciplined Intelligence: Critical Inquiry and Canadian Thought in the Victorian Era*. McGill-Queens Univ. Pr. 1979 $24.00 pap. $10.95. A brilliant examination of the Anglo-Canadian mind and the British influence that shaped Canadian society in the Victorian era. An important, though not easy to follow, book on the history of ideas in Canada, a subject traditionally overlooked by students of culture and philosophy.

Mowat, Farley. *The Great Betrayal*. Little, Brown 1977 pap. $5.95. An angry brief by a world-famous naturalist and writer against the exploitation and destruction of the Canadian Arctic by oil and gas interests.

Owram, Doug. *Promise of Eden: The Canadian Expansionist Movement and the Idea of the West, 1856–1900*. Univ. of Toronto Pr. 1980 pap. $12.50. A study of Canadians' attempts to conquer the British Northwest, a region that up to 1856 had been dismissed as inhospitable. A well-written research book detailing a fascinating period and concluding that it was the northwest wilderness that conquered the pioneers and not the opposite.

Read, Colin. *The Rising in Western Upper Canada, 1837–38: The Duncombe Revolt and After*. Univ. of Toronto Pr. 1982 $40.00 pap. $14.95. A reconstruction of the famous 1837 revolt and fiasco when Canadians who favored a political system similar to the United States during the Jacksonian era tried to take over the government. Using contemporary sources, the author fleshes out the rebels. Good reading.

Steltzer, Ulli, and Catherine Kerr. *Coast of Many Faces*. Univ. of Washington Pr. 1979 pap. $22.95. A book of black-and-white photographs of the people and places of Canada's West Coast with commentaries from the people who live there. This volume gives the reader a firsthand sense of everyday life in the small communities of the area.

Taylor, Charles. *Radical Tories: The Conservative Tradition in Canada*. Univ. of Toronto Pr. 1982 $14.95. A readable, interesting exploration of the conservative thinkers who have shaped modern Canada. Although the politicians interviewed in this book differ in their solution to their country's problem, one sentiment is clear: They do not want Canada to be overrun by the United States.

Thorburn, H. *Party Politics in Canada*. Prentice-Hall 4th ed. 1979 pap. $11.95. A collection of well-written essays on contemporary politics and new developments in the Canadian party system. A standard work of political science.

Warner, William. *Distant Water: The Fate of the North Atlantic Fisherman*. Little, Brown 1983 $17.45; Penguin 1984 pap. $7.95. A brilliant book about international fishing in the North Sea. An account of several voyages in leviathan factory trawlers and the adventure and conflict of the fishing industry.

Wearing, Joseph. *The L-Shaped Party: The Liberal Party of Canada, 1958–1980*. McGraw-Hill 1981 o.p. A very detailed modern history, from the late 1950s to the present, of the party of Canada's famed and colorful former prime minister, Pierre Trudeau.

Wilson, Edmund. *O Canada: An American's Notes on Canadian Culture*. Farrar 1965 $4.95; Octagon repr. of 1966 ed. 1976 lib. bdg. $18.00. The unique American literary critic's random but often incisive notes are certainly a pleasure to read. Wilson tends to overdramatize and romanticize, but as with all his works, this volume is thought-provoking and exciting.

Young, Brian. *George-Etienne Cartier: Montreal Bourgeois*. McGill-Queens Univ. Pr. 1981 $23.95 pap. $11.95. Readable biography of one of the fathers of the confederation that attempts to present Cartier as a highly successful businessman who turned politician not only to benefit his country but also himself.

LATIN AMERICA

The lands we now call Latin America have always held foreigners in thrall. As the Indies, New Spain, El Dorado, or America's Backyard, Latin America has lured, fascinated, and captured conquistador, priest, pirate, explorer, soldier, diplomat, and missionary alike. From Columbus in his search for the Indies, through Cortez, Pizarro, and Sir Walter Raleigh to William Walker and his private army, from U.S. Marines in Nicaragua and the Dominican Republic to the CIA in Cuba and Chile, the rest of the world has come to Latin America. Spain, Portugal, England, France, Holland, and the United States have all attempted in their various ways to possess these lands. In the end, they were all themselves possessed by what they came to conquer.

The lure of Latin America still exists for politicians, businessmen, missionaries, scholars, adventurers, travelers, and writers. The Cuban Revolution and radical policies of Fidel Castro, the election and later violent overthrow of the Marxist government of Salvador Allende, the Sandinista Revolution in Nicaragua, and the violence and terror in Guatemala and El Salvador have all focused the attention of the world on Latin America, the Golden Land. A new interest has also stirred in the Golden Cities of the past, in the

Olmecs, Maya, Aztecs, Incas, and other pre-Columbian peoples, paralleling the rise in interest in the contemporary affairs of the area.

This intense fascination, almost obsession, with Latin America among people in the United States and Western Europe has produced a flood of published materials, words from the titles and subtitles of which reflect a continuing conflict between Latin America and the foreigner and among the Latin Americans themselves: "Sons of the Shaking Earth," "A Rain of Darts," "Red Gold," "Endless War," "Open Veins," "Cry of the People," "Prisoner without a Name," "Murder of Chile," "Bitter Fruit," "Weakness and Deceit," "Secret War," "Land or Death," "Labyrinth of Solitude," and the last and final "Loss of El Dorado." The following list attempts a record of the best efforts in the English language to understand, explain, and communicate the fascination of Latin America to its neighbors to the north.

General Surveys, Bibliographies, and Reference Works

Bibliographic Guide to Latin American Studies. G. K. Hall annual 1985 lib. bdg. $395.00. Designed for libraries and researchers, this work lists material cataloged at the Library of Congress and in the Latin American collection of the University of Texas. Arranged in dictionary style (authors, titles, and subjects interfiled), this reference work can be used effectively by the general reader.

Crow, John A. *The Epic of Latin America.* Univ. of California Pr. 1980 $46.50 pap. $14.95. A standard history, written for the general audience in a simple, if somewhat prosaic, style. Provides a good overview for Latin American history.

Esquenazi Mayo, Roberto, and Michael C. Meyer, eds. *Latin American Scholarship since World War II: Trends in History, Political Science, Literature, Geography, and Economics.* Univ. of Nebraska Pr. 1971 $25.50. Essays by 19 eminent Latin Americanists on recently published research in various areas of Latin American studies, this work provides direction to the student and the general reader. Supplements the important collection by Howard F. Cline, *Latin American History: Essays on Its Study and Teaching, 1889–1965,* now unfortunately out of print.

Griffin, Charles C., ed. *Latin America: A Guide to the Historical Literature.* Univ. of Texas Pr. 1981 o.p. The standard bibliography of Latin American history, with contributions by 37 scholars. Containing good narrative introductions and annotations, this volume is indispensable for the student or researcher, but must be supplemented by use of the *Hispanic American Historical Review* and the *Latin American Research Review,* both important journals in the field.

Herring, Hubert, and Helen B. Herring. *A History of Latin America.* Knopf 3d ed. 1968 $29.00. A graceful, well-written introduction with facts, figures, and dates throughout, presenting a thoughtful interpretation of the history of Latin America.

Martin, Dolores M., and others, eds. *Handbook of Latin American Studies.* Univ. Pr. of Florida vols. 38–40 1977–78 ea. $40.00–$47.50; Univ. of Texas Pr. vols. 42–45 1982–83 text ed. ea. $65.00. A very selective, very important annual bibliography of major monographs and periodical articles, including evaluative comments by scholars. A major reference source.

Tannenbaum, Frank. *Ten Keys to Latin America.* Random (Vintage) 1966 pap. $4.95. A contemporary classic, which, though written two decades ago, is still thought-provoking and fresh in its interpretations and presentation.

Wauchope, Robert, and others, eds. *Handbook of Middle American Indians.* Univ. of

Texas Pr. 15 vols. 1964–75 Supplements 1981–to date, consult publisher for individual volumes and prices. A colossal, comprehensive reference work on all aspects of pre-Spanish life in Mesoamerica, for the scholar and serious researcher. This monumental undertaking is unique in the field of Latin American studies.

Williams, Eric. *From Columbus to Castro: The History of the Caribbean, 1492–1969.* Harper 1971 $13.95; Random (Vintage) 1983 pap. $8.95. A subjective history seen from the Caribbean perspective by a controversial political figure, writing straightforwardly and intelligently.

Wolf, Eric. *Sons of the Shaking Earth.* Univ. of Chicago Pr. 1959 $15.00; Univ. of Chicago Pr. (Phoenix Bks.) pap. $6.00. One of the most exciting, most significant books ever written on what is now known as Mexico and Central America. Concentrates on pre-Columbian cultures, but provides considerable insight into modern life in Middle America. Although more than 25 years old, this volume should still be required reading for anyone interested in Latin America.

Pre-Columbian Peoples and Culture

Alcina-Franch, José. *Pre-Columbian Art.* Trans. by I. Maris Paris, Abrams 1983 $125.00. A massive work, aesthetically oriented, with stunning photographs. A great source book for the entire field, with plans, descriptions, and photographs of principal archaeological sites included. An expensive, but well-done production.

Berdan, Frances. *The Aztecs of Central Mexico: An Imperial Society.* Holt text ed. 1982 pap. $9.95. An introductory outline, anthropological in focus, of Aztec society, that includes socioeconomic and political analyses as well.

Bernal, Ignacio. *The Olmec World.* Trans. by Doris Heyden and Fernando Horcasitas, Univ. of California Pr. 1969 pap. $7.95. A clear synthesis of information on Mesoamerica's first "real" culture, noted for the colossal sculptures of stone and delicate jade carvings it left behind.

Bingham, Hiram. *Lost City of the Incas.* Atheneum text ed. 1963 pap. $4.95; Greenwood repr. of 1948 ed. 1981 lib. bdg. $35.00. A classic exploration and discovery tale, recounting Bingham's discovery of the lost Incan capital of Machu Picchu in 1911.

Brundage, Burr Cartwright. *Empire of the Inca.* Fwd. by Arnold J. Toynbee, *Civilization of the Amer. Indian Ser.* Univ. of Oklahoma Pr. repr. of 1963 ed. 1974 $24.95 1985 pap. $10.95. A straightforward political history, based on archaeological records and accounts, of the Spanish conquistadores. The same author's *Lords of Cuzco*, now out of print, gives a detailed account of the workings of Inca bureaucracy in its last days.

———. *A Rain of Darts: The Mexica Aztecs.* Texas Pan-Amer. Ser. Univ. of Texas Pr. 1972 $20.00. A clear and exceedingly well-written account of the Mexica Aztecs and their capital Technochtitlan. Precise and scholarly, but eminently readable.

Cobo, Bernabe. *History of the Inca Empire: Customs, Legends, History and Sociology.* Trans. by Roland Hamilton, fwd. by John H. Rowe, *Texas Pan-Amer. Ser.* Univ. of Texas Pr. text ed. 1979 $20.00 1983 pap. $8.95. Cobo, a seventeenth-century Jesuit, used early written sources for his charming narrative history, originally completed in 1653 as *Historia del Nuevo Mundo*, of which this volume is one part. Cobo's treatise was the most comprehensive work on the Incas until the twentieth century.

Coe, Michael D. *The Maya. Ancient People and Places Ser.* Thames & Hudson 3d ed. 1984 pap. $9.95. A standard work of introduction by the great pre-Columbian scholar and professor of anthropology at Yale University. Coe's work has been inspirational and exemplary for others in the field.

————. *Mexico*. Holt 2d ed. text ed. 1977 pap. $8.95; *Ancient Peoples and Places Ser.* Thames & Hudson 3d ed. rev. 1984 $19.95 pap. $9.95. A clear, concise history of the pre-Spanish peoples of Mexico from the early hunters through the Olmecs, Toltecs, and Mixtecs to the Aztecs. A good starting place for the general reader.

Garcilaso-de-la-Vega, El Inca. *Royal Commentaries of the Incas and a General History of Peru*. Trans. by Harold V. Livermore, Univ. of Texas Pr. 2 vols. 1966 $75.00. Originally written in the late sixteenth or early seventeenth century, these works are elegies of the son of an Incan princess and a conquistador. Despite their age and prejudices on the part of Garcilaso, both volumes present accounts that pay attention to detail and historical fact. The *Royal Commentaries* tells of the growth of the Incan Empire, and the *General History* supplies Garcilaso's version of the conquest in comparison to those of the conquistadores.

Hammond, Norman. *Ancient Maya Civilization*. Rutgers Univ. Pr. 1982 $30.00. The best available general introduction and overview of Mayan history and culture, Hammond's work is elegantly written and a pleasure to read.

Henderson, John S. *The World of the Ancient Maya*. Cornell Univ. Pr. 1981 $29.95 1983 pap. $13.95. A good introduction, with lucid and free-flowing, nontechnical prose.

Morley, Sylvanus G., George W. Brainerd, and Robert J. Sharer. *The Ancient Maya*. Stanford Univ. Pr. 4th ed. rev. 1983 $28.50. A standard scholarly work, full of factual information on history, society, and material culture. This volume, originally published in 1946 and revised in 1956, has fortunately been updated and revised by Robert J. Sharer who incorporated new theories and research. An impressive historical work with a solid tradition behind it.

Pasztory, Esther. *Aztec Art*. Abrams 1983 $60.00. An excellent survey, classifying and describing Aztec art both as an individual work and by style and function. This volume displays a sensitivity to the interaction among art, culture, and history. Superior illustrations.

Pearce, Kenneth. *The View from the Top of the Temple: Ancient Maya Civilization and Modern Maya Culture*. Univ. of New Mexico Pr. 1984 $24.95 pap. $12.95. A superior work of imagination and scholarship, combining anthropological and archaeological approaches to Mayan culture with a vivid account of the contemporary Maya of the Yucatan, Mexico, and Guatemala. A very unusual, immensely enjoyable work.

Perera, Victor, and Robert D. Bruce. *The Last Lords of Palenque: The Lacandon Mayas of the Mexican Rain Forest*. Little, Brown 1982 $17.95; Univ. of California Pr. 1984 pap. $7.95. A fascinating journalistic account of the lives and beliefs of the last of the Maya, full of human interest.

Soustelle, Jacques. *Daily Life of the Aztecs on the Eve of the Spanish Conquest*. Stanford Univ. Pr. 1961 pap. $8.95. A good synthesis of research and investigation of the peoples believed by many to be the "mother" civilization of the Americas. Also recommended for information on the Olmecs is a collection of scholarly essays entitled *The Olmec and Their Neighbors*, unfortunately out of print.

Stephens, John L. *Incidents of Travel in Central America, Chiapas and Yucatan*. Dover 2 vols. repr. of 1841 ed. 1969 pap. ea. $6.50; Peter Smith 2 vols. $28.50. These two delightful volumes were hugely popular nineteenth-century travel and discovery narratives. Stephens, an American traveler, archaeologist, and diplomat, and Catherwood, an English artist, brought the Mayan civilization to the attention of the outside world through their words and pictures. Both volumes are full of insight and adventure. Other classics of exploration and archaeology in Latin America are very nicely excerpted in Robert Wauchope's *They Found the Buried Cities*, which is now out of print.

Stierlin, Henri. *The Art of the Incas and Its Origins*. Trans. by Billy Ross and Peter Ross, Rizzoli 1983 $50.00
———. *The Art of the Maya: From the Olmecs to the Toltec-Maya*. Trans. by Peter Graham, Rizzoli 1981 $50.00. *The Art of the Incas and Its Origins* and *The Art of the Maya*, two nicely produced volumes, elegantly synthesize and reevaluate Incan and Mayan art, concentrating on important groups of works. Reproductions are well done.

Vaillant, George C. *Aztecs of Mexico: Origin, Rise, and Fall of the Aztec Nation*. Gannon lib. bdg. $13.50; ed. by Suzannah B. Vaillant, Penguin rev. ed. 1955 pap. $6.95. A standard history for the nonspecialist, presenting a clearly written overview and sensitive recreation of Aztec society, economy, crafts, religion, and warfare. Other recommended books on the Aztecs, unfortunately out of print, are Miguel Leon-Portilla's *Aztec Thought and Culture* and the chronicle of the sixteenth-century Dominican Fray Diego Duran, *The Aztecs*.

Discovery and Conquest

Diaz del Castillo, Bernal. *Discovery and Conquest of Mexico*. Ed. by Gerano Garcia, trans. by A. P. Maudslay, intro. by I. A. Leonard, Farrar 1956 pap. $10.95. A primary source document, edited and translated from the Spanish, of one of Cortez's conquistadores, who wrote this account in his old age in the sixteenth century. A detailed, nostalgic, violent, and certainly prejudiced tale of the Aztecs and their conquerors. Also valuable are the lengthy epistles or reports of Cortez himself, translated with notes and commentary as *Letters from Mexico*. The best edition, edited by A. R. Pagden, is now unfortunately out of print.

Hemming, John. *The Conquest of the Incas*. Harcourt 1970 $15.00 1973 pap. $9.95. An excellent, fast-paced modern history, scholarly, yet accessible to the general reader. Hemming provides an accurate, well-rounded account of Incan society as well as of Pizarro and the conquerors.

Las Casas, Bartolome de. *In Defense of the Indians*. Trans. and ed. by Stafford Poole, Northern Illinois Univ. Pr. 1974 $25.00. An account of the nature and being of the pre-Columbian peoples, a defense of their rights as human beings, and a plea for the conservation of their culture, this work is only part of the writings of the great sixteenth-century friar known as the Apostle of the Indies. Lewis Hanke's famous work describing the main legal, religious, and humanitarian controversies of the Spanish Conquest and occupation, *The Spanish Struggle for Justice in the Conquest of America*, centers on Las Casas and his thought, but is shamefully out of print.

Leon-Portilla, Miguel, ed. *The Broken Spears: The Aztec Account of the Conquest of Mexico*. Trans. by Lysander Kemp, Beacon 1962 pap. $46.95. An anthology of accounts written by the Aztecs themselves, detailing their own view of the Spaniards and their conquest. A fascinating and important book.

Lockhart, James. *The Men of Cajamarca: A Social and Biographical Study of the First Conquerors of Peru*. Latin Amer. Monographs Univ. of Texas Pr. 1972 $22.50. A very intense, in-depth study of the 168 Spaniards who captured the Incan emperor Atahualpa at Cajamarca. A remarkable book, scholarly, serious, and eminently readable.

Morison, Samuel E. *Admiral of the Ocean Sea: A Life of Christopher Columbus*. Little,

Brown 1942 $24.95; Northeastern Univ. Pr. repr. of 1942 ed. text ed. 1983 pap. $10.95. The most famous biography of Columbus, this work must be read by anyone interested in the origins of Latin America. Stunningly written, reading like a novel, this work is still full of historical data and useful interpretation.

Padden, R. C. *The Hummingbird and the Hawk: Conquest and Sovereignty in the Valley of Mexico, 1503–1541.* Harper 1970 pap. $7.25; Ohio State Univ. Pr. 1967 $6.75. An elegant historical recreation of the rise of the Aztec society and Empire and the formation of early colonial societies from the conflict between the conquerors and the native American culture. A very special historical work.

Parry, John H., and Robert G. Keith, eds. *New Iberian World: A Documentary History of the Discovery and Settlement of Latin America to the Early 17th Century.* Times Bks. 5 vols. 1984 $500.00. An anthology of writings, a comprehensive collection of source materials, more than two-thirds of which have been newly translated, with introductions and commentaries. Sources include chronicles, laws, political treatises, religious tracts, personal narratives, and government documents. An impressive, useful reference book, but unaccountably expensive.

Prescott, William H. *The Conquest of Mexico and Peru.* Ed. by Roger Howell, Irvington text ed. $22.50. The great nineteenth-century American historian's spectacular accounts of the Spanish Conquest, these volumes are colorful, fascinating reading, if superseded by modern historical interpretations and scholarship.

Ricard, Robert. *The Spiritual Conquest of Mexico.* Peter Smith 1983 $15.00. A classic study, originally published in 1933, of the activity of the church in the conquest of the New World.

Sahagún, Bernardino de, ed. *The War of Conquest: How It Was Waged Here in Mexico.* Trans. by Arthur J. Anderson and Charles E. Dibble, Univ. of Utah Pr. 1978 $15.00 pap. $7.95. An account of the conquest, by the sixteenth-century Franciscan missionary and scholar Sahagún, that quotes extensively from Aztec accounts. Sahagún's scholarship and fascination with the lives of those he converted led him to produce a masterwork on Aztec society, actually never published until 1956. It is known as the *Historia General* and is written in the Aztec language Nahuatl. This volume is part of a monumental 12-volume English translation of Sahagún's *Florentine Codex.*

Sauer, Carl O. *The Early Spanish Main.* Univ. of California Pr. repr. of 1966 ed. pap. $8.95. A study of the discovery and exploration of the Caribbean islands, Central America, and northern South America, from 1492 to 1519. Sauer, a prominent American geographer, writes in an unusual, individualistic manner.

Varner, John G., and Jeannette J. Varner. *Dogs of the Conquest.* Univ. of Oklahoma Pr. 1983 $19.95. A well-researched and enjoyable account of the use of dogs as lethal weapons in the conquest. An unusual book with interest for the general reader.

Colonial History

Bethell, Leslie, ed. *The Cambridge History of Latin America: Colonial Latin America.* Cambridge Univ. Pr. 2 vols. 1985 ea. $65.00–$75.00. *Colonial Latin America* represents the first two volumes of an eight-volume history of Latin America that will no doubt be considered a definitive work. These volumes deal with the Spanish colonies in 34 topical chapters from Leon-Portilla's "Mesoamerica before 1519" to Robert Stevenson's "The Music of Colonial Brazil." Each chapter is by a recognized authority and presents a synthesis of information including excellent bibliographic essays.

Boxer, C. R. *The Golden Age of Brazil, 1695–1750: Growing Pains of a Colonial Soci-*

ety. Univ. of California Pr. 1962 $34.50. A solid political and economic study of the early Portuguese Empire in the New World.

Gibson, Charles. *The Aztecs under Spanish Rule: A History of the Indians of the Valley of Mexico, 1519–1810*. Stanford Univ. Pr. 1964 $45.00 pap. $15.95. A most important, classic work that examines the changes in Indian life after the defeat of the Aztecs. This work is also a broad and masterful survey of one part of Latin American society in the colonial period.

Haring, C. H. *The Spanish Empire in America*. Harcourt 1963 pap. $4.95; Peter Smith $10.25. A solid introduction to the organization and functioning of colonial institutions.

Lafaye, Jacques. *Quetzacoatl and Guadalupe: The Formation of Mexican National Consciousness, 1513–1813*. Trans. by Benjamin Keen, intro. by Octavio Paz, Univ. of Chicago Pr. 1977 lib. bdg. $22.00. A difficult but rewarding study of the formation of Mexican culture, through the melding of the complex beliefs of Spanish Roman Catholicism with Aztec religion, and the desire of the colonials for a complete break with "Old Spain."

Lockhart, James. *Spanish Peru, 1532–1560: A Colonial Society*. Univ. of Wisconsin Pr. 1968 $30.00 pap. $12.50. An excellent microstudy, focusing on the period of violence, unrest, and political chaos, but showing the economic and political development of the colonial system throughout it all. Primarily aimed toward scholars, imaginatively using sixteenth-century notary records, this is a fascinating piece of work.

Lockhart, James, and Enrique Ott. *Letters and People of the Spanish Indies*. *Cambridge Latin Amer. Studies* 1976 $39.50 pap. $11.95. A fascinating collection of letters written to relatives, friends, and superiors in Spain from people in the sixteenth-century Caribbean. Excellent commentary by the editors.

Lockhart, James, and Stuart Schwartz. *Early Latin America: A History of Colonial Spanish America and Brazil*. *Cambridge Latin Amer. Studies* 1983 $49.50 pap. $14.95. An excellent new synthesis of ideas treating the history of Spanish and Portuguese colonial America with a unified view. Accessible to both the scholar and the general reader.

MacLachlan, Colin M., and Jaime E. Rodriguez O. *The Forging of the Cosmic Race: A Reinterpretation of Colonial Mexico*. Univ. of California Pr. 1980 $28.50 pap. $7.95. A new interpretation of Mexico's colonial heritage that challenges the theory of Spain as an exploitative power, draining colonial resources. MacLachlan advocates the belief that the colonial system developed prosperity and capitalism for Mexican society as well as the mother country.

MacLeod, Murdo J. *Spanish Central America: A Socioeconomic History, 1520–1720*. Univ. of California Pr. 1985 lib. bdg. $27.50 pap. $9.95. A classic study of the social and economic structure of colonial Central America, emphasizing the destructive results of reliance on a single-crop agricultural system.

Phelan, John L. *The People and the King: The Comunero Revolution in Colombia, 1781*. Univ. of Wisconsin Pr. 1978 $29.50. A scholarly interpretation of the Comunero Rebellion, which began Colombia's war for independence. Through the examination of census information and contemporary accounts, the author pieces together striking "biographies" of the rebellion's leaders.

Modern Latin America: General Works

Aguilar, Luis E., ed. *Marxism in Latin America*. Temple Univ. Pr. 2d ed. rev. 1978 $27.95 pap. $9.95. A collection of writings by Marxists, Communists, and Socialists, revealing many different leftist approaches to the problems of Latin American society.

Anna, Timothy E. *Spain and the Loss of America*. Univ. of Nebraska Pr. 1983 $26.50. An important study of the breakup of the Spanish Empire between 1810 and 1825. Anna emphasizes the economic, military, and administrative structures of the Spanish governance of the New World.

Blasier, Cole. *The Giant's Rival: The USSR and Latin America*. Pitt Latin Amer. Ser. Univ. of Pittsburgh Pr. 1983 $14.95 text ed. pap. $7.95. A well-researched account of Soviet involvement in Latin America, emphasizing the crucial role of Cuba in world affairs.

Burns, E. Bradford. *The Poverty of Progress: Latin America in the Nineteenth Century*. Univ. of California Pr. 1980 $18.95 1983 pap. $6.95. A thoughtful interpretation of Brazilian history, proposing the theory that Western ideas of progress superimposed on Latin America are to a large extent the cause of current poverty. Other cultural strains, such as the Afro-American, are viewed as more positive and natural for Latin America.

Chace, James. *Endless War: How We Got Involved in Central America and What Can Be Done*. Random (Vintage) 1984 pap. $3.95. An examination of the Central American policies of the Reagan administration and an analysis of U.S. intervention from the nineteenth century to the present.

Chaney, Elsa M. *Supermadre: Women in Politics in Latin America*. Latin Amer. Monographs Univ. of Texas Pr. text ed. 1979 $17.50. Sociological analysis of the roles women have played as writers, in the work force, and as homemakers. Women's participation in these areas will grow as they begin to learn the lessons of "politics of food."

Ciricione, Joseph, ed. *Central America and the Western Alliance*. Holmes & Meier 1985 $24.50. Published conference proceedings examining the current state of Central America as viewed from an international perspective.

Debray, Regis. *Revolution in the Revolution? Armed Struggle and Political Struggle in Latin America*. Fwd. by Paul M. Sweezy, Greenwood repr. of 1967 ed. 1980 lib. bdg. $24.75; trans. by Bobbye Ortiz, intro. by Roberto F. Retamar, Grove repr. of 1967 ed. pap. $1.50. A classic Marxist analysis of politics and exploitation in Latin America.

De Madariaga, Salvadore. *Bolivar*. Greenwood repr. of 1952 ed. 1979 lib. bdg. $42.50. A highly controversial biography of the famous liberator. De Madariaga sees Bolivar as a renegade and produces a scholarly volume debunking the myths surrounding the liberator.

Elkin, Judith L. *Jews of the Latin American Republics*. Univ. of North Carolina Pr. 1980 $22.50. A historical study covering Brazil, Argentina, Mexico, and the Caribbean from colonial times to the present. Impressive.

Galeano, Eduardo. *Open Veins of Latin America: Five Centuries of the Pillage of a Continent*. Trans. by Cedric Belfrage, Monthly Review 1973 pap. $8.00. An important book for developing an understanding of Latin America's anti-Yankee sentiments.

Johnson, John J. *The Military and Society in Latin America*. Stanford Univ. Pr. 1964 $25.00. A milestone in the study of Latin American politics, stressing the important role of the military and the officer class as a political force.

Kandell, Jonathan. *Passage through El Dorado: The Conquest of the World's Last Great Wilderness*. Morrow 1984 $15.95. A perceptive, readable book on the journey of the author in the Amazon basin, using seldom-traveled routes. A sad story of economic development and the destruction of some of the world's most beautiful natural terrain.

Kirkpatrick, Jeane J. *Dictatorships and Double Standards: Rationalism and Reason in Politics.* Simon & Schuster 1982 $14.95; Simon & Schuster (Touchstone Bks.) 1983 pap. $7.95. Of immense importance for the understanding of the foreign policy of the Reagan administration, not solely in Latin America but throughout the world. Should be required reading for all students and general readers.

Knight, Franklin W. *The Caribbean: The Genesis of a Fragmented Nationalism. Latin Amer. Histories Ser.* Oxford 1978 $22.50 pap. $8.50. An analysis of the forces of decentralization and artificial divisions in the Caribbean hindering development. A very well written work, best in its coverage of the colonial and post-independence periods.

Lernoux, Penny. *The Cry of the People: United States Involvement in the Rise of Fascism, Torture, and Murder and the Persecution of the Catholic Church in Latin America.* Doubleday 1980 $14.95; Penguin 1982 pap. $7.95. A passionate account of the Roman Catholic church's role in Latin America, chronicling that institution's increasingly progressive social and political involvement in Latin America. An indictment of the governments of the area and U.S. foreign policy. A harrowing presentation of repressive violence and the continuing violation of human rights.

Manach, Jorge. *Martí: Apostle of Freedom.* Devin $6.50. A very popular biography of the poet, revolutionary, and architect of Cuba's War of Independence from Spain. Detailed descriptions of the Cuban community of New York and Tampa in the earlier part of the century.

Martí, José. *Our America: Writings on Latin America and the Struggle for Cuban Independence.* Trans. by Elinor Randall, Monthly Review 1978 $16.50 1979 pap. $7.50. Martí was the advocate of the creation of one Latin American nation and one of the most popular and revered figures in the history of Latin America. This anthology introduces his thought and political philosophy as well as his observations and perceptions about life in the Americas.

Newfarmer, Richard, ed. *From Gunboats to Diplomacy: New U.S. Policies for Latin America.* Johns Hopkins Univ. Pr. 1984 $25.00 pap. $11.95. Engaging essays examining the relations between the United States and Latin America.

Rodriguez O., Jaime E. *The Emergence of Spanish America: Vincente Rocafuerte and Spanish Americanism, 1808–1832.* Univ. of California Pr. 1976 $42.50. A superb analysis of independence and the years following, when leaders, especially Vincente Rocafuerte, statesman and president of Ecuador, sought to unite the Americas into one commonwealth.

Sigmund, Paul E. *Multinationals in Latin America: The Politics of Nationalization.* Univ. of Wisconsin Pr. 1980 $27.50 pap. $10.95. An important in-depth study of the controversial issue of the presence of foreign corporations in developing countries. Thoughtfully explores the varying attitudes of all Americans to private business in Latin America. Particular discussion centers on foreign corporations in Cuba, Mexico, and Peru.

Skidmore, Thomas E., and Peter H. Smith. *Modern Latin America.* Oxford 1984 $22.50 pap. $12.95. A solid introductory survey, emphasizing economic history and demography, and focusing on regional political and cultural differences in Argentina, Chile, Brazil, Peru, Mexico, Cuba, and Central America.

Véliz, Claudio. *The Centralist Tradition of Latin America.* Princeton Univ. Pr. 1980 $29.00 pap. $12.50. A lucid, provocative essay, exploring the factors that have erected a preference and tendency for centralist domination and authoritarian regimes in Latin America.

Woodward, Ralph L., Jr. *Central America: A Nation Divided*. Oxford 1976 text ed. pap. $8.95. A concise study, full of statistics and maps, detailing the economic and political woes of this area.

Wynia, G. W. *The Politics of Latin American Development*. Cambridge Univ. Pr. 2d ed. 1984 $39.50 pap. $11.95. A refreshing new introductory treatment of Latin American political and economic systems, viewing various political structures as games with particular and specific players and rules. A very unusual work.

Modern Latin America: Individual Countries

ARGENTINA

Barnes, John. *Evita, First Lady: A Biography of Eva Peron*. Grove 1978 $12.95 1981 pap. $4.95. A good biography of one of the most famous or infamous Argentinians in the history of that country. For the most part, Barnes stays to the facts, keeping away from the overpowering legend of the woman.

Calvert, Peter. *The Falklands Crisis: The Rights and the Wrongs*. St. Martin's 1982 $20.00. A pro-British account of the Falklands/Malvinas incident, with a good analysis of Argentinian military thinking.

Kirkpatrick, Jeane J. *Leader and Vanguard in Mass Society: A Study of Peronist Argentina*. MIT 1971 $30.00. An important study of Argentinian politics between 1955 and 1966 focusing on the analysis of nondemocratic politics. Kirkpatrick, former U.S. ambassador to the United Nations and Reagan adviser, has exerted considerable influence on U.S. foreign policy.

Page, Joseph A. *Peron: A Biography*. Random 1983 $25.00. A successful attempt at understanding the complex and enigmatic leader who dominated Argentinian politics for more than a quarter-century.

Scobie, James R. *Argentina: A City and a Nation*. Latin Amer. Histories Ser. Oxford 2d ed. text ed. 1971 pap. $8.95. A socioeconomic study of Argentina, skillfully combining economic analyses with political interpretations. Colorful vignettes of Argentinian life make the many facts and statistics easier to digest.

Timerman, Jacobo. *Prisoner without a Name, Cell without a Number*. Trans. by Toby Talbot, Knopf 1981 $12.50; Random (Vintage) 1982 pap. $2.95. The autobiographical and philosophical work of a journalist imprisoned and tortured by the Argentinian military junta. A controversial, powerful work.

BOLIVIA

Klein, Herbert S. *Bolivia: The Evolution of a Multi-Ethnic Society*. Latin Amer. Histories Ser. Oxford text ed. 1982 $22.50 pap. $9.95. An excellent, general overview of the economic, social, and political history of Bolivia with emphasis on the twentieth century.

Malloy, James M. *Bolivia: The Uncompleted Revolution*. Pitt Latin Amer. Ser. Univ. of Pittsburgh Pr. 1970 $19.95. A detailed analysis of the 1952 Bolivian Revolution.

Nash, June. *We Eat the Mines and the Mines Eat Us: Dependency and Exploitation in Bolivian Tin Mines*. Columbia Univ. Pr. 1979 $30.00 pap. $14.00. A sensitive study based on 16 months of fieldwork and interviews, this volume explores in detail the lives and beliefs of Bolivian miners, providing the reader with excellent background on contemporary Bolivian society.

BRAZIL

Burns, E. Bradford. *A History of Brazil*. Columbia Univ. Pr. 2d ed. 1980 $40.00 pap. $14.00. Well-written history of Brazil from discovery to the present, emphasizing unique developments, such as the nonviolent transition from monarchy to republic.

Da Cunha, Euclides. *Rebellion in the Backlands*. Trans. by Samuel Putnam, Univ. of Chicago Pr. 1957 pap. $5.95. Brazil's great classic, a chronicle of the war against a fanatic messiah who challenged the Brazilian republic in the later nineteenth century. Written by a participant in the campaign, this volume is often described as the South American *War and Peace*.

Stone, Roger D. *Dreams of Amazonia*. Viking 1985 $17.95. A moving protest against the development of the Amazonian forests by the Brazilian government and various business interests.

CHILE

Chavkin, Samuel. *The Murder of Chile: Eyewitness Account of the Coup, the Terror and the Resistance Today*. Dodd 1982 $13.95. A compelling account of the last hours of Allende, expertly told, almost reproducing in the reader the terror felt by those imprisoned in the stadium and the panic of the city after the coup.

Loveman, Brian. *Chile: The Legacy of Hispanic Capitalism*. Latin Amer. Histories Ser. Oxford 1979 $22.50 text ed. pap. $8.95. A general history of Chile, putting forth the thesis that, despite the Marxist experiment of the 1970s, the natural form of Chilean development is democratic capitalism. A scholarly work, emphasizing socioeconomic trends, especially in its analysis of the working classes and the poor.

Smirnow, Gabriel. *The Revolution Disarmed: Chile, 1970–1973*. Monthly Review 1981 pap. $7.50. A perceptive analysis of Allende's government, examining its accomplishments and carefully studying its flaws. A methodical and thoughtful book.

COLOMBIA

Martz, John D. *Colombia*. Greenwood repr. of 1962 ed. 1975 lib. bdg. $19.75. A political narrative of modern Colombia with a very good introductory chapter and very readable style.

COSTA RICA

Bell, John P. *Crisis in Costa Rica: The 1948 Revolution*. Latin Amer. Monographs. Univ. of Texas Pr. 1971 $13.95. A sound study of the revolution that brought José Figueres to power in Costa Rica. Figueres, the architect of modern Costa Rica, came into power in 1948 through revolution, was later elected to the presidency, survived an invasion in the 1950s, and through his reforms made Costa Rica the democracy it is today.

Biesanz, Richard. *The Costa Ricans*. Prentice-Hall 1982 pap. $22.95. An important introduction to Costa Rica, the only nation in Latin America not to have an armed force, and one of the most peaceful and prosperous.

CUBA

Franqui, Carlos. *Diary of the Cuban Revolution*. Trans. by Elaine Kerrigan, Viking 1980 $25.00. A history of the Cuban Revolution by a participant, drawing on diaries, letters, recorded conversations, and interviews.

————. *Family Portrait with Fidel: A Memoir.* Trans. by Alfred Macadam, Random 1984 $17.95; Random (Vintage) 1984 pap. $8.95. No other book captures the contradictory nature of Castro as does this memoir by one of his former lieutenants. The book is fascinating, covering events not covered by other writers in such detail.

Philipson, Lorrin, and Rafael Llerena. *Freedom Flights.* Random 1981 $12.95. More than 16,000 Cubans have left their home illegally, crossing the Florida straits in small boats and makeshift embarkations. This collection tells the stories of many of those who survived through this escape route.

Santamaria, Haydee. *Moncada.* Intro. by Robert Taber, Lyle Stuart 1980 $8.95. A modest volume that narrates the story of a daring raid that launched Castro into history in 1953, by one of the participants in that raid. A personal, vivid book.

Thomas, Hugh. *Cuba: The Pursuit of Freedom, 1762–1969.* Harper 1971 $33.65. This mammoth book by a respected scholar is regarded by most critics as the best general history of Cuba ever published, though sadly in need of an update.

Wyden, Peter. *The Bay of Pigs: The Untold Story.* Simon & Schuster (Touchstone Bks.) 1980 $10.95. An objective rendering of the CIA-planned invasion of Cuba in 1961, probably one of the most famous incidents in modern U.S. history as well as Cuban history. This volume presents both points of view, invaders' and defenders'.

THE DOMINICAN REPUBLIC

Calder, Bruce J. *The Impact of Intervention: The Dominican Republic during the U.S. Occupation of 1916–1924. Texas Pan-Amer. Ser.* Univ. of Texas Pr. text ed. 1984 $22.50. The U.S. invasion of the Dominican Republic in the 1960s has tended to make historians forget the longer occupation of the island by U.S. forces nearly 60 years ago. This excellent account of that event is both scholarly and accessible to the general reader.

Gutierrez, Carlos Maria. *The Dominican Republic: Rebellion and Repression.* Monthly Review 1973 pap. $2.95. A journalistic account of life on the island under the U.S. occupation of the 1960s. A provoking, highly readable account.

Wiarda, Howard J. *Dictatorship and Development: The Methods of Control in Trujillo's Dominican Republic.* Univ. Pr. of Florida 1968 $10.00 pap. $6.00. A well-written analysis based upon personal observations rather than actual research. A good introduction.

ECUADOR

Cueva, Agustin. *The Process of Political Domination in Ecuador.* Transaction Bks. 1981 $19.95. This topically arranged volume with brief chapters describing political events serves as a good introduction to modern Ecuadorian political history.

Fitch, John S., III, ed. *The Military Coup d'Etat as a Political Process: Ecuador, 1948– 1966.* Johns Hopkins Univ. Pr. text ed. 1977 $22.50. A stimulating analysis of Latin American politics, using the model of the coup as an integral, predictable element in Ecuadorian politics, drawing conclusions for the rest of Latin America.

EL SALVADOR

Bonner, Raymond. *Weakness and Deceit: U.S. Policy and El Salvador.* Times Bks. 1984 $16.95. An angry, strong book by a *N.Y. Times* reporter, this volume gives a firsthand view of the turmoil and terror in El Salvador and a critique of U.S. foreign policy in that country.

Brockman, James R. *The Word Remains: A Life of Oscar Romero.* Orbis Bks. 1982 pap. $12.95. A biography of the archbishop of San Salvador, martyred in 1980 by right-wing terrorists, this volume provides insight into the political climate of the country and a tempered account of Romero's efforts to bring peace to his country.

Didion, Joan. *El Salvador.* Simon & Schuster 1983 $12.95; Washington Square Pr. 1983 pap. $5.95. While Didion's book might not add new research findings to the study of Salvadoran politics, her pen captures the aura of terror and fear in the lives of a people whose society is torn by civil war and political terrorism.

Montgomery, Tommie S. *Revolution in El Salvador: Origins and Evolution.* Intro. by Ramon Quiroz, Westview Pr. 2d ed. 1985 lib. bdg. $32.50 text ed. pap. $14.95. A good history of various insurrectionary groups in El Salvador.

GUATEMALA

Schlesinger, Stephen, and Stephen Kinzer. *Bitter Fruit: The Untold Story of the American Coup in Guatemala.* Doubleday 1982 pap. $8.95. Journalists Schlesinger and Kinzer provide a fascinating account of the CIA-planned overthrow of the government of Jacopo Arbenz in 1954. Their exposition of the role of the United States in this particular case serves as a basis for conclusions regarding subsequent U.S. involvement in Central America.

Sexton, James D., ed. *Son of Tecun Uman: A Maya Indian Tells His Life Story.* Univ. of Arizona Pr. 1981 $19.95 pap. $12.95. The diaries of a Mayan and the recorded conversations he had with the author form an autobiographical narrative of a world not much changed since the sixteenth century.

HAITI

James, Cyril L. *Black Jacobins: Toussaint L'Ouverture and the San Domingo Revolution.* Random (Vintage) 1963 pap. $5.95. A famous, impassioned rebellion that influenced the United States and the rest of the Americas throughout the nineteenth and twentieth centuries is the subject of this work, written with color and a faithfulness to historical facts. A classic.

Schmidt, Hans R., Jr. *The United States Occupation of Haiti, 1915–1934.* Rutgers Univ. Pr. 1971 $30.00. Fearing German occupation of the island, President Woodrow Wilson sent the marines to Haiti, where what was intended to be a short stay became a 19-year occupation. A good, scholarly study of this important part of Haitian history, with reflections on the U.S. role in the Caribbean throughout the century.

JAMAICA

Craton, Michael M. *Searching for the Invisible Man: Slaves and Plantation Life in Jamaica.* Harvard Univ. Pr. 1978 $35.00. A beautifully illustrated, well-researched, and well-documented recreation of the life on Jamaican plantations, a typical Caribbean colonial institution.

MEXICO

Guzmán, Martín L. *The Eagle and the Serpent.* Trans. by Harriet de Onís, Peter Smith $10.25. A chronicle of the Mexican Revolution by a participant that is a classic both as history and literature.

Katz, Friedrich. *The Secret War in Mexico: Europe, the United States, and the Mexican*

Revolution. Univ. of Chicago Pr. 1981 lib. bdg. $30.00 pap. $15.00. An important book examining the direct and covert participation of foreign powers in the Mexican Revolution.

Meyer, Michael C., and William L. Sherman. *The Course of Mexican History.* Oxford 2d ed. 1983 $18.95. A superior historical survey. Treats Mexican history comprehensively and is written with a concise, serious style. Excellent bibliographies for further reading are included.

Parkinson, Roger. *Zapata: A Biography.* Stein & Day 1975 $35.00 1980 pap. $6.95. A well-written biography of the Mexican rebel who led the 1910–1919 peasant rebellion and is the hero of modern Mexico. A good historical exploration rather than just the retelling of another legend.

Paz, Octavio. *Labyrinth of Solitude, the Other Mexico, and Return to the Labyrinth of Solitude, Mexico and the U.S., and the Philanthropic Ogre.* Trans. by Rebecca Philips, Grove 1985 $22.50; trans. by Lysander Kemp, Grove (Everyman's) 1985 pap. $9.95. A poet, essayist, and diplomat, Paz has written the best study of the Mexican people available. Written with beauty, mastery, force, and insight, this book is classifiable as history, but stands among the best books of the twentieth century on any subject.

Simpson, Lesley B. *Many Mexicos: Silver Anniversary Edition.* Univ. of California Pr. 1966 $28.95 pap. $8.95. One of the best books ever written on Mexico, a general history and appreciation of great popularity.

Vasconcelos, José. *A Mexican Ulysses: An Autobiography.* Trans. by Rex W. Crawford, Greenwood repr. of 1963 ed. 1972 lib. bdg. $60.00. Vasconcelos, teacher, statesman, and mystic, was one of the most important cultural forces behind the Mexican Revolution. In his autobiography, he discusses his attempt to create a political philosophy of general culture. The biography is more useful, however, for his glimpses into the life of the Mexican Revolution and the history of Mexico.

NICARAGUA

Cabestrero, Teófilo. *Ministers of God, Ministers of the People: Testimonies of Faith from Nicaragua.* Trans. by Robert R. Barr, Orbis Bks. 1983 pap. $6.95. Ernesto Cardenal, Miguel d'Escoto, and others are priests devoted to their religion. They are also revolutionaries devoted to the Sandinista regime. This volume offers rare glimpses of the faith of revolutionary Roman Catholics in Latin America.

Diederich, Bernard. *Somoza and the Legacy of U.S. Involvement in Central America.* Dutton 1981 $19.75. A historical record of the collapse under fire of the Somoza regime, with an exploration of previous U.S. policy in Nicaragua.

Rosset, Peter, and John Vandermeer. *The Nicaragua Reader: Documents of a Revolution under Fire.* Grove 1983 $22.50 pap. $8.95. A well-rounded collection of essays and articles with varying points of view.

Selser, Gregorio. *Sandino.* Trans. by Cedric Belfrage, Monthly Review 1982 pap. $7.50. One of the few available biographies of the hero of the Nicaraguan Revolution, the rebel who challenged the U.S. Marines in the 1930s.

Walker, Thomas W. *Nicaragua: The Hand of Sandino.* Nations of Contemporary Latin Amer. Westview Pr. 1982 lib. bdg. $25.00 pap. $11.50. The best available general history of Nicaragua and the Sandinista Revolution.

Wall, James T. *Manifest Destiny Denied: America's First Intervention in Nicaragua.* Univ. Pr. of Amer. 1981 lib. bdg. $24.75 text ed. pap. $12.25. The story of William Walker, a lawyer and a writer, who with his private army attempted to conquer Nicaragua in the 1850s.

PANAMA

McCullough, David. *The Path between the Seas: The Creation of the Panama Canal, 1870–1914.* Simon & Schuster 1977 $17.50; Simon & Schuster (Touchstone Bks.) 1978 pap. $12.50. A wonderful book. McCullough has packaged facts, anecdotes, memoranda, correspondence, and official documents into a fast-paced narrative that describes the building of the canal, an adventure that at the time had no equal.

PARAGUAY

Lewis, Paul H. *Paraguay under Stroessner.* Univ. of North Carolina Pr. 1980 $22.50. A carefully researched study documenting Stroessner's rise to power, viewing the general as the culmination of a tradition of "strong men" shaped by Paraguayan power politics.

Phelps, Gilbert. *The Tragedy of Paraguay.* St. Martin's 1975 $26.00. From 1864 to 1870 Paraguay fought a war with both Argentina and Brazil, which resulted in the death of nearly half the country's population. This balanced work is the story of that tragic war and the nineteenth-century dictator Solano, who led his country into battle.

Warren, Harris G. *Paraguay: An Informal History.* Greenwood repr. of 1949 ed. 1982 lib. bdg. $45.00. An excellent, if not up-to-date, history of Paraguay, skillfully combining comment and documentary quotation.

PERU

Blanco, Hugo. *Land or Death: The Peasant Struggle in Peru.* Path Pr. 1972 $20.00 pap. $5.95. An important work in the history of revolutionary movements of Latin America. The Trotskyite Blanco writes of his attempts at organizing the Quechua Indians into a political movement.

Dobyns, Henry F., and Paul L. Doughty. *Peru: A Cultural History. Latin Amer. Histories Ser.* Oxford 1976 $22.50 pap. $9.95. A well-researched, easy-to-read overview of Peruvian history.

Mariátequi, José C. *Seven Interpretive Essays on Peruvian Reality.* Trans. by Marjory Urquidi, Univ. of Texas Pr. 1971 pap. $9.95. A major book dealing with the problems of Peruvian society, by the Marxist thinker who died in 1930, proclaiming the kinship of socialism and the Indigenous Reform movement of Peru. A very important document in Peruvian political history.

Werlich, David P. *Peru: A Short History.* Southern Illinois Univ. Pr. 1978 $24.95. Written for the general reader, this volume chronicles Peru from precolonial times to the early 1970s.

PUERTO RICO

Carr, Raymond. *Puerto Rico: A Colonial Experiment. Twentieth-Century Fund Study* New York Univ. Pr. 1984 $25.00; Random (Vintage) 1984 pap. $9.95. A controversial study of the not so easily definable relations between the United States and Puerto Rico. Perhaps the most important book on the island.

Marqués, René. *The Docile Puerto Rican: Essays.* Trans. by Barbara B. Aponte, Temple Univ. Pr. 1976 $19.95. A work that will sadden and anger the reader, this is a literary and sociological tour-de-force by the major Puerto Rican author, playwright, and essayist, a psychoanalysis of the Puerto Rican people.

Morales Carrión, Arturo M. *Puerto Rico: A Political and Cultural History.* Norton 1983 $19.50 1984 text ed. pap. $8.95. A well-researched and documented history by a distinguished historian and former assistant secretary of state for Latin America.

Trinidad

Naipaul, V. S. *The Loss of El Dorado.* Random 1984 $4.95. This world-renowned author has not only written about the emergence of modern Trinidad, but has also provided an insightful analysis of colonialism and colonialists. Full of perception and wit, this book is superbly written.

Uruguay

Finch, M. H. *A Political Economy of Uruguay since 1870.* St. Martin's 1981 $29.95. An examination of the problems afflicting modern Uruguay, written as a political and economic study for the nonspecialist.

Porzecanski, Arturo C. *Uruguay's Tupamaros: The Urban Guerilla. Special Studies in International Politics and Government* Irvington 1973 $29.00. A short book, full of documentation provided from the guerrilla side, on one of the twentieth century's most famous guerrilla movements.

Venezuela

Levine, Daniel H. *Religion and Politics in Latin America: The Catholic Church in Venezuela and Colombia.* Princeton Univ. Pr. 1981 pap. $11.50. An outstanding work on the church in Latin America, emphasizing the variety of opinions and political views within Latin American Roman Catholicism. A very thoughtful work, particularly good on the church in Venezuela.

Lombardi, John V. *People and Places in Colonial Venezuela.* Indiana Univ. Pr. 1976 $25.00. An excellent general history of Venezuela, covering colonial times to the present.

CHAPTER 9

British History

John P. McCarthy

In history a great volume is unrolled for our instruction, drawing the materials of future wisdom from the past errors and infirmities of mankind.
—EDMUND BURKE, *Reflections on the Revolution in France*

Until the twentieth century the writing of British history was generally constructed around a limited number of themes: the struggle for popular rights, usually through the courts and Parliament, against arbitrary monarchy; the cause of English religious liberty against Continental, and especially papal, absolutism; and the Anglo-Saxon proclivity toward local free and democratic practices in spite of the imposition of the Norman yoke of despotism. Admittedly, like all popular historical consciousness, this approach was filled with contradictions. For instance, it was the greatly strengthened monarchy of the sixteenth century that broke the religious link with Rome. Furthermore, both conservatives defending an existing order and radical reformers seeking change would try to shroud themselves with the Anglo-Saxon cloak: the former as champions of tradition and the latter as the radical restorers of ancient liberties.

This approach to history, which became perfected in the nineteenth century when the writing of history became professionalized, has been labeled the "Whig Interpretation of History." Herbert Butterfield defined it as "the tendency in many historians to write on the side of Protestants and Whigs, to praise revolutions, provided they have been successful, to emphasize certain principles of progress in the past and to produce a story which is the ratification if not the glorification of the present" (*The Whig Interpretation of History*). Expectedly, such historical attitudes were prevalent during the late nineteenth-century era of imperialism and social Darwinism.

This Whig history has not disappeared in the middle and late twentieth century, especially in more popular writers of history like Winston Churchill and A. L. Rowse, particularly if the writings are celebrations of Britain's and mankind's triumph over nazism. But even among the professional historical specialists whose works correct earlier errors, there is "the tendency to patch the new research into the old story even when the research in detail has altered the bearings of the whole subject" (Butterfield). According to Butterfield, such should be expected since "it is part and parcel of the

Whig interpretation of history that it studies the past with reference to the present. . . . The Whig historian stands in the summit of the 20th century, and organizes his scheme of history from the point of view of his own day."

This tendency is borne out even in twentieth-century departures from earlier Whig orthodoxy, such as the Marxist or socialist analyses of the Reformation and the Industrial Revolution by R. H. Tawney, L. B. Stone, Eric Hobsbawm, and Edward Palmer Thompson. In addition, extensive interest has developed in social history, that is, the examination of the lives of ordinary people rather than the great figures of an era. Naturally these social historians are in no small part influenced by the issues of their (and present) times. Hence, there are many studies of women, of sexual behavior, and of leisure activities, and proportionately fewer of kings and generals.

The first section of this bibliography is a general reference section that is divided into a listing of bibliographic sources and then reference books and general histories that cover the eight periods into which this chapter divides British history: Roman and Anglo-Saxon (to 1066), Norman and Angevin (to 1216), Late Medieval (to 1485), Tudor (to 1603), Stuart (to 1714), Hanoverian (to 1837), Victorian (to 1901), and Twentieth-Century Britain. Books dealing with material pertaining to more than one of these chronological periods are listed in the period to which they devote most attention.

GENERAL REFERENCE

Bibliographies

Altholz, Josef L. *Victorian England, 1837–1901. Bibliographical Handbooks of the Conference on British Studies* Cambridge Univ. Pr. 1970 $17.50

Altschul, Michael. *Anglo-Norman England, 1066–1154. Bibliographical Handbooks of the Conference on British Studies* Cambridge Univ. Pr. 1969 $17.50

Brown, Lucy M., and Ian Christie. *Bibliography of British History, 1789–1851.* Oxford 1977 $110.00

Chaloner, W. H., and R. C. Richardson. *Bibliography of British Social and Economic History.* Manchester 1984 $37.50

Cook, Christopher, and John Stevenson. *Longman Atlas of Modern British History: A Visual Guide to British Society and Politics, 1700–1970.* Longman text ed. 1978 pap. $13.95

Graves, Edgar B., ed. *A Bibliography of English History to 1485.* Oxford 1975 $135.00

Hanham, H. J., ed. *Bibliography of British History, 1851–1914.* Oxford 1976 $145.00

Havighurst, A. F. *Modern England: 1901–1970. Bibliographical Handbooks of the Conference on British Studies* Cambridge Univ. Pr. 1976 $17.95

Kanner, Barbara, ed. *The Women of England from Anglo-Saxon Times to the Present: Interpretive Bibliographical Essays.* Shoe String (Archon) 1979 $30.00

Levine, Mortimer, ed. *Bibliographical Handbook on Tudor England: 1485–1603. Bibliographical Handbooks of the Conference on British Studies* Cambridge Univ. Pr. 1968 $17.95

Pargellis, Stanley, and D. J. Medley. *Bibliography of British History: The Eighteenth Century, 1714–1789.* Rowman repr. of 1951 ed. 1977 $30.00

Read, Conyers, ed. *Bibliography of British History: Tudor Period, 1485–1603.* Rowman 2d ed. repr. of 1959 ed. 1978 $35.00

Stevenson, Bruce, comp. *Reader's Guide to Great Britain: A Bibliography.* Bowker o.p.; Rowman 1977 $32.50

Wilkinson, B. *The High Middle Ages in England, 1154–1377. Bibliographical Handbooks of the Conference on British Studies* Cambridge Univ. Pr. 1978 $19.95

Reference Books and General Histories

Beckett, James G. *Making of Modern Ireland, 1603–1923.* Knopf 1966 $17.95

Beresford, M. W., and J. K. S. St. Joseph. *Medieval England: An Aerial Survey. Cambridge Air Studies* 2d ed. 1979 $37.50

Bossy, John. *The English Catholic Community, 1570–1850.* Oxford 1976 $34.95

Butler, David E., ed. *British Political Facts, 1900–1974.* Ed. by Anne Sloman, St. Martin's 4th rev. ed. 1975 $35.00

Checkland, Sydney. *British Public Policy, 1776–1939: An Economic and Social Perspective.* Cambridge Univ. Pr. $54.50

Clarkson, Leslie A. *Death, Disease and Famine in Pre-Industrial England.* St. Martin's 1975 $21.50

Cockburn, J. S. *Crime in England.* Princeton Univ. Pr. 1977 $36.00

Cook, Christopher, and Keith Brendan. *British Historical Facts, 1830–1900.* St. Martin's text ed. repr. 1975 $29.95

Cullen, L. M. *Economic History of Ireland since 1660.* David & Charles pap. $14.95

Darby, H. C., ed. *A New Historical Geography of England after 1600.* Cambridge Univ. Pr. 1978 $70.00

———. *A New Historical Geography of England before 1600.* Cambridge Univ. Pr. 1978 $59.50 pap. $23.95

Dickinson, W. Croft. *Scotland from the Earliest Times to 1603.* Ed. by Archibald A. Duncan, Oxford 3d. ed. text ed. 1977 $49.95

Douglas, David C., and G. W. Greenaway, eds. *English Historical Documents, 1042–1189.* Oxford 2d ed. 1981 vol. 2 $105.00

Duncan, A. A. *Scotland: The Making of the Kingdom. Edinburgh History of Scotland Ser.* Barnes & Noble text ed. 1975 $37.50

Edwards, Ruth D. *An Atlas of Irish History.* Methuen 2d ed. 1981 $21.00 pap. $9.50

Falkus, Malcolm, and John Gillingham, eds. *Historical Atlas of Britain.* Continuum 1981 $35.00

Flinn, M. W. *British Population Growth, 1700–1850. Studies in Economic and Social History* Humanities Pr. text ed. 1970 pap. $4.00

Freeman-Grenville, G. S. *Atlas of British History.* Rowman 1979 $16.50 pap. $8.95

Girouard, Mark. *Life in the English Country House: A Social and Architectural History.* Penguin 1980 pap. $12.95; Yale Univ. Pr. 1978 $37.50

———. *The Return to Camelot: Chivalry and the English Gentleman.* Yale Univ. Pr. 1981 $40.00

Harvie, Christopher. *Scotland and Nationalism: Scottish Society and Politics, 1707–1977.* Allen & Unwin text ed. 1977 $21.00 pap. $9.95

Jolliffe, John E. *Constitutional History of Medieval England: From the English Settlement to 1485.* Norton Lib. 1967 pap. $8.95

Kanner, Barbara, ed. *The Women of England from Anglo-Saxon Times to the Present: Interpretive Bibliographical Essays.* Shoe String (Archon) 1979 $30.00

Kee, Robert. *The Green Flag.* Delacorte 1972 $15.00. A moderate study of a passionate subject—Ireland.

Keir, David L. *Constitutional History of Modern Britain since 1485.* Norton 1967 pap. $6.95

Kellas, James G. *Modern Scotland: The Nation since 1870.* Allen & Unwin text ed. pap. $9.95

Knowles, David. *Monastic Order in England.* Cambridge Univ. Pr. 2d ed. 1963 $87.50. A monk himself, Knowles is the authority on religious and monastic orders in English history.

———. *The Religious Orders in England.* Cambridge Univ. Pr. 3 vols. vol. 1 (1948) $54.50 pap. $18.95 vol. 2 (1955) $64.50 pap. $21.95 vol. 3 (1979) $69.50 pap. $23.95

Knowles, David, and R. Neville Hadcock. *Medieval Religious Houses in England and Wales.* Cambridge Univ. Pr. 1972 $47.95; St. Martin's 2d ed. 1972 $29.95

Lawrence, Clifford H., ed. *The English Church and the Papacy in the Middle Ages.* Fordham Univ. Pr. 1965 $20.00

Lloyd, T. O. *The British Empire, 1558–1983.* Short Oxford History of the Modern World Ser. 1984 $29.95 pap. $13.95

Lyon, Bryce. *A Constitutional and Legal History of Medieval England.* Norton 2d ed. 1980 $16.95

Lyons, F. S. *Ireland since the Famine.* Fontana 1973 pap. o.p. Authoritative and encyclopedic study of Ireland since the 1840s.

McCaffrey, Lawrence J. *Ireland: From Colony to Nation State.* Prentice-Hall 1979 $22.95 pap. $18.95

Mitchell, Brian R., and Phyllis Deane. *Abstract of British Historical Statistics.* Cambridge Univ. Pr. 1962 $80.00

Norman, E. R. *Church and Society in England, 1770–1970: A Historical Survey.* Oxford 1976 $59.00. Presentation by an orthodox churchman.

O'Farrell, P. J. *England and Ireland since 1800.* Oxford text ed. 1975 pap. $5.95. A study of conflicting national attitudes.

———. *Ireland's English Question: Anglo-Irish Relations, 1534–1970. Fabric of British History Ser.* Schocken 1972 $11.50 pap. $4.95. Study of attitudes since the sixteenth century.

Oxford History of England. Ed. by Sir George Clark, Oxford 15 vols. Write publisher for individual volumes and prices.

Pelling, Henry. *A History of British Trade Unionism.* St. Martin's 3d ed. 1977 $25.00

Pinchbeck, Ivy, and Margaret Hewitt. *Children in English Society.* Univ. of Toronto Pr. 2 vols. vol. 1 (1970) $22.50 vol. 2 (1973) $17.50

Powicke, Frederick M., and E. B. Fryde, eds. *Handbook of British Chronology. Royal Historical Society Ser.* Rowman 1961 $18.50

Schlatter, Richard. *Recent Views on British History: Essays on Historical Writings since 1966.* Rutgers Univ. Pr. 1984 $50.00

Smith, George. *Dictionary of National Biography from the Earliest Times to 1900.* Ed. by Stephen Leslie and Sidney Lee, Oxford 22 vols. 1882–1953 supp. 1 $998.00 supp. 2 $89.00 supp. 3 $72.00 supp. 4 $89.00 supp. 5 $89.00. One of the most important reference works.

Stewart, A. T. *The Narrow Ground.* Faber 1977 $14.95. A historical view of Ulster Unionist consciousness.

Webb, Robert K. *Modern England: From the Eighteenth Century to the Present.* Harper text ed. 1980 pap. $18.95. One of the best histories of modern England.

Wrigley, E. A. *The Population History of England, 1541–1871: A Reconstruction. Studies in Social and Demographic History* Harvard Univ. Pr. text ed. 1982 $65.00

BEFORE THE NORMAN CONQUEST, PRE-1066

The Anglo-Saxon Chronicle. Ed. by Simon Taylor, Biblio Dist. text ed. 1983 $30.00; ed. by Charles Plummer, Oxford 2 vols. repr. of 1899 ed. $105.00. Fundamental narrative source of early English history, consisting of annals composed in various monasteries, done in earnest during King Alfred's reign (871–899) and continuing until the end of King Stephen's reign. Taken as a whole, it is the first history of a Western nation in its own language.

Ashe, Geoffrey. *Kings and Queens of Early Britain.* Methuen 1984 $16.95

Barlow, Frank. *The English Church, 1000–1066: A Constitutional History.* Shoe String (Archon) 1963 $10.00

Birley, Anthony. *The People of Roman Britain.* Univ. of California Pr. 1980 $35.00

Blair, P. H. *An Introduction to Anglo-Saxon England.* Cambridge Univ. Pr. 2d ed. 1977 $59.50 pap. $14.95. One of the best works on the period.

Brooke, Christopher. *From Alfred to Henry III, 871–1272. Norton Lib.* 1966 pap. $7.95

Duckett, Eleanor S. *Alfred the Great: The King and His England.* Univ. of Chicago Pr. 1956 $15.00 1958 pap. $6.95. Excellent study of one of the first kings of a united English people.

———. *Anglo-Saxon Saints and Scholars.* Shoe String (Archon) repr. of 1947 ed. 1967 $26.00

Fisher, D. J. *The Anglo-Saxon Age. History of England Ser.* Longman 1973 $12.95

Frere, Sheppard. *Britannia: A History of Roman Britain.* Routledge & Kegan rev. ed. 1978 $32.00. Carefully researched and well-organized update of earlier research on Roman Britain.

Laing, Lloyd. *Celtic Britain. Britain before the Conquest Ser.* Academy Chicago 1983 pap. $7.95; Scribner 1979 $15.95

Laing, Lloyd, and Jennifer Laing. *Anglo-Saxon England. Britain before the Conquest Ser.* Academy Chicago 1983 pap. $7.95

Loyn, H. R. *The Vikings in Britain.* St. Martin's 1977 $15.95

Mayr-Harting, Henry. *The Coming of Christianity to England. Fabric of British History Ser.* Schocken 1972 $12.50

Morris, John. *The Age of Arthur.* Scribner 1973 $17.50

Richmond, I. A. *Roman Britain.* Penguin 1978 pap. $4.95

Rosenthal, Joel T. *Angles, Angels and Conquerors, 400–1154.* Knopf 1973 vol. 1 $10.00. The first volume in the Knopf (Borzoi) *History of England.*

Salway, Peter. *Roman Britain. Oxford History of England Ser.* 1981 $49.95

Sawyer, P. H. *From Roman Britain to Norman England.* St. Martin's 1979 $27.50

Stenton, Frank M. *Anglo-Saxon England.* Gordon 1977 lib. bdg. $79.95; *Oxford History of England Ser.* 3d ed. 1971 $39.00

Thomas, Charles. *Christianity in Roman Britain to A.D. 500.* Univ. of California Pr. 1981 $40.00

Whitelock, Dorothy. *The Beginnings of English Society.* Penguin 1952 pap. $4.95

NORMAN AND ANGEVIN ENGLAND, 1066–1216

Barlow, Frank. *The Feudal Kingdom of England: 1042–1216.* Longman 3d ed. text ed. 1972 pap. $12.50

Brown, R. Allen. *Origins of English Feudalism. Historical Problems: Studies and Documents* Allen & Unwin 1973 pap. $8.95. Origins of the sociopolitical system that characterized the era.

Darby, H. C., ed. *Domesday England. Domesday Geography of England Ser.* Cambridge Univ. Pr. 1977 $85.00. England when inquests were made for purposes of royal taxation.

Denny, Norman, and Josephine Filmer-Sankey. *The Bayeux Tapestry: The Norman Conquest, 1066.* Merrimack 1984 $15.00. The tapestry celebrates the Norman conquest of England.

Finn, R. Weldon. *The Norman Conquest and Its Effects on the Economy.* Shoe String (Archon) 1970 $25.00

Gibson, Margaret. *Lanfranc of Bec.* Oxford 1978 $45.00. Perceptive study of the archbishop of Canterbury, who was a close associate and ally of William the Conqueror.

Holt, James C. *Magna Carta and the Idea of Liberty.* Krieger 1982 pap. $7.50; *Major Issues in History Ser.* Wiley text ed. 1972 pap. $6.50

Howarth, David. *Ten Sixty Six: The Year of the Conquest.* Penguin 1981 pap. $5.95; Viking 1978 $13.95 ·

Jones, Thomas M. *The Becket Controversy.* Wiley 1970 o.p. An analysis of the twelfth-century church-state clash that continues to intrigue scholars, poets, and playwrights.

Kealey, Edward J. *Roger of Salisbury: Viceroy of England.* Univ. of California Pr. 1972 $37.00. A biography of the leading churchman and political official of the early twelfth century.

Knowles, David. *Thomas Becket.* Stanford Univ. Pr. 1971 $15.00

Loyn, H. R. *The Norman Conquest.* Hutchinson 3d ed. 1984 $18.25 pap. $10.95

Powicke, F. M. *Stephen Langton.* Kelley repr. of 1927 ed. lib. bdg. $12.50. The archbishop of Canterbury who mediated between King John and Pope Innocent, and between John and his nobles. The latter confrontation resulted in the signing of the Magna Carta.

Stenton, Doris M. *English Justice between the Norman Conquest and the Great Charter, 1066–1215.* Amer. Philosophical Society 1964 $4.00

——. *English Society in the Early Middle Ages, 1066–1307.* Gannon lib. bdg. $11.50; Penguin (Pelican) 1952 pap. $4.95

Stenton, F. M. *The First Century of English Feudalism, 1066–1166.* Greenwood 2d ed. repr. of 1961 ed. 1979 lib. bdg. $24.75

Van Caenegem, R. C. *The Birth of the English Common Law.* Cambridge Univ. Pr. 1973 $32.50

Warren, W. L. *Henry II. Eng. Monarchs Ser.* Univ. of California Pr. 1973 $48.50 pap. $11.95. One of the greatest kings of England.

——. *King John.* Univ. of California Pr. rev. ed. 1982 pap. $8.95. Henry II's son, who had to sign the Magna Carta.

THE LATER MIDDLE AGES, 1216–1485

Barber, Richard. *Edward Prince of Wales and Aquitaine: A Biography of the Black Prince.* Scribner 1978 $17.50. The royal warrior who fought in the Hundred Years War.

Bellamy, John. *Crime and Public Order in the Later Middle Ages. Studies in Social History* Univ. of Toronto Pr. 1973 $22.50

Bolton, J. L. *The Medieval English Economy, 1150–1500. Rowman & Littlefield Univ. Lib.* 1980 $25.00 pap. $16.00

Chancellor, John. *The Life and Times of Edward I.* Intro. by Antonia Fraser, *Kings and Queens of England Ser.* Biblio Dist. 1981 $17.50. The great lawgiver and summoner of Parliaments in the late thirteenth century.

Chrimes, S. B. *An Introduction to the Administrative History of Mediaeval England. Studies in Mediaeval History* Blackwell 3d ed. 1966 pap. $9.95

Dobson, R. B. *The Peasants' Revolt of Thirteen Eighty One.* Humanities Pr. repr. of 1970 ed. text ed. 1982 $30.50 pap. $14.50

Fowler, Kenneth. *The Age of Plantagenet and Valois.* Merrimack 1967 o.p. The era of the Hundred Years War.

————, ed. *Hundred Years War.* St. Martin's text ed. 1971 $17.95

Fryde, Natalie. *The Tyranny and Fall of Edward II, 1321–1326.* Cambridge Univ. Pr. 1979 $39.50

Goodman, Anthony. *The Wars of the Roses: Military Activity and English Society, 1452–1497.* Routledge & Kegan 1981 $30.00. The struggle for the throne of England in the fifteenth century.

Gottfried, Robert S. *Epidemic Disease in Fifteenth-Century England: The Medical Response and the Demographic Consequences.* Rutgers Univ. Pr. 1978 $25.00

Griffiths, Ralph A. *The Reign of Henry VI.* Univ. of California Pr. 1981 $40.00. A biography of the last Lancastrian king.

Hatcher, John. *Plague, Population and the English Economy, 1348–1530. Studies in Economic and Social History* Humanities Pr. 1977 pap. $5.50

Holmes, George A. *The Estates of the Higher Nobility in Fourteenth-Century England.* AMS Pr. repr. of 1957 ed. $28.50

————. *The Good Parliament.* Oxford 1975 o.p. Rebellious Parliament of 1376.

————. *The Later Middle Ages. History of England Ser.* Norton 1966 pap. $6.95

Keen, Maurice. *The Outlaws of Medieval Legend. Studies in Social History* Routledge & Kegan 1977 $26.95; Univ. of Toronto Pr. rev. ed. 1978 $15.00. Robin Hood et al.

Kendall, Paul M. *Yorkist Age: Daily Life during the Wars of the Roses. Norton Lib.* repr. of 1962 ed. 1970 pap. $7.95

————, ed. *Richard III: The Great Debate.* Allen & Unwin text ed. 1955 $25.00; *Norton Lib.* repr. of 1955 ed. 1975 pap. $10.95. A different look at the villainously regarded monarch of the late fifteenth century.

King, Edmund. *England, 1175–1425.* Scribner 1979 $9.95

Lander, J. R. *Conflict and Stability in Fifteenth Century England.* Humanities Pr. 3d ed. repr. of 1969 ed. 1977 pap. $12.00

————. *Crown and Nobility, 1450–1509.* McGill-Queens Univ. Pr. 1976 lib. bdg. $25.00

————. *Government and Community: England, 1450–1509. New History of England Ser.* Harvard Univ. Pr. 1980 $27.50 1981 pap. $9.95

Leff, G. *Paris and Oxford Universities in the 13th and 14th Centuries: An Institutional and Intellectual History.* Krieger repr. of 1968 ed. 1975 $18.50

Myers, A. R. *England in the Late Middle Ages.* Gannon lib. bdg. $11.50; Penguin (Pelican) 1952 pap. $4.95

Oman, Charles. *The Great Revolt of 1381. British History Ser.* Haskell repr. of 1906 ed. lib. bdg. $39.95

Postan, M. M. *The Medieval Economy and Society: An Economic History of Britain, 1100–1500.* Univ. of California Pr. 1973 $31.50

Prestwick, Michael. *The Three Edwards: War and State in England, 1272–1377.* St. Martin's 1980 $27.50

————. *War, Politics and Finance under Edward I.* Rowman 1972 $17.50

Ross, Charles. *Edward IV. Eng. Monarchs Ser.* Univ. of California Pr. 1975 $48.50

———. *Richard III. Eng. Monarchs Ser.* Univ. of California Pr. 1982 24.50 1983 pap.
$8.95
Senior, Michael. *The Life and Times of Richard II.* Ed. by Antonia Fraser, *Kings and Queens of England Ser.* Biblio Dist. text ed. 1981 $17.50
Wilkinson, Bertie. *Later Middle Ages in England: 1216–1485. History of England Ser.* Longman text ed. 1977 pap. $12.95
Ziegler, Philip. *Black Death.* Harper repr. of 1969 ed. 1971 pap. $4.95. The causes and influence of the fourteenth-century plague, by an eminent scholar.

THE TUDORS, 1485–1603

Andrews, Kenneth R. *Trade, Plunder and Settlement: Maritime Enterprise and the Genesis of the British Empire, 1480–1630.* Cambridge Univ. Pr. 1985 $49.50 pap. $16.95
Beer, Barrett L. *Northumberland: The Political Career of John Dudley, Earl of Warwick and Duke of Northumberland.* Kent State Univ. Pr. 1974 $15.00. Prominent political operator of the Tudor era.
Bindoff, S. T. *Tudor England.* Gannon lib. bdg. $11.50; Penguin (Pelican) 1950 pap. $4.95
Chambers, Jonathan D. *Population, Economy, and Society in Pre-Industrial England.* Intro. by W. A. Armstrong, *Oxford Pap. Ser.* 1972 pap. $4.95
Cressy, David. *Literacy and the Social Order.* Cambridge Univ. Pr. 1980 $32.50. The effects of the introduction of the printing press on education and the social-class structure.
Cross, Claire. *Church and People, 1450–1600. Fontana Lib. of Eng. History* Humanities Pr. text ed. 1976 $35.50. Discussion of an era when religion and politics were inseparable.
Davis, Ralph. *English Overseas Trade, 1500–1700. Studies in Economic and Social History* Humanities Pr. 1973 pap. $4.00
Dickens, Arthur G. *The English Reformation. Fabric of British History Ser.* Schocken 1968 pap. $7.95
Donaldson, G. *The Scottish Reformation.* Cambridge Univ. Pr. $47.50
Edwards, R. Dudley. *Church and State in Tudor Ireland: A History of Penal Laws against Irish Catholics, 1534–1603.* Russell repr. of 1935 ed. 1972 $18.00. An analysis of the traditional conflict in Ireland, where the Reformation was only the surface, under the Tudors.
Erickson, Carolly. *The First Elizabeth.* Summit 1983 $19.95 1984 pap. $9.95
Greenblatt, Stephen J. *Sir Walter Raleigh: The Renaissance Man and His Roles.* Yale Univ. Pr. 1973 o.p.
Hexter, J. H. *Reappraisals in History: New Views on History and Society in Early Modern Europe.* Univ. of Chicago Pr. 2d ed. 1979 lib. bdg. $20.00 pap. $8.00. Significant critique of prevailing historical interpretations.
Hoskins, W. G. *The Age of Plunder: The England of Henry VIII, 1500–1547. Social and Economic History of England Ser.* Longman text ed. 1976 pap. $11.95
Hughes, Philip E., ed. *Faith and Works: Cranmer and Hooker on Justification.* Morehouse 1982 pap. $5.95
———. *The Reformation in England.* Macmillan 1951 o.p. Scholarly Catholic analysis.
Jones, Whitney Richard David. *The Mid-Tudor Crisis, 1539–1563.* Macmillan 1973 o.p.

Jordan, W. K. *Edward VI, the Threshold of Power: The Dominance of the Duke of Northumberland, 1549–1553.* Harvard Univ. Pr. (Belknap Pr.) 1970 $30.00. The son of Henry VIII—the child king—who died before he reached his maturity.

——. *Edward VI, the Young King: The Protectorship of the Duke of Somerset.* Harvard Univ. Pr. (Belknap Pr.) 1968 $30.00

Lane, Peter. *Elizabethan England. Visual Sources Ser.* David & Charles 1981 $14.95

Levine, Mortimer. *Tudor Dynastic Problems, 1462–1571. Historical Problems: Studies and Documents* Allen & Unwin text ed. 1973 pap. $8.95. These problems were the key to much of what happened in this period.

Loades, D. M. *Politics and the Nation, 1450–1660: Obedience, Resistance and Public Order.* Ed. by Y. R. Elton, *Fontana Lib. of Eng. History* Humanities Pr. text ed. 1974 $22.25; Watts 1974 pap. $4.95

——. *The Reign of Mary Tudor: Politics, Government and Religions in England, 1553–1558.* St. Martin's 1979 $29.95. The attempt by Queen Mary to undo the Reformation.

MacCaffrey, Wallace. *The Shaping of the Elizabethan Regime.* Princeton Univ. Pr. 1971 $40.00

Mattingly, Garrett. *The Armada.* Houghton Mifflin pap. $9.95. History told in the grand style.

Read, C. *Lord Burghley and Queen Elizabeth.* Knopf 1960 o.p. The chief minister of Queen Elizabeth, their personal relationship and public policy.

——. *Mr. Secretary Cecil and Queen Elizabeth.* Knopf 1955 o.p. The son of Burghley, who was secretary of state under Elizabeth and engineered James I's succession to the throne.

Ridley, Jasper. *Statesman and Saint: Wolsey and More—A Study in Contrast.* Viking 1983 $20.75. Henry VIII, "saint"?

——. *Thomas Cranmer.* Darby repr. of 1962 ed. 1983 lib. bdg. $65.00. Major engineer of the Reformation.

Scarisbrick, J. J. *Henry VIII. Eng. Monarchs Ser.* Univ. of Calif. Pr. 1968 $37.50 pap. $6.95

Simpson, Alan. *Wealth of Gentry, 1540–1660. Midway Repr. Ser.* Univ. of Chicago Pr. repr. of 1962 ed. 1975 pap. o.p. The new wealth of a new class in a new age.

Smith, Lacey B. *Elizabeth Tudor: Biography of a Queen. Lib. of World Biography* Little, Brown 1975 $8.95 pap. $7.70

——. *Henry VIII: The Mask of Royalty.* Academy Chicago repr. of 1973 ed. 1982 pap. $5.95; Merrimack 1980 $17.95

Smith, Ralph Bernard. *Land and Politics in the England of Henry VIII.* Oxford 1970 o.p. The relationship between land and politics is regarded by some schools of historical thought as the central issue of the Tudor era.

Thomas, Keith. *Religion and the Decline of Magic.* Scribner text ed. 1971 pap. o.p.

Tittler, Robert. *Nicholas Bacon: The Making of a Tudor Statesman.* Ohio Univ. Pr. 1976 $15.00. Bacon was an important jurist and opponent of Mary Stuart.

Van Cleave Alexander, Michael. *The First of the Tudors: A Study of Henry VII and His Reign.* Rowman 1980 $27.50

Wernham, R. B. *Before the Armada: The Emergence of the English Nation, 1485–1588. Norton Lib.* repr. of 1966 ed. 1972 pap. $6.95

——. *The Making of Elizabethan Foreign Policy, 1558–1603.* Univ. of California Pr. 1981 $17.50 pap. $5.75

Youings, Joyce. *The Dissolution of the Monasteries. Historical Problems: Studies and Documents* Allen & Unwin text ed. 1971 pap. $12.50. An explanation of the dissolution of the monasteries, a process that created a vested interest in the Reformation.

THE STUARTS, 1603–1714

Childs, John. *The Army, James II and the Glorious Revolution*. St. Martin's 1981 $27.50

Fletcher, A. J. *The Outbreak of the English Civil War*. New York Univ. Pr. 1981 $47.50; State Mutual Bk. 1981 $60.00

Fraser, Antonia. *Cromwell*. Knopf 1973 o.p.

———. *Royal Charles: Charles II and the Restoration*. Dell (Delta Bks.) repr. of 1979 ed. 1980 pap. $8.95; Knopf 1979 $16.95

Gregg, Edward. *Queen Anne*. Routledge & Kegan 1984 $29.95 pap. $9.95

Hibbard, Caroline M. *Charles I and the Popish Plot*. Univ. of North Carolina Pr. 1983 $28.00

Horwitz, Henry. *Parliament, Policy and Politics in the Reign of William III*. Univ. of Delaware Pr. $35.00

Howell, Roger, Jr. *Cromwell. Lib. of World Biography* Little, Brown 1977 $8.95

Hunt, William. *The Puritan Moment: The Coming of Revolution in an English County*. Harvard Univ. Pr. text ed. 1983 $36.00 1984 pap. $8.95

Jacob, Margaret C. *The Newtonians and the English Revolution, 1689–1720*. Cornell Univ. Pr. 1976 $27.50

Jones, James Rees. *Country and Court: England, 1658–1714. New History of England Ser.* Harvard Univ. Pr. 1978 $22.50 pap. $7.95. A recent general history taking newer areas of research and inquiry into account.

———. *The Revolution of 1688 in England. Revolutions in the Modern World Ser.* Norton text ed. 1973 pap. $5.95. The event that parallels 1776 in Anglo-American constitutional liberalism. "General readers will find the whole work uniquely intelligent, for compared with . . . the works of Maurice Ashley and John Carswell, the Revolution is not treated as a working out of manifest destiny, nor are there any questions begged as in the classic coverage of G. M. Trevelyan" (*Choice*).

Kenyon, J. P. *The Popish Plot*. St. Martin's 1972 o.p. An analysis of the anti-Catholic paranoia that helped found the Whig party.

———. *Stuart England*. Penguin (Pelican) 1978 pap. $4.95; St. Martin's 1978 $22.50

Kishlansky, Mark A. *The Rise of the New Model Army. Cambridge Pap. Lib.* 1979 $19.95 1983 pap. $14.95. The revolutionary army of the parliamentary-Puritan cause.

Laslett, Peter. *The World We Have Lost: England before the Industrial Revolution*. Scribner 3d ed. 1984 $19.95 text ed. pap. $12.95. Pioneering approach to understanding preindustrial English society.

Lee, Maurice, Jr. *Government by Pen: The Scotland of James VI and I*. Univ. of Illinois Pr. 1980 $19.50. Under James, the separate kingdom of Scotland began to share a monarchy with England, Wales, and Ireland.

MacCormack, John R. *Revolutionary Politics in the Long Parliament*. Harvard Univ. Pr. text ed. 1973 $20.00. The Parliament that rose against Charles I, but was overtaken by its own extremists.

Manning, Brian. *The English People and the English Revolution, 1640–1649*. Holmes & Meier text ed. 1976 $25.00

Miller, John. *James II: A Study in Kingship*. Wayland 1978 o.p. A study of failure.

Prall, Stuart E. *The Bloodless Revolution: England, 1688.* Peter Smith $6.00; Univ. of Wisconsin Pr. repr. of 1972 ed. 1985 pap. $9.95

Riley, P. W. *The Union of England and Scotland: A Study in Anglo-Scottish Politics of the Eighteenth Century.* Rowman 1978 $26.50

Thirsk, Joan. *The Restoration. Problems and Perspectives in History* Longman text ed. 1975 pap. $4.95. The return of the Stuart monarchy after Cromwell's defeat.

Underdown, David. *Pride's Purge: Politics in the Puritan Revolution.* Allen & Unwin text ed. repr. of 1971 ed. 1985 pap. $13.50; Oxford 1971 $37.50. The exclusion of the moderates from the Long Parliament.

Walzer, Michael, ed. *Regicide and Revolution: Speeches Made at the Trial of Louis XVI.* Trans. by Marian Rothstein, *Studies in the History and Theory of Politics* Cambridge Univ. Pr. 1974 $29.95

————. *The Revolution of the Saints: A Study in the Origins of Radical Politics.* Harvard Univ. Pr. text ed. 1982 pap. $7.95. The ultimate in revolutionary fanaticism: the belief that only the "saved" should rule.

Wedgwood, Cicely V. *King's Peace.* Macmillan (Collier Bks.) 1969 pap. o.p. This and *The King's War* (o.p.), *Thomas Wentworth, First Earl of Stafford: A Revaluation* (o.p.), and *The Trial of Charles I* (o.p.) remain the standard account of the English Civil War and the reign of Charles I.

Weston, Corinne, and Janelle R. Greenberg. *Subjects and Sovereigns: The Grand Controversy over Legal Sovereignty in Stuart England.* Cambridge Univ. Pr. 1981 $47.50

Willson, D. H. *King James VI and I.* Jonathan Cape 1956 o.p. A celebrated biography of "the wisest fool in Christendom."

Wilson, Charles. *England's Apprenticeship, 1603–1763. Social and Economic History of England Ser.* Longman text ed. 1965 pap. $17.95. The economic preliminary to the Industrial Revolution and British world ascendancy.

Woolrych, Austin. *Commonwealth to Protectorate.* Oxford 1982 $49.95. Constitutional evolution under Cromwell.

Worden, B. *The Rump Parliament, 1648–1653.* Cambridge Univ. Pr. 1974 $49.50 pap. $19.95

Zagorin, Perez. *The Court and the Country: The Beginning of the English Revolution.* Atheneum text ed. repr. of 1969 ed. 1971 pap. $3.25

Zaller, Robert. *The Parliament of 1621: A Study in Constitutional Conflict.* Univ. of California Pr. 1971 $24.50. The Parliament that wanted support for the Protestants in the Continental war, wanted to curb and control royal expenditures, and impeached Lord Chancellor Francis Bacon.

THE HANOVERIANS, 1714–1837

Anstey, Roger, and A. P. Antippas. *The Atlantic Slave Trade and British Abolition, 1760–1810. Cambridge Commonwealth Ser.* Humanities Pr. 1975 $22.50. The effort to curb one of the horrors of European expansion.

Ayling, Stanley. *The Elder Pitt: Earl of Chatham.* McKay 1976 o.p. A new appraisal of the maker of the British empire.

————. *John Wesley.* Abingdon 1983 $16.95. The founder of Methodism.

Brock, Michael. *The Great Reform Act.* Ed. by Joel Hurstfield, Humanities Pr. text ed. 1974 pap. $12.25. Brief treatment of the first step toward the democratization of Britain.

Brooke, John. *King George III*. Academy Chicago repr. of 1972 ed. 1974 pap. $4.95
Brown, Earl K. *Women of Mr. Wesley's Methodism. Studies in Women and Religion*
Mellen 1984 $49.95
Brown, Peter D. *William Pitt, Earl of Chatham*. Allen & Unwin 1978 text ed. $32.50.
Browning, Reed. *The Duke of Newcastle*. Yale Univ. Pr. 1975 $35.00. One of the great
Whig patrons and political managers under George II.
Chambers, Jonathan D. *Population, Economy, and Society in Pre-Industrial England*.
Intro. by W. A. Armstrong, *Oxford Pap. Ser.* 1972 pap. $4.95
Chambers, Jonathan D., and Gordon E. Mingay. *The Agricultural Revolution*. David
& Charles 1975 pap. $16.95. The transformation that enabled Britain to feed a
greatly expanded population.
Christie, Ian R., and Benjamin W. Labaree. *Empire or Independence, 1760–1776: A
British American Dialogue. Norton Lib.* 1977 pap. $5.95. British and U.S. exami-
nation of the prelude to the American Revolution.
Cookson, J. E. *Lord Liverpool's Administration: The Crucial Years, 1815–1822*. Shoe
String (Archon) 1975 $30.00. An administration beset by an insane king, a rakish
regent, the threat of revolution, and a prime minister who was part leader and
head of government rather than the king's servant.
Cunningham, Hugh. *Leisure in the Industrial Revolution, 1780–1880*. St. Martin's
1980 $26.00
Davis, Ralph. *The Industrial Revolution and British Overseas Trade*. Humanities Pr.
text ed. 1978 $21.00 pap. $10.75
Deane, Phyllis. *The First Industrial Revolution*. 1966. Cambridge Univ. Pr. 2d ed.
1980 $47.50 pap. $12.95
Derry, John W. *Castlereagh. British Political Biography Ser.* St. Martin's 1976 o.p.
Statesman of the Congress of Vienna era.
———. *Charles James Fox*. David & Charles 1972 $37.50. An outspoken Whig, who
was a friend of the radicals, the Americans, and the French.
———. *English Politics and the American Revolution*. St. Martin's text ed. 1977
$14.95
Dickinson, H. T. *Liberty and Property: Political Ideology in Eighteenth Century Britain*.
Holmes & Meier text ed. 1978 $49.50
———. *Walpole and the Whig Supremacy. Men and Their Times Ser.* Verry 1973 o.p.
The first prime minister and the man who guaranteed Whig ascendancy and the
heritage of the Glorious Revolution.
Dobson, C. R. *Masters and Journeymen: A Prehistory of Industrial Relations*. Rowman
1980 $24.75. Labor relations before the Industrial Revolution.
Drescher, Seymour. *Econocide: British Slavery in the Era of Abolition*. Univ. of Pitts-
burgh Pr. 1977 $21.95
Emsley, Clive. *British Society and the French Wars, 1793–1815*. Rowman 1979 $19.50
Endelman, Todd M. *The Jews of Georgian England, 1714–1830: Tradition and Change
in a Liberal Society*. Jewish Publication Society 1979 $14.50
Goodwin, Albert. *The Friends of Liberty: The English Democratic Movement in the Age
of the French Revolution*. Harvard Univ. Pr. text ed. 1979 $32.50. Inevitably re-
garded as a subversive movement, especially when England was at war with
revolutionary France.
Hartwell, R. M. *The Industrial Revolution and Economic Growth*. Methuen 1971 o.p.
Sympathetic account of the ultimately benevolent effect of the Industrial Revolution.
Hedley, Olwen. *Queen Charlotte*. Transatlantic 1976 $15.00. The wife of George III.
Hibbert, Christopher. *George IV: Prince of Wales, 1752–1811*. Harper 1972 o.p.

————. *George IV: Regent and King, 1811–1830.* Harper 1974 vol. 2 $15.00. The rakish and unpleasant son of the religious and dutiful George III.

Hilton, Boyd. *Corn, Cash, Commerce: The Economic Policies of the Tory Government, 1815–1830. Oxford Historical Monographs* 1978 $17.95

Hoffman, Ross J. *The Marquis: A Study of Lord Rockingham, 1730–1782.* Fordham Univ. Pr. 1973 $35.00. Important Whig leader, patron of Edmund Burke, and leader of loyal opposition to George III.

Kronenberger, Louis. *The Extraordinary Mr. Wilkes.* Doubleday 1974 o.p. The radical demagogue of the 1760s and 1770s.

Marcus, Geoffrey. *Heart of Oak: A Survey of British Sea Power in the Georgian Era.* Oxford 1975 $27.50

Marshall, Dorothy. *Eighteenth Century England, 1714 to 1784. History of England Ser.* Longman 2d ed. 1975 pap. $14.50

Marshall, P. J. *East India Fortunes: The British in Bengal in the Eighteenth Century.* Oxford Univ. Pr. 1976 $45.00

McLynn, F. J. *The Jacobite Army in England, 1745.* Humanities Pr. text ed. 1983 $29.00. Bonnie Prince Charlie's forces.

Mingay, Gordon E. *English Landed Society in the Eighteenth Century.* Univ. of Toronto Pr. 1963 $20.00

————. *The Gentry: The Rise and Fall of a Ruling Class. Themes in British Social History* Longman text ed. 1976 pap. $10.95

O'Gorman, Frank. *The Rise of Party in England: The Rockingham Whigs, 1760–1782.* Allen & Unwin text ed. 1975 $32.50. The loyal opposition to George III.

Owen, John B. *Eighteenth Century: 1714–1815.* Norton Lib. repr. 1976 pap. $8.95; *History of England Ser.* Rowman 1975 $13.75; Van Nostrand 1974 $27.50

Pawson, Eric. *The Early Industrial Revolution.* Barnes & Noble text ed. 1979 $21.50; David & Charles 1979 $29.95

Peters, Marie. *Pitt and Popularity: The Patriot Minister and London Opinion during the Seven Years War.* Oxford 1980 $55.00

Rudé, George. *Hanoverian London, 1714–1808. History of London Ser.* Univ. of California Pr. 1971 $40.00

Sack, James J. *The Grenvillites, 1801–29: Party Politics and Factionalism in the Age of Pitt and Liverpool.* Univ. of Illinois Pr. 1979 $20.00

Semmel, Bernard. *The Methodist Revolution.* Basic Bks. 1973 $12.95. Religious development with its enormous social, economic, and political implications.

Speck, W. A. *Stability and Strife: England, 1714–1760. New History of England Ser.* Harvard Univ. Pr. 1977 $15.00 pap. $7.95

Summerson, John. *Georgian London.* MIT 3d ed. 1978 $30.00; Penguin repr. of 1962 ed. 1979 pap. $4.95

Taylor, A. J. P., ed. *The Standard of Living in Britain in the Industrial Revolution. Debates in Economic History Ser.* Methuen 1975 pap. $12.95

Thomas, Peter D. *Lord North. British Political Biography Ser.* St. Martin's 1975 $25.00. George III's prime minister during the American Revolution.

THE VICTORIAN AGE, 1837–1901

Altick, Richard D. *Victorian People and Ideas.* Norton 1974 pap. $8.95. Interesting and perceptive glimpses of the age.

Arnstein, Walter L. *Protestant versus Catholic in Mid-Victorian England: Mr. Newdegate and the Nuns.* Univ. of Missouri Pr. text ed. $20.00

Briggs, Asa. *Age of Improvement, 1783 to 1867. History of England Ser.* Longman text
 ed. 1959 pap. $13.95. A pace-setting general history of the period. Briggs's ap-
 proaches and themes have been followed by many other historians.
Brundage, Anthony. *The Making of the New Poor Laws: The Politics of Inquiry, Enact-
 ment, and Implementation, 1832–1839.* Rutgers Univ. Pr. 1978 $22.50. A rational,
 but heartless welfare system.
Buckland, Patrick. *Irish Unionism.* Gill & MacMillan 2 vols. 1972–73 o.p. The history of those in Ireland who wanted to maintain the union with Britain.
Clark, G. Kitson. *Churchmen and the Condition of England, 1832–1885.* Methuen
 1973 o.p. A sympathetic account of churchmen and their interest in the social
 question.
———. *Making of Victorian England.* Atheneum text ed. 1967 pap. $6.95. A most im-
 portant interpretation of the era.
Conacher, J. B. *The Peelites and the Party System, 1846–52. Lib. of Politics and Society
 Ser.* Shoe String (Archon) 1972 $17.50. The breakaway conservatives who would
 form coalitions with the Whigs.
Cook, Christopher. *A Short History of the Liberal Party, 1900–1975.* Merrimack 2d ed.
 1984 $24.00; St. Martin's 1976 $19.95
Curtis, L. Perry, Jr. *Apes and Angels: The Irishman in Victorian Caricature.* Smithsonian 1971 $8.95
Donnelly, James S. *Landlord and Tenant in Nineteenth Century Ireland.* Gill & Mac-
 Millan 1973 o.p. An issue often subject to simplistic analysis is very ably han-
 dled in this work.
Edwards, R. Dudley, ed. *The Great Famine: Studies in Irish History, 1845–1852.* Pref.
 by E. R. Green, Russell repr. of 1957 ed. 1976 $30.00. The definitive scholarly
 analysis.
Emy, H. V. *Liberals, Radicals and Social Politics, 1892–1914.* Cambridge Univ. Pr.
 1973 $42.50. Liberalism's move from laissez-faire to collectivism.
Farwell, Byron. *The Great Anglo-Boer War.* Harper 1976 $16.95
Fergusson, Thomas G. *British Military Intelligence, 1870–1914: The Development of a
 Modern Intelligence Organization.* Univ. Publications of Amer. 1984 $25.00
Feuchtwanger, E. J. *Gladstone. British Political Biography Ser.* St. Martin's 1975
 $25.00. Study of one of the Victorian greats.
Freeden, Michael. *The New Liberalism: An Ideology of Social Reform.* Oxford 1978 o.p.
 An assessment of turn-of-the-century collectivist liberalism.
Gallagher, J. A. *The Decline, Revival and Fall of the British Empire.* Cambridge Univ.
 Pr. 1982 $32.50. Gallagher is a thoughtful revisionist historian of British imperi-
 alism.
Gilbert, Alan D. *Religion and Society in Industrial England. Themes in British Social
 History* Longman text ed. 1976 pap. $12.95
Halstead, John P. *The Second British Empire: Trade, Philanthropy, and Good Govern-
 ment, 1820–1890. Contributions in Comparative Colonial Studies* Greenwood
 1983 lib. bdg. $35.00
Hamer, D. A. *Liberal Politics in the Age of Gladstone and Roseberry: A Study in Leader-
 ship and Policy.* Oxford 1972 $24.95
Harrison, John F. *The Second Coming: Popular Millenarianism, 1780–1850.* Rutgers
 Univ. Pr. 1979 $27.50
Hayes, Paul M. *The Nineteenth Century, 1814–1880. Modern British Foreign Policy
 Ser.* St. Martin's 1975 $26.00
Hibbert, Christopher. *The Great Mutiny: India, 1857.* Penguin 1980 pap. $7.95; Vi-
 king 1978 $15.95. Lively account of the Indian uprising.

Holcombe, Lee. *Victorian Ladies at Work: Middle Class Working Women in England and Wales, 1850–1914*. Shoe String (Archon) 1973 $19.00. A study of women who challenged the confinements of their era.

Holmes, J. Derek. *More Roman Than Rome: English Catholicism in the Nineteenth Century*. Patmos Pr. 1978 $21.95

Jones, Raymond A. *The British Diplomatic Service, 1815–1914*. Humanities Pr. text ed. 1983 $17.75

Joyce, Patrick. *Work, Society, and Politics: The Culture of the Factory in Later Victorian England*. Rutgers Univ. Pr. 1980 $30.00

Koss, Stephen E. *The Rise and Fall of the Political Press in Britain: The Twentieth Century*. Univ. of North Carolina Pr. 1984 $34.00

Krein, David F. *Last Palmerston Government: Foreign Policy, Domestic Politics, and the Genesis of "Splendid Isolation."* Iowa State Univ. Pr. 1978 pap. $9.50. Palmerston was the personification of "John Bull."

Laqueur, Thomas W. *Religion and Respectability: Sunday Schools and English Working Class Culture, 1780–1850*. Yale Univ. Pr. 1976 $37.50

Larkin, Emmet. *The Making of the Roman Catholic Church in Ireland, 1850–1860*. Univ. of North Carolina Pr. 1980 $30.00. The revival of organizational and devotional discipline after more than a century of persecution and disorder.

Lee, Joseph. *The Modernisation of Irish Society, 1848–1914*. Irish Bk. Ctr. 1973 pap. $9.95

Le May, G. H. *The Victorian Constitution*. St. Martin's 1979 $27.50

Lyons, F. S. *Charles Stewart Parnell*. Oxford 1977 $25.00. Definitive biography of the constitutional nationalist Irish leader.

MacDonagh, Oliver. *Early Victorian Government, 1830–1870*. Holmes & Meier 1977 text ed. $29.50. Decisive analysis, setting the premises for other historians.

———. *Ireland: The Union and Its Aftermath*. Allen & Unwin text ed. 1977 pap. $9.95. Develops the fundamental questions for other historians.

McCaffrey, Lawrence J. *Ireland: From Colony to Nation State*. Prentice-Hall 1979 $22.95 pap. $18.95. Balanced picture.

McCartney, Donal, ed. *The World of Daniel O'Connell*. Irish Bks. 1980 pap. $8.95

Mingay, Gordon E. *Rural Life in Victorian England*. Holmes & Meier text ed. 1978 o.p.

Mokyr, Joel. *Why Ireland Starved: A Quantitative and Analytical History of the Irish Economy, 1800–1850*. Allen & Unwin text ed. 1983 $29.95 1985 pap. $11.95. Computerized use of social statistics in an attempt to explain why the famine was so severe.

Moore, David C. *The Politics of Deference: A Study of the Mid-Nineteenth Century English Political System*. Barnes & Noble text ed. 1977 o.p. Examination of the willingness of most English people to be ruled by those judged to be their "betters."

Nowlan, Kevin B., and Maurice R. O'Connell, eds. *Daniel O'Connell: Portrait of a Radical*. Irish Bks. 1984 pap. $8.50. Essays on different aspects of the great Irish political figure.

O'Ferrall, Fergus. *Daniel O'Connell*. Gill & MacMillan 1981 o.p. The constitutional leader of the Irish Catholics.

Pakenham, Thomas. *The Boer War*. Random 1979 $20.00

Pelling, Henry. *Popular Politics and Society in Late Victorian Britain*. Humanities Pr. text ed. 1979 $26.50 pap. $13.50; St. Martin's 1968 $22.50

Read, Donald, ed. *Edwardian England: Reassessments*. Rutgers Univ. Pr. text ed. $25.00 pap. $9.95

Richter, Donald C. *Riotous Victorians*. Ohio Univ. Pr. text ed. 1981 $14.95 pap. $7.95

Robbins, Keith. *The Eclipse of a Great Power: Modern Britain, 1870–1975*. Longman text ed. 1983 $33.00 pap. $14.95

———. *John Bright*. Routledge & Kegan 1979 $25.00. The early and mid-Victorian radical and free trader.

Roberts, David. *Paternalism in Early Victorian England*. Rutgers Univ. Pr. 1979 $30.00

Royle, Edward. *Radicals, Secularists and Republicans: Popular Freethought in Britain, 1866 to 1915*. Rowman 1980 $29.50

Ruse, Michael. *The Darwinian Revolution: Science Red in Tooth and Claw*. Univ. of Chicago Pr. 1979 $20.00 pap. $10.95

Stansky, Peter. *Gladstone: A Progress in Politics*. Intro. by J. H. Plumb, Little, Brown 1979 $9.95; Norton 1981 pap. $4.95

Thomis, Malcolm I. *Responses to Industrialisation: The British Experience, 1780–1850*. Shoe String (Archon) 1976 $18.50

Thomis, Malcolm I., and Peter Holt. *Threats of Revolution in Britain, 1789–1848*. Shoe String (Archon) 1977 $16.50

Townshend, Charles. *Political Violence in Ireland: Government and Resistance since 1848*. Oxford 1983 $39.95 1985 pap. $12.95

Trench, Charles C. *The Great Dan: A Biography of Daniel O'Connell*. Jonathan Cape 1984. Good popular biography of the Irish political leader.

Ward, John T. *Chartism*. Humanities Pr. text ed. 1973 $15.50. A study of the first mass political movement in England.

Woodham-Smith, Cecil B. *Great Hunger*. Dutton 1980 pap. $8.95; Harper 1963 $16.95. Popular but solid account of the Irish famine.

Ziegler, Philip. *Melbourne*. Atheneum 1982 pap. $10.95; Knopf 1976 $15.00. Victoria's first prime minister.

THE TWENTIETH CENTURY

Bartlett, C. J. *A History of Postwar Britain, 1945–74*. Longman text ed. 1977 pap. $13.95

Bedarida, François. *A Social History of England, 1851–1975*. Methuen 1979 $14.95 pap. $13.95

Beer, Samuel H. *Modern British Politics: Parties and Pressure Groups in the Collectivist Age*. Norton repr. of 1965 ed. 1982 pap. $7.95

Branson, Noreen. *Britain in the Nineteen Twenties*. Ed. by Eric J. Hobsbawm, *History of British Society Ser*. Univ. of Minnesota Pr. 1976 $20.00

Cook, Christopher. *Age of Alignment: Electoral Politics in Britain, 1922–1929*. Univ. of Toronto Pr. 1975 $27.50

Cowling, Maurice. *The Impact of Hitler: British Politics and British Policy, 1933–1940. Cambridge Studies in the History and Theory of Politics* 1975 $64.50; Univ. of Chicago Pr. (Phoenix Bks.) 1977 pap. $7.95

———. *Impact of Labour, Nineteen Twenty to Nineteen Twenty Four: The Beginning of Modern British Politics. Cambridge Studies in the History and Theory of Politics* 1971 $49.95

Eatwell, Roger. *The Labour Governments, 1945–1951*. David & Charles 1979 $35.00 pap. $14.95

Fanning, Ronan. *Independent Ireland. Helicon History of Ireland Ser*. Irish Bk. Ctr. 1983 $22.95 pap. $9.95. Ireland since 1922.

Gilbert, Alan D. *The Making of Post Christian Britain*. Longman text ed. 1980 $23.00

Gilbert, Bentley B. *Britain since 1918*. St. Martin's 2d ed. 1980 $23.50

Grigg, John. *The People's Champion, 1902–1911*. Univ. of California Pr. 1979 $40.00

——. *The Young Lloyd George*. Univ. of California Pr. repr. of 1973 ed. 1978 $34.50

Hachey, Thomas E. *British and Irish Separatism: From the Fenians to the Free State, 1867–1922*. Catholic Univ. Pr. 1984 pap. $8.95

Harkness, David. *Northern Ireland since Nineteen Twenty*. Helicon History of Ireland Ser. Irish Bk. Ctr. 1983 $22.95 pap. $9.95

Harrison, Brian. *Separate Spheres: The Opposition to Woman Suffrage in Britain*. Holmes & Meier repr. text ed. 1978 $39.50

Havighurst, Alfred F. *Britain in Transition: The Twentieth Century*. Univ. of Chicago Pr. 1979 $25.00 text ed. pap. $9.95

Hayes, Paul. *The Twentieth Century, 1880–1939*. Modern British Foreign Policy Ser. St. Martin's 1978 $25.00

James, Robert R. *The British Revolution, 1880–1939*. Knopf 1977 o.p.

Kennedy, Paul. *The Realities behind Diplomacy: Background Influences on British External Policy, 1865–1980*. Allen & Unwin text ed. 1981 $27.50 1983 pap. $9.95

——. *The Rise of the Anglo-German Antagonism: 1860–1914*. Allen & Unwin text ed. 1980 $60.00 1982 pap. $19.50

Koss, Stephen. *Nonconformity in Modern British Politics*. Shoe String (Archon) 1975 $18.50

Lee, J. M. *The Churchill Coalition, 1940–1945*. Shoe String (Archon) 1980 $20.00

Lloyd, T. O. *Empire to Welfare State: English History, 1906–1976*. Short Oxford History of the Modern World Ser. 2d ed. 1979 $37.50 pap. $13.95

Marwick, Arthur. *British Society since 1945*. Pelican Social History of Britain Ser. Allen Lane 1984 $15.95; Penguin Social History of Britain Ser. 1983 pap. $4.95; Viking 1984 $15.95

McKibbin, Ross. *The Evolution of the Labour Party, 1910–1924*. Oxford Historical Monographs repr. of 1974 ed. 1983 pap. $14.95

Meacham, Standish. *A Life Apart: The English Working Class, 1890–1914*. Harvard Univ. Pr. 1977 $18.50

Moore, Roger. *The Emergence of the Labour Party, 1880-1924*. Humanities Pr. text ed. 1978 $18.75

Morgan, Kenneth O. *Consensus and Disunity: The Lloyd George Coalition Government, 1918 to 1922*. Oxford text ed. 1979 $44.00

——. *Wales in British Politics, Eighteen Sixty Eight to Nineteen Twenty Two*. Humanities Pr. 3d ed. text ed. 1980 $19.00

Murphy, John. *Ireland in the Twentieth Century*. Irish Bk. Ctr. 1975 pap. $7.95

O'Day, Alan, ed. *The Edwardian Age: Conflict and Stability, 1900–1914*. Shoe String (Archon) 1979 $18.50

O'Malley, Padraig. *Uncivil Wars: Ireland Today*. Houghton Mifflin 1983 $20.00 1984 pap. $9.95. The best analysis of the Northern Irish situation.

Pelling, Henry. *A Short History of the Labour Party*. St. Martin's 5th ed. text ed. 1977 pap. $10.95

Phillips, Gregory D. *The Diehards: Aristocratic Society and Politics in Edwardian England*. Harvard Univ. Pr. 1979 $18.50. The last stand against democracy.

Pugh, Martin. *Electoral Reform in War and Peace, 1906–1918*. Routledge & Kegan 1978 $20.00

Ramsden, John. *The Age of Balfour and Baldwin, 1902–1940*. History of the Conservative Party Ser. Longman text ed. 1978 $44.00

Read, Donald, ed. *Edwardian England: Reassessments*. Rutgers Univ. Pr. text ed. $25.00

Rose, Richard. *Governing without Consensus: An Irish Perspective.* Beacon 1971 pap. $6.95. Sociopolitical explanation of the Northern Irish problem.

Rowland, Peter. *David Lloyd George: A Biography.* Macmillan 1976 o.p.

Sampson, Anthony. *The Changing Anatomy of Britain.* Random 1983 $17.95; Random (Vintage) 1984 pap. $8.95. Ideal introduction for the layman, and very useful for the scholar as well.

Sked, Alan, and Christopher Cook. *Post War Britain: A Political History.* Penguin Nonfiction Ser. 1985 pap. $7.95

Thompson, Paul. *The Edwardians: The Remaking of British Society.* Academy Chicago 1977 pap. $6.50; Indiana Univ. Pr. 1975 $15.00

Townshend, Charles. *The British Campaign in Ireland, 1919–1921.* Oxford Historical Monographs 1978 pap. $15.95

Ward, Alan J. *The Easter Rising: Revolution and Irish Nationalism.* Harlan Davidson text ed. 1980 pap. $8.95. Analysis of the Irish rebellion.

Wiener, Martin. *English Culture and the Decline of the Industrial Spirit, 1850–1980.* Cambridge Univ. Pr. 1981 $24.95 pap. $8.95

ACTON, LORD JOHN E. 1834–1902

Regius professor at Cambridge University and editor of the *Rambler*, a monthly Roman Catholic publication, Acton was a liberal Catholic during a period of strong ultramontanism in the English Church. In 1859 he was elected to Parliament as a liberal. He was a strong critic of political and ecclesiastical tyranny and the concentration of power. The architect of the *Cambridge Modern History*, Acton died after publication of the first volume. Although an influential historian, he never finished a book. The publications listed below are collections of essays and lectures.

BOOKS BY ACTON

Collected Works. Gordon $600.00

Lectures on Modern History. 1906. Ed. by E. Golin, Peter Smith $10.50

History of Freedom, and Other Essays. Ed. by John N. Figgis and R. V. Laurence, AMS Pr. repr. of 1910 ed. $24.50; *Essay Index Repr. Ser.* Ayer repr. of 1907 ed. $26.50

Lectures on the French Revolution. Ed. by John N. Figgis and R. V. Laurence, AMS Pr. repr. of 1910 ed. $24.50

Essays on Church and State. Peter Smith $11.00

Essays on Freedom and Power. Peter Smith $12.00

BOOKS ABOUT ACTON

Himmelfarb, Gertrude. *Lord Acton: A Study in Conscience and Politics.* Univ. of Chicago Pr. (Phoenix Bks.) 1962 pap. $1.50

Mathew, David, *Lord Acton and His Times.* Univ. of Alabama Pr. 1968 $22.50

Schuettinger, Robert L. *Lord Acton: Historian of Liberty.* Open Court 1976 $12.50

ASHTON, THOMAS S. 1889–1968

Ashton is one of the major historians of the Industrial Revolution in Britain. He approaches it from a positive perspective, seeing it as an ultimately benevolent development reflective of human creativity and enterprise.

BOOKS BY ASHTON

Iron and Steel in the Industrial Revolution. Kelley repr. of 1924 ed. $25.00
Economic and Social Investigations in Manchester, 1833–1933. Kelley repr. of 1934 ed. $19.50
An Economic History of England: The Eighteenth Century. Methuen 1972 pap. $13.95
Eighteenth-Century Industrialist: Peter Stubs of Warrington. Kelley 1939 $17.50
Industrial Revolution: 1760–1830. Oxford 1948 pap. $4.95

BAGEHOT, WALTER. 1826–1877

Bagehot was a Victorian liberal and editor of *The Economist.* Essentially a conservative liberal, he was appreciative of the organic and evolutionary character of political institutions, but similarly sympathetic to necessary change and reform. He was also a noted literary critic.

BOOKS BY BAGEHOT

Collected Works of Walter Bagehot. Ed. by John Stevas St. Norman, intro. by Jacques Barzun, Harvard Univ. Pr. 1968 vols. 3 and 4 $70.00
Biographical Studies. Ed. by Richard H. Hutton, AMS Pr. repr. of 1881 ed. $12.50; Richard West repr. of 1895 ed. 1973 $15.00; Scholarly repr. of 1889 ed. 1972 $12.00
Estimates of Some Englishmen and Scotchmen. Darby repr. of 1858 ed. 1980 lib. bdg. $47.50; Folcroft repr. of 1858 ed. 1974 lib. bdg. $45.00
The English Constitution. 1864. Intro. by R. H. Crossman, Cornell Univ. Pr. 1966 pap. $7.95; *Classics of Eng. Legal History in the Modern Era Ser.* Garland repr. of 1867 ed. 1978 lib. bdg. $61.00; *World's Class. Ser.* Oxford 1968 $12.95. Study of effective and ineffective institutions of government.
Lombard Street: A Description of the Money Market. 1873. Ed. by Mira Wilkins, *International Finance Ser.* Ayer repr. of 1917 ed. 1978 lib. bdg. $30.00; intro. by Frank C. Genovese, Hyperion Pr. repr. of 1962 ed. 1979 $19.00; ed. by Hartley Withers, Orion repr. of 1927 ed. 1984 pap. $9.95. Influential study of the British banking system.
Physics and Politics. 1875. Greenwood repr. of 1956 ed. 1973 lib. bdg. $15.00; Sharon Hill 1881 $30.00. Pathbreaking study of the relationship between the natural and the social sciences.
Economic Studies. 1880. Ed. by Richard H. Hutton, Kelley 2d ed. repr. of 1898 ed. $25.00; Scholarly repr. 1976 $11.50

BOOKS ABOUT BAGEHOT

Buchan, Alastair. *Spare Chancellor: The Life of Walter Bagehot.* Michigan State Univ. Pr. 1960 $5.00
Irvine, William. *Walter Bagehot.* Shoe String (Archon) repr. of 1939 ed. 1970 $19.50. The standard biography.
Sisson, C. H. *The Case of Walter Bagehot.* Humanities Pr. text ed. 1972 $11.00

BEDE (or Baeda, Beda) THE VENERABLE, SAINT. 673–735

One of the outstanding scholars of eighth-century Europe, Bede taught Greek, Latin, Hebrew, and theology at the monastery at Jarrow. He concentrated on the advance of Christian faith in England. While sharing the pious beliefs of his time, he was a discriminating scholar who acknowledged his sources and was a critical reporter.

BOOK BY BEDE

The Ecclesiastical History of England. Ed. by John A. Giles, *Bohn's Antiquarian Lib.* AMS Pr. repr. of 1849 ed. $34.50

BOOK ABOUT BEDE

Browne, G. F. *The Venerable Bede: His Life and Writings.* Folcroft repr. of 1919 ed. 1972 lib. bdg. $30.00

BELLOC, HILAIRE. 1870–1953

A political radical, Belloc was a historian and a liberal member of Parliament for South Salford. He attacked the fundamental premises of Whig history and the idealization of Anglo-Saxon England. Instead, he emphasized the importance of such Continental influences as the Church and the Normans on English institutions. He was a Catholic apologist and defender of the monarchy against the Whig oligarchy of the modern era. With Cecil Chesterton, he founded the *Eye Witness*, a weekly newspaper.

BOOKS BY BELLOC

The Servile State. 1912. Liberty Fund 1977 $8.00 pap. $3.00
Warfare in England. Darby repr. of 1912 ed. 1983 lib. bdg. $35.00
How the Reformation Happened. 1928. Peter Smith $11.00
James the Second. Select Bibliographies Repr. Ser. Ayer repr. of 1928 ed. $20.00
Wolsey. 1930. Arden Lib. repr. of 1933 ed. 1978 lib. bdg. $20.00
Cranmer. Eng. Biographies Ser. Haskell repr. of 1931 ed. 1972 lib. bdg. $55.95
Essays of a Catholic. Essay Index Repr. Ser. Ayer repr. of 1931 ed. $18.00
William the Conqueror. 1933. Darby repr. of 1938 ed. 1983 lib. bdg. $35.00
Milton. Greenwood repr. of 1935 ed. lib. bdg. $24.75
Characters of the Reformation. Essay Index Repr. Ser. Ayer repr. of 1936 ed. $24.00
The Crisis of Civilization. Greenwood repr. of 1937 ed. 1973 lib. bdg. $19.75
Great Heresies. Essay Index Repr. Ser. Ayer repr. of 1938 ed. $18.00
Elizabethan Commentary. Haskell repr. of 1942 ed. 1969 lib. bdg. $49.95

BOOKS ABOUT BELLOC

Braybrook, Patrick. *Some Thoughts on Hilaire Belloc: Ten Studies.* Haskell repr. of 1969 ed. lib. bdg. $48.59; Richard West 1973 $17.50
Markel, Michael H. *Hilaire Belloc. Twayne's Eng. Authors Ser.* G. K. Hall 1982 lib. bdg. $16.95
McCarthy, John P. *Hilaire Belloc: Edwardian Radical.* Liberty Fund 1979 $8.00 pap. $3.00
Speaight, Robert. *Life of Hilaire Belloc. Biography Index Repr. Ser.* Ayer repr. of 1957 ed. $29.00; Darby repr. of 1957 ed. 1981 lib. bdg. $35.00
Wilson, A. N. *Hilaire Belloc.* Atheneum 1984 $17.95

BUCKLE, HENRY T. 1821–1862

Buckle was a nineteenth-century liberal who intended to write a history of civilization that encompassed the entire human experience instead of the traditional emphases on political and military history. He gave a minimal role to government in the history of human advancement, which, he believed, was the consequence of the growth of knowledge and thought. That growth he connected to such material factors as climate and soil and their effect on the production and distribution of wealth. Although he only completed two volumes of his *History of Civilization in England,* the work influenced English liberal historians by its emphasis on the masses instead of individuals, and historians of science by its understanding of the relationship between nature and history.

BOOK BY BUCKLE

History of Civilization in England. 1857–61. Ed. by Clement Wood, intro. by H. Kohn, *Milestones of Thought Ser.* Ungar abr. ed. $12.00 pap. $4.95

BURKE, EDMUND. 1729–1797

Burke was a Whig spokesman and member of Parliament who criticized the potential aggrandizement of monarchical power by George III and sympathized with American and Irish grievances. He is best remembered for his adamant condemnation of the French Revolution, and his essay on the latter is the bible of political conservatism. He is one of the giants of English history and a very eloquent writer. (See also Chapter 4 in this volume.)

BOOKS BY BURKE

Works. Somerset 12 vols. repr. of 1899 ed. $695.00

Selected Works. Ed. by Walter J. Bate, Greenwood repr. of 1960 ed. 1975 lib. bdg. $25.50

Correspondence of Edmund Burke. Univ. of Chicago Pr. 9 vols ea. $32.00

Correspondence of Edmund Burke: Index. Ed. by Barbara Lowe, Univ. of Chicago Pr. 1978 vol. 10 $40.00

The Writings and Speeches of Edmund Burke: Party, Parliament and the American Crisis, 1766–1774. Ed. by Paul Langford, Oxford text ed. 1981 vol. 2 $120.00

Letters, Speeches and Tracts on Irish Affairs. Ed. by Matthew Arnold, AMS Pr. repr. of 1881 ed. $36.00

Selected Letters of Edmund Burke. Ed. by Walter J. Bate, Greenwood repr. of 1960 ed. 1975 lib. bdg. $25.50; ed. by Harvey C. Mansfield, Jr., Univ. of Chicago Pr. 1984 lib. bdg. $27.50

Selected Writings and Speeches. Ed. by J. P. Stanlis, Peter Smith $11.50

Two Speeches on Conciliation with America and Two Letters on Irish Questions. Century Bookbindery 1983 $35.00

A Philosophical Enquiry into the Origin of Our Idea of the Sublime and the Beautiful. 1756. Ed. by James T. Boulton, Univ. of Notre Dame Pr. 1968 pap. $6.95

A Vindication of Natural Society. 1756. Intro. by Frank N. Pagano, Liberty Fund repr. of 1757 ed. 1982 $8.50 text ed. pap. $4.50

Account of the European Settlements in America. 1758. AMS Pr. 2 vols. repr. of 1808 ed. ea. $15.50 set $30.00; Ayer 2 vols. in 1 repr. of 1777 ed. $53.00

A Letter to the Sheriffs of Bristol: A Speech at Bristol on Parliamentary Conduct; A Letter to a Noble Lord. 1777. Ed. by William Murison, AMS Pr. repr. of 1920 ed. $34.00

On the American Revolution. Ed. by E. R. Barkan, Peter Smith 2d ed. $10.25
Reflections on Revolution in France. 1790. Penguin 1982 pap. $3.95

CHURCHILL, WINSTON S. 1874–1965 (NOBEL PRIZE 1953)

Prime minister from 1940–45 and again from 1951–55, Churchill was both a maker and a writer of British history. As a war leader, statesman, and historian, he was a man of humor and courage. Descended from prominent historical figures, he received the Nobel Prize for *The Second World War* and Houghton Mifflin received the Carey-Thomas Award for its publication.

BOOKS BY CHURCHILL

Liberalism and the Social Problem. British History Ser. Haskell repr. of 1909 ed. 1972 lib. bdg. $53.95
Great Contemporaries. Essay Index Repr. Ser. Ayer repr. of 1937 ed. $23.00; Univ. of Chicago Pr. (Phoenix Bks.) 1976 pap. $4.95
While England Slept: A Survey of World Affairs, 1932–1938. Pref. by Randolph S. Churchill, Ayer repr. of 1938 ed. $23.00; Irvington repr. of 1938 ed. 1982 lib. bdg. $22.00
The Second World War: Chartwell Edition. 1948–53. Houghton Mifflin 6 vols. 1983 ea. $22.95 set $300.00
A History of the English-Speaking Peoples. 1956–58. Dodd 4 vols. pap. ea. $8.95 set $35.00. In his review, Sir Harold Nicholson wrote: "The narrative is so lucid, the treatment so unbiased, the events so vividly portrayed and the style so memorable, that the book leaves a fixed impress on the mind. It is a work of research and reflection; it is both massive and readable, authoritative and exciting, instructive and pleasurable, stimulating and abundantly fair" (*N.Y. Times*).

BOOKS ABOUT CHURCHILL

Churchill, Randolph S. *Winston S. Churchill.* Houghton Mifflin 3 vols. 1966–67 ea. $15.00. The companion to Volume 1, parts 1 and 2, is $25.00; the companion to Volume 2, parts 1–3, is $45.00.
Gilbert, Martin. *Winston S. Churchill.* Houghton Mifflin. See publisher's catalog for volumes and prices.
Thompson, Reginald W. *Churchill and the Montgomery Myth.* Evans 1968 $5.95

CLAPHAM, JOHN H. 1873–1946

One of the foremost economic historians of the Industrial Revolution, Clapham taught at Cambridge University. He described the Industrial Revolution from a positive perspective and challenged the prevailing popular unsympathetic view developed by turn-of-the-century reformers.

BOOKS BY CLAPHAM

An Economic History of Modern Britain. 1931–38. Cambridge Univ. Pr. 3 vols. 2d rev. ed. See publisher's catalog for prices.
A Concise Economic History of Britain: From the Earliest Times to 1750. AMS Pr. repr. of 1949 ed. 1976 $25.00

CLARENDON, EDWARD HYDE, 1st Earl. 1609–1674

Clarendon was a monarchist and Stuart official who first opposed and then served Charles I. During the Civil War, he accompanied the future Charles II into exile, and after the Restoration, served as lord chancellor. Unpopular with the Restoration court, he was eventually dismissed and fled England to spend the remainder of his life in exile.

BOOK BY CLARENDON

Selections from the History of the Rebellion and the Civil Wars, and the Life by Himself. Ed. by G. Huehns, intro. by Hugh Trevor-Roper, Oxford 1978 $13.95. Written from Clarendon's own experiences and from original documents, this is an invaluable account of the British Civil War.

COBBETT, WILLIAM. 1763–1835

Cobbett was a populist radical, who condemned the oligarchy and gentry for their dominance of England in modern history. He was the champion of a free peasantry and advocated the notion that English liberty had been suborned by the Norman yoke and later by the modern oligarchy.

BOOK BY COBBETT

Parliamentary History of England from the Norman Conquest in 1066 to the Year 1803. AMS Pr. 36 vols. repr. of 1920 ed. ea. $62.50 set $2,250.00

ELTON, GEOFFREY R. 1921–

Elton is a Cambridge University constitutional historian and a scholar of Tudor administrative history. His studies have emphasized the development of modern governmental machinery, under the direction of Thomas Cromwell—one of the major figures of Henry VIII's reign—as the central feature of the Tudor era.

BOOKS BY ELTON

The Tudor Revolution in Government. 1953. Cambridge Univ. Pr. 1959 $54.00 pap. $17.50

The Tudor Constitution: Documents and Commentary. 1960. Cambridge Univ. Pr. 2d ed. 1982 $64.50 pap. $18.95

Policy and Police: The Enforcement of the Reformation in the Age of Cromwell. Cambridge Univ. Pr. 1972 $47.50

Reform and Renewal: Thomas Cromwell and the Common Weal. Cambridge Univ. Pr. 1973 pap. $10.95

Annual Bibliography of British and Irish History. Humanities Pr. text ed. 1976–82 ea. $23.00–$38.00

Essays on Tudor and Stuart Politics and Government: Papers and Reviews, 1973–1981. Cambridge Univ. Pr. 1982 vol. 3 $49.50

FORTESCUE, SIR JOHN. 1394–1476

A late medieval jurist, Fortescue championed the concept of government by consent rather than royal absolutism. Naturally, his ideas were central to the advocates of parliamentary rights in later centuries.

BOOK BY FORTESCUE

The Governance of England: Otherwise Called the Difference between an Absolute and a Limited Monarchy. Hyperion Pr. repr. of 1885 ed. 1979 $29.50. Written c.1471 with the title *Difference between an Absolute and Limited Monarchy*, it was first published posthumously in 1714.

FREEMAN, EDWARD A. 1823–1892

Freeman was one of the late Victorian Germanists who traced the strength of English institutions to the Anglo-Saxons who extirpated the Britonic and Roman influence in England, and from whose instincts and practices later institutions emerged.

BOOKS BY FREEMAN

Historical Essays. AMS Pr. 4 vols. repr. of 1871–92 ed. $170.00
History of the Norman Conquest of England: Its Causes and Its Results. AMS Pr. 5 vols. repr. of 1879 ed. $295.00
Reign of William Rufus and the Accession of Henry the First. AMS Pr. 2 vols. repr. of 1882 ed. $85.00

FROUDE, JAMES A. 1818–1894

A vigorous Protestant nationalist whose writings celebrate the Tudor triumph against Continental despotism and "popery," Froude was sympathetic to Henry VIII and a critic of Elizabeth I. A typical proponent of standard attitudes of his era, Froude was a close friend of THOMAS CARLYLE (see Vol. 1).

BOOKS BY FROUDE

History of England from the Fall of Wolsey to the Defeat of the Spanish Armada. 1856–70. AMS Pr. 12 vols. repr. of 1870 ed. $540.00
English in Ireland in the Eighteenth Century. AMS Pr. 3 vols. repr. of 1881 ed. $90.00
Thomas Carlyle: A History of His Life in London, 1834–1881. Richard West 2 vols. repr. of 1884 ed. $65.00; Scholarly 2 vols. repr. of 1881 ed. 1971 $59.00
Thomas Carlyle: A History of the First Forty Years of His Life. Richard West 2 vols. repr. of 1882 ed. 1973 $65.00; Scholarly 2 vols. repr. 1981 lib. bdg. $59.00
Oceana; or England and Her Colonies. Black Heritage Lib. Collection Ser. Ayer repr. of 1886 ed. $18.75
English in the West Indies; or The Bow of Ulysses. Greenwood repr. of 1888 ed. $18.75
The Earl of Beaconsfield. Select Bibliographies Repr. Ser. Ayer repr. of 1890 ed. $19.00; Richard West repr. of 1890 ed. $25.00
The Divorce of Catherine of Aragon. AMS Pr. 2d ed. repr. of 1891 ed. $31.50; Norwood repr. of 1891 ed. $15.00; Sharon Hill 1891 $30.00
Lectures on the Council of Trent, Delivered at Oxford, 1892–3. Associated Faculty Pr. repr. of 1901 ed. 1969 $25.00
The Life and Letters of Erasmus and the Unknown Historical Significance of the Protestant Reformation. Amer. Class. College Pr. 2 vols. 1984 $147.55; AMS Pr. repr. of 1895 ed. $24.50; Richard West repr. 1903 $24.00
English Seaman in the Sixteenth Century. Richard West repr. of 1909 ed. $25.00
The Reign of Mary Tudor. Norwood repr. $25.00
The Spanish Armada. Coronado Pr. 1972 pap. $1.00

BOOKS ABOUT FROUDE

Dunn, Waldo H. *Froude and Carlyle: A Study of the Froude-Carlyle Controversy.* Associated Faculty Pr. repr. of 1933 ed. 1969 $29.00

Goetzman, Robert. *James Anthony Froude: A Bibliography of Studies. Reference Lib. of the Humanities* Garland 1977 lib. bdg. $25.00

GARDINER, SAMUEL R. 1829–1902

An amateur historian, Gardiner wrote the most minutely detailed, almost day-by-day account of the political events and wars of the seventeenth century. His thorough research on the Civil War was based on an examination of sources in domestic and foreign archives. He was generally sympathetic to the Cromwellians and Parliament.

BOOKS BY GARDINER

The Thirty Years' War: 1618–1648. Arden Lib. repr. of 1891 ed. 1977 lib. bdg. $20.00; Greenwood repr. of 1903 ed. lib. bdg. $15.00; *British History Ser.* Haskell repr. of 1903 ed. lib. bdg. $49.95; Norwood repr. of 1889 ed. $25.00; Scholarly repr. of 1912 ed. 1972 $9.00

The First Two Stuarts and the Puritan Revolution, 1603–1660. Arden Lib. repr. of 1891 ed. 1977 lib. bdg. $25.00; Peter Smith $5.25; Richard West repr. of 1911 ed. 1978 lib. bdg. $20.00

Cromwell's Place in History. Select Bibliographies Repr. Ser. Ayer repr. of 1897 ed. $15.00; Norwood repr. of 1897 ed. $15.00

What the Gunpowder Plot Was. AMS Pr. repr. of 1897 ed. $11.50; Scholarly 1971 $9.00

History of England, 1603–1656. AMS Pr. 18 vols. in 3 sections repr. of 1903 ed. $475.00

Oliver Cromwell. Charles River Bks. repr. of 1909 ed. 1977 $25.00; Folcroft repr. of 1925 ed. 1980 lib. bdg. $30.00; Richard West repr. 1980 lib. bdg. $30.00

GASH, NORMAN. 1912–

Gash studies the motives and machinations behind the politics of the Age of Peel (the 1830s and the 1840s) as explanations of the political pronouncements, doctrines, and developments of that time.

BOOKS BY GASH

Politics in the Age of Peel. Humanities Pr. 2d ed. text ed. 1977 $24.00; *Norton Lib.* repr. of 1953 ed. 1971 pap. $2.95

Reaction and Reconstruction in English Politics, 1832 to 1852. Greenwood repr. of 1965 ed. 1981 lib. bdg. $27.50

Sir Robert Peel: The Life of Sir Robert Peel after 1830. Rowman 1972 $25.00

Aristocracy and People: Britain, Eighteen Fifteen to Eighteen Sixty Five. New History of England Ser. Harvard Univ. Pr. 1980 $20.00 pap. $9.95

GEOFFREY OF MONMOUTH. 1100?–1154

A twelfth-century cleric, Geoffrey was bishop of St. Asaph. His writings contributed to the magnification of the Norman kings and are one of the chief sources of material on the Arthurian legend.

BOOK BY GEOFFREY OF MONMOUTH

The History of the Kings of Britain. Ed. by Charles W. Dunn, trans. by Sebastian Evans, Dutton 1958 pap. $3.95; trans. by Lewis Thorpe, *Classic Ser.* Penguin 1977 pap. $3.95

BOOK ABOUT GEOFFREY OF MONMOUTH

Leckie, R. William, Jr. *The Passage of Dominion: Geoffrey of Monmouth and the Periodization of Insular History in the Twelfth Century.* Univ. of Toronto Pr. 1981 $22.00

HALEVY, ELIE. 1870–1937

A French historian, Halévy was an authority on nineteenth-century England. He idealized liberal advancement without revolution and emphasized the importance of Benthamite radicalism and Protestant Evangelicalism in the advance of liberal and humane institutions and practices in Britain. He also stressed the role of Methodism in restraining the potential working-class revolution.

BOOKS BY HALEVY

Birth of Methodism in England. Trans. by Bernard Semmel, Univ. of Chicago Pr. 1971 $6.00
The Growth of Philosophic Radicalism. 1901–04. Faber 3d ed. 1972 pap. $6.95; Kelley repr. of 1952 ed. $25.00
History of the English People in the Nineteenth Century. 1912–30. Peter Smith 5 vols. o.p.

HAMMOND, JOHN L. 1872–1949, and HAMMOND, BARBARA. 1873–1962

The Hammonds were early twentieth-century radical historians. Their committed research indicted oligarchic exploitation of the peasantry, the worker, and the artisan on the eve of and during the Industrial Revolution.

BOOKS BY JOHN L. HAMMOND

The Village Labourer, 1760–1832: A Study in the Government of England before the Reform Bill. Kelley repr. of 1913 ed. $20.00; ed. by Gordon E. Mingay, Longman text ed. 1978 $22.00 pap. $12.95
The Skilled Labourer, 1760–1832. Kelley repr. of 1919 ed. $20.00; Longman text ed. 1979 $24.00
Gladstone and the Irish Nation. Biblio Dist. repr. of 1938 ed. 1964 $36.00; Greenwood repr. of 1938 ed. 1974 lib. bdg. $45.00; Shoe String (Archon) 1964 $10.00

BOOKS BY JOHN L. HAMMOND AND BARBARA HAMMOND

The Town Labourer, 1760–1832: The New Civilization. Arden Lib. repr. of 1917 ed. 1979 lib. bdg. $25.00; Century Bookbindery repr. of 1932 ed. 1980 lib. bdg. $25.00; Kelley repr. of 1917 ed. $20.00; ed. by John Lovell, Longman text ed. 1978 $21.00 pap. $11.50; pref. by Asa Briggs, Peter Smith $10.25
Lord Shaftesbury. Select Bibliographies Repr. Ser. Ayer repr. of 1923 ed. $23.50; Biblio Dist. 1969 $29.50; Darby 1981 $35.00; Folcroft 1923 $10.00; Shoe String (Archon) 4th ed. repr. of 1936 ed. 1969 $21.50
The Rise of Modern Industry. World History Ser. Haskell 1974 lib. bdg.

HILL, CHRISTOPHER. 1912–

Master of Balliol College, Oxford, Hill is a neo-Marxist whose work examines the role of economic factors in the events of the seventeenth century. He places particular emphasis on the grievances and treatment of the poorer and outcast sectors of society.

BOOKS BY HILL

Intellectual Origins of the English Revolution. Oxford 1965 $12.00 1980 text ed. pap. $15.95

English Revolution, 1640. Beekman 1966 pap. $4.95

Good Old Cause: English Revolution of 1640–1660. Ed. by Edmund Dell, Biblio Dist. 2d rev. ed. 1969 $32.50

God's Englishman: Oliver Cromwell and the English Revolution. Harper 1972 pap. $7.50

The World Turned Upside Down. Penguin (Pelican) repr. of 1972 ed. 1984 pap. $5.95

Change and Continuity in Seventeenth-Century England. Harvard Univ. Pr. 1975 $20.00

Some Intellectual Consequences of the English Revolution. Univ. of Wisconsin Pr. 1980 $17.50 pap. $7.95

The Century of Revolution, 1603–1714. Norton 2d ed. text ed. 1982 $19.95 pap. $5.95

The Experience of Defeat: Milton and Some Contemporaries. Viking 1984 $20.00

HOBSBAWM, ERIC J. 1917–

Hobsbawm is a neo-Marxist historian of the Industrial Revolution who pays particular attention to the inequities toward the lower classes, especially in law and politics.

BOOKS BY HOBSBAWM

Primitive Rebels. Norton Lib. 1965 pap. $5.95

Bandits. Pageant of History Ser. Delacorte 1969 $4.50

Revolutionaries. New Amer. Lib. (Meridian) repr. 1975 pap. $3.95

Captain Swing: A Social History of the Great English Agricultural Uprising of 1830. Norton Lib. repr. of 1968 ed. 1975 pap. $7.95

Industry and Empire. Vol. 3 in *Pelican Economic History of Britain.* Penguin 1970 pap. $5.95

Peasants in History: Essays in Honour of Daniel Thorner. Oxford 1980 $19.95

The Invention of Tradition. Past and Present Publications Ser. Cambridge Univ. Pr. 1983 $29.95 pap. $9.95

Age of Revolution, 1789–1848. New Amer. Lib. $4.50

LECKY, W. E. H. 1838–1903

A foremost Victorian Whig-liberal, Lecky wrote an encyclopedic study of eighteenth-century England and Ireland that is a reflection of his own political beliefs.

BOOKS BY LECKY

Historical and Political Essays. Essay Index Repr. Ser. Ayer repr. of 1908 ed. $20.00; Folcroft 1973 lib. bdg. $25.00

History of European Morals from Augustus to Charlemagne. European Sociology Ser.
   1869. Ayer 2 vols. in 1 3d ed. repr. 1975 $66.00
History of England in the Eighteenth Century. 1878–90. AMS Pr. 7 vols. rev. ed. repr.
   of 1893 ed. $210.00
History of Ireland in the Eighteenth Century. AMS Pr. 5 vols. repr. of 1893 ed $57.50;
   ed. by L. P. Curtis, Jr., *Classics of British Historical Lit. Ser.* Univ. of Chicago Pr.
   (Phoenix Bks.) abr. ed. 1972 pap. $3.95
Democracy and Liberty. Intro. by William Murchison, Liberty Fund repr. of 1896 ed.
   1981 $20.00
Leaders of Public Opinion in Ireland. Europe 1815–1945 Ser. Da Capo 2 vols. repr. of
   1903 ed. 1973 lib. bdg. $79.50

MACAULAY, THOMAS BABINGTON, 1st Baron. 1800–1859

Macaulay's history is the classic statement of Whig history: the celebration of the Glorious Revolution for preserving the constitutional foundations on which English liberty developed. The book covers the years 1685 to 1702. Although his history has been praised for its narrative style and extensive research, it has been criticized for its lack of objectivity.

BOOK BY MACAULAY

History of England from the Accession of James II. 1849–61. Ed. by C. H. Firth, AMS
   Pr. 6 vols. repr. of 1915 ed. ea. $45.00 set $270.00

BOOKS ABOUT MACAULAY

Firth, C. H. *Commentary on Macaulay's "History of England."* Biblio Dist. 1964 $30.00
Roberts, Sydney C. *Lord Macaulay: The Pre-Eminent Victorian.* Arden Lib. repr. of
   1927 ed. 1978 $6.00

MAITLAND, FREDERIC WILLIAM. 1850–1906

Maitland was a legal historian, who founded the Selden Society for the publication of early English documents. A formative medievalist, he emphasized the significance of the Normans and of the monarchy in general in the development of constitutional and social structures.

BOOKS BY MAITLAND

Selected Essays. Ed. by H. D. Hazeltine, *Essay Index Repr. Ser.* Ayer repr. of 1936 ed.
   $17.50
Doomsday Book and Beyond. Ed. by Roy M. Mersky and J. Myron Jacobstein, *Classics in Legal History Repr. Ser.* Hein repr. of 1897 ed. 1970 lib. bdg. $32.50
Roman Canon Law in the Church of England. Burt Franklin repr. of 1898 ed. 1969
   $21.00
Constitutional History of England. Cambridge Univ. Pr. text ed. repr. of 1908 ed.
   $75.00 pap. $21.95
Forms of Action at Common Law. 1909. Cambridge Univ. Pr. text ed. 1936 pap. $9.95
A Sketch of English Legal History. AMS Pr. repr. of 1915 ed. 1976 $17.45

BOOKS ABOUT MAITLAND

Cameron, James R. *Frederic William Maitland and the History of English Law.* Greenwood repr. of 1961 ed. 1977 lib. bdg. $19.75

Fifoot, C. H. *Frederic William Maitland: A Life. Studies in Legal History* Harvard Univ. Pr. 1971 $22.50

NAMIER, SIR LEWIS B. 1888–1966

Namier was a Polish-Jewish émigré. His specialized studies of eighteenth-century English political and diplomatic history set the pattern for later studies in that and other eras. He prepared detailed biographical studies of individual members of several Parliaments to study mid-eighteenth-century England. He concluded that the underlying motives behind political action were especially familial and oligarchic connections and the quest for position and place, rather than great events and issues.

BOOKS BY NAMIER

Skyscrapers, and Other Essays. Essay Index Repr. Ser. Ayer repr. of 1931 ed. $14.50
In the Margin of History. Essay Index Repr. Ser. Ayer repr. of 1939 ed. $18.00
Conflicts: Studies in Contemporary History. Essay Index Repr. Ser. Ayer repr. of 1942 ed. $18.00; Darby repr. of 1942 ed. 1982 lib. bdg. $30.00; Telegraph Bks. repr. of 1942 ed. 1982 lib. bdg. $30.00
Structure of Politics at the Accession of George III. 1929. St. Martin's 2d ed. 1957 $14.95
Facing East: Essays on Germany, the Balkans, and Russia in the Twentieth Century. Gannon 1947 lib. bdg. $17.50
England in the Age of the American Revolution. St. Martin's 2d ed. 1974 pap. $27.50
Europe in Decay, 1936–40. 1950. Peter Smith $10.75
Personalities and Powers. Greenwood repr. of 1955 ed. 1974 lib. bdg. $15.00
Vanished Supremacies. Select Bibliographies Reprint Ser. Ayer repr. of 1958 ed. $12.50
Crossroads of Power. Essay Index Repr. Ser. Ayer repr. of 1962 ed. $15.00

NEALE, SIR JOHN. 1890–1975

Neale, a professor at London University, is an expert on Tudor politics, especially the more minute details of the reign of Elizabeth I. He explains events and developments largely in terms of family connection and patronage.

BOOKS BY NEALE

The Age of Catherine De Medici. Harper pap. $3.95; Merrimack 1978 pap. $6.50
Queen Elizabeth I: A Biography. 1934. Doubleday (Anchor) 1957 pap. $6.50; St. Martin's 1959 $16.95

PARIS, MATTHEW. 1200–1259

Paris was a monk, who served as historiographer of the convent of St. Albans. In the first part of his history of civilization, he largely rewrote the history prepared by his predecessor, Roger of Wendover. In the second part, from 1235 to 1259, however, he used his own experiences and research. He recounted the struggles of his time between the king and the barons, favoring the barons and the principles of responsible government.

Book by Paris

English History: From the Year 1235 to 1259. Trans. by John A. Giles, AMS Pr. 3 vols. repr. of 1852 ed. $85.00

PLUMB, J(OHN) H(AROLD). 1911–

A professor of history at Cambridge University, Plumb is the definitive authority on England's first prime minister, Robert Walpole. He presents a balanced study of the era of Whig supremacy and the earlier Hanoverian period, 1714–1760. Says Crane Brinton, "Plumb writes firmly and well in the British academic tradition of his master, G. M. Trevelyan" (*N.Y. Herald Tribune*).

Books by Plumb

England in the Eighteenth Century, 1714–1815. Gannon lib. bdg. $11.50; Penguin (Pelican) 1950 pap. $4.95
Studies in Social History. Essay Index Repr. Ser. Ayer repr. of 1955 ed. $22.00
Sir Robert Walpole. 1956–61. Kelley 2 vols. repr. of 1961 ed. o.p.
Men and Centuries. Greenwood repr. of 1963 ed. 1979 lib. bdg. $24.75
Growth of Political Stability in England, 1675–1725. Humanities Pr. 1977 repr. of 1967 ed. text ed. pap. $13.25
The English Heritage. Forum Pr. text ed. 1978 pap. $15.95
Georgian Delights: The Pursuit of Happiness. Little, Brown 1980 $12.95

POLLARD, ALBERT FREDERICK. 1869–1948

Pollard was a major student of the Tudor era. His more conventionally written biographies and studies are still standard accounts in constitutional, social, political, and economic history. He also served as one of the editors of the *Dictionary of National Biography.*

Books by Pollard

England under Protector Somerset. Russell repr. of 1900 ed. 1966 $9.00
History of England from the Accession of Edward Sixth to the Death of Elizabeth: Fifteen Forty Seven to Sixteen Hundred Three. AMS Pr. repr. of 1910 ed. $22.50; Greenwood repr. of 1910 ed. 1969 lib. bdg. $20.00; Kraus repr. of 1910 ed. $35.00
Reign of Henry Seventh from Contemporary Sources. AMS Pr. 3 vols. repr. of 1914 ed. $95.00
Tudor Studies, Presented by the Board of Studies in History in the University of London to Albert Frederick Pollard. Russell repr. of 1924 ed. 1970 $11.50
Thomas Cranmer and the English Reformation, 1489–1556. AMS Pr. repr. of 1927 ed. $42.50
Wolsey. Greenwood repr. of 1953 ed. 1978 lib. bdg. $32.25

POWICKE, FREDERICK MAURICE. 1879–1963

Powicke was a foremost authority on thirteenth-century England. He particularly emphasized the confrontation between the kings and the nobility as an explanation of events.

Books by Powicke

Stephen Langton. Kelley repr. of 1927 ed. lib. bdg. $12.50

The Christian Life in the Middle Ages and Other Essays. Greenwood repr. of 1935 ed.
  lib. bdg. $22.50
Ways of Medieval Life and Thought. Biblo & Tannen 1949 $10.00
Modern Historians and the Study of History: Essays and Papers. Greenwood repr. of
  1955 ed. 1976 lib. bdg. $18.25
Thirteenth Century, 1216–1307. Oxford History of England Ser. 2d ed. 1962 $37.95

ROWSE, A(LFRED) L(ESLIE). 1903–

Rowse has defined history as "life looked back over in the perspective of
time." He is an authority on Elizabeth I. Rowse offers a mid-twentieth-cen-
tury version of Whig and Protestant-nationalist history.

BOOKS BY ROWSE

On History: A Study of Present Tendencies. 1927. Folcroft 1973 lib. bdg. $10.00
*The English Spirit: Essays in History and Literature (Swift, Carlyle, Shakespeare, Words-
  worth).* Arden Lib. repr. of 1944 ed. 1977 lib. bdg. $30.00; Folcroft repr. of 1946
  ed. 1977 lib. bdg. $20.00
The England of Elizabeth (The Elizabethan Age). 1952. Univ. of Wisconsin Pr. repr.
  1978 $25.00 pap. $12.50
An Elizabethan Garland. AMS Pr. repr. of 1953 ed. $15.00
The Early Churchills: An English Family. Greenwood repr. of 1956 ed. 1974 lib. bdg.
  $21.75
The Churchills. Greenwood repr. of 1958 ed. 1974 lib. bdg. $23.50. An abridgment of
  The Early Churchills and *The Later Churchill* (o.p.).
The Elizabethans and America. Greenwood repr. of 1959 ed. 1978 lib. bdg. $23.50;
  Norwood repr. of 1959 ed. 1984 lib. bdg. $40.00
Sir Walter Raleigh: His Family and Private Life. Greenwood repr. of 1962 ed. 1975 lib.
  bdg. $20.50
The Elizabethan Renaissance: The Life of the Society. Scribner 1972 $20.00
Eminent Elizabethans. Univ. of Georgia Pr. 1983 $19.00
Memories of Men and Women, American and British. Univ. Pr. of Amer. 1983 lib. bdg.
  $15.25 text ed. pap. $9.75

SAYLES, GEORGE OSBORNE. 1901–   , and RICHARDSON, HENRY GERALD. 1884–d.(?)

Sayles and Richardson are students of medieval administrative history.
They de-emphasize the common law and the legislative and policy role of
Parliament that earlier Whig historians stressed. Instead, they assert the im-
portant role of the monarchy and of Parliament as a judicial body.

BOOKS BY SAYLES AND RICHARDSON

The Governance of Medieval England. Columbia Univ. Pr. 1963 $29.00
The English Parliament in the Middle Ages. Hambledon 1981 $42.00

BOOKS BY SAYLES

The Medieval Foundations of England. A. S. Barnes 1961 o.p.
The King's Parliament of England. Norton 1974 $7.95 text ed. pap. $6.95

STONE, LAWRENCE. 1919–

Stone teaches history at Princeton University. With his semi-Marxist perspective, he examines class relationships and ambitions as explanatory factors in sixteenth- and seventeenth-century English history.

BOOKS BY STONE

Crisis of the Aristocracy, 1558–1641. Oxford 1965 $45.00
The Causes of the English Revolution. Harper 1972 pap. $3.95
Family and Fortune: Studies in Aristocratic Finance in the Sixteenth and Seventeenth Centuries. Oxford 1973 $24.95
The Family, Sex and Marriage: England 1500–1800. Harper 1977 $30.00
The Past and the Present. Routledge & Kegan 1981 $21.95
An Open Elite? England, 1540–1880. Oxford 1984 $29.95

STUBBS, WILLIAM. 1825–1901

Stubbs taught history at Oxford University until he was made bishop of Chester. He was a classic nineteenth-century Germanist historian, who traced English liberty to the organic development of Anglo-Saxon concepts of the law, and folk will to its later manifestations in the form of baronial revolt and the appearance of Parliament.

BOOKS BY STUBBS

The Constitutional History of England. Ed. by James Cornford, *Classics of British Historical Lit. Ser.* Univ. of Chicago Pr. 2d ed. 1979 lib. bdg. $27.00
Historical Introduction to the Rolls Series. AMS Pr. repr. of 1902 ed. $11.50
Lectures on Early English History. Ed. by Arthur Hassall, Rothman repr. of 1906 ed. 1980 lib. bdg. $35.00

BOOK ABOUT STUBBS

Shaw, William A. *Bibliography of the Historical Works of Dr. Creighton, Dr. Stubbs, Dr. S. R. Gardiner, and the Late Lord Acton.* Burt Franklin 1969 $17.50

TAWNEY, RICHARD H. 1880–1962

A pioneering socialist, who studied the economic motivation and the rise of modern capitalism, Tawney saw a direct link between modern capitalist wealth and the cause of the Reformation and the revolt of Parliament in the sixteenth and seventeenth centuries. Tawney was active in the British Labour party and served on numerous government bodies dealing with education and economic policies.

BOOKS BY TAWNEY

The Acquisitive Society. 1920. Harcourt 1955 pap. $4.95
British Labour Movement. Greenwood repr. of 1925 ed. 1969 lib. bdg. $15.00
Religion and the Rise of Capitalism. 1926. Peter Smith $10.50
Business and Politics under James I: Lionel Cranfield as Merchant and Minister. Russell repr. of 1958 ed. 1976 $20.00
Equality. Intro. by R. M. Titmuss, Barnes & Noble 1964 pap. $8.95
Social History and Literature. Folcroft 1977 lib. bdg. $10.00

THOMPSON, EDWARD PALMER. 1924–

Thompson is a contemporary neo-Marxist. He has studied especially the development of a working-class consciousness in the early years of the Industrial Revolution.

BOOKS BY THOMPSON

Making of the English Working Class. Random (Vintage) 1966 pap. $11.95
Whigs and Hunters. Pantheon 1976 pap. $7.95
(and others). *Albion's Fatal Tree: Crime and Society in Eighteenth-Century England.*
    Pantheon 1976 pap. $8.95

TOUT, THOMAS FREDERICK. 1855–1929

An authority on medieval history, Tout wrote a detailed study of governmental administration in the thirteenth and fourteenth centuries that helped adjust the overemphasis that historians had been giving to the development of Parliament in that period. As a result of Tout's work, the constructive role of the monarchy was more fully appreciated.

BOOKS BY TOUT

Political History of England from the Ascension of Henry 3rd to the Death of Edward
    3rd: 1216–1377. Political History of England Ser. AMS Pr. repr. of 1905 ed.
    $22.50; Kraus repr. of 1905 ed. $35.00
Chapters in the Administrative History of Medieval England. 1920–33. Manchester vol.
    1 (1930) $40.00 vol. 2 (1920) $40.00 vol. 3 (1928) $40.00 vol. 4 (1928) $40.00 vol. 5
    (1930) $40.00 vol. 6 (1933) $40.00

TREVELYAN, GEORGE MACAULAY. 1876–1962

The grandnephew of Macaulay, regius professor at Cambridge, and master of Trinity College, Trevelyan is probably the most widely read twentieth-century historian of Britain. His very well written, thorough, and numerous books adhere to the traditional Whig perspective.

BOOKS BY TREVELYAN

Early History of Charles James Fox. AMS Pr. repr. of 1880 ed. $31.00; Folcroft 1973
    lib. bdg. $15.00
England in the Age of Wycliffe. Intro. by J. A. Tuck, AMS Pr. 3d ed. repr. of 1900 ed.
    $34.50; Rowman repr. of 1899 ed. 1973 pap. $6.00
England under the Stuarts. 1907. Methuen 21st ed. 1966 pap. $17.95
Life of John Bright. Greenwood repr. of 1913 ed. 1971 lib. bdg. $20.00; Richard West
    1913 $17.00
Lord Grey of the Reform Bill: Being the Life of Charles, Second Earl Grey. Greenwood
    repr. of 1920 ed. lib. bdg. $19.75
England under Queen Anne. AMS Pr. 3 vols. repr. of 1930–34 ed. $149.50
Grey of Fallodon: Being the Life of Sir Edward Grey. Afterword by Viscount Grey,
    AMS Pr. repr. of 1937 ed. $41.50
The English Revolution, 1688–1689. 1938. Oxford 1965 pap. $5.95
English Social History: A Survey of Six Centuries, Chaucer to Queen Victoria. 1942. Mc-
    Kay 1965 pap. $2.95

TREVOR-ROPER, HUGH R(EDWALD). 1914–

Regius professor of modern history at Oxford University, Trevor-Roper is a meticulous researcher and an eloquent and prolific writer. His books cover all of British history from medieval to contemporary days.

BOOKS BY TREVOR-ROPER

The Last Days of Hitler. Arden Lib. repr. of 1947 ed. 1979 lib. bdg. $37.50; Macmillan (Collier Bks.) 3d ed. 1962 pap. $4.95
Historical Essays. 1956. Gannon 1966 lib. bdg. $15.00
The European Witch Craze in the Sixteenth and Seventeenth Centuries and Other Essays. Harper 1969 pap. $5.50
Plunder of the Arts in the Seventeenth Century. Transatlantic 1972 $8.75

WILLIAM OF MALMESBURY. c.1096–1143.

William of Malmesbury was a Norman monk whose writing, which celebrated the Norman conquest, was a history of the kings of England from 449 to 1127.

BOOK BY WILLIAM OF MALMESBURY

Chronicle of the Kings of England from the Earliest to King Stephen. Ed. by John A. Giles, trans. by J. Sharpe, AMS Pr. repr. of 1847 ed. $27.50

CHAPTER 10

World History

David L. Hicks

> . . . the memory and knowledge of the past is the instruction of the present and the warning of the future. . . .
>
> —Louis Le Roy, *On the Vicissitudes of Affairs*

Though a historian of minor accomplishment himself, Le Roy states here the universal opinion held by his more distinguished contemporaries and by almost all historians from the Renaissance to the present day. The principal use of history was to instruct. History might amuse and edify, but it was intended above all to inform people of the present generation of the experience of the past so that they might act wisely in the future.

The nineteenth century was the time when historians were most closely listened to. Macaulay in England, Michelet in France, Treitschke in Germany, Mahan in the United States—all of them deeply influenced the thinking and actions of their literate countrymen. Indeed, Alfred Thayer Mahan was probably the first historian whose ideas had worldwide impact. His historical justification for sea power convinced Theodore Roosevelt in the United States, Kaiser Wilhelm in Germany, and the emperor and his military advisers in Japan to build big navies.

Today, there are no Mahans writing history, and to some degree the influence of the historian on public and private policy has waned since the great days of the nineteenth century. One important reason is that contemporary historians tend to be particularists, concerned with small subjects and without the broad vision or powers of synthesis of a Mahan. True wisdom, however, is still founded on what they tell us of the past. Many of their books are contained in this chapter on world history.

BOOKS ON THE WRITING AND PHILOSOPHY OF HISTORY

The selections here are only a handful of the many works on the meaning and purpose of history and how to do research and write on a historical subject. The basic principles of modern historical scholarship were set down during the Italian Renaissance, but from that time until the later nineteenth century, historians wrote mostly about past politics. In the last 100 years, political history has gone out of style, eclipsed particularly by economic and social history. Since World War II, the quantitative method of the French *Annales* school has dominated European historiography. In going beyond pure political history, contemporary historians have been obliged to use in their research such other disciplines as economics and sociology. The list below includes books that discuss all branches of contemporary historical writing.

Aron, Raymond. *Introduction to the Philosophy of History: An Essay on the Limits of Historical Objectivity.* 1938. Trans. by George J. Irwin, Greenwood repr. of 1961 ed. 1976 lib. bdg. $24.75. (See Aron's main listing in this chapter.)

Barnes, Harry E. *A History of Historical Writing.* Dover 2d ed. repr. of 1937 ed. 1962 pap. $7.50; Peter Smith 2d ed. rev. $12.00. A standard treatment, but unconventional in approach.

Barzun, Jacques. *Clio and the Doctors: History, Psycho History, Quanto History.* Univ. of Chicago Pr. (Phoenix Bks.) 1974 pap. $3.45

Barzun, Jacques, and Henry F. Graff. *The Modern Researcher.* Harcourt 4th ed. text ed. 1985 pap. in progress. Despite the more general title, this concentrates on historical research. The authors are historians who long conducted a course in historiography and historical method at Columbia University.

Becker, Carl L. *Everyman His Own Historian: Essays on History and Politics.* Times Bks. 1972 pap. $2.95. A small classic.

Benjamin, Jules R. *A Student's Guide to History.* St. Martin's 3d ed. text ed. 1983 pap. $6.95. Contains an extremely useful bibliography of reference works, as well as excellent advice on research and writing.

Berkhofer, Robert F., Jr. *A Behavioral Approach to Historical Analysis.* Macmillan (Free Pr.) text ed. 1971 pap. $7.95

Burke, Peter. *The Renaissance Sense of the Past. Documents of Modern History Ser.* St. Martin's 1970 pap. $19.95. A documentary study of how the modern "sense of history" developed during the period 1350–1650.

Butterfield, Herbert. *Man on His Past.* Cambridge Univ. Pr. $37.50 pap. $10.95. A classic by a distinguished historian of science. Several nineteenth-century historians, including Ranke, Burckhardt, and Arton, are discussed.

Cantor, Norman F., and Richard I. Schneider. *How to Study History.* Harlan Davidson pap. $7.95

Carr, Edward H. *What Is History?* Random (Vintage) 1967 pap. $4.95. A leading historian of the Russian Revolution reflects on history.

Cohen, Morris R. *The Meaning of Human History.* Open Court 2d ed. 1961 $24.95 pap. $7.95

Daniels, Robert. *Studying History: How and Why.* Prentice-Hall 3d ed. text ed. 1981 pap. $12.95. A useful methodological handbook.

Elton, G. R. *Political History.* Basic Bks. text ed. 1970 $7.95; *History and Historiography Ser.* Garland 1985 lib. bdg. $20.00

Fischer, David H. *Historian's Fallacies: Toward a Logic of Historical Thought.* Harper 1970 $10.00 pap. $7.50

Gay, Peter. *Style in History.* McGraw-Hill Pap. repr. of 1974 ed. 1976 pap. $3.95. "It can be read with profit and pleasure by anyone from the undergraduate level up who is interested in the history of historical thought" (*Choice*).

Gooch, G. P. *History and Historians in the 19th Century.* 1913. Beacon 1959 o.p. Although old-fashioned in its purely political approach, this remains a classic. (See Gooch's main listing in this chapter.)

Halperin, S. William, ed. *Essays in Modern European Historiography. Class. Euro-*

pean Historians Ser. Univ. of Chicago Pr. (Phoenix Bks.) 1972 pap. $3.45. "Ana-
lytical biographies of 16 important historians who lived roughly between 1880–
1960. Each biography is written by a competent scholar" (*Choice*).

Hughes, H. Stuart. *History as Art and as Science: Twin Vistas on the Past. History and
Historiography Ser.* Garland 1985 lib. bdg. $20.00; *Midway Repr. Ser.* Univ. of Chi-
cago Pr. text ed. 1975 pap. $5.50

Le Roy-Ladurie, Emmanuel. *The Territory of the Historian.* Trans. by Ben Reynolds
and Sian Reynolds, Univ. of Chicago Pr. repr. of 1973 ed. 1979 lib. bdg. $21.00
1982 pap. $10.95

Lewis, Bernard. *History Remembered, Recovered, Invented.* Princeton Univ. Pr. 1975.
$12.00 pap. $6.95. "Three types of history are defined: traditional, the discovery
and analysis of historical data by academic scholarship, and the construction of
history for a particular end" (*LJ*).

Lifton, Robert J., and Eric Olson, eds. *Explorations in Psychohistory: The Wellfleet Papers of Erik Erikson, Robert Jay Lifton and Kenneth Kenniston.* Simon & Schuster
1975 $9.95 pap. $3.95. "This collection of papers by a most distinguished gathering of thinkers is an important and potentially influential contribution in the
emergence of the new discipline of psychohistory . . . [which] represents, for
all the follies of its lesser [practitioners], an attempted breakthrough into exploring the human condition" (*LJ*).

Meyerhoff, Hans, ed. *The Philosophy of History in Our Times.* Garland 1985 lib. bdg.
$35.00

Nevins, Allan. *History and Historians.* Scribner 1975 o.p. "Appealing models of historical craftsmanship" (*LJ*). (See Nevins's main listing in Chapter 7.)

Plumb, J. H. *The Death of the Past.* Humanities Pr. text ed. 1978 $12.50

Rowse, A. L. *The Use of History. History and Historiography Ser.* Garland 1985 lib.
bdg. $25.00

Shafer, Robert J., ed. *A Guide to Historical Method.* Dorsey 3d ed. 1980 pap. $15.50

Stoianovich, Traian. *French Historical Method: The "Annales" Paradigm.* Cornell
Univ. Pr. 1976 $27.50

Thompson, J. W. *A History of Historical Writing.* Peter Smith 2 vols. $42.00. The most
thorough study of modern European historiography.

Toynbee, Arnold J. *A Study of History.* Oxford 12 vols. 1939–61 ea. $25.00–$37.50.
(See Toynbee's main listing in this chapter.)

GENERAL REFERENCE WORKS

The atlases, encyclopedias, bibliographies, and other reference works listed
below cover all of the areas of the world included in this chapter. Additional works will be found under specific areas and countries.

The American Bibliography of Slavic and East European Studies, for 1967. Ed. by Kenneth E. Naylor, Ohio State Univ. Pr. 1973 pap. $3.25

Aufricht, Hans. *Guide to League of Nations Publications.* AMS Pr. repr. of 1951 ed.
$32.50

Bibliographic Guide to Soviet and East European Studies. G. K. Hall 1981 3 vols. lib.
bdg. $310.00 1982 3 vols. lib. bdg. $310.00 1984 3 vols. lib. bdg. $350.00

Boehm, Eric H., and others, eds. *Historical Periodicals Directory. Clio Periodicals Directories Ser.* ABC-Clio 3 vols. 1982 lib. bdg. ea. $87.50

Catchpole, Brian. *A Map History of the Modern World.* Heinemann 3d ed. text ed. 1982 pap. $7.00

Chambers Atlas of World History. State Mutual Bk. 1980 $36.00

Chew, Allen F. *An Atlas of Russian History: Eleven Centuries of Changing Borders.* Yale Univ. Pr. text ed. 1967 pap. $10.95

Davies, C. Collin. *An Historical Atlas of the Indian Peninsula.* Oxford 2d ed. 1959 pap. $5.95

Demographic Yearbook. 1952–to date. Ed. by the United Nations, International Pubns. annual 34th ed. 1984 $85.00

Ferguson, Eugene S., ed. *Bibliography of the History of Technology.* MIT 1968 $17.50

Florinsky, Michael T. *Encyclopedia of Russia and the Soviet Union.* McGraw-Hill 1961 o.p. The author is a historian.

Foreign Affairs 50-Year Index, 1922–1972. Ed. by Robert J. Palmer, Bowker 1973 o.p.

Gailey, Harry A., Jr. *The History of Africa in Maps.* Denoyer-Geppert repr. 1979 pap. $6.95

Gould, Julius, and W. J. Kolb. *UNESCO Dictionary of the Social Sciences.* Macmillan (Free Pr.) 1964 $40.00

Gutkind, P., and J. B. Webster, eds. *A Select Bibliography of Traditional and Modern Africa. Program of Eastern African Studies* Syracuse Univ. Pr. 1968 o.p.

Hale, J. R., ed. *A Concise Encyclopedia of the Italian Renaissance. World of Art Ser.* Oxford 1981 $19.95 pap. $9.95. Useful articles, emphasizing art and artists.

Heravi, Mehdi. *Concise Encyclopedia of the Middle East.* Public Affairs Pr. 1979 $12.00 pap. $6.50

Hucker, Charles O. *China: A Critical Bibliography.* Univ. of Arizona Pr. 1962 pap. $3.95

International Encyclopedia of the Social Sciences. Ed. by David L. Sills, Macmillan (Free Pr.) 17 vols. in 8 1977 $310.00 with *Biographical Supplement* 1979 set $340.00

Israel, Fred L., ed. *Major Peace Treaties of Modern History, 1648–1967.* Chelsea House 4 vols. 1967 o.p. 1980 vol. 5 $60.00. Text of treaties from Westphalia (1648) to Tashkent, between India and Pakistan (1966).

Jones, David L. *Books in English on the Soviet Union, 1917–1973: A Bibliography.* Garland 1975 lib. bdg. $43.00

Kinder, Herman, and Werner Hilgemann. *The Anchor Atlas of World History.* Doubleday 2 vols. 1975–78 pap. ea. $6.95

Langer, William L., ed. *An Encyclopedia of World History.* Houghton Mifflin 5th ed. 1972 $32.00. A book such as this is necessarily limited, this one largely to political subjects.

Mallory, Walter H., ed. *Political Handbook of the World: Parliaments, Parties and Press as of January 1, 1931.* Elliots Bks. text ed. $49.50

McEvedy, Colin. *The Atlas of Modern History to 1815.* Penguin 1973 pap. $5.95

McInnis, Raymond G., ed. *Social Science Research Handbook.* Garland 1985 lib. bdg. $40.00

Mitchell, B. R. *European Historical Statistics, 1750–1970.* Columbia Univ. Pr. 1975 $60.00; *Cultural Atlas Ser.* Facts on File 1980 lib. bdg. $85.00

Muir, Ramsey. *Muir's Historical Atlas: Ancient, Medieval and Modern.* Ed. by R. E. Treharne and Harold Fullard, Barnes & Noble 10th ed. repr. of 1911 ed. 1964 $23.50

National Geographic Society. *National Geographic Atlas of the World.* National Geographic Society 5th ed. 1981 $44.95

News Dictionary. Facts on File 1981 $14.95

Nunn, G. Raymond, ed. *Asia Reference Works: A Select Annotated Guide*. Wilson repr. of 1971 ed. text ed. 1980 $59.00

Paetow, Louis J. *A Guide to the Study of Medieval History*. Kraus rev. ed. repr. of 1931 ed. $55.00. The basic handbook for all medieval historians.

Palmer, Alan. *The Penguin Dictionary of Modern History, 1789–1945*. Penguin 1984 pap. $6.95

Pearcy, G. Etzel, and Elvyn A. Stoneman. *Handbook of New Nations*. Crowell 1968 $11.49

Rider, K. J. *The History of Science and Technology: A Select Bibliography*. Oryx 2d ed. 1970 pap. $7.00

Roach, John, ed. *A Bibliography of Modern History*. Cambridge Univ. Pr. 1968 o.p. Compiled to accompany the *New Cambridge Modern History*, but useful as a separate volume.

Rogers, A. Robert. *The Humanities: A Selective Guide to Information Sources*. Libraries Unlimited 2d ed. 1980 lib. bdg. $33.00

Shapiro, D., ed. *A Select Bibliography on Russian History, 1801–1917*. Blackwell 1962 o.p.

Shepherd, William R. *Shepherd's Historical Atlas*. Barnes & Noble 9th ed. rev. 1980 $35.95; Harper 9th ed. repr. of 1964 ed. 1973 $22.50. A classic atlas by one of the first historians of the expansion of Europe.

Tregonning, Kennedy G. *Southeast Asia: A Critical Bibliography*. Univ. of Arizona Pr. 1969 pap. $4.95

Voight, M., and J. Treyz, comps. *Books for College Libraries*. Amer. Lib. Association 6 vols. 2d ed. 1975 pap. $80.00

Wagar, W. Warren. *Books in World History: A Guide for Teachers and Students*. Indiana Univ. Pr. 1973 $4.95

White, Carl M. *Sources of Information in the Social Sciences: A Guide to the Literature*. Amer. Lib. Association 2d ed. text ed. 1973 $30.00

Wiener, Philip P., ed. *Dictionary of the History of Ideas*. Scribner 5 vols. 1980 pap. $75.00

WORLD HISTORY: GENERAL WORKS

Very few works can with any degree of accuracy be called "world histories," whatever their title. Most are, in fact, histories of the Western world with the rest of the world tacked on, and those that try for better balance are superficial and not very useful. The subject is simply too vast for a single work. Those listed here are the best and/or most recent of a generally unsatisfactory lot, and readers are advised to refer to specific areas and countries.

Braudel, Fernand. (See Braudel's main listing in this chapter.)

Brinton, C. Crane, and John B. Christopher. 1955. *A History of Civilization: 1648 to the Present*. Prentice-Hall 6th ed. 1984 pap. $18.95

Burns, Edward M., and Philip L. Ralph. *World Civilizations*. Norton 2 vols. in 1 1982 $25.95

Clough, S. B. *European History in a World Perspective*. Heath 3 vols. text ed. 1975 ea. $7.95–$14.95. The focus is on Europe.

Cornwell, R. D. *World History in the Twentieth Century*. Longman 2d ed. text ed. 1981 pap. $10.95

Freeman-Grenville, G. S. *A Chronology of World History: A Calendar of Principal Events from 3000 BC to AD 1976*. Rowman 2d ed. 1978 $45.00

Geiger, Theodore. *The Conflicted Relationship: The West and the Transformation of Asia, Africa and Latin America. Atlantic Policy Studies Ser.* McGraw-Hill 1967 o.p.

Goff, Richard, and others. *The Twentieth Century: A Brief Global History*. Random text ed. 1983 pap. $13.95

Grigg, David B. *The Agricultural Systems of the World: An Evolutionary Approach. Cambridge Geographical Studies* 1974 pap. $21.95

McKay, John P. *A History of World Societies*. Houghton Mifflin 2 vols. text ed. 1983 ea. $27.95 pap. ea. $18.95. One of the better attempts at a true world history.

McNeill, William H. *The Rise of the West: A History of the Human Community*. Univ. of Chicago Pr. (Phoenix Bks.) 1970 pap. $9.95. A pioneering attempt to present Western history in a world setting. The prime example of how such an attempt leads to superficiality. (See McNeill's main listing in this chapter.)

Palmer, Robert R., and Joel Colton. *A History of the Modern World*. Knopf 2 vols. 6th ed. text ed. 1983 $29.00 pap. $18.00. Many times revised, this has become a classic among college history texts, but is readable and useful to general readers.

Shafer, Boyd C. *Europe and the World in the Age of Expansion*. Univ. of Minnesota Pr. 10 vols. vols. 1–9 1974–84 ea. $12.50–35.00 vol. 10 in progress. This could be the exception to the rule that world histories must be superficial.

Stavrianos, Leften. *A Global History: The Human Heritage*. Prentice-Hall 3d ed. text ed. 1983 pap. $20.95

Strayer, Joseph R., and Hans W. Gatzke. *The Mainstream of Civilization*. Harcourt 7 vols. 4th ed. 1984 lib. bdg. ea. $15.95–$27.95. A reasonably successful textbook, but the emphasis remains on Europe.

Thomas, Hugh. *A History of the World*. Harper repr. of 1979 ed. 1982 pap. $12.95. A particularly notable example of Eurocentrism, but good for what it is.

Walbank, T. Walter, and others. *Civilization Past and Present*. Scott, Foresman 2 vols. 7th ed. 1976 o.p. A good and popular college textbook, but again the focus is on Europe.

WAR AND THE PROBLEMS OF PEACE
IN THE MODERN WORLD

Included here are books on various aspects of war and diplomacy in the nineteenth century and particularly in the twentieth century. An attempt has been made to provide coverage of major areas of the world, and additional titles will be found in the area listings. But, given European dominance of the world during the last 200 years, the emphasis is necessarily on Europe. A number of books cited are directed at the military and diplomatic problems peculiar to the nuclear age.

Adamthwaite, Anthony. *The Lost Peace: International Relations in Europe, 1918–1939*. St. Martin's 1981 $25.00

Albrecht-Carrié, Rene. *A Diplomatic History of Europe: Since the Congress of Vienna*. Harper rev. ed. text ed. 1973 pap. $23.50. Characterized by sound scholarship and carefully drawn conclusions.

Allison, Graham T. *Essence of Decision: Explaining the Cuban Missile Crisis*. Little, Brown 1971 pap. $10.95

Baer, George W. *Test Case: Italy, Ethiopia and the League of Nations.* Hoover Institution 1977 $15.95. A scholarly study of a subject too often overlooked.

Baker, Paul R. *The Atomic Bomb: The Great Decision.* Holt 2d ed. text ed. 1976 pap. $12.95. An excellent collection of articles pro and con.

Baldwin, Hanson W. *Battles Lost and Won: Great Campaigns of World War II.* Avon 1967 o.p.; Harper 1966 o.p. Popular and readable but this and the title below are accurate and useful books by a noted war correspondent.

——. *World War I: An Outline History.* Harper 1962 $12.45

Blumenson, Martin. *The Patton Papers.* Houghton Mifflin 2 vols. 1972–74 ea. $35.00– $39.50

Buchanan, A. Russell, ed. *The United States and World War Two: Military and Diplomatic Documents.* Documentary History of the U.S. Ser. Univ. of South Carolina Pr. 1972 $19.95

Calvocoressi, Peter, and Guy Wint. *Total War: The Story of World War II.* Pantheon 1972 $15.00 1980 pap. $6.95

Carr, Edward H. *International Relations between the Two World Wars, 1919–1939.* St. Martin's 1969 $22.50

Chamberlain, Neville. *In Search of Peace.* Essay Index Repr. Ser. Ayer repr. of 1939 ed. $18.00

Collier, Basil. *Japan at War: An Illustrated History of the War in the Far East, 1931–45.* Hippocrene Bks. 1977 $14.95

——. *The Second World War: A Military History.* Peter Smith $18.00

Craig, William. *Enemy at the Gates.* Ballantine repr. 1974 pap. $1.95. "Craig spent five years interviewing survivors of the battle—Germans, Russians, Italians, Rumanians, Austrians, and Hungarians—as well as studying documents, letters, monographs from both sides of the struggle. . . . [He] has brought us a vivid and detailed account of this titanic struggle" (*Choice*).

Craven, Wesley F., and James L. Cate. *The Army Air Forces in World War II.* Ed. by James Gilbert, Ayer 7 vols. repr. of 1948 ed. 1979 lib. bdg. ea. $42.00 set $294.00

Davis, Lynn E., and others. *The Cold War Begins: Soviet-American Conflict over Eastern Europe.* Princeton Univ. Pr. 1974 $38.50

Eisenhower, John S. *The Bitter Woods: A Comprehensive Study of the War in Europe.* Putnam 1969 o.p. A study of the German and Allied commands during the European campaign of World War II with emphasis on the Battle of the Bulge. "With an amazing—I almost said overwhelming—grasp of detail, John Eisenhower, a West Pointer and former professional Army officer, tells us what was happening everywhere, at almost every level, within the German as well as the Allied lines" (Charles Poore, *N.Y. Times*).

Falls, Cyril. *The Great War, 1914–1918.* Capricorn Bks. 1961 o.p. A classic study.

Feis, Herbert. *Churchill, Roosevelt, Stalin: The War They Waged and the Peace They Sought.* Princeton Univ. Pr. 2d ed. 1967 $60.00 pap. $14.50

——. *Road to Pearl Harbor: The Coming of the War between the United States and Japan.* Princeton Univ. Pr. 1950 pap. $10.50

Fischer, Fritz. *Germany's Aims in the First World War.* Norton 1968 pap. $8.95

——. *War of Illusions: German Policies from 1911 to 1914.* Trans. by Marion Jackson, Norton 1975 $9.95

——. *World Power or Decline: The Controversy over Germany's Aims in the First World War.* Trans. by Lancelot L. Farrar and others, Norton 1974 pap. $3.95

Freedman, Lawrence. *The Evolution of Nuclear Strategy.* St. Martin's 1981 $35.00 1982 pap. $10.95

Fuller, John F. *The Conduct of War, 1789–1961: A Study of the Impact of the French,*

Industrial and Russian Revolutions on War and Its Conduct. Greenwood repr. of 1961 ed. 1981 lib. bdg. $30.00

Fussell, Paul. *The Great War and Modern Memory.* Oxford 1975 $17.95 pap. $8.95. A brilliant study on how World War I is remembered—and forgotten.

Gaddis, John L. *The United States and the Origins of the Cold War, 1941–1947. Contemporary Amer. History Ser.* Columbia Univ. Pr. 1972 $32.50 pap. $11.00

George, Alexander L. *The Chinese Communist Army in Action: The Korean War and Its Aftermath.* Columbia Univ. Pr. 1967 pap. $11.00

Gimbel, John. *The Origins of the Marshall Plan.* Stanford Univ. Pr. 1976 $27.50

Greenfield, Kent R. *American Strategy in World War II: A Reconsideration.* Greenwood repr. of 1963 ed. 1979 lib. bdg. $25.00; Krieger 1982 pap. $7.50

Gulick, Edward V. *Europe's Classical Balance of Power: A Case History of the Theory and Practice of One of the Great Concepts of European Statecraft.* Greenwood repr. 1982 lib. bdg. $35.00

Hillgruber, Andreas. *Germany and the Two World Wars.* Trans. by William C. Kirby, Harvard Univ. Pr. text ed. 1981 $14.50

Holloway, David. *The Soviet Union and the Arms Race.* Yale Univ. Pr. 2d ed. 1984 $20.00 pap. $7.95

Irving, David. *Hitler's War.* Viking 1977 $19.95

Jackson, W. G. F. *Overlord: Normandy, 1944.* Ed. by Noble Frankland and Christopher Dowling, *Politics and Strategy of the Second World War Ser.* Univ. of Delaware Pr. 1979 $18.50. A book on tactics and strategy by a distinguished military historian.

Joll, James. *The Origins of the First World War.* Longman text ed. 1984 pap. $14.95

Keegan, John. *The Face of Battle: A Study of Agincourt, Waterloo and the Somme.* Penguin 1983 pap. $5.95; Random (Vintage) repr. of 1976 ed. 1977 pap. $5.95; Viking 1976 $13.95. Keegan looks at war in an entirely new way, here through the battles of Agincourt, Waterloo, and the Somme.

———. *Six Armies in Normandy: From D-Day to the Liberation of Paris.* Penguin 1983 pap. $6.95

Kelleher, Catherine M. *Germany and the Politics of Nuclear Weapons. Institute of War and Peace Studies* Columbia Univ. Pr. 1975 $30.00

Kennan, George F. (See Kennan's main entry in this chapter.)

Kissinger, Henry. *The White House Years.* Little, Brown 1979 $24.95. Controversial memoirs by a controversial figure.

Koch, H. W., ed. *Origins of the First World War.* Taplinger 1972 pap. $3.95

Kohl, Wilfrid L. *French Nuclear Diplomacy.* Princeton Univ. Pr. 1971 $36.00

La Feber, Walter. *America, Russia, and the Cold War.* Random 4th ed. text ed. 1980 pap. $10.95

Langhorne, Richard. *The Collapse of the Concert of Europe, 1890–1914.* St. Martin's 1981 $22.50. Diplomacy in the decades before World War I.

Lewin, Ronald. *The War on Land: The British Army in World War II.* Morrow 1970 $8.95

Liddell Hart, Basil H. *History of the First World War.* Cassell 1970 o.p.

———. *History of the Second World War.* Putnam 1980 pap. $10.95. This and the *History of the First World War* are masterworks by this century's most distinguished military historian.

Mandelbaum, Michael. *The Nuclear Question.* Cambridge Univ. Pr. 1979 $24.95 pap. $9.95

Milward, Alan S. *War, Economy and Society, 1939–1945.* Peter Smith 1983 $13.25; Univ. of California Pr. 1977 pap. $6.95

Morison, Samuel Eliot. *The Two-Ocean War: A Short History of the United States Navy in the Second World War*. Atlantic Monthly Pr. 1963 $19.95. (See Morison's main listing in Chapter 7.)

Morris, A. J. *The Scaremongers: The Advocacy of War and Rearmament, 1896–1914*. Routledge & Kegan 1984 $38.95

Nicolson, Harold. *Peacemaking 1919*. Peter Smith 1984 $17.00

Petrie, Charles A. *Diplomatic History, 1713–1933*. AMS Pr. repr. of 1946 ed. $35.00. A good, solid account of a sometimes confusing subject.

Pipes, Richard. *U.S.-Soviet Relations in the Era of Détente: A Tragedy of Errors*. Westview Pr. 1981 lib. bdg. $28.50 text ed. pap. $11.95

Pogue, Forrest C. *George C. Marshall*. Viking 3 vols. 1963–73 ea. $19.95. An exemplary biography, thoroughly researched and judicious in its conclusions.

Prins, Gwyn, ed. *The Nuclear Crisis Reader*. Random (Vintage) 1984 pap. $6.95

Quester, George H. *Nuclear Proliferation: Breaking the Chain*. Univ. of Wisconsin Pr. 1981 $27.50 text ed. pap. $9.95

Ranger, Robin. *Arms and Politics, 1958–1978*. Westview Pr. text ed. 1979 pap. $17.00

Remak, J. *The Origins of the Second World War*. Prentice-Hall (Spectrum Bks.) 1976 pap. $4.95

Ridgway, Matthew B. *The Korean War*. Doubleday 1967 o.p. An intelligent assessment by a leading participant.

Rommel, Erwin. *Rommel Papers*. Ed. by Basil H. Liddell Hart, *Quality Pap. Ser.* Da Capo 1982 $9.95. The "Desert Fox" is fully revealed in these skillfully edited memoirs.

Scott, Harriet F., and William F. Scott. *The Armed Forces of the USSR*. Westview Pr. 3d ed. lib. bdg. $32.50 text ed. pap. $14.95

Sherwin, Martin J. *A World Destroyed: The Atomic Bomb and the Grand Alliance*. Random (Vintage) repr. of 1975 ed. 1977 pap. $5.95

Strahan, Hew. *European Armies and the Conduct of War*. Allen & Unwin text ed. 1983 $28.50 pap. $12.50

Talbott, Strobe. *Deadly Gambits: The Reagan Administration and the Stalemate in Nuclear Arms Control*. Knopf 1984 $17.95. An account of the arms control controversy within the Reagan administration by a correspondent for *Time* magazine.

Toland, John. *Battle: The Story of the Bulge*. New Amer. Lib. (Signet Class.) 1982 pap. $3.95

——. *The Last One Hundred Days*. Bantam 1966 $20.00 pap. $5.95

——. *Rising Sun: The Decline and Fall of the Japanese Empire: 1936–1945*. Bantam 1971 pap. $5.95; Random 1970 $25.00

Tuchman, Barbara. *The Guns of August*. Bantam 1976 pap. $4.95. A detailed account of the first month of World War I. (See Tuchman's main listing in this chapter.)

Tunney, Christopher. *Biographical Dictionary of World War II*. St. Martin's 1973 $8.95. Includes more than 400 short biographies of the major participants.

Uldricks, Teddy J. *Diplomacy and Ideology: The Origins of Soviet Foreign Relations, 1917–1930*. Sage 1979 $25.00 pap. $12.50

Walters, F. P. *The League of Nations*. Oxford 1965 o.p. The standard account.

Watt, Donald C. *Too Serious a Business: European Armed Forces and the Coming of the Second World War*. Univ. of California Pr. 1975 $29.50

Weigley, Russell F. *The American Way of War: A History of U.S. Military Strategy and Policy*. Indiana Univ. Pr. 1977 pap. $9.95

——. *History of the United States Army*. Indiana Univ. Pr. enl. ed. 1984 pap. $10.95; Macmillan 1967 $29.95

————. *Towards an American Army: Military Thought from Washington to Marshall.* Greenwood repr. of 1962 ed. 1974 lib. bdg. $37.50

Weill, Herman N. *European Diplomatic History, 1815–1914: Documents and Interpretations.* Exposition Pr. 1972 $15.00 pap. $5.00

Werth, Alexander. *Russia at War.* Carroll & Graf 1984 pap. $13.95

Woolsey, R. James, and Michael Quinlan, eds. *Nuclear Arms: Ethics, Strategy, Politics.* ICS Pr. 1984 $22.95 pap. $8.95

Wright, Gordon. *The Ordeal of Total War, 1939–1945.* Harper pap. $5.95. The impact of World War II on European politics and society.

Young, Peter. *Short History of World War Two, 1939–1945. Apollo Eds.* Crowell 1972 pap. $5.50. Useful, but sometimes lacking in significant detail.

EUROPE: GENERAL

Included in this section are works concerned for the most part with economic and social trends and conditions, and with ideological and political movements affecting Europe as a whole from the sixteenth century to the present. Works on war and diplomacy will be found earlier in this chapter.

Abendroth, Wolfgang. *A Short History of the European Working Class.* Trans. by Nicholas Jacobs and others, Monthly Review 1972 pap. $5.95

Anderson, M. S. *Europe in the Eighteenth Century, 1713–1783. General History of Europe Ser.* Longman 2d ed. text ed. 1976 pap. $12.95

Arendt, Hannah. (See Arendt's main listing in this chapter.)

Aries, Philippe. *Centuries of Childhood: A Social History of Family Life.* Random 1965 pap. $6.95

————. *Western Attitudes toward Death from the Middle Ages to the Present.* Johns Hopkins Univ. Pr. text ed. 1974 $7.50 pap. $4.95. Two brilliant books by one of the most creative social historians of his generation.

Barraclough, Geoffrey. *An Introduction to Contemporary History.* Gannon lib. bdg. $10.50; Penguin 1968 pap. $4.95. A useful synthesis by a distinguished historian.

Baumer, Franklin L. *Modern European Thought: Continuity and Change in Ideas, 1600–1950.* Macmillan 1978 $15.95

Bezucha, Robert J. *Modern European Social History: A Collection of Essays. Civilization and Society Ser.* Heath 1972 $8.95

Boggs, Carl, and David Plotke, eds. *The Politics of Eurocommunism: Socialism in Transition.* South End Pr. 1980 $15.00 pap. $6.50

Braudel, Fernand. (See Braudel's main listing in this chapter.)

Breunig, Charles. *The Age of Revolution and Reaction, 1789–1850.* Norton 2d ed. 1977 $12.95 pap. $7.95

Bridenthal, Renate, and Claudia Koonz. *Becoming Visible: Women in European History.* Houghton Mifflin text ed. 1977 pap. $15.95. Some problems of women's history.

Burke, Peter. *Popular Culture in Early Modern Europe.* Harper 1978 pap. $7.95

————, ed. *Economy and Society in Early Modern Europe: Essays from Annales.* Harper 1972 o.p. Important studies out of the influential French school of history.

Cambridge Economic History of Europe. Cambridge Univ. Pr. 7 vols. 1941–65 write publisher for individual volumes and prices. Separate volumes from the Middle Ages to the present. Generally commendable essays.

Churchill, Winston. (See Churchill's main listing in Chapter 9.)

Cipolla, Carlo M. *Before the Industrial Revolution: European Economy and Society, 1000–1700*. Norton 2d ed. rev. 1980 $16.95 text ed. pap. $6.95

——, ed. *The Fontana Economic History of Europe*. Barnes & Noble 6 vols. 1974–77 ea. $23.50. Consists of separate chapters by specialists.

Clough, Shepard B. *European Economic History (The Economic Development of Western Civilization)*. McGraw-Hill 3d ed. text ed. 1975 $41.00. A standard survey recently brought up-to-date.

Craig, Gordon A. *Europe, 1815–1914*. Holt 3d ed. text ed. 1972 $19.95

Doyle, William. *Old European Order, 1660–1800*. Short Oxford History of the Modern World Ser. 1978 $39.95 pap. $15.95

Feis, Herbert. *Europe the World's Banker, 1870–1914*. Kelley repr. of 1930 ed. $27.50

Felice, Renzo de. *Interpretations of Fascism*. Trans. by Brenda H. Everett, Harvard Univ. Pr. 1977 $16.50

Firestone, Shulamith. *The Dialectic of Sex*. Morrow repr. of 1973 ed. 1974 pap. $5.95. More problems of women's history.

Ford, Franklin L. *Europe, 1780–1830*. General History of Europe Ser. Longman text ed. 1971 pap. $11.95

Forster, Robert, ed. *Family and Society*. Trans. by Patricia Ranum, *Selections from the Annales* Johns Hopkins Univ. Pr. text ed. 1976 $20.00

Forster, Robert, and Orest Ranum, eds. *Biology of Man in History. Selections from the Annales* Johns Hopkins Univ. Pr. text ed. 1975 $18.50 pap. $4.95.

——. *Food and Drink in History*. Trans. by Elborg Forster and Patricia Ranum, *Selections from the Annales* Johns Hopkins Univ. Pr. text ed. 1979 $14.00 pap. $4.95. Useful collections of articles from *Annales*.

Foucault, Michel. *Discipline and Punish: The Birth of the Prison*. Trans. by Alan Sheridan, Pantheon 1978 $10.95; Random (Vintage) repr. 1979 pap. $6.95

——. *A History of Sexuality: An Introduction*. Trans. by Robert Hurley, Pantheon 1978 $8.95; Random (Vintage) repr. of 1978 ed. 1980 pap. $4.95. Unique and brilliant synthesis by a great contemporary social historian. Few recent historical works have had so strong an impact on intellectuals in general as this.

——. *Madness and Civilization: A History of Insanity in the Age of Reason*. Random (Vintage) 1973 pap. $4.95

Freeman, Jo, ed. *Women: A Feminist Perspective*. Mayfield 3d ed. text ed. 1984 pap. $15.95

Gay, Peter. *The Enlightenment: An Interpretation—the Science of Freedom*. Norton Lib. 2 vols. repr. of 1966–69 ed. 1977 pap. ea. $9.95–$11.95. A controversial but stimulating study by one of the most prolific contemporary historians.

Gilbert, Felix. *End of the European Era: 1890 to the Present*. Norton 2d ed. 1979 $24.95 text ed. pap. $9.95

Gillis, John R. *Youth and History: Tradition and Change in European Age Relations, 1770 to Present*. Studies in Social Discontinuity Academic Pr. rev. ed. 1981 $10.50

Ginzburg, Carlo. *The Cheese and the Worms: The Cosmos of a Sixteenth-Century Miller*. Trans. by John Tedeschi and Anne Tedeschi, Johns Hopkins Univ. Pr. text ed. 1980 $17.50

Griffith, William E., ed. *The European Left: Italy, France, and Spain*. Lexington Bks. 1979 $29.50

Hay, Denys. *Europe in the Fourteenth and Fifteenth Centuries*. General History of Europe Ser. Longman text ed. 1966 pap. $13.50

Hodgart, Alan. *The Economics of European Imperialism*. Foundations of Modern History Ser. Norton 1978 $7.95 pap. $4.95

Hughes, H. Stuart. *Consciousness and Society: The Reorientation of European Social Thought, 1890–1930.* Octagon repr. of 1958 ed. 1976 lib. bdg. $26.00; Random (Vintage) 1961 pap. $4.95

————. *The Sea Change: The Migration of Social Thought, 1930–1965.* Harper 1975 $10.00; McGraw-Hill 1977 pap. $4.95

Joll, James. *Europe since 1870: An International History.* Harper text ed. 1973 pap. $21.50. An excellent general survey, covering social and economic as well as political history.

Jones, E. L. *The European Miracle: Environments, Economies and Geopolitics in the History of Europe and Asia.* Cambridge Univ. Pr. text ed. 1981 $39.50 pap. $11.95. A different approach, stressing the unique factors in European development to explain Europe's world influence.

Kann, Robert A. *A History of the Habsburg Empire, 1526–1918.* Univ. of California Pr. 1974 $55.00 pap. $12.95. A useful general survey.

Landes, David S. *Unbound Prometheus: Technological Change and Industrial Development in Western Europe from 1750 to the Present.* Cambridge Univ. Pr. $49.50 pap. $13.95. A study unique in scope and for that reason most valuable.

Langer, William L., ed. *The Rise of Modern Europe.* Harper consult publisher for individual volumes and prices. This famous series, known to several generations of graduate history students as the *Langer Series*, was begun a half century ago and was intended to cover the period 1350 to the present. Many of the volumes are dated in their emphasis on political history, but all of them are well-written and stimulating syntheses, useful to both student and general reader.

Laqueur, Walter. *Europe since Hitler: The Rebirth of Europe.* Penguin rev. ed. 1982 pap. $6.95

Le Roy-Ladurie, Emmanuel. *Times of Feast, Times of Famine: A History of Climate since the Year 1000.* Doubleday 1971 o.p. An exemplary study by a leading historian of the *Annales* school.

Lichtheim, George. *A Short History of Socialism.* Praeger 1970 o.p. The standard study.

Maier, Charles S., ed. *The Origins of the Cold War and Contemporary Europe.* Watts 1978 pap. $7.95

Mattingly, Garrett. (See Mattingly's main listing in this chapter.)

McKay, Derek, and H. M. Scott. *The Rise of the Great Powers: The Great Powers and European States Systems, 1648–1815.* Longman text ed. 1983 $30.00 pap. $11.95

Mitterauer, Michael, and Reinhard Sieder. *The European Family: Patriarch to Partnership, 1400 to the Present.* Trans. by Karla Oosterveen and Manfred Horzinger, Univ. of Chicago Pr. 1982 lib. bdg. $25.00 1984 pap. $9.95. Brings together the large body of work done in recent years in family history.

Moore, Barrington, Jr. *Social Origins of Dictatorship and Democracy.* Beacon 1966 pap. $9.95

Mosse, George L. *Masses and Man: Nationalist and Fascist Perceptions of Reality.* Fertig 1980 $35.00

Mundy, John. *Europe in the High Middle Ages, 1150–1309. General History of Europe Ser.* Longman text ed. pap. $15.95

The New Cambridge Modern History. Cambridge Univ. Pr. 14 vols. $695.00. Separate volumes from the Renaissance to the present. Some of the separate essays are excellent, many others disappointing. Does not replace the old *Cambridge Modern History* for factual detail.

Oxford History of Modern Europe. Oxford 7 vols. consult publisher for individual volumes and prices

Parry, J. H. *The Age of Reconnaissance: Discovery, Exploration, and Settlement, 1450–1650*. Univ. of California Pr. 1981 pap. $8.95 1982 $26.50. An excellent survey of European expansion overseas and the creation of the first empires from the Portuguese beginnings to the establishment of the Dutch in the Far East.

Paxton, Robert O. *Europe in the 20th Century*. Harcourt text ed. 1975 $23.95. A good, solid text.

Pollard, Sidney. *European Economic Integration, 1815–1970*. Ed. by Geoffrey Barraclough, *Lib. of European Civilization Ser.* Harcourt text ed. 1974 pap. $11.95; Transatlantic 1974 $8.75

————. *Peaceful Conquest: The Industrialization of Europe, 1760–1970*. Oxford 1981 pap. $19.95

Rupp, Leila J. *Mobilizing Women for War: German and American Propaganda, 1939–1945*. Princeton Univ. Pr. 1978 $25.00

Schmitt, Hans A. *European Union: From Hitler to De Gaulle*. Krieger pap. $5.95

————, ed. *U.S. Occupation in Europe after World War II*. Univ. Pr. of Kansas text ed. 1978 pap. $7.95

Schmitt, Hans A., and W. Walton Butterworth. *The Path to European Union: From the Marshall Plan to the Common Market*. Greenwood repr. of 1962 ed. 1981 lib. bdg. $25.00

Silverman, Dan P. *Reconstructing Europe after the Great War*. Harvard Univ. Pr. text ed. 1982 $25.00

Skocpol, Theda. *States and Social Revolutions*. Cambridge Univ. Pr. 1979 pap. $11.95

Stearns, Peter N. *European Society in Upheaval: Social History since 1750*. Macmillan 2d ed. text ed. 1975 pap. consult publisher for price

Stone, Norman. *Europe Transformed, 1878–1919*. Harvard Univ. Pr. text ed. 1984 $20.00 pap. $7.95

Stromberg, Roland N. *Europe in the Twentieth Century*. Prentice-Hall text ed. 1980 pap. $23.95. An excellent, widely used text.

————. *European Intellectual History since 1789*. Prentice-Hall 3d ed. 1981 pap. $18.95

Talmon, J. R. *Romanticism and Revolt, 1815–1848. Lib. of World Civilization* Norton text ed. 1979 pap. $5.95

Taylor, Telford. *Munich: The Price of Peace*. Random 1980 pap. $8.95

Thompson, J. M. *European History, 1494–1789*. Harper 1969 o.p. Useful, though a bit old-fashioned in its approach.

Vaughan, Richard. *Twentieth Century Europe: Paths to Unity*. Barnes & Noble text ed. 1979 $23.50

Weber, Eugene, ed. *Twentieth-Century Europe*. Forum Pr. text ed. 1980 pap. $6.95

Wegs, J. Robert. *Europe since 1945: A Concise History*. St. Martin's text ed. 1984 pap. $11.95. A particularly good survey with critical bibliographies.

Woolf, S. J., ed. *Fascism in Europe*. Methuen 1981 $26.00 pap. $9.95. Interpretive essays on various countries.

EUROPE: SEPARATE STATES

France

Ambler, John S., ed. *The French Socialist Experiment*. Institute for the Study of Human Issues text ed. 1984 $27.50 pap. $12.95

Anderson, R. D. *France, 1870–1914: Politics and Society*. Routledge & Kegan 1977 $22.50 1984 pap. $8.95. A good, up-to-date survey.

Ashley, Maurice. *Louis the Fourteenth and the Greatness of France.* Macmillan (Free Pr.) 1965 pap. $11.95

Beauroy, Jacques, and others. *The Wolf and the Lamb: Popular Culture in France from the Old Regime to the Twentieth Century.* Anma Libri 1977 pap. $24.50

Bernstein, Samuel. *French Political and Intellectual History.* Transaction Bks. text ed. 1983 pap. $24.95

Bertier de Sauvigny, Guillaume de, and David H. Pinkney. *History of France.* Trans. by James Friguglietti, Forum Pr. rev. & enl. ed. text ed. 1983 $29.95 pap. $19.95

Briggs, Robin. *Early Modern France, 1560–1715.* Oxford 1977 $14.95 pap. $7.95. Incorporates recent scholarship that has modified many of the older views of this period.

Cerny, Philip G. *Social Movements and Protest in France.* St. Martin's 1982 $25.00

Cobb, Richard. *French and Germans, Germans and French: A Personal Interpretation of France under Two Occupations.* Univ. Pr. of New England 1983 $15.95

Cobban, Alfred. *A History of Modern France.* Penguin 3 vols. 1966 pap. ea. $3.95. The standard work in English, covering the period from 1715 to the 1960s.

Crozier, Brian. *De Gaulle.* Scribner 1974 o.p. A good biography, critical of De Gaulle.

Derfler, Leslie. *The Third French Republic, 1870–1940.* Krieger text ed. 1982 pap. $5.95

Frears, J. R. *France in the Giscard Presidency.* Allen & Unwin text ed. 1981 pap. $10.95

Goodwin, Albert. *The French Revolution.* Hutchinson 5th ed. 1984 pap. $8.95. Of the many books on the subject, this is perhaps the most readable and the easiest for the nonexpert to understand.

Goubert, Pierre. *The Ancien Regime: French Society, 1600–1750.* Trans. by Steve Cox, Harper 1974 pap. $5.95

Grosser, Alfred. *French Foreign Policy under De Gaulle.* Greenwood repr. of 1967 ed. 1977 lib. bdg. $20.00

Hanley, David L., A. P. Kerr, and Neville H. Waites. *Contemporary France: Politics and Society since 1945.* Routledge & Kegan rev. ed. 1984 pap. $17.95

Horne, Alistair. *The French Army and Politics, 1870–1970.* Bedrick Bks. 1984 $12.95

————. *A Savage War of Peace: Algeria, 1954–1962.* Penguin 1979 pap. $5.95; Viking 1978 $19.95

Hughes, Judith M. *To the Maginot Line: The Politics of French Military Preparations in the 1920's.* Harvard Univ. Pr. 1971 $18.50

Johnson, R. W. *The Long March of the French Left.* St. Martin's 1981 $27.50

Kedward, H. R. *Resistance in Vichy France.* Oxford 1978 $34.95

Kuisel, Richard F. *Capitalism and the State in Modern France: Renovation and Economic Management in the Twentieth Century.* Cambridge Univ. Pr. 1981 $44.50

Lefebvre, Georges. *Coming of the French Revolution.* Trans. by Robert R. Palmer, Princeton Univ. Pr. 1947 pap. $6.95

————. *Napoleon from 18 Brumaire to Tilsit, 1799–1807.* Trans. by Henry F. Stockhold, Columbia Univ. Pr. 1969 $32.00

————. *Napoleon from Tilsit to Waterloo, 1807–1815.* Trans. by J. E. Anderson, Columbia Univ. Pr. 1969 $32.00

Lichtheim, George. *Marxism in Modern France.* Columbia Univ. Pr. 1966 $32.00 pap. $11.00

MacRae, D., Jr. *Parliament Parties and Society in France: 1946–1958.* St. Martin's 1967 $19.95. A good study of 12 crucial years in the history of postwar France.

Micaud, Charles A. *French Right and Nazi Germany, 1933–1939.* Octagon 1964 lib. bdg. $18.50

Mousnier, Roland E. *The Institutions of France under the Absolute Monarchy, 1598–1789: Society and the State.* Trans. by Brian Pearce, Univ. of Chicago Pr. repr. of 1974 ed. 1980 $55.00

Neale, J. E. *The Age of Catherine de Medici.* Merrimack 1978 pap. $6.50

Paxton, Robert O. *Vichy France: Old Guard and New Order, 1940–1944.* Columbia Univ. Pr. 1982 $27.50 pap. $9.50

Pickles, Dorothy. *The Fifth French Republic.* Greenwood repr. of 1960 ed. 1976 lib. bdg. $16.25

———. *Problems of Contemporary French Politics.* Methuen 1982 $22.00 pap. $9.95

Sobel, Robert. *French Revolution: A Concise History and Interpretation.* Peter Smith $11.00

Talbott, John. *The War without a Name: France in Algeria, 1954–1962.* Knopf 1980 $12.95

Thompson, J. L. *Louis Napoleon and the Second Empire.* Columbia Univ. Pr. 1983 $39.00 pap. $13.00

Tint, Herbert. *France since 1918.* David & Charles 1970 $24.00 pap. $12.50

Williams, Philip M. *Crisis and Compromise: Politics in the Fourth Republic.* Shoe String (Archon) 1964 $11.00

Williams, Philip M., and Martin Harrison. *Politics and Society in De Gaulle's Republic.* Greenwood repr. of 1960 ed. 1979 lib. bdg. $24.75

Wright, Gordon. *France in Modern Times.* Norton 3d ed. repr. of 1981 ed. $24.95 pap. $15.95. Contains an excellent bibliography.

Young, Robert J. *French Foreign Policy, 1918–1945: A Guide to Research and Research Materials.* Ed. by Christoph M. Kimmich, Scholarly Resources 1981 lib. bdg. $20.00

———. *In Command of France: French Foreign Policy and Military Planning, 1933–1940.* Harvard Univ. Pr. 1978 $20.00

Zeldin, Theodore. *France, 1848–1945: Anxiety and Hypocrisy.* Oxford 2 vols. 1973–77 ea. $45.00–$49.00 pap. ea. $9.95. A thorough survey, with extremely useful bibliographies.

Germany

Abraham, David. *The Collapse of the Weimar Republic: Political Economy and Crisis.* Princeton Univ. Pr. 1981 $36.00 pap. $14.50

Baker, Kendall L., and others. *Germany Transformed: Political Culture and the New Politics.* Harvard Univ. Pr. text ed. 1981 $25.00. A study of postwar Germany's democracy.

Bendersky, Joseph W. *A History of Nazi Germany.* Nelson-Hall text ed. 1984 $22.95 pap. $10.95

Bracher, Karl D. *The German Dictatorship: The Origins, Structure, and Effects of National Socialism.* Intro. by Peter Gay, Holt text ed. 1972 pap. $15.95

Bullock, Alan. *Hitler: A Study in Tyranny.* Harper 1964 $16.95 pap. $11.50. Still the best biography.

Bulow, Bernhard H. *Imperial Germany.* Trans. by Marie A. Lewenz, Greenwood repr. of 1914 ed. 1979 lib. bdg. $24.75

Carsten, Franz L. *Reichswehr and Politics: 1918–1933.* Oxford 1966 $39.95: Univ. of California Pr. repr. of 1966 ed. 1974 pap. $8.50. This work on the German army in the 1920s is particularly illuminating.

Conradt, David P. *The German Polity. Comparative Studies of Political Life Ser.* Longman text ed. 1984 pap. $13.95

Craig, Gordon A. *Germany, 1865–1945. History of Modern Europe Ser.* Oxford 1978 $27.50 pap. $15.95
———. *Politics of the Prussian Army, 1640–1945.* Oxford repr. of 1956 ed. 1964 pap. $9.95. A classic study, well deserving of its high repute.
Detwiler, Donald S., ed. *World War Two German Military Studies.* Garland 10 pts. in 23 vols. 1979 lib. bdg. ea. $67.00
Eyck, Eric. *Bismarck and the German Empire. Norton Lib.* 1964 pap. $7.95. Although somewhat dated, this remains a valuable study of the Iron Chancellor.
———. *A History of the Weimar Republic.* Trans. by Harlan P. Hanson and Robert G. L. Waite, Harvard Univ. Pr. 2 vols. 1962–63 $30.00
Feuchtwanger, E. J., ed. *Upheaval and Continuity: A Century of German History.* Univ. of Pittsburgh Pr. 1974 pap. $6.95
Fischer, Fritz. *Germany's Aims in the First World War.* Norton 1968 pap. $8.95
Gay, Peter. *Freud, Jews and Other Germans: Masters and Victims in Modernist Culture.* Oxford 1979 pap. $8.95
———. *Weimar Culture: The Outsider as Insider.* Greenwood repr. of 1968 ed. 1981 lib. bdg. $24.25; Harper 1970 pap. $4.95. An extremely perceptive analysis by a distinguished scholar.
Gimbel, John. *The American Occupation of Germany: Politics and the Military, 1945–1949.* Stanford Univ. Pr. 1968 $27.50
Henderson, W. O. *The Rise of German Industrial Power, 1834–1914.* Univ. of California Pr. 1976 $35.00 pap. $8.50
Hiden, John. *Germany and Europe, 1919–1939.* Longman text ed. 1978 pap. $10.50
Hildebrand, Klaus. *The Foreign Policy of the Third Reich.* Univ. of California Pr. 1974 $30.00 pap. $7.95
Hiscocks, Richard. *The Adenauer Era.* Greenwood repr. of 1966 ed. 1976 lib. bdg. $19.25
Hitler, Adolf. *Mein Kampf.* Trans. by Ralph Manheim, Houghton Mifflin $17.95 pap. $9.95. Obviously, this should be read by anyone wanting to understand the Nazi era.
Holborn, Hajo. *A History of Modern Germany.* Princeton Univ. Pr. 3 vols. 1982 pap. ea. $7.95–$8.95. Covers the period from the late fifteenth century to the end of World War II with grace and superb scholarship.
Irving, David. *Hitler's War.* Viking 1977 $19.95
Koch, H. W. *A Constitutional History of Germany in the Nineteenth and Twentieth Centuries.* Longman 1984 $17.95
Laqueur, Walter. *Weimar: A Cultural History.* Putnam 1976 $4.95
Mosse, George L. *The Crisis of German Ideology: Intellectual Origins of the Third Reich.* Fertig repr. of 1964 ed. 1981 $27.50
———. *The Nationalization of the Masses: Political Symbolism and Mass Movements in Germany from the Napoleonic Wars through the Third Reich.* Fertig 1975 $27.50
Nettl, J. P. *Rosa Luxemburg.* Oxford 1966 o.p. This is the standard biography.
Prittie, Terence. *Willy Brandt: Portrait of a Statesman.* Schocken 1974 $10.50. A good biography, though somewhat uncritical.
Quigley, Hugh, and R. J. Clark. *Republican Germany: A Political and Economic Study, 1919–1928.* Gordon 1976 lib. bdg. $69.95
Ritter, Gerhard. *The Sword and the Scepter: The Problem of Militarism in Germany.* Trans. by Heinz Norden, Univ. of Miami Pr. 4 vols. 1969–73 ea. $19.95 set $69.95

Ryder, A. J. *Twentieth-Century Germany: From Bismarck to Brandt.* Columbia Univ. Pr. 1972 $34.00 pap. $15.00. A useful survey with good bibliographies.

Schoenbaum, David. *Hitler's Social Revolution: Class and Status in Nazi Germany, 1933–1939.* Intro. by Henry Turner, Doubleday (Anchor) pap. $3.50; Norton repr. 1980 pap. $7.95

Seabury, Paul. *The Wilhelmstrasse: A Study of German Diplomats under the Nazi Regime.* Greenwood repr. of 1954 ed. 1976 lib. bdg. $17.25

Shirer, William L. *The Berlin Diary: The Journal of a Foreign Correspondent, 1934–1941.* Penguin 1979 pap. $5.95

Smith, Bradley F. *Reaching Judgment at Nuremberg: The Untold Story of How the Nazi War Criminals Were Judged.* New Amer. Lib. 1979 o.p. The most balanced assessment of the war crime trials.

Speer, Albert. *Inside the Third Reich.* Macmillan 1981 pap. $9.95

Stern, Fritz R. *The Politics of Cultural Despair: A Study in the Rise of the Germanic Ideology. California Lib. Repr. Ser.* Univ. of California Pr. repr. 1974 $37.50 pap. $7.95. A perceptive analysis of Germany in the late nineteenth century.

The Weimar Republic: A Historical Bibliography. ABC-Clio 1984 lib. bdg. consult publisher for price

Weinberg, Gerhard L. *The Foreign Policy of Hitler's Germany: Diplomatic Revolution in Europe, 1933–1936.* Univ. of Chicago Pr. 1970 pap. $10.95

———. *The Foreign Policy of Hitler's Germany: Starting World War II, 1937–1939.* Univ. of Chicago Pr. 1980 $44.00

Italy

Beales, D. *The Risorgimento and the Unification of Italy.* Longman text ed. 1982 pap. $8.95

Blackmer, Donald L. *Unity in Diversity: Italian Communism and the Communist World. Studies in Communism, Revisionism and Revolution* MIT 1968 $32.50

Blackmer, Donald L., and Sidney Tarrow, eds. *Communism in Italy and France.* Princeton Univ. Pr. 1975 $57.00

Bosworth, Richard. *Italy and the Approach of the First World War.* St. Martin's 1984 $22.50

Cannistraro, Philip V., ed. *Historical Dictionary of Fascist Italy.* Greenwood 1982 lib. bdg. $49.95

Clark, Martin. *Modern Italy, 1871–1982.* Longman text ed. 1984 $35.00 pap. $19.95

de Grand, Alexander J. *Italian Fascism: Its Origins and Development.* Univ. of Nebraska Pr. 1982 $16.50 pap. $7.95

Delzell, Charles F. *Italy in the Twentieth Century.* Amer. Historical Association text ed. 1981 pap. $3.50

Fermi, Laura. *Mussolini.* Univ. of Chicago Pr. (Phoenix Bks.) 1966 pap. $13.00

Hughes, Serge. *The Fall and Rise of Modern Italy.* Greenwood repr. of 1967 ed. 1983 lib. bdg. $39.75

Kogan, Norman. *A Political History of Post-War Italy: From the Old to the New Center Left.* Praeger 1981 $27.95

Mack Smith, Denis. *Italy: A Modern History.* Univ. of Michigan Pr. rev. & enl. ed. 1969 $19.95. The standard history of Italy in English. It is a good, solid book, emphasizing political history.

Mussolini, Benito. *The Political and Social Doctrine of Fascism.* Gordon $59.95. A collection of Il Duce's writings and speeches.

Sarti, Roland. *Fascism and the Industrial Leadership in Italy, 1919–1940: A Study in the Expansion of Private Power under Fascism.* Univ. of California Pr. 1971 $37.50
Seton-Watson, Christopher. *Italy from Liberalism to Fascism, 1870–1925.* Methuen 1967 $65.00
Wiskemann, Elizabeth. *Italy since 1945.* St. Martin's 1972 $22.50
Zuckerman, Alan S. *The Politics of Faction: Christian Democratic Rule in Italy.* Yale Univ. Pr. text ed. 1979 $26.50

Spain and Portugal

Alba, Victor. *Transition in Spain from Franco to Democracy.* Trans. by Barbara Lotito, Transaction Bks. 1978 $14.95
Arnold, David. *The Age of Discovery, 1400–1600.* Methuen 1984 pap. $3.95
Beevor, Antony. *The Spanish Civil War.* Bedrick Bks. 1983 $19.95
Bruce, Neil. *Portugal: The Last Empire.* Halsted Pr. 1975 $11.95
Carr, Raymond. *Spain, 1808–1974. History of Modern Europe Ser.* Oxford 2d ed. 1982 pap. $17.95. The standard history of the period in English.
Carr, Raymond, and Juan P. Fusi. *Spain: Dictatorship to Democracy.* Allen & Unwin 2d ed. text ed. 1981 pap. $10.95
Castro, Americo. *The Spaniards: An Introduction to Their History.* Trans. by Willard F. King and Selma Margaretten, Univ. of California Pr. 1980 pap. $15.95
Chapman, Charles E. *A History of Spain Founded on the Historia de España y de la Civilización Española of Rafael Altamira.* Darby repr. of 1938 ed. lib. bdg. $75.00
Clarence-Smith, Gervase. *The Third Portuguese Empire.* Manchester Univ. Pr. 1985 $29.00
Collins, Roger. *Early Medieval Spain: Unity in Diversity, 400–1000.* St. Martin's 1983 $27.50
de Olivera Marques, Antonia H. *History of Portugal.* Columbia Univ. Pr. 2 vols. 1972 ea. $28.00–$30.00
Diffie, Bailey W., and George D. Winius. *Foundations of the Portuguese Empire, 1415–1850.* Ed. by Boyd C. Shafer, *Europe and the World in the Age of Expansion Ser.* Univ. of Minnesota Pr. 1978 $25.00 pap. $5.95
Elliott, J. H. *Imperial Spain, 1469–1716.* New Amer. Lib. 1977 pap. $8.95
Graham, Lawrence S., and Harry M. Makler, eds. *Contemporary Portugal: The Revolution and Its Antecedents.* Univ. of Texas Pr. text ed. 1979 $27.50 pap. $12.95
Harrison, Joseph. *An Economic History of Modern Spain.* Holmes & Meier text ed. 1978 $32.50
Herr, Richard. *An Historical Essay on Modern Spain.* Univ. of California Pr. 1974 pap. $8.95
———. *Spain. Modern Nations in Historical Perspective Ser.* Prentice-Hall 1971 $12.95
Jackson, Gabriel. *Spanish Republic and the Civil War, 1931–1939.* Princeton Univ. Pr. 1965 $46.00 pap. $12.50. A well-balanced study.
Kamen, Henry. *Concise History of Spain.* Scribner 1973 $3.95
Kay, H. *Salazar and Modern Portugal.* Eyre & Spottiswood 1970 o.p. Of the few histories of Portugal in English, this, for all its limitations, is the best.
Livermore, Harold U. *New History of Portugal.* Cambridge Univ. Pr. 2d ed. 1977 $59.50 pap. $16.95
Lynch, John. *Spain under the Habsburgs.* New York Univ. Pr. 2 vols. 2d ed. rev. 1984 pap. ea. $15.00
Mitchell, David. *The Spanish Civil War.* Watts 1983 $18.95

O'Callaghan, Joseph F. *A History of Medieval Spain.* Cornell Univ. Pr. 1983 pap. $22.95

Payne, Stanley G. *Falange: A History of Spanish Fascism.* Stanford Univ. Pr. 1961 $25.00 pap. $8.95. The best study of Spain's Fascist party.

———. *A History of Spain and Portugal.* Univ. of Wisconsin Pr. 2 vols. text ed. 1973 ea. $25.00. The coverage is broad, but the author makes use of the most recent scholarship.

———. *Spanish Revolution. Revolutions in the Modern World Ser.* Norton text ed. 1969 pap. $6.95

Thomas, Hugh. *Spanish Civil War.* Harper rev. ed. 1977 $27.50. A provocative and well-informed study.

Scandinavia and the Low Countries

Andersson, Ingvar. *A History of Sweden.* Trans. by Carolyn Hannay, Greenwood repr. of 1968 ed. 1975 lib. bdg. $27.25

Derry, T. K. *A History of Modern Norway, 1814–1972.* Oxford 1973 $42.00

———. *A History of Scandinavia: Norway, Sweden, Denmark, Finland and Iceland.* Amer.-Scandinavian Foundation 1979 $25.00

Eckstein, Harry. *Division and Cohesion in Democracy: A Study of Norway. Center of International Studies Ser.* Princeton Univ. Pr. 1966 $30.00 pap. $8.95

Geyl, Pieter. *The Revolt of the Netherlands, 1555–1609.* Barnes & Noble text ed. 1980 $21.50 pap. $7.95. One of the many splendid works by the master Dutch historian of this century.

Hovde, B. J. *Scandinavian Countries, 1720–1865.* Associated Faculty Pr. 2 vols. repr. of 1948 ed. $62.50

Lijphart, Arend. *The Politics of Accommodation: Pluralism and Democracy in the Netherlands.* Univ. of California Pr. new ed. 1976 $30.00

Rustow, Dankwart A. *Politics of Compromise: A Study of Parties and Cabinet Government in Sweden.* Greenwood repr. of 1955 ed. lib. bdg. $15.00

Vexler, Robert I. *Scandinavia: Denmark, Norway, Sweden, 1319–1974; A Chronology and Fact Book.* Oceana 1977 $8.50

Vlekke, Bernard H. *Evolution of the Dutch Nation.* Roy 1945 o.p. The standard survey in English, covering Dutch history from the beginning to the end of World War II.

Eastern Europe

Barber, Noel. *Seven Days of Freedom: The Hungarian Uprising, 1956.* Stein & Day 1975 $2.95

Burks, R. V. *East European History: An Ethnic Approach.* Amer. Historical Association text ed. 1973 pap. $1.50

Jelavich, C., and B. Jelavich. *The Establishment of the Balkan National States, 1804–1920. History of East Central Europe Ser.* Univ. of Washington Pr. 1977 $25.00

Jones, Christopher D. *Soviet Influence in Eastern Europe: Political Autonomy and the Warsaw Pact.* Praeger 1981 $35.95 pap. $16.95

Kaser, M. C., and E. A. Radice. *The Economic History of Eastern Europe, 1919–1975.* Oxford 2 vols. 1984 ea. $39.95

Okey, Robin. *Eastern Europe, 1740–1980: Feudalism to Communism.* Univ. of Minnesota Pr. 1982 $29.50 pap. $12.95

Rothschild, Joseph. *East Central Europe between the Two World Wars. History of East Central Europe Ser.* Univ. of Washington Pr. 1974 pap. $12.95

Rusinow, Dennison. *The Yugoslav Experiment, 1948–1974*. Univ. of California Pr. 1978 $43.50 pap. $9.50

Smith, Alan H. *The Planned Economies of Eastern Europe*. Holmes & Meier text ed. 1983 $34.50

Stavrianos, Leften S. *The Balkans since 1453*. Holt 1963 o.p. The standard English survey, very well done.

Wolff, Robert L. *The Balkans in Our Time*. Harvard Univ. Pr. rev. ed. text ed. 1974 $30.00; Norton rev. ed. text ed. 1978 pap. $11.95

Woodhouse, C. M. *Struggle for Greece, 1941–1949*. Beekman 1979 $29.95. A solid study of one of the lesser-known conflicts of World War II.

Zinner, Paul E. *Communist Strategy and Tactics in Czechoslovakia, 1918–48*. Greenwood repr. of 1963 ed. 1976 lib. bdg. $22.50

RUSSIA AND THE SOVIET UNION

Abraham, Richard, and Lionel Kochan. *The Making of Modern Russia*. St. Martin's 1984 $25.00

Alexander, John T. *Emperor of the Cossacks: Pugachev and the Frontier Jacquerie, 1773–1775*. Coronado Pr. 1973 pap. $6.00

Auty, Robert, and D. Obolensky, eds. *Companion to Russian Studies: An Introduction to Russian History*. Cambridge Univ. Pr. 1976 vol. 1 $52.50

Avrich, Paul, ed. *The Anarchists in the Russian Revolution. Documents of Revolution Ser*. Cornell Univ. Pr. 1973 pap. $7.95

————. *Kronstadt, 1921. Norton Lib*. 1974 pap. $5.95

Azrael, Jeremy R., ed. *Soviet Nationality Policies and Practices*. Praeger 1978 $44.95

Barghoorn, Frederick C. *Soviet Foreign Propaganda*. Princeton Univ. Pr. 1964 $33.00

Barratt, Glynn R. *Voices in Exile: The Decembrist Memoirs*. McGill-Queens Univ. Pr. 1974 $18.50

Barron, John. *KGB Today: The Hidden Hand*. Berkley Publishing 1985 pap. $4.95. An interesting and enlightening study of the Soviet secret police.

Benois, Alexandre. *The Russian School of Painting*. Longwood repr. of 1916 ed. 1979 lib. bdg. $30.00

Bialer, Seweryn, ed. *Stalin and His Generals: Soviet Military Memoirs of World War II*. Westview Pr. 1984 $38.50

Bradley, John. *Allied Intervention in Russia, 1917–1920*. Univ. Pr. of Amer. text ed. 1984 pap. $12.75

Breslauer, George W. *Khrushchev and Brezhnev as Leaders: Building Authority in Soviet Politics*. Allen & Unwin text ed. 1982 $28.50 pap. $12.95

Brown, Emily C. *Soviet Trade Unions and Labor Relations*. Harvard Univ. Pr. 1966 $22.50

Brzezinski, Zbigniew K. *Soviet Bloc: Unity and Conflict*. Harvard Univ. Pr. rev. & enl. ed. 1967 $32.50 pap. $11.00

Carr, Edward H. *A History of Soviet Russia*. Macmillan 7 vols. 1951–64 ea. $12.95–$14.95. A good, standard history in English.

————. *The Russian Revolution from Lenin to Stalin, 1917–1929*. Macmillan (Free Pr.) 1979 $16.95

Chamberlin, William Henry. *The Russian Revolution*. Grosset & Dunlap 2 vols. 1965 o.p. Chamberlin's history is one of the most comprehensive and popular studies of the Russian Revolution.

————. *Russia's Iron Age*. Ayer repr. of 1934 ed. 1970 $23.50

Charques, Richard D. *Short History of Russia.* Dutton 1958 pap. $3.95

Chew, Allen F. *An Atlas of Russian History: Eleven Centuries of Changing Borders.* Yale Univ. Pr. text ed. 1967 pap. $10.95. Comprehensive maps of Russia and Russian territory over 11 centuries.

Churchward, L. G. *The Soviet Intelligentsia: An Essay on the Social Structure and Roles of the Soviet Intellectuals during the 1960's.* Routledge & Kegan 1973 $23.95

Clubb, O. Edmund. *China and Russia: "The Great Game." Studies of the East Asian Institute* Columbia Univ. Pr. 1970 $35.00 pap. $14.00

Cohen, Stephen F. *Bukharin and the Bolshevik Revolution: A Political Biography, 1888–1938.* Knopf 1973 $15.00; Oxford repr. of 1973 ed. 1980 pap. $11.95; Random (Vintage) 1974 pap. $3.95

———. *Rethinking the Soviet Experience: Politics and History since 1917.* Oxford 1985 $17.95

Cohen, Stephen F., and others, eds. *The Soviet Union since Stalin.* Indiana Univ. Pr. 1980 $22.50 pap. $8.95

Colton, Timothy J. *Commissars, Commanders, and Civilian Authority: The Structure of Soviet Military Politics.* Harvard Univ. Pr. 1979 $25.00

Connor, Walter D. *Deviance in Soviet Society: Crime, Delinquency, Alcoholism.* Columbia Univ. Pr. 1972 $31.00

———. *Socialism, Politics and Equality: Hierarchy and Change in Eastern Europe and the USSR.* Columbia Univ. Pr. 1979 $34.00 pap. $14.50

Conquest, Robert. *The Great Terror: Stalin's Purge of the Thirties.* Macmillan (Collier Bks.) rev. ed. 1973 o.p. "The author knows practically everything about this blood-chilling story. He tells it all, and tells it extraordinarily well. Most wholeheartedly recommended to libraries" (*LJ*).

Crankshaw, Edward. *Khrushchev: A Career.* Penguin 1971 pap. $3.95

Cressey, George B. *Soviet Potentials: A Geographic Appraisal.* Syracuse Univ. Pr. 1962 pap. $5.95

Daniels, Robert V. *Red October: Bolshevik Revolution of 1917.* Beacon 1984 $10.95.

D'Encausse, Helene C. *Decline of an Empire: The Soviet Socialist Republic in Revolt.* Harper 1981 pap. $5.95

Deutscher, Isaac. *The Prophet Armed: Trotsky, 1879–1921.* Oxford repr. of 1954 ed. 1980 pap. $9.95. This and the following two books are the standard biography of Trotsky.

———. *The Prophet Unarmed: Trotsky, 1921–1929.* Oxford repr. of 1959 ed. 1980 pap. $9.95

———. *The Prophet Outcast: Trotsky, 1929–1940.* Oxford repr. of 1968 ed. 1980 pap. $9.95.

———. *Stalin: A Political Biography.* Oxford 2d ed. pap. $14.95

———. *Unfinished Revolution: Russia 1917–1967.* Oxford 1967 $14.95 pap. $6.95

Dukes, Paul. *October and the World: Perspectives on the Russian Revolution.* St. Martin's 1979 $20.00

———. *Russia under Catherine the Great.* Oriental Research 2 vols. 1978 $24.00

Dziewanowski, M. K. *A History of Soviet Russia.* Prentice-Hall 2d ed. text ed. 1985 pap. $22.95

Elwood, Ralph C., ed. *Reconsiderations on the Russian Revolution.* Slavica 1976 $14.95

Engel, Barbara A., and Clifford N. Rosenthal, eds. *Five Sisters: Women against the Tsar.* Knopf 1975 $8.95; Schocken 1977 pap. $6.95

Engle, Eloise, and Lauri A. Paananen. *The Winter War: The Russo Finnish Conflict, 1939–1940.* Scribner 1973 $7.95; Westview Pr. repr. of 1973 ed. 1985 $10.00

Fainsod, Merle. *How Russia Is Ruled.* Harvard Univ. Pr. rev. ed. 1963 $30.00
Feis, Herbert. *Churchill, Roosevelt, Stalin: The War They Waged and the Peace They Sought.* Princeton Univ. Pr. 2d ed. 1967 $60.00 pap. $14.50
Ferro, Marc. *October 1917.* Routledge & Kegan 1980 $35.00
Filene, Peter G. *Americans and the Soviet Experiment, 1917–1933.* Harvard Univ. Pr. 1967 $22.50. American attitudes toward the Russian Revolution.
Fischer, Louis. *The Road to Yalta: Soviet Foreign Relations, 1944–1945.* Harper 1972 o.p. "Fischer, an expert and provocative writer, portrays clearly the leading figures of the time, especially Churchill and Stalin" (*Choice*).
———. *Russia's Road from Peace to War: Soviet Foreign Relations, 1917–1941.* Greenwood repr. of 1969 ed. 1979 lib. bdg. $37.50
Fisher, Alan W. *The Crimean Tartars.* Hoover Institution 1978 $14.95
Fitzpatrick, Sheila. *Education and Social Mobility in the Soviet Union: 1921–1934. Soviet and East European Studies* Cambridge Univ. Pr. 1979 $42.50
———. *The Russian Revolution.* Oxford 1982 $19.95
Gasiorowska, Xenia. *The Image of Peter the Great in Russian Fiction.* Univ. of Wisconsin Pr. 1979 $30.00
Gilison, Jerome M. *The Soviet Image of Utopia.* Johns Hopkins Univ. Pr. 1974 $18.50
Gill, Graeme J. *Peasants and Government in the Russian Revolution.* Barnes & Noble text ed. 1979 $26.50
Golder, Frank A. *Russian Expansion on the Pacific, 1641–1850.* Peter Smith $8.50
Granick, David. *The Red Executive: A Study of the Organization Man in Russian Industry.* Ed. by Lewis A. Coser and Walter W. Powell, *Perennial Works in Sociology Ser.* Ayer repr. of 1960 ed. 1979 lib. bdg. $26.50
Griffith, W. E., ed. *The Soviet Empire: Expansion and Detente.* Lexington Bks. 1976 $26.50
Hahn, Werner G. *The Politics of Soviet Agriculture: 1960–1970.* Johns Hopkins Univ. Pr. 1972 $25.00
Haimson, Leopold H., ed. *The Mensheviks: From the Revolution of 1917 to the Outbreak of the Second World War. History of Menshevism Ser.* Univ. of Chicago Pr. text ed. 1975 $22.50
Hammond, Thomas T., ed. *Soviet Foreign Relations and World Communism: A Selected, Annotated Bibliography of 7,000 Books in 30 Languages.* Princeton Univ. Pr. 1965 $88.00
Hayward, Max, and Leopold Labedz, eds. *Literature and Revolution in Soviet Russia, 1917–1962.* Greenwood repr. of 1963 ed. 1976 lib. bdg. $24.75
Herzen, Alexander. *My Past and Thoughts: The Memoirs of Alexander Herzen.* Gordon 6 vols. $600.00; trans. by J. D. Duff, Russell repr. of 1923 ed. 1967 2 pts. in 1 vol. $10.00; ed. by Dwight MacDonald, Univ. of California Pr. 1981 $34.00 pap. $9.95. A wealthy Russian of the nineteenth century gives a most interesting first-hand account of Russian history in his time.
Hough, Jerry F., and Merle Fainsod. *How the Soviet Union Is Governed: An Extensively Revised and Enlarged Edition by Jerry F. Hough of Merle Fainsod's "How Russia Is Ruled."* Harvard Univ. Pr. text ed. 1979 $25.00
Hunczak, Taras, ed. *Russian Imperialism: From Ivan the Great to the Revolution.* Intro. by Hans Kohn, Rutgers Univ. Pr. 1974 $35.00
Institute for the Study of the U.S.S.R. *Prominent Personalities in the U.S.S.R.: A Biographic Directory Containing 6,015 Biographies.* Ed. by Edward L. Crowley and others, Scarecrow Pr. 1968 o.p.
———. *Who Was Who in the U.S.S.R.: A Biographic Directory Containing 5,015 Biogra-*

phies of Prominent Soviet Historical Personalities. Ed. by Heinrich E. Schulz and Paul K. Urban, Scarecrow Pr. 1972 o.p.

Johnson, Priscilla, and Leopold Labedz, eds. *Khrushchev and the Arts: The Politics of Soviet Culture, 1962–1964.* MIT 1965 $17.50. "[Johnson's] analysis, together with the valuable documents and notes that comprise the remainder of this useful study, furnish both raw material and orientations helpful to social scientists and to interested citizens generally" (*Public Opinion Quarterly*).

Katkov, George. *Russia 1917: The February Revolution.* Greenwood repr. of 1967 ed. 1979 lib. bdg. $37.50

————. *Russia 1917: The Kornilov Affair, Kerensky and the Breakup of the Russian Army.* Longman text ed. 1980 $27.00

Keep, John. *The Russian Revolution: A Study in Mass Mobilization. Revolutions in the Modern World Ser.* Norton 1977 $19.50. An interesting and different perspective on the Revolution. An important book in this field.

Kennan, George F. (See Kennan's main listing in this chapter.)

Kerner, Robert J. *Urge to the Sea: The Course of Russian History—The Role of Rivers, Portages, Ostrogs, Monasteries, and Furs.* Russell repr. of 1942 ed. 1971 $14.00

Khrushchev, Nikita S. *Khrushchev Remembers: The Last Testament.* Ed. by Strobe Talbot, commentary by Edward Crankshaw, Little, Brown 1971 o.p. Memoirs, opinions, ideology of the late Soviet leader.

Kliuchevskii, Vasilii O. *A History of Russia.* Trans. by C. J. Hogarth, Russell 5 vols. repr. of 1911–31 ed. o.p.

————. *Peter the Great.* Trans. by Liliana Archibald, Beacon 1984 pap. $10.53

————. *The Rise of the Romanovs.* St. Martin's 1970 o.p. Classic works by a distinguished historian.

Knei-Paz, Baruch. *The Social and Political Thought of Leon Trotsky.* Oxford 1978 pap. $17.95

Kochan, Lionel, and Richard Abraham. *The Making of Modern Russia.* Penguin (Pelican) rev. ed. 1983 pap. $7.95

Lane, David. *Politics and Society in the U.S.S.R.* New York Univ. Pr. 2d ed. 1978 pap. $17.50

Lenin. (See Lenin's main listing in this chapter.)

Lewin, Moshe. *Lenin's Last Struggle.* Monthly Review 1978 pap. $8.00

————. *Russian Peasants and Soviet Power: A Study of Collectivization.* Norton repr. 1975 pap. $5.95

Lewis, Robert A., and others. *Nationality and Population Change in Russia and the USSR: An Evaluation of Census Data, 1897–1970.* Praeger text ed. 1976 $31.95

Lincoln, W. Bruce. *Nicholas I: Emperor and Autocrat of All the Russias.* Indiana Univ. Pr. 1978 pap. $8.95

————. *The Romanovs: Autocrats of All the Russias.* Doubleday (Dial) 1981 $24.95 1983 pap. $14.95

Madariaga, Isabel de. *Russia in the Age of Catherine the Great.* Yale Univ. Pr. 1982 $50.00 pap. $15.95

Makepeace, R. W. *Marxist Ideology and Soviet Criminal Law.* Barnes & Noble 1980 $27.50

Manning, Roberta T. *The Crisis of the Old Order in Russia: Gentry and Government.* Princeton Univ. Pr. 1982 $47.50

Massie, Robert K. *Nicholas and Alexandra.* Atheneum 1967 $24.50; Dell 1985 pap. $5.95. A well-written, romanticized account.

Massie, Suzanne. *Land of the Firebird.* Simon & Schuster (Touchstone Bks.) repr. of 1980 ed. 1982 pap. $25.00

Mawdsley, Evan. *The Russian Revolution and the Baltic Fleet: War and Politics, February 1917–April 1918. Studies in Russian and East European History Ser.* Barnes & Noble text ed. 1978 $26.50

Mazour, Anatole G. *Modern Russian Historiography.* Greenwood rev. ed. 1975 lib. bdg. $27.50

McAuley, Alastair. *Economic Welfare in the Soviet Union: Poverty, Living Standards, and Inequality.* Univ. of Wisconsin Pr. 1979 $37.50

McCagg, William O., Jr. *Stalin Embattled: 1943–1948.* Wayne State Univ. Pr. 1978 $18.95

McCauley, Martin, ed. *The Russian Revolution and the Soviet State, 1917–1921: Documents. Studies in Russian and East European History Ser.* Barnes & Noble text ed. 1975 $26.50. Documents of the Russian Revolution.

——. *The Soviet Union since 1917.* Longman text ed. 1981 $30.00 pap. $13.95

McClelland, J. C. *Autocrats and Academics: Education, Culture, and Society in Tsarist Russia.* Univ. of Chicago Pr. 1979 lib. bdg. $14.00

Medvedev, Roy A., and others. *Let History Judge: The Origins and Consequences of Stalinism.* Knopf 1971 $15.00; Random (Vintage) 1973 pap. $9.95

Micunovic, Veljko. *Moscow Diary.* Trans. by David Floyd, Doubleday 1980 $15.95

Miller, Margaret. *The Rise of the Soviet Consumer.* Transatlantic pap. $2.50

Mirsky, D. *Russia: A Social History.* Ed. by C. G. Seligman, Greenwood 1983 lib. bdg. $39.75

Nettl, J. P. *Soviet Achievement. History of European Civilization Lib.* Harcourt text ed. 1968 pap. $7.95

Nove, Alec. *An Economic History of the U.S.S.R.* Penguin rev. ed. 1972 pap. $5.95. The books by Nove are standard works on the Soviet economy.

——. *The Soviet Economic System.* Allen & Unwin 2d ed. text ed. 1981 pap. $13.50

——. *Stalinism and After.* Allen & Unwin text ed. 1975 $7.50

Nowak, Frank. *Medieval Slavdom and the Rise of Russia.* Greenwood repr. of 1930 ed. lib. bdg. $15.00

Pearson, Michael. *The Sealed Train: Lenin's Eight-Month Journey from Exile to Power.* Putnam 1975 o.p. "A vivid account of the famous and controversial episode of the Russian Revolution—Lenin's passage through Germany to Russia after the overthrow of the Czar in February 1917" (*LJ*).

Pethybridge, Roger. *The Social Prelude to Stalinism.* St. Martin's 1974 $25.00

Pipes, Richard. *Formation of the Soviet Union: Communism and Nationalism, 1917–1923.* Harvard Univ. Pr. rev. ed. 1964 $22.50

——. *Russia Under the Old Regime.* Scribner text ed. 1975 pap. $14.95. "We put away this book with a feeling of gratitude for the fresh insights it gives us into the broad sweep of Russian history, its unique dilemmas and its pathos" (*N.Y. Times*).

Pushkarev, Sergei G., comp. *Dictionary of Russian Historical Terms from the Eleventh Century to 1917.* Ed. by George Vernadsky, Yale Univ. Pr. 1970 $18.50

Rauch, George von. *The Baltic States: Estonia, Latvia, Lithuania—The Years of Independence, 1917–1940.* Univ. of California Pr. 1974 $24.75

——. *History of Soviet Russia.* Trans. by Peter Jacobsohn and Annette Jacobsohn, Irvington 6th ed. text ed. 1982 pap. $14.95

Reed, John. *Ten Days That Shook the World.* Gordon 1982 lib. bdg. $75.00; intro. by John Lawson and N. K. Krupskaya, International Publishing 1967 pap. $3.50; New Amer. Lib. 1982 pap. $3.50; intro. by A. J. P. Taylor and V. I. Lenin, Penguin 1979 pap. $3.95; ed. by Bertram D. Wolfe, Random (Vintage) 1960 pap.

$4.95. "Classic example of journalism so perceptive that it approximates history" (Granville Hicks, *SR*).

Riasanovsky, Nicholas V. *A History of Russia*. Oxford 4th ed. 1984 $39.95 pap. $24.95. A solid, traditional history concerning all of Russian history.

Rigby, T. H. *Lenin's Government. Soviet and East European Studies* Cambridge Univ. Pr. 1979 $59.50

Robinson, Geroid T. *Rural Russia under the Old Regime: A History of the Landlord-Peasant World and a Prologue to the Peasant Revolution of 1917*. Univ. of California Pr. 1967 pap. $9.95

Rousset, David. *The Legacy of the Bolshevik Revolution: A Critical History of the USSR*. St. Martin's 1982 vol. 1 $27.50; Schocken 1982 vol. 1 pap. $12.95

Rubin, Ronald I. *The Unredeemed: Anti-Semitism in the Soviet Union*. Times Bks. 1972 $10.00

Ruud, Charles A. *Fighting Words: Imperial Censorship and the Russian Press, 1804–1906*. Univ. of Toronto Pr. 1982 $35.00

Ryavec, Karl W., ed. *Soviet Society and the Communist Party*. Univ. of Massachusetts Pr. 1978 $12.00

Sakharov, Andrei D. *Progress, Coexistence and Intellectual Freedom*. Norton 1968 o.p. "Here is the boldest, most courageous and most starkly expressed statement by a living Russian—or for that matter, by anyone—on the absolute need in a nuclear world for an end to prenuclear politics, partisanship, patriotism, propaganda, and for the real beginnings of freedom, coexistence and even cooperation between the two giants, the United States and Soviet Russia. . . . A tremendously important and luminous book" (*PW*).

Salisbury, Harrison E. *The 900 Days: The Siege of Leningrad*. Avon 1970 pap. $2.50; Harper 1969 $16.95. "This is an account of one of the most horrible, and also one of the most heroic, episodes in human history. . . . [Mr. Salisbury] has read all the published sources, not only the official histories, but also the reminiscences of which there are a lot" (C. P. Snow, *N.Y. Times*).

——, ed. *Soviet Union: The Fifty Years*. Harcourt 1967 $10.00

Seton-Watson, Hugh. *Russian Empire, 1801–1917. History of Modern Europe Ser*. Oxford 1967 $42.50

Shub, David. *Lenin: A Biography. Pelican Ser*. Penguin 1976 pap $3.95

Smirnov, Georgi. *Soviet Man: The Making of a Socialist Type of Personality*. Beekman 1975 $15.00

Solzhenitsyn, Aleksandr I. *The Gulag Archipelago*. Trans. by Thomas P. Whitney, Harper 3 vols. vol. 1 (1974) $20.14 vol. 2 (1975) $20.14 pap. $4.33; trans. by Harry Willetts, vol. 3 (1978) $20.14 1979 pap. $2.95

Stalin, Joseph. (See Stalin's main listing in this chapter.)

Tatu, Michel. *Power in the Kremlin: From Khrushchev to Kosygin*. Trans. by Helen Katel, Viking 1969 o.p. "A combination of lucid journalistic style, an instinct for relevant minute details, and a rare understanding of the personal as well as the ideological aspects of Soviet politics contribute to an academically fully acceptable study of remarkable quality" (*Choice*).

Thomson, Gladys S. *Catherine the Great and the Expansion of Russia*. Ed. by A. L. Rowse, Greenwood repr. of 1947 ed. 1985 lib. bdg. $45.00

Treadgold, Donald W. *Twentieth-Century Russia*. Houghton Mifflin 5th ed. 1981 pap. $22.50. A solid, well-written text.

Trotsky, Leon. (See Trotsky's main listing in this chapter.)

Tucker, Robert C. *Stalin as Revolutionary, 1879–1929: A Study in History and Personality*. Norton 1973 $12.95 pap. $10.95

————, ed. *Stalinism: Essays in Historical Interpretation. Norton Lib.* repr. of 1977 ed. 1978 $19.95 pap. $10.95

Ulam, Adam B. *The Bolsheviks.* Macmillan (Collier Bks.) 1968 pap. $8.95

————. *Expansion and Coexistence: Soviet Foreign Policy, 1917–1973.* Holt 2d ed. text ed. 1974 pap. $18.95. "This big, informative work by a Russian expert at Harvard is close to enthralling" (*New Yorker*).

Vernadsky, George. *A History of Russia.* Yale Univ. Pr. rev. ed. 1961 pap. $11.95. The classic history of Russia in English. (See Vernadsky's main listing in this chapter.)

————. *The Origins of Russia.* Greenwood repr. of 1959 ed. 1975 lib. bdg. $20.75

Vishnevskaya, Galina. *Galina: A Russian Story.* Trans. by Guy Daniels, Harcourt 1984 $19.95. An autobiography by the exiled Russian soprano. This is an in-depth first-hand account of life in Russia as well as a commentary on Russian culture and arts.

Volin, Lazar A. *A Century of Russian Agriculture: From Alexander II to Khrushchev. Russian Research Ctr. Studies* Harvard Univ. Pr. 1970 $37.50

Wesson, Robert G. *Lenin's Legacy: The Story of the CPSU.* Ed. by Richard F. Staar, Hoover Institution 1978 pap. $9.95. A history of the Communist party in the Soviet Union.

Westwood, J. N. *Endurance and Endeavour: Russian History, 1812–1980. Short Oxford History of the Modern World Ser.* 2d ed. 1981 $34.95 pap. $14.95

Wildman, Allan K. *The End of the Russian Imperial Army: The Old Army and the Soldier's Revolt (March–April 1917).* Princeton Univ. Pr. 1979 $36.00

Wistrich, Robert. *Trotsky: Fate of a Revolutionary.* Rowman 1980 $19.00; Stein & Day 1982 $14.95

Yaney, George L. *The Systematization of Russian Government: Social Evolution in the Domestic Administration of Imperial Russia, 1711–1905.* Univ. of Illinois Pr. 1973 $27.50

Zaleski, Eugene. *Stalinist Planning for Economic Growth, 1933–1952.* Ed. by Maria-Christine MacAndrew and John H. Moore, Univ. of North Carolina Pr. 1980 $50.00

HISTORY OF THE JEWS

This section contains general works on Jews and Judaism, with emphasis on the modern period. Works specifically on Israel are to be found in a later section.

Ackroyd, Peter R. *Exile and Restoration: A Study of Hebrew Thought in the Sixth Century B.C. Old Testament Lib.* Westminster 1968 $14.95. "A masterly survey of the period running from the eve of the exile to the end of the Sixth Century BC" (*TLS*).

Agus, Jacob B., and others. *The Jewish People: History, Religion, Literature.* Ayer 41 bks. 1973 $1,106.50

Antin, Mary. *The Promised Land: A Study of Israel and the Jewish People.* Ed. by Annette K. Baxter, Ayer repr. of 1969 ed. 1980 lib. bdg. $24.00

Arendt, Hannah. *Eichmann in Jerusalem: A Report of the Banality of Evil.* 1963. Penguin rev. ed. 1977 pap. $6.95; Peter Smith 1983 $11.25. The author covered the trial for the *New Yorker* and the series of articles in that magazine form the bulk of this book. (See Arendt's main listing in this chapter.)

Aschheim, Steven E. *Brothers and Strangers: The East European Jew in German and German-Jewish Consciousness, 1800–1923.* Univ. of Wisconsin Pr. text ed. 1982 $25.00. An excellent insight into German and German-Jewish ideology.

Avi-Hai, Avraham. *Ben-Gurion: State Builder.* Transaction Bks. 1974 $12.95. This is a good biography of the Israeli leader.

Bakan, David. *Sigmund Freud and the Jewish Mystical Tradition.* Beacon 1975 pap. $4.95

Baron, Salo W. *A Social and Religious History of the Jews.* Columbia Univ. Pr. 17 vols. 2d ed. rev. & enl. ea. $40.00. A masterpiece, still incomplete, by the greatest living historian of the Jews.

Beck, Evelyn T. *Kafka and the Yiddish Theatre: Its Impact on His Work.* Univ. of Wisconsin Pr. 1971 $27.50. An interesting study of Eastern European Jewish cultural traditions.

Bein, Alex. *Theodor Herzl: A Biography of the Founder of Modern Zionism.* Trans. by Maurice Samuel, Atheneum 1970 pap. $4.75. A good biography of a founder of Zionism.

Ben Gurion, David. *Israel: Years of Challenge.* Holt 1963 $5.00

——. *Letters to Paula.* Univ. of Pittsburgh Pr. 1972 o.p. Very personal works by the great Israeli leader.

——, ed. *The Jews in Their Land.* Doubleday 1974 $9.95

Ben-Sasson, Haim, and others, eds. *A History of the Jewish People.* Harvard Univ. Pr. 1976 $60.00

Bettelheim, Bruno. *The Informed Heart: Autonomy in a Mass Age.* Avon 1971 pap. $3.95; Macmillan (Free Pr.) 1960 $17.95

Black, Edwin. *The Transfer Agreement: The Untold Story of the Secret Pact between the Third Reich and Jewish Palestine.* Macmillan 1984 $19.95

Bridger, David, and Samuel J. Wolk. *The New Jewish Encyclopedia.* 1925. Behrman 1962 o.p. A concise encyclopedia with definitions concerning Jewish religion and liturgy, places, and people in Jewish history.

Byrnes, R. F. *Antisemitism in Modern France.* Fertig 1969 o.p. A very interesting study of anti-Semitism in twentieth-century France.

Caplan, Neil. *Palestine Jewry and the Arab Question, 1917–1925.* Biblio Dist. 1978 $28.50

Chazan, Robert, and Marc L. Raphael, eds. *Modern Jewish History: A Source Reader.* Schocken text ed. 1974 pap. $9.95

Chesler, Evan R. *The Russian Jewry Reader.* Anti-Defamation League pap. $2.45

Cohen, Hayim J. *Jews of the Middle East (1860–1972).* Transaction Bks. 1973 $12.95. "The history of the Jews in the Middle East is without doubt the most neglected subject in modern Jewish historiography. It is for this reason that any book which deals with this subject in a serious and scholarly manner is to be welcomed" (*Choice*).

Cohen, Michael J. *Palestine, Retreat from the Mandate: The Making of British Policy, 1936–45.* Holmes & Meier text ed. 1978 $35.00

Cohen, Naomi. *American Jews and the Zionist Idea.* Ktav pap. $8.95

Cuddihy, John Murray. *The Ordeal of Civility: Freud, Marx, Levi-Strauss, and the Jewish Struggle with Modernity.* Basic Bks. 1974 o.p. "Analyzes Jewish assimilation in post-18th-century Europe and America as a subcultural microcosm of the general global process of modernization" (*LJ*).

Davidowicz, Lucy S., ed. *The Golden Tradition: Jewish Life and Thought in Eastern Europe.* Schocken 1984 pap. $11.95. "For the excellence of the selections and the high quality of the translation, this book is highly recommended" (*LJ*).

————. *A Holocaust Reader.* Behrman 1976 o.p.

Davis, Moshe, ed. *The Yom Kippur War: Israel and the Jewish People.* Intro. by Ephraim Katzir, Ayer 1974 $11.00

Deutscher, Isaac. *The Non-Jewish Jew and Other Essays.* Alyson 1982 pap. $5.95. An expert on Soviet affairs analyzes the question of being a Jew.

Dimont, Max I. *The Indestructible Jews.* New Amer. Lib. (Signet Class.) 1973 pap. $2.50. Dimont writes that "Jewish history consists of a unique series of events that has preserved the Jews as Jews in exile to fulfill their avowed mission of ushering in the brotherhood of Man" (*LJ*).

————. *Jews, God and History.* New Amer. Lib. (Signet Class.) 1972 pap. $3.95

Dinnerstein, L. *The Leo Frank Case.* Columbia Univ. Pr. 1968 $25.00

Eban, Abba. *My Country.* Random 1972 $15.00. A collection of Eban's speeches.

Ehrmann, Eliezar L. *Readings in Jewish History: From the American Revolution to the Present.* Ktav $8.95

Einstein, Albert. *The World as I See It: Ideas and Opinions.* Citadel Pr. 1979 pap. $2.95

Eisenberg, Azriel. *Jewish Historical Treasures.* Bloch Publishing 1969 $10.00. "From nearly four millennia of Jewish history the author has chosen . . . objects, artifacts, manuscripts, and instruments with the purpose of illuminating Jewish life through the ages" (*LJ*).

Elon, Amos. *The Israelis: Founders and Sons.* Penguin 1983 pap. $5.95. Popular studies.

Encyclopedia Judaica. Macmillan 16 vols. 1972 o.p.

Fine, Morris, ed. *The American Jewish Year Book.* Ed. by Milton Himmelfarb and others, Jewish Publication Society 1980 $15.00

Finkelstein, Louis, ed. *The Jews.* Schocken 3 vols. 4th ed. 1970–71 pap. ea. $6.95–$7.95

Fishman, Priscilla, ed. *The Jews of the United States.* Pref. by Arthur Hertzberg, Times Bks. 1974 $8.95. "One of a number of by-products of the new Encyclopedia Judaica" (*Choice*).

Friedlander, Albert H., ed. *Out of the Whirlwind: A Reader of Holocaust Literature.* Schocken 1976 $10.95

Friedlander, Henry, and Milton Sybil, eds. *The Holocaust: Ideology, Bureaucracy and Genocide.* Kraus 1981 lib. bdg. $45.00

Friedman, Isaiah. *Germany, Turkey, and Zionism, 1897–1918.* Oxford 1977 $59.00

Gilbert, Martin. *Atlas of the Arab-Israeli Conflict.* Macmillan 1975 o.p. "This concise book of 101 diligently prepared maps covers the creation and continuing existence of the state of Israel" (*Choice*).

Graetz, Heinrich. *The Structure of Jewish History and Other Essays.* Ktav $20.00 pap. $11.95

Grant, Michael. *Jews in the Roman World.* Scribner 1973 $20.00. Grant traces Jewish history from the Maccabean uprising to the Christianization of the Roman Empire, concentrating on Roman Palestine.

Greenberg, Louis. *The Jews in Russia: The Struggle for Emancipation.* Fwd. by Alfred Levin, AMS Pr. 2 vols. in 1 repr. of 1965 ed. $27.50; ed. by Mark Wishnitzer, Schocken 2 vols. in 1 1976 pap. $11.95. A basic work on the subject covering the period 1772–1917.

Halpern, Ben. *Idea of the Jewish State. Middle Eastern Studies* Harvard Univ. Pr. rev. ed. 1969 $30.00

Hertzberg, Arthur. *French Enlightenment and the Jews.* Columbia Univ. Pr. 1968 $32.00

————, ed. *The Zionist Idea: A Historical Analysis and Reader.* Atheneum text ed. 1969 pap. $7.95; Greenwood repr. of 1959 ed. $23.50

Herzl, Theodor. *The Diaries of Theodor Herzl.* Peter Smith $15.00

Hilberg, Raoul. *The Destruction of the European Jews.* Harper 1979 pap. $11.50; Holmes & Meier text ed. 1984 $105.00

Howe, Irving. *World of Our Fathers.* Bantam 1981 pap. $3.95; Harcourt 1976 $14.95; Pocket Bks. repr. of 1978 ed. pap. $6.95; Simon & Schuster (Touchstone Bks.) 1983 pap. $12.95

Hyman, Louis. *The Jews of Ireland from Earliest Times to the Year 1910.* Irish Academic Pr. 1972 o.p. "The first fully documented history of the Jews of Ireland which traces the origins of the Irish Jewish community from the 11th century until the beginning of the 20th" (*Choice*).

Hyman, Paula. *From Dreyfus to Vichy: The Transformation of French Jewry, 1906–1939.* Columbia Univ. Pr. 1979 $25.00

The Jewish Encyclopedia. Ed. by I. Singer, Gordon 12 vols. 1976 lib. bdg. $998.95

Kahn, Roger. *The Passionate People.* International Publishing 1969 $7.50

Kaplan, Chaim A. *A Scroll of Agony: The Warsaw Diary of Chaim A. Kaplan.* Trans. by Abraham Katsh, Macmillan 1981 pap. $6.95

Katz, Jacob. *From Prejudice to Destruction: Anti-Semitism, 1700–1933.* Harvard Univ. Pr. 1980 $25.00 1982 pap. $7.95

————. *Out of the Ghetto: The Social Background of Jewish Emancipation, 1770–1870.* Harvard Univ. Pr. 1973 $17.50; Schocken repr. of 1973 ed. 1978 pap. $6.95

Kertzer, Morris N. *What Is a Jew?* Bloch Publishing rev. ed. repr. of 1953 ed. 1973 $7.95; Macmillan (Collier Bks.) 1978 pap. $4.95

Klein, Dennis B. *Jewish Origins of the Psychoanalytic Movement.* Praeger 1981 $33.95. A provocative, scholarly study.

Kochan, Lionel, ed. *The Jews in Soviet Russia since 1917.* Oxford 3d ed. 1978 pap. $7.95

Laqueur, Walter. *A History of Zionism.* Holt 1972 $11.95; Schocken repr. 1976 $12.95. "An extremely important book that could be qualified as unique" (*Journal of Modern History*).

Levin, Nora. *The Holocaust: The Destruction of European Jewry, 1933–1945.* Schocken 1973 pap. $12.95

————. *While Messiah Tarried: Jewish Socialist Movements, 1871–1917.* Schocken 1977 $24.50 1979 pap. $10.95

Litvinoff, Barnet, ed. *The Essential Chaim Weizmann: The Man, the Statesman, the Scientist.* Holmes & Meier text ed. 1983 $24.50. An important collection of Weizmann's work.

Lumer, Hyman, ed. *Lenin on the Jewish Question.* International Publishing 1974 $7.50 pap. $2.75. Contains all Lenin's key writings on the Jewish question.

Mann, Jacob. *Texts and Studies in Jewish History and Literature.* Ktav 2 vols. rev. ed. 1970 $79.50

Marrus, Michael R. *The Politics of Assimilation: The French Jewish Community at the Time of the Dreyfus Affair.* Oxford 1980 pap. $19.95

Marrus, Michael R., and Robert O. Paxton. *Vichy France and the Jews.* Basic Bks. 1981 $29.95; Schocken repr. of 1981 ed. 1983 pap. $12.95

McCagg, William O. *Jewish Nobles and Geniuses in Modern Hungary.* East European Monographs East European Quarterly 1973 $15.00

Meir, Golda. *A Land of Our Own: An Oral Autobiography.* Ed. by Marie Syrkin, Putnam 1973 o.p.

————. *My Life*. Dell 1976 pap. o.p. A gripping, well-written autobiography and an excellent study of Jews and the birth of Israel.

Memmi, Albert. *The Liberation of the Jew*. Trans. by Judy Hyun, Viking 1967 $10.00. A Tunisian Jew examines the problems of being Jewish in the modern world.

Mendelsohn, Ezra. *The Jews of East Central Europe between the World Wars*. Indiana Univ. Pr. 1983 $27.50

————. *Zionism in Poland: The Formative Years, 1915–1926*. Yale Univ. Pr. text ed. 1982 $40.00

Mendes-Flohr, Paul R., and Jehuda Reinharz. *The Jews in the Modern World: A Documentary History*. Oxford 1980 $35.00 text ed. pap. $16.95

Meyer, Michael A. *The Origins of the Modern Jew: Jewish Identity and European Culture in Germany, 1749–1824*. Wayne State Univ. Pr. repr. of 1967 ed. 1972 $9.95 pap. $5.95

————, ed. *Ideas of Jewish History*. Lib. of Jewish Studies Behrman 1974 $15.95

Michaelis, Meir. *Mussolini and the Jews: German-Italian Relations and the Jewish Question in Italy, 1922–1945*. Oxford 1978 $55.00. This is an interesting study of the Jews in Italy under Mussolini.

Mosse, George L. *The Crisis of German Ideology: Intellectual Origins of the Third Reich*. Fertig repr. of 1964 ed. 1981 $27.50; Putnam 1964 pap. $3.95

————. *Germans and Jews*. Fertig 1984 $23.50

————. *Toward the Final Solution: A History of European Racism*. Fertig 1978 $27.50; Harper 1980 pap. $4.95; Univ. of Wisconsin Pr. repr. of 1978 ed. text ed. 1985 pap. $12.95.

Niewyk, Donald L. *The Jews in Weimar Germany*. Louisiana State Univ. Pr. 1980 $22.50

Patai, Raphael. *Israel between East and West: A Study in Human Relations*. Greenwood rev. ed. 1970 lib. bdg. $29.95

Patai, Raphael, and Jennifer Wing. *The Myth of the Jewish Race*. Scribner 1975 $6.95

Poppel, Stephen M. *Zionism in Germany, 1897–1933: The Shaping of a Jewish Identity*. Jewish Publication Society 1977 $7.95

Porath, Jonathan D. *Jews in Russia: The Last Four Centuries*. United Synagogue Bk. 1973 pap. $3.75

Reinharz, Jehuda. *Fatherland or Promised Land: The Dilemma of the German Jews, 1893–1914*. Univ. of Michigan Pr. 1975 $16.95

Reitlinger, Gerald. *The Final Solution*. A. S. Barnes rev. ed. 1961 pap. $4.95. Reitlinger has written an excellent book on the Jews, Hitler, and the Holocaust.

Rodinson, Maxime. *Israel: A Colonial Settler State*. Trans. by David Thorstad, intro. by Peter Buch, Monad Pr. 1973 pap. $3.95. This book "places the history of Zionism and Israel in the perspective of European expansion and colonialism in the Third World and upholds the view . . . [that Israel is] a 'colonial settler state' imposed by force on an unwilling Palestinian population" (*Choice*).

Rothenberg, Joshua. *The Jewish Religion in the Soviet Union*. Ktav 1971 $15.00

Sachar, Howard M. *The Course of Modern Jewish History*. Dell (Delta Bks.) rev. & enl. ed. 1977 pap. $12.95

Sanders, Ronald. *The High Walls of Jerusalem: A History of the Balfour Declaration and the Birth of the British Mandate for Palestine*. Holt 1983 $24.95

Sartre, Jean-Paul. *Anti-Semite and Jew*. Schocken 1967 pap. $4.95

Schleunes, Karl A. *The Twisted Road to Auschwitz: Nazi Policy toward German Jews, 1933–1939*. Univ. of Illinois Pr. o.p. Schleunes has become one of the most important historians of Jewish studies, and *The Twisted Road to Auschwitz* is one of the most respected works on the topic.

Scholem, Gershom. *Major Trends in Jewish Mysticism.* Schocken 3d ed. 1961 pap. $8.95

———. *On Jews and Judaism in Crisis: Selected Essays.* Ed. by Werner J. Dannhauser, Schocken repr. 1978 $16.50 pap. $7.95

Schorske, Carl. *Fin-de-Siècle Vienna: Politics and Culture.* Knopf 1980 $16.95; Random 1981 pap. $9.95. "Seven separate studies on Vienna at the turn of the century—politics and culture including a study of Jews, anti-semitism. . . . Not only is it a splendid exploration of several aspects of early modernism in their political context; it is an indicator of how the discipline of intellectual history is currently practiced by its most able and ambitious craftsman. It is also a moving vindication of historical study itself, in the face of modernism's defiant suggestion that history is obsolete" (David A. Hollinger, *History Book Club Review*).

Sklare, Marshall, ed. *America's Jews.* Random 1971 pap. $9.95

———. *The Jewish Community in America.* Lib. of Jewish Studies Behrman text ed. 1974 $15.95

Snyder, Louis L. *The Dreyfus Case: A Documentary History.* Rutgers Univ. Pr. 1973 $27.00. The standard study.

Sokel, Walter H. *The Writer in Extremis: Expressionism in Twentieth Century German Literature.* Stanford Univ. Pr. 1959 $20.00

Sokolow, Nahum. *History of Zionism, 1600–1918.* Ktav 2 vols. in 1 rev. ed. 1969 $45.00

Stein, Leonard. *The Balfour Declaration.* Humanities Pr. repr. of 1961 ed. text ed. 1983 $36.50

Steiner, Jean Francis. *Treblinka.* Intro. by Terrence Des Pres, New Amer. Lib. 1979 pap. $3.95. The best-selling account of the abortive prisoners' revolt in the Treblinka concentration camp.

Tal, Uriel. *Christians and Jews in Germany: Religion, Politics, and Ideology in the Second Reich, 1870–1914.* Trans. by Noah J. Jacobs, Cornell Univ. Pr. 1975 $32.50

Wavell, Archibald P. *The Palestine Campaigns. Select Bibliographies Repr. Ser.* Ayer repr. of 1931 ed. 1972 $34.00. The British general writes of his World War II experiences.

Weinryb, Bernard. *The Jews of Poland: A Social and Economic History of the Jewish Community in Poland from 1100–1800.* Jewish Publication Society 1973 pap. $10.00

Weizmann, Chaim. *Trial and Error: The Autobiography of Chaim Weizmann.* Greenwood repr. of 1949 ed. 1972 lib. bdg. $35.00

Wiesel, Elie. *Jews of Silence.* New Amer. Lib. (Plume) pap. $1.95

———. *Legends of Our Time.* Avon repr. of 1968 ed. 1970 pap. $2.50; Schocken repr. of 1968 ed. 1982 pap. $6.95

Wiesenthal, Simon. *The Murderers among Us: The Simon Wiesenthal Memoirs.* 1967. Ed. by Joseph Wechsberg, Bantam 1973 o.p. Memoirs of a man who dedicated himself to tracking down Nazi war criminals, 900 of whom he brought to justice.

Wilson, Stephen. *Ideology and Experience: Anti-Semitism in France at the Time of the Dreyfus Affair.* Fairleigh Dickinson Univ. Pr. 1982 $60.00

Wistrich, Robert S., ed. *The Left against Zion: Communism, Israel, and the Middle East.* Biblio Dist. 1979 $25.00 pap. $9.95

———. *Revolutionary Jews from Marx to Trotsky.* Fwd. by James Joll, Barnes & Noble text ed. 1976 $19.50

THE MIDDLE EAST: GENERAL

Included in this section are works concerned with general Middle Eastern political history and with economic and social trends and conditions. More specific works are listed under "Separate States," and works on Islam as a belief and way of life are to be found in the section titled "Islam as Idea and Religion."

Ashtor, Eliyahu. *The Medieval Near East: Social and Economic History.* State Mutual Bk. 1978 $60.00

Beaumont, Peter, and others. *The Middle East: A Geographical Study.* Wiley 1976 $59.95 pap. $31.95

Brown, L. Carl, ed. *From Medina to Metropolis: Heritage and Change in the Near Eastern City.* Darwin Pr. text ed. 1973 pap. $17.95

Carter, Jimmy. *The Blood of Abraham: Insights into the Middle East.* Houghton Mifflin 1985 $15.95

Choucri, Nazli, and Vincent Ferraro. *International Politics of Energy Interdependence.* Lexington Bks. 1976 $23.95

Clarke, J. I., and W. B. Fisher. *Populations of the Middle East and North Africa: A Geographical Approach.* Holmes & Meier text ed. 1972 $44.50

Congressional Quarterly, Inc. *Middle East: U.S. Policy, Israel, Oil and the Arabs.* Congressional Quarterly 5th ed. 1981 pap. $10.00

Cook, M. A., ed. *Studies in the Economic History of the Middle East: From the Rise of Islam to the Present Day.* Oxford 1970 $29.95

Costello, V. F. *Urbanization in the Middle East. Urbanization in Developing Countries Ser.* Cambridge Univ. Pr. 1977 $22.95 pap. $9.95

Davis, E. *Challenging Colonialism: Bank Misr and Egyptian Industrialization, 1920–1941.* Princeton Univ. Pr. 1982 $23.50

Fallon, N. *Middle East Oil Money and Its Future Expenditure.* Crane Russak 1976 $19.50; State Mutual Bk. 1976 $19.00

Freedman, Robert O., ed. *The Middle East since Camp David.* Westview Pr. 1984 o.p.

———. *Soviet Policy toward the Middle East since 1970.* Praeger rev. ed. 1978 $37.50

Golan, Galia. *Yom Kippur and After. Soviet and East European Studies* Cambridge Univ. Pr. 1977 $52.50

Haddad, George M. *Revolutions and Military Rule in the Middle East: Egypt, Sudan, Yemen.* Speller 3 vols. ea. $10.00–$12.50

Halpern, Manfred. *Politics of Social Change in the Middle East and North Africa.* Princeton Univ. Pr. 1963 pap. $12.50

Hershlag, Z. Y. *Introduction to the Modern Economic History of the Middle East.* Humanities Pr. repr. of 1964 ed. text ed. 1980 $66.50

Hitti, Philip K. *Islam and the West: A Historical Cultural Survey.* Krieger 1979 pap. $5.95

———. *A Short History of the Near East.* Van Nostrand 1966 o.p. The best survey.

Hourani, Albert. *Arabic Thought in the Liberal Age, 1798–1939.* Cambridge Univ. Pr. 1983 $49.50 pap. $14.95

Issawi, Charles, ed. *The Economic History of the Middle East: A Book of Readings. Midway Repr. Ser.* Univ. of Chicago Pr. 1976 pap. $19.00

———. *An Economic History of the Middle East and North Africa. Economic History of the Modern World Ser.* Columbia Univ. Pr. 1984 pap. $12.50

Jacoby, Neil H. *Multinational Oil: A Study in Industrial Dynamics. Studies of the Modern Corporation Ser.* Macmillan 1974 $17.95 pap. $3.95

Karpat, Kemal H., ed. *Political and Social Thought in the Contemporary Middle East.* Praeger rev. ed. 1982 $37.95 pap. $16.95

Kormoss, I. B., ed. *Oxford Regional Economic Atlas: Western Europe.* Oxford 1971 $19.95 pap. $6.95

Landen, Robert G. *The Emergence of the Modern Middle East: Selected Readings.* Van Nostrand text ed. 1970 pap. $8.95

Lenczowski, George. *The Middle East in World Affairs.* Cornell Univ. Pr. 4th ed. 1980 $42.50 pap. $18.95

Lerner, Daniel. *The Passing of Traditional Society.* Macmillan (Free Pr.) 1964 pap. $2.45

Levy, Reuben. *A Baghdad Chronicle. Studies in Islamic History* Porcupine Pr. repr. of 1929 ed. 1978 lib. bdg. $25.00

Lippman, Thomas W. *Islam: Politics and Religion in the Muslim World.* Foreign Policy Association 1982 pap. $3.00

Longrigg, Stephen H. *Middle East.* Aldine 2d ed. 1970 $29.95

Mansfield, Peter. *The Middle East: A Political and Economic Survey.* Oxford 5th ed. 1980 $35.00

———. *The Ottoman Empire and Its Successors.* St. Martin's 1973 $18.95 pap. $9.95

Mitchell, Richard P. *An Annotated Bibliography on the Modern History of the Near East.* Ctr. for Northeast and North African Studies text ed. 1980 pap. $2.00

Owen, Roger. *Middle East in the World Economy, 1800–1914.* Methuen 1981 $45.00

Pfeiffer, Charles C., and Howard F. Vos. *The Wycliffe Historical Geography of the Bible Lands.* Moody 1967 $19.95

Rosof, Patricia J., and others. *The Middle East and North Africa: Medieval and Modern History.* Haworth Pr. text ed. 1983 $22.95

Said, Edward W. *Orientalism.* Pantheon 1978 $15.00; Random (Vintage) 1979 pap. $6.95

Shwadran, Benjamin. *The Middle East, Oil, and the Great Powers.* Transaction Bks. 3d ed. 1973 $19.95; Westview Pr. repr. of 1955 ed. 1985 pap. $42.50

Vatikiotis, P. J. *Conflict in the Middle East.* Allen & Unwin text ed. 1971 $27.50; Rowman 1971 $15.00

Vita, Finzi Claudio. *Mediterranean Valleys: Geological Change in Historical Times.* Cambridge Univ. Pr. 1969 $34.50

Wiet, Gaston. *Baghdad: Metropolis of the Abbasid Caliphate.* Trans. by Seymour Feiler, *Centers of Civilization Ser.* Univ. of Oklahoma Pr. 1971 $5.95

Yale, William. *Near East: A Modern History. History of the Modern World Ser.* Univ. of Michigan Pr. rev. & enl. ed. 1968 $10.00

ISLAM AS IDEA AND RELIGION

Abdalati, Hammudah. *The Family Structure in Islam.* Amer. Trust 1976 $10.95

Afzal-Ur-Rehman. *Economic Doctrines of Islam.* Kazi 4 vols. $24.50

Ahmed, Ziauddin, and others. *Money and Banking in Islam.* New Era 1983 pap. $12.95

Ali, Abdullah. *The Spirit and the Future of Islam.* Institute for Economic & Political World Strategic Studies 2 vols. 1983 $187.50

Berger, Morroe. *Islam in Egypt Today: Social and Political Aspects of Popular Religion.* Cambridge Univ. Pr. 1970 $29.95

Brett, Michael, and Werner Forman. *The Moors: Islam in the West.* Merrimack 1984 $20.00

Bukhsh, S. K. *The Renaissance of Islam.* Kazi 1981 $29.00

Charnay, J. P. *Islamic Culture and Socio-Economic Change. Social, Economic and Political Studies of the Middle East* Humanities Pr. text ed. 1981 pap. $16.25

Christopher, John B. *The Islamic Tradition. Major Traditions in World Civilization Ser.* Harper text ed. 1972 pap. $11.50

Dawasha, Adeed, ed. *Islam in Foreign Policy.* Cambridge Univ. Pr. 1984 $24.95

Dessouki, Ali. *Islamic Resurgence in the Arab World.* Praeger 1982 $34.95

Donaldson, Dwight M. *The Shi'ite Religion: A History of Islam in Persia and Irak.* AMS Pr. repr. of 1933 ed. $49.50

Esposito, John L. *Women in Muslim Family Law. Contemporary Issues in the Middle East Ser.* Syracuse Univ. Pr. text ed. 1982 pap. $10.95

Farah, Caeser E. *Islam: Beliefs and Observances.* Barron 3d ed. text ed. pap. $4.50

Geertz, Clifford. *Islam Observed: Religious Development in Morocco and Indonesia.* Univ. of Chicago Pr. (Phoenix Bks.) 1971 pap. $5.00; Yale Univ. Pr. 1968 $10.00

Gibb, H. A. R., and J. H. Kramers, eds. *Shorter Encyclopedia of Islam.* Cornell Univ. Pr. 1957 $85.00

Hitti, Philip K. *Islam: A Way of Life.* Regnery-Gateway 1971 pap. $6.95

Holt, Peter M., and others, eds. *Cambridge History of Islam.* Cambridge Univ. Pr. 2 vols. 1970 $178.00 pap. $62.00

Hopwood, Derek. *Middle East and Islam: A Bibliographical Introduction.* International Publishing 1972 $30.00

Hughes, Thomas P. *A Dictionary of Islam.* Gordon 2 vols. 1980 lib. bdg. $199.95

Israeli, R., ed. *Islam in Asia: Southeast and East Asia.* Westview Pr. 1984 $27.50

Keddie, Nikki R., ed. *Scholars, Saints and Sufis: Muslim Religious Institutions since 1500.* Univ. of California Pr. 1972 pap. $8.95

Khalidi, Tarif. *Classical Arab Islam: The Heritage and Culture of the Golden Age.* Darwin Pr. 1984 $17.95

Khumayni, Ruh A. *Islam and Revolution: Writings and Declarations of Imam Khomeini.* Trans. by Hamid Algar, Mizan Pr. 1981 $24.95

Levy, Reuben. *The Social Structure of Islam.* Cambridge Univ. Pr. 1957 $65.00

Lewis, Bernard. *The Muslim Discovery of Europe.* Norton 1982 $19.95

——. *Race and Colour in Islam.* Octagon repr. 1980 lib. bdg. $14.00

Lewis, Bernard, and others, eds. *Encyclopedia of Islam.* Humanities Pr. 5 vols. 1960–78 ea. $185.75–275.50

Lewis, I. M., ed. *Islam in Tropical Africa.* Indiana Univ. Pr. 2d ed. 1980 pap. $10.95

Piscatori, James P., ed. *Islam in the Political Process.* Cambridge Univ. Pr. 1983 $39.50 pap. $14.95

Planhol, Xavier De. *World of Islam.* Cornell Univ. Pr. 1959 pap. $7.95

Rahman, Fazlur. *Islam and Modernity: Transformation of an Intellectual Tradition.* Univ. of Chicago Pr. 1982 lib. bdg. $15.00

Roberts, Robert. *The Social Laws of the Qoran.* Apt Bks. text ed. 1982 $11.95

Rodinson, Maxime. *Islam and Capitalism.* Trans. by Brian Pearce, Univ. of Texas Pr. 1978 pap. $9.95

Siddigri, A. H. *The Islamic Concept of Religion and Its Revival.* Kazi 1981 $19.00

Smith, Wilfred C. *Islam in Modern History.* Princeton Univ. Pr. 1957 $33.00 pap. $8.95

Trimingham, J. Spencer. *The Influence of Islam upon Africa. Arab Background Ser.* Longman 2d ed. text ed. 1980 $27.00

——. *Islam in East Africa.* Ayer repr. of 1964 ed. 1980 lib. bdg. $18.00

Udovitch, A. L., ed. *Islamic Middle East, 700–1900: Studies in Economic and Social History.* Darwin Pr. 1981 $29.95

THE MIDDLE EAST: SEPARATE STATES

Israel

Bain, Kenneth R. *The March to Zion: United States Policy and the Founding of Israel.* Texas A & M Univ. Pr. 1980 $15.95

Bell, J. Bowyer. *Terror out of Zion: The Fight for Israeli Independence, 1929–1949.* Univ. Pr. repr. of 1979 ed. rev. ed. 1984 $17.95

Ben Gurion, David, ed. *The Jews in Their Land.* Doubleday 1974 $9.95

Berler, Alexander. *New Towns in Israel.* Transaction Bks. 1970 $14.95

Dayan, Moshe. *Breakthrough: A Personal Account of the Egypt-Israel Peace Negotiations.* Knopf 1981 $15.00

————. *Diary of the Sinai Campaign.* Greenwood repr. of 1967 ed. 1979 lib. bdg. $24.75; Schocken 1967 pap. $1.95. Dayan's personal account of the 1965 war with the Arabs.

Elazar, Daniel J., and Janet Aviad. *Religion and Politics in Israel: The Interplay of Judaism and Zionism.* Amer. Jewish Committee 1981 pap. $2.50

Evenari, Michael, and Nephtali Tadmor. *The Negev: The Challenge of a Desert.* Harvard Univ. Pr. 2d ed. text ed. 1982 $35.95

Feldman, Lily G. *The Special Relationship between West Germany and Israel.* Allen & Unwin text ed. 1984 $35.00

Freedman, Robert O. *Israel in the Begin Era.* Praeger 1982 $35.95

————, ed. *World Politics and the Arab-Israeli Conflict.* Pergamon 1979 $46.00

Gayron, Daniel. *Israel after Begin.* Houghton Mifflin 1984 $13.95

Herzog, Chaim. *The War of Atonement, October 1973.* Little, Brown 1975 $15.95

Hopkins, I. W. *Jerusalem: A Study in Urban Geography.* Ed. by Charles F. Pfeiffer, *Baker Studies in Biblical Archaeology* 1970 pap. $2.95

Horowitz, Dan, and Moshe Lissak. *Origins of the Israeli Polity: Palestine under the Mandate.* Trans. by Charles Hoffman, Univ. of Chicago Pr. 1979 lib. bdg. $22.00

Kedourie, Elie, and Sylvia G. Haim, eds. *Palestine and Israel in the Nineteenth and Twentieth Centuries.* Biblio Dist. 1982 $39.50

Kollek, Teddy, and Moshe Pearlman. *Jerusalem: A History of Forty Centuries.* Random 1968 o.p.

Krausz, Ernest, ed. *Politics and Society in Israel.* Transaction Bks. text ed. 1984 $29.95 pap. $9.95

Kutcher, Arthur. *The New Jerusalem: Planning and Politics.* MIT 1974 pap. $7.95

Leon, D. *Kibbutz: New Way of Life.* Pergamon 1969 $19.50 pap. $7.75

Orni, Efraim, and Elisha Ofrat. *Geography of Israel.* Jewish Publication Society 3d ed. $13.95

Reinharz, Jehuda. *Chaim Weizmann: The Making of a Zionist Leader.* Oxford 1985 $29.95

Roberts, Samuel J. *Survival or Hegemony? The Foundations of Israeli Foreign Policy.* *Studies in International Affairs* Johns Hopkins Univ. Pr. 1974 $15.00

Sachar, Howard M. *A History of Israel: From the Rise of Zionism to Our Time.* Knopf 1979 $12.95

Safran, Nadav. *United States and Israel.* Amer. Foreign Policy Lib. Harvard Univ. Pr. 1963 $15.00

Schiff, Ze'ev, and Ehud Ya'ari. *Israel's Lebanon War.* Trans. by Ina Freidman, Simon & Schuster 1984 $17.95

Weizman, Ezer. *The Battle for Peace.* Bantam 1981 $15.95

Egypt

Abdel-Fadil, M. *Development, Economic Distribution and Social Change in Rural Egypt, 1952–1970.* Cambridge Univ. Pr. 1976 pap. $17.95

Abu-Lughod, Janet. *Cairo: 1001 Years of the City Victorious.* Princeton Univ. Pr. 1971 $55.00

Aliboni, R., and others. *Egypt's Economic Potential.* Croon Helm 1984 $28.00

Baker, Raymond W. *Egypt's Uncertain Revolution under Nasser and Sadat.* Harvard Univ. Pr. 1978 $17.50

Berque, Jacques. *Egypt.* Faber 1972 $37.50

Bowie, Robert R. *Suez, 1956. International Crisis and the Role of Law Ser.* Oxford 1974 pap. $5.95

Budge, Ernest A. *A Short History of the Egyptian People.* Norwood 1980 lib. bdg. $30.00

Dykstra, Darrell I. *Egypt in the Nineteenth Century: The Impact of Europe upon a Non-Western Society.* Ctr. for Northeast and North African Studies text ed. 1979 pap. $5.00

Gilsenan, Michael. *Saint and Sufi in Modern Egypt: An Essay in the Sociology of Religion. Monographs in Social Anthropology* Oxford 1973 $34.00

Harik, Iliya F. *Political Mobilization of Peasants: A Study of an Egyptian Community.* Indiana Univ. Pr. 1974 $12.50

Harris, Christina. *Nationalism and Revolution in Egypt: The Role of the Muslim Brotherhood.* Hyperion Pr. repr. of 1964 ed. 1981 $24.75

Heikal, Mohamed. *The Sphinx and the Commissar: The Rise and Fall of Soviet Influence in the Arab World.* Harper 1979 $12.95. An analysis of Egyptian relations with the Soviet Union.

Holt, Peter M. *Egypt and the Fertile Crescent, 1516–1922: A Political History.* Cornell Univ. Pr. 1969 pap. $9.95

———, ed. *Political and Social Change in Modern Egypt: Historical Studies from the Ottoman Conquest to the United Arab Republic.* Oxford 1968 $23.00

Hussein, Mahmoud. *Class Conflict in Egypt, 1945–1970.* Trans. by Alfred Ehrenfeld and others, Monthly Review 1973 $13.95 1974 pap. $6.50

Landes, David S. *Bankers and Pashas: International Finance and Economic Imperialism in Egypt.* Harvard Univ. Pr. 1980 pap. $8.95

Mabro, Robert. *The Egyptian Economy, 1952–1972. Economies of the World Ser.* Oxford text ed. 1974 $24.00

———. *The Industrialization of Egypt, 1939–1973: Policy and Performance.* Oxford 1976 $37.00

Richmond, John. *Egypt, 1798–1952: Her Advance toward Modern Identity.* Columbia Univ. Pr. 1977 $25.00

al-Sadat, A. *In Search of Identity: An Autobiography.* Harper 1978 $14.37 1979 pap. $7.64. Excellent autobiography of the late president of Egypt.

al-Sayyid-Marsot, Afaf L. *Egypt's Liberal Experiment, 1922–1936.* Univ. of California Pr. 1977 $36.50

Shoukri, Ghali. *Egypt: Portrait of a President—Sadat's Road to Jerusalem.* Biblio Dist. 1982 $30.00

Vatikiotis, P. J. *The Egyptian Army in Politics.* Greenwood repr. of 1961 ed. 1975 lib. bdg. $25.50

———. *Nasser and His Generation.* St. Martin's 1978 $29.95

Waterbury, John. *The Egypt of Nasser and Sadat: The Political Economy of Two Regimes. Princeton Studies on the Near East* 1983 $45.00 pap. $12.50

Wheelock, Keith. *Nasser's New Egypt. Foreign Policy Research Institute Ser.* Greenwood repr. of 1960 ed. 1975 lib. bdg. $18.25

Iran and Iraq

Adams, Robert McC. *Land Behind Baghdad: A History of Settlement on the Diyala Plains.* Univ. of Chicago Pr. 1965 $22.00

Amirsadeghi, Hossein, ed. *Twentieth-Century Iran.* Holmes & Meier text ed. 1977 $45.00

Barth, Frederik. *Nomads of South Persia: The Basseri Tribe of the Khamseh Confederacy.* Universitet text ed. 1965 $10.00

Batatu, John. *The Old Social Classes and the Revolutionary Movements of Iraq: A Study of Iraq's Old Landed and Commercial Classes and of Its Communists, Ba'thists and Free Officers. Princeton Studies on the Near East* 1979 $120.00 pap. $29.50

Bonnie, Michael E., and Nikki R. Keddie, eds. *Continuity and Change in Modern Iran.* State Univ. of New York Pr. text ed. 1981 pap. $11.95

Cambridge History of Iran. Cambridge Univ. Pr. 5 vols. 1968–83 ea. $74.50–$135.00

Elwell-Sutton, L. P. *Persian Oil: A Study in Power Politics.* Greenwood repr. of 1955 ed. 1975 lib. bdg. $21.50; Hyperion Pr. repr. of 1955 ed. 1976 $19.50

Fesharaki, Fereidun. *The Development of the Iranian Oil Industry: International and Domestic Aspects.* Praeger text ed. 1976 $32.95

Fischer, Michael M. *Iran: From Religious Dispute to Revolution. Harvard Studies in Cultural Anthropology* 1982 pap. $7.95

Ghareeb, Edmund. *The Kurdish Question in Iraq. Contemporary Issues in the Middle East Ser.* Syracuse Univ. Pr. 1981 $22.00 pap. $12.95

Hasan-Ibn-Hasan, Fasa'l. *A History of Persia under Quajar Rule.* Trans. by Herbert Busse, Columbia Univ. Pr. 1972 $34.00

Hooglund, Eric J. *Land and Revolution in Iran, 1960–1980. Modern Middle East Ser.* Univ. of Texas Pr. text ed. 1982 $19.95

Irving, Clive. *Crossroads of Civilization: Three Thousand Years of Persian History.* Barnes & Noble text ed. 1979 $21.50

Ismael, Tareq Y. *Iraq and Iran: Roots of Conflict. Contemporary Issues in the Middle East Ser.* Syracuse Univ. Pr. 1982 $24.00 pap. $12.95

Issawi, Charles. *Economic History of Iran, 1800–1914.* Ed. by William R. Polk, *Publications of the Ctr. for Middle Eastern Studies* Univ. of Chicago Pr. 1971 $25.00

Katouzian, Homa. *The Political Economy of Modern Iran: Despotism and Pseudo-Modernism.* New York Univ. Pr. 1981 $50.00 pap. $20.00

Keddie, Nikki R. *Religion and Politics in Iran: Shi'ism from Quietism to Revolution.* Yale Univ. Pr. text ed. 1983 $27.50

Keddie, Nikki R., and Yann Richard. *Roots of Revolution: An Interpretive History of Modern Iran.* Yale Univ. Pr. text ed. 1981 $32.50 pap. $7.95

Koury, Enver M., and Charles G. MacDonald, eds. *Revolution in Iran: A Reappraisal.* Institute of Middle Eastern & North African Affairs 1982 pap. $7.00

Langley, Kathleen M. *The Industrialization of Iraq. Middle Eastern Monographs Ser.* Harvard Univ. Pr. 1961 pap. $4.50

Longrigg, Stephen H. *Iraq, 1900–1950. Arab Background Ser.* International Bk. Ctr. 1968 $16.00

Looney, Robert E. *Economic Origins of the Iranian Revolution.* Pergamon text ed. 1982 $36.00

al-Marayati, Abid A. *Diplomatic History of Modern Iraq.* Speller 1960 $6.00

Marri, Phebe. *The Modern History of Iraq.* Westview Pr. 1984 lib. bdg. $30.00

Moshiri, Farrokh. *The State and Social Revolution in Iran: A Theoretical Perspective.* Peter Lang text ed. 1984

Penrose, Edith, and E. F. Penrose. *Iraq: Economics, Oil and Politics. Nations of the Modern World Ser.* Westview Pr. 1978 lib. bdg. $42.50

Purser, B. H., ed. *The Persian Gulf.* Springer-Verlag 1973 $53.00

Ramazani, Rouhollah K. *Iran's Foreign Policy, 1941–1973: A Study of Foreign Policy in Modernizing Nations.* Univ. Pr. of Virginia 1975 $20.00

Roux, Georges. *Ancient Iraq.* Penguin 1980 pap. $5.95

Sanasarian, Eliz. *Women's Rights Movement in Iran: Mutiny, Appeasement, and Repression from 1900 to Khomeini.* Praeger 1982 pap. $12.95

Siddique, Kaukab. *Islamic Revolution: The Iranian Experiment.* Ed. by Nadrat Naeem, Amer. Society for Education & Religion 1984 pap. $3.50

Sykes, Perry. *A History of Persia.* Gordon 1976 lib. bdg. $69.95

Tahir-Kheli. *The Iran-Iraq War: Old Conflicts, New Weapons.* Praeger 1983 $26.95

Wilber, Donald N. *Iran Past and Present: From Monarchy to Islamic Republic.* Princeton Univ. Pr. 9th ed. 1981 o.p.

Saudi Arabia and the Arabs

Antonius, George. *The Arab Awakening: The Story of the Arab National Movement.* Gordon 1976 lib. bdg. $75.00; International Bk. Ctr. $22.00

Berger, Morroe. *The Arab World Today.* Octagon repr. of 1962 ed. 1980 lib. bdg. $34.50

———. *The New Metropolis in the Arab World.* Octagon 1973 lib. bdg. $20.00

Fenelon, K. G. *The United Arab Emirates: An Economic and Social Survey.* Longman 2d ed. text ed. 1977 $15.00

Glassman, Jon D. *Arms for Arabs: The Soviet Union and War in the Middle East.* Johns Hopkins Univ. Pr. 1976 $22.50

Glubb, John Bagot. *A Short History of the Arab People.* Stein & Day 1970 pap. $5.95

Hitti, Philip K. *History of the Arabs.* St. Martin's 10th ed. 1970 pap. $16.95

Holden, David, and Richard Johns. *The House of Saud: The Rise and Rule of the Most Powerful Dynasty in the Arab World.* Holt 1981 $19.95

Hopwood, Derek, ed. *The Arabian Peninsula: Society and Politics. Studies on Modern Asia and Africa* Allen & Unwin text ed. 1972 $32.50

Hourani, Albert. *Arabic Thought in the Liberal Age, 1798–1939.* Cambridge Univ. Pr. 1983 $49.50 pap. $14.95

———. *Minorities in the Arab World.* AMS Pr. repr. of 1947 ed. $25.00

Issawi, Charles. *The Arab World's Legacy.* Darwin Pr. 1981 $17.95

Khouri, Fred J. *The Arab-Israeli Dilemma.* Syracuse Univ. Pr. 2d ed. 1976 pap. $8.95

Khuri, Raif. *Modern Arab Thought: Channels of the French Revolution to the Arab East.* Ed. by Charles Issawi, trans. by Ihsan Abbas, Kingston 1983 $29.00

Mack, John E. *A Prince of Our Disorder: The Life of T. E. Lawrence.* Little, Brown 1978 $15.00 pap. $7.95

Patai, Raphael. *The Arab Mind.* Scribner 1983 $24.95 pap. $12.95. "In 16 chapters Patai discusses a number of topics, among them Arab child rearing practices, Bedouin ethos, sexual behavior, the role of Islam and of the Arabic language . . . Arab unity and the Arab's reactions to and relations with the West" (*Choice*).

Patwardhan, Vinayak N., and William J. Darby. *The State of Nutrition in the Arab Middle East.* Vanderbilt Univ. Pr. 1972 $15.00

Pesce, Angelo. *Jiddah: Portrait of an Arabian City.* State Mutual Bk. repr. 1977 $59.95

Polk, William R. *The Arab World (The United States and the Arab World)*. Amer. Foreign Policy Lib. Harvard Univ. Pr. 4th ed. text ed. 1980 $27.50 pap. $10.00

Sherbiny, Nalem A. *Arab Oil: Impact on Arab Countries and Global Implications*. Ed. by Mark A. Tessler, Praeger 1976 $39.95

Young, Hubert W. *The Independent Arab*. AMS Pr. repr. of 1933 ed. $21.50

Turkey

Alderson, Anthony D. *The Structure of the Ottoman Dynasty*. Greenwood repr. of 1956 ed. 1982 lib. bdg. $49.75

Bailey, Frank E. *British Policy and the Turkish Reform Movement: A Study in Anglo-Turkish Relations, 1826–1853*. Fertig repr. of 1942 ed. 1970 $27.50

Bisbee, Eleanor. *The New Turks: Pioneers of the Republic, 1920–1950*. Greenwod repr. of 1951 ed. 1975 $21.75

Davis, P. H., ed. *Flora of Turkey and the East Aegean Islands*. Edinburgh Univ. Pr. 6 vols. 1956–79 ea. $52.50–$125.00; Columbia Univ. Pr. vol. 7 $125.00

Findley, Carter V. *Bureaucratic Reform in the Ottoman Empire: The Sublime Porte, 1789–1922*. Princeton Univ. Pr. 1980 $36.00

Geyikdaqi, Mehmet Y. *Political Parties in Turkey: The Role of Islam*. Praeger 1984 $25.95

Hasluck, F. W. *Christianity and Islam under the Sultans*. Octagon 2 vols. repr. of 1929 ed. lib. bdg. $66.00

Hirsch, Eva. *Poverty and Plenty on the Turkish Farm: An Economic Study of Turkish Agriculture in the 1950's*. Modern Middle East Ser. Columbia Univ. Pr. 1970 pap. $20.00

Howard, Harry N. *Turkey, the Straits, and U.S. Foreign Policy*. Middle East Institute Sponsor Ser. Johns Hopkins Univ. Pr. 1975 $30.00. "An excellent, serious, well-documented analysis of US involvement with and interest in the historic Turkish straits" (*LJ*).

Issawi, Charles. *The Economic History of Turkey, 1800–1914*. Publications of the Ctr. for Middle Eastern Studies Univ. of Chicago Pr. 1981 lib. bdg. $23.00

Kent, Marian, ed. *The Great Powers and the End of the Ottoman Empire*. Allen & Unwin text ed. 1984 $29.95

Kinross, Lord. *The Ottoman Centuries: The Rise and Fall of the Turkish Empire*. Morrow 1979 pap. $10.95

Lewis, Bernard. *The Emergence of Modern Turkey*. Royal Institute of International Affairs Ser. Oxford 1968 pap. $7.95. The best modern survey.

———. *Studies in Classical and Ottoman Islam (7th–16th Centuries)*. State Mutual Bk. 1980 $68.00

Miller, William. *The Ottoman Empire and Its Successors, 1801–1927*. Biblio Dist. new ed. 1966 $39.50; Octagon 1966 lib. bdg. $43.00

Paine, Suzanne. *Exporting Workers: The Turkish Case*. Cambridge Univ. Pr. 1974 $37.50 pap. $19.95

Shaw, S. J. *History of the Ottoman Empire and Modern Turkey*. Cambridge Univ. Pr. 2 vols. 1977 $102.50 pap. $39.50

Vucinich, W. S. *The Ottoman Empire: Its Record and Legacy*. Krieger 1979 pap. $5.95

Webster, D. E. *The Turkey of Ataturk: Social Process in the Turkish Reformation*. AMS Pr. repr. of 1939 ed. $20.00

Weiker, Walter F. *The Modernization of Turkey from Ataturk to the Present Day*. Holmes & Meier text ed. 1981 $42.50

Other States, Areas, and People

Bradsher, Henry S. *Afghanistan and the Soviet Union.* Duke Univ. Pr. 1983 $32.50

Castle, Wilfrid T. *Syrian Pageant: The History of Syria and Palestine, 100 B.C. to A.D. 1945.* Gordon 1977 lib. bdg. $59.95

Demir, Soliman. *The Kuwait Fund and the Political Economy of Arab Regional Development.* Praeger text ed. 1976 $37.95

Dupree, Louis. *Afghanistan.* Princeton Univ. Pr. 1973 $60.00 pap. $12.50

el-Fathaly, Omar I., and Monte Palmer. *Political Development and Social Change in Libya.* Lexington Bks. 1980 $26.50

Fletcher, Arnold. *Afghanistan: Highway of Conquest.* Greenwood repr. of 1965 ed. 1982 lib. bdg. $35.00

Gall, Sandy. *Behind Russian Lines: An Afghan Journal.* St. Martin's 1984 $22.50

Hawley, Donald. *Oman and Its Renaissance.* International Bk. Ctr. 1980 $55.00

————. *The Trucial States.* Allen & Unwin 1971 $12.95

Loizos, Peter. *The Greek Gift: Politics in a Cypriot Village.* St. Martin's 1975 $32.50

Longrigg, Stephen H. *Syria and Lebanon under French Mandate.* Octagon 1972 lib. bdg. $29.00

el-Mallakh, Ragaei. *Economic Development and Regional Cooperation: Kuwait. Publications of the Ctr. for Middle Eastern Studies* Univ. of Chicago Pr. 1968 $11.50

Newell, Nancy P., and Richard S. Newell. *The Struggle in Afghanistan.* Cornell Univ. Pr. 1982 pap. $7.95

Nikolaos, Van Dam. *The Struggle for Power in Syria: Sectarianism, Regionalism and Tribalism in Politics, 1961–1978.* St. Martin's 1979 $26.00

Quandt, William B. *The Politics of Palestinian Nationalism.* Univ. of California Pr. 1973 $25.50 pap. $7.95

Said, Edward W. *The Question of Palestine.* Random (Vintage) 1980 pap. $3.95

Vatikiotis, P. J. *Politics and the Military in Jordan: A Study of the Arab Legion, 1921–1957.* Biblio Dist. 1967 $30.00

Wai, Dunstan M., ed. *The Southern Sudan: The Problem of National Integration.* Biblio Dist. 1973 $29.50

Wenner, Manfred W. *Modern Yemen, 1918–1966. Studies in Historical and Political Science* Johns Hopkins Univ. Pr. 1967 $18.50

AFRICA

The selections here cover all of Africa south of the Sahara, including the black nations and South Africa. No attempt has been made to list books that might more properly be listed under such other major headings as anthropology or archaeology. Rather, the books treat African history from the prehistoric period to the present. One must recognize, of course, that research into African history before the colonial period depends heavily on anthropological and archaeological methods.

Albright, D. E. *Communism in Africa.* Indiana Univ. Pr. 1980 $12.95

Allen, Chris, and Gavin Williams, eds. *Sub-Saharan Africa.* Monthly Review 1982 $18.00 pap. $8.00

Arojan, Lois A., and Richard P. Mitchell. *The Modern Middle East and Northern Africa.* Macmillan text ed. 1984 consult publisher for price

Austin, Dennis. *Politics in Africa.* Univ. Pr. of New England text ed. 1984 $16.00 pap. $8.95

Baylies, Carolyn, and others, eds. *The Dynamics of the One-Party State in Zambia.* Manchester Univ. Pr. 1984 $35.00

Bennett, G. *Kenya: A Political History.* Oxford 1963 o.p. A good survey, clarifying many of the complex historical issues.

Betts, Raymond F., ed. *The Scramble for Africa. Problems in European Civilization* Heath 2d ed. 1972 o.p. Articles by experts on Europe's nineteenth-century rush to colonize.

Bissell, Richard E., and Michael Radu, eds. *Africa in the Post-Decolonization Era.* Transaction Bks. 1984 $29.95 pap. $9.95

Bohannan, Paul, and Philip D. Curtin. *Africa and Africans.* Natural History Pr. 1971 $6.50. An excellent book for the neophyte in African history.

Bonner, Phillip. *Kings, Commoners, Concessionaires: Evolution and Dissolution of the Swazi State.* Cambridge Univ. Pr. 1983 $49.50

Bovill, Edward W., and Robin Hallett. *The Golden Trade of the Moors. Oxford Pap. Ser.* 2d ed. 1968 pap. $7.95. Although now a bit dated, this remains the classic study of old African trade centering on the great city of Timbuktu.

Bowman, Larry W. *Politics in Rhodesia: White Power in an African State.* Harvard Univ. Pr. text ed. 1973 $15.00

Bryant, Arthur T. *The Zulu People as They Were before the White Man Came.* Greenwood repr. of 1949 ed. $31.00

Brzezinski, Zbigniew K., ed. *Africa and the Communist World.* Hoover Institution 1963 $10.00. Occasionally misinformed, but mostly useful articles.

Callaghy, Thomas M., ed. *South Africa in Southern Africa: The Intensifying Vortex of Violence.* Praeger 1983 $45.00

Campling, Elizabeth. *Africa in the Twentieth Century. Twentieth-Century World History Ser.* David & Charles 1980 $14.95

Cartey, Wilfred, and Martin Kilson, eds. *The Africa Reader: Colonial Africa.* Random (Vintage) 2 vols. 1970 pap. ea. $3.95. A useful introduction.

Cassell, Abayomi. *Liberia: History of the First African Republic.* Irvington 2 vols. 1984 ea. $28.50

Christopher, A. J. *Colonial Africa: An Historical Geography.* Barnes & Noble 1984 $28.50

Coapland, Reginald. *The Exploitation of East Africa.* State Mutual Bk. 1967 $5.95. A study of one aspect of European colonialism.

Coleman, James S. *Nigeria: Background to Nationalism.* Univ. of California Pr. 1971 $45.00

Crahan, Margaret, and Franklin W. Knight, eds. *Africa and the Caribbean: Legacies of a Link. Studies in Atlantic History and Culture Ser.* Johns Hopkins Univ. Pr. 1979 $15.00

Crowder, Michael. *The Cambridge History of Africa.* Cambridge Univ. Pr. 1984 vol. 8 $84.50

——. *West African Resistance: The Military Response to Colonial Occupation.* Holmes & Meier text ed. 1971 $35.00. Aspects of the African struggle against colonialism.

Curtin, Philip D. *The Atlantic Slave Trade: A Census.* Univ. of Wisconsin Pr. 1969 pap. $10.95. One of the most scholarly treatments of the subject.

Curtin, Philip D., and others. *African History.* Little, Brown text ed. 1978 pap. $15.95. Probably the best general text, covering all of Africa, including North Africa, from the late Stone Age to the end of the colonial era.

Davenport, T. R. *South Africa: A Modern History.* Univ. of Toronto Pr. 1977 $35.00 pap. $10.95. A reasonable, well-balanced account.

Davidson, Basil. *Africa in History: Themes and Outlines.* Macmillan (Collier Bks.) rev. & enl. ed. 1974 pap. $6.95
———. *The African Genius: An Introduction to Social and Cultural History.* Little, Brown 1970 pap. $6.95
———. *The African Slave Trade.* Little, Brown rev. & enl. ed. 1981 $16.95
———. *Modern Africa.* Longman 1983 pap. $7.95
Denoon, Donald, and Balaam Nyeko. *Southern Africa since 1800.* Longman 2d ed. text ed. 1984 pap. $14.95. A generally sound survey.
Ekundare, R. O. *An Economic History of Nigeria, 1860–1960.* Holmes & Meier text ed. 1973 $35.00. A solid, generally reliable survey.
Elphick, R., and H. Giliomee, eds. *The Shaping of South African Society.* Longman 1980 $30.00 text ed. pap. $12.95. Articles emphasizing the unique social character of South Africa.
Emerson, Rupert, and Martin Kilson, eds. *The Political Awakening of Africa.* Greenwood repr. of 1965 ed. 1981 lib. bdg. $19.75
First, Ruth. *South-West Africa.* Peter Smith $11.00
Fleming, Francis. *Southern Africa.* Scholarly repr. 1981 lib. bdg. $19.00
Forde, C. Daryll, and P. M. Kaberry, eds. *West African Kingdoms in the Nineteenth Century.* Oxford 1967 pap. $14.95. Extremely useful in understanding the African background of modern African history.
Gailey, Harry A., Jr. *The History of Africa.* Krieger 2 vols. text ed. 1981 pap. ea. $11.50–$14.50
———. *The History of Africa in Maps.* Denoyer-Geppert 1979 pap. $6.95
Gann, L. H., and Peter Duignan, eds. *Colonialism in Africa, 1870–1960.* Cambridge Univ. Pr. 5 vols. 1969–73 o.p. A massive collaborative work that covers the subject thoroughly.
Gerhart, Gail M. *Black Power in South Africa: The Evolution of an Ideology. Perspectives on Southern Africa Ser.* Univ. of California Pr. 1978 pap. $7.95
Ghai, Dharam, and Samir Radwin, eds. *Agrarian Policies and Rural Poverty in Africa.* International Labour Office 1983 $21.40
Gibson, Richard. *African Liberation Movements: Contemporary Struggles against White Minority Rule.* Oxford 1972 pap. $4.95. An excellent, informative survey.
Gutteridge, W. F. *Military Regimes in Africa. Studies in African History* Methuen 1975 pap. $9.95. Unfortunately dated by events.
Guy, J. J. *Destruction of the Zulu Kingdom.* Longman 1979 o.p. An excellent book, treating a significant tragedy with insight.
Hallett, Robin. *Africa since 1875: A Modern History. History of the Modern World Ser.* Univ. of Michigan Pr. 1974 $15.00. A competent survey.
Hargreaves, J. D. *The End of Colonial Rule in West Africa: Essays in Contemporary History.* Barnes & Noble text ed. 1979 $25.00
Harrison, David. *The White Tribe of Africa: South Africa in Perspective.* Univ. of California Pr. 1982 $16.95
Hopkins, A. G. *An Economic History of West Africa. Economic History of the Modern World Ser.* Columbia Univ. Pr. 1973 $28.00 pap. $12.50
Houghton, D. Hobart. *The South African Economy.* Oxford 1976 $18.95. The best book on the subject.
Howard, Rhoda. *Colonialism and Underdevelopment in Ghana.* Holmes & Meier text ed. 1978 $35.00
Hull, Richard. *African Cities and Towns before the European Conquest.* Norton 1976 pap. $5.95. An excellent book, well written and perceptive, intended for the informed lay reader.

Iliffe, John. *The Emergence of African Capitalism.* Univ. of Minnesota Pr. 1984 $29.50 pap. $10.95

International Scientific Committee for the Drafting of a General History of Africa. *A General History of Africa.* Unipub 2 vols. 1981 ea. $35.00. Volumes 3–8 will be published over a period of three years.

Isaacman, Allen, and Barbara Isaacman. *Mozambique: Sowing the Seeds of Revolution.* Westview Pr. 1984 lib. bdg. $26.50 text ed. pap. $12.50. The only study of its kind in English.

Johnson, Samuel. *The History of the Yorubas: From the Earliest Times to the Beginning of the British Protectorate.* Routledge & Kegan repr. of 1921 ed. 1969 $32.50

July, Robert W. *A History of the African People.* Scribner 4th ed. 1985 $30.00. Suffers from the author's attempt to cover too much.

Kalu, Ogbu U. *The History of Christianity in West Africa.* Longman text ed. 1981 $28.00

Kaniki, M. H., ed. *Tanzania under Colonial Rule.* Longman text ed. 1980 pap. $10.95

Karis, Thomas, and Gwendolyn M. Carter, eds. *From Protest to Challenge: A Documentary History of Politics in South Africa, 1882–1964.* Hoover Institution 2 vols. 1972–73 ea. $14.50–$17.50. Indispensable to the serious student of South African history.

Kruger, D. W. *The Making of a Nation: A History of the Union of South Africa, 1910–1961.* International Specialized Bk. 1982 $13.50

Latimer, Elizabeth W. *Europe in Africa in the Nineteenth Century.* Greenwood repr. of 1895 ed. $24.75

Legum, Colin. *Pan-Africanism: A Short Political Guide.* Greenwood repr. of 1962 ed. 1976 lib. bdg. $22.75

Lodge, Tom. *Black Politics in South Africa since 1945.* Longman 1983 $30.00 pap. $11.95

Maquet, Jacques. *Africanity: The Cultural Unity of Black Africa.* Oxford 1972 pap. $6.95. Interesting, but suffers from the attempt to justify a faulty premise.

———. *Civilizations of Black Africa.* Oxford 1972 pap. $7.95

Marais, Johannes S. *The Cape Coloured People, 1652–1937.* AMS Pr. repr. of 1939 ed. $27.50. An attempt to define one of the "non-White" groups in South Africa from a historical viewpoint.

Marks, Shula B., and Anthony Atmore, eds. *Economy and Society in Pre-Industrial South Africa.* Longman text ed. 1981 $25.00 pap. $11.95. An excellent collection of articles.

Mason, Philip. *The Birth of a Dilemma: Conflict and Settlement of Rhodesia.* Greenwood repr. of 1958 ed. 1982 lib. bdg. $39.75

Mattiessen, Peter. *The Tree Where Man Was Born.* Dutton 1983 pap. $8.95

Mbiti, John S. *African Religions and Philosophy.* Doubleday (Anchor) 1970 pap. $6.50. A useful survey of a large and complex subject.

McKay, Vernon. *Africa in World Politics.* Greenwood repr. of 1963 ed. lib. bdg. $19.75

McKenzie, J. M. *The Partition of Africa.* Methuen 1983 pap. $3.95

Nattrass, Jill. *The South African Economy: Its Growth and Change.* Oxford 1981 pap. $14.95. An excellent introduction to the subject.

Nickerson, Jane S. *Short History of North Africa.* Biblo & Tannen 1961 $9.00

Obbo, Christine. *African Women: Their Struggle for Economic Independence.* Biblio Dist. 1980 pap. $8.95; State Mutual Bk. 1982 $35.00. Interesting, but too broad in concept.

Odendaal, Andre. *Black Protest Politics in South Africa to 1912.* Barnes & Noble 1984 $28.50

Ogot, Berthwell A., ed. *War and Society in Africa*. Biblio Dist. 1972 $30.00 pap. $12.50. African rivalries before the coming of the Europeans.

Oliver, Roland, and Anthony Atmore. *Africa since 1800*. Cambridge Univ. Pr. 3d ed. 1981 $37.50 pap. $11.95

O'Meara, Dan. *Volkskapitalisme: Class, Capital and Ideology in the Development of Afrikaner Nationalism, 1934–1948*. Cambridge Univ. Pr. 1983 $44.50

Palmer, Robin, and Neil Parsons, eds. *The Roots of Rural Poverty in Central and Southern Africa*. Univ. of California Pr. 1978 $35.00 pap. $9.50

Patterson, Sheila. *The Last Trek: A Study of the Boer People and the Afrikaner Nation*. Greenwood repr. of 1957 ed. 1982 lib. bdg. $27.50

Penrose, Ernest Francis, ed. *European Imperialism and the Partition of Africa*. Biblio Dist. 1975 $30.00. The politics of empire-building by European powers in the nineteenth century.

Phillips, Claude S. *The African Political Dictionary*. ABC-Clio 1983 lib. bdg. $30.00 pap. $14.25

Ranger, T. O., ed. *Aspects of Central African History*. Heinemann text ed. 1968 $12.00. Several articles on a variety of topics.

Rosof, Patricia J., and others. *The Middle East and North Africa: Medieval and Modern History*. Haworth Pr. text ed. 1983 $22.95

Rotberg, Robert I., ed. *Namibia: Political and Economic Prospects*. Lexington Bks. 1982 $20.00. Articles defining and offering solutions for some of Namibia's recent problems.

Sagay, J. O., and D. A. Wilson. *Africa: A Modern History, 1800–1975*. Holmes & Meier text ed. 1981 $29.50 pap. $16.50

Samkange, Stanlake. *Origins of Rhodesia*. Heinemann text ed. 1969 $15.00

Saunders, Christopher, ed. *Black Leaders in Southern African History*. Heinemann text ed. 1979 $17.95 pap. $7.50. Suffers from overenthusiasm for the "leadership" qualities of some of the leaders.

Schneider, H. K. *The African: An Ethnological Account*. Prentice-Hall 1981 pap. $18.95. This kind of study is essential to understanding the people and events in modern African history.

Sillery, Anthony. *Botswana: A Short Political History*. Harper 1974 o.p. An excellent, clearly written summary.

Slade, Ruth. *King Leopold's Congo*. Greenwood repr. of 1962 ed. 1974 lib. bdg. $15.75. A study of Belgian policy in the decades before World War II.

Snowden, Frank M., Jr. *Blacks in Antiquity: Ethiopians in the Greco-Roman Experience*. Harvard Univ. Pr. (Belknap Pr.) 1970 pap. $8.95. Popular in approach, but informative and interesting.

Stevens, Christopher. *The Soviet Union and Black Africa*. Holmes & Meier text ed. 1976 $35.00

Stoneman, Colin, ed. *Zimbabwe's Inheritance*. St. Martin's 1982 $27.50. Rhodesian tradition in Rhodesia's successor state.

Trimingham, J. Spencer. *The Influence of Islam upon Africa*. Arab Background Ser. Longman 2d ed. text ed. 1980 $27.00

Vansina, Jan. *Kingdoms of the Savanna*. Univ. of Wisconsin Pr. 1966 pap. $12.50. Central Africa in the period before European colonization.

Wai, Dunstan M. *The African-Arab Conflict in the Sudan*. Holmes & Meier text ed. 1981 $35.50

Warner, Philip. *Dervish: The Rise and Fall of an African Empire*. Taplinger 1974 $10.95

Weinstein, Warren, and Thomas H. Henriksen, eds. *Soviet and Chinese Aid to African*

Nations. Praeger Special Studies 1980 $33.95. Some articles are speculative, others dated by events.

Welch, Claude E., Jr., ed. *Soldier and State in Africa: A Comparative Analysis of Military Intervention and Political Change.* Northwestern Univ. Pr. 1970 $13.25. The phenomenon of the military dictator is analyzed.

Willett, Frank. *African Art. World of Art Ser.* Oxford 1971 pap. $9.95; Thames & Hudson text ed. 1985 pap. $9.95. A good survey of a subject essential to an understanding of African history.

Wills, A. J. *An Introduction to the History of Central Africa.* Oxford 4th ed. 1984 $37.50 pap. $18.95

Wilson, Monica, and Leonard M. Thompson, eds. *A History of South Africa to 1870.* Westview Pr. 1983 lib. bdg. $37.50 text ed. pap. $14.50. Originally published as Volume 1 of *The Oxford History of South Africa.*

———. *The Oxford History of South Africa: South Africa, 1870–1966.* Oxford text ed. 1971 vol. 2 $11.95. Companion to volume listed above.

Zartman, I. William, ed. *The Political Economy of Nigeria.* Praeger 1983 $33.95 pap. $15.95. Extremely useful articles.

ASIA: GENERAL

As in earlier sections, this one on Asia begins with a listing of general works on all of Asia and works concerned with more than one country or area. This section is followed by listings for separate states and areas.

Allworth, Edward A., ed. *Central Asia: A Century of Russian Rule.* Columbia Univ. Pr. 1967 $39.00

Almond, Gabriel A., and G. Bingham Powell, Jr. *Comparative Politics Today: A World View.* Little, Brown 2d ed. text ed. 1980 $21.95 3d ed. text ed. 1984 $24.95

Bingham, Woodbridge, and others. *A History of Asia.* Allyn & Bacon 2 vols. 2d ed. text ed. 1974 ea. $15.95

Bloodworth, Dennis. *An Eye for the Dragon: Southeast Asia Observed, 1954–1970.* Farrar 1970 $8.95

Cady, John F. *The History of Postwar Southeast Asia: Independence Problems.* Univ. of Ohio Pr. 1975 $26.00 pap. $12.00

Case, C. M. *South Asian History, 1750–1950: A Guide to Periodicals, Dissertations and Newspapers.* Princeton Univ. Pr. 1967 $60.00

Clyde, Paul H., and Burton F. Beers. *Far East: A History of Western Impacts and Eastern Responses (1830–1975).* Prentice-Hall 6th ed. 1976 $33.95

Coedes, G. *Indianized States of Southeast Asia.* Ed. by Walter F. Vella, trans. by Susan B. Cowing, Univ. of Hawaii Pr. 1968 $17.50

———. *The Making of Southeast Asia.* Trans. by H. M. Wright, Univ. of California Pr. 1969 $18.50 1983 pap. $8.95

Dodge, Ernest S. *Islands and Empires: Western Impact on the Pacific and East Asia.* Univ. of Minnesota Pr. 1976 $17.50 1978 pap. $5.95. This is an interesting history of the European impact upon the Pacific islands and East Asia.

Fairbank, John K., and Albert M. Craig. *East Asia: Tradition and Transformation.* Houghton Mifflin 2d ed. text ed. 1978 $30.95. (See Fairbank's main listing in this chapter.)

Fisher, Charles. *South East Asia.* Methuen 2d ed. 1966 $65.00

Gratton, Clinton Hartley. *The Southwest Pacific to 1900.* Univ. of Michigan Pr. 1963

$15.00. This scholarly yet readable work covers the cultural history of Australia, New Zealand, the islands—mainly the Fijis, Samoa, New Caledonia, and New Guinea—and Antarctica.

Hall, D. G. *A History of South East Asia.* St. Martin's 4th ed. 1981 $37.50 pap. $15.95

Harrison, John A. *The Founding of the Russian Empire in Asia and America.* Univ. of Miami Pr. 1982 $10.95

Henderson, William, ed. *Southeast Asia: Problems of United States Policy.* MIT text ed. 1964 pap. $10.00

Hodgson, Marshall G. *The Gunpowder Empires and Modern Times.* Vol. 3 in *The Venture of Islam.* Univ. of Chicago Pr. (Phoenix Bks.) 1977 pap. $9.50

Iriye, Akira. *After Imperialism: The Search for a New Order in the Far East, 1921–1931.* Atheneum text ed. 1969 pap. $5.95. By a Japanese who became a U.S. citizen, an "impressive work" (*LJ*).

Kearney, Robert N., ed. *Politics and Modernization in South and Southeast Asia.* Schenkman 1975 pap. $7.95

Lach, Donald F., and Edmund S. Wehrle. *International Politics in East Asia since World War Two.* Praeger text ed. 1975 $29.95 pap. $8.95

Matthew, Helen G., ed. *Asia in the Modern World.* New Amer. Lib. 1963 pap. $1.25

Michael, F., and G. Taylor. *The Far East in the Modern World.* Holt 3d ed. text ed. 1975 $18.95

Myrdal, Gunnar. *Asian Drama: An Inquiry into the Poverty of Nations.* Kraus 3 vols. repr. of 1968 ed. $30.00; Pantheon 3 vols. 1968 pap. $10.00; Random (Vintage) 1972 pap. $4.95

Pearn, B. R. *An Introduction to the History of South East Asia.* Humanities Pr. text ed. 1965 pap. $3.50

Peffer, Nathaniel. *The Far East: A Modern History.* Ed. by Claude A. Buss, *History of the Modern World Ser.* Univ. of Michigan Pr. rev. & enl. ed. 1968 $15.00

Pye, Lucian W. *Southeast Asia's Political Systems. Comparative Asian Government Ser.* Prentice-Hall 2d ed. text ed. 1974 $10.95 pap. $7.95

Steinberg, David J., and others. *In Search of Southeast Asia: A Modern History.* Univ. of Hawaii Pr. repr. of 1971 ed. text ed. 1985 pap. $14.95

Ward, Barbara. *Interplay of East and West: Points of Conflict and Cooperation.* 1957. *Norton Lib.* 1962 pap. $1.25. (See Ward's main listing in this chapter.)

Welty, Paul T. *The Asians: Their Heritage and Their Destiny.* Harper 5th ed. text ed. 1976 pap. $9.50

Wilcox, Wayne Ayres. *The Emergence of Bangladesh: Problems and Opportunities for a Redefined American Policy in South Asia.* Amer. Enterprise Institute 1973 pap. $4.25

Zabriskie, E. H. *American-Russian Rivalry in the Far East, 1895–1914.* Greenwood repr. of 1946 ed. 1973 lib. bdg. $15.00

ASIA: SEPARATE STATES AND AREAS

China

Baker, Hugh. *Chinese Family and Kinship.* Columbia Univ. Pr. 1979 $27.50 pap. $10.50

Baum, Richard. *Prelude to Revolution: Mao, the Party, and the Peasant Question, 1962–66.* Columbia Univ. Pr. 1975 $23.00

Bennett, Gordon A., and Ronald N. Montaperto. *Red Guard: The Political Biography of Dai Hsiao Ai.* Peter Smith $11.00

Bernstein, Thomas P. *Up to the Mountains and Down to the Villages: The Transfer of Youth from Urban to Rural China.* Yale Univ. Pr. 1977 $30.00

Berton, Peter, and Eugene Wu. *Contemporary China: A Research Guide.* Hoover Institution 1967 $25.00. Contains 2,226 entries of books, periodicals, and theses published mainly after 1949 in Communist China and after 1945 in Taiwan.

Bloodworth, Dennis. *The Chinese Looking Glass.* Farrar rev. ed. 1980 $15.00 pap. $8.95

Bonavia, David. *The Chinese.* Harper 1980 $14.37; Penguin rev. ed. 1983 pap. $5.95

Cell, C. P., ed. *Revolution at Work: Mass Campaigns in China. Studies in Social Discontinuity* Academic Pr. 1977 $42.50

Chang, Parris H. *Power and Policy in China.* Pennsylvania State Univ. Pr. 2d ed. enl. 1978 $24.95 text ed. pap. $12.50

Ch'en, Jerome. *Mao and the Chinese Revolution: With Thirty-Seven Poems by Mao Tsetung.* Oxford 1967 pap. $6.95

Ch'en, Jerome, and Nicholas Tarling, eds. *Studies in the Social History of China and South-East Asia.* Cambridge Univ. Pr. 1970 $54.50

Chen, Lung Chu, and Harold D. Lasswell. *Formosa, China, and the United Nations: Formosa in the World Community.* St. Martin's 1967 $8.95

Clayre, Alasdair. *The Heart of the Dragon.* Houghton Mifflin 1985 $29.95

Clubb, O. Edmund. *Twentieth-Century China.* Columbia Univ. Pr. 3d ed. 1978 $35.00 pap. $14.00

Creel, H. G. *Confucius and the Chinese Way.* Peter Smith $6.00

Eastman, Lloyd E. *The Abortive Revolution: China Under Nationalist Rule, 1927–1937. Harvard East Asian Monographs* text ed. 1974 $25.00

Ebrey, Patricia B., ed. *Chinese Civilization and Society: A Sourcebook.* Macmillan (Free Pr.) 1981 $19.95 text ed. pap. $12.95

Eckstein, A. *China's Economic Revolution.* Cambridge Univ. Pr. 1977 $59.50 pap. $15.95

Esherick, Joseph W. *Reform and Revolution in China: The 1911 Revolution in Hunan and Hubei.* Univ. of California Pr. 1976 $34.00

Fitzgerald, Charles P. *China: A Short Cultural History.* Praeger 3d ed. text ed. 1954 pap. $7.95; Quaker City Bks. 1942 $20.00

Gittings, John. *A Chinese View of China.* Pantheon 1973 $6.95 pap. $2.95

———. *The Role of the Chinese Army. Royal Institute of International Affairs Ser.* Greenwood repr. of 1967 ed. 1981 lib. bdg. $32.50; Oxford 1967 $19.95

Goodrich, L. Carrington. *A Short History of the Chinese People.* Harper pap. $6.50

Hebert, Jacques, and Pierre E. Trudeau. *Two Innocents in Red China.* Oxford 1968 $5.50. A lighthearted account of the authors' visit to Communist China in 1960.

Heng, Liang, and Judith Shapiro. *Son of the Revolution.* Intro. by Jerome A. Cohen, Knopf 1983 $15.00; Random (Vintage) 1984 pap. $5.95

Ho, Ping-Ti, and Tang Tsou, eds. *China in Crisis: China's Heritage and the Communist Political System.* Fwd. by Charles U. Daly, Univ. of Chicago Pr. 2 vols. 1968 ea. $11.50–$12.50; Univ. of Chicago Pr. (Phoenix Bks.) 1970 pap. ea. $3.45–$3.95

Houn, Franklin W. *Short History of Chinese Communism: Completely Updated.* Prentice-Hall rev. ed. 1973 $8.95; Prentice-Hall (Spectrum Bks.) pap. $3.95

Hsieh, Alice L. *Communist China's Strategy in the Nuclear Era.* Greenwood repr. of 1962 ed. 1976 lib. bdg. $18.75

Jacobsen, C. G. *Sino-Soviet Relations since Mao: The Chairman's Legacy.* Praeger 1981 $33.95

Jungk, Robert. *China and the West: Mankind Evolving.* Humanities Pr. text ed. 1970 $10.50

Karnow, Stanley. *Mao and China: From Revolution to Revolution*. Penguin 1984 pap. $7.95; Viking 1972 $15.00

Karol, K. S. *China: The Other Communism*. Trans. by Tom Baistow, Hill & Wang rev. ed. 1968 pap. $3.95. A comparison of communism in China and Russia by a former Soviet citizen.

Klein, Donald W., and Anne B. Clark. *Biographical Dictionary of Chinese Communism, 1921–1965*. Harvard East Asian Ser. 2 vols. 1970 $65.00

Lall, Arthur. *How Communist China Negotiates*. Columbia Univ. Pr. 1968 $25.00 pap. $12.00. The former Indian ambassador to the United Nations describes Chinese diplomacy during the 14-month conference in Laos, 1961–1962.

Lifton, Robert J. *Revolutionary Immortality: Mao Tse-tung and the Chinese Revolution*. Peter Smith $5.25

——. *Thought Reform and the Psychology of Totalism*. Norton Lib. 1963 pap. $9.95

Mao Tse-tung. *Quotations from Chairman Mao Tse-tung*. China Bks. 2d ed. 1967 $1.95

Meisner, Maurice J. *Li Ta-Chao and the Origins of Chinese Marxism*. Atheneum text ed. 1970 pap. $6.95

Meskill, John, ed. *An Introduction to Chinese Civilization*. Heath text ed. 1973 pap. $16.95; *Companion to Asian Studies Ser.* Columbia Univ. Pr. 1973 $37.50

Myrdal, Jan. *China: The Revolution Continued*. Random (Vintage) 1972 pap. $2.95

——. *Report from a Chinese Village*. Pantheon Village Ser. 1981 pap. $6.95; Random (Vintage) 1972 pap. $6.95

Needham, Joseph. *Science and Civilization in China*. Cambridge Univ. Pr. 5 vols. consult publisher for individual volumes and prices

Overmeyer, Daniel L. *Folk Buddhist Religion: Dissenting Sects in Late Traditional China*. Harvard East Asian Ser. 1967 $15.00

Parish, William L., and Martin K. Whyte. *Village and Family in Contemporary China*. Univ. of Chicago Pr. (Phoenix Bks.) 1978 lib. bdg. $30.00 pap. $12.00

Pye, Lucian W. *The Spirit of Chinese Politics: A Psychocultural Study of the Crisis in Political Development*. MIT 1968 $12.50

Rawski, Evelyn S. *Education and Popular Literacy in Ch'ing China*. Michigan Studies on China Univ. of Michigan Pr. text ed. 1979 $16.50

Rice, Edward E. *Mao's Way*. Univ. of California Pr. 1972 pap. $4.95

Salisbury, Harrison E. *Orbit of China*. Harper 1967 $10.00

——. *To Peking and Beyond: A Report on the New Asia*. Times Bks. 1973 $7.95

Schiffrin, Harold Z. *Sun Yat-Sen and the Origins of the Chinese Revolution*. Univ. of California Pr. 1968 $33.50

Schram, Stuart R. *Mao Zedong: A Preliminary Reassessment*. St. Martin's 1983 $22.50. "An engrossing account of the momentous Chinese revolution and the man who bought it off. [This] can be read with profit by specialist and layman alike" (*N.Y. Times*).

——, ed. *Chairman Mao Talks to the People: Talks and Letters, 1956–1971*. Pantheon 1975 pap. $6.95

Schurmann, Franz. *Ideology and Organization in Communist China*. Univ. of California Pr. 2d ed. enl. 1968 pap. $7.95

Seymour, James D., ed. *The Fifth Modernization: China's Human Rights Movement, 1978–1979*. Intro. by Mab Huang, E. M. Coleman text ed. 1980 $19.50

Short, Philip. *The Dragon and the Bear: Inside China and Russia Today*. Morrow 1983 $19.95

Snow, Edgar. *The Long Revolution*. Random (Vintage) 1973 pap. $1.95

——. *Red China Today: The Other Side of the River*. Random rev. ed. 1971 $25.00

———. *Red Star Over China.* Bantam 1978 pap. $4.95; Grove rev. ed. 1968 $10.00 pap. $8.95

Solinger, Dorothy. *Regional Government and Political Integration in Southwest China, 1949–1954: A Case Study.* Univ. of California Pr. 1977 $41.00

Spence, Jonathan. *The Death of Woman Wang.* Penguin 1979 pap. $5.95; Viking 1978 $12.95

Terrill, Ross. *800,000,000: The Real China.* Dell (Delta) 1972 o.p.

Trager, Frank N., ed. *Communist China, 1949–1969: A Twenty Year Appraisal.* Ed. by William Henderson, New York Univ. Pr. 1970 $12.00

Tsou, Tang. *America's Failure in China, 1941–1950.* Univ. of Chicago Pr. (Phoenix Bks.) 1967 vol. 2 pap. $3.95

———, ed. *China in Crisis: China's Policies in Asia and America's Alternatives.* Fwd. by Charles U. Daly, Univ. of Chicago Pr. 1968 vol. 2 $15.00. An assessment of the Open Door policy in China.

Tuchman, Barbara. *Stilwell and the American Experience in China, 1911–45.* Bantam 1972 pap. $5.95; Macmillan 1971 $21.95. (See Tuchman's main listing in this chapter.)

Vogel, Ezra F. *Canton under Communism: Programs and Politics in a Provincial Capital, 1949–1968.* Harvard East Asian Ser. 1969 $22.50 pap. $8.95

Wakeman, Frederic, Jr. *The Fall of Imperial China. Transformation of Modern China Ser.* Macmillan (Free Pr.) 1975 $10.95 text ed. pap. $8.95

———. *History and Will: Philosophical Perspectives of Mao Tse-tung's Thought.* Univ. of California Pr. 1976 pap. $9.50

Wang, James C. *Contemporary Chinese Politics: An Introduction.* Prentice-Hall 2d ed. text ed. 1985 pap. $17.95

Wang, Yi-C. *Chinese Intellectuals and the West, 1872–1949.* Univ. of North Carolina Pr. 1966 $19.50

Whiting, Allen S., and Robert F. Dernberger. *China's Future: Foreign Policy and Economic Development in the Post Mao Era.* McGraw-Hill 1977 $18.50

Whyte, Martin K. *Small Groups and Political Rituals in China.* Univ. of California Pr. 1974 $31.00

Wilson, Dick. *The Long March, 1935.* Avon repr. 1973 pap. $1.95; Penguin 1982 pap. $6.95; Viking 1972 $8.95

Wylie, Raymond F. *The Emergence of Maoism: Mao Tse-tung, Ch'en Po Ta, and the Search for Chinese Theory, 1935–1945.* Stanford Univ. Pr. 1980 $27.50

Young, Arthur N. *China's Nation Building Effort, 1927–1937: The Financial and Economic Record.* Hoover Institution 1971 $22.50

Japan

Akita, George. *Foundations of Constitutional Government in Modern Japan, 1868–1900.* Harvard Univ. Pr. 1967 $18.50

Barnet, Richard J. *The Alliance: America, Europe, Japan—Makers of the Post-War World.* Simon & Schuster 1983 $19.95

Beasley, W. G. *The Meiji Restoration.* Stanford Univ. Pr. 1972 $35.00

———. *The Modern History of Japan.* St. Martin's 3d ed. 1981 $27.50

Benedict, Ruth. *The Chrysanthemum and the Sword: Patterns of Japanese Culture.* Houghton Mifflin $8.95; New Amer. Lib. 1967 pap. $7.95

Borg, Dorothy, and Okamoto Shumpei, eds. *Pearl Harbor as History: Japanese-American Relations, 1931–1941. Studies of the East Asian Institute* Columbia Univ. Pr. 1973 $50.00 pap. $18.00

Bowen, Roger W. *Rebellion and Democracy in Meiji Japan: A Study of Commoners in the Popular Rights Movement*. Univ. of California Pr. 1980 $36.50

Brzezinski, Zbigniew K. *The Fragile Blossom: Crisis and Change in Japan*. Harper 1972 $10.00

Burkman, Thomas W., ed. *The Occupation of Japan: The International Context*. MacArthur Memorial 1984 pap. $10.00

Chapman, J. W., and R. Drifte, eds. *Japan's Quest for Comprehensive Security: Defense, Diplomacy and Dependence*. St. Martin's 1983 $25.00

Cooper, Michael. *Introduction to Japanese History and Culture*. Pergamon 1971 pap. $3.94

Curtis, Gerald. *Election Campaigning Japanese Style*. Kodansha 1984 pap. $5.95

Dore, Ronald P. *British Factory, Japanese Factory: The Origins of National Diversity in Employment Relations*. Univ. of California Pr. 1973 $31.00 pap. $9.95

Dower, J. W. *Empire and Aftermath: Yoshida Shigeru and the Japanese Experience, 1878–1954*. Harvard East Asian Monographs text ed. 1979 $30.00

———. *Japanese History, Politics, and Society: A Bibliographic Guide*. Wiener 1984 consult publisher for price

Dunn, Charles J. *Everyday Life in Traditional Japan*. Tuttle 1977 pap. $5.25

Duus, Peter. *The Rise of Modern Japan*. Houghton Mifflin text ed. 1976 $22.50

Earl, David M. *Emperor and Nation in Japan: Political Thinkers of the Tokugawa Period*. Greenwood repr. of 1964 ed. 1981 lib. bdg. $25.00

Elison, George. *Deus Destroyed: The Image of Christianity in Early Modern Japan*. Harvard East Asian Ser. 1974 $37.50

Fairbank, John K., and Albert M. Craig. *East Asia: Tradition and Transformation*. Houghton Mifflin 2d ed. text ed. 1978 $30.95

Fletcher, Miles. *The Search for a New Order: Intellectuals and Fascism in Prewar Japan*. Univ. of North Carolina Pr. 1982 $24.00

Fukutake, Tadashi. *Japanese Society Today*. Columbia Univ. Pr. 2d ed. 1981 pap. $9.50

Gibney, Frank. *Japan: The Fragile Superpower*. New Amer. Lib. rev. ed. 1985 pap. $8.95; Norton rev. ed. 1979 $12.95

Hackett, Roger F. *Yamagata Aritomo in the Rise of Modern Japan, 1838–1922*. Harvard East Asian Ser. 1971 $15.00

Hall, Ivan P. *Mori Arinori*. Harvard East Asian Ser. 1973 $32.50

Hall, John W. *Government and Local Power in Japan: A Study Based on the Bizen Province, 500–1700*. Princeton Univ. Pr. 1981 $30.00 pap. $14.50

———. *Japan*. Dell (Delta) 1971 pap. $10.95

Hall, John W., and others, eds. *Japan before Tokugawa: Political Consolidation in Economic Growth, 1500 to 1650*. Princeton Univ. Pr. 1981 $33.00

———. *Studies in the Institutional History of Early Modern Japan*. Intro. by J. R. Strayer, Princeton Univ. Pr. 1968 $33.00 pap. $11.50

Hanley, Susan B., and Kozo Yamamura. *Economic and Demographic Change in Preindustrial Japan, 1600–1868*. Princeton Univ. Pr. 1978 $44.00 pap. $16.50

Jones, Francis C. *Japan's New Order in East Asia: Its Rise and Fall, 1937–45*. AMS Pr. repr. of 1954 ed. $40.00

Komuta, Kensaburo. *Japan's Economy in World Perspective*. Ed. by Molleen Matsumura, Alin Foundation 1983 $7.95

Kosaka, Masataka. *A History of Postwar Japan*. Kodansha 1982 pap. $6.25

Kosaka, Masataka, and Edwin O. Reischauer. *One Hundred Million Japanese*. Kodansha 1972 $10.50

Lee, Thomas B., ed. *Modern History of China and Japan.* Irvington text ed. 1972 pap. $6.95

Leonard, Jonathan N. *Early Japan.* Time-Life 1968 $13.95

Lifton, Robert J. *Death in Life: Survivors of Hiroshima.* Basic Bks. 1982 $18.75 pap. $10.50

Livingston, Jon, and Felicia Oldfather. *The Japan Reader.* Pantheon 2 vols. 1974 pap. ea. $10.95

Lockwood, William W. *The Economic Development of Japan: Growth and Structural Change, 1868–1938.* Princeton Univ. Pr. rev. ed. 1969 $35.00 pap. $7.95

Mason, Richard, and John Caiger. *A History of Japan.* Macmillan (Free Pr.) 1973 $10.95

Matsumura, Gentaro. *The Emperor's Island: The Story of Japan.* Univ. of Chicago Pr. (Phoenix Bks.) 1977 pap. $6.95

Mizuno, Soji. *Early Foundations for Japan's Twentieth-Century Economic Emergence.* Vantage 1981 $8.95

Morton, W. Scott. *Japan: Its History and Culture.* Apollo Eds. Crowell 1975 pap. $2.95; McGraw-Hill 1984 $7.95

Myers, Ramon H., and Mark R. Peattie, eds. *The Japanese Colonial Empire, 1895–1945.* Princeton Univ. Pr. 1984 $47.50

Neumann, William L. *America Encounters Japan: From Perry to MacArthur.* Johns Hopkins Univ. Pr. 1963 $28.50

O'Connor, Edmund. *Japan's Modernization.* Ed. by Malcolm Yapp and Marget Killingray, Greenhaven Pr. repr. of 1977 ed. 1980 lib. bdg. $6.95 text ed. pap. $2.45

Ohkawa, Kazushi, and Henry Rosovsky. *Japanese Economic Growth: Trend Acceleration in the Twentieth Century.* Stanford Univ. Pr. 1973 $25.00

Ozaki, Robert S., and Walter Arnold, eds. *Japan's Foreign Relations: A Global Search for Economic Security.* Westview Pr. 1984 $27.00 text ed. pap. $12.95

Packard, George R. *Protest in Tokyo: The Treaty Crisis of 1960.* Greenwood repr. of 1966 ed. 1978 lib. bdg. $32.25

Pascale, Richard T., and Anthony G. Althos. *The Art of Japanese Management: Applications for American Executives.* Simon & Schuster 1981 $11.95; Warner Bks. 1982 pap. $4.95

Plummer, Katherine. *The Shogun's Reluctant Ambassadors.* Tuttle 1984 pap. $8.25

Pyle, Kenneth B. *The Making of Modern Japan: An Introduction.* Heath text ed. 1977 pap. $7.95

Reischauer, Edwin O. *Japan: The Story of a Nation.* Knopf rev. ed. 1974 $15.95 text ed. pap. $12.00

Royama, Masamichi. *Foreign Policy of Japan, 1914–1939.* Greenwood repr. of 1941 ed. 1973 lib. bdg. $15.00

Sansom, George. *A History of Japan, 1615–1867.* Stanford Univ. Pr. 1963 $17.50 pap. $7.95

———. *A History of Japan, 1334–1615.* Stanford Univ. Pr. 1961 $25.00 pap. $10.95

———. *A History of Japan to 1334.* Stanford Univ. Pr. 1958 $25.00 pap. $10.95

———. *Japan: A Short Cultural History.* Stanford Univ. Pr. 1952 rev. ed. $32.50 pap. $10.95

Smith, Thomas C. *The Agrarian Origins of Modern Japan.* Stanford Univ. Pr. 1959 $20.00 pap. $6.95

Statler, Oliver. *Japanese Inn: A Reconstruction of the Past.* Univ. of Hawaii Pr. repr. of 1961 ed. 1982 pap. $8.95. A very readable study of Japanese culture.

Storry, Richard. *The Double Patriots: A Study of Japanese Nationalism.* Greenwood repr. of 1957 ed. 1973 lib. bdg. $21.50

————. *Japan and the Decline of the West in Asia*. St. Martin's 1979 $22.50

Thayer, Nathaniel B. *How the Conservatives Rule Japan. Studies of the East Asian Institute* Princeton Univ. Pr. 1969 $33.00

Toland, John. *The Rising Sun: The Decline and Fall of the Japanese Empire: 1936–1945*. Bantam 1971 pap. $5.95; Random 1970 $25.00

Turnbull, S. R. *The Samurai: A Military History*. Seven Hills Bks. repr. of 1977 ed. 1983 $29.95

Vogel, Ezra F. *Japan's New Middle Class: The Salary Man and His Family in a Tokyo Suburb*. Univ. of California Pr. enl. ed. 1971 $29.50

Warshaw, Steven, and C. David Bromwell. *Japan Emerges: A Concise History of Japan from Its Origin to the Present*. Univ. Pr. of Amer. text ed. 1983 pap. $7.75

Wolfe, Robert. *Americans as Proconsuls: United States Military Government in Germany and Japan, 1944–1952*. Southern Illinois Univ. Pr. 1984 $27.50

Wray, Harry, and Hilary Conroy, eds. *Japan Examined: Perspectives on Modern Japanese History*. Univ. of Hawaii Pr. 1983 lib. bdg. $22.50 text ed. pap. $12.95

Yamamura, Kozo. *Economic Policy in Postwar Japan: Growth versus Economic Democracy*. Univ. of California Pr. 1967 $30.00

The Indian Subcontinent

Ahmed, Abkar S. *Religion and Politics in Muslim Society: Order and Conflict in Pakistan*. Cambridge Univ. Pr. 1983 $39.50

Basham, A. L. *The Wonder That Was India: A Survey of the History and Culture of the Indian Sub Continent before the Coming of the Muslims*. Merrimack 1983 $34.95; Taplinger 1968 $13.50

Bhattacharya, Sachchidananda. *A Dictionary of Indian History*. Greenwood repr. of 1972 ed. 1977 lib. bdg. $58.50

Bondurant, Joan V. *Conquest of Violence: The Gandhian Philosophy of Conflict*. Univ. of California Pr. rev. ed. 1965 $25.00. "One of the most exciting political theory books in recent years. The work has two merits: first, it gives us the clearest and most powerful statement to date of the central ideas of Gandhi's political thought; second, it forces us to consider these ideas not as historical or cultural curiosities, but as a challenge to the main body of Western political philosophy" (*Pacific Affairs*).

Bowles, Chester. *View from New Delhi: Selected Speeches and Writings*. Yale Univ. Pr. 1969 $22.50

Brown, D. M. *The Nationalist Movement: Indian Political Thought from Ranade to Bhave*. Peter Smith 1962 $7.00. ". . . a good introduction to a greater understanding of Indian political thought in its own milieu" (*American Political Science Review*).

Brown, Judith M. *Modern India: The Origins of an Asia Democracy. Short Oxford History of the Modern World Ser*. 1984 $32.50 pap. $12.95

Brown, W. Norman. *The United States and India, Pakistan, Bangladesh. Amer. Foreign Policy Lib*. Harvard Univ. Pr. 3d ed. 1972 $27.50 pap. $8.95

The Cambridge History of India. Cambridge Univ. Pr. 6 vols. 1955–70 o.p.

Chaudhuri, Nirad C. *The Autobiography of an Unknown Indian*. Univ. of California Pr. 1968 $21.50

Chhabra, G. S. *Advanced Study in the History of Modern India*. Verry 3 vols. 1972 $40.00

Crane, Robert I. *A History of South Asia*. Amer. Historical Association text ed. 1973 pap. $1.50

Danvers, Frederick C. *Portuguese in India*. Octagon 2 vols. 1966 lib. bdg. $72.00

Das, M. N. *Partition and Independence of India.* Humanities Pr. text ed. 1983 $23.00
Dayal, Baghubir, and A. E. Barrow. *An Outline of Indian History and Culture.* Apt Bks. text ed. 1983 vol. 1 $8.95
Gandhi, Mohandas K. *Delhi Diary: Daily Talks at Prayer Meetings, 1947–1948.* Greenleaf Bks. 1982 $7.50
———. *Gandhi: An Autobiography.* Beacon 1983 $18.95
———. *Nonviolence in Peace and War, 1942.* Intro. by Paul F. Power, Garland 2 vols. lib. bdg. ea. $38.00 set $76.00
Ghose, Sankar. *Socialism and Communism in India.* Verry 1971 $8.25
Hallissey, Robert C. *The Rajput Rebellion against Aurangzeb: A Study of the Mughal Empire in Seventeenth Century India.* Univ. of Missouri Pr. 1977 $13.00
Horn, Robert C. *Soviet-Indian Relations: Issues & Influence.* Praeger 1982 $39.95 pap. $13.95
Last, Murray. *The Sokoto Caliphate. Ibadan History Ser.* Humanities Pr. text ed. 1967 pap. $8.00
Majumdar, R. C., and P. N. Chopra. *Main Currents of Indian History.* Humanities Pr. text ed. 1980 $9.50
Malleson, G. B. *Historical Sketch of the Native States of India.* South Asia Bks. repr. of 1975 ed. 1984 $38.00
Menon, A. Sreedhara. *Social and Cultural History of India: Kerala.* Orient Bk. Dist. text ed. 1979 $20.00
Nanda, B. R. *Gokhale, Gandhi and the Nehrus: Studies in Indian Nationalism.* St. Martin's 1974 $19.95
Nayar, Kuldip. *India after Nehru.* International Bk. Dist. 1975 $9.00
Organ, Troy W. *Hinduism.* Barron text ed. 1974 pap. $6.95
Pemble, John. *The Raj, the Indian Mutiny, and the Kingdom of Oudh, 1801–1859.* Fairleigh Dickinson Univ. Pr. 1978 $27.50
Rudolph, Lloyd I., and Susanne H. Rudolph. *The Modernity of Tradition: Political Development in India. Midway Repr. Ser.* Univ. of Chicago Pr. text ed. 1984 pap. $13.00
Smith, Vincent. *The Oxford History of India.* Ed. by Percival Spear, Oxford 4th ed. 1981 pap. $12.95
Spear, Percival. *India: A Modern History. History of the Modern World Ser.* Univ. of Michigan Pr. rev. & enl. ed. 1972 $15.00
———. *The Oxford History of Modern India, 1740–1975.* Oxford 2d ed. 1978 pap. $10.95
Srinivas, M. N. *Social Change in Modern India.* Univ. of California Pr. 1966 o.p. "The most complete available analysis of the dynamics of the Indian caste system" (*American Sociological Review*). "For persons with an interest in modern India, this book is nothing less than required reading" (*Journal of Asian Studies*).
Tames, Richard. *India and Pakistan in the Twentieth Century. Twentieth-Century World History Ser.* David & Charles 1981 $14.95
Tandon, Prakash. *Punjabi Century, 1857–1947.* Fwd. by Maurice Zinkin, Univ. of California Pr. 1968 pap. $5.95. ". . . Tandon builds a clear picture of the caste system and the pattern of Hindu family behavior" (*TLS*).
Venkata Ramanappa, M. N. *Outlines of South Indian History.* International Bk. Dist. 1976 $7.50
Wilber, Donald N. *Pakistan. Area and Country Survey Ser.* Human Relations Area Files 1964 $18.00
Wilcox, Wayne A. *Pakistan: The Consolidation of a Nation.* Columbia Univ. Pr. 1963 $28.50

Wiser, William, and Charlotte Wiser. *Behind Mud Walls, 1930–1960*. Univ. of California Pr. rev. ed. 1972 $19.50 pap. $7.95. "[An] important first-hand account of two phenomena which are characteristics of modern India—namely, the impact upon village life of the new ways which have come with independence; and the social and personal disorganization which tends to afflict the young amidst the rapid growth of urbanization" (*TLS*).

Wolpert, Stanley. *A New History of India*. Oxford 2d ed. 1982 $29.95 text ed. pap. $10.95

Other States and Areas

Bender, David L., and others. *The Vietnam War: Opposing Viewpoints*. Greenhaven Pr. 1984 lib. bdg. $11.95 text ed. pap. $5.95

Boettcher, Thomas D. *Vietnam: The Valor and the Sorrow*. Little, Brown 1985 $24.45 pap. $14.45

Butler, David. *The Fall of Saigon: Scenes from the Sudden End of a Long War*. Simon & Schuster 1985 $18.95

Buttinger, Joseph. *Vietnam: The Unforgettable Tragedy*. Horizon Pr. 1976 $8.95

Choy, Bong-Youn. *Korea: A History*. Tuttle 1971 $21.50

Conroy, Hilary. *The Japanese Seizure of Korea, 1868–1910: A Study of Realism and Idealism in International Relations*. Univ. of Pennsylvania Pr. 1974 pap. $11.95

Fall, Bernard B. *Hell in a Very Small Place: The Siege of Dien Bien Phu*. Quality Pap. Ser. Da Capo repr. of 1967 ed. 1985 pap. $11.95

———. *The Two Viet-Nams: A Political and Military Analysis*. Westview Pr. 1984 pap. $36.00

Fitzgerald, Frances. *Fire in the Lake: The Vietnamese and the Americans in Vietnam*. Little, Brown 1972 $15.00; Random (Vintage) 1973 pap. $4.95

Griffis, William E. *Corea: The Hermit Nation*. AMS Pr. 9th ed. rev. & enl. repr. of 1911 ed. $37.50

Harrison, James P. *The Endless War: Fifty Years of Struggle in Vietnam*. Macmillan (Free Pr.) text ed. 1982 $17.95

Henthorn, William E. *History of Korea*. Macmillan (Free Pr.) 1971 $17.00 text ed. pap. $11.95

Hersh, Seymour M. *My Lai Four: A Report on the Massacre and Its Aftermath*. Random 1970 $10.95

Ho Tai, Hue-Tam. *Millenarianism and Peasant Politics in Vietnam*. Harvard Univ. Pr. text ed. 1983 $30.00

Honey, P. J. *Communism in North Vietnam: Its Role in the Sino Soviet Dispute*. Greenwood repr. of 1963 ed. 1973 lib. bdg. $15.00. "A fascinating picture of the struggle between the pro-Peking and pro-Moscow factions" (*N.Y. Times*).

Kendrick, Alexander. *The Wound Within: America in the Vietnam Years, 1945–1974*. Little, Brown 1975 pap. $9.95

Kwak, Tai-Hwan, and John Chay, eds. *U.S.-Korean Relations, 1882–1982*. Westview Pr. 1983 lib. bdg. $27.50

Kwak, Tai-Hwan, and others. *The Two Koreas in World Politics*. Westview Pr. 1984 lib. bdg. $25.00

Lamb, Alastair. *Mandarin Road to Old Hue: Narratives of Anglo Vietnamese Diplomacy from the 17th Century to the Eve of the French Conquest*. Shoe String (Archon) 1970 $25.00.

Lee, Ki-Baik. *A New History of Korea*. Trans. by Edward W. Wagner and Edward J. Schultz, Harvard Univ. Pr. text ed. 1984 $25.00

Mackie, J., ed. *Indonesia: The Making of a Nation.* Univ. of Queensland Pr. 1981 pap. $10.00

McCarthy, Mary. *Hanoi.* Harcourt 1968 pap. $1.45

———. *Vietnam.* Harcourt 1967 pap. $.95

Neher, Clark D., ed. *Modern Thai Politics from Village to Nation.* Schenkman 1981 $22.50 text ed. pap. $12.50

Neill, Wilfred T. *Twentieth-Century Indonesia.* Columbia Univ. Pr. 1973 $35.00 pap. $15.00

Pike, Douglas. *The Viet Cong: The Organization and Techniques of the National Liberation Front of South Vietnam. Studies in Communism, Revisionism and Revolution* MIT 1966 $25.00. By an official of the USIA, stationed for several years in Saigon, who had access to captured NLP documents and intelligence sources.

Reid, Anthony. *The Blood of the People: Revolution and the End of Traditional Rule in Northern Sumatra.* Oxford text ed. 1979 $37.50

Ricklefs, M. C. *A History of Modern Indonesia.* Indiana Univ. Pr. 1981 $22.50

Roy, Jules. *The Battle of Dienbienphu.* Carroll & Graf 1984 pap. $8.95; Harper 1965 $15.00. A bitter analysis, by a French writer, of France's catastrophic defeat in 1954.

Salisbury, Harrison E. *Behind the Lines: Hanoi, December 23–January 7.* Harper 1967 $10.00. The Pulitzer Prize-winning reporter of the *N.Y. Times* writes of his visit to North Vietnam's capital, in an adaptation of his original articles. Awarded the Sidney Hillman Foundation Award in 1967 for outstanding achievement in mass communications.

Schell, Jonathan. *The Military Half: An Account of Destruction in Quang Ngai and Quang Tin.* Knopf 1968 o.p. *The Military Half* and *The Village of Ben Suc*, both by Schell, present similar treatment from the same quarter in two northern provinces of South Vietnam in the summer of 1967.

———. *The Village of Ben Suc.* Knopf 1967 o.p. The destruction of a village 30 miles from Saigon by the U.S. military, and the forced evacuation of its 3,500 inhabitants to refugee camps, is described by a correspondent for the *New Yorker.*

Soebadio, H., and C. Sarvaas. *Dynamics of Indonesian History.* Elsevier 1978 $80.75

Sullivan, Marianna P. *France's Vietnam Policy: A Study in French-American Relations.* Greenwood 1978 lib. bdg. $25.00

Taylor, Keith W. *The Birth of Vietnam.* Univ. of California Pr. text ed. 1983 $38.50

Terwiel, B. J. *A History of Modern Thailand. Histories of Southeast Asia Ser.* Univ. of Queensland Pr. text ed. 1984 $29.95 pap. $17.95

Tinker, Hugh. *The Union of Burma. Royal Institute of International Affairs Ser.* Oxford 4th ed. 1967 $13.00

Vlekke, Bernard H. M. *Nusantara: A History of the East Indian Archipelago.* Ed. by Mira Wilkins, *European Business Ser.* Ayer repr. of 1943 ed. 1977 lib. bdg. $38.50

Wright, Edward R., ed. *Korean Politics in Transition.* Univ. of Washington Pr. 1975 $20.00

Wyatt, David K. *Thailand: A Short History.* Yale Univ. Pr. 1984 $27.50

———

ARENDT, HANNAH. 1906–1975

A victim of nazism who fled Germany in 1933, Hannah Arendt was well equipped to write her superb *The Origins of Totalitarianism*, which David Riesman called "an achievement in historiography. . . . I happen to think such an experience in understanding our times as this book provides in itself a social force not to be underestimated" (*Commentary*). Her study of Eichmann at his trial, part of which appeared originally in the *New Yorker*, was a painfully searching investigation into what made this Nazi persecutor tick. *Men in Dark Times* includes essays on Hermann Broch, Walter Benjamin, and Bertolt Brecht, as well as an interesting characterization of Pope John XXIII.

Born in Hanover, Germany, Arendt received her doctorate from Heidelberg. On leaving Germany in the 1930s, she went to France where she helped with the resettlement of Jewish children in Palestine. She emigrated to the United States in 1941 and became an American citizen in 1951. She was research director of the Conference on Jewish Relations, chief editor of Schocken Books, executive director of Jewish Cultural Reconstruction in New York City, a visiting professor at several universities, including the University of California, Princeton, Columbia, and the University of Chicago, and university professor on the graduate faculty of the New School for Social Research. She won a number of grants and fellowships and in 1967 received the Sigmund Freud Prize of the German Akademie für Sprache und Dichtung for her fine scholarly writing.

BOOKS BY ARENDT

The Origins of Totalitarianism. 1951. Harcourt 1973 pap. $7.95; Peter Smith 1983 $15.00

The Human Condition. 1958. Univ. of Chicago Pr. (Phoenix Bks.) 1970 pap. $10.95

Between Past and Future: Eight Exercises in Political Thought. 1961. Penguin enl. ed. 1977 pap. $5.95; Peter Smith 1983 $11.25

Eichmann in Jerusalem: A Report of the Banality of Evil. 1963. Penguin rev. ed. 1977 pap. $6.95; Peter Smith 1983 $11.25

On Revolution. Pelican Ser. Greenwood repr. of 1963 ed. 1982 lib. bdg. $35.00; Penguin 1977 pap. $5.95

Men in Dark Times. Harcourt 1968 $6.50 1970 pap. $4.95

On Violence. Harcourt 1970 pap. $2.95

Crises of the Republic. Harcourt 1972 $6.95

BOOKS ABOUT ARENDT

Kateb, George. *Hannah Arendt: Politics, Conscience, Evil. Philosophy and Society Ser.* Rowman 1984 $24.95

Tolle, Gordon J. *Human Nature under Fire: The Political Philosophy of Hannah Arendt.* Univ. Pr. of Amer. 1982 lib. bdg. $25.00 text ed. pap. $10.50

Whitfield, Stephen J. *Into the Dark: Hannah Arendt and Totalitarianism.* Temple Univ. Pr. 1980 $29.95

Young-Bruehl, Elisabeth. *Hannah Arendt: For Love of the World.* Yale Univ. Pr. 1982 $32.50 1983 pap. $14.95

ARON, RAYMOND. 1905–

Raymond Aron is a political scientist, sociologist, economist, and philosopher, who has a far-ranging mind and pen that have explored every facet of human society. He analyzes the world political scene in his contributions to *Le Figaro*, the French conservative newspaper, in his books and radio commentary, and as a teacher at *L'école pratique des hautes etudes* in Paris. An expert in international relations, he has used his influence in favor of a French alliance with the United States.

As a man of the center, he has been critical of both left and right. "His 1957 book *Opium of the Intellectuals*, which berated Marxism and the French intellectual elite, played a significant role in the debate between Marxists and non-Marxists in France" (*N.Y. Times*).

Peace and War was widely reviewed here and abroad. George Steiner wrote: "There have always been those who hold . . . that man's political, public existence can, given sufficient knowledge and practical insight, be both understood and ameliorated . . . . This rationalist tradition springs from Aristotelian logic and the confident sanity of Roman law . . . . In its modern guise, though, it is preeminently French and reflects the long drama of reason from Descartes to Camus . . . . Today, its representative heir is Raymond Aron" (*New Yorker*). Martin Wight described it in the *Observer* as a "noble, temperate and magisterial book."

Not every critic was so favorable, although the space given to Aron by, for example, J. P. Nettl, in the *N.Y. Review of Books*, demonstrates that even if Aron "is not a profound or original thinker" he "is the product of a mood, the answer to a need" and therefore a necessary present concern. Professor Aron visited the United States in 1969 as professor-at-large, Cornell University.

BOOKS BY ARON

German Sociology. 1935. Trans. by Mary Bottomore and Thomas Bottomore, ed. by Lewis A. Coser and Walter W. Powell, Ayer repr. of 1964 ed. lib. bdg. 1979 $13.00; Greenwood repr. of 1957 ed. 1979 lib. bdg. $18.75

Introduction to the Philosophy of History: An Essay on the Limits of Historical Objectivity. 1938. Trans. by George J. Irwin, Greenwood repr. of 1961 ed. 1976 lib. bdg. $24.75

The Century of Total War. 1951. Greenwood repr. of 1954 ed. 1981 lib. bdg. $28.75

The Opium of the Intellectuals. 1955. Trans. by Terence Kilmartin, Greenwood 1977 lib. bdg. $24.25; Norton Lib. 1962 pap. $3.45

(and August Heckscher). *Diversity of Worlds.* Intro. by Arnold Wolfers, Greenwood repr. of 1957 ed. 1973 lib. bdg. $22.50

War and Industrial Society. Trans. by Mary Bottomore, Greenwood repr. of 1959 ed. 1980 lib. bdg. $18.75

Peace and War: A Theory of International Relations. 1962. Krieger repr. of 1966 ed. 1981 $46.50

The Great Debate: Theories of Nuclear Strategy. 1963. Trans. by Ernst Pawel, Greenwood repr. of 1965 ed. 1981 lib. bdg. $27.50

Main Currents in Sociological Thought: Montesquieu, Comte, Marx, Tocqueville, the Sociologists, and the Revolution of 1848. 1967. Doubleday 1968 pap. $5.95

On War. Trans. by Terence Kilmartin, Norton Lib. 1968 pap. $3.45

Marxism and the Existentialists. Harper 1969 o.p.

Essay on Freedom. Norton 1970 o.p.

The Imperial Republic: The United States and the World, 1945–1973. 1973. Prentice-Hall 1975 $9.95; Univ. Pr. of Amer. repr. of 1973 ed. 1982 lib. bdg. $29.00 text ed. pap. $14.75

Politics and History: Selected Essays. Ed. and trans. by Miriam Conant, Macmillan
    (Free Pr.) 1978 $24.95; Transaction Bks. 1984 pap. $12.95
In Defense of Decadent Europe. Univ. Pr. of Amer. text ed. 1984 pap. $9.75

BARNETT, A(RTHUR) DOAK. 1921–

Born of American parents in Shanghai, Doak Barnett has spent much
time in China. After receiving his M.A. from Yale University, he became a
correspondent in Hong Kong for the *Chicago Daily News* (1947–50 and
1952–53). He was public affairs officer at the U.S. consulate-general in
Hong Kong (1951–52) and later an associate of the American Universities
Field Staff for Asian areas.

He was chairman of the foreign area studies department at the U.S. State
Department's Foreign Service Institute, professor of political science at Columbia University, and chairman of the Contemporary China Studies Committee of Columbia's East Asian Institute. A member of, or consultant for,
many organizations engaged in China studies, Barnett is, of course, one of
the best-known experts in the United States on China.

BOOKS BY BARNETT

Communist Economic Strategy: The Rise of Mainland China. Greenwood repr. of 1959
    ed. 1976 lib. bdg. $19.25
Communist China and Asia: Challenge to American Policy. Random 1960 o.p.
China on the Eve of the Communist Takeover. Westview Pr. repr. of 1963 ed. 1985
    $31.00. "Why and how was mainland China lost to the Communists. Here is a
    highly readable book that throws a great deal of light on the matter. [Professor
    Barnett] reveals enough of the Communists' doctrinaire ignorance and authori-
    tarianism to indicate why their regime, by now, has become the most rigid, xe-
    nophobic dictatorship the Middle Kingdom has ever known" (*N.Y. Times*).
Communist China: The Early Years, 1949–55. Praeger 1964 o.p. A collection of previ-
    ously published articles, "this book deals with . . . the period of 'transition to so-
    cialism' and the first two years of the first Five Year Plan . . . . Written in an
    easy style with caution and modesty, a lack of dogmatism and an obvious zest
    for digging up facts, these articles stand the test of time very well indeed" (*N.Y.
    Times*).
*Cadres, Bureaucracy, and Political Power in Communist China. Studies of the East
    Asian Institute* Columbia Univ. Pr. 1967 $29.50. ". . . describes the operations of
    the Communist system with skill and ingenuity . . . . There is no better account
    of how the Communist government actually operated in 1965" (Oscar Handlin).
China after Mao: With Selected Documents. Princeton Univ. Pr. 1967 $30.00 pap.
    $9.95. Based on the Walter E. Edge Lectures given at Princeton University in
    1966.
(ed.). *Chinese Communist Politics in Action. Studies in Chinese Government and Poli-
    tics* Univ. of Washington Pr. 1969 pap. $7.95
(and others, eds.). *The United States and China: The Next Decade.* Praeger 1970 o.p.
A New U.S. Policy toward China. Brookings 1971 $9.95 pap. $3.95
Uncertain Passage: China's Transition to the Post Mao Era. Brookings 1974 $22.95
    pap. $8.95
China's Economy in Global Perspective. Brookings 1981 $32.95 pap. $16.95

The FX Decision: Another Crucial Moment in U.S.-China-Taiwan Relations. Studies in Defense Policy Brookings 1981 pap. $6.95
U.S. Arms Sales: The China-Taiwan Tangle. Studies in Defense Policy Brookings 1982 pap. $6.95

BRAUDEL, FERNAND. 1902–

Perhaps the most admired and respected European historian of the present generation, Fernand Braudel, through his unique interests and methodology, has made the *Annales* school of history the most influential of all contemporary schools of history. His monumental *The Mediterranean and the Mediterranean World in the Age of Philip Second* was the first attempt to study a historic period (the sixteenth century) and an area (the lands bordering the Mediterranean Sea) in their totality, from climatic conditions to social structures, from ethnic origins to trade routes. His work has inspired dozens of younger historians, the best of whom have trained under him at *L'école pratique des hautes politiques* in Paris, of which he is director.

BOOKS BY BRAUDEL

The Mediterranean and the Mediterranean World in the Age of Philip Second. 1949–73. Trans. by Sian Reynolds, Harper 2 vols. 2d ed. rev. 1976 pap. ea. $12.02–$12.45
Capitalism and Material Life, 1400–1800. 1967. Trans. by Miriam Kochan, Harper 1973 $14.95 1974 pap. $8.95
Afterthoughts on Material Civilization and Capitalism. Trans. by Patricia M. Ranum, *Symposia in Comparative History Ser.* Johns Hopkins Univ. Pr. 1977 pap. $4.45
On History. Trans. by Sarah Matthews, Univ. of Chicago Pr. 1980 lib. bdg. $17.00
The Perspectives of the World: Civilization and Capitalism. Harper 1984 vol. 3 $38.00 1982 pap. $8.50

BRINTON, C(LARENCE) CRANE. 1898–1968

A History of Civilization is a good, workmanlike history of mankind from the prehistoric era to the present by a team of scholars led by Crane Brinton, a leading member of Harvard's history department for half a century. The emphasis is on cultural, intellectual, and economic development, with frequent quotations from contemporary writings, poetry, orations, and documents. In the introduction, "The Uses of History," the authors maintain that history "can be for any of us who want to study it, a kind of extension in space and time of our own experience, a deepening and widening of our own little private histories."

Born in Winsted, Connecticut, Brinton graduated from Harvard and took his Ph.D. in 1923 from Oxford. He spent the rest of his life, until retirement shortly before his death, teaching at Harvard.

BOOKS BY BRINTON

Political Ideas of the English Romanticists. Russell repr. of 1926 ed. 1962 $15.00
The Jacobins: An Essay in the New History. Russell repr. of 1930 ed. 1961 $19.00
English Political Thought in the Nineteenth Century. 1933. Gannon 1962 lib. bdg. $13.50; Peter Smith $5.00

A Decade of Revolution, 1789–1799. Rise of Modern Europe Ser. Greenwood repr. of
    1934 ed. 1983 lib. bdg. $45.00
The Anatomy of Revolution. 1938. Peter Smith $13.50; Random (Vintage) rev. ed.
    1965 pap. $4.95
United States and Britain. 1945. Greenwood repr. of 1948 ed. lib. bdg. $15.00
From Many, One: The Process of Political Integration. Greenwood repr. of 1948 ed.
    1971 lib. bdg. $15.00
Ideas and Men: The Story of Western Thought. 1950. Prentice-Hall 2d ed. 1963 $26.95
The Temper of Western Europe. Greenwood repr. of 1953 ed. lib. bdg. $15.00
(and others). *A History of Civilization.* 1955. Prentice-Hall 2 vols. 6th ed. 1984 pap.
    ea. $18.95
(ed.). *The Portable Age of Reason Reader.* Viking 1956 o.p.
The Lives of Talleyrand. Norton Lib. 1963 pap. $4.95
Shaping of Modern Thought. Prentice-Hall (Spectrum Bks.) 1963 pap. $3.95
(and others). *Civilization in the West.* 1964. Prentice-Hall 2 vols. 3d ed. text ed. 1973
    ea. $18.95 pap. ea. $11.95
The Americans and the French. Amer. Foreign Policy Lib. Harvard Univ. Pr. 1968 o.p.
    "An outspoken discussion of Anglo-French relations since the Second World
    War" (*PW*).

BURCKHARDT, JACOB (CHRISTOPH). 1818–1897

Burckhardt is universally recognized as one of the greatest historians of
the nineteenth century and the greatest historian of the Italian Renaissance.
In his major works he developed the branch of history known as
Kulturgeschichte (roughly translated as "history of culture") and brilliantly
demonstrated its potentialities to contemporaries whose interest had traditionally been in purely political history. In the most influential of his works,
The Civilization of the Renaissance in Italy, Burckhardt defined the Italian
Renaissance as the beginning of modern times, its protagonists as the first
modern men. Though questioned and modified by later historians, particularly by medievalists, the definition remains generally valid today.

Burckhardt was Swiss and taught all his professional life at the University of Basel. Several of his published works were compiled from his lecture
notes.

BOOKS BY BURCKHARDT

The Age of Constantine the Great. 1853. Trans. by Moses Hadas, Univ. of California
    Pr. 1982 pap. $7.95
The Cicerone: An Art Guide to Painting in Italy for the Use of Travellers and Students.
    1855. Ed. by Sydney J. Freedberg, *Connoisseurship Criticism and Art History Ser.*
    Garland 1979 lib. bdg. $36.00. A history of Italian art, mainly during the Renais-
    sance.
The Civilization of the Renaissance in Italy. 1860. Intro. by B. Nelson and C. Trinkaus,
    Harper 2 vols. pap. ea. $3.80; Merrimack 1983 $13.95; intro. by Hajo Holborn,
    Modern Lib. 1954 $6.95; Peter Smith 2 vols. $28.00
Reflections on History (Force and Freedom). 1905. Liberty Fund 1979 $9.00 pap. $5.00
History of Greek Culture. Trans. by Palmer Hilty, Ungar 1963 $30.00
The Architecture of the Italian Renaissance. Ed. by Peter Murray, Univ. of Chicago Pr.
    1984 lib. bdg. $50.00

CARLYLE, THOMAS. 1795–1881

Carlyle moved to London in 1834 "to be near necessary works of reference for the projected 'French Revolution.' " Finally completed in 1837, his book was received with great acclaim. Although it vividly recreates scenes of the Revolution, it is not a factual account but a poetic rendering of an event in history. He spent 13 years (1852–65) on his massive *History of Friedrich II of Prussia, Called Frederick the Great,* a survey of a "hero" in accordance with his conviction, expressed in *On Heroes, Hero-Worship and the Heroic in History,* that the work of the world is accomplished by natural leaders.

BOOKS BY CARLYLE

Works. Scholarly 30 vols. 1896–1901 $555.00
Selected Works, Reminiscences and Letters. Ed. by Julian Symons, Harvard Univ. Pr. 1970 o.p.
The French Revolution. 1837. Biblio Dist. (Everyman's) 2 vols. in 1 repr. of 1906 ed. 1980 $15.95
On Heroes, Hero-Worship and the Heroic in History. 1841. Ed. by Carl Niemeyer, Univ. of Nebraska Pr. (Bison) 1966 pap. $6.95
History of Friedrich II of Prussia, Called Frederick the Great. 1858–65. Ed. by John Clive, *Class. European Historians Ser.* Univ. of Chicago Pr. 1969 o.p.

BOOKS ABOUT CARLYLE

Chesterton, Gilbert K. *Thomas Carlyle.* Arden Lib. repr. of 1902 ed. 1980 lib. bdg. $10.00; Haskell repr. 1973 lib. bdg. $37.95
Clubbe, John B. *Two Reminiscences of Thomas Carlyle.* Duke Univ. Pr. 1974 $12.75
Dyer, Isaac W. *Bibliography of Thomas Carlyle's Writings and Annotations.* Burt Franklin repr. of 1928 ed. 1967 $23.50
Froude, James A. *Thomas Carlyle: A History of His Life in London, 1834–1881.* Richard West 2 vols. repr. of 1884 ed. $65.00; Scholarly 2 vols. repr. of 1881 ed. 1971 $59.00
————. *Thomas Carlyle: A History of the First Forty Years of His Life.* Richard West 2 vols. repr. of 1882 ed. 1973 $65.00
Gascoyne, David. *Thomas Carlyle.* British Bk. Ctr. o.p.
Kaplan, Fred. *Thomas Carlyle: A Biography.* Cornell Univ. Pr. 1983 $35.00
Neff, Emery. *Carlyle and Mill.* Octagon 1964 lib. bdg. $26.00
Ralli, Augustus. *Guide to Carlyle.* Haskell repr. of 1920 ed. 1970 lib. bdg. $79.95
Rosenberg, Phillip. *The Seventh Hero: Thomas Carlyle and the Theory of Radical Activism.* Harvard Univ. Pr. 1974 $16.50
Tarr, Rodger L. *Thomas Carlyle: A Bibliography of English-Language Criticism, 1824–1974.* Univ. Pr. of Virginia 1976 $15.00
Young, Louise M. *Thomas Carlyle and the Art of History.* Arden Lib. repr. of 1939 ed. 1980 lib. bdg. $30.00; Folcroft repr. of 1939 ed. $20.00; Octagon repr. of 1939 ed. 1971 lib. bdg. $18.00

CROCE, BENEDETTO. 1866–1952

The philosopher and historian who "emerged from almost twenty years of semi-imprisonment under the Fascist regime to become one of the members of the new Italian government" wrote on a variety of historical and literary subjects, including a critical analysis of Shakespeare. But his most influential work is on the philosophy of history, the essentials of which may be found in Robin G. Collingwood, *The Idea of History.*

BOOKS BY CROCE

Philosophy of Giambattista Vico. Trans. by Robin G. Collingwood, Russell repr. of 1913 ed. $20.00

History: Its Theory and Practice. 1916. Trans. by Douglas Ainslie, Russell repr. of 1920 ed. 1960 $16.00

Autobiography. Trans. by Robin G. Collingwood, *Select Bibliographies Repr. Ser.* Ayer repr. of 1927 ed. $13.00

A History of Italy, 1871–1915. 1929. Trans. by Cecilia M. Ady, Russell 1963 o.p.

The History of Europe in the Nineteenth Century. 1933. Harcourt 1963 o.p.

History as the Story of Liberty. 1938. Trans. by Sylvia Sprigge, Regnery-Gateway pap. $5.95; Univ. Pr. of Amer. repr. of 1970 ed. text ed. 1984 pap. $13.50

My Philosophy and Other Essays on the Moral and Political Problems of Our Time. Trans. by E. F. Caritt, AMS Pr. repr. of 1949 ed. $18.75

Philosophy, Poetry, History: An Anthology of Essays. Trans. by Cecil Sprigge, Oxford 1966 o.p.

The History of the Kingdom of Naples. 1970. Intro. by H. Stuart Hughes, *Class. European Historians Ser.* Univ. of Chicago Pr. (Phoenix Bks.) 1972 pap. $2.95

Historical Materialism and the Economics of Karl Marx. Transaction Bks. 1981 $29.95 text ed. pap. $6.95

The Philosophy of History. Foundation Class. 1983 $89.75

The Philosophy of Politics. Amer. Class. College Pr. 1984 $77.85

Sentiment and Romance in the Poetry by Shakespeare. Amer. Class. College Pr. 1983 $89.85

What Is Living and What Is Dead in the Philosophy of Hegel. Garland 1984 lib. bdg. $30.00

BOOKS ABOUT CROCE

Benham, Allen R. *Clio and Mr. Croce.* Folcroft repr. of 1928 ed. lib. bdg. $10.00

Bosanquet, Bernard. *Croce's Aesthetic.* Gordon 1974 lib. bdg. $59.95

Carr, H. Wildon. *Philosophy of Benedetto Croce: The Problem of Art and History.* Russell repr. of 1917 ed. 1969 $8.50

———. *Time and History in Contemporary Philosophy with Special Reference to Bergson and Croce.* Gordon 1974 lib. bdg. $59.95

Collingwood, Robin G. *The Idea of History.* Ed. by T. M. Knox, Oxford 1946 pap. $9.95. The most influential statement of Croce's view of how a historian studies history.

de Gennaro, Angelo A. *Philosophy of Benedetto Croce: An Introduction.* Greenwood repr. of 1961 ed. lib. bdg. $15.00

DURANT, WILL(IAM) (JAMES). 1885–1981, and ARIEL DURANT. 1898–1981

Will Durant began his massive *Story of Civilization* in 1927, and by the time the seventh volume was published in 1961 his wife Ariel's assistance had earned her title-page recognition as coauthor. The Durants brought popular history to the intelligent lay reader, a fact that Orville Prescott noted: "To introduce and to popularize is not less worthy an enterprise than to unearth some hitherto unknown facts or to present some new and controversial theory. Many professional historians believe that it is, and some have looked down their noses at the Durants. The truth is that the art of history includes both kinds of writing and needs both. The scholar who delves into obscure archives is essential; without him ignorance would prevail. But the writer who can make history available to the general reader is necessary too" (*SR*).

Born in North Adams, Massachusetts, Will Durant earned his undergraduate degree at St. Peter's College in New Jersey. He eventually taught at the libertarian Ferrer Modern School in New York, where he met his wife, then Ada Kaufman, one of his pupils whom he later preferred to call Ariel. Durant earned his Ph.D. in philosophy from Columbia University, where he studied under John Dewey, among others. The Durants made several world tours to visit the countries they treated in their history and received countless honorary degrees. In 1968 they received the Pulitzer Prize for *Rousseau and Revolution*, the final volume of their magnum opus. Explaining why they stopped at this point in history, they wrote: "We find ourselves exhausted on reaching the French Revolution. We know that this event did not end history, but it ends us."

BOOKS BY THE DURANTS

The Story of Civilization. Simon & Schuster 10 vols. 1935–67 ea. $29.95–$32.95

Renaissance. Simon & Schuster 1953 $29.95

Rousseau and Revolution. Simon & Schuster 1967 $32.95

The Lessons of History. Simon & Schuster 1968 $13.95. "A modest, balanced and helpful statement of the beliefs and values that have resulted from the Durants' immersion in historical investigation these many years. Here are their fair-mindedness, their respect for human dignity, their exaltation of reason, their horror of bigotry and their faith in education as the clue to the betterment of the human condition" (*N.Y. Times*).

Interpretations of Life. 1970. Simon & Schuster (Touchstone Bks.) 1976 pap. $4.95. Includes essays on Faulkner, Hemingway, O'Neill, Pound, Sartre, Mann, and Kafka.

The Pleasures of Philosophy. Simon & Schuster (Touchstone Bks.) pap. $10.75

FAIRBANK, JOHN K(ING). 1907–

John K. Fairbank, long the director of Harvard's East Asian Research Center, has had a distinguished academic career in the field of Asian studies, in which his books are of the first importance. Born in South Dakota, he took his Harvard A.B. in 1929 and his Ph.D. at Oxford in 1936. During World War II he worked for the Office of Strategic Services in Washington, D.C., was special assistant to the U.S. ambassador in Chungking (1942–43), was attached to Washington's Office of War Information (1944–45) and director of the U.S. Information Service in China (1945–46). He has been at Harvard, except for these intervals, since 1936.

Fairbank was a leading exponent of the movement in the United States to reestablish diplomatic relations with China. People in the United States need, he believes, much broader knowledge of things Asian as part of their general knowledge and as the specialized equipment of scholars, civil servants, and statesmen.

BOOKS BY FAIRBANK

(and Kwang-Ching Liu). *Modern China: A Bibliographical Guide to Chinese Works, 1898–1937.* Harvard Univ. Pr. 1950 o.p. "The books described in this bibliography are in the Chinese language, and deal with affairs in China since the Reform Movement of 1898. The titles are given in Chinese characters and in romanized form, although all annotations are in English. Students of Chinese affairs, burdened by a difficult language and a voluminous literature, will welcome this convenient and lucid guide. Even those who do not read the language can glean from it much valuable information. It is a challenge to improved scholarship on China in the West" (*U.S. Quarterly Booklist*). "This is a splendid bibliography with abundant notes explaining the merit of each particular item, and doing it very intelligently. It is in fact a catalogue raisonné of a section of the very rich Harvard-Yenching Library, and its existence will greatly increase the practical value of that library" (*Isis*).

Trade and Diplomacy on the China Coast: The Opening of the Treaty Ports, 1842–1854. Harvard Univ. Pr. 2 vols. in 1 1954 $18.00; Stanford Univ. Pr. 1953 pap. $10.95

(and Teng Ssu-Yu). *Ch'ing Administration: Three Studies.* Harvard Yenching Institute Studies 1960 pap. $5.00

(and Robert Bowie). *Communist China, 1955–59: Policy Documents with Analysis.* Center for International Affairs Ser. Harvard Univ. Pr. 1962 pap. $18.00

(and Edwin O. Reischauer). *A History of East Asian Civilization.* Houghton Mifflin 2 vols. 1965 o.p.

China: The People's Middle Kingdom and the U.S.A. Harvard Univ. Pr. (Belknap Pr.) 1967 $10.00. "John K. Fairbank has an admirable mission: to make Every man an expert on China. To this end, he has assembled a collection of eleven of his speeches and previously published popular articles, most of quite recent vintage . . . . In his ability to capture centuries of Chinese history in a brief essay, he is without peer" (*Journal of American History*).

(ed.). *Chinese World Order: Traditional China's Foreign Relations.* Harvard East Asian Ser. 1968 pap. $8.95

The United States and China. 1971. Harvard Univ. Pr. 4th ed. enl. text ed. 1983 $20.00 pap. $7.95

China Perceived: Images and Policies in Chinese American Relations. Knopf 1974 $8.95; Random (Vintage) 1976 pap. $3.95

Chinese-American Interactions: A Historical Summary. Rutgers Univ. Pr. 1974 o.p. "These essays preserve the casually inserted personal reminiscence, the deliberate understatement, and the ironic aside that mark Fairbank's lectures" (*LJ*).

(ed.). *The Missionary Enterprise in China and America.* Studies in Amer. East Asian Relations Harvard Univ. Pr. text ed. 1975 $25.00. "This collection of essays . . . is based on careful research and it will start the reader's imagination along a number of paths of speculation" (*TLS*).

(and Albert M. Craig). *East Asia: Tradition and Transformation.* Houghton Mifflin 2d ed. text ed. 1978 $30.95

(and Edwin O. Reischauer). *China: Tradition and Transformation.* Houghton Mifflin text ed. 1978 $21.95

(and Kwang-Ching Liu). *History of China: Late Ch'ing.* Cambridge History of China 1980 $95.00

Chinabound: A Fifty-Year Memoir. Harper 1983 pap. $9.62

GOOCH, G(EORGE) P(EABODY). 1873–1968

"As one of the two historians to whom the British Government confided the task of editing for publication the British official documents bearing on the First World War . . . Gooch is, of course, steeped in the international politics of the time" (*Manchester Guardian*). He contributed several chapters to the *Cambridge Modern History* and served in Parliament from 1906 to 1910. His autobiography, *Under Six Reigns*, extends in time from Queen Victoria to Elizabeth II and restates the proud creed of the liberal scholar who dares to embrace all men and all history and to seek their common verities. "Gooch was widely known not only as a historian but also as an authority on methods used to deal with history as a branch of knowledge. He was an opponent of the school that holds that history can be dealt with as a science" (*N.Y. Times*). He was editor of the British *Contemporary Review* from 1911 to 1960.

BOOKS BY GOOCH

English Democratic Ideas in the Seventeenth Century. 1898. Cambridge Univ. Pr. 1927 o.p.

Annals of Politics and Culture, 1492–1899. History, Economics and Social Science Ser. Burt Franklin repr. of 1905 ed. 1971 lib. bdg. $22.50

History and Historians in the 19th Century. 1913. Beacon 1959 o.p.

Germany and the French Revolution. Biblio Dist. repr. of 1920 ed. 1965 $35.00

Franco-German Relations, 1871–1914. Russell repr. of 1923 ed. 1967 $5.00

Studies in Modern History. Essay Index Repr. Ser. Ayer repr. of 1931 ed. $20.00

Courts and Cabinets. Essay Index Repr. Ser. Ayer repr. of 1946 ed. $25.00

Frederick the Great: The Ruler, the Writer, the Man. 1947. Shoe String 1962 o.p.

Studies in German History. Russell repr. of 1948 ed. 1969 $14.00

Maria Theresa and Other Studies. Shoe String (Archon) repr. of 1951 ed. 1965 $23.50

Catherine the Great and Other Studies. Shoe String (Archon) repr. of 1954 ed. 1966 $19.50

Louis the XV: The Monarchy in Decline. Greenwood repr. of 1956 ed. 1976 lib. bdg. $21.50

Under Six Reigns. Shoe String (Archon) repr. of 1958 ed. 1971 $22.00

GUERARD, ALBERT L(EON). 1880–1959

Born and educated in France, Guérard came to the United States as a college teacher of French in 1906 and did much to interpret the civilization of his native land. He wrote many excellent volumes which combine erudition and "esprit" with literary elegance. His *France in the Classical Age* (o.p.) has long been a classic. His autobiography, *Personal Equation* (1948), is out of print, as is his *Testament of a Liberal* (1956).

BOOKS BY GUERARD

French Civilization in the Nineteenth Century. History of French Civilization Ser. Cooper Square Pr. repr. of 1918 ed. 1971 o.p.

French Civilization from Its Origins to the Close of the Middle Ages. Cooper Square Pr. repr. of 1921 ed. $25.00

Beyond Hatred: The Democratic Ideal in France and America. Greenwood repr. of
     1925 ed. $19.75
France in the Classical Age: The Life and Death of an Ideal. 1928. Gannon 1970 o.p.
France: A Short History. Norton 1946 $8.50
Napoleon III: A Great Life in Brief. 1955. Greenwood repr. of 1966 ed. 1979 lib. bdg.
     $22.50
Napoleon I. Knopf 1956 o.p.
France: A Modern History. 1959. Rev. and enl. by Paul A. Gagnon, Univ. of Michigan
     Pr. 1969 $15.00

KENNAN, GEORGE F(ROST). 1904–

   After his graduation from Princeton University in 1925, George Kennan
entered the Foreign Service. His diplomatic posts have always found him in
critical spots at crucial times. In 1933 he helped reopen the U.S. embassy in
Moscow after long-delayed recognition by the United States of the
U.S.S.R.—and witnessed Stalin's purge trials. As secretary of legation in
Prague in 1938 he watched the German army occupy the city, and in 1939,
when he was assigned to the Berlin embassy, the onset of World War II kept
him confined with other Americans for six months. He was Ambassador
Averell Harriman's chief aide in Russia from 1944 to 1946, helped imple-
ment the Marshall Plan, and was briefly U.S. ambassador to the Soviet
Union in 1952. In 1953 he became a member of the Institute for Advanced
Study, Princeton, N.J. He has also taught at the University of Chicago and
at Oxford. He emerged from official retirement (1961–63) to be U.S. ambassador to Yugoslavia.
   Within the limitations of his official roles, he has been a vocal critic of
U.S. foreign policy. In 1947 his article for *Foreign Affairs*, signed "Mr. X,"
recommended a U.S. policy of containment toward Russia. (In this, as in
other matters, he often failed to convince his superiors of the wisdom of his
advice at a given moment.) Later, he called the Johnson administration's
Vietnam policy a "massive miscalculation and error of policy, an error for
which it is hard to find any parallels in our history." It is, he continued, "so
destructive to civilian life that no conceivable political outcome could justify the attendant suffering and destructiveness."

BOOKS BY KENNAN

American Diplomacy, 1900–1950. 1951. Univ. of Chicago Pr. 1970 pap. $5.50
The Realities of American Foreign Policy. 1954. Norton 1966 o.p.
Soviet-American Relations, 1917–1920: The Decision to Intervene. 1956–58. Norton 2
     vols. 1984 pap. ea. $12.95. Volume 1 won the 1957 Pulitzer Prize for history and
     the National Book Award.
Russia, the Atom and the West. Greenwood repr. of 1958 ed. 1974 lib. bdg. $15.00
Soviet Foreign Policy, 1917–1941. Greenwood repr. of 1960 ed. 1978 lib. bdg. $20.00;
     Krieger text ed. 1979 pap. $5.95
Russia and the West under Lenin and Stalin. New Amer. Lib. 1961 pap. $3.95
On Dealing with the Communist World. Harper 1964 o.p.
From Prague after Munich: Diplomatic Papers, 1938–39. Princeton Univ. Pr. 1968
     $30.00 pap. $8.95. These are letters, official reports, and diary entries written by

Kennan as U.S. secretary of legation in Prague during the German occupation of Czechoslovakia. "An invaluable eyewitness account and analysis of the dismemberment and destruction of a nation as recorded at the time by a particularly knowledgeable, articulate and sensitive observer" (*N.Y. Times*). "They reveal an accurate eye and a keen judgment. Above all, Kennan was aware of what he now describes as 'one of humanity's oldest and most recalcitrant dilemmas: the dilemma of a limited collaboration with evil, in the interests of its ultimate mitigation, as opposed to the uncompromising, heroic but suicidal resistance to it, at the expense of the ultimate weakening of the forces capable of acting against it' " (*SR*).

Memoirs. Little-Atlantic 2 vols. 1967–72 o.p. Volume 1 is "a remarkably candid, beautifully written and utterly fascinating intellectual career autobiography of a distinguished diplomat and scholar. . . . There is material here for a dozen books. There are accounts of serpentine negotiations and portraits of the colleagues and statesmen who took part in them and shaped the political world of our time . . . . This is, in short, a major history" (*N.Y. Times*). It won the 1968 National Book Award and Pulitzer Prize. Volume 2 covers "the origins of the Korean War; the cold war mystique of Acheson and Dulles; Moscow in 1952 in the last months of Stalin; how Kennan got thrown out of the Soviet Union for an unguarded remark in a Berlin airport; the McCarthy attack on old friends; the convulsion of the cold warriors over Kennan's Reith Lectures proposing disengagement in central Europe; and his service in Yugoslavia under Kennedy" (*N.Y. Times Bk. Review*).

Marquis de Custine and His Russia in 1839. Princeton Univ. Pr. 1971 $18.00

The Nuclear Delusion: Soviet-American Relations in the Atomic Age. Pantheon 1983 $13.95 pap. $4.95

The State Department Policy Planning Staff Papers. Ed. by Anna K. Nelson, Garland 1983 lib. bdg. $125.00

Russia Leaves the War. Norton 1984 pap. $12.95

KOHN, HANS. 1891–1971

The Idea of Nationalism (1944, o.p.) established its author as the outstanding authority on the problem of nationalism. Hans Kohn, who has been called "one of the great teachers of our day," received his doctorate from the German University in his native city of Prague. Taken prisoner by the Russians in World War I, he was sent to Turkestan and Siberia, where he witnessed the Russian Revolution and Civil War. Afterward he settled in Jerusalem and wrote several books on the history and politics of the Middle East. He came to the United States in 1931 and, after a period of lecturing at the New School for Social Research in New York, he became professor of modern European history at Smith College in 1934. In 1949 he went to City College, New York, where he was made emeritus professor in 1962. *Living in a World Revolution* is a highly personal book in which he discusses the impact on himself and on Western civilization of two world wars, the Russian Revolution, and the dissolution of European colonialism.

BOOKS BY KOHN

The History of Nationalism in the East. 1928. Scholarly repr. of 1929 ed. $49.00

Nationalism and Imperialism in the Hither East. 1931. Fertig repr. of 1932 ed. $29.50

Nationalism in the Soviet Union. 1932. AMS Pr. repr. of 1933 ed. $15.00
Western Civilization in the Near East. AMS Pr. repr. of 1936 ed. $10.00
Revolutions and Dictatorships. Essay Index Repr. Ser. Ayer repr. of 1939 ed. $25.50
Not by Arms Alone: Essays on Our Time. Essay Index Repr. Ser. Ayer repr. of 1940 ed.
    $15.00
The Idea of Nationalism: A Study in Its Origin and Background. 1944. Macmillan 1961
    o.p.
Prophets and People: Studies in Nineteenth Century Nationalism. Octagon repr. of
    1946 ed. 1975 lib. bdg. $18.50
Political Ideologies of the Twentieth Century. 1949. Peter Smith o.p.
Pan-Slavism: Its History and Ideology. Porcupine Pr. repr. of 1953 ed. lib. bdg. $25.00
Nationalism: Its Meaning and History. 1955. Krieger repr. of 1965 ed. 1982 text ed.
    pap. $6.95; Peter Smith rev. ed. $5.50
The Making of the Modern French Mind. 1955. Peter Smith $5.25
A Basic History of Modern Russia: Political, Cultural and Social Trends. Van Nostrand
    1957 o.p.
The Mind of Germany: The Education of a Nation. Harper 1960 o.p.
The Age of Nationalism: The First Era of Global History. Greenwood repr. of 1962 ed.
    1976 lib. bdg. $19.75
(ed.). *The Mind of Modern Russia: Historical and Political Thought of Russia's Great
    Age.* Harper 1962 o.p.
Reflections on Modern History: The Historian and Human Responsibility. Greenwood
    repr. of 1963 ed. 1978 lib. bdg. $26.75
Living in a World Revolution: My Encounters with History. 1964. Simon & Schuster
    (Touchstone Bks.) 1970 pap. $2.95
Absolutism and Democracy, 1814–1852. Van Nostrand 1965 o.p.
(and Wallace Sokolsky). *African Nationalism in the Twentieth Century. Anvil Ser.* Van
    Nostrand 1965 o.p.
Nationalism and Realism: 1852–1879. Krieger 1968 pap. $6.95; Peter Smith $5.75
(and Daniel Walden). *Readings in American Nationalism.* Van Nostrand 1970 o.p.

LATOURETTE, KENNETH S(COTT). 1884–1968

Latourette was an authority on the Far East, a sound historian, and a de-
voutly religious person, who never "perverted history in the interests of his
religious convictions." The author of more than 80 books on religious and
oriental topics, he served briefly as a missionary in China and helped direct
mission activities throughout his lifetime. He was ordained in the Baptist
ministry in 1918 and was professor of missions and oriental history at Yale
after 1927, becoming emeritus in 1953. He was decorated by the Chinese
government with the Order of Jade in 1938.

BOOKS BY LATOURETTE

History of Early Relations between the United States and China, 1784–1844. 1917.
    Kraus o.p.
A History of Japan. 1918. Macmillan 1957 o.p.
History of Christian Missions in China. Russell repr. of 1929 ed. 1967 $22.50
The Chinese: Their History and Culture. 1934. Macmillan 2 vols. in 1 4th ed. rev. 1964
    o.p.
A History of the Expansion of Christianity. 1937–45. Zondervan 7 vols. ea. $8.95

(ed.). *Gospel, the Church and the World. Essay Index Repr. Ser.* Ayer repr. of 1946 ed. $18.00

A Short History of the Far East. 1946. Macmillan 4th ed. text ed. 1964 o.p.

A History of Christianity. 1953. Harper 2 vols. rev. ed. 1975 pap. ea. $10.53–$11.49

Christianity in a Revolutionary Age. Greenwood 5 vols. repr. of 1958–62 ed. 1973 lib. bdg. $160.50; Zondervan 5 vols. ea. $5.95

China. Prentice-Hall 1964 o.p.

Christianity through the Ages. Harper pap. $7.64; Peter Smith $16.25

LENIN, NIKOLAI (born VLADIMIR ILYICH ULYANOV). 1870–1924

The man who was probably the single most effective influence behind the Russian Revolution of 1917 was described in 1894 by his contemporary A. N. Potresov as "a great force. But at the same time with a quality of one-sidedness, a kind of single note simplification, a quality of over-simplifying the complexities of life." Believing fervently in the Marxist "rule of the proletariat," Lenin dedicated his life to revolution with a notable lack of personal vanity or ambition and a singular ruthlessness of purpose. "The most highly charged utilitarian who ever came out of the laboratory of history," Trotsky wrote of him in 1924.

Born in Simbirsk, now called after him Ulyanovsk, the son of middle-class parents, Lenin's early training was in law. After his brother's execution for involvement in a plot against Czar Alexander III, he dedicated himself entirely to revolutionary causes. He was exiled several times to Siberia, and in 1900 he went to live in London, where he headed the Bolshevik revolutionary party. He returned to his homeland at the time of the abortive revolution of 1905, but went abroad again in 1907, writing and speaking in Marxist terms to promote the uprising of the Russian working classes. At the outbreak of the 1917 revolution (during World War I he had been living in Switzerland), he returned to Russia and with the victory of the Bolsheviks over the Kerensky government assumed the powerful post of chairman of the Council of People's Commissars. He played the major role (he was by now also chairman of the Communist party) in suppressing the Christian churches, establishing the Third International, and laying the groundwork for the present form of the Soviet Union. When he died from a stroke in 1924, Stalin became his successor.

BOOKS BY LENIN

Complete Collected Works. Imported Pubns. 45 vols. 1980 ea. $3.25 set $135.00

Selected Works. Imported Pubns. 3 vols. 1977 $15.00

The Essentials of Lenin. Russian Studies: Perspectives on the Revolution Ser. Hyperion Pr. 2 vols. repr. of 1947 ed. 1974 $70.00

Lenin on Politics and Revolution: Selected Writings. Trans. and ed. by James E. Connor, Pegasus 1968 o.p.

Letters of Lenin. Ed. and trans. by Elizabeth Hill and Doris Mudie, Hyperion Pr. repr. of 1937 ed. 1973 $32.40

What Is to Be Done? Burning Questions of Our Movement. 1902. Ed. by James S. Allen, International Publishing 1969 pap. $2.50. Lenin's pamphlet on the role of the revolutionary party.

Imperialism: The Highest Stage of Capitalism. 1916. China Bks. 1965 pap. $2.25; International Publishing 1969 pap. $1.75. Lenin's famous treatise on imperialism as the result of finance, capital, and monopoly.

The State and Revolution. 1917. China Bks. 1965 pap. $2.25; Greenwood repr. of 1935 ed. 1978 lib. bdg. $22.50; International Publishing 1932 pap. $1.50

Lenin on the United States. Ed. by C. Leiteizen and James S. Allen, International Publishing 1970 pap. $3.65

BOOKS ABOUT LENIN

Bachman, John E. *Lenin and Trotsky.* Ed. by I. E. Cadenhead, Barron 1974 o.p.

Balabanoff, Angelica. *Impressions of Lenin.* Trans. by Isotta Cesari, intro. by Bertram D. Wolfe, Univ. of Michigan Pr. 1964 pap. $1.75. Memoirs by one of the early leaders of Soviet Russia.

Deutscher, Isaac. *Lenin's Childhood.* Oxford 1970 $9.95

Everdale, Carl P. *The Contributions of Lenin and Mao Tse-tung to the Communist Theories Advanced by Marx and Engels.* Institute for Economic & Political World Strategic Studies 2 vols. 1982 $187.45

Fischer, Louis. *The Life of Lenin.* Harper 1964 o.p. Fischer met Lenin in 1922 on his first visit to Russia and is a leading expert on the U.S.S.R.

Gerson, Leonard D., ed. *Lenin and the Twentieth Century: A Bertram D. Wolfe Retrospective.* Hoover Institution 1984 lib. bdg. $27.95

Hill, Christopher. *Lenin and the Russian Revolution.* Penguin 1978 pap. $3.95

Institute of Marxism-Leninism. *Lenin: A Biography.* Imported Pubns. 1983 $11.95

Krupskaya, N. K. *Memories of Lenin.* Beekman 1970 o.p.

Lewin, Moshe. *Lenin's Last Struggle.* Monthly Review 1978 pap. $8.00

Page, Stanley W. *The Geopolitics of Leninism.* East European Quarterly 1982 $20.00

Pearson, Michael. *The Sealed Train: Lenin's Eight-Month Journey from Exile to Power.* Putnam 1975 o.p.

Polan, A. J. *Lenin and the End of Politics.* Univ. of California Pr. text ed. 1984 $22.50 pap. $9.95

Rosmer, Alfred. *Moscow Under Lenin.* Trans. by Ian Birchall, intro. by Tamara Deutscher, Monthly Review 1973 $8.95 pap. $3.75

Theen, Rolf H. *Lenin: Genesis and Development of a Revolutionary.* Princeton Univ. Pr. 1980 $18.00 pap. $6.95

Trotsky, Leon. *Lenin: Notes for a Biographer.* Trans. by Tamara Deutscher, Putnam 1971 o.p.

————. *The Young Lenin.* Trans. by Max Eastman, Doubleday 1972 o.p.

Wolfe, Bertram D. *The Bridge and the Abyss: The Troubled Friendship of Maxim Gorky and V. I. Lenin.* Greenwood repr. of 1967 ed. 1983 lib. bdg. $32.50

MAHAN, ALFRED THAYER. 1840–1914

Mahan was the greatest U.S. military historian and one of the most influential of all nineteenth-century historians. Son of an instructor at West Point, whose precepts were followed by generals on both sides in the Civil War, he attended Annapolis and saw duty in the South Atlantic and Gulf of Mexico against the Confederacy. He taught briefly at Annapolis, but spent most of his academic career at the newly founded Naval War College. Mahan's two major works, *The Influence of Sea Power upon History, 1660–1783*, published in 1890, and *The Influence of Sea Power upon the French Revolution and Empire, 1793–1812*, published two years later, attributed the dominance of

Great Britain in world politics during the eighteenth and nineteenth centuries to its invincible navy. His ideas were picked up by Theodore Roosevelt in the United States, by Admiral von Tirpitz in Germany, and by Admiral Togo in Japan, and used to justify the building of large U.S., German, and Japanese fleets. Indeed, Mahan was assigned some of the blame for the naval race before World War I. He wrote other books on sea power, was a founder of the Navy League, and fought throughout his life for a Panama Canal. He is the spiritual father of the modern U.S. Navy.

BOOKS BY MAHAN

The Gulf and Inland Waters: The Navy in the Civil War. Select Bibliographies Repr. Ser. Ayer repr. of 1883 ed. $21.50

The Influence of Sea Power upon History, 1660–1783. Hill & Wang 1957 pap. $12.95; Little, Brown repr. of 1890 ed. $17.50

The Influence of Sea Power upon the French Revolution and Empire, 1793–1812. 1892. Greenwood 2 vols. repr. of 1898 ed. 10th ed. 1968 lib. bdg. $32.25; Scholarly 2 vols. repr. of 1898 ed. $34.00

Admiral Farragut. Greenwood repr. of 1895 ed. 1969 lib. bdg. $15.00; Haskell repr. of 1895 ed. 1969 lib. bdg. $49.95; Scholarly repr. of 1892 ed. 1970 $10.00

The Interest of America in Sea Power: Present and Future. Select Bibliographies Repr. Ser. Ayer repr. of 1897 ed. $21.00

The Life of Nelson: The Embodiment of British Sea Power. Foundation Class. 4 vols. repr. of 1897 ed. $657.50; Greenwood 2 vols. repr. of 1897 ed. 1968 lib. bdg. $28.75; Haskell 2 vols. repr. of 1897 ed. 1969 lib. bdg. $69.96; Scholarly 2 vols. in 1 repr. of 1897 ed. $27.00

Lessons of the War with Spain. Select Bibliographies Repr. Ser. Ayer repr. of 1899 ed. $21.00

Problem of Asia. Associated Faculty Pr. repr. of 1900 ed. 1971 $19.50

Story of the War in South Africa, 1899–1900. Greenwood repr. of 1900 ed. lib. bdg. $15.00

Types of Naval Officers, Drawn from the History of the British Navy. Essay Index Repr. Ser. Ayer repr. of 1901 ed. $22.75; *Essay Index Repr. Ser.* Irvington repr. of 1901 ed. lib. bdg. $19.75

Retrospect and Prospect. Associated Faculty Pr. repr. of 1902 ed. 1968 $20.50

Sea Power in Its Relations to the War of 1812. Greenwood 2 vols. repr. of 1905 ed. 1969 lib. bdg. $28.75; Haskell 2 vols. repr. of 1905 ed. 1969 lib. bdg. $79.95

From Sail to Steam: Recollections of Naval Life. Da Capo repr. of 1907 ed. 1968 lib. bdg. $37.50

Naval Strategy. Greenwood repr. of 1911 ed. 1975 lib. bdg. $34.25

Armaments and Arbitration; or The Place of Force in the International Relations of States. Associated Faculty Pr. repr. of 1912 ed. 1973 $23.50

Major Operations of the Navies in the War of American Independence. Greenwood repr. of 1913 ed. 1968 lib. bdg. $19.50

The Panama Canal and Sea Power in the Pacific. Amer. Class. College Pr. 1977 $97.45; Institute of Economic & Political World Strategic Studies repr. of 1913 ed. 1983 $115.75

The Decline of the United States and the Safety of the Free World. Amer. Class. College Pr. 2 vols. 1978 $167.75

Europe, Russia, the United States and the Problem of Asia. Amer. Class. College Pr. 1984 $147.45

Naval Power and Naval War. Institution of Economic & Political World Strategic Studies 1983 $187.45

BOOKS ABOUT MAHAN

Livesay, W. E. *Mahan on Sea Power.* Univ. of Oklahoma Pr. 1947 o.p.
Seager, Robert. *Alfred Thayer Mahan: The Man and His Letters.* Naval Institute Pr. 1977 $24.95

MATTINGLY, GARRETT. 1900–1961

While a graduate student at Harvard in the early 1920s, Garrett Mattingly composed a sonnet a day to teach himself to write English well. He developed a wonderfully elegant style, which complemented his unusually original historical ideas.

Mattingly taught at Northwestern and Long Island universities, and was on leave from Columbia as Eastman Professor at Oxford when he died. For an appreciation of his life and a critique of his work, see the articles by Leo Gershoy and J. H. Hexter in C. H. Carter, ed., *From the Renaissance to the Counter Reformation: Essays in Honor of Garrett Mattingly* (o.p.).

BOOKS BY MATTINGLY

Catherine of Aragon. AMS Pr. repr. of 1942 ed. $32.50
Renaissance Diplomacy. Houghton Mifflin 1971 pap. $4.95; Russell repr. of 1955 ed. 1970 $12.00
The Armada. 1959. Houghton Mifflin 1962 pap. $9.95. This book was awarded a special Pulitzer Prize.

McNEILL, WILLIAM H(ARDY). 1917–

Arnold Toynbee has acclaimed McNeill's *The Rise of the West*, which took nine years to write, as "the most lucid presentation of world history in narrative form that I know." It won the 1963 National Book Award for history and the Gordon J. Laing Prize of the University of Chicago. The author, born in Canada, was chairman of the Department of History at the University of Chicago. His one-volume *A World History*, which gives equal space to Asia and the West, was greeted as a work of major importance by Toynbee, Hans Kohn, Geoffrey Bruun, Stringfellow Barr, and John Barkham, among others. He was one of the editors of the *Readings in World History Series* published by Oxford.

BOOKS BY McNEILL

History of Western Civilization: A Handbook. 1948. Univ. of Chicago Pr. rev. ed. text ed. 1969 pap. $14.00
America, Britain and Russia: Their Cooperation and Conflict, 1941–1946. Johnson Repr. repr. of 1953 ed. $60.00
Past and Future. Univ. of Chicago Pr. (Phoenix Bks.) 1954 o.p.
The Rise of the West: A History of the Human Community. 1963. Univ. of Chicago Pr. (Phoenix Bks.) 1970 pap. $9.95
Europe's Steppe Frontier, 1500–1800: A Study of the Eastward Movement in Europe. 1964. *Midway Repr. Ser.* Univ. of Chicago Pr. 1975 pap. $13.00

A World History. Oxford 3d ed. 1979 $29.95 text ed. pap. $16.95. "He makes the interactions between different civilizations, in all periods of history, the main theme
of his book . . . . In fact, he makes a complicated story lucid" (Arnold Toynbee).
Includes an excellent portfolio of colored maps.

The Contemporary World, 1914–Present. 1968. Scott, Foresman rev. ed. 1975 pap.
$9.95

Ecumene: Story of Humanity. Harper 1973 o.p.

The Shape of European History. Oxford 1974 $16.95 pap. $5.95

Venice: The Hinge of Europe, 1081–1797. Univ. of Chicago Pr. 1974 $10.75

Plagues and People. Doubleday (Anchor) 1977 pap. $5.50

The Metamorphosis of Greece since World War II. Univ. of Chicago Pr. 1978 $12.95

The Human Condition: An Ecological and Historical View. Princeton Univ. Pr. 1980
$12.50

The Pursuit of Power: Technology, Armed Force and Society since A.D. 1000. Univ. of
Chicago Pr. 1982 $20.00

The Great Frontier: Freedom and Hierarchy in Modern Times. Princeton Univ. Pr. 1983
$13.95

NEHRU, JAWAHARLAL. 1889–1964

Nehru, architect of India's freedom and prime minister from independence in 1947 until his death in 1964, wrote widely on Indian nationalist activities. Educated at Harrow and Cambridge, he returned to India in 1912
and joined Gandhi's movement in 1919, was second to him in influence, and
succeeded him as leader of the National Congress party in 1942. He served
seven terms in jail from 1921 to 1934. During one stretch of imprisonment,
1930–33, Nehru passed the time by writing letters to his young daughter
about man's whole history—enough letters to fill a 1,000-page volume, published as *Glimpses of World History* (1942, o.p.). It "retains all of Nehru's
philosophical reflections about history, with enough glimpses to illustrate
the main course of development in both East and West and their relations
today" (*N.Y. Times*).

Much loved and often criticized, Nehru, nurtured by his long periods of
contemplation and inaction in prison, was at once revolutionary, philosopher, and practical politician. He was perhaps the last great example of the
leader who through experience and training—and great literary ability—
understood equally, and interpreted through his speeches and writings, the
ancient East and modern West.

BOOKS BY NEHRU

Selected Works of Jawaharlal Nehru. Ed. by S. Gopal, South Asia Bks. 10 vols. 1972–
78 ea. $12.75–$16.00

Speeches, 1946–1964. Verry 5 vols. o.p.

Nehru on World History. 1942. Ed. by Saul K. Padover, Indiana Univ. Pr. abr. ed.
1962 pap. $2.45

The Discovery of India. 1946. Ed. by Robert I. Crane, Doubleday (Anchor) 1960 o.p.

Independence and After. Essay Index Repr. Ser. Ayer repr. of 1950 ed. $26.50

Mahatma Gandhi. Asia Publishing House 1966 o.p.

India's Quest: Being Letters on Indian History. Asia Publishing House 1967 o.p.

A Bunch of Old Letters: Written Mostly to Jawaharlal Nehru, and Some Written by Him. Asia Publishing House 2d ed. 1960 o.p.

BOOKS ABOUT NEHRU

Benudhar, Pradham. *The Socialist Thought of Jawaharlal Nehru.* South Asia Bks. 1974 o.p.

Butler, Lord C. H. *Jawaharlal Nehru.* Cambridge Univ. Pr. 1967 $1.95

Chakraborty, A. K. *Jawaharlal Nehru's Writings.* South Asia Bks. 1981 $15.00

Chhibber, V. N. *Jawaharlal Nehru: Man of Letters.* Verry 1970 o.p.

Copeland, Ian. *Jawaharlal Nehru of India, 1889–1964. Leaders of Asia Ser.* Univ. of Queensland Pr. 1980 pap. $3.00

Darbari, J., and R. Darbari. *Commonwealth and Nehru.* Humanities Pr. text ed. 1984 $13.00

Edwardes, Michael. *Nehru: A Pictorial Biography.* Viking 1963 o.p. This portrait based in part on material supplied by Nehru's family includes many pictures never before printed.

Gopal, Ram. *The Mind of Jawaharlal Nehru.* Apt Bks. text ed. 1980 pap. $3.95

————. *Trials of Jawaharlal Nehru.* Biblio Dist. 1964 $24.00; Humanities Pr. text ed. 1962 $6.50

Range, Willard. *Jawaharlal Nehru's World View: A Theory of International Relations.* Univ. of Georgia Pr. 1961 o.p. Range analyzes Nehru's published writings, speeches, and interviews. Although some of the author's conclusions are susceptible to argument, his book is helpful in the understanding of a very complex person.

Seton, Marie. *Panditji: A Portrait of Jawaharlal Nehru.* Taplinger 1967 o.p. The author, observing Nehru from the standpoint of an admiring family friend, "is very self-consciously a Boswell" (*N.Y. Times*).

SCHEVILL, FERDINAND. 1868–1954

A popular and respected teacher at the University of Chicago, from which he retired in 1937, Schevill wrote a number of books, the best known of which is *A History of Florence* (o.p.), still the most useful general history in any language.

BOOKS BY SCHEVILL

Siena: The History of a Medieval Commune. Peter Smith $5.50; Richard West repr. of 1909 ed. 1979 lib. bdg. $40.00

The History of the Balkan Peninsula: From the Earliest Times to the Present Day. Eastern European Collection Ser. Ayer repr. of 1922 ed. 1970 $38.50

First Century of Italian Humanism. World History Ser. Haskell repr. of 1928 ed. 1970 pap. $40.00; Russell repr. of 1928 ed. 1967 $5.00

A History of Florence: From the Founding of the City through the Renaissance. Ungar rev. ed. 1961 o.p.

The Medici. Arden Lib. repr. of 1950 ed. 1981 lib. bdg. $35.00; Peter Smith $5.00

Six Historians. Univ. of Chicago Pr. 1956 o.p.

SPENGLER, OSWALD. 1880–1936

Like Toynbee's great *A Study of History, The Decline of the West* has as its theme the rise and decline of civilizations, but unlike Toynbee, Spengler believed that present occidental civilization had reached its period of decadence and was about to be conquered by the Mongolian people of Asia. Spengler was a teacher of mathematics, who wrote his book in extreme poverty in Munich during World War I. He revised it in the period of despair following the war, and the 1923 edition brought him wealth and fame. At first, because of his dislike of "non-Aryan" peoples, he was popular with the Nazis, but he refused to participate in their anti-Semitic activities. He was allowed to stay in Germany and to keep his property, but the last years of his life were spent under the cloud of official disfavor.

BOOKS BY SPENGLER

Selected Essays. Trans. by Donald O. White, Regnery-Gateway 1967 o.p.

Aphorisms. Trans. by Gisela K. O'Brien, Regnery-Gateway 1967 o.p.

The Decline of the West. 1918–22. Knopf 2 vols. 1945 ea. $20.00

The Hour of Decision. 1933. Trans. by Charles F. Atkinson, AMS Pr. repr. of 1934 ed. $27.50

World History: The Destiny-Idea and the Causality-Principle. Foundation Class. repr. 1984 $137.55

STALIN, JOSEPH (VISSARIONOVICH). 1879–1953

Stalin first became interested in Marxism while he was (briefly) studying for the priesthood. After various periods of arrest and escape or imprisonment, he became a follower of Lenin in the split between the Mensheviks and Bolsheviks in 1903. Originally called Dzhugashvili, he took the name Stalin, "man of steel," about 1913; he was then an editor of the embryo Communist paper *Pravda.* After the October 1917 Revolution, he became people's commissar for nationalities, the leading member of the triumvirate that ruled the U.S.S.R. after Lenin's death. During the period of his dictatorship, which followed, many of his former comrades perished in the purges.

Although Stalin signed a mutual nonaggression agreement with Nazi Germany in 1939, Germans attacked Russia in 1941. During the war and after the Allied victory he met with Churchill, Roosevelt, and Truman at the Teheran, Yalta, and Potsdam conferences. At his death, he received the funeral of a state hero and was buried next to Lenin in Moscow's Red Square. In 1961, after Nikita Khrushchev had denounced Stalin and his policies, Stalin's body was moved to the cemetery for heroes near the Kremlin Wall. In March 1969, *Pravda* began issuing excerpts from the new novel *They Fought for Their Country* by Mikhail Sholokhov, which imply that Stalin was unaware of the activities of his secret police in pursuing the purges of the 1930s.

In 1967 his daughter Svetlana Alliluyeva caused a sensation when she abandoned the U.S.S.R. and her two nearly grown children, to seek haven in the United States, where she settled for many years before returning in 1984 to the Soviet Union. In 1986 she left the U.S.S.R. and returned to the United States, expressing her intent to remain in the country permanently. Her *Twenty Letters to a Friend* cast new light on Stalin's private life and her mother's suicide. In the book she refrains from expressing active hostility to her father and believes that he was to some extent deceived by Beria, chief of his secret police.

Of the many biographical studies of Stalin, one of the most fascinating is that by Leon Trotsky. In the introduction to the 1967 edition, Bertram D. Wolfe writes: "In all literature there is no more dramatic relationship between author and subject . . . . It is like Robespierre doing a life of Fouche, Kurbsky of Ivan the Terrible, Muenzer of Martin Luther."

BOOKS BY STALIN

Works. Ed. by Robert H. McNeal, Hoover Institution 3 vols. 1967 o.p.
Foundations of Leninism. 1939. China Bks. 1965 $4.95 pap. $2.50
Dialectical and Historical Materialism. International Publishing 1940 pap. $.75
Great Patriotic War of the Soviet Union. Greenwood repr. of 1945 ed. lib. bdg. $15.00
Economic Problems of Socialism in the U.S.S.R. China Bks. pap. $1.25
Marxism and the Problems of Linguistics. China Bks. pap. $1.25
Correspondence with Churchill and Attlee. Putnam 1965 o.p.
Correspondence with Roosevelt and Truman. Putnam 1965 o.p.

BOOKS ABOUT STALIN

Alliluyeva, Svetlana. *Twenty Letters to a Friend: A Memoir.* Trans. by Priscilla Mac-Millan, Harper 1967 $11.49. Recollections by Stalin's daughter of the period up to her father's death.
Antonov-Ovseyenko, Anton. *The Time of Stalin: Portrait of a Tyranny.* Harper 1983 pap. $8.61
Bialer, Seweryn, ed. *Stalin and His Generals: Soviet Military Memoirs of World War II. Encore Ed. Ser.* Westview Pr. 1984 $38.50
Conquest, Robert. *The Great Terror: Stalin's Purge of the Thirties.* Macmillan (Collier Bks.) rev. ed. 1973 o.p.
Deutscher, Isaac. *Stalin: A Political Biography.* Oxford 2d ed. pap. $14.95. "Highly valuable for its patient and frequently illuminating analysis of the first eight volumes of Stalin's 'Collected Works.'. . . It is by any test stylistically a skillful and well written book" (Bertram D. Wolfe).
Payne, Robert. *The Rise and Fall of Stalin.* Simon & Schuster 1965 o.p. A readable and exciting narrative.
Taubman, William. *Stalin's American Policy.* Norton 1983 pap. $7.95
Trotsky, Leon. *Stalin: An Appraisal of the Man and His Influence.* Intro. by Bertram D. Wolfe, Stein & Day 1970 o.p. The classic biography of Trotsky's victorious rival.
Tucker, Robert C. *Stalin as Revolutionary, 1879–1929: A Study in History and Personality.* Norton 1973 $12.95 pap. $10.95
Urban, George. *Stalinism.* St. Martin's 1982 $25.00

SYMONDS, JOHN ADDINGTON. 1840–1893

Symonds, an English poet, essayist, and literary historian, spent much of his life on the Continent and wrote many travel books and biographies; he is also known for his remarkable translation of CELLINI's autobiography. His major work, *The Renaissance in Italy,* is a classic collection of sketches in cultural history.

BOOKS BY SYMONDS

Letters and Papers. 1923. Ed. by Horatio F. Brown, Richard West o.p.

The Renaissance in Italy. 1875–86. Peter Smith 3 vols. ea. $10.75 set $32.25
A Short History of the Renaissance in Italy. Cooper Square Pr. repr. of 1894 ed. $22.50

BOOKS ABOUT SYMONDS

Babington, Percy L. *Bibliography of the Writings of John Addington Symonds.* Burt Franklin repr. of 1925 ed. 1967 $24.50
Brooks, Van Wyck. *John Addington Symonds: A Biographical Study.* Scholarly 1971 $21.00
Brown, Horatio F. *Letters and Papers of John Addington Symonds.* Richard West repr. of 1923 ed. $25.00

TAYLOR, A(LAN) J(OHN) P(ERCIVALE). 1906–

Fritz Stern wrote of this British historian and his *The Struggle for Mastery in Europe, 1848–1918*, in the *Political Science Quarterly:* "There is something Shavian about A. J. P. Taylor and his place among academic historians; he is brilliant, erudite, witty, dogmatic, heretical, irritating, insufferable, and withal inescapable. He sometimes insults and always instructs his fellow-historians, and never more so than in his present effort to reinterpret the diplomatic history of Europe from 1848 to the end of the First World War.... After a brilliant introduction, in which he defines the balance of power and assesses the relative and changing strength of the Great Powers, Mr. Taylor presents a chronological survey, beginning with the diplomacy of war, 1914–1918.... [He] writes on two levels. He narrates the history of European diplomacy and compresses it admirably into a single volume. Imposed upon the narrative is his effort to probe the historical meaning of given actions and conditions.... He has a peculiar sense of inevitability, growing out of what he regards the logic of a given development, as well as a delicate feeling for live options and alternatives. Mr. Taylor suggests that fear, not aggression, was the dominant impulse of pre-war diplomacy."

The Origins of the Second World War, again controversial and lively, starts from the premise (in Taylor's words) that "the war of 1939, far from being premeditated, was a mistake, the result on both sides of diplomatic blunders." The *New Statesman* said of it: "Taylor is the only English historian now writing who can bend the bow of Gibbon and Macaulay. [This is] a masterpiece: lucid, compassionate, beautifully written in a bare, sparse style, and at the same time deeply disturbing."

English History, 1919–1945, a volume in the *Oxford History of England Series*, has been widely praised. The *N.Y. Review of Books* greeted it as "an astonishing tour de force." ALLAN NEVINS, while disagreeing with Taylor's account of the origins of World War II, found *English History* the "best" of Mr. Taylor's books to date, "a volume of high merit, rich in insight and offering a marvelously full, but compact, record of perhaps the most eventful period in all English history."

BOOKS BY A. J. P. TAYLOR

Germany's First Bid for Colonies, 1884–1885: A Move in Bismarck's European Policy. Norton Lib. repr. of 1938 ed. 1970 pap. $1.25; Shoe String (Archon) repr. of 1938 ed. 1967 $13.50

The Course of German History. 1945. Putnam 1962 o.p.

From Napoleon to Stalin: Comments on European History. AMS Pr. repr. of 1950 ed. $28.50

The Struggle for Mastery in Europe: 1848–1918. History of Modern Europe Ser. Oxford 1954 $42.00 pap. $12.95. "What makes this the best study of European diplomacy since W. L. Langer's volumes on the post-1870 period is his ability to keep the major developments of the period clearly before his readers, while at the same time providing them with circumstantial and absorbing accounts of the policies and ambitions of individual powers and statesmen, the changing diplomatic alignments, and the crises and wars which filled the period" (*SR*).

Bismarck: The Man and the Statesman. 1955. Random (Vintage) 1967 pap. $4.95

Beaverbrook. Simon & Schuster $12.95

The Origins of the Second World War. 1961. Atheneum 1983 pap. $9.95; Fawcett 1978 pap. $2.25

The First World War: An Illustrated History. 1963. Peter Smith $6.00

English History, 1919–1945. Oxford History of England Ser. 1965 $32.50 pap. $7.95

From Sarajevo to Potsdam. History of European Civilization Lib. Harcourt text ed. 1966 pap. $11.95

TAYLOR, HENRY OSBORN. 1856–1941

Henry Osborn Taylor lectured at Harvard, but was best known for his masterpiece *The Medieval Mind* (o.p.), the subject of his lifetime study. Its sequel, *Thought and Expression in the Sixteenth Century*, published in 1920 is out of print as is *Prophets, Poets and Philosophers of the Ancient World.*

BOOKS BY HENRY OSBORN TAYLOR

Ancient Ideals: A Study of Intellectual and Spiritual Growth from Early Times to the Establishment of Christianity. 1896. Norwood 2 vols. repr. 1900 ed. $100.00; Telegraph Bks. 2 vols. repr. of 1900 ed. 1982 lib. bdg. $100.00; Ungar 2 vols. 1964 $32.50

The Classical Heritage of the Middle Ages. 1901. Ungar 1958 o.p.

The Medieval Mind: A History of the Development of Thought and Emotion in the Middle Ages. 1911. Harvard Univ. Pr. 2 vols. 4th ed. rev. 1959 o.p.

TOYNBEE, ARNOLD J(OSEPH). 1889–1975

Toynbee has always been a controversial historian, who made sweeping generalizations about history that were often criticized by other scholars. Of himself, he wrote: "What I am trying to do is explain to Western people that they are only a small minority of the world—the great world is Asia and Africa—outside the West."

His *Study of History* took him 40 years of steady labor, and at 80 he was still going strong and continuing to work a seven-day week. " 'I suppose that one day I might stop, and if I stopped I might suddenly crumple,' he said. 'It is very important to keep going.' " Rather than revise the whole ten-volume set (the *Historical Atlas and Gazetteer* is Volume 11), Toynbee decided to correct errors and refute his critics in *Reconsiderations* (Volume 12 of *A Study of History*).

East to West: A Journey round the World (1958, o.p.) is a collection of world portraits of contemporary affairs and conditions in ancient setting, and *Between Oxus and Jumna* (1961, o.p.) serves as an unsurpassed travel guide to a little-known, rugged area encompassing Afghanistan, western Pakistan, and northwest India.

BOOKS BY TOYNBEE

The Western Question in Greece and Turkey: A Study in the Contrast of Civilizations. Fertig repr. of 1922 ed. 2d ed. 1970 $35.00

The World after the Peace Conference. Johnson Repr. repr. of 1925 ed. pap. $9.00

The Islamic World since the Peace Settlement. Johnson Repr. repr. of 1927 ed. $50.00

A Study of History: The Disintegrations of Civilization. Royal Institute of International Affairs Ser. Oxford 12 vols. 1939–61 ea. $25.00–$37.50

Civilization on Trial (and *The World and the West*). New Amer. Lib. 1958 pap. $4.95

Hitler's Europe. Johnson Repr. repr. of 1954 ed. $60.00 pap. $54.00

The Industrial Revolution. 1956. Peter Smith $10.25

An Historian's Approach to Religion. 1956. Oxford 2d ed. 1979 $22.50

America and the World Revolution and Other Lectures. Oxford 1962 o.p.

Hannibal's Legacy. Oxford 2 vols. 1965 $74.50

Change and Habit: The Challenge of Our Time. Oxford 1966 $11.95

Acquaintances. Oxford 1967 $18.95. Biographical sketches of people Toynbee knew.

Experiences. Oxford 1969 $22.50. Autobiographical reminiscences intended as a sequel to *Acquaintances.* "He tells of his youth, his career and some personal affairs, always with an eye on more generally valid observations. Then he draws up a balance sheet of human affairs, and finally shows himself from a new angle: as a poet . . . . Those of us who have been privileged to know him personally will treasure Toynbee's autobiographical chapters especially. For a wider circle of readers—and this brilliant volume deserves many thousands of them—his balance sheet of human affairs in his lifetime may be even more fascinating" (Felix E. Hirsch, *N.Y. Times*).

Some Problems of Greek History. Oxford 1969 o.p.

Cities on the Move. Oxford 1970 $15.95

Constantine Porphyrogenitus and His World. Oxford 1973 $45.00

Mankind and Mother Earth: A Narrative History of the World. Oxford 1976 $37.50. Toynbee's last book, published posthumously. It emphasizes the interaction of man with his environment and with his fellow man from the beginnings of human life until the 1970s.

BOOKS ABOUT TOYNBEE

Gargan, Edward T., ed. *The Intent of Toynbee's History.* Loyola Univ. Pr. 1961 $5.00

Geyl, Pieter. *Debates with Historians.* World Publishing 1958 o.p. Includes a brilliant and devastating critique of Toynbee by the greatest Dutch historian of this century.

Ortega y Gasset, Jose. *An Interpretation of Universal History.* Trans. by Mildred Adams, Norton 1973 $8.95 1984 pap. $7.95. A series of lectures on Toynbee's *A Study of History.*

Stromberg, Roland N. *Arnold J. Toynbee: Historian for an Age in Crisis.* Southern Illinois Univ. Pr. 1972 o.p.

TROTSKY, LEON (pseud. of Lev Davydovich Bronstein). 1879–1940

The son of Jewish parents, Trotsky became a member of a Marxist circle in 1896. Imprisoned many times, he escaped from Siberia by using the name of a jailer called Trotsky on a false passport. During World War I, he lived in Switzerland, France, and New York City, where he edited the newspaper *Novy Mir* (*New World*). He went back to Russia in 1917 and joined Lenin in the first, abortive, July Revolution of the Bolsheviks. A key organizer of the successful October Revolution, he was people's commissar for foreign affairs in the Lenin regime. Antagonism developed between Trotsky and Stalin during the Civil War of 1918–20; he also had differences with Lenin over control of the workers' union.

Exiled by Stalin after Lenin's death, Trotsky fled across Siberia (carrying with him source material on his experiences in the revolution) to Norway, France, and finally Mexico, where he began work on the biography of his bitter enemy Stalin in a heavily barred and guarded home in Coyoacan. He realized he was racing against time and was able to complete 7 of the 12 chapters before a member of the Soviet secret police managed to work his way into the household by posing as a convert to Trotskyism. Through the latter's agency, Trotsky was killed with a pickax at the desk where he was writing "Stalin," and the manuscript was spattered with its author's blood. The construction of the remaining 5 chapters was accomplished by the translator Charles Malamuth (a son-in-law of Jack London) from notes, work sheets, and fragments. Malamuth's translation of the initial chapters had been completed and checked by Trotsky before his death.

BOOKS BY TROTSKY

Writings. Ed. by George Breitman and others, Pathfinder Pr. 9 vols. 1970–74 ea. $30.00 pap. ea. $9.95

Literature and Revolution. c.1925. Univ. of Michigan Pr. 1960 $6.95

The Third International after Lenin. 1930. Intro. by G. Horowitz, Pathfinder Pr. 1970 pap. $8.95

The Russian Revolution: The Overthrow of Tzarism and the Triumph of the Soviets. 1932. Trans. by Max Eastman, Doubleday (Anchor) abr. ed. 1959 pap. $7.95

The Stalin School of Falsification. 1932. Trans. by George Saunders, Pathfinder Pr. 1980 lib. bdg. $27.00 pap. $7.95

The First Five Years of the Communist International. 1945. Ed. by John G. Wright and David Salner, Monad Pr. 2 vols. 2d ed. 1973 ea. $25.00 pap. ea. $7.95

Marxism in Our Time. 1970. Pathfinder Pr. 1972 pap. $1.25

Europe and America: Two Speeches on Imperialism. Trans. by John G. Wright, Pathfinder Pr. 1971 o.p.

The Trotsky Papers, 1917–1922. Ed. by Jan M. Meijer, *Russian Ser.* Mouton 2 vols. 1964–71 ea. $106.75–$113.00. Letters, messages, and the like from Trotsky's official Soviet period.

Trotsky's Diary in Exile, 1935. Trans. by Elena Zarudnaya, Atheneum text ed. 1964 pap. $3.95; intro. by Jean van Heijenoort, Harvard Univ. Pr. 1976 $15.00

My Life: Authorized Translation and Edition. Intro. by Joseph Hansen, Pathfinder Pr. 1970 pap. $8.95; Peter Smith $10.75

BOOKS ABOUT TROTSKY

Day, R. B. *Leon Trotsky and the Politics of Economic Isolation. Soviet and East European Studies* Cambridge Univ. Pr. 1973 $24.95

Deutscher, Isaac. *The Prophet Armed: Trotsky, 1879–1921.* Oxford repr. of 1954 ed. 1980 pap. $9.95

——. *The Prophet Unarmed: Trotsky, 1921–1929.* Oxford repr. of 1959 ed. 1980 pap. $9.95

——. *The Prophet Outcast: Trotsky, 1929–1940.* Oxford repr. of 1968 ed. 1980 pap. $9.95

Hansen, Joseph. *Leon Trotsky: The Man and His Works.* Pathfinder Pr. 1969 $2.45

Mandel, Ernest. *Trotsky: A Study in the Dynamic of His Thought.* Schocken 1980 $18.00 pap. $6.75

Molyneux, John. *Leon Trotsky's Theory of Revolution.* St. Martin's 1981 $25.00

Stokes, Curtis. *The Evolution of Trotsky's Theory of Revolution.* Univ. Pr. of Amer. 1982 lib. bdg. $26.25 text ed. pap. $11.00

Wolfe, Bertram D. *Three Who Made a Revolution.* Stein & Day 1984 $24.95 pap. $12.95. The best book in its field in any language.

Wolfenstein, E. Victor. *Revolutionary Personality: Lenin, Trotsky, Gandhi. Center of International Studies Ser.* Princeton Univ. Pr. 1971 $33.00

TUCHMAN, BARBARA (WERTHEIM). 1912–

Tuchman is a daughter of Maurice Wertheim, a New York banker, art collector, and founder of the Theatre Guild, and granddaughter of Henry Morgenthau, Sr. *The Guns of August*, her dramatic retelling of the events of the first 30 days of World War I, was a runaway bestseller in 1962 and won for its author a Pulitzer Prize. Of her earlier book on the same subject, the *N.Y. Times* said: "The value and importance of her book lies in her brilliant use of well known materials, her sureness of insight, and her competent grasp of a complicated chapter of diplomatic history."

BOOKS BY TUCHMAN

The Zimmerman Telegram. 1958. Ballantine 1985 pap. $7.95. A key incident in World War I.

The Guns of August. Bantam 1976 pap. $4.95; Macmillan 1962 $19.95

The Proud Tower. Bantam 1972 pap. $4.95; Macmillan 1966 $17.95

Stilwell and the American Experience in China, 1911–1945. Bantam 1972 pap. $5.95; Macmillan 1971 $21.95

Notes from China. Macmillan (Collier Bks.) 1972 pap. $2.95

A Distant Mirror: The Calamitous Fourteenth Century. Ballantine 1980 pap. $8.95; Knopf 1978 $25.00. Granted that the fourteenth century is a most difficult period to deal with, this book is still particularly disappointing in that it neglects Italy, where the Renaissance was just beginning, almost entirely.

Practicing History: Selected Essays. Ballantine 1982 pap. $7.95; Knopf 1981 $6.50

Bible and Sword: England and Palestine from the Bronze Age to Balfour. Ballantine 1984 $9.95

The March of Folly: From Troy to Vietnam. Ballantine 1985 pap. $9.95; Knopf 1984 $18.95. The "folly" is war. An interesting approach through case histories, but too often the facts take second place to the overall preconception.

VERNADSKY, GEORGE. 1887–1973

Professor Emeritus George Vernadsky of Yale was a Russian émigré who settled in the United States and became one of the foremost historians on the subject of his native land. His life, he said, fell into three periods. The first was his youth in Moscow, taking his degree from the University of Moscow, teaching Russian history at the University of Petrograd (1914–17) in the stimulating intellectual atmosphere of the former St. Petersburg, and finally studying and teaching in the Urals and Crimea, where, he said, even the revolution did not unduly disturb the universities. His second period was seven years in exile, spent teaching in Constantinople, Athens, Prague, and Paris. In 1927, he was invited to Yale; he came to the United States and remained in New Haven for the rest of his academic career, gradually producing a monumental body of work on Russian history. "While the transition from one span of my life to another was more or less painful," he said, "the more I think of the course of my life, the more I find that in many respects I should be grateful to Fate for this tortuous path, since it gave me the variety and richness of experience, and since in each of the three paths I was fortunate to meet so many kind and congenial friends."

Vernadsky's major work is the five-volume *A History of Russia*. Planned as a collaboration between Vernadsky and Michael Karpovich of Harvard, it was originally intended to run to nine volumes, but Karpovich's death in 1959 ended the possibility of his doing the later sections, and no further volumes appeared. Nevertheless, for the period it covers (to the time of the Renaissance and Reformation in Europe), it is the definitive work. Vernadsky's shorter *A History of Russia* brings the history of Russia up to the nuclear age.

BOOKS BY VERNADSKY

Lenin: Red Dictator. AMS Pr. repr. of 1931 ed. $18.50

A History of Russia:

> *Ancient Russia*. Pref. by Michael Karpovich, Yale Univ. Pr. 1943 $30.00. "It is impossible within the limits of a review to suggest all the ideas, outlooks, insights which 'Ancient Russia' provides .... Despite the remoteness of the centuries treated, the reader will find insights of every kind into the Russia of our day. And all who are interested in Russian history will recognize in 'Ancient Russia' a notable achievement of scholarship and interpretation" (Bertram D. Wolfe, *N.Y. Herald Tribune*).

> *Kievan Russia*. 1948. Yale Univ. Pr. 1973 pap. $11.95. "This volume is an outstanding contribution to the understanding of an important period of Russian history. It is bound to have a marked influence on Western opinion about the year in Russian history it treats in such a masterly manner" (*SR*).

> *The Mongols and Russia*. Yale Univ. Pr. 1953 o.p. "A volume distinguished by mature scholarship and based on thorough research and keen synthesis ..." (R. J. Kerner, *SR*).

> *Russia at the Dawn of the Modern Age*. Yale Univ. Pr. 1959 o.p. "The moment one begins to read a careful, scholarly history of Russia, such as the great work which Professor Vernadsky has in progress, the superficiality of so many of our current concepts about Russia becomes apparent" (Harrison Salisbury, in *SR*).

The Tsardom of Moscow, 1547–1682. Yale Univ. Pr. 2 vols. 1969 o.p. "Vernadsky is
  the most prolific student of Russian history in the United States, past or present,
  and he richly deserves our gratitude for the remarkable erudition and energy he
  has consistently brought to his writings" (S. H. Baron, *American Historical Review*).
(ed.). *Medieval Russian Laws.* 1947. Octagon 1965 lib. bdg. $18.50
A History of Russia. Yale Univ. Pr. rev. ed. 1961 pap. $11.95

WARD, BARBARA (LADY JACKSON). 1914–1981

An outstanding authority on world political, social, and economic issues,
Barbara Ward (Lady Jackson) has written many books for the general reader.
Her *Five Ideas That Change the World* are nationalism, industrialism, colonialism, communism, and internationalism. *India and the West* defined the urgency of India's desperate economic requirements and outlined a specific program for their accomplishment. Of it Edward Weeks wrote in the *Atlantic:*
"Ward's new book . . . is in many respects the most important she has ever
written. The qualities which she brings to her writing—her gift for historical
analysis, her explanation of difficult economic problems, and her reasonable
faith in the initiative of the free world—were never more needed."

The Rich Nations and the Poor Nations, which President Lyndon Johnson
remarked "excites and inspires me" and Adlai Stevenson found "exceedingly
important," was described by Eric F. Goldman as "wondrously lucid, richly
informed and trenchantly argued, tough-minded but never failing to assume that intelligence and will can move human society forward" (*N.Y.
Times Bk. Review*).

Born in Yorkshire, Ward was educated in England, Paris, and Germany.
At Somerville College, Oxford, she took first-class honors in philosophy, politics, and economics. She became an editor of the *Economist* in 1939. In
1958, she was appointed a Carnegie Fellow and Visiting Scholar in International Economic Development at Harvard University. Ten years later, she
became Albert Schweitzer Professor of International Economic Development at Columbia University. In January 1967 she was appointed by Pope
Paul VI to the Pontifical Commission of Justice and Peace.

BOOKS BY WARD

Interplay of East and West: Points of Conflict and Cooperation. 1957. *Norton Lib.* 1962
  pap. $1.25
Five Ideas That Change the World. Greenwood repr. of 1959 ed. 1984 lib. bdg. $25.00;
  Norton 1959 pap. $6.95
India and the West: Pattern for a Common Policy. Norton 1961 o.p.
The Rich Nations and the Poor Nations. Norton Lib. 1962 pap. $4.95
Nationalism and Ideology. Norton 1966 pap. $2.50.
Spaceship Earth. Columbia Univ. Pr. 1966 $25.00 pap. $11.00
The Lopsided World. Norton 1968 $3.95 pap. $1.95. The needs of the poor nations and
  the urgency for rich nations to help meet them.
(and Rene Dubos). *Only One Earth: The Care and Maintenance of a Small Planet.* Nor-
  ton 1983 pap. $5.95
(and others, eds.). *The Widening Gap: Development in the 1970's.* Columbia Univ. Pr.
  1971 $30.00

CHAPTER 11

Music and Dance

Michael A. Keller

Music is not an illusion, but revelation rather. Its triumphant power
resides in the fact that it reveals to us beauties we find nowhere
else, and that the apprehension of them is not transitory, but a
perpetual reconcilement of life.
  —Peter Ilyich Tchiakovsky, in *An Encyclopedia of Quotations about Music*

On with the dance! let joy be unconfined;
No sleep till morn, when Youth and Pleasure meet
To chase the glowing Hours with flying feet.
                    —Byron, *Childe Harold's Pilgrimage*

Music and dance have always been a part of the human environment. The beginnings of these art forms predate written history. They have served as part of religious, ceremonial, and work activities, as well as providing aesthetic pleasure. From the work songs of the pyramid builders to the background elevator tunes of the present era, music and the movement to its rhythm, or dance, have been common to every segment of society. For much of history, however, experiencing a professional performance has been an infrequent occurrence for most people. Modern technology has radically changed this situation so that music to suit a wide variety of tastes is readily and inexpensively available. Radio, television, and home entertainment systems are pouring forth a continual blanket of music. Nor are people restricted by location—portable radios and cassette and CD players allow them to enjoy their favorite sounds everywhere. More people hear and see Pavarotti in one television show than attended all of Caruso's performances, and Baryshnikov has danced for larger audiences than Nijinsky would have dreamed possible.

These technological changes have sparked an interest in the greater understanding of music and dance—history, criticism, and personalities. The volumes listed below not only cover the more traditional forms of opera, classical music, and ballet, but include jazz, ethnic music and dance, and contemporary music and dance. Nearly all of the books selected incorporate references to sources and are replete with reasonably good bibliographies, indexes, glossaries, illustrations, and other aids to the reader.

MUSIC

History and Criticism

Abraham, Gerald. *A Hundred Years of Music*. Biblio Dist. 4th ed. 1974 $40.50 pap. $13.50. Covers music from Beethoven to Schoenberg.

Adorno, Theodor W. *Introduction to the Sociology of Music*. Trans. by E. B. Ashton, Continuum 1976 $16.95. Twelve essays dealing with the social contexts of music and its listeners, espousing a complex philosophical view that incorporates method and substance.

Austin, William W. *Music in the 20th Century, from Debussy through Stravinsky*. Norton 1966 $24.95. Provocative history of music in the first two-thirds of the twentieth century. Outstanding bibliography.

Barzun, Jacques. *Critical Questions: On Music and Letters, Culture and Biography, 1940–1980*. Ed. by Bea Friedland, Univ. of Chicago Pr. 1982 lib. bdg. $22.50 1984 pap. $8.95. An anthology of reprinted articles on a wide variety of subjects aimed at the culturally informed reader.

Bukofzer, Manfred F. *Music in the Baroque Era: From Monteverdi to Bach*. Norton 1974 $20.95. Thoughtful survey through style criticism rather than detailed analysis of individual pieces of music. The standard history of the period.

Chase, Gilbert. *America's Music: From the Pilgrims to the Present*. Fwd. by Douglas Moore, Greenwood 2d rev. ed. repr. of 1966 ed. 1981 lib. bdg. $45.00. American music up to about 1960.

Crocker, Richard L. *A History of Musical Style*. McGraw-Hill text ed. 1966 $19.95. Covers the development of Western musical style, stressing the continuity of basic musical principles. Particularly strong in earlier periods.

Dahlhaus, Carl. *Esthetics of Music*. Trans. by William W. Austin, Cambridge Univ. Pr. 1982 $29.95 pap. $10.95. "A systematic and historical survey and critique of the chief esthetic theories about European music" (Translator's introduction).

Dichter, Harry, and Elliot Shapiro. *Early American Sheet Music, 1768–1889*. Dover repr. of 1941 ed. 1977 pap. $7.95; Peter Smith $17.25. The classic study of music, mostly popular, published on a few "sheets" of paper and widely distributed before the age of the phonograph eclipsed the age of the parlor piano.

Einstein, Alfred. *Music in the Romantic Era*. Norton 1947 $14.95. The history of the romantic movement as manifested in music.

Grout, Donald J. *A History of Western Music*. Norton 3d ed. text ed. 1980 $24.95. The standard one-volume history of music used in thousands of colleges and graduate schools. Copiously but appropriately illustrated. Carefully selected bibliography. Chronology, glossary.

Hamm, Charles. *Music in the New World*. Norton 1983 $25.00. A history of the importation, imitation, and synthesis of music in America. References to currently available recordings.

Hitchcock, H. Wiley. *Music in the United States: A Historical Introduction*. Prentice-Hall 2d ed. text ed. 1974 pap. $15.95. Seeks to assess many styles of American music.

Hoppin, Richard H., ed. *Anthology of Medieval Music*. Norton 1978 $12.95 pap. $7.95

Kerman, Joseph. *Contemplating Music: Challenges to Musicology*. Harvard Univ. Pr. 1985 $15.00. A book addressing the historical and philosophical orientation of the scholarly field of musicology. Intended to be challenging and provocative to scholars, it will reveal much about the profession for those others who might wish to know why and how various attitudes and techniques may have influenced the program notes and books they read about the music they hear.

———. *Listen*. Worth 3d ed. 1980 $26.95. Essentially a text on music appreciation that includes thumbnail biographies, time lines, and a glossary.

Lang, Paul H., ed. *Music in Western Civilization*. Norton 1940 $34.95

Mellers, Wilfrid. *Music in a New Found Land: Two Hundred Years of American Music*. Stonehill 1975 o.p. A cosmopolitan and selective history of 200 years of American music, from Billings and Beiderbeck to Coltrane and Cage.

The New Oxford History of Music. Oxford 10 vols. 1954–85 ea $49.95. Lengthy surveys by leading scholars within broad topical areas: Ancient and Oriental Music; Early Medieval Music from 1300; Ars Nova and the Renaissance; The Age of Humanism; Opera and Church Music; The Growth of Instrumental Music; The Age of Enlightenment; The Age of Beethoven; Romanticism; Modern Age. A volume of tables, bibliographies, and indexes has not yet been published, but is clearly needed.

Newlin, Dika. *Bruckner, Mahler, Schoenberg*. Norton rev. ed 1978 $14.95. Discusses the continuity of the Viennese musical tradition, beginning with mid-nineteenth century Bruckner and ending with mid-twentieth century Schoenberg. Newlin's main concern was to demonstrate the connections between Schoenberg and Mahler and to point out the necessity of understanding Mahler in order to appreciate Schoenberg. The same necessity was thought to exist for Bruckner and Mahler.

Pauly, Reinhard G. *Music in the Classic Period*. Prentice-Hall 2d ed. text ed. 1973 pap. $17.95

Peyser, Joan. *Twentieth-Century Music: The Sense Behind the Sound*. Intro. by Jacques Barzun, Schirmer Bks. 1980 pap. $5.95. Music from Wagner to Varese.

Plantinga, Leon. *Romantic Music: A History of Musical Style in Nineteenth-Century Europe*. Norton 1985 $21.95

Porter, Andrew. *Music of Three Seasons, 1974–1977*. Farrar 1978 pap. $14.95. Gathered from the "Musical Events" column of the *New Yorker*.

———. *Music of Three More Seasons, 1977–1980*. Knopf 1981 $22.95. Gathered from the "Musical Events" column of the *New Yorker*.

———. *A Musical Season: A Critic from Abroad in America*. Viking 1974 o.p. Cogent, well-crafted, witty remarks on performances, musicians, musical events.

Rauchhaupt, Ursula von, ed. *The Symphony*. Thames & Hudson 1973 o.p. Anthology of essays, copiously illustrated, originally issued to accompany a record. Refers to both the musical genre and the orchestral organization.

Reese, Gustave. *Music in the Middle Ages*. Norton 1940 $24.95. This remains the standard history, with many bibliographic references.

———. *Music in the Renaissance*. Norton rev. ed. 1959 $29.95. The standard history of music from 1350 to c.1650, with lavish bibliographic references. Dated but essential.

Rosen, Charles. *The Classical Style: Haydn, Mozart, Beethoven*. Norton Lib. 1972 pap. $8.95; Viking 1971 $12.50. Focusing on the three giant figures of the period, Rosen, a concert pianist and polymath scholar, describes musical conventions, techniques, and vocabulary.

———. *Sonata Forms*. Norton repr. of 1980 ed. 1986 pap. $9.95. This book relates the sonata to eighteenth-century social and musical conditions and then briefly considers post–eighteenth century sonata forms.

Sachs, Curt. *The Commonwealth of Art: Style in the Fine Arts, Music and the Dance*. Norton 1946 o.p. A major study of history and culture, "this book . . . is to show that, and how, all arts unite in one consistent evolution to mirror man's diversity in space and time and the fate of his soul" (Introduction).

————. *Rhythm and Tempo: A Study in Music History*. Norton 1953 o.p. The best of a handful of English works on the subject.

————. *The Rise of Music in the Ancient World: East and West*. Norton 1943 o.p. "An exposure to the roots from which the music of the West has grown" (Preface).

Southern, Eileen. *The Music of Black Americans: A History*. Norton 2d ed. 1983 $25.00 text ed. pap. $12.95. An introductory history and guide to the musical contributions of Afro-Americans, incorporating elements of social, political, and economic history.

Strunk, Oliver. *Source Readings in Music History from Classical Antiquity throughout the Romantic Era*. 1950. Norton 1965 $24.95. Documents crucial to the history of Western music, with extensive annotations and footnotes to make the contexts clear.

Stuckenschmidt, H. H. *Twentieth-Century Music*. McGraw-Hill 1969 pap. $3.95

Tovey, Donald F. *Essays in Musical Analysis*. Oxford 6 vols. $32.95. Formative essays on a large number of works in the standard repertory. Essentially program notes for the informed concert-goer. Glossary and index in Volume 6.

Weiss, Piero, and Richard Taruskin. *Music in the Western World: A History in Documents*. Schirmer Bks. text ed. 1984 pap. $16.95. An excellent selection of translated source documents bringing much of music history into perspective through the words of the major figures and their observers.

Reference

Apel, Willi. *Harvard Dictionary of Music*. Harvard Univ. Pr. (Belknap Pr.) rev. & enl. ed. 1969 $25.00. Authoritative entries on terms in music. Brief bibliographies.

Arnold, Denis, ed. *The New Oxford Companion to Music*. Oxford 2 vols. 1983 $95.00. A dictionary of terms, titles, people, forms, places, and periods of musical significance. Oriented to the general reader and complete in itself, the work has a British slant.

ASCAP Biographical Dictionary. Bowker 4th ed. 1980 $41.95 o.p. Most composers and authors licensed by ASCAP completed questionnaires that serve as the basis for the approximately 10,000 entries.

Ayre, Leslie. *The Gilbert and Sullivan Companion*. Intro. by Martyn Green, Dodd 1972 $12.50; New Amer. Lib. (Plume) 1976 pap. $4.95. A brief essay on the careers of Gilbert and Sullivan, followed by a dictionary of works, people, places, characters, songs, and favorite lines in their productions.

Bane, Michael. *Who's Who in Rock*. Dodd 1982 pap. $10.95; Facts on File 1981 $17.95. Crucial facts on the 1,200 individuals and groups most famous in rock and closely related genres.

Barlow, Harold, and Sam Morgenstern, eds. *A Dictionary of Musical Themes*. Intro. by J. Erskine. Crown rev. ed. 1976 $14.95. Themes of orchestral literature in original keys displayed in musical notation.

————. *A Dictionary of Opera and Song Themes*. 1970. Crown rev. ed. 1976 $15.95. A list by composer of famous vocal themes.

Block, Adrienne F., and Carol Neuls-Bates, eds. *Women in American Music: A Bibliography of Music and Literature*. Greenwood 1979 lib. bdg. $39.95. A classified bibliography including abstracts of the literature about women in American music.

Brody, Elaine, and Claire Brook. *The Music Guide to Austria and Germany*. Dodd 1976 $10.00 Musical Baedeker arranged by city, covering for each guides and services, opera houses and concert houses, concert series, libraries and museums, conservatories and schools, musical landmarks, musical organizations, and the businesses of music. Lesser cities less extensively covered. Helpful appendixes.

———. *The Music Guide to Belgium, Luxembourg, Holland and Switzerland.* Dodd 1977 $10.00

———. *The Music Guide to Great Britain.* Dodd 1976 $10.00

———. *The Music Guide to Italy.* Dodd 1978 $10.00

Brook, Barry S. *Thematic Catalogs in Music: An Annotated Bibliography.* Pendragon 1972 lib. bdg. $32.00. Covers works arranging a variety of bodies of music by composer(s), by manuscript(s), by publisher(s), and so on, in systematic order and providing positive identification by reference to musical concepts or themes. Citations are in musical notation.

Bull, Storm. *Index to Biographies of Contemporary Composers.* Scarecrow Pr. 2 vols. 1964–74 $27.50–$30.00. A tabular index to periodical articles and dictionary entries in approximately 185 sources on composers active in the twentieth century up to 1973.

Claghorn, Charles E. *Biographical Dictionary of American Music.* Parker Publishing 1973 $13.95. Includes entries for lyricists, librettists, and hymnists, as well as other musicians.

———. *Biographical Dictionary of Jazz.* Prentice-Hall 1983 $25.00

Cobbett's Cyclopedic Survey of Chamber Music. Ed. by Walter Wilson Cobbett, Oxford 2 vols. 1929 supp. ed. by Colin Mason, 1963 o.p. A dictionary of articles about "ensemble music suited for playing in a room." The chamber musician's standard reference work.

Cohen, Aaron I. *International Encyclopedia of Women Composers.* Bowker 1981 $159.95. Brief biographical sketches of more than 5,000 women composers, most with lists of works.

Craig, Warren. *Sweet and Lowdown: America's Popular Song Writers.* Scarecrow Pr. 1978 $37.50. A biographical dictionary with an index to song titles and an index to musicals.

Davies, John H. *Musicalalia: Sources of Information in Music.* Pergamon 1966 o.p. Organized by categories of researcher (e.g., listener, singer, collector). An excellent little book.

De Lerma, Dominique René. *Bibliography of Black Music; Reference Materials.* Greenwood 2 vols. 1981 lib. bdg. ea. $29.95–$35.00. Volume 1 concerns reference materials in classified order; Volume 2 treats Afro-American idioms (i.e., musical traditions and styles); Volume 3 covers geographical studies arranged by country and cultural groups, including a section on acculturation. Includes 80,000 entries.

Diamond, Harold J. *Music Criticism: An Annotated Guide to the Literature.* Scarecrow Pr. 1979 $21.00. An annotated index to critical and analytical writings about musical compositions drawn from many sources. Clearly not comprehensive, but very helpful.

Duckles, Vincent. *Music Reference and Research Materials: An Annotated Bibliography.* Macmillan (Free Pr.) 3d ed. text ed. 1974 $19.95. Describes more than 1,900 music reference works, principally works concerned with Western music. A fourth edition is in progress.

Eisler, Paul E. *World Chronology of Music History.* Oceana 6 vols. 1972–80 lib. bdg. ea. $45.00. Entries by year, month, and day for large and small events and achievements.

Erickson, J. Gunnar, and others. *Musician's Guide to Copyright*. Scribner rev. ed. $14.95. Basic and clearly presented information about the 1972 copyright law as it relates to the music industry.

Fink, Robert, and Robert Ricci. *The Language of Twentieth-Century Music*. Schirmer Bks. 1975 $17.95. Definitions of the basic terms of twentieth-century musical styles: computer and electronic music, film music, jazz, and so on. There is a topical listing of terms and bibliographies arranged by style.

Fuld, James J. *The Book of World Famous Music: Classical, Popular and Folk*. Crown rev. & enl. ed. 1971 $15.00. Entries by title include information about compositions, origins, variants, sources, and first and early editions. A compendium of basic historical information about hundreds of well-known melodies, preceded by a long introduction drawing together considerable information about publishing and copyrighting music in a most convenient form. The music reference librarian's secret weapon.

Gray, Michael H., and Gerald D. Gibson. *Bibliography of Discographies*. Bowker 1977–83 ea. $25.00–49.95. Authoritative guides to the literature about sound recordings. Since most of this literature is hidden in periodicals and as back matter in monographs, this work is of crucial importance. Thousands of references.

Green, Stanley. *Encyclopedia of the Musical Theatre*. Da Capo repr. of 1976 ed. 1980 pap. $10.95; Dodd 1976 $17.50. Alphabetical array of short articles on the facts about the most important people, productions, and songs of the musical theater in New York and London. Avoids vaudeville, Gilbert and Sullivan, one-act or one-person shows, and similar genres. Includes lists of awards.

———. *The World of Musical Comedy*. A. S. Barnes 4th ed. rev. 1980 $30.00; Da Capo repr. of 1980 ed. 4th ed. 1984 pap. $16.95

Heyer, Anna H. *Historical Sets: Collected Editions, and Monuments of Music*. Amer. Lib. Association 2 vols. 3d ed. 1981 $175.00. Covers complete editions of the works of individual composers, and major published collections of music. Reveals the wealth of music not ordinarily accessible through library catalogs, but nevertheless in library collections.

Hughes, Andrew. *Medieval Music: The Sixth Liberal Art*. Univ. of Toronto Pr. 1980 $37.50. A classified and annotated bibliography of approximately 2,300 works about medieval music.

International Who's Who in Music. 1935–to date. Gale 10th ed. 1985 $85.00. More than 8,000 biographical entries submitted by the subjects.

Jablonski, Edward. *The Encyclopedia of American Music*. Doubleday 1982 $24.95. Divided into seven sections based on historical periods in American music, with an essay on the significant events and developments of each period followed by a discussion of concepts and biographies of people and ensembles.

Julian, John, ed. *A Dictionary of Hymnology: Origin and History of Christian Hymns*. Gordon 4 vols. 1977 lib. bdg. $600.00; Kregel 2 vols. repr. of 1977 ed. 1985 $120.00. Systematic, classic reference work.

Kallmann, Helmutt, and others, eds. *Encyclopedia of Music in Canada*. Univ. of Toronto Pr. 1981 $85.00. Covers the activities and contributions of Canadian individuals and organizations to music.

Kinkle, Roger D. *The Complete Encyclopedia of Popular Music and Jazz, 1900–1950*. Crown 4 vols. 1974 $100.00. A complex, authoritative work that includes people who were active before 1950. The first volume provides a chronological list of important musical works. There are two volumes of biographies of individuals and groups, including short discographies. The last volume is a compendium of lists, indexes, and a brief bibliography.

Krummel, Donald W., and others. *Resources of American Musical History: A Directory of Source Materials from Colonial Times to World War II*. Univ. of Illinois Pr. 1981 $70.00. A bicentennial project that lists collections of research materials by city and state.

Kutsch, K. J., and Leo Riemens. *A Concise Biographical Dictionary of Singers, from the Beginning of Recorded Sound to the Present*. Trans. by Harry Earl Jones, Chilton 1969 o.p.

Lewine, Richard, and Alfred Simon. *Songs of the Theater: A Definitive Index to the Songs of the Musical Stage*. Wilson 1984 $70.00. A comprehensive index to more than 17,000 songs from 1,200 Broadway and off-Broadway shows.

Michaelides, Solon. *The Music of Ancient Greece: An Encyclopedia*. Faber 1978 $39.00. Entries on persons, terms, places, and instruments.

Music Industry Directory. Marquis 7th ed. 1983 $67.50. Basic information on organizations, competitions, and awards, education, resources, performance, management, and commercial aspects of the industry. Poorly indexed. Lengthy directory of American music publishers.

Musical Instruments of the World; An Illustrated Encyclopedia by the Diagram Group. Facts on File 1978 $29.95. Copiously illustrated, with instruments only briefly described.

Nulman, Mary. *Concise Encyclopedia of Jewish Music*. Feldheim $9.95. More than 500 entries covering all facets of Jewish music.

Parsons, Denys. *The Directory of Tunes and Musical Themes*. Spencer, Brown 1975 o.p. Indexes more than 14,000 themes using the direction of successive pitches in each theme, so that one need not know how to read music to identify the origin of the theme.

Pavlakis, Christopher. *The American Music Handbook*. Macmillan (Free Pr.) 1974 $25.00. Compendium of information on all areas of organized musical activity in the United States, with overwhelming emphasis on classical music.

Randel, Don M. *Harvard Concise Dictionary of Music*. Harvard Univ. Pr. (Belknap Pr.) 1978 $15.00 pap. $7.95. Biographical information, definitions of terms, entries on compositions and instruments. The best pocket-size dictionary of music.

Roche, Jerome, and Elizabeth Roche. *A Dictionary of Early Music, from the Troubadours to Monteverdi*. Oxford 1981 $17.95. A compact work with entries on instruments, forms, terms, and composers from c.1100 to c.1650.

Roxon, Lillian. *Rock Encyclopedia*. Workman 1969 o.p. Musicians, groups, terms, and concepts. Many discographies.

Sachs, Harvey. *Virtuoso, the Instrumentalist as Superstar: The Life and Art of Niccolo Paganini, Franz List, Anton Rubenstein, Ignace Jan Paderewski, Fritz Kreisler, Pablo Casals, Wanda Landowski, Vladimir Horowitz [and] Glenn Gould*. Thames & Hudson 1982 $18.95. Short biographies.

Sadie, Stanley, ed. *The New Grove Dictionary of Music and Musicians*. Grove 20 vols. 6th ed. 1980 $2,100.00. The crowning achievement of Anglo-American musical scholarship in the mid-twentieth century. Really an encyclopedia about music, the work features signed articles about people, terms, instruments, cities and countries, forms and genres, and virtually all facets of the art form. Most articles are followed by bibliographies of the most relevant secondary sources. Lists of varying extensiveness follow entries on individual composers. Widely but not uncritically accepted as the fundamental music reference work around the world.

Shapiro, Nat, ed. *An Encyclopedia of Quotations about Music*. Da Capo repr. of 1977 ed. 1981 pap. $7.95; Doubleday 1978 $10.00. Aphorisms quoted and identified by name and source and indexed by keywords. Arranged in topical order.

Shaw, Arnold, ed. *Dictionary of American Pop/Rock.* Schirmer Bks. 1982 $12.95. Concise entries on people, places, terms, titles, and jargon of rock and other popular musical styles.

Shemel, Sidney, and M. William Krasilovsky. *This Business of Music.* Watson-Guptill 5th ed. 1985 $19.95. Contracts, deals, agreements, agents, licensing, records, copyright, payola, performing rights organizations, foreign rights, arrangements, infringements, sources of information and assistance, forms, and taxation revealed.

Simpson, Claude M. *The British Broadside Ballad and Its Music.* Rutgers Univ. Pr. 1966 $45.00. An analytic survey of the genre arranged by title.

Slonimsky, Nicholas. *Music since 1900.* 1937. Scribner 1985 $30.00. A chronological survey of twentieth-century music up to 1969 with a section quoting documents and letters on musical subjects in the same period. Glossary.

——, ed. *Baker's Biographical Dictionary of Musicians.* Schirmer Bks. 6th ed. 1978 $85.00. Brief but authoritative entries on musical figures throughout history. Includes lists of works and occasional short bibliographies. The preface is a charming but thorough essay on the problems of writing biographies of musicians.

Southern, Eileen. *Biographical Dictionary of Afro-American and African Musicians.* Greenwood 1982 lib. bdg. $55.00. Short pieces on black musicians' professional lives.

Stambler, Irwin, and Grelun Landon. *The Encyclopedia of Folk, Country, and Western Music.* St. Martin's 2d ed. 1983 $50.00. Long entries on performers, institutions, ensembles. Lists of awards.

Thompson, Kenneth. *St. Martin's Dictionary of Twentieth-Century Composers, 1910–1971.* St. Martin's 1973 $30.00. Lengthy essays on 32 of the most respected composers of the first half of the twentieth century.

Vinton, John, ed. *The Dictionary of Contemporary Music.* Dutton 1974 $25.00. Covering composers, styles, terms, schools, and instruments of twentieth-century concert music in the Western tradition. Many entries on composers were based on information supplied by the composers themselves.

Who's Who in American Music: Classical. Bowker 1985 $125.00. Information supplied by the subjects. Geographic and professional classifications and indexes.

Zaimont, Judith Lang, and Karen Famera, eds. *Contemporary Concert Music by Women: A Directory of the Composers and Their Works.* Greenwood 1981 lib. bdg. $27.50. Entries include photographs and samples of orthography with classified lists of compositions.

Zaimont, Judith Lang, and others, eds. *The Musical Woman: An International Perspective.* Greenwood 1984 $49.95. A chronicle of women's achievements in music around the world as composers, conductors, critics, scholars, and entrepreneurs, but not as solo performers.

Music Appreciation

Barzun, Jacques, ed. *Pleasures of Music: An Anthology of Writings about Music and Musicians from Cellini to Bernard Shaw.* Univ. of Chicago Pr. abr. ed. 1977 $15.00 pap. $4.95

Downes, Edward. *The New York Philharmonic Guide to the Symphony.* Walker 1976 $25.00. Anthology of program notes for pieces frequently appearing in symphonic programs. Sensitive and supportive but not critical. Cites main themes in musical notation.

Machlis, Joseph. *The Enjoyment of Music: An Introduction to Perceptive Listening.* Norton 5th ed. 1984 text ed. $24.95. A classic, dated, but clear introduction to the resources and some of the principal musical styles of Western music.

Types of Music

CONTEMPORARY MUSIC

Anhalt, Istvan. *Alternative Voices: Essays on Contemporary Vocal and Choral Composition.* Univ. of Toronto Pr. 1984 $35.00. Covering the works of Berio, Ligeti, and Lutoslawski.

Blesh, Rudi, and Harriet Janis. *They All Played Ragtime.* Music Sales rev. ed. pap. $9.95. Definitive history of one of the precursors of jazz.

Brown, Peter, and Steven Gaines. *The Love You Make: An Insider's Story of the Beatles.* McGraw-Hill 1983 $14.95; New Amer. Lib. (Signet Class.) 1984 pap. $4.50

Dutton, Gregory Battcock. *Breaking the Sound Barrier: A Critical Anthology of the New Music.* Dutton 1981 pap. $7.00. Thirty essays on the styles characterizing art music since 1960.

Griffiths, Paul. *Concise History of Avant Garde Music: From Debussy to Boulez.* World of Art Ser. Oxford 1978 pap. $9.95

Mellers, Wilfrid. *The Twilight of the Gods: The Music of the Beatles.* Schirmer Bks. 1975 pap. $8.95; Viking 1974 $7.95

Pollock, Bruce. *When Rock Was Young: A Nostalgic Review of the Top Forty Era.* Holt 1981 pap. $6.95. Covers the first decade (1955–65) of rock and roll. The breezy style is appropriate to the proponents of the style.

Schwartz, Elliott. *Electronic Music: A Listener's Guide.* Da Capo repr. of 1975 ed. 1985 lib. bdg. $29.50. An introduction to electronic music through the music itself. Includes a section of observations by composers of electronic music. Bibliography, discography, indexes.

Shaw, Arnold. *Honkers and Shouters: The Golden Years of Rhythm and Blues.* Macmillan (Collier Bks.) 1978 pap. $9.95. Rhythm and blues as an indigenous black musical style, separate from rock and soul music.

Stambler, Irwin. *Encyclopedia of Pop, Rock, and Soul.* St. Martin's 1975 $19.95 1977 pap. $14.95. Lengthy entries on famous artists and groups with lists of awards.

Tjepkema, Sandra L. *A Bibliography of Computer Music: A Reference for Composers.* Univ. of Iowa Pr. text ed. 1981 $24.00. "A comprehensive listing of books, articles, dissertations and papers relating to the use of computers by composers of music."

ETHNIC MUSIC

Buchner, Alexander. *Folk Music Instruments of the World.* Crown 1972 o.p. An illustrated survey.

Collaer, Paul. *Music of the Americas.* Praeger 1971 o.p. Covers the music of the indigenous peoples of the New World.

Kunst, Jaap. *Ethnomusicology: A Study of Its Nature, Its Problems, Methods and Representative Personalities to Which Is Added a Bibliography.* Scholarly repr. 3d ed. 1959 $39.00. A seminal study.

Malm, William P. *Music Cultures of the Pacific, the Near East and Asia.* Prentice-Hall

2d ed. text ed. 1977 pap. $17.95. An introductory work, with definitions of many regional terms.

May, Elizabeth, ed. *Musics of Many Cultures: An Introduction*. Univ. of California Pr. 1980 $42.00 pap. $19.95. Twenty essays written by specialists, but intended for the general reader. Filmography.

McAllester, David P., ed. *Readings in Ethnomusicology*. Johnson Repr. 1971 o.p. Twenty-three essays by scholars on notation and classification, history, functionalism, and regional studies.

Merriam, Alan P. *The Anthropology of Music*. Northwestern Univ. Pr. 1964 $23.95 pap. $10.95. Provides a theory and methodology for the study of music as human behavior, based on the fusion of methods of cultural anthropology and ethnomusicology. Extensive bibliography.

Nettl, Bruno. *Folk and Traditional Music of the Western Continents*. Prentice-Hall 2d ed. 1973 pap. $18.95. Includes chapters on the music of Latin America.

Reck, David B. *Music of the Whole Earth*. Scribner 1977 $19.95 pap. $16.95. An illustrated study of nonart, non-Western music.

Sachs, Curt. *The Wellsprings of Music*. Ed. by Jaap Kunst, Da Capo repr. of 1977 ed. pap. $4.95. A masterfully woven tapestry of the musical world, placing Western classical music in the fabric of the rest of musical culture.

Titon, Jeff Todd, and others. *Worlds of Music: An Introduction to the Music of the World's Peoples*. Schirmer Bks. 1984 $18.95. Chapters on North America, Africa, Europe, and India. Recorded examples.

FILM MUSIC

Evans, Mark. *Soundtrack: The Music of the Movies*. Da Capo repr. of 1975 ed. 1979 pap. $6.95

Limbacher, James L., ed. *Film Music: From Violins to Video*. Scarecrow Pr. 1974 $37.50. Reprinted essays on film music, mostly by film composers. Bibliography on film music.

Prendergast, Roy M. *Film Music: A Neglected Art*. Norton Lib. 1978 pap. $7.95. "The first attempt at a comprehensive look at the history, aesthetics, and techniques of film music" (Preface).

JAZZ

Balliett, Whitney. *American Singers*. Oxford 1979 $19.95. Portraits of American popular and jazz singers.

————. *Dinosaurs in the Morning: Forty-One Pieces on Jazz*. Greenwood repr. of 1962 ed. 1978 lib. bdg. $27.50. An anthology of previously published reviews and essays by one of the most distinguished of the New York jazz critics.

————. *Night Creatures: A Journal of Jazz, 1975–80*. Oxford 1981 $19.95. Another anthology of previously published reviews and essays.

Chilton, John. *Who's Who of Jazz*. Da Capo 4th ed. 1985 $25.00 pap. $11.95. Entries for more than 1,000 jazz musicians born before 1920.

Coker, Jerry. *Listening to Jazz*. Prentice-Hall 1982 pap. $6.95. A basic appreciation text.

Dance, Stanley. *The World of Swing*. Da Capo 1979 pap. $7.95. Covers big band jazz of the 1930s and later.

Feather, Leonard. *The Encyclopedia of Jazz*. Horizon Pr. 1960 $25.00. Chronology, with brief entries on jazz people, and short concluding essays.

Giddins, Gary. *Rhythm-a-ning: Jazz Tradition and Innovation in the '80s*. Oxford 1985

$17.95. A chronicle of the jazz scene in the 1980s taken from the author's *Village Voice* column.

Gridley, Mark C. *Jazz Styles: History and Analysis.* 1978. Prentice-Hall 2d ed. text ed. 1985 pap. $18.95. A chronological introduction to jazz written for those who have no experience with jazz. The basic facts about the important figures of jazz and their musical contributions are clearly presented.

Grime, Kitty. *Jazz Voices.* Merrimack 1984 $24.95

Hefele, Bernhard. *Jazz Bibliography: An International Literature on Jazz, Blues, Spirituals, Gospel, and Ragtime Music with a Selected List of Works on the Social and Cultural Background from the Beginning to the Present.* Saur 1981 lib. bdg. $36.00. A classified bibliography providing excellent coverage up to about 1980.

Hodeir, André. *Jazz: Its Evolution and Essence.* Trans. by David Noakes, Da Capo repr. of 1956 ed. 1975 lib. bdg. $29.50; trans. by David Noakes, Grove rev. ed. 1980 pap. $3.95. The classic essay dealing with the principal styles, personalities, and problems of jazz.

Meadows, Eddie S. *Jazz Reference and Research Materials: A Bibliography.* Garland 1981 lib. bdg. $43.00. A thorough survey of books and articles on jazz.

Placksin, Sally. *American Women in Jazz: Nineteen Hundred to the Present: Their Words, Lives, and Music.* Putnam 1982 o.p.

Rose, Al, and Edmond Souchon. *New Orleans Jazz: A Family Album.* Louisiana State Univ. Pr. 3d ed. rev. & enl. text ed. 1984 $35.00 pap. $19.95; Pelican 1981 $17.50. A "who was who" with pictures, including a section on ensembles and a number of illustrated essays.

Russell, Ross. *Jazz Styles in Kansas City and the Southwest.* Univ. of California Pr. 1982 $22.50 pap. $8.95. Kansas City was one of the three provincial centers of jazz development between 1920 and 1940. Jazz then spread throughout the United States and became recognized widely as a national style.

Sales, Grover. *Jazz: America's Classical Music.* Prentice-Hall 1984 $18.95 pap. $9.95. The principles of jazz explicated for the layperson. Includes good descriptions of the music and the performers.

Shapiro, Nat, ed. *Hear Me Talkin' to Ya: The Story of Jazz by the Men Who Made It.* Ed. by Nat Hentoff, Dover 1966 pap. $5.95; Peter Smith $14.00

Simon, George T. *The Big Bands.* Fwd. by Frank Sinatra, Macmillan (Collier Bks.) rev. & enl. ed. 1975 pap. $9.95; Schirmer Bks. 4th ed. 1981 $20.00 pap. $11.95

Stearns, Marshall. *Winslow: The Story of Jazz.* Oxford 1956 $22.50 pap. $9.95. A classic history of the genre.

Williams, Martin. *The Jazz Heritage.* Oxford 1985 $17.95. Reexaminations of jazz artists after reissues of some of their recordings. Profiles of jazz artists and some consideration of theoretical matters.

———. *Jazz Masters in Transition, 1957–1969.* Da Capo repr. of 1970 ed. 1980 $25.00 1982 pap. $7.95

———. *The Jazz Tradition.* Oxford rev. ed. 1983 $18.95 pap. $6.95. Essays on jazz masters and jazz matters. Williams is the producer of the splendid Smithsonian jazz albums.

———. *Where's the Melody: A Listener's Introduction to Jazz.* Da Capo repr. of 1966 ed. 1983 pap. $7.95

NON-WESTERN MUSIC

Berliner, Paul F. *The Soul of Mbira: Music and Traditions of the Shona People of Zimbabwe.* Univ. of California Pr. 1978 $36.50 pap. $6.95. A study of African musical culture from the frame of reference of the mbira, the so-called finger piano. A good attempt to break from the colonialist mentality so often found in studies of non-Western music by Westerners.

Kaufman, Walter. *Musical References in the Chinese Classics*. Information Coordinators 1976 $15.00. Includes essays, translations, and original Chinese texts of the sources.

Nketia, Joseph H. *The Music of Africa*. Norton 1974 pap. $8.95. A survey of the broad musical traditions of Africa, set in their historical, social, and cultural contexts.

Wade, Bonnie C. *Music in India: The Classical Traditions*. Prentice-Hall 1979 o.p. An introduction to the fundamental aspects of two classical Indian traditions, the Hindustani and the Karnatic.

OPERA

Grout, Donald J. *A Short History of Opera*. Columbia Univ. Pr. 2d ed. 1965 $28.00. A comprehensive, if compact, history of opera as a musical genre. Fundamental.

Kerman, Joseph. *Opera as Drama*. Greenwood repr. of 1956 ed. 1981 lib. bdg. $25.00. In a discussion of operas by Monteverdi, Purcell, Mozart, Verdi, Wagner, and Stravinsky, among others, Kerman demonstrates that opera is a hybrid art form requiring appreciation and understanding from a number of viewpoints.

Loewenburg, Alfred, ed. *Annals of Opera, 1597–1940*. Rowman 2 vols. in 1 3d ed. rev. 1984 $55.00. The classic chronological reference to opera. Each entry includes names of librettist and composer, sources of plot, name of theater and city of first and subsequent productions, and other significant information. Does not include synopses of plots.

Martin, George W. *The Opera Companion*. Dodd 1979 pap. $13.95. Short essays on a variety of operatic subjects, a glossary of operatic terms, and synopses of commonly produced operas.

Moore, Frank L. *Crowell's Handbook of World Opera*. Intro. by Darius Milhaud, Greenwood repr. of 1961 ed. 1974 lib. bdg. $43.00. Packed with useful information.

Orrey, Leslie, and Gilbert Chase, eds. *The Encyclopedia of Opera*. Scribner 1976 $22.50. Approximately 3,000 entries on operas, operatic people, and places particularly relevant to opera today.

Traubner, Richard. *Operetta: A Theatrical History*. Doubleday 1983 $29.95. An undocumented history of light opera from the 1850s to the 1950s. International scope. Illustrated, musical examples. Bibliography.

Tuggle, Robert. *The Golden Age of Opera*. Fwd. by Anthony A. Bliss, Holt 1983 $35.00. Concerning the Metropolitan Opera, its singers and productions.

Conductors

Holmes, J. L. *Conductors on Record*. Greenwood 1982 lib. bdg. $49.95. Entries include lists of works recorded by each conductor.

Matheopoulous, Helena Maestro. *Encounters with Conductors of Today*. Harper 1982 $23.99. Essays on and interviews with 24 of the best-known musical directors. The Von Karajan interview is especially long and revealing.

Musical Instruments

Baines, Anthony, ed. *Musical Instruments Through the Ages*. Walker 1975 $15.00

Boyden, David D. *History of Violin Playing, from Its Origins to 1761 and Its Relationship to the Violin and Violin Music*. Oxford 1965 $89.00. The definitive study.

Campbell, Margaret. *The Great Violinists*. Doubleday 1981 $19.95. Sensitive encapsu-

lated histories of famous violinists beginning with Corelli and including some
who play principally chamber music.

Gill, Dominic, ed. *The Book of the Piano*. Cornell Univ. Pr. 1981 $48.50. A book of
well-illustrated essays.

————. *The Book of the Violin*. Rizzoli 1984 $35.00. A collection of well-illustrated
essays.

Good, Edwin M. *Giraffes, Black Dragons and Other Pianos: A Technological History
from Cristofori to the Modern Concert Grand*. Stanford Univ. Pr. 1982 $32.50. A
chronological treatment of the "advances" or changes made on the piano in its
various stages of development.

Kaiser, Joachim. *Great Pianists of Our Time*. Trans. by David Wooldridge and
George Unwin. Herder Bk. Ctr. 1971 o.p. Brief biographical sketches.

Kehler, George. *The Piano in Concert*. Scarecrow Pr. 2 vols. 1982 $87.50. Contains
2,000 biographical sketches of important pianists of the nineteenth and twentieth centuries with chronological lists of compositions in their repertories.

Lenz, Wilhelm von. *The Great Piano Virtuosos of Our Time: A Classic Account of Studies with Liszt, Chopin, Tausig, and Henselt*. Ed. by Philip Reder, Da Capo repr. of
1899 ed. 1973 lib. bdg. $21.50

Loesser, Arthur. *Men, Women and Pianos*. Simon & Schuster 1964 pap. $4.95. A popu-
lar but charming account filled with quotations from contemporary sources and
tracing the history of the piano from its inception to the mid-twentieth century.

Mach, Elyse. *Great Pianists Speak for Themselves*. Intro. by George Solti, Dodd 1980
$9.95. Essays by the most famous pianists, each preceded with a biographical
sketch and a photographic portrait.

Marcuse, Sibyl. *Musical Instruments: A Comprehensive Dictionary*. Norton Lib. repr.
of 1964 ed. 1975 pap. $7.95. Brief entries covering instruments of all times and
places.

Matthews, Denis, ed. *Keyboard Music*. Taplinger 1978 $12.50 pap. $7.95. An anthology of essays by distinguished historians of keyboard music. An excellent, brief
survey.

Sachs, Curt. *The History of Western Instruments*. Norton 1940 o.p. Covers Western
and non-Western instruments chronologically.

Schwarz, Boris. *Great Masters of the Violin, from Corelli to Stern, Zukerman, and
Perlman*. Fwd. by Yehudi Menuhin, Simon & Schuster 1983 $24.00

Singers

Breslin, Herbert H., ed. *The Tenors*. Macmillan 1974 o.p. Essays on Richard Tucker,
Jon Vickers, Franco Corelli, Placido Domingo, and Luciano Pavarotti by established opera critics.

Hines, Jerome. *Great Singers on Great Singing*. Doubleday 1982 $17.95; Limelight
Eds. 1984 pap. $8.95. Interviews with many of the great singers.

Kutsch, K. J., and Leo Riemens. *A Concise Biographical Dictionary of Singers, from
the Beginning of Recorded Sound to the Present*. Trans. and annot. by Harry Earl
Jones, Chilton 1969 o.p. The standard reference tool on the subject.

Mordden, Ethan. *Demented: The World of the Opera Diva*. Watts 1984 $16.95. A re-
cital of the almost incredible difficulties of being a prima donna.

Pleasants, Henry. *The Great American Popular Singers*. Simon & Schuster 1985
$19.95 pap. $9.95. Biographical entries.

————. *The Great Singers, from Jenny Lind to Callas and Pavarotti*. Simon & Schuster
rev. ed. 1981 o.p.

Rasponi, Lanfranco. *The Last Prima Donnas*. Knopf 1982 $22.50; Limelight Eds. 1985 $12.95. Conversations between the author and some of the greatest first ladies of the opera in the twentieth century.

ARMSTRONG, LOUIS. 1900–1971

"Satchmo" was the nickname for one of the most innovative American jazz trumpeters of his era. He began his career in the unsavory districts of New Orleans, was quickly noted for his improvisational style, and raised the importance of solo performances in jazz. Armstrong's raspy baritone voice and brilliant trumpet playing combined to make an unforgettable musical signature appreciated all over the world. He also appeared in Broadway shows and in films.

BOOKS BY ARMSTRONG

Swing That Music. Intro. by Rudy Vallee, Longman 1936 o.p.
Satchmo: My Life in New Orleans. Prentice-Hall 1954 o.p.
Louis Armstrong: A Self-portrait. The interview by Richard Meryman. Eakins repr. 1971 pap. $3.95

BOOKS ABOUT ARMSTRONG

Hoskins, Robert. *Louis Armstrong: Biography of a Musician*. Holloway 1980 o.p. Back matter includes filmography and discography.
Jones, Max, and John Chilton. *Louis: The Louis Armstrong Story, 1900–1971*. Mayflower Bks. repr. 1975 o.p.

BACH, JOHANN SEBASTIAN. 1685–1750

Most famous member of an illustrious family of German musicians, Johann Sebastian Bach achieved a reputation as an organist in his own lifetime, but was "rediscovered" by Felix Mendelssohn as the supreme synthesizer of compositional practices in the high baroque. His cantatas, organ preludes, and fugues, the mass in B minor, the passions, and the Brandenburg concerti are regarded by some as the most sublime music ever composed.

BOOKS ABOUT BACH

David, Hans T., and Arthur Mendel, eds. *The Bach Reader*. Norton Lib. rev. ed. 1966 pap. $12.95. A collection of contemporaneous and early documents on Bach's life and music, up to the "rediscovery" of Bach by Mendelssohn and others in the late 1820s.
Forkel, Johann N. *Johann Sebastian Bach: His Life, Art and Work*. Trans. by Charles S. Terry, Da Capo repr. of 1920 ed. 1970 lib. bdg. $35.00
Geiringer, Karl, and Irene Geiringer. *Johann Sebastian Bach: The Culmination of an Era*. Oxford 1966 $22.50
Grew, Eva, and Sidney Grew. *Bach*. Biblio Dist. repr. of 1947 ed. 1977 $13.50; Little, Brown 1979 pap. $7.95
Schwendowius, Barbara, and Wolfgang Domling, eds. *Johann Sebastian Bach: Life, Times, Influence*. Trans. by John Coombs and others, European Amer. Music 1978 $45.00; Heinman 1977 $45.00; Yale Univ. Pr. 1984 $35.00

BARTÓK, BÉLA. 1881–1945

Pianist, critic, ethnomusicologist, and composer, Bartók is Hungary's leading composer of the twentieth century. He is also known for his travels
throughout Hungary to collect folk music. With the outbreak of World War
II, he left Europe and settled in the United States, supported by royalties
from his compositions and by the American patroness Elizabeth Sprague
Coolidge. His works are extremely complex, and Bartók was not fully appreciated during his life. The *Mikrocosmos* for piano, the *Concerto for Orchestra*,
and *Music for Strings, Percussion, and Celeste* are among his most famous
works.

BOOK BY BARTÓK

Béla Bartók: Essays. Ed. by Benjamin Suchoff, St. Martin's 1976 o.p. Bartók's repu-
    tation as a composer completely overshadows his achievements as ethno-
    musicologist, teacher, critic, and pianist. These essays demonstrate his broad
    range of interests.

BOOKS ABOUT BARTÓK

Milne, Hammish. *Bartók: His Life and Times.* Midas Bks. 1981 $40.00
Stevens, Halsey. *Life and Music of Béla Bartók.* Oxford repr. of 1964 ed. rev. ed. 1967
    pap. $6.95

BASIE, WILLIAM (COUNT). 1904–1984

Count Basie was the most famous and long-lived jazz composer identified
with the big band style. He worked in vaudeville before moving to Kansas
City in the mid-1930s. Basie's piano style is recognizable by the predomi-
nance of the right hand. He formed his own band in 1935 and achieved international fame. In 1981, he received national recognition at Kennedy Center.
He is the composer of such popular classics as "April in Paris," "Jumpin' at
the Woodside," "Broadway," and the "One O'Clock Jump."

BOOKS ABOUT BASIE

Dance, Stanley. *The World of Count Basie.* Da Capo repr. 1985 pap. $10.95
Horricks, Raymond. *Count Basie and His Orchestra, Its Music and Its Musicians.*
    1937. Greenwood repr. of 1957 ed. 1972 lib. bdg. $22.50

BEETHOVEN, LUDWIG VAN. 1770–1827

Beethoven was born in Berlin, where he began studying music at the age
of 4 and published his first works at age 11. In 1792, he moved to Vienna
and studied briefly with Haydn and Albrechtsberger. His compositions revolutionized music with their dramatic use of harmonic and rhythmic motives. Beethoven was the first major composer to attempt to live off his compositions without continuous employment in a noble court or a church. His
symphonies, string quartets, and the *Missa Solemnis* compete in importance
only with his piano sonatas. Although deafness began to afflict him in 1801,
it did not affect his creative genius. His funeral was attended by thousands
of admirers.

BOOKS ABOUT BEETHOVEN

Arnold, Denis, and Nigel Fortune, eds. *The Beethoven Reader*. Norton 1971 $25.00. Essays by Beethoven specialists still striving to fill in gaps in the history and understanding of Beethoven and his music.

Solomon, Maynard. *Beethoven*. Schirmer Bks. 1977 $19.95 1979 pap. $10.95. Significantly illuminates the composer's psychological development, the evolution of his personal relationships, and the connections between his life and his music.

Tovey, Donald F. *A Companion to Beethoven's Pianoforte Sonatas*. AMS Pr. repr. of 1931 ed. $30.00

Tyson, Alan, ed. *Beethoven Studies*. Norton 1973 $10.00. Eight essays by leading Beethoven scholars bringing new light on Beethoven's problems.

———. *Beethoven Studies II*. Oxford 1977 $34.95

———. *Beethoven Studies III*. Cambridge Univ. Pr. 1982 $57.50

BELLINI, VINCENZO. 1801–1835

Bellini was an opera composer whose works, especially *Norma* and *I Puritanni*, are produced regularly by the world's major opera companies. Bellini is highly regarded as a composer of great melodies in the bel canto style.

BOOK ABOUT BELLINI

Orrey, Leslie. *Bellini*. Biblio Dist. 1969 $13.50; Little, Brown repr. of 1969 ed. 1973 pap. $7.95

BERG, ALBAN. 1885–1935

Berg was a student of Arnold Schoenberg and the composer of two magnificently powerful operas, *Wozzeck* and *Lulu*. He composed using the 12-tone system, but infused it with classical forms and occasional lapses into tonal harmonies.

BOOKS ABOUT BERG

Carner, Mosco. *Alban Berg: The Man and the Work*. Holmes & Meier 2d rev. ed. text ed. 1983 $42.50

Jarman, Douglas. *The Music of Alban Berg*. Univ. of California Pr. 1978 $49.50 1983 pap. $11.95

Monson, Karen. *Alban Berg*. Houghton Mifflin 1979 $15.00

BERIO, LUCIANO. 1925–

Berio is a contemporary Italian composer who uses a wide variety of resources in his compositions. Berio quotes passages from other composers' works in his music and incorporates theatrical elements freely. His *Sequenzi* and *Chemins*, series of compositions for various voices and instruments, require performers to push their technique to the limits.

BOOK BY BERIO

Two Interviews with Rossana Dalmonte and Balint Andras Varga. Trans. and ed. by David Osmond-Smith, Boyars 1985 $19.95. Wide-ranging discussions of Berio's aesthetic views as well as his views on technical matters and the avant-garde musical scene. Short biography.

BERLIOZ, HECTOR. 1803–1869

Composer and critic, Berlioz never mastered any instrument and was largely a self-taught composer. He received the Prix de Rome for the *Symphonie fantastique,* his most ambitious and well-known work. Although despondent in later years as a result of a broken marriage and financial problems, he composed the dramatic symphony *Romeo and Juliet.* Many of his compositions are programmatic music, representing a known story or sequence of ideas.

BOOKS ABOUT BERLIOZ

Barzun, Jacques. *Berlioz and His Century: An Introduction to the Age of Romanticism.* Univ. of Chicago Pr. 1982 pap. $9.95
Holoman, D. Kern. *The Creative Process in the Autograph Musical Documents of Hector Berlioz.* Ed. by George Buelow, UMI Research 1980 $49.95
MacDonald, Hugh. *Berlioz Orchestral Music.* Biblio Dist. text ed. 1983 $17.95; Univ. of Washington Pr. 1969 pap. $4.95
Rushton, Julian. *The Musical Language of Berlioz.* Cambridge Univ. Pr. 1984 $49.50

BERNSTEIN, LEONARD 1918–

Bernstein's career reveals many talents and styles. He is a gifted pianist, a sought-after conductor, and a very successful composer. *West Side Story* is one of the best known of his works and it has had a marked influence on the composition of Broadway musicals following it. He also composed a mass, the short opera *Trouble in Tahiti,* and the ballet *Fancy Free.* His recordings of the Mahler symphonies helped to renew interest in that composer's life and works worldwide. He has directed many famous American orchestras, including the New York Philharmonic.

BOOKS BY BERNSTEIN

Bernstein on Broadway. Intro. by Adolph Green, Schirmer Bks. 1981 $29.95 pap. $19.95
Findings. Simon & Schuster 1982 o.p.
The Unanswered Question: Six Talks at Harvard. Harvard Univ. Pr. 1976 $25.00 pap. $12.50

BRAHMS, JOHANNES. 1833–1897

Brahms was a composer, pianist, and conductor. Born in Hamburg, he made his debut as a pianist at the age of 14. In 1853, he met Robert Schumann, who published an article in the Viennese *Neue Zeitschrift für Musik* stating that Brahms was a genius. In 1862, he moved to Vienna, where he conducted the Singakademie and the Gesellschaft der Musikfreunde, and composed. His music shows respect for the form and structure of the eighteenth century; his style is romantic, but his form is classic.

Books about Brahms

Latham, Peter. *Brahms*. Biblio Dist. repr. 1975 $13.50; Little, Brown repr. 1975 pap.
$7.95
May, Florence. *The Life of Johannes Brahms*. Intro. by Ralph Hill, Paganiniana 2
vols. repr. 1981 $19.95; Scholarly 2 vols. 1976 lib. bdg. $69.00
Schumann, Clara, and Johannes Brahms. *Brahms Letters, 1853–1896*. Ed. by
Berthold Litzmann, Hyperion Pr. 2 vols. in 1 repr. of 1927 ed. 1980 $39.50

BRITTEN, LORD BENJAMIN. 1913–1976

Britten was one of Britain's most remarkable composers. He was a conscientious objector, and his *War Requiem* is a moving tribute to the victims of war everywhere. His operas, among them *Peter Grimes, Billy Budd, Albert Herring*, and *The Turn of the Screw*, display his ability to deal with a wide variety of themes and resources. He is the first British composer to have been elevated to the peerage.

Books about Britten

Brett, Philip, ed. *Benjamin Britten: Peter Grimes*. Cambridge Univ. Pr. 1983 $32.50
pap. $9.95. A collection of essays for the serious amateur or scholar concerning
the history, analysis, and interpretation of this opera.
Evans, Peter. *The Music of Benjamin Britten*. Univ. of Minnesota Pr. 1979 $29.50. A review of the composer's entire creative output.
Kennedy, Michael. *Britten*. Biblio Dist. 1981 $22.50
Palmer, Christopher, ed. *The Britten Companion*. Cambridge Univ. Pr. 1984 $34.50
pap. $11.95. Essays by scholars and critics covering Britten's musical life, based
in part on materials in the Britten-Pears Library and Archive.
White, Eric W. *Benjamin Britten: His Life and Operas*. Ed. by John Evans. Univ. of
California Pr. rev. ed. text ed. 1983 $30.00 pap. $12.95
Whittall, Arnold. *The Music of Britten and Tippett: Studies in Themes and Techniques*.
Cambridge Univ. Pr. 1982 $44.50

BRUCKNER, ANTON. 1824–1896

Bruckner was an Austrian symphonist, choral composer, and organist.
His first major work was an *Ave Maria* for seven voices. After hearing a performance of Wagner's *Tannhauser* in 1863, he became a Wagner disciple. In the last third of his life, he composed nine symphonies and numerous sacred works. He was a devout Roman Catholic and a famous music teacher in Vienna.

Book about Bruckner

Watson, Derek. *Bruckner*. Biblio Dist. text ed. 1975 $13.50; Little, Brown repr. 1975
$11.00

CAGE, JOHN. 1912–

A modernist composer, Cage is known for his unusual theories and experimental compositions. He studied with Henry Cowell and with Schoenberg. He invented the "prepared piano" (the attachment of materials such as metal and wood to a piano's strings, thus simulating the sound of percussion instruments), for which he composed his *Bacchanale* and *Sonatas and Interludes*. His most famous piece, *4'3"*, consists of silence punctuated by whatever random sounds happen to occur. Cage has applied the *I Ching* and a variety of aleatoric principles to his compositions. For many years, he was associated with Merce Cunningham and has also written music for the dance.

BOOK BY CAGE

Silence: Lectures and Writings of John Cage. Wesleyan Univ. Pr. 1961 pap. $10.95

CALLAS, MARIA. 1923–1977

An American soprano of Greek parentage, Callas was known as much for her dramatic interpretations of operatic roles as for her singing. Her personal life and her relationships with employers were equally fiery and well publicized. She was widely praised for her performance in the movie *Medea*.

BOOKS ABOUT CALLAS

Meneghini, Giovannibattista. *My Wife Maria Callas.* Trans. by Henry Wisneski, Farrar 1982 $16.50 pap. $8.95
Stassinopoulis, Arianna. *Maria Callas: The Woman behind the Legend.* Ballantine 1982 pap. $3.75

CHARLES, RAY. 1930–

Ray Charles is one of the most popular contemporary composers and singers. Originally a rhythm and blues artist, he has added "soul," country and western, and jazz styles to his compositional repertory. "Georgia on My Mind" and "I Can't Stop Loving You" are among his classics.

BOOK BY CHARLES

(and David Ritz). *Brother Ray.* Doubleday 1978 $9.95

CHOPIN, FREDERIC. 1810–1849

Born in Poland, Chopin published his first work, a rondo for two pianos, when he was 14 years of age. He eventually settled in Paris, where his admirers included Liszt, Bellini, and Berlioz. He effectively removed the bonds of the symphonic and choral traditions on the piano, allowing it to flower fully as a solo instrument. For ten years he had a stormy relationship with novelist George Sand. His sickly and dependent personal life contrasts dramatically with his musical compositions, which require brilliant technique to navigate their elaborate melodic and harmonic figurations.

BOOKS ABOUT CHOPIN

Liszt, Franz. *Frederic Chopin.* Trans. by Edward N. Waters, Vienna House repr. of 1963 ed. 1973 pap. $10.00
Marek, George R., and Maria Gordon-Smith. *Chopin.* Harper 1978 $14.95
Walker, Alan, ed. *The Chopin Companion: Profiles of the Man and the Musician.* Norton 1973 pap. $7.95

COLTRANE, JOHN. 1926–1967

A virtuoso jazz tenor saxophonist, Coltrane was one of the pantheon of jazz improvisers. Influenced by Lester Young, he attracted attention when he played with Miles Davis. He studied African and Asian music to add to his reservoir of techniques and styles. He was a very influential jazz musician.

Books about Coltrane

Cole, Bill. *John Coltrane*. Schirmer Bks. 1976 $14.95 1978 pap. $10.95
Simpkins, C. O. *Coltrane: A Biography*. Herndon House o.p.
Thomas, J. C. *Chasin the Trane: The Music and Mystique of John Coltrane*. Da Capo 1976 pap. $7.95

COPLAND, AARON. 1900–

Copland is a distinguished American composer and conductor. Supported early in his career by Koussevitzky, Copland employed folk elements in many of his compositions, among them *Billy the Kid*, *Applachian Spring*, and *Rodeo*. Copland has exerted enormous influence on the development of younger American composers by sponsoring concert series, festivals, artistic colonies, and competitions.

Books by Copland

Music and Imagination. Harvard Univ. Pr. 1952 pap. $3.95
What to Listen for in Music. McGraw-Hill rev. ed. 1957 $16.95; New Amer. Lib. rev. ed. 1964 pap. $2.75
Copland on Music. Da Capo repr. of 1960 ed. 1976 lib. bdg. $29.50; Norton Lib. 1963 pap. $7.95
(and Vivian Perlis). *Copland: 1900 through 1942*. St. Martin's 1984 $24.95

DAVIS, MILES. 1926–

A jazz trumpeter and composer, Davis was part of the group that invented bebop. He was known as a "cool" player favoring lyrical and harmonically ambiguous elements. Later he incorporated more unusual styles, adding electronics and hard rock sounds to his more recent compositions.

Books about Davis

Carr, Ian. *Miles Davis: A Critical Biography*. Fwd. by Len Lyons, Morrow 1982 $14.95 1984 pap. $6.95
Cole, Bill. *Miles Davis: A Musical Biography*. Morrow 1974 $7.95 pap. $5.95
Nisenson, Eric. *Round about Midnight: A Portrait of Miles Davis*. Doubleday (Dial) 1982 pap. $10.95

DEBUSSY, CLAUDE. 1862–1918

A distinguished French composer, Debussy is regarded as the chief musical figure in the early twentieth-century impressionist school centered in Paris. His piano and orchestral pieces employ Asian and Russian musical elements; he used numerous unresolved dissonances and consecutive parallel fourths and fifths, and perfected a modal compositional technique involving musical "cells." *La Mer* and *Prélude à l'Après-midi d'un faune* are filled with examples of his use of stunning orchestral coloration.

BOOK BY DEBUSSY

The Poetic Debussy: A Collection of His Song Texts and Selected Letters. Trans. by Richard Miller, ed. by Margaret G. Cobb, Northeastern Univ. Pr. 1981 $22.95

BOOKS ABOUT DEBUSSY

Holloway, Robin. *Debussy and Wagner.* Da Capo repr. of 1979 ed. text ed. 1982 pap. $16.50
Wenk, Arthur B. *Claude Debussy and the Poets.* Univ. of California Pr. 1976 $49.50

DVORÁK, ANTONIN. 1841–1904

A Bohemian composer, Dvorák first achieved success with his *Slavonic Dances.* In 1892, he came to the United States to be director of the National Conservatory of Music in New York. His peripatetic career (he traveled extensively) and the honors bestowed on him by numerous nations are paralleled in his compositions by their cosmopolitan use of national and folk melodies and the free flowing new melodies he composed. His most famous symphony, *From the New World* (also called *The New World Symphony*), deliberately demonstrates the fertile base American composers might have utilized to enrich their country's music. His chamber music is exquisite. He returned to Prague and was appointed director of the Prague Conservatory.

BOOKS ABOUT DVORÁK

Butterworth, Neil. *Dvorák: His Life and Times.* Paganiniana repr. of 1980 ed. 1981 $12.95
Clapham, John. *Dvorák.* Norton 1979 $19.95
Robertson, Alec. *Dvorák.* Biblio Dist. repr. of 1964 ed. 1969 $13.50: Little, Brown repr. of 1974 ed. 1977 pap. $7.95

ELLINGTON, EDWARD KENNEDY (DUKE). 1899–1974

Ellington was a jazz pianist, composer, and bandleader, and his skill as pianist and bandleader is surpassed only by the impressive depth and quality of his compositions and those of people working closely with him. *Mood Indigo* and *Sophisticated Lady*, the *Black and Tan Fantasy* and *Black, Brown and Beige*, and the two sacred concerts, among his best-known compositions, give some idea of the range of his work.

BOOKS BY ELLINGTON

Music Is My Mistress. Da Capo 1976 pap. $7.95; Doubleday 1973 $14.95
(and Stanley Dance). *Duke Ellington in Person: An Intimate Memoir.* Da Capo 1979 pap. $5.95; Houghton Mifflin 1978 $10.95

BOOKS ABOUT ELLINGTON

Dance, Stanley. *The World of Duke Ellington.* Fwd. by Duke Ellington, Da Capo repr. of 1970 ed. 1980 pap. $7.95
George, Don. *Sweet Man: The Real Duke Ellington.* Putnam 1981 $6.95

FOSTER, STEPHEN (COLLINS). 1826–1864

An American composer, Foster wrote both the words and the music to many of his 189 songs, among them "Old Folks at Home," "Oh! Susanna," "Jeanie with the Light Brown Hair," and "Beautiful Dreamer." His music was greatly influenced by black minstrel shows. The gentleness of many of Foster's songs was not characteristic of his life. He was constantly in need of money, his marriage was most unhappy, and he died penniless in New York's Bellevue Hospital.

BOOKS ABOUT FOSTER

Austin, William W. *Susanna, Jeanie and the Old Folks at Home: The Songs of Stephen C. Foster from His Times to Ours.* Macmillan 1975 $17.95. A ground-breaking exploration of the various meanings of Foster's songs in their social and historical contexts.

Howard, John Tasker. *Stephen Foster, America's Troubadour.* Arden Lib. repr. of 1943 ed. 1982 lib. bdg. $50.00

GERSHWIN, GEORGE. 1898–1937

One of the most original and popular American composers, Gershwin was an almost immediate success with his song "Swanee." His opera *Porgy and Bess,* written for black singers using Afro-American musical styles, is a real masterpiece. *Rhapsody in Blue,* for piano and jazz orchestra, is another ground-breaking piece, incorporating jazz and blues sources and idioms in the classical concerto style. His song "I Got Rhythm" has been performed thousands of times in hundreds of ways by jazz musicians. His brother, Ira, wrote the lyrics for many of his songs.

BOOKS ABOUT GERSHWIN

Armitage, Merle. *George Gershwin: Man and Legend. Biography Index Repr. Ser.* Ayer repr. of 1958 ed. $16.50

Schwartz, Charles. *Gershwin: His Life and Music.* Da Capo repr. of 1973 ed. 1979 pap. $7.95

HANDEL, GEORGE FRIDERIC. 1685–1759

An English composer of German birth, Handel was trained in Saxony, traveled to Italy, and eventually settled in England, finding notoriety and success in each location as a composer of operas and chamber music, and as an organist. In England, his success as court composer and, for a time, as a composer and producer of operas was overshadowed by the composition of his masterpiece, the *Messiah,* the oratorios, and the various occasional pieces.

BOOKS ABOUT HANDEL

Deutsch, Otto. *Handel: A Documentary Biography.* Da Capo repr. of 1954 ed. 1974 lib. bdg. $75.00

Flower, Newman. *Handel: His Personality and His Times.* Academy Chicago repr. of 1923 ed. 1972 pap. $5.95

Harris, Ellen T. *Handel and the Pastoral Tradition.* Oxford 1980 $45.00

Hogwood, Christopher. *Handel.* Thames & Hudson 1985 $19.95. Extensive quotations from contemporaneous documents.

HAYDN, JOSEPH. 1732–1809

An Austrian composer, Haydn in his life and career spanned several musical eras. He is best known now for his symphonies and quartets, but his sacred works and operas are just as accomplished. His influence on Mozart and Beethoven was important. Haydn's music on first hearing seems clear and direct, but it is filled with subtlety, invention, and emotion, all in classical proportions.

Books about Haydn

Geiringer, Karl, and Irene Geiringer. *Haydn: A Creative Life in Music.* Univ. of California Pr. 3d ed. rev. 1983 $24.95 pap. $8.95
Robbins-Landon, H. C. *Haydn: Chronicle and Works.* Indiana Univ. Pr. 5 vols. 1977–81 $325.00

HINDEMITH, PAUL. 1895–1963

Hindemith was a German composer and conductor of great originality. His career began with the study of violin and viola, and he held important positions in German ensembles before the Nazi era. Eventually he made his way to the United States and was a professor at Yale. Hindemith's musical style is uniquely his own. He sought in each piece to find the style, musical vocabulary, and thematic material most suitable for the intended use of the piece. He was immensely prolific and eclectic as a composer, writer, and teacher.

Book by Hindemith

A Composer's World: Horizons and Limitations. Peter Smith $11.25

Book about Hindemith

Skelton, Geoffrey. *Paul Hindemith: The Man behind the Music.* Taplinger 1977 $10.00

HOROWITZ, VLADIMIR. 1904–

Horowitz, an American pianist of Russian birth, has for so long been the pianist of the first place in the first rank that his rare appearances in the past two decades have become landmark musical events. He is best known for his performances of great romantic piano literature, especially the music of Liszt, Tchaikovsky, Chopin, and that of his friend Rachmaninoff.

Book about Horowitz

Plaskin, Glenn. *Horowitz: A Biography of Vladimir Horowitz.* Morrow 1983 $19.95 1984 pap. $10.95

IVES, CHARLES EDWARD. 1874–1954

Ives was an American composer who learned music at home and then studied it at Yale. He was a prosperous insurance man, but continued to compose as an avocation. His *Concord* Sonata for piano, *Three Places in New*

England for orchestra, and 114 songs are real masterpieces featuring many unusual musical elements.

Book by Ives

Essays before a Sonata, the Majority, and Other Writings. Ed. by Howard Boatwright, *Norton Lib.* repr. of 1962 ed. 1970 pap. $6.95. The composer's thoughts on the *Concord Sonata*, the work so representative of his highest achievements, the influence of the Concord transcendentalists preceding him, and the American cultural scene that formed his context.

Books about Ives

Cowell, Henry, and Sidney Cowell. *Charles Ives and His Music.* Da Capo repr. of 1969 ed. 1981 $29.50; Oxford repr. of 1966 ed. 1969 pap. $4.95
Hitchcock, H. Wiley. *Ives. Oxford Studies of Composers* 1977 pap. $9.95
Perlis, Vivian. *Charles Ives Remembered: An Oral History. Norton Lib.* repr. of 1974 ed. 1976 pap. $3.95; fwd. by Aaron Copeland, Yale Univ. Pr. 1974 $20.00
Rossiter, Frank. *Charles Ives and His America.* Liveright 1975 $15.00

JOPLIN, SCOTT. 1868–1917

Joplin, an American composer and pianist, is synonymous with ragtime, but he also composed operas and ballets of great merit. His fame has come only in the last 20 years due to the reprinting of most of his piano works in an edition by Vera Brodsky Lawrence published by the New York Public Library. His compositions include "The Entertainer" and "Fig Leaf Rag."

Books about Joplin

Gammond, Peter. *Scott Joplin and the Ragtime Era.* St. Martin's rev. ed. 1975 $8.95 1977 pap. $3.95
Haskins, James S., and Kathleen Benson. *Scott Joplin.* Doubleday 1978 $8.95

LISZT, FRANZ. 1811–1886

A Hungarian composer and pianist, Liszt studied with Salieri in Vienna and was a child prodigy. He was a product of and contributor to the most advanced romantic sensibilities. As a musician, he greatly influenced the advancement of pianistic technique and the use of chromatic harmonies. He was an ardent supporter of Wagner, a brilliant improviser, and a composer of great gifts. He spent much time in Rome, was a friend of the pope, and took the vows of four minor orders. His music exercised a great influence on the direction of musical history.

Books about Liszt

Huneker, James G. *Franz Liszt.* AMS Pr. repr. of 1924 ed. $24.50
Searle, Humphrey. *Music of Liszt.* Dover 1966 pap $4.95
Sitwell, Sacheverell. *Liszt.* Dover pap. $7.50
Walker, Alan. *Franz Liszt: The Virtuoso Years, 1811–1847.* Knopf 1983 $25.00
Westerby, Herbert. *Liszt, Composer, and His Piano Works.* Greenwood repr. of 1936 ed. lib. bdg. $22.50

MAHLER, GUSTAV. 1860–1911

The life of Mahler, who was born in Austria, revolved almost entirely around his conducting career. In 1908, he became conductor at the Metropolitan Opera House in New York, and in 1909, of the New York Philharmonic. His compositions are regarded as the last and most extensive of the romantic period. While his symphonies did not receive much approbation in his lifetime, they have achieved real prominence in recent years.

BOOK BY MAHLER

Selected Letters of Gustav Mahler. Trans. by Elaine Wilkins and Ernest Kaiser, ed. by Knud Martner and Alma Mahler, Farrar 1979 $30.00

BOOKS ABOUT MAHLER

Cooke, Deryck. *Gustav Mahler: An Introduction to His Music.* Cambridge Univ. Pr. 1980 $27.95 pap. $8.95
De La Grange, Henry-Louis. *Mahler.* Doubleday 1973 $17.50
Mitchell, Donald. *Gustav Mahler: The Early Years.* Ed. by David Mathews. Univ. of California Pr. 1980 $30.00. Extensively documented bibliography.

MENDELSSOHN, FELIX. 1809–1847

A German composer and conductor whose brief life resulted in many great works, Mendelssohn wrote songs, sonatas, cantatas, organ works, concertos, and symphonies. His first masterpiece, the overture to *A Midsummer Night's Dream,* was produced when he was only 17. His symphonies and incidental music are remarkable in that they were composed by someone so young. Mendelssohn is also responsible for the revival of interest in Bach's vocal and choral music by having performed the *St. Matthew Passion* in Berlin in 1829.

BOOKS ABOUT MENDELSSOHN

Finson, John W., and R. Larry Todd, eds. *Mendelssohn and Schumann: Essays on Their Music and Its Context.* Duke Univ. Pr. 1984 lib. bdg. $32.75
Radcliffe, Philip. *Mendelssohn.* Biblio Dist. repr. rev. ed. 1976 $13.50; Little, Brown rev. ed. repr. of 1954 ed. 1976 pap. $7.95

MONTEVERDI, CLAUDIO. 1567–1643

One biographer has termed Monteverdi "the creator of modern music." As an Italian composer of vocal music, his importance and influence are undeniable. His operas, including his masterpiece *Orfeo,* are distinguished by the flexible use of music to advance and comment on the dramatic action. His madrigals show imaginative use of dissonance.

BOOKS ABOUT MONTEVERDI

Arnold, Denis. *Monteverdi.* Biblio Dist. rev. ed. 1975 $13.50; Little, Brown repr. of 1963 ed. 1975 pap. $7.95
Arnold, Denis, and Nigel Fortune, eds. *Monteverdi Companion. Norton Lib.* 1972 pap. $5.95

Redlich, Hans F. *Claudio Monteverdi: Life and Works* .Trans. by Kathleen Dale, Greenwood repr. of 1952 ed. lib. bdg. $19.50

Schrade, Leo. *Monteverdi: Creator of Modern Music*. Da Capo repr. of 1950 ed. 1979
lib. bdg. $39.50

MOZART, WOLFGANG AMADEUS. 1756–1791

Born in Austria, Mozart's life and musical career were brief and fiery. He
was a child prodigy, and could compose whole symphonies and operas in his
head, needing only to write them out for performance. His gifts as a composer of endless streams of melodies, beautifully harmonized, are astounding. His symphonies and concerti are brilliant. The chamber music is stunning. Among his operas are *Don Giovanni, The Magic Flute*, and *The Marriage
of Figaro*. Mozart's brief life has produced nearly two centuries of deserved
adulation from the trained musician, the music scholar, and the unsophisti-
cated listener.

BOOKS ABOUT MOZART

Anderson, Emily, trans. and ed. *The Letters of Mozart and His Family*. Norton 2d ed.
rev. 1986 $50.00

Biancolli, Louis, ed. *The Mozart Handbook: A Guide to the Man and His Music*. Greenwood repr. of 1954 ed. 1976 lib. bdg. $45.00

Blom, Eric. *Mozart*. Biblio Dist. rev. ed. repr. of 1974 ed. 1976 $13.00; Little, Brown
rev. ed. repr. of 1974 ed. 1978 pap. $7.95

Deutsch, Otto E. *Mozart: A Documentary Biography*. Stanford Univ. Pr. 1966 $42.50

Hildesheimer, Wolfgang. *Mozart*. Random (Vintage) 1983 pap. $8.95

Landon, Howard C., and Donald Mitchell, eds. *The Mozart Companion*. Greenwood
repr. of 1956 ed. 1981 lib. bdg. $29.75

MUSSORGSKY, MODEST. 1839–1881

Mussorgsky was firmly entrenched in the nationalist Russian music
school of Borodin and Rimski-Korsakov. His friend Rimski-Korsakov "assisted" the half-trained Mussorgsky in completing and arranging his works.
The original versions are making a small comeback and deserve serious attention. He was a great colorist; the opera *Boris Godunov*, among other
works, is a good example of his art.

BOOKS ABOUT MUSSORGSKY

Brown, Malcòlm H., ed. *Mussorgsky: In Memoriam, 1881–1981*. UMI Research 1982
$44.95

Calvocoressi, M. D. *Mussorgsky*. Biblio Dist. rev. ed. 1974 $13.50; ed. by Gerald Abra-
ham, Little, Brown rev. ed. repr. of 1946 ed. 1974 pap. $7.95

Orlova, Alexandra. *Mussorgsky's Days and Works: A Biography in Documents*. Trans.
by Roy Guenther, ed. by Malcolm Brown, UMI Research 1983 $74.95

PARKER, CHARLIE ("BIRD"). 1920–1955

Parker was a jazz saxophonist and composer from Kansas City who
quickly made his way to New York, where he formed a quartet with Dizzy

Gillespie. Parker helped bring bebop into the world, but will always be re-membered for his incredible improvisatory and compositional gifts.

BOOKS ABOUT PARKER

Priestly, Brian. *Charlie Parker*. Ed. by John L. Smith, Hippocrene Bks. 1984 $6.95
Reisner, Robert G., ed. *Bird: The Legend of Charlie Parker*. Da Capo repr. of 1962 ed. 1975 lib. bdg. $22.50 pap. $9.95
Russell, Ross. *Bird Lives: The High Life and Hard Times of Charlie (Yardbird) Parker*. McKay 1973 $10.95

PORTER, COLE. 1891–1964

Porter began his musical career at Yale, writing light songs and college music. He wrote the words and music for *Can Can, Kiss Me Kate*, and *Silk Stockings*, all of which are distinguished by their sophisticated and engaging songs. His most popular songs include "Night and Day, "Let's Do It," and "In the Still of the Night."

BOOKS ABOUT PORTER

Eells, George. *The Life That He Led: A Biography of Cole Porter*. Putnam 1967 o.p.
Kimball, Robert, ed. *The Complete Lyrics of Cole Porter*. Fwd. by John Updike, Knopf 1983 $30.00; Random (Vintage) 1984 pap. $14.95
———. *The Unpublished Cole Porter*. Simon & Schuster 1975 o.p.
Schwartz, Charles. *Cole Porter: A Biography*. Da Capo 1979 pap. $6.95

PROKOFIEV, SERGE. 1891–1953

Prokofiev studied with Liadov and Rimski-Korsakov, but developed his own identity as a modernist Russian composer. During the Russian Revolution, he came to the United States. From about 1918 until 1932, he concertized, but finally returned to Russia, where he composed some of his best-known works, including *Peter and the Wolf, Romeo and Juliet*, and *War and Peace*. Among his works are seven symphonies, seven concerti, nine so-natas, and chamber music. He used sharp rhythms, and although his later works were not as strident as those of his earlier years, they remained vigorous and powerful. He won the Stalin Prize during World War II, but was denounced in 1948 for his Western musical thinking. He returned to favor in 1951 and won the Stalin Prize a second time. His music is lively, with a sharp mix of traditional and modern elements.

BOOK BY PROKOFIEV

Prokofiev by Prokofiev: A Composer's Memoir. Doubleday 1979 $14.00

BOOKS ABOUT PROKOFIEV

Seroff, Victor. *Sergei Prokofiev: A Soviet Tragedy*. Taplinger rev. of 1968 ed. 1979 $14.95 pap. $7.95
Shostakovich, Dmitri, and others. *Sergei Prokofiev: Materials, Articles, Interviews*. Imported Pubns. 1978 $9.45. Prokofiev in his own words, those of his colleagues, including Dmitri Shostakovich; published in a translation authorized by the Soviet Union.

PUCCINI, GIACOMO. 1858–1924

The operas of the Italian composer Puccini quickly won esteem and have become part of the standard repertory of the world's leading opera companies. *La Bohème, Turandot, Madama Butterfly, Tosca,* and *La Fanciulla del West* demonstrate his ability to create an intense psychodrama from the first notes of the first act. He was a true successor to Verdi.

BOOKS ABOUT PUCCINI

Ashbrook, William. *The Operas of Puccini.* Fwd. by Roger Parker, Cornell Univ. Pr. repr. 1985 $29.95 pap. $9.95
Carner, Mosco. *Puccini: A Critical Biography.* Holmes & Meier rev. ed. text ed. 1977 $55.00
Osborne, Charles. *The Complete Operas of Puccini: A Critical Guide.* Atheneum 1982 $15.95

PURCELL, HENRY. 1659-1695

Purcell was associated with the royal court his entire life and he is generally counted with Dowland and Britten among England's greatest composers. His opera *Dido and Aeneas* shows his skill as a dramatist, contrapuntist, and melodist. His anthems, court orders, and consorts reveal mastery of composition for instrumental and mixed ensembles.

BOOKS ABOUT PURCELL

Westrup, Jack A. *Purcell.* Rev. by Nigel Fortune, Biblio Dist. rev. ed. 1980 $19.75
Zimmerman, Franklin B. *Henry Purcell: His Life and Times, 1659–1695.* Univ. of Pennsylvania Pr. 2d ed. rev. 1983 $37.50 pap. $19.95

RACHMANINOFF, SERGE. 1873–1943

Russian-born, Rachmaninoff's early career was as a pianist, but Tchaikovsky recognized his importance as a conductor and encouraged him to continue composing. By the age of 24, Rachmaninoff had composed the opera *Aleko* and the famous C-sharp Minor Prelude. His piano concertos are regarded by many as models of the late romantic formulation of that genre. His music was eclectic in style, and his belief that the music existed to reveal beauty left him opposed to Russian nationalist composers. In 1909, he first traveled to the United States. He became an exile as a result of the Russian Revolution and lived in Switzerland and the United States.

BOOKS ABOUT RACHMANINOFF

Bertensson, Sergei, and Jay Leyda. *Sergei Rachmaninoff: A Lifetime in Music.* New York Univ. Pr. 1956 $25.00
Norris, Geoffrey. *Rakhmaninoff.* Biblio Dist. 1976 $13.50; Littlefield 1978 pap. $7.95
Piggott, Patrick. *Rachmaninoff.* Faber 1978 $9.95
Walker, Robert. *Rachmaninoff: His Life and Times.* Paganiniana expanded ed. 1981 $12.95

RAVEL, MAURICE. 1875–1937

Born in France, Ravel reveals in his compositions many of the currents active in Paris in the early twentieth century. His coloristic effects and occasional use of whole-tone scales and tritones place him with Debussy and the impressionists. The sense of proportion and austere aspects of some pieces reflect his interest in and reverence for music of the past. He wrote the ballet *Daphnis and Chloe* and the opera *L'Heure espagnole*.

BOOKS ABOUT RAVEL

Demuth, Norman. *Ravel.* Hyperion Pr. repr. of 1947 ed. 1979 $22.45
Myers, Rollo H. *Ravel: His Life and Works.* Greenwood repr. of 1960 ed. 1973 lib. bdg. $22.50
Nichols, Roger. *Ravel.* Biblio Dist. 1977 $13.50
Orenstein, Arbie. *Ravel: Man and Musician.* Columbia Univ. Pr. 1975 $25.00

SCHOENBERG, ARNOLD. 1874–1951

An American of Austrian birth, Schoenberg composed initially in a highly developed romantic style, but eventually turned to painting and expressionism. At first, he was influenced by Wagner and tried to write in a Wagnerian style. He attracted the attention of Alban Berg and Anton Webern, with whom he created a new compositional method based on using all 12 half-steps in each octave as an organizing principle, the so-called 12-tone technique. His importance to the development of twentieth-century music is incredible, but the music he composed using this new method is not easily accessible to most concertgoers.

BOOK BY SCHOENBERG

Style and Idea: Selected Writings of Arnold Schoenberg. Ed. by Leonard Stein, Faber repr. 1982 $45.00

BOOKS ABOUT SCHOENBERG

Leibowitz, Rene. *Schoenberg and His School: The Contemporary Stage of the Language of Music.* Da Capo repr. of 1949 ed. 1975 pap. $5.95
Rosen, Charles. *Arnold Schoenberg.* Viking 1975 $9.95
Stuckenschmidt, H. H. *Arnold Schoenberg.* Greenwood repr. of 1960 ed. 1979 lib. bdg. $19.75; Schirmer Bks. 1978 $20.00

SCHUBERT, FRANZ. 1797–1828

Schubert was born in Vienna, and his brief and difficult life is not at all reflected in his astounding outpouring of lieder cycles, symphonies, and chamber and church music. The song cycles and many of the piano works show that Schubert was a poet in music, conveying a wide range of emotions and meanings through these forms.

BOOKS ABOUT SCHUBERT

Deutsch, Otto E. *Schubert: A Documentary Biography.* Trans. by Eric Blom, Da Capo repr. of 1946 ed. 1977 lib. bdg. $75.00

Fischer-Dieskau, Dietrich. *Schubert's Songs: A Biographical Study.* Knopf 1977
 $13.95; trans. by Kenneth S. Whitton, Limelight Eds. 1984 pap. $8.95
Hutchings, Arthur. *Schubert.* Biblio Dist. 1978 $13.50; Little, Brown rev. ed. repr. of
 1973 ed. 1978 pap. $7.95

SHOSTAKOVICH, DMITRI. 1906–1975

A true child of the Russian Revolution, Shostakovich suffered his entire
life from a childhood of malnutrition and disease. He was, nevertheless, a
composer of powerful and advanced music. As a symphonist he is hardly
surpassed in his own time. Shostakovich was alternately reviled and hailed
by the leadership of the Soviet Union, but his own output is remarkably consistent in style, technique, and emotional content.

BOOKS BY SHOSTAKOVICH

Testimony: The Memoirs of Dmitri Shostakovich. Trans. by Antonina W. Bouis, ed. by
 Solomon Volkov, Harper 1979 $15.00. The review by Laurel Fay in the *Russian
 Review*, October 1980, raises some questions about this work's authenticity.
Shostakovich: About Himself and His Times. Imported Pubns. 1981 $12.00.
 Shostakovich's articles reprinted by a Russian publisher and translated into En-
 glish.

BOOK ABOUT SHOSTAKOVICH

Kay, Norman. *Shostakovich.* Oxford 1972 pap. $7.95

STRAUSS, RICHARD. 1864–1949

Born in Munich, Strauss is a bridge between mid-nineteenth century romanticism and mid-twentieth century eclecticism. The tone poems, especially *Macbeth, Don Juan, Till Eulenspiegel lustige Streiche,* and *Tod und
Verklarung,* are rich tapestries of motives, harmonic complexity and
extramusical associations. Among his operas are *Guntram, Elektra,* and *Der
Rosenkavalier.*

BOOKS BY STRAUSS

Recollections and Reflections. Trans. by L. J. Lawrence, Greenwood repr. of 1953 ed.
 1974 lib. bdg. $22.50
A Confidential Matter: The Letters of Richard Strauss and Stefan Zweig, 1931–1935.
 Fwd. by Edward E. Lowinsky, Univ. of California Pr. 1977 $17.95
*A Working Friendship: The Correspondence between Richard Strauss and Hugo von
 Hofmannsthal.* Trans. by Hans Hammelmann and Ewald Osers, Vienna House
 1974 pap. $17.50

BOOKS ABOUT STRAUSS

Hartmann, Rudolf. *Richard Strauss: The Staging of His Operas and Ballets.* Oxford
 1981 $45.00
Schuh, Willi. *Richard Strauss: A Chronicle of the Early Years, 1864–1898.* Trans. by
 Mary Whittall, Cambridge Univ. Pr. 1982 $67.50

STRAVINSKY, IGOR. 1882–1971

An American composer of Russian birth, Stravinsky's life and works can hardly be described in a few words, so cosmopolitan were his perambulations and contributions and so influential and powerful his music. He studied with Rimski-Korsakov, and wrote music for the Ballet Russe at the request of Diaghilev. The results included *L'Oiseau de feu, Petrushka,* and *Le Sacre du printemps.* After leaving Russia, his style changed and he turned to the past for inspiration. In his classical idiom, he wrote concerti for piano and violin, *Oedipus Rex,* and the *Symphony of Psalms.*

BOOKS BY STRAVINSKY

Igor Stravinsky: An Autobiography. Norton Lib. 1962 pap. $5.95; October 1966 $6.95
Stravinsky Petrushka. Ed. by Charles Hamm, Norton 1967 pap. $7.95
Poetics of Music in the Form of Six Lessons. Pref. by G. Seferis, Harvard Univ. Pr. 1970 $12.50 pap. $4.95
Themes and Conclusions. Univ. of California Pr. 1982 pap. $8.95
(and Robert Craft). *Conversation with Igor Stravinsky.* Univ. of California Pr. 1980 pap. $4.95
(and Robert Craft). *Expositions and Developments.* Univ. of California Pr. 1981 pap. $6.95
(and Robert Craft). *Memories and Commentaries.* Univ. of California Pr. 1981 pap. $5.95
(and Robert Craft). *Dialogues.* 1968. Univ. of California Pr. 1982 pap. $6.95

BOOKS ABOUT STRAVINSKY

Libman, Lillian. *And Music at the Close: Stravinky's Last Years, a Personal Memoir.* Beekman 1972 $18.00; Norton 1972 $12.50
Stravinsky, Theodore. *Catherine and Igor Stravinsky.* Boosey & Hawkes 1973 $30.00
Stravinsky, Vera, and Robert Craft. *Stravinsky: In Pictures and Documents.* Simon & Schuster 1979 o.p.
Van den Toorn, Pieter C. *The Music of Igor Stravinsky.* Yale Univ. Pr. text ed. 1983 $40.00
White, Eric W. *Stravinsky: The Composer and His Works.* Univ. of California Pr. 2d ed. 1980 $30.00 1985 pap. $10.95. A short biography with a lengthy "register of works" providing copious information and a description of each work. Appendixes of documents, arrangements, bibliographic sources.

TCHAIKOVSKY, PETER ILYICH. 1840–1893

The life of the great Russian composer Tchaikovsky must have been filled with psychological torment and indecision, but his music never reflects these problems. The ballet *Romeo and Juliet* is one of the calmest and most lyrical works in the ballet repertory. Tchaikovsky's symphonies and operas include numerous dramatic elements as well as reflections of his well-developed sense of fatalism. His masterpieces include the Fourth Symphony, the opera *Eugen Onegin,* and the Violin Concerto.

BOOK BY TCHAIKOVSKY

Letters to His Family: An Autobiography. Trans. by Galina Von Meck, ed. by Percy M. Young, Stein & Day 1982 $25.00 pap. $12.95

Books about Tchaikovsky

Brown, David. *Tchaikovsky: The Crisis Years.* Norton 2 vols. 1979–83 ea. $24.95–$25.00
Garden, Edward. *Tchaikovsky.* Biblio Dist. 1973 $13.50
Volkoff, Vladimir. *Tchaikovsky: A Self-Portrait.* Taplinger 1975 $15.00
Wiley, Roland J. *Tchaikovsky's Ballets: Swan Lake, Sleeping Beauty, Nutcracker.* Oxford 1985 $39.95

THOMSON, VIRGIL. 1896–

The musical development of this American composer and critic received much of its force from his association with Gertrude Stein in Paris in the 1920s. His opera *Four Saints in Three Acts* is a masterpiece of contrast, treating the buffalike plot with hymnlike seriousness. Thomson's music and prose are subtle, humorous, and well crafted, but underneath it all is a profound philosopher.

Books by Thomson

The State of Music 1939. Greenwood repr. of 1939 ed. 1974 lib. bdg. $15.00
American Music since 1910. Holt 1971 pap. o.p.
Virgil Thomson. Da Capo 1977 pap. $6.95; Dutton 1985 pap. $1.95
A Virgil Thomson Reader. Intro. by John Rockwell, Dutton 1984 pap. $11.95; Houghton Mifflin 1981 $25.00. A selection of writings about music by one of the most wise and witty of the composer-critics. Includes two interviews and a bibliography of Thomson's writings.

TIPPETT, MICHAEL. 1905–

Tippett was educated entirely in England. He has been acutely involved with political and social events, but has maintained his well-developed neo-romantic style of composition. Tippett prefers large forms and writes his own librettos. He is an inheritor of the best British tradition of composing understandable but deeply emotional music.

Books about Tippett

Bowen, Meirion. *Michael Tippett.* Universe text ed. 1982 $15.00
Kemp, Ian. *Tippett: The Composer and His Music.* Da Capo 1985 $37.50
Matthews, David. *Michael Tippett: An Introductory Story.* Faber 1980 pap. $7.95
White, Eric W. *Tippett and His Operas.* Pref. by Andrew Porter, Da Capo repr. of 1979 ed. 1981 $23.50
Whittall, Arnold. *The Music of Britten and Tippett: Studies in Themes and Techniques* Cambridge Univ. Pr. 1982 $44.50

VERDI, GIUSEPPE. 1813–1901

Verdi has finally achieved the level of universal respect that his great dramatic works deserve. During his own lifetime, he was successful and lionized, particularly in his native Italy, but the appeal of Wagner and his followers led some to disregard Verdi as a mere melodist. *La Traviata, Macbeth, Rigoletto, Don Carlos, Aida,* and the other operas are standards now, but Verdi's sacred music and songs deserve more recognition.

BOOKS ABOUT VERDI

Baldini, Gabriele. *The Story of Giuseppe Verdi*. Intro. by Julian Budden, Cambridge Univ. Pr. 1980 $47.50 pap. $13.95

Budden, Julian. *The Operas of Verdi*. Oxford 3 vols. 1978–1981 pap. ea. $15.00

————. *Verdi*. Biblio Dist. 1985 $26.95

Busch, Hans, trans. *Verdi's Aida: The History of an Opera in Letters and Documents*. Univ. of Minnesota Pr. 1978 $40.00 pap. $15.00

Conati, Marcello, ed. *Encounters with Verdi*. Trans. by Richard Stokes, fwd. by Julian Budden, Cornell Univ. Pr. 1984 $25.00

Kimbell, David R. *Verdi in the Age of Italian Romanticism*. Cambridge Univ. Pr. 1981 $84.50 1985 pap. $19.95

Martin, George. *Verdi: His Music, Life and Times*. Da Capo repr. of 1963 ed. 1979 $49.50

Porter, Andrew, and David Rosen, eds. *Verdi's Macbeth: A Source Book*. Norton text ed. 1984 $39.95

Walker, Frank. *The Man Verdi*. Knopf repr. of 1962 ed. $15.00; Univ. of Chicago Pr. repr. of 1962 ed. 1982 pap. $9.95

Weaver, William, ed. *Verdi: A Documentary Study*. Thames & Hudson 1977 $37.50

Weaver, William, and Martin Chusid, eds. *The Verdi Companion*. Norton 1979 $22.95

VIVALDI, ANTONIO. 1678–1741

Vivaldi was a prolific Italian composer of concerti, but he also wrote numerous operas, chamber works, and sacred works. *The Four Seasons* is a work of genuine genius, but his prolixity apparently did not permit him to recapitulate this quality often. Vivaldi's works were well known and have been used as the basis of numerous works by other composers, including Bach.

BOOK ABOUT VIVALDI

Talbot, Michael. *Vivaldi*. Biblio Dist. 1978 $13.50

WAGNER, RICHARD. 1813–1883

One of the most influential German composers, Wagner transferred the center of the operatic world from Italy to Germany. In his first opera, *Die Feen*, as in all his operas, he was his own librettist. As a result of the success of *Rienzi* and *The Flying Dutchman*, he was appointed artistic director of the Saxon Court, in which capacity he composed *Tannhauser* and *Lohengrin*. His music is dramatic and builds to amazing climaxes. He symbolizes the synthesis of all the arts in opera—caring about the dramatic content and scenery as well as the music. He married Cosima, the daughter of Liszt, and in 1876 he opened the Festival Theater in Bayreuth, which was dedicated to the preservation of his operas.

BOOKS BY WAGNER

My Life. Trans. by Andrew Gray, ed. by Mary Whittall, Cambridge Univ. Pr. 1983 $39.50; Scholarly 2 vols. repr. of 1936 ed. $89.00 pap. $59.00

The Ring of the Nibelungen. Trans. by Andrew Porter, Norton 1977 $17.50 pap. $6.95

BOOKS ABOUT WAGNER

Chancellor, John. *Wagner*. Little, Brown 1978 $12.95

Digaetani, John L., ed. *Penetrating Wagner's Ring: An Anthology*. Da Capo repr. of 1978 ed. 1983 lib. bdg. $45.00; Fairleigh Dickinson Univ. Pr. 1978 $25.00

Gregor-Dellin, Martin. *Richard Wagner: His Life, His Work, His Century*. Trans. by J. Maxwell Brownjohn, Harcourt 2 vols. 1983 $25.00

Hodson, Phillip. *Who's Who in Wagner: An A to Z Look at His Life and Work*. Macmillan 1984 $14.95. Information about people, places, and ideas central to Wagner's life and works.

Hollinrake, Roger. *Nietzsche, Wagner and the Philosophy of Pessimism*. Allen & Unwin text ed. 1982 $35.00

James, David B. *Wagner and the Romantic Disaster*. Hippocrene Bks. 1983 $22.50

Large, David C., and William Weber, eds. *Wagnerism in European Culture and Politics*. Cornell Univ. Pr. 1984 $34.50 pap. $14.95

McCreless, Patrick P. *Wagner's Siegfried: Its Drama, History, and Music*. Ed. by George Buelow, UMI Research 1982 $44.95

Osborne, Charles. *Richard Wagner and His World*. Scribner 1977 $3.95

———. *The World Theater of Wagner: A Celebration of 150 Years of Wagner Productions*. Macmillan 1982 $36.50

Skelton, Geoffrey. *Richard and Cosima Wagner: Biography of a Marriage*. Houghton Mifflin 1982 $14.95

Westernhagen, Curt von. *Wagner: A Biography, 1813–1833*. Trans. by Mary Whittall, Cambridge Univ. Pr. 1981 pap. $16.95

WEBERN, ANTON VON. 1883–1945

Perhaps the most severe of the Second Viennese School of composers, Webern studied musicology, but quickly became a follower of Schoenberg. His remaining works are practically gossamer in their adherence to the most rigid interpretation of the rules for composition using 12 tones.

BOOKS ABOUT WEBERN

Kolneder, Walter. *Anton Webern: An Introduction to His Works*. Trans. by Humphrey Searle. Greenwood repr. of 1968 ed. 1982 lib. bdg. $25.00; trans. by Humphrey Searle, Univ. of California Pr. 1968 $18.50

Moldenhauer, Hans, and Demar Irvine, eds. *Anton von Webern: Perspectives*. Da Capo repr. of 1966 ed. 1978 lib. bdg. $27.50

Moldenhauer, Hans, and Rosaleen Moldenhauer. *Anton von Webern: A Chronicle of His Life and Work*. Knopf 1978 $25.00

XENAKIS, IANNIS. 1922–

Xenakis is an avant-garde Greek composer, who attempts to apply mathematical constructs to musical composition. In this age of technology, his work captivates many other composers and may prove to be one of the formative generators of compositional technique in the late twentieth century.

BOOKS BY XENAKIS

Formalized Music: Thought and Mathematics in Composition. Indiana Univ. Pr. 1971 $25.00

Arts, Sciences, Alloys. Trans. by Sharon Kanach, Pendragon 1985 lib. bdg. $36.00

BOOK ABOUT XENAKIS

Bois, Mario. *Iannis Xenakis, the Man and His Music: A Conversation with the Composer and a Description of His Works.* Greenwood repr. of 1967 ed. 1980 lib. bdg. $25.00

DANCE

History and Criticism

Buckle, Richard. *Buckle at the Ballet: Selected Ballet Writings.* Atheneum 1980 $19.95. Collected articles of the ballet critic for the *Sunday Times* (London), from 1959 to 1975, arranged by subject, and indexed.

Clarke, Mary, and Pam Thomas. *A History of Dance.* Outlet 1981 $9.98. Covers the globe and all periods rather briefly, but with real authority. Copiously illustrated.

Cohen, Selma J. *Next Week, Swan Lake: Reflections on Dance and Dances.* Wesleyan Univ. Pr. 1982 $18.50 1986 pap. $10.95. Concerned with the identity of certain works, genres, and dance itself. Reviews historic, dramatic, stylistic, and personal problems of the art. Focused on Western concert dance.

Croce, Arlene. *Going to the Dance.* Knopf 1982 $20.00 pap. $8.95. Articles collected from this most perceptive critic's writings in the *New Yorker* from the previous five years.

Haskell, Arnold L. *Balletomania: Story of an Obsession.* AMS Pr. repr. of 1934 ed. $19.50; Knopf 1977 $12.50. Story of a personal odyssey to achieve a depth of understanding that can be described as intoxicating. Annotated after nearly four decades more experience as a dance critic and followed by new pieces on recent developments.

Jowitt, Deborah. *The Dance in Mind: Profiles and Reviews, 1977–83.* Photographs by Lois Greenfield, Godine 1985 $19.95. Selected pieces by the dance critic of the *Village Voice.*

Kirstein, Lincoln. *Dance: A Short History of Classic Theatrical Dancing.* Dance Horizons repr. 1969 pap. $11.50; Greenwood repr. of 1935 ed. lib. bdg. $19.50. A dated, but thorough, history of the Western tradition.

Martin, John. *Introduction to the Dance.* Dance Horizons pap. $7.95. A consideration of the dance in history and society, intending to awaken or verbalize responses to dance as a means of communication. A classic.

Nevell, Richard. *A Time to Dance: American Country Dancing from Hornpipes to Hot Hash.* St. Martin's 1977 $10.00

Sachs, Curt. *World History of the Dance.* Trans. by Bessie Schoenberg, *Norton Lib.* 1963 pap. $8.95

Terry, Walter. *How to Look at Dance.* Photographs by Jack Vartoogian and Linda Vartoogian, Morrow 1982 $14.95. Covers all styles of art and popular dance.

———. *I Was There: Selected Dance Reviews and Articles, 1936–1976.* Princeton Bk. 1978 $17.95. The best writings of the American dean of dance critics.

Reference

Cobbett-Steinberg, Steven, ed. *The Dance Anthology.* New Amer. Lib. (Plume) 1980 $10.95. Essays and articles on a variety of themes by some of the most thoughtful writers on the dance, many of them choreographers, dancers, and musicians. Chronology, dance family trees, and a guide to dance literature. A fine book.

Cohen-Stratyner, Barbara Naomi. *Biographical Dictionary of Dance.* Schirmer Bks. 1982 lib. bdg. $75.00. Profiles 2,900 dance persons in classical and popular dance. Lists of works and bibliographies.

Copeland, Roger, and Marshall Cohen. *What Is Dance: Readings in Theory and Criticism.* Oxford 1983 $25.00 pap. $12.95. A widely diversified collection of good writings about dance examining fundamental questions of dance aesthetics.

Koegler, Horst. *The Concise Oxford Dictionary of Ballet.* 1977. Oxford 2d ed. 1982 pap. $14.95. Crisp entries on all aspects of ballet (people, works, companies, terms, and ethnic and social dancing), including modern dance. Occasional bibliographies.

Lawson, Joan. *The Principles of Classical Dance.* Photographs by Anthony Crickmay, Knopf 1980 $12.95. Photographs accompanying brief explications of the rules of movement for ballet.

McDonagh, Don. *The Complete Guide to Modern Dance.* Doubleday 1976 $15.95. Brief entries on major figures in modern dance with analyses of the most characteristic of their productions. End papers show "extended choreographic families in a single graphic representation."

Raffe, W. G., and M. E. Purdon. *Dictionary of the Dance.* A. S. Barnes repr. 1975 o.p. Covers all periods and places with entries on terms, genres, locations, costumes, sets, and themes. No biographical materials, but there is a bibliography as well as geographical and subject indexes.

Sharp, Harold, and Marjorie Z. Sharp. *Index to Characters in the Performing Arts.* Scarecrow Pr. 4 pts. 1966–73 ea. $17.50–$45.00. Identifies characters, lists creative persons, and gives dates and places of first performances.

The Simon and Schuster Book of the Ballet. Intro. by Mario Psai, Simon & Schuster 1980 $24.95. A chronological, illustrated catalog of ballets.

Van Zile, Judy A. *Dance in India: An Annotated Guide to Source Materials.* Asian Music text ed. 1973 pap. $7.50. A comprehensive listing of source materials in English.

Wilson, G. B. L. *A Dictionary of Ballet.* Theatre Arts 3d ed. rev. & enl. 1971 o.p. Covers Western dance with very brief entries on persons, dances, terms.

Ballet

Balanchine, George, and Jeffrey Bairstow. *Balanchine's Complete Stories of the Great Ballets.* Doubleday 1977 $27.50. Basic facts, plot summaries, and notes on approximately 450 ballets. Brief concluding essays and a glossary.

Beaumont, Cyril. *Ballets of Today: Being a Second Supplement to the Complete Book of Ballets.* Putnam 1954 o.p. Descriptions of ballets, each followed by short critical commentary.

———. *Ballets Past and Present: Being a Third Supplement to the Complete Book of Ballets.* Putnam 1955 o.p. Descriptive of ballets as in *Ballets of Today.*

———. *Complete Book of Ballets: A Guide to the Principal Ballets of the Nineteenth and Twentieth Centuries.* Putnam 1938 o.p. A classic work featuring summaries of the plots and basic facts of the most famous ballets.

Guest, Ivor. *Adventures of a Ballet Historian, an Unfinished Memoir.* Dance Horizons 1982 $20.00. Includes a bibliography of works by this prolific writer of dance books.

Lee, Carol. *An Introduction to Classical Ballet.* Erlbaum 1983 $22.50. A dry but solid work on the historical and technical foundations of classical ballet intended for the developing professional, but worth attention by the serious balletomane.

Percival, John. *Modern Ballet*. Outlet 1980 o.p. An illustrated summary of artistic developments in ballet.

American Dance

Mazo, Joseph H. *Prime Movers: The Makers of Modern Dance in America*. Morrow 1977 $12.50 1978 pap. $6.95; Princeton Bk. repr. of 1977 ed. text ed. 1983 pap. $12.95. Extensive essays on nine of modern dance's principal exponents.

Stearns, Marshall, and Jean Stearns. *Jazz Dance: The Story of American Vernacular Dance*. Schirmer Bks. 1979 pap. $12.95. Deals with American dancing that is performed to and with the rhythms of jazz.

Ethnic Dance

Emery, Lynne Fauley. *Black Dance in the United States from 1619 to 1970*. Ayer repr. of 1972 ed. 1980 lib. bdg. $34.00. A comprehensive study of the dance forms of black Americans. A scholarly but readable work replete with quotations, footnotes, and an extensive bibliography.

Royce, Anya P. *The Anthropology of Dance*. Indiana Univ. Pr. 1977 pap. $7.95. Explores the meanings and symbolisms of dance in general and of ethnic and tribal groups in particular.

Zoete, Beryl de, and Walter Spies. *Dance and Drama in Bali*. 1938. Oxford repr. 1973 o.p. A classic exposition of Balinese dance and thus on non-Western dance, revealing the important and recurring links between drama and dance.

Dance Companies

Barnes, Clive. *Inside American Ballet Theatre*. Intro. by Justin Colin, Da Capo repr. of 1977 ed. 1983 pap. $11.95; Dutton 1977 pap. $9.95. An annotated photographic essay.

Bland, Alexander. *The Royal Ballet: The First Fifty Years*. Doubleday 1981 $39.95. A history of the ballet company that began life as the Sadler's Wells Ballet.

Cameron, Judy, photographer. *The Bolshoi Ballet*. Intro. by Walter Terry, Harper 1975 $17.50

Doeser, Linda. *Ballet and Dance: The World's Major Companies*. St. Martin's 1978 $15.00. Descriptions of dance companies from all over the world, but the focus is on European, Russian, and American companies.

Gregory, John, and Alexander Ukladnikov. *Leningrad's Ballet: Maryinsky to Kirov*. Universe 1982 $15.00. An introduction to the history, traditions, and life of the famous Kirov Ballet Company.

Newman, Barbara. *Striking a Balance: Dancers Talk about Dancing*. Houghton Mifflin 1982 $17.95 pap. $10.95. Transcribed conversations with ballet dancers.

Walker, Katherine Sorley. *DeBasil's Ballets Russes*. Atheneum 1983 $19.95. A chronicle of the Ballet Russe de Monte Carlo. Extensive appendixes.

Choreographers

Hastrup, Baird. *Choreographer and Composer.* Twayne 1983 o.p. A modern history of the complementary roles of the chief creators of dance. Discusses working relationships and the creative process.

Regosin, Elinor. *The Dance Makers: Conversations with American Choreographers.* Walker 1980 o.p. A dozen interviews with legendary and budding choreographers.

ASHTON, FREDERICK. 1904–

Ashton is perhaps the most influential contemporary British dancer and choreographer. He has been incredibly prolific, creating more than 60 works, and serving as director of the Royal Ballet in the 1960s. Not only involved with ballet, he has choreographed musicals and collaborated with both Benjamin Britten and Virgil Thomson.

BOOK ABOUT ASHTON

Vaughan, David. *Frederick Ashton and His Ballets.* Knopf 1977 $25.00. Synopses of ballets and transcriptions of choreographic notes of the great British choreographer.

BALANCHINE, GEORGE. 1904–1983

Dancer, choreographer, and the major influence on ballet in this century, Balanchine was born in Russia, enjoyed a career there, worked with Diaghilev, came to the American Ballet in 1934 and exercised his talents in the United States until his death. In 1948 he became principal choreographer and artistic director of the New York City Ballet. He refined and expanded the vocabulary of dance.

BOOKS ABOUT BALANCHINE

Kirstein, Lincoln. *Portrait of Mr. B: Photographs of George Balanchine with an Essay.* Photographs by Jonathan Cott and Edwin Denby, fwd. by Peter Martins, Viking 1984 $30.00 pap. $12.95. Includes photographs from 1904 to 1983, and essays by Jonathan Cott and Edwin Denby.

Maiorano, Robert, and Valerie Brooks. *Balanchine's Mozartiana: The Making of a Masterpiece.* Freundlich 1985 $17.95. Balanchine at work.

Taper, Bernard. *Balanchine.* Times Bks. rev. ed. 1984 $19.95

Volkov, Solomon. *Balanchine's Tchaikovsky: Interviews with George Balanchine.* Trans. by Antonina W. Bouis, Simon & Schuster 1985 $19.95

BARYSHNIKOV, MIKHAIL. 1948–

Baryshnikov came to the United States after a successful career with the Kirov Ballet. Immediately upon his defection in 1974 he danced for the National Ballet of Canada and the American Ballet. He has also appeared in Hollywood films.

BOOK ABOUT BARYSHNIKOV

Smakov, Gennady. *Baryshnikov: From Russia to the West*. Farrar 1981 $17.95 pap.
$10.95

BOURNONVILLE, AUGUST. 1805–1879

The son of a famous dancer and choreographer, Bournonville created
more than 60 dances in his career in Copenhagen, utilizing techniques and
subjects he had learned in Paris as well as those of the Danish scene. Dance
historians consider him to be one of the most important, if not the most important, choreographers of the nineteenth century.

BOOK BY BOURNONVILLE

My Theatre Life. Trans. by Patricia McAndrew, Wesleyan Univ. Pr. 1979 $40.00. The
autobiography of the nineteenth-century ballet choreographer and impresario.

CUNNINGHAM, MERCE. 1919–

Cunningham's career has spanned the early years of the American modern dance movement (through his connection with Martha Graham) to the
postmodernist developments (through his association with John Cage). His
works require new intellectuality and strength of the performers, and demand that audiences observe dance in new ways. A seminal figure, who recently received a life achievement award at the Kennedy Center.

BOOK BY CUNNINGHAM

Changes: Notes on Choreography. Ed. by Frances Starr, Ultramarine, o.p. Typographi-
cally difficult book that gives a unique view of the creative impulse in modern
dance.

BOOK ABOUT CUNNINGHAM

Klosty, James, ed. *Merce Cunningham*. Dutton 1975 pap. $8.95. Fifteen essays by
composers, dancers, and other artists who worked with Cunningham inter-
spersed with candid photographs of the Merce Cunningham Dance Company.

DIAGHILEV, SERGEI. 1872–1929

This famous Russian impressario changed the taste in Paris, and thus in
the world, in the second two decades of the twentieth century. He was an
avant-gardist of the first order and worked with such luminaries as
Balanchine and Stravinsky, and Fokine and Nijinsky early in their careers
to develop new sounds and sights distinctly different from traditional fare.
An extraordinarily complex figure, Diaghilev in his life and life-style gener-
ated a number of books that focus on serious faults exhibited by him and
his colleagues.

BOOKS ABOUT DIAGHILEV

Buckle, Richard. *Diaghilev*. Atheneum 1979 $22.50 1984 pap. $14.95
MacDonald, Nesta. *Diaghilev Observed by Critics in England and the United States,
1911–1929*. Dance Horizons 1975 $27.50 pap. $14.95. Transmits contemporane-

ous accounts of Diaghilev's performances and activities. Arranged chronologically and by performance.

DUNCAN, ISADORA. 1878–1927

A native of San Francisco, Duncan was influenced by a Greek revivalist movement that, among other effects, brought the Greek Theatre to the University of California at Berkeley campus. She was a modernist whose philosophical and stylistic utterances and examples were more visible and well known than her dancing. Duncan was a feminist and lived her life as the legend it became.

BOOK BY DUNCAN

My Life. Liveright 1955 pap. $7.95. Once considered scandalous, the autobiography lays bare aspects of the life and crusade of the artist in her advocacy of serious modern dance.

FONTEYN, DAME MARGOT. 1919–

Fonteyn is thought by her many critics to have been the best British dancer of the mid-twentieth century. Except for a brief period and several tours, she has worked entirely with the Royal Ballet and its precursors.

BOOK BY FONTEYN

Margot Fonteyn: Autobiography. Knopf 1976 $16.95

GRAHAM, MARTHA. 1894–

Not only is Martha Graham correctly identified as a pioneer of modern dance, she must also be termed the progenitor of modern dancers and modern dance companies. More than 35 of her students and dancers have become choreographers or directors of dance companies. Graham studied at the Denishawn School from the age of 16 and was dancing with the Denishawn Company by 1923. So long was her career that critics discern four major style periods.

BOOK BY GRAHAM

The Notebook of Martha Graham. Harcourt 1973 $27.50

BOOKS ABOUT GRAHAM

McDonagh, Don. *Martha Graham.* Praeger 1974 o.p. The first extensive biography.
Terry, Walter. *Frontiers of Dance: The Life of Martha Graham.* Crowell 1975 o.p.

KIRSTEIN, LINCOLN. 1907–

Kirstein became involved in the dance as a spectator at first and then moved to writing about dance, an occupation that has continued throughout his life. He has also served as a dance company manager. The New York City Ballet has been Kirstein's best-known managerial appointment, but some of his earlier posts must have been almost as exciting. He was the founding director of *The Dance Index.*

BOOK BY KIRSTEIN

Ballet: Bias and Belief. Intro. by Nancy Reynolds, Dance Horizons $25.00

MASSINE, LEONIDE. 1895–1979

This Russian ballet dancer and choreographer was trained at the Imperial Theatre in Moscow, worked successively for Diaghilev as dancer and choreographer, and frequently danced his own works. He employed facial and body gestures from vaudeville, the circus, and the cinema in his works.

BOOK BY MASSINE

Massine on Choreography: Theory and Exercises in Composition. Faber 1977 $45.00

NIJINSKY, VASLAV. 1890–1950

Considered by many the greatest male dancer of the twentieth century, Nijinsky danced for only 12 years. He began his studies in Moscow, continued them at the Imperial School of Dancing in St. Petersburg, and was brought to Western audiences by Diaghilev. He apparently had prodigious technical skills coupled with intelligence, taste, and bearing. In 1917 he suffered a mental breakdown, and never fully recovered.

BOOK ABOUT NIJINSKY

Krasovskaya, Vera. *Nijinsky.* Trans. by John E. Bowlt, Schirmer Bks. 1979 $17.95.
Literary, not scientific, biography.

NUREYEV, RUDOLPH. 1938–

Perhaps the most widely recognized ballet star today, Nureyev was trained in the Soviet Union and danced with the Kirov Ballet. His defection in 1961 was the first of the modern defections that have plagued the Kirov. He has performed with all of the world's greatest ballet companies and continues to dance brilliantly in classical and modern styles.

BOOK BY NUREYEV

Nureyev: An Autobiography with Pictures. Dutton 1963 $8.95

BOOK ABOUT NUREYEV

Barnes, Clive. *Nureyev.* Helene Obolensky 1982 $35.00

PAVLOVA, ANNA. 1881–1931

Pavlova was a child star in St. Petersburg at the Imperial School and worked with Fokine before the Diaghilev tours. Many consider her to have been the definition of the perfect female dancer.

BOOKS ABOUT PAVLOVA

Lazzarini, John, and Roberta Lazzarini. *Pavlova: Repertoire of a Legend.* Schirmer Bks. 1980 $35.00. An annotated photographic biography.
Money, Keith. *Anna Pavlova: Her Life and Art.* Knopf 1982 $55.00. Extensive; includes translations of newspaper and journal articles.

ST. DENIS, RUTH. 1880–1968

St. Denis was heavily influenced by Delsarte and David Belasco. Exoticism, richness, and magnificence characterize her creations. It has been suggested that St. Denis adopted elements of foreign cultures and incorporated them in her dances with no particular comprehension of either the cultures or the place of the abstracted elements.

Book by St. Denis

Ruth St. Denis: An Unfinished Life. AMS Pr. repr. of 1939 ed. $42.50. Autobiographical, but with substantial material on the precursors of modern dance.

Book about St. Denis

Shelton, Suzanne. *Divine Dancer: A Biography of Ruth St. Denis.* Doubleday 1981 $15.95

SHAWN, TED. 1891–1972

Shawn married Ruth St. Denis, and, in collaboration with her, developed a dancing style that amalgamated a kind of exhibitionistic ballroom style with Greek and Asian influences. In the 1930s, he was influenced by modernist dancing from Germany and created a number of powerful pieces for all-male companies on themes associated with power, force, and energy. Jacob's Pillow, the summer dance mecca for many Easterners, was established by Ted Shawn and His Men Dancers.

Book about Shawn

Terry, Walter. *Ted Shawn: Father of American Dance.* Dial 1976 o.p.

CHAPTER 12

Art and Architecture

Adolf K. Placzek

> Only through art can we get outside of ourselves and know another's view
> of the universe which is not the same as ours. . . .
> —MARCEL PROUST, *The Maxims of Marcel Proust*

The enormous increase in writing on art and in illustrated art books is a phenomenon of the twentieth century. It reflects not only the central role of art in the human experience, but also a growing interest in past beauty, a critical concern with the varied, fast-changing, and often problematic art of the present, and a wondering about the future. Everything we see and touch is to some degree art: a table, a picture, a house, a whole city. It started with cave drawings, but it will not end with skyscraper design. Art books existed in antiquity: in Greece, in Rome, and of course in China. In the Western world, writing on art started in earnest with the Italian Renaissance (although the medieval scholastics had much to say about beauty). A particularly rich literature developed on architecture (Alberti, who also wrote magnificently on painting and sculpture; Serlio; Palladio; Vignola). With the advent of sophisticated printing techniques, as engraving and etching replaced the more simple woodcut, the book with illustrations took over. Often the book on art was itself a work of art. The eighteenth century was particularly rich in art publications of the most elaborate kind. The nineteenth century witnessed the rise of new graphic techniques, lithography above all, followed by the great breakthrough into photography. All of this resulted in a vast new literature in the arts. Great encyclopedias and their more modest cousins, dictionaries, came into being. Pattern books and how-to books—with deep roots in the past— appeared in great numbers, with all the new styles, materials, and techniques they could now offer. The nineteenth century also saw the beginning of art history as a discipline and as a branch of art literature—art not as a present-day activity, but as a treasure of the past, a key to the past, an historic phenomenon. Art theory is another branch of art literature. What is art all about? Why art? What is great art? (And, for that matter, what is bad art?) Closely related to art theory is art criticism, particularly in the twentieth century, where a history of contemporary art is of necessity also a critique and a selection. The biography of artists is another important category of art literature, with a tradition going back to Vasari and the Renaissance.

Architecture stands somewhat apart, because it is both an art and a utilitarian pursuit; only some buildings are art, but all must be structurally sound. The books on architecture listed in this chapter deal with architecture primarily as an art; titles on architectural engineering are not included, although of course most books on architecture contain some practical elements—as does the very first of all such treatises, by the Roman Vitruvius in the first century B.C.

The literature on the decorative arts (furniture, glass, metalwork, etc.) also stresses practical considerations. Titles in this field are listed separately from painting and sculpture. Although the list is by no means exhaustive, most of the basic books are included, as well as many of those dealing with a specific area, such as furniture design. In this literature, theory and criticism seem less central, and many of the publications are directed to the amateur, the lover of art objects, the collector.

The books listed in this chapter are more than a cross-section. They represent a broad selection of the most important books encompassing *all* the arts—painting, sculpture, architecture, the graphic arts, and decoration—as well as those on the specifics of theory, history, style, country, and social background: criticism as well as practice.

The most comprehensive history of art in the English language is the *Pelican History of Art*. Each volume is by a different eminent author and deals with a different specific subject (for example, *Architecture: 19th and 20th Centuries*, by Henry-Russell Hitchcock, or *Art and Architecture in Italy, 1600–1800*, by Rudolf Wittkower). These volumes—nearly 50 by now—are not listed individually. A good art library should have all of them. They are available in paperback as well as in hardcover. The most comprehensive encyclopedia of the arts in English is the *Encyclopedia of World Art* (McGraw-Hill); for current periodical literature see the *Art Index*.

ART: GENERAL READING LIST

Arnheim, Rudolf. *Art and Visual Perception: A Psychology of the Creative Eye.* 1954. Univ. of California Pr. 2d ed. rev. & enl. 1974 $28.50 pap. $10.95

Arntzen, Etta, and Robert Rainwater. *Guide to the Literature of Art History.* Amer. Lib. Association 1981 $75.00. The most comprehensive bibliography of art literature. A highly scholarly tool.

The Art Index: A Cumulative Author and Subject Index to a Selected List of Fine Arts Periodicals and Museum Bulletins. Wilson vols. 1–8 (1929–53) ea. $70.00 vols. 9–18 (1953–70) ea. $125.00. "The most up-to-date continuing bibliography of periodical literature on Art and a basic tool for Art research" (Etta Arntzen).

Canadian Centre for Films on Art for the Federation of Arts. *Films on Art.* Watson Guptill 1977 $17.95

Dreyfuss, Henry, ed. *Symbol Sourcebook: An Authoritative Guide to International Graphic Symbols.* McGraw-Hill 1972 $59.95; Van Nostrand 1984 pap. $18.50.

Ehrenzweig, Anton. *The Hidden Order of Art: A Study of the Psychology of Artistic Imagination. California Lib. Repr. Ser.* Univ. of California Pr. 1976 pap. $8.95. A study in the psychology of artistic imagination.

Encyclopedia of World Art. Publishers Guild 15 vols. 1959 $995.00. A joint enterprise of McGraw-Hill and Italian publishers. The most comprehensive and far-ranging encyclopedia in the arts.

Gardner, Helen. *Art through the Ages.* Harcourt 2 vols. text ed. 6th ed. o.p. The most useful of the older general surveys, many times reprinted and widely read.

Gealt, Adelheid M. *Looking at Art.* Bowker 1983 $29.95 pap. $19.95. A visitor's guide to museum collections.

Gombrich, E. H. *Art and Illusion: A Study in the Psychology of Pictorial Presentation. Bollingen Ser.* Princeton Univ. Pr. 2d ed. 1961 $60.00 pap. $14.50. An important text of art theory.

———. *The Story of Art.* Cornell Univ. Pr. 13th ed. rev. ed. 1980 $25.00 pap. $14.95; Prentice-Hall 14th ed. text ed. 1985 pap. $19.95. One of the most learned and sophisticated general texts.

Gowing, Lawrence. *The Encyclopedia of Visual Art.* Prentice-Hall 2d ed. 1983 $100.00. Volume 1 is a history of art. Volume 2 is a biographical dictionary of artists that is international in scope and richly illustrated.

Hall, James. *Dictionary of Subjects and Symbols in Art.* Ed. by Kenneth Clark, *Icon Eds.* Harper 2d ed. rev. 1979 pap. $8.95

Hauser, Arnold. *The Social History of Art.* 1951. Random (Vintage) 4 vols. 1957–58 ea. $3.95–$5.95; trans. by Kenneth Norcott, Univ. of Chicago Pr. 1982 lib. bdg. $37.50. Economic and social forces are stressed.

Holt, Elizabeth G., ed. *A Documentary History of Art: The Middle Ages and the Renaissance.* Princeton Univ. Pr. 2 vols. repr. of 1947 ed. 1981 vol. 1 $27.50 vol. 2 $30.00 pap. ea. $9.95. An expansion and revision of literary sources of art history; an anthology of text from Theophilus to Goethe. A selection of original texts.

Honour, Hugh, and John Fleming. *The Visual Arts: A History.* Prentice-Hall 1983 $39.00 pap. $23.95. A particularly fine survey.

Hudson, Kenneth, and Ann Nicholls, eds. *The Dictionary of World Museums.* 1975. Facts on File 2d ed. 1981 $75.00

Janson, H. W. *History of Art.* 1962. Abrams 2d ed. rev. 1977 $37.50; Prentice-Hall text ed. rev. & enl. ed. 1969 $14.95. Among the most usable and indeed widely used one-volume texts.

Janson, H. W., and Dora Jane Janson. *Key Monuments of the History of Art.* Abrams 1959 o.p. A visual survey.

Jobes, Gertrude. *Dictionary of Mythology, Folklore and Symbols.* Scarecrow Pr. 3 vols. 1961 $85.00

Levey, Michael. *A History of Western Art.* World of Art Ser. Oxford 1968 pap. $9.95

Mayer, Ralph, ed. *Dictionary of Art Terms and Techniques.* Barnes & Noble 1981 pap. $6.95; Crowell 1969 $14.37

Murray, Peter, and Linda Murray, eds. *The Penguin Dictionary of Art and Artists.* Penguin 1984 pap. $6.95. Highly useful small volume, often reprinted.

Myers, Bernard S. *Art and Civilization.* McGraw-Hill text ed. 2d ed. 1967 $39.95

———, ed. *McGraw-Hill Dictionary of Art.* McGraw-Hill 1969 o.p. Comprehensive, wide-ranging, and richly illustrated; intended as a great dictionary rather than an encyclopedia.

The Official Museum Directory. National Register 1984 $77.00

Osborne, Harold. *Oxford Companion to Art.* Oxford 1970 $45.00. An important aid.

Pevsner, Nikolaus, ed. *Pelican History of Art.* Penguin 1953–to date. 42 vols. The most comprehensive history of art and architecture published in English. Each volume is by a different author on a distinct subject, such as Rudolf Wittkower,

Art and Architecture in Italy, 1600–1750 (pap. 1973), or John Wilmerding, *American Art* (1976).

Phaidon Encyclopedia of Art and Artists. Dutton 1978 o.p. A comprehensive and authoritative guide for both student and general reader.

RILA, ed. *International Directory of the Literature of Art.* J. Paul Getty Trust 1975 vol. 1. An abstracting and indexing service for current publication in the history of art. Important bibliographic tool for current literature.

Saff, Donald, and Deli Sacilotto. *Printmaking: History and Process.* Holt text ed. 1978 $26.95

Spencer, Harold. *Readings in Art History.* Scribner 2 vols. text ed. 3d ed. 1976 pap. ea. $11.95. Readings from the writings of outstanding art historians.

Thames and Hudson Dictionary of Art and Artists. Ed. by Herbert Read and Nikos Stangos, Thames & Hudson rev. ed. 1985 $19.95. Useful, small volume, particularly well illustrated.

Wölfflin, Heinrich. *Principles of Art History: The Problem of the Development of Style in Later Art.* Ill. by M. D. Hottinger, Dover pap. $4.95; Peter Smith $13.50. Influential book on the basic pairs of concepts in Western art, such as painterly versus linear, sculptural versus planar, etc.

ART: SPECIAL ASPECTS

Andreae, Bernard. *The Art of Rome.* Abrams 1978 $125.00

Baigell, Matthew. *Dictionary of American Art.* Harper 1979 $17.95 pap. $8.95

Berenson, Bernhard. *Italian Painters of the Renaissance.* Foundation Class. 2 vols. repr. of 1897 ed. 1982 $145.50. A list of the principal artists and their works by the famous connoisseur and master attributor.

Boase, Thomas S., ed. *English Art, 1100–1216. Oxford History of Eng. Art Ser.* 1953 $32.50. A comprehensive scholarly history, strong on text, of "what more accurately should be called British Art," by leading scholars.

Brown, Milton W., and others, eds. *American Art, Painting, Sculpture, Architecture, Decorative Arts.* Abrams 1979 $45.00. Wide-ranging, richly illustrated by several major scholars.

Carpenter, Rhys. *Greek Sculpture.* 1960. Univ. of Chicago Pr. (Phoenix Bks.) repr. 1971 pap. $11.95

Clark, Kenneth. *The Art of Humanism.* Harper 1983 $19.23

Coomaraswamy, Ananda K. *History of Indian and Indonesian Art.* 1965. Peter Smith $13.75

Crowe, Joseph A., G. B. Cavalcaselle, and Douglas Langston. *A History of Painting in Italy, Umbria, Florence, and Siena from the Second to the Sixteenth Century.* AMS Pr. repr. of 1914 ed. $245.00; Scholarly 6 vols. repr. of 1903 ed. 1972 $500.00. The first and still usable comprehensive survey in English.

Delevoy, Robert L. *Symbolists and Symbolism.* Rizzoli 1982 pap. $17.50

Du Bourguet, Pierre. *Early Christian Art.* Morrow 1971 o.p.

Evans, Joan. *Art in Mediaeval France, 987–1498.* Oxford 1969 o.p. A masterly survey of the subject.

Findlay, James A., comp. *Modern Latin American Arts: A Bibliography. Art Reference Collection Ser.* Greenwood 1983 lib. bdg. $35.00

Freedberg, Sydney J. *Painting of the High Renaissance in Rome and Florence.* Hacker 2 vols. repr. of 1961 ed. rev. ed. 1985 lib. bdg. $120.00

Gilbert, Creighton. *History of Renaissance Art.* Harper 1973 pap. $7.95

Gray, Basil, ed. *The Arts of India.* Cornell Univ. Pr. 1981 $55.00. Rich in illustrations.

Haftmann, Werner. *Painting in the Twentieth Century.* Praeger 2 vols. 2d ed. enl. 1965 o.p. An authoritative and thorough text.

Hamilton, George H. *Nineteenth and Twentieth Century Art: Painting, Sculpture, Architecture.* Abrams 1970 $40.00; Prentice-Hall text ed. 1972 $31.95

Igoe, Lynn Moody, and James Igoe, eds. *Two Hundred and Fifty Years of Afro-American Art: An Annotated Bibliography.* Bowker 1981 $149.95

Kanof, Abram. *Jewish Ceremonial Art and Religious Observance.* Abrams 1969 o.p.

Karpel, Bernard, ed. *Arts in America: A Bibliography.* Smithsonian 4 vols. 1979–80 $190.00. The most comprehensive in the field, including film, theater, photography, dance, as well as the graphic arts and architecture.

Kelemen, Pal. *Baroque and Rococo in Latin America.* 1951. Dover pap. $10.00; Peter Smith 2 vols. 2d ed. $20.00. The authoritative work in English.

Lee, Sherman E. *A History of Far Eastern Art.* Abrams 1982 $45.00; Prentice-Hall text ed. rev. ed. 1974 $24.95. Rich in illustrations.

Madsen, Stephan T. *Sources of Art Nouveau.* Trans. by Christopherson Ragnar, *Architecture and Decorative Arts Ser.* Da Capo repr. of 1956 ed. 1975 lib. bdg. $49.59; *Quality Pap. Ser.* Da Capo 1976 pap. 8.95

Maillard, Robert. *New Dictionary of Modern Sculpture.* Amiel 1971 $12.50

Moholy-Nagy, Laszlo. *Vision in Motion.* Theobald 1947 $16.50. The pioneer Bauhaus, painter-photographer's statement "on the interrelatedness of art and life." A modern document.

Munsterberg, Hugo. *The Arts of China.* Tuttle 1972 $29.50

———. *The Arts of Japan: An Illustrated History.* Tuttle 1958 $29.50 1972 pap. $13.50

Osborne, Harold, ed. *The Oxford Companion to Twentieth-Century Art.* Oxford 1981 $45.00

Panofsky, Erwin. *Early Netherlandish Painting.* Harper 2 vols. 1974 vol. 1 $12.95 vol. 2 $11.95. The most scholarly and authoritative work.

Papadopoulo, Alexandre. *Islam and Muslim Art.* Intro. by Lucien Mazenod, trans. by Robert E. Wolf, photographs by Jean Mazenod, Abrams 1979 $125.00

A Pictorial Encyclopedia of the Oriental Arts. Crown 1969 o.p. Compiled from the oriental section of the *Encyclopedia of World Art.*

Read, Herbert. *A Concise History of Modern Painting. World of Art Ser.* Oxford 1974 pap. $9.95; Thames & Hudson text ed. 1985 pap. $9.95. "Enlarged and updated third edition."

Rewald, John. *History of Impressionism.* 1946. New York Graphic Society 1980 $40.00 pap. $22.50

Rice, D. Talbot. *Art of the Byzantine Era. World of Art Ser.* Oxford 1963 pap. $9.95; Thames & Hudson 1985 text ed. pap. $9.95

Richter, Gisela M. *Sculpture and Sculptors of the Greeks.* Yale Univ. Pr. 4th ed. rev. & enl. 1971 $47.50. The most authoritative book in English on the subject.

Robertson, Martin. *History of Greek Art.* 1973. Cambridge Univ. Pr. 2 vols. 1976 $135.00

Selz, Peter. *Art in Our Times: A Pictorial History, 1890–1980.* Abrams 1981 $45.00; Harcourt text ed. 1981 pap. $22.95

Siren, Osvald. *Chinese Painting: Leading Masters and Principles.* Hacker 7 vols. repr. of 1956 ed. 1974 lib. bdg. $300.00. The most scholarly and wide-ranging survey.

Strong, Eugenia. *Roman Sculpture from Augustus to Constantine. Art Histories Collection Ser.* Ayer repr. of 1907 ed. $33.00; Hacker 1971 lib. bdg. $25.00

Taft, Lorado. *The History of American Sculpture. Art Histories Collection Ser.* Ayer repr. of 1924 ed. $38.50

Voyce, Arthur. *The Art and Architecture of Medieval Russia.* Univ. of Oklahoma Pr. 1967 pap. $14.95. The most authoritative work in English on the subject.

Zarnecki, George. *Art of the Medieval World: Architecture, Sculpture, Painting, the Sacred Arts.* Abrams 1976 $40.00; Prentice-Hall 1976 $30.95

ART: BIOGRAPHY

Bachmann, Donna G., and Sherry Piland. *Women Artists: An Historical, Contemporary and Feminist Bibliography.* Scarecrow Pr. 1978 $20.00

Canaday, John. *Lives of the Painters.* Norton 4 vols. 1969 $24.95

Cummings, Paul, ed. *Dictionary of Contemporary American Artists.* St. Martin's 4th ed. 1982 $50.00

Davis, Lenwood G., and Janet L. Sims. *Black Artists in the United States: An Annotated Bibliography of Books, Articles, and Dissertations on Black Artists, 1779–1979.* Greenwood 1980 lib. bdg. $35.00

Fielding, Mantle. *Dictionary of American Painters, Sculptors, and Engravers.* Ed. by Genevieve Doran, Associated Bk. enl. ed. 1974 $17.50; Modern Bks. rev. ed. repr. of 1926 ed. 1975 $17.50; Wallace-Homestead $25.00

Harris, Ann S., and Linda Nochlin. *Women Artists: Fifteen Fifty to Nineteen Fifty.* Knopf 1977 pap. $19.95

Podro, Michael. *The Critical Historians of Art.* Yale Univ. Pr. 1982 $32.50 pap. $9.95. On the major art historians and their writings.

Rubinstein, Charlotte S. *American Women Artists: From Early Indian Times to the Present.* G. K. Hall 1982 lib. bdg. $39.95

Vasari, Giorgio. *Lives of the Most Eminent Painters, Sculptors and Architects.* AMS Pr. 10 vols. repr. of 1915 ed. ea. $42.50 set $425.00. One of the great source books of Italian Renaissance art, with the ever-fresh biographies of most of the great masters—Michelangelo, Raphael, and many others.

Waterhouse, Ellis. *The Dictionary of British Eighteenth Century Painters.* Antique Collectors' Club 1981 $79.50

Wittkower, Rudolf, and Margot Wittkower. *Born under Saturn: The Character and Conduct of Artists.* Norton Lib. repr. of 1963 ed. 1969 pap. $9.95. A documented history from antiquity to the French Revolution.

Wood, Christopher. *The Dictionary of Victorian Painters.* Antique Collectors Club 1978 $74.50; Apollo 1979 $74.50; Gale 2d ed. rev. 1978 $140.00

ARCHITECTURE: GENERAL READING LIST

Copplestone, Trewin, ed. *World Architecture: An Illustrated History from the Earliest Times.* 1963. Crescent Bks. repr. 1981 o.p. A monumental, beautifully illustrated survey.

Fletcher, Banister. *History of Architecture.* Ed. by J. C. Palmes, Scribner 18th ed. text ed. 1975 $65.00. The basic textbook, richly illustrated.

Giedion, Sigfried. *The Beginnings of Architecture: The Eternal Present—A Contribution on Constancy and Change. Bollingen Ser.* Princeton Univ. Pr. vol. 2 repr. of 1964 ed. 1981 $60.00 pap. $19.00. Prehistory, Egypt, Sumer, and more.

Gloag, John. *The Architectural Interpretation of History.* St. Martin's 1977 $18.95

Harris, Cyril M. *Dictionary of Architecture and Construction*. McGraw-Hill 1975 $49.50. Excellent work on technical terms, including construction.

——. *Historic Architecture Sourcebook*. McGraw-Hill 1977 $34.95. Strong on historic terms and definitions. Detailed, richly illustrated.

Pevsner, Nikolaus, John Fleming, and Hugh Honour. *A Dictionary of Architecture*. Overlook Pr. 1976 $27.95. Biographical as well as historical, with less emphasis on technical terms. Of great all-around use.

Rasmussen, Steen E. *Experiencing Architecture*. 1959. MIT 2d ed. 1962 pap. $5.95. A good introduction to the theory of architectural appreciation.

Summerson, John. *The Classical Language of Architecture*. MIT 1966 pap. $4.95. The most lucid explanation of the so-called orders and the classical tradition they represent.

ARCHITECTURE: SPECIAL ASPECTS

Benevolo, Leonardo. *History of Modern Architecture*. MIT 2 vols text ed. 1971 pap. $25.00

Blumenson, John C. *Identifying American Architecture: A Pictorial Guide to Styles and Terms, 1600–1945*. Fwd. by Nikolaus Pevsner, Norton rev. ed. 1981 $13.95. A pictorial guide to styles and terms.

Fitch, James M. *Historic Preservation*. McGraw-Hill 1982 $41.50. A basic manual on a rather new subject.

Giedion, Sigfried. *Space, Time and Architecture: The Growth of a New Tradition*. 1941. Harvard Univ. Pr. 1966 5th ed. rev. & enl. $35.00. The most influential book on the development of modern architecture.

Hamlin, Talbot. *Greek Revival Architecture in America*. Intro. by D. L. Arnaud, Dover repr. of 1944 ed. pap. $7.50; Peter Smith $15.00

Hatje, Gerd, ed. *Encyclopedia of Modern Architecture* (*Knaurs Lexikon der Modernen Architektur*). Abrams 1964 o.p. A useful one-volume survey on an international basis.

Hitchcock, Henry-Russell. *American Architectural Books: A List of Books, Portfolios, and Pamphlets on Architecture and Related Subjects Published in America before 1895*. Ed. by Adolf K. Placzek, *Architectural and Decorative Arts Ser.* Da Capo repr. of 1946 ed. 1976 lib. bdg. $21.50. A comprehensive bibliography of architecture books published in America up to 1895. This edition includes also a highly useful chronological list by William H. Jordy.

——. *German Renaissance Architecture*. Princeton Univ. Pr. 1981 $75.00

Jordy, William H., and William H. Pierson, Jr. *American Buildings and Their Architects*. 1970–73. Doubleday (Anchor) 4 vols. 1976 pap. ea. $10.95. A fifth volume is in preparation.

Kaufmann, Emil. *Architecture in the Age of Reason: Baroque and Post Baroque in England, Italy and France*. Intro. by J. Hudnut, Dover repr. of 1955 ed. 1968 pap. $7.00; Shoe String (Archon) repr. of 1955 ed. 1966 $19.50. Baroque and postbaroque in England, Italy, and France.

Le Corbusier. *Towards a New Architecture (Vers une architecture)*. 1923. Holt 1976 o.p. The influential manifesto by one of the masters of modern architecture.

Liang Ssu-ch'eng. *A Pictorial History of Chinese Architecture*. Ed. by Wilma Fairbank, MIT 1984 $30.00. A study of the development of its structure system and the evolution of types.

Morrison, Hugh. *Early American Architecture: From the First Colonial Settlement to the National Period.* Oxford text ed. 1953 $19.95

Palladio, Andrea. *The Four Books of Architecture.* 1570. Ed. by Isaac Ware, intro. by Adolf K. Placzek, Dover text ed. repr. of 1738 ed. 1960 pap. $10.00; Peter Smith $21.00. One of the great books of classical architecture. The rich illustrations in this reprint derive from the English edition of 1738.

Pevsner, Nikolaus. *Outline of European Architecture.* Penguin 1950 pap. $11.95. The best-written and most fundamental book on the subject.

Poppeliers, John, and Nancy B. Schwartz. *What Style Is It? A Guide to American Architecture.* Preservation Pr. text ed. 2d ed. 1984 $7.95

Roos, Frank J., Jr. *Bibliography of Early American Architecture: Writings on Architecture Constructed before 1860 in Eastern and Central U.S..* Univ. of Illinois Pr. 1968 $15.00

Roth, Leland M. *A Concise History of American Architecture. Icon Eds.* Harper 1980 pap. $11.95

Ruskin, John. *The Seven Lamps of Architecture.* 1849. Farrar 1961 pap. $7.95. The manifesto of Victorian architecture.

Scully, Vincent. *Shingle Style and the Stick Style: Architectural Theory and Design from Richardson to the Origins of Wright. Publications in the History of Art Ser.* Yale Univ. Pr. rev. ed. 1971 $32.50 pap. $14.95

Sharp, Dennis. *Sources of Modern Architecture: A Bibliography. Architectural Association Papers Ser.* Wittenborn 1967 pap. $9.50

Smith, G. E. Kidder. *The Architecture of the United States.* Doubleday (Anchor) 3 vols. 1981 ea. $29.95 pap. ea. $14.95. Volume 1 has an introduction by Albert Bush Brown, Volume 2 by Frederick Nichols, and Volume 3 by David Gebhart. The most comprehensive guide to buildings and structures throughout the United States. Numerous illustrations.

Vitruvius. *The Ten Books on Architecture.* Trans. by Morris H. Morgan, Dover text ed. 1960 pap. $5.50; Peter Smith $12.25. Written in the first century A.D. by a Roman architect, this book has remained the main source for Greco-Roman architectural thinking. Hundreds of later editions in all major languages exist.

Whiffen, Marcus. *American Architecture since 1780: A Guide to the Styles.* MIT 1969 $25.00 pap. $7.95. Most useful for its definitions and descriptions of styles.

Wittkower, Rudolf. *Architectural Principles in the Age of Humanism. Warburg Institute Studies.* Kraus repr. of 1949 ed. $16.00; Norton 1971 pap. $6.95. Originally published in 1949, this learned treatise has remained an influential interpretation of Renaissance architecture and its ideas.

ARCHITECTURE: BIOGRAPHY

Colvin, H. C. *A Biographical Dictionary of British Architects, 1600–1840.* Facts on File $75.00. The most thorough listing of British architects and their works.

Emanuel, Muriel, ed. *Contemporary Architects.* St. Martin's 1980 $70.00. Strong on the younger generation of architects.

Placzek, Adolf K., ed. *Macmillan Encyclopedia of Architects.* 4 vols. 1982 $275.00. The most comprehensive biographical work across the ages, with thorough essays on the major architects.

Richards, James M., ed. *Who's Who in Architecture: From 1400 to the Present.* Holt 1977 $19.95

Torre, Susana, ed. *Women in American Architecture: A Historic and Contemporary Perspective.* Watson Guptill 1977 $26.50

Withey, Henry F., and Elsie Rathburn Withey. *Biographical Dictionary of American Architects (Deceased).* New Age 1956 o.p. In spite of inaccuracies, the most detailed listing of American architects, particularly minor ones.

DECORATIVE ARTS

Anthony, Edgar W. *History of Mosaics.* Hacker repr. of 1935 ed. 1968 $40.00

Aronson, Joseph. *The Encyclopedia of Furniture.* Crown rev. ed. 1965 $15.95

Barber, Edwin. *The Pottery and Porcelain of the United States and Marks of American Potters.* Wallace-Homestead $20.00

Beazley, J. D. *Attic Red-Figure Vase-Painters.* Oxford 3 vols. 2d ed. $149.00. The authoritative work on the subject.

Boger, Louise, and H. Batterson Boger. *Dictionary of Antiques and the Decorative Arts.* 1967. Scribner rev. ed. 1979 $35.00

Chaffers, William. *Marks and Monograms on European and Oriental Pottery and Porcelain.* 1965. Borden $39.95. The basic reference tool.

Edwards, Ralph. *The Dictionary of English Furniture.* Antique Collectors' Club 3 vols. 1983 $295.00

Evans, Joan. *Pattern: A Study of Ornament in Western Europe from 1180 to 1900.* Da Capo 2 vols. 1976 ea. $9.95; Hacker 2 vols. repr. of 1931 ed. 1975 lib. bdg. $75.00. A scholarly survey.

Gloag, John. *A Short Dictionary of Furniture.* Allen & Unwin 1976 pap. $14.95. Containing 1,767 terms used in Britain and America.

Hamlin, A. D. *A History of Ornament Ancient and Medieval.* Cooper Square Pr. 2 vols. repr. of 1916 ed. 1973 lib. bdg. $85.00; Longwood Pr. repr. of 1916 ed. 1978 lib. bdg. $40.00. Still the most scholarly survey in English.

Harthan, John. *The History of the Illustrated Book: The Western Tradition.* Thames & Hudson 1981 $60.00

Haywood, Helene, ed. *World Furniture: An Illustrated Survey.* McGraw-Hill 1965 o.p. Massive, richly illustrated world survey.

Honour, Hugh, and John Fleming. *Dictionary of the Decorative Arts.* Harper 1977 $29.95

Jones, Owen. *Grammar of Ornament.* 1856. Van Nostrand 1982 $60.00. The greatest nineteenth-century illustrated album on ornaments.

Kampler, Fritz, and Klaus G. Beye. *Glass: A World History.* New York Graphic Society 1966 o.p. The story of 4,000 years of fine glassmaking.

Mayor, A. Hyatt. *Prints and People: A Social History of Printed Pictures.* New York Graphic Society 1971 $20.00; Princeton Univ. Pr. 1980 $45.00 pap. $14.50

Mehlman, Felice. *Phaidon Guide to Glass.* Prentice-Hall 1983 $12.95 pap. $6.95

Nutting, Wallace. *Furniture Treasury.* Macmillan 1949 3 vols. $29.95. Volumes 1 and 2 are in one volume. A standard set.

Osborne, Harold, ed. *The Oxford Companion to the Decorative Arts.* Oxford 1975 $49.95

Savage, George, and Harold Newman. *Illustrated Dictionary of Ceramics.* Van Nostrand 1974 $24.95

Ware, Dora, and Maureen Stafford. *An Illustrated Dictionary of Ornament.* St. Martin's 1975 $15.00 1984 pap. $12.95

Weibel, Adele C. *Two Thousand Years of Textiles.* Hacker repr. of 1952 ed. 1972 $75.00

Weinberger, Norman S. *Encyclopedia of Comparative Letterforms for Artists and Designers.* Art Direction 1971 $24.95

Wills, Geoffrey, comp. *A Concise Encyclopedia of Antiques.* Van Nostrand 1975 $15.00

The reader who wishes to learn about an individual artist will naturally start with his biography. Biographies may be either by contemporaries (like Vasari or Condivi or Michelangelo) or by the more critical and systematic authors of later times. Not infrequently an artist will write (or, so to speak, invent) his own biography—autobiography is an ancient and honored branch of art literature. Beyond the autobiographical, the writing of great artists on their art—and on art in general—is of prime importance. It may be noted that some artists/architects are also articulate and prolific writers; others, apart from what they express through their art, are almost silent. Michelangelo wrote superb poetry; Rembrandt hardly a word; Frank Lloyd Wright wrote reams; H. H. Richardson nothing. Some, particularly modern artists, write extensively about their theories or, as it were, programs for society; some have defined ideologies; others act like tongue-tied craftsmen. Some write extraordinary diaries (Dürer, for example); others wonderfully revealing letters (Van Gogh).

What else should one look for? Records of the artist's work—complete records if possible. It should be remembered that some artists were masters in several media (like Michelangelo: supreme architect, sculptor, painter). Book selection must reflect that. And to be of use to the reader, a book must represent the artist's work pictorially: excellence of reproduction in an art book is an important consideration—although it cannot be conveyed on a catalog card or bibliographic entry. A catalog of the entire *oeuvre* (as it is often called) of an artist, or a major part of it, with annotations, datings, ascriptions, etc., is called a *catalogue raisonné.* Where available, such a catalog constitutes a basic element in the literature on a given artist. (Many of those, recording the works of European masters, are of course not in English and are therefore not included in the following selective bibliography.)

Evaluation, criticism, and reappraisal are other areas in the literature on artists. So also are aesthetic analysis and even description of images—although, here, an illustration is indeed worth a thousand words. There are, too, the books that put an individual artist into the context of his time—like "Michelangelo and his world"—and those that deal with a special aspect, such as "Michelangelo and religion" (the titles are fictitious). Further, for most great masters, there are books on major works (*chefs d'oeuvre,* as art historians often call them)—such as, let us say, the many books on Michelangelo's Sistine Chapel or, in the case of a contemporary artist, on Picasso's *Guernica.*

While not all the categories mentioned are covered for each artist in the bibliography, they should provide a framework to guide the readers in their selection. Exhibition catalogs are valuable for special studies. Some are important scholarly tools; some are ephemeral; others cover only certain aspects or certain collections. Thus, exhibition catalogs are not listed here for general use.

Thirty-four artists and architects were chosen for inclusion. All are of the first rank or near it. The selection was focused first on the towering figures of the Italian Renaissance—Michelangelo, Leonardo, Raphael, and Titian—together with some of the great artists of the sixteenth and seventeenth centuries in other Western countries—Germany, Spain, France—in the persons of Dürer, Velazquez, and Poussin; then the Netherlands: there are the great figures of Rembrandt and Rubens and the fascinating Bruegel. Somewhat lesser artists command interest because of their colorful writing: Cellini was included as an example. The great time of the eighteenth century in England is represented by bibliographies on Wren, Reynolds, and Gainsborough, to which, for France, Watteau is added; early nineteenth-century England, the time of the great romantic poets, by Constable and Turner. Then come the modern: the great impressionists—or some of them—from Manet and Monet to the great triad Cezanne, Gauguin, and Van Gogh, and on to Matisse and Picasso. The leading architects of modernism are also listed: Le Corbusier, Mies van der Rohe, and Gropius, as are the three master architects who made U.S. architecture such an exciting story—Richardson, Sullivan, and Wright.

It is remarkable how vast a literature some artists and architects have around them. Today, the examples would be Wright and Picasso. On others, there is often surprisingly little from which to choose; they may still have to wait for reevaluation or rediscovery. Many more monographs need to be written. Art literature, art criticism, and indeed art biography are fields in full development.

BERNINI, GIANLORENZO. 1598–1680

Sculptor and architect, Bernini was the formative master of the Roman baroque. Son of a fine sculptor, his own originality and power soon became evident. He ceased to treat marble as a block and concentrated on the multiplicity of viewpoints from which a figure could be experienced. The drama and richness of his sculpture—in marble, stucco, and stone—is extraordinary. Subsequent neoclassicism disapproved of him, but his fame has returned and will endure. Bernini was also baroque Rome's greatest architect. He created the mighty square and colonnades in front of St. Peter's and the baldacchino in the basilica. He was also a painter and writer of note. Of a tempestuous temperament, he was deeply religious. The mystical-sensuous *Ecstasy of St. Theresa* is among his most famous sculptures.

Books about Bernini

Baldinucci, Filippo. *The Life of Bernini*. 1682. Trans. by Catherine Enggrass, Pennsylvania State Univ. Pr. 1966 o.p. One of the main contemporary sources.

Borsi, Franco. *Bernini*. Rizzoli 1984 $75.00. The most detailed and richly illustrated
   of recent Bernini literature.
Hibbard, Howard. *Bernini*. Penguin. repr. 1966 pap. $7.95
Selected Drawings of Gian Lorenzo Bernini. Dover 1977 pap. $6.50
Wallace, Robert. *World of Bernini. Lib. of Art Ser*. Silver Burdett 1970 $19.94

BRUEGEL THE ELDER, PIETER. c.1525–1569

Pieter Bruegel was the founder and greatest figure of an extraordinary
family of Flemish painters. Because of his realistic subject matter, he is often called the "Peasant" Bruegel. His son, Pieter II (c.1564–1638) (who made
numerous copies of his father's great paintings), is called the "Hell"
Bruegel; another son, Jan (1568–1625), carries the name "Velvet" Bruegel.
Pieter Bruegel, himself no peasant, but a learned humanist who had traveled to France and—importantly–to Renaissance Italy, is famous for his
stark peasant scenes. These include dramatic pictures of historical events
like the terrible *Massacre of the Innocents*, which is believed to depict the
Spanish atrocities in the Netherlands. He was also a great painter of landscapes, into which he put scenes of peasant life (*Ice Skating*) or of mythological events (*The Fall of Icarus*).

BOOKS ABOUT BRUEGEL

Gibson, Walter S. *Bruegel*. Oxford 1977 $19.95 pap. $9.95; *World of Art Ser*. Thames
   & Hudson 1985 pap. $9.95
Hughes, Robert, ed. *The Complete Paintings of Bruegel*. Abrams 1970 o.p.
Klein, H. Arthur, ed. *Graphic Worlds of Peter Bruegel the Elder: Reproducing Sixty-
   Four Engravings and a Woodcut after Designs by Peter Bruegel the Elder*. Dover
   1963 pap. $6.95
Lavalleyi, Jacques. *Pieter Bruegel the Elder and Lucas Van Leyden: The Complete En-
   gravings, Etchings, and Woodcuts*. Abrams 1967 o.p.

CELLINI, BENVENUTO. 1500–1571

Cellini today is more famous for his autobiography than for his statue of
Perseus. His autobiography has been called the most unflinching in all literature. His unhesitating confession of hate, theft, murder, and sensuality has
sometimes seemed shocking. The story of his many dishonorable adventures
reads like a picaresque novel. Yet this autobiography is a valuable picture of
its time. The manuscript of Cellini's autobiography was circulated for more
than 150 years before it was printed in 1730. During that time it was frequently copied, and many different texts of it exist at the present day.

BOOKS BY CELLINI

Life of Benvenuto Cellini. 1730. Biblio Dist. (Everyman's) 1979 $5.00
The Autobiography of Benvenuto Cellini. Ed. by Alessandro Nova, St. Martin's 1984
   $19.95
Treatises on Goldsmithing and Sculpture. Trans. by C. R. A. Ashbee, Dover 1966 pap.
   $3.00; Peter Smith $4.50

CEZANNE, PAUL. 1839–1906

Paul Cézanne, who was one of the most influential and powerful painters of the postimpressionist phase, led the way to twentieth-century cubism and abstract art. He was born in Aix-en-Provence, the son of a prosperous banker. It was his close friend, the novelist EMILE ZOLA (see Vol. 2), who steered him to art and persuaded him to study in Paris. He was at first closely allied with his fellow-painters, Pissaro and other impressionists, but gradually drew apart from them in his painstaking and dedicated search for a new style. In 1886, he retired to Provence, where, as he was financially independent, he could totally concentrate on his art. The careful balance of tones, building form with color into almost geometrical (indeed, almost cubist) compositions, distinguishes his work. A firm grounding in the great French classical tradition turned him away from the romantic and impressionist toward the abstract art of the future. Cézanne, particularly in his later years, was a solitary man, not an intellectual, and he wrote very little. His watercolors are often as masterful as his oil paintings.

BOOK BY CÉZANNE

Letters. Ed. by John Rewald, Hacker 5th ed. 1984 $60.00

BOOKS ABOUT CÉZANNE

Badt, Kurt. *The Art of Cézanne.* Hacker repr. of 1965 ed. 1985 lib. bdg. $50.00
Chappuis, Adrien. *The Drawings of Paul Cézanne: A Catalogue raisonné.* New York Graphic Society 2 vols. 1973 $175.00
Loran, Erle. *Cézanne's Composition: Analysis of His Form with Diagrams and Photographs of His Motifs.* 1943. Univ. of California Pr. 3d ed. 1963 $25.00
Murphy, Richard W. *World of Cézanne. Lib. of Art Ser.* Silver Burdett 1968 $19.94
Rewald, John. *Paul Cézanne: The Watercolors—A Catalogue raisonné.* New York Graphic Society 1984 $150.00
Roberts, Jane. *The World View of Paul Cézanne: A Psychic Interpretation.* Prentice-Hall 1977 $9.95 pap. $4.95
Rubin, William. *Cézanne: The Late Work.* New York Graphic Society 1977 $45.00
Schapiro, Meyer. *Paul Cézanne.* Abrams 1952 $40.00
Shiff, Richard. *Cézanne and the End of Impressionism: A Study of the Theory, Technique and Critical Evaluation of Modern Art.* Univ. of Chicago Pr. 1984 lib. bdg. $29.95
Wechsler, Judith. *The Interpretation of Cézanne.* UMI Research 1981 $34.95

CONSTABLE, JOHN. 1776–1837

John Constable, together with J. M. W. Turner, was one of the two greatest English landscape painters of the nineteenth century. It was his deep love of nature ("The sound of water . . . willows, old rotten planks . . . I love those things. These scenes made me a painter") that inspired him: Changing clouds, trees, rivers, the effect of light and atmosphere were his lifelong inspiration. But he was also a master of careful formal composition, which he developed from his many wonderfully spontaneous sketches, and of a fresh and looser technique, which influenced the French impressionists. His life was relatively uneventful: he was financially secure, became successful, and kept at his work with remarkable concentration. He is distinguished from Turner by a certain restraint both in his subject matter and his technique.

BOOK BY CONSTABLE

John Constable's Correspondence. Ed. by R. B. Beckett, *Suffolk Records Society* Boydell & Brewer 6 vols. repr. 1962–68 ea. $13.50–$16.50

BOOKS ABOUT CONSTABLE

Badt, Kurt. *John Constable's Clouds.* 1950. Trans. by Stanley Godman, Saifer repr. 1971 $12.50

Boydell and Brewer, eds. *John Constable's Discourses.* State Mutual Bk. 1980 $35.00

Day, Harold A. *John Constable, R. A., 1776–1837: Drawings—The Golden Age. East Anglican Painters Ser.* Wittenborn 1976 $25.00

Fleming-Williams, Ian. *Constable: Landscape Watercolours and Drawings.* Merrimack $22.95

Fleming-Williams, Ian, and Leslie Parris. *The Discovery of Constable.* Holmes & Meier text ed. 1984 $39.50

Reynolds, Graham. *Constable: The Natural Painter.* Academy Chicago repr. of 1965 ed. 1980 pap. $3.95

Taylor, Basil. *Constable Paintings, Drawings and Watercolours.* State Mutual Bk. 2d ed. 1975 $50.00

Walker, John. *Constable.* Abrams 1979 $40.00

DÜRER, ALBRECHT. 1471–1528

Albrecht Dürer was the commanding figure of the German Renaissance. Born in Nuremburg, the son of a goldsmith, he was apprenticed at age 15 to a painter and printmaker, where he learned the precision of detail that is one of the hallmarks of his great art, both in his woodcuts and in his drawings (*The Hare* is a famous example). As a young man, he traveled widely throughout Germany and also to Italy, where he was profoundly affected by the emerging art of the High Renaissance, of which he became the primary exponent in the North. He settled in Nuremburg, which he left in 1520 for a trip to the Netherlands, the diaries of which are among the most interesting documents in the history of art. Dürer was a fine painter, but one of the greatest graphic artists of all time. He left more than 350 woodcuts, 100 engravings, and approximately 900 drawings and watercolors. As a humanist artist of his time, he was also deeply concerned with art theory and wrote treatises on measurement, fortification, proportion, and on artistic theory itself.

BOOK BY DÜRER

Albrecht Dürer: Sketchbook of His Journey to the Netherlands, 1520–21. Praeger 1971 o.p. With extracts from his diary.

BOOKS ABOUT DÜRER

The Complete Paintings of Dürer. Trans. by Alistair Sims, Abrams 1968 o.p.

Dodgson, Campbell. *Albrecht Dürer: Engravings and Etchings.* Da Capo repr. of 1926 ed. 1967 $27.50

Maximilian's Triumphal Arch: Woodcuts by Albrecht Dürer and Others. Peter Smith $13.75

Panofsky, Erwin, *Life and Art of Albrecht Dürer*. Princeton Univ. Pr. 1955 $40.00 pap.
    $19.50. Among the most important contributions to the extensive Dürer litera-
    ture.
Russell, Francis. *World of Dürer. Lib. of Art Ser.* Silver Burdett 1967 $19.94. Part of
    the Time-Life Library of Art.
Strauss, Walter L. *The Complete Drawings of Albrecht Dürer: A Complete Catalogue rai-
    sonné.* Abaris Bks. 6 vols. $540.00
———, ed. *The Complete Engravings, Etchings, and Dry Points of Albrecht Dürer.*
    Dover 1972 pap. $7.50; Peter Smith $15.00
———, ed. and trans. *The Human Figure: The Complete "Dresden Sketchbook."* Peter
    Smith $14.50
Wölfflin, Heinrich, ed. *Drawings of Albrecht Dürer*. Trans. by Stanley Appelbaum,
    Dover 1970 pap. $6.00

GAINSBOROUGH, THOMAS. 1727–1788

Thomas Gainsborough was perhaps the greatest painter of eighteenth-century England. He came from a simpler, more provincial background than
his famous rival Sir Joshua Reynolds. His masters were the Dutch landscape painters of the seventeenth century, rather than those of the Italian
Renaissance whom Reynolds adored. Gainsborough was a superb portrait-
ist, with an impeccable technique and a warm sympathy for his sitters. The
Blue Boy in San Marino, California, is his most popular painting. His lifelong love, however, was landscape painting, rather than portraiture, and
here he led the way to the nineteenth century.

BOOK BY GAINSBOROUGH

Letters. Ed. by Mary Woodall, New York Graphic Society rev. ed. 1963 o.p.

BOOKS ABOUT GAINSBOROUGH

Hayes, John. *Drawings of Thomas Gainsborough*. Yale Univ. Pr. 2 vols. 1971 $100.00
———. *Gainsborough as Printmaker*. Yale Univ. Pr. 1972 $35.00. Published for the
    Paul Mellon Centre for Studies in British art.
———. *The Landscape Paintings of Thomas Gainsborough: A Critical Text and Cata-
    logue raisonné*. Cornell Univ. Pr. 2 vols. 1983 $150.00
Leonard, Jonathan N. *World of Gainsborough. Lib. of Art Ser.* Silver Burdett 1969
    $19.94. Part of the Time-Life Library of Art.

GAUGUIN, PAUL. 1848–1903

Paul Gauguin, together with Van Gogh and Cézanne, was one of the great
masters of postimpressionism. His life story, prototypical of the artist-rebel,
was the subject of novels and films, such as W. SOMERSET MAUGHAM's *The
Moon and Sixpence* (see Vol. 1). Born in Paris, he spent his youth with his Peruvian mother's family in Peru and went to sea as a 16 year old. He then became a stockbroker in Paris, painting in his spare time. His early paintings
were impressionist. In 1883, he broke with his bourgeois life and eventually
separated from his family. In 1888 he visited Van Gogh in Arles with disas-
trous results. In 1891, he went to Tahiti. Apart from a short return to Paris,
he spent the rest of his life in the South Sea Islands, in poverty, poor health,

and recurring struggles with the colonial authorities. Gauguin, in art, sought to return to nature and truth. Inspired by the primitive peoples among whom he was living, he covered his canvases with stark forms, rhythmic patterns, and strong color, going far beyond naturalistic representation. Through this, his influence on modern art was powerful. His book *Noa Noa* is a moving account of his thoughts and life.

BOOKS BY GAUGUIN

Paul Gauguin: Letters to His Wife and Friends. Ed. by Maurice Malingue, trans. by Henry J. Stenning, AMS Pr. repr. of 1949 ed. 1983 $30.00

The Intimate Journals of Paul Gauguin. Pref. by E. Gauguin, Routledge & Kegan 1985 pap. $14.95

Noa Noa: The Tahitian Journal. Fine Arts Ser. Dover repr. of 1919 ed. 1985 pap. $3.95; Farrar 1957 pap. $5.95; trans. by O. F. Theis, Richard West repr. of 1920 ed. 1978 $25.00. His life in the South Pacific, important for its discussion of his aesthetic principles.

BOOKS ABOUT GAUGUIN

Goldwater, Robert. *Gauguin.* 1957. Abrams 1984 $19.95

Gray, Christopher. *Sculpture and Ceramics of Paul Gauguin.* Hacker repr. of 1963 ed. 1980 lib. bdg. $75.00

Longstreet, Stephen, ed. *Drawings of Gaugin.* Borden $9.95 pap. $3.95

GOYA Y LUCIENTES, FRANCISCO JOSÉ DE. 1746–1828

Francisco José de Goya y Lucientes was the great Spanish painter and graphic artist whose fame rests not only on his superb painterly abilities, but also on the darkness and drama of the subject matter he recorded. Born in Saragossa, he settled in Madrid in 1774. His early paintings are gay and almost rococo in feeling (e.g., his tapestry cartoons in the Prado). In 1789 he was appointed official court painter—a position once held by Diego Velazquez, whom he admired and emulated. In 1794 Goya became deaf, and his mood changed profoundly. He began to draw and etch. The *Caprichos* (1796–98), aquatinted etchings, date from that period: satirical, grotesque, and nightmarish scenes. His famous, unsparingly realistic *Family of King Charles IV* (How did he get away with it?) was painted in 1800. When in 1808 Spain was taken over by Napoleon, a terrible civil war ensued. Goya, torn between his Francophile liberalism and his Spanish patriotism, more than all else hated the cruelties of war. The 65 etchings *Los Desastres de la Guerra* are among the most moving antiwar documents in all art. Technically, Rembrandt's influence was powerful. Fourteen large mysterious murals, the so-called *Black Paintings*, were painted toward the end of Goya's life. He spent his last years in Bordeaux, in voluntary exile from the Spanish Bourbon regime.

BOOKS ABOUT GOYA

The Complete Etchings, Aquatints and Lithographs of Goya. Abrams 1962 o.p.

The Complete Etchings of Goya. Fwd. by Aldous Huxley, Crown 1943 o.p. Contains the *Caprichos* and the disasters of war.

Drawings of Goya. Borden $9.95 pap. $3.95

Gudiol, José. *Goya.* Abrams 1965 $40.00
Harris, Tomas. *Goya: Lithographs and Engravings.* Intro. by Anthony Blunt, Wofsy
    Fine Arts 2 vols. repr. of 1964 ed. 1983 $175.00. Vol. 2 contains the catalogue rai-
    sonné.
Schickel, Richard. *World of Goya. Lib. of Art Ser.* Silver Burdett 1968 $19.94

GROPIUS, WALTER. 1883–1969

Walter Gropius, as leader of the famous Bauhaus, as teacher, and as de-
signer, was a dominant figure of twentieth-century architecture. Born in Berlin of a family with great architectural tradition, he strove—in the years after
World War I—to bring architecture into harmony with the new industrial
age and with the social needs of the times. He was one of the founders of the
Deutsche Werkbund (1907), whose aim was the modern design of everyday objects. In 1919, he became director of the Weimar School of Design, which he
reorganized and renamed the Bauhaus; its goal was to educate designers
who would create functional, rational, and socially responsive architecture
and objects of art for daily use. In 1925, the Bauhaus moved to Dessau,
where, for its new quarters, Gropius designed buildings in a clean, functional, highly innovative style. The Bauhaus was suppressed by the Nazis in
1933, and Gropius fled to England. There he practiced architecture with the
architect Maxwell Fry. In 1937 he came to the United States where he headed
the highly influential department of architecture at Harvard University until
1952. A firm and articulate believer in teamwork, he founded the Architects
Collaborative, which designed, among many other buildings, the U.S. Embassy in Athens and the Pan American Building in New York. Working with a
team of young architects, Gropius designed the Harvard Graduate Center. He
also wrote several books, among them *The Scope of Total Architecture.*

BOOKS BY GROPIUS

The Scope of Total Architecture. 1952. Macmillan (Collier Bks.) 1962 o.p. Gropius's
    own statements on the totality of modern architecture.
New Architecture and the Bauhaus. MIT 1965 pap. $5.95
Apollo in the Democracy. Trans. by Ise Gropius, McGraw-Hill 1968 o.p.

BOOK ABOUT GROPIUS

Wingler, Hans. *Bauhaus: Weimar, Dessau, Berlin, Chicago.* MIT 1969 $150.00 pap.
    $25.00. The most comprehensive volume, not only on Gropius, but also on the
    teachings and activities of the famous and influential Bauhaus in its various lo-
    cations.

LE CORBUSIER (pseud. of Charles Edouard Jeanneret-Gris). 1887–1965

Le Corbusier can be called the leading architect of modern architecture.
Born of Swiss parentage near Geneva, but a lifelong Parisian by choice, he
started his practice in 1922, and in 1923 published his startling manifesto of
what he called "the aesthetics of modern life," *Vers une architecture (Towards a New Architecture).* He worked first at simplifying and liberating
house design through the revolutionary use of new materials—reinforced
concrete above all—and new technical ideas for mass production, which he

applied in the so-called Dom-Ino and the Citrohan House. In his widely influential book *La Ville radieuse (The Radiant City)* he laid down his urbanistic ideas: a city of high-rise buildings set among trees and grass. His designs for large building groups were as influential as were his domestic designs. Among them there are the famous housing project in Marseilles (the Unité d'habitation), his League of Nations project in Geneva (unexecuted), and, toward the end of his life, the startling designs for the capital city of Punjab, Chandigarh. He also participated—controversially—in the designs for the U.N. headquarters in New York. In his last years, Le Corbusier turned away from the geometry and pure logic of his first designs and adopted sculptural and dramatic forms (as in Chandigarh). The almost mystical complexities of the Pilgrim Church of Ronchamps in the French Jura opened another chapter in the history of twentieth-century architecture.

Books by Le Corbusier

Le Corbusier Sketchbooks. Notes by Françoise de Franclieu, MIT (Architectural History Foundation and Fondation Le Corbusier) 4 vols. 1981–82 ea. $165.00. Le Corbusier as a painter and master of drawing.

Ideas of Le Corbusier: Architecture and Urban Planning. Trans. by Jacques Guiton and Margaret Guiton, Braziller 1981 $25.00 pap. $9.95

Towards a New Architecture (Vers une architecture). 1927. Praeger 1970 o.p. One of the most influential books on modern architecture.

The Radiant City (La ville radieuse). 1935. Trans. by Pamela Knight, Viking 1967 $35.00. Vastly influential on city planning.

The Modulor and Modulor 2. Harvard Univ. Pr. 1980 pap. $12.95

Books about Le Corbusier

Besset, Maurice. *Le Corbusier.* Rizzoli 1976 $50.00

Blake, Peter. *The Master Builders: Le Corbusier, Mies van der Rohe, Frank Lloyd Wright.* Norton Lib. 1976 pap. $7.95

Evenson, Norma. *Le Corbusier: The Machine and the Grand Design.* 1969. Braziller $7.95

Jencks, Charles. *Le Corbusier and the Tragic View of Architecture.* Harvard Univ. Pr. 1974 $16.50 pap. $9.50

Jordan, Robert F. *Le Corbusier.* Lawrence Hill 1972 $10.00

Papadaki, Stamo, ed. *Le Corbusier: Architect, Painter, Writer.* Macmillan 1948 o.p. An important early book.

Sekler, Eduard F., and William Curtis. *Le Corbusier at Work: The Genesis of the Carpenter Center for the Visual Arts.* Intro. by Barbara Norfleet, pref. by J. L. Sert, Harvard Univ. Pr. 1978 $35.00

Serenyi, Peter. *Le Corbusier in Perspective. Artists in Perspective Ser.* Prentice-Hall 1975 $8.95; Prentice-Hall (Spectrum Bks.) pap. $3.95

von Moos, Stanislaus. *Le Corbusier: Elements of a Synthesis.* MIT 1979 $42.50 pap. $9.95

Walden, Russell. *The Open Hand: Essays on Le Corbusier.* MIT 1977 $40.00 pap. $9.95

LEONARDO DA VINCI. 1452–1519

Often called the Universal Man, this towering genius in science, engineering, aeronautics, technology—in fact, in almost all the pursuits of man—was also one of the greatest painters, as well as a sculptor, an architect, and a town planner. Born in Vinci, Leonardo was apprenticed as a 14 year old to the sculptor-painter Andrea Verrocchio in Florence. In 1482, he went to Milan as a military engineer, sculptor, and architect, and remained there for 17 years. While in Milan, he designed the crossing tower of the Milan cathedral and, among many other works, painted *The Last Supper,* a mural in the Church of Santa Maria delle Grazie (1496–97); this is one of his greatest creations and a main work of Western art. During these creative years in Milan, he also composed his *Treatise on Painting* and filled his ever-fascinating, inexhaustible notebooks. In 1499, on the fall of his patron Lodovico Sforza, he returned to Florence. The *Mona Lisa* dates from that period (1503–06). After a short and unsuccessful time in Rome (1513–16), he settled in France under the patronage of Francis I. He died in Amboise at the age of 67. A supposedly lost manuscript was rediscovered at the National Library in Madrid in 1965 and published in 1974.

BOOKS BY LEONARDO DA VINCI

The Notebooks of Leonardo da Vinci. Ed. by Irma A. Richter, *World's Class. Ser.* Oxford 1982 pap. $4.95; ed. by Jean Paul Richter, Peter Smith 2 vols. $36.00

Codex Atlanticus: A Facsimile of the Restored Manuscript. Johnson Repr. 12 vols. $12,000.00. A vast publishing venture, beautifully reproducing Leonardo's greatest manuscript, but at a very high price.

The Madrid Codices of Leonardo da Vinci. Trans. by Ladislao Reti, McGraw-Hill 1974 $1,250.00. Leonardo's recently refound codex, long considered lost. An expensive purchase, but of major importance.

Leonardo da Vinci Drawings. Dover 1983 pap. $2.50

BOOKS ABOUT LEONARDO DA VINCI

Clark, Kenneth. *Leonardo da Vinci: An Account of His Development as an Artist.* Gannon lib. bdg. $11.50; Penguin 1976 pap. $4.95

Cooper, Margaret. *Inventions of Leonardo da Vinci.* Macmillan 1968 $9.95

Eissler, Kurt R. *Leonardo da Vinci: Psychoanalytic Notes on the Enigma.* International Univ. Pr. text ed. 1961 $35.00. A study into the validity of criticism of Freud's book.

Freud, Sigmund. *Leonardo da Vinci: A Study in Psychosexuality.* Random (Vintage) 1966 pap. $2.95

Goldscheider, Ludwig. *Leonardo da Vinci: Life and Work, Paintings and Drawings.* 1943. New York Graphic Society 8th ed. 1967 o.p. This classic has Vasari's life as the main text, with da Vinci's letters, other documents concerning him, a chronology, and a bibliography. Reproduces all Leonardo's paintings and 80 drawings; 62 text illustrations; 135 large plates of which 43 are in color.

Hart, Ivor B. *World of Leonardo da Vinci.* Kelley repr. 1962 $35.00. "This interesting book will long remain a standard work on Leonardo as scientist and engineer" (*N.Y. Times*).

Heydenreich, Ludwig H. *Leonardo: The Last Supper.* Ed. by John Fleming and Hugh Honour, Viking 1974 $16.95

Panofsky, Erwin. *Codex Huygens and Leonardo da Vinci's Art Theory.* Greenwood repr. of 1940 ed. 1971 lib. bdg. $22.50; *Warburg Institute Studies* Kraus repr. of 1940 ed. $32.00

Pedretti, Carlo. *Leonardo: A Study in Chronology and Style.* Johnson Repr. $24.95 pap. $14.95

Philipson, Martin, ed. *Leonardo da Vinci: Aspects of the Renaissance Genius.* Braziller 1966 o.p. Thirteen studies on Leonardo. Contributors include Bernard Berenson, Herbert Read, George Sarton, Giorgio de Santillana, Kenneth Clark, and K. R. Eissler. Chronology. Notes on contributors. "Should be useful for many years to come" (*LJ*).

Wallace, Robert. *World of Leonardo. Lib. of Art Ser.* Silver Burdett 1966 $19.94

Wohl, Hellmut. *Leonardo da Vinci.* McGraw-Hill 1967 $24.95

MANET, EDOUARD. 1832–1883

Edouard Manet is one of the fathers of impressionism and of the new naturalism in painting. With pictures like the *Absinthe Drinkers* and the famous *Déjeuner sur l'herbe*—a naked woman picnicking in the woods with three fully dressed men—he caused a storm of criticism. In 1863, together with his friends Monet, Renoir, Sisley, and Pissarro, he led the influential Salon des Refusés (Salon of the Rejected), which ushered in the new art of impressionism. Strongly influenced by the Venetian Renaissance masters Giorgione and Titian, but even more by the Spain of Velazquez and Goya, he was thoroughly aware of the traditions of the past. Yet he was one of the great innovators in painting, in subject matter as well as in technique. His later years were marred by ill health. For him official recognition came too late; he died at the age of 51, a disappointed man. Among his later great paintings are *In the Conservatory* and *The Bar at the Folies-Bergères.*

BOOKS ABOUT MANET

The Complete Paintings of Manet. Intro. by Phoebe Pool, notes by Sandra Orienti, Abrams 1967

Hamilton, George H. *Manet and His Critics. Norton Lib.* repr. of 1954 ed. 1969 pap. $3.95

Hanson, Anne C. *Manet and the Modern Tradition.* Yale Univ. Pr. 1977 $45.00 pap. $15.95

Reff, Theodore. *Manet and Modern Paris: One Hundred Paintings, Drawings, Prints, and Photographs by Manet and His Contemporaries.* Univ. of Chicago Pr. 1983 $39.95

Schneider, Pierre. *World of Manet, 1832–1883. Lib. of Art Ser.* Silver Burdett 1968 $19.94

MATISSE, HENRI. 1869–1954

Henri Matisse is, next to Picasso, the greatest and most versatile artist of modernism. His long career embraced most of the currents of postimpressionist art, in all of which he created highly personal works of remarkable beauty and subtlety. Born in Picardie, France, he came to Paris as a youth and studied under conventional masters like Bouguereau, and then moved to impressionism. From impressionism, he turned to Cézanne and soon to the exaltation of pure color that characterized the *Fauves* (*The Wild Beasts*) whose leading master he became. He went through an expressionist phase and was also much affected by black and Near Eastern art. In that period, flat decorative patterns in brilliant colors predominated. *La Danse* and *La Musique* are examples. In 1914 he went to live on the Riviera, where he remained for the rest of his long life. Here the great series of *Odalisques* occupied him until the 1930s. His last major work was the decoration of a convent chapel at Venice. Matisse was also a book illustrator of originality, a highly individual sculptor, and a creator of extraordinary paper cutouts.

BOOKS ABOUT MATISSE

Barr, Alfred H., Jr. *Matisse: His Art and His Public.* Ayer repr. of 1951 ed. $30.00

Elderfield, John. *Henri Matisse Cutouts.* Braziller 1978 $22.50 pap. $14.95

Flam, Jack D., ed. *Matisse on Art.* Dutton 1978 pap. $11.95

Gowing, Lawrence. *Matisse.* Oxford 1979 $19.95

Jacobus, John. *Matisse.* Abrams 1973 $40.00 1984 $19.95

Lieberman, William S. *Matisse: Fifty Years of His Graphic Art.* Braziller repr. of 1956 ed. 1981 $30.00 pap. $12.95

Russell, John. *World of Matisse. Lib. of Art Ser.* Silver Burdett 1969 $19.94

Schneider, Pierre. *Matisse.* Trans. by Bridget S. Romer, Rizzoli 1984 $95.00. The recent major study.

Watkins, Nicholas. *Matisse.* Oxford 1985 $39.95. Clearly written and accessible introduction.

MICHELANGELO BUONARROTI. 1475–1564

Michelangelo was one of the greatest artists the human race has produced. As sculptor, painter, and architect, he personified the climax of the Italian High Renaissance, and even its transition to mannerism and baroque. He was born near Florence in 1475, to a noble but poor family, Buonarroti, was trained as a fresco painter by the great Ghirlandaio, but soon turned to sculpture. The lovely *Pieta* in St. Peter's in Rome is one of his earliest masterpieces; the *David* in Florence came soon after. In 1505, Michelangelo went to Rome, where he worked for Pope Julius II, a powerful and tempestuous patron of the arts, by whom he was asked to design a vast tomb with 40 figures. The project, with which he struggled for years, was gradually cut down until only the majestic *Moses* and the two *Slaves* remained. For Michelangelo, this was one of the great tragedies of his life. It was, however, Julius II who commissioned him to paint the vast cycle of frescoes on the ceiling of the Sistine Chapel—one of the greatest works ever created by human hand, done entirely by Michelangelo alone, working under incredible difficulties, literally lying on his back on a high scaffold for years (1508–12). Many years later (1536), he added the huge dramatic fresco of the *Last Judgment* on the altar wall of the same chapel. In Florence, he created the Medici Chapel with the famous sculptured figures of *Day* and *Night, Dawn* and *Evening*. In 1541, at the age of 71, he became chief architect of the incomplete church of St. Peter's in Rome, on which he worked tirelessly until his death in 1564 at the age of 89; the basilica's mighty dome is his creation. In his later years, he also wrote sublime poetry, into which he poured the innermost heart of a lonely, melancholy, and intensely religious genius.

BOOK BY MICHELANGELO

Complete Poems and Selected Letters of Michelangelo. Trans. with a fwd. by Creighton Gilbert, Vintage 1970 o.p.

BOOKS ABOUT MICHELANGELO

Clements, Robert J. *Michelangelo's Theory of Art.* New York Univ. Pr. 1961 $17.50

The Complete Paintings of Michelangelo. Intro. by L. D. Ettlinger, Abrams 1969 o.p.

Condivi, Ascanio. *The Life of Michelangelo.* Trans. by Alice S. Wohl, Louisiana State Univ. Pr. 1976 $25.00. Together with Vasari's *Lives,* the main contemporary source.

Grimm, Hermann F. *Life of Michelangelo.* Trans. by Fanny E. Bunnett, Greenwood 2 vols. repr. of 1900 ed. lib. bdg. $48.00; Scholarly 2 vols. $59.00. One of the greatest biographies.

Hartt, Frederick, ed. *Michelangelo. Lib. of Great Painters Ser.* Abrams 1965 $40.00. 1984 $19.95

Hibbard, Howard. *Michelangelo.* Harper 1975 $20.00 1976 pap. $9.95

Seymour, Charles, ed. *Michelangelo: The Sistine Chapel. Critical Studies in Art History* Norton 1972 pap. $7.95

Stone, Irving, ed. *Drawings of Michelangelo.* Borden $9.95 pap. $3.95

Summers, David. *Michelangelo and the Language of Art.* Princeton Univ. Pr. 1981 pap. $21.00

Tolnay, Charles Q. de. *Michelangelo.* 1943–68. Princeton Univ. Pr. 6 vols. Vols. 1 & 2 (1969) ea. $85.00 Vol. 3 (1970) $85.00 Vol. 4 (1970) $87.00 Vol. 5 (1970) $85.00 Vol. 6 (1970) $40.00. The most comprehensive work on the great master.

MIES VAN DER ROHE, LUDWIG. 1886–1969

Mies van der Rohe, a father of modern architecture, was the great master of steel-and-glass construction. Born in Aachen, Germany, he soon became a leading force in the experimental architecture in the restless period after 1918. He designed revolutionary expressionist glass skyscrapers which, however, were never built. A classic rationalism then took over: the German Pavilion for the Barcelona Exhibition of 1929 (now destroyed) is the most famous example of geometrical, unadorned design, with all the component parts clearly revealed.

In 1930 he built the fine Tugendhat house in Brno, Czechoslovakia. He was director of the Bauhaus from 1930 until it was closed by the Nazis in 1933. He emigrated to the United States in 1937 and there began a second great career: the prototypical skeleton-frame skyscrapers are the outcome, among which are the Lake Shore Drive Apartments in Chicago (1948–50) and, most famous of them all, the Seagram Building in New York City (1957–58). Two of Mies's sayings have become almost proverbial: "less is more" and "God is in the detail."

BOOKS ABOUT MIES VAN DER ROHE

Glaeser, Ludwig, ed. *Ludwig Mies van der Rohe: Drawings in the Collection of the Museum of Modern Art.* MIT 1974 $25.00

Honey, Sandra, and others. *Mies van der Rohe.* Rizzoli 1979 o.p.

Johnson, Philip C. *Mies van der Rohe.* New York Graphic Society 1978 pap. $9.95

MONET, CLAUDE. 1840–1926

Claude Monet was probably the greatest painter of the impressionist group and, throughout his long life, its most unswerving representative. He was devoted to the representation of visual impressions, of light and color, rather than sharp forms in dramatic compositions. He spent little time studying the old masters, but worked with Courbet, admired Manet, and was aware of Turner and of Japanese art. He lived much of his life in poverty, becoming known only gradually. He liked to paint series—or variations—on the same theme, like the *Poplars* and the *Haystacks* and the *Rouen Cathedral*. In 1883, he settled at Giverny, where he made himself an elaborate garden. He spent the rest of his life there and it was there that he painted—again and again—his famous *Waterlilies*. His late works—with blindness setting in—with their almost abstract patterns anticipate abstract expressionism.

BOOKS ABOUT MONET

Gordon, Robert, and Andrew Forge. *Monet*. Abrams 1983 $75.00

Seitz, William C. *Claude Monet: Seasons and Moments. Museum of Modern Art Publications in Repr. Ser.* Ayer repr. of 1960 ed. 1970 $17.00

———. *Monet*. Abrams 1984 $19.95

Tucker, Paul H. *Monet at Argenteuil*. Yale Univ. Pr. 1982 $30.00 1984 pap. $14.95

Wildenstein, Daniel. *Monet's Years at Giverny: Beyond Impressionism*. Abrams 1978 $22.50 pap. $12.50

PICASSO, PABLO. 1881–1973

Pablo Ruiz y Picasso, Spanish painter, graphic artist, and sculptor, is generally considered the most revolutionary, influential, and versatile artist of the twentieth century. He was born in Malaga, son of a painter, and studied in Barcelona. His extraordinary talent showed at an early age: before he was 14, he had already produced a masterwork in the classic tradition. His early paintings (1901–04) of the so-called Blue Period (in which blues dominate the color scheme) deal with outcasts, beggars, sick children, and circus people. The *Old Guitarist* is the most famous of his Blue Period paintings. In Paris, he developed a lighter palette—the so-called Rose Period. *The Boy with Horse* stands out. In his so-called Negro Period (1907–09), he concerned himself with elementary forms. During those same years he turned to the incipient cubist movement. *Les Demoiselles d'Avignon*, in its semiabstract geometric forms, was a revolutionary step toward twentieth-century modernism, which he, together with Braque and Matisse, really set in motion. Picasso went through the entire vocabulary of cubism, its analytical as well as its synthetic phase. After 1918 he was also hailed as an initiator of surrealism. The horrors of the Spanish civil war affected him deeply. *Guernica* depicts the destruction of the ancient Basque capital by Nazi bombers, with almost mythological power. *Night Fishing at Antibes* is another masterwork of that period. In his later years he experimented with ceramics and did highly original sculptures—the famous *Goat*—and collages. He also produced a flood of drawings, lithographs, engravings, and even stage designs. He remained creative to the last day of his life.

BOOKS ABOUT PICASSO

Arnheim, Rudolf. *The Genesis of a Painting: Picasso's Guernica.* Univ. of California
   Pr. repr. of 1962 ed. 1980 $36.50 pap. $10.95
Ashton, Dore. *Picasso on Art.* Penguin 1977 pap. $6.95
Barr, Alfred H., Jr. *Picasso: Fifty Years of His Art.* Ayer repr. of 1955 ed. $14.95; New
   York Graphic Society rev. & enl. 1974 pap. $14.95
Cabanne, Pierre. *Pablo Picasso: His Life and Times.* Trans. by Harold J. Salemson,
   Morrow 1977 $19.95 2d ed. repr. of 1977 ed. 1979 pap. $6.95
Elgar, Frank, and Robert Maillard. *Picasso.* Amiel rev. ed. 1972 $15.00
Hilton, Timothy. *Picasso. World of Art Ser.* Oxford 1975 pap. $9.95; Thames & Hud-
   son 1985 pap $9.95
Jaffe, Hans Ludwig. *Picasso.* Abrams 1964 $40.00 1984 $19.95; Doubleday 1980
   $14.95
Oates, Whitney J., ed. *From Sophocles to Picasso.* Greenwood repr. of 1962 ed. 1973
   lib. bdg. $18.75. The present-day vitality of the classical tradition.
O'Brian, Patrick. *Picasso: A Biography.* Putnam 1976 $12.95
Penrose, Roland. *Picasso: His Life and Works.* Univ. of California Pr. 1981 $25.00
   pap. $10.95
Picasso Lithographers: Sixty-One Works. Dover 1980 pap. $2.00
Schiff, Gert. *Picasso: The Last Years.* Braziller 1984 $35.00 pap. $17.50
Stein, Gertrude. *Matisse, Picasso and Gertrude Stein: With Two Shorter Stories.* Ultra-
   marine repr. of 1933 ed. 1972 $35.00. Published in cooperation with the Mu-
   seum of Modern Art.
Zervos, Christian. *Picasso's Complete Work.* Wofsy Fine Arts 33 vols. $250.00

POUSSIN, NICOLAS. 1564–1665

   Nicolas Poussin is the most important and accomplished painter in
French classical art. He was born in Normandy, trained in Paris, and—like
so many artists before him—went to Italy to perfect his art. He remained in
Rome for the rest of his life, except for one short return to Paris (1640–42).
Poussin strove, above all, for order, solemnity, clarity, the heroic (even his
landscape paintings are labeled as "heroic landscapes"), and faithfulness to
Greek and Roman ideals. He subordinated color to composition and form.
In spite of his long years in Rome, he never broke with the France of DES-
CARTES (see Vol. 4) and CORNEILLE (see Vol. 2), and his influence on subse-
quent French art, from David through Cézanne, has been great.

BOOKS ABOUT POUSSIN

Hibbard, Howard. *Poussin: The Holy Family on the Steps.* Viking 1974 o.p.
Longstreet, Stephen, ed. *The Drawings of Nicolas Poussin.* Borden $9.95 pap. $3.95
Wright, Christopher. *Poussin Paintings: A Catalogue raisonné.* Alpine 1984 $75.00

RAPHAEL (Raffaello Sanzio). 1483–1520

   Raphael was, with Michelangelo and Leonardo, one of the three masters
of the High Renaissance; he was also the youngest and died prematurely after a life of incredible creativity and accomplishment. He was the son of a
painter, Giovanni Santi, and his actual name was Raffaello Santi of Sanzio.
He was trained in Florence, but spent most of his short life in Rome. There he
created his major works, famous for the harmony and elegance of their de-

sign. Above all, there are the frescoes for the papal apartments in the Vatican (*The Stanze*), which he painted at exactly the time Michelangelo was painting the Sistine Chapel (1508–12); among them are such masterpieces as the *School of Athens* and the *Disputà*. His oil painting, the *Sistine Madonna*, is justly famous. Raphael—in the Renaissance manner—was also an accomplished architect and, in his last years, architect-in-chief of St. Peter's.

BOOKS ABOUT RAPHAEL

Beck, James. *Raphael*. Abrams 1976 $40.00
The Complete Paintings of Raphael. Abrams 1969 o.p.
The Complete Works of Raphael. Reynal 1969 o.p.
Joannides, Paul. *The Drawings of Raphael: With a Complete Catalog*. Univ. of California Pr. 1983 $110.00
Jones, Roger, and Nicholas Penny. *Raphael*. Yale Univ. Pr. 1983 $35.00
Pope-Hennessy, John. *Raphael*. New York Univ. Pr. 1970 $40.00

REMBRANDT HARMENSZ VAN RIJN. 1606–1669

Rembrandt is the greatest painter of the Dutch School and one of the greatest painters of all time. With a glowing sense of color, he was often somber with a tragic view of reality and the human condition, and a wonderful eye for light and darkness. He was prodigiously creative: more than 600 paintings, more than 300 etchings (many of them masterpieces), and approximately 2,000 drawings (including many exquisite landscape sketches) have been counted. Biblical and historical subjects take up a large part of his work, but he was also a marvelous portrait painter, as we see in the portraits of his mother, his first and second wives, and his son, but above all in his searching self-portraits, done at various stages of his life—from the hopeful, lighthearted youth to the disillusioned but unflinching and deeply introspective old man. There are more than 60 self-portraits—a record unique in the history of art. Born in Leiden, in the Netherlands, he moved to Amsterdam in 1631, where he spent the rest of his life. In his youth he loved luxury and the pleasures of life; later he became increasingly austere. Rembrandt was highly successful in his early years, but prevailing taste and his own style developed in very different directions. He died a poor and isolated man in 1669. The *Night Watch* and *The Anatomy Lesson of Dr. Tulp* (both in Amsterdam) are among his most famous pictures. Among the etchings, the *Hundred Guilder Print* stands out.

BOOKS ABOUT REMBRANDT

Clark, Kenneth. *Rembrandt and the Italian Renaissance*. Ed. by Seymour Slive, New York Univ. Pr. 1966 $45.00
Haak, Bob. *Rembrandt Drawings*. Trans. by Elizabeth Willems-Treeman, Overlook Pr. 1976 $12.95 1977 pap. $5.95
Held, Julius S. *Rembrandt Fecit: A Selection of Rembrandt's Etchings*. S. & F. Clark 1981 pap. $4.00
———. *Rembrandt's Aristotle and Other Rembrandt Studies*. Princeton Univ. Pr. 1969 $25.00
Hind, Arthur M. *Catalogue of Rembrandt's Etchings*. Da Capo 2 vols. in 1 repr. of 1923 ed. lib. bdg. $49.50

Munz, Ludwig, and Bob Haak. *Rembrandt.* Abrams 1984 $19.95
Rosenberg, Jakob. *Rembrandt: Life and Work.* Cornell Univ. Pr. rev. ed. 1980 pap.
    $14.95
Slive, Seymour, ed. *Drawings of Rembrandt.* Dover 2 vols. pap. ea. $8.95
Wright, Christopher. *Rembrandt Self-Portraits.* Viking 1982 $25.00

RENOIR, PIERRE AUGUSTE. 1841–1919

Pierre Auguste Renoir, together with Monet, was one of the two leading painters of the impressionist school. He was close to Monet, but also influenced by the realism of Courbet and the light palette of the rococo painters Watteau, Fragonard, and Boucher. The human figure—and human flesh—was one of his main interests, as it was also with Manet (but not with Monet). He preferred bright colors in pink, orange, red, and cheerful subjects. His output was amazing—nearly 6,000 pictures, many of them in U.S. collections. He achieved great success during his lifetime. His last years were spent in the south of France. Though crippled by arthritis, he continued to paint and even do some sculpture.

Books about Renoir

Gaunt, William. *Renoir.* Merrimack 1983 $27.50 pap. $18.95
Hanson, Lawrence. *Renoir: The Man, the Painter, and His World.* Beekman 1972
    $14.95
Pach, Walter. *Renoir.* Abrams 1984 $19.95
Renoir, Jean. *Renoir, My Father.* Trans. by Randolph Weaver and Dorothy Weaver,
    Little, Brown 1962 pap. $3.95. The famous filmmaker son's recollection of his
    great father.
Rewald, John, ed. *Renoir Drawings.* AMS Pr. repr. of 1946 ed. $50.00
Stella, Joseph G. *The Graphic Work of Renoir: A Catalogue raisonné.* Schram text ed.
    1975 pap. $30.00
White, Barbara. *Renoir: His Life, Art and Letters.* Abrams 1984 $67.50

REYNOLDS, SIR JOSHUA. 1723–1792

Sir Joshua Reynolds was the most influential and important painter of Georgian England, the first President of the Royal Academy, and, so to speak, the greatest establishment figure in English art. Born into a cultured family (unlike most artists of his day), he was a learned man, in touch with the leading literary men of the time, Dr. SAMUEL JOHNSON (see Vol. 1) among them. He received thorough training in Italy (1750–52), where he studied the works of Michelangelo, Raphael, and Titian. He thus became a confirmed neoclassicist, but some influences from the baroque style of Rubens are also discernible. His *Discourses*, held at the academy and widely disseminated in print, are the most important documents of eighteenth-century classicism in art, and exercised great influence. As a painter, he excelled in portraiture. Many members of the high aristocracy of his time were painted by him in the grand manner, which he combined with subtlety and sensitivity. His technique was often faulty, and many of his pictures have cracked or lost much of their color. He was extraordinarily prolific until blindness struck him in his last year, as it did MILTON (see Vol. 1) and Handel.

BOOKS BY REYNOLDS

Letters by Joshua Reynolds. Ed. by Frederick W. Hilles, AMS Pr. repr. of 1929 ed. $23.00

Discourses on Art. Ed. by Robert R. Wark, Yale Univ. Pr. 1975 o.p. Published for the Paul Mellon Centre for Studies in British Art.

BOOKS ABOUT REYNOLDS

Steegman, John. *Sir Joshua Reynolds.* Folcroft repr. of 1932 ed. 1977 lib. bdg. $17.50
Waterhouse, Ellis. *Reynolds.* Praeger 1973 o.p.

RICHARDSON, HENRY HOBSON. 1836–1886

Henry Hobson Richardson, the most influential American architect of the late nineteenth century, studied at Harvard University and then, like many of his American contemporaries, at the Ecole des Beaux Arts in Paris (1859–62). However, he did not remain a Beaux-Arts man, but developed a personal style of originality and power, based on Romanesque precedents: bold round arches, arcades, massive walls, often roughly rusticated, all with a very individual touch. The style—the so-called Richardsonian Romanesque, or simply Richardsonian—had enormous influence throughout the land. Richardson was aware of the practical and functional: his Marshall Field Warehouse in Chicago (now demolished) was in effect a totally modern storehouse. His great Trinity Church in Boston and his massive Allegheny Court House and Jail are among his most famous buildings. Richardson also designed libraries and railroad stations. He strongly influenced Louis Henry Sullivan and even Frank Lloyd Wright, and pointed the way to the future in American architecture.

BOOKS ABOUT RICHARDSON

Hitchcock, Henry-Russell. *The Architecture of Henry Hobson Richardson and His Times.* 1936. MIT 1966 o.p.

Ochsner, Jeffrey Karl. *H. H. Richardson: Complete Architectural Works.* MIT 1982 $55.00 pap. $25.00. The definitive catalogue raisonné.

O'Gorman, James F. *H. H. Richardson and His Office: Selected Drawings.* MIT 1979 $55.00

Scully, Vincent. *Shingle Style and the Stick Style: Architectural Theory and Design from Richardson to the Origins of Wright. Publications in the History of Art Ser.* Yale Univ. Pr. rev. ed. 1971 $32.50 pap. $14.95

Van Rensselaer, Mariana G. *Henry Hobson Richardson and His Works.* Intro. by William Morgan, Dover repr. of 1888 ed. 1979 pap. $6.00

RODIN, AUGUSTE. 1840–1917

Auguste Rodin, the most celebrated sculptor of the late nineteenth century, was born in Paris. He worked originally as a mason, but soon devoted himself to sculpture. His great master was Michelangelo ("he freed me from academicism"). He was a supreme realist as well as a romantic; his first major work, *The Age of Bronze,* seemed so lifelike that he was even accused of having cast it from a living model (there are more than 150 recasts of it). Many of his sculptures are extremely popular and widely reproduced—such as *The Kiss, The Thinker,* and the haunting *Burghers of Calais.* One of his innovations was the torso or the fragment as a complete work of art. His main work is the vast *Gates of Hell*. Many of his works, or recasts of them, are in U.S. collections.

BOOK BY RODIN

Cathedrals of France. Trans. by Elisabeth C. Geissbuhler, pref. by Herbert Read, Black Swan rev. ed. 1981 $25.00. In Rodin's own words.

BOOKS ABOUT RODIN

Champigneulle, Bernard. *Rodin*. Trans. by J. Maxwell Brownjohn, *World of Art Ser.* Oxford 1980 pap. $9.95
Elsen, Albert E. *Rodin Rediscovered*. National Gallery of Art pap. $7.00; New York Graphic Society 1981 $42.50
Hale, William H. *World of Rodin*. *Lib. of Art Ser.* Wiley 1969 $15.95
Rilke, Rainer Maria. *Rodin*. Haskell 1974 lib. bdg. $39.95. The great German poet's recollection and appreciation of the master, as whose secretary he served.
Tancock, John L. *The Sculpture of Auguste Rodin: The Collection of the Rodin Museum, Philadelphia*. Philadelphia Museum of Art 1976 $40.00

RUBENS, PETER PAUL. 1577–1640

Peter Paul Rubens, Flemish baroque painter, son of a prominent Antwerp lawyer, was the most prolific, influential, and brilliant artist of his time, but also a scholar, entrepreneur, and diplomat. He served in this latter capacity in 1629, negotiating a peace between Spain and England. He spent several of his early years in Italy, where he learned much of his great art from the Italian Renaissance. In 1608, he settled in his hometown of Antwerp, where, assisted in his vast output by many assistants, he lived a sumptuous life. Great commissions came to him. The *Life of Maria Medici* (21 canvases, now in the Louvre) stands out, as do the ceilings at Whitehall in London. His style is exuberant, dramatic, and of an incomparable sureness of touch, whether depicting a female nude or a great historic event.

BOOKS ABOUT RUBENS

Burchard, Ludwig, comp. *Corpus Rubenianum Ludwig Burchard: An Illustrated Catalogue raisonné of the Work of Peter Paul Rubens Based on the Material Assembled by the Late Dr. Ludwig Burchard in Twenty-Six Parts*. Oxford part I (1968) $74.00 part II (1978) 2 vols. $148.00 part VIII (1972–73) 2 vols. $148.00 part IX (1971) $74.00 part X (1978) $74.00 part XVI (1972) $74.00 part XVIII (1982) $74.00 part XIX (1982) $74.00 part XXI (1978) 2 vols. $148.00 part XXIV (1978) $74.00 part XXV (1983) $74.00. A monumental work, also containing scholarly monographs on individual works or groups of works by Rubens.
Downes, Kerry. *Rubens*. Hippocrene 1984 $29.50
Held, Julius S. *The Oil Sketches of Peter Paul Rubens: A Critical Catalogue*. Princeton Univ. Pr. 2 vols. 1980 $150.00
Held, Julius S., and others. *Rubens and His Circle*. Princeton Univ. Pr. 1901 $38.50
Jaffe, Michael. *Rubens and Italy*. Cornell Univ. Pr. 1977 $85.00
Wedgwood, Cicely V. *World of Rubens*. *Lib. of Art Ser.* Silver Burdett 1967 $19.94. Time-Life Library of Art.

SULLIVAN, LOUIS HENRY. 1856–1924

Louis Henry Sullivan, American architect, was a key figure in the development of modern architecture; he is often, loosely, called the Father of the Skyscraper. He was also an eloquent writer on the new style as he envisioned it. Sullivan was born in Boston, studied at the Massachusetts Institute of Technology and briefly in Paris. He started his practice in Chicago, together with the architect Dankmar Adler. The massive Auditorium Building, innovative in the clarity and power of its design, is the chief building of the so-called Chicago School of Architecture and a memorial to their noteworthy collaboration; they parted company in 1894. On his own, Sullivan had already designed one of the earliest masterpieces of skyscraper architecture in the United States, the Wainwright Building in St. Louis. His next great skyscraper design was the Guaranty Building in Buffalo. Sullivan was a difficult and lonely man, beset by personal problems; in his later years, his practice dwindled, but he still created some buildings of great beauty—small banks in the Midwest—the Farmer's Bank at Owatonna, Minnesota, being the most famous. Sullivan was a master of ornament, although he aimed at clear forms and questioned the role of decoration. The famous slogan "form follows function," which he coined, has been variously interpreted, but it has become part of the vocabulary of modern architecture. Frank Lloyd Wright was Sullivan's assistant from 1887 to 1893 and considered him his *lieber meister* (dear master); he paid him eloquent tribute in his book *Genius and the Mobocracy.* Sullivan himself was a highly poetic and persuasive writer, above all in his *Kindergarten Chats* (1918) and his *Autobiography of an Idea* (1924).

Books by Sullivan

The Autobiography of an Idea. Dover repr. of 1924 ed. pap. $6.00. The master's own story.
Kindergarten Chats and Other Writings. Documents of Modern Art. Dover repr. of 1947 ed. 1980 pap. $5.00; Peter Smith $13.50; Wittenborn repr. 1976 pap. $12.50

Books about Sullivan

Condit, Carl W. *Chicago School of Architecture.* Univ. of Chicago Pr. (Phoenix Bks.) 1973 pap. $10.95
Connely, Willard. *Louis Sullivan: A Biography.* Horizon Pr. 1971 $5.95. A fine biography.
Morrison, Hugh. *Louis Sullivan: Prophet of Modern Architecture.* Greenwood repr. of 1935 ed. 1971 lib. bdg. $21.75; *Norton Lib.* 1962 pap. $5.95; Peter Smith 1958 $12.00. The pioneer biography of a pioneer architect.
Sprague, Paul E. *The Drawings of Louis Henry Sullivan: A Catalogue of the Frank Lloyd Wright Collection at the Avery Architectural Library.* Fwd. by Adolf K. Placzek, Princeton Univ. Pr. 1979 $50.00
Wright, Frank L. *Genius and the Mobocracy.* Horizon Pr. 1971 $25.00. Wright's eloquent tribute to his *lieber meister* (dear master).

TITIAN (Tiziano Vecelli). c.1487–1576

Titian was the greatest painter of the Venetian school of painting, which spanned the centuries from Bellini and Giorgione through Veronese and

Tintoretto to Tiepolo. Titian represents the High Renaissance. In a shimmering, color-rich, sensuous style, he painted mythological, historical, religious, and erotic subjects—the whole range of the sixteenth-century imagination. He was also a portrait painter of rare psychological power and sympathy (his several portraits of the lonely and harassed emperor, Charles V, stand out as much as do his pictures of various fleshy Venetian beauties). The art of the 80 year old became mysterious and spiritual, much like the late paintings of Rembrandt. Titian was much honored by his contemporaries during a long life, spent mostly in Venice.

Books about Titian

All the Paintings of Titian. Ed. by Francesco Valcanover, Hawthorne Bks. 4 vols. 1964 o.p.
Hope, Charles. *Titian.* Harper 1980 $29.95
Rosand, David. *Titian.* Abrams 1978 $40.00
———. *Titian: His World and His Legacy.* Columbia Univ. Pr. 1982 $55.00
Williams, Jay. *The World of Titian, c.1488–1576. Lib. of Art Ser.* Silver Burdett 1968 $19.94. Part of the Time-Life Library of Art.

TURNER, JOSEPH MALLORD WILLIAM. 1775–1851

Joseph Mallord William Turner, with Constable, was one of the two greatest English landscape painters, and one of the greatest romantic artists of all time. He was also a major precursor of impressionism. Steam, breaking waves, fire, the luminosity of the air, and above all light itself, were his subject matter. The son of a London barber, he showed a precocious talent and made an early career, which enabled him to travel to France, Switzerland, and Italy. The Swiss Alps and the beauty of Venice nourished his vision. His enormous originality attracted criticism, but he found a powerful supporter in John Ruskin, who considered him the greatest of the "modern painters." He was freer in his composition than Constable, as he was in his impressionist technique, and in his subject matter, which included such dramatic scenes as the famous *Shipwreck*, or *Steam and Speed*, or *The Snowstorm*. He worked extensively for engravers and published a *Liber Studiorum* (1807–19) of his own landscape engravings, in defense, as it were, of his art. The variety, spontaneity, and beauty of his drawings and watercolor sketches are almost unequaled. There are no less than 20,000 of them. Personally, Turner was a hardheaded and taciturn man who, in his later years, turned into a recluse.

Book by Turner

Collected Correspondence of J. M. W. Turner with an Early Diary and a Memoir by George Jones. Ed. by John Gage, Oxford text ed. 1980 $45.00

Books about Turner

Butlin, Martin, and Evelyn Joll. *The Paintings of J. M. W. Turner.* Yale Univ. Pr. rev. ed. 1984 $195.00
Finberg, Alexander J. *The Life of J. M. W. Turner.* Oxford 2d ed. rev. 1961 o.p.
———. *Turner's Sketches and Drawings.* Schocken 1968 o.p.
Gage, John. *Turner: Rain, Steam and Speed. Art in Context Ser.* Viking 1972 $16.95

Hermann, Luke. *Turner: Paintings, Watercolors, Prints and Drawings.* New York
    Graphic Society 1975 $42.50
Reynolds, Graham. *Turner. World of Art Ser.* Oxford 1969 pap. $9.95; Thames & Hud-
    son text ed. 1985 pap. $9.95
Selz, Jean. *Turner.* Crown 1975 $7.95

VAN GOGH, VINCENT. 1853–1890

Vincent Van Gogh was one of the great postimpressionist masters and because of the power and accessibility of his work and the tragedy and dedication of his life, almost a legend as an artist. The son of a Dutch parson, he was
largely self-taught. Ascetic and intensely spiritual, he viewed art as almost a
religious vocation. He painted incessantly and left a vast volume of work, but
sold only one picture during his lifetime. In 1888, he went to Arles in search of
the glowing sunlight, there breaking from the somber, earthbound realism of
his early style to the brilliant colors, passionate thick brushstrokes, and
incredible joyousness of that later time. He became insane and shot himself in
1890. His letters to his brother Theo are a moving and fascinating account of
his working processes and the agony and drama of his daily life.

BOOKS BY VAN GOGH

The Complete Letters of Vincent Van Gogh. New York Graphic Society repr. of 1958
    ed. 1978 $85.00. "Nothing that one can say about the quality of these letters is
    enough. They are the most important documents connected with modern art in
    existence" (*New Statesman*).
The Letters of Vincent Van Gogh. Ed. by Mark Roskill, Atheneum 1963 pap. $7.95
Dear Theo: The Autobiography of Vincent Van Gogh. Ed. by Irving Stone, New Amer.
    Lib. (Signet Class.) repr. of 1946 ed. 1969 pap. $3.95

BOOKS ABOUT VAN GOGH

Complete Van Gogh: Paintings, Drawings, Sketches. Outlet 1984 $39.95
Hagen, Osjkar. *Vincent Van Gogh.* Gordon $59.95
Hammacher, A. M. *Van Gogh: Twenty-Five Masterworks.* Abrams 1984 pap. $14.95
Hammacher, A. M., and Renilde Hammacher. *Van Gogh: A Documentary Biography.*
    Macmillan 1982 $36.50
Nagera, Humberto. *Vincent Van Gogh: A Psychological Study.* International Univ. Pr.
    text ed. 1967 text ed. $22.50
Schapiro, Meyer. *Van Gogh.* Abrams 1984 $19.95
Stone, Irving. *Lust for Life.* Doubleday 1954 $15.95; New Amer. Lib. (Plume) 1984
    pap. $8.95; *Enriched Class. Ed. Ser.* Pocket Bks. 1977 pap. $2.95
Wallace, Robert. *The World of Van Gogh. Lib. of Art Ser.* Silver Burdett 1969 $19.94

VELAZQUEZ, DIEGO RODRIGUEZ DE SILVA. 1599–1660

Velazquez was the greatest painter of the Spanish Renaissance. Born in
Seville, where he also worked in his early years, he became the court
painter in Madrid in 1623. He remained in the service of Philip IV for the
rest of his life, portraying his king in many psychologically searching and
moving portraits. He visited Italy in 1629–31, but the roots of his art were
firmly Spanish. Court life was not his only concern. Deeply human pictures
of the humble and of street life are among his greatest (for example, *The Wa-*

ter Carrier of Seville, The Old Woman Cooking Eggs). One of the outstanding historical paintings of all time is the *Surrender of Breda. Las Meninas* (*The Maids of Honor*), a court painting full of subtle allusions, is probably his best-known work. Picasso painted 44 variations on its theme. Although his work was neglected in the eighteenth century, Velazquez exerted a strong influence on later nineteenth-century painting.

BOOKS ABOUT VELAZQUEZ

Brown, Dale. *The World of Velazquez. Lib. of Art Ser.* Silver Burdett 1969 $19.94. Part of the Time-Life Library of Art.
Harris, Enriqueta. *Velazquez.* Cornell Univ. Pr. 1982 $48.50

WATTEAU, JEAN-ANTOINE. 1684–1721

Watteau, the representative painter of the French rococo (together with Fragonard and Boucher), was born in Valenciennes and spent most of his life in Paris. He was strongly influenced by the two great Venetian painters, Veronese and Titian, and above all, by Rubens. Soft colors, delicate curves, joie de vivre, mixed with a certain dreamlike melancholy, characterize most paintings of this great artist. He suffered from tuberculosis and died at the age of 37. Although he was classed as a *Peintre de Fêtes Galantes*, there is an underlying seriousness in his work. His most famous picture is the *Embarcation for the Island of Cythera* (Louvre). His use of color anticipated much of impressionism.

BOOKS ABOUT WATTEAU

Longstreet, Stephen, ed. *Drawings.* Borden $9.95 pap. $3.95
Posner, Donald. *Watteau.* Cornell Univ. Pr. 1983 $75.00
Schneider, Pierre. *World of Watteau. Lib. of Art Ser.* Silver Burdett 1967 $19.94

WREN, SIR CHRISTOPHER. 1632–1723

Wren was the greatest English classical architect. He was originally destined to be a scientist and held the Chair of Astronomy at Oxford University before he was 30. NEWTON (see Vol. 5) considered him one of the best mathematicians of the day. Soon he applied his genius, however untrained, to architecture. The Sheldonian Theatre at Oxford is the work of a brilliant amateur. He went to France to view architecture in 1665. The London fire of 1666 was his great opportunity. For the restoration of the city, he produced a magnificent town plan with radiating streets—hardly the work of an amateur—and concerned himself with the rebuilding of 51 city churches and of the great St. Paul's Cathedral. The latter, with its vast dimensions and majestic dome, is one of his crowning achievements. Among numerous works, he built the library of Trinity College, Cambridge, a highly sophisticated design, and the great Greenwich Hospital. Order, grandeur, harmony, and a scientific ingenuity characterize Wren's buildings.

BOOKS ABOUT WREN

Bennett, James A. *The Mathematical Science of Christopher Wren.* Cambridge Univ. Pr. 1983 $29.95

Downes, Kerry. *The Architecture of Wren*. Universe text ed. 1982 $37.50. The most au-
thoritative and up-to-date treatment.
Furst, Viktor. *The Architecture of Sir Christopher Wren*. Somerset repr. of 1956 ed.
$49.00
Gray, Ronald D. *Christopher Wren and St. Paul's Cathedral*. Cambridge Univ. Pr. 1980
pap. $4.95

WRIGHT, FRANK LLOYD. 1867–1959

Wright is widely considered the greatest American architect and certainly
one of the most influential. Throughout a career of nearly 70 years he produced
masterpiece after masterpiece, each different and boldly new and yet each
with the unmistakable touch of Wright's genius in the treatment of material,
the detailing, and the overall concept. Born in Wisconsin of Welsh ancestry, he
began his career in Chicago as chief assistant to Louis Henry Sullivan, who influenced his early thinking on the American architect as harbinger of democracy and on the organic nature of the true architecture. Out of these ideas he
developed the so-called prairie house of which the Robie House in Chicago and
the Avery Coonley House in Riverdale, Illinois, are outstanding examples.
Public buildings followed: the Larkin Administration Building in Buffalo
(destroyed) and the Unity Temple in Oak Park, Illinois, the former probably
the most original and seminal office building up to that time (1905). The
Midway Gardens in Chicago and the Imperial Hotel in Tokyo (both gone)
followed. Personal tragedy, misunderstanding, and neglect dogged his middle
years, but he prevailed and in his later life gathered enormous success and
fame. The masterworks of his mature years are the Johnson Wax Building in
Racine, Wisconsin, and Fallingwater, Bear Run, Pennsylvania—with its bold
cantilevered balconies over a running stream probably the most admired and
pictured private house in American architecture; then, toward the end of his
life, the Guggenheim Museum in New York City. Wright's own houses (to
which he joined architectural studios) must be mentioned: Taliesin West, a
true Shangri-la in the Arizona desert, to which he turned from the severe
winters in Wisconsin where he had built his extraordinary Taliesin East.
Wright was also a prolific and highly outspoken writer, ever polemical, ever
ready to propagate his ideas and himself. All his books reflect a passionate
dedication to his beliefs—in organic architecture, in democracy, in creativity.

BOOKS BY WRIGHT

An Autobiography. Horizon Pr. 1976 $25.00. His life and discussion of his buildings
with 20 pages of photographs.
The Early Work of Frank Lloyd Wright. Intro. by Grant C. Manson, *Architecture Ser.*
Dover repr. 1983 pap. $7.50; Horizon Pr. $25.00. The first English translation
from the German in which it was first published. Photographs and plans.
Writings and Buildings. Ed. by Edgar Kaufmann and Ben Raeburn, Horizon Pr.
$9.95. A selection from his writings and designs from the early 1890s to 1959,
with 150 illustrations.
The Future of Architecture. Horizon Pr. $17.50; New Amer. Lib. pap. $6.95. A collection of his later major writings. Beginning with the widely discussed "Conversa-

tion" (1953), in which he explains his aims and contributions, it includes several rare works originally published in separate editions.

An American Architecture. Ed. by Edgar Kaufmann, Horizon Pr. $25.00

The Natural House. Horizon Pr. $14.95. An infinite variety of houses for people of limited means; with practical comments, a restatement of Wright's principles and beliefs.

A Testament. Horizon Pr. $25.00. Sets forth his memories, his ideas, his hopes for the future.

Living City. Horizon Pr. repr. of 1958 ed. 1984 $25.00; New Amer. Lib. pap. $6.95. A lyrical and completely rewritten version of his *When Democracy Builds* (o.p.)

Genius and the Mobocracy. Horizon Pr. 1971 $25.00. Wright's eloquent tribute to Louis Henry Sullivan, his *lieber meister* (dear master).

BOOKS ABOUT WRIGHT

Brooks, H. Allen, ed. *Prairie School Architecture: Studies from the Western Architect.* Univ. of Toronto Pr. 1975 $35.00; Van Nostrand 1983 pap. $19.95

Hitchcock, Henry-Russell. *In the Nature of Materials: The Buildings of Frank Lloyd Wright, 1887–1941.* Da Capo repr. of 1942 ed. 1975 pap. $12.95. The main book on the early works of Frank Lloyd Wright. Still a basic document.

Meehan, Patrick J., ed. *The Master Architect: Conversations with Frank Lloyd Wright.* Wiley 1984 $29.95

Scully, Vincent, Jr. *Frank Lloyd Wright.* Masters of World Architecture Ser. Braziller 1960 pap. $7.95

Smith, Norris K. *Frank Lloyd Wright: A Study in Architectural Content.* Amer. Life Foundation text ed. rev. ed. 1978 pap. $10.00

Storrer, William A. *The Architecture of Frank Lloyd Wright: A Complete Catalog.* MIT 2d ed. 1978 pap. $11.95. The most useful catalog.

Sweeney, Robert L. *Frank Lloyd Wright: An Annotated Bibliography.* Fwd. by Adolf K. Placzek, *Art and Architecture Bibliographies Ser.* Hennessey 1978 $29.95. The most comprehensive bibliography of writings by and about Wright.

Twombly, Robert C. *Frank Lloyd Wright: His Life and His Architecture.* Wiley 1979 $29.95

Wright, Olgivanna L. *Shining Brow: Frank Lloyd Wright.* Horizon Pr. pap. $5.95

CHAPTER 13

The Mass Media

Sandra Grilikhes

He gave man speech, and speech created thought
Which is the measure of the universe
—SHELLEY, *Prometheus Unbound*

For masterpieces are not single and solitary births; they are the outcome of
many years of thinking in common, of thinking by the body of the people, so
that the experience of the mass is behind a single voice.
—VIRGINIA WOOLF, *A Room of One's Own*

Among the several hundred definitions of communications to be found, one
might choose Jurgen Ruesch's notion that communication is a process that
links discontinuous parts of the living world to one another. Of a certainty,
today's world of communication attempts to measure the universe in ways
never before conceived.

The complex technological world of satellites, cable, telecommunications,
and computers has become so astonishingly commonplace that it is no
longer considered sufficient to be merely print literate. Certainly, different
kinds of demands are made on the individual by reading, listening, or looking at images. Yet television and video literacy and computer literacy have
become *de rigueur* necessities of contemporary and future life. It is no longer
acceptable to sit passively before the television set without understanding
the methods and manner of its manipulation, as well as its art. The same
sort of need for literacy applies to the motion picture—past, present, and future—as well.

It has always been known that the cognitive activity required by the reading of great literature exercises the intellect in many excellent ways. New
applications of this kind of intellectual and aesthetic activity are being developed in order that citizens can participate knowledgeably and discrimi-
natively in their culture, society, and government. The tremendous, all-
reaching effects of the mass media must be matched by a public that can
understand the history, effects, and art of those media, so that all of the
citizenry can clearly perceive the means utilized by the media to mold,
sway, and change opinion.

The titles selected for inclusion here serve as an introduction to history
and criticism in the field and suggest the breadth of the burgeoning fields of
communication that change even as this chapter is written. These titles are

tools with which to get at the heart of the matter of the mass media in all their richness and variability; to learn their rules, to determine their prejudices and whims (which are only prejudices and whims of those who wield decision-making power in the media), and to develop the means to meet the media with the power of understanding that can be gained by active reason in order to create the technologically literate public that is so necessary.

Some of the key contemporary figures have not yet become the subject of published books, but material on them can be found readily in articles and essays.

COMMUNICATIONS

Reference Books

Anderson, Elliott, and Mary Kinzie, eds. *The Little Magazine in America: A Modern Documentary History.* Pushcart Pr. 1978 $35.00

Beecham, C. Robert. *Resource Book for International Communications.* Transnational Communication Ctr. 1983 $5.00

Blum, Eleanor. *Basic Books in the Mass Media: An Annotated, Selected Booklist Covering General Communications, Book Publishing, Broadcasting, Film, Magazines, Newspapers, Advertising, Indexes, and Scholarly and Professional Periodicals.* Univ. of Illinois Pr. 2d ed. 1980 $27.50. "[This] book is a key research tool and library buying guide for the lasting books of the 1970's that cover broad communications issues. (Single-agency histories and biographies remain excluded.) Books revised since the first edition get slightly rewritten notes, with comparative comments. Only a few classics from the first edition remain. . . . [Blum] has essentially created a new book which may be used alone, or, preferably, in random with the earlier collection" (A. Z. Bass, *LJ*).

Broadcasting/Cablecasting Yearbook. Broadcasting Publications annual 1984 $80.00. A comprehensive directory "of radio, television, cable and other electronic mass communication media—how they evolved, how they work, how they are regulated" (Introduction).

Burrelle's Black Media Directory, 1984. Burrelle's Media Directories 1983 $35.00

Burrelle's Hispanic Media Directory, 1984. Burrelle's Media Directories 1983 $35.00

Burrelle's Women's Media Directory, 1984. Burrelle's Media Directories 1983 $35.00

DeFleur, Melvin, and Shearon Lowery. *Milestones in Mass Communication Research.* Longman text ed. 1983 pap. $14.95

Friedman, Leslie. *Sex-Role Stereotyping in the Mass Media: An Annotated Bibliography. Reference Lib. of Social Science Ser.* Garland 1977 lib. bdg. $42.00

Gerbner, George, and Marsha Siefert, eds. *World Communications: A Handbook.* Longman 1984 consult publisher for information. "The selection of articles for this handbook reflects a joining of research and policy. When possible we have provided studies that assess communications situations along with policy statements or informed views on these same issues" (Preface).

Gillmor, Donald M., and Jerome A. Barron. *Mass Communications Law, Cases and Comment. Amer. Casebook Ser.* West 3d ed. text ed. 1979 $19.95

Gitter, George, and Robert Grunin, eds. *Communication: A Guide to Information Sources.* Gale 1980 $60.00

Gross, Lynne S. *The New Television Technologies.* William C. Brown text ed. 1983 pap. consult publisher for price

Halpern, Jeanne W. *Computers and Composing: How the New Technologies Are Changing Writing.* Southern Illinois Univ. Pr. 1984 $8.50

Joyce, William L., ed. *Printing and Society in Early America.* Ed. by David D. Hall, Richard D. Brown, and John B. Hench, Amer. Antiquarian Society text ed. 1983 $32.50

Langman, Larry. *The Video Encyclopedia.* Garland 1983 lib. bdg. $21.00

Longley, Dennis, and Michael Shain, eds. *Dictionary of Information Technology.* Wiley 1982 $42.25

Longman Dictionary of the Mass Media and Communication. Longman 1982 pap. $13.95

McCavitt, William E. *Radio and Television: A Selected, Annotated Bibliography.* Scarecrow Pr. 1982 $15.00

Obudho, Constance E., ed. *Human Nonverbal Behavior: An Annotated Bibliography.* Greenwood 1979 lib. bdg. $29.95

Putnam, Linda L., and Michael E. Pacanowsky, eds. *Communication and Organizations: An Interpretive Approach. Sage Focus Eds.* 1983 $28.00 pap. $14.00

Rosenberg, Jerry M. *Dictionary of Computers, Data Processing, and Telecommunications.* Wiley 1984 $29.95 pap. $14.95

Sapan, Joshua. *Making It in Cable TV: Career Opportunities in Today's Fastest Growing Media Industry.* Putnam 1984 pap. $7.95

Shearer, Benjamin F., and Marilyn Huxford, eds. *Communications and Society: A Bibliography on Communications Technologies and Their Social Impact.* Greenwood 1983 lib. bdg. $35.00

Television and Cable Factbook 1984. Television Digest annual 2 vols. $147.00. "The authoritative reference for the Television, Cable and Electronics Industries" (Publisher's description).

Weik, Martin H. *Communications Standard Dictionary.* Van Nostrand text ed. 1982 $42.50

World Communications: A 200-Country Survey of Press, Radio, Television, and Film. Gower Pr. 1975 $27.50

General Works

Abel, Elie, ed. *What's News: The Media in American Society.* Institute of Contemporary Studies text ed. 1981 $18.95 pap. $7.95. "One way to create a book on ethics/responsibility of the mass media is to assemble a stable of 12 authorities and have each write a chapter on such topics as why the family owned newspaper is vanishing from the American scene; how the proliferation of new communication technologies may be changing our society; whether, in the computer age, the individual's right to privacy is endangered. . . . The pedigrees of the writers are impressive . . . . [and] Elie Abel . . . binds the whole thing together. . . . However, the book exhibits the weakness of its genre: unevenness of quality. All the chapters delve into subjects that have been treated before [and] . . . . several authors represented . . . have little to add to the discussion" (*Choice*).

Arno, Andrew, and Wymal Dissanayake. *The News Media in National and International Conflict. Special Study.* Westview Pr. 1984 pap. $25.00

Bagdikian, Ben H. *The Media Monopoly.* Beacon 1984 $16.95 pap. $8.95. The author contends that the nation's media "have congealed into huge communications complexes to the extent that more than half of our major newspapers, magazines, radio and television operations, book publishers, and movie producers are controlled by just fifty corporations. . . . Instead of serving the public interest, he charges, the media increasingly serve the very private interests of their corporate owners and, more broadly, of the corporate power structure" (*Columbia Journalism Review*).

Books, Libraries, and Electronics: Essays on the Future of Written Communication. Knowledge Industry 1982 $24.95

Butler, Matilda, and William Paisley, eds. *Women and the Mass Media: A Sourcebook for Research and Action.* Human Sciences Pr. text ed. 1980 $34.95 pap. $14.95

Codding, George A., Jr. *The International Telecommunication Union: An Experiment in International Cooperation. International Propaganda and Communications Ser.* Ayer repr. of 1952 ed. 1972 $27.50

Cole, Barry, and Mal Oettinger. *Reluctant Regulators: The FCC and the Broadcast Audience.* Addison-Wesley 1978 $10.95

Communications and the Future. Bethesda World Future Society 1982 $14.50

Communications Technology in Education and Training: Proceedings of the Fourth National Conference on Communications Technology. Information Dynamics 1982 $20.00

Compaine, Benjamin M. *Understanding New Media: Trends and Issues in Electronic Distribution of Information.* Ballinger 1984 $29.95

———, ed. *Who Owns the Media? Concentration of Ownership in the Mass Communication Industry. Communications Lib. Ser.* Knowledge Industry 2d ed. 1982 $45.00. "Each industry is treated by a well-known expert in the area and the result is a volume that should become the standard reference on this topic.... Can be used by novices to the area of study as an accurate first introduction to the economic structure of any one of the industries covered. Excellent bibliography and index. Highly recommended to libraries at all levels" (*Choice*).

Cornish, Edward, ed. *Communications Tomorrow: The Coming of the Information Society.* Transaction Bks. text ed. 1982 pap. $6.95

Czitrom, Daniel J. *Media and the American Mind: From Morse to McLuhan.* Univ. of North Carolina Pr. 1982 $19.95 pap. $7.95

Danziger, Kurt. *Interpersonal Communication.* Pergamon text ed. 1976 pap. $14.00

Davison, W. Phillips, James Boylan, and Frederick T. C. Yu. *Mass Media: Systems and Effects.* Praeger text ed. 1976 pap. $17.95

DeFleur, Melvin, and Sandra J. Ball-Rokeach. *Theories of Mass Communication.* Longman 1981 pap. $16.45

Diamond, Edwin, Norman Sandler, and Milton Mueller. *Telecommunications in Crisis: The First Amendment, Technology, and Deregulation.* Cato Institute 1983 pap. $6.00

Dominick, Joseph. *The Dynamics of Mass Communication.* Random text ed. 1983 pap. $19.95

Duke, Judith S. *Religious Publishing and Communications. Communications Lib. Ser.* Knowledge Industry 1980 $29.95

Edelstein, Alex S. *Comparative Communication Research.* Pref. by Wilbur Schramm, Sage 1982 $17.95 pap. $9.95

Editor and Publisher International Yearbook. Editor and Publisher annual 1984 $33.00. "The encyclopedia of the newspaper industry" (Publisher's description).

Feagans, Lynne, and Roberta Golinkoff. *The Origins and Growth of Communication.* Ablex 1984 $39.50

Fischer, Heinz-Dietrich, and John C. Merrill, eds. *International and Intercultural Communication.* Hastings 2d ed. 1976 pap. $12.50

Geller, Evelyn. *Forbidden Books in American Public Libraries, 1876–1939: A Study in*

Cultural Change. Contributions in Librarianship and Information Science Ser. Greenwood 1984 lib. bdg. $29.95

Gerbner, George, ed. *Mass Media Policies in Changing Cultures.* Wiley 1977 $37.50

Greenfield, Patricia. *Mind and Media: The Effects of Television, Video Games, and Computers. Developing Child Ser.* Harvard Univ. Pr. text ed. 1984 $12.50 pap. $4.95

Gumpert, Gary, and Robert Cathcart, eds. *Inter/Media: Interpersonal Communication in a Media World.* Oxford 2d ed. 1982 pap. $14.95

Gumperz, John J. *Discourse Strategies. Studies in Interactional Sociolinguistics* Cambridge Univ. Pr. 1982 $34.50 pap. $11.95. "What unifies these chapters (several of which have appeared in other forms elsewhere) into a complete text is the mix of theoretical background skillfully interwoven into fabric of the research findings. . . . The book's central hypothesis is 'that utterance can be understood in numerous ways, and that people . . . interpret a given utterance based on their definition of what is happening at the time of interaction.' "

Gurevitch, Michael, ed. *Culture, Society and the Media.* Methuen 1982 pap. $13.95

Hamelink, Cees J. *Cultural Autonomy in Global Communications.* Longman 1983 $15.00

Havick, John J., ed. *Communications Policy and the Political Process. Contributions in Political Science Ser.* Greenwood 1983 lib. bdg. $29.95

Hedebro, Goran. *Communication and Social Change in Developing Nations: A Critical View.* Iowa State Univ. Pr. 1982 $7.95

Hoffman, Lance J., ed. *Computers and Privacy in the Next Decade.* Academic Pr. 1980 $24.00

Hoggart, Richard, and Janet Morgan, eds. *The Future of Broadcasting.* Holmes & Meier text ed. 1982 $29.50

Horsfield, Peter. *Religious Television: The Experience in America. Communication and Human Values Ser.* Longman text ed. 1984 $15.00

Howitt, Dennis. *The Mass Media and Social Problems. International Ser. in Experimental Social Psychology* Pergamon 1982 pap. $13.00

Irwin, Manley R. *Telecommunications America: Markets without Boundaries.* Greenwood 1984 lib. bdg. $29.95

Jamieson, Kathleen H., and Karlyn K. Campbell. *The Interplay of Influence: Mass Media and Their Public in News, Advertising, Politics.* Wadsworth text ed. 1982 pap. $11.95

Katz, Elihu, ed. *Mass Media and Social Change. Sage Studies in International Sociology* 1981 $28.00 pap. $14.00

Key, Mary R., ed. *The Relationship of Verbal and Non-Verbal Communication. Contributions to the Sociology of Language Ser.* Mouton text ed. 1980 $30.00

Lehman, Maxwell, ed. *Communication Technologies and the Information Flow.* Pergamon 1981 pap. $10.95

Mander, Mary S. *Communications in Transition.* Praeger 1983 $33.95

McAnany, Emile, and Jorge Schnitman, eds. *Communication and Social Structure: Critical Studies in Mass Media Research.* Praeger 1981 $37.95

McQuail, Dennis. *Communication Models for the Study of Mass Communications.* Longman 1982 pap. $8.95

Meadow, Robert G. *Politics as Communications.* Ablex 1980 $27.50

Middleton, Karen P. *The Economics of Communication.* Pergamon 1980 $28.00

Nimmo, Dan. *Political Communication and Public Opinion in America.* Scott, Foresman 1978 pap. $14.50

Ploman, Edward. *Space, Earth and Communication.* Greenwood 1984 $27.50

Poyatos, Fernando. *New Perspectives in Non-Verbal Communication.* Pergamon 1983 $39.00

Robinson, Glen O., ed. *Communications for Tomorrow: Policy Perspectives for the 1980's.* Aspen Institute 1978 $8.95

Rogers, Everett M. *Communication Networks.* Macmillan (Free Pr.) 1981 $24.95

Roloff, Michael E. *Interpersonal Communication: The Social Exchange Approach.* Sage 1980 $12.50

Salomon, Gavriel. *Communication and Education.* Sage 1981 $24.00

Schiller, Herbert. *Information and the Crisis Economy.* Ablex 1984 $22.50

Schramm, Wilbur. *Men, Women, Messages and Media.* Harper 1982 pap. $12.50

Schwartz, Tony. *Media: The Second God.* Doubleday 1983 pap. $7.95. "[This] book contains many valuable and interesting observations on the creating and producing of commercials for radio and television, along with some intriguing ideas about the power of media and how to control it" (*LJ*).

Sigel, Efrem, ed. *Videotext: The Coming Revolution in Home-Office Information Retrieval.* Knowledge Industry 1980 $27.95. "A factual, concise, cool headed guide to social/personal consequences of the widespread use of new, telecommunications-based information forms" (John Adams, *School Library Journal*).

Singh, Indu B., ed. *Telematics in the Year 2000.* Ablex 1983 $29.50

Slack, Jennifer. *Communication Technologies and Society.* Ablex 1982 $24.50

Snow, Robert P. *Creating Media Culture.* Sage 1983 $28.00

Sorrels, Bobbye. *The Nonsexist Communicator.* Prentice-Hall 1983 $16.95

Stanley, Robert H., ed. *The Broadcast Industry: An Examination of Major Issues.* Hastings 1975 $7.95

Sweeney, G. P. *Information and the Transformation of Society.* Elsevier 1982 $51.00

Theobald, Robert. *Beyond Despair: A Policy Guide to the Communication Era.* Seven Locks Pr. 1981 $8.95

Tolchin, Susan. *Dismantling America: The Rush to Deregulate.* Houghton Mifflin 1983 $16.95

Tuchman, Gaye, and others, eds. *Hearth and Home: Images of Women in the Mass Media.* Oxford 1978 pap. $11.95

Turow, Joseph. *Media Industries: The Production of News and Entertainment.* Longman 1984 $29.95

Williams, Frederick. *Communications Revolution.* Sage 1982 $25.00

JOURNALISM

History and Criticism

Calvocoressi, Peter. *Freedom to Publish.* Humanities Pr. 1980 pap. $15.50

Compaine, Benjamin M. *The Newspaper Industry in the 80's.* Knowledge Industry 1980 $24.00

Curry, Jane L. *Press Control around the World.* Praeger 1982 $33.95

Desmond, Robert Williams. *Information Process: World News Reporting to the 20th Century.* Univ. of Iowa Pr. 1978 $22.50

Diamond, Edwin. *Good News, Bad News.* MIT 1978 pap. $6.95. The author argues that "television is not as powerful as the industry thinks it is. . . . A former Newsweek editor and now an MIT political scientist, [he] . . . explores the interdependence of TV and politics and of TV news and entertainment, with a . . . look at the relationship of news weeklies and newspapers to TV" (*LJ*).

Emery, Edwin. *Press and America*. Prentice-Hall 1984 pap. $6.95

Fischer, Heinz-Dietrich, ed. *Outstanding International Press Reporting*. De Gruyter 1984 vol. 1 $46.70

Fox, Walter. *Writing the News: Print Journalism in the Electronic Age*. Hastings 1977 $6.50

Ghiglione, Loren, ed. *The Buying and Selling of America's Newspapers*. Berg 1984 $21.95

Golding, Peter, and Philip Elliot. *Making the News*. Longman 1980 $35.00

Goodwin, H. Eugene. *Groping for Ethics in Journalism*. Iowa State Univ. Pr. 1983 pap. $16.95

Hartley, John. *Understanding News*. Methuen 1982 pap. $7.95

Hellman, John. *Fables of Fact: The New Journalism as New Fiction*. Univ. of Illinois Pr. 1981 $12.95

Hutt, Allen. *The Changing Newspaper: Typographic Trends in Britain and America, 1622–1972*. Beil $29.50

Hynds, Ernest C. *American Newspapers in the Nineteen Eighties. Studies in Media Management* Hastings rev. ed. 1980 $18.95 pap. $9.95

Kessler, Lauren. *The Dissident Press*. Sage 1984 $17.50 pap. $8.95

Kurian, George Thomas. *World Press Encyclopedia*. Facts on File 2 vols. 1981 $120.00 set

Lang, Gladys Engel. *The Battle for Public Opinion*. Columbia Univ. Pr. 1983 pap. $13.50

Marzio, Peter C. *The Men and Machines of American Journalism: A Pictorial Essay*. Smithsonian 1973 pap. $5.95

Merrill, John Calhoun, and Harold A. Fisher. *The World's Great Dailies: Profiles of Fifty Newspapers*. Hastings 1980 pap. $10.50

Milner, Anita C. *Newspaper Indexes: A Location and Subject Guide for Researchers*. Scarecrow Pr. 3 vols. 1977–82 ea. $16.00

National News Council. *In the Public Interest—III, 1979–1983*. National News Council 1984 $10.00

Nord, David Paul. *Newspapers and New Politics*. UMI Research 1981 $39.00

Paneth, Donald. *The Encyclopedia of American Journalism*. Facts on File 1983 $49.95

Pickett, Calder. *Voices of the Past: Key Documents in the History of American Journalism*. Grid 1977 pap. $18.95

Righter, Rosemary. *Whose News? Politics, the Press, and the Third World*. Times Bks. 1978 o.p.

Rosenberg, Jerry M. *Inside the Wall Street Journal*. Macmillan 1982 $16.95. "An insightful look at the 100-year-old Dow Jones company, with special emphasis on *The Wall Street Journal.* . . .The author shows that the *Journal* has always been an apostle of free enterprise and business expansion without questioning too deeply the implications of oligarchic capitalism. . . . The firm's emergence as a multimedia conglomerate of global penetration is examined in the context of new technologies and changing administrative philosophies" (*Choice*).

Schudson, Michael. *Discovering the News: A Social History of American Newspapers*. Basic Bks. 1978 $13.95. "Schudson sees news as a product packaged for consumers and sold for profit. Its market is society, and when society changes, news changes. The rise of a democratic market society in the 1830s altered the news in America, pushing newspapers to mass circulation and pressing journalists to entertain or to inform. After World War I, objectivity became the journalists' ideology. But judgment affects fact and news is influenced by its changing sources, subjects, and audience" (*LJ*).

Shaw, David. *Press Watch: A Provocative Look at How Newspapers Report the News.* Macmillan 1984 $15.95

Smith, Anthony, ed. *Newspapers and Democracy: International Essays on a Changing Medium.* MIT 1980 $5.00. Includes 14 essays grouped into four main parts: technology and the press, the press and the state in the established democracies, press and state in the newer democracies, and editorial content and control.

The Sociology of Journalism and the Press. Rowman 1980 pap. $18.95

Talese, Gay. *The Kingdom and the Power.* Dell 1981 pap. $3.50. "Seldom has anyone been so successful in making a newspaper [the *New York Times*] come alive as a human institution" (*N.Y. Times Bk. Review*).

Walker, Martin. *Powers of the Press.* Pilgrim Pr. 1983 $20.00

Journalists

Abrams, Alan E., ed. *Journalists Biographies Master Index.* Gale 1979 $85.00

American Newspaper Journalists. Volumes 23, 25, and 29 in the *Dictionary of Literary Biography.* Gale 1983–84 ea. $85.00–$88.00. Covers the years 1873–1950.

Anderson, Jack, and James Boyd. *Confessions of a Muckraker: The Inside Story of Life in Washington.* Random 1979 $12.95. "For more than two decades, the muckrakers battled foes from Forrestal to Nixon, from MacArthur to McCarthy. Among his stories, the author interjects sober reflections on the role of the press, concluding . . . that there were occasions on which the advocacy journalism he practiced may have overstepped the bounds of propriety. Anderson's readable and entertaining account offers an enlightening historical perspective on the journalistic tradition in which he continues to be engaged" (Wes Daniels, *LJ*).

Berges, Marshall. *The Life and Times of Los Angeles: A Newspaper, a Family, and a City.* Atheneum 1984 $17.50

Bray, Howard. *The Pillars of the Post: The Making of a News Empire in Washington.* Norton 1980 $7.95. "Bray's well-researched chronicle exposes the inner workings of the operation under publishers Meyer, Phil Graham, Katherine Graham, and now Donald Graham. This comprehensive study deals with the Post's major newsmaking events—the Pentagon Papers, Watergate, and the violent press strike. It provides an insightful look into journalism and its role in modern times" (M. S. Leach, *LJ*).

Brendon, Piers. *The Life and Death of the Press Barons.* Atheneum 1983 $14.95. "[This is] an extremely skillful assemblage. . . . The range of sources behind [this book] is eclectic and interesting, and some of the best material (notably on Pulitzer and Hearst) comes from unpublished manuscript sources. What emerges is on one level a gallery of eccentrics, and on another a series of studies in the tactics of power. . . . Horace Greeley comes through as most politically powerful; the elder James Gordon Bennett as most sinister; Joseph Pulitzer as most pathetic. The personalized nature of these judgments is inevitable; Brendon reiterates that his subjects were too individual to fit into any pattern and that the fate of their newspapers was dictated by their personalities and their fortunes" (*TLS*).

Friendly, Fred W. *The Good Guys, the Bad Guys, and the First Amendment: Free Speech versus Fairness in Broadcasting.* Random 1976 pap. $3.95

Hart, Jack R. *The Information Empire: The Rise of the Los Angeles Times and the Times Mirror Corporation.* Univ. Pr. of Amer. 1981 $27.75

Hess, Stephen. *The Washington Reporters.* Brookings 1981 $22.95

Johnstone, John Wallace Claire, and others. *News People: A Sociological Portrait of American Journalists and Their Work.* Univ. of Illinois Pr. 1976 $17.50

Marzio, Peter C. *The Men and Machines of American Journalism: A Pictorial Essay.*
    Smithsonian 1973 pap. $5.95
Marzolf, Marion. *Up from the Footnote: A History of Women Journalists.* Hastings
    1977 pap. $12.95
Meeker, Richard H. *Newspaperman: S. I. Newhouse and the Business of News.* Tick-
    nor & Fields 1983 $17.95
Roberts, Chalmers M. *The Washington Post: The First 100 Years.* Houghton Mifflin
    1977 $15.95
Schlipp, Madelon G., ed. *Great Women of the Press.* Southern Illinois Univ. Pr. 1983
    $27.50
Weiner, Richard. *Syndicated Columnists.* Public Relations 3d ed. 1979 $15.00

BROADCAST JOURNALISM

History and Criticism

Barrett, Marvin, ed. *Broadcast Journalism, 1979–81: The 8th Alfred I. DuPont Colum-
    bia University Survey.* Everest House 1982 $15.95
Campaign '84: Advertising and Programming Obligations of the Electronic Media.
    Practising Law Institute 1984 $35.00
Diamond, Edwin. *The Spot: The Rise of Political Advertising on Television.* MIT 1984
    $17.50
Gibson, Martin L. *Editing in the Electronic Era.* Iowa State Univ. Pr. 1979 $25.00
Graber, Doris. *Crime News and the Public.* Praeger 1980 $34.95
Hill, George H. *Religious Broadcasting, 1920–83: A Selectively Annotated Bibliogra-
    phy.* Garland 1984 $36.00
Hoover, Stewart M. *The Electronic Giant: A Critique of Telecommunications from a
    Christian Perspective.* Brethren Pr. 1982 pap. $6.95
Hulteng, John L. *The News Media: What Makes Them Tick?* Prentice-Hall 1979 $12.95
Lesher, Stephen. *Media Unbound: Impact of Television Journalism on the Public.*
    Houghton Mifflin 1982 $13.95. "[Lesher's] point is not that the quality of Ameri-
    can journalism has declined, but that its intrinsic faults have become more glar-
    ing as its power has increased. And that TV news in particular has come to
    dominate—and distort—the public's perception of events. . . . Most of his book
    is devoted to examples of shortcomings, from coverage of the Tet offensive and
    the invasion of Afghanistan to the Iran hostage crisis and Three Mile Island.
    There is plenty of ammunition for media-haters here. But Lesher opposes any at-
    tempt to constrain the press 'by law or fiat.' As a journalist himself, he simply
    wants to warn: Let the Viewer Beware" (*Christian Science Monitor*).
MacKuen, Michael. *More than News: Media Power in Public Affairs.* Sage 1981 $24.00
Madsen, Axel. *Sixty Minutes: The Power and the Politics.* Dodd 1984 $16.95
Nimmo, Dan, and James E. Combs. *Nightly Horrors: Crisis Coverage on Television Net-
    work News.* Univ. of Tennessee Pr. 1985 $18.95
Porter, William E. *Assault on the Media: The Nixon Years.* Univ. of Michigan Pr. 1976
    $12.95 pap. $6.95
Presidency and the Mass Media in the Age of Television. Univ. Pr. of Amer. 1978 pap.
    $13.00
Ranney, Austin. *Channels of Power: The Impact of Television on American Politics.* Ba-
    sic Bks. 1983 $14.95 1985 pap. $6.95

Robinson, Michael J. *Over the Wire and on T.V.: CBS and UPI in Campaign '80.* Basic Bks. 1983 $24.95

Sterling, Christopher H., and John M. Kittross. *Stay Tuned: A Concise History of American Broadcasting.* Wadsworth 1978 $25.95

Van Gerpen, Maurice. *Privileged Communication and the Press: The Citizen's Right to Know Versus the Law's Right to Confidential News Source Evidence.* Greenwood 1979 $27.50. This is a review of the issues surrounding news source confidentiality.

Videotex and the Press. Learned Information 1982 $30.00

Weaver, David H. *Videotex Journalism: Teletext Viewdata and the News.* Erlbaum 1983 $18.00

Westin, A. V. *Newswatch: How TV Decides the News.* Simon & Schuster 1982 pap. $6.95. This is an "explanation of the components of television network news, written by a veteran producer and correspondent. Emphasizing that teamwork is the most important factor in a successful broadcast, Westin draws on personal experience and the recollections of anchorpersons such as Mike Wallace to describe how reporters, anchors, producers, camera operators, and correspondents cooperate to produce informative reports under great deadline pressure" (*LJ*).

Broadcast Journalists

Cronkite, Walter. *Challenges of Change.* Public Affairs Pr. 1971 pap. $7.50

Fang, Irving E. *Those Radio Commentators.* Iowa State Univ. Pr. 1977 $14.95

Gelfman, Judith S. *Women in Television News.* Columbia Univ. Pr. 2d ed. 1976 $20.00

Lewis, Carolyn Diana. *Reporting for Television.* Columbia Univ. Pr. 1984 $18.50

Lichello, Robert. *Edward R. Murrow: Broadcaster of Courage.* Ed. by D. Steve Rahmas, SamHar Pr. 1972 $3.50

Matusow, Barbara. *The Evening Stars: The Making of the Network News Anchors.* Houghton Mifflin 1983 $14.95

Rather, Dan (with Mickey Hershkowitz). *The Camera Never Blinks: Adventures of a TV Journalist.* Ballantine 1984 pap. $2.95

Reasoner, Harry. *Before the Colors Fade.* Knopf 1981 $11.50; Morrow 1983 pap. $5.70

Sevareid, Arnold Eric. *Conversations with Eric Sevareid.* Public Affairs Pr. 1977 pap. $6.00

Wallace, Mike. *Close Encounters.* Morrow 1984 $17.95 pap. $4.50

Winfield, Betty H., and Lois B. DeFleur. *Edward R. Murrow Heritage: Challenge for the Future.* Iowa State Univ. Pr. text ed. 1985 $21.50

RADIO AND TELEVISION

History and Criticism

Adler, Richard P., ed. *All in the Family: A Critical Appraisal.* Praeger 1979 $39.95. A thoroughgoing study that presents reviews, research material, sample scripts, and a total assessment of the impact of the program on U.S. culture. Includes a symposium on the meaning of "All in the Family," and an excellent bibliography.

———. *Understanding Television: Essays on Television as a Social and Cultural Force.* Praeger 1981 $39.50 text ed. pap. $18.95

Altheide, David L. *Creating Reality: How TV News Distorts Events. Sage Lib. of Social Research* 1976 $24.00 pap. $12.00

Belville, H. M., Jr. *Audience Ratings: Radio, Television and Cable.* Erlbaum 1985 $39.95. A history and a look at future trends.

Bluem, A. William. *Documentary in American Television.* Hastings 1964 o.p. A classic in the field.

Brown, Les. *Keeping Your Eye on Television.* Seabury 1979 pap. $4.95

———. *Les Brown's Encyclopedia of Television.* Zoetrope 1982 $29.95

———, ed. *Fast Forward: The New Television and American Society.* Andrews, McMeel & Parker 1983 $9.95

Buckman, Peter. *All for Love: A Study in Soap Opera.* Merrimack 1985 $15.95

Busby, Linda J., and Donald L. Parker. *The Art and Science of Radio.* Allyn & Bacon text ed. 1984 $21.00

Cantor, Muriel G. *Prime-Time Television: Content and Control.* Sage 1980 $17.50. "The book is free of excess sociological jargon and the material reads easily. . . . A most useful introduction to and overview of a very complex subject" (*Choice*).

———. *The Soap Opera.* Sage 1983 $17.50

Cass, Ronald A. *Revolution in the Wasteland: Value and Diversity in Television.* Univ. Pr. of Virginia 1981 $10.00. This book "explores the economics of television programming, regulatory policies, and the nature of the concepts of value and diversity. . . . Cass predicts that . . . cable television, pay television, satellites, video discs, and videocassettes will satisfy demands for greater variety and more valuable programs. The newest of these technologies—videodiscs and videocassettes—are likely to remain outside the purview of the FCC and some minor relaxation of commercial television regulation will accompany the growth of audiences for these unregulated delivery mechanisms" (Publisher's note). Index.

Cassata, Mary B. *Life on Daytime Television.* Ablex 1983 $29.50

Castleman, Harry, and Walter J. Podrazik. *Watching TV: Four Decades of American Television.* McGraw-Hill 1982 $22.50

Cole, Barry, ed. *Television Today.* Oxford 1981 pap. $9.95. "Cole anthologizes and introduces almost 80 *TV Guide* essays. . . . Authors include, among others, historians Schlesinger and Boorstin and futurists Asimov and Toffler. Also represented are the views of the network executives [concerning] present realities such as Nielsen ratings and the F.C.C." (*LJ*).

Comstock, George. *Television in America.* Sage 1980 $17.50. Comstock "examines the ability of TV news to elevate the trivial to the apparently significant; to project information and attitudes in the guise of entertainment; to, paradoxically, both accelerate maturation (by learning things more rapidly) and arrest it (by not exploring the implications of what has been learned); and, finally, to assess the probable impact of TV on attention span and family life" (*Choice*).

Conrad, Peter. *Television: The Medium and Its Manners.* Routledge & Kegan 1982 $12.95

Coppa, Frank J., ed. *Screen and Society: The Impact of Television upon Aspects of Contemporary Civilization.* Nelson-Hall 1979 $20.95

Cowan, Geoffrey. *See No Evil: The Backstage Battle over Sex and Violence on Television.* Simon & Schuster 1980 $4.95. An excellent survey of censorship on television, with a substantial section on Norman Lear.

Cross, Donna Woolfolk. *Mediaspeak: How Television Makes Up Your Mind.* Coward-McCann 1983 $13.95. "The author seeks to show that television's program content, including that of news shows, promotes establishment values, and that viewers are being brainwashed by the medium's pervasive sameness" (*LJ*).

Cullingford, Cedric. *Children and Television*. St. Martin's 1984 $22.50

DeLuca, Stuart M. *Television's Transformation: The Next 25 Years*. Barnes & Noble 1980 $9.95

Drake, Harold L. *Humanistic Radio Production*. Univ. Pr. of Amer. 1982 $22.25

Dunning, John. *Tune in Yesterday: The Ultimate Encyclopedia of Old-Time Radio, 1926–76*. Prentice-Hall 1976 pap. $8.95

Esslin, Martin. *The Age of Television*. Freeman 1981 pap. $10.95

Fornatale, Peter, and Joshua E. Mill. *Radio in the Television Age*. Overlook Pr. 1980 $17.95. "This is a history of radio in the 1950s, 1960s, and 1970s, told in chronological order, with two major facets—radio news and non-commercial radio— treated separately within the text. . . . It is our hope that this book will provoke a greater awareness of how and why people use radio, and how they might seek to improve it" (Preface).

Frank, Ronald E., and Marshall G. Greenberg. *The Public's Use of Television*. Sage 1980 $27.50. This study is an investigation of individual interests and activities, relating needs and behavior primarily with respect to television, but also covering radio, newspapers, magazines, books and movies. The authors "conducted over 2,400 personal interviews throughout the United States, breaking the TV viewer's interests into 18 categories covering over 130 special interest areas ranging from sports to religion" (Publisher's note).

Gianakos, Larry J. *Television Drama Series Programming: A Comprehensive Chronicle*. Scarecrow Pr. 1980 $25.00

Goethals, Gregor T. *The TV Ritual: Worship at the Video Altar*. Beacon 1981 pap. $6.97. It is the author's thesis that "television today supplies our society with many of the religious elements once supplied only by the church. . . . [He] proposes that today the sacramental power of images in American society has been most effectively taken over by commercial television" (*Christian Century*). Index.

Hammond, Charles M. *The Image Decade: Television Documentary, 1965–1975*. Hastings 1981 $23.50. This book deals "with the art and practice of TV documentary in terms of concepts, programs, producers, reporters and events. . . . Each discussion will tell you what TV news and theme documentaries accomplished when they turned to look at the emergence of minorities and women, at the American family, education, urban life, Vietnam, or Washington. . . . This study is only about news and theme documentaries—not the networks themselves or even their respective total news operations" (Introduction).

Harris, Jay S., and others, eds. *TV Guide: The First 25 Years*. Simon & Schuster rev. ed. 1980 pap. $9.95

Head, Sydney W. *Broadcasting in America*. Houghton Mifflin 1982 $24.95

Hedinsson, Elias. *TV, Family and Society: The Social Origins and Effects of Adolescents' TV Use*. Humanities Pr. 1981 $29.95

James, Watson C. *Television in Transition*. Crain 1983 $74.95

Johnston, Jerome, and James S. Ettema. *Positive Images: Breaking Stereotypes with Children's Television*. Sage 1982 $24.00

Kaplan, E. Ann, ed. *Regarding Television: Critical Approaches*. Amer. Film Institute 1983 $25.00. An anthology.

Krasnow, Erwin G. *The Politics of Broadcast Regulation*. St. Martin's 1982 $18.95

Levinson, Richard, and William Link. *Stay Tuned: An Inside Look at the Making of Prime-Time Television*. St. Martin's 1981 $11.95. "This book aims for the heart of the competitive, prime-time TV entertainment jungle, and it scores with thoughtful, insightful, serious, oftentimes humorous power punches. It serves as . . . a rich sociological study that elevates good reading for entertainment to the rarity of being an absorbing and valuable textbook. This book is highly recommended reading for all levels—viewers as well as non-viewers, industry professionals, students and teachers" (*Choice*).

Lichty, Lawrence W., and Malachi C. Topping. *American Broadcasting: A Source Book on the History of Radio and Television. Studies in Public Communication* Hastings 1975 $26.50 text ed. pap. $15.00

Liebert, R. *The Early Window: The Effects of Television on Children and Youth.* Pergamon 1982 $28.00

Linsky, Marvin, ed. *Television and the Presidential Elections.* Lexington Bks. 1983 $20.00

MacDonald, J. Fred. *Blacks and White TV: Afro-Americans in Television since 1948.* Nelson-Hall 1983 $23.95

Macy, John W. *To Irrigate a Wasteland: The Struggle to Shape a Public Television System in the United States.* Univ. of California Pr. 1974 $17.95. "Written by the man who best knows the problems of public programming, the book should become required reading for university radio and television students as well as for anyone who is interested in . . . public broadcasting" (*Choice*).

McCavitt, William E. *Radio and Television: A Selected Annotated Bibliography.* Scarecrow Pr. supp. 1 (1977–81) 1982 $14.00

Mitz, Rick. *The Great TV Sitcom Book.* Putnam 1983 pap. $12.95

Mosco, Vincent. *Broadcasting in the United States: Innovative Challenge and Organizational Control.* Ablex 1979 $19.50

Murray, John P. *Television and Youth.* Boys Town Ctr. 1980 pap. $10.00

Newcomb, Horace. *Television: The Critical View.* Oxford 3d ed. 1982 pap. $9.95

Paulu, Burton. *Radio and Television Broadcasting in Eastern Europe.* Univ. of Minnesota Pr. 1974 $25.00

Quinlan, Sterling. *Inside ABC: American Broadcasting Company's Rise to Power.* Hastings 1979 $12.95. This history of the television network is written by a former ABC station manager. He writes of ABC's "creation by government bureaucracy, of its survival of takeover attempts by Howard Hughes and by ITT [and] of the . . . personal stories of executive suite power struggles. . . . Quinlan was Vice President and General Manager of ABC's Chicago station for eleven of the seventeen years he was with the company" (Publisher's note). Bibliography and index.

Rader, Benjamin. *In Its Own Image: How Television Has Transformed Sports.* Macmillan (Free Pr.) 1984 $15.95

Reed, Maxine K. *Career Opportunities in Television and Video.* Facts on File 1982 $19.95

Reiss, David S. *M A S H: The Exclusive Inside Story of TV's Most Popular Show.* Bobbs 1980 pap. $9.95

Rubin, Bernard, ed. *Small Voices and Great Trumpets: Minorities and the Media.* Praeger 1980 $33.95

Rx Television: Enhancing the Preventive Impact of TV. Haworth Pr. 1983 $22.95

Sass, Lauren R. *Television: The American Medium in Crisis.* Facts on File 1979 $19.95

Sklar, Robert. *Prime-Time America: Life on and behind the Television Screen.* Oxford 1980 $19.95. "This collection of Sklar's television criticism from *American Film* and *Chronicle Review* magazines is divided into three major areas: culture and values on TV, the people and practice of the industry, and reviews of specific programs" (*LJ*).

Skornia, Harry J. *Television and the News: A Critical Appraisal.* Pacific Bks. 1968 pap. $3.95

Steinberg, Cobbett. *TV Facts.* Facts on File rev. ed. 1984 $19.95

Television and Aggression: A Panel Study. Academic Pr. 1982 $39.50

Terrace, Vincent. *Radio's Golden Years: The Encyclopedia of Radio Programs, 1930– 1960.* A. S. Barnes 1981 $15.00

————. *Television, 1970–1980.* A. S. Barnes 1981 $22.50

TV Guide Index 1978–80. Triangle supp. 1982 pap. $30.00

TV Guide Twenty-Five Year Index. Triangle 1979 $60.00

Wertheim, Arthur F. *Radio Comedy.* Oxford 1979 $27.50

Williams, Frederick. *Children, Television, and Sex-Role Stereotyping.* Praeger 1981 $29.95. "In the public television series Freestyle a boy is portrayed holding a doll; a girl is shown taking charge of a basketball team that beats a boys' squad. Accompanying the development of Freestyle was a federally funded research project on the effects of such television viewing on sex-role stereotyping. This book is the report of that research" (*Choice*). Bibliography and indexes.

Winick, Mariann, and Charles Winick. *Television Experience: What Children See.* Sage 1979 $24.00

Woolery, George W. *Children's Television: The First Thirty-Five Years, 1946–1981.* Scarecrow Pr. 1983 $27.50

World Radio TV Handbook. Billboard Bks. 1983 pap. $17.50

Radio and Television Artists

Bedell, Sally. *Up the Tube: Prime-Time Television in the Silverman Years.* Viking 1981 $13.95. "As a chief executive for CBS from 1970 to 1975, ABC from 1975–1978, and NBC from 1978 to the present, Fred Silverman has dominated American evening television programming for the past ten years. *TV Guide* writer Bedell chronicles the industry during what she views as a decade of decline" (*LJ*).

Paley, William S. *As It Happened: A Memoir.* Doubleday 1979 o.p. The autobiography of the founder of the Columbia Broadcasting System. Paley "includes descriptions of his early ventures in the family tobacco business, his purchase of a foundering radio network in 1928, the heyday of radio and television programming, and controversies with Edward R. Murrow, Daniel Schorr, the CIA, and others" (*LJ*).

Scheuer, Steven. *Who's Who in Television and Video.* Facts on File 1983 $49.95

Wilk, Max. *The Golden Age of Television.* Delacorte 1976 $10.00

FILM

The proliferation of film books during the past ten years attests to the popularity of both film itself and the growth of interest in it—as popular entertainment, as an art form, and as the subject of serious analytic discourse.

Film societies that sponsor avant-garde films, foreign films, or musicals abound. Special-interest groups in schools, community centers, adult centers, and libraries have vital ongoing film programs. Film courses, both inside and outside the university and college setting, have burgeoned. In colleges, film series are shown in such diverse departments as English, History, History of Art or Architecture, Romance Languages, City Planning, Social Work, and Cinema Study. Finally, the easy availability of rental video films, which can be shown on home video cassette recorders, has made film widely available in contemporary Western society.

The books included in this section cover the early development, history and criticism, and future development of the lively, economically healthy, and growing film industry.

Reference Works

Andrew, Dudley. *Major Film Theories: An Introduction.* Oxford 1976 pap. $6.95

Armour, Robert A. *Film: A Reference Guide.* Amer. Popular Culture Ser. Greenwood 1980 lib. bdg. $29.95

Arnheim, Rudolf. *Film as Art.* Univ. of California Pr. 1960 pap. $4.95

Austin, Bruce A. *The Film Audience: An International Bibliography of Research.* Scarecrow Pr. 1983 $16.50

Berger, Arthur A., ed. *Film in Society.* Transaction Bks. 1980 $10.95

Brady, Anna, and Carolyn N. Weiner, eds. *Union List of Film Periodicals: Holdings of Selected American Collections.* Greenwood 1984 $35.00. Contains access by subject and title and information on how to obtain specific issues through library visit or interlibrary loan.

Cadden, Tom Scott. *What a Bunch of Characters! An Entertaining Guide to Who Played What in the Movies.* Prentice-Hall 1984 pap. $9.95. More than 2,600 roles played by 50 of Hollywood's most famous stars.

Champlin, Charles. *The Movies Grow Up, 1940–1980.* Ohio Univ. Pr. 1981 $25.95

Cowie, Peter, ed. *International Film Guide.* A. S. Barnes 9 vols. 1974–80 ea. $7.95 1981 pap. $9.95 1983 pap. $10.95. "Eminently useful . . . well on its way to becoming the authoritative reference source on the growing edge of cinema" (*SR*).

Enser, A. G. *Filmed Books and Plays: A List of Books and Plays from Which Films Have Been Made, 1928–1983.* Lexington Bks. 1985 $44.00

The Film Index: A Bibliography. Vol. 1, *Film as Art.* Arno repr. of 1941 ed. 1966 $24.00; Vol. 2, *Film as Industry* Kraus 1984 $95.00; Vol. 3, *Film in Society* Kraus 1985 $85.00. An exhaustive bibliography of film literature and a guide to filmmakers and films from the days of silent cinema through 1936. Superb indexing.

Film Literature Index, 1973–78, 1980–83. Filmdex 10 vols. $225.00. Author-subject periodical index to the international literature of film. Published quarterly, with annual cumulation.

Foreman, Alexa L. *Women in Motion.* Bowling Green 1983 $19.95

Garbicz, Adam, and Jacek Klinowski. *Cinema, the Magic Vehicle: A Guide to Its Achievement.* Schocken 2 vols. repr. of 1975 ed. 1983 pap. ea. $12.50

Green, Stanley. *Encyclopedia of the Musical Film.* Oxford 1981 $35.00

Halliwell, Leslie. *The Filmgoer's Companion.* Farrar (Hill & Wang) 8th ed. 1984 $42.50

Hardy, Phil. *The Film Encyclopedia.* Morrow vol. 1 1984 $25.00

Heinzkill, Richard. *Film Criticism: An Index to Critics' Anthologies.* Scarecrow Pr. 1975 o.p.

Katz, Ephraim. *The Film Encyclopedia.* Perigee 1982 $14.95

Kindem, Gorham, ed. *The American Movie Industry: The Business of Motion Pictures.* Southern Illinois Univ. Pr. 1982 pap. $17.95

Leonard, William T. *The Theatre: Stage to Screen to Television.* Scarecrow Pr. 1981 2 vols. $74.50. A catalog of film and television adaptations of original theater works.

Less, David. *The Movie Business.* Random 1981 pap. $5.95

Limbacher, James L., ed. *Feature Films: A Directory of Feature Films on 16mm and Videotape Available for Rental, Sale, and Lease.* Bowker 8th ed. 1985 $75.00

Magill, Frank N., ed. *Magill Survey of Cinema.* Salem Pr. 4 vols. 1980 $200.00. Synopses of the plots of a substantial number of the best-known films.

Manchel, Frank. *Film Study: A Resource Guide.* Fairleigh Dickinson Univ. Pr. 1973 $27.50

Mast, Gerald. *The Movies in Our Midst.* Univ. of Chicago Pr. 1982 $37.50

Monaco, James. *Who's Who in American Film Now.* Zoetrope 1981 $19.95 pap. $7.95

Nash, Jay R., and Stanley R. Ross, eds. *The Motion Picture Guide.* Cinebooks (dist. by R. R. Bowker) 1985–86. 12 vols. $750.00 annual suppl. $150.00

New York Times Film Reviews, 1913–1968. N.Y. Times 11 vols. & appendix 1913–68 $840.00

Niver, Kemp R. *Motion Pictures from the Library of Congress Paper Print Collection.* Univ. of California Pr. 1967 $70.00. A "unique and authoritative study" describing, "often with casts and credits . . . some 3,000 films released in the U.S. between 1894 and 1912" (*SR*).

O'Donnell, Monica M. *Contemporary Theatre, Film and Television: A Biographical Guide.* Gale 1984 vol. 1 $90.00 1985 vol. 2 $90.00

Pitts, Michael R. *Horror Film Stars.* MacFarland 1981 $16.95

Rehrauer, George. *The Macmillan Film Bibliography.* Macmillan 1982 2 vols. $120.00. A major source for film bibliographies in all areas.

Sadoul, Georges. *Dictionary of Films.* Univ. of California Pr. 1972 $36.50

Salem, James. *The Screenplay from the Jazz Singer to Dr. Strangelove.* Part 4 in *A Guide to Critical Reviews.* Scarecrow Pr. 1972 2 vols. $45.00

Schatz, Thomas. *Hollywood Genres.* Temple Univ. Pr. 1981 $29.95

Sharff Stefan. *The Elements of Cinema: Toward a Theory of Cinesthetic Impact.* Columbia Univ. Pr. 1982 $26.50

Singer, Michael, ed. *Film Directors: A Complete Guide.* Lone Eagle 1982 $32.95

Statistics on Film and Cinema, 1955–1977. UNESCO 1981 pap. $5.25

Sullivan, Kaye. *Films for, by and about Women.* Scarecrow Pr. 1980 $27.50

Talbot, Daniel, ed. *Film: An Anthology.* Univ. of California Pr. 2d ed. 1966 $3.95. A small treasure trove of classic articles on film.

Vincent, Carl, ed. *General Bibliography of Motion Pictures.* Arno 1972 $17.00

Willis, John, ed. *Screen World.* (Orig. *Daniel Blum's Screen World*). Crown vols. 33–35 1981–84 ea. $19.95

History and Criticism

The American Indian: Stereotypes of Native Americans in Films. N.J. State Museum 1980 $5.95

Armes, Roy. *A Critical History of British Cinema.* Oxford 1978 $27.50

———. *Patterns of Realism: Neo-realism in Italian Cinema.* Garland 1984 $60.00

Atkins, Thomas R., ed. *Sexuality in the Movies.* Quality Pap. Ser. Da Capo repr. of 1975 ed. 1984 pap. $12.95; Indiana Univ. Pr. 1975 $6.95

Balio, Tino, ed. *United Artists: The Company Built by the Stars.* Univ. of Wisconsin Pr. 1976 $22.50. "The history, which treats those years in which the founders controlled the company, is based on the rich corporate records of United Artists. . . . [This] is the first full and scholarly history of a major film company" (Publisher's note).

Barnouw, Erik, and Sukrahmaryan Krishnaswamy. *Indian Film*. Oxford 2d ed. 1980 $19.95

Bazin, Andre. *What Is Cinema?* Trans. by Hugh Gray, Univ. of California Pr. 2 vols. 1967–71 ea. $19.95 pap. $5.95. Translations of significant essays, the first to appear since his death in 1958. Bazin was the most important French film critic of his time.

Blum, Daniel. *A New Pictorial History of the Talkies*. Rev. by John Kobal, Putnam 1982 pap. $9.95

———. *A Pictorial History of the Silent Screen*. Putnam 1982 $9.95

Brownlow, Kevin. *The Parade's Gone By*. Univ. of California Pr. 1976 pap. $9.95. This is a serious book about the silent film in America, with interesting discussions of technique.

Cagin, Seth. *Hollywood Films of the Seventies*. Harper 1984 pap. $9.95

Clarens, Carlos. *Classics of the Horror Film*. Citadel Pr. 1974 $14.00 pap. $9.95

———. *Crime Movies: From Griffith to the Godfather and Beyond*. Norton 1980 pap. $9.95

Curran, James, and Vincent Porter, eds. *British Cinema History*. Barnes & Noble 1984 $32.50

DeGrazia, Edward, and Roger K. Newman. *Banned Films: Movies, Censors, and the First Amendment*. Bowker 1982 $29.95 pap. $19.95

Everson, William K. *The Bad Guys: A Pictorial History of the Movie Villain*. Citadel Pr. 1968 pap. $8.95. "A most remarkable rogue's gallery of men you love to hate. . . . The text is written with wit, charm and erudition" (*LJ*).

Faber, Stephen. *Hollywood Dynasties*. Delilah Bks. 1984 $16.95

Fielding, Raymond. *The Technique of Special Effects Cinematography*. Hastings rev. & enl. ed. 1982 $26.95

Franklin, Joe. *Classics of the Silent Screen*. Citadel Pr. 1983 pap. $9.95

Fulton, Albert R. *Motion Pictures: The Development of an Art from Silent Films to the Age of Television*. Univ. of Oklahoma Pr. rev. ed. 1980 $21.95

Geduld, Harry M. *The Birth of the Talkies: From Edison to Jolson*. Indiana Univ. Pr. 1975 $15.00. "The story of the invention of the technology necessary for the talking picture as we know it today" (*LJ*).

Huss, Roy, and Norman Silverstein. *The Film Experience: Elements of Motion Picture Art*. Dell 1969 pap. $6.95. Examines the art of such directors as Griffith, Lang, Welles, and Antonioni.

Insdorf, Annette. *Indelible Shadows: Film and the Holocaust*. Random 1983 $7.95

Jacobs, Lewis. *The Rise of the American Film: A Critical History*. Teachers College Pr. 1968 $24.95 pap. $15.95

———, ed. *The Emergence of Film Art: The Evolution and Development of the Motion Picture as Art, from 1900 to the Present*. Hopkinson & Blake 1979 $24.95. "Jacobs' new anthology is distinguished by the same qualities of clear organization and selective discrimination that have made his previous *Introduction to the Art of the Movies* an invaluable source of information. Covering the whole spectrum of the cinema, he succeeds again in condensing a great amount of substantial material into an easily manageable format" (George Amberg).

Jarvie, Ian C. *Movies as Social Criticism: Aspects of Their Social Psychology*. Scarecrow Pr. 1978 $15.00

Jowett, Garth, and James M. Linton. *Movies as Mass Communication*. Sage 1980 $17.50

Kael, Pauline. *Taking It All In: A Collection of Movie Reviews*. Holt 1984 pap. $14.95

Kaminsky, Stuart M. *American Film Genres*. Nelson-Hall 2d ed. rev. 1984 lib. bdg. $25.95 text ed. pap. $12.95

Kane, Kathryn. *Visions of War: Hollywood Combat Films of World War II*. Univ. of Michigan Pr. 1982 $39.95

Kaplan, E. Ann. *Women and Film: Both Sides of the Camera*. Methuen 1983 pap. $10.95. An important and pivotal selection of essays. The author is an authority in the field.

Kinwood, Roy. *Fifty Years of Serial Thrills*. Scarecrow Pr. 1983 $15.00

———. *Kino: A History of the Russian and Soviet Film*. Macmillan (Collier Bks.) 1973 $40.00 pap. $12.95. "A meticulous study of the pre-Soviet and early Soviet silent films with some coverage of the wartime period" (*Journal of the Society of Motion Picture and TV Engineers*).

Lasky, Betty. *RKO: The Biggest Little Major of Them All*. Prentice-Hall 1984 $14.95. A history, somewhat subjective, of the long-defunct major studio.

Leyda, Jay. *Dianying: An Account of Films and the Film Audience in China*. MIT 1972 $25.00 pap. $6.95

Limbacher, James L. *Sexuality in World Cinema*. Scarecrow Pr. 2 vols. 1983 $72.50

Low, Rachel. *The History of the British Film, 1918–1929*. Vol. 4. Bowker 1971 o.p. "A definitive history of the British film industry" (*Choice*).

May, John R., and Michael Byrd, eds. *Religion in Film*. Univ. of Tennessee Pr. 1982 $16.50

Michael, Paul. *The Academy Awards, 1927–1982*. Crown 4th ed. 1982 $17.95

Monaco, James. *American Film Now: The People, the Power, the Money, the Movies*. New Amer. Lib. 2d ed. 1984 $24.95

Murray, Edward. *Nine American Film Critics: A Study of Theory and Practice*. Ungar 1975 $16.50 pap. $6.95. "An analysis of nine writers chosen as 'representative' American film critics" (*LJ*).

Nesteby, James R. *Black Images in American Films, 1896–1954: The Interplay between Civil Rights and Film Culture*. Univ. Pr. of Amer. 1982 lib. bdg. $26.00 text ed. pap. $13.00

Nilsen, Vladimir. *The Cinema as a Graphic Art*. Farrar (Hill & Wang) 1984 $60.00. An important study on the use of the camera in filmmaking.

Sarris, Andrew. *Politics and Cinema*. Columbia Univ. Pr. 1978 $23.00

Schnitman, Jorge A. *Film Industries in Latin America: Dependency and Development*. Ablex 1984 $22.50

Silet, Charles L. *The Pretend Indians: Images of Native Americans in the Movies*. Iowa State Univ. Pr. 1980 pap. $10.95

Spottiswoode, Raymond. *The Focal Encyclopedia of Film and Television: Techniques*. Hastings 1974 $74.95

Stephenson, Ralph. *The Animated Film*. International Film Guide Ser. A. S. Barnes rev. ed. 1981 pap. $5.95

Taylor, Richard. *Film Propaganda: Nazi Germany and Soviet Russia*. Barnes & Noble 1979 $26.50

Thomas, Tony. *Harry Warren and the Hollywood Musical*. Citadel Pr. 1975 $17.95

Torrence, Bruce T. *Hollywood: The First 100 Years*. Zoetrope 1982 $24.95

Tyler, Parker. *A Pictorial History of Sex in Films*. Citadel Pr. 1974 $14.95

Walsh, Andrea. *Women's Film and Female Experience: 1940–50*. Praeger 1984 $22.95

Wasko, Janet. *Movies and Money: Financing the American Film Industry*. Ablex 1982 $27.50

Film Artists

Almendros, Nestor. *A Man with a Camera*. Pref. by François Truffaut, Farrar 1984 $15.95. Autobiography of a leading independent cinematographer.

Coursodon, J. P., and Pierre Sauvage. *American Directors*. McGraw-Hill 2 vols. 1983 ea. $21.95 pap. ea. $11.95

Crist, Judith, ed. *Take 22: Moviemakers on Moviemaking*. Viking 1984 $25.00. Twenty-two interviews with major stars and directors from the U.S. film industry.

Di Orio, Al. *Barbara Stanwyck: A Biography*. Coward-McCann 1984 $15.95

Downing, David. *Jack Nicholson*. Stein & Day 1984 $14.95

Dyer, Richard. *Stars*. British Film Institute 1979 pap. $7.95

Edmonds, I. G., and Reiko Mimura. *The Oscar Directors*. A. S. Barnes 1980 $17.95

Harmetz, Aljean. *The Making of the Wizard of Oz: Movie Magic and Studio Power in the Prime of MGM and the Miracle of Production*. Limelight Eds. repr. of 1977 ed. 1984 pap. $8.95

Higham, Charles. *Sisters: The Story of Olivia de Havilland and Joan Fontaine*. Coward-McCann 1984 $15.95

Kuhn, Annette. *Women's Pictures: Feminism and Cinema*. Routledge & Kegan 1982 pap. $10.50

Monaco, James. *Alain Resnais*. Oxford 1978 $22.50 1979 pap. $8.95. An important book about the pivotal French New Wave director.

Murray, Edward. *Nine American Film Critics: Study of Theory and Practice*. Ungar 1975 $16.50 pap. $6.95

Parish, James R. *Film Directors Guide: Western Europe*. Scarecrow Pr. 1976 $16.50

Pollock, Dale. *Skywalking: The Life and Films of George Lucas*. Harmony 1983 $15.95. "A very informative look at a success story that is as improbable as it is dramatic" (*LJ*).

Rotha, Paul. *Robert J. Flaherty: A Biography*. Univ. of Pennsylvania Pr. 1983 $25.00

Simmons, Garner. *Peckinpah: A Portrait in Montage*. Univ. of Texas Pr. 1984 $8.95

Thomson, David. *Biographical Dictionary of Film*. Morrow 2d ed. rev. 1981 $15.95

Truett, Evelyn Mack. *Who Was Who on Screen*. Bowker 3d ed 1984 $65.00 pap. $24.95

Windeler, Robert. *Burt Lancaster*. St. Martin's 1984 $12.95

ALLEN, WOODY. 1935–

[SEE Volume 1, Chapter 16.]

ANTONIONI, MICHELANGELO. 1912–

Michelangelo Antonioni of Italy, a former film critic and screenwriter, made his first feature film in 1954. He broke away from the neorealism then in vogue and, in a style rigorously disciplined, distinguished himself as an original artist by his concern with the interior states of isolated man. His subjects are often from the prosperous middle class and his only social criticism oblique. *L'Accentura*, his sixth film, established his fame. He is the director of *Blow-Up*, set in mod London. *Zabriski Point* concerns contemporary American youth and its politics.

BOOK BY ANTONIONI

Blow-Up. Modern Film Scripts Ser. Simon & Schuster 1970 $10.95 pap. $6.95

BOOKS ABOUT ANTONIONI

Lyons, Robert J. *Michelangelo Antonioni's Neo-Realism: A World View. Dissertations on Film Ser.* Ayer 1976 lib. bdg. $17.00

Rifkin, Ned. *Antonioni's Visual Language.* Ed. by Diane Kirkpatrick, *Studies in Cinema* UMI Research 1982 $39.95

BERGMAN, INGMAR. 1918–

Ingmar Bergman, Swedish screenwriter, playwright, and stage and film director and producer, is a major figure among contemporary "complete filmmakers." *The Seventh Seal* was the first of many films, sometimes poetic, often bleak and uncompromising in theme, that brought him international recognition. His subject is almost invariably the cosmic relationships of man and God, life and death. Always interesting although not always counted as wholly successful in what he has set out to do, Bergman has been one of those chiefly responsible for the present popularity of film among the student generation.

BOOKS BY BERGMAN

Four Screenplays: Smiles of a Summer Night, The Seventh Seal, Wild Strawberries, The Magician. Trans. by Lars Malmstrom and David Kushner, Simon & Schuster 1984 $50.00

The Seventh Seal. Lorrimer Classic Screenplay Ser. Ungar pap. $6.95

Wild Strawberries. Simon & Schuster 1969 $10.95 pap. $6.95

Persona and Shame. Grossman 1984 pap. $6.95

BOOKS ABOUT BERGMAN

Cowie, Peter. *Ingmar Bergman: A Critical Biography.* Scribner 1982 $19.95

Donner, Jorn. *The Personal Vision of Ingmar Bergman.* Trans. by Holger Lundbergh, Bks. for Libraries 1964 $20.25

Gibson, Arthur. *The Silence of God: Creative Response to the Films of Ingmar Bergman.* Mellen 1978 $9.95

Jones, G. William. *Talking with Ingmar Bergman.* Southern Methodist Univ. Pr. 1984 $25.00

Livingston, Paisley. *Ingmar Bergman and the Rituals of Art.* Cornell Univ. Pr. 1982 $24.50

Manvell, Roger. *Ingmar Bergman: An Appreciation. Dissertations on Film Ser.* Ayer 1980 $18.00

Marker, Lise-Lone, and Frederick J. Marker. *Ingmar Bergman. Directors in Perspective Ser.* Cambridge Univ. Pr. 1982 $39.50 pap. $12.95

Mosley, Philip. *Ingmar Bergman: The Cinema as Mistress.* Boyars 1981 $16.00

BOGART, HUMPHREY. 1899–1957

Bogart first achieved national acclaim as Duke Mantee in the film version of *The Petrified Forest* in 1936. After that success he played a succession of gangster (or other tough-guy) roles until he was able to shake off that image. Critics respected his outstanding performance in *The Maltese Falcon* and *Casablanca*, although he often made light of his talents. "He can drop his accurate English and fall into the clipped jargon of the underworld; he can snarl or cringe, and all apparently without effort" (*Current Biography*). He won an Academy Award in 1951 for his performance in *The African Queen*. Since his death, his films have found a tremendous following.

BOOKS ABOUT BOGART

McCarty, Clifford. *Bogey: The Films of Humphrey Bogart*. Citadel Pr. 1970 pap. $7.95
Pettigrew, Terrence. *Bogart: A Definitive Study of His Film Career*. Proteus 1981 pap. $8.95

BUÑUEL, LUIS. 1900–1983

Luis Buñuel made his first films with Salvador Dali, whom he met among other surrealists at Madrid University in the 1920s. *L'Age d'Or*, the second of these films, is considered a masterpiece and a major key to his later works. After 14 years of relative silence, he won the 1951 Cannes Film Festival director's prize for *Los Olvidados* and again for *Nazarin* in 1958. *Viridiana* and *Belle de Jour* established him as a major presence on the European film scene. Buñuel's films are often morbid and violent, sometimes macabre. His more recent films include *The Discreet Charm of the Bourgeoisie* and *The Phantom of Liberty*. His art does not purport to be subjective statement; most often he is merely carrying out producer's assignments.

BOOKS BY BUÑUEL

Belle de Jour. Modern Film Scripts Ser. Simon & Schuster 1970 $10.95 pap. $6.95
Tristana. Modern Film Scripts Ser. Simon & Schuster 1971 $10.95 pap. $6.95
Exterminating Angel: Los Olvidados and Nazarin. Modern Film Scripts Ser. Simon & Schuster 1972 $10.95 pap. $6.95
Luis Buñuel: Three Screen Plays. Cinema Class. Ser. Garland 1984 lib. bdg. $40.00

BOOKS ABOUT BUÑUEL

Aranda, Francisco. *Luis Buñuel: A Critical Biography*. Ed. by David Robinson, Da Capo repr. of 1975 ed. 1976 lib. bdg. $25.00 pap. $6.95
Buache, Freddy. *The Cinema of Luis Buñuel. International Film Guide Ser.* A. S. Barnes 1973 pap. $4.95
Durgnat, Raymond. *Luis Buñuel*. Univ. of California Pr. expanded rev. ed. 1978 pap. $4.95. "Mr. Durgnat eloquently explores the ambiguities and complexities of Buñuel's themes and symbols so that the flavor and character of his art vividly emerges. This is a splendidly conceived and executed critique of a film maker who is both poet and moralist, Freudian and Marxist, humanist and cynic" (*LJ*). Durgnat says of his subject: "Over thirty-six years from the hothouse of Parisian Surrealism through the wilderness of cheap Mexican comedies, to his grande epoque of international celebrity, [Buñuel's] films have explored a body of attitudes and experiences remarkable for its consistency."
Higginbotham, Virginia. *Luis Buñuel. Filmmakers Ser.* G. K. Hall 1979 lib. bdg. $13.50

CHAPLIN, SIR CHARLES (SPENCER). 1889–1977

Born in England, Charlie Chaplin acted in, directed, produced, and wrote his own films. In England he appeared in London music halls and then joined a pantomime group. During a tour of the United States, he came to the attention of Mack Sennett. Creator of the beloved "legendary tramp" for the Keystone Company, Chaplin remained with the company from 1914 to 1915. He founded United Artists in 1919 with D. W. Griffith, Douglas Fairbanks, and Mary Pickford. Among his most famous productions are *The Gold Rush, City Lights*, and *The Great Dictator*. In 1952, following criticism of his political and personal opinions, Chaplin settled in Switzerland.

BOOK BY CHAPLIN

My Autobiography. Simon & Schuster 1964 pap. $4.95

BOOKS ABOUT CHAPLIN

Bowman, Wodgeson. *Charlie Chaplin: His Life and Art.* Haskell 1974 $13.95

Francis, David, and Raoul Sobel. *Chaplin: Genesis of a Clown.* Charles River Bks. $5.95

Gehring, Wes D. *Charlie Chaplin: A Bio-Bibliography.* Greenwood 1983 $35.00

Huff, Theodore. *Charlie Chaplin.* Ayer repr. of 1951 ed. 1972 $30.00

Kamin, Dan. *Charlie Chaplin's One-Man Show.* Scarecrow Pr. 1984 $29.50

Manvell, Roger. *Chaplin.* Little, Brown 1974 $8.95 pap. $3.95

Molyneaux, Gerard. *Charles Chaplin's City Lights: Its Production and Dialectical Structure.* Ed. by Garth S. Jowett, *Dissertations on Film Ser.* Garland 1982 lib. bdg. $50.00

Robinson, David. *Chaplin: The Mirror of Opinion.* Indiana Univ. Pr. 1983 $19.50 pap. $9.50

Smith, Julian. *Chaplin. Filmmakers Ser.* G. K. Hall 1984 lib. bdg. $15.95

COCTEAU, JEAN. 1889–1963

A leader of the Paris avant-garde of the 1920s and 1930s, Cocteau began his film career—one of many outlets of his multiple talents—working in a surrealistic mode. Among his more famous productions are *Blood of a Poet* and *Beauty and the Beast*, an exciting surrealistic version of Perrault's fairy tale. At the age of 70 he directed his own "testament" in the film *Testament d'Orphée*. His early discovery of the "poetry" possible in the medium has had a revolutionary influence on the development of, for example, Godard—and of the underground film. (See also Volume 2, Chapter 9.)

BOOKS BY COCTEAU

Beauty and the Beast: Diary of a Film. Dover 1972 pap. $5.00

Cocteau on the Film. Trans. by Vera Traill, Dover 1972 $25.00

Cocteau on the Film: Conversations with Jean Cocteau Recorded by André Fraigneau. Cinema Class. Ser. Garland 1984 lib. bdg. $25.00

Cocteau's World. Humanities Pr. text ed. 1972 $21.25

Books about Cocteau

Ashton, Dore, and others. *Jean Cocteau and the French Scene.* Ed. by Alexandra Anderson, Abbeville Pr. 1984 $19.95

Crosland, Margaret. *Jean Cocteau.* Darby repr. of 1955 ed. lib. bdg. $30.00

Evans, Arthur B. *Jean Cocteau and His Films of Orphic Identity.* Art Alliance 1974 $22.50

DISNEY, WALT. 1901–1966

Walt Disney first gained fame with his cartoon creations, Mickey Mouse and Donald Duck, and with feature-length animated films like *Snow White and the Seven Dwarfs, Fantasia, Pinocchio, Bambi, Alice in Wonderland,* and *Lady and the Tramp.* In the 1950s he filmed a number of nature films that were very popular and informative—*Seal Island, Nature's Half Acre, The Living Desert,* and *The Vanishing Prairie.* His production company was also successful with television shows like "The Mickey Mouse Club," "Davy Crockett," and "The Wonderful World of Disney." He won numerous Academy Awards and other honors.

Books about Disney

Finch, Christopher. *The Art of Walt Disney: Companion Edition.* Abrams 1975 $15.95

Lynn, Gartley, and Elizabeth Leebron. *Walt Disney: A Guide to References and Resources.* G. K. Hall 1979 lib. bdg. $31.50

Maltin, Leonard. *The Disney Films.* Crown rev. ed. 1984 pap. $10.95

Thomas, Frank, and Ollie Johnston. *Disney Animation: The Illusion of Life.* Abbeville Pr. text ed. 1981 $75.00

EISENSTEIN, SERGEI. 1898–1948

Potemkin, a silent film that appeared in 1925, was the great Russian film director's first brilliant "mass epic," originally commissioned just after the 1918 Russian Revolution to commemorate the 1905 anti-Czarist uprising. In it, he developed his "shock-attraction" technique, of which the most famous example is the slaughter on the great flight of steps in Odessa and the slow descent of a baby in its carriage through the carnage. For a while Eisenstein worked in Hollywood. He often found himself at odds with the Soviet government, but in his brief life he brought glory to the Soviet people, particularly in *Potemkin, Ten Days That Shook the World, Alexander Nevsky,* and part I of *Ivan the Terrible.* Part II was withheld by the Soviet Film Trust because of government disfavor and later released; part III was never completed.

Books by Eisenstein

Film Form. Harcourt 1969 pap. $6.95

Film Sense. Harcourt 1969 pap. $5.95

Film Essays with a Lecture. Trans. by Jay Leyda, Praeger 1970 $25.00 pap. $6.95

Notes of a Film Director. Trans. by X. Danko, Dover rev. ed. 1970 $9.25

Immoral Memories: An Autobiography. Houghton Mifflin 1983 $19.95

Ivan the Terrible. Lorrimer Class. Screenplay Ser. Ungar $12.95 pap. $8.95

BOOKS ABOUT EISENSTEIN

Leyda, Jay, and Zina Voynow. *Eisenstein at Work.* Pantheon 1982 $20.00 pap. $15.95
Nizhny, Vladimir. *Lessons with Eisenstein.* Farrar (Hill & Wang) 1962 pap. $5.95
Thompson, K. *Eisenstein's Ivan the Terrible: A Neoformalist Analysis.* Princeton Univ.
     Pr. 1981 $35.00 pap. $12.50

FELLINI, FEDERICO. 1920–

Federico Fellini is known for his unique style, developed early in his career, with its ornate visual effects, uninhibited sentiment, mischievous humor, and private romantic fantasy. He first attracted attention abroad with *I Vitelloni* and with *La Strada,* which focuses on the poor, but in a deeply sensitive manner, touched with poetry. The latter brought him international success, as did *La Dolce Vita,* with its portrait of the rich and rootless in a decadent Rome, and the autobiographical *8½.* Fellini's penchant for obscurity, his symbolism and sharp satire (of the church, for example) have made him from time to time controversial, but his imaginative impact is uncontested.

BOOKS ABOUT FELLINI

Benderson, Albert E. *Critical Approaches to Federico Fellini's "8½."* Dissertations on
     Film Ser. Ayer 1974 $15.00
Bonandella, Peter. *Federico Fellini: Essays in Criticism.* Oxford 1978 pap. $8.95
Burke, Frank. *Federico Fellini: "Variety Lights" to "La Dolce Vita."* Filmmakers Ser.
     G. K. Hall 1984 lib. bdg. $19.95
Price, Barbara, and Theodore Price. *Federico Fellini: An Annotated International Bibli-*
     ography. Scarecrow Pr. 1978 $17.50
Stubbs, John C., and others, eds. *Federico Fellini: A Guide to References and Re-*
     sources. G. K. Hall 1978 lib. bdg. $33.50

FIELDS, W(ILLIAM) C(LAUDE). 1879–1946

W. C. Fields was a vaudevillian for many years and later joined the Ziegfield Follies. He entered films in 1925, working mainly for Paramount. He wrote many of his later filmscripts under a pseudonym (sometimes using the name Otis Criblecoblis) and is known for his comic roles in films such as *The Bank Dick, My Little Chickadee,* and *Never Give a Sucker an Even Break.*

BOOK ABOUT FIELDS

Deschner, Donald. *Films of W. C. Fields.* Citadel Pr. $12.00 pap. $7.95

FORD, JOHN. 1895–1973

Ford directed almost 200 feature films. He won Academy Awards for *The Informer* (1935), *The Grapes of Wrath* (1940), *How Green Was My Valley* (1941), and *The Quiet Man* (1952). His legendary Westerns often starred John Wayne, Ward Bond, and Victor McLaglen.

BOOKS ABOUT FORD

Bogdanovich, Peter. *John Ford*. Univ. of California Pr. expanded rev. ed. 1978 pap. $4.95. Based on on-the-scene interviews with the director, this volume represents an "almost ideal approach to John Ford" (*LJ*).

McBride, Joseph, and Michael Wilmington. *John Ford*. Da Capo 1975 $22.50

Place, J. A. *The Western Films of John Ford*. Citadel Pr. 1974 $12.00. "The critiques of Ford's 17 Westerns emphasize the element of legend and romance that sweeps through all of his works be it *Stagecoach*—called by many critics the best Western ever made—or *She Wore a Yellow Ribbon*" (*LJ*).

GODARD, JEAN-LUC. 1930–

Jean-Luc Godard is hailed as the most original director of the 1960s. A former critic for *Les Cahiers du Cinema*, Godard has become a liberating force for young filmmakers, his work being popular chiefly among the small, youthful coterie he seeks to attract. In 1959 he made his directorial debut with *Breathless*, which broke new ground and was an immediate international success. Sometimes criticized for an "iconoclastic" and "anarchistic" use of his medium, the New Wave director produces films that are fast-moving, choppy, witty, informal—indeed, a wild collage of contrasting modes. But he has them under absolute control and is, says critic Stanley Kauffmann, a "director to the medium born." His other films include *Alphaville*, *La Chinoise*, and *Weekend*.

BOOKS BY GODARD

Alphaville. Trans. by Peter Whitehead, *Modern Film Scripts Ser.* Simon & Schuster 1968 $10.95 pap. $6.95

Pierrot LeFou. Modern Film Scripts Ser. Simon & Schuster 1969 $10.95 pap. $6.95

Le Petit Soldat. Modern Film Scripts Ser. Simon & Schuster 1971 $10.95 pap. $6.95

Weekend and Wind from the East. Modern Film Scripts Ser. Simon & Schuster 1972 $17.95 pap. $8.95

BOOKS ABOUT GODARD

Kreidl, John. *Jean-Luc Godard. Filmmakers Ser.* G. K. Hall 1980 lib. bdg. $13.50

Lesage, Julia. *Jean-Luc Godard: A Guide to References and Resources*. G. K. Hall 1979 lib. bdg. $47.00

MacCabe, Colin. *Godard: Images, Sounds, Politics*. Indiana Univ. Pr. 1980 $22.50

GRIFFITH, D(AVID) W(ARK). 1875–1948

D. W. Griffith began his career as an actor and writer with the Biograph Company. With *The Birth of a Nation* in 1915, he became the father of filmmaking in the United States. He is responsible for developing many innovative techniques, including the long shot, the closeup, the full shot, the fade-in, the fade-out, and the montage, and in 1921, he was the first to use dialogue in a feature film. With Chaplin, Douglas Fairbanks, and Mary Pickford, he was one of the founders of United Artists in 1919. Today *The Birth of a Nation* is considered by many to be reactionary.

BOOKS ABOUT GRIFFITH

Brown, Karl. *Adventures with D. W. Griffith*. Ed. by Kevin Brownlow, Da Capo 1976 pap. $6.95; Farrar 1973 $10.00. "Brown writes with humor, humanity, and historical sense—but more important, . . . in a prose that attempts to recapture something of what it was to be 17 and in on the birth of movie art" (*Choice*).

Fleener-Marzec, Nickieann. *D. W. Griffith's The Birth of a Nation: Controversy, Suppression, and the First Amendment as It Applies to Filmic Expression, 1915–1973*. Ed. by Garth S. Jowett, *Dissertations on Film Ser.* Ayer 1980 lib. bdg. $56.50

Henderson, Robert M. *D. W. Griffith: His Life and Work*. Oxford 1972 $50.00

Niver, Kemp R. *D. W. Griffith: His Biograph Films in Perspective*. Historical Films 1974 $15.00

Williams, Martin. *Griffith: First Artist of the Movies*. Oxford 1980 $17.95

HARDY, OLIVER. 1892–1957

[SEE LAUREL, STAN, in this section.]

HITCHCOCK, ALFRED. 1899–1980

Born in England, Alfred Hitchcock was a director, writer, and producer of suspense films, beginning in the 1930s. Often, he played a small role in his films. He reached prominence with his *39 Steps* in 1935. Three years later, he began working in the United States. Hitchcock's techniques, first encountered by a wide public in *The Lady Vanishes* in 1938, greatly influenced directors of the 1950s and 1960s. He was one of those rare artists who was at once experimental and commercially popular from the start. Some of Hitchcock's successes include *Vertigo*, *Psycho*, and *The Birds*.

BOOKS ABOUT HITCHCOCK

Durgnat, Raymond. *The Strange Case of Alfred Hitchcock; or The Plain Man's Hitchcock*. MIT 1974 pap. $9.95

Haley, Michael. *The Alfred Hitchcock Album*. Prentice-Hall 1981 $17.95 pap. $9.95

Noble, Peter. *Alfred Hitchcock*. Gordon 1979 lib. bdg. $69.95

Phillips, Gene D. *Alfred Hitchcock. Filmmakers Ser.* G. K. Hall 1984 lib. bdg. $16.95

Rohmer, Eric, and Claude Chabrol. *Hitchcock: The First Forty-Four Films. Ungar Film Lib.* 1979 $12.95 pap. $6.95

Rotham, William. *Hitchcock: The Murderous Gaze*. Harvard Univ. Pr. 1982 pap. $10.95

Truffaut, François. *Hitchcock*. Simon & Schuster 1969 pap. $11.95 rev. ed. 1984 $19.95. "One of the most revealing and engrossing books on film art, technique and history ever put together" (*N.Y. Times*).

KUBRICK, STANLEY. 1928–

Stanley Kubrick is an American film director with an extremely diversified list of films to his credit. His work includes *2001: A Space Odyssey*, *Paths of Glory*, *Lolita*, *Doctor Strangelove*, and *A Clockwork Orange*. According to *Time*, "He enjoys the rare right to final cut of his film without studio advice or interference. . . . About his work Kubrick is the most self-conscious and rational of men. His eccentricities—secretiveness, a great need for privacy— are caused by his intense awareness of time's relentless passage."

BOOKS ABOUT KUBRICK

Ciment, Michel. *Kubrick*. Trans. by Gilbert Adair, Holt 1983 $25.00
Coyle, Wallace. *Stanley Kubrick: A Guide to Reference and Resources*. G. K. Hall 1980
     lib. bdg. $27.50
Nelson, Thomas A. *Kubrick: Inside a Film Artist's Maze*. Indiana Univ. Pr. 1983
     $37.50 pap. $9.95
Walker, Alexander. *Stanley Kubrick Directs*. Harcourt enl. ed. 1972 pap. $8.95

KUROSAWA, AKIRA. 1910–

Kurosawa is generally recognized as the best of the Japanese filmmakers.
He was the first native of his country to gain international recognition in
this field—for *Rashomon*, which received first prize at the Venice Film Festival in 1951, and *The Magnificent Seven*. Since 1960 Kurosawa has headed
his own production company in Tokyo.

BOOKS BY KUROSAWA

Ikiru. Lorrimer Classic Screenplay Ser. Ungar $10.95 pap. $8.95
Seven Samurai. Lorrimer Classic Screenplay Ser. Ungar $12.95 pap. $9.95

BOOK ABOUT KUROSAWA

Richie, Donald. *The Films of Akira Kurosawa*. Univ. of California Pr. rev. ed. 1984
     pap. $12.95. "It can be said confidently that this is the best study yet made of a
     film director's work" (*LJ*). The volume is handsomely and lavishly illustrated
     with stills from the films of this Japanese director, the most famous of which
     are *Rashomon* and *Yojimbo*. The book includes an excellent filmography.

LAUREL, STAN. 1890–1965, and OLIVER HARDY. 1892–1957

One of the most popular American comedy teams, Laurel and Hardy have
an enduring popularity. Laurel began as a music hall performer in London
and later appeared in vaudeville as a comic; Hardy began as a silent screen
actor in Hollywood. The two met by chance in 1926 and began their partnership, first with many short films. The pair won an Academy Award in 1933
for best short subject for *The Music Box*.

BOOKS ABOUT LAUREL AND HARDY

Barr, Charles. *Laurel and Hardy*. Univ. of California Pr. 1968 pap. $2.95
Everson, Bill. *Films of Laurel and Hardy*. Citadel Pr. 1969 $12.00 pap. $9.95
Guiles, Fred L. *Stan: The Life of Stan Laurel*. Stein & Day 1980 $12.95
Scagnetti, Jack. *Laurel and Hardy Scrapbook*. Jonathan David 1982 pap. $8.95

THE MARX BROTHERS

The Marx Brothers—Groucho, Chico, Harpo, and Zeppo (who left the
group in 1933)—were the zany comic team of the 1930s and 1940s who won
popular as well as "highbrow" success with their brilliant combination of
pantomime, verbal wit, and slapstick. Chico performed at the piano, the
mute Harpo at his harp, while Groucho did the fast talking. Their fans remember particularly *Animal Crackers, A Night at the Opera, A Day at the*

Races, and *Monkey Business*. During the 1950s, Groucho had a popular television quiz program, called "You Bet Your Life."

BOOKS BY THE MARX BROTHERS

Monkey Business and Duck Soup. Class. Film Scripts Ser. Simon & Schuster 1972 pap. $10.95
Groucho and Me. Manor Bks. 1978 pap. $1.95. Autobiography of Groucho Marx.

BOOK ABOUT THE MARX BROTHERS

Eyles, Allen. *The Marx Brothers: Their World of Comedy*. A. S. Barnes 1966 pap. $4.95

MONROE, MARILYN. 1926–1962

Monroe first achieved star billing in 1952 in several films for RKO; less than a year later she was the highest-paid actress in Hollywood. She later starred in *Gentlemen Prefer Blondes, How to Marry a Millionaire, The Seven Year Itch*, and *River of No Return*. Married and divorced several times, she died of an overdose of barbiturates in 1962.

BOOKS ABOUT MONROE

Conway, Michael, and Mark Ricci. *The Films of Marilyn Monroe*. Citadel Pr. 1968 $12.00 pap. $7.95
Spada, James, and George Zeno. *Monroe: Her Life in Pictures*. Doubleday 1982 $14.95
Speriglio, Milo A. *Marilyn Monroe: Murder Cover-Up*. Seville 1983 pap. $7.95
Taylor, Roger. *Marilyn Monroe in Her Own Words*. Delilah Bks. 1983 pap. $6.95

TRUFFAUT, FRANÇOIS. 1932–1984

Truffaut was at one time critic for the avant-garde magazine *Les Cahiers du Cinema*. An admirer of American feature films, he was much influenced by Hitchcock. His own films, among which *The Four Hundred Blows* is one of the most popular, employ the New Wave techniques of a personally expressive camera. Truffaut's other films include *Shoot the Piano Player* and *Day for Night*.

BOOK BY TRUFFAUT

Jules and Jim. Trans. by Nicholas Fry, *Modern Film Scripts Ser*. Simon & Schuster 1968 $10.95 pap. $6.95

BOOKS ABOUT TRUFFAUT

Insdorf, Annette. *François Truffaut*. Filmmakers Ser. G. K. Hall 1978 lib. bdg. $12.50; fwd. by Warren French, Morrow 1979 pap. $4.95
Walz, Eugene P. *François Truffaut: A Guide to References and Resources*. G. K. Hall 1982 lib. bdg. $37.50

VISCONTI, LUCHINO. 1906–1976

Visconti achieved worldwide fame as one of the triumvirate (with Fellini and Antonioni) of great Italian directors. He has been called the father of the Italian neorealistic school. "Just as Visconti combines his aristocratic heritage with a deep social commitment, so does his art blend extreme realism with a sense of the colorful and the spectacular" (*Contemporary Biography*). His films include *La Terra Treme*, *The Damned*, and *Death in Venice*.

BOOKS BY VISCONTI

Luchino Visconti—Three Screenplays: White Nights, Rocco and His Brothers, The Job. Trans. by Judith Green, Grossman 1970 $40.00

Luchino Visconti—Two Screenplays: La Terra Treme, Senso. Trans. by Judith Green, Grossman 1971 $35.00

VON STERNBERG, JOSEPH. 1894–1969

Born in Vienna, von Sternberg came to the United States at 17 and went to Hollywood, where he took on various writing and directorial tasks. His greatest successes were *Morocco*, *Shanghai Express*, and *American Tragedy*. He returned to Germany to direct his most famous film, *The Blue Angel*, starring Marlene Dietrich and Emil Jannings.

BOOKS BY VON STERNBERG

(and Heinrich Mann). *The Blue Angel. Class. Film Scripts Ser.* Simon & Schuster 1968 $13.50 pap. $7.95

Shanghai Express and Morocco. Class. Film Scripts Ser. Simon & Schuster 1972 $12.95 pap. $8.95

Macao. RKO Class. Screenplay Ser. Ungar 1984 $14.95 pap. $8.95

BOOKS ABOUT VON STERNBERG

Baxter, Peter. *Sternberg. British Film Institute Bks.* Univ. of Illinois Pr. 1980 $14.50 pap. $7.95

Weinberg, Herman G. *Joseph von Sternberg.* Dutton 1976 $30.00

VON STROHEIM, ERICH. 1885–1957

The Austrian-born film figure was known abroad and on the Hollywood scene as an uncompromising artist. An actor during and after World War I, usually playing the sadistic seducer or the villainous German officer, he directed his first film in 1919. *Greed* in 1925 was the climax at once of his style of fastidious realism and of his career-long battle with his producers, who objected to the expense of his work and to the all-too-modern morality of his films. When, in the 1940s, producers became unwilling to employ his directing talents, von Stroheim returned to acting. He was nominated for the 1950 Academy Award for best supporting actor in *Sunset Boulevard*.

BOOK BY VON STROHEIM

Greed: A Reconstruction of the Complete Erich von Stroheim Film from Stills. Ed. by Herman G. Weinberg, Arno 1972 $50.00; Dutton 1973 pap. $9.95

BOOKS ABOUT VON STROHEIM

Finler, Joel. *Stroheim.* Univ. of California Pr. 1968 pap. $2.45

Noble, Peter. *Hollywood Scapegoat: The Biography of Erich von Stroheim.* Arno 1972 $18.00

Weinberg, Herman G. *Stroheim: A Pictorial Record of His Films.* Peter Smith $10.25. "A work of lasting value" (*Choice*).

WELLES, ORSON. 1915–1985

Welles was an innovative American actor, director, and producer. In 1938, he created a national sensation with his radio broadcast adaptation of H. G. Wells's *War of the Worlds.* In 1941, he wrote, produced, directed, and starred in his most famous film, *Citizen Kane,* regarded by many critics as the best film in motion picture history. His later films were less successful.

BOOK BY WELLES

Trial. Modern Film Scripts Ser. Simon & Schuster 1970 $10.95 pap. $6.95

BOOKS ABOUT WELLES

Cantril, Hadley. *Invasion from Mars: A Study in the Psychology of Panic.* Harper 1966 o.p.; Princeton Univ. Pr. 1982 $27.00 pap. $9.95
Higham, Charles. *The Films of Orson Welles.* Univ. of California Pr. 1970 $19.95
McBride, Joseph. *Orson Welles.* Secker & Warburg 1972 $11.95

CHAPTER 14

Folklore and Humor

Wendell Tripp

> Within all human societies, whether savage or civilized, we may naturally
> expect to find old beliefs, old customs, old memories, which are relics of an
> unrecorded past. Such sayings and doings, wherever found . . . have the
> common "note," that they are sanctioned and perpetuated . . . by habit and
> tradition. And the scientific study of folklore consists in bringing modern
> scientific methods . . . to bear upon forms of Tradition, just as they have
> been brought to bear upon other phenomena.
> —CHARLOTTE S. BURNE, *The Handbook of Folklore*

The term "Folk-Lore" was coined in 1864 by an Englishman, William J.
Thoms, to replace "popular antiquities" or "popular literature" as a more
precise description for the study of the manners, customs, songs and tales,
and beliefs of the general population. The British Folk-Lore Society was established in 1878 and the American Folk-Lore Society ten years later. By
the end of the century, folklore had become a distinct, if inconsistently defined, field of learning in the major countries of the world.

U.S. and British folklorists, as the term "lore" suggests, tended to emphasize literary traditions, while European practitioners extended the study to
include a people's culture in general—from architectural styles to law, religion, education, and other established functions of national life. Germans,
in fact, preferred the term *Volkskunde*, to include physical as well as oral
manifestations of tradition.

In the decades before World War II, folklore in the United States remained a vaguely defined discipline. Most of its practitioners came from
other fields of study, especially anthropology, literature, social history, philosophy, sociology, and musicology. Many were amateur students of various
traditions, and despite the efforts of individual leaders, the field lacked order and cohesiveness. Certain universities began to offer courses in folklore,
but the instructor was usually a member of the school's English or anthropology department. This situation changed rapidly during the 1940s, especially after the war, when an increasing number of colleges established folklore as an undergraduate major and then as a program of graduate study.
Indiana University granted the first Ph.D. in folklore in 1953. Several other
universities—including the University of California at Los Angeles, George
Washington University, the University of Pennsylvania, and the University
of Texas—created doctoral programs. Professional folklorists developed so-

phisticated indexing systems and systems of classification, applied rigorous guidelines to the collecting of data, and employed statistics and other scientific tools in the analysis of raw data. The 1970s witnessed, in the words of the late Richard M. Dorson, a "folklore boom" (*Journal of the Folklore Institute*), and if the boom has subsided the field remains vigorous, certainly well established, in the 1980s.

Because it became a generic term, "folklore" to the general public often connotes mere nostalgia or a belief in something untrue. Certain popular writers and singers have compounded the confusion by actually creating folktales and folk songs, a practice that Dorson labels "fakelore." Folklorists themselves still do not agree on a general theory of folklore. Some consider it a humanity, others a social science, still others consider it one of the behavioral sciences. Some folklorists still specialize in oral and literary tradition, others study such specific topics as styles in houses or barns or quilts, or less concrete topics like group behavior. Some emphasize the historical context of their data; others believe that all source material provides its own context. They agree completely, however, on the need for precision and accuracy in collecting data, and intellectual honesty in analyzing it. They are not antiquarians. Their work as a whole deals not with isolated curiosities, but with events and patterns that shed light on the human condition.

GENERAL WORKS AND REFERENCE TITLES

The works in this section offer an introduction to the field of folklore and include histories of the subject, guides to folklore methodology, anthologies, textbooks, bibliographies, and encyclopedias. Reference works on single types of folklore, such as folk song or legend, will be found in the subsequent sections of this chapter.

General Works

Bett, Henry. *Nursery Rhymes and Tales: Their Origin and History.* Folcroft lib. bdg. $17.50; Gale repr. of 1924 ed. 1968 $34.00; Gordon $59.95

Brunvand, Jan H. *Folklore: A Handbook for Study and Research.* St. Martin's 1976 text ed. pap. $6.95. Written for college students, but useful to anyone interested in learning the history and methods of folklore and folklorists.

Clarkson, Atelia, and Gilbert B. Cross. *World Folktales: A Scribner Resource Collection.* Scribner 1984 $19.95 pap. $12.95

Coffin, Tristram P., and Hennig Cohen, eds. *Folklore in America.* Doubleday (Anchor) 1970 pap. $4.95

Cox, George W. *An Introduction to the Science of Comparative Mythology and Folklore.* 1881. Gale repr. of 1883 ed. 1968 $34.00; Gordon lib. bdg. $69.95. Still a useful analysis of mythology based on examination of Asian and European myths.

Dorson, Richard M. *America in Legend: Folklore from the Colonial Period to the Present.* Pantheon 1973 pap. $12.95. Fully documented and written in a readable style that makes the book useful to professions and to the general reader.

———. *Folklore and Fakelore: Essays toward a Discipline of Folk Studies.* Harvard Univ. Pr. 1976 $22.50

————, ed. *Folklore and Folklife: An Introduction.* Univ. of Chicago Pr. 1972 $16.50
1982 pap. $10.00. This book "maintains a professional, research-oriented tone
and still manages to be exciting, readable, and filled with quaint and interesting facts" (*LJ*).

————. *Handbook of American Folklore.* Intro. by W. Edson Richmond, Indiana Univ.
Pr. 1983 $35.00. A monumental collection of essays by leading scholars. Dis-
cusses the relationship between anthropology and literature in folklore. Includes tributes to such pioneers as Thompson, Leach, Boatright, Halpert, and
Hand.

Dundes, Alan. *Interpreting Folklore.* Indiana Univ. Pr. 1980 $25.00 pap. $9.95. Thirteen essays by Dundes that offer interpretations of folklore terms, methods, and
applications.

————. *The Study of Folklore.* Prentice-Hall text ed. 1965 $21.95

Goldstein, Kenneth S. *A Guide for Field Workers in Folklore.* Pref. by Hamish Henderson, Gale repr. 1964 $35.00 pap. $20.00. This "first systematic guide to field collecting techniques published in the United States . . . serves as an introduction
to the materials and problems of folklore collection and documentation for the
beginner and the amateur . . ." (B. A. Botkin, *N.Y. Folklore Quarterly*).

Newall, Venetia J., ed. *Folklore Studies in the Twentieth Century: Proceedings of the
Centenary Conference of the Folklore Society.* Rowman 1980 $85.00

Propp, Vladimir. *Theory and History of Folklore. Theory and History of Lit. Ser.* Intro.
by Anatoly Liberman, Univ. of Minnesota Pr. 1984 $29.50 pap. $12.95

Quimby, Ian M., and Scott T. Swank, eds. *Perspectives on American Folk Art.* Norton
$21.95 pap. $9.95

Richmond, Winthrop E., ed. *Studies in Folklore: In Honor of Distinguished Service
Professor Stith Thompson.* Greenwood repr. of 1957 ed. 1972 o.p.

Toelken, Barre. *The Dynamics of Folklore.* Houghton Mifflin 1979 $21.95. Directed to
classroom use, but attractively illustrated, clearly written, and offers any reader
an introduction to the subject and to the methods and concerns of modern folklorists.

Yoder, Don, ed. *American Folklife.* Univ. of Texas Pr. 1976 $22.50. Includes 12 essays
by Don Yoder, Ward H. Goodenough, James Marston Fitch, Fred B. Kniffen, Leslie P. Greenhill, William B. Knipmeyer (whose essay was edited, with an introduction by Henry Glassie), Gerald L. Davis, Warren E. Roberts, David J. Winslow, James L. Evans, Walter L. Robbins, and Jacob D. Elder.

General Reference

Baughman, Ernest W. *Type and Motif Index of the Folktales of England and North
America.* Humanities Pr. 1966 $56.00

Bronner, Simon J. *American Folk Art: A Guide to Sources. Reference Lib. of the Humanities* Garland 1984 lib. bdg. $30.00

Daniels, Cora L., and C. M. Stevans, eds. *Encyclopedia of Superstitions, Folklore and
the Occult Sciences of the World.* Gale 3 vols. repr. of 1903 ed. 1971 $107.00

Flanagan, Cathleen C., and John T. Flanagan. *American Folklore: A Bibliography,
1950–1974.* Scarecrow Pr. 1977 $22.50

Jobes, Gertrude. *Dictionary of Mythology, Folklore and Symbols.* Scarecrow Pr. 3 vols.
1961 $85.00

Jones, Steven S. *Folklore and Literature in the U.S.: An Annotated Bibliography of Studies of Folklore in American Literature.* Ed. by Alan Dundes, *Folklore Bibliographies
Ser.* Garland 1984 lib. bdg. $35.00

FOLK SONG AND DANCE

The works listed in this section include general reference books on the subjects of folk song and folk dance, as well as books on geographical and national collections of song and dance, and critical studies of song and dance as genre. Some U.S. regional and ethnic titles are included here, but see also the section "U.S. Regional and Ethnic Folklore," which includes "Afro-American Folklore."

Banerji, P. *Aesthetics of Indian Folk Dance.* Humanities Pr. 1983 $33.50

Baring-Gould, Sabine. *A Garland of Country Song: English Folk Songs with Their Traditional Melodies.* Arden Lib. repr. of 1895 ed. 1980 lib. bdg. $15.00; Folcroft repr. of 1895 ed. 1976 lib. bdg. $15.00; Gordon $59.95

Bartok, Bela. *The Hungarian Folk Song.* Ed. by Benjamin Suchoff, trans. by M. D. Calvocoressi, *Bartok Studies in Musicology* State Univ. of New York Pr. 1980 $59.50 pap. $19.50

Blom, Jan B., and others, eds. *Norwegian Folk Music.* Columbia Univ. Pr. 1981 $65.00

Brand, Oscar. *The Ballad Mongers: Rise of the Modern Folk Song.* Greenwood repr. of 1962 ed. 1979 lib. bdg. $22.50. "A lively, gossipy, informative off-the-cuff personal history of the folksong revival, its sources and popularity. The book gains in immediacy what it loses in objectivity from folksinger, composer and impresario Brand's involvement in all popular phases of the movement" (B. A. Botkin, *N.Y. Folklore Quarterly*).

Breathnach, Breandan. *Folk Music and Dances of Ireland.* Irish Bk. Ctr. rev. ed. 1977 pap. $5.95; Irish Bks. repr. of 1971 ed. 1983 pap. $6.95

Buffington, Albert F. *Pennsylvania German Secular Folk Songs.* Pennsylvania German Society 1974 $15.00

Causley, Charles, ed. *Modern Folk Ballads.* Pocket Poets Ser. Dufour 1966 pap. $2.00

Child, Francis J. *English and Scottish Popular Ballads.* Dover 5 vols. 1965 pap. ea. $7.50. Child's aim was to include "every obtainable version of every extant English or Scottish ballad, with the fullest possible discussion of related songs or stories in the popular literature of all nations." He had nearly completed it—in ten parts—at his death.

Christeson, R. P. *The Old Time Fiddler's Repertory: 245 Traditional Tunes.* Univ. of Missouri Pr. 1973 pap. $15.95

Cohen, Anne B. *Poor Pearl, Poor Girl: The Murdered Girl Stereotype in Ballad and Newspaper.* Amer. Folklore Society Memoir Ser. Univ. of Texas Pr. 1973 pap. $5.95. An exhaustive study of ballads that were based on the murder and beheading of a pregnant woman from Greencastle, Indiana. A good example of a modern folklorist at work as Cohen explores historical and cultural influences.

Cohen, Norm. *Long Steel Rail: The Railroad in American Folksong. Music in Amer. Life Ser.* Univ. of Illinois Pr. 1984 pap. $17.50. "Cohen's narrative and interpretations, his discographical detail, the song texts and tune transcriptions, together with a variety of illustrative materials and extensive bibliography make this book an indispensable one for all scholars of railroad history and folklore as well as for those of blues and hillbilly music" (Ivan Tribe, *Journal of Amer. Folklore*).

Cook, Harold E. *Shaker Music: A Manifestation of American Folk Culture.* Bucknell Univ. Pr. 1973 $25.00

Ferris, William, and Mary L. Hart, eds. *Folk Music and Modern Sound.* Univ. Pr. of Mississippi 1981 pap. $7.95

Forucci, Samuel L. *A Folk Song History of America: America through Its Songs.* Prentice-Hall 1984 $22.95 pap. $14.95

Fowke, Edith. *Lumbering Songs from the Northern Woods. Amer. Folklore Society Memoir Ser.* Univ. of Texas Pr. 1970 $9.95

Gilbert, Cecile. *International Folk Dance at a Glance.* Burgess 2d ed. 1974 $11.95

Glassie, Henry, and others. *Folksongs and Their Makers.* Bowling Green 1971 pap. $5.00

Green, Archie. *Only a Miner: Studies in Recorded Coal Mining Songs. Music in Amer. Life Ser.* Univ. of Illinois Pr. 1972 $20.00 text ed. pap. $8.95. "Few scholars are simultaneously disciplined in labor history, pop lore, American folk balladry, and hillbilly/blues discography, and Green does an admirable job of holding the reader's interest and providing him with the necessary background, whether he be expert or novice in the fields concerned . . ." (Norm Cohen, *Journal of Amer. Folklore*).

Hague, Eleanor, comp. *Spanish-American Folk-Songs.* Kraus repr. of 1917 ed. $15.00. Ninety-five Spanish folk songs from California, Arizona, Mexico, Cuba, Puerto Rico, and Central and South America.

Indiana University, Folklore Institute, Archives of Traditional Music. *A Catalog of Phonorecording of Music and Oral Data Held by the Archives of Traditional Music.* G. K. Hall 1976 $31.50

Isaku, Patia R. *Mountain Storm, Pine Breeze: Folk Song in Japan.* Univ. of Arizona Pr. 1981 $12.95 pap. $6.50

Jackson, George P. *Another Sheaf of White Spirituals.* Ed. by Kenneth S. Goldstein, pref. by Dan Yoder, *Publications in Folksong and Balladry Ser.* Folklorica Pr. repr. of 1952 ed. 1982 pap. $15.95; Wildman Pr. 1982 pap. $15.95

Joukowsky, Anatol M. *The Teaching of Ethnic Dance.* Ayer repr. of 1965 ed. 1980 lib. bdg. $19.00

Karpeles, Maud, and Cecil J. Sharp, eds. *Eighty Appalachian Folk Songs.* Faber 1983 pap. $5.95

Kennedy, Peter, ed. *Folksongs of Britain and Ireland.* Schirmer Bks. 1975 $35.00

Kidson, Frank, and Mary Neal. *English Folk-Song and Dance.* 1915. Rowman 1972 $10.00

Lawless, Ray M. *Folksingers and Folksongs in America: A Handbook of Biography, Bibliography and Discography.* Greenwood repr. of 1965 ed. 1981 lib. bdg. $49.50. An indispensable volume for libraries, this edition includes corrections, a supplement, new biographies, descriptions of books and magazines in the field, a selective list of records, and other material.

Leach, R., and R. Palmer, eds. *Folk Music in School. Resources of Music Ser.* Cambridge Univ. Pr. 1978 $19.95 pap. $9.95

Lifton, Sarah. *Listener's Guide to Folk Music.* Facts on File 1983 $11.95

Lomax, Alan. *The Folk Songs of North America.* Doubleday 1960 pap. $14.95

——, ed. *The Folk Song Style and Culture.* Transaction Bks. repr. of 1968 ed. 1978 pap. $6.95

Malone, Bill C. *Country Music, U.S.A.: A Fifty Year History. Amer. Folklore Society Memoir Ser.* Univ. of Texas Pr. 1969 pap. $9.95

Parsons, Kitty. *Gloucester Sea Ballads.* Fermata 2d ed. rev. repr. of 1947 ed. 1981 pap. $4.95

Pawlowska, Harriet. *Merrily We Sing: One Hundred Five Polish Folksongs.* Wayne State Univ. Pr. 1961 $12.95 1983 pap. $11.95

Rubin, Ruth, ed. *A Treasury of Jewish Folksong.* Piano settings by Ruth Post; ill. by T. Herzl Rome, Schocken 1976 $12.50

———. *Voices of a People: The Story of Yiddish Folksong.* Jewish Publication Society repr. of 1973 ed. 1979 pap. $8.95. "Both a social history of Yiddish folk songs and a song-history of East European Jewry, from the Shtetl or small town of the Czarist Pale to U.S. and Palestinian immigration, the Soviet Union, Nazi concentration camps, and the Warsaw Ghetto. Transliterated texts and literal translations, without tunes" (B. A. Botkin, *N.Y. Folklore Quarterly*).

Sandberg, Larry, and Dick Weissman. *The Folk Music Sourcebook.* Knopf 1976 pap. $7.95

Seeger, Pete. *The Incompleat Folksinger.* Simon & Schuster 1972 pap. $5.95

Slobin, Mark, ed. *Old Jewish Folk Music: The Collections and Writings of Moshe Beregovski.* Univ. of Pennsylvania Pr. 1982 $42.50 pap. $17.95

Stambler, Irwin, and Grelun Landon. *Encyclopedia of Folk, Country and Western Music.* St. Martin's 1982 $50.00

Warner, Anne. *Traditional American Folk Songs from the Anne and Frank Warner Collection.* Fwd. by Alan Lomax, Syracuse Univ. Pr. 1984 $48.00 pap. $25.95

Wolfe, Charles K. *Kentucky Country: Folk and Country Music of Kentucky.* Univ. Pr. of Kentucky 1982 $16.00. Analyzes the evolution of country music in the context of regional history and culture.

FOLKTALE, LEGEND, AND MYTH

Tales, legends, and myths, although related to fiction, are derivations of actual events or efforts to explain events. In a sense, they are interpretations or perceptions of historical happenings. They, therefore, provide information relating to the cultural history of a group or nation, and they enable folklorists to study group attitudes and customs. Legends and myths are, in fact, the only source of information about groups of people who left no written records.

This section includes anthologies and critical studies of tales, legends, and myths, and mythology in general, and works relating to individual countries; it includes a selected few U.S. ethnic titles (see the section on U.S. Regional and Ethnic Folklore for additional references). The most complete series of folktales is the University of Chicago's *Folktales of the World Series*, edited by Richard M. Dorson. See also Dorson's *Folktales Told around the World.*

Abrahams, Roger D. *The Man-of-Words in the West Indies: Performance and the Emergence of Creole Culture.* Johns Hopkins Univ. Pr. 1983 $24.50 pap. $12.95. "... a significant volume of essays—significant because they show one man's development and refinement of a folkloristic theory, significant because the theory is representative of the performance-centered school of folkloristics, and significant because through his analysis, Abrahams touches the very core of the British West Indian cultural system and places West Indian creativity within a cultural and historical framework" (Jane C. Beck, *Journal of Amer. Folklore*).

Aiken, Riley. *Mexican Folktales from the Borderland.* SMU Pr. 1980 $10.00

Ainsworth, Catherine H. *Folktales of America.* Clyde Pr. 2 vols. 1981 pap. ea. $10.00

———. *Polish-American Folktales.* Clyde Pr. 1977 $10.00

Algarin, Joanne P. *Japanese Folk Literature: A Core Collection.* Bowker 1982 $29.95. A comprehensive annotated bibliography of English-language sources of Japanese folk literature, with an introduction that discusses the historiography of Japanese folk literature. The bibliography is divided into three parts: works on folklore, folktale anthologies, and classic folktales.

Asbjornsen, Peter C., and Moe Jorgen. *Norwegian Folk Tales.* Ill. by T. Kittelsen and Erik Werenskiold, Pantheon 1982 pap. $5.95

Bergeret, Annie, and Mabel Tennaille. *Tales from China. World Folktale Lib.* Silver Burdett $12.68

Bin Gorion, Micha J., and Emanuel Bin Gorion, eds. *Mimekor Yisrael: Classical Jewish Folktales.* Trans. by I. M. Lask, Indiana Univ. Pr. 3 vols. 1976 $100.00

Botkin, B. A., ed. *Treasury of American Folklore.* Fwd. by Carl Sandburg, Outlet 1984 $7.98

Briggs, Katherine M. *British Folktales.* Pantheon 1980 pap. $5.95

Buchan, David. *Scottish Tradition: A Collection of Scottish Folklore.* Routledge & Kegan 1984 $25.00

Cavendish, Richard, ed. *Legends of the World.* Ill. by Eric Fraser, Schocken 1982 $29.95. Forty-three essays written by 34 experts.

Coburn, Jewell R. *Encircled Kingdom: Legends and Folktales of Laos.* Burn, Hart 1979 $12.50

Cocchiara, Giuseppe. *The History of Folklore in Europe.* Trans. by John N. McDaniel, Institute for the Study of Human Issues 1981 $16.95

Curtin, Jeremiah. *Myths and Folktales of the Russians, Western Slavs, and Magyars.* Gordon 1977 $59.95

Danaher, Kevin. *Folktales of the Irish Countryside.* Irish Bks. repr. of 1976 ed. 1982 pap. $5.95

Degh, Linda, ed. *Studies in East European Folk Narrative.* Univ. of Texas Pr. 1978 $25.00

Delarue, Paul. *The Borzoi Book of French Folk Tales. Folklore of the World Ser.* Ayer 1980 $45.00

Domotor, Tekla. *Hungarian Folk Beliefs.* Indiana Univ. Pr. 1983 $20.00. Accounts of witch trials, werewolves, snakes, dragons, healers, and magical happenings. Helps "the discerning reader to realize the similarities among cultures with respect to folk beliefs" (*Choice*).

Dorson, Richard M. *Folktales Told around the World.* Univ. of Chicago Pr. 1978 pap. $15.00. Surprisingly, this volume was not well received by professional folklorists, but it is wide-ranging and readable.

Drower, Ethel A. *Folk Tales of Iraq.* AMS Pr. 1978 $30.50

El-Shamy, Hasan M., ed. *Folktales of Egypt.* Fwd. by Richard M. Dorson, *Folktales of the World Ser.* Univ. of Chicago Pr. 1980 lib. ed. $25.00 pap. $8.95. A vast amount of information pertaining to tale types and motifs with good suggestions for additional tale types.

Fowke, Edith. *Folklore of Canada.* McClelland 1977 $10.95. Includes a few examples of all folklore genres, "regardless of the worth, interest, or accuracy of available materials," and tries to "give equal representation to all parts of Canada. Only Manitoba and the Yukon Territory are left out entirely" (Richard S. Tallman, *Journal of Amer. Folklore*).

Georges, Robert A. *Greek-American Folk Beliefs and Narratives: Survivals and Living Tradition.* Ed. by Richard M. Dorson, *Folklore of the World Ser.* Ayer repr. 1980 lib. bdg. $22.00

Gilard, Hazel A. *A Giant Walked among Them*. Golden Quill Pr. 1977 $8.00. Half tall tales of Paul Bunyan.

Glassie, Henry. *Passing the Time in Ballymenone: Culture and History of an Ulster Community*. Amer. Folklore Society Ser. Univ. of Pennsylvania Pr. 1982 $35.00. "Through the tales, songs, fiddle and whistle tunes, house plans and decorations, daily labor, calendar and custom, belief and behavior, Glassie seeks the history and values of the community as perceived by its citizens, and liberally seasons those with his own analyses and philosophizing" (D. K. Wilgus, *Journal of Amer. Folklore*).

Gordon, Raoul, ed. *The Folklore of Puerto Rico*. Gordon 1976 lib. bdg. $59.95

Green, Lila. *Tales from Africa*. Ill. by Jerry Pinkey, *World Folktale Lib*. Silver Burdett 1979 $12.68

————. *Tales from Hispanic Lands*. Ill. by Donald Silverstein, *World Folktale Lib*. Silver Burdett 1979 $12.68

Greenway, John. *Tales from the United States*. Ill. by Susan Perl, *World Folktale Lib*. Silver Burdett 1979 $12.68

Haggart, James A. *Israel in Folklore*. Artisan Sales 1981 pap. $5.00

Hall, Edwin S., Jr. *The Eskimo Storyteller: Folktales from Noatak, Alaska*. Univ. of Tennessee Pr. 1975 $27.50. A collection of 188 folktales printed exactly as narrated by two elders of a Noatak village in northwestern Alaska.

Kightly, Charles. *The Folk Heroes of Britain*. Thames & Hudson 1982 $19.95 1984 pap. $10.95

Klein, Barbro S. *Legends and Folk Beliefs in a Swedish American Community: A Study in Folklore and Acculturation*. Ed. by Richard M. Dorson, *Folklore of the World Ser*. Ayer 2 vols. repr. 1980 lib. bdg. $78.00

Kongas-Maranda, Elli Kaija. *Finnish American Folklore: Quantitative and Qualitative Analysis*. Ed. by Richard M. Dorson, *Folklore of the World Ser*. Ayer repr. 1980 lib. bdg. $51.50

Leach, Maria, and Jerome Fried, eds. *Funk and Wagnalls Standard Dictionary of Folklore, Mythology, and Legends*. Harper 1984 pap. $24.95

Lindow, John. *Swedish Legends and Folktales*. Univ. of California Pr. 1978 $12.95

Luthi, Max. *The European Folktale: Form and Nature*. Trans. by John D. Niles, *Translations in Folklore Studies Ser*. Institute for the Study of Human Issues text ed. 1982 $16.50. Still an insightful and provocative interpretation.

Marshall, Sybil. *Everyman's Book of English Folktales*. Ill. by John Lawrence, Biblio Dist. 1981 $17.50

Miller, Joseph C. *The African Past Speaks: Essays on Oral Tradition and History*. Shoe String (Archon) 1980 $27.50

Monteiro, Mariana. *Legends and Popular Tales of the Basque People*. Ayer repr. of 1887 ed. $15.00; Gordon 1976 lib. bdg. $59.95

Monter, William. *Ritual, Myth and Magic in Early Modern Europe*. Ohio Univ. Pr. 1984 $24.95

Myles, Colette G., ed. *The Butterflies Carried Him Home and Other Indian Tales*. Ill. by Yava Aarow, Artmans Pr. 1981 $4.95

Norton, Eloise S. *Folk Literature of the British Isles: Readings for Librarians, Teachers, and Those Who Work with Children and Young Adults*. Scarecrow Pr. 1978 lib. bdg. $15.00

Noy, Dov. *Studies in Jewish Folklore*. Ktav 1981 $25.00

Oinas, Felix J., ed. *Heroic Epic and Saga: An Introduction to the World's Great Folk Epics*. Indiana Univ. Pr. 1978 $29.95. Fifteen essays that examine the major epics of the ancient Near East and ancient and medieval Europe to reveal the common source of formal literature and folklore.

Paredes, Americo, ed. *Folktales of Mexico. Folktales of the World Ser.* Univ. of Chicago Pr. 1970 pap. $6.95. ". . . a welcome collection of Mexican folktales that still abound in oral literature . . ." (Terrence Hansen, *Western Folklore*).

Robertson, R. MacDonald. *Selected Highland Folktales.* David & Charles 1977 $12.50

Robinson, H. S., and K. Wilson. *The Encyclopedia of Myths and Legends of All Nations.* Ed. by Barbara L. Picard, Sportshelf repr. of 1974 ed. text ed. rev. 1978 $24.50

Segall, Jacob, ed. *Roumanian Folktales Retold from the Original.* Gordon 1977 lib. bdg. $59.95

Sheohmelian, O. *Three Apples from Heaven: Armenian Folk Tales.* Ed. by Arra Avakian and others, trans. by O. Sheohmelian, ill. by Adrina Zanazanian, Ararat Pr. 1982 pap. $6.95

Slater, Candace. *Stories on a String: The Brazilian Literature de Cordel.* Univ. of California Pr. 1982 $30.00

Stoddard, Florence J. *As Old as the Moon: Cuban Legends and Folklore of the Antillas.* Gordon 1976 lib. bdg. $59.95

Strickland, Walter W. *Panslavonic Folklore.* AMS Pr. 1980 $25.00

Thompson, Stith. *The Folktale.* AMS Pr. repr. of 1946 ed. $34.00; Univ. of California Pr. $32.50 pap. $8.95. Includes two appendixes, "Important Works on the Folktale" and "Principal Collections of Folktales," as well as indexes of tale types and motifs.

Todd, Loreto. *Some Day Been Dey: West African Pidgin Folktale.* Routledge & Kegan 1979 pap. $18.50

Toor, Frances. *Mexican Folkways.* Gordon 1976 lib. bdg. $59.95

Toth, Marian D. *Tales from Thailand: Folklore, Culture, and History.* Tuttle 1983 $14.50

Van Duong, Quyen, and Jewell R. Coburn. *Beyond the East Wind: Legends and Folktales of Vietnam.* Burn Hart 1976 $12.50

Wheeler, Post. *Tales from the Japanese Storytellers as Collected in the Ho Dan Zo.* Ed. by Harold G. Henderson, Tuttle 1974 pap. $3.95

Wolkstein, Diane, ed. *The Magic Orange Tree: And Other Haitian Folktales.* Ill. by Elsa Henriquez, Knopf 1978 $7.95; Schocken repr. of 1978 ed. 1980 pap. $5.95

Zeitlin, Steven J., Amy J. Kotkin, and Holly Cutting Baker. *A Celebration of American Family Folklore: Tales and Traditions from the Smithsonian Collection.* Smithsonian 1982 o.p. The first of its kind to be published, this is an excellent source book for general readers and professionals, prepared by the founders of the Family Folklore Program at the Smithsonian Institution. Includes customs, family albums, and stories about courtship, feuds, and heroism.

U.S. REGIONAL AND ETHNIC FOLKLORE

Arranged by region—New England, Mid-Atlantic, South, Midwest, West—with additional sections on U.S. Indian Folklore and Afro-American Folklore, this section includes titles relating to all aspects of the general subject: ballads and songs, folktales, legends, riddles, haunts, superstitions, tall tales, ethnography, ethnomusicology, linguistics, humor, and more.

New England

Aldrich, Lawson. *The Cheechako: Facts, Fables and Recipes.* Down East 1982 pap. $7.95

Beck, Jane C., ed. *Always in Season: Folk Art and Traditional Culture in Vermont.* Photographs by Erik Borg, fwd. by Ellen Lovell McCullock, pref. by Elaine Eff, Vermont Council on the Arts 1982 pap. $14.95

Benes, Peter, ed. *Foodways in the Northeast.* Boston Univ. Pr. 1982 pap. $8.00. Essays on the preparation and serving of food in the Northeast, mainly in Massachusetts and mainly before 1800. The essays, by archeologists, historians, and museum curators, deal with implements, diet, costs of food, and customs relating to food.

Cahill, Robert E. *New England's Strange Sea Sagas. Collectible Class. Ser.* Chandler-Smith 1984 pap. $3.95

Deindorfer, Robert G., ed. *America's One Hundred One Most High Falutin', Big Talkin' Knee Slappin', Golly Whoppers and Tall Tales: The Best of the Burlington Liars' Club.* Workman 1980 pap. $3.95

Dorson, Richard M. *Jonathan Draws the Long Bow: New England Popular Tales and Legends.* Russell Pr. repr. of 1946 ed. 1970 $11.50

Flanders, Helen H., and George Brown. *Vermont Folksongs and Ballads.* 1931. Gale 1968 $45.00

Flanders, Helen H., and Marguerite Olney, eds. *Ballads Migrant in New England. Granger Index Repr. Ser.* Ayer repr. of 1953 $17.00

Gray, Roland P., ed. *Songs and Ballads of the Maine Lumberjacks.* Gale repr. of 1924 ed. 1969 $35.00

Huntington, Gale. *Vineyard Tales.* Tashmoo 1980 pap. $7.95

Jagendorf, Moritz A. *New England Bean Pot: American Folk Stories to Read and to Tell.* Vanguard 1978 $7.95. For younger readers.

Kittredge, George L. *The Old Farmer and His Almanack.* Corner House repr. of 1904 ed. 1974 $18.50

——. *Witchcraft in Old and New England.* Atheneum repr. of 1929 ed. text ed. 1972 pap. $4.75; Russell repr. of 1929 ed. 1958 $18.00

Silitch, Clarissa M., ed. *The Old Farmer's Almanac Book of Old Fashioned Puzzles.* Yankee Bks. 1976 pap. $5.95

The Mid-Atlantic States

Ainsworth, Catherine H. *Legends of New York State. Folklore Bks.* Clyde Pr. 1983 $10.00

Bethke, Robert D. *Adirondack Voices: Woodsmen and Woods Lore.* Univ. of Illinois Pr. 1981 $12.50. "This book is a product of contemporary ways of thinking about folklore: it is about interaction, changing situations, and the many-sided potential for meaning that expressive forms have. It is not a book heavy with the technical terms forged by those who have given us ways to so conceive of folklore, nor is it a book that calls attention to, or that deeply explores, its own good insights; but it is a lovely book for all that, a book full of wonderful observation and fine detail" (Deborah Kodish, *Journal of Amer. Folklore*).

Cazden, Norman, and others. *Folk Songs of the Catskills.* Intro. by Pete Seeger, State Univ. of New York Pr. 1982 $69.50 pap. $19.95. Brings together 178 texts, including several recited examples, and accompanying tunes mainly from the farming, lumbering, and former rafting region of Delaware and Sullivan counties.

Gardner, E. E. *Folklore from the Schoharie Hills, New York.* 1937. Ayer 1977 $29.00. A central New York classic.

Glimm, James Y. *Flatlanders and Ridgerunners: Folktales from the Mountains of Northern Pennsylvania.* Univ. of Pittsburgh Pr. 1983 $11.95 pap. $5.95

Jones, Louis C. *Three Eyes on the Past: Exploring New York State Folk Life.* Syracuse Univ. Pr. 1982 pap. $12.95. A "wonderfully informal but disjointed book. It begins with rich material drawn from his experience, focusing on the title article—an excellent guide for any local historian. He then turns to folklore in the state of New York, embodying material drawn from his *Things That Go Bump in the Night* (1959) and essays that incorporate his abiding love for his native region" (*Choice*).

Kauffman, Henry J. *Pennsylvania Dutch American Folk Art.* Dover rev. & enl. ed. pap. $5.50; Peter Smith rev. & enl. ed. $13.50

Leach, Macedward, and Henry Glassie. *A Guide for Collectors of Oral Traditions and Folk Cultural Material in Pennsylvania.* Pennsylvania Historical and Museum Commission 1973 pap. $2.00

Levine, Gaynell S., ed. *Languages and Lore of the Long Island Indians.* Pref. by James Truex, Ginn Pr. 1981 pap. $15.00

Litchen, Frances. *Folk Art Motifs of Pennsylvania.* Dover 1976 pap. $4.50; Peter Smith $12.00

Thompson, Harold. *Body, Boots, and Britches.* Intro. by Thomas F. O'Donnell, Syracuse Univ. Pr. 2d ed. 1979 $18.00 pap. $9.95. The best-known work by a pioneer folklorist, this is the beginning book for pleasurable examination of folklore in New York State.

Welles, E. R., and J. P. Evans. *Legend of Sleepy Hollow, Rip Van Winkle, President Van Buren and Brom.* Learning Inc. 1984 pap. $4.00

The South

Brown, Frank C. *The Frank C. Brown Collection of North Carolina Folklore.* Ed. by Newman I. White, Duke Univ. Pr. 7 vols. 1952–64 ea. $25.00 set $150.00

Browne, Ray, ed. *A Night with the Hants and Other Alabama Experiences.* Intro. by Carlos Drake, Bowling Green 1976 $12.95 pap. $6.95

Carey, George. *A Faraway Time and Place: Lore of the Eastern Shore.* Ed. by Richard M. Dorson, *International Folklore Ser.* Ayer repr. of 1971 ed. 1977 lib. bdg. $22.00. An impressive collection of stories from the white watermen in the region between the Nanticoke and Pocomoke Rivers on the lower eastern shore of the Chesapeake.

———. *Maryland Folk Legends and Folk Songs.* Tidewater 1971 pap. $4.00. "Perhaps the most important contribution of the book is the section on 'Urban and Modern Legends,' one of the most succinct presentations of the subject available. Here we find a good sampling of the grisly beliefs that reflect the anxieties of today's 'youth culture' " (John Burrison, *Journal of Amer. Folklore*).

Carpenter, Cal. *The Walton War and Tales of the Great Smoky Mountains.* Copple 1980 pap. $5.95

Chase, Richard. *Jack Tales.* Houghton Mifflin 1943 $10.95. ". . . Southern Appalachian versions of the 'Jack' cycle of folktales of the British-American trickster hero, the poor, unpromising, lazy, and often unscrupulous boy who wins out by his cleverness, sharpwittedness and luck, as in 'Jack and the Beanstalk' and 'Jack the Giant-Killer' " (B. A. Botkin, *N.Y. Folklore Quarterly*).

Clarke, Kenneth, and Mary Clarke. *The Harvest and the Reapers: Oral Traditions of Kentucky.* Univ. Pr. of Kentucky 1974 $6.95

Combs, Josiah H. *Folk Songs of the Southern United States.* Ed. by D. K. Wilgus, *Amer. Folklore Society Bibliographical and Special Ser.* Univ. of Texas Pr. 1967 $15.95. From the original French *Folk Songs du Midi des Etats-Unis* and the English-language manuscript on which it was based. Includes music.

Cuthbert, John A. *West Virginia Folk Music.* West Virginia Univ. Pr. 1982 $10.00

Davis, Hubert J. *Myths and Legends of the Great Dismal Swamp.* Ill. by Sarah Codd, Johnson Publishing 1981 $7.50

Fraser, Walter J., Jr., and Winfred B. Moore, Jr., eds. *The Southern Enigma: Essays on Race, Class, and Folk Culture. Contributions in Amer. History Ser.* Greenwood lib. bdg. $35.00

Gainer, Patrick W. *Witches, Ghosts and Signs: Folklore of the Southern Appalachians.* Seneca Bks. 1975 $7.95

Gilmore, Robert K. *Ozark Baptizings, Hangings, and Other Diversions: Theatrical Folkways of Rural Missouri, 1885–1910.* Fwd. by Robert Flanders, Univ. of Oklahoma Pr. 1984 $14.95

Goehring, Eleanor E. *Tennessee Folk Culture: An Annotated Bibliography.* Univ. of Tennessee Pr. text ed. 1982 $16.50

Harden, John. *Tar Heel Ghosts.* Univ. of North Carolina Pr. 1980 $9.95 pap. $4.95

LaPin, Dierdre, and Louis Guida. *Hogs in the Bottoms: Family Folklore in Arkansas.* August House 1982 pap. $15.95

Montell, William L. *Ghosts along the Cumberland: Deathlore in the Kentucky Foothills.* Univ. of Tennessee Pr. 1975 $16.50

Randolph, Vance. *Ozark Folksongs.* Ed. by Norm Cohen, *Music in Amer. Life Ser.* Univ. of Illinois Pr. 1982 $35.00 pap. $14.95; intro. by W. K. McNeil, Univ. of Missouri Pr. 4 vols. repr. of 1949 ed. 1980 text ed. ea. $32.00 pap. ea. $12.95

———. *Pissing in the Snow and Other Ozark Folktales.* Avon 1977 pap. $3.95; Univ. of Illinois Pr. 1976 $8.95. ". . . a book of real significance for anyone interested at all in scatological lore. The antiquity of some of the tales, in their first printed form, is easily ascertained, and others can be dated tentatively because of their topicality, some might say" (Ken Periman, *Journal of Amer. Folklore*).

Rhyne, Nancy. *Tales of the South Carolina Low Country.* Blair 1982 pap. $5.95

Rosenbaum, Art, and Margo Rosenbaum. *Folk Visions and Voices: Traditional Music and Song in North Georgia.* Fwd. by Pete Seeger, Univ. of Georgia Pr. 1983 $27.50

The Midwest

Baker, Ronald L. *Hoosier Folk Legends.* Indiana Univ. Pr. 1982 $15.00 pap. $7.95

Brewster, Paul G., ed. *Ballads and Songs of Indiana.* Ed. by Kenneth S. Goldstein and Winthrop E. Richmond, *Publications in Folksong and Balladry Ser.* Folklorica Pr. repr. of 1940 ed. 1982 pap. $15.95; Wildman Pr. pap. $15.95

Degh, Linda, ed. *Indiana Folklore: A Reader.* Indiana Univ. Pr. $20.00 pap. $7.95. A selection of articles reprinted from the *Journal of Indiana Folklore.*

Gard, Robert E., and L. G. Sorden. *Wisconsin Lore.* Stanton & Lee 1971 $8.95

Kane, Grace F. *Myths and Legends of the Mackinacs and the Lake Region.* Black Letter 2d ed. repr. of 1897 ed. 1972 o.p.

Koch, William E. *Folklore from Kansas: Customs, Beliefs, and Superstitions.* Univ. Pr. of Kansas 1980 $19.95 pap. $12.95. Useful for a "researcher with a good deal of knowledge in the fields of customs, belief, and superstition. Those with a little less knowledge or with a less item-oriented research interest will be aware of the lack of analysis, references, and supplemental materials . . ." (Jennie A. Chin, *Journal of Amer. Folklore*).

Mittlefehldt, Pamela. *Minnesota Folklife: An Annotated Bibliography.* Ed. by I. Karon Sherarts, pref. by Ellen J. Stekert, Minnesota Historical Society 1979 pap. $3.50

Neely, Charles. *Tales and Songs of Southern Illinois.* Richard West repr. of 1938 ed. 1978 $30.00

Pound, Louise, *Nebraska Folklore.* Greenwood repr. of 1960 ed. 1976 lib. bdg. $22.50

Stout, Earl J., ed. *Folklore from Iowa. Amer. Folklore Society Memoir Ser.* Kraus repr. of 1936 ed. $34.00

Thomas, Rosemary H. *It's Good to Tell You: French Folk Tales from Missouri.* Univ. of Missouri Pr. 1981 $24.00

Welsch, Roger. *Shingling the Fog and Other Plains Lies.* Univ. of Nebraska Pr. 1980 $13.50 pap. $4.95. "The tall tale is the most collected, published, and abused form of folk narrative in North America. [This book] . . . extends the collection and publication of the genre to include a sizable corpus of authentic tales from the Great Plains, primarily Nebraska; the abuses in this latest collection are of omission, and are certainly outweighed by the accurate depiction of the tall tale and the tall tale tradition in a book directed toward a popular rather than a professional audience" (Richard S. Tallman, *Journal of Amer. Folklore*).

——, comp. *A Treasury of Nebraska Pioneer Folklore.* Ill. by Jack Brodie, Univ. of Nebraska Pr. 1966 $9.95. Compiled mainly from the 30 *Nebraska Folklore Pamphlets* prepared by the W.P.A. Writers Program from 1927 to 1940.

The West

Bauman, Richard, and Roger D. Abrahams, eds. *And Other Neighborly Names: Social Process and Cultural Image in Texas Folklore.* Univ. of Texas Pr. text ed. 1981 $25.00

Bratcher, James T. *Analytical Index to Publications of the Texas Folklore Society.* SMU Pr. 36 vols. 1973 ea. $15.95

Brett, Bill. *There Ain't No Such Animal and Other East Texas Tales.* Ill. by Harvey Johnson, Texas A & M Univ. Pr. 1979 $9.95

Campa, Arthur L. *Sayings and Riddles in New Mexico.* Borgo Pr. 1982 lib. bdg. $22.95

Cannon, Hal, ed. *Utah Folk Art: A Catalog of Material Culture.* Brigham Young Univ. Pr. 1980 pap. $10.95

Dobie, J. Frank. *Coronado's Children: Tales of Lost and Buried Treasures of the Southwest.* Ill. by Ben C. Mead, Darby repr. of 1931 ed. 1982 lib. bdg. $50.00; ill. by Charles Shaw, fwd. by Frank H. Wardlaw, Univ. of Texas Pr. repr. of 1930 ed. 1978 $14.95 pap. $8.95

——. *The Longhorns.* Ill. by Tom Lea, Little, Brown 1941 $17.45; Univ. of Texas Pr. repr. 1980 pap. $9.95

——. *Tales of Old-Time Texas.* Little, Brown 1955 $12.45

——. *A Vaquero of the Brush Country.* Ill. by Justice C. Gruelle, pref. by Lawrence C. Powell, Univ. of Texas Pr. repr. of 1960 ed. 1981 pap. $7.95. Partly from the reminiscences of John Young. "Discusses the practices of the open range, characteristics of ranch people, the cowboy's belongings; includes tales of longhorns, razorbacks, mustangs and other range yarns, as well as authentic lore of the bloody border and the cattle trail" (B. A. Botkin, *N.Y. Folklore Quarterly*).

——, ed. *Legends of Texas. Texas Folklore Society Publications* Pelican 2 vols. repr. of 1924 ed. 1975 pap. ea. $3.95; SMU Pr. repr. of 1924 ed. 1964 $15.95

Helm, Mike. *Oregon's Ghosts and Monsters.* Rainy Day Pr. 1983 pap. $7.95

Judson, Katherine. *Myths and Legends of the Pacific Northwest.* Shorey Indian Ser. repr. of 1910 ed. 1980 pap. $12.95

Kilpatrick, Jack, and Anna Kilpatrick. *Friends of Thunder, Folktales of Oklahoma.* SMU Pr. repr. of 1964 ed. 1977 pap. $9.95

Lee, Hector. *Heroes, Villains, and Ghosts: Folklore of Old California.* Ill. by Judy Sutcliffe, Capra Pr. 1984 pap. $8.95

Lingenfelter, Richard E., and others, eds. *Songs of the American West.* Univ. of California Pr. 1968 $37.00

Maclean, Angus. *Cuentos: Based on the Folk Tales of the Spanish Californians.* Panorama West 1979 $9.95 pap. $5.95

Paredes, Americo. *A Texas-Mexican Cancionero: Folksongs of the Lower Border.* Univ. of Illinois Pr. 1975 pap. $7.95

Robb, John D. *Hispanic Folk Music of New Mexico and the Southwest: A Self-Portrait of the People.* Univ. of Oklahoma Pr. 1980 $42.50

Russell, Bert. *Calked Boots and Other Northwest Writings.* Lacon 4th ed. 1979 $9.95 pap. $5.95

Schwartz, Henry. *Kit Carson's Long Walk and Other True Tales of Old San Diego.* Ill. by Amy Schwartz, Association of Creative Writers 1980 pap. $3.95

Taylor, Lonn, and Ingrid Maar. *The American Cowboy.* Harper 1983 $48.08

Thorp, N. Howard, ed. *Songs of the Cowboys.* Univ. of Nebraska Pr. (Bison) repr. of 1908 ed. 1984 $15.95 pap. $5.95. Twenty-three songs, reprinted in facsimile, with the original or reconstructed texts, variants, and tunes. Includes historical and critical notes, a bibliography for each song, a lexicon, and a general bibliography.

Trimble, Marshall. *Arizona Adventure: Action Packed True Tales of Early Arizona.* Golden West 1982 pap. $5.00

U.S. Indian Folklore

Bemister, Margaret. *Thirty Indian Legends of Canada.* Merrimack 1983 pap. $8.95

Boatright, Mody C., ed. *The Sky Is My Tipi.* Texas Folklore Society Publications SMU Pr. repr. of 1949 ed. 1966 $9.95

Boyer, L. Bryce. *Childhood and Folklore: A Psychoanalytic Study of Apache Personality.* Psychohistory Pr. 1979 $16.95 pap. $8.95. Written from a psychoanalytical approach, this book "is generally clear and intelligible to the layman. . . . The folklorist interested in the psychological functions of narrative can learn much. It should serve as a model for future studies, but will be difficult to equal" (J. L. Fischer, *Journal of Amer. Folklore*).

Choate, F. *The Indian Fairy Book: From the Original Legends.* Gordon 1977 lib. bdg. $59.95

Clark, Ella E. *Indian Legends from the Northern Rockies.* Civilization of the Amer. Indian Ser. Univ. of Oklahoma Pr. repr. of 1966 ed. 1977 $17.95

————. *Indian Legends of the Pacific Northwest.* Univ. of California Pr. 1953 pap. $5.95

Clements, William M., and Frances M. Malpezzi. *Native American Folklore, 1879–1979: An Annotated Bibliography.* Ohio Univ. Pr. (Swallow) text ed. 1984 $34.95. A bibliography of more than 5,000 entries about native Americans north of Mexico. Includes narratives, songs, chants, prayers, formulas, orations, and proverbs. Covers music, dance, games, and ceremonials.

Coffin, Tristram P., ed. *Indian Tales of North America: An Anthology for the Adult*

Reader. Amer. Folklore Society Bibliographical and Special Ser. Univ. of Texas Pr. 1961 pap. $6.95

Cushing, Frank H. *Zuni Folk Tales.* AMS Pr. repr. of 1901 ed. $35.50; Gordon 1977 lib. bdg. $59.95

Eastman, Mary. *Dahcotah: Or, Life and Legends of the Sioux around Fort Snelling.* Pref. by C. M. Kirkland, *Mid-Amer Frontier Ser.* Ayer repr. of 1849 ed. 1975 $18.00

Erodes, Richard, and Alfonso Ortiz. *American Indian Myth and Legends.* Pantheon 1984 $19.45

Gossen, Gary H. *Chamulas in the World of the Sun: Time and Space in a Maya Oral Tradition.* Harvard Univ. Pr. text ed. 1974 $18.50; ill. by Marian L. Calixto, Waveland Pr. text ed. repr. of 1974 ed. 1984 pap. $9.95

Grinnell, George B. *Blackfoot Lodge Tales: The Story of a Prairie People.* Corner House repr. of 1892 ed. 1972 $16.95; Univ. of Nebraska Pr. (Bison) 1962 pap. $5.95

Jacobs, Melville. *Content and Style of an Oral Literature: Clackamas Chinook Myths and Tales.* Univ. of Chicago Pr. 1959 $17.50

Jagendorf, Moritz A. *Tales from the First Americans.* Ill. by Jack Endewelt, *World Folktale Lib.* Silver Burdett 1979 $12.68

Merriam, Alan P. *Ethnomusicology of the Flathead Indians.* Viking Fund Publications in Anthropology Ser. Aldine repr. of 1967 ed. o.p. ". . . an important work in the literature of primitive music, both for Professor Merriam's insight into Indian beliefs, social thought, customs, and intellectual responsiveness, and for the major contribution he makes towards the developing techniques of ethnomusicology" (*LJ*).

Norman, Howard, trans. *Where the Chill Came From: Cree Windigo Tales and Journeys: 1982.* North Point Pr. $17.50 pap. $9.00

Salomon, J. H. *The Book of Indian Crafts and Indian Lore.* Gordon 1977 $69.95

Schorer, C. E., ed. *Indian Tales of C. C. Trowbridge: Collected from Wyandots, Miamis and Shawanoes.* Green Oak Pr. 1985 $12.95

Spencer, Katherine. *Reflections of Social Life in the Navaho Origin Myth. Univ. of New Mexico Publications in Anthropology* AMS Pr. repr. of 1947 ed. 1983 $20.00

Talashoma, Herschel, and Ekkehart Malotki, eds. *Hopitutuwutsi-Hopi Tales: A Bilingual Collection of Hopi Indian Stories.* Univ. of Arizona Pr. 1983 $24.50 pap. $14.50

Thompson, Stith, ed. *Tales of the North American Indians.* Indiana Univ. Pr. 1966 pap. $9.95. Ninety-six tales arranged according to type, with "comparative notes, to show the extent of the distribution of each tale and each motif, [presented] . . . as to be obvious to the general reader" (Introduction).

Wood, Marion. *Spirits, Heroes and Hunters from North American Indian Mythology.* Ill. by John Sibbick, *World Mythologies Ser.* Schocken 1982 $15.95

Afro-American Folklore

Abrahams, Roger D. *Deep Down in the Jungle: Negro Narrative Folklore from the Streets of Philadelphia.* Aldine text ed. rev. ed. 1970 $29.95 pap. $14.95. ". . . a selected body of obscene folk narrative collected in a single four-block Negro neighborhood in Philadelphia and consisting of playing the dozens, toasts, and jokes. In addition to the treatment of the specific sociological and psychological patterns of urban neighborhood and (mother-centered) family life [and related material], there is much insightful comment on types of the Negro contest hero developed in this gang subculture" (B. A. Botkin, *N.Y. Folklore Quarterly*).

Bell, Michael J. *The World from Brown's Lounge: An Ethnography of Black Middle Class Play.* Univ. of Illinois Pr. 1983 $14.95. A "study of speech play among blacks who frequent a neighborhood bar in Philadelphia [that] effectively shows how folklore study can move beyond its customary conceptual and methodological parameters to provide insight into . . . 'the aesthetics of ordinary experience' " (William Clements, *Journal of Amer. Folklore*).

Christensen, A. M. *Afro-American Folklore: Told round Cabin Fires on the Sea Islands of South Carolina.* Greenwood repr. of 1892 ed. $10.00

Courlander, Harold. *Negro Folk Music, U.S.A.* Columbia Univ. Pr. repr. 1963 pap. $12.00

——. *A Treasury of African Folklore.* Crown 1975 $14.95

Dance, Daryl C. *Shuckin' and Jivin': Folklore from Contemporary Black Americans.* Indiana Univ. Pr. 1978 $25.00 pap. $7.95. ". . . further evidence of the vitality, imagination, variety, and strength of the black folk tradition in America; it joins a list of previous general collections of Afro-American folklore that includes Hurston, Brewer, and Hughes and Bontemps, and, although still not the ideal collection, it in many ways improves on its predecessors. One improvement is that *Shuckin' and Jivin'* is unexpurgated; all of the material is rendered in the language in which it is normally told, much of it obscene" (Patrick Mullen, *Journal of Amer. Folklore*).

Epstein, Dena J. *Sinful Tunes and Spirituals: Black Folk Music to the Civil War. Music in Amer. Life Ser.* Univ. of Illinois Pr. 1977 pap. $9.95

Hughes, Langston. *Book of Negro Humor.* Dodd 1965 $8.95. From African prototypes and memories of slavery to "The Jazz Folk" and "Harlem Jive," from "Black Magic and Chance" to "The Problem," from work songs, sermons, and spirituals to songs, poetry, and prose "in the folk manner," the book explores the integral relationship between Negro folklore, life, and literature. Like the slaves, writes Arna Bontemps in his introduction, whose folktales "were actually projections of personal experiences and hopes and defeats in terms of symbols," today's "Negro writers, and the many others who have used the Negro as subject . . . continue to dip into the richness of Negro folk life."

Hurston, Zora N. *Mules and Men.* Greenwood repr. of 1935 ed. $19.75; ill. by Miguel Covarrubias, Indiana Univ. Pr. repr. 1978 $17.50 pap. $6.95

Jackson, Bruce, ed. *The Negro and His Folklore in Nineteenth Century Periodicals. Amer. Folklore Society Bibliographic and Special Ser.* Univ. of Texas Pr. text ed. repr. of 1967 ed. 1977 pap. $14.50. ". . . brings into sharp focus the social and aesthetic values of Negro folklore as seen by white contemporaries from slavery to freedom. Of the 18 periodicals from which the 35 articles, sketches, and reviews have been selected, only one—the *Southern Workman*, established in 1871 at Hampton Institute—represents the (late) emergence of the Negro as collector and student of his own folklore as well as its creator and subject. For the rest, the book deals with development of changing white attitudes toward the Negro and his folklore, varying from 'paternalistic condescension' and caricature to sympathetic interest. In tracing this development . . . Jackson supplies a critical and historical perspective" (B. A. Botkin, *N.Y. Folklore Quarterly*).

Joyner, Charles. *Down by the Riverside: A South Carolina Slave Community. Blacks in the New World Ser.* Univ. of Illinois Pr. 1984 $24.95

Kebede, Ashenafi. *Roots of Black Music: The Vocal, Instrumental and Dance Heritage of Africa and Black America.* Prentice-Hall 1982 $16.95 pap. $7.95

Klotman, Phyllis R., and others, eds. *Humanities through the Black Experience.* Kendall-Hunt text ed. 1977 pap. $12.95

Levine, Lawrence W. *Black Culture and Black Consciousness: Afro-American Folk Thought from Slavery to Freedom.* Oxford repr. 1977 $27.50 pap. $12.95

Livingston, Jane, and John Beardsley. *Black Folk Art in America, 1930–1980.* Fwd. by Peter C. Marzio, Univ. Pr. of Mississippi 1982 pap. $20.00

Osofsky, Gilbert, ed. *Puttin' on Ole Massa: The Slave Narratives of Henry Bibb, William W. Brown, and Solomon Northrup.* Harper 1969 pap. $7.95. Osofsky was one of the first historians to realize that folkoristic sources were necessary for writing the history of peoples, white and black, who left no written record.

Owen, Mary A. *Voodoo Tales, as Told among the Negroes of the Southwest.* Intro. by C. G. Leland, *Black Heritage Lib. Collection Ser.* Ayer repr. of 1893 ed. $17.00; Greenwood repr. of 1893 ed. $13.00

Puckett, N. Niles. *Folk Beliefs of the Southern Negro.* Greenwood repr. of 1926 ed. 1968 $22.50

Skowronski, Joann. *Black Music in America: A Bibliography.* Scarecrow Pr. 1981 $37.50

Smith, Michael P. *Spirit World: Pattern in the Expressive Folk Culture of Afro-American New Orleans.* New Orleans Urban Folklife Alliance 1984 pap. $14.00

Spalding, Henry D. *Encyclopedia of Black Folklore and Humor.* Intro. by J. Mason Brewer, Jonathan David rev. ed. 1979 $16.95. A collection of anecdotes, stories, songs, poems, proverbs, and superstitions, and a few recipes for soul food.

Szwed, John F., and Roger D. Abrahams. *Afro-American Folk Culture: An Annotated Bibliography of Materials from North, Central and South America and the West Indies. Publications of the Amer. Folklore Society* Institute for the Study of Human Issues 2 pts. text ed. 1978 $60.00

Talley, Thomas W. *Negro Folk Rhymes, Wise and Otherwise: A Study.* Folcroft repr. of 1922 ed. 1980 lib. bdg. $40.00

Thompson, Rose. *Hush Child, Can't You Hear the Music.* Ed. by Charles Beaumont, *Brown Thrasher Original Ser.* Univ. of Georgia Pr. 1982 $12.50

Waters, Donald J. *Strange Ways and Sweet Dreams: Afro-American Folklore from the Hampton Institute.* G. K. Hall 1983 lib. bdg. $52.00

MISCELLANEOUS AND APPLIED FOLKLORE

The application of folklore to other disciplines—history, literature, psychology, sociology, linguistics—is a major occupation of many present-day folklorists, and many of the titles in this section deal with these applications. The titles deal with everyday life and the supernatural, including art and crafts, material culture, proverbs, riddles, beliefs, and customs, as well as with urban folklore, an emerging field of its own.

Baker, Donald. *Functions of Folk and Fairy Tales.* Association for Childhood Education International 1981 pap. $2.00

Baker, Margret. *Folklore of the Sea.* David & Charles 1979 $16.95. Baker's observation that sailors are the most superstitious beings in existence is confirmed by this work. "Beginning with the rituals surrounding shipbuilding itself, Baker sails along through the esoteric seas of phantom ships, strange seagoing custom, sea-serpents, and weather gods" (Mark Norton Schatz, *Journal of Amer. Folklore*).

Ben, Amos D., and K. Goldstein, eds. *Folklore: Performance and Communication. Approaches to Semiotics Ser.* Mouton text ed. 1975 pap. $60.00

Bishop, Robert. *American Folk Sculpture.* Dutton 1983 pap. $19.95

Bluestein, Gene, and Winfred Bernhard. *The Voice of the Folk: Folklore and American Literary Theory.* Univ. of Massachusetts Pr. 1972 pap. $6.95. In this theoretical discussion of the relationship between folk literature and more traditional literary criticism, Bluestein's "key literary figures are Emerson and Whitman, and his point of view is enriched in the final pages by his ability to draw upon Negro folksong (spirituals, blues, and jazz) and even the rock and roll music of the 1960s" (John Flanagan, *Journal of Amer. Folklore*).

Boatright, Mody C. *Folklore of the Oil Industry.* SMU Pr. 1984 pap. $9.95

Botkin, B. A. *Sidewalks of America: Folklore, Legends, Sagas, Traditions, Customs, Songs, Stories, and Sayings of City Folk.* Greenwood repr. of 1954 ed. 1976 lib. bdg. $34.75

Brunvand, Jan H. *The Choking Doberman and Other "New" Urban Legends.* Norton 1984 $13.95

———. *The Vanishing Hitchhiker: American Urban Legends and Their Meanings.* Norton 1981 $14.95 1982 pap. $5.95. Directed to the general reader, this book effectively demonstrates the narrative process and established folkloristic techniques. "The text literally interweaves communication patterns and technological developments and so legitimizes American urban legends and their meanings. The first introductory chapter, 'New Legends for Old,' is an especially useful overview of the genre, of its performance contexts, of its possibility as cultural symbol, and of the need for analysis" (Janet L. Langlois, *Journal of Amer. Folklore*).

Cahill, Holger. *American Folk Art: The Art of the Common Man in America, 1750–1900. Museum of Modern Art Publications in Repr. Ser.* Ayer repr. of 1932 ed. 1970 $20.00

Camp, John. *Magic, Myth and Medicine.* Taplinger 1974 $8.50

Coffin, Tristram P. *Uncertain Glory: Folklore and the American Revolution.* Gale 1971 $35.00

Dickson, Paul, and Joseph Goulden. *There Are Alligators in Our Sewers and Other American Credos.* Delacorte 1983 $11.95; Dell 1984 pap. $5.95

Dorson, Richard M. *American Folklore and the Historian.* Univ. of Chicago Pr. 1971 o.p.

Dundes, Alan, and Carl R. Pagter. *Work Hard and You Shall Be Rewarded: Urban Folklore from the Paperwork Empire.* Indiana Univ. Pr. 1978 pap. $5.95. A collection of expressions with annotations and interpretive comments that claims to be the first systematic book-length published collection of such material. "The authors argue for the folkloric nature of their graphic materials despite the fact that these expressions are neither drawn from rural, non-literate, lower-class sources nor transmitted by oral means. Rather the materials are held to qualify as folklore because they are traditional in that they lack recognized authorship and exhibit variation in their form and content as they are encountered in multiple versions over time and space. Only someone with the most narrow-minded conception of what folklore is can quibble over the legitimacy of these traditional graphic materials as folkloric" (Thomas A. Burns, *Journal of Amer. Folklore*).

Eadie, John W. *Classical Traditions in Early America.* Trillium Pr. 1976 pap. $10.00

Glassie, Henry. *All Silver and No Brass: An Irish Christmas Mumming.* Indiana Univ. Pr. 1976 $12.50; Univ. of Pennsylvania Pr. 1983 $8.95. "In an occupation built upon the examination of interpersonal expression at close range it is ironic, if not downright embarrassing, that so much of what folklorists do remains shrouded in the same mists of romanticism and curious speculation as the subjects and objects he regularly studies. Consequently, as a book which includes among its several goals 'an honest presentation of how and why the folklorist practices his craft.' Henry Glassie's *All Silver and No Brass* will be welcomed and appreciated by folklorists and general readers alike. . . . The mumming of which Glassie writes is the annual performance of a rhymed drama by groups of costumed young men in the homes of Northern Irish communities during the week following Christmas" (Charles Camp, *Journal of Amer. Folklore*).

————. *Pattern in the Material Folk Culture of the Eastern United States. Amer. Folklore Society Ser.* Univ. of Pennsylvania Pr. repr. of 1968 ed. rev. ed. 1971 $22.50 pap. $9.95

Granger, Byrd H. *Motif Index for Lost Mines and Treasures, Applied to Redaction of Arizona Legends, and to Lost Mines and Treasure Legends Exterior to Arizona.* Univ. of Arizona Pr. text ed. 1978 $17.50

Hand, Wayland D. *Magical Medicine: The Folkloric Component of Folk Medicine in the Folk Belief, Custom, and Ritual of Non-Primitive Peoples.* Univ. of California Pr. 1981 $29.50

Herbert, S. *Child-Lore: A Study in Folklore and Psychology.* Gordon 1976 $59.95

Herzfeld, Michael. *Ours Once More: Folklore Ideology, and the Making of Modern Greece.* Univ. of Texas Pr. 1982 $22.50

Hobsbawm, Eric, and Terence Ranger, eds. *The Invention of Tradition.* Cambridge Univ. Pr. 1983 $29.95 pap. $9.95

Knapp, Mary, and Herbert Knapp. *One Potato, Two Potato: The Secret Education of American Children.* Norton text ed. 1978 pap. $6.95. A significant and extensive collection from children, mainly in the United States, that is "deserving of serious attention by educators, parents, and folklorists" (Gary Alan Fine, *Journal of Amer. Folklore*).

Marling, Karal A. *The Colossus of Roads: Myth and Symbol along the American Highway.* Univ. of Minnesota Pr. 1984 $27.50 pap. $12.95

Rinzler, Carol A. *The Dictionary of Medical Folklore.* Crowell 1979 $14.37

Scheub, Harold. *African Oral Narratives, Proverbs, Riddles, Poetry and Song: An Annotated Bibliography. Reference Publications Ser.* G. K. Hall 1977 lib. bdg. $47.00

Schneiderman, Leo. *The Psychology of Myth, Folklore and Religion.* Nelson-Hall text ed. 1981 $29.95 pap. $9.95

Slobin, Mark. *Tenement Songs: The Popular Music of Jewish Immigrants. Music in Amer. Life Ser.* Univ. of Illinois Pr. 1982 $18.95. Shows the influence of folklore on related disciplines.

Using Folk Tales in Multicultural Education. Univ. of Connecticut School of Education 1982 $1.50. A slender pamphlet but the suggestions are sound.

Wernecke, Herbert H. *Christmas Customs around the World.* Westminster 1979 pap. $5.95

Zipes, Jack. *Breaking the Magic Spell: Radical Theories of Folk and Fairy Tales.* Methuen 1984 pap. $9.95; Univ. of Texas Pr. text ed. 1979 $15.00. ". . . deals mostly with the German Romantics in their social, political, and economic context, but he also writes of other fringes of folklore in the final two essays, 'The Utopian Function of Fairy Tales and Fantasy: Ernst Bloch the Marxist and J. R. R. Tolkien the Catholic' and 'On the Use and Abuse of Folk and Fairy Tales with Children: Bruno Bettelheim's Moralistic Magic Wand'" (Steve Siporin, *Journal of Amer. Folklore*).

————. *The Trials and Tribulations of Little Red Riding Hood: Versions of the Tale in Socio-Cultural Context.* Bergin & Garvey 1983 $34.95 pap. $16.95. Presents the texts, with commentary, of the tale in a variety of versions—from France, Germany, England, the United States, and other countries.

FOLK AND POPULAR HUMOR

In a certain sense, no distinction exists between folk and popular humor. All humor is composed of discernible motifs and various basic situations. Folk humor, in its various forms, is of uncertain origin, is often vulgar (but so is popular humor these days), lives in the collective mind of segments of the public, and has been communicated through time by oral means. Popular humor is usually prepared by professionals and disseminated through the printed or electronic media. The two forms obviously blend. The following list includes samples of both types and analyses of both.

Asimov, Isaac. *Isaac Asimov's Treasury of Humor*. Houghton Mifflin 1979 pap. $8.95

Billington, Ray Allen. *Limericks Historical and Hysterical: Plagiarized, Arranged, Annotated and Some Written by Ray Allen Billington*. Norton 1981 $9.95

Boas, Guy. *An Anthology of Wit*. Arden Lib. repr. of 1934 ed. 1977 lib. bdg. $10.00; Telegraph Bks. repr. of 1934 ed. 1983 lib. bdg. $40.00

Bombeck, Erma. *Motherhood: The Second Oldest Profession*. Dell 1984 pap. $3.95; McGraw-Hill 1984 $12.95. One of several books in print by a genuinely original wit and spokesperson for a maturing generation.

Bond, Simon. *One Hundred and One More Uses for a Dead Cat*. Crown 1982 pap. $3.95

Cohen, Hennig, and William B. Dillingham, eds. *Humor of the Old Southwest*. Univ. of Georgia Pr. repr. of 1964 ed. 2d ed. text ed. 1975 pap. $10.00

Cohen, Stanley J., and Robert Wool. *How to Survive on Fifty Thousand to One Hundred Fifty Thousand Dollars a Year*. Houghton Mifflin 1984 $13.95

Davies, John, ed. *Everyman's Book of Nonsense*. Fwd. by Spike Milligan, Biblio Dist. 1981 $13.95 text ed. 1982 pap. $3.95

Dickson, Paul. *Jokes: Outrageous Bits, Atrocious Puns, and Ridiculous Routines for Those Who Love Jests*. Ill. by Don Addis, Delacorte 1984 $13.95

Dorson, Richard M. *Man and Beast in American Comic Legend*. Intro. by Alan Dundes, afterword by Jeff Dorson, Indiana Univ. Pr. 1983 $20.00. "The last work of the man who did more than anyone else to see folklore studies recognized as a legitimate field of study at American universities. During his long career Richard M. Dorson published more than two dozen books. None of them exceeds this one in entertaining content. . . . [It] contains ten portraits of American legendary creatures, among these the Windham Frogs, the Hoopsnake, Bigfoot, and that rare high-plains creature the Jackalope. Augmenting this American bestiary are portraits of eight legendary American liars: Jim Bridger, Oregon Smith, Hathaway Jones, and others. The descriptions of man and beast are equally interesting and will be of great interest not only to folklorists but to all those who enjoy tall tales well told" (*Choice*).

Downs, Robert B., ed. *Bear Went Over the Mountain: Tall Tales of American Animals*. Gale repr. of 1964 ed. 1971 $40.00. A spirited compilation of more than 63 lying, humorous, and fantastic tales of U.S. animals, arranged according to region—Yankee, southern, Ozark, Texan, and western—with the addition of animal-fable and shaggy-dog types.

Eastman, Max. *Enjoyment of Laughter*. Darby repr. of 1937 ed. 1981 lib. bdg. $25.00

Elliot, Bob, and Ray Goulding. *From Approximately Coast to Coast: It's the Bob and Ray Show*. G. K. Hall lib. bdg. $14.95

Ephron, Delia. *How to Eat Like a Child: And Other Lessons in Not Being a Grownup*. Ballantine pap. $5.95; Viking 1978 $7.95

Ervin, Sam J., Jr. *Humor of a Country Lawyer*. Univ. of North Carolina Pr. 1983 $12.95

Esar, Evan. *The Comic Encyclopedia*. Doubleday 1978 $12.50

——. *Twenty Thousand Quips and Quotes*. Doubleday 1968 $15.95. A collection of single-sentence quips and quotes organized in 2,000 categories. "... a wealth of material for studying the relation of the 'detached saying' to the proverbial saying and of native to sophisticated American Humor, from the quips of the horse-sense cracker-box philosopher and newspaper paragrapher to those of our sophisticated wisecrackers and zany comedians. Behavioral scientists would do well to harken to Esar's suggestion that they look into this mirror of 'contemporary prejudices' and public attitudes" (B. A. Botkin, *N.Y. Folklore Quarterly*).

Fisher, Seymour, and Rhoda L. Fisher. *Pretend the World Is Funny and Forever: A Psychological Analysis of Comedians, Clowns, and Actors*. Erlbaum text ed. 1981 $29.95

Gruner, Charles R. *Understanding Laughter: The Workings of Wit and Humor*. Nelson-Hall 1978 o.p.

Holland, Norman N. *Laughing: A Psychology of Humor*. Cornell Univ. Pr. 1982 $19.95. "Holland summarizes a tremendous amount of philosophy, physiology, anthropology, history, and psychology. The review is broad and, as far as experimental psychology is concerned, unsympathetic. The experimental study of humor is derided for being too quantitative. Consequently the second half of the book is concerned with qualitative analysis ..." (*Choice*).

Inge, M. Thomas. *The Frontier Humorists: Critical Views*. Shoe String (Archon) 1975 $19.50

Koon, George W., ed. *A Collection of Classic Southern Humor Fiction and Occasional Fact by Some of the South's Best Story Tellers*. Peachtree 1984 $12.95 pap. $8.95

Kujoth, Jean S. *Subject Guide to Humor: Anecdotes, Facetiae and Satire from 365 Periodicals, 1968–74*. Scarecrow Pr. 1976 $15.00

Legman, Gershon. *No Laughing Matter: An Analysis of Sexual Humor*. Indiana Univ. Pr. 2 vols. repr. of 1968 ed. 1982 ea. $37.50 set $75.00. "The jokes of this First Series, which have been called 'the clean dirty jokes' will be followed by a Second Series, already completed, of 'the dirty dirty jokes' " (Publisher's note). "Under the mask of humor," writes Legman, "our society allows infinite aggressions, by everyone and against everyone.... Erotic humor is far and away the most popular of all types."

——. *No Laughing Matter: Rationale of the Dirty Joke*. Breaking Point 1975 $18.00; Crown 1976 $9.98. "Legman applies his heavily psychoanalytical theory and extreme Freudian approach to the deep feelings of hostility, guilt, and aggressiveness which lead a person to tell such jokes.... Despite Legman's extremely conventional Freudian interpretation of dirty jokes and the great length of his work, *No Laughing Matter* remains as a singular landmark in the study of erotic humor and should not be overlooked by any serious folklorist" (Christine Hoffman, *Journal of Amer. Folklore*).

Logue, Christopher. *Sweet and Sour: An Anthology of Comic Verse*. David & Charles 1983 $14.95

Loveland, Marion F. *America Laughs: A Sampler*. Collegium text ed. 1978 pap. $8.50

Meine, Franklin J. *Tall Tales of the Southwest.* Scholarly repr. of 1946 ed. 1971 $49.00

Moody, Raymond A., Jr. *Laugh after Laugh: The Healing Power of Humor.* Headwaters Pr. 1978 $7.95

Morris, Rosamund, ed. *Masterpieces of Humor.* Hart 1983 pap. $3.95

Shore, Sammy. *The Warmup: Life as a Warmup Comic.* Ed. by Pat Golbitz, Morrow 1984 $15.95

Spalding, Henry, ed. *Joys of Italian Humor and Folklore.* Jonathan David 1980 $16.95

Truchtenberg, Stanley. *American Humorists, 1800–1950. Dictionary of Literary Biography Ser.* Gale 2 vols. 1982 $170.00

POPULAR CULTURE

A relatively new area of study, which flowered in U.S. colleges in the 1960s, popular culture has been defined by Ray B. Browne, editor of the *Journal of Popular Culture* (founded in 1967), as "all aspects of the world we inhabit. . . . Our total life picture." It relates to the everyday world around us, what we do while awake, what we dream about when asleep. Popular culture today is usually disseminated by the mass media. The relationship between popular culture and folklore is obvious, and many individuals work in both fields.

Brantlinger, Patrick. *Bread and Circuses: Theories of Mass Culture as Social Decay.* Cornell Univ. Pr. 1984 $24.95

Donakowski, Conrad L. *A Muse for the Masses: Ritual and Music in an Age of Democratic Revolution, 1770–1870.* Univ. of Chicago Pr. 1977 lib. bdg. $27.50. "In a brilliant and wide-ranging discussion, Donakowski traces the development of the musical artist as propagandizer, as hero and as servant, and the development of music's use as decoration, communication and insulation in a way calculated to irritate the reader to further thought and study. As one reflects on the uses and misuses of music and communal ritual in today's secular and religious world, Donakowski's treatment of a turbulent period offers insight and illumination that is both pertinent and provocative" (Carl Schalk, *Christian Century*).

Dorfman, Ariel. *The Empire's Old Clothes: What the Lone Ranger, Babar, and Other Innocent Heroes Do to Our Minds.* Trans. by Clark Hensen, Pantheon 1983 $14.45 pap. $9.95. A "commentary on the exploitation of Third World countries by industrialized, Western powers, and the role that children's literature (including comic-book characters like Donald Duck) plays in teaching children not to rebel and to become part of the consumer economy" (*LJ*).

Fishburn, Katherine. *Women in Popular Culture: A Reference Guide. Amer. Popular Culture Ser.* Greenwood 1982 lib. bdg. $29.95. A history and bibliography of women in popular culture from colonial days to the present. Includes chapters on popular literature, magazines, film, television, advertising, and on theories of women in popular culture. In addition, appendixes list selected periodicals, bibliographies, a chronology of important dates, and research centers.

Fishwick, Marshall W. *Common Culture and the Great Tradition: The Case for Renewal. Contributions to the Study of Popular Culture Ser.* Greenwood 1982 lib. bdg. $27.50

Fraser, W. Hamish. *The Coming of the Mass Market, 1850–1914.* Shoe String (Archon) 1981 $27.50

Hoffman, Frank W. *Popular Culture and Libraries.* Shoe String (Archon) 1984 $29.50 pap. $18.50

Landrum, Larry N., ed. *American Popular Culture: A Guide to Information Sources.* Amer. Studies Information Guide Gale 1982 $58.00. "Landrum . . . has listed and briefly annotated more than 2,000 information sources in the wide-ranging field of popular culture. There is a cross-referenced, cross-indexed subject index and also a name index of both author and other personal name entries. Chapters bear such standard headings as bibliographies and indexes, general works, and anthologies, as well as the less decipherable 'material culture.' The latter includes fashion and architecture. There are also the obligatory chapters on sports, games, music, dance, theater, and literature. Also included are leisure, media, public art, and advertising. A chapter on entertainments refers to the circus, magic, and burlesque" (*Choice*).

Schroeder, Fred E. *Five Thousand Years of Popular Culture: Popular Culture before Printing.* Bowling Green 1980 $17.95 pap. $9.95

————. *Twentieth-Century Popular Culture in Museums and Libraries.* Bowling Green 1981 $30.00

Staples, Shirley. *Male Female Comedy Teams in American Vaudeville, 1865–1932.* Ed. by Bernard Beckerman, *Theater and Dramatic Studies* UMI Research 1984 $44.95. A doctoral dissertation that relates the origin and rise of vaudeville and the many individuals who took part. Shows, to some extent, the reflection of contemporary life in vaudeville routines.

Toll, Robert C. *The Entertainment Machine: American Show Business in the Twentieth Century.* Oxford 1982 $35.00 pap. $12.95. In this history of show business, Toll presents the "thesis that technology has created the changes in the popular styles of entertainment in America. . . . Divided into public (theater and movies) and home (phonograph, radio, television) entertainment, the book discusses the difference between pleasing an audience directly and through an advertising sponsor. The last chapters focus on six main genres: Westerns, popular music, musicals, crime, sex, and comedy" (*LJ*).

Warshow, Robert. *Immediate Experience: Movies, Comics, Theatre and Other Aspects of Popular Culture.* Intro. by Lionel Trilling, Atheneum repr. text ed. 1970 pap. $3.25

CHAPTER 15

Travel and Exploration

Charles R. Goeldner

As the Spanish proverb says, "He who would bring home the wealth of the Indies must carry the wealth of the Indies with him." So it is in traveling; a man must carry knowledge with him, if he would bring home knowledge.
—SAMUEL JOHNSON, Boswell's *Life of Johnson*

It is hard to know if today's traveler differs markedly from those *Innocents Abroad* MARK TWAIN (see Vol. 1) satirized in his 1869 book. Twain described the group he accompanied around the world as passive viewers of selected stops on tours and gullible listeners to the outrageous tales of tour guides. Although tourism is not new, considerable evidence suggests that changes are in the wind as the twenty-first century approaches. Probably the most obvious change lies in the sheer increase in numbers of tourists, a phenomenon arising from a variety of causes: Returning servicemen have tasted the joys of travel; pictures taken from spacecraft and satellite communications make our world seem smaller; jet travel puts world travel within the means of a greater number of people; and the expansion of businesses into worldwide enterprises allows globe-trotting executives to combine business and pleasure. In short, travel has become a prime goal for an increasing number of people, ranging from the budget-minded student to the wealthy retiree.

So, books provide information about historical aspects of different locales as well as advice on how to "see and enjoy" the best aspects of a country. Some professional travelers glamorize their trips for the guidance of the vacationer, while literary travelers write about their love for the places they have visited. Some travelers go to new places for sheer adventure. While space reigns as the new frontier, it is still out of the reach of ordinary travelers. Instead, people seek adventure exploring the ocean in scuba diving, in retracing historic routes, and in mountain climbing. There are those like Thor Heyerdahl, Francis Chichester, Sir Edmund Hillary, Robert Falcon Scott, and Jacques Cousteau, who deliberately travel with only the basic necessities of life in order to feel the challenge of pitting themselves against the forces of nature.

Libraries and bookstores abound with travel guides. Names like Mobil, Berlitz, Michelin, Nagel, Fodor, Fielding, and Frommer represent only a few of the countless number of available travel guides. In the past, guides were meagerly illustrated and encyclopedic in tone; today's are colorfully illustrated and engagingly written. Those wishing assistance in selecting a travel guide can consult one of four bibliographies to guidebooks. The first is Jon O. Heise (with Dennis O'Reilly), *The Travel Book: Guide to the Travel Guides.* An update of the 1978 edition, the book provides a guide to Africa, Asia, Australia, the Caribbean, Europe, Latin America, and the Pacific Islands. Annotations are incisive and readable. The other three are John A. Post and Jeremiah B. Post, *Travel in the United States: A Guide to Information Sources;* Susan Nueckel, *Selected Guide to Travel Books;* Maggy Simony, *Traveler's Reading Guide: Background Books, Novels, Travel Literature, and Articles.* Because these guidebooks can easily be found in libraries and bookstores, only limited mention will be made of them in the reference section of the chapter.

Most of the references in this chapter deal with accounts of trips, adventures, and exploration. These are the aspects of travel and adventure that interest the majority of readers. There is also another side of travel. Because travel and tourism are a growing industry throughout the world, a brief list of references on the scholarly aspect of travel is presented to provide a picture of the industry, its magnitude, and its impact.

SCHOLARLY REFERENCE BOOKS

Bosselman, Fred P. *In the Wake of the Tourist: Managing Special Places in Eight Countries.* Conservation Foundation 1978 $15.00. Examines the impact of tourism in Israel, Mexico, France, Australia, the Netherlands, England, Germany, and Japan.

Gee, Choy Y., and James C. Makens. *Travel Industry.* AVI text ed. 1984 $26.50. Provides a basic understanding of travel and tourism and provides insights into the development and operation of the various components of the travel industry.

Goeldner, Charles R., and Karen Duea. *Bibliography of Tourism and Travel Research Studies, Reports and Articles.* Business Research Division, Univ. of Colorado 9 vols. 1980 $60.00. This bibliography is a research resource on travel, recreation, and tourism.

————. *Travel Trends in the United States and Canada.* Business Research Division, Univ. of Colorado text ed. 1984 pap. $45.00. This document is published every three years and provides useful statistics on a variety of travel-related areas. Data have been compiled from 260 sources.

Gunn, Clare A. *Tourism Planning.* Crane Russak 1979 $22.50. Describes opportunities for greater expansion of tourism on the state and regional scale, without damage to delicate natural resources.

Lundberg, Donald E. *The Tourist Business.* Van Nostrand 5th ed. 1985 pap. $22.95. Explores the travel industry and covers travel modes, the role of travel agents, why people travel, the economic and social impact of tourism, tourist destination development, and travel research.

Lundberg, Donald E., and Carolyn Lundberg. *International Travel and Tourism.* Tourism Hospitality Ser. Wiley 1984 $23.95. The perspective of this book is American—why Americans go abroad, where they go, how they get there, and how they get around once they have arrived. It was written as a textbook for international travel.

McIntosh, Robert W., and Charles R. Goeldner. *Tourism: Principles, Practices and Philosophies.* Wiley 5th ed. 1984 $29.95. This classic introduction to tourism provides a broad global perspective with emphasis on planning and developing tourism. It investigates the cultural, economic, sociological, and psychological aspects of tourism. New material in this edition includes chapters on consumer markets, airline deregulation, and consumerism. Appendix material features careers in tourism and data sources.

Mill, Robert C., and others. *The Tourism System: An Introductory Text.* Prentice-Hall text ed. 1985 $25.95

National Tourism Policy Study Final Report. Committee of Commerce, Science and Transportation, U.S. Senate 1978 consult publisher for information. Prepared by Arthur D. Little, Inc., this report presents the findings of the final phase of the National Tourism Policy Study. The study was designed to develop a proposed national tourism policy for the United States; to define appropriate roles for the federal government, the states, cities, private industry, and consumers in carrying out, supporting, and contributing to the national tourism policy; and to recommend organizational, programmatic, and legislative strategies for implementing the proposed national tourism policy.

Organization for Economic Cooperation and Development. *Tourism Policy and International Tourism in OECD Member Countries, 1981.* OECD annual text ed. 1984 pap. $19.00. Annual report on tourism statistics in OECD countries.

Rosenow, John E., and Gerreld L. Pulsipher. *Tourism: The Good, the Bad, and the Ugly.* Century Three 1979 $17.95; Media Products & Marketing 1983 pap. $12.95. This book about travel in the United States emphasizes tourism's role in preserving the diversity of the country and improving the quality of community life.

Waters, Somerset R. *Travel Industry World Yearbook: The Big Picture.* Child & Waters annual 1985 vol. 29 pap. $49.00. Presents a compact, up-to-date review of the latest happenings in the world of tourism.

GENERAL REFERENCE WORKS

Adams, Percy G. *Travel Literature and the Evolution of the Novel.* Univ. Pr. of Kentucky 1983 $30.00. "... especially illuminating on two traveler-novelists, Defoe and Smollett, and in his chapter on prose styles" (*Choice*).

————. *Travelers and Travel Liars, 1600–1800.* Dover 1962 o.p. About real accounts that contain untruths, armchair trips made to seem real, and the different impressions made when different people describe the same places or events.

Barish, Frances. *Frommer's Guide for the Disabled Traveler: United States, Canada and Europe.* Simon & Schuster 1984 pap. $10.95

Barthelme, Donald. *Overnight to Many Distant Cities. Contemporary Amer. Fiction Ser.* Penguin 1985 pap. $5.95; Putnam 1983 $13.95

Blum, Ethel. *The Total Traveler by Ship: The Cruise Traveler's Handbook. Compleat Traveler's Guides Ser.* Burt Franklin 3d ed. 1981 pap. $8.95

Borders, Earl, Jr. *The Bus Trip Handbook.* Home Run Pr. 1985 pap. $8.95

Business Traveler's, Inc. *The Business Traveler's Survival Guide.* Watts 1981 pap. $9.95

Canning, John. *Fifty True Mysteries of the Sea.* Stein & Day 1984 pap. $3.95

Carlson, Raymond, ed. *National Directory of Free Vacation and Travel Information.* Pilot Books rev. ed. 1984 pap. $3.95

Casson, Lionel. *Travel in the Ancient World.* Allen & Unwin 1974 $15.00

Clark, James I. *Three Years on the Ocean*. Raintree 1982 pap. $9.27

Clark, Merrian E., and Bonnie Wilson. *Ford's Freighter Travel Guide: Sept. 1980–81*. Ford's Travel 63rd ed. rev. 1984 pap. $7.50

Council on International Education Exchange. *Work, Study, Travel Abroad, 1984–1985*. St. Martin's 1984 pap. $6.95

Cox, Edward G. *Reference Guide to the Literature of Travel, Including Voyages, Geographical Descriptions, Adventures, Shipwrecks and Expeditions*. Greenwood 3 vols. repr. of 1935–1949 ed. lib. bdg. $82.00. These definitive bibliographies list in chronological order from the earliest date to the year 1800 all books on foreign travel printed in Great Britain, together with translations from foreign tongues. The final chapters, "General Reference Books" and "Bibliographies," include books to 1936.

Delogu, Orlando E., ed. *United Nations List of National Parks and Equivalent Reserves, 1980. Environmental Policy and Law Papers* Unipub 1980 pap. $8.00. "Details more than 1,350 national parks and nature reserves in 140 member countries of the United Nations" (Publisher's note).

D'Oyley, Elizabeth, ed. *Great Travel Stories of All Nations*. Arden Lib. repr. of 1932 ed. 1979 lib. bdg. $40.00; Sharon Hill repr. of 1932 ed $35.00

Durrell, Lawrence. *The Spirit of Place: Letters and Essays on Travel*. Ed. by Alan G. Thomas, Dutton 1971 $10.00; Leete's Island Bks. 1984 pap. $8.95

Gellhorn, Martha. *Travels with Myself and Another*. Dodd 1979 $8.95; Hippocrene Bks. 1984 pap. $9.95

Guggenheim, Hans G. *Around the World in Eighty Ways*. Exposition Pr. 1982 pap. $6.00

Halliburton, Richard. *Complete Book of Marvels*. Darby 1981 lib. bdg. $30.00. Descriptions and illustrations of many natural and man-made wonders of the Occident and the Orient in a classic work—Golden Gate Bridge, Niagara Falls, Machu Picchu, Matterhorn, Colossus, Mt. Everest, Angkor, and others.

————. *The Royal Road to Romance*. Folcroft repr. of 1925 ed. 1978 lib. bdg. $35.00; Greenwood repr. of 1925 ed. lib. bdg. $25.75

Hamalian, Leo, ed. *Ladies on the Loose: Women Travellers of the Eighteenth and Nineteenth Centuries*. Dodd 1981 $11.95

Herbert, Anthony B. *The International Traveler's Security Handbook*. Hippocrene Bks. 1984 $19.95

Herrmann, Paul. *The Great Age of Discovery*. Trans. by Arnold J. Pomerans, Greenwood repr. of 1958 ed. 1974 $27.50. An unusual presentation, spanning five centuries, from Columbus to Livingstone in Africa.

Hindleu, Geoffrey. *Tourists, Travellers, and Pilgrims*. Hutchinson 1983 $9.95. A tour of five centuries of European history as experienced by ambassadors, writers, and an assortment of odd travelers who recorded their impressions of the hazards and delights of traveling. Hindleu manages this integration of history seen through a wide variety of eyes with both charm and wit.

Huxley, Aldous. *Along the Road: Notes and Essays of a Tourist*. Ayer repr. of 1925 ed. $16.00

Jakle, John A. *The Tourist: Travel in Twentieth Century North America*. Univ. of Nebraska Pr. 1985 $24.95 pap. $12.95

Jenkins, Peter. *A Walk across America*. Fawcett 1979 pap. $3.95

Jenkins, Peter, and Barbara Jenkins. *The Walk West: A Walk across America 2*. Fawcett 1983 pap. $3.95; Morrow 1981 $14.95. "One heck of an adventure. . . . Peter and Barbara are a good couple to travel with whose enthusiasm is infectious. Their prose is crisp and full of humor" (*Washington Post*).

Keay, John. *Eccentric Travelers.* Tarcher 1984 $12.95. "Strange men and improbable journeys are the subjects of this collection of essays. There are seven travellers . . . including Manning in Tibet, Palgrave in Arabia, the naturalist Waterton in South America, and the blind Holman crossing Russia and Siberia in the winter" (*LJ*).

Kowet, Don. *The Jet Lag Book: How to Rest Your Mind and Body and Beat the Fatigue and Confusion of Jet Lag.* Crown 1983 pap. $4.95

Lockwood, Allison. *Passionate Pilgrims.* Cornwall Bks. 1981 $30.00

Lubbock, Basil. *The China Clippers.* Foundation Class. 2 vols. repr. of 1922 ed. 1984 $187.55; State Mutual Bk. 1981 $45.00

MacCannell, Dean. *The Tourist: A New Theory of the Leisure Class.* Schocken 1976 pap. $6.95

Mendel, Roberta. *A Survival Manual for the Independent Woman Traveler.* Pin Prick 1982 $12.95

Mortimer, Charles G. *Travels of Charlie.* East Ridge Pr. 1975 pap. $6.95

Naylor, Penelope. *The Woman's Guide to Business Travel.* Hearst Bks. 1981 $14.95

Parry, J. H. *The Discovery of the Sea.* Univ. of California Pr. 1982 $26.50 pap. $8.95. ". . . describes the evolution of shipbuilding, navigation, geographical knowledge and trade and politics that made possible the voyages by European seafarers at the end of the fifteenth century and the beginning of the sixteenth [which] established beyond dispute that all the world's seas were connected" (Publisher's note).

Penrose, Boies. *Travel and Discovery in the Renaissance, 1420–1620.* Atheneum 1962 text ed. pap. $4.95. Factually sound, clearly written history with good bibliographies.

——. *Urbane Travelers, 1591–1635.* Octagon repr. 1970 lib. bdg. $19.50

Pletcher, Barbara A. *Travel Sense: A Guide for Business and Professional Women.* Kampmann 1980 $9.95

Portnoy, Sanford, and Joan Portnoy. *How to Take Great Trips with Your Kids.* Harvard Common Pr. 1984 $14.95 pap. $8.95

Pratson, Frederick. *Consumer's Guide to Package Travel around the World.* Globe Pequot 1984 pap. $10.95

Rebuffat, Gaston. *Men and the Matterhorn.* Trans. by Eleanor Brockett, Oxford 1973 $22.50. Written with love by a skilled writer and French mountaineer.

——. *On Ice and Snow and Rock.* Trans. by Patrick Evans, Oxford 1971 $19.50. "This is a book devoted to the equipment and techniques of mountain climbing . . . but it is also an important book that will be classic in the literature of mountains and mountain climbing" (*LJ*).

Rimington, Critchell, ed. *The Sea Chest: A Yachtsman's Reader.* Norton 1975 $14.95

Rosenthal, A. M., and P. Arthur Gelb, eds. *The Sophisticated Traveler: Winter, Love It or Leave It.* Villard 1984 $14.95. An uncommon guide to winter travel containing an array of travel writing by such authors as Joyce Carol Oates, Peter Benchley, John Updike, and William Buckley, Jr.

Rugoff, Milton, ed. *Great Travelers.* Simon & Schuster 2 vols. 1960 $12.50. This handsomely produced and illustrated anthology provides a catholic variety of firsthand accounts, skillfully chosen and organized.

Savage, Michael D., and others. *How to Go around the World Overland.* Surf 1984 pap. $14.95

Searles, John B. *An Insider's Guide to the Travel Game: How to Get the Most for Your Travel Dollar.* Rand-Rofua 1983 pap. $7.95

Shutt, V. Gladys. *Hey Traveller! Wanna Ride?* Vantage 1983 $10.95

Silverberg, Robert. *The Longest Voyage: Circumnavigations in the Age of Discovery*. Bobbs 1972 $10.00. "This book is about the early (1519–1617) circumnavigations of the world. The voyages of Magellan and Drake are described . . . as are the lesser known around-the-world cruises of Thomas Cavendish, Oliver van Noort, Joris van Spillbergen, and William Schouten and Jacob Le Maire . . . also information about pre-Magellan voyages, the European colonization of the Far East, the search for Terra Australis, and the mysterious Patagonian giants" (*LJ*).

Sinor, John. *Small Escapes under the Sun*. Alive Publications 1981 pap. $4.95

Sobek's International Explorer's Society. *One Thousand Journeys to the Rivers, Lands and Seas of Seven Continents*. Crown 1984 pap. $11.95

Sonntag, Ida. *Don't Drink the Water*. Chris Mass 1980 $7.95

Sykes, Percy M. *A History of Exploration from the Earliest Times to the Present Day*. Greenwood repr. of 1949 ed. 1976 lib. bdg. $49.50

Turner, A. C. *Traveller's Health Guide*. Bradt 1984 $7.95

Twain, Mark. *Innocents Abroad*. Harper repr. of 1869 ed. $12.95; New Amer. Lib. (Signet Class.) pap. $3.95

Warden, Herbert W., 3rd, ed. *In Praise of Sailors: A Nautical Anthology of Art, Poetry, and Prose*. Abrams 1978 o.p.

Williams, Neville. *Contraband Cargoes: Seven Centuries of Smuggling*. Shoe String (Archon) 1961 $16.00

Yapp, Peter. *Traveller's Dictionary of Quotations*. Routledge & Kegan 1985 $19.95

THE AMERICAS: NORTH AND SOUTH

Abbey, Edward. *Beyond the Wall: Essays from the Outside*. Holt 1984 $14.45 pap. $7.70. This collection of ten essays ranges from deserts of the Southwest and the Baja Peninsula of Mexico to the desertlike Arctic permafrost tundra of Alaska's Kongakut River.

Adventure Roads North. Alaska Northwest 1983 $14.95

Audubon, John J. *Delineations of American Scenery and Character*. Amer. Environmental Studies Ayer repr. of 1926 ed. 1970 $14.50. A reprint of Audubon's travel essays as a collection. In the original version, these essays were meant as fillers, to serve as relief between Audubon's photos and his descriptions of wildlife. However, they present a picture of North American eastern frontier life from 1808 to 1834, by a man who was as keen an observer of men as of wildlife.

Brower, Kenneth. *The Starship and the Canoe*. Harper 1983 pap. $5.72; Holt 1978 $8.95. The story of Freeman Dyson, the well-known quantum physicist, and his son, George, a strong conservationist. While Freeman Dyson was experimenting with the possibilities of atomic propulsion in connection with spacecraft, his son, George, was living in a tree house and working as a canoe maker in Canada. Brower draws a marvelous comparison between the technologically oriented and the natural adventurer.

Cahn, Robert, and Robert Glenn Ketchum. *American Photographers and the National Parks*. Viking 1981 $75.00. "The work of 37 artists, these photographs comprise a record of the changing ways people have seen and used the parks. The pictures are arranged chronologically . . ." (*N.Y. Review of Books*).

Carmer, Carl, ed. *Tavern Lamps Are Burning: Literary Journeys Through Six Regions and Four Centuries of New York State*. McKay 1964 $10.00. An anthology of British and American writing describing regions of New York State.

Carter, William E. *First Book of Bolivia.* Watts 1963 $4.90. William Carter went to Bolivia as a traveler and remained for approximately 20 years. His writing is that of a man fond of his adopted country, yet still fairly objective.

Champlain, Samuel De. *Narrative of a Voyage to the West Indies and Mexico in the Years 1599–1602.* Ed. by Norton Shaw, trans. by Alice Wilmere, Burt Franklin repr. of 1859 ed. $26.00

Chickering, William H. *Within the Sound of These Waves: The Story of the Kings of Hawaii Island, Containing a Full Account of the Death of Captain Cook, together with the Hawaiian Adventures of George Vancouver and Sundry Other Mariners.* Greenwood repr. of 1941 ed. 1971 lib. bdg. $24.75

Cook, James H. *Fifty Years on the Old Frontier as Cowboy, Hunter, Guide, Scout, and Ranchman.* Intro. by Charles King, Univ. of Oklahoma Pr. 5th ed. 1981 pap. $9.95. This volume has been a favorite for its thoughtful perspective on the U.S. western frontier, as seen through the eyes of Captain James Cook, after he retired from the sea. His ranch in Nebraska was host to paleontologists, anthropologists, and others.

Cumming, William P., and others. *The Exploration of North America, 1630–1776.* Putnam 1974 o.p. "Extracts from journals, letters, and manuscripts compiled from the observations of explorers, missionaries, fur trappers, and others from 1630 until the period of the Revolution" (*Booklist*).

Frome, Michael. *The National Parks.* Rand McNally rev. ed. 1981 pap. $9.95

Harner, Michael J. *The Jivaro: People of the Sacred Waterfalls.* Doubleday (Anchor) 1972 pap. $3.95; *California Lib. Repr. Ser.* Univ. of California Pr. text ed. 1983 $30.00 pap. $7.95. About a tribe in Ecuador.

Henfrey, Colin. *Manscapes: An American Journey.* Harvard Common Pr. 1973 $7.95. "An English prose virtuoso's tour of the U.S. in the late 1960's presents often shocking, sometimes predictable, but always germane reactions to what has become of the contemporary American experience" (*Booklist*).

Johnson, Beth. *Yukon Wild: The Adventures of Four Women Who Paddled 2,000 Miles through America's Last Frontier.* Berkshire Traveller 1984 pap. $10.95

Lamar, Howard, and Leonard Thompson, eds. *The Frontier in History: North America and Southern Africa Compared.* Yale Univ. Pr. 1981 text ed. $40.00 pap. $8.95

Limerick, Jeffrey, Nancy Ferguson, and Richard Oliver. *America's Grand Resort Hotels.* Pantheon 1979 $20.00

Meisch, Lynn. *A Traveler's Guide to El Dorado and the Inca Empire.* Penguin Handbooks Ser. rev. ed. 1984 pap. $14.95. A very practical guidebook with sections on travel arrangements, food, clothing, border crossings, communications, history, and mythology. A must for anyone interested in following the old route to El Dorado.

Moon, William L. *Blue Highways: A Journey into America.* Fawcett 1984 pap. $3.95. From calendars to deluxe cafes, Cajun music, Trappist monks to hang-gliders, Moon took a circular trip around the United States and pictures what is gone and nearly gone from the United States, as well as presenting a wry, sophisticated view of what he saw.

Mowat, Farley. *Canada North.* Little, Brown 1968 $4.95

Muir, John. *Travels in Alaska.* AMS Pr. repr. of 1915 ed. $19.50; Houghton Mifflin 1979 pap. $7.95; Scholarly repr. of 1915 ed. $39.00. An explorer with a genuine love of the wilderness, the vanishing edge, Muir manages to capture Alaska in the 1800s better than any other writer.

National Geographic Society. *Wilderness USA.* National Geographic Society 3d ed. 1975 $9.95

Ogburn, Charlton. *The Southern Appalachians: A Wilderness Quest.* Morrow 1975 $14.95 pap. $5.95

Olson, Sigurd F. *Open Horizons.* Knopf 1969 $11.50. "Sigurd Olson's beautifully written book (he has written five others on the Far North) [describes] his youth on a far-northern Wisconsin farm and the love of the lakes, forests and rivers that brought him back, after college, to learn the rugged life of a wilderness guide. Olson is a philosopher as well as a remarkable writer on nature. . . . A spellbinder" (*PW*).

———. *Wilderness Days.* Knopf 1972 $22.95

Phelan, Nancy. *The Chilean Way.* British Bk. Ctr. 1974 $16.50

Severin, Timothy. *The Golden Antilles.* Knopf 1970 $8.95. "Severin traces in almost minute detail the life of the myth of El Dorado in the minds of British explorers after 1595 . . ." (*Best Sellers*).

Simon, Kate. *Mexico: Places and Pleasures.* Crowell 1979 $16.30 pap. $7.95; Harper 1984 pap. $7.64

Stanton, William. *The Great United States Exploring Expedition of 1838–1842.* Univ. of California Pr. 1975 $30.00. ". . . a complex tale of political intrigue, adventure, shipwreck, personality conflicts, professional jealousy—with some ludicrous episodes. . . . [The expedition] marked a turning point in American science, when gentlemen naturalists were replaced by professionals and specialists" (*PW*).

Stevenson, Robert L. *Travels in Hawaii.* Univ. of Hawaii Pr. 1973 $10.50

Sutton, Horace. *Travelers: The American Tourist from Stage Coach to Space Shuttle.* Morrow 1980 $12.50. "Sutton approaches his subject with the enthusiasm of a busload of Rotarians at the Place Pigalle. His description of Americans on the road, whether to the watering holes of pre-Revolutionary New England or to the glamour spots of postwar southern France, are unfailingly witty and unflinchingly honest . . ." (*N.Y. Times Bk. Review*).

Taylor, Charles. *Six Journeys: A Canadian Pattern.* Univ. of Toronto Pr. 1977 $11.95

Theroux, Paul. *The Old Patagonian Express: By Train through the Americas.* Houghton Mifflin 1979 pap. $2.50

Tilden, Freeman. *The National Parks.* Knopf rev. ed. 1968 pap. $10.95

———. *The State Parks: Their Meaning in American Life.* Fwd. by Conrad L. Wirth, Knopf 1962 $8.95. Companion volume to *The National Parks*.

U.S. National Park Service. *Explorers and Settlers: Historic Places Commemorating the Early Exploration and Settlement of the United States.* Finch Pr. 1968 $15.00. "Part 1 of the present volume covers in a fine narrative style the extension of European civilization into the New World. Part 2 is a splendid survey of historic sites and buildings, copiously illustrated" (*LJ*).

Wilson, Earl J. *The Mexican Caribbean: Twenty Years of Underwater Exploration.* Exposition Pr. 1982 $10.00

Wright, Billie. *Four Seasons North: A Journal of Life in the Alaskan Wilderness.* Harper 1973 $9.95. One of the best books about northern Alaska available, full of descriptions of the Brooks Range, the Nuamiut Eskimos, and so on.

Zochert, Donald. *Walking in America.* Knopf 1974 $10.00

Zwinger, Ann. *Run, River, Run: A Naturalist's Journey Down One of the Great Rivers of the West.* Harper 1975 o.p. "Zwinger explored the Green River from its headwaters to its confluence with the Colorado, and her narrative is punctuated with quotations from earlier explorers, as well as with bits of information from a variety of disciplines (history, archaeology, botany . . .)" (*LJ*).

EUROPE

Baker, Daisy. *More Travels in a Donkey Trap.* International Specialized Bk. 1977 $9.95. "The author describes her travels with a donkey and cart about the countryside of her cottage in Devon, England. She reminisces about the past as she remembers her childhood in the country, her period as between-maid to the bishop's daughters, her first love during the First World War, and her marriage" (Publisher's note).

Baker, Paul R. *The Fortunate Pilgrims: Americans in Italy, 1800–1860.* Harvard Univ. Pr. 1964 $5.95

Bradley, David. *Lion Among Roses: A Memoir of Finland.* Holt 1965 o.p. "Penetrates heart and mind" (*LJ*).

Brett, David. *High Level: The Alps from End to End.* David & Charles 1983 $23.50

Burckhardt, Jacob. *The Cicerone: An Art Guide to Painting in Italy for the Use of Travellers and Students.* Ed. by Sydney J. Freedburg, *Connoisseurship, Criticism and Art History Ser.* Garland 1979 lib. bdg. $36.00

Connery, Donald S. *The Scandinavians.* Simon & Schuster 1972 $9.95. Connery, "a free-lance writer, has done surprisingly well from limited sources and personal observations; he dwells too much on some popular notions of contemporary Scandinavia but dispels most myths about sex, suicides and sin" (*LJ*).

Denham, H. M. *The Adriatic: A Sea Guide to Venice, the Italian Shore and the Dalmatian Coast.* Norton 1977 $19.95. "Unique and charming" (*LJ*).

———. *The Ionian Islands to Rhodes: A Sea Guide.* Norton 1976 $19.95

Durrell, Lawrence. *The Greek Islands.* Penguin 1980 pap. $14.95; Viking 1978 $25.00. One hundred outstanding color photos complement the writing, which describes sun-washed, history-laden islands. Evocative description—myth, architectural, and archaeological details are woven with the author's personal reminiscences.

Fermor, Patrick L. *Roumeli: Travels in Northern Greece. Travel Lib.* Penguin 1984 pap. $5.95

Fussell, P. *Abroad: British Literary Traveling between the Wars.* Oxford 1980 $19.95. "The English travel books of the 20s and 30s were . . . written in the Indian summer of what is now a dead form. Evelyn Waugh, Graham Greene, Norman Douglas, D. H. Lawrence, Robert Byron were the last masters of the art which was to be killed off by politics and the tourist industry" (*N.Y. Times Bk. Review*).

Gould, John. *Europe on a Saturday Night.* Down East repr. of 1968 ed. 1979 pap. $3.95. The entertaining travels of a Maine couple.

Gregory, Lady. *The Voyages of St. Brendan: The Navigator and Stories of the Saints of Ireland.* British-Amer. Bks. pap. $4.95

Hall, Ellen, and Emily Hall. *The Halls of Ravenswood.* Ed. by A. R. Mills, Transatlantic 1968 $6.95. The yearly travels of a Victorian family.

Hillaby, John. *A Walk through Britain.* Houghton Mifflin 1978 $7.95 pap. $4.95. The author's journey on foot from Land's End in southwestern Cornwall to John O'Groat's in northeastern Scotland during the spring and summer of 1966. "Hillaby's interest in and knowledge of natural life and prehistory give his book a lively theme and a distinctive flavor in which there is not a trace of the trite or commonplace. He also pleads convincingly for better conservation and recreation practices" (*LJ*).

Ingstad, Helge. *Westward to Vinland.* Trans. by Erik J. Friis, St. Martin's 1969 $8.95. Ingstad's account of Norse ruins in Newfoundland.

Kimbrough, Emily. *Floating Island.* Book & Tackle 1984 pap. $7.50. An account of a 12-day barge trip by a group of Americans through the canals of central France.

Laxalt, Robert. *In a Hundred Graves: A Basque Portrait.* Basque Bk. Ser. Univ. of Nebraska Pr. 1972 $8.00

———. *Sweet Promised Land.* Harper 1957 $10.00. An old Nevada sheepherder returns to his native village in the Pyrenees for a visit.

Liberman, Alexander. *Greece, Gods, and Art.* Intro. by Robert Graves, commentaries by Iris C. Love, Viking 1968 o.p. This "does more to bring the reader close to ancient Greece than would a dozen weary jet flights and bus journeys. A superb technical and imaginative performance" (Lewis Mumford).

McCarthy, Mary. *The Stones of Florence.* Harcourt 1976 $39.95

———. *Venice Observed.* Harcourt 1963 pap. $3.95. The novelist's brilliant pen explores past and present aspects of the Queen of the Adriatic.

McGough, Elizabeth. *On Your Own in Europe: A Teenager's Travel Guide.* Morrow 1978 pap. $5.50

Mead, William E. *The Grand Tour in the Eighteenth Century.* Ayer repr. of 1914 ed. $27.50; Richard West repr. of 1914 ed. 1973 $13.50

Michener, James A. *Iberia: Spanish Travels and Reflections.* Fawcett 1985 pap. $5.95; Random 1968 $29.95. "Michener unfolds a dazzling panorama of Spanish history, character, customs, and art; he discusses sex and bull-fighting, food and wine, picnics, pilgrimages, bird sanctuaries, cathedrals, museums, palaces. Scattered throughout are bright bits about fleabag hotels and delightful rogues" (*SR*).

Middleton, Dorothy. *Victorian Lady Travellers.* Academy Chicago repr. of 1965 ed. 1982 $12.95 pap. $6.95

Mullins, Edwin. *The Pilgrimage to Santiago.* Taplinger 1974 $12.95

Oakes, George W. *Turn Left at the Pub.* Congdon & Weed 1985 $8.95; McKay 1977 $5.95

Oakes, George W., and Alexander Chapman. *Turn Right at the Fountain.* Holt 4th ed. rev. 1981 $16.95 pap. $9.95

Parkes, Joan. *Travel in England in the Seventeenth Century.* Greenwood repr. of 1925 ed. lib. bdg. $20.50; Oxford repr. of 1925 ed. $15.95

Pillement, Georges. *Unknown Greece.* International Pubns. 2 vols. 1973 o.p. A guide to the less familiar regions of Greece. The author has written similar texts for France, Italy, Portugal, Sardinia and Corsica, Sicily, Spain, Turkey, and Yugoslavia.

Pritchett, Victor S. *London Perceived.* Harcourt 1966 pap. $3.95

Simon, Kate. *Italy: The Places in Between.* Harper rev. & enl. ed. 1984 $16.30 pap. $7.64

Skelton, R. A. *The Vinland Map and the Tartar Relation.* Fwd. by Alexander O. Vietor, Yale Univ. Pr. 1965 $35.00. Contains a reproduction of the map suggesting that the Norsemen discovered America about 1000 A.D.

Symons, Arthur. *Cities and Sea-Coasts and Islands.* Richard West repr. of 1918 ed. 1978 lib. bdg. $25.00. The author believes that one cannot write about an area or city unless it has aroused some intense emotion, whether love or hate. Each of the areas he covers has in some way moved him, and for this reason he is able to provide an insight, a feeling of atmosphere, for those cities in Europe that he selected, which many other travel books lack.

Theroux, Paul. *The Kingdom by the Sea: A Journey around Great Britain.* Washington Square Pr. 1984 pap. $4.95

Thublon, Colin. *Where Nights Are Longest: Travels by Car through Western Russia.* Random 1984 $16.95

Walzer, Mary M. *A Travel Guide for the Disabled: Western Europe.* Van Nostrand 1982 $11.95

Williamson, James A. *The Ocean in English History: Being the Ford Lectures.* Greenwood repr. of 1941 ed. 1979 lib. bdg. $24.75

AFRICA, ASIA, AND OCEANIA

Ackerley, J. R. *Hindoo Holiday: An Indian Journal.* Penguin 1984 pap. $5.95

Ames, Evelyn. *A Glimpse of Eden.* Houghton Mifflin 1967 o.p. The experiences of the author and her husband photographing East African wildlife are the substance of this "poetic, moving and memorable book" (*LJ*).

Candlin, Enid Saunders. *A Traveler's Tale: Memories of India.* Macmillan 1974 o.p. "The parameters of Eastern and Western civilization touch but do not mesh in this picture of the Indian sub-continent when British colonial rule ebbed in the aftermath of World War II" (*Booklist*).

Chiang, Yee. *The Silent Traveller in Japan.* Norton 1972 $15.00. "Japan and things Japanese as revealed by this distinguished Chinese scholar, artist and poet are experienced in a new dimension, for he sees them in relation to things Western and things Chinese" (Publisher's note).

Dedmon, Emmett. *China Journal.* Rand McNally 1973 o.p. "The author, who is Editorial Director of the *Chicago Sun Times* was one of the first American journalists to tour contemporary China. [He] shares his experiences and insights on this country's unique political and social organization" (Publisher's note).

Dunmore, John. *The Nineteenth Century.* Vol. 2 in *French Explorers in the Pacific.* Oxford 1969 $22.00

Edgar, Neal L., and Wendy Y. Ma, eds. *Travel in Asia: A Guide to Information Sources. Geography and Travel Information Guide Ser.* Gale 1982 $60.00

Fernea, Elizabeth W. *Guests of the Sheik: An Ethnology of an Iraqi Village.* Doubleday (Anchor) repr. 1969 pap. $5.95. Life in a tribal settlement on the edge of a village in southern Iraq.

Fernea, Robert A., and Georg Gerster. *Nubians in Egypt: Peaceful People.* Univ. of Texas Pr. 1973 $23.50

Godden, Jon, and Rumer Godden. *Shiva's Pigeons: An Experience of India.* Viking 1972 $25.00. "A fascinating and revealing document which . . . reflects and interreflects the ever-changing patterns of colors of an India where their spirits, like Shiva's pigeons, haunt the places they love" (Publisher's note).

Hillaby, John. *Journey to the Jade Sea.* Academy Chicago 1982 pap. $5.95

Kane, Robert S. *Africa A to Z.* Doubleday 1972 $9.95. This author has written many such guides, including *Asia A to Z* and *South Pacific A to Z.*

Kazantzakis, Nikos. *Japan-China: A Journal of Two Voyages to the Far East.* Trans. by George C. Papageotes, Creative Arts Bks. 1982 pap. $9.95

Lattimore, Owen, and Eleanor Lattimore. *Silks, Spices and Empire: Asia Seen through the Eyes of Its Discoverers.* Ed. by Evelyn S. Nef, Delacorte 1968 o.p. A fascinating anthology of writings collected by the noted orientalist and his wife.

Locke, John C., ed. *First Englishmen in India.* AMS Pr. repr. of 1930 ed. $18.00

Mowat, Farley. *The Siberians.* Little, Brown 1971 $8.95; Penguin 1972 pap. $3.95. A report of two long visits this Canadian author made to Siberia in 1966 and 1969 in which he shows that Siberia has recently become a productive and modern country.

Murphy, Dervla. *In Ethiopia with a Mule.* Transatlantic 1970 $9.95

——. *Tibetan Foothold.* Transatlantic 1967 $8.95

——. *The Waiting Land: A Spell in Nepal.* Transatlantic 1969 $12.50. "The 'spell' of the subtitle refers to what the author feels and transmits to her readers, a spell conjured by the friendly hardy people, their customs, and the unspeakable beauty of the country. Miss Murphy, a traveler who breaks all barriers of space, language, religion, food, comfort, and bacteria, writes with love, style, and wit" (*LJ*).

National Geographic Society. *Journey into China.* National Geographic Society 5th ed. 1984 $19.95

Newby, Eric. *A Short Walk in the Hindu Kush.* Intro. by Evelyn Waugh, Penguin 1981 pap. $5.95. Like many other amateur mountaintop walkers, Newby had the ambition to be more than a tourist and to reach places where few Englishmen had been before.

Panter-Downes, Mollie. *Ooty Preserved: A Victorian Hill Station in India.* Farrar 1967 $4.95

Perham, Margery. *African Apprenticeship: An Autobiographical Journey in Southern Africa.* 1929. Holmes & Meier 1974 o.p. "Here we see the beginning of her lifetime career and interest in Africa. . . . For all levels of libraries with an African interest" (*Choice*).

Rotberg, Robert I. *Africa and Its Explorers: Motives, Methods and Impacts.* Harvard Univ. Pr. 1970 o.p. Essays by nine Africanists on seven British and two German explorers of the nineteenth century—Barth, Livingstone, Burton, Speke, Baker, Rohlf, Stanley, Cameron, and Thomson.

Salisbury, Charlotte. *China Diary: After Mao.* Ed. by Beth Walker, Walker 1979 $9.95

Severin, Timothy. *The African Adventure.* Dutton 1973 o.p. "The adventures of a variety of explorers, military men, missionaries and sportsmen as they encounter the huge African continent. . . . Severin examines the explorers' varying motives and personalities, basing his account on their numerous publications, covering several centuries and all parts of the continent" (*LJ*).

Swaan, Wim. *Japanese Lantern.* Taplinger 1970 $8.95. A cultural guide in the form of essays.

Theroux, Paul. *The Great Railway Bazaar: By Train through Asia.* Houghton Mifflin 1975 $18.95; Washington Square Pr. repr. 1985 pap. $7.95. An account of a four-month railroad journey across Asia. "Perhaps not since Mark Twain's 'Following the Equator' (1897) have a wanderer's leisurely impressions been hammered into such wry, incisive mots. . . . By word and the seat of his pants Theroux has paid nostalgic homage to the pre-jet era, when men optimistically hoped to bind up the world with bands of steel" (*Time*).

THE ARCTIC AND ANTARCTICA

Cameron, Ian. *The Mountains at the Bottom of the World.* Avon 1974 pap. $1.25

Metzger, Charles R. *The Silent River: A Pastoral Elegy in the Form of a Recollection of Arctic Adventure.* Omega 1984 pap. $7.95

Mowat, Farley, and David Blackwood. *The Wake of the Great Sealers.* Little, Brown 1974 $19.95. The story of the Newfoundland men of the nineteenth and early twentieth centuries who set out in flimsy ships to hunt seals on the treacherous North Atlantic ice fields; lavishly illustrated.

Neatby, L. H. *Discovery in Russian and Siberian Waters*. Ohio Univ. Pr. 1973 $15.00. "A most fascinating and well-written account of Arctic exploration beginning with the mid-19th century" (*LJ*).

Wilson, Edward. *Diary of the Discovery Expedition to the Antarctic Regions, 1901–1904*. Ed. by Ann Savours, fwd. by the Duke of Edinburgh, Humanities Pr. 1967 $24.75. "Edward Wilson, who died with Scott on their return from the South Pole in 1912, first visited the Antarctic some 10 years earlier, keeping a personal and detailed diary, describing the day-to-day work, and the adventures of the scientific expedition. The author, surgeon and scientist of the expedition, was himself a remarkable man, which becomes evident on reading this book. It is illustrated with 47 of Wilson's exquisite watercolors, numerous pencil sketches throughout the text and 5 maps" (*LJ*).

———. *Diary of the "Terra Nova" Expedition to the Antarctic: 1910–1912*. Ed. by H. R. King, Humanities Pr. text ed. 1972 $21.50. "The tragic story of Scott's last expedition to the Antarctic . . . as seen through the eyes of Scott's second in command and scientific director" (*LJ*). "The pictures reproduced in this volume are remarkable by any standard. . . . A hundred reproductions appear in this handsome publication" (*TLS*).

INDIVIDUAL TRAVELS AND EXPLOITS

Adamson, J. H., and H. F. Folland. *The Shepherd of the Ocean: Sir Walter Raleigh and His Times*. Gambit 1969 o.p. "Raleigh's story has probably never been better told" (Edward Wagenknecht).

Anderson, Charles R., ed. *Journal of a Cruise to the Pacific Ocean, 1842–1844, in the Frigate United States with Notes on Herman Melville*. AMS PR. repr. of 1937 ed. $16.50

Anderson, Frank J. *Submarines, Diving, and the Underwater World: A Bibliography*. Shoe String 1975 $25.00

Beasley, David. *Through Paphlagonia with a Donkey: An Adventure in the Turkish Isfendyars*. Davus 1983 pap. $9.95 1984 $30.00

Bernard, Miguel A. *The Lights of Broadway and Other Essays: Reflections of a Filipino Traveler*. Cellar 1981 pap. $4.50 text ed. pap. $4.75

Biennes, Ranulph. *To the Ends of the Earth: The Transglobe Expedition, the First Pole-to-Pole Circumnavigation of the Globe*. Arbor House 1983 $17.95 pap. $9.95

Buckley, William F., Jr. *Atlantic High: A Celebration*. Doubleday 1982 $22.50. The book is "filled with a variety of delectable morsels—anecdotes, yarns, jokes, reflections, discussions, and diary jottings, touching on everything that interests a small group of educated upper-middle-class men who are sailing together. . . . So much more than a book about a sailing trip" (*Bk. Review Digest*).

Burgess, Robert F. *The Cave Divers*. Florida Class. 1982 $9.95

Champlain, Samuel De. *The Voyages and Explorations of Samuel De Champlain, 1604–1616*. AMS Pr. 2 vols. repr. of 1922 ed. $55.00

Cousteau, Jacques, and Alexis Sivirine. *Jacques Cousteau's Calypso*. Abrams 1983 $37.50. The volume focuses on the vessel itself, beginning in 1942 with its construction as a minesweeper for the British navy and continuing through many changes in its evolution into a modern research vessel. "Beautifully illustrated . . . a most attractive artistic production as well as a useful reference for those interested in the anatomy and equipment of ships, particularly research vessels" (*Choice*).

Darwin, Charles R. *Diary of the Voyage of H.M.S. Beagle*. Ed. by Nora Barlow, Kraus repr. of 1933 ed. 1969 $25.00

———. *Journal of Researches into the Natural History and Geology of the Countries Visited during the Voyage of the H.M.S. Beagle round the World, under the Command of Capt. Fitz Roy R.N.* AMS Pr. 2 vols. 1972 $42.50; Norwood repr. of 1892 ed. 1977 lib. bdg. $30.00

Dunlop, Bill, and Frank M. Drigotas, Jr. *One Man Alone across the Atlantic in a Nine-foot Boat*. Down East 1983 pap. $8.95

Fletcher, Colin. *The Complete Walker III*. Knopf 3d ed. 1984 $20.00 pap. $11.95

———. *New Complete Walker*. Knopf 1974 $14.95. A book for the stroller, the hiker, and the backpacker. Fletcher's *The Complete Walker* and its revised version (above) contain practical tips for the hiker and the backpacker, and backpacking equipment analysis. In addition, the book is laced with thoughtful insights on the philosophy of walking.

Fowler, Richard. *Amazing Journey of Space Ship H-30*. EDC 1984 pap. $8.95

Fremont, John Charles. *Report of the Exploring Expedition to the Rocky Mountains in the Year 1842: And to Oregon and North California in the Years 1843–44*. 1845. Univ. Microfilms 1966 $7.75

Graham, Robin L., and Derek Gill. *Dove*. Harper 1972 $14.95. The true story of a 16-year-old boy who sailed his 24-foot sloop around the world for five years and 33,000 miles to discover adventure and love.

Grant, George M. *Ocean to Ocean: Sandford Fleming's Expedition through Canada in 1872*. Tuttle repr. 1967 $3.95. "A stirring account of a small party's journey from Halifax in the east to Victoria in the west in search of a transcontinental railway route. A first-person story of the exhilarations and the hardships of the trip, it compares well with its nearest American counterpart, 'The Journals of Lewis and Clark' " (*N.Y. Times*).

Henderson, Richard. *Singlehanded Sailing: The Experiences and Techniques of the Lone Voyagers*. International Marine 1976 $22.50

Hiscock, Eric C. *Voyaging under Sail*. Oxford 2d ed. 1970 $25.00

Johnson, William H. *The World's Discoverers: The Story of Bold Voyages by Brave Navigators during a Thousand Years*. Gordon 1977 lib. bdg. $59.95

Keay, John. *When Men and Mountains Meet: The Explorers of the Western Himalayas, 1820–75*. Shoe String 1981 $19.50; Transatlantic 1978 $28.50

Kennedy, James Y. *South Seas Odyssey: An Escape*. Contemporary Bks. 1977 $8.95

Kingsley, Mary. *Travels in West Africa: Congo Français, Corsico and Cameroons*. 1897. Biblio Dist. 3d ed. rev. 1965 $37.50; Merrimack 1983 pap. $10.95. "This is one of the classic writings on African exploration. . . . It was a sensational success, and a second popular edition appeared in 1900. . . . Mary Kingsley, niece of the novelist Charles, kept house in Cambridge for her father, a physician and amateur anthropologist. Upon his death in 1892 she inherited a small estate and a taste for adventure which led her, quite by chance, to West Africa. Her explorations and account of her first two trips, in 1893 and 1895, were remarkable achievements. And, with far-reaching effects, her intelligent, humanitarian approach to the study of African culture demolished forever the concept of 'savage Africa' and its 'childlike natives' " (*LJ*).

Ledyard, John. *Journey through Russia and Siberia, 1787–1788: The Journal and Selected Letters*. Ed. by Stephen D. Watrous, Univ. of Wisconsin Pr. 1966 o.p. "John Ledyard was one of the most amazing explorers of all time. A Connecticut Yankee, he first saw the Pacific Northwest with Captain Cook in the 1770's and dreamed of returning there. Enlisting the aid of men like Jefferson, Lafayette, Banks, he conceived the idea of journeying eastward across Europe and Siberia, thence shipping to Alaska and walking across North America to New York. This well-researched, ably edited book describes his journey almost to the Pacific Coast of Siberia, before Catherine the Great ordered him returned to Europe" (*LJ*).

Linblad, Lars-Eric, and John G. Fuller. *Passport to Anywhere: The Story of Lars-Eric Linblad.* Time Bks. 1983 $20.75

Lincoln, Joseph C. *Soaring on the Wind: A Photographic Essay on the Sport of Soaring.* Northland 1973 $15.00

Martin, Sheila. *Seatramps: Five Years of Ocean Life.* Merrimack 1978 $12.95

Morris, Jan. *Journeys.* Oxford 1984 $12.95 1985 pap. $6.95. "Her latest journey takes her to . . . Vienna, Stockholm, Peking and Shanghai, Aberdeen in Scotland, Calcutta, and Wells, England. One of the 5 American stopovers is Las Vegas. . . . [She] may at times see more than is there, but a good travel writer has to. She may be the best we have" (*N.Y. Times Bk. Review*).

Muir, John. *The Cruise of the Corwin: Journal of the Arctic Expedition of 1881 in Search of De Long and the Jeannette.* Berg repr. of 1917 ed. 1974 lib. bdg. $19.95; Scholars Reference Lib. 1918 $30.00

Obregon, Mauricio. *Argonauts to Astronauts.* Harper 1980 $15.00. "The great explorers of the surface of the earth . . . are cited here for widening the horizons of the known world. . . ." [The author's] thesis is that with the space frontier we have come full circle. Astronauts are now the leading edge of knowledge and adventure that will open our world in much the same way that ancient explorers did theirs. Fresh insight into the history of exploration with an air of controlled excitement that should intrigue young adult readers" (*School Lib. Journal*).

Pike, Zebulon Montgomery. *The Journals of Zebulon Montgomery Pike, with Letters and Related Documents.* Ed. by Donald Jackson, *Amer. Exploration and Travel Ser.* Univ. of Oklahoma Pr. 2 vols. 1966 $47.50

Rishel, Virginia. *Wheels to Adventure: Bill Rishel's Western Routes.* Howe Brothers 1983 pap. $9.95

Roberts, David. *Great Exploration Hoaxes.* Ed. by Herbert Michaelman, Crown 1981 $10.95; Sierra 1982 $12.95

————. *The Mountain of My Fear.* Vanguard 1968 $14.95. The story of the first scaling of the western face of Alaska's Mount Huntington by four Harvard students in 1965.

Roth, Hal. *Two against Cape Horn.* Norton 1978 $18.95

————. *Two on a Big Ocean.* Norton 1978 $17.95. "This book describes the 19 months the Roths spent circumnavigating the Pacific Ocean, from San Francisco to Tahiti and the South Seas, then to Japan, the sub-Arctic Aleutians and the mountainous Alaskan and Canadian coasts. In their 35-foot sailboat Whisper they traveled 18,538 miles, called at 75 ports, made hundreds of new friends, and gained a new understanding of the sea and the people who live beside it" (Publisher's note).

Rotman, Jeffrey L., and Barry W. Allen. *Beneath Cold Seas: Exploring Temperate Waters of North America.* Van Nostrand 1983 $19.95

Sayre, Woodrow Wilson. *Four against Everest.* Prentice-Hall 1964 o.p. "Sayre's amazing ascent with three companions almost to the top of Everest was a tremendous test and magnificent achievement of the human spirit. With the sublime confidence of amateurs, without governmental permission or the help of Sherpas, and scorning oxygen as offensive to aesthetic principles and good sportsmanship, they faced unseen hazards but survived.... The chapter 'Why Men Climb' is a masterpiece" (*LJ*).

Speke, John H. *Journal of the Discovery of the Source of the Nile*. Biblio Dist. (Everyman's) repr. of 1906 ed. 1969 $12.95

Steinbeck, John. *Travels with Charley in Search of America*. Penguin 1980 pap. $3.95. In late summer 1960, Steinbeck set out from Sag Harbor, New York, in a three-quarter-ton pickup truck with a small cabin built on it. He traveled over the face of America with his ten-year-old poodle of indifferent health named Charley.

Teilhard de Chardin, Pierre. *Letters from a Traveller*. Ed. by Claude Aragonnes, intros. by Julian Huxley, Pierre Leroy, S.J., and Claude Aragonnes, Harper 1962 o.p. These are selections from letters written between 1923 and 1955 by Father Teilhard de Chardin, one of the world's leading paleontologists. His travels took him to China, Java, India, Ethiopia, South Africa, and the United States. A person of keen perception and spiritual insight, "He describes vividly the exotic lands where he searched for prehistoric man."

Zweig, Paul. *The Adventurer: The Fate of Adventure in the Western World*. Basic Bks. 1974 $12.50; Princeton Univ. Pr. 1981 $24.00 pap. $7.50

BORROW, GEORGE (HENRY). 1803–1881

Borrow was employed by the (Protestant) Bible Society to distribute Bibles in Catholic Spain in 1835. He encountered much opposition and was on one occasion imprisoned for three weeks. The famous account of his experience has little to do with the Bible and much to do with the people, land, and perils of his journey. Borrow is as racy in his descriptions of places as of people. *Lavengro* (1851) and its sequel, *The Romany Rye* (1857), are like novels in their interest and excitement. They are stories of gypsies, rich in gypsy lore, superstitions, and customs. Borrow spent many years in close association with Spanish gypsies and translated the Gospel of St. Luke into their language. His linguistic abilities were remarkable; he gives much space to word derivations, particularly in *Lavengro*. His books abound in pugnacious passages; his attacks on Sir Walter Scott, on prizefighters, and on "papists" are indicative of some of his sharp prejudices. But he wrote marvelously, and those who admire him are his devotees for life.

BOOKS BY BORROW

Works. Ed. by Clement Shorter, AMS Pr. 16 vols. repr. of 1924 ed. $300.00

Life, Writings and Correspondence; An Account of the Gypsy-Scholar, Traveler, Linguist and Agent for the British and Foreign Bible Society, 1803–1881. Ed. by William Ireland Knapp, Gale 2 vols. repr. of 1899 ed. 1967 $55.00

The Bible in Spain. Intro. by Walter Starkie, Biblio Dist. (Everyman's) 1961 $5.00

Lavengro: The Scholar, the Gypsy, the Priest. Intro. by Walter Starkie, Biblio Dist. (Everyman's) 1961 $8.95 pap. $2.95

Romany Rye. Biblio Dist. (Everyman's) repr. of 1906 ed. text ed. 1969 $8.95 pap. $3.95; Oxford 1984 pap. $7.95

BOOKS ABOUT BORROW

Bigland, Eileen. *In the Steps of George Borrow.* Telegraph Bks. repr. of 1951 ed. 1982 lib. bdg. $50.00

Jenkins, Herbert, ed. *Life of George Borrow.* Associated Faculty Pr. repr. of 1912 ed. 1970 $25.50

Walling, Robert A. *George Borrow: The Man and His Works.* Folcroft repr. of 1908 ed. 1977 lib. bdg. $30.00

BURTON, SIR RICHARD (FRANCIS). 1821–1890

Sir Richard Burton, the explorer, adventurer, translator, and student of Eastern sexual customs, continues to draw writers "as a honey pot draws bears," says Thomas Lask. Orville Prescott has written (*SR*): "One of the great explorers of the nineteenth century, Burton disguised himself as a Pathan dervish and doctor in order to penetrate the forbidden cities of Medina and Mecca. He was the first European to reach Harar, the religious capital of Somaliland. He was the discoverer of Lake Tanganyika, and explored in the Congo, the Cameroons, Dahomey, and Brazil. He was a pioneer ethnologist and anthropologist. He was a linguist of dazzling ability, speaking twenty-nine languages and eleven dialects. He wrote forty-three books on his travels, two volumes of poetry, and translated (in addition to *The Arabian Nights*) six volumes of Portuguese literature, two of Latin poetry, and four of Neapolitan, African, and Hindu folklore."

BOOKS BY BURTON

Sindh and the Races That Inhabit the Valley of the Indus. Intro. by H. T. Lambrick, *Oxford in Asia Historical Repr. Ser.* repr. of 1851 ed. 1974 $14.50

The Look of the West, 1860. Univ. of Nebraska Pr. (Bison) 1963 pap. $3.75

The Lake Region of Central Africa: A Picture of Exploration. Scholarly repr. of 1860 ed. 1972 $69.00

The City of the Saints. AMS Pr. repr. of 1862 ed. $29.00. Burton's account of his overland journey in 1860 to the home of the Mormons in Salt Lake City.

Wanderings in West Africa from Liverpool to Fernando Po. Johnson Repr. 2 vols. repr. of 1863 ed. 1971 $42.00

Nile Basin. Intro. by Robert O. Collins. *Middle East in the Twentieth Century Ser.* Da Capo 2d ed. repr. of 1864 ed. 1967 $25.00

Wit and Wisdom from West Africa: A Book of Proverbial Philosophy, Idioms, Enigmas, and Laconisms. Biblo & Tannen repr. of 1865 ed. 1969 $16.00; Greenwood repr. of 1865 ed. $24.75

Explorations of the Highlands of Brazil, with a Full Account of the Gold and Diamond Mines. Greenwood repr. of 1869 ed. 1968 lib. bdg. $32.75

Zanzibar: City, Island, and Coast. Johnson Repr. repr. of 1872 ed. 2 vols. $70.00

Two Trips to Gorilla Land and the Cataracts of the Congo. Johnson Repr. repr. of 1876 ed. 2 vols. in 1 $45.00

Personal Narrative of a Pilgrimage to Al Madinah and Meccah. Ed. by Isabel Burton, Dover 2 vols. repr. of 1893 ed. pap. ea. $7.95; Peter Smith 2 vols. repr. $28.50

The Erotic Traveler. Ed. by Edward Leigh, Putnam 1967 o.p. "Subtitled 'an astonishing exploration of bizarre sex rites and customs by the great adventurer,' this is sexual anthropology at its most exotic" (*Virginia Kirkus Service*).

BOOKS ABOUT BURTON

Brodie, Fawn M. *The Devil Drives: A Life of Sir Richard Burton*. Norton 1967 $15.95 1984 pap. $9.95. "Richard Burton's career was a bizarre adventure full of failures as well as achievements. It has been told often, but never with such scholarly zeal and judicious detachment as in *The Devil Drives*, by Fawn M. Brodie. . . . She is diligent in research, deft in keeping her narrative moving briskly, and unshockable when confronted by material that can still raise eyebrows even in our outspoken age" (Orville Prescott, *SR*).

Burton, Isabel. *The Life of Captain Sir Richard Burton*. Longwood 2 vols. repr. of 1898 ed. 1977 lib. bdg. $60.00

Burton, Jean. *Sir Richard Burton's Wife* Richard West 1942 $20.00

Dearden, Seton. *The Arabian Night: A Study of Sir Richard Burton*. Richard West repr. of 1936 ed. $25.00

Penzer, Norman M. *An Annotated Bibliography of Sir Richard Francis Burton*. Burt Franklin repr. of 1923 ed. 1970 $20.00

Stisted, Georgiana M. *True Life of Captain Sir Richard Burton*. Greenwood repr. of 1896 ed 1969 $20.00

Wright, Thomas. *Life of Sir Richard Burton*. Research and Source Works Ser. Burt Franklin 2 vols. repr. of 1906 ed. 1968 $35.50

BYRD, RICHARD E(VELYN). 1888–1957

Rear Admiral Byrd was a U.S. naval officer and aviator—the only person who had flown over both poles and one of the first men to fly the Atlantic. During World War I, he was lieutenant commander of the U.S. air forces in Canada. *Skyward* (1928, o.p.) tells of the first airplane flight made over the North Pole with Floyd Bennett in 1926. *Little America* (1930, o.p.) is a detailed record of Byrd's flight over the South Pole. *Alone* is his remarkable tale of fortitude during his self-imposed isolation at Advance Base in the Antarctic in 1934. In spring 1947 Byrd returned from his fifth and largest polar expedition, the largest exploring expedition ever organized—13 ships manned by 4,000 men, entirely naval in personnel.

"America's strategic concept of polar defense is an outgrowth of Admiral Byrd's five exploration ventures into the Arctic and Antarctic. . . . He was in over-all command of the Naval task force that, between 1955 and 1959, was to prepare, supply and maintain a series of scientific stations in Antarctica. . . . He was placed by President Eisenhower in charge of all Antarctic activities of the United States" (*N.Y. Times*).

Byrd received a special medal of the National Geographic Society from President Herbert Hoover in 1930, the Legion of Merit for "outstanding services" from President Franklin D. Roosevelt in 1945, and the Defense Department's Medal of Freedom in 1957. It is thought that he impaired his health seriously while on the 1933–34 expedition. He was buried with full military honors in the Arlington National Cemetery.

BOOKS BY BYRD

Discovery: The Story of the Second Byrd Antarctic Expedition. Intro. by Claude A. Swanson, *Select Bibliographies Repr. Ser.* Ayer repr. of 1935 ed. $36.00; Gale repr. of 1935 ed. 1971 $47.00

Alone. Island repr. of 1938 ed. 1984 $16.95

BOOKS ABOUT BYRD

Bernard, Raymond. *Hollow Earth.* Barker Bks. 1969 pap. $9.95; Citadel Pr. 1976 pap. $3.95; University Bks. 1969 $6.95

Rose, Lisle A. *Assault on Eternity: Richard E. Byrd and the Exploration of Antarctica, 1946–47.* Naval Institute Pr. 1980 $19.95

CLARK, WILLIAM. 1770–1838

[SEE LEWIS, MERIWETHER, in this chapter.]

COLUMBUS, CHRISTOPHER (Cristoforo Colombo). 1446–1506

A man of imagination, dreams, and perseverance, Columbus, the Genoese, persuaded King Ferdinand and Queen Isabella of Spain to sponsor his search for the Orient through a Western route. Columbus made four voyages to the New World, always landing in the West Indies and believing he was very close to the "Island of Cipango" (Japan). Difficulties with his crew and with his native subjects led to his dismissal as Spanish governor of the islands, although King Ferdinand remained an admirer of his nautical prowess.

Fernando Colon (Ferdinand Columbus), his son, wrote *The Life of the Admiral Christopher Columbus.* "It is greatly to Ferdinand's credit as an honest biographer that, while trying to show what a hard, sad life his father led, he included so much evidence to suggest that Columbus enjoyed it" (*New Yorker*).

BOOKS BY COLUMBUS

Christopher Columbus: His Life, His Works, His Remains, as Revealed by Original Printed and Manuscript Records. Ed. by John Boyd Thatcher, AMS Pr. 3 vols. repr. of 1903–04 ed. 1967 o.p.

Journal (during His First Voyage, 1492–1493): And Documents Relating to the Voyages of John Cabot and Gasper Corte Real. Ed. by Clements R. Markham, *Hakluyt Society Ser.* Burt Franklin repr. 1972 lib. bdg. $29.50

Journal of the First Voyage to America. Select Bibliographies Repr. Ser. Ayer repr. of 1924 ed. 1972 $16.00

Four Voyages to the New World. Intro. by John E. Fagg, Peter Smith $16.75

Letter to Rafael Sanchez. Johnson Repr. repr. of 1493 ed. $5.00

BOOKS ABOUT COLUMBUS

Colon, Fernando. *The Life of Admiral Christopher Columbus.* Trans. and ed. by Benjamin Kenn, Rutgers Univ. Pr. 1959 $10.00

Garner, Richard L., and Donald C. Henderson. *Columbus and Related Family Papers, 1451–1902: An Inventory of the Boal Collection.* Pennsylvania State Univ. Pr. 1974 pap. $5.95

Irving, Washington. *The Life and Voyages of Christopher Columbus: To Which Are*

Added Those of His Companions. AMS Pr. repr. of 1893 ed. $49.50; Darby repr. of 1868 ed. 1983 lib. bdg. $200.00

Morison, Samuel E. *Admiral of the Ocean Sea.* Little, Brown 1942 $24.95; Northeastern Univ. Pr. text ed. 1983 pap. $10.95

Olson, Julius E., ed. *Northmen, Columbus and Cabot, 985–1503.* Ed. by Edward G. Bourne, Barnes & Noble repr. of 1906 ed. 1967 $21.50

COOK, CAPTAIN JAMES. 1728–1779

Captain Cook's voyages round the world resulted in the discovery of the Sandwich Islands, the eastern coast of Australia, called New South Wales, and other important geographical information. He was killed by savages in Hawaii. An obelisk was erected there in his memory in 1874. Cook's *Voyages* was written partly by himself and continued by Captain James King after Cook's death.

"It is not too easy at this distance to appreciate fully the impact which Cook's voyages had on the intellectual world of his day. In a period of acute international tension . . . the exploring ships went out, incidentally, with safe conducts from belligerents, and the published reports quickly translated into the principal languages aroused immense enthusiasm. . . . In many ways Cook's second voyage was the high point of his career as an explorer and scientist" (*LJ*). In fall 1960, it was reported that a faded manuscript and logbook of Cook's first and second voyages were sold to a London bookseller for $148,400. In early 1969 an expeditionary party of the Academy of Natural Sciences of Philadelphia located some of Captain Cook's cannons in waters ten fathoms deep off the coast of Australia.

Books by Cook

Journal of H.M.S. Endeavour, 1768–1771. Genesis ltd. ed. 1977 $460.00

The Explorations of Captain James Cook in the Pacific, as Told by Selections of His Own Journals, 1768–1779. Ed. by A. Grenfell Price, intro. by Percy G. Adams, Dover pap. $6.00; Peter Smith $14.00

Authentic Narrative of a Voyage Performed by Captain Cook and Captain Clerke in His Majesty's Ships Resolution and Discovery during the Years 1776–1780: In Search of a North-West Passage between the Continents of Asia and America. 1782. Ed. by William Ellis, Da Capo 2 vols. 1969 o.p.

Voyages of Discovery. Ed. by John Barrow, Biblio Dist. (Everyman's) 1976 $10.95

Books about Cook

Beaglehole, J. C. *The Life of Captain James Cook.* Stanford Univ. Pr. 1974 $29.50

Conner, Daniel, and Lorraine Miller. *Master Mariner: Captain James Cook and the Peoples of the Pacific.* Univ. of Washington Pr. 1978 $25.00

Elliot, T. C., ed. *Captain Cook's Approach to Oregon.* Oregon Historical Society 1974 pap. $1.00

Fisher, Robin, and Hugh Johnston, eds. *Captain James Cook and His Times.* Univ. of Washington Pr. 1979 $19.95

Mitchell Library, Sydney. *Bibliography of Captain James Cook, Circumnavigator.* Burt Franklin repr. of 1928 ed. 1967 $20.50

Vaughan, Thomas, and C. M. Murray Oliver. *Captain Cook, R.N.: The Resolute Mariner.* Oregon Historical Society 1974 $11.95 pap. $4.95
Villiers, Alan. *Captain James Cook: A Definitive Biography.* Scribner 1970 $20.00

DANA, RICHARD HENRY, JR. 1815–1882

Two Years before the Mast (1840), the diary of what happened on the brig *Pilgrim* in its voyages round the Horn in 1834–36—a brig only 86 feet long and registering 180 tons—is a book so preeminent in the literature of the sea that England at one time gave a copy of it to every sailor in the Royal Navy.

The author "broke away from Harvard without a degree to become a common sailor," says Allan Nevins (*SR*). He had "a gift for close observation and character portrayal" and was "an appreciative student of nature," but wrote only one fascinating novel, although he tried others. Of the *Journal*, Nevins writes: "Robert F. Lucid, who presents the text with admirable care and illuminating annotations, remarks that Dana himself would emphatically agree that his journal does not rank with the diaries of Boswell or Pepys as a document of self-revelation, but adds that it does reveal a great deal about the character of the man." Dana kept the journal from 1841 to 1860. Dana's *Autobiographical Sketch, 1814–1842* (o.p.) is a brief account of his first 27 years. One of his later activities was "helping to found the Free Soil Party and rescue runaway slaves" (Nevins).

BOOKS BY DANA

Two Years before the Mast. Biblio Dist. (Everyman's) repr. of 1912 ed. 1972 $12.95 pap. $3.50; Buccaneer Bks. repr. 1981 lib. bdg. $18.95; ed. by Thomas Philbrick, *Penguin Amer. Lib. Ser.* 1981 pap. $4.95
To Cuba and Back. Ed. by C. Harvey Gardiner, Southern Illinois Univ. Pr. 1966 o.p. "During Dana's lifetime *To Cuba and Back* was as popular as his *Two Years before the Mast.* It became the standard guidebook for English speaking travelers and was still in print on the eve of World War I. Now a historical curiosity, it is of interest primarily to students of Dana and of Cuban history and to devotees of older travel books. . . . Its bibliographical and biographical introductions and the supervision of its reprinting have been done by an authority in his field. But Professor Gardiner has tampered with the text (omitting some pages, modernizing certain English spellings, consolidating shorter paragraphs) and in so doing has eliminated the audience for which this work and indeed the entire series seem most suited—the serious student and scholar. In its mutilated and modernized form this perceptive, entertaining, and compelling 19th-century view of Cuba will appeal primarily to the layman" (*LJ*).
The Journal of Richard Henry Dana, Jr. Ed. by Robert F. Lucid, Harvard Univ. Pr. 3 vols. 1968 o.p.

BOOKS ABOUT DANA

Adams, Charles F. *Richard Henry Dana.* Gale 2 vols. repr. of 1890 ed. 1968 $45.00
Gale, Robert L. *Richard Henry Dana. Twayne's U.S. Authors Ser.* G. K. Hall 1969 lib. bdg. $13.50
Shapiro, Samuel. *Richard Henry Dana, Jr.* Michigan State Univ. Pr. 1961 $5.00

FREUCHEN, PETER. 1886–1957

Peter Freuchen made his first trip to the Arctic in 1906. Off and on for more than two generations he lived, hunted, and traveled with the Eskimos, understanding them better than any other man of our generation. His first wife was an Eskimo, about whom he wrote *Ivalu, the Eskimo Wife.*

"Fliers enroute from Fort Churchill to distant Arctic air bases can still trace their course by landmarks he first put on the map." He aided refugees from the Nazis during the late 1930s and was active in the Underground movement after Denmark was occupied and before his own escape to Sweden. In 1957 he won the Gold Medal of the International Benjamin Franklin Society for his "service to mankind in opening new frontiers."

BOOKS BY FREUCHEN

The Peter Freuchen Reader. Ed. and trans. by Dagmar Freuchen, pref. by David Loth, Simon & Schuster 1965 o.p. "Included here are selections from *Vagrant Viking, Book of the Seven Seas, Arctic Adventure,* and *Eskimo,* plus a few pieces translated from Danish . . ." (LJ).

Arctic Adventure: My Life in the Frozen North. AMS Pr. repr. of 1935 ed. $32.50; Darby repr. of 1935 ed. 1982 lib. bdg. $35.00

(and David Loth). *Peter Freuchen's Book of the Seven Seas.* Simon & Schuster 1966 $9.95

Book of the Eskimos. Fawcett 1977 pap. $2.95

Ivalu, the Eskimo Wife. Trans by Janos Jusztis and Edward P. Erich, AMS Pr. repr. of 1935 ed. $20.00

GUNTHER, JOHN. 1901–1970

A war correspondent during World War II, John Gunther later devoted all his time to writing and is famous for his *Inside* books. Following his fourth visit to Russia in 1956, he presented important as well as trivial facts in *Inside Russia Today* (1958, o.p.). "The greatest service Mr. Gunther has done is to bring Russia down to a level we can all understand and talk and argue about" (*N.Y. Times*). In 1958 he received the Geographic Society of Chicago Publication Award for his *Inside* books.

Inside U.S.A. (1951) and *Inside Africa* (1955) are out of print. He wrote several biographies and a deeply moving account of the death of his young son of a brain tumor. His *Procession* (1965, o.p.) is a group of sketches of international political figures drawn from his *Inside* books and from articles. *Inside Australia,* completed and edited by William Forbis, was published posthumously.

BOOKS BY GUNTHER

Inside Europe Today. Harper rev. ed. 1962 $12.50. In this book, Gunther "has made a conscientious effort to interview some of the most important statesmen. . . . He has been conspicuously successful with Adenauer and Macmillan. He has gathered a lot of pertinent observations and characteristic stories about many others, like de Gaulle, Salazar and Tito. He draws also an intriguing pen-portrait of Khrushchev after the collapse of the Paris 'Summit' " (*LJ*).

Inside South America. Harper 1967 o.p. "Guntherization, as it must to all continents, has come again to South America, in another marvelous plum pudding of a book" (*N.Y. Times*).

A Fragment of Autobiography: The Fun of Writing the Inside Books. Harper 1962 o.p. Gunther is, on a serious level, probably the best known of all American writers on foreign affairs. His books are friendly in approach, authoritative, and fair-minded. In his lively and informative *A Fragment of Autobiography*, he begins with *Inside Europe* (1936, o.p.), then takes each of his books in turn and "describes how he chose his topics, the preparations he made for his travels, the information he sought, and how he wrote his manuscripts."

John Gunther's Inside Australia. Completed and ed. by William Forbis, Harper 1972 o.p.

HAKLUYT, RICHARD. 1552–1616

Hakluyt wrote not of his own travels but of other men's. He was an English divine who took such patriotic pride in the achievements of his countrymen that he devoted his life to preserving the records of all English voyages. They are in three parts—to Russia, to India, and to America. The Hakluyt Society, which republishes records of early voyages and travels, perpetuates his labors as well as his memory.

BOOKS BY HAKLUYT

Divers Voyages Touching the Discovery of America and the Islands Adjacent. 1582. Ed. by John W. Jones, Burt Franklin repr. $30.50

Principall Navigations, Voyages, Traffiques and Discoveries of the English Nation. AMS Pr. 12 vols. repr. of 1905 ed. $265.00; Kelley 12 vols. 3d ed. repr. of 1903 ed. $350.00

Hakluyt's Voyages to the New World: A Selection. Ed. by David F. Hawke, Bobbs 1972 pap. $3.40

Voyages and Discoveries. Ed. by Jack Beeching *Penguin Eng. Lib. Ser.* 1972 pap. $5.95

Voyages and Documents. Ed. by Janet Hampden, *World Class. Ser.* Oxford 1958 $9.50

BOOK ABOUT HAKLUYT

Parks, George B. *Richard Hakluyt and the English Voyages.* Folcroft repr. of 1928 ed. 1984 lib. bdg. $100.00; Ungar 2d ed. 1961 $13.50

HARRER, HEINRICH. 1912–

In 1939 Harrer was a member of the Nanga Parbat Expedition that was interned in India by the British at the outbreak of World War II. He escaped by way of Tibet, and during his seven years there he was unofficial tutor to the Dalai Lama in Lhasa and taught him geography, arithmetic, and English. Harrer is an Austrian, and during his years at the College and University of Graz he climbed hundreds of walls and ridges in the Alps, some for the first time.

BOOKS BY HARRER

Seven Years in Tibet. Intro. by Peter Fleming, Tarcher repr. of 1954 ed. 1982 pap. $8.95

Tibet Is My Country. Trans. by Edward Fitzgerald, Dutton 1961 o.p. The oral autobiography of Thubten Jugme Norbu, brother of the Dalai Lama.

HEYERDAHL, THOR. 1914–

"This is an enthralling book," Hamilton Lasso wrote in the *New Yorker* of *Kon-Tiki*, "and I don't think I can be very far off in calling it the most absorbing sea tale of our time." Heyerdahl, a Norwegian ethnologist, conceived the theory—not then accepted by other scientists—that Polynesia may have been originally settled by men who crossed the 4,000 miles of ocean from Peru in rafts made of balsa logs. *Kon-Tiki* is the story of how he and five others built the raft, as men of the Stone Age could build it, and traveled in it from Peru to a small island east of Tahiti—a "most fascinating description of intelligent courage."

Heyerdahl believes that he has at last solved the problem of how natives raised the great statues on Easter Island and has written a most absorbing account of it in *Aku-Aku* (1958). He has adduced further corroboration of his theory from the findings in *The Archaeology of Easter Island*.

In spring 1969, Heyerdahl was engaged in a new experiment—planning to cross the Atlantic from Morocco to Yucatan in a 12-ton papyrus boat that he and others built themselves in the manner of the ancient Egyptians. In spite of general skepticism as to whether the boat, called the *Ra*, could make the journey without sinking when it became thoroughly water-soaked, Heyerdahl and six others set out in full confidence. They hoped to demonstrate that Egyptians might have made the journey in this manner four or five thousand years ago and thus were the precursors of the Incas and Mayas. In July 1969, however, they were forced to abandon their attempt 600 miles short of their goal, near the Virgin Islands, after a series of storms had crippled the *Ra*. They left it drifting in the hope that it might reach Barbados on its own. Their second attempt in *Ra II* was successful.

BOOKS BY HEYERDAHL

Kon-Tiki: Across the Pacific by Raft. 1948. Trans. by F. H. Lyon, *Enriched Class. Ed. Ser.* Pocket Bks. 1973 pap. $3.95; Washington Square Pr. 1980 pap. $3.95

(and Edwin L. Ferdon, Jr.). *The Archaeology of Easter Island: Reports of the Norwegian Archaeological Expedition to Easter Island and the East Pacific.* Univ. of New Mexico Pr. 1961 o.p. In this superb work the editors and staff give full accounts of topography, climatology, flora and fauna, dwellings, artifacts, and, incidentally, the solution to several perplexing problems. Although intended for informed scientists and students of archaeology and anthropology, this book has a wider appeal.

The Ra Expeditions. New Amer. Lib. (Signet) 1972 pap. $1.95

FATU-HIVA: Back to Nature on a Pacific Island. New Amer. Lib. (Signet) 1976 pap. $2.25. Heyerdahl's "recollection of this colorful period in the infancy of his absorbing career is an attention riveting escape book as well as a revealing, if unnecessarily preachy, essay on what white men have done to a once happy South Sea island, and how the island retaliated against a white couple attempting to settle there. . . . It is a valuable contribution to the knowledge of Polynesia" (*N.Y. Times*).

The Art of Easter Island. Doubleday 1976 $35.00

BOOK ABOUT HEYERDAHL

Blassingame, Wyatt. *Thor Heyerdahl: Viking Scientist.* Lodestar Bks. 1979 $7.95

HILLARY, SIR EDMUND. 1919–

Sir Edmund Hillary wrote the chapter "Final Assault" in *The Conquest of Everest* (o.p.) by Sir John Hunt. Queen Elizabeth knighted both of them during the coronation festivities of 1953. Before the Everest triumph, Hillary had written several books about his adventures on other famous expeditions.

In June 1960, Hillary announced that in the fall he would attempt an ascent of the 27,790-foot Malaka Peak in Nepal about 20 miles east of Everest. He had two objectives: "first, to determine the effects of high altitude on climbers not equipped with oxygen equipment and, second, to make further efforts to track down the 'Abominable Snowman' " (*N.Y. Times*). The results, which were negligible, are told in *High in the Thin Cold Air* (1962, o.p.), which Hillary coauthored with Desmond Doig. This expedition did, however, establish a school at Khumjung, which made up for some of the other disappointments.

BOOKS BY HILLARY

(and Vivian Fuchs). *The Crossing of Antarctica: The Commonwealth Trans-Antarctic Expedition 1955–1958.* Greenwood repr. of 1959 ed. o.p.
Nothing Venture, Nothing Win. Putnam 1975 $12.95. "The tough, cheery, occasionally irascible New Zealander tells his life story . . ." (*PW*). ". . . an exciting adventure yarn, particularly when he's describing his early mountaineering exploits" (*LJ*).

BOOK ABOUT HILLARY

Kelly, Robert. *For Those in Peril: The Life and Times of Sir William Hillary Founder of the R.N.L.J.* State Mutual Bk. 1979 $25.00

KINGLAKE, ALEXANDER (WILLIAM). 1809–1891

The Cambridge History of English Literature regards *Eothen* as "perhaps the best book of travel in the English language." It consists of letters which Kinglake wrote home while making an extensive tour of the East in 1840. It was four years before he could find a publisher. He became the historian of the Crimea in 1863. "Eothen" is a Greek word meaning "from the early dawn" or "from the East."

BOOKS BY KINGLAKE

Eothen. 1844. Intro. by Harold Spender. Dutton 1954 o.p.
The Invasion of the Crimea. AMS Pr. 9 vols. repr. of 1888 ed. 1972 $337.50; Arden Lib. 8 vols. repr. of 1863 ed. 1978 lib. bdg. $300.00

BOOK ABOUT KINGLAKE

Tuckwell, W. *A. W. Kinglake: A Biographical and Literary Study.* Richard West repr. of 1902 ed. $20.00

LAWRENCE, T(HOMAS) E(DWARD) (T. E. Shaw). 1888–1935

T. E. Lawrence was a soldier, author, archaeologist, traveler, and translator. He was best known as Lawrence of Arabia, the man who freed the Arabs from the Turks in World War I. The manuscript of his *The Seven Pillars of Wisdom* (1926) was lost when two-thirds finished and he rewrote the book from memory in 1919. Because it expressed certain personal and political opinions that Lawrence did not wish to publicize, it was offered for sale in 1926 in England at a prohibitive price. To ensure copyright in the United States it was reprinted here by Doran (now Doubleday) and ten copies offered for sale at $20,000 each, a price "high enough to prevent their ever being sold." In 1935 Lawrence was killed when the motorbike given him by George Bernard Shaw went out of control on an English lane. Doubleday then brought out a limited edition and a trade edition, substantially the same as the rare 1926 edition. *Revolt in the Desert* (o.p.) is an abridgment of *The Seven Pillars*, which the author made to pay the printing expenses of the original. *The Mint*, an account of his service with the Royal Air Force, was published posthumously in an edition of 50 copies, ten of which were offered for sale at a price of half a million dollars each, to ensure no copies being sold. In 1950 a popular edition, in 1955 a limited edition, and in 1963 a paperback edition were published. After the war Lawrence enlisted in the Air Corps as Private Ross; in 1927 he became legally T. E. Shaw, under which name he was buried.

Earlier biographers, including Lowell Thomas and Robert Graves, were enthusiastic and laudatory. Twenty years after Lawrence's death, Richard Aldington wrote *Lawrence of Arabia: A Biographical Enquiry*, which "set off a fury of charge and countercharge." But Lawrence's saga had become legend. In tribute to this adventurous, enigmatic genius, who shunned fame, wealth, and power, King George V wrote, "His name will live in history." Public interest in "the elusive, mysterious and complex young Irishman" who led the Arab revolt was revived by *Lawrence of Arabia*, 1962's most honored film.

In recent years the picture of Lawrence has changed again with the revelation of his illegitimacy, his readiness to embroider the truth, and other quirks and neuroses; but there were English witnesses to many of his accomplishments and the disagreements among those who knew him have hindered efforts to discredit him in any definitive manner; even the Arabs view him with their Arab pride at stake. He remains enigmatic and eccentric and is likely to be the subject of more research and many volumes before the truth about him is fully understood.

BOOKS BY LAWRENCE

The Evolution of a Revolt: Early Postwar Writings of T. E. Lawrence. Ed. by Rodelle Weintraub, Pennsylvania State Univ. Pr. 1967 $19.95. Newspaper and journal articles from 1918 to 1921.

The Essential T. E. Lawrence: Selections from His Writings. 1951. Ed. by David Garnett, Viking 1963 o.p.

The Seven Pillars of Wisdom. Doubleday 1966 $10.00; Penguin 1976 pap. $7.95

The Mint. Norton Lib. 1963 pap. $4.95

BOOKS ABOUT LAWRENCE

Aldington, Richard. *Lawrence of Arabia: A Biographical Enquiry*. Greenwood repr. of 1955 ed. 1976 lib. bdg. $31.50

Clements, Frank *T. E. Lawrence: A Reader's Guide*. Shoe String (Archon) 1973 $17.50

Kiernan, Reginald H. *Lawrence of Arabia*. Folcroft repr. of 1935 ed. 1977 lib. bdg. $27.50; Richard West repr. of 1935 ed. 1980 lib. bdg. $25.00

Lawrence, A. W. *T. E. Lawrence by His Friends*. Richard West repr. of 1937 ed. $35.00

Liddell Hart, Basil H. *T. E. Lawrence in Arabia and After*. Greenwood repr. of 1934 ed. 1979 lib. bdg. $27.50. An early biography, but a good one.

Meyers, Jeffrey. *T. E. Lawrence: A Bibliography. Reference Lib. of the Humanities*. Garland 1975 lib. bdg. $19.00

Richards, Vyvyan. *Portrait of T. E. Lawrence. Eng. Biography Ser*. Haskell 1975 lib. bdg. $41.95

Robinson, Edward. *Lawrence: The Story of His Life*. Folcroft repr. of 1935 ed. 1979 lib. bdg. $27.00; Norwood repr. of 1935 ed. 1980 lib. bdg. $25.00; Richard West repr. of 1935 ed. $20.00

LEWIS, MERIWETHER. 1774–1809, and WILLIAM CLARK. 1770–1838

The Lewis and Clark expedition was one of the earliest crossings of the United States. Eager to expand the country, President THOMAS JEFFERSON appointed Lewis, formerly his private secretary, to seek a Northwest passage to the Orient. Lewis and his partner, William Clark, were both seasoned soldiers, expert woodsmen, and boatmen. They both kept journals and so did 4 sergeants and 1 private in the party of 43 men. They started from St. Louis in 1804 up to the Missouri River, across the Rockies, and down to the Pacific coast at the mouth of the Columbia River. The Indian maiden Sacajawea (the Bird Woman), wife of one of the members, gave them valuable help on the hazardous journey, which lasted two years, four months, and ten days, and cost the U.S. government a total of $38,722.25. Lewis was the better educated of the two captains and his account has more force, but Clark was a superb observer who wrote in an ingenious phonetic spelling of his own invention.

The official edition of the *Journals* did not appear until 1814, when they were edited in two volumes by Nicholas Biddle and Paul Allen. This text, a paraphrase of the journals, was used in various editions until 1904, when Reuben G. Thwaites edited an eight-volume edition, published in 1904–05. Bernard De Voto's edition follows the original text, but omits or summarizes the less important passages, making the journals available in all their original freshness.

Early in 1960 it was announced in the *N.Y. Times* that 67 notes written by Clark had been given by Frederick W. Beinecke of New York to the Yale University Library. "The documents, finger-smudged, blotted and blurred with cross-outs, list personal observations previously unknown to historians. . . . The documents, consisting of old letters, envelopes and scraps of paper, were the subject of an unusual legal fight. After the Clark notes were found in an attic in St. Paul, Minnesota, in 1952, the United States moved to obtain them. The Government contended the documents were part of the official records of Clark while he served the United States. The Federal Court of Appeals in

St. Louis dismissed the suit on Jan. 23, 1958. The court test was closely watched by libraries, museums and the American Philosophical Society. Had the Government been upheld, the custody of similar historical documents would have been jeopardized. . . ."

Shortly after the end of the expedition, Lewis was appointed governor of the Territory of Upper Louisiana. When he at last took up his post he was mysteriously killed—or took his own life—in the lonely wilderness.

BOOKS BY LEWIS AND CLARK

Atlas of the Lewis and Clark Expedition. Ed. by Gary E. Mouton, *Journals of the Lewis and Clark Expedition Ser.* Univ. of Nebraska Pr. 1983 $10.00

History of the Expedition under the Command of Captains Lewis and Clark. 1814. Ed. by Elliott Coues. Peter Smith 3 vols. repr. $45.00

The Original Journals of the Lewis and Clark Expedition, 1804–1806. Ed. by Reuben G. Thwaites, Ayer 8 vols. repr. of 1904–05 ed. $224.00

Journals of Lewis and Clark: A New Selection. Ed. by Bernard De Voto, Houghton Mifflin 1963 pap. $10.95; ed. by John Bakeless, New Amer. Lib. 1964 pap. $3.95. This well-edited collection of source materials is intended to complement the *Journals*, drawing together many letters, orders, invoices, and similar documents now scattered in both published and unpublished form. There are many detailed and informative annotations that make this volume fascinating and important reading.

BOOKS ABOUT LEWIS AND CLARK

Allen, John L. *Passage through the Garden: Lewis and Clark and the Image of the American Northwest.* Univ. of Illinois Pr. 1975 $32.95

Cutright, Paul R. *A History of the Lewis and Clark Journals.* Univ. of Oklahoma Pr. 1976 $22.50

Fisher, Vardis. *Suicide or Murder.* O L Holmes 1978 pap. $2.95

Flandrau, Grace. *Lewis and Clark Expedition.* Shorey repr. of 1927 ed. pap. $5.95

Hawke, David F. *Those Tremendous Mountains: The Story of the Lewis and Clark Expedition.* Norton 1980 $12.95

Jackson, Donald, ed. *Letters of the Lewis and Clark Expedition with Related Documents, 1783–1854.* Univ. of Illinois Pr. 1979 $49.50

Ronda, James. *Lewis and Clark among the Indians.* Univ. of Nebraska Pr. 1984 $24.95

Smith, Betsey. *The Lewis and Clark Expedition. Turning Points in Amer. History Ser.* Silver Burdett 1984 $14.96

Wheeler, Olin D. *The Trail of Lewis and Clark, 1804–1904.* AMS Pr. 2 vols. repr. of 1904 ed. $57.50

LINDBERGH, CHARLES A(UGUSTUS). 1902–1974

Charles Lindbergh's " 'The Spirit of St. Louis' is a magnificent book. . . . It is a historic document, revealing not only a fascinating individual, but a nation in the throes of whelping an industry which would one day become a source of its power" (*SR*). *We* was published shortly after the first historic solo, nonstop, transatlantic flight to Paris in 1927. *The Spirit of St. Louis* (1953) is the contemplative, almost hour-by-hour, account of that flight. The first low-priced edition was published to coincide with the release of the motion picture starring James Stewart. During World War II, Lindbergh flew combat missions in the Pacific. Later he worked with Pan American Airways and the National Naval Medical Center. In 1967 the *N.Y. Times* celebrated the fortieth anniversary of Lindbergh's transatlantic flight by reprinting the pilot's original account as it appeared in that newspaper on May 23, 1927. Afflicted with incurable cancer, Lindbergh elected to spend his last days at his retreat in the Hawaiian Islands, where he was buried with private ceremonies in an unmarked grave.

BOOKS BY LINDBERGH

We. Putnam 1927 $7.95

The Spirit of St. Louis. Avon 1985 pap. $5.95

The Wartime Journals of Charles A. Lindbergh. Harcourt 1970 $19.95. Covers the years 1937–45.

Boyhood on the Upper Mississippi: A Reminiscent Letter. Minnesota Historical Society 1972 $4.50

BOOKS ABOUT LINDBERGH

Cole, Wayne S. *Charles A. Lindbergh and the Battle Against American Intervention in World War II.* Harcourt 1974 $10.00

Foster, John T. *The Flight of the Lone Eagle: Charles Lindbergh Flies Nonstop from New York to Paris.* Watts $6.45

Ross, Walter. *The Last Hero: Charles A. Lindbergh.* Woodhill 1979 pap. $1.75. "...compelling throughout.... One of the best things about it is that Mr. Ross, in spite of what must have been repeated temptation, never grovels in hero-worship before his subject.... Surely his simplicity and stubborn drive explain much about Lindbergh, and Ross's book illuminates the surprising ways these trials have kept the hero from ever looking back" (London Wainwright, *Life*).

LIVINGSTONE, DAVID. 1813–1873

One of the most remarkable explorers of the nineteenth century, the Scotsman Livingstone sought first as a missionary and devout Christian to end the slave trade in Africa and then to locate the source of the Nile. In these attempts, he lost his wife, who caught a fever on an expedition in which she joined him. He discovered Victoria Falls and the lands between Nyasa and Tanganyika, encountering other hardships and tragedies in his double quest, but was much beloved by Africans who knew him. He never abated in his efforts in their behalf. His association with Sir Henry Morton Stanley is well known. The latter had been sent to find him by an American newspaper when Livingstone was feared lost; the formal approach of Stanley's first remark on finding him in a remote African village, "Dr. Livingstone, I presume," amused the world and the greeting became a byword. Stanley was with him in northern Tanganyika when he died. *Missionary Travels* (1857) is essentially the contemporary record of Livingstone's two journeys to northwestern Rhodesia in 1851–53. These letters furnish "priceless source material not only for the student of religious history but for the anthropologist and sociologist.... Completely devoted to the cause of Christ, Livingstone was also a realist and a man of unusual intelligence" (*LJ*).

Books by Livingstone

Missionary Travels and Researches in South Africa. Select Bibliographies Repr. Ser. Ayer repr. of 1857 ed. 1972 $52.00

The Zambesi Expedition, 1858–1863. Ed. by J. P. Wallis, Humanities Pr. 2 vols. 1956 o.p.

Narrative of an Expedition to the Zambesi and Its Tributaries: And of the Discovery of Lakes Shirwa and Nyasa, 1858–1864. Johnson Repr. repr. of 1866 ed. $48.00

Livingstone's Africa: Perilous Adventures and Extensive Discoveries in the Interior of Africa. Black Heritage Lib. Collection Ser. Ayer repr. of 1872 ed. $25.25; Irvington repr. of 1872 ed. text ed. $24.25

Last Journals of David Livingstone in Central Africa from 1865 to His Death. Ed. by Horace Waller, Greenwood 2 vols. repr. of 1874 ed. 1968 lib. bdg. $35.00

Livingstone's Missionary Correspondence, 1841–1856. Ed. by Isaac Schapera, Univ. of California Pr. 1961 $24.00

The David Livingstone Family Letters. Ed. by Isaac Schapera, Greenwood 2 vols. repr. of 1959 ed. 1975 lib. bdg. $31.50; Humanities Pr. 2 vols. 1959 text ed. $11.00

Some Letters from Livingstone, 1840–1872. Greenwood repr. of 1940 ed. $22.50

Books about Livingstone

Blaikie, William G. *Personal Life of David Livingstone.* Greenwood 1880 $22.00

Martelli, George. *Livingstone's River.* Simon & Schuster 1970 $7.50

Pachai, Bridglal, ed. *Livingstone, Man of Africa: Memorial Essays, 1873–1973.* Longman 1973 text ed. $9.00

Ransford, Oliver. *David Livingstone: The Dark Continent.* St. Martin's 1978 $27.50

Stanley, Henry M. *How I Found Livingstone.* Greenwood repr. of 1913 ed. $26.00

MORTON, H(ENRY CANOVA) V(OLLAM). 1892–1979

H. V. Morton began writing as an undergraduate in England. By the time he was 19, he became assistant editor of the *Birmingham Gazette and Express.* Later he joined the staff of the *Daily Mail* in London. Returning home from the British Army after World War I, he realized how little he actually knew his country. His explorations led him to write a travel series published by Dodd. He has been called "perhaps the greatest living authority on the material being of the British Isles—that is to say, on their landscape, buildings, monuments, customs and history." As a devout churchman, he has also written several books on biblical personages and places. He was an experienced and worldly traveler who had a "unique talent for capturing the essence of lives long past."

Books by Morton

H. V. Morton's Britain. Dodd 1969 o.p. Selections from his *In Search* books on England, Scotland, Ireland, and Wales.

In the Steps of the Master. Dodd 1984 pap. $12.95; Folcroft 1935 lib. bdg. $32.59

A Traveller in Rome. Dodd 1984 pap. $12.95

A Traveller in Southern Italy. Dodd 1969 $10.00. "Well written, well illustrated and really a fine example of the bookmaker's art, this book presents the whole of northern Italy with much skill. The result is a literary feast through the regions of Lombardy and Emilia, the cities of Venice and Florence. Morton is incapable of mere good writing; he is superb. A walk through Verona or a visit to the Pitti

Palace or Dante's tomb is turned into a masterpiece of mood mingled with perception. Morton is so effective in evoking the past that it remains no farther away in time than the last ticking of a clock" (*LJ*).

PARK, MUNGO. 1771–1806

One of the earliest of African explorers, the Scotsman Mungo Park discovered the Niger River and his explorations helped to map the interior of Africa. His classic account of his adventures was originally published as *Travels in the Interior Districts of Africa* (1799). On a second expedition he was lost.

BOOKS BY PARK

Travels in the Interior Districts of Africa. Scholarly repr. of 1813 ed. $27.00
Journal of a Mission to the Interior of Africa. Scholarly $21.00

BOOKS ABOUT PARK

Lupton, Kenneth. *Mungo Park: The African Traveler.* Oxford 1979 $32.50
Thomson, Joseph. *Mungo Park and the Niger.* Argosy repr. of 1890 ed. 1970 $15.00

PEARY, ROBERT E(DWIN). 1856–1920

Robert E. Peary, the American who discovered the North Pole, first became interested in Arctic exploration after a trip into the interior of Greenland in 1886. Later trips there funded by the Philadelphia Academy of Natural Sciences proved that Greenland is an island and resulted in his account *Northward over the Great Ice.*

Nearest the Pole tells of his Arctic trip when the "farthest north" record was set about 200 miles from the North Pole. On April 6, 1909, he finally reached the North Pole after a voyage in the specially built ship *Roosevelt* and a long trek over ice via dogsled. *The North Pole* published in 1910 is his account of that final trip. He retired from the U.S. Navy in 1911 with the rank of rear admiral, but again served his country during World War I.

BOOKS BY PEARY

Northward over the Great Ice: A Narrative of Life and World among the Shores and upon the Interior Ice Cap of Northern Greenland in the Years 1886 and 1891–1897. AMS Pr. 2 vols. repr. of 1898 ed. o.p.
Nearest the Pole: A Narrative of the Polar Expedition of the Peary Arctic Club in the S.S. Roosevelt, 1905–1906. AMS Pr. repr. of 1907 ed. o.p.
The North Pole: Its Discovery in 1909 under the Auspices of the Peary Arctic Club. Arden Lib. repr. of 1910 ed. lib. bdg. $45.00

BOOK ABOUT PEARY

Hunt, William R. *To Stand at the Pole: The Dr. Cook-Admiral Peary North Pole Controversy.* Stein & Day 1982 $19.95

POLO, MARCO. 1254?–1324?

Marco Polo was the pioneer explorer of central Asia and China. His contemporaries refused to believe his story, but time has fully credited the veracity of all he wrote. *The Travels* (1300–24) was written while he was a prison inmate in Genoa during the war between Venice and Genoa. It was dictated to a fellow prisoner entirely in French and almost immediately translated into many languages.

BOOKS BY POLO

The Book of Marco Polo. Ed. and trans. by Henry Yule, AMS Pr. 3 vols. 3d ed. repr. of 1920 ed. $97.50

The Travels of Marco Polo. Trans. by Ronald Latham, Abaris Bks. 1982 $35.00; Biblio Dist. (Everyman's) 1954 $7.50; Harmony Raine repr. 1982 lib. bdg. $18.95; ed. by Manuel Komroff, Liveright 1953 $6.95

The Description of the World. AMS Pr. 2 vols. repr. of 1938 ed. $65.00

BOOKS ABOUT POLO

Hart, Henry H. *Marco Polo: Venetian Adventurer.* Univ. of Oklahoma Pr. 1967 $17.95

Komroff, Manuel, ed. *Contemporaries of Marco Polo. Black and Gold Lib.* Liveright 1937 $6.95

Olschki, Leonardo. *Marco Polo's Asia: An Introduction to His "Description of the World" Called "Il Milione."* Trans. by John A. Scott, Univ. of California Pr. 1960 $42.50

Ross, E. Denison. *Marco Polo and His Books.* Folcroft repr. of 1934 ed. lib. bdg. $10.00

Rugoff, Milton. *The Travels of Marco Polo.* New Amer. Lib. (Signet Class.) 1982 pap. $3.50

SCOTT, ROBERT FALCON. 1868–1912

After an initial expedition to Antarctica, the British Robert Scott reached the South Pole in 1912 only to find that the Norwegian explorer Amundsen had beaten him by a month. Scott and his party perished in a blizzard on the return trip. It was not until the following spring that their bodies and scientific documents were recovered. The documents were published in two books that are valuable as records of scientific research and as human documents. *Scott's Last Expedition* (1913) is his own classic diary of the tragedy together with scientific material gathered on the journey. "Captain Scott kept a precise diary of the bitter days of his last journey South. His hands and feet crippled by frostbite, his eyes and mind befuddled by Antarctic blizzard, he traveled on to final defeat—and, in a way, magnificent triumph. Coming to the South Pole area itself, Scott was overwhelmed to learn that he had been preceded by the Norwegian. He knew full well the shattering implications in terms of personal and national prestige. But, gentleman to the end, he dutifully picked up Amundsen's message to the world (left at the South Pole in case Amundsen did not make it home successfully), and this eventually was conveyed to the King of Norway as proof that the Norwegian had beaten the Briton. Scott's was an act that could have been performed only by a man of honor. It is on the return trip that Scott's diary reaches a poignancy seldom matched in exploration writing" (*SR*).

Books by Scott

The Voyage of the Discovery. Greenwood 2 vols. repr. of 1905 ed. 1969 lib. bdg. $57.00; Transatlantic 1951 $18.00

Scott's Last Expedition: Captain Scott's Own Story. Intro. by Peter Scott, Transatlantic 1923 $8.95

Books about Scott

Nickles, Sylvie. *Scott and the Discovery of the Antarctic.* Grossman 1972 o.p.

Wilson, Edward. *Diary of the Discovery Expedition to the Antarctic Regions, 1901–1904.* Ed. by Ann Savours, fwd. by the Duke of Edinburgh, Humanities Pr. 1967 $24.75

SLOCUM, JOSHUA. 1844–1909

Captain Joshua Slocum, the intrepid mariner who has been called the Thoreau of the Sea, set out in April 1896 to sail around the world alone in a small sloop he had reclaimed from a derelict and named *The Spray.* The voyage took three years, two months, and two days. He told the story of this trip in *Sailing Alone Around the World. American Authors and Books, 1640–1940* makes the statement that he started another voyage on November 14, 1909 and was never heard from again. He was legally declared dead as of that date.

Books by Slocum

The Voyages of Joshua Slocum. Ed. by Walter Magnes Teller, Sheridan repr. of 1958 ed. 1985 $22.50. Includes all the published works, hitherto unpublished correspondence, a checklist, and a selected bibliography.

Sailing Alone Around the World. Dover repr. of 1900 ed. 1956 pap. $3.95; Norton rev. ed. 1984 $17.95

The Voyage of the Liberdade (and *Sailing Alone*). Macmillan (Collier Bks.) 1970 pap. $3.50

Books about Slocum

Slocum, Victor. *Captain Joshua Slocum.* State Mutual Bk. 1982 $40.00

Teller, Walter M. *Joshua Slocum.* Rutgers Univ. Pr. 1971 $25.00

SNOW, EDWARD (ROWE). 1902–1982

Author, historian, and adventurer, Edward Snow was descended from a long line of sea captains and spent several years of his early life sailing around the world. The *N.Y. Times* called him "just about the best chronicler of the days of sail alive today."

Books by Snow

The Islands of Boston Harbor: 1630–1971. Dodd repr. of 1971 ed. 1984 pap. $9.95

Ghost, Gales and Gold. Dodd 1972 $6.95

The Lighthouses of New England, 1716-1973. Dodd 1984 pap. $9.95

Supernatural Mysteries and Other Tales: New England to the Bermuda Triangle. Dodd 1974 $7.95

Marine Mysteries and Dramatic Disasters of New England. Dodd 1976 $8.95

Pirates, Shipwrecks, and Historic Chronicles. Dodd 1981 $10.95

STANLEY, SIR HENRY MORTON. 1841–1904

Stanley was a U.S. traveler born in Wales, educated in the poorhouse, and adopted by a New Orleans merchant who gave him his name. He fought in the Confederate army and after the war became a newspaper correspondent. He was commissioned by the *N.Y. Herald* to go in search of Livingstone in 1871.

Stanley based one of his most popular books, *Through the Dark Continent*, on a series of diaries in which he recorded the progress of his expedition of 1874–77. He presented the day-to-day account of his journeys undertaken to discover the sources of the Nile and Congo rivers, his circumnavigation of Lakes Victoria and Tanganyika, and his dangerous trip down the Congo River to Boma. (See also David Livingstone in this chapter.)

BOOKS BY STANLEY

How I Found Livingstone. Greenwood repr. of 1913 ed. $26.00
Coomassie and Magdala: The Story of Two British Campaigns in Africa. Select Bibliographies Repr. Ser. Ayer repr. of 1874 ed. $32.00
My Kalulu, Prince, King, and Slave: A Story of Central Africa. Greenwood repr. of 1874 ed. $21.25
Through the Dark Continent, or The Sources of the Nile, around the Great Lakes of Equatorial Africa, and down the Livingstone River to the Atlantic Ocean. Greenwood 2 vols. repr. of 1878 ed. 1968 lib. bdg. $60.75
The Congo and the Founding of Its Free State. Scholarly 2 vols. repr. of 1885 ed. $75.00
The Story of Emin's Rescue as Told in Stanley's Letters. Ed. by J. S. Keltie, Greenwood repr. of 1890 ed. $17.50
Autobiography. Ed. by Dorothy Stanley, Greenwood repr. of 1909 ed. lib. bdg. $28.50

BOOKS ABOUT STANLEY

Buel, J. W. *Heroes of the Dark Continent. Black Heritage Lib. Collection Ser.* Ayer repr. of 1889 ed. $32.75
Farwell, Byron. *The Man Who Presumed: A Biography of Henry M. Stanley.* Greenwood repr. of 1957 ed. 1974 lib. bdg. $19.25
Feather, A. G. *Stanley's Story, or Through the Wilds of Africa. Africa History Ser.* Metro Bks. repr. of 1890 ed. 1969 lib. bdg. $29.00
Tames, R. *Henry Morton Stanley. Clarendon Biography Ser.* Newbury Bks. pap. $3.50; Seven Hills Bks. pap. $3.50

STARK, FREYA (MADELINE). 1893–

Freya Stark was brought up in northwestern Italy. After 1914 she became a wartime censor and then a nurse. She studied Arabic with a Capuchin monk in San Remo and after 1927 began wanderings into remote parts of the Middle East—alone, usually in poverty, and often ill. She was in the British government service, chiefly at Aden, Cairo, and Baghdad, from 1939 to 1945, and married S. H. Perowne in 1947. In 1952 she traveled about the western coast of Turkey looking at 55 ruined sites.

"Most of all she delighted in southern Arabia, but her passion for Persia comes out in clear, crisp descriptions. . . . For her light gleams from the ancient temples and the incense found in a Himyaritic tomb still smells sweetly" (*N.Y. Times*). The *Atlantic* called her *Rome on the Euphrates* (o.p.) "an illuminating history of the Roman frontier in Asia Minor and the Middle East. The story sprawls across the events of eight centuries from west Africa from the Battle of Magnesia in 189 B.C. to the death of Justinian in 565 A.D. The author is not a professional historian, but she has worked through the basic sources with care, and she knows how to tell an interesting story." The *New Statesman* wrote: "Stark can astonish us no more. She has long been the first of contemporary English travel writers." Harold Nicolson said, "She has written the best travel books of her generation and her name will survive as an artist in prose."

BOOKS BY STARK

The Journey's Echo. Transatlantic $16.95

The Valley of the Assassins: And Other Persian Travels. Norwood repr. of 1934 ed. 1978 lib. bdg. $20.00

East Is West. Transatlantic $19.50

Alexander's Path. Transatlantic 1975 $28.50. "From Caria to Cilicia, Miss Stark recreates (although not on foot) the route that Alexander the Great, conqueror of Asia Minor, took in his march through Lycia and Pamphylia. An excellent and absorbing travel book that rewards the reader with its magical mingling of the ancient and the modern" (*PW*).

Zodiac Arch. Transatlantic 1975 $16.95. "Stark is a writer to be savored. She is known not only for her novels but for numerous books of travel and history which communicate her distinctive hallmark, a controlled and sensitive style that is at once immediate in its evocations of scene and keenly interpretive, with flashes of gentle wit. . . . Her new volume . . . is a collection of essays, remembrances and interpretations of journeys she has made and thoughts arising from her travels" (*PW*).

Minaret of Djam: An Excursion in Afghanistan. Transatlantic 1972 $19.50

The Southern Gates of Arabia: A Journey to the Hadhramaut. Lib. of Travel Class. Tarcher 1983 $9.95; Transatlantic 1972 $28.50

STEFANSSON, VILHJALMUR. 1879–1962

Stefansson, Canadian born of Icelandic parentage and the last of the dog-sled explorers, spent many years in the Arctic. His books aim to combat popular misconceptions about the Far North. They show that it is a good place for colonization, that human life can be supported there on a diet of seal alone, and that it has possibilities for commercial usefulness. Stefansson's "findings changed man's prevailing concepts. By 'humanizing' the icy north, he became known as the man who robbed the Arctic Circle of all its terrors and most of its discomforts" (*Boston Globe*). As far back as 1915 he suggested the feat that the atom-powered *Nautilus* accomplished—submerging under the Arctic ice on the Pacific side and emerging, after two months, on the Atlantic. The whole fascinating search for a northwest passage is told with scholarly authority in his *Northwest to Fortune* (1958). "Clearly and lovingly written, the book brings color and even warmth to regions which for so many of us have seemed wrapped in cold, fog, and ice" (*Christian Science Monitor*).

BOOKS BY STEFANSSON

The Stefansson-Anderson Arctic Expedition of the American Museum of Natural History: Preliminary Ethnological Report. 1914. AMS Pr. repr. of 1919 ed. $42.50
Hunters of the Great North. AMS Pr. repr. of 1922 ed. $27.50
Adventures in Error. Gale repr. of 1936 ed. 1970 $40.00
Unsolved Mysteries of the Arctic. Intro. by Stephen Leacock, *Essay Index Repr. Ser.* Ayer repr. of 1938 ed. $25.50
Iceland: The First American Republic. Pref. by Theodore Roosevelt, Greenwood repr. of 1939 ed. 1971 lib. bdg. $17.75
The Friendly Arctic: The Story of Five Years in Polar Regions. Greenwood repr. of 1943 ed. lib. bdg. $56.25
Northwest to Fortune. Greenwood repr. of 1958 ed. 1974 lib. bdg. $22.50

BOOK ABOUT STEFANSSON

Diubaldo, Richard J. *Stefansson and the Canadian Arctic*. McGill-Queens Univ. Pr. 1978 $21.95

VAN DER POST, LAURENS. 1906–

Colonel Laurens Van der Post, a distinguished British subject born in South Africa, has "spent most of his adult life with one foot in Africa and one in England." The beautifully composed *Venture to the Interior* is much more than an account of the planned journey from London to Nyasaland in South Africa, the climbing of Mianje, and the exploration of Nyika. It catches the "unique and indefinable spirit of the ancient continent" and explores the interiors of men's minds. His *The Heart of the Hunter* points the way toward a rediscovery of the positive values in our own lives.

BOOKS BY VAN DER POST

Venture to the Interior. Greenwood repr. of 1951 ed. 1973 lib. bdg. $15.00; Harcourt 1979 pap. $7.95
The Lost World of the Kalahari. Harcourt repr. of 1958 ed. 1977 pap. $7.95. An account of an expedition into the remote Kalahari Desert to study the few remaining communities of the Bushmen.
The Heart of the Hunter. Harcourt 1980 pap. $4.95. This study of the heart and soul of the African Bushmen started in *The Lost World of the Kalahari*.
Patterns of Renewal. Pendle Hill 1962 pap. $2.30
A View of All the Russias. Morrow 1964 $7.95. "This is a fine piece of impressionistic writing, sensitive and perceptive, occasionally accurate, with a strong feeling for nature and many vivid descriptions of landscapes (especially Asian ones), all made to order for the armchair traveler or the nostalgic Russian exile, but hardly the fare for the reader in search of information and insight" (*LJ*).

VESPUCCI, AMERIGO. 1451–1512

The Renaissance Florentine explored the American coast from Florida to Patagonia. He was the first to declare South America a separate continent rather than a part of Asia. As a navigator-mathematician he measured the earth's circumference more exactly than anyone before him and devised an accurate system for ascertaining longitude. His accounts were published in 1507 by Martin Waldseemuller, German geographer, who suggested the new lands be named "America."

Book by Vespucci

Letters and Other Documents Illustrative of His Career. Trans. and ed. by Clements R. Markham, *Hakluyt Society Ser.* Burt Franklin repr. of 1894 ed. $26.00

Books about Vespucci

Arciniegas, German. *Amerigo and the New World.* Octagon repr. of 1955 ed. lib. bdg. $27.50

Pohl, Frederick J. *Amerigo Vespucci, Pilot Major.* 1944. Octagon 1966 $21.50

Name Index

In addition to authors, this index includes the names of persons mentioned in connection with titles of books written, whether they appear in introductory essays, general bibliographies at the beginnings of chapters, discussions under main headings, or "Books About" sections. Persons mentioned in passing—to indicate friendships, relationships, and so on—are generally not indexed. Editors are not indexed unless there is no specific author given; such books include anthologies, bibliographies, yearbooks, and the like. Translators, writers of introductions, forewords, afterwords, etc., are not indexed except for those instances where the translator seems as closely attached to a title as the real author, e.g., FitzGerald's translation of the *Rubáiyát of Omar Khayyám*. Main name headings appear in boldface as do the page numbers on which the main entries appear.

Aaron, Daniel, 263
Aaron, Richard I., 164
Abbey, Edward, 618
Abdalati, Hammudah, 433
Abdel-Fadil, M., 436
Abel, Elie, 562
Abendroth, Wolfgang, 410
Abernathy, M. Glenn, 280
Abraham, David, 415
Abraham, Gerald, 485
Abraham, Henry J., 297
Abraham, Richard, 420, 423
Abrahams, Roger D., 595, 602, 604, 606
Abrahamson, James L., 302
Abrams, Alan E., 567
Abrams, Philip, 188
Abramson, Jeffrey, 175, 178
Abu-Lughod, Janet, 436
Achtert, Walter S., 22
Ackerley, J. R., 623
Ackerman, Bruce, 155
Ackroyd, Peter R., 426
Acton, John E., 384
Adams, Abigail, 82
Adams, Anthony, 223

Adams, Charles F., 633
Adams, Charles Francis, 81, 83
Adams, George R., 253
Adams, Gerard F., 128
Adams, Henry, 305. *See also* Volume 1
Adams, Herbert B., 342
Adams, James Truslow, 83, 261, 306, **307**
Adams, John, 81, 130
Adams, John Quincy, 81, 83, 305
Adams, Larry L., 325
Adams, Percy G., 615
Adams, Robert McC., 437
Adams, Sherman, 62
Adams, Willi Paul, 294
Adamson, J. H., 625
Adamthwaite, Anthony, 406
Adcock, F. E., 244, 249
Adler, Mortimer J., 20, 150, 223, 260
Adler, Richard P., 569
Adorno, T. W., 175
Adorno, Theodor W., 485

Afzal-Ur-Rehman, 433
Agar, Herbert, 308
Agger, Robert E., 191
Agmon, Tamir, 131
Agresto, John, 151, 294
Aguilar, Luis E., 357
Agus, Jacob B., 426
Ahmed, Abkar S., 452
Ahmed, Ziauddin, 433
Aiken, Riley, 595
Ainsworth, Catherine H., 595, 599
Airasian, Peter W., 227
Akers, Charles W., 83
Akita, George, 449
Alba, Victor, 418
Albert, Peter J., 266
Albrecht-Carrié, Rene, 406
Albright, D. E., 440
Alcina-Franch, José, 353
Alden, John R., 265
Alderson, Anthony D., 439
Aldington, Richard, 638, 639
Aldous, Joan, 195
Aldred, Cyril, 239
Aldrich, Lawson, 599

Alexander, Charles C., 285
Alexander, Fred, 343
Alexander, Herbert E., 297
Alexander, John T., 420
Alexander, Shana, 51
Algarin, Joanne P., 596
Ali, Abdullah, 433
Aliboni, R., 436
Alkire, Leland G., Jr., 9
Allen, Barry W., 627
Allen, Chris, 440
Allen, David Grayson, 264
Allen, F. Sturges, 33
Allen, John L., 640
Allen, Woody. *See* Volume 1
Allibone, Samuel A., 20
Alliluyeva, Svetlana, 475, 476
Allison, Graham T., 406
Allport, Gordon W., 170, 174, **175,** 190, 196
Allworth, Edward A., 445
Almendros, Nestor, 578
Almond, Gabriel A., 154, 155, 445
Almy, Millie, 235
Alpert, Harry, 206
Alsop, Joseph, 91, 277
Altbach, Philip G., 223
Altheide, David L., 570
Altholz, Josef L., 368
Althos, Anthony G., 451
Altick, Richard D., 49, 379
Altschul, Michael, 368
Ambler, John S., 413
Ambrose, Stephen E., 62, 280, 302
Ames, Evelyn, 623
Ames, John G., 12
Amirsadeghi, Hossein, 437
Ammer, Christine, 124
Ammer, Dean, 124
Ammianus Marcellinus, 249
Anderson, Charles R., 625
Anderson, Dennis, 31
Anderson, Elliott, 561
Anderson, Emily, 509
Anderson, Frank J., 625
Anderson, J. K., 246
Anderson, J. R., 171
Anderson, Jack, 567
Anderson, Jervis, 285
Anderson, M. S., 410
Anderson, Martin, 129
Anderson, R. D., 413
Andersson, Ingvar, 419

Andreae, Bernard, 529
Andrew, Dudley, 574
Andrewes, Antony, 239
Andrews, Kenneth R., 374
Anhalt, Istvan, 492
Anna, Timothy E., 358
Anstey, Roger, 377
Anthony, Edgar W., 534
Antin, Mary, 426
Antippas, A. P., 377
Antonioni, Michelangelo, 578
Antonius, George, 438
Antonov-Ovseyeneko, Anton, 476
Apel, Willi, 487
Apostle, Richard A., 196
Apps, Jerold W., 224
Apter, David E., 154
Aptheker, Herbert, 212, 260, 319
Aranda, Francisco, 580
Archdeacon, Thomas J., 289
Arciniegas, German, 649
Arendt, Hannah, 426, **455**
Arensberg, Conrad M., 110
Argyle, Michael, 172
Aries, Philippe, 195, 410
Aristotle 246. *See also* Volume 4
Arjomand, Said A., 198
Armes, Roy, 575
Armitage, Merle, 505
Armour, Robert A., 574
Armstrong, Louis, 497
Armstrong, Scott, 302
Arndt, H. W., 128
Arnheim, Rudolf, 174, 527, 549, 574
Arno, Andrew, 562
Arnold, David, 418
Arnold, Denis, 487, 499, 508
Arnold, Walter, 451
Arnold, William J., 173
Arnopoulos, Sheila M., 349
Arnstein, Walter L., 379
Arntzen, Etta, 527
Arojan, Lois A., 440
Aron, Raymond, 155, 157, 205, 280, 402, **456**
Aronson, Elliot, 170, 171
Aronson, Joseph, 534
Arora, Shirley L., 45
Arrian, 246
Arrianus, Flavius. *See* Arrian
Arrington, Leonard, 51

Arrow, Kenneth J., 124, **132**
Arsenault, Raymond, 315
Asbell, Bernard, 78
Asbjornsen, Peter C., 596
Aschheim, Steven E., 427
Ash, Lee, 10
Ashbrook, William, 511
Ashe, Geoffrey, 371
Asher, Herbert B., 152, 297
Ashley, Maurice, 414
Ashton, Dore, 549, 582
Ashton, Frederick, 521
Ashton, Thomas S., 384
Ashtor, Eliyahu, 432
Asimov, Isaac, 609
Aslanian, Carol B., 224
Atkins, Beryl T., 39
Atkins, Thomas R., 575
Atkinson, John W., 173
Atmore, Anthony, 443, 444
Auchincloss, Louis, 306
Audubon, John J., 618
Aufricht, Hans, 403
Augustine. *See* Volume 4
Austin, Bruce A., 574
Austin, Dennis, 440
Austin, Michel M., 241, 243
Austin, William W., 485, 505
Auty, Robert, 420
Avato, Rose M., 16
Avi-Hai, Avraham, 427
Aviad, Janet, 435
Avrich, Paul, 224, 420
Axelrad, P., 45
Axelsen, J., 39
Ayling, Stanley, 377
Ayre, Leslie, 487
Azrael, Jeremy R., 420

Babington, Percy L., 477
Babkin, Boris P., 184
Bach, Johann Sebastian, 497
Bach, Robert L., 195
Bacheller, Martin A., 18
Bachman, John E., 470
Bachmann, Donna G., 531
Badger, Reid, 285
Badian, E., 241
Badt, Kurt, 538, 539
Baeda, Saint, or Beda. *See* Bede the Venerable, Saint
Baer, George W., 407
Bagdikian, Ben H., 562
Bagehot, Walter, 385
Bagnall, Roger, 241

Baigell, Matthew, 529
Bailey, Frank E., 439
Bailey, Frederick G., 105, 107
Bailey, Kenneth D., 100
Bailey, Thomas A., 253, 297, 302, 336
Bailyn, Bernard, 260, 261, 265, 298
Bain, Kenneth R., 435
Baines, Anthony, 495
Bair, Frank E., 17
Bairstow, Jeffrey, 519
Bakan, David, 170, 427
Baker, Daisy, 621
Baker, Donald, 606
Baker, Holly Cutting, 598
Baker, Hugh, 446
Baker, Kendall L., 415
Baker, Leonard, 51
Baker, Margret, 606
Baker, Paul R., 407, 621
Baker, Ray S., 96
Baker, Raymond W., 436
Baker, Ronald L., 601
Baker, Russell, 51
Baker, William S., 94
Balabanoff, Angelica, 470
Balanchine, George, 519, **521**
Baldini, Gabriele, 516
Baldinucci, Filippo, 536
Baldwin, Hanson W., 407
Baldwin, Roger, 35
Bales, Robert F., 172, 188
Balio, Tino, 575
Ball-Rokeach, Sandra J., 190, 563
Balliett, Whitney, 493
Baltes, Paul B., 172
Bandura, Albert, 173
Bane, Michael, 487
Banerji, P., 593
Banks, Ann, 277
Banner, Lois W., 289
Banton, Michael, 109
Baraka, Amiri, 51
Baram, Michael S., 129
Baranov, A. N., 19
Barber, Bernard, 196, 199
Barber, Edwin, 534
Barber, Noel, 419
Barber, Richard, 372
Barber, Sotirios A., 295
Barbrook, Alec, 289
Barghoorn, Frederick C., 420
Baring-Gould, Sabine, 593

Barish, Frances, 615
Barker, Robert, 182
Barker, Roger G., 191
Barkham, John, 472
Barlow, Frank, 371
Barlow, Harold, 487
Barnard, Alan, 104
Barnard, Chester I., 127, 197
Barnard, Henry, 229
Barnes, Catherine A., 298
Barnes, Clive, 520, 524
Barnes, Harry E., 187, 402
Barnes, John, 360
Barnet, Richard J., 302, 303, 449
Barnett, A. Doak, 75, **458**
Barnhart, Clarence L., 25, 27, 30
Barnhart, Robert K., 25, 27, 30
Barnouw, Erik, 576
Baron, Salo W., 427
Barone, Michael, 15
Barr, Alfred H., Jr., 546, 549
Barr, Charles, 586
Barr, Stringfellow, 472
Barraclough, Geoffrey, 410
Barratt, Glynn R., 420
Barrett, Marvin, 568
Barron, Gloria J., 336
Barron, Jerome A., 561
Barron, John, 420
Barrow, A. E., 453
Barth, Frederik, 437
Barth, Gunther, 285
Barth, Roland S., 224
Barthelme, Donald, 615
Bartlett, C. J., 382
Bartlett, Irving H., 268
Bartlett, John, 20
Bartlett, Richard, 289
Bartók, Béla, 498, 593
Baryshnikov, Mikhail, 521
Barzun, Jacques, 22, 180, 402, 485, 491, 500
Basham, A. L., 452
Basie, William, 498
Batatu, John, 437
Bate, W. Jackson, 51
Bateson, Gregory, 105, 119
Bateson, Mary C., 51, 120
Baughman, Ernest W., 592
Baum, Richard, 446
Bauman, Richard, 602
Baumer, Franklin L., 410
Baxter, Maurice G., 95

Baxter, Peter, 588
Baylies, Carolyn, 441
Baym, M. I., 306
Bazin, Andre, 576
Beaglehole, J. C., 632
Beale, Howard K., 336
Beales, D., 417
Bean, Frank D., 195, 197
Beard, Charles A., 91, 151, 295, **308**
Beard, Mary R., 308
Beardsley, John, 606
Beasley, David, 625
Beasley, W. G., 449
Beattie, J. H., 113
Beattie, John, 103
Beauchamp, Tom L., 101
Beaumont, Cyril, 519
Beaumont, Gustave de, 341
Beaumont, Peter, 432
Beauroy, Jacques, 414
Beazley, J. D., 534
Beccaria, Cesare Bonesana, 193
Beck, Evelyn T., 427
Beck, James, 550
Beck, Jane C., 599
Becker, Carl L., 87, 161, 295, **310,** 402
Becker, Gary S., 124, 126, 195
Becker, Howard, 187, 194
Becker, Robert A., 287
Beckett, James G., 369
Bedarida, François, 382
Bedau, Hugo A., 193
Bede the Venerable, Saint, 385
Bedell, Sally, 573
Beecham, C. Robert, 561
Beer, Barrett L., 374
Beer, Samuel H., 382
Beerbohm, Max, 60
Beers, Burton F., 445
Beers, Henry A., 336
Beers, Henry P., 258
Beethoven, Ludwig van, 498
Beevor, Antony, 418
Bein, Alex, 427
Bell, Daniel, 102, 154, **204,** 289
Bell, J. Bowyer, 435
Bell, James K., 30
Bell, John P., 361
Bell, Michael J., 605
Bellah, Robert N., 102, 198

Bellamy, John, 372
Bellini, Vincenzo, 499
Belloc, Hilaire, 386
Beloff, Max, 87
Belville, H. M., Jr., 570
Bemis, Samuel Flagg, 83, **311**
Bemister, Margaret, 603
Ben, Amos D., 606
Ben-David, Joseph, 189, 198, 199, 215
Ben Gurion, David, 427, 435
Ben-Sasson, Haim, 427
Ben-Yehuda, Eliezer, 42
Bender, David L., 454
Bendersky, Joseph W., 415
Benderson, Albert E., 583
Bendiksen, Robert, 195
Bendix, Reinhard, 150, 201, 221
Benedict, Ruth, 105, 106, 110, **111,** 449
Benes, Peter, 599
Benet, Stephen V., 95
Benevolo, Leonardo, 532
Bengtson, Hermann, 238
Benham, Allen R., 462
Benjamin, Jules R., 402
Bennett, G., 441
Bennett, Gordon A., 446
Bennett, James A., 557
Bennett, Lerone, Jr., 255, 265
Bennis, Warren, 224
Benois, Alexandre, 420
Bensman, Joseph, 192
Benson, Kathleen, 507
Benson, Lee, 253, 309, 343
Bent, Silas, 69
Bentham, Jeremy, 158
Bentley, Harold W., 45
Benudhar, Pradham, 474
Berberi, Dilaver, 42
Berckmans, Tracey R., 101
Berdan, Frances, 353
Berelson, Bernard, 99, 100, 152, 190
Berenson, Bernhard, 529
Beresford, M. W., 369
Berg, Alban, 499
Berger, Adolf, 244
Berger, Arthur A., 574
Berger, Bennett, 203
Berger, Charles R., 171
Berger, Morroe, 433, 438
Berger, Raoul, 298

Bergeret, Annie, 596
Berges, Marshall, 567
Bergevin, Paul, 224
Bergman, Ingmar, 579
Bergman, Peter, 38
Bergson, Abram, 130, 156
Berio, Luciano, 499
Berkhofer, Robert F., Jr., 402
Berkin, Carol, 265
Berkowitz, Leonard, 170
Berle, Adolf A., Jr., 127
Berler, Alexander, 435
Berlin, Ira, 270
Berlin, Isaiah, 141
Berliner, Paul F., 494
Berlioz, Hector, 500
Berman, Larry, 280
Berman, William C., 79
Bernal, Ignacio, 353
Bernard, Jessie, 203
Bernard, Miguel A., 625
Bernard, Raymond, 631
Bernard, Richard M., 280
Bernd, Joseph L., 295
Bernhard, Winfred, 607
Bernini, Gianlorenzo, 536
Berns, Walter, 152
Bernstein, Barton J., 79
Bernstein, Carl, 280, 284
Bernstein, Leonard, 500
Bernstein, Richard J., 231
Bernstein, Samuel, 414
Bernstein, Thomas P., 447
Berque, Jacques, 436
Berrey, Lester V., 31
Berry, Mary F., 289
Bertensson, Sergei, 511
Bertier de Sauvigny, Guillaume de, 414
Berton, Peter, 447
Berton, Pierre, 349
Berulfsen, B., 44
Berwanger, Eugene H., 274
Besset, Maurice, 543
Besterman, Theodore, 114
Bestor, Arthur, 203
Bethell, Leslie, 356
Bethke, Robert D., 599
Bett, Henry, 591
Bettelheim, Bruno, 178, 427
Betteridge, Harold, 40
Bettman, Otto L., 274
Betts, Raymond F., 441
Bever, Thomas, 171
Beye, Klaus G., 534
Bezucha, Robert J., 410

Bhagwati, Jagdish, 130
Bhattacharya, Sachchidananda, 452
Biagi, Adele, 43
Bialer, Seweryn, 420, 476
Biancolli, Louis, 509
Biard, Jean Dominique, 39
Bickel, Alexander M., 298
Bickerman, Elias J., 238
Biennes, Ranulph, 625
Biers, William R., 242
Biesanz, Richard, 361
Bigland, Eileen, 629
Billias, George A., 253, 262
Billington, Ray Allen, 289, 343, 344, 609
Bin Gorion, Emanuel, 596
Bin Gorion, Micha J., 596
Bindoff, S. T., 374
Binet, Alfred, 173, **176**
Bingham, Hiram, 353
Bingham, Woodbridge, 445
Binstock, Robert H., 189
Birley, Anthony, 371
Birren, James E., 189
Bisbee, Eleanor, 439
Bishop, Jim, 71, 89
Bishop, Robert, 607
Bishop, William W., Jr., 155
Bissell, Richard E., 441
Bjork, Daniel W., 181
Black, Duncan, 153
Black, Edwin, 427
Black, G. J., 336
Black, Max, 214
Blackmer, Donald L., 417
Blackmur, R. P., 306
Blackwood, David, 624
Blaikie, William G., 642
Blair, P. H., 371
Blair, Roger D., 129
Blake, Peter, 543
Blalock, Hubert M., 100, 188
Blanco, Hugo, 365
Blanco, Richard L., 258
Bland, Alexander, 520
Blasier, Cole, 358
Blassingame, John W., 270, 289
Blassingame, Wyatt, 637
Blau, Judith R., 198
Blau, Peter M., 196, 197, 201, 203
Blaug, Mark, 124, 140, 145
Bleaney, Michael, 138
Blesh, Rudi, 492

Blessington, John P., 234
Blissett, Marlan, 301
Block, Adrienne F., 487
Block, N. J., 173
Blom, Eric, 509
Blom, Jan B., 593
Bloodworth, Dennis, 445, 447
Bloom, Benjamin S., 224
Bloomfield, Leonard, 108, **112**
Blos, Peter, 172
Bluem, A. William, 570
Bluestein, Gene, 607
Blum, D. Steven, 164, 325
Blum, Daniel, 576
Blum, Eleanor, 561
Blum, Ethel, 615
Blum, John M., 96, 262, 275, 278, 336
Blumenson, John C., 532
Blumenson, Martin, 407
Blumer, Herbert, 196
Blunden, Edmund C., 66
Boardman, John, 242
Boas, Franz, 112
Boas, Guy, 609
Boase, Thomas S., 529
Boatner, Mark M., III, 257
Boatright, Mody C., 603, 607
Bocchetta, Vittore E., 43
Boden, Margaret, 173
Boehm, David A., 14
Boehm, Eric H., 403
Boettcher, Thomas D., 454
Bogart, Humphrey, 579
Bogart, Leo, 156, 190
Bogdanovich, Peter, 584
Boger, H. Batterson, 534
Boger, Louise, 534
Boggs, Carl, 410
Boggs, R. S., 46
Bogue, Allan G., 272, 301
Bogue, Donald J., 197
Bogus, Ronald, 34
Bohannan, Paul, 193, 441
Bohm-Bawerk, Eugen von, 126
Bohrn, Harald, 213
Bois, Mario, 518
Boller, Paul F., 260, 298
Bolt, Christine, 289
Bolton, J. L., 372
Bombeck, Erma, 609
Bomse, Marguerite D., 46
Bonandella, Peter, 583

Bonavia, David, 447
Bond, Otto F., 46
Bond, Simon, 609
Bondurant, Joan V., 452
Bonner, Phillip, 441
Bonner, Raymond, 362
Bonnie, Michael E., 437
Bonnifield, Paul, 287
Bonomi, Patricia U., 266
Bontemps, Arna, 289
Boorman, Scott A., 75
Boorstin, Daniel J., 87, 161, 252, 260, 262, **312**
Booth, Charles, 191, **204**
Borders, Earl, Jr., 615
Bordley, James, III, 289
Borg, Dorothy, 449
Borgatta, Edgar F., 188
Boring, Edwin G., 169, 177
Bork, Robert H., 127
Bornet, Vaughn D., 70, 280
Borning, Bernard C., 309
Bornstein, Marc H., 170
Borrow, George, 628
Borsi, Franco, 537
Boruch, Robert F., 101
Bosanquet, Bernard, 462
Bosselman, Fred P., 614
Bossy, John, 369
Boswell, James. *See* Volume 1
Bosworth, Joseph, 37
Bosworth, Richard, 417
Bothwell, Robert, 349
Botkin, B. A., 596, 607
Bottomore, Tom, 157, 187
Bottrall, Margaret, 49
Bournonville, August, 522
Bourricaud, François, 214
Bovill, Edward W., 441
Bowder, Diana, 241
Bowen, Catherine Drinker, 49, **55,** 64, 151, 317
Bowen, James, 224
Bowen, Meirion, 515
Bowen, Roger W., 450
Bower, Gordon H., 171, 173
Bower, Robert T., 101
Bower, T. G., 172
Bowers, Claude G., 86, 88
Bowers, David G., 189
Bowersock, G. W., 66, 240
Bowie, Robert R., 436, 464
Bowle, John, 160
Bowler, R. Arthur, 266
Bowles, Chester, 452

Bowley, Marian, 145
Bowman, Larry W., 441
Bowman, Wodgeson, 581
Boxer, C. R., 356
Boyd, Anne M., 12
Boyd, James, 567
Boyden, David D., 495
Boyer, Ernest L., 224
Boyer, L. Bryce, 603
Boylan, James, 563
Bracher, Karl D., 415
Bracken, Susan, 16
Bradbury, Katherine L., 202
Bradlee, Benjamin C., 72
Bradley, David, 621
Bradley, Henry, 27
Bradley, John, 420
Bradsher, Henry S., 440
Brady, Anna, 574
Bragdon, H. W., 96
Brahms, Johannes, 500, 501
Brainerd, George W., 354
Bram, Leon L., 3
Brams, Steven J., 147
Brand, Oscar, 593
Branson, Noreen, 382
Brant, Irving, 90
Brantlinger, Patrick, 611
Branyan, Robert L., 281
Bratcher, James T., 602
Braudel, Fernand, 459
Bray, Howard, 567
Braybrook, Patrick, 386
Breathnach, Breandan, 593
Brebner, John Bartlet, 347
Brecht, Arnold, 149
Breen, T. H., 264
Breit, William, 124
Breitweiser, Mitchell R., 64
Bremer, Howard F., 83, 94
Bremner, Robert H., 272, 281
Brendan, Keith, 369
Brendon, Piers, 567
Breslauer, George W., 420
Breslin, Herbert H., 496
Brett, Bill, 602
Brett, David, 621
Brett, Michael, 433
Brett, Philip, 501
Breuer, Joseph, 178
Breunig, Charles, 410
Brew, J. O., 103
Brewer, Annie M., 6
Brewster, K. G., 26
Brewster, Paul G., 601

Brickell, Henry M., 224
Bridenbaugh, Carl, 264, 266, 268
Bridenthal, Renate, 410
Bridger, David, 427
Briggs, Asa, 380
Briggs, Katherine M., 596
Briggs, Robin, 414
Brill, Alida, 151
Brim, Orville G., Jr., 172, 202
Brinkley, Alan, 278
Brinton, C. Crane, 302, 396, 405, **459**
Briscoe, Mary L., 49
Brito, Dagobert, 194
Britten, Benjamin, 501
Brock, Michael, 377
Brock, William R., 262
Brockman, James R., 363
Broder, David, 298
Broderick, Francis L., 319
Brodie, Fawn M., 51, 88, 161, 630
Brodinsky, Ben, 224
Brody, Elaine, 487, 488
Brody, Hugh, 349
Brogan, D. W., 89
Bromwell, C. David, 452
Bronner, Simon J., 592
Bronstein, Lev Davydovich. *See* Trotsky, Leon
Brook, Barry S., 488
Brook, Claire, 487, 488
Brooke, Christopher, 371
Brooke, John, 378
Brooks, H. Allen, 559
Brooks, Robert C., 159
Brooks, Valerie, 521
Brooks, Van Wyck, 477
Broom, Leonard, 188
Broun, Anne S., 267
Brower, Kenneth, 618
Brown, A. A., 124
Brown, D. M., 452
Brown, Dale, 557
Brown, David, 515
Brown, Dee, 274, 275
Brown, Earl K., 378
Brown, Emily C., 420
Brown, Frank C., 600
Brown, George, 599
Brown, Horatio F., 477
Brown, Judith M., 452
Brown, Karl, 585
Brown, L. Carl, 432

Brown, Les, 570
Brown, Lester R., 194
Brown, Lucy M., 368
Brown, Malcolm H., 509
Brown, Marjorie J., 7
Brown, Michael S., 204
Brown, Milton W., 529
Brown, Peter, 240, 244, 492
Brown, Peter D., 378
Brown, R. Allen, 371
Brown, R. F., 46
Brown, Robert, 100
Brown, Robert E., 151, 309
Brown, Roger H., 268
Brown, Seyom, 303
Brown, Stuart G., 73, 93
Brown, W. Norman, 452
Browne, G. F., 386
Browne, Ray, 600
Brownell, Blaine A., 277
Browning, Reed, 378
Brownlow, Kevin, 576
Brubaker, Timothy H., 189
Bruce, Neil, 418
Bruce, Robert D., 354
Bruckner, Anton, 501
Brueckner, John H., 39
Bruegel the Elder, Pieter, 537
Bruggencate, K. Ten, 39
Brugger, Robert J., 253
Brundage, Anthony, 380
Brundage, Burr Cartwright, 353
Bruner, Jerome S., 174, 224
Brunvand, Jan H., 591, 607
Bruun, Geoffrey, 472
Bryant, Arthur T., 441
Bryce, James, 102, 152, 153, **159,** 342
Brzezinski, Zbigniew K., 420, 441, 450
Buache, Freddy, 580
Buchan, Alastair, 385
Buchan, David, 596
Buchanan, A. Russell, 407
Buchanan, James M., 132, 138, 153
Buchner, Alexander, 492
Buckhout, Robert, 169
Buckland, Patrick, 380
Buckland, W. W., 244
Buckle, Henry T., 386
Buckle, Richard, 518, 522
Buckley, William F., Jr., 51, 298, 625

Buckman, Peter, 570
Budden, Julian, 516
Budge, Ernest A., 436
Buel, J. W., 646
Buffington, Albert F., 593
Bukhsh, S. K., 434
Bukofzer, Manfred F., 485
Bulas, Kazimierz, 44
Bull, Storm, 488
Bullitt, William, 96
Bullock, Alan, 415
Bullock, Henry Allen, 290
Bulmer, Martin, 101, 187
Bulow, Bernhard H., 415
Buñuel, Luis, 580
Bunzel, John H., 298
Bunzel, Ruth, 103
Burawoy, Michael, 126
Burch, Philip H., 281
Burchard, John, 322
Burchard, Ludwig, 553
Burchfield, Robert W., 28
Burckhardt, Jacob, 460, 621
Burford, Alison, 243
Burgess, Ernest W., 195, 213
Burgess, Robert F., 625
Burke, Edmund, 159, 387
Burke, Frank, 583
Burke, Peter, 402, 410
Burke, Robert E., 258
Burkman, Thomas W., 450
Burks, R. V., 419
Burnham, Walter D., 156, 298
Burns, Arthur F., 143
Burns, E. Bradford, 358, 361
Burns, Edward M., 405
Burns, James M., 91, 262
Burns, Richard Dean, 259
Burrow, John W., 123
Burt, Ronald, 188, 201
Burton, David H., 336
Burton, Isabel, 630
Burton, Jean, 630
Burton, Richard, 629
Busby, Linda J., 570
Busch, Hans, 516
Bushman, Richard L., 264, 323
Butler, David, 454
Butler, David E., 369
Butler, Lord C. H., 474
Butler, Matilda, 563
Butlin, Martin, 555
Butt, Archibald W., 336
Butterfield, Herbert, 402

Butterworth, Neil, 504
Butterworth, W. Walton, 413
Buttinger, Joseph, 454
Buttress, F. A., 11
Byrd, Michael, 577
Byrd, Richard E., 630
Byrne, Josefa H., 32
Byrnes, R. F., 427

Cabanne, Pierre, 549
Cabestrero, Teófilo, 364
Cadden, Tom Scott, 574
Cadenheard, I. E., 336
Cady, John F., 445
Caesar, Julius, 249
Cage, John, 501
Cagin, Seth, 576
Cahill, Holger, 607
Cahill, Robert E., 599
Cahn, Robert, 618
Cahn, Sammy, 35
Cahn, Steven M., 224
Caiger, John, 451
Calder, Bruce J., 362
Caldwell, Bruce J., 125
Calhoun, John Caldwell, 83
Callaghy, Thomas M., 441
Callahan, North, 60
Callas, Maria, 502
Callwood, June, 347
Calvert, G. H., 46
Calvert, Peter, 360
Calvin, Allen, 224
Calvocoressi, M. D., 509
Calvocoressi, Peter, 407, 565
Cameron, Averil, 243
Cameron, David, 160
Cameron, Ian, 624
Cameron, James R., 394
Cameron, Judy, 520
Camp, John, 607
Campa, Arthur L., 602
Campbell, Alistair, 37
Campbell, Angus, 102, 153, 196
Campbell, Carl, 130
Campbell, Colin, 131
Campbell, D'Ann, 278
Campbell, Karlyn K., 564
Campbell, Margaret, 495
Campbell, Rex R., 292
Campbell, Rosemary, 131
Campling, Elizabeth, 441
Canaday, John, 531
Canavan, Francis P., 160

Cancro, Robert, 173
Candlin, Enid Saunders, 623
Cannell, Charles F., 101
Canning, John, 615
Cannistraro, Philip V., 417
Cannon, Hal, 602
Cantor, Muriel G., 570
Cantor, Norman F., 402
Cantril, Hadley, 190, 589
Capers, Gerald M., 84
Caplan, David, 171
Caplan, Neil, 427
Caplovitz, David, 128
Caplow, Theodore, 198, 208
Cappon, Lester J., 255
Capps, Walter H., 281
Carcopino, Jerome, 243
Carey, George, 600
Carlson, Raymond, 615
Carlyle, Thomas, 461
Carmer, Carl, 618
Carner, Mosco, 499, 511
Caro, Robert A., 70, 281
Carpenter, Cal, 600
Carpenter, Finley, 185
Carpenter, Francis B., 89
Carpenter, Rhys, 529
Carpenter, Ronald H., 344
Carr, Edward H., 150, 402, 407, 420
Carr, H. Wildon, 462
Carr, Ian, 503
Carr, Raymond, 365, 418
Carrington, Henry B., 255
Carroll, John E., 349
Carroll, Peter N., 262, 281
Carrow, Milton M., 129
Carruth, Gordon, 257
Carsten, Franz L., 415
Carter, C. H., 472
Carter, Gwendolyn M., 443
Carter, Jimmy, 334, 432
Carter, Paul A., 276
Carter, William E., 619
Carterette, Edward C., 174
Cartey, Wilfred, 441
Cartwright, Dorwin, 172
Carver, Terrell, 134
Cary, Francine Curro, 325
Casanova. See Volume 1
Case, C. M., 445
Cass, Ronald A., 570
Cassara, Ernest, 259
Cassata, Mary B., 570
Cassell, Abayomi, 441
Casson, Lionel, 243, 615

Castillo, Carlos, 46
Castle, Wilfrid T., 440
Castleman, Harry, 570
Castro, Americo, 418
Catchpole, Brian, 404
Cate, James L., 407
Cathcart, Robert, 564
Catlin, George, 290
Catton, Bruce, 67, 89, 313, 315
Catton, William B., 89, 262, 313, 315
Causley, Charles, 593
Cavalcaselle, G. B., 529
Cavendish, Richard, 596
Cazden, Norman, 599
Cecil, David. See Volume 1
Cell, C. P., 447
Cellini, Benvenuto, 537
Ceplair, Larry, 285
Cerny, Philip G., 414
Cézanne, Paul, 538
Chabrol, Claude, 585
Chace, James, 358
Chaffers, William, 534
Chakraborty, A. K., 474
Chalfant, Edward, 306
Chaloner, W. H., 368
Chamberlain, Neville, 407
Chamberlin, William Henry, 420
Chambers, Jonathan D., 374, 378
Champigneulle, Bernard, 553
Champlain, Samuel De, 619, 625
Champlin, Charles, 574
Chancellor, John, 372, 517
Chaney, Elsa M., 358
Chang, Parris H., 447
Channing, Steven A., 270
Chao, Yuen R., 38
Chaplin, Charles, 581
Chaplin, J. P., 170
Chapman, Alexander, 622
Chapman, Charles E., 418
Chapman, Hester W., 56
Chapman, J. W., 450
Chapman, John W., 169
Chapman, Robert L., 33
Chappuis, Adrien, 538
Charles, Ray, 502
Charnay, J. P., 434
Charnwood, Lord, 336
Charques, Richard D., 421
Charvat, William, 334

Chase, Gilbert, 485, 495
Chase, Richard, 600
Chaudhuri, Nirad C., 452
Chavkin, Samuel, 361
Chay, John, 454
Chazan, Robert, 427
Checkland, Sydney, 369
Ch'en, Jerome, 447
Chen, Lung Chu, 447
Cherlin, Andrew, 195
Chesler, Evan R., 427
Chesnut, Mary Boykin
    Miller, 51, 272
Chesnutt, Charles W., 85
Chessman, G. Wallace, 336
Chesterfield, Philip. *See*
    Volume 1
Chesterton, Gilbert K., 461
Chew, Allen F., 404, 421
Chhabra, G. S., 452
Chhibber, V. N., 474
Chi, Wen-Shun, 38
Chiang, Yee, 623
Chichester, Francis, 613
Chickering, William H., 619
Child, Francis J., 593
Child, Irvin L., 106
Childe, V. Gordon, 107
Childers, Peter G., 173
Childs, John, 376
Chilton, John, 493, 497
Chinard, Gilbert, 83, 88
Chirot, Daniel, 200
Choate, F., 603
Chomsky, Noam, 108
Chopin, Frederic, 502
Chopra, P. N., 453
Choucri, Nazli, 155, 432
Choy, Bong-Youn, 454
Chrimes, S. B., 373
Christensen, A. M., 605
Christensen, Larry B., 170
Christeson, R. P., 593
Christie, Ian R., 368, 378
Christie, Richard, 165
Christopher, A. J., 441
Christopher, John B., 405,
    434
Church, Elihu Dwight, 259
Churchill, Randolph S., 388
Churchill, Winston S., 388
Churchward, L. G., 421
Churgin, Jonah R., 224
Chusid, Martin, 516
Cicero, Marcus Tullius, 249
Cicourel, Aaron V., 188

Cigler, Allan J., 298
Ciment, Michel, 586
Cipolla, Carlo M., 411
Ciricione, Joseph, 358
Claghorn, Charles E., 488
Clapham, John, 504
Clapham, John H., 388
Clarence-Smith, Gervase,
    418
**Clarendon, Edward Hyde,
389**
Clarens, Carlos, 576
Clark, A. H., 133
Clark, Anne B., 448
Clark, Ella E., 603
Clark, G. Kitson, 380
Clark, Grenville, 155
Clark, Harry H., 331
Clark, J. M., 40
Clark, James I., 616
Clark, John Bates, 132
Clark, John M., 133
Clark, Kenneth, 529, 544,
    550
Clark, Kenneth B., 196
Clark, Lincoln H., 128
Clark, Martin, 417
Clark, Merrian E., 616
Clark, R. J., 416
Clark, Ronald W., 64
Clark, Terry Nicholas, 189,
    215
Clark, W. E., 107
Clark, William, 639
Clarke, J. I., 432
Clarke, Kenneth, 601
Clarke, Mary, 518, 601
Clarkfield, Gerard H., 303
Clarkson, Atelia, 591
Clarkson, Leslie A., 369
Clay, Henry, 84
Clayre, Alasdair, 447
Clecak, Peter, 285
Clements, Frank, 639
Clements, Robert J., 547
Clements, William M., 603
Clift, Dominique, 349
Clinard, Marshall B., 193
Cline, Howard F., 334
Clough, Ralph N., 303
Clough, S. B., 405, 411
Cloward, Richard A., 201
Clubb, Jerome M., 298
Clubb, O. Edmund, 421, 447
Clubbe, John B., 461
Clyde, Paul H., 445

Coapland, Reginald, 441
Cobb, Richard, 414
Cobban, Alfred, 414
Cobbett, Walter Wilson, 488
Cobbett, William, 389
Cobbett-Steinberg, Steven,
    518
Cobo, Bernabe, 353
Coburn, Jewell R., 596, 598
Cocchiara, Giuseppe, 596
Cochran, Thomas C., 268
Cockburn, J. S., 369
Cockshut, A. O., 49
Cocteau, Jean, 581
Codding, George A., Jr., 563
Coe, Michael D., 353, 354
Coedes, G., 445
Coffin, Tristram P., 591, 603,
    607
Cohen, A. K., 193
Cohen, Aaron I., 488
Cohen, Anne B., 593
Cohen, Arthur A., 75, 232
Cohen, Edward E., 244
Cohen, Hayim J., 427
Cohen, Hennig, 591, 609
Cohen, J. M., 20
Cohen, Lester H., 266
Cohen, M. J., 20
Cohen, Mark Nathan, 107
Cohen, Marshall, 519
Cohen, Michael J., 427
Cohen, Morris R., 402
Cohen, Naomi, 427
Cohen, Norm, 593
Cohen, Selma J., 518
Cohen, Stanley J., 609
Cohen, Stephen F., 421
Cohen, Wilbur J., 135
Cohen-Stratyner, Barbara
    Naomi, 519
Cohn, Adrian, 30
Coit, Margaret L., 84
Coker, Jerry, 493
Colburn, David R., 288
Cole, Barry, 563, 570
Cole, Bill, 503
Cole, G. D. H., 157
Cole, H. S. D., 194
Cole, Jonathan R., 199, 203
Cole, Margaret I., 148
Cole, Michael, 171
Cole, Stephen, 199
Cole, Wayne S., 278, 641
Coleman, James S., 191, 192,
    196, 211, 441

Coleman, William D., 349
Coles, Robert, 178
Colinari, John, 43
Collaer, Paul, 492
Collier, Basil, 407
Collier, Peter, 287
Collingwood, Robin G., 462
Collins, Bruce, 272, 300
Collins, Randall, 192
Collins, Roger, 418
Collison, Mary, 20
Collison, Robert, 20
Colombo, Cristoforo. See Columbus, Christopher
Colon, Fernando, 631
Colton, Calvin, 85
Colton, Joel, 406
Colton, Timothy J., 421
Coltrane, John, 503
Columbus, Christopher, 631
Colvin, H. C., 533
Combs, James E., 568
Combs, Jerald A., 303
Combs, Josiah H., 601
Commager, Henry Steele, 88, 224, 261, 263, **314**, 316, 329, 330
Commons, John R., 126, **133**
Compaine, Benjamin M., 190, 563, 565
Comstock, George, 570
Comte, Auguste, 205
Conacher, J. B., 380
Conati, Marcello, 516
Conder, John, 307
Condit, Carl W., 554
Condivi, Ascanio, 547
Cone, Carl B., 160
Conkin, Paul K., 286, 287
Connell, Evan S., 51
Connely, Willard, 554
Conner, Daniel, 632
Connery, Donald S., 621
Connor, W. Robert, 245
Connor, Walter D., 421
Conquest, Robert, 421, 476
Conrad, John P., 194
Conrad, Peter, 194, 570
Conradt, David P., 415
Conroy, Hilary, 452, 454
Constable, John, 538
Contosta, David R., 307
Conway, Michael, 587
Conway, Moncure D., 331
Conwell, Chic, 193

Cook, Christopher, 368, 369, 380, 382, 384
Cook, Darian, 272
Cook, Harold E., 593
Cook, James, 619, **632**
Cook, M. A., 432
Cooke, Alistair, 93, 262
Cooke, Deryck, 508
Cooke, Jacob E., 86
Cookson, J. E., 378
Cooley, Charles H., 205
Coomaraswamy, Ananda K., 529
Cooper, John Milton, 336
Cooper, Margaret, 544
Cooper, Michael, 450
Copeland, Ian, 474
Copeland, Roger, 519
Copland, Aaron, 503
Coppa, Frank J., 570
Copplestone, Trewin, 531
Corden, W. M., 130
Cordier, Andrew W., 68
Corn, Joseph J., 287
Cornish, Edward, 563
Cornwell, R. D., 405
Corwin, Edward S., 153, 295, 299
Coser, Lewis A., 188, 189, 190, 192, 198, 201, 211, 215, 216
Costain, Thomas B., 348
Costello, John, 278
Costello, V. F., 432
Cott, Nancy F., 290
Coulson, Jessie, 28, 37, 45
Courlander, Harold, 605
Coursodon, J. P., 578
Cousteau, Jacques, 613, 625
Cowan, Geoffrey, 570
Cowell, Frank R., 216
Cowell, Henry, 507
Cowell, Sidney, 507
Cowie, A. P., 32
Cowie, Peter, 574, 579
Cowling, Maurice, 382
Cox, Edward G., 616
Cox, George W., 591
Cox, John H., 273
Cox, LaWanda, 272, 273
Coyle, Wallace, 266, 586
Crabb, Cecil V., Jr., 303
Craft, Robert, 514
Crahan, Margaret, 441
Craig, Albert M., 445, 450, 464

Craig, Gordon A., 411, 416
Craig, Warren, 488
Craig, William, 407
Craigie, William A., 25, 27
Crane, Diana, 199
Crane, Robert I., 452
Crane, Verner W., 64
Crankshaw, Edward, 52, 74, 421
Cranston, Maurice, 164
Cranz, Galen, 290
Craton, Michael M., 363
Craven, Avery O., 270
Craven, Wesley F., 407
Crawford, Michael, 241
Creel, H. G., 447
Creighton, Donald G., 347
Cremin, Lawrence A., 222, 225, 290
Cressey, Donald R., 193
Cressey, George B., 421
Cressy, David, 374
Crews, Frederick B., 22
Crick, Bernard, 149
Crist, Judith, 578
Croce, Arlene, 518
Croce, Benedetto, 461
Crocker, Richard L., 485
Cronkite, Walter, 569
Cronon, E. David, 259
Crook, J. A., 244
Crosland, Charles A., 157
Crosland, Margaret, 582
Cross, Claire, 374
Cross, Donna Woolfolk, 570
Cross, Gilbert B., 591
Crosskey, W. W., 295
Crossman, R. S., 168
Crouch, Tom D., 287
Crow, John A., 352
Crowder, Michael, 441
Crowe, Joseph A., 529
Crowley, Dale P., 43
Crozier, Brian, 414
Crozier, Michel, 150
Crunden, Robert M., 276
Cuddihy, John Murray, 427
Cueva, Agustin, 362
Cullen, L. M., 369
Cullingford, Cedric, 571
Cumming, William P., 619
Cummings, Paul, 531
Cunliffe, Marcus, 94
Cunningham, Hugh, 378
Cunningham, Merce, 522
Curran, James, 576

Current, Richard N., 89, 95, 262
Curry, Jane L., 565
Curry, Leonard P., 270
Curti, Merle, 285
Curtin, Jeremiah, 596
Curtin, Philip D., 441
Curtis, Charles P., Jr., 143
Curtis, Gerald, 450
Curtis, L. Perry, Jr., 380
Curtis, William, 543
Cushing, Frank H., 604
Cuthbert, John A., 601
Cutright, Paul R., 640
Cuyas, Arturo, 46
Cyert, Richard M., 197
Czitrom, Daniel J., 563

Dabney, Virginius, 88
Da Cunha, Euclides, 361
Daghlian, Philip B., 49
Dahl, Robert A., 151, 152, 153, 191
Dahlhaus, Carl, 485
Dahrendorf, Ralf, 192
Dallek, Robert, 92, 277, 303
Dallin, Alexander, 157
Daly, Herman E., 128
Dalzell, Robert F., Jr., 95
Dam, Hari N., 325
Dana, Richard Henry, Jr., 633
Danaher, Kevin, 596
Dance, Daryl C., 605
Dance, Stanley, 493, 498, 504
Daniels, Cora L., 592
Daniels, Jonathan, 79
Daniels, Robert, 402, 421
Dann, John C., 266
D'Antonio, William V., 195
Danvers, Frederick C., 452
Danziger, Kurt, 563
Darbari, J., 474
Darbari, R., 474
Darby, H. C., 369, 372
Darby, William J., 438
Darnay, Brigitte T., 6
Darwin, Charles R., 171, 626
Dary, David, 285
Das, M. N., 453
Daube, David, 244
Davenport, Herbert J., 140
Davenport, T. R., 441
David, Hans T., 497

Davidowicz, Lucy S., 427, 428
Davidson, Basil, 268, 442
Davidson, Marshall B., 262
Davies, C. Collin, 404
Davies, J. K., 239
Davies, John, 609
Davies, John H., 488
Davies, Peter, 36
Davies, Thomas, 65
Davis, Allen F., 285
Davis, Allison, 110
Davis, Burke, 94
Davis, David Brion, 268
Davis, E., 432
Davis, Hubert J., 601
Davis, Jefferson, 315
Davis, Joseph S., 128
Davis, Lenwood G., 531
Davis, Lynn E., 281, 407
Davis, Miles, 503
Davis, Moshe, 428
Davis, P. H., 439
Davis, Ralph, 374, 378
Davis, Varina, 315
Davison, W. Phillips, 563
Dawasha, Adeed, 434
Dawson, Nelson Lloyd, 278
Dawson, Warren R., 114
Day, Harold A., 539
Day, James M., 175
Day, R. B., 481
Dayal, Baghubir, 453
Dayan, Moshe, 435
Deane, Herbert A., 162
Deane, Phyllis, 124, 370, 378
Dearden, Seton, 630
De Beer, Gavin R., 66
DeBenedetti, Charles, 285
Debo, Angie, 290
Debray, Regis, 358
Debussy, Claude, 503
Decarie, Therese G., 184
DeConde, Alexander, 70, 258, 303
Dedmon, Emmett, 623
Deering, Christopher J., 301
DeFleur, Lois B., 569
DeFleur, Melvin, 190, 561, 563
de Ford, Miriam Allen, 14
de Funiak, William Q., 30
de Gamez, Tanya, 47
de Gennaro, Angelo A., 462
Degh, Linda, 596, 601
Degler, Carl N., 290

de Grand, Alexander J., 417
De Grazia, Alfred, 339
DeGrazia, Edward, 576
DeGregorio, William A., 255
Deighton, Lee C., 35
Deindorfer, Robert G., 599
De La Grange, Henry-Louis, 508
Delany, Martin R., 290
Delarue, Paul, 596
De Lerma, Dominique René, 488
Delevoy, Robert L., 529
Delogu, Orlando E., 616
Deloria, Vine, Jr., 195, 290
DeLuca, Stuart M., 571
Delzell, Charles F., 417
De Madariaga, Salvadore, 358
De Marco, Joseph P., 319
Dembo, Tamara, 182
de Mello Vianna, Fernando, 46
D'Emilio, John, 201
Demir, Soliman, 440
de Morais, Armando, 44
Demuth, Norman, 512
D'Encausse, Helene C., 421
Denham, H. M., 621
Dennett, Tyler, 336
Denny, Norman, 372
Denoon, Donald, 442
De Novo, John A., 303
Denzin, Norman K., 202
de Olivera Marques, Antonia H., 418
Derfler, Leslie, 414
Dernberger, Robert F., 449
Derow, Peter, 241
Derry, John W., 378
Derry, T. K., 419
Deschner, Donald, 583
Desmond, Robert Williams, 565
Dessouki, Ali, 434
Detwiler, Donald S., 416
Deutsch, Karl W., 153, 155, 190
Deutsch, Morton, 170, 192
Deutsch, Otto E., 505, 509, 512
Deutscher, Isaac, 421, 428, 470, 476, 481
Deveraux, George, 106
De Voto, Bernard, 270, **316**
Dewey, John, 230, 463

Dews, Peter B., 185
Diaghilev, Sergei, 522
Diamond, Edwin, 563, 565, 568
Diamond, Harold J., 488
Diaz del Castillo, Bernal, 355
Dicey, Albert V., 151, 156
Dichter, Harry, 485
Dick, Everett, 275, 290
Dickens, Arthur G., 374
Dickinson, H. T., 378
Dickinson, W. Croft, 369
Dickson, Paul, 607, 609
Dickson, William J., 172, 204
Didion, Joan, 363
Diederich, Bernard, 364
Dietze, Gottfried, 295
Diffie, Bailey W., 418
Digaetani, John L., 517
Diggins, John P., 285
Diggs, Ellen Irene, 14
Dillingham, William B., 609
Dimont, Max I., 428
Dinkin, Robert J., 266
Dinnerstein, L., 428
Dio Chrysostom, 247
Di Orio, Al, 578
Disney, Walt, 582
Dissanayake, Wymal, 562
Diubaldo, Richard J., 648
Divine, Robert A., 62, 70, 281, 303
Dixon, J. I., 46
Dobb, Maurice, 124
Dobbs, Charles M., 281
Dobie, J. Frank, 602
Dobson, C. R., 378
Dobson, John M., 276
Dobson, R. B., 373
Dobson, W. A., 38
Dobyns, Henry F., 365
Dobzhansky, Theodosius, 107
Dodge, Ernest S., 445
Dodgson, Campbell, 539
Doeser, Linda, 520
Dohrenwend, Barbara S., 200
Dohrenwend, Bruce P., 200
Dolan, Edwin G., 132
Dollard, John, 100, 105, 170, 174, **176**
Dominick, Joseph, 563
Domling, Wolfgang, 497
Domotor, Tekla, 596
Donakowski, Conrad L., 611

Donald, David, 259, 270, 274
Donaldson, Dwight M., 434
Donaldson, G., 374
Doniach, N. S., 38
Donnelly, James S., 380
Donner, Jorn, 579
Donohue, Christine N., 14
Donovan, Robert J., 79, 281
Dore, Ronald P., 450
Dorfman, Ariel, 611
Dorfman, Joseph, 124, 133, 143, 220
Dornbusch, Charles E., 259
Dorson, Richard M., 105, 591, 592, 596, 599, 607, 609
Doughty, Howard, 332
Doughty, Paul L., 365
Douglas, David C., 369
Douglas, Jack D., 194
Douglas, Mary, 102, 107
Douglass, Frederick, 85, 273
Dover, K. J., 243
Dower, J. W., 450
Downes, Edward, 491
Downes, Kerry, 553, 558
Downing, David, 578
Downs, Anthony, 152
Downs, Robert B., 230, 609
Doyle, William, 411
D'Oyley, Elizabeth, 616
Drake, Harold L., 571
Drake, Milton, 15
Drescher, Seymour, 342, 378
Dreyfuss, Henry, 527
Drifte, R., 450
Drigotas, Frank M., Jr., 626
Driver, Harold E., 110, 116, 290
Drower, Ethel A., 596
Drucker, Peter F., 128
Dry, Murray, 297
Duberman, Martin, 83
Dubois, Marguerite-Marie, 39
Du Bois, Shirley G., 319
Du Bois, W. E. B., 317
Dubos, Rene, 483
Du Bourguet, Pierre, 529
Duckett, Eleanor S., 371
Duckles, Vincent, 488
Duea, Karen, 614
Duesenberry, James S., 128
Duffus, Robert L., 220
Dugger, Ronnie, 71, 281
Duignan, Peter, 442

Duke, Daniel L., 225
Duke, Judith S., 563
Dukes, Paul, 421
Dulles, Foster R., 303
Dumbauld, Edward, 295
Duncan, A. A., 369
Duncan, Greg J., 130
Duncan, Isadora, 523
Duncan, Otis D., 100, 101, 200, 202, 203
Dundes, Alan, 105, 592, 607
Dundy, Elaine, 52
Dunlop, Bill, 626
Dunmore, John, 623
Dunn, Charles J., 450
Dunn, Waldo H., 391
Dunning, John, 571
Dupaquier, Jacques, 140
Dupree, Louis, 440
Durand, Micheline, 46
Durant, Ariel, 462
Durant, Will, 462
Dürer, Albrecht, 539
Durgnat, Raymond, 580, 585
Durham, James C., 341
Durham, Philip, 290
Durkheim, Emile, 109, 169, 188, 194, **206**
Durrell, Lawrence, 616, 621
Dutton, Gregory Battcock, 492
Duus, Peter, 450
Dvořák, Antonin, 504
Dworkin, Gerald, 173
Dyer, Isaac W., 461
Dyer, Richard, 578
Dyer, Thomas G., 336
Dykstra, Darrell I., 436
Dziewanowski, M. K., 421

Eadie, John W., 607
Earl, David M., 450
Eastin, Roy B., 14
Eastman, Lloyd E., 447
Eastman, Mary, 604
Eastman, Max, 610
Easton, David, 149, 153
Eaton, Clement, 85, 268, 315
Eatwell, Roger, 382
Eban, Abba, 428
Ebbinghaus, Hermann, 177
Ebrey, Patricia B., 447
Eccles, William J., 348
Eckenrode, Hamilton J., 315
Eckert, Ross D., 127

Eckstein, A., 447
Eckstein, Harry, 419
Edel, Leon, 49, 60. *See* main
  entry Volume 1
Edelhart, Mike, 20
Edelstein, Alex S., 563
Eden, Anthony, 61
Edgar, Neal L., 623
Edmonds, I. G., 578
Edmonds, Michael, 60
Edmunds, David, 290
Edwardes, Michael, 474
Edwards, George C., 299
Edwards, I. E., 238, 239
Edwards, Paul, 7, 99
Edwards, R. Dudley, 374,
  380
Edwards, Ralph, 534
Edwards, Ruth D., 369
Eells, George, 510
Egan, Kieran, 229
Eggan, Fred, 110
Ehrenberg, Victor, 239
Ehrenzweig, Anton, 527
Ehrlich, Eugene, 27, 155
Ehrmann, Eliezar L., 428
Einstein, Albert, 428
Einstein, Alfred, 485
Eisenach, Eldon J., 142
Eisenberg, Azriel, 428
**Eisenhower, Dwight David,
  61**
Eisenhower, John S., 407
Eisenstadt, Shmuel N., 189,
  196
Eisenstein, Sergei, 582
Eisler, Paul E., 488
Eisner, Elliot W., 225
Eissler, Kurt R., 544
Ekundare, R. O., 442
Elazar, Daniel J., 151, 435
Elder, Glen H., Jr., 172, 189
Elderfield, John, 546
Elgar, Frank, 549
Eliade, Mircea, 109
Elison, George, 450
Elkin, Judith L., 358
Elkind, David, 235
**Ellington, Edward Kennedy,
  504**
Elliot, Bob, 610
Elliot, Jean, 349
Elliot, Philip, 566
Elliot, T. C., 632
Elliott, J. H., 418
Elliott, Martha J., 151

Ellul, Jacques, 199
Elon, Amos, 428
Elphick, R., 442
Elsen, Albert E., 553
**Elton, Geoffrey R., 253, 389,
  402**
Elwell-Sutton, L. P., 437
Elwood, Ralph C., 421
Emanuel, Muriel, 533
Embree, John F., 110
Emerson, Rupert, 442
Emery, Donald W., 36
Emery, Edwin, 566
Emery, H. G., 26
Emery, Lynne Fauley, 520
Emery, Walter B., 239
Emsley, Clive, 378
Emy, H. V., 380
Endelman, Todd M., 378
Engel, Barbara A., 421
Engels, Friedrich, 133
Engerman, Stanley L., 287
England, R. W., Jr., 193
Engle, Eloise, 421
English, John, 349
Englung, Steven, 285
Enser, A. G., 574
Epenshade, Edward B., Jr.,
  18
Ephron, Delia, 610
Epstein, Barbara Leslie, 290
Epstein, Dena J., 605
Epsy, Willard R., 33
Erasmus, Charles J., 203
Erenberg, Lewis A., 285
Erickson, Carolly, 52, 374
Erickson, J. Gunnar, 489
Erikson, Erik H., 172, 177
Erikson, Kai T., 191, 194
Erman, Adolf, 239
Erodes, Richard, 604
Ervin, Sam J., Jr., 610
Esar, Evan, 610
Escarpit, Robert, 189
Escott, Paul D., 315
Esherick, Joseph W., 447
Esposito, John L., 434
Esquenazi Mayo, Roberto,
  352
Esslin, Martin, 571
Estes, William K., 174
Esthus, Raymond A., 337
Ethridge, James M., 6
Ettema, James S., 571
Evans, Arthur B., 582
Evans, Bergen, 20, 30

Evans, Charles, 259
Evans, Cornelia, 30
Evans, J. A., 245
Evans, J. P., 600
Evans, Joan, 529, 534
Evans, Mark, 493
Evans, Morgan O., 118
Evans, Peter, 501
Evans, Richard I., 176, 184
**Evans-Pritchard, E. E., 108,
  110, 112**
Evelyn, John. *See* Volume 1
Evenari, Michael, 435
Evenson, Norma, 543
Everdale, Carl P., 470
Everett, Frank E., 316
Everson, William K., 576,
  586
Ewald, William Bragg, 281
Eyck, Eric, 416
Eyles, Allen, 587

Faber, Doris, 78
Faber, Stephen, 576
Fainsod, Merle, 422
**Fairbank, John K., 445, 450,
  463**
Fairfield, Roy P., 295
Falkus, Malcolm, 369
Fall, Bernard B., 454
Fallon, N., 432
Falls, Cyril, 407
Famera, Karen, 491
Fang, Irving E., 569
Fanning, Ronan, 382
Fant, Maureen B., 244
Farah, Caeser E., 434
Farley, Reynolds, 195, 196
Farmer, John S., 32
Farnham, Charles H., 332
Farrand, Max, 151, 295
Farrell, R. B., 41
Farwell, Byron, 380, 646
Fasel, George, 160
Fass, Paula S., 277
el-Fathaly, Omar I., 440
Fausold, Martin L., 70
Fauve, Chamoux A., 140
Fay, Bernard, 64
Feagans, Lynne, 563
Feather, A. G., 646
Feather, Leonard, 493
Featherman, David L., 201
Fehrenbacher, Don E., 89,
  270

Fei, Hsiao Tung, 110
Feifel, Herman, 195
Feingold, Henry L., 92
Feinman, Ronald L., 276
Feis, Herbert, 407, 411, 422
Feldberg, Michael, 270
Feldman, Lily G., 435
Felice, Renzo de, 411
Fellini, Federico, 583
Fellman, Michael, 271
Fenelon, K. G., 438
Fenno, Richard F., 299
Ferdon, Edwin L., Jr., 636
Ferguson, E. James, 259
Ferguson, Eugene S., 404
Ferguson, John, 244
Ferguson, Nancy, 619
Fergusson, Rosalind, 22
Fergusson, Thomas G., 380
Fermi, Laura, 417
Fermor, Patrick L., 621
Fernald, James C., 33
Fernea, Elizabeth W., 623
Fernea, Robert A., 623
Ferrar, H., 39
Ferraro, Vincent, 432
Ferreira, Julio A., 44
Ferrell, Robert H., 79, 281
Ferris, William, 594
Ferro, Marc, 422
Fesharaki, Fereidun, 437
Festinger, Leon, 171, 197
Feuchtwanger, E. J., 380, 416
Field, Harry, 191
Fielding, Mantle, 531
Fielding, Raymond, 576
Fields, W. C., 583
Fifoot, C. H., 395
Filene, Peter G., 422
Filmer-Sankey, Josephine, 372
Finberg, Alexander J., 555
Finch, Christopher, 582
Finch, M. H., 366
Findlay, James A., 529
Findley, Carter V., 439
Findling, John E., 258
Fine, John V. A., 239
Fine, Morris, 428
Finegold, Leo, 45
Finer, Herman, 153
Fink, Robert, 489
Finkelman, Paul, 270
Finkelstein, Louis, 428
Finler, Joel, 588

Finley, John H., Jr., 245
Finley, Moses I., 239, 240, 243
Finn, Chester E., Jr., 225
Finn, R. Weldon, 372
Finson, John W., 508
Finsterbusch, Kurt, 188
Firestone, Shulamith, 411
First, Ruth, 442
Firth, C. H., 394
Firth, Raymond, 104, 105, 107, 108, 109, 110, **113,** 119
Fischer, Claude S., 196
Fischer, David H., 402
Fischer, Fritz, 407, 416
Fischer, Heinz-Dietrich, 563, 566
Fischer, Louis, 422, 470
Fischer, Michael M., 437
Fischer-Dieskau, Dietrich, 513
Fischhoff, Baruch, 199
Fishburn, Katherine, 611
Fisher, Alan W., 422
Fisher, Charles, 445
Fisher, D. J., 371
Fisher, Harold A., 566
Fisher, Herbert A., 159
Fisher, Irving, 131, **134**
Fisher, Irving Norton, 134
Fisher, Louis, 295
Fisher, Mary, 260
Fisher, Nigel, 75
Fisher, Rhoda L., 610
Fisher, Robin, 632
Fisher, Seymour, 610
Fisher, Vardis, 640
Fisher, W. B., 432
Fishman, Priscilla, 428
Fishwick, Marshall W., 611
Fitch, James M., 532
Fitch, John S., III, 362
Fitzgerald, Charles P., 447
Fitzgerald, Frances, 291, 454
Fitzhardinge, L. F., 240
Fitzhugh, William, 264
Fitzpatrick, Sheila, 422
Flam, Jack D., 546
Flanagan, Cathleen C., 592
Flanagan, John T., 592
Flanagan, Owen J., Jr., 170
Flanders, Helen H., 599
Flandrau, Grace, 640
Flanigan, William J., 301

Fleener-Marzec, Nickieann, 585
Fleming, Francis, 442
Fleming, John, 528, 532, 534
Fleming, Thomas J., 88
Fleming-Williams, Ian, 539
Flesch, Rudolf, 22
Fletcher, A. J., 376
Fletcher, Arnold, 440
Fletcher, Banister, 531
Fletcher, Colin, 626
Fletcher, Miles, 450
Flexner, James T., 86, 94
Flexner, Stuart B., 33, 36
Flinn, M. W., 369
Florinsky, Michael T., 404
Flower, Elizabeth, 285
Flower, Newman, 505
Fogel, Robert W., 253, 287
Foley, Michael, 282
Folland, H. F., 625
Follett, Wilson, 30
Foner, Eric, 273, 331
Fonteyn, Margot, 523
Foote, Shelby, 273
Foote, Wilder, 68
Forcey, Charles, 325
Ford, Franklin L., 411
Ford, John, 583
Ford, Paul L., 64, 86, 94
Forde, C. Daryll, 108, 442
Foreman, Alexa L., 574
Forge, Andrew, 548
Forkel, Johann N., 497
Forman, George E., 235
Forman, Werner, 433
Formisano, Ronald P., 268
Fornara, Charles W., 241
Fornatale, Peter, 571
Forster, Klaus, 19
Forster, Robert, 411
Forsythe, Robert S., 317
Fortes, Meyer, 109, 113, 122
Fortescue, John, 389
Fortune, Nigel, 499, 508
Fortune, R. F., 110
Forucci, Samuel L., 594
Foster, George M., 104
Foster, John T., 641
Foster, Mark S., 277
Foster, Stephen, 505
Foucault, Michel, 169, 411
Fowke, Edith, 594, 596
Fowler, F. G., 30, 32
Fowler, Henry W., 28, 30, 31, 32, 37

Fowler, Kenneth, 373
Fowler, Richard, 626
Fowler, William M., Jr., 266
Fox, Dixon R., 338, 344
Fox, Richard Wightman, 287
Fox, Stephen R., 291
Fox, Walter, 566
Foy, Felician, 16
Frady, Marshall, 291
Francis, David, 581
Frank, Anne, 62
Frank, Ronald E., 571
Frank, Tenney, 243
Frankfort, Henri, 239
Franklin, Benjamin, 63
Franklin, Joe, 576
Franklin, John Hope, 256, **319**
Franklyn, Julian, 35
Franqui, Carlos, 361, 362
Fraser, Antonia, 52, 376
Fraser, W. Hamish, 611
Fraser, Walter J., Jr., 291, 601
Frassanito, William A., 273
Frazer, James George, 109, **114**
Frazier, E. Franklin, 287
Frears, J. R., 414
Freedberg, Sydney J., 529
Freeden, Michael, 380
Freedman, Anne, 197
Freedman, Lawrence, 407
Freedman, Maurice, 114
Freedman, Robert O., 432, 435
Freehling, Alison G., 270
Freeman, Derek, 119, 120
Freeman, Donald, 348
Freeman, Douglas Southall, 56, 94
Freeman, Edward A., 390
Freeman, Howard E., 101
Freeman, Jo, 201, 411
Freeman, William, 32
Freeman-Grenville, G. S., 369, 406
Freidel, Frank, 92, 273
Freire, Paulo, 225
Fremont, John Charles, 626
French, John R. P., Jr., 203
Frenkel, Jacob A., 130
Frere, Sheppard, 371
Freuchen, Peter, 634
Freud, Sigmund, 96, **178,** 544

Freyre, Gilberto, 196
Fried, Jerome, 597
Friedel, Frank, 256
Friedlander, Albert H., 428
Friedlander, Henry, 428
Friedman, Isaiah, 428
Friedman, Lawrence J., 270
Friedman, Leon, 256
Friedman, Leslie, 561
Friedman, Milton, 126, 130, 131, **135**
Friedman, Morton P., 174
Friedman, Rose, 135
Friedrich, Carl J., 150, 151, 152, 153
Friendly, Fred W., 151, 567
Frier, Bruce W., 244
Frisbie, W. Parker, 195, 197
Frisby, David, 216
Frisch, Ragnar, 125
Frome, Michael, 619
Fromm, Erich, 178
Froude, James A., 390, 461
Fry, Gladys-Marie, 271
Fryde, E. B., 370
Fryde, Natalie, 373
Frye, Northrop, 349
Fuchs, Victor R., 102
Fuchs, Vivian, 637
Fukutake, Tadashi, 450
Fuld, James J., 489
Fuller, John F., 407
Fuller, John G., 627
Fuller, R. Buckminster, 225
Fulton, Albert R., 576
Fulton, Robert J., 195
Funk, Charles E., 36
Funk, Charles E., Jr., 36
Furlong, William Rea, 291
Furst, Viktor, 558
Furth, Hans G., 184, 235
Fusi, Juan P., 418
Fussell, Paul, 408, 621
Futch, Ovid L., 273

Gable, John A., 337
Gaddis, John L., 278, 303, 408
Gage, John, 555
Gagné, Robert M., 174
Gailey, Harry A., Jr., 404, 442
Gainer, Patrick W., 601
Gaines, Steven, 492
Gainsborough, Thomas, 540

Galbraith, John Kenneth, 102, 127, **135**
Gale, Robert L., 332, 633
Galeano, Eduardo, 358
Gall, Sandy, 440
Gallagher, Hugh G., 52, 92
Gallagher, J. A., 380
Galvan, Roberto A., 46
Gambs, John S., 136
Gammond, Peter, 507
Gandhi, Mohandas K., 453.
    See main entry Volume 4
Gann, L. H., 442
Gans, Herbert J., 191, 202
Garbicz, Adam, 574
García de Paredes, Angel, 46
García-Pelayo y Gross, Ramon, 46
Garcilaso-de-la-Vega, El Inca, 354
Gard, Robert E., 601
Garden, Edward, 515
Gardiner, Alan H., 239
Gardiner, C. Harvey, 334
Gardiner, Samuel R., 391
Gardner, E. E., 600
Gardner, Helen, 528
Gardner, Howard, 116, 173, 185, 189
Gardner, James B., 253
Gardner, John W., 225
Gardner, Joseph L., 337
Gardner, Lloyd C., 303
Garfield, James, 89
Gargan, Edward T., 342, 479
Garibaldi, Antoine, 225
Garms, Walter I., 225
Garner, Richard L., 631
Garnett, Angelica, 52
Garraty, John A., 262, 295
Garrett, N., 260
Garrick, David, 65
Garrison, William Lloyd, 291
Gascoyne, David, 461
Gash, Norman, 391
Gasiorowska, Xenia, 422
Gaskell, Elizabeth Cleghorn.
    See Volume 1
Gasparis, Priscilla de, 101
Gaston, Jerry, 200, 210
Gatzke, Hans W., 406
Gauguin, Paul, 540
Gaunt, William, 344, 551
Gauthier, David P., 160
Gay, Peter, 178, 253, 402, 411, 416

Gay, Robert M., 23
Gayer, A. D., 134
Gaylin, Willard, 193
Gayron, Daniel, 435
Gealt, Adelheid M., 528
Geduld, Harry M., 576
Gee, Choy Y., 614
Geertz, Clifford, 104, 105, 109, **114,** 199, 434
Geertz, Hildred, 114
Gehring, Wes D., 581
Geiger, George R., 231
Geiger, Theodore, 406
Geiringer, Irene, 497, 506
Geiringer, Karl, 497, 506
Gelb, Norman, 266
Gelb, P. Arthur, 617
Gelber, Leonard, 258
Gelfman, Judith S., 569
Geller, Evelyn, 563
Gellhorn, Martha, 616
Gennep, Arnold van, 109
Genovese, Eugene D., 287
Geoffrey of Monmouth, 391
George, Alexander L., 96, 408
George, Don, 504
George, Henry, 131
George, Juliette L., 96
Georges, Robert A., 596
Gephart, Ronald M., 259
Gerber, Barbara L., 40
Gerbner, George, 561, 564
Gerhart, Gail M., 442
Gershoy, Leo, 472
Gershwin, George, 505
Gerson, Leonard D., 470
Gerster, Georg, 623
Getty, Ian A., 349
Geyikdaqi, Mehmet Y., 439
Geyl, Pieter, 419, 479
Ghai, Dharam, 442
Ghareeb, Edmund, 437
Ghiglione, Loren, 566
Ghose, Sankar, 453
Giametti, A. Bartlett, 225
Gianakos, Larry J., 571
Gibaldi, Joseph, 22
Gibb, H. A. R., 434
Gibbon, Edward, 66, 240
Gibbons, Don C., 194
Gibney, Frank, 31, 450
Gibson, Arthur, 579
Gibson, Charles, 357
Gibson, Gerald D., 489
Gibson, H., 69

Gibson, James J., 174
Gibson, Margaret, 372
Gibson, Martin L., 568
Gibson, Richard, 442
Gibson, Ronald, 316
Gibson, Walter S., 537
Gibson, William M., 337
Giddens, Anthony, 188, 201, 221
Giddins, Gary, 493
Giedion, Sigfried, 531, 532
Gieryn, Thomas, 199, 211
Gilard, Hazel A., 597
Gilbert, Alan D., 380, 382
Gilbert, Bentley B., 383
Gilbert, Cecile, 594
Gilbert, Creighton, 530
Gilbert, Felix, 411
Gilbert, James, 282
Gilbert, Martin, 388, 428
Gilbert, Neil, 127
Giliomee, H., 442
Gilison, Jerome M., 422
Gill, Derek, 626
Gill, Dominic, 496
Gill, Graeme J., 422
Gillingham, John, 369
Gillis, John R., 411
Gillispie, Charles C., 100
Gillmor, Donald M., 561
Gilmore, Robert K., 601
Gilsenan, Michael, 436
Gimbel, John, 408, 416
Ginzberg, Eli, 128
Ginzburg, Carlo, 411
Girouard, Mark, 369
Gitter, George, 561
Gittings, John, 447
Glaeser, Ludwig, 547
Glare, P. G., 44
Glaser, Barney G., 195
Glaser, William A., 197
Glass, D. V., 140
Glassie, Henry, 594, 597, 600, 607, 608
Glassman, Jon D., 438
Glazer, Nathan, 195, 202
Glimm, James Y., 600
Gloag, John, 531, 534
Glock, Charles Y., 101, 197
Glubb, John Bagot, 438
Gluckman, Max, 113, 192
Gochberg, Herbert S., 40
Godard, Jean-Luc, 584
Godden, Jon, 623
Godden, Rumer, 623

Godolphin, Frances R. B., 240
Goebel, Julius, Jr., 86
Goehlert, Robert U., 13, 156, 256, 259
Goehring, Eleanor E., 601
Goeldner, Charles R., 614, 615
Goethals, Gregor T., 571
Goetzman, Robert, 391
Goetzmann, William H., 271
Goff, Richard, 406
Goffman, Erving, 108, 194, 197, **206**
Gogh, Vincent van. See Van Gogh, Vincent
Golan, Galia, 432
Goldberg, Nathan, 42
Goldberger, Arthur, 101
Goldenberg, Edie, 299
Golder, Frank A., 422
Golding, Peter, 566
Goldman, Eric F., 71, 483
Goldman, Ralph M., 299
Goldscheider, Ludwig, 544
Goldschmid, Harvey J., 127
Goldschmidt, Walter R., 112
Goldsmith, M. M., 160
Goldstein, Doris, 342
Goldstein, Kenneth S., 592, 606
Goldstine, Herman H., 147
Goldthorpe, John H., 127
Goldwater, Robert, 541
Goldwin, Robert A., 151
Golinkoff, Roberta, 563
Gollin, Gillian, 199
Gombrich, E. H., 528
Gooch, Anthony, 46
Gooch, G. P., 402, **465**
Good, Anthony, 104
Good, Edwin M., 496
Goode, Kenneth G., 262
Goode, William J., 195, 196
Goodenough, Ward H., 107, 121
Goodlad, John I., 225
Goodman, Anthony, 373
Goodman, Elliot R., 157
Goodman, John C., 132
Goodman, Louis W., 196
Goodman, Paul, 268
Goodnow, Frank J., 150
Goodrich, Frances, 63
Goodrich, L. Carrington, 447
Goodwin, Albert, 378, 414

Goodwin, H. Eugene, 566
Gopal, Ram, 474
Gorden, Raymond L., 101
Gordon, Lincoln, 302
Gordon, Michael, 291
Gordon, Raoul, 597
Gordon, Robert, 548
Gordon-Smith, Maria, 502
Gorer, Geoffrey, 110
Gorham, Charles, 341
Gorham, William, 202
Goslin, David A., 202
Gosnell, Harold F., 166, 282, 337
Gossen, Gary H., 604
Gottfried, Robert S., 373
Gottman, Jean, 202
Gottschalk, Louis, 101, 104
Gottschalk, Walter, 42
Goubert, Pierre, 414
Gough, Kathleen, 108
Gouinlock, James, 231
Gould, John, 621
Gould, Julius, 100, 404
Gould, Stephen J., 107, 173
Goulden, Joseph, 607
Goulding, Ray, 610
Govan, Gilbert E., 316
Gove, Philip Babcock, 29
Gowing, Lawrence, 528, 546
Goya y Lucientes, Francisco José de, 541
Graber, Doris, 299, 568
Graetz, Heinrich, 428
Graff, Henry F., 256, 402
Graham, Lawrence S., 418
Graham, Martha, 523
Graham, Otis L., Jr., 92
Graham, Robin L., 626
Grambs, Jean D., 225
Granger, Byrd H., 608
Granick, David, 422
Grant, Curtis, 333
Grant, George M., 626
Grant, Michael, 428
Grant, Ulysses S., 67
Grantham, Dewey, 337
Gratton, Clinton Hartley, 445
Graubard, Stephen R., 160
Graunt, John, 198
Graves, Edgar B., 368
Graves, Robert, 638
Gray, Basil, 530
Gray, Christopher, 541
Gray, Edward, 46

Gray, J. A., 171, 184
Gray, Michael H., 489
Gray, Roland P., 599
Gray, Ronald D., 558
Green, Archie, 594
Green, Julien, 52
Green, Lila, 597
Green, Mark J., 299
Green, Stanley, 489, 574
Greenaway, G. W., 369
Greenberg, Bradley S., 72
Greenberg, Janelle R., 377
Greenberg, Joseph H., 108
Greenberg, Louis, 428
Greenberg, Marshall G., 571
Greenberg, Milton, 258
Greenblatt, Stephen J., 374
Greene, Maxine, 226
Greenfield, Kent R., 408
Greenfield, Patricia, 564
Greenhall, Agnes, 3
Greenstein, F. I., 149, 282
Greenway, John, 597
Gregg, Edward, 376
Gregor-Dellin, Martin, 517
Gregory, John, 520
Gregory, Lady, 621
Grew, Eva, 497
Grew, Sidney, 497
Gridley, Mark C., 494
Griffin, Anne, 349
Griffin, Charles C., 352
Griffin, Grace Gardner, 311
Griffis, William E., 454
Griffith, D. W., 584
Griffith, W. E., 411, 422
Griffiths, Paul, 492
Griffiths, Ralph A., 373
Grigg, David B., 406
Grigg, John, 383
Grim, Ronald E., 259
Grime, Kitty, 494
Grimm, Hermann F., 547
Grinnell, George B., 604
Grob, Gerald N., 253, 262, 291
Grodzins, Morton, 151
Gropius, Walter, 542
Grose, Francis, 32
Grosjean, François, 226
Gross, John, 22
Gross, Lynne S., 561
Grosser, Alfred, 414
Grout, Donald J., 485, 495
Grove, Walter R., 194
Grube, Joel W., 190

Gruber, Katherine, 7
Grunbaum, Adolf, 175
Gruner, Charles R., 610
Grunin, Robert, 561
Gudiol, José, 542
Guenzel, Pamela J., 101
Guerard, Albert L., 465
Guest, Ivor, 519
Guetzkow, Harold, 101
Guggenheim, Hans G., 616
Guida, Louis, 601
Guiles, Fred L., 586
Guilford, Joy P., 173
Gulick, Edward V., 408
Gumpert, Gary, 564
Gumperz, John J., 108, 564
Gunn, Clare A., 614
Gunther, John, 634
Gura, Philip F., 264
Guralnik, David B., 28
Gurevitch, Michael, 564
Gurney, O. R., 239
Gurvich, George, 188
Gustafson, Milton O., 256
Guterbock, Thomas M., 153
Guth, DeLloyd J., 72
Guthrie, James W., 225
Gutierrez, Carlos Maria, 362
Gutkind, Peter C., 104, 404
Gutteridge, W. F., 442
Guy, J. J., 442
Guzmán, Martín L., 363

Haak, Bob, 550, 551
Haas, Ernst B., 155
Haavelmo, Trygve, 126
Hachey, Thomas E., 383
Hacker, Andrew, 256
Hacker, Louis M., 321
Hackett, Albert, 63
Hackett, Roger F., 450
Hadcock, R. Neville, 370
Haddad, George M., 432
Hadden, Jeffrey K., 202
Haftmann, Werner, 530
Hagan, William T., 291
Hagedorn, Hermann, 337
Hagen, Osjkar, 556
Haggart, James A., 597
Hagood, Patricia, 10
Hagstrom, Jerry, 257
Hague, Eleanor, 594
Hahn, Werner G., 422
Haim, Sylvia G., 435
Haiman, Franklyn S., 150

Haimson, Leopold H., 422
Hakluyt, Richard, 635
Halberstam, David, 72, 73, 303
Hale, J. R., 404
Hale, Judson, 16
Hale, Nathan G., Jr., 179
Hale, William H., 553
Halévy, Elie, 392
Haley, Alex, 52
Haley, Michael, 585
Hall, Alice J., 18
Hall, Calvin S., 175, 179
Hall, D. G., 446
Hall, David D., 264
Hall, Edwin S., Jr., 597
Hall, Ellen, 621
Hall, Emily, 621
Hall, Frances A., 43
Hall, G. Stanley, 172, 179
Hall, Ivan P., 450
Hall, James, 528
Hall, James L., 7
Hall, Jerome, 193
Hall, John R., 37
Hall, John W., 450
Hall, Kermit L., 259
Hall, Peter Dobkin, 285
Hall, Robert A., Jr., 43
Hall, Robert E., 130, 131
Halle, Louis J., 304
Hallett, Judith P., 244
Hallett, Robin, 441, 442
Halliburton, Richard, 616
Hallissey, Robert C., 453
Halliwell, Leslie, 574
Hallo, William W., 239
Hallowell, A. Irving, 105
Halpenny, Frances, 347
Halperin, Morton H., 157
Halperin, S. William, 402
Halpern, Ben, 428
Halpern, Jeanne W., 562
Halpern, Manfred, 432
Halsey, William D., 26
Halstead, John P., 380
Ham, Christopher, 156
Hamalian, Leo, 616
Hamelink, Cees J., 564
Hamer, D. A., 380
Hamilton, Alexander, 86, 151, 294, 295
Hamilton, George H., 530, 545
Hamilton, Holman, 316
Hamilton, Mary A., 148

Hamilton, Peter, 214
Hamlin, A. D., 534
Hamlin, Talbot, 532
Hamm, Charles, 485
Hammacher, A. M., 556
Hammacher, Renilde, 556
Hammarskjold, Dag, 67
Hammond, Barbara, 392
Hammond, Charles M., 571
Hammond, John L., 392
Hammond, N. G. L., 241
Hammond, Norman, 354
Hammond, Phillip E., 199
Hammond, Thomas T., 422
Hampden-Turner, Charles, 170
Hand, Wayland D., 608
Handel, George Frideric, 505
Handlin, Lilian, 89, 322
Handlin, Mary, 322
Handlin, Oscar, 89, 100, 195, 321, 343
Hands, A. R., 243
Hanham, H. J., 368
Hanley, David L., 414
Hanley, Susan B., 450
Hansen, Alvin, 136, 138, 143
Hansen, Joseph, 481
Hanson, Anne C., 545
Hanson, Lawrence, 551
Harbert, Earl N., 307
Harbison, Winfred A., 296
Harden, John, 601
Harding, Vincent, 291
Hardy, C. De Witt, 323
Hardy, Oliver, 586
Hardy, Phil, 574
Hare, A. Paul, 172
Hareven, Tamara K., 78, 172, 291
Hargreaves, J. D., 442
Hargrove, Erwin C., 299
Harik, Iliya F., 436
Haring, C. H., 357
Haring, Douglas G., 106
Harkness, David, 383
Harlan, Louis R., 52, 237
Harmetz, Aljean, 578
Harner, Michael J., 619
Harrer, Heinrich, 635
Harris, Ann S., 531
Harris, Christina, 436
Harris, Cyril M., 532
Harris, Ellen T., 505
Harris, Enriqueta, 557
Harris, Frank. See Volume 1

Harris, H. A., 243
Harris, Jay S., 571
Harris, Mark Jonathan, 278
Harris, Marvin, 102, 105
Harris, Seymour E., 138
Harris, Tomas, 542
Harris, William H., 288
Harris, William V., 244
Harrison, Brian, 383
Harrison, David, 442
Harrison, James P., 454
Harrison, John A., 446
Harrison, John F., 380
Harrison, Joseph, 418
Harrison, Martin, 415
Harrod, Roy F., 138
Hart, Henry H., 644
Hart, Herbert L., 155, 158
Hart, Ivor B., 544
Hart, Jack R., 567
Hart, Jeffrey, 282
Hart, Mary L., 594
Harter, Lafayette G., Jr., 133
Harthan, John, 534
Hartley, John, 566
Hartmann, H. I., 203
Hartmann, Rudolf, 513
Hartmann, Susan, 79
Hartt, Frederick, 547
Hartwell, R. M., 378
Harvey, A. McGehee, 289
Harvey, David, 141
Harvey, James C., 71
Harvey, Paul, 239
Harvie, Christopher, 369
Hasan-Ibn-Hasan, Fasa'l, 437
Haskell, Arnold L., 518
Haskins, James S., 507
Hasluck, F. W., 439
Hassler, Warren W., Jr., 304
Hastrup, Baird, 521
Hatch, Jane M., 14
Hatcher, John, 373
Hatje, Gerd, 532
Hattaway, Herman, 273
Hauser, Arnold, 189, 528
Hauser, Robert M., 201
Havard, William C., 295
Havick, John J., 564
Havighurst, A. F., 368, 383
Hawke, David F., 331, 640
Hawkins, Hugh, 237, 319
Hawkridge, David G., 226
Hawley, Amos H., 192
Hawley, Donald, 440
Hawley, Ellis Wayne, 277

Hawtrey, R. G., 126
Hay, Denys, 411
Hay, John, 89
Hayakawa, S. I., 33
Haydn, Joseph, 506
Hayek, Friedrich A. von, 126, **136,** 150
Hayes, E. Nelson, 116
Hayes, John, 540
Hayes, Paul, 380, 383
Hayes, Tanya, 116
Haynes, Richard F., 80
Hayward, Max, 422
Haywood, Helene, 534
Hazlitt, William C., 22
Head, Sydney W., 571
Heale, Michael J., 268
Healy, William, 193
Hebert, Jacques, 447
Hecht, Marie B., 86
Heckscher, August, 457
Hedebro, Goran, 564
Hedinsson, Elias, 571
Hedley, Olwen, 378
Hefele, Bernhard, 494
Heikal, Mohamed, 436
Heilbroner, Robert L., 130
Heimart, Alan, 327
Heims, Steve J., 147
Heinz, John P., 198
Heinzkill, Richard, 574
Heise, Jon O., 614
Held, Julius S., 550, 553
Heller, Francis H., 282
Heller, Walter H., 131
Hellman, John, 566
Helm, Mike, 603
Hemming, John, 355
Hench, John B., 265
Henderson, Donald C., 631
Henderson, Hubert, 128
Henderson, John S., 354
Henderson, L. J., 143
Henderson, Richard, 626
Henderson, Robert M., 585
Henderson, Ronald W., 196
Henderson, W. O., 134, 416
Henderson, William, 446
Hendrickson, Robert, 36
Henfrey, Colin, 619
Heng, Liang, 447
Henley, W. E., 32
Henriksen, Thomas H., 444
Henry, Jules, 102
Henslin, James M., 196
Henthorn, William E., 454

Heravi, Mehdi, 404
Herberg, Will, 199
Herbert, Anthony B., 616
Herbert, Eugenia W., 65
Herbert, S., 608
Hermann, Luke, 556
Herndon, William H., 89
Herodotus, 245
Herold, J. Christopher, 57
Herr, Richard, 342, 418
Herring, George C., 282
Herring, Helen B., 352
Herring, Hubert, 352
Herrmann, Paul, 616
Hersh, Seymour M., 454
Hershkowitz, Mickey, 569
Hershlag, Z. Y., 432
Herskovits, Melville Jean, 107, 112, **115,** 291
Hertzberg, Arthur, 428, 429
Herzen, Alexander, 422
Herzfeld, Michael, 608
Herzl, Theodor, 429
Herzog, Chaim, 435
Hess, Beth B., 202
Hess, Stephen, 299, 567
Hesseltine, William B., 67, 89
Hession, Charles H., 136
Hewitt, Margaret, 370
Hexter, J. H., 374, 472
Heydenreich, Ludwig H., 544
Heyer, Anna H., 489
Heyerdahl, Thor, 636
Hibbard, Caroline M., 376
Hibbard, Howard, 537, 547, 549
Hibbert, Christopher, 378, 379, 380
Hickman, Bert, 131
Hicks, John R., 124, 129, **137**
Hiden, John, 416
Higginbotham, Virginia, 580
Higham, Charles, 578, 589
Higham, John, 253, 286
Hilberg, Raoul, 429
Hildebrand, Klaus, 416
Hildesheimer, Wolfgang, 52, 509
Hilgard, Ernest J., 173
Hilgard, Ernest R., 180
Hilgemann, Werner, 404
Hill, Christopher, 393, 470
Hill, Frank E., 330
Hill, George H., 568
Hill, Martha, 128

Hill, Michael J., 156
Hillaby, John, 621, 623
Hillary, Edmund, 637
Hillgruber, Andreas, 408
Hilton, Boyd, 379
Hilton, Timothy, 549
Himmelfarb, Gertrude, 384
Himmelfarb, Milton, 15
Hinckley, Barbara, 299
Hind, Arthur M., 550
Hindemith, Paul, 506
Hindleu, Geoffrey, 616
Hines, Jerome, 496
Hinnant, Charles H., 160
Hinsdale, Burke A., 233
Hionides, Harry T., 42
Hirsch, Eva, 439
Hirsch, Mark D., 321
Hirsch, Walter, 198
Hirschi, Travis, 193
Hirschman, Albert O., 129, 150
Hiscock, Eric C., 626
Hiscocks, Richard, 416
Hitchcock, Alfred, 585
Hitchcock, H. Wiley, 485, 507
Hitchcock, Henry-Russell, 527, 532, 552, 559
Hitler, Adolf, 416
Hitti, Philip K., 432, 434, 438
Ho, Ping-Ti, 447
Ho Tai, Hue-Tam, 454
Hoagland, Edward, 349
Hobbes, Thomas, 153, **160**
Hobsbawm, Eric J., 150, **393,** 608
Hochman, Stanley, 258
Hochschild, Jennifer L., 154
Hodeir, André, 494
Hodgart, Alan, 411
Hodges, John C., 22
Hodgson, Godfrey, 282
Hodgson, Marshall G., 446
Hodson, H. V., 16
Hodson, Phillip, 517
Hoequist, Charles, Jr., 33
Hoff-Wilson, Joan, 78
Hoffer, Peter C., 268
Hoffman, Daniel N., 269
Hoffman, Frank W., 612
Hoffman, Lance J., 564
Hoffman, Nancy, 226
Hoffman, Ronald, 266
Hoffman, Ross J., 379

Hoffmann, Stanley, 155
Hofstadter, Richard, 101, 226, 254, 261, 269, 299, 310, **323,** 344
Hoggart, Richard, 564
Hogwood, Christopher, 506
Hoijer, Harry, 123
Holborn, Hajo, 416
Holcombe, Lee, 381
Holden, David, 438
Holland, James G., 185
Holland, Norman N., 610
Hollander, Samuel, 145, 146
Holler, Frederick L., 149
Holliday, J. S., 271
Hollingshead, August B., 192
Hollinrake, Roger, 517
Holloway, David, 408
Holloway, Robin, 504
Holmes, George A., 373
Holmes, J. Derek, 381
Holmes, J. L., 495
Holmes, John W., 350
Holmes, Oliver Wendell, Jr., 68
Holoman, D. Kern, 500
Holroyd, Michael, 60
Holsti, Ole R., 282
Holt, Elizabeth G., 528
Holt, James C., 372
Holt, John, 226
Holt, Pat M., 303
Holt, Peter M., 382, 434, 436
Holzer, Harold, 89, 273
Homans, George C., 143, 172
Honey, Maureen, 278
Honey, P. J., 454
Honey, Sandra, 547
Honour, Hugh, 528, 532, 534
Hooglund, Eric J., 437
Hook, J. N., 291
Hook, Sidney, 231
Hoover, C. B., 127
Hoover, Herbert, 69
Hoover, Stewart M., 568
Hope, Charles, 555
Hopkins, A. G., 442
Hopkins, I. W., 435
Hopkins, Terence K., 101
Hoppin, Richard H., 485
Hopwood, Derek, 434, 438
Horgan, Paul, 89, **324**
Horn, Robert C., 453
Horne, Alistair, 414
Horowitz, Dan, 435
Horowitz, David, 287, 300

Horowitz, Francis D., 172
Horowitz, Irving Louis, 212
Horowitz, Vladimir, 506
Horricks, Raymond, 498
Horsfield, Peter, 564
Horwitz, Henry, 376
Hoselitz, Bert F., 100
Hoskins, Robert, 497
Hoskins, W. G., 374
Hotten, John Campden, 256
Hough, Jerry F., 422
Houghton, D. Hobart, 442
Houghton, Walter E., 11
Houle, Cyril O., 226
Houn, Franklin W., 447
Hourani, Albert, 432, 438
Hovde, B. J., 419
Hovland, Carl I., 174
Howard, Harry N., 439
Howard, Jane, 120
Howard, John Tasker, 505
Howard, Moss, 173
Howard, Rhoda, 442
Howarth, David, 372
Howe, Irving, 291, 429
Howe, Mark DeWolfe, 69
Howell, Roger, Jr., 376
Howey, Richard S., 142
Howitt, Dennis, 564
Howland, Harold, 337
Howland, Marguerite S., 257
Hsieh, Alice L., 447
Hsu, Francis L., 106
Hubbard, Linda S., 9
Hucker, Charles O., 404
Hudson, Kenneth, 528
Huff, Theodore, 581
Huggins, Nathan I., 85
Hughes, Andrew, 489
Hughes, Emmet J., 62
Hughes, H. Stuart, 403, 412
Hughes, Judith M., 414
Hughes, Langston, 605
Hughes, Philip E., 374
Hughes, Robert, 537
Hughes, Serge, 417
Hughes, Thomas P., 434
Huizinga, Johan, 105
Hulbert, James R., 25
Hull, Clark L., 179
Hull, Richard, 442
Hulteng, John L., 568
Hume, Robert A., 307
Hunczak, Taras, 422
Huneker, James G., 507
Hunsinger, Walter W., 21

Hunt, Gaillard, 90
Hunt, John, 637
Hunt, William, 376
Hunt, William R., 643
Hunter, Floyd, 192
Hunter, Monica, 104
Huntington, Gale, 599
Huntington, Samuel P., 198
Hurn, Christopher J., 226
Hurston, Zora N., 605
Hurt, R. Douglas, 288
Hurwitz, Howard L., 337
Huss, Roy, 576
Hussein, Mahmoud, 436
Hutchings, Arthur, 513
Hutchins, Robert M., 231
Hutchinson, William K., 259
Hutt, Allen, 566
Huxford, Marilyn, 191, 562
Huxley, Aldous, 616
Huxley, Julian, 107
Hyman, Herbert H., 202
Hyman, Louis, 429
Hyman, Paula, 429
Hymes, Dell, 108
Hynds, Ernest C., 566
Hyneman, Charles S., 269

Iacocca, Lee, 52
Igoe, James, 530
Igoe, Lynn Moody, 530
Iliffe, John, 443
Illich, Ivan, 226
Ilyichov, L. F., 134
Immerwahr, Henry R., 245
Inge, M. Thomas, 610
Ingstad, Helge, 621
Inhelder, Barbel, 184, 185
Insdorf, Annette, 576, 587
Iribas, Juan L., 46
Iriye, Akira, 446
Irland, Lloyd C., 129
Irvine, Demar, 517
Irvine, William, 385
Irving, Clive, 437
Irving, David, 408, 416
Irving, Washington, 631
Irwin, Manley R., 564
Isaacman, Allen, 443
Isaacman, Barbara, 443
Isaku, Patia R., 594
Ismael, Tareq Y., 437
Israel, F. L., 256, 340, 404
Israeli, R., 434

Issawi, Charles, 432, 437, 438, 439
Ives, Charles Edward, 506
Izard, Carroll E., 171

Jablonski, Edward, 489
Jackall, Robert, 203
Jackman, Mary R., 102
Jackman, Robert W., 102
Jackson, Bruce, 605
Jackson, David J., 188
Jackson, Donald, 640
Jackson, Donald Dale, 271
Jackson, Gabriel, 418
Jackson, George P., 594
Jackson, Joan S., 14
Jackson, John E., 300
Jackson, Kenneth T., 256
Jackson, Lady. See Ward, Barbara
Jackson, Nancy E., 228
Jackson, W. G. F., 408
Jacob, Margaret C., 376
Jacobs, Jane, 202, 350
Jacobs, Lewis, 576
Jacobs, Melville, 604
Jacobs, Wilbur R., 344
Jacobsen, C. G., 447
Jacobus, John, 546
Jacoby, Neil H., 432
Jacoby, Susan, 226
Jacoway, Elizabeth, 288
Jaeger, Werner, 246
Jaffe, Hans Ludwig, 549
Jaffe, Michael, 553
Jaffe, Philip J., 278
Jagendorf, Moritz A., 599, 604
Jahoda, Marie, 179
Jakle, John A., 616
James, Cyril L., 363
James, David B., 517
James, Edward T., 50
James, Janet W., 50
James, Robert R., 383
James, T. G. H., 239
James, Watson C., 571
James, William, 180, 235
Jamieson, Kathleen H., 564
Jamieson, Perry D., 273
Jandy, Edward C., 205
Janes, Jodith, 6
Janis, Harriet, 492
Janowitz, Morris, 190, 198, 282

Janson, Dora Jane, 528
Janson, H. W., 528
Jarman, Douglas, 499
Jarvie, Ian C., 576
Jay, John, 86, 151, 294, 295
Jeanneret-Gris, Charles Edouard. See Le Corbusier
Jefferson, Thomas, 86, 160
Jeffery, Lillian H., 240
Jeffrey, Julie Roy, 275
Jeffrey, William, Jr., 295
Jeffreys-Jones, Rhodri, 300
Jelavich, B., 419
Jelavich, C., 419
Jencks, Charles, 543
Jencks, Christopher, 201, 215, 226
Jenkins, Barbara, 616
Jenkins, Elizabeth, 58
Jenkins, Herbert, 629
Jenkins, Peter, 616
Jenness, Diamond, 350
Jensen, Arthur R., 173
Jensen, Merrill, 296
Jensen, Richard, 275
Jervis, Robert, 157
Jevons, William Stanley, 137
Jezer, Marty, 282
Jingrong, Wu, 39
Joannides, Paul, 550
Jobes, Gertrude, 528, 592
Johnpoll, Bernard, 282, 341
Johnpoll, Lillian, 282
Johns, Richard, 438
Johnson, Beth, 619
Johnson, Burges, 35
Johnson, Charles B., 40
Johnson, Daniel M., 292
Johnson, Donald B., 261
Johnson, Elizabeth S., 138
Johnson, Harry G., 138
Johnson, John J., 358
Johnson, John W., 286
Johnson, Lyndon Baines, 70
Johnson, Philip C., 547
Johnson, Priscilla, 423
Johnson, R. W., 414
Johnson, Samuel, 443. See main entry Volume 1
Johnson, Thomas H., 261, 262, 327
Johnson, William H., 626
Johnston, Donald, 22
Johnston, Hugh, 350, 632
Johnston, Jerome, 571
Johnston, John, 125

Johnston, Ollie, 582
Johnstone, John Wallace Claire, 567
Joll, Evelyn, 555
Joll, James, 408, 412
Jolliffe, John E., 369
Jolowicz, H. F., 244
Joncich, Geraldine, 236
Jones, A. H., 240
Jones, Archer, 273
Jones, B. J., 44
Jones, C. P., 247
Jones, Charles O., 300
Jones, Christopher D., 419
Jones, David L., 404
Jones, E. L., 412
Jones, Ernest, 179
Jones, Esnor, 223
Jones, Everett L., 290
Jones, Francis C., 450
Jones, G. William, 579
Jones, James Rees, 376
Jones, John F., 194
Jones, Louis C., 600
Jones, Max, 497
Jones, Owen, 534
Jones, Raymond A., 381
Jones, Roger, 550
Jones, Steven S., 592
Jones, Thomas M., 372
Jones, Trevor, 41
Jones, V. C., 337
Jones, Whitney Richard David, 374
Jongmans, D. G., 104
Joplin, Scott, 507
Jordan, David P., 66
Jordan, Robert F., 543
Jordan, Teresa, 292
Jordan, W. K., 375
Jordan, Winthrop D., 292
Jordy, William H., 307, 532
Jorgen, Moe, 596
Josephson, Matthew, 58
Josephus, Flavius, 247
Joukowsky, Anatol M., 594
Jowett, Garth, 576
Jowitt, Deborah, 518
Joyce, Patrick, 381
Joyce, William L., 562
Joyner, Charles, 605
Judson, Katherine, 603
Juergens, George, 276
Jules-Rosette, Bennetta, 109, 199
Julian, John, 489

July, Robert W., 443
Jungk, Robert, 447
Juster, F. Thomas, 188, 200

Kaberry, P. M., 442
Kadish, Sanford H., 100, 193
Kaegi, Walter E., 240
Kael, Pauline, 576
Kagan, Jerome, 170, 172, 173
Kahn, Alfred E., 129
Kahn, Herman, 157
Kahn, Roger, 429
Kahrl, George M., 66
Kaiser, Joachim, 496
Kaledin, Eugenia, 286, 307
Kallich, Martin, 60
Kallmann, Helmutt, 489
Kalu, Ogbu U., 443
Kamen, Henry, 418
Kamin, Dan, 581
Kaminsky, Stuart M., 577
Kammen, Michael, 254, 266
Kampler, Fritz, 534
Kanawada, Leo V., 278
Kandell, Jonathan, 358
Kane, Grace F., 601
Kane, Joseph Nathan, 15, 256
Kane, Kathryn, 577
Kane, Robert S., 623
Kaniki, M. H., 443
Kann, Robert A., 412
Kanner, Barbara, 368, 369
Kanof, Abram, 530
Kanter, Rosabeth M., 203
Kaplan, Chaim A., 429
Kaplan, E. Ann, 571, 577
Kaplan, Fred, 461
Kaplan, Harold, 307
Kaplan, Louis, 49
Kapp, Ernst, 246
Kapuscinski, Ryszard, 52
Kardiner, Abram, 106
Karis, Thomas, 443
Karl, Barry D., 102, 166, 277
Karnow, Stanley, 75, 448
Karol, K. S., 448
Karpat, Kemal H., 433
Karpel, Bernard, 530
Karpeles, Maud, 594
Karsten, Peter, 304
Kaser, M. C., 419
Kateb, George, 456
Katkov, George, 423

Katona, George, 128
Katouzian, Homa, 437
Kattenburg, Paul M., 282
Katz, Bill, 8
Katz, Elihu, 191, 208, 564
Katz, Ephraim, 574
Katz, Friedrich, 363
Katz, Jacob, 429
Katz, Linda Sternberg, 8
Katzman, David M., 292
Katzmann, Robert A., 127
Kauffman, Henry J., 600
Kaufman, Allen, 271
Kaufman, Herbert, 154
Kaufman, Walter, 495
Kaufmann, Emil, 532
Kay, H., 418
Kay, Norman, 513
Kazantzakis, Nikos, 623
Kealey, Edward J., 372
Kearney, Robert N., 446
Kearns, Doris, 71, 283
Keating, Barry P., 128
Keating, Maryann O., 128
Keay, John, 617, 626
Kebede, Ashenafi, 605
Keddie, Nikki R., 434, 437
Kedourie, Elie, 435
Kedward, H. R., 414
Kee, Robert, 278, 369
Keefe, William J., 300
Keegan, John, 408
Keen, Maurice, 373
Keep, John, 423
Keeton, G. W., 17
Kegan, Robert, 173
Kegley, Charles W., Jr., 304
Kehler, George, 496
Kehoe, Alice B., 292
Keir, David L., 369
Keith, Jennie, 109, 189
Keith, Robert G., 356
Kelemen, Pal, 530
Kellaghan, Thomas, 227
Kellas, James G., 370
Kelleher, Catherine M., 408
Keller, Howard H., 41
Keller, Morton, 337
Kelley, Harold H., 174
Kelley, Robert L., 286
Kelly, Alfred H., 296
Kelly, Robert, 637
Kelsen, Hans, 151
Kemp, Ian, 515
Kendall, Patricia, 198, 210
Kendall, Paul M., 50, 373

Kendrick, Alexander, 454
Kendrick, Benjamin B., 321
Kenen, Peter B., 130
Kennan, George F., 304, **466**
Kennedy, David M., 277
Kennedy, James Y., 626
Kennedy, John Fitzgerald, 71, 300
Kennedy, Michael, 501
Kennedy, Paul, 383
Kennedy, Peter, 594
Kennedy, Robert F., 72
Kennedy, Thomas C., 310
Kenney, E. J., 241
Kennington, Alice, 7
Kent, J. P., 242
Kent, Marian, 439
Kenton, Edna, 348
Kenyon, J. P., 376
Kenyon, John S., 31
Kerber, Linda K., 286, 292
Kerman, Joseph, 485, 486, 495
Kerner, Robert J., 423
Kerr, A. P., 414
Kerr, Catherine, 350
Kerr, Clark, 140, 226
Kertzer, David L., 109, 189
Kertzer, Morris N., 429
Kessler, Lauren, 566
Kessler-Harris, Alice, 288
Ketcham, Ralph, 90, 300
Ketchum, Robert Glenn, 618
Kett, Joseph F., 292
Key, Mary R., 564
Key, V. O., Jr., 152, 153, 154, 156, **161**
Keynes, John Maynard, 124, 125, 127, 130, **138**
Keynes, Milo, 138
Khalidi, Tarif, 434
Khouri, Fred J., 438
Khrushchev, Nikita S., 73, 423
Khumayni, Ruh A., 434
Khuri, Raif, 438
Kidson, Frank, 594
Kidwell, David S., 131
Kiernan, Reginald H., 639
Kiewiet, D. Roderick, 153
Kightly, Charles, 597
Killian, Lewis, 190
Kilpatrick, Anna, 603
Kilpatrick, Jack, 603
Kilpatrick, William Heard, 232

Kilson, Martin, 441, 442
Kimball, Robert, 510
Kimball, Ruth, 33
Kimbell, David R., 516
Kimbrough, Emily, 622
Kindem, Gorham, 574
Kinder, Herman, 404
King, Edmund, 373
King, M., 39
King, P., 39
King, W. Francis H., 21
Kinglake, Alexander, 637
Kingsley, Mary, 626
Kinkle, Roger D., 489
Kinross, Lord, 439
Kinwood, Roy, 577
Kinzer, Stephen, 363
Kinzie, Mary, 561
Kirk-Greene, C. W. E., 40
Kirkpatrick, Jeane J., 359,
   360
Kirstein, Lincoln, 518, 521,
   523
Kirzner, Israel M., 146
Kishlansky, Mark A., 376
Kissinger, Henry, 283, 304,
   408
Kittredge, George L., 599
Kittross, John M., 569
Klapper, Joseph, 191
Klausner, Samuel Z., 194
Klehr, Harvey, 278
Klein, Barbro S., 597
Klein, Dennis B., 429
Klein, Donald W., 448
Klein, Ernest, 36
Klein, Ethel, 203
Klein, H. Arthur, 537
Klein, Herbert S., 360
Klineberg, Otto, 173, **181**
Klinowski, Jacek, 574
Kliuchevskii, Vasilii O., 423
Kloe, Donald R., 34
Klosty, James, 522
Klotman, Phyllis R., 605
Kluckhohn, Clyde, 105, 115
Knapp, Herbert, 608
Knapp, Mary, 608
Knei-Paz, Baruch, 423
Knight, Frank H., 125, **139**
Knight, Franklin W., 359,
   441
Knollenberg, Bernhard, 94,
   266
Knott, Thomas A., 31
Knowles, David, 370, 372

Knowles, Malcolm M., 226
Knox, John, 348
Koch, Adrienne, 88, 90
Koch, H. W., 408, 416
Koch, Sigmund, 180
Koch, William E., 601
Kochan, Lionel, 420, 423,
   429
Koegler, Horst, 519
Koenig, Louis W., 300
Koffka, Kurt, 174
Kogan, Norman, 417
Kohl, Herbert, 226, 227
Kohl, Wilfrid L., 408
Kohler, Wolfgang, 175
Kohn, Hans, 467, 472
Kohn, Melvin L., 201, 204
Kolb, W. J., 100, 404
Kollek, Teddy, 435
Kolneder, Walter, 517
Kolodny, Annette, 264, 292
Komroff, Manuel, 644
Komuta, Kensaburo, 450
Kongas-Maranda, Elli Kaija,
   597
Koon, George W., 610
Koonz, Claudia, 410
Koopmans, Tjalling C., 125
Kormoss, I. B., 433
Korn, Francis, 116
Kornhauser, Ruth R., 193
Kornhauser, William, 152,
   190, 198
Kosaka, Masataka, 450
Koss, Stephen, 381, 383
Kotkin, Amy J., 598
Koury, Enver M., 437
Kovach, Joseph K., 169, 177
Kowet, Don, 617
Koyre, Alexandre, 168
Kraay, Colin, 242
Kracauer, Siegfried, 189, 191
Kramer, Rita, 234
Kramers, J. H., 434
Krasilovsky, M. William, 491
Krasnow, Erwin G., 571
Krasovskaya, Vera, 524
Kraus, Michael, 334
Krauss, Ellis S., 193
Krausz, Ernest, 435
Kraut, Alan M., 271, 292
Kraut, John A., 330
Kreidl, John, 584
Krein, David F., 381
Krishnaswamy,
   Sukrahmaryan, 576

Kroeber, Alfred L., 103, 105,
   115
Kroeber, Theodora, 116
Kronenberger, Louis, 379
Kropotkin, Peter, 150
Kruger, D. W., 443
Krummel, Donald W., 490
Krupskaya, N. K., 470
Kruskal, William H., 100
Kubrick, Stanley, 585
Kuhn, Annette, 578
Kuhn, Thomas S., 199
Kuhrt, Amelie, 243
Kuisel, Richard F., 414
Kujoth, Jean S., 610
Kunst, Jaap, 492
Kuper, Hilder, 110
Kuper, Leo, 122, 193
Kurian, George Thomas, 15,
   566
Kurosawa, Akira, 586
Kurtz, Michael L., 72
Kurz, Mordecai, 132
Kuschner, David S., 235
Kushima, John J., 271
Kutcher, Arthur, 435
Kutler, Stanley I., 304
Kutsch, K. J., 490, 496
Kuznets, Simon, 129
Kwak, Tai-Hwan, 454

Labaree, Benjamin W., 378
Labedz, Leopold, 422, 423
Labov, William, 108
Lacey, W. K., 244
Lach, Donald F., 446
Ladd, Everett C., Jr., 300
Lafaye, Jacques, 357
La Feber, Walter, 275, 408
Laing, Jennifer, 371
Laing, Lloyd, 371
Laird, Charlton, 34
Laistner, M. M. W., 240
Lall, Arthur, 448
Lamar, Howard, 619
Lamb, Alastair, 454
Lamphere, Louise, 203
Lanctot, Gustave, 347
Land, Kenneth C., 188, 200
Landau, Sidney, 28, 34
Landen, Robert G., 433
Lander, J. R., 373
Landes, David S., 412, 436
Landon, Grelun, 491, 595
Landon, Howard C., 509

Landrum, Larry N., 612
Landy, Eugene E., 32
Landynski, Jacob W., 296
Lane, David, 423
Lane, Hana Umlauf, 17
Lane, Peter, 375
Lane, Robert E., 154
Lang, Gladys Engel, 566
Lang, Mabel, 245
Lang, Paul H., 486
Langbaum, Francesco L. V., 40
Langer, William L., 404, 412
Langhorne, Richard, 408
Langley, Kathleen M., 437
Langman, Larry, 562
Langston, Douglas, 529
Lannie, Vincent P., 230
Lansing, John B., 125
LaPalombara, Joseph G., 150
LaPin, Dierdre, 601
Laqueur, Thomas W., 381
Laqueur, Walter, 149, 151, 412, 416, 429
Large, David C., 517
Larkin, Emmet, 381
Larsen, Lawrence H., 281
Larson, Gary O., 286
Las Casas, Bartolome de, 355
Lasch, Christopher, 102
Lash, Joseph P., 68, 78, 92
Laska, Shirley, 202
Laski, Harold J., 162
Lasky, Betty, 577
Laslett, Peter, 376
Lass, A. H., 22
Lasso, Hamilton, 636
Lasswell, Harold D., 154, 156, 163, 175, 447
Lasswell, Marcia, 196
Lasswell, Thomas E., 196
Last, Murray, 453
Latham, Earl, 296
Latham, Peter, 501
Latham, R. E., 44
Latimer, Elizabeth W., 443
Latourette, Kenneth S., 468
Latsis, Spiro J., 125
Lattimore, Eleanor, 623
Lattimore, Owen, 623
Laufer, William S., 175
Laumann, Edward O., 198
Laurel, Stan, 586
Lavalleyi, Jacques, 537
Lawless, Ray M., 594

Lawrence, A. W., 639
Lawrence, Clifford H., 370
Lawrence, T. E., 638
Lawson, Joan, 519
Laxalt, Robert, 622
Lazarsfeld, Paul F., 102, 130, 151, 153, 188, 191, 198, 207, 210, 218
Lazzarini, John, 524
Lazzarini, Roberta, 524
Leach, Edmund R., 104, 105, 111
Leach, Macedward, 600
Leach, Maria, 597
Leach, R., 594
Leakey, Mary, 53
Lears, T. J. Jackson, 287
Leary, William M., 259
Le Bon, Gustave, 190
Leckie, R. William, Jr., 392
Leckie, Robert, 304
Leckie, William H., 275
Lecky, W. E. H., 393
Le Corbusier, 532, 542
Ledyard, John, 626
Lee, Carol, 519
Lee, Hector, 603
Lee, J. M., 383
Lee, Joseph, 381
Lee, Ki-Baik, 454
Lee, Maurice, Jr., 376
Lee, R. Alton, 283
Lee, Sherman E., 530
Lee, Thomas B., 451
Leebron, Elizabeth, 582
Leeper, Robert W., 182
Lees-Milne, James, 77
Lefebvre, Georges, 414
Leff, G., 373
Lefkowitz, Mary R., 244
Leftwich, Richard H., 127
Leggett, Glenn, 23
Legman, Gershon, 610
Legum, Colin, 443
Lehman, Maxwell, 564
Leibowitz, Rene, 512
Leidy, W. Philip, 13, 256
Leites, Nathan, 190, 191
Lekachman, Robert, 139
Le May, G. H., 381
Lenczowski, George, 433
Lender, Mark E., 292
Lenin, Nikolai, 469
Lenz, Wilhelm von, 496
Leon, D., 435

Leon-Portilla, Miguel, 355
Leonard, Jonathan N., 451, 540
Leonard, Thomas C., 304
Leonard, Thomas M., 15
Leonard, William T., 574
Leonardo da Vinci, 543
Leontief, Wasily, 125
Lerner, Daniel, 156, 163, 200, 433
Lerner, Gerda, 292
Lerner, Max, 342
Lerner, Richard M., 173
Lernoux, Penny, 359
Le Roy-Ladurie, Emmanuel, 403, 412
Lesage, Julia, 584
Lesher, Stephen, 568
Leslie, Louis A., 36
Less, David, 575
Lessa, William A., 109
Leuchtenburg, William E., 263, 278, 300, 329
Levenson, J. C., 307
Levering, Ralph B., 283
Levey, Judith, 3
Levey, Michael, 528
Lévi-Strauss, Claude, 106, 108, 109, 116
Levich, Richard, 131
Levin, Henry M., 203
Levin, Meyer, 63
Levin, N. Gordon, Jr., 96, 277
Levin, Nora, 429
Levine, Adeline G., 194
Levine, Daniel H., 366
Levine, Gaynell S., 600
Levine, Lawrence W., 606
Levine, Mortimer, 368, 375
Levine, Robert A., 106
Levinson, Richard, 571
Levitan, Sar A., 130, 283
Levy, Reuben, 433, 434
Levy, Samuel L., 145
Lewin, Kurt, 174, 181, 193
Lewin, Moshe, 423, 470
Lewin, Ronald, 408
Lewine, Richard, 490
Lewis, Bernard, 403, 434, 439
Lewis, Carolyn Diana, 569
Lewis, David, 286
Lewis, I. M., 434
Lewis, Jan, 269
Lewis, Lloyd, 67

Lewis, Meriwether, 639
Lewis, Naphtali, 240, 242, 243
Lewis, Norman, 34
Lewis, Oscar, 117, 122, 192
Lewis, Paul H., 365
Lewis, Robert A., 423
Lewis, Ruth M., 117
Lewis, W. Arthur, 130
Leyda, Jay, 511, 577, 583
Liang Ssu-ch'eng, 532
Liberman, Alexander, 622
Libman, Lillian, 514
Lichello, Robert, 569
Lichtheim, George, 141, 412, 414
Lichtheim, Miriam, 239
Lichty, Lawrence W., 572
Liddell, H. G., 42
Liddell Hart, Basil H., 408, 639
Lieberman, William S., 546
Liebert, R., 572
Lienhardt, Samuel, 201
Lifton, Robert J., 75, 403, 448, 451
Lifton, Sarah, 594
Lightfoot, Sara L., 227
Lightman, Marjorie, 78
Lijphart, Arend, 419
Lillard, Paula P., 234
Limbacher, James L., 493, 575, 577
Limerick, Jeffrey, 619
Lin Yutang, 39
Linblad, Lars-Eric, 627
Lincoln, Abraham, 88
Lincoln, Charles E., 195
Lincoln, Joseph C., 627
Lincoln, W. Bruce, 423
Lindbergh, Charles A., 640
Lindblom, Charles E., 130, 156
Linden, Carl A., 74
Lindow, John, 597
Lindsay, A. D., 152
Lindzey, Gardner, 104, 170, 175, 176, 181
Lingeman, Richard, 292
Lingenfelter, Richard E., 603
Link, Arthur S., 96, 259, 262, 276
Link, William, 571
Linsky, Marvin, 572
Linton, James M., 576
Linton, Ralph, 104

Lippman, Thomas W., 433
Lippmann, Walter, 156, **163, 324**
Lipset, Seymour M., 102, 154, 156, 201, 211, 323
Lipson, Leon, 155
Lipton, Gladys, 43, 46
Lisio, Donald J., 70
Lissak, Moshe, 435
Liszt, Franz, 502, **507**
Litchen, Frances, 600
Little, William, 28, 37
Litvinoff, Barnet, 429
Litwack, Leon F., 273
Liu, Kwang-Ching, 464
Livermore, Harold U., 418
Livesay, W. E., 472
Livingood, James W., 316
Livingston, Jane, 606
Livingston, Jon, 451
Livingston, Paisley, 579
Livingstone, David, 641
Livy, 250
Llerena, Rafael, 362
Lloyd, T. O., 370, 383
Loader, Colin, 209
Loades, D. M., 375
Locke, John, 154, **164**
Locke, John C., 623
Lockhart, James, 355, 357
Lockhart, John Gibson. *See* Volume 1
Lockwood, Allison, 617
Lockwood, William W., 451
Lodge, Henry C., 94
Lodge, Tom, 443
Loehlin, John C., 173
Loesser, Arthur, 496
Loewenburg, Alfred, 495
Lofland, L., 202
Logue, Christopher, 610
Loh, Wallace D., 155
Loizos, Peter, 440
Lomax, Alan, 594
Lombardi, John V., 366
Lomperis, Timothy J., 304
Long, Barbara, 256
Long, E. B., 256
Longley, Dennis, 562
Longrigg, Stephen H., 433, 437, 440
Longstreet, Stephen, 541, 549, 557
Longyear, Marie, 23
Loomis, Burdell A., 298
Loomis, Charles P., 192

Looney, Robert E., 437
Lopez, Claude-Anne, 65
Lopreato, Joseph, 107
Loran, Erle, 538
Lorber, Judith, 198
Lord, James, 53
Lorenz, Konrad, 171, **182**
Loth, David, 634
Loubser, Jan J., 214
Louchheim, Katie, 278
Loveland, Marion F., 610
Loveman, Brian, 361
Low, Rachel, 577
Lowenthal, Leo, 189
Lowery, Shearon, 561
Lowi, Theodore J., 154
Lowie, Robert H., 110, 111
Lowitt, Richard, 258, 279
Loyn, H. R., 371, 372
Lubbock, Basil, 617
Luchetti, Cathy, 292
Lukacs, John, 262
Lukes, Steven, 206
Lumer, Hyman, 429
Lundberg, Carolyn, 614
Lundberg, Donald E., 614
Lundberg, Ferdinand, 296
Lunt, Paul S., 110
Lupton, Kenneth, 643
Luria, A. R., 171
Lurie, Leonard, 300
Luskin, John, 325
Lussier, Antoine S., 349
Luthi, Max, 597
Luttwak, Edward N., 244
Lutz, Donald S., 269
Lynch, John, 418
Lynch, K. L., 198
Lynd, Helen Merrell, 192, **208**
Lynd, Robert S., 192, **208**
Lynd, Staughton, 296
Lynn, Gartley, 582
Lyon, Bryce, 370
Lyon, Melvin, 307
Lyons, F. S., 370, 381
Lyons, Robert J., 579
Lyttle, Clifford, 195

Ma, Wendy Y., 623
Maar, Ingrid, 603
Mabro, Robert, 436
Macaulay, Thomas Babington, 394
MacCabe, Colin, 584

MacCaffrey, Wallace, 375
MacCannell, Dean, 617
Maccoby, Eleanor E., 173
MacCormack, John R., 376
MacDonagh, Oliver, 381
MacDonald, A. M., 25
MacDonald, Charles G., 437
MacDonald, Hugh, 500
MacDonald, J. Fred, 572
MacDonald, Nesta, 522
MacDonald, William L., 242
MacDowell, Douglas M., 244
MacGregor, James C., 347
Mach, Elyse, 496
Machiavelli, Niccolò, 165
Machlis, Joseph, 492
Machlup, Fritz, 125, 126, 137
Mack, John E., 53, 438
Mack, Mary Peter, 158
Mack-Smith, Denis, 417
MacKendrick, Paul, 242
Mackie, J., 455
Mackin, Ronald, 32
MacKuen, Michael, 568
MacLachlan, Colin M., 357
Maclean, Angus, 603
Maclear, Michael, 283
MacLeod, Duncan J., 266
MacLeod, Murdo J., 357
MacLeod, Robert B., 169
Macmillan, Harold, 74
MacMullen, Ramsay, 243, 244
MacRae, Duncan, Jr., 156, 414
Macy, John W., 572
Madariaga, Isabel de, 423
Madaus, George F., 227
Madge, John H., 188
Madina, Maan A., 38
Madison, James, 86, **90,** 151, 294, 295
Madsen, Axel, 568
Madsen, Stephan T., 530
Magdol, Edward, 293
Mager, N. H., 26
Mager, S. K., 26
Magid, Henry M., 162
Magill, Frank N., 21, 575
Mahan, Alfred Thayer, 470
Mahler, Gustav, 508
Mahler, Vincent A., 130
Maier, Charles S., 412
Maier, Pauline, 266
Maillard, Robert, 530, 549

Main, Jackson Turner, 264, 296
Maine, Henry Sumner, 117
Maiorano, Robert, 521
Maitland, Frederic William, 394
Maizlish, Stephen E., 271
Majumdar, R. C., 453
Makens, James C., 614
Makepeace, R. W., 423
Makler, Harry M., 418
Malcolm, Janet, 179
Malinowski, Bronislaw, 104, 106, 108, 109, 111, **118**
Malkiel, Burton G., 131
el-Mallakh, Ragaei, 440
Malleson, G. B., 453
Mallory, Walter H., 404
Mallowan, M. E. L., 239
Malloy, James M., 360
Malm, William P., 492
Malone, Bill C., 594
Malone, Dumas, 53, 88, 161
Malone, Michael P., 254
Malotki, Ekkehart, 604
Malpezzi, Frances M., 603
Malthus, Thomas Robert, 139
Maltin, Leonard, 582
Manach, Jorge, 359
Manchel, Frank, 575
Manchester, William, 72, 279, 283
Mandel, Ernest, 481
Mandelbaum, Michael, 408
Mander, Mary S., 564
Mane, Robert, 307
Manet, Edouard, 545
Mann, Heinrich, 588
Mann, Horace, 233
Mann, Jacob, 429
Mannheim, Karl, 154, 199, **208**
Manning, Brian, 376
Manning, Roberta T., 423
Manosevitz, Martin, 175
Mansfield, Harvey C., Jr., 165
Mansfield, Peter, 433
Manvell, Roger, 579, 581
Mao Tse-tung, 75, 448
Maquet, Jacques, 443
Marais, Johannes S., 443
al-Marayati, Abid A., 437
March, James G., 197
Marcus, Geoffrey, 379

Marcus, George E., 152
Marcuse, Herbert, 141
Marcuse, Sibyl, 496
Marcy, Michel, 40
Marek, George R., 502
Mariátequi, José C., 365
Markel, Michael H., 386
Marker, Frederick J., 579
Marker, Lise-Lone, 579
Marks, Frederick W., III, 337
Marks, Georgette A., 40
Marks, Lawrence E., 175
Marks, Shula B., 443
Markson, Elizabeth W., 202
Marling, Karal A., 608
Marquès, René, 365
Marri, Phebe, 438
Marriott, McKim, 105, 192
Marrou, H. I., 245
Marrus, Michael R., 429
Marsh, Margaret, 150
Marshall, Alfred, 125, **140**
Marshall, Dorothy, 379
Marshall, P. J., 379
Marshall, Sybil, 597
Martelli, George, 642
Martí, José, 359
Martin, Dolores M., 352
Martin, Donald L., 131
Martin, Fenton S., 13, 256
Martin, George, 495, 516
Martin, James Kirby, 266, 292
Martin, John, 518
Martin, John B., 93
Martin, Kingsley, 162
Martin, Michael, 258
Martin, Paul S., 293
Martin, Phyllis, 31
Martin, Ralph G., 72, 283
Martin, Samuel, 43
Martin, Sheila, 627
Martis, Kenneth C., 156
Martz, John D., 361
Marvin, Francis S., 205
Marwick, Arthur, 383
The Marx Brothers, 586
Marx, Karl, 126, 129, 134, **140**
Marzio, Peter C., 566, 568
Marzolf, Marion, 568
Maslowski, Peter, 304
Mason, Edward S., 128
Mason, Philip, 443
Mason, Richard, 451
Masotti, Louis H., 202

Massie, Robert K., 53, 423
Massie, Suzanne, 423
Massine, Leonide, 524
Mast, Gerald, 575
Masters, Roger D., 169
Matheopoulous, Helena Maestro, 495
Mathew, David, 384
Mathews, Jane D., 292
Mathews, Mitford McLeod, 26
Matisse, Henri, 545
Matsumura, Gentaro, 451
Matthaei, Julie A., 288
Matthew, Helen G., 446
Matthew, William, 50
Matthews, David, 515
Matthews, Denis, 496
Matthews, Richard K., 269
Mattiessen, Peter, 443
Mattingly, Garrett, 317, 375, 472
Matusow, Allen J., 283
Matusow, Barbara, 569
Maurer, David J., 259
Maurois, André. *See* Volume 1
Mauss, Armand L., 201
Mauss, Marcel, 107
Mawdsley, Evan, 424
Mawson, C. O. Sylvester, 34
Maxwell, Christine, 36
May, Elizabeth, 493
May, Ernest R., 304
May, Florence, 501
May, Isobel, 43
May, John R., 577
Mayer, Adrian C., 105
Mayer, J. P., 342
Mayer, Ralph, 528
Mayhew, David R., 156
Mayo, Bernard, 88
Mayo, Henry B., 152
Mayor, A. Hyatt, 534
Mayr-Harting, Henry, 371
Mazo, Joseph H., 520
Mazour, Anatole G., 424
Mazuzan, George T., 70
Mbiti, John S., 443
McAllester, David P., 493
McAnany, Emile, 564
McAuley, Alastair, 424
McBride, Joseph, 584, 589
McCaffrey, Lawrence J., 370, 381

McCagg, William O., 424, 429
McCaig, I. R., 32
McCandless, Byron, 291
McCarrick, Earlean M., 260
McCarthy, John D., 201
McCarthy, John P., 386
McCarthy, Joseph, 72
McCarthy, Martha M., 227
McCarthy, Mary, 300, 455, 622
McCartney, Donal, 381
McCarty, Clifford, 580
McCauley, Martin, 424
McCavitt, William E., 562, 572
McClelland, David C., 174
McClelland, J. C., 424
McClelland, Peter D., 125
McClosky, Herbert, 151
McClure, Ruth, 78
McClymer, John F., 276
McConnell, John W., 124
McCormick, Richard L., 276
McCormick, Richard P., 300
McCoy, Drew R., 288
McCraw, Thomas K., 129
McCreless, Patrick P., 517
McCullough, David, 276, 337, 365
McDonagh, Don, 519, 523
McDonald, Forrest, 88, 94, 152, 296
McElvaine, Robert S., 279
McEvedy, Colin, 404
McFeely, William S., 53, 67
McGill, Ralph, 344
McGough, Elizabeth, 622
McIlvaine, Betsy, 13
McInnis, Raymond G., 404
McIntosh, Robert W., 615
McKay, Alexander G., 242
McKay, Derek, 412
McKay, John P., 406
McKay, Robert B., 300
McKay, Vernon, 443
McKee, Delber, 337
McKenzie, J. M., 443
McKenzie, R. D., 213
McKibbin, Ross, 383
McKillop, A. B., 350
McLellan, David, 134
McLuhan, Marshall, 191
McLynn, F. J., 379
McNair, Arnold D., 244
McNaught, Kenneth, 347

McNaughton, William, 39
McNeill, William H., 406, 472
McNulty, Paul J., 131
McPherson, James M., 273
McQuail, Dennis, 564
McWhiney, Grady, 273
Meacham, Standish, 383
Mead, George Herbert, 196, 209
Mead, Margaret, 103, 104, 107, 110, 111, 119, 173
Mead, William E., 622
Meadow, Robert G., 564
Meadows, Donella H., 194
Meadows, Eddie S., 494
Meagher, Sylvia, 72
Means, Barbara, 171
Means, Gardiner C., 127
Medici, Lorenzo de, 165
Medley, D. J., 368
Medvedev Roy A., 74, 424
Mee, Charles L., Jr., 279
Meehan, Patrick J., 559
Meeker, Richard H., 568
Meeks, Wayne A., 243
Meghan, R. Wander, 92
Mehlman, Felice, 534
Meier, August, 237, 256, 320
Meiggs, Russell, 240
Meine, Franklin J., 611
Meir, Golda, 429, 430
Meisch, Lynn, 619
Meisner, Maurice J., 448
Mellaart, James, 239
Mellers, Wilfrid, 486, 492
Mellor, John W., 126, 129
Mellow, James R., 53
Meltzer, Milton, 293
Memmi, Albert, 430
Mencken, H. L., 21
Mendel, Arthur, 497
Mendel, Roberta, 617
Mendeloff, John, 129
Mendelsohn, Ezra, 430
Mendelssohn, Felix, 508
Mendes-Flohr, Paul R., 430
Meneghini, Giovannibattista, 502
Menger, Carl, 141
Menon, A. Sreedhara, 453
Merk, Frederick, 263
Merriam, Alan P., 493, 604
Merriam, Charles E., 166, 337
Merrill, John C., 563, 566

Merritt, Jeffrey, 15, 256
Merton, Robert K., 188, 189, 197, 198, 200, 201, 208, 209, **210,** 218
Meskill, John, 448
Messer, Robert L., 283
Messinger, Heinz, 41
Metzger, Charles R., 624
Metzger, Walter, 101
Meyer, Michael A., 430
Meyer, Michael C., 352, 364
Meyer, Reinhold, 242
Meyerhoff, Hans, 403
Meyers, Jeffrey, 639
Micaud, Charles A., 414
Michael, F., 446
Michael, Paul, 577
Michaelides, Solon, 490
Michaelis, Meir, 430
Michelangelo Buonarroti, 546
Michels, Robert, 153, **211**
Michener, James A., 622
Micunovic, Veljko, 424
Middlekauff, Robert, 266
Middleton, Dorothy, 622
Middleton, Karen P., 564
Miers, Earl S., 67
Mies van der Rohe, Ludwig, 547
Milavsky, J. Ronald, 171, 191
Milgram, Stanley, 174
Mill, Harriet T., 142, 203
Mill, John Stuart, 142, 154, 203
Mill, Joshua E., 571
Mill, Robert C., 615
Millar, Fergus, 240
Miller, David H., 254
Miller, David L., 210
Miller, Elizabeth W., 260
Miller, George A., 169, 180
Miller, James, 169
Miller, James C., III, 129
Miller, John, 376
Miller, John C., 88, 269
Miller, Joseph C., 597
Miller, Lorraine, 632
Miller, Margaret, 424
Miller, Merle, 71, 80, 283
Miller, Nathan, 92, 279
Miller, Neal E., 174, 177, 178
Miller, Perry, 261, **326**
Miller, William, 263, 439
Millett, Allan R., 304

Millis, Walter, 327
Mills, C. Wright, 102, **211**
Mills, Theodore M., 172
Milne, Hammish, 498
Milner, Anita C., 566
Miłosz, Czesław, 157
Milward, Alan S., 408
Mimura, Reiko, 578
Mingay, Gordon E., 378, 379, 381
Minor, Michael J., 188
Mintz, Sidney W., 293
Miroff, Bruce, 72
Mirrielees, Edith, 317
Mirsky, D., 424
Mitchell, B. R., 370, 404
Mitchell, Broadus, 86, 267, 296
Mitchell, David, 418
Mitchell, Donald, 508, 509
Mitchell, G. Duncan, 100
Mitchell, James, 4
Mitchell, Louise, 296
Mitchell, Richard P., 433, 440
Mitchell, Wesley C., 143
Mitterauer, Michael, 412
Mitterling, Philip I., 260
Mittlefehldt, Pamela, 602
Mitz, Rick, 572
Mitzman, Arthur, 221
Miura, Akira, 44
Mizuno, Soji, 451
Modell, Judith, 111
Modgil, Celia, 235
Modgil, Sohan, 235
Modglin, Nel, 35
Moehring, Eugene P., 340
Moholy-Nagy, Laszlo, 530
Mokyr, Joel, 381
Moldenhauer, Hans, 517
Moldenhauer, Rosaleen, 517
Molyneaux, Gerard, 581
Molyneux, John, 481
Monaco, James, 575, 577, 578
Monet, Claude, 548
Money, Keith, 524
Monroe, Marilyn, 587
Monson, Karen, 499
Montagu, Ashley, 171, 183
Montagu, Mary Wortley. *See* Volume 1
Montanaro, John S., 39
Montaperto, Ronald N., 446
Monteiro, Mariana, 597

Montell, William L., 601
Monter, William, 597
Montesquieu, Charles de Secondat, 166
Montessori, Maria, 233
Monteverdi, Claudio, 508
Montgomery, Tommie S., 363
Moody, Raymond A., Jr., 611
Moon, William L., 619
Moore, Barrington, Jr., 412
Moore, David C., 381
Moore, Frank L., 495
Moore, Henry L., 131
Moore, Jack B., 319
Moore, Roger, 383
Moore, Sally F., 203
Moore, Wilbert E., 188, 200
Moore, Winfred B., Jr., 291, 601
Morales-Carrión, Arturo M., 365
Mordden, Ethan, 496
Morehead, Joe, 13, 256
Morehead, Philip D., 34
Morgan, Edmund S., 88, 94, 269
Morgan, H. Wayne, 293
Morgan, James N., 125
Morgan, Janet, 564
Morgan, Joy E., 233
Morgan, Kenneth O., 383
Morgan, Lewis Henry, 111, **120**
Morgan-Witts, Max, 289
Morgenstern, Oskar, 125, 147
Morgenstern, Sam, 487
Morgenthau, Hans J., 300, 305
Morgenthau, Henry, Sr., 481
Morishima, Michio, 129
Morison, Samuel Eliot, 263, **328,** 355, 409, 632
Morley, Sylvanus G., 354
Morris, A. J., 409
Morris, Charles R., 283
Morris, Edmund, 337
Morris, Jan, 627
Morris, John, 371
Morris, Mary, 31, 36
Morris, Richard B., 258, 261, 267, 314
Morris, Robert C., 227
Morris, Rosamund, 611
Morris, William, 25, 31, 36
Morrison, Hugh, 533, 554

Morse, John T., Jr., 83
Mortimer, Charles G., 617
Morton, H. V., 642
Morton, W. L., 347
Morton, W. Scott, 451
Mosca, Gaetano, 157
Mosco, Vincent, 572
Moshiri, Farrokh, 438
Mosley, Philip, 579
Moss, Norman, 30, 32
Mosse, George L., 412, 416, 430
Mossman, Jennifer, 9
Motta, Giuseppe, 43
Moulton, Harold K., 42
Moulton, Jenni H., 41
Moulton, Phillips P., 81
Mousnier, Roland E., 415
Mowat, Farley, 350, 619, 623, 624
Mowry, George E., 277, 337
Moynihan, Daniel P., 195
Mozart, Wolfgang Amadeus, 509
Mrozek, Donald J., 293
Mueller, Milton, 563
Muenchhausen, Friedrich von, 267
Muessig, Raymond H., 315
Muir, John, 619, 627
Muir, Ramsey, 404
Mulder, John M., 97
Muller, V. K., 45
Mullin, Gerald, 271
Mullins, Edwin, 622
Mumford, Lewis, 202
Mundy, John, 412
Muñoz, Olivia, 46
Munsterberg, Hugo, 530
Munz, Ludwig, 551
Murdock, George P., 104, 108, 109, 1 **120**
Murphey, Murray G., 285
Murphy, Bruce A., 296
Murphy, Dervla, 624
Murphy, Eloise C., 337
Murphy, Gardner, 169, 177
Murphy, John, 383
Murphy, Paul L., 277
Murphy, Richard W., 538
Murphy, Walter F., 152
Murray, C. J., 328
Murray, Charles, 102
Murray, Edward, 577, 578
Murray, Henry A., 175, **183**
Murray, James A. H., 27

Murray, John P., 572
Murray, Linda, 528
Murray, Oswyn, 240
Murray, Peter, 528
Murrin, John M., 264
Musgrave, Peggy, 132
Musgrave, Richard, 132
Mussen, P. H., 173
Musso, Louis, III, 337
Mussolini, Benito, 417
Mussorgsky, Modest, 509
Myerhoff, Barbara G., 203
Myers, A. R., 373
Myers, Bernard S., 528
Myers, Ramon H., 451
Myers, Robert Manson, 273
Myers, Rollo H., 512
Myles, Colette G., 597
Myrdal, Gunnar, 148, 196, **212,** 446
Myrdal, Jan, 448

Nachtigal, Paul M., 227
Nadel, S. F., 109, 111
Nagel, Ernest, 101
Nagel, Paul C., 83, 307
Nagera, Humberto, 556
Naipaul, V. S., 366
Nair, Kusum, 126
Naisbitt, John, 102
Namias, June, 293
Namier, Lewis B., 395
Nanda, B. R., 453
Nasaw, David, 227
Nash, George H., 70, 277
Nash, Jay R., 575
Nash, June, 360
Nathan, Joe, 227
Nathanson, Jerome, 231
Nattrass, Jill, 443
Navasky, Victor S., 73
Nayar, Kuldip, 453
Naylor, Kenneth E., 403
Naylor, Penelope, 617
Neal, Mary, 594
Neal, Steve, 279
Neale, John, 395, 415
Neaman, Judith, 31
Neatby, L. H., 625
Nebylitsyn, V. D., 171
Needham, Joseph, 448
Neely, Charles, 602
Neely, Mark E., Jr., 89, 258
Neff, Emery, 461
Neher, Clark D., 455

Nehru, Jawaharlal, 473
Neill, A. S., 227
Neill, Wilfred T., 455
Nelkin, Dorothy, 200, 204
Nelson, Douglas, 15
Nelson, Michael, 299, 300
Nelson, Thomas A., 586
Nelson, William E., 275
Nesteby, James R., 577
Nettl, Bruno, 493
Nettl, J. P., 416, 424
Neu, Charles E., 337
Neuberger, E., 124
Neuenschwander, John A., 267
Neuls-Bates, Carol, 487
Neuman, A. R., 230
Neumann, Franz L., 157
Neumann, Sigmund, 157
Neumann, William L., 451
Nevell, Richard, 518
Nevins, Allan, 90, 260, 263, 314, **330,** 403, 633
Newall, Venetia J., 592
Newby, Eric, 624
Newcomb, Benjamin H., 65
Newcomb, Horace, 572
Newell, Nancy P., 440
Newell, Richard S., 440
Newfarmer, Richard, 359
Newhouse, Dora, 34
Newlin, Dika, 486
Newman, Barbara, 520
Newman, Cardinal John Henry. *See* Volume 4
Newman, Harold, 534
Newman, Roger K., 576
Nicholas, Barry, 244
Nicholls, Ann, 528
Nichols, Roger, 512
Nicholson, Margaret, 31
Nickerson, Jane S., 443
Nickles, Harry, 31
Nickles, Sylvie, 645
Nicolson, Harold, 76, 409
Nicolson, Nigel, 77
Nie, Norman H., 153
Niebuhr, H. Richard, 199
Niewyk, Donald L., 430
Nijinsky, Vaslav, 524
Nikolaos, Van Dam, 440
Nilsen, Vladimir, 577
Nimmo, Dan, 564, 568
Nisenson, Eric, 503
Niver, Kemp R., 575, 585
Nizhny, Vladimir, 583

Nketia, Joseph H., 495
Noble, David W., 262
Noble, Peter, 585, 588
Nobles, Gregory H., 264
Nochlin, Linda, 531
Noelle-Neumann, Elisabeth, 156
Noory, Samuel J., 36
Nord, David Paul, 566
Nordhaus, W., 125
Nore, Ellen, 310
Norman, E. R., 370
Norman, Howard, 604
Norris, Geoffrey, 511
North, Robert, 155
Norton, Aloysius A., 338
Norton, Eloise S., 597
Novak, Michael, 102, 127, 152
Novak, Richey, 41
Novak, William, 52
Nove, Alec, 424
Nowak, Frank, 424
Nowlan, Kevin B., 381
Noy, Dov, 597
Nueckel, Susan, 614
Nugent, Walter, 293
Nulman, Mary, 490
Nunn, G. Raymond, 405
Nureyev, Rudolph, 524
Nutting, Teresa, 40
Nutting, Wallace, 534
Nyeko, Balaam, 442
Nyhart, J. D., 129

Oakes, George W., 622
Oakes, James, 271
Oates, Stephen B., 50, 53, 90, 271, 274, 283
Oates, Whitney J., 549
Obbo, Christine, 443
Obolensky, D., 420
Obregon, Mauricio, 627
O'Brian, Patrick, 549
O'Brien, Jacqueline, 10
Obudho, Constance E., 562
O'Callaghan, Joseph F., 419
Ochsner, Jeffrey Karl, 552
O'Connell, Maurice R., 381
O'Connor, Edmund, 451
O'Day, Alan, 383
Odendaal, Andre, 443
O'Donnell, Kenneth P., 72
O'Donnell, Monica M., 575
O'Driscoll, Gerald P., Jr., 146

Oettinger, Mal, 563
O'Farrell, P. J., 370
O'Ferrall, Fergus, 381
Offner, Arnold, 279
Ofrat, Elisha, 435
O'Gara, Gordon C., 338
Ogborn, William F., 200
Ogbu, John U., 227
Ogburn, Charlton, 620
Ogburn, William Fielding, 213
O'Gorman, Frank, 379
O'Gorman, James F., 552
Ogot, Berthwell A., 444
Ohkawa, Kazushi, 451
Oinas, Felix J., 597
Okey, Robin, 419
Oldfather, Felicia, 451
O'Leary, Timothy J., 121
Oleszek, Walter J., 300
Oliver, Andrew, 83
Oliver, C. M. Murray, 633
Oliver, Richard, 619
Oliver, Roland, 444
Olney, Marguerite, 599
Olschki, Leonardo, 644
Olson, Eric, 403
Olson, Julius E., 632
Olson, Mancur, 129
Olson, Sigurd F., 620
Olwell, Carol, 292
O'Malley, Padraig, 383
Oman, Charles, 373
O'Meara, Dan, 444
O'Neil, Robert M., 227
O'Neill, William L., 283
Onions, Charles T., 27, 28, 37
Onuf, Peter S., 267
O'Reilly, Dennis, 614
Orenstein, Arbie, 512
Organ, Troy W., 453
Orlov, Ann, 100, 195
Orlova, Alexandra, 509
Orni, Efraim, 435
Orren, Gary, 201
Orrey, Leslie, 495, 499
Orszagh, Laszlo, 42
Ortega y Gasset, José, 189, 190, 479
Ortiz, Alfonso, 604
Ortiz, Flora I., 227
Osborn, George C., 97
Osborne, Charles, 511, 517
Osborne, Harold, 528, 530, 534
Osofsky, Gilbert, 606

O'Toole, G. J. A., 276
Ott, Enrique, 357
Overacker, Louise, 166
Overmeyer, Daniel L., 448
Owen, John B., 379
Owen, Mary A., 606
Owen, Roger, 433
Owram, Doug, 350
Ozaki, Robert S., 451

Paananen, Lauri A., 421
Pacanowsky, Michael E., 562
Pach, Walter, 551
Pachai, Bridglal, 642
Pachter, Marc, 50
Packard, George R., 451
Packard, Rosa C., 234
Padden, R. C., 356
Padover, Saul K., 50, 161, 296
Paetow, Louis J., 405
Page, Joseph A., 360
Page, Monte M., 173
Page, Stanley W., 470
Pagter, Carl R., 607
Paine, Suzanne, 439
Paine, Thomas, 331
Paisley, William, 563
Pakenham, Thomas, 381
Paley, William S., 573
Palladio, Andrea, 533
Pallottino, Massimo, 242
Palmer, Alan, 21, 405
Palmer, Christopher, 501
Palmer, David R., 267
Palmer, Monte, 440
Palmer, R., 594
Palmer, Robert R., 406
Palmer, Robin, 444
Paludan, Philip Shaw, 274
Paneth, Donald, 566
Panofsky, Erwin, 530, 540, 544
Panter-Downes, Mollie, 624
Papadaki, Stamo, 543
Papadopoulo, Alexandre, 530
Papert, Seymour, 227
Paredes, Americo, 598, 603
Pareto, Vilfredo, 143
Pargellis, Stanley, 368
Paris, Matthew, 395
Paris, Ruth, 35
Parise, Frank, 14
Parish, James R., 578
Parish, Peter J., 274

Parish, William L., 448
Park, Mungo, 643
Park, Robert Ezra, 202, **213**
Parker, Charlie, 509
Parker, Donald L., 570
Parker, Edwin B., 72
Parker, Theodore, 326
Parker, Thomas, 15, 305
Parkes, Joan, 622
Parkinson, Roger, 364
Parkman, Francis, 316, **331,** 348
Parks, George B., 635
Parmet, Herbert S., 72, 283
Parnes, Herbert S., 131
Parnwell, E. C., 46
Parrington, Vernon L., 254
Parris, Leslie, 539
Parry, J. H., 356, 413, 617
Parsons, Denys, 490
Parsons, Kitty, 594
Parsons, Neil, 444
Parsons, Talcott, 106, 107, 140, 144, 196, 201, 204, 206, **214,** 221, 228
Partington, Paul G., 319
Partnow, Elaine, 21
Partridge, Eric, 31, 32, 33, 37
Pascal, Roy, 50
Pascale, Richard T., 451
Passmore, John, 194, 228
Pasztory, Esther, 354
Patai, Raphael, 430, 438
Pater, Alan F., 21
Pater, Jason R., 21
Patinkin, Don, 139
Patrick, Rembert W., 316
Patterson, James T., 263, 288
Patterson, Sheila, 444
Patwardhan, Vinayak N., 438
Paulu, Burton, 572
Pauly, Reinhard G., 486
Pavitt, K. L., 194
Pavlakis, Christopher, 490
Pavlov, Ivan Petrovich, 174, **183**
Pavlova, Anna, 524
Pawel, Ernst, 53
Pawlowska, Harriet, 594
Pawson, Eric, 379
Paxton, John, 17, 149
Paxton, Robert O., 413, 415, 429
Payne, Robert, 476
Payne, Stanley G., 419

Paz, Octavio, 116, 364
Pearce, Kenneth, 354
Pearcy, G. Etzel, 405
Pearlman, Michael, 276
Pearlman, Moshe, 435
Pearn, B. R., 446
Pearson, Hesketh. *See* Volume 1
Pearson, Michael, 424, 470
Peary, Robert E., 643
Pease, Otis A., 333
Peattie, Mark R., 451
Pechman, Joseph A., 131
Peck, Harry T., 335
Peckham, Howard H., 261, 267
Pedretti, Carlo, 545
Peffer, Nathaniel, 446
Peirce, Neal R., 257
Pelling, Henry, 370, 381, 383
Pells, Richard H., 102, 286
Pemble, John, 453
Pennock, J. Roland, 150
Penny, Nicholas, 550
Penrose, Boies, 617
Penrose, Edith, 438
Penrose, Ernest Francis, 438, 444
Penrose, Roland, 549
Penzer, Norman M., 630
Pepys, Samuel. *See* Volume 1
Percival, John, 520
Perera, Victor, 354
Perham, Margery, 624
Perkins, Dexter, 92
Perkins, Edwin J., 288
Perkinson, Henry J., 228
Perlis, Vivian, 503, 507
Perloff, Harvey S., 136
Perrett, Geoffrey, 277
Perrow, Charles, 200
Perry, Lewis, 271, 286
Pesce, Angelo, 438
Pessen, Edward, 301
Peters, Marie, 379
Petersen, Renée, 198
Petersen, Svend, 301
Petersen, William, 140, 198
Peterson, Merrill D., 88, 161
Peterson, Richard L., 131
Pethybridge, Roger, 424
Petrie, Charles A., 409
Petrocik, John R., 153, 279
Pettigrew, Terrence, 580
Pettigrew, Thomas F., 197

Pevsner, Nikolaus, 528, 532, 533
Peyser, Joan, 486
Pfeffer, Leo, 301
Pfeiffer, Charles C., 433
Pheby, John, 27, 41
Phelan, John L., 357
Phelan, Nancy, 620
Phelps, Edmund S., 131, 132
Phelps, Gilbert, 365
Philipson, Lorrin, 362
Philipson, Martin, 545
Phillips, Claude S., 444
Phillips, E. D., 243
Phillips, Gene D., 585
Phillips, Gregory D., 383
Phillips, Robert S., 3
Phythian, Brian, 33
Piaget, Jean, 173, 174, **184, 234**
Piattelli, Palmarini Massimo, 185
Picasso, Pablo, 548
Pickett, Calder, 566
Pickles, Dorothy, 415
Pierce, L. C., 225
Piers, Maria W., 178
Pierson, George W., 342
Pierson, William H., Jr., 532
Piggott, Patrick, 511
Pigou, A. C., 139, 140
Pike, Douglas, 455
Pike, Zebulon Montgomery, 627
Piland, Sherry, 531
Pillement, Georges, 622
Pinchbeck, Ivy, 370
Pinkerton, Edward C., 37
Pinkney, David H., 414
Pious, Richard M., 301
Pipes, Richard, 409, 424
Piscatori, James P., 434
Pitkin, Hanna F., 165
Pitt, David C., 104
Pitts, Michael R., 575
Piven, Frances F., 201
Place, J. A., 584
Placksin, Sally, 494
Placzek, Adolf K., 533
Planhol, Xavier De, 434
Plano, Jack C., 258
Plantinga, Leon, 486
Plaskin, Glenn, 506
Plato, 167
Platt, Gerald, 228
Pleasants, Henry, 496

Pleck, Elizabeth H., 290
Pletcher, Barbara A., 617
Pliny the Younger, 250
Ploman, Edward, 564
Ploski, Harry, 16
Plotke, David, 410
Plumb, J. H., 396, 403
Plummer, Katherine, 451
Plutarch, 247
Podgorecki, Adam, 155
Podrazik, Walter J., 570
Podro, Michael, 531
Poge, George R., 85
Poggi, Gianfranco, 342
Pogonowski, Iwo, 44
Pogue, Forrest C., 409
Pohl, Frederick J., 649
Polan, A. J., 470
Polanyi, Karl, 107, **144**
Polk, William R., 439
**Pollard, Albert Frederick,
396**
Pollard, Edward A., 316
Pollard, Sidney, 413
Pollock, Bruce, 492
Pollock, Dale, 578
Polo, Marco, 643
Polsby, Nelson W., 149, 154,
156, 192, 301
Polybius, 248
Pomeroy, Sarah B., 244
Poore, Benjamin Perley, 14
Pope-Hennessy, John, 550
Poppel, Stephen M., 430
Poppeliers, John, 533
Popper, Karl R., 168
Porath, Jonathan D., 430
Porter, Andrew, 486, 516
Porter, Cole, 510
Porter, David L., 279
Porter, Glenn, 258
Porter, Kenneth Wiggins,
271
Porter, Vincent, 576
Porter, William E., 568
Portes, Alejandro, 195
Portnoy, Joan, 617
Portnoy, Sanford, 617
Porzecanski, Arturo C., 366
Posner, Donald, 557
Post, Jeremiah B., 614
Post, John A., 614
Postan, M. M., 373
Postman, Leo, 174, 175, 190
Postman, Neil, 228
Potresov, A. N., 469

Potter, David M., 333
Poulton, Helen, 257
Pouncey, Peter, 245
Pound, Louise, 602
Pound, Roscoe, 155
Poussin, Nicolas, 549
Powell, David, 34
Powell, G. Bingham, Jr., 445
Powell, Lawrence N., 274
Powell, Walter W., 193
Powicke, Frederick Maurice,
370, 372, **396**
Poyatos, Fernando, 565
Prall, Stuart E., 377
Prange, Gordon W., 279
Pratson, Frederick, 617
Pred, Allan R., 272
Prendergast, Roy M., 493
Prescott, Orville, 462
**Prescott, William Hickling,
334,** 356
Prestwick, Michael, 373
Price, Barbara, 583
Price, David E., 301
Price, Derek de Solla,
200
Price, Theodore, 583
Priestly, Brian, 510
Pring, J. T., 42
Pringle, H. F., 338
Prins, Gwyn, 409
Pritchett, C. Herman, 152,
296
Pritchett, Victor S., 622
Prittie, Terence, 416
Procopius, 248
Proctor, Paul, 26
Prokofiev, Serge, 510
Propp, Vladimir, 592
Prothro, Edwin T., 171
Proudhon, Pierre J., 150
Prucha, Francis P., 293
Prude, Jonathan, 288
Prussen, Ronald W., 283
Puccini, Giacomo, 511
Puckett, N. Niles, 606
Pugh, Martin, 383
Pulsipher, Gerreld L., 615
Purcell, Gary R., 9
Purcell, Henry, 511
Purdon, M. E., 519
Purser, B. H., 438
Pusey, Nathan M., 228
Pushkarev, Sergei G., 424
Putnam, Linda L., 562
Pye, Lucian W., 446, 448

Pyle, Kenneth B., 451
Pym, Barbara, 53

Quandt, William B., 440
Quarles, Benjamin, 85, 267,
274
Quennell, Peter. *See* Volume
1
Quester, George H., 409
Quigley, Hugh, 416
Quigley, John M., 132
Quimby, Ian M., 592
Quinlan, Michael, 410
Quinlan, Sterling, 572
Quinley, Harold E., 197
Quint, Howard H., 263

Rachmaninoff, Serge, 511
Radcliffe, Philip, 508
Radcliffe-Brown, A. R., 104,
108, 109, 111, **121**
Rader, Benjamin, 572
Radice, E. A., 419
Radu, Michael, 441
Radwin, Samir, 442
Rae, John, 146
Raffe, W. G., 519
Ragazzini, Giuseppe, 43
Rahman, Fazlur, 434
Raiffa, Howard, 193
Raimo, John, 257
Rainwater, Robert, 527
Rajak, Tessa, 247
Rakove, Jack N., 267
Ralli, Augustus, 461
Ralph, Philip L., 405
Ramazani, Rouhollah K.,
438
Ramsden, John, 383
Randall, James G., 274
Randall, Willard, 65
Randel, Don M., 490
Randolph, Vance, 601
Range, Willard, 474
Ranger, Robin, 409
Ranger, T. O., 444, 608
Rankin, Nigel, 45
Ranney, Austin, 568
Ransford, Oliver, 642
Ransom, Roger L., 124, 288
Ranum, Orest, 411
Rapaport, David, 175, 179
Raph, Jane, 185
Raphael, 549

Raphael, Marc L., 427
Rasmussen, Steen E., 532
Rasponi, Lanfranco, 497
Rather, Dan, 569
Rattenbury, Judith, 101
Rauch, George von, 424
Rauchhaupt, Ursula von, 486
Ravel, Maurice, 512
Ravitch, Diane, 228, 293
Rawley, James A., 274
Rawlings, Hunter R., III, 245
Rawski, Evelyn S., 448
Ray, Arthur J., 348
Read, Colin, 350
Read, Conyers, 368, 375
Read, Donald, 381, 383
Read, Herbert, 530
Reagan, Michael, 152
Real, James, 328
Reasoner, Harry, 569
Rebuffat, Gaston, 617
Reck, David B., 493
Redfern, James, 46
Redfield, Robert, 105, 106, 122, 192
Redford, Emmette S., 301
Redlich, Hans F., 509
Reed, John, 424
Reed, Maxine K., 572
Rees, Alan M., 6
Reese, Gustave, 486
Reeves, Richard, 342
Reff, Theodore, 545
Regosin, Elinor, 521
Rehrauer, George, 575
Reich, Warren T., 100
Reichard, Gary W., 281
Reid, Anthony, 455
Reid, Stuart, 34
Reinharz, Jehuda, 430, 435
Reischauer, Edwin O., 450, 451, 464
Reisner, Robert G., 510
Reiss, Albert J., Jr., 202
Reiss, David S., 572
Reitlinger, Gerald, 430
Remak, J., 409
Rembrandt Harmensz van Rijn, 550
Remini, Robert Vincent, 272
Renoir, Jean, 551
Renoir, Pierre Auguste, 551
Renty, Ivan de, 46
Renz, Loren, 7
Repplier, Agnes, 348
Reps, John W., 275

Resek, Carl, 120
Reuter, Frank T., 267
Reutter, Edmund E., Jr., 228
Rewald, John, 530, 538, 551
Reynolds, Barbara, 42, 43
Reynolds, Graham, 539, 556
Reynolds, Joshua, 551
Reynolds, L. D., 241
Reynolds, Lloyd G., 129, 131
Reynolds, Paul R., 23
Rezneck, Samuel, 267
Rhodes, James Ford, 263
Rhyne, Nancy, 601
Riasanovsky, Nicholas V., 425
Ricard, Robert, 356
Ricardo, David, 144
Ricci, Mark, 587
Ricci, Robert, 489
Rice, Bradley R., 280
Rice, D. Talbot, 530
Rice, Edward E., 76, 448
Rice, Howard C., 267
Rice, Kym S., 264
Richard, Yann, 437
Richards, James M., 533
Richards, Vyvyan, 639
Richardson, E. L., 44
Richardson, Emeline, 242
Richardson, Henry Gerald, 397
Richardson, Henry Hobson, 552
Richardson, Lewis Fry, 157
Richardson, R. C., 368
Richie, Donald, 586
Richmond, I. A., 371
Richmond, John, 436
Richmond, P. G., 185
Richmond, Winthrop E., 592
Richter, Donald C., 381
Richter, Gisela M., 530
Richter, M., 167
Ricklefs, M. C., 455
Rickman, John, 110
Rider, K. J., 405
Ridgon, Susan M., 117
Ridgway, Matthew B., 409
Ridley, Jasper, 375
Ridolfi, Roberto, 165
Rieber, R. W., 169, 187
Riecken, Henry W., 101
Rieff, Philip, 175, 179
Riemens, Leo, 490, 496
Riesman, David, 102, 214, 220, 226, 455

Rifkin, Ned, 579
Rigby, T. H., 425
Righter, Rosemary, 566
Riis, Jacob A., 338
Riker, William H., 155
Riley, Matilda W., 188, 189
Riley, P. W., 377
Rilke, Rainer Maria, 553
Rimington, Critchell, 617
Rinzler, Carol A., 608
Ripley, Randall B., 301
Rips, Rae E., 12
Rishel, Virginia, 627
Ritter, Gerhard, 416
Ritz, David, 502
Roach, John, 405
Robb, John D., 603
Robbins, Celia Dame, 21
Robbins, Keith, 382
Robbins, Lionel, 125
Robbins, Richard, 193
Robbins-Landon, H. C., 506
Roberts, Chalmers M., 568
Roberts, David, 382, 627
Roberts, Donald F., 191
Roberts, Jane, 538
Roberts, Robert, 434
Roberts, Samuel J., 435
Roberts, Sydney C., 394
Robertson, Alec, 504
Robertson, James Oliver, 254
Robertson, Martin, 530
Robertson, R. MacDonald, 598
Robinson, David, 581
Robinson, Edgar E., 70
Robinson, Edward, 639
Robinson, Geroid T., 425
Robinson, Glen O., 565
Robinson, H. S., 598
Robinson, Halbert B., 228
Robinson, James A., 156
Robinson, Joan, 127
Robinson, Michael J., 569
Robson, John M., 142
Roche, Elizabeth, 490
Roche, Jerome, 490
Rock, Irvin, 175
Rockwood, Raymond O., 310
Rodale, J. I., 34
Rodin, Auguste, 552
Rodinson, Maxime, 430, 434
Rodriguez O., Jaime E., 357, 359
Roe, Ann, 107

Roedell, Wendy C., 228
Roethlisberger, F. J., 172, 204
Roffman, Howard, 72
Rogers, A. Robert, 405
Rogers, Everett M., 200, 565
Rogow, Arnold A., 163
Rogowski, Ronald, 154
Rohmer, Eric, 585
Roland, Charles P., 274
Roller, David C., 258
Roloff, Michael E., 171, 565
Romasco, Albert U., 70, 279
Rommel, Erwin, 409
Ronda, James, 640
Room, Adrian, 19, 35
Roos, Frank J., Jr., 533
Roosevelt, Eleanor, 77
Roosevelt, Elliott, 92
Roosevelt, Franklin D., 91
Roosevelt, Kermit, 338
Roosevelt, Theodore, 335, 471
Rosaldo, Michelle Zimbaliste, 203
Rosand, David, 555
Rose, Al, 494
Rose, Anne C., 286
Rose, Jerry, 190
Rose, Lisle A., 631
Rose, Peter I., 202
Rose, Richard, 384
Rose, Willie Lee, 274
Rose-Innes, Arthur, 38
Rosen, Charles, 486, 512
Rosen, David, 516
Rosen, Frederick, 158
Rosenau, James N., 155, 282
Rosenbaum, Art, 601
Rosenbaum, Margo, 601
Rosenbaum, Patricia, 202
Rosenberg, Emily S., 288
Rosenberg, Jakob, 551
Rosenberg, Jerry M., 562, 566
Rosenberg, Morris, 170
Rosenberg, Phillip, 461
Rosenberg, Rosalind, 203
Rosenblatt, Paul, 81
Rosenblum, Nancy L., 158
Rosengarten, Theodore, 53
Rosenman, Samuel I., 92
Rosenmuller, J., 147
Rosenof, Theodore D., 259
Rosenow, John E., 615
Rosenthal, A. M., 617

Rosenthal, Clifford N., 421
Rosenthal, Joel T., 371
Rosmer, Alfred, 470
Rosof, Patricia J., 433, 444
Rosovsky, Henry, 451
Rosow, Irving, 202
Ross, Charles, 373, 374
Ross, Dorothy, 179
Ross, E. Denison, 644
Ross, Irwin, 80
Ross, Ishbel, 316
Ross, John A., 100, 198
Ross, Stanley R., 575
Ross, Walter, 641
Rosset, Peter, 364
Rossi, Alice S., 203
Rossi, Ino, 117
Rossi, Peter H., 101
Rossiter, Clinton, 86, 301
Rossiter, Frank, 507
Rostovtzeff, Mikhail, 240
Rotberg, Robert I., 444, 624
Roth, Hal, 627
Roth, Leland M., 533
Roth, Robert J., 231
Rotha, Paul, 578
Rotham, William, 585
Rothbard, Murray N., 146
Rothenberg, Joshua, 430
Rothman, Ellen K., 293
Rothschild, Joan, 203
Rothschild, Joseph, 419
Rotman, Jeffrey L., 627
Rotraud, K. E. I., 40
Rousseau, Jean Jacques, 168
Rousset, David, 425
Roux, Georges, 438
Rowan, Richard L., 131
Rowe, Frank, 284
Rowe, John C., 307
Rowland, Peter, 384
Rowse, A. L., 397, 403
Rowse, Arthur E., 93
Roxon, Lillian, 490
Roy, Jules, 455
Royama, Masamichi, 451
Royce, Anya P., 520
Royle, Edward, 382
Rubens, Peter Paul, 553
Rubin, Barry, 151
Rubin, Bernard, 572
Rubin, Richard L., 301
Rubin, Ronald I., 425
Rubin, Ruth, 595
Rubin, Stephen, 129
Rubin, William, 538

Rubinfeld, Daniel L., 132
Rubinstein, Charlotte S., 531
Rudé, George, 379
Rudler, Gustave, 40
Rudolph, Lloyd I., 453
Rudolph, Susanne H., 453
Rudwick, Elliot M., 319
Rue, John E., 76
Ruffner, Frederick G., Jr., 20
Ruffner, James A., 9, 17
Rugoff, Milton, 617, 644
Rumney, Jay, 217
Rupp, Leila J., 413
Ruse, Michael, 382
Rushton, Julian, 500
Rusinow, Dennison, 420
Ruskin, John, 533
Russell, Bert, 603
Russell, D. A., 248
Russell, Francis, 540
Russell, James E., 236
Russell, John, 546
Russell, Ross, 494, 510
Russett, Bruce M., 163
Rustow, Dankwart A., 419
Rutland, Robert A., 269, 296
Rutman, Anita H., 265
Rutman, Darrett B., 265
Ruud, Charles A., 425
Ryavec, Karl W., 425
Ryder, A. J., 417

Sabin, Joseph, 257
Sachar, Howard M., 430, 435
Sachs, Curt, 486, 487, 493, 496, 518
Sachs, Harvey, 490
Sacilotto, Deli, 529
Sack, James J., 379
al-Sadat, A., 436
Sadie, Stanley, 490
Sadoul, Georges, 575
Saff, Donald, 529
Safran, Nadav, 435
Sagay, J. O., 444
Sahagún, Bernardino de, 356
Sahlins, Marshall D., 106, 107
Said, Edward W., 433, 440
St. Clair, Oswald, 145
Ste-Croix, G. E. M. de, 239
St. Denis, Ruth, 525
St. Joseph, J. K. S., 369
Sakharov, Andrei D., 425
Salem, James, 575

Sales, Grover, 494
Salinger, Pierre, 73
Salisbury, Charlotte, 624
Salisbury, Harrison E., 305, 425, 448, 455
Sallust, 250
Salomon, Gavriel, 565
Salomon, J. H., 604
Salvatore, Nick, 53
Salway, Peter, 371
Salzinger, Kurt, 169
Samkange, Stanlake, 444
Sampson, Anthony, 75, 384
Samuels, Ernest, 307
Samuelson, Paul A., 125
Sanasarian, Eliz, 438
Sandberg, Larry, 595
Sandburg, Carl, 59, 90
Sanders, Ronald, 430
Sandler, Norman, 563
Sansom, George, 451
Santamaria, Haydee, 362
Sanzio, Raffaello. *See* Raphael
Sanzone, John, 152
Sapan, Joshua, 562
Sapir, Edward, 106, 108, **122**
Sarris, Andrew, 577
Sarti, Roland, 418
Sartori, Giovanni, 152
Sartre, Jean-Paul, 430
Sarvaas, C., 455
Sass, Lauren R., 572
Sassoon, Siegfried. *See* Volume 1
Sauer, Carl O., 356
Saum, Lewis O., 272
Saunders, A. N. W., 240
Saunders, Christopher, 444
Sauvage, Pierre, 578
Savage, George, 534
Savage, Henry, 263
Savage, Michael D., 617
Savage, William W., 286
Savaiano, Eugene, 47
Sawey, Orlan, 317
Sawyer, P. H., 371
Sayles, George Osborne, 397
Sayre, John, 156, 259
Sayre, Wallace S., 154
Sayre, Woodrow Wilson, 627
Sayres, Sohnya, 102
al-Sayyid-Marsot, Afaf L., 436
Scagnetti, Jack, 586
Scammell, Michael, 54

Scarborough, John, 243
Scarisbrick, J. J., 375
Scavenius, H., 44
Scavnicky, Gary E. A., 47
Schachner, Nathan, 86
Schaie, K. Warner, 172, 189
Schambra, William A., 151
Schank, Roger C., 173
Schapiro, Meyer, 538, 556
Schapsmeier, Edward, 325
Schapsmeier, Frederick, 325
Schatz, Thomas, 575
Schell, Jonathan, 455
Schellenberg, James A., 182, 210
Schelling, Thomas C., 155, 157
Scheub, Harold, 608
Scheuer, Steven, 573
Schevill, Ferdinand, 474
Schickel, Richard, 542
Schiff, Gert, 549
Schiff, Ze'ev, 435
Schiffrin, Harold Z., 448
Schiller, Dan, 286
Schiller, Herbert, 565
Schlachter, Gail Ann, 9
Schlatter, Richard, 370
Schleifer, James T., 342
Schlesinger, Arthur M., 268, 338
Schlesinger, Arthur M., Jr., 54, 72, 73, 92, 257, 284, 301, 317, **339**
Schlesinger, Stephen, 363
Schleunes, Karl A., 430
Schlipp, Madelon G., 568
Schmeckebier, Laurence F., 14
Schmidt, Hans R., Jr., 363
Schmitt, Hans A., 413
Schmittroth, John, Jr., 4, 7
Schmookler, Jacob, 129
Schnabel, Ernst, 63
Schnaiberg, Allan, 194
Schneider, David M., 108
Schneider, H. K., 444
Schneider, Joseph W., 194
Schneider, Pierre, 545, 546, 557
Schneider, Richard I., 402
Schneider, William, 156
Schneiderman, Leo, 608
Schnitman, Jorge, 564, 577
Schoch, Henry A., 338
Schoenbaum, David, 417

Schoenberg, Arnold, 512
Schoenberg, Sandra Perlman, 202
Schoffler, Herbert, 41
Scholem, Gershom, 431
Schooler, Carmi, 201, 204
Schorer, C. E., 604
Schorske, Carl, 431
Schrade, Leo, 509
Schram, Stuart R., 76, 448
Schramm, Wilbur, 191, 565
Schramm, Wilbur J., 333
Schroeder, Fred E., 612
Schubert, Franz, 512
Schudson, Michael, 566
Schuettinger, Robert L., 384
Schuh, Willi, 513
Schultz, Theodore W., 126
Schulzinger, Robert D., 305
Schumann, Clara, 501
Schumpeter, Joseph A., 124, 127, 129, 131, 134, 142, 152, 157
Schur, Norman W., 30
Schurmann, Franz, 448
Schurz, Carl, 85
Schwartz, Anna J., 131, 135
Schwartz, Benjamin I., 76
Schwartz, Bernard, 296, 301
Schwartz, Charles, 505, 510
Schwartz, Elliott, 492
Schwartz, Henry, 603
Schwartz, Nancy B., 533
Schwartz, Stuart, 357
Schwartz, Theodore, 120
Schwartz, Tony, 565
Schwartzenberger, G., 17
Schwarz, Boris, 496
Schwebel, Milton, 185
Schwendowius, Barbara, 497
Scobie, James R., 360
Scott, Donald M., 261
Scott, H. M., 412
Scott, Harriet F., 409
Scott, John P., 171
Scott, R., 42
Scott, Robert Falcon, 644
Scott, William F., 409
Scullard, H. H., 241
Scully, Vincent, 533, 552, 559
Seabury, Paul, 417
Seager, Robert, 472
Sear, Frank, 242
Searle, Humphrey, 507
Searles, John B., 617

Sears, Donald A., 23
Sears, Robert R., 170, 177, 179
Sedgwick, Henry D., 333
Seeger, Pete, 595
Seeley, John R., 192
Segal, Julius, 170
Segall, Jacob, 598
Seidler, Murray B., 341
Seitz, William C., 548
Sekler, Eduard F., 543
Seldes, George, 21
Seligman, E. R. A., 100
Sellin, Thorsten, 193
Selser, Gregorio, 364
Seltzer, Leon E., 19
Selye, Hans, 171
Selz, Jean, 556
Selz, Peter, 530
Selznick, Gertude J., 197
Selznick, Philip, 188, 197
Semmel, Bernard, 379
Senior, Michael, 374
Senior, Nassau William, 145
Sennett, Richard, 127, 202
Serenyi, Peter, 543
Seroff, Victor, 510
Service, Elman R., 106, 107
Seton, Marie, 474
Seton-Watson, Christopher, 418
Seton-Watson, Hugh, 425
Sevareid, Arnold Eric, 569
Severin, Timothy, 620, 624
Sévigné, Mme de. *See* Volume 2
Sewall, Gilbert T., 228
Sewall, Jonathan, 82
Sewell, William H., 201
Sexton, James D., 363
Seymour, Charles, 547
Seymour, James D., 448
Seymour-Ure, Colin, 154
Shackleton, Robert, 167
Shafer, Boyd C., 406
Shafer, Byron E., 284
Shafer, Robert J., 403
Shaikh, Shafi, 38
Shain, Michael, 562
Shakow, David, 175, 179
El-Shamy, Hasan M., 596
Shanas, Ethel, 189
Shapiro, D., 405
Shapiro, Elliot, 485
Shapiro, Judith, 447
Shapiro, Martin, 297

Shapiro, Nat, 490, 494
Shapiro, Samuel, 633
Shapiro, William E., 3
Sharer, Robert J., 354
Sharff, Stefan, 575
Sharp, Cecil J., 594
Sharp, Dennis, 533
Sharp, Harold, 519
Sharp, Marjorie Z., 519
Sharpe, Myron E., 136
Shaw, Arnold, 491, 492
Shaw, David, 567
Shaw, Harry, 31
Shaw, Nate, 293
Shaw, Peter, 83
Shaw, Ralph, 260
Shaw, S. J., 439
Shaw, T. E. *See* Lawrence, T. E.
Shaw, William A., 398
Shawn, Ted, 525
Shearer, Benjamin F., 191, 562
Sheehy, Eugene P., 10
Shelanski, Vivien B., 195, 197
Sheldon, Eleanor B., 200
Shelton, Suzanne, 525
Shemel, Sidney, 491
Sheohmelian, O., 598
Shepherd, Jack, 307
Shepherd, William G., 127
Shepherd, William R., 405
Sheppard, Helen E., 4
Sherbiny, Nalem A., 439
Sherman, William L., 364
Sherwin, Martin J., 409
Shi, David E., 59, 103, 286
Shibutani, Tamotsu, 190
Shiff, Richard, 538
Shils, Edward, 190, 200, 215
Shirer, William L., 417
Shoemaker, Richard H., 260
Sholokhov, Mikhail, 475
Shore, Sammy, 611
Short, James F., Jr., 188, 193
Short, Philip, 448
Shostakovich, Dmitri, 510, 513
Shoukri, Ghali, 436
Shoup, Carl S., 145
Showman, Richard, 256
Shub, David, 425
Shubik, Martin, 125
Shumpei, Okamoto, 449
Shutt, V. Gladys, 617

Shuy, Roger, 108
Shwadran, Benjamin, 433
Shweder, Richard A., 106
Shy, John, 260
Sibley, Elbridge, 100
Sicherman, Barbara, 50
Siddigri, A. H., 434
Siddique, Kaukab, 438
Sieder, Reinhard, 412
Siefert, Marsha, 561
Siegal, Bernard J., 104
Siegman, Gita, 5, 6
Sigel, Efrem, 565
Sigmund, Paul E., 359
Silberman, Charles E., 193
Silbey, Joel H., 301
Silet, Charles L., 577
Silitch, Clarissa M., 599
Silk, Leonard, 124
Sillery, Anthony, 444
Sills, David L., 8, 100, 195, 197, 404
Silver, Carole, 31
Silver, Eric, 54
Silverberg, Robert, 618
Silverman, Dan P., 413
Silverman, Kenneth, 54
Silverstein, Norman, 576
Simey, Margaret B., 205
Simey, Thomas S., 205
Simic, Zivajin, 45
Simmel, Georg, 193, 215, 219
Simmons, Garner, 578
Simon, Alfred, 490
Simon, George T., 494
Simon, Herbert A., 150, 173, 197
Simon, John B., 228
Simon, Kate, 293, 620, 622
Simony, Maggy, 614
Simpkins, C. O., 503
Simpson, Alan, 375
Simpson, Claude M., 491
Simpson, George E., 115
Simpson, George G., 107
Simpson, J. A., 22
Simpson, Lesley B., 364
Simpson, Smith, 305
Simpson, Thomas D., 131
Simpson, William Kelly, 239
Sims, Janet L., 531
Sindler, Allan P., 301
Singer, Andre, 113
Singer, David, 15
Singer, J. D., 155

Singer, Michael, 575
Singh, Indu B., 565
Sinor, John, 618
Siren, Osvald, 530
Sisson, C. H., 385
Sitwell, Osbert. *See* Volume 1
Sitwell, Sacheverell, 507
Sivirine, Alexis, 625
Sizler, Theodore R., 228
Sjoberg, Gideon, 202
Skeat, Walter W., 37
Sked, Alan, 384
Skelton, Geoffrey, 506, 517
Skelton, R. A., 622
Skey, Malcolm, 43
Skidmore, Thomas E., 359
Skillin, Marjorie E., 23
Skinner, B. F., 174, **185**
Sklar, Robert, 572
Sklare, Marshall, 431
Skocpol, Theda, 126, 201, 413
Skolnick, Jerome H., 155
Skornia, Harry J., 573
Skotheim, Robert Allen, 286, 310, 311, 329
Skowronski, Joann, 606
Slack, Jennifer, 565
Slade, Ruth, 444
Slater, Candace, 598
Slater, Philip, 103
Slive, Seymour, 551
Sloan, Irving J., 257
Slobin, Mark, 595, 608
Slocum, Joshua, 645
Slocum, Victor, 645
Slonimsky, Nicholas, 491
Slusser, Robert M., 74
Smakov, Gennady, 522
Small, Kenneth A., 202
Smelser, Neil J., 107, 190, 201, 204
Smirnitsky, A. I., 45
Smirnov, Georgi, 425
Smirnow, Gabriel, 361
Smith, Adam, 125, 126, **145**
Smith, Alan H., 3, 420
Smith, Anthony, 567
Smith, Betsey, 640
Smith, Bradley F., 417
Smith, Charlotte C., 311
Smith, Constance, 197
Smith, Curt, 284
Smith, Dwight L., 260, 347
Smith, Edward C., 149, 297

Smith, G. E. Kidder, 533
Smith, Gene, 67, 70, 97
Smith, George, 370
Smith, George H., 309
Smith, Joseph H., 86
Smith, Julian, 581
Smith, Kenneth, 140
Smith, Kerry V., 129
Smith, Lacey B., 375
Smith, Logan P., 37
Smith, Michael P., 606
Smith, Morton, 238
Smith, Norris K., 559
Smith, Page, 83, 268, 269, 272, 274, 297
Smith, Peter H., 359
Smith, Ralph Bernard, 375
Smith, Ralph E., 204
Smith, Richard N., 70
Smith, Samuel, 170
Smith, Steven S., 301
Smith, Thomas C., 451
Smith, Vincent, 453
Smith, Wilfred C., 434
Smith, Wilson, 226
Smithies, Arthur, 132
Snipp, C. Matthew, 195
Snodgrass, Anthony M., 240
Snow, Edgar, 448, 449
Snow, Edward, 645
Snow, Robert P., 565
Snowden, Frank M., Jr., 239, 444
Snyder, Louis L., 431
Sobel, Lester A., 18
Sobel, Raoul, 581
Sobel, Robert, 255, 415
Soebadio, H., 455
Sohn, Louis, 155
Sokel, Walter H., 431
Sokolow, Nahum, 431
Sokolsky, Wallace, 468
Solinger, Dorothy, 449
Solomon, Arthur P., 202
Solomon, Maynard, 499
Solzhenitsyn, Aleksandr I., 425
Sombart, Werner, 219
Somers, Gerald G., 133
Somit, Albert, 149
Sonntag, Ida, 618
Sorden, L. G., 601
Sorel, Georges, 150
Sorensen, Theodore C., 72, 302
Sorokin, Pitirim A., 200, **216**

Sorrels, Bobbye, 565
Souchon, Edmond, 494
Soustelle, Jacques, 354
Southern, Eileen, 487, 491
Southworth, Herman M., 126
Sowell, Thomas, 293
Spada, James, 587
Spain, August O., 84
Spain, Daphne, 202
Spalding, Henry, 606, 611
Sparkes, Ivan G., 35
Speaight, Robert, 386
Spear, Percival, 453
Speck, W. A., 379
Spector, Ronald, 279
Speer, Albert, 417
Speke, John H., 628
Spence, Jonathan, 449
Spence, Kenneth W., 174
Spencer, Harold, 529
Spencer, Herbert, 217
Spencer, Katherine, 604
Spencer, Robert F., 104
Spengler, Oswald, 474
Sperber, Hans, 258
Speriglio, Milo A., 587
Spicer, Edward H., 105
Spiegel-Rosing, Ina, 200
Spier, Leslie, 123
Spies, Walter, 520
Spindler, George D., 104
Spiro, Melford E., 119
Spottiswoode, Raymond, 577
Sprague, Paul E., 554
Spuhler, J. N., 173
Spykman, Nicholas J., 216
Srinivas, M. N., 453
Ssu-Yu, Teng, 464
Stadter, Philip A., 247, 248
Stafford, Maureen, 535
Stahl, Fred A., 47
Stalin, Joseph, 475
Stambler, Irwin, 491, 492, 595
Stampp, Kenneth M., 272
Stanley, Henry Morton, 641, 642, **646**
Stanley, Robert H., 565
Stansky, Peter, 382
Stanton, Frank N., 207
Stanton, William, 620
Staples, Shirley, 612
Stark, Freya, 646
Starr, Chester G., 239
Starr, Isidore, 320

Starr, Paul, 198, 293
Stassinopoulis, Arianna, 502
Statler, Oliver, 451
Statt, David, 170
Stavrianos, Leften, 406, 420
Stearns, Jean, 520
Stearns, Marshall, 494, 520
Stearns, Peter N., 413
Steegman, John, 552
Steel, Ronald, 54, 164, 325
Stefansson, Vilhjalmur, 647
Steffen, Jerome O., 254
Stegner, Wallace, 317
Stein, Arthur A., 305
Stein, Elizabeth P., 66
Stein, Gertrude, 549
Stein, Leonard, 431
Stein, Maurice R., 203
Steinbeck, John, 628
Steinberg, Cobbett, 573
Steinberg, David J., 446
Steinberg, Stephen, 195, 197
Steiner, Gary A., 99, 191
Steiner, George, 116, 117
Steiner, Jean Francis, 431
Steiner, Maurice, 103
Steiner, Roger J., 40
Steiner, Stanley, 294
Steinglass, F., 38
Steinmetz, Sol, 25, 27, 30
Steintrager, James, 158
Stella, Joseph G., 551
Steltzer, Ulli, 350
Stelzer, Irwin M., 127
Stenton, Doris M., 372
Stenton, F. M., 371, 372
Stephen, Leslie, 143, 158
Stephens, John L., 354
Stephenson, Ralph, 577
Sterling, Christopher H., 569
Sterling, John C., 95
Stern, Bernhard J., 120
Stern, Fritz R., 417
Stern, Henry R., 41
Sterne, Emma G., 319
Stevans, C. M., 592
Stevens, Christopher, 444
Stevens, Halsey, 498
Stevenson, Adlai E., 92
Stevenson, Bruce, 369
Stevenson, Burton Egbert, 21
Stevenson, Elizabeth, 307
Stevenson, John, 368
Stevenson, Robert L., 620
Steward, Bright, 341

Steward, Julian, 106, 107, 116
Stewart, A. T., 370
Stick, David, 265
Stiegel, Frederick F., 284
Stierlin, Henri, 355
Stigler, George J., 124, 126, 142
Stikoff, Harvard, 284
Stillwell, Richard, 241
Stinchcombe, Arthur L., 193
Stisted, Georgiana M., 630
Stites, Frances N., 269
Stocking, George W., Jr., 103, 112
Stoddard, Florence J., 598
Stoessinger, John G., 305
Stoianovich, Traian, 403
Stokes, Curtis, 481
Stone, Alan, 288
Stone, George W., Jr., 66
Stone, Irving, 547, 556
Stone, Julius, 118, 155
Stone, Lawrence, 398
Stone, Norman, 413
Stone, Philip J., 101
Stone, Roger D., 361
Stoneman, Colin, 444
Stoneman, Elvyn A., 405
Storing, Herbert J., 297
Storrer, William A., 559
Storry, Richard, 451, 452
Story, Norah, 348
Story, Ronald, 260
Storzer, Gerald H., 40
Stott, William, 279
Stouffer, Samuel A., 151, 217
Stourzh, Gerald, 65
Stout, Earl J., 602
Strachey, Lytton, 60
Strahan, Hew, 409
Strasser, Susan, 288
Stratton, Clarence, 31
Strauss, Anselm L., 195
Strauss, Leo, 160, 165, 168
Strauss, Richard, 513
Strauss, Walter L., 540
Stravinsky, Igor, 514
Stravinsky, Theodore, 514
Stravinsky, Vera, 514
Strayer, Joseph R., 406
Street, Brian V., 113
Strickland, Walter W., 598
Strike, Kenneth A., 229
Strode, Hudson, 315, 316

Stromberg, Roland N., 413, 479
Strong, Eugenia, 530
Strousse, Jean, 54
Strout, Cushing, 310, 311
Strozier, Charles B., 274
Strunk, Oliver, 487
Strunk, William, Jr., 23
Stuart, Reginald C., 269
Stubbs, John C., 583
Stubbs, William, 398
Stuckenschmidt, H. H., 487, 512
Styron, William, 344
Suelzle, Marijean, 196
Suetonius, 250
Sullivan, Gerald, 284
Sullivan, John L., 152
Sullivan, Kaye, 575
Sullivan, Louis Henry, 554
Sullivan, Marianna P., 455
Sulloway, Frank J., 179
Summers, David, 547
Summerson, John, 379, 532
Susman, Warren I., 103
Sutch, Richard, 288
Sutherland, Anne, 195
Sutherland, Edwin H., 193
Suttles, Gerald D., 192
Sutton, Horace, 620
Swaan, Wim, 624
Swank, Scott T., 592
Swanson, Bert, 191
Swanson, Donald C., 42
Sweeney, G. P., 565
Sweeney, Robert L., 559
Swindler, William F., 297
Swingewood, Alan, 188
Switzer, Richard, 40
Sybil, Milton, 428
Syed, Anwar H., 325
Sykes, J. B., 25
Sykes, Percy M., 618
Sykes, Perry, 438
Syme, Ronald, 241, 249, 250, 251
Symonds, John Addington, 476
Symons, Arthur, 622
Sztompka, Piotr, 211
Szwed, John F., 606

Tacitus, Cornelius, 251
Tadmor, Nephtali, 435
Taeuber, Conrad, 218

Taeuber, Irene B., 218
Taft, Donald R., 193
Taft, Lorado, 531
Tahir-Kheli, Shirin, 438
Tal, Uriel, 431
Talashoma, Herschel, 604
Talbot, Daniel, 575
Talbot, Michael, 516
Talbott, John, 415
Talbott, Strobe, 409
Talese, Gay, 567
Talley, Thomas W., 606
Talmon, J. R., 413
Tames, Richard, 453, 646
Tancock, John L., 553
Tandon, Prakash, 453
Tanenhaus, Joseph, 149
Tannenbaum, Frank, 352
Tannenbaum, Percy H., 191
Tanur, Judith M., 100
Taper, Bernard, 521
Tarbell, Ida M., 90
Tarde, Gabriel, 174
Tariello, Frank, 275
Tarling, Nicholas, 447
Tarr, Rodger L., 461
Tarrow, Sidney, 417
Taruskin, Richard, 487
Tate, A., 316
Tate, Thad W., 264
Tatu, Michel, 425
Taubman, William, 476
Tawney, Richard H., 398
Tax, Sol, 107, 126
Taylor, A. J. P., 379, 477
Taylor, Basil, 539
Taylor, Charles, 351, 620
Taylor, Charles L., 149
Taylor, Eugene, 181
Taylor, G., 446
Taylor, George R., 344
Taylor, Henry Osborn, 478
Taylor, James C., 189
Taylor, James L., 44
Taylor, John F. A., 229
Taylor, Keith W., 455
Taylor, Lonn, 603
Taylor, Richard, 577
Taylor, Roger, 587
Taylor, Ronald, 42
Taylor, Telford, 413
Tchaikovsky, Peter Ilyich, 514
Teaford, Jon C., 275
Tehan, Arline B., 307

Teilhard de Chardin, Pierre, 628
Teller, Walter M., 645
Tennaille, Mabel, 596
Terkel, Studs, 280
Terrace, Vincent, 573
Terrill, Ross, 76, 449
Terry, Walter, 518, 523, 525
Terwiel, B. J., 455
Teschner, Richard V., 46
Teska, P. T., 171
Thayer, Nathaniel B., 452
Theen, Rolf H., 470
Theobald, Robert, 565
Theodorson, Achilles G., 188
Theodorson, George A., 188
Thernstrom, Stephan, 100, 195, 263, 288
Theroux, Paul, 620, 622, 624
Thielens, Wagner, Jr., 102, 151, 198, 208
Thirsk, Joan, 377
Thomas, Benjamin P., 90
Thomas, Charles, 371
Thomas, Emory M., 274
Thomas, Frank, 582
Thomas, Gordon, 289
Thomas, Hugh, 362, 406, 419
Thomas, J. C., 503
Thomas, Keith, 375
Thomas, Lawrence L., 44
Thomas, Lowell, 638
Thomas, Milton H., 330
Thomas, Norman, 340
Thomas, Pam, 518
Thomas, Peter D., 379
Thomas, Rosemary H., 602
Thomas, Tony, 577
Thomas, W. I., 204, 218
Thomis, Malcolm I., 382
Thompson, Della, 45
Thompson, Edward Palmer, 399
Thompson, Harold, 600
Thompson, J. L., 415
Thompson, J. M., 413
Thompson, J. W., 403
Thompson, K., 583
Thompson, Kenneth, 491
Thompson, Leonard, 445, 619
Thompson, Paul, 384
Thompson, Reginald W., 388
Thompson, Rose, 606
Thompson, Stith, 598, 604
Thoms, William J., 590

Thomson, David, 578
Thomson, Gladys S., 425
Thomson, Joseph, 643
Thomson, Virgil, 515
Thorburn, H., 351
Thorndike, Edward L., 235
Thorp, N. Howard, 603
Thorpe, William, 287
Thublon, Colin, 623
Thucydides, 245
Thurow, Lester, 125
Thursfield, Richard E., 230
Ticknor, George, 335
Tilden, Freeman, 620
Tilly, Charles, 200
Timberlake, Michael, 203
Timerman, Jacobo, 360
Timmons, Christine, 31
Tinbergen, Jan, 130
Tinbergen, Nikolaas, 171, 185
Tindall, George B., 263
Tinen, James, 20
Tingley, Donald F., 260
Tinker, Hugh, 455
Tint, Herbert, 415
Tippett, Michael, 515
Tipton, Steven M., 102
Tirpitz, Admiral von, 471
Tiryakian, Edward A., 154, 217
Titian, 554
Titon, Jeff Todd, 493
Tittler, Robert, 375
Tjepkema, Sandra L., 492
Tobin, James, 126
Tocqueville, Alexis de, 103, 152, 341
Todd, Loreto, 598
Todd, R. Larry, 508
Toelken, Barre, 592
Togo, Admiral, 471
Toland, John, 280, 409, 452
Tolchin, Susan, 565
Toll, Robert C., 612
Tolle, Gordon J., 456
Tolnay, Charles Q. de, 547
Tönnies, Ferdinand, 192, 219
Toor, Frances, 598
Topping, Malachi C., 572
Torre, Susana, 534
Torrence, Bruce T., 577
Toth, Marian D., 598
Toth, Susan A., 54
Tout, Thomas Frederick, 399
Tovey, Donald F., 487, 499

Towell, Julie E., 4
Townshend, Charles, 382, 384
Toynbee, Arnold J., 403, 474, **478**
Trachtenberg, Alan, 287
Trager, Frank N., 449
Trager, George L., 123
Trami, Eugene P., 338
Traubner, Richard, 495
Traugott, Michael, 299
Treadgold, Donald W., 425
Tregonning, Kennedy G., 405
Treiman, Donald J., 203
Trench, Charles C., 382
Trevelyan, George Macaulay, 399
Trevor-Roper, Hugh R., 400
Treyz, J., 405
Tribe, Laurence H., 152
Trimble, Marshall, 603
Trimingham, J. Spencer, 434, 444
Tripp, Rhoda Thomas, 21
Trittschuh, Travis, 258
Troeltsch, Ernst, 199
Trotsky, Leon, 469, 470, 476, **480**
Trow, Martin A., 211
Trowbridge, Rob, 16
Troy, Thomas F., 305
Troyat, Henri, 54
Truchtenberg, Stanley, 611
Trudeau, Pierre E., 447
Truett, Evelyn Mack, 578
Truffaut, François, 585, **587**
Truman, David B., 154
Truman, Harry S., 79
Truman, Margaret, 80
Trump, D. H., 239
Tsou, Tang, 447, 449
Tuchman, Barbara, 409, 449, **481**
Tuchman, Gaye, 565
Tucker, Glenn, 274
Tucker, Paul H., 548
Tucker, Robert C., 425, 426, 476
Tucker, Robert W., 305
Tuckwell, W., 637
Tufte, Edward R., 101
Tuggle, Robert, 495
Tugwell, Rexford G., 92
Tullock, Gordon, 132, 153
Tunney, Christopher, 409
Turabian, Kate L., 23

Turnbull, S. R., 452
Turner, A. C., 618
Turner, E. G., 242
Turner, Frederick Jackson, 254, **342**
Turner, Joseph Mallord William, 555
Turner, Julius, 153
Turner, Ralph, 170, 190
Turner, Victor, 109
Turow, Joseph, 565
Tuttle, William H., Jr., 292
Tuttle, William M., Jr., 319
Twain, Mark, 618
Twombly, Robert C., 559
Twyman, Robert, 258
Tyack, David B., 229
Tyler, Parker, 577
Tylor, Edward Burnett, 106, **123**
Tyson, Alan, 499

Udelson, Joseph H., 287
Udovitch, A. L., 434
Uhr, Carl G., 148
Ujifusi, Grant, 15
Ukladnikov, Alexander, 520
Ulam, Adam B., 426
Uldricks, Teddy J., 409
Ulyanov, Vladimir Ilyich. *See* Lenin, Nikolai
Underdown, David, 377
Unruh, John D., 272
Urban, George, 476
Urdang, Laurence, 14, 15, 20, 21, 31, 33, 257
Urofsky, Melvin I., 276
Urquhart, Brian, 68

Vaillant, George C., 355
Van Caenegem, R. C., 372
Van Cleave Alexander, Michael, 375
Van den Bark, Melvin, 31
Van den Haag, Ernst, 194
Van den Toorn, Pieter C., 514
Vandermeer, John, 364
Van der Post, Laurens, 648
Van Deusen, Glyndon G., 85
Van Doren, Carl, 65, 268
Van Doren, Charles, 20, 260
Van Duong, Quyen, 598
Van Dusen, Albert E., 265

Van Gerpen, Maurice, 569
Van Gogh, Vincent, 556
Van Rensselaer, Mariana G., 552
Vansina, Jan, 444
Van Til, William, 233
Van Wagoner, Merrill Y., 38
Van Zile, Judy A., 519
Varner, Jeannette J., 356
Varner, John G., 356
Vasari, Giorgio, 531
Vasconcelos, José, 364
Vatikiotis, P. J., 433, 436, 440
Vaughan, Alden T., 265
Vaughan, David, 521
Vaughan, Richard, 413
Vaughan, Robert G., 302
Vaughan, Thomas, 633
Veblen, Thorstein, 128, **219**
Vecelli, Tiziano. *See* Titian
Vecsey, Christopher T., 254
Velazquez de la Cadena, Mariano, 46
Velazquez, Diego Rodriguez de Silva, 556
Véliz, Claudio, 359
Venables, Robert W., 254
Venkata Ramanappa, M. N., 453
Verba, Sidney, 153, 154, 201
Verbrugghe, Gerald, 242
Verdi, Giuseppe, 515
Vermeule, Emily T., 240
Vernadsky, George, 426, **482**
Vespucci, Amerigo, 648
Vexler, Robert I., 419
Vidal-Naquet, Pierre, 243
Vidich, Arthur J., 192
Villa Rojas, Alfonso, 122
Villiers, Alan, 633
Vincent, Carl, 575
Vinovskis, Maris, 291
Vinterberg, L., 39
Vinton, John, 491
Viorst, Milton, 284
Visconti, Luchino, 587
Vishnevskaya, Galina, 426
Vita, Finzi Claudio, 433
Vitek, Alexander J., 45
Vitruvius, 533
Vitzthum, Richard C., 254
Vivaldi, Antonio, 516
Vlekke, Bernard H., 419, 455
Vogel, Ezra F., 449, 452
Vogler, David, 302

Vogt, Evon Z., 109
Voight, M., 405
Vojta, George, 128
Vold, George B., 194
Volin, Lazar A., 426
Volkoff, Vladimir, 515
Volkov, Solomon, 521
Von Holst, Hermann, 84
Von Leyden, W., 160
Von Mises, Ludwig, 146
von Moos, Stanislaus, 543
Von Neumann, John, 125, **146**
Von Sternberg, Joseph, 588
Von Stroheim, Erich, 588
Vos, Howard F., 433
Voyce, Arthur, 531
Voynow, Zina, 583
Vucinich, W. S., 439

Wachs, Harry, 235
Wade, Bonnie C., 495
Wade, Mason, 333
Wagar, W. Warren, 405
Wagenknecht, Edward, 276
Wagner, Richard, 516
Wahlke, John C., 156
Wai, Dunstan M., 440, 444
Waites, Neville H., 414
Wakelyn, John L., 293
Wakeman, Frederic, Jr., 76, 449
Walbank, F. W., 240, 248
Walbank, T. Walter, 406
Walden, Daniel, 468
Walden, Russell, 543
Waldman, Michael, 299
Waldo, Dwight, 150
Walford, Albert J., 11
Walker, Alan, 502, 507
Walker, Alexander, 586
Walker, Frank, 516
Walker, J., 35
Walker, John, 539
Walker, Katherine Sorley, 520
Walker, Martin, 567
Walker, Robert, 511
Walker, Samuel, 294
Walker, Thomas W., 364
Wall, James T., 364
Wallace, Amy, 14
Wallace, Anthony, 106, 109, 289
Wallace, Irving, 14

Wallace, Michael, 261, 324
Wallace, Mike, 569
Wallace, Robert, 537, 545, 556
Wallace-Hadrill, Andrew, 251
Wallechinsky, David, 14, 15
Wallerstein, Immanuel, 101, 129
Walling, Robert A., 629
Walpole, Horace. *See* Volume 1
Walras, Leon, 125
Walsh, Andrea, 577
Walter, Claire, 15
Walters, F. P., 409
Walters, R. H., 173
Walters, Ronald G., 269
Walworth, Arthur, 97
Walz, Eugene P., 587
Walzer, Mary M., 623
Walzer, Michael, 377
Wang, James C., 449
Wang, Yi-C., 449
Ward, Alan J., 384
Ward, Barbara, 446, **483**
Ward, Geoffry C., 92
Ward, John T., 382
Warden, Herbert W., 3rd, 618
Ware, Dora, 535
Ware, Susan, 280
Warner, Anne, 595
Warner, Philip, 444
Warner, W. Lloyd, 110, 128
Warner, William, 351
Warren, Harris G., 70, 365
Warren, W. L., 372
Warshaw, Steven, 452
Warshow, Robert, 612
Wasby, Stephen L., 302
Washburn, Wilcomb E., 261
Washington, Booker T., 85, **236**
Washington, George, 93
Wasko, Janet, 577
Wasserman, Paul, 5, 6, 7, 10
Waterbury, John, 436
Waterhouse, Ellis, 531, 552
Waters, Donald J., 606
Waters, Somerset R., 615
Watkins, Mary Michelle, 9
Watkins, Nicholas, 546
Watson, Derek, 501
Watson, G. R., 244
Watson, John B., 174, **186**

Watson, Robert I., 170, 179
Watt, Donald C., 409
Watteau, Jean-Antoine, 557
Wauchope, Robert, 352
Wavell, Archibald P., 431
Wayne, Stephen J., 299, 302
Wearing, Joseph, 351
Weaver, David H., 569
Weaver, Donald B., 170
Weaver, Suzanne, 127
Weaver, William, 516
Webb, Beatrice, 147
Webb, Bernard, 316
Webb, Eugene J., 101
Webb, Robert K., 370
Webb, Sidney, 147
Webb, Stephen, 265
Weber, Eugene, 413
Weber, Marianne, 221
Weber, Max, 101, 197, 199, 203, 219, **220**
Weber, William, 517
Webern, Anton von, 517
Webster, D. E., 439
Webster, Daniel, 94
Webster, J. B., 404
Webster, T. B. L., 240
Wechsler, Judith, 538
Wedgwood, Cicely V., 377, 553
Weems, Mason L., 94
Wegs, J. Robert, 413
Wehr, Hans, 38
Wehrle, Edmund S., 446
Weibel, Adele C., 535
Weigley, Russell F., 280, 409, 410
Weik, Martin H., 562
Weiker, Walter F., 439
Weill, Herman N., 410
Weinberg, Alvin M., 195
Weinberg, Gerhard L., 417
Weinberg, Herman G., 588, 589
Weinberg, Martha W., 156
Weinberg, Meyer, 294
Weinberger, Norman S., 535
Weiner, Carolyn N., 574
Weiner, Richard, 568
Weingast, David E., 326
Weinryb, Bernard, 431
Weinstein, Warren, 444
Weiss, Nancy J., 280
Weiss, Piero, 487
Weissberg, Robert, 156
Weissman, Dick, 595

Weitenkampf, Frank, 330
Weitzman, Lenore J., 196
Weitzman, Martin L., 131
Weizman, Ezer, 435
Weizmann, Chaim, 431
Welch, Claude E., Jr., 445
Wellborn, Charles, 326
Welles, E. R., 600
Welles, Orson, 589
Wellisch, Hans H., 11
Wells, Colin, 241
Wells, Robert V., 294
Welsch, Roger, 602
Welty, Eudora, 54
Welty, Paul T., 446
Wenk, Arthur B., 504
Wenner, Manfred W., 440
Wentworth, Harold, 33
Werlich, David P., 365
Wernecke, Herbert H., 608
Wernham, R. B., 375
Werth, Alexander, 410
Wertheim, Arthur F., 573
Wertheim, Maurice, 481
Wertheimer, Barbara Mayer, 289
Wesley, John. *See* Volume 4
Wesson, Robert G., 426
West, James, 110
West, Rebecca, 276
Westerby, Herbert, 507
Westernhagen, Curt von, 517
Westin, A. V., 569
Westoff, Charles F., 198
Weston, Corinne, 377
Westrup, Jack A., 511
Westwood, J. N., 426
Wheeler, Olin D., 640
Wheeler, Post, 598
Wheeler, Stanton, 155
Wheelock, Keith, 437
Whelan, Christopher, 155
Whelpton, Pascal K., 198
Whiffen, Marcus, 533
White, Barbara, 551
White, Carl M., 405
White, E. B., 23
White, Eric W., 501, 514, 515
White, K. D., 243
White, Leonard, 166
White, Leslie A., 106, 107
White, Lynn, Jr., 67
White, Morton M., 339
White, Robert W., 183
White, Theodore H., 284
Whitehead, David, 241

Whitelock, Dorothy, 371
Whitfield, Francis J., 44
Whitfield, Jane S., 35
Whitfield, Stephen J., 456
Whiting, Allen S., 449
Whiting, Barbara J., 22
Whiting, John W., 106
Whitnah, Donald R., 257
Whitney, David C., 16
Whittall, Arnold, 501, 515
Whitten, Mary E., 22
Whorf, Benjamin L., 123
Whyte, Martin K., 448, 449
Whyte, William F., 172, 192
Wiarda, Howard J., 362
Wick, Adele E., 194
Wicker, Tom, 71, 72
Wickersham, John, 242
Wicksell, Knut, 148
Widenor, William C., 305
Wiecek, William M., 303
Wiener, Martin, 384
Wiener, Philip P., 11, 405
Wiesel, Elie, 431
Wiesenthal, Simon, 431
Wiet, Gaston, 433
Wilber, Donald N., 438, 453
Wilcox, Clair, 127
Wilcox, Wayne A., 446, 453
Wildavsky, Aaron, 102, 150, 301
Wildenstein, Daniel, 548
Wildman, Allan K., 426
Wilensky, Harold L., 198
Wiley, Bell I., 274, 316
Wiley, Roland J., 515
Wilk, Max, 573
Wilkins, Charlotte W., 311
Wilkinson, B., 369, 374
Willett, Frank, 445
William of Malmesbury, 400
Williams, Edwin B., 27, 47
Williams, Eric, 353
Williams, Frederick, 109, 229, 565, 573
Williams, Gavin, 440
Williams, George W., 263
Williams, James, 16
Williams, Jay, 555
Williams, Martin, 494, 585
Williams, Neville, 618
Williams, Philip M., 415
Williams, Robert B., 231
Williams, T. Harry, 90, 262, 305
Williams, Victoria, 229

Williams, William Appleman, 305
Williamson, James A., 623
Willigan, Dennis J., 198
Willis, John, 575
Willmott, Peter, 108
Wills, A. J., 445
Wills, Garry, 94, 270, 297
Wills, Geoffrey, 535
Willson, D. H., 377
Wilmington, Michael, 584
Wilshire, Bruce, 181
Wilson, A. N., 386
Wilson, Bonnie, 616
Wilson, Charles, 377
Wilson, D. A., 444
Wilson, Dick, 76, 449
Wilson, E. A., 45
Wilson, Earl J., 620
Wilson, Edmund, 332, 351
Wilson, Edward, 625, 645
Wilson, Edward O., 171, 174
Wilson, Frank P., 22
Wilson, G. B. L., 519
Wilson, John F., 168
Wilson, K., 598
Wilson, Logan, 198
Wilson, Monica, 445
Wilson, N. G., 241
Wilson, Stephen, 431
Wilson, Woodrow, 95
Wiltse, Charles M., 84
Wiltshire, David, 217
Winch, Robert F., 196
Windeler, Robert, 578
Winfield, Betty H., 569
Wing, Jennifer, 430
Winget, Lynn W., 47
Wingler, Hans, 542
Winick, Charles, 104, 573
Winick, Mariann, 573
Winius, George D., 418
Winner, Langdon, 200
Wint, Guy, 407
Wirth, Louis, 192
Wiser, Charlotte, 454
Wiser, William, 454
Wish, Harvey, 254
Wishy, Bernard, 261
Wiskemann, Elizabeth, 418
Wissler, Clark, 111, 294
Wistrich, Robert, 426, 431
Witherspoon, Alexander M., 31
Withey, Elsie Rathburn, 534
Withey, Henry F., 534

Withey, Lynne, 83
Wittfogel, Karl A., 157
Wittkopf, Eugene R., 304
Wittkower, Margot, 531
Wittkower, Rudolf, 527, 531, 533
Wofford, Harris, 72, 73
Wohl, Hellmut, 545
Wolf, Arthur P., 199
Wolf, C. P., 195, 197
Wolf, Eric, 353
Wolf, Theta H., 176
Wolfe, Alan, 127
Wolfe, Bertram D., 470, 476, 481
Wolfe, Charles K., 595
Wolfe, J. N., 137
Wolfe, Robert, 452
Wolfenstein, E. Victor, 481
Wolfenstein, Martha, 190, 191
Wolff, Kurt H., 206, 216
Wolff, Robert L., 420
Wolff, Robert P., 141
Wölfflin, Heinrich, 529, 540
Wolfgang, Marvin, 193, 194
Wolfson, Nicholas, 128
Wolin, Sheldon S., 149
Wolk, Samuel J., 427
Wolkstein, Diane, 598
Woll, Peter, 150
Wolman, Benjamin B., 170
Wolpert, Stanley, 454
Wood, Christopher, 531
Wood, Gordon S., 268
Wood, John C., 140, 145, 146
Wood, Marion, 604
Woodcock, George, 348
Woodham-Smith, Cecil B., 382
Woodhouse, C. M., 420
Woodward, Bob, 280, 284, 302
Woodward, C. Vann, 254, 302, **344**
Woodward, Ralph L., Jr., 360
Woodward, W. E., 94
Wool, Robert, 609
Woolery, George W., 573
Woolf, Harry, 101
Woolf, Leonard. *See* Volume 1
Woolf, S. J., 413

Woolman, John, 80
Woolrych, Austin, 377
Woolsey, R. James, 410
Worden, B., 377
Worsley, Peter, 105
Wray, Harry, 452
Wren, Christopher, 557
Wright, Benjamin F., 326
Wright, Billie, 620
Wright, Christopher, 549, 551
Wright, Edward R., 455
Wright, Frank Lloyd, 554, **558**
Wright, Gordon, 410, 415
Wright, Herbert F., 191
Wright, Olgivanna L., 559
Wright, Quincy, 158
Wright, Richard, 294
Wright, Thomas, 630
Wrigley, E. A., 370
Wrone, David R., 72
Wrong, Dennis, 221
Wu, Eugene, 447
Wundt, Wilhelm, 186
Wyatt, David K., 455
Wyden, Peter, 362
Wylie, Raymond F., 449
Wyman, Mark, 275
Wynar, Bohdan S., 4, 11
Wynia, G. W., 360

Xenakis, Iannis, 517
Xenophon, 246

Ya'ari, Ehud, 435
Yale, William, 433
Yamamura, Kozo, 450, 452
Yandle, Bruce, 129
Yaney, George L., 426
Yang, Lien-Sheng, 38
Yapp, Peter, 618
Yazawa, Melvin, 265
Yellowitz, Irwin, 289
Yergin, Daniel, 305
Yoder, Don, 592
Youings, Joyce, 375
Young, Alfred F., 268
Young, Arthur N., 449
Young, Brian, 351
Young, Frank W., 110
Young, Hubert W., 439

Young, Louise M., 461
Young, Michael, 108
Young, Mildred B., 81
Young, Peter, 410
Young, Robert J., 415
Young, Ruth E., 43
Young-Bruehl, Elisabeth, 456
Yu, Frederick T. C., 563

Zablocki, Benjamin, 203
Zabriskie, E. H., 446
Zacher, Mark W., 68
Zagorin, Perez, 377
Zaimont, Judith Lang, 491
Zald, Mayer N., 201
Zaleski, Eugene, 426
Zaller, Robert, 377
Zander, Alvin, 172
Zarnecki, George, 531
Zaroulis, Nancy, 284
Zartman, I. William, 445
Zeigler, Philip, 54
Zeisel, Hans, 101, 155
Zeitlin, Irving, 188, 342
Zeitlin, Steven J., 598
Zeldin, Theodore, 415
Zeltner, Philip M., 231
Zenderland, Leila, 254
Zeno, George, 587
Zervos, Christian, 549
Zetterbaum, Marvin, 342
Ziegler, Philip, 374, 382
Zimmerman, Franklin B., 511
Zinn, Howard, 263
Zinner, Paul E., 420
Zipes, Jack, 608
Znaniecki, Florian, 190, 198, 204, 218, 219
Zochert, Donald, 620
Zoete, Beryl de, 520
Zorbaugh, Harvey, 192
Zotter, Josefa, 42
Zuckerman, Alan S., 418
Zuckerman, Harriet, 200
Zurcher, Arnold, 149
Zviadadze, Givi, 30
Zweig, Paul, 628
Zwinger, Ann, 620
Zysman, John, 132

Title Index

Titles of all books discussed in *The Reader's Adviser* are indexed here, except broad generic titles such as "Complete Works," "Selections," "Poems," "Correspondence." Also omitted is any title listed with a main-entry author that includes that author's name, e.g., *Collected Prose of T. S. Eliot*, and titles under "Books About," e.g., *Eliot's Early Years* by Lyndall Gordon. The only exception to this is Shakespeare (Volume 2), where all works by and about him are indexed. To locate all titles by and about a main-entry author, the user should refer to the Name Index for the author's primary listing (given in boldface). Whenever the name of a main-entry author is part of a title indexed here, the page reference is to a section other than the primary listing. In general, subtitles are omitted. When two or more identical titles by different authors appear, the last name of each author is given in parentheses following the title.

ASCAP Biographical Dictionary, 487
Abe Lincoln Grows Up, 59
Abigail Adams, 83
The Abolition of War, 327, 328
The Abortive Revolution, 447
Above the Battles, 304
Abraham Lincoln and the Union, 322
Abraham Lincoln: Citizen of New Salem, 324
The Abraham Lincoln Encyclopedia, 258
Abraham Lincoln: The Man behind the Myth, 274
Abraham Lincoln: The Prairie Years, 59
Abraham Lincoln: The Prairie Years and the War Years, 59
Abraham Lincoln: The War Years, 59

Abroad: British Literary Traveling between the Wars, 621
Absolutism and Democracy, 1814–1852, 468
The Absorbent Mind, 234
The Absorption of Immigrants, 196
Abstract of British Historical Statistics, 370
Abstracting and Indexing Services Directory, 4
Abundance for What?, 215
Academic American Encyclopedia, 2
The Academic Man, 198
The Academic Mind, 102, 151, 198, 208
The Academic Revolution, 215, 226
The Academic Scribblers, 124
The Academy Awards, 1927–1982, 577
Acceptable Risk, 199

Accessories after the Fact, 72
Accident at Three Mile Island, 195, 197
Account of the European Settlements in America, 387
Acculturation, 115
Acculturation in Seven Indian Tribes, 104
The Achievement Motive, 174
The Achieving Society, 174
Acquaintances, 479
The Acquisitive Society, 398
Acronyms, Initialisms, and Abbreviations Dictionary 1986–87, 4
Across the Wide Missouri, 270, 316
The Adams Chronicles (1750–1900), 307
The Adams Family, 308
Adaptation and Intelligence, 235
The Adenauer Era, 416

Adirondack Voices, 599
Administrative Behavior,
   150, 197
The Administrative State,
   150
Admiral Farragut, 471
Admiral of the Ocean Sea,
   328, 329, 355, 632
Adolescence: Its Psychology
   and Its Relations to
   Physiology, Anthropology,
   Sociology, Sex, Crime,
   Religion and Education,
   172, 179
The Adriatic, 621
Advanced Study in the
   History of Modern India,
   452
Adventure Roads North, 618
The Adventurer, 628
Adventures for Another
   World, 265
Adventures in Error, 648
Adventures in Freedom, 322
Adventures of a Ballet
   Historian, an Unfinished
   Memoir, 519
The Adventures of a
   Biographer, 49, 55
Aesthetics of Indian Folk
   Dance, 593
The Affluent Society, 102,
   135
Afghanistan, 440
Afghanistan and the Soviet
   Union, 440
Afghanistan: Highway of
   Conquest, 440
Africa: A Modern History,
   1800–1975, 444
Africa A to Z, 623
Africa and Africans, 441
Africa and Its Explorers, 624
Africa and the Caribbean,
   441
Africa and the Communist
   World, 441
Africa in History, 442
Africa in the Post-
   Decolonization Era, 441
Africa in the Twentieth
   Century, 441
Africa in World Politics, 443
Africa: Its People and Their
   Culture History, 121
The Africa Reader, 441

Africa since 1800, 444
Africa since 1875, 442
The African, 444
The African Adventure, 624
African Apprenticeship,
   624
The African-Arab Conflict in
   the Sudan, 444
African Art, 445
African Cities and Towns
   before the European
   Conquest, 442
The African Genius, 442
African History, 441
African Homicide and
   Suicide, 193
African Liberation
   Movements, 442
African Nationalism in the
   Twentieth Century, 468
African Oral Narratives,
   Proverbs, Riddles, Poetry
   and Song, 608
The African Past Speaks, 597
The African Political
   Dictionary, 444
African Political Systems,
   113
African Religions and
   Philosophy, 443
The African Slave Trade, 442
African Systems of Kinship
   and Marriage, 108
African Women, 443
Africanity, 443
Afro-American Folk Culture,
   606
Afro-American Folklore, 605
Afro-American History: A
   Bibliography, 260
After Imperialism: The
   Search for a New Order in
   the Far East, 446
After Secession, 315
Afterthoughts on Material
   Civilization and
   Capitalism, 459
Against Mediocrity, 225
Against the Stream, 212
Age and Anthropological
   Theory, 109, 189
The Age of Alexander, 248
Age of Alignment: Electoral
   Politics in Britain, 1922–
   1929, 382
The Age of Arthur, 371

The Age of Balfour and
   Baldwin, 1902–1940, 383
The Age of Catherine De
   Medici, 395, 415
The Age of Constantine the
   Great, 460
The Age of Discovery, 1400–
   1600, 418
Age of Improvement, 1783 to
   1867, 380
The Age of Jackson, 339
The Age of Nationalism, 468
The Age of Plantagenet and
   Valois, 373
The Age of Plunder, 374
The Age of Reason, 331
The Age of Reconnaissance,
   413
The Age of Reform, 269, 323
The Age of Revolution and
   Reaction, 1789–1850, 410
Age of Revolution, 1789–
   1848, 393
The Age of Roosevelt, 339
The Age of Television
   (Bogart), 190
The Age of Television
   (Esslin), 571
Aggression, 171
Aggression: A Social
   Psychological Analysis,
   170
Aging and Old Age, 202
Aging and Society, 189
Aging from Birth to Death,
   189
The Agrarian Origins of
   Modern Japan, 451
Agrarian Policies and Rural
   Poverty in Africa, 442
The Agricola and the
   Germania, 251
Agricultural Development
   and Economic Growth,
   126
The Agricultural Revolution,
   378
The Agricultural Systems of
   the World, 406
Aku-Aku, 636
Al Smith and His America,
   322
Alain Resnais, 578
Albion's Fatal Tree, 399
Album of American History,
   261, 307, 308

Alexander's Path, 647
Alfred the Great, 371
Alice James, 54
Alienation and Charisma, 203
Alistair Cooke's America, 262
All Faithful People, 198, 208
All for Love, 570
All God's Dangers, 53, 293
All in the Family, 569
All Our Children Learning, 224
All Passion Spent, 77
All Romanized English-Japanese Dictionary, 43
All Silver and No Brass, 607
All the President's Men, 280
Allen's Synonyms and Antonyms, 33
The Alliance: America, Europe, Japan, 449
Allied Intervention in Russia, 1917–1920, 420
Allusions—Cultural, Literary, Biblical, and Historical, 20
The Almanac of American History, 257, 340
The Almanac of American Politics, 15
Almanacs of the United States, 15
Alone, 630, 631
Along the Road, 616
Alphaville, 584
Alterations of Personality, 176
Alternative Voices: Essays on Contemporary Vocal and Choral Composition, 492
Alternatives to Regulation, 129
Always in Season, 599
Always the Young Strangers, 60
Amazing Journey of Space Ship H-30, 626
Ambassador's Journal, 136
America: A History, 322
America: A Narrative History, 263
America and the Image of Europe, 312

America and the World Revolution and Other Lectures, 479
America Arms for a New Century, 302
America at 1750, 323
America, Britain and Russia, 472
America Encounters Japan, 451
America Faces the Future, 309
America Goes to War, 313
America: History and Life, 253
America in Legend, 591
America in Midpassage, 309
America in Our Time, 282
America in Search of Itself, 284
America in the Twenties, 277
America in the Twentieth Century, 263
America Laughs, 610
America Now, 102
America Revised, 291
America, Russia, and the Cold War, 408
America the Quotable, 20
America through British Eyes, 330
America through Women's Eyes, 309
America To-Day, 340
The American, 308
American Architectural Books, 532
An American Architecture, 559
American Architecture since 1780, 533
American Art, Painting, Sculpture, Architecture, Decorative Arts, 529
American as Reformer, 339
American Bibliography, 259
American Bibliography, 1801–1819, 260
The American Bibliography of Slavic and East European Studies, 403
American Book of Days, 14
American Book Publishing Record, 4
The American-British, British-American

Dictionary with Helpful Hints to Travelers, 30
American Broadcasting, 572
American Buildings and Their Architects, 532
American Bureaucracy, 150
American Caesar, 279
The American Campaigns of Rochambeau's Army, 1780–1783, 267
American Capitalism (Galbraith), 127, 135
American Capitalism (Hacker), 321
American City Government, 309
The American Civil War, 274
American Civilization, 312
The American College Dictionary, 25
The American Commonwealth, 102, 159
The American Compromise, 254
The American Constitution, 296
The American Constitutional System, 152
American Counterpoint, 345
The American Cowboy, 603
An American Dilemma, 196, 212, 217
American Diplomacy in the Twentieth Century, 305
American Diplomacy, 1900–1950, 466
American Diplomatic History, 303
American Directors, 578
American Domestic Priorities, 132
American Economic History: A Guide to Information Sources, 259
American Education: The Colonial Experience, 1607–1783, 225
American Education: The National Experience, 1783–1876, 225, 290
American Epoch, 262
The American Family in Social-Historical Perspective, 291
American Federalism, 151
American Film Genres, 577

American Film Now, 577
American Folk Art, 592, 607
American Folk Sculpture, 607
American Folklife, 592
American Folklore (Dorson), 105
American Folklore (Flanagan and Flanagan), 592
American Folklore and the Historian, 607
American Foreign Policy, 304
American Foreign Policy: A Documentary History, 303
American Foreign Policy and the Blessings of Liberty, and Other Essays, 311
American Foreign Policy in the Making, 1932–1940, 309
American Foreign Policy: Patterns and Process, 304
American Foreign Relations, 253
American Heritage Book of Great Historic Places, 313
American Heritage Book of the Revolution, 313
The American Heritage Desk Dictionary, 25
The American Heritage Dictionary of the English Language, 25
American Heritage Picture History of the Civil War, 313
American Heroine, 285
American Higher Education, 226
American Higher Education, 1945–1970, 228
The American Historian, 254
American Historians, 1607–1865, 253
American History: A Survey, 262
American History: Retrospect and Prospect, 253
American Humorists, 1800–1950, 611
American Ideals and Other Essays, 336
American Ideals versus the New Deal, 69

American Immigration Collection, Series 1, 322
The American Indian, 111
The American Indian and the United States, 261
American Indian Environments, 254
American Indian Leaders, 290
American Indian Myth and Legends, 604
The American Indian Reader, 289
The American Indian: Stereotypes of Native Americans in Films, 575
American Indians, 291
The American Inquisition, 304
American Intellectual Histories and Historians, 286, 310, 311, 329
American Interests and Policies in the Middle East, 1900–1939, 303
The American Jewish Yearbook, 15, 428
American Jews and the Zionist Idea, 427
American Journey, 342
American Leadership in World Affairs, 282
American Legal Culture, 1908–1940, 286
American Library Directory, 4
American Military Thought, 328
The American Mind, 314
The American Movie Industry, 574
The American Music Handbook, 490
American Music since 1910, 515
American Myth, American Reality, 254
The American Nation, 262
The American Negro, 115
American Newspaper Journalists, 567
American Newspapers in the Nineteen Eighties, 566
The American Occupation of Germany, 416

The American Occupational Structure, 203
The American People and Foreign Policy, 155
The American People in the Twentieth Century, 322
American Photographers and the National Parks, 618
American Policy toward Communist China, 1949–1969, 303
The American Political Dictionary, 258
American Political Terms, 258
The American Political Tradition, 299, 323
American Political Writing during the Founding Era, 1760–1805, 269
American Politics and Public Policy (Burnham and Weinberg), 156
American Politics and Public Policy (Sindler), 301
American Popular Culture, 612
The American Presidency, 301
The American Presidency: A Historical Bibliography, 258
The American President, 154
American Press Opinion, 330
An American Primer, 260, 312
American Profile, 1900–1909, 276
American Puritans, 326
American Reference Books Annual, 2, 4
American Reformers, 1815–1860, 269
The American Republic, 323
The American Revolution, 260
The American Revolution: Changing Perspectives, 266
The American Revolution: Explorations in the History of American Radicalism, 268
The American Revolution, 1775–1783, 265
The American Revolution Reconsidered, 267

American-Russian Relations, 1781–1947, 305
American-Russian Rivalry in the Far East, 1895–1914, 446
The American Science of Politics, 149
The American Secretaries of State and Their Diplomacy, 1776–1925, 311
American Singers, 493
American Social History as Recorded by British Travellers, 330
The American Soldier, 217, 218
The American South, 345
The American Spirit (Bailey), 253
The American Spirit (Beard and Beard), 309
American State Politics, 162
The American States during and after the Revolution, 1775–1798, 330
American Statesmen, 340
American Statistics Index, 12
American Strategy in World War II, 408
The American Style of Foreign Policy, 303
The American System, 151
The American Thesaurus of Slang, 31
American Thought: The Civil War to World War I, 326
American Transcendentalists, 327
The American University, 228
The American University as an Instrument of Republican Culture, 321
An American Utopian, 211
American Violence, 261, 324
The American Voter, 153
The American Way of War, 409
The American West, 254
American Women Artists, 531
American Women in Jazz, 494

The Americans (Boorstin), 262, 312
The Americans (Handlin), 321, 322
The Americans and the French, 460
Americans and the Soviet Experiment, 1917–1933, 422
Americans as Proconsuls, 452
Americans in Transition, 224
The Americans: The Colonial Experience, 312
The Americans: The Democratic Experience, 312
The Americans: The National Experience, 312
America's Ascent, 276
America's Failure in China, 1941–1950, 449
America's Families, 261
America's Foreign Policy, 1945–1976, 305
America's Frontier Heritage, 289
America's Grand Resort Hotels, 619
America's Great Frontiers and Sections, 343
America's Jews, 431
America's Longest War, 282
America's Music, 485
America's One Hundred One Most High Falutin', Big Talkin' Knee Slappin', Golly Whoppers and Tall Tales, 599
America's Quest for the Ideal Self, 285
America's Struggle against Poverty, 1900–1980, 288
The Anabasis, 246
The Anabasis of Alexander and the Indica, 247
The Analysis of Behavior, 185
The Analytical Greek Lexicon Revised, 42
Analytical Index to Publications of the Texas Folklore Society, 602
Analyzing Electoral History, 298
Anarchism, 150

Anarchist Women, 150
The Anarchists in the Russian Revolution, 420
The Anatomy of Racial Attitudes, 196
The Anatomy of Revolution, 460
The Anchor Atlas of World History, 404
The Ancien Regime: French Society, 1600–1750, 414
Ancient Athenian Maritime Courts, 244
The Ancient Economy, 243
Ancient Egyptian Literature, 239
The Ancient Egyptians, 239
Ancient Greece and Rome, 241
The Ancient Greeks: A Critical History, 239
The Ancient Greeks: An Introduction to Their Life and Thought, 240
The Ancient History of Western Civilization, 238
Ancient Ideals, 478
Ancient Iraq, 438
Ancient Judaism, 199, 220
Ancient Law, 117, 118
The Ancient Maya, 354
Ancient Maya Civilization, 354
The Ancient Near East, 239
Ancient Russia, 482
Ancient Society, 120
And Keep Your Powder Dry, 110, 119
And Music at the Close, 514
And Other Neighborly Names, 602
The Andaman Islanders, 111, 121
Andrew Jackson and the Course of American Freedom, 1822–1832, 272
Angles, Angels and Conquerors, 400–1154, 371
Anglo-Norman England, 1066–1154, 368
The Anglo-Saxon Age, 371
The Anglo-Saxon Chronicle, 371
An Anglo-Saxon Dictionary, 37
Anglo-Saxon England, 371

Anglo-Saxon Saints and Scholars, 371
The Animal in Its World, 186
The Animated Film, 577
The Annals of America, 260
The Annals of Imperial Rome, 251
Annals of Opera, 1597–1940, 495
Annals of Politics and Culture, 1492–1899, 465
An Annotated Bibliography on the Modern History of the Near East, 433
Annual Bibliography of British and Irish History, 389
The Annual Register 1984, 16
Annual Review of Anthropology, 104
Annual Review of Psychology, 170
Annual Review of Sociology, 188
Another Chance, 282
Another Part of the Twenties, 276
Another Sheaf of White Spirituals, 594
Anthology of Medieval Music, 485
An Anthology of Wit, 609
Anthropological Approaches to the Study of Religion, 109
An Anthropologist at Work, 104, 111, 119
Anthropologists in the Field, 104
Anthropology: An Introduction to the Study of Man and Civilization, 123
Anthropology and Modern Life, 112
Anthropology: Culture, Patterns, and Processes, 115
The Anthropology of Dance, 520
The Anthropology of Music, 493
Anthropology Today, 103
The Antifederalists, 296

Anti-Intellectualism in American Life, 269, 323
Anti-Politics in America, 298
Anti-Semite and Jew, 430
Anti-Semitism in America, 197
Antisemitism in Modern France, 427
Antislavery Reconsidered, 271
The Antitrust Paradox, 127
Apes and Angels, 380
Apollo in the Democracy, 542
An Apology for Printers, 64
Appleton's New Cuyas Dictionary, 46
Applied Network Analysis, 188
Applied Science and Technology Index, 2
Approaches to the Study of Social Structure, 201
Approaches to Writing, 324
Aptitude Testing, 180
The Arab Awakening, 438
The Arab-Israeli Dilemma, 438
The Arab Mind, 438
Arab Oil, 439
The Arab World, 439
The Arab World Today, 438
The Arab World's Legacy, 438
The Arabian Night, 630
The Arabian Nights, 629
The Arabian Peninsula, 438
Arabic-English Dictionary of the Modern Literary Language, 38
Arabic Thought in the Liberal Age, 1798–1939, 432, 438
The Archaeology of Easter Island, 636
The Archaeology of Greece, 242
Archaic and Classical Greece, 241
Archaic and Classical Greek Coins, 242
Archaic Egypt, 239
Archaic Greece: The Age of Experiment, 240
Archaic Greece: The City-States c.700–500 B.C, 240

Architects and Firms, 198
The Architectural Interpretation of History, 531
Architectural Principles in the Age of Humanism, 533
Architecture in the Age of Reason, 532
Architecture: 19th and 20th Centuries, 527
The Architecture of the Italian Renaissance, 460
The Architecture of the Roman Empire, 242
The Architecture of the United States, 533
Arctic Adventure, 634
Argentina, 360
Argonauts of the Western Pacific, 111, 118
Argonauts to Astronauts, 627
Aristocracy and People, 391
Arizona Adventure, 603
The Armada, 375, 472
Armaments and Arbitration, 471
The Armed Forces of the USSR, 409
The Armies of the Streets, 272
Arms and Independence, 266
Arms and Insecurity, 157
Arms and Men, 327, 328
Arms and Politics, 1958–1978, 409
Arms and the State, 328
Arms for Arabs, 438
The Army Air Forces in World War II, 407
The Army, James II and the Glorious Revolution, 376
The Army of the Potomac, 313
Around the World in Eighty Ways, 616
Art and Architecture in Italy, 1600–1800, 527
The Art and Architecture of Medieval Russia, 531
Art and Civilization, 528
Art and Illusion, 528
The Art and Science of Negotiation, 193
The Art and Science of Radio, 570

Art and Visual Perception, 174, 527
Art in Mediaeval France, 987–1498, 529
Art in Our Times, 530
Art Index, 2, 527
Art, Mind, and Brain, 189
The Art of Autobiography in Nineteenth and Twentieth Century England, 49
The Art of Biography, 50
The Art of Diplomacy, 302
The Art of Easter Island, 636
The Art of Humanism, 529
The Art of Japanese Management, 451
The Art of Rome, 529
Art of the Byzantine Era, 530
The Art of the Incas and Its Origins, 355
The Art of the Maya, 355
Art of the Medieval World, 531
The Art of War, 165
Art through the Ages, 528
Artificial Intelligence and Natural Man, 173
Arts and Humanities Citation Index, 4
Arts in America, 530
The Arts of China, 530
The Arts of India, 530
The Arts of Japan, 530
Arts, Sciences, Alloys, 517
As He Saw It, 92
As It Happened, 573
As Long as the Sun Shines and Water Flows, 349
As Old as the Moon, 598
Asia in the Modern World, 446
Asia Reference Works, 405
Asian Drama, 212, 446
The Asians, 446
Aspects of Caste in South India, Ceylon and North West Pakistan, 105
Aspects of Central African History, 444
Aspects of Death in Early Greek Art and Poetry, 240
Assault on Eternity, 631
Assault on the Media, 568
Asset Accumulation and Economic Activity, 126

Associations' Publications in Print 1984–1985, 4
Asylums: Essays on the Social Situation of Mental Patients and Other Inmates, 197, 207
At Dawn We Slept, 279
At Ease, 62
At General Howe's Side, 1776–1778, 267
At Odds, 290
Athenian Culture and Society, 240
The Athenian Empire, 240
Atlantic High, 625
The Atlantic Slave Trade, 441
The Atlantic Slave Trade and British Abolition, 1760–1810, 377
The Atlas of American History (Adams), 307
Atlas of American History (Jackson), 256
Atlas of British History, 369
Atlas of Early American History, 255
An Atlas of Irish History, 369
The Atlas of Modern History to 1815, 404
An Atlas of Russian History, 404, 421
Atlas of the Arab-Israeli Conflict, 428
The Atomic Bomb, 407
Attack and Die, 273
Attic Red-Figure Vase-Painters, 534
Audience Ratings, 570
Augustan History, 249
Augustine of Hippo, 244
The Authoritarian Personality, 175
Authority in the Modern State, 162
The Autobiography of an Idea, 554
The Autobiography of an Unknown Indian, 452
The Autobiography of LeRoi Jones-Amiri Baraka, 51
Autocrats and Academics, 424
Autonomous Technology, 200

Awards, Honors, and Prizes, 5
Awareness of Dying, 195
The Awesome Power, 80
The Azande, 113
Aztec Art, 354
The Aztecs of Central Mexico, 353
Aztecs of Mexico, 355
The Aztecs under Spanish Rule, 357

Back to the City, 202
Backwoods Utopia, 203
The Bad Guys: A Pictorial History of the Movie Villain, 576
The Bagatelles from Passy, 64
Baghdad, 433
A Baghdad Chronicle, 433
Baker's Biographical Dictionary of Musicians, 491
Balanchine's Complete Stories of the Great Ballets, 519
The Balfour Declaration, 431
Balinese Character, 119
The Balkans in Our Time, 420
The Balkans since 1453, 420
The Ballad Mongers, 593
Ballads and Songs of Indiana, 601
Ballads Migrant in New England, 599
Ballet and Dance, 520
Ballet: Bias and Belief, 524
Balletomania, 518
Ballets of Today, 519
Ballets Past and Present, 519
The Baltic States, 424
Bandits, 393
Bankers and Pashas, 436
Banned Films, 576
Banners at Shenandoah, 313
Barbara Stanwyck, 578
The Barnhart Dictionary of New English since 1963, 25, 30
Baroque and Rococo in Latin America, 530
Bartholomew World Atlas, 18

Bartlett's Familiar Quotations, 20
Basic Books in the Mass Media, 561
Basic Documents in American History, 261
The Basic English-Chinese, Chinese-English Dictionary, 38
A Basic History of Modern Russia, 468
Basic Japanese Conversation Dictionary, 43
Basic Skills: A Guide for Parents and Teachers on the Subjects Most Vital to Education, 226
Basic Skills: A Plan for Your Child, A Program for All Children, 227
Basic Writings in the History of Psychology, 170
The Battle for Peace, 435
The Battle for Public Opinion, 566
The Battle of Dienbienphu, 455
Battle: The Story of the Bulge, 409
Battles Lost and Won: Great Campaigns of World War II, 407
Bauhaus, 542
The Bay of Pigs, 362
The Bayeux Tapestry, 372
Bear Went Over the Mountain, 609
Beauty and the Beast, 581
Beaverbrook, 478
The Becket Controversy, 372
Becoming American, 289
Becoming Visible: Women in European History, 410
Been in the Storm So Long, 273
Before Color Prejudice, 239
Before Philosophy, 239
Before the Armada, 375
Before the Colors Fade, 569
Before the Industrial Revolution, 411
Before the Mayflower, 265
Before the Trumpet, 92
Begin, 54

Beginners' Dictionary of Chinese-Japanese Characters, 38
The Beginnings of Architecture, 531
The Beginnings of English Society, 371
The Beginnings of National Politics, 267
The Beginnings of the American People, 310
Behavior: An Introduction to Comparative Psychology, 186
Behavior and Evolution, 107
Behavior in Public Places, 194
The Behavior of Organisms, 174, 185
A Behavior System, 180
The Behavioral and Social Sciences, 99
A Behavioral Approach to Historical Analysis, 402
A Behavioral Theory of the Firm, 197
Behaviorism, 174, 186
Behemoth, 157
Behind Mud Walls, 1930–1960, 454
Behind Russian Lines, 440
Behind the Lines: Hanoi, December 23–January 7, 455
Behind the Mirror, 182
Being an Anthropologist, 104
Bell and Cohn's Handbook of Grammar, Style and Usage, 30
Belle de Jour, 580
Ben-Gurion, 427
Beneath Cold Seas, 627
Benefit-Cost Analysis of Social Regulation, 129
Berlin Crisis of 1961, 74
The Berlin Diary, 417
The Best and the Brightest, 72, 303
Between Oxus and Jumna, 479
Between Past and Future, 456
Beyond Boom and Crash, 130

Beyond Despair: A Policy Guide to the Communication Era, 565
Beyond Freedom and Dignity, 185
Beyond Geography, 343
Beyond Hatred, 466
Beyond Human Scale, 128
Beyond Positivism, 125
Beyond Separate Spheres, 203
Beyond Suffrage, 280
Beyond the East Wind, 598
Beyond the Melting Pot, 195
Beyond the Nation-State, 155
Beyond the Wall, 618
Beyond the Welfare State, 212
Bias in Mental Testing, 173
Bible and Sword, 481
The Bible in Spain, 628
Bibliographic Guide to Latin American Studies, 352
Bibliographic Guide to Soviet and East European Studies, 403
Bibliographic Index, 5
Bibliographical Handbook on Tudor England, 368
Bibliographies in American History, 1942–1978, 258
A Bibliography of American Autobiographers, 49
A Bibliography of American Autobiography, 1945–1980, 49
Bibliography of Black Music, 488
Bibliography of British History (Pargellis and Medley), 368
Bibliography of British History (Read), 368
Bibliography of British History, 1789–1851, 368
Bibliography of British History, 1851–1914, 368
Bibliography of British Social and Economic History, 368
A Bibliography of Computer Music, 492
Bibliography of Discographies, 489

Bibliography of Early
American Architecture,
533
A Bibliography of English
History to 1485, 368
A Bibliography of Modern
History, 405
Bibliography of the History
of Technology, 404
Bibliography of Tourism and
Travel Research Studies,
Reports and Articles, 614
The Big Bands, 494
Big Science, Little Science,
200
Big Structures, Large
Processes, Huge
Comparisons, 200
Biographical Dictionary of
Afro-American and African
Musicians, 491
Biographical Dictionary of
American Architects
(Deceased), 534
Biographical Dictionary of
American Music, 488
A Biographical Dictionary of
British Architects, 1600–
1840, 533
Biographical Dictionary of
Chinese Communism,
1921–1965, 448
Biographical Dictionary of
Dance, 519
Biographical Dictionary of
Film, 578
Biographical Dictionary of
Jazz, 488
Biographical Dictionary of
World War II, 409
Biographical Directory of
American Colonial and
Revolutionary Governors,
1607–1789, 257
Biographical Directory of
the American Congress,
1774–1971, 255
Biographical Directory of
the United States
Executive Branch, 1774–
1977, 255
Biography Index, 2, 5, 50
Biography News, 50
A Biography of the
Constitution of the United
States, 296

Biography: The Craft and
the Calling, 49, 55
Biological and Agricultural
Index, 2
Biological Bases of
Individual Behavior, 171
Biological Studies of Mental
Processes, 171
Biology and Knowledge, 235
Biology of Man in History,
411
Bird, 510
Bird Lives, 510
The Birth of a Dilemma, 443
Birth of Methodism in
England, 392
The Birth of the Bill of
Rights, 1776–1791, 296
The Birth of the English
Common Law, 372
The Birth of the Nation, 268,
338
The Birth of the Talkies, 576
The Birth of Vietnam, 455
Bismarck (Crankshaw), 52
Bismarck (Taylor), 478
Bismarck and the German
Empire, 416
Bitter Fruit, 363
The Bitter Heritage, 339
The Bitter Woods, 407
Black Artists in the United
States, 531
Black Bourgeoisie, 287
Black Boy, 294
Black Byzantium, 111
Black Chronology, 14
Black Colleges and
Universities, 225
Black Culture and Black
Consciousness, 606
Black Dance in the United
States from 1619 to 1970,
520
Black Death, 374
A Black Diplomat in Haiti,
85
Black Folk Art in America,
1930–1980, 606
Black Folk Then and Now,
318
Black Images in American
Films, 1896–1954, 577
Black Jacobins, 363
Black Leaders in Southern
African History, 444

Black Leaders of the
Twentieth Century, 256,
320
Black Market, 193
Black Migration in America,
292
Black Mother, 268
Black Music in America, 606
The Black Muslims in
America, 195
Black North in 1901, 318
Black Politics in South
Africa since 1945, 443
Black Power in South Africa,
442
Black Protest Politics in
South Africa to 1912, 443
Black Reconstruction in
America, 1860–1880, 318
Blackberry Winter, 120
Blackfoot Lodge Tales, 604
Blacks and White TV, 572
Blacks and Whites, 195, 196
The Blacks in America,
1492–1977, 257
Blacks in Antiquity, 239, 444
The Blast of War, 1939–
1945, 74
The Blood of Abraham, 432
The Blood of the People, 455
The Bloodless Revolution,
377
Blooming, 54
Bloomsbury, 60
Blossoms in the Dust, 126
Blow-Up, 579
The Blue and the Gray, 314
The Blue Angel, 588
Blue Highways, 619
Body, Boots, and Britches,
600
The Boer War, 381
Bogey, 580
The Bold and Magnificent
Dream, 313
Bolivar, 358
Bolivia: The Evolution of a
Multi-Ethnic Society, 360
Bolivia: The Uncompleted
Revolution, 360
The Bolsheviks, 426
The Bolshoi Ballet, 520
Bon Ton, 65
Bonaparte in Egypt, 57
The Book of Abigail and
John, 82

The Book of America, 257
The Book of Calendars, 14
The Book of Indian Crafts
  and Indian Lore, 604
The Book of Lists #3, 14
Book of Negro Humor, 605
The Book of Similes, 35
The Book of Slang, 31
Book of the Eskimos, 634
The Book of the Piano, 496
The Book of the Violin, 496
The Book of World Famous
  Music: Classical, Popular
  and Folk, 489
Book Review Digest, 2, 5
Book Review Index, 5
Booker T. Washington, 52
Booker T. Washington and
  His Critics, 319
Books for College Libraries,
  405
Books in English on the
  Soviet Union, 1917–1973,
  404
Books in Print, 5
Books in Series, 5
Books in World History,
  405
Books, Libraries, and
  Electronics, 563
Books: The Culture and
  Commerce of Publishing,
  189, 190
Booms and Depressions, 134
Born under Saturn, 531
The Borzoi Book of French
  Folk Tales, 596
Boss Platt and His New York
  Machine, 337
Boston's Immigrants, 322
Botswana, 444
Bowker's Complete
  Sourcebook of Personal
  Computing 1985, 5
Boyhood on the Upper
  Mississippi, 641
The Brandeis/Frankfurter
  Connection, 296
Breach of Faith, 284
Bread and Circuses, 611
Breaking the Magic Spell,
  608
Breaking the Sound Barrier,
  492
Breakthrough: A Personal
  Account of the Egypt-

Israel Peace Negotiations,
  435
The Brethren, 302
The Bridge and the Abyss,
  470
Brierfield, 316
Brigham Young: American
  Moses, 51
Bringing Back the Parties,
  301
Britain: An Official
  Handbook, 16
Britain in the Nineteen
  Twenties, 382
Britain in Transition, 383
Britain since 1918, 383
Britain through American
  Eyes, 315
Britannia, 371
Britannica Book of English
  Usage, 31
Britannica Book of the Year,
  16
Britannica Junior
  Encyclopaedia for Boys
  and Girls, 2
British and Irish
  Separatism, 383
British Autobiographies, 50
British Books in Print, 6
The British Broadside Ballad
  and Its Music, 491
The British Campaign in
  Ireland, 1919–1921, 384
British Cinema History,
  576
The British Diplomatic
  Service, 1815–1914, 381
The British Empire, 1558–
  1983, 370
British Factory, Japanese
  Factory, 450
British Folktales, 596
British Historical Facts,
  1830–1900, 369
British Labour Movement,
  398
British Military Intelligence,
  1870–1914, 380
British Policy and the
  Turkish Reform
  Movement, 439
British Political Facts, 1900–
  1974, 369
British Population Growth,
  1700–1850, 369

British Public Policy, 1776–
  1939, 369
The British Revolution,
  1880–1939, 383
British Society and the
  French Wars, 1793–1815,
  378
British Society since 1945,
  383
The Broadcast Industry, 565
Broadcast Journalism, 1979–
  81, 568
Broadcasting/Cablecasting
  Yearbook, 561
Broadcasting in America,
  571
Broadcasting in the United
  States, 572
The Broken Spears, 355
Brother Ray, 502
Brothers and Strangers, 427
Bruckner, Mahler,
  Schoenberg, 486
Brueckner's French
  Contextuary, 39
Buckle at the Ballet, 518
The Budgetary Process in
  the United States, 132
The Buffalo Soldiers, 275
Builders of the Bay Colony,
  329
Bukharin and the Bolshevik
  Revolution, 421
The Bull Moose Years, 337
A Bunch of Old Letters, 474
The Burden of Southern
  History, 344, 345
Bureaucracy and Political
  Development, 150
The Bureaucratic
  Phenomenon, 150
Bureaucratic Reform in the
  Ottoman Empire, 439
Burrelle's Black Media
  Directory, 1984, 561
Burrelle's Hispanic Media
  Directory, 1984, 561
Burrelle's Women's Media
  Directory, 1984, 561
Burt Lancaster, 578
Bury My Heart at Wounded
  Knee, 274
The Bus Trip Handbook, 615
Business and Politics under
  James I, 398
Business-Cycle Theory, 136

Business Cycles, 131, 143
Business Cycles and
  National Income, 136, 143
Business Periodicals Index, 2
The Business Traveler's
  Survival Guide, 615
The Butterflies Carried Him
  Home and Other Indian
  Tales, 597
The Buying and Selling of
  America's Newspapers,
  566
Byzantium and the Decline
  of Rome, 240

CIS Congressional
  Committee Hearings
  Index, 12
CIS/Index and CIS Annual,
  12
CIS U.S. Serial Set Index, 13
CQ Almanac, 16
Cadres, Bureaucracy, and
  Political Power in
  Communist China, 458
Cairo, 436
Calculus of Consent, 132, 153
Calked Boots and Other
  Northwest Writings, 603
Call to Greatness, 93
The Calling of Sociology,
  215
The Cambridge Ancient
  History, 238
Cambridge Economic
  History of Europe, 410
The Cambridge History of
  Africa, 441
The Cambridge History of
  India, 452
Cambridge History of Iran,
  437
Cambridge History of Islam,
  434
The Cambridge History of
  Latin America, 356
The Cambridge Italian
  Dictionary, 42
Cambridge Modern History,
  384, 465
The Camera Never Blinks,
  569
Campaign '84, 568
Campaigning for Congress,
  299

The Campaigns of
  Alexander, 247
Canada, 347
Canada North, 619
Canada since 1945, 349
Canadian Almanac and
  Directory, 16, 347
Canadian Books in Print, 6
The Canadian Centenary
  Series, 347
The Canadian Frontier,
  1534–1821, 348
The Canadians, 348
Cannibals and Kings, 105
Canton under Communism,
  449
The Cape Coloured People,
  1652–1937, 443
Capital, 126, 129, 133, 140,
  141
Capital and Employment,
  126
Capital and Growth, 129,
  137
Capital and Interest, 126
Capital Punishment in the
  United States, 193
Capitalism and Freedom,
  126, 135
Capitalism and Material
  Life, 1400–1800, 459
Capitalism and Modern
  Social Theory, 221
Capitalism and the
  Historians, 137
Capitalism and the State in
  Modern France, 414
Capitalism and the Welfare
  State, 127
Capitalism, Slavery, and
  Republican Values, 271
Capitalism, Socialism and
  Democracy, 127, 152, 157
Captain Swing, 393
The Captive Mind, 157
Career Change in Midlife,
  203
Career Opportunities in
  Television and Video, 572
Career Patterns in
  Education, 227
The Caribbean, 359
Carmichael's Manual of
  Child Psychology, 173
The Carter Years, 280

The Case for the League of
  Nations, 96
Cassell's Compact French-
  English, English-French
  Dictionary, 39
Cassell's Concise Spanish
  Dictionary (Spanish-
  English and English-
  Spanish), 46
Cassell's German-English,
  English-German
  Dictionary, 40
Cassell's Italian Dictionary,
  43
Cassell's New German
  Dictionary (German-
  English and English-
  German), 40
Cassell's Spanish-English,
  English-Spanish
  Dictionary, 46
Caste and Class in a
  Southern Town, 105, 176,
  177
Caste and Kinship in Central
  India, 105
Caste and the Economic
  Frontier, 105, 107
Castlereagh, 378
Catal Huyuk, 239
Catalog of Books Relating to
  the Discovery and Early
  History of North and
  South America, 259
A Catalog of Phonorecording
  of Music and Oral Data
  Held by the Archives of
  Traditional Music, 594
A Catalogue of the Books of
  John Quincy Adams
  Deposited in the Boston
  Athenaeum, 306
Cathedrals of France, 553
Catherine of Aragon, 472
Catherine the Great, 54
Catherine the Great and
  Other Studies, 465
Catherine the Great and the
  Expansion of Russia, 425
Catholic Almanac 1985, 16
Causal Inferences in
  Nonexperimental
  Research, 100
Causes of Delinquency, 193
The Causes of the English
  Revolution, 398

The Cave Divers, 625
A Celebration of American
    Family Folklore, 598
Celtic Britain, 371
Centennial History, 313
Center and Periphery, 215
Central America, 360
Central America and the
    Western Alliance, 358
Central Asia, 445
Central Problems in Social
    Theory, 188
The Centralist Tradition of
    Latin America, 359
Centuries of Childhood, 195,
    410
Centuries of Santa Fe, 324
A Century of Political
    Cartoons, 330
Century of Progress, 309
The Century of Revolution,
    1603–1714, 393
A Century of Russian
    Agriculture, 426
The Century of Total War,
    457
Chaim Weizmann, 435
Chairman Mao Talks to the
    People, 448
The Challenge of Anne
    Boleyn, 56
The Challenge to Liberty, 69
Challenges of Change, 569
Challenging Colonialism,
    432
Chambers Atlas of World
    History, 404
Chambers Twentieth
    Century Dictionary, 25
Chamulas in the World of
    the Sun, 604
Chan Kom, 122
Chance or Destiny, 322
A Chance to Learn, 294
Change and Continuity in
    Seventeenth-Century
    England, 393
Change and Habit, 479
Changes: Notes on
    Choreography, 522
The Changing American
    Voter, 153
The Changing Anatomy of
    Britain, 384
The Changing Culture of an
    Indian Tribe, 104

The Changing Newspaper,
    566
Changing of the Guard, 298
The Changing Population of
    the United States, 218
Channels of Power, 568
Chapters in the
    Administrative History of
    Medieval England, 399
The Character and Influence
    of the Indian Trade in
    Wisconsin, 343
Characters of the
    Reformation, 386
Charities and Social Aid in
    Greece and Rome, 243
Charles Beard and the
    Constitution, 151
Charles I and the Popish
    Plot, 376
Charles James Fox, 378
Charles Stewart Parnell,
    381
Charles Sumner and the
    Coming of the Civil War,
    270
Chartism, 382
Chasin the Trane, 503
Checklist of United States
    Public Documents 1789–
    1909, 12
The Cheechako, 599
The Cheese and the Worms,
    411
Chicago Lawyers, 198
The Chicago Manual of
    Style, 22
Chicago School of
    Architecture, 554
The Chicago School of
    Sociology, 187
The Chief Executive, 300
The Child and Reality, 235
The Child and the
    Curriculum, 231
Child Development and
    Education, 235
The Child in the Family, 234
Child-Lore, 608
Child Training and
    Personality, 106
Childhood and Folklore, 603
Childhood and Society, 172,
    177, 178
Childhood Socialization, 202
Children and Television, 571

Children in English Society,
    370
The Children of Pride, 273
The Children of Sánchez,
    117
Children of the Uprooted,
    321, 322
Children, Television, and
    Sex-Role Stereotyping, 573
Children's Television, 573
The Child's Conception of
    Number, 235
The Child's Conception of
    Physical Causality, 235
The Child's Conception of
    the World, 184, 235
The Child's Construction of
    Knowledge, 235
Chile, 361
The Chilean Way, 620
China, 469
China: A Critical
    Bibliography, 404
China: A Short Cultural
    History, 447
China after Mao, 458
China and Russia, 421
China and the West, 447
The China Clippers, 617
China Diary, 624
China in Crisis, 447, 449
China Journal, 623
China on the Eve of the
    Communist Takeover, 458
China Perceived, 464
China: The Other
    Communism, 448
China: The People's Middle
    Kingdom and the U.S.A.,
    464
China: The Revolution
    Continued, 448
China: Tradition and
    Transformation, 464
Chinabound, 464
China's Economic
    Revolution, 447
China's Economy in Global
    Perspective, 458
China's Future, 449
China's Nation Building
    Effort, 1927–1937, 449
The Chinese (Bonavia),
    447
The Chinese (Latourette),
    468

Chinese-American Interactions, 464
Chinese Civilization and Society, 447
The Chinese Communist Army in Action, 408
Chinese Communist Politics in Action, 458
Chinese-English Dictionary of Contemporary Usage, 38
Chinese-English Dictionary of Modern Usage, 39
Chinese/English Phrase Book For Travellers, 39
Chinese Exclusion versus the Open Door Policy, 1900–1906, 337
Chinese Family and Kinship, 446
Chinese Intellectuals and the West, 1872–1949, 449
The Chinese Looking Glass, 447
Chinese Painting, 530
A Chinese View of China, 447
Chinese World Order, 464
Ch'ing Administration, 464
The Choice before Us, 341
The Choices, 340, 341
The Choking Doberman and Other "New" Urban Legends, 607
Choreographer and Composer, 521
The Christian Life in the Middle Ages and Other Essays, 397
Christianity and Islam under the Sultans, 439
Christianity in a Revolutionary Age, 469
Christianity in Roman Britain to A.D. 500, 371
Christianity through the Ages, 469
Christians and Jews in Germany, 431
Christmas Customs around the World, 608
Christopher Columbus, Mariner, 328, 329
Chronicle of the Kings of England from the Earliest to King Stephen, 400

A Chronology of World History, 406
The Chrysanthemum and the Sword, 110, 111, 449
Church and People, 1450–1600, 374
Church and Society in England, 1770–1970, 370
Church and State in Tudor Ireland, 374
The Churchill Coalition, 1940–1945, 383
Churchill, Roosevelt, Stalin, 407, 422
The Churchills, 397
Churchmen and the Condition of England, 1832–1885, 380
The Cicerone, 460, 621
Cincinnatus, 94, 270
The Cinema as a Graphic Art, 577
Cinema, the Magic Vehicle, 574
Cities and Sea-Coasts and Islands, 622
Cities and the Wealth of Nations, 202
Cities in Revolt, 264
Cities on the Move, 479
City (Park), 202
The City (Weber), 203
The City in History, 202
The City of the Saints, 629
City People, 285
The Civic Culture, 154
The Civic Culture Revisited, 154
Civil Liberties Under Attack, 314
The Civil War (Caesar), 249
The Civil War (Catton), 313
The Civil War: A Narrative, 273
The Civil War and Reconstruction, 274
Civil War Books, 260
The Civil War Day by Day, 256
The Civil War Dictionary, 257
Civilization in the West, 460
The Civilization of the Renaissance in Italy, 460
Civilization on Trial, 479

Civilization Past and Present, 406
Civilizations of Black Africa, 443
Class and Class Conflict in Industrial Society, 192
Class Awareness in the United States, 102
Class Conflict in Egypt, 1945–1970, 436
Class Conflict, Slavery, and the United States Constitution, 296
The Class Struggle in the Ancient Greek World, 239
Classical and Foreign Quotations, 21
Classical Arab Islam, 434
A Classical Dictionary of the Vulgar Tongue, 32
The Classical Heritage of the Middle Ages, 478
The Classical Language of Architecture, 532
The Classical Style, 486
Classical Traditions in Early America, 607
Classics of the Horror Film, 576
Classics of the Silent Screen, 576
Classrooms in the Crossfire, 227
Clio and the Doctors, 402
Close Encounters, 569
The Cloud of Danger, 304
The Coal Question, 138
Coast of Many Faces, 350
Cobbett's Cyclopedic Survey of Chamber Music, 488
Codex Atlanticus, 544
The Cognitive Computer, 173
Cognitive Development, 171
Cognitive Sociology, 188
The Cold War, 164, 325
The Cold War as History, 304
The Cold War Begins, 281, 407
The Cold War, 1945–1972, 283
The Collapse of the Concert of Europe, 1890–1914, 408
The Collapse of the Weimar Republic, 415

A Collection of Classic
  Southern Humor Fiction
  and Occasional Fact by
  Some of the South's Best
  Story Tellers, 610
Collective Behavior, 190
Collective Violence, 193
Collectivist Economic
  Planning, 136
The College-Bred Negro
  American, 318
Collier's Encyclopedia, 2
Collins Contemporary Greek
  Dictionary, 42
Collins Gem Dictionary of
  Synonyms, 33
Collins-Robert French-
  English Dictionary, 39
Colombia, 361
Colonial Africa, 441
Colonial Merchants and the
  American Revolution,
  1763–1776, 338
Colonialism and
  Underdevelopment in
  Ghana, 442
Colonialism in Africa, 1870–
  1960, 442
Color and Democracy, 318
Color and Race, 320
The Colossus of Roads, 608
Columbia-Lippincott
  Gazetteer of the World, 19
The Comic Encyclopedia,
  610
Coming Apart, 283
Coming Fury, 313
Coming of Age in Samoa,
  119, 173
The Coming of Christianity
  to England, 371
The Coming of Industrial
  Order, 288
The Coming of Post-
  Industrial Society, 204,
  289
The Coming of the Civil
  War, 270
Coming of the French
  Revolution, 414
The Coming of the Mass
  Market, 1850–1914, 611
The Coming to Power,
  340
Commercial Atlas and
  Marketing Guide, 18

Commissars, Commanders,
  and Civilian Authority,
  421
Commitment and
  Community, 203
Committees in Congress, 301
Common Culture and the
  Great Tradition, 611
Common Errors in English
  and How to Avoid Them,
  31
A Common Faith, 231
The Common Law, 68, 69
The Common School and the
  Negro American, 318
Common Sense, 331
Common Sense and Other
  Political Writings, 331
Common Sense, the Rights
  of Man, and Other
  Essential Writings, 331
Commonwealth, 322
The Commonwealth of Art,
  486
The Commonwealth of
  Learning, 224, 314, 315
Commonwealth to
  Protectorate, 377
Communication: A Guide to
  Information Sources, 561
Communication and
  Education, 565
Communication and
  Organizations, 562
Communication and
  Persuasion, 174
Communication and Social
  Change in Developing
  Nations, 564
Communication and Social
  Structure, 564
Communication Models for
  the Study of Mass
  Communications, 564
Communication Networks,
  565
Communication
  Technologies and Society,
  565
Communication
  Technologies and the
  Information Flow, 564
Communications and
  Society, 191, 562
Communications and the
  Future, 563

Communications for
  Tomorrow, 565
Communications in
  Transition, 564
Communications Policy and
  the Political Process, 564
Communications Revolution,
  565
Communications Standard
  Dictionary, 562
Communications Technology
  in Education and
  Training, 563
Communications Tomorrow,
  563
Communism, Conformity
  and Civil Liberties, 151,
  218
Communism in Africa,
  440
Communism in Italy and
  France, 417
Communism in North
  Vietnam, 454
Communist China,
  458
Communist China and Asia,
  458
Communist China, 1955–59,
  464
Communist China, 1949–
  1969, 449
Communist China's Strategy
  in the Nuclear Era, 447
Communist Economic
  Strategy, 458
The Communist Manifesto,
  133, 134, 141
Communist Strategy and
  Tactics in Czechoslovakia,
  1918–48, 420
The Communist World and
  Ours, 325
Community and Society,
  192, 219
Community Conflict, 191,
  192
Community Power and
  Political Theory, 154, 192
Community Power
  Structure, 192
Companion to Russian
  Studies, 420
The Comparative Approach
  to American History, 254,
  345

Comparative Communication Research, 563

Comparative Frontiers, 254

Comparative Higher Education Abroad, 223

Comparative Methods in Psychology, 170

Comparative Politics Today, 445

Comparative Studies of How People Think, 171

The Complete Anti-Federalist, 297

Complete Book of Ballets, 519

Complete Book of Marvels, 616

The Complete Book of the Olympics, 15

The Complete Book of U.S. Presidents, 255

The Complete Encyclopedia of Popular Music and Jazz, 1900–1950, 489

The Complete Guide to Modern Dance, 519

Complete Presidential Press Conferences, 1933–1945, 91

The Complete Walker III, 626

A Composer's World, 506

A Comprehensive Bibliography of American Constitutional and Legal History, 1896–1979, 259

A Comprehensive Etymological Dictionary of the English Language, 36

Comprehensive Index to the Publications of the United States Government 1881–1893, 12

A Comprehensive Persian-English Dictionary, 38

The Compromised Scientist, 181

The Computer and the Brain, 147

Computer Processing of Social Science Data Using OSIRIS IV, 101

Computers and Composing, 562

Computers and Privacy in the Next Decade, 564

The Concept of Law, 155

The Concept of the Corporation, 128

A Concise Anglo-Saxon Dictionary, 37

A Concise Biographical Dictionary of Singers, from the Beginning of Recorded Sound to the Present, 490, 496

The Concise Cambridge Italian Dictionary, 43

The Concise Columbia Encyclopedia, 3

Concise Dictionary of American History, 258

A Concise Dictionary of English Idioms, 32

Concise Dictionary of English Slang, 33

Concise Dictionary of Spoken Chinese, 38

A Concise Economic History of Britain, 388

A Concise Encyclopedia of Antiques, 535

Concise Encyclopedia of Jewish Music, 490

A Concise Encyclopedia of the Italian Renaissance, 404

Concise Encyclopedia of the Middle East, 404

Concise Etymological Dictionary of the English Language, 37

A Concise History of American Architecture, 533

Concise History of Avant Garde Music, 492

A Concise History of Modern Painting, 530

Concise History of Spain, 418

The Concise Oxford Dictionary of Ballet, 519

The Concise Oxford Dictionary of Current English, 25

The Concise Oxford Dictionary of Proverbs, 22

The Concise Oxford Dictionary of Quotations, 20

The Concise Oxford English-Arabic Dictionary of Current Usage, 38

The Concise Oxford French Dictionary, 39

Concise Usage and Abusage, 31

The Condition, Elevation, Emigration, and Destiny of the Colored People of the United States, 290

The Condition of the Working Class in England, 133

Conditioned Reflexes, 174, 183

The Conditions of Learning, 174

Conditions of World Order, 155

The Conduct of War, 1789–1961, 407

Conductors on Record, 495

The Confederacy, 274

The Confederate Nation, 1861–1865, 274

Confederate Women, 274

Confederates, 313

Confederation, Constitution, and Early National Period, 1781–1815, 259

Confessions and Self-Portraits, 50

Confessions of a Muckraker, 567

The Confidence Gap, 156

A Confidential Matter, 513

Configurations of Culture Growth, 105, 115

Conflict and Consensus, 193

Conflict and Crisis, 79, 281

Conflict and Stability in Fifteenth Century England, 373

Conflict and the Web of Group Affiliations, 193, 216

The Conflict in Education in a Democratic Society, 232

Conflict in Japan, 193

Conflict in the Middle East, 433

Conflict Sociology, 192

The Conflicted Relationship, 406

Conflicts, 395

Confucius and the Chinese Way, 447

The Congo and the Founding of Its Free State, 646

Congress and Foreign Policy Making, 156

Congress and Law-Making, 256

Congress and the American People, 300

Congress and the Court, 152

Congress and the Presidency, 339

Congress and the Waning of the New Deal, 279

Congress: Process and Policy, 301

Congress: The Electoral Connection, 156

The Congressional Directory, 257

Congressional Government, 96

Congressional Index, 13

Congressional Procedures and the Policy Process, 300

Congressional Record, 12

The Conquest of Everest, 637

The Conquest of Gaul, 249

The Conquest of Mexico and Peru, 356

The Conquest of the Incas, 355

Conquest of Violence: The Gandhian Philosophy of Conflict, 452

Conquistadors in North American History, 324

Conscience in Politics, 93

Consciousness and Society, 412

Consensus and Disunity, 383

Conservatism in America, 301

Considerations on Representative Government, 154

The Conspiracy of Catiline, 250

The Conspiracy of Pontiac, 332

Constancy and Change in Human Development, 172

Constantine Porphyrogenitus and His World, 479

Constituencies and Leaders in Congress, 300

The Constitution: A Documentary and Narrative History, 297

The Constitution between Friends, 295

The Constitution of Liberty, 137

The Constitution of Society, 201

The Constitution of the United States and Related Documents, 297

The Constitution of the United States: With Case Summaries, 297

The Constitution: That Delicate Balance, 151

A Constitutional and Legal History of Medieval England, 370

Constitutional Choices, 152

Constitutional Government and Democracy, 151, 152, 153

Constitutional History of England, 394, 398

A Constitutional History of Germany in the Nineteenth and Twentieth Centuries, 416

Constitutional History of Medieval England, 369

Constitutional History of Modern Britain since 1485, 369

Constitutional Law of the Federal System, 296

Constitutional Reason of State, 151

Consumer Behavior, 128

The Consumer Health Information Source Book, 6

Consumer Sourcebook, 6

Consumer's Guide to Package Travel around the World, 617

A Consumers', Researchers', and Students' Guide to Government Publications, 13

Contemplating Music, 485

Contemporary American History, 1877–1913, 309

Contemporary Architects, 533

Contemporary Authors, 50

Contemporary China, 447

Contemporary Chinese Politics, 449

Contemporary Concert Music by Women, 491

Contemporary France, 414

The Contemporary International Economy, 130

Contemporary Portugal, 418

Contemporary Theatre, Film and Television, 575

The Contemporary World, 1914–Present, 473

Content Analysis in Communications Research, 100

Content and Style of an Oral Literature, 604

A Continuing Task, 322

Continuities in Cultural Evolution, 107, 119

Continuities in Social Research, 210, 218

Continuities in the Language of Social Research, 207

Continuity and Change in Modern Iran, 437

Contraband Cargoes, 618

A Contribution to a Critique of Political Economy, 141

Contribution to the Theory of the Trade Cycle, 137

The Control of Trusts, 132

Controversy: Politics of Technical Decisions, 200

A Convenant with Power, 303

Conversations with Eric Sevareid, 569

Coomassie and Magdala, 646

Cooperation and Competition among Primitive Peoples, 119

The Co-operative Movement in Great Britain, 148

Copyright Handbook, 22

Coral Gardens and Their Magic, 119

Corea: The Hermit Nation, 454

Corn, Cash, Commerce, 379
Coronado's Children, 602
The Corporation in Modern
    Society, 128
The Corporation in the
    Emergent American
    Society, 128
Corpus Rubenianum Ludwig
    Burchard, 553
Correspondence of the
    French Ministers to the
    United States, 1791–1797,
    343
Correspondence with
    Churchill and Attlee, 476
Correspondence with
    Roosevelt and Truman,
    476
Cortina/Grosset Basic French
    Dictionary, 40
Cortina/Grosset Basic
    German Dictionary, 42
Cortina/Grosset Basic Italian
    Dictionary, 42
The Costa Ricans, 361
The Counter-Revolution of
    Science, 137
Country and Court: England,
    1658–1714, 376
Country Life in Classical
    Times, 243
Country Music, U.S.A., 594
Course of American
    Economic Growth and
    Development, 321
The Course of Empire, 316,
    317
The Course of German
    History, 478
The Course of Mexican
    History, 364
The Course of Modern
    Jewish History, 430
The Court and the Country,
    377
Courts and Cabinets, 465
Cowboy Culture, 285
The Cowboy Hero, 286
Cowgirls, 292
Cracks in the Constitution,
    296
Craftsmen in Greek and
    Roman Society, 243
Cranmer, 386
Creating Media Culture, 565
Creating Reality, 570

Creating Rosie the Riveter,
    278
The Creation of the
    American Republic, 1776–
    1787, 268
Crestwood Heights, 192
Crime and Custom in Savage
    Society, 118
Crime and Public Order in
    the Later Middle Ages, 372
Crime and Punishment:
    Changing Attitudes in
    America, 193
Crime in England, 369
Crime Movies, 576
Crime News and the Public,
    568
Crime of the Century, 72
The Crimean Tartars, 422
Criminal Violence, Criminal
    Justice, 193
Criminology, 193
Crises of the Republic, 456
Crisis and Compromise, 415
Crisis in Costa Rica, 361
The Crisis in Keynesian
    Economics, 137
The Crisis of Civilization,
    386
The Crisis of Confidence, 340
Crisis of Fear, 270
The Crisis of German
    Ideology, 416, 430
The Crisis of Power, 303
Crisis of the Aristocracy,
    1558–1641, 398
The Crisis of the Old Order
    in Russia, 423
Criteria for the Life History,
    with Analyses of Six
    Notable Documents, 100,
    176, 177
The Critical Historians of
    Art, 531
A Critical History of British
    Cinema, 575
The Critical Period in
    American Religion, 1875–
    1900, 338
Critical Questions, 485
Cromwell (Fraser), 376
Cromwell (Howell), 376
Cromwell's Place in History,
    391
The Crossing of Antarctica,
    637

Crossroads of Civilization,
    437
Crossroads of Liberalism,
    325
Crossroads of Power, 395
The Crowd, 190
Crowell's Handbook of
    World Opera, 495
Crown and Nobility, 1450–
    1509, 373
The Cruise of the Corwin,
    627
Crusade in Europe, 62
Crusaders and
    Compromisers, 271
Crusaders and Pragmatists,
    305
The Cry of the People, 359
Cuba, 362
Cuentos, 603
Cultural Autonomy in Global
    Communications, 564
The Cultural Contradictions
    of Capitalism, 204
Cultural Materialism, 105
The Cultural Pattern in
    American Politics, 286
Culture: A Critical Review of
    Concepts and Definitions,
    115
Culture against Man, 102
Culture and Behavior, 105
Culture and Experience, 105
Culture and Its Creators,
    189, 215
Culture and Personality, 106
Culture and Practical
    Reason, 106
Culture and Society, 121
Culture as History, 103
Culture, Behavior, and
    Personality, 106
Culture Conflict and Crime,
    193
The Culture of Cities, 202
The Culture of Consumption,
    287
The Culture of Narcissism,
    102
Culture, Society and the
    Media, 564
Culture Theory, 106
Cumulative Book Index, 6
Curious Naturalists, 186
Current Biography Yearbook
    1985, 50

The Current Crisis in
American Politics, 298
Current Index to Journals in
Education, 6
Custer Died for Your Sins,
290
Custom and Conflict in
Africa, 113, 192

Dahcotah: Or, Life and
Legends of the Sioux
around Fort Snelling, 604
Dahomey, 115
Daily Life in Ancient Rome,
243
Daily Life of the Aztecs on
the Eve of the Spanish
Conquest, 354
The Damned and the
Beautiful, 277
Dance: A Short History of
Classic Theatrical
Dancing, 518
Dance and Drama in Bali,
520
The Dance Anthology, 518
Dance in India, 519
The Dance in Mind, 518
The Dance Makers, 521
Dangerous Currents, 125
Daniel O'Connell (Nowlan
and O'Connell), 381
Daniel O'Connell (O'Ferrall),
381
Daniel Webster, 268
Danish-English, English-
Danish Dictionary, 39
The Dark Ages, 282
Dark Ghetto, 196
Dark Horse, 279
Dark Princess, 318
The Darwinian Revolution,
382
David Lloyd George, 384
Day by Day: The 40's, 15
Day by Day: The 50's, 15,
256
Day by Day: The 60's, 15
The Day the Bubble Burst,
289
Days of Sorrow and Pain, 51
Dead Ends, 155
Deadly Gambits, 409
Dear Bess, 79
Dear Theo, 556

Dearest Friend, 83
Death and Identity, 195
Death, Disease and Famine
in Pre-Industrial England,
369
Death in Life: Survivors of
Hiroshima, 451
Death in the Dark, 308
A Death in the Sánchez
Family, 117
The Death of a President, 72
The Death of the Past, 403
The Death of Woman Wang,
449
The Death Penalty, 194
The Death Penalty in
America, 193
DeBasil's Ballets Russes, 520
Debates with Historians, 479
A Decade of Revolution,
1789–1799, 460
Deceived with Kindness, 52
Decision to Prosecute, 127
De Cive or the Citizen, 160
The Declaration of
Independence: A Study in
the History of Political
Ideas, 87, 161, 295, 310
The Declaration of
Independence and the
Constitution, 296
The Declaration of
Independence and What It
Means Today, 295
The Decline and Fall of the
Roman Empire, 240
Decline of an Empire, 421
Decline of Radicalism, 312
The Decline of the United
States and the Safety of
the Free World, 471
The Decline of the West, 474,
475
The Decline, Revival and
Fall of the British Empire,
380
Deep Down in the Jungle,
604
Deep South, 110
The Defeat of America, 315
Defense of the Constitution
of Government of the
United States of America,
82
Defining the Basics of
American Education, 224

De Gaulle, 414
Degradation of the
Democratic Dogma, 306
Delay in Court, 155
Delhi Diary, 453
Delineations of American
Scenery and Character,
618
Delinquent Boys, 193
Demented: The World of the
Opera Diva, 496
Democracy: An American
Novel, 306
Democracy and Classical
Greece, 239
Democracy and Education,
231
Democracy and Liberty, 394
Democracy in America, 103,
152, 159, 208, 341
Democracy in Crisis, 162
Democracy in Jonesville,
110
The Democratic and the
Authoritarian State, 157
Democratic Theory, 152
Demographic Yearbook, 404
Demography of Racial and
Ethnic Groups, 195, 197
Departing Glory, 337
Dependency Approaches to
International Political
Economy, 130
Dervish: The Rise and Fall
of an African Empire, 444
Descent from Glory, 83, 307
Deschooling Society, 226
The Description of the
World, 644
Design and Truth in
Autobiography, 50
The Destruction of the
European Jews, 429
Destruction of the Zulu
Kingdom, 442
Detachment and the Writing
of History, 310
Deus Destroyed, 450
Development and Scope of
Higher Education in the
United States, 323
Development, Economic
Distribution and Social
Change in Rural Egypt,
1952–1970, 436
Development in Infancy, 172

The Development of
  Academic Freedom in the
  United States, 101
Development of American
  Political Science, 149
The Development of Sex
  Differences, 173
The Development of the
  English Biography, 77
The Development of the
  Iranian Oil Industry, 437
The Development of
  Thought, 184
Developmental Planning,
  130
Developmental Psychology:
  Historical and
  Philosophical Perspectives,
  173
Deviance and
  Medicalization, 194
Deviance in Soviet Society,
  421
The Devil Drives, 630
Devil Theory of War, 309
The Dialectic of Sex, 411
Dialectical and Historical
  Materialism, 476
Dianying, 577
The Diaries of Theodor
  Herzl, 429
The Diary of George
  Templeton Strong, 1835–
  1875, 330
Diary of Philip Hone, 1828–
  1851, 330
Diary of the Cuban
  Revolution, 361
Diary of the Discovery
  Expedition to the
  Antarctic Regions, 1901–
  1904, 625, 645
Diary of the Sinai
  Campaign, 435
Diary of the "Terra Nova"
  Expedition to the
  Antarctic, 625
Diary of the Voyage of
  H.M.S. Beagle, 626
Diccionario Inglés, 46
Diccionario Moderno
  Español-Inglés, 46
Dictatorship and
  Development, 362
Dictatorships and Double
  Standards, 359

Dictionaries, Encyclopedias,
  and Other Word-Related
  Books, 6
Dictionary and Thesaurus of
  the Hebrew Language, 42
Dictionary of American Art,
  529
Dictionary of American
  Biography, 50
Dictionary of American
  Diplomatic History, 258
Dictionary of American
  English on Historical
  Principles, 25
A Dictionary of American-
  English Usage, 31
Dictionary of American
  History, 258, 307
Dictionary of American
  Painters, Sculptors, and
  Engravers, 531
Dictionary of American
  Politics, 149
Dictionary of American Pop/
  Rock, 491
Dictionary of American
  Slang, 33
A Dictionary of
  Americanisms on
  Historical Principles, 26
Dictionary of Anthropology,
  104
Dictionary of Antiques and
  the Decorative Arts, 534
A Dictionary of Architecture,
  532
Dictionary of Architecture
  and Construction, 532
Dictionary of Art Terms and
  Techniques, 528
A Dictionary of Ballet, 519
Dictionary of Behavioral
  Science, 170
Dictionary of Books Relating
  to America from Its
  Discovery to the Present
  Time, 257
The Dictionary of British
  Eighteenth Century
  Painters, 531
Dictionary of Business and
  Economics, 124
Dictionary of Canadian
  Biography, 347
A Dictionary of Catch
  Phrases, 32

A Dictionary of Clichés, 31
Dictionary of Collective
  Nouns and Group Terms,
  35
A Dictionary of Collective
  Onomatopoeic Sounds,
  Tones and Noises in
  English and Spanish, 34
Dictionary of Computers,
  Data Processing, and
  Telecommunications, 562
Dictionary of Contemporary
  American Artists, 531
Dictionary of Contemporary
  American English, 30
A Dictionary of
  Contemporary American
  Usage, 30
A Dictionary of
  Contemporary and
  Colloquial Usage, 32
The Dictionary of
  Contemporary Music, 491
Dictionary of Demography,
  198
The Dictionary of Do's and
  Don'ts, 31
A Dictionary of Early Music,
  from the Troubadours to
  Monteverdi, 490
The Dictionary of English
  Furniture, 534
Dictionary of Films, 575
Dictionary of Foreign
  Quotations, 20
Dictionary of German
  Synonyms, 41
A Dictionary of Hymnology,
  489
A Dictionary of Indian
  History, 452
Dictionary of Information
  Technology, 562
A Dictionary of Islam, 434
The Dictionary of Medical
  Folklore, 608
Dictionary of Medieval Latin
  from British Sources, 44
A Dictionary of Modern
  English Usage, 31
Dictionary of Modern French
  Idioms, 40
A Dictionary of Modern
  Written Arabic, 38
A Dictionary of Musical
  Themes, 487

Dictionary of Mythology, Folklore and Symbols, 528, 592
Dictionary of National Biography, 50, 370
A Dictionary of Opera and Song Themes, 487
Dictionary of Politics, 149
Dictionary of Problem Words and Expressions, 31
Dictionary of Pronunciation, 36
Dictionary of Psychology (Chaplin), 170
Dictionary of Psychology (Statt), 170
Dictionary of Quotations, 20
A Dictionary of Rhyming Slang, 35
Dictionary of Russian Historical Terms from the Eleventh Century to 1917, 424
Dictionary of Scientific Biography, 100
A Dictionary of Slang and Unconventional English, 33
A Dictionary of Spanish Terms in English, with Special Reference to the American Southwest, 45
Dictionary of Spoken Russian, 45
Dictionary of Subjects and Symbols in Art, 528
A Dictionary of the Chinese Particles, with a Prolegomenon in Which the Problems of the Particles Are Considered, 38
Dictionary of the Dance, 519
Dictionary of the Decorative Arts, 534
Dictionary of the History of Ideas, 11, 405
A Dictionary of the Social Sciences, 100
Dictionary of the Spanish and English Languages, 46
A Dictionary of the Underworld, British and American, 32
The Dictionary of Victorian Painters, 531

The Dictionary of World Museums, 528
Dictionary: Polish-English, English-Polish, 44
The Diehards, 383
A Different Valor, 316
The Diffusion of Innovations, 200
Dilemmas of Democracy, 342
The Dimensions of Liberty, 322
Dimensions of Tolerance, 151
Dinosaurs in the Morning, 493
Diplomacy and Ideology: The Origins of Soviet Foreign Relations, 1917–1930, 409
Diplomacy in Ancient Greece, 244
The Diplomacy of the American Revolution, 311
A Diplomatic History of Europe, 406
Diplomatic History of Modern Iraq, 437
A Diplomatic History of the American People, 302
Diplomatic History, 1713–1933, 409
Directory of Directories, 6
Directory of Publishing Opportunities in Journals and Periodicals, 22
Directory of Special Libraries and Information Centers, 6
The Directory of Tunes and Musical Themes, 490
Discipline and Punish: The Birth of the Prison, 411
A Disciplined Intelligence, 350
Disclosing the Past, 53
Discourse Strategies, 564
Discourses on Art, 552
The Discoverers, 312
Discovering America, 1700–1875, 263
Discovering the News, 566
Discovery, 631
Discovery and Conquest of Mexico, 355

Discovery in Russian and Siberian Waters, 625
The Discovery of India, 473
The Discovery of the Child, 234
The Discovery of the Sea, 617
Dismantling America, 565
A Disquisition on Government, 84
Dissent in Three American Wars, 329
The Dissident Press, 566
The Dissolution of the Monasteries, 375
A Distant Mirror, 481
Distant Water, 351
The Distribution of Wealth, 132, 133
Divers Voyages Touching the Discovery of America and the Islands Adjacent, 635
Diversity in International Communism, 157
Diversity of Worlds, 457
Divine Dancer, 525
Division and Cohesion in Democracy, 419
Division and Reunion: 1829–1889, 96
Division and the Stresses of Reunion, 1845–1876, 333
The Division of Labor in Society, 206
Divisions on a Ground, 349
Divisions throughout the Whole, 264
The Divorce of Catherine of Aragon, 390
The Divorce Revolution, 196
Dizionario Commerciale Inglése-Italiano, Italiano-Inglése, 43
Dizionario Inglése-Italiano, Italiano-Inglése, 43
The Docile Puerto Rican, 365
The Doctrines of American Foreign Policy, 303
Documentary Expression and Thirties America, 279
A Documentary History of American Industrial Society, 133
A Documentary History of Art, 528

Documentary History of the Constitution of the United States of America, 1786–1870, 295

A Documentary History of the Negro People in the United States, 260

Documentary in American Television, 570

Documents Catalog, 13

Documents of American History, 261, 314

Documents Relating to New England Federalism, 1800–1815, 306

Dogs of the Conquest, 356

The Dollar and the International Monetary System, 136

Domesday England, 372

The Dominican Republic, 362

Donovan and the CIA, 305

Don't Drink the Water, 618

Doomsday Book and Beyond, 394

The Double Patriots: A Study of Japanese Nationalism, 451

The Doubleday Roget's Thesaurus in Dictionary Form, 34

Dove, 626

Down and Out in the Great Depression, 279

Down by the Riverside, 605

The Dragon and the Bear, 448

The Drawing of America, 262

Dream and Reality, 304

A Dream of Wings, 287

Dreams of Amazonia, 361

The Dred Scott Case, 270

The Dreyfus Case, 431

Drift and Mastery, 325

Drift Toward Dissolution, 270

Drinking in America, 292

Drugs in America, 293

Du Système Penitentiaire aux Etats-Unis et de son Application en France, 341

The Duke of Newcastle, 378

The Dusk of Dawn, 318

The Dust Bowl (Bonnifield), 287

The Dust Bowl (Hurt), 288

Dutch-English and English-Dutch, 39

Dutch-English Dictionary, 39

Dutch-English, English-Dutch Dictionary, 39

Dutch Schools of New Netherland and Colonial New York, 233

Dwight D. Eisenhower: Soldier and Statesman, 283

The Dynamic of Social Movements, 201

A Dynamic Theory of Personality, 182

The Dynamics of Bureaucracy, 197

The Dynamics of Culture Change, 104, 119

The Dynamics of Folklore, 592

Dynamics of Indonesian History, 455

The Dynamics of Mass Communication, 563

The Dynamics of the One-Party State in Zambia, 441

Dynamics of World Power, 340

Eagle against the Sun, 279

The Eagle and the Serpent, 363

The Earl of Beaconsfield, 390

Early American Architecture, 533

Early American Proverbs and Proverbial Phrases, 22

Early American Sheet Music, 1768–1889, 485

Early American Taverns, 264

Early Americans, 268

Early Christian Art, 529

The Early Churchills, 397

Early Foundations for Japan's Twentieth-Century Economic Emergence, 451

Early Greece, 240

Early History of Charles James Fox, 399

The Early History of Rome, 250

The Early Industrial Revolution, 379

Early Japan, 451

Early Latin America, 357

Early Medieval Spain, 418

Early Mesopotamia and Iran, 239

Early Modern France, 1560–1715, 414

Early Netherlandish Painting, 530

The Early Spanish Main, 356

Early Victorian Government, 1830–1870, 381

The Early Window, 572

The Earnest Men, 272

East Asia, 445

East Asia and U.S. Security, 303

East Asia: Tradition and Transformation, 450, 464

East Central Europe between the Two World Wars, 419

East European History, 419

East India Fortunes, 379

East Is West, 647

East to West, 479

The Easter Rising, 384

Eastern Europe, 1740–1980, 419

Easy Chair, 317

The Ebony Handbook, 255

Ebony Pictorial History of Black America, 255

Eccentric Travelers, 617

The Ecclesiastical History of England, 386

The Eclipse of a Great Power: Modern Britain, 1870–1975, 382

The Eclipse of Community, 203

Econocide: British Slavery in the Era of Abolition, 378

Econometric Methods, 125

Econometric Models of Cyclical Behavior, 131

Economic and Demographic Change in Preindustrial Japan, 1600–1868, 450

Economic and Environmental Impacts of

a U.S. Nuclear
Moratorium, 1985–2010,
195
Economic and Social
History of Ancient Greece,
243
Economic and Social
Investigations in
Manchester, 1833–1933,
385
Economic Anthropology,
107, 115
The Economic Approach to
Human Behavior, 124
Economic Basis of Politics,
309
The Economic Consequences
of the Peace, 138
Economic Co-operation
among Negro Families,
318
Economic Cycles,
131
Economic Development and
Regional Cooperation:
Kuwait, 440
The Economic Development
of Japan, 451
Economic Doctrines of
Islam, 433
Economic Growth, Capital
Gains and Income
Distribution, 130
Economic Growth in the
Third World, 1850–1980,
129
Economic Growth of
Nations, 129
The Economic History of
Eastern Europe, 1919–
1975, 419
An Economic History of
England, 385
Economic History of Iran,
1800–1914, 437
Economic History of Ireland
since 1660, 369
An Economic History of
Modern Britain, 388
An Economic History of
Modern Spain, 418
An Economic History of
Nigeria, 1860–1960,
442
The Economic History of the
Middle East, 432

An Economic History of the
Middle East and North
Africa, 432
An Economic History of the
U.S.S.R., 424
The Economic History of
Turkey, 1800–1914, 439
An Economic History of
West Africa, 442
An Economic History of
Women in America, 288
An Economic Interpretation
of the Constitution of the
United States, 151, 295,
309
The Economic Mind in
American Civilization,
1606–1933, 124, 143
The Economic Organization,
125, 139
Economic Origins of the
Iranian Revolution, 437
Economic Policy in Postwar
Japan, 452
Economic Problems of
Socialism in the U.S.S.R.,
476
Economic Stabilization in
an Unstable World, 136
Economic Studies, 385
Economic Survey Methods,
125
An Economic Survey of
Ancient Rome, 243
Economic Theory in
Retrospect, 124, 140
An Economic Theory of
Democracy, 152
The Economic Value of
Education, 126
Economic Welfare in the
Soviet Union, 424
Economics, 125
The Economics of
Agricultural Development,
126
The Economics of Collective
Action, 133
The Economics of
Communication, 564
The Economics of European
Imperialism, 411
The Economics of Imperfect
Competition, 127
Economics of Public Policy,
132

The Economics of
Regulation, 129
The Economists, 124
Economy and Society, 107,
204
Economy and Society in
Early Modern Europe, 410
Economy and Society in Pre-
Industrial South Africa,
443
The Economy, Liberty, and
the State, 127
The Economy of Colonial
America, 288
Ecumene, 473
Edison, 58
Editing in the Electronic
Era, 568
Editor and Publisher
International Yearbook,
563
Education, 236
Education and Popular
Literacy in Ch'ing China,
448
Education and Social
Mobility in the Soviet
Union, 422
Education and the
Democratic Ideal, 224
Education for a Changing
Civilization, 233
Education Index, 2, 6, 225
Education of Black Peoples,
1906–1960, 318
The Education of Mrs. Henry
Adams, 286, 307
Education Today, 231
The Educational
Imagination, 225
Educational Psychology,
236
Edward IV, 373
Edward Prince of Wales and
Aquitaine, 372
Edward R. Murrow, 569
Edward R. Murrow
Heritage, 569
Edward S. Corwin's
Constitution and What It
Means Today, 295
Edward VI, the Threshold of
Power, 375
Edward VI, the Young King,
375
The Edwardian Age, 383

Edwardian England, 381, 383
The Edwardians, 384
The Effects of Mass Communication, 191
Efforts for Social Betterment among Negro Americans, 318
Egypt, 436
Egypt and the Fertile Crescent, 1516–1922, 436
Egypt in the Nineteenth Century, 436
The Egypt of Nasser and Sadat, 436
Egypt of the Pharoahs, 239
Egypt: Portrait of a President—Sadat's Road to Jerusalem, 436
Egypt, 1798–1952, 436
The Egyptian Army in Politics, 436
The Egyptian Economy, 1952–1972, 436
The Egyptians, 239
Egypt's Economic Potential, 436
Egypt's Liberal Experiment, 1922–1936, 436
Egypt's Uncertain Revolution under Nasser and Sadat, 436
Eichmann in Jerusalem, 426, 456
800,000,000: The Real China, 449
Eight Issues in American History, 333
Eighteenth Century England, 1714 to 1784, 379
Eighteenth-Century Industrialist, 385
Eighteenth Century: 1714–1815, 379
Eighty Appalachian Folk Songs, 594
Eisenhower, 280
The Eisenhower Administration, 1953–1961, 281
Eisenhower and the Cold War, 281
Eisenhower the President, 281
Eisenhower's Lieutenants, 280

El Diccionario del Español Chicano, 46
El-Hi Textbooks and Serials in Print, 1985, 6
El Mundo de los Negocios, 46
El Salvador, 363
The Elder Pitt, 377
Eleanor and Franklin, 92
Election Campaigning Japanese Style, 450
Elections and the Political Order, 153
Electoral Reform in War and Peace, 1906–1918, 383
The Electronic Giant, 568
Electronic Music, 492
The Elementary Forms of the Religious Life, 109, 206
The Elementary Structures of Kinship, 108, 116
Elementary Structures Reconsidered, 116
The Elements of Cinema, 575
The Elements of Law, 160
Elements of Pure Economics, 125
Elements of Social Organization, 109, 113
Elements of Style, 23
Elizabeth and Essex, 60
Elizabeth and Leicester, 58
Elizabeth the Great, 58
Elizabeth Tudor, 375
Elizabethan Commentary, 386
Elizabethan England, 375
An Elizabethan Garland, 397
The Elizabethan Renaissance, 397
The Elizabethans and America, 397
Elmtown's Youth and Elmtown Revisited, 192
The Elusive Republic, 288
Elvis and Gladys, 52
The Emancipation Proclamation, 320
The Emergence of African Capitalism, 443
The Emergence of Bangladesh, 446
The Emergence of Film Art, 576

The Emergence of Maoism, 449
Emergence of Modern America, 1865–1978, 330
The Emergence of Modern Turkey, 439
The Emergence of Spanish America, 359
The Emergence of the Labour Party, 1880-1924, 383
The Emergence of the Modern Middle East, 433
Emile, 168
Eminent Elizabethans, 397
Eminent Victorians, 60
Emotions, Cognition, and Behaviour, 171
The Emperor, 52
Emperor and Nation in Japan, 450
The Emperor in the Roman World, 240
Emperor of the Cossacks, 420
The Emperor's Island, 451
Empire and Aftermath, 450
The Empire of Reason, 315
Empire of the Air, 58
Empire of the Inca, 353
Empire or Independence, 1760–1776, 378
Empire to Welfare State, 383
The Empire's Old Clothes, 611
Encircled Kingdom, 596
Encounters, 207
Encounters with Conductors of Today, 495
Encyclopaedia Britannica, 2
Encyclopaedia of the Social Sciences, 100
The Encyclopedia Americana, 3
Encyclopedia Buying Guide, 2
Encyclopedia Judaica, 428
Encyclopedia of American Economic History, 258
The Encyclopedia of American Facts and Dates, 257
Encyclopedia of American Foreign Policy, 258
Encyclopedia of American History, 258

The Encyclopedia of American Journalism, 566

The Encyclopedia of American Music, 489

Encyclopedia of Associations, 7

Encyclopedia of Bioethics, 100

Encyclopedia of Black Folklore and Humor, 606

Encyclopedia of Comparative Letterforms for Artists and Designers, 535

Encyclopedia of Crime and Justice, 100, 193

The Encyclopedia of Folk, Country, and Western Music, 491, 595

The Encyclopedia of Furniture, 534

The Encyclopedia of Homonyms, "Sound-Alikes," 34

Encyclopedia of Information Systems and Services, 7

Encyclopedia of Islam, 434

The Encyclopedia of Jazz, 493

Encyclopedia of Modern Architecture, 532

Encyclopedia of Music in Canada, 489

The Encyclopedia of Myths and Legends of All Nations, 598

The Encyclopedia of Opera, 495

Encyclopedia of Philosophy, 7, 99

Encyclopedia of Pop, Rock, and Soul, 492

An Encyclopedia of Quotations about Music, 490

Encyclopedia of Russia and the Soviet Union, 404

The Encyclopedia of Southern History, 258

Encyclopedia of Superstitions, Folklore and the Occult Sciences of the World, 592

Encyclopedia of the American Revolution, 257

Encyclopedia of the Musical Film, 574

Encyclopedia of the Musical Theatre, 489

The Encyclopedia of Visual Art, 528

Encyclopedia of World Art, 527

An Encyclopedia of World History, 404

Encyclopedic Dictionary of Roman Law, 244

The End of an Alliance, 283

An End of Arms, 327

The End of Colonial Rule in West Africa, 442

The End of Ideology, 102, 154, 204

End of the European Era, 411

The End of the Russian Imperial Army, 426

Endeavors in Psychology, 183

Endless War, 358

The Endless War: Fifty Years of Struggle in Vietnam, 454

Endurance and Endeavour: Russian History, 426

Enemies of the Roman Order, 243

The Enemy among Us, 284

Enemy at the Gates, 407

The Enemy Within, 73

The Engineers and the Price System, 220

England and Ireland since 1800, 370

England, 1175–1425, 373

England in the Age of the American Revolution, 395

England in the Age of Wycliffe, 399

England in the Eighteenth Century, 1714–1815, 396

England in the Late Middle Ages, 373

The England of Elizabeth (The Elizabethan Age), 397

England under Protector Somerset, 396

England under Queen Anne, 399

England under the Stuarts, 399

England's Apprenticeship, 1603–1763, 377

English and Scottish Popular Ballads, 593

English-Arabic Vocabulary, 38

English Art, 1100–1216, 529

The English Catholic Community, 1570–1850, 369

The English Church and the Papacy in the Middle Ages, 370

The English Church, 1000–1066, 371

The English Constitution, 385

English Culture and the Decline of the Industrial Spirit, 1850–1980, 384

English Democratic Ideas in the Seventeenth Century, 465

The English Duden, 41

English English, 30

The English Fact in Quebec, 349

English Folk-Song and Dance, 594

English-French Glossary, 40

The English Heritage, 396

English Historical Documents, 1042–1189, 369

English History: From the Year 1235 to 1259, 396

English History, 1919–1945, 477, 478

English in Ireland in the Eighteenth Century, 390

English in the West Indies, 390

English-Italian, Italian-English Dictionary, 43

English Justice between the Norman Conquest and the Great Charter, 1066–1215, 372

English Landed Society in the Eighteenth Century, 379

The English Language, 37

English Loanwords in Japanese, 44

English Overseas Trade, 1500–1700, 374

The English Parliament in the Middle Ages, 397

The English People and the English Revolution, 1640–1649, 376

English Political Pluralism, 162

English Political Thought in the Nineteenth Century, 459

English Politics and the American Revolution, 378

English Poor Law History, 148

English Proverbs & Proverbial Phrases, 22

The English Reformation, 374

The English Revolution, 1688–1689, 399

English Revolution, 1640, 393

English-Russian Dictionary, 45

English Seaman in the Sixteenth Century, 390

An English-Serbocroatian Dictionary, 45

English Social History, 399

English Society in the Early Middle Ages, 1066–1307, 372

The English Spirit, 397

The English Utilitarians, 143, 158

Enjoyment of Laughter, 610

The Enjoyment of Music: An Introduction to Perceptive Listening, 492

The Enlightenment, 411

The Entertainment Functions of Television, 191

The Entertainment Machine, 612

The Environment: From Surplus to Scarcity, 194

Environmental Diplomacy, 349

Eothen, 637

The Epic of America, 307, 308

The Epic of Latin America, 352

Epidemic Disease in Fifteenth-Century England, 373

Equality, 398

Equality in America, 201

Equality of Educational Opportunity, 196

Equilibrium, Stability, and Growth, 129

The Era of Reform Eighteen Thirty to Eighteen Sixty, 315

The Erotic Traveler, 629

Errand into the Wilderness, 327

The Eskimo Storyteller, 597

Essay and General Literature Index, 7

An Essay Concerning Human Understanding, 164

An Essay on Crimes and Punishments, 193

Essay on Freedom, 457

An Essay on the Nature and Significance of Economic Science, 125

Essays before a Sonata, the Majority, and Other Writings, 507

Essays in Biography, 138

Essays in Eighteenth-Century Biography, 49

Essays in International Economic Theory, 130

Essays in International Economics, 130

Essays in Modern European Historiography, 402

Essays in Musical Analysis, 487

Essays in Positive Economics, 135

Essays in Social Anthropology, 113

Essays in Sociological Theory, 214

Essays in the Earlier History of American Corporations, 128

Essays of a Catholic, 386

Essays on American Antebellum Politics, 1840–1860, 271

Essays on Behavioral Economics, 128

Essays on Church and State, 384

Essays on Freedom and Power, 384

Essays on General Politics, Commerce and Political Economy, 64

Essays on Politics and Culture, 142

Essays on Sociology and Social Psychology, 209

Essays on the Sociology of Knowledge, 199, 209

Essays on Tudor and Stuart Politics and Government, 389

Essence of Decision, 406

The Essential Chaim Weizmann, 429

Essentials of Economic Theory as Applied to Modern Problems of Industry and Public Policy, 132

The Establishment of the Balkan National States, 1804–1920, 419

The Estates of the Higher Nobility in Fourteenth-Century England, 373

Esther, 306

Esthetics of Music, 485

Estimates of Some Englishmen and Scotchmen, 385

Ethical Issues in Social Science Research, 101

Ethics: An Investigation of the Facts and Laws of the Moral Life, 187

Ethics and Educational Policy, 229

Ethics in Social Research, 101

Ethnic America, 293

Ethnic Information Sources of the U.S., 7

The Ethnic Myth, 195

Ethnicity: Theory and Experience, 195

Ethnographic Bibliography of North America, 121

Ethnomusicology, 492

Ethnomusicology of the Flathead Indians, 604

The Etruscans, 242

The Etruscans: Their Art and Civilization, 242
An Etymological Dictionary of the English Language, 37
Eugene V. Debs, 53
Europa Yearbook, 16
Europe and America, 480
Europe and the World in the Age of Expansion, 406
Europe in Africa in the Nineteenth Century, 443
Europe in Decay, 1936–40, 395
Europe in the Eighteenth Century, 1713–1783, 410
Europe in the Fourteenth and Fifteenth Centuries, 411
Europe in the High Middle Ages, 1150–1309, 412
Europe in the 20th Century (Paxton), 413
Europe in the Twentieth Century (Stromberg), 413
Europe on a Saturday Night, 621
Europe, 1780–1830, 411
Europe, 1789–1920, 343
Europe, 1815–1914, 411
Europe, Russia, the United States and the Problem of Asia, 471
Europe since 1870, 412
Europe since Hitler, 412
Europe since 1945, 413
Europe the World's Banker, 1870–1914, 411
Europe Transformed, 1878–1919, 413
European Armies and the Conduct of War, 409
European Diplomatic History, 1815–1914, 410
European Discovery of America, 329
European Economic History, 411
European Economic Integration, 1815–1970, 413
The European Family, 412
The European Folktale, 597
European Historical Statistics, 1750–1970, 404

European History in a World Perspective, 405
European History, 1494–1789, 413
European Imperialism and the Partition of Africa, 444
European Intellectual History since 1789, 413
The European Left, 411
The European Miracle, 412
The European Revolution and Correspondence with Gobineau, 342
European Society in Upheaval, 413
European Union, 413
The European Witch Craze, 400
Europe's Classical Balance of Power, 408
Europe's Steppe Frontier, 1500–1800, 472
Evaluation: A Systematic Approach, 101
The Eve of the Revolution, 310
Evening Post, 330
The Evening Stars, 569
Everyday Life in Traditional Japan, 450
Everyday Spanish Idioms, 46
Everyman a Phoenix, 49
Everyman His Own Historian, 310, 402
Everyman's Book of English Folktales, 597
Everyman's Book of Nonsense, 609
Everything in Its Path, 191, 194
Everything to Live For, 324
Evita, First Lady, 360
Evolution and Culture, 106, 107
Evolution and Modification of Behavior, 171, 182
Evolution and Society, 123
The Evolution of a Revolt, 638
The Evolution of Culture, 106, 107
The Evolution of Economic Ideas, 124
The Evolution of Nuclear Strategy, 407

The Evolution of Societies, 214
The Evolution of Society, 217
Evolution of the Dutch Nation, 419
The Evolution of the Labour Party, 1910–1924, 383
Evolution: The Main Synthesis, 107
The Evolving Self, 173
Excavating in Egypt, 239
Excellence: Can We Be Equal and Excellent Too?, 225
Exchange and Power in Social Life, 196
Exchange Rates and International Macroeconomics, 130
Executive Privilege, 298
Exile and Restoration, 426
Exit, Voice, and Loyalty, 150
Expansion and Coexistence: Soviet Foreign Policy, 426
Experience and Education, 231
Experience and Nature, 231
The Experience of Defeat, 393
Experiences, 479
Experiencing Architecture, 532
Experimental Methodology, 170
Explaining America, 297
Explanation in Social Science, 100
The Exploitation of East Africa, 441
Exploration and Empire, 271
The Exploration of North America, 1630–1776, 619
Explorations in Cultural Anthropology, 121
Explorations in General Theory in Social Science, 214
Explorations in Personality, 175, 183
Explorations in Psychohistory, 403
Explorations of the Highlands of Brazil, 629
Explorers and Settlers, 620
The Exploring Spirit, 312

Exporting Workers: The Turkish Case, 439
Expositions and Developments, 514
The Expression of the Emotions in Man and Animals, 171
Exterminating Angel, 580
The Extraordinary Mr. Wilkes, 379
An Eye for the Dragon, 445

FDR: An Intimate History, 279
FDR, 1882–1945, 277
FDR's Splendid Deception, 52
The FX Decision, 459
Fabian Essays in Socialism, 147
Fables of Fact, 566
The Face of Battle, 408
Facing East, 395
Facing Life, 322
Facing the Dictators, 61
Factor Analysis and Measurement in Sociological Research, 188
Facts about the Presidents, 15, 256
Facts for Socialists, from the Political Economists and Statisticians, 148
Facts on File, 14
The Facts on File Dictionary of Proverbs, 22
Facts on File Yearbooks, 16
Fads and Foibles in Modern Sociology and Related Sciences, 216
Fair Science, 203
Faith and Works, 374
Falange: A History of Spanish Fascism, 419
The Falklands Crisis, 360
The Fall and Rise of Modern Italy, 417
The Fall of Imperial China, 449
The Fall of Public Man, 127
The Fall of Saigon, 454
The Fall of the Roman Republic, 248
Families and Religions, 195
The Family, 195

The Family among the Australian Aborigines, 108
Family and Fortune, 398
Family and Kinship in East London, 108
Family and Population in Nineteenth-Century America, 291
Family and Society, 411
The Family: From Traditional to Companionship, 195
Family Growth in Metropolitan America, 198
The Family in Classical Greece, 244
Family Names, 291
Family Portrait, 56
Family Portrait with Fidel, 362
Family Relationships in Later Life, 189
The Family, Sex and Marriage, 398
Family, Socialization and Interaction Process, 196, 214
The Family Structure in Islam, 433
Family Word Finder, 33
Famous First Facts, 15
Far East: A History of Western Impacts and Eastern Responses (1830–1975), 445
The Far East: A Modern History, 446
The Far East in the Modern World, 446
Far from Cibola, 324
A Faraway Time and Place, 600
Farewell to the Party of Lincoln, 280
Fascism and the Industrial Leadership in Italy, 1919–1940, 418
Fascism in Europe, 413
Fast Forward, 570
The Fate of Midas and Other Essays, 300
Fatherland or Promised Land, 430
Fathers and Daughters in Roman Society, 244
FATU-HIVA, 636

Fear in Battle, 176
Feature Films, 575
The Federalist (Dietze), 295
The Federalist (Hamilton, Madison, and Jay), 86, 295
The Federalist: A Classic on Federalism and Free Government, 295
The Federalist Era, 1789–1801, 269
The Federalist Papers (Fairfield), 295
Federalist Papers (Hamilton, Madison, and Jay), 86, 90, 151
The Federalists vs. the Jeffersonian Republicans, 268
The Female Experience, 292
The Female World, 203
The Feudal Kingdom of England, 371
Fiction Catalog, 7
Field Theory in Social Science, 182
Fifth Avenue, 293
The Fifth French Republic, 415
The Fifth Modernization, 448
Fifty Basic Civil War Documents, 314
Fifty True Mysteries of the Sea, 615
Fifty Years of Serial Thrills, 577
Fifty Years on the Old Frontier as Cowboy, Hunter, Guide, Scout, and Ranchman, 619
Fighting Words: Imperial Censorship and the Russian Press, 425
Film: A Reference Guide, 574
Film: An Anthology, 575
Film as Art, 574
The Film Audience, 574
Film Criticism, 574
Film Directors, 575
Film Directors Guide, 578
The Film Encyclopedia (Hardy), 574
The Film Encyclopedia (Katz), 574
Film Essays with a Lecture, 582

The Film Experience, 576
Film Form, 582
Film in Society, 574
The Film Index, 574
Film Industries in Latin
    America, 577
Film Literature Index, 1973–
    78, 1980–83, 574
Film Music: A Neglected Art,
    493
Film Music: From Violins to
    Video, 493
Film Propaganda, 577
Film Sense, 582
Film Study, 575
Filmed Books and Plays, 574
The Filmgoer's Companion,
    574
Films for, by and about
    Women, 575
Films on Art, 527
Fin-de-Siècle Vienna, 431
The Final Days, 284
The Final Solution, 430
Financial Institutions,
    Markets, and Money, 131
Financing Politics, 297
Find It in Fowler, 31
Findings, 500
Finnish American Folklore,
    597
Fire-Bell in the Night, 322
Fire in the Lake, 454
Fire in the Streets, 284
The Fires of Jubilee, 271
The First American
    Constitutions, 294
First Book of Bolivia, 619
The First Century of English
    Feudalism, 1066–1166, 372
First Century of Italian
    Humanism, 474
The First Elizabeth, 52, 374
First Englishmen in India,
    623
First Essay on Population,
    139
The First Five Years of the
    Communist International,
    480
First Generation, 293
The First Industrial
    Revolution, 378
First Lady of the South, 316
First Lectures in Political
    Sociology, 211

The First New Nation, 102,
    154
The First of the Tudors,
    375
First-Person America, 277
The First Two Stuarts and
    the Puritan Revolution,
    1603–1660, 391
The First Urban Christians,
    243
The First World War, 478
Firsthand Report, 62
Fiscal Policy and Business
    Cycles, 136
Five Families, 117
Five Ideas That Change the
    World, 483
Five Sisters: Women against
    the Tsar, 421
Five Thousand Americans,
    128
Five Thousand Years of
    Popular Culture, 612
Flames across the Border,
    349
Flatlanders and
    Ridgerunners, 600
Flight and Rebellion, 271
The Flight of the Lone Eagle,
    641
Floating Island, 622
Flora of Turkey and the East
    Aegean Islands, 439
The Focal Encyclopedia of
    Film and Television, 577
Folk and Traditional Music
    of the Western Continents,
    493
Folk Art Motifs of
    Pennsylvania, 600
Folk Beliefs of the Southern
    Negro, 606
Folk Buddhist Religion, 448
The Folk Culture of Yucatan,
    105, 106, 122, 192
The Folk Heroes of Britain,
    597
Folk Literature of the British
    Isles, 597
Folk Music and Dances of
    Ireland, 593
Folk Music and Modern
    Sound, 594
Folk Music in School, 594
Folk Music Instruments of
    the World, 492

The Folk Music Sourcebook,
    595
A Folk Song History of
    America, 594
The Folk Song Style and
    Culture, 594
The Folk Songs of North
    America, 594
Folk Songs of the Catskills,
    599
Folk Songs of the Southern
    United States, 601
Folk Tales of Iraq, 596
Folk Visions and Voices,
    601
Folklore, 606
Folklore: A Handbook for
    Study and Research, 591
Folklore and Fakelore, 591
Folklore and Folklife, 592
Folklore and Literature in
    the U.S., 592
Folklore from Iowa, 602
Folklore from Kansas, 601
Folklore from the Schoharie
    Hills, New York, 600
Folklore in America, 591
Folklore of Canada, 596
The Folklore of Puerto Rico,
    597
Folklore of the Oil Industry,
    607
Folklore of the Sea, 606
Folklore Studies in the
    Twentieth Century, 592
Folksingers and Folksongs in
    America, 594
Folksongs and Their Makers,
    594
Folksongs of Britain and
    Ireland, 594
The Folktale, 598
Folktales of America, 595
Folktales of Egypt, 596
Folktales of Mexico, 598
Folktales of the Irish
    Countryside, 596
Folktales of the World
    Series, 595
Folktales Told around the
    World, 595, 596
Folkways, 121
Follett Vest-Pocket French
    Dictionary, 40
Follett Vest-Pocket Italian
    Dictionary, 43

The Fontana Economic History of Europe, 411
Food and Drink in History, 411
The Food Crisis in Prehistory, 107
Food in the Social Order, 107
Foodways in the Northeast, 599
For the Common Defense, 304
For Those in Peril, 637
For Victory in Peaceful Competition with Capitalism, 73
Forays and Rebuttals, 316
Forbidden Books in American Public Libraries, 1876–1939, 563
The Force of Women in Japanese History, 308
Ford, 330
Ford's Freighter Travel Guide, 616
Foreign Affairs, 61
Foreign Affairs 50-Year Index, 1922–1972, 404
Foreign Policy and the Free Society, 328
The Foreign Policy of Hitler's Germany: Diplomatic Revolution in Europe, 1933–1936, 417
The Foreign Policy of Hitler's Germany: Starting World War II, 1937–1939, 417
Foreign Policy of Japan, 1914–1939, 451
The Foreign Policy of the Third Reich, 416
Foreign Travelers in America, 1810–1935, 340
The Forging of the Cosmic Race, 357
The Forgotten Frontier, 275
Formalized Music, 517
Formation of the Soviet Union, 424
Formative Years, 306
Formosa, China, and the United Nations, 447
Forms of Action at Common Law, 394
Forms of Talk, 108, 207

Formula of His Own, 307
Forthcoming Books, 7
The Fortunate Pilgrims, 621
Fortune Is a Woman, 165
The Fossil Evidence for Human Evolution, 107
The Foundation Directory, 7
Foundations of Constitutional Government in Modern Japan, 1868–1900, 449
Foundations of Leninism, 476
Foundations of Method, 233
The Foundations of Psychoanalysis, 175
The Foundations of Sovereignty, and Other Essays, 162
Foundations of the Portuguese Empire, 1415–1850, 418
Founding of Harvard College, 329
The Founding of New England, 307
The Founding of the Russian Empire in Asia and America, 446
Four against Everest, 627
Four American Party Leaders, 337
Four Americans, 336
The Four Books of Architecture, 533
Four Days, 72
Four Fine Gentlemen, 56
Four Portraits and One Subject, 317
Four Seasons North, 620
Four Speeches Hitherto Unpublished or Unknown, 89
Four Voyages to the New World, 631
The Fourth President, 90
The Fragile Blossom: Crisis and Change in Japan, 450
A Fragment of Autobiography, 635
A Fragment on Government, 158
Frame Analysis, 207
Frames of Mind, 173

The Framing of the Constitution of the United States, 151
France: A Modern History, 466
France: A Short History, 466
France and England in North America, 331, 332, 348
France, 1848–1945, 415
France, 1870–1914, 413
France in Modern Times, 415
France in the Classical Age, 465, 466
France in the Giscard Presidency, 414
France since 1918, 415
France's Vietnam Policy, 455
Francis Bacon, 55
Franco-German Relations, 1871–1914, 465
The Frank C. Brown Collection of North Carolina Folklore, 600
The Frankfurt School and Critical Theory, 187
Franklin D. Roosevelt and American Foreign Policy, 1932–1945, 277
Franklin D. Roosevelt and the New Deal, 1932–1940, 278
Franklin D. Roosevelt's Diplomacy and American Catholics, Italians, and Jews, 278
Frederick the Great, 465
The Free and the Unfree, 262
The Free Black in Urban America, 1800–1850, 270
The Free Negro in North Carolina, 1790–1860, 320
Free to Choose, 135
Free to Teach, 227
Freedom and Its Limitations in American Life, 334
Freedom and Order (Commager), 314
Freedom and Order (Eden), 61
Freedom and Reform, 139
Freedom and Responsibility in the American Way of Life, 310
Freedom Flights, 362

Freedom in Contemporary
Society, 329
Freedom, Loyalty, Dissent,
314
Freedom to Publish, 565
Freedom with Justice, 102
Fremont, 330
French and Germans,
Germans and French, 414
The French Army and
Politics, 1870–1970, 414
French Civilization from Its
Origins to the Close of the
Middle Ages, 465
French Civilization in the
Nineteenth Century, 465
French Enlightenment and
the Jews, 428
French False Friends, 40
French Foreign Policy, 1918–
1945, 415
French Foreign Policy under
De Gaulle, 414
French Historical Method:
The "Annales" Paradigm,
403
French Nuclear Diplomacy,
408
French Political and
Intellectual History, 414
The French Revolution
(Carlyle), 461
The French Revolution
(Goodwin), 415
French Revolution (Sobel),
415
French Right and Nazi
Germany, 1933–1939, 414
The French Socialist
Experiment, 413
Freud, Jews and Other
Germans, 416
Freud: The Mind of the
Moralist, 175
The Friendly Arctic, 648
Friends and Fiddlers, 55
The Friends of Liberty, 378
Friends of Thunder,
Folktales of Oklahoma,
603
From Africa to the United
States and Then, 262
From Alfred to Henry III,
871–1272, 371
From Approximately Coast
to Coast, 610

From Birth to Maturity, 173
From Caligari to Hitler, 191
From Colonies to
Commonwealth, 265
From Columbus to Castro,
353
From Dreyfus to Vichy, 429
From Generation to
Generation, 189
From Gunboats to
Diplomacy, 359
From Honey to Ashes, 116
From Many, One, 460
From Medina to Metropolis,
432
From Napoleon to Stalin,
478
From Nationalism to
Revolutionary Islam, 198
From Prague after Munich,
466
From Prejudice to
Destruction: Anti
Semitism, 429
From Protest to Challenge: A
Documentary History of
Politics in South Africa,
443
From Roman Britain to
Norman England, 371
From Sail to Steam, 471
From Sarajevo to Potsdam,
478
From Slavery to Freedom,
319, 320
From Solon to Socrates, 239
From Streetcar to
Superhighway, 277
From the Gracchi to Nero,
241
From the Old South to the
New, 291
From the Renaissance to the
Counter Reformation, 472
Frommer's Guide for the
Disabled Traveler, 615
The Frontier, 254
The Frontier Humorists, 610
The Frontier in American
History, 254, 343
The Frontier in History, 619
Frontier Thesis, 344
Frontier Women, 275
Frontiers of American
Culture, 308
Frontiers of Change, 268

Frontiers of Dance, 523
Frustration and Aggression,
170, 176, 177
Frustration and Aggression:
An Experiment with
Young Children, 182
Functionalism Historicized,
103
Functions of Folk and Fairy
Tales, 606
The Functions of Social
Conflict, 192, 215, 216
The Functions of the
Executive, 127, 197
Fundamental Principles of
the Sociology of Law, 155
Fundamentals of Learning,
236
Funk & Wagnalls
Comprehensive Standard
International Dictionary,
26
Funk & Wagnalls Modern
Guide to Synonyms and
Related Words, 33
Funk & Wagnalls New
Encyclopedia, 3
Funk & Wagnalls Standard
College Dictionary, 26
Funk & Wagnalls Standard
Desk Dictionary, 26
Funk and Wagnalls
Standard Dictionary of
Folklore, Mythology, and
Legends, 597
Funk & Wagnalls Standard
Handbook of Synonyms,
Antonyms and
Prepositions, 33
Furniture Treasury, 534
The Future Comes, 309
The Future of Architecture,
558
The Future of Broadcasting,
564
The Future of Government
in the United States, 166
The Future of Socialism,
157
The Future of the
International Monetary
System, 131

Galina: A Russian Story,
426

Game Theory and Related Approaches to Social Behavior, 125
Gandhi, 453
Gandhi's Truth, 178
A Garland of Country Song, 593
Gemeinschaft und Gesellschaft, 219
Gender Advertisements, 207
Gender and the Life Course, 203
Gender Politics, 203
General Anthropology, 112
General Bibliography of Motion Pictures, 575
A General History of Africa, 443
The General Inquirer, 101
General Interviewing Techniques, 101
General Science Index, 2
The General Theory of Employment, Interest and Money, 124, 127, 130, 138, 141
The General Theory of Law and State, 151
The Genesis of a Painting, 549
Genesis of the Frontier Thesis, 344
Genetic Epistemology, 235
Genius and the Mobocracy, 554, 559
The Genius of American Politics, 312
The Genius of George Washington, 269
Genocide, 193
The Gentry, 379
Geography of Israel, 435
George C. Marshall, 409
George-Etienne Cartier, 351
George IV: Prince of Wales, 1752–1811, 378
George IV: Regent and King, 1811–1830, 379
George Washington, 56, 57
George Washington Williams, 320
Georgetown University Round Table on Languages and Linguistics, 108
Georgian Delights, 396

Georgian London, 379
The German Dictatorship, 415
A German-English Dictionary of Idioms, 42
The German Ideology, 134
The German People, 110
The German Polity, 415
German Renaissance Architecture, 532
German Root Lexicon, 41
German Sociology, 457
A German Word Family Dictionary, 41
Germans and Jews, 430
Germany and Europe, 1919–1939, 416
Germany and the French Revolution, 465
Germany and the Politics of Nuclear Weapons, 408
Germany and the Two World Wars, 408
Germany, 1865–1945, 416
Germany Transformed, 415
Germany, Turkey, and Zionism, 1897–1918, 428
Germany's Aims in the First World War, 407, 416
Germany's First Bid for Colonies, 1884–1885, 477
Gestalt Psychology, 175
Gettysburg: A Journey in Time, 273
Gettysburg: The Final Fury, 314
The Ghetto, the Gold Coast and the Slum, 192
Ghost, Gales and Gold, 645
Ghosts along the Cumberland, 601
Giacometti, 53
A Giant Walked among Them, 597
The Giant's Rival, 358
Gift: Forms and Functions of Exchange in Archaic Societies, 107
The Gift of Black Folk, 318
Gifted Young Children, 228
The Gilbert and Sullivan Companion, 487
Giraffes, Black Dragons and Other Pianos, 496
Give Us Good Measure, 348
Gladstone, 380

Gladstone: A Progress in Politics, 382
Gladstone and the Irish Nation, 392
Glass, 534
A Glimpse of Eden, 623
A Glimpse of Sion's Glory, 264
Glimpses of World History, 473
A Global History, 406
The Glorious Cause, 266
The Glory and the Dream, 283
The Glory Road, 313
A Glossary of Spanish Literary Composition, 46
Gloucester Sea Ballads, 594
Goddesses, Whores, Wives and Slaves, 244
God's Englishman, 393
God's Fool, 52
Going to the Dance, 518
Gokhale, Gandhi and the Nehrus, 453
The Gold Coast and the Slum, 192
Gold Dust, 271
The Golden Age of American Anthropology, 103
The Golden Age of Brazil, 1695–1750, 356
The Golden Age of Opera, 495
The Golden Age of Television, 573
The Golden Antilles, 620
The Golden Bough, 109, 114
The Golden Trade of the Moors, 441
The Golden Tradition, 427
The Good Guys, the Bad Guys, and the First Amendment, 567
The Good High School, 227
Good News, Bad News, 565
Good Old Cause, 393
The Good Old Days—They Were Terrible, 274
The Good Parliament, 373
The Good Society, 325
Goode's World Atlas, 18
Gospel, the Church and the World, 469
Gouverneur Morris, 336

The Governance of England, 390

The Governance of Medieval England, 397

Governing New York City, 154

Governing without Consensus, 384

Government Agencies, 257

Government and Community, 373

Government and Local Power in Japan, 450

Government by Pen, 376

The Government of Associations, 197

Government Publications and Their Use, 14

The Governmental Process, 154

Governmental Secrecy and the Founding Fathers, 269

Governments, Markets, and Growth, 132

Grammar of Ornament, 534

A Grammar of Politics, 162

The Grand Strategy of the Roman Empire, 244

The Grand Tour in the Eighteenth Century, 622

Grant, 53

Grant, Lee, Lincoln and the Radicals, 313

Grant Moves South, 313

Grant Takes Command, 313

The Great Age of Discovery, 616

The Great American Fair, 285

The Great American Popular Singers, 496

The Great American Values Test, 190

The Great Anglo-Boer War, 380

The Great Awakening, 327

The Great Betrayal, 350

Great Contemporaries, 388

The Great Dan: A Biography of Daniel O'Connell, 382

The Great Debate: Theories of Nuclear Strategy, 457

Great Dissenters, 341

Great Exploration Hoaxes, 627

The Great Explorers, 329

The Great Famine, 380

The Great Father, 293

The Great Frontier, 473

Great Harry, 52

Great Heresies, 386

Great Hunger, 382

Great Issues in American History, 324

Great Masters of the Violin, from Corelli to Stern, Zukerman, and Perlman, 496

The Great Mutiny, 380

Great Patriotic War of the Soviet Union, 476

Great Pianists of Our Time, 496

Great Pianists Speak for Themselves, 496

The Great Piano Virtuosos of Our Time, 496

The Great Powers and the End of the Ottoman Empire, 439

The Great Psychologists from Aristotle to Freud, 170, 179

The Great Railway Bazaar, 624

The Great Reform Act, 377

The Great Republic, 261

The Great Revolt of 1381, 373

Great River, 324

The Great Secession Winter of 1860–61 and Thirteen Other Essays, 306

The Great Singers, from Jenny Lind to Callas and Pavarotti, 496

Great Singers on Great Singing, 496

The Great Television Race, 287

The Great Terror: Stalin's Purge of the Thirties, 421, 476

The Great Transformation, 144

Great Travel Stories of All Nations, 616

Great Travelers, 617

The Great Treasury of Western Thought, 20

The Great TV Sitcom Book, 572

The Great United States Exploring Expedition of 1838–1842, 620

Great Villiers, 56

The Great Violinists, 495

The Great War and Modern Memory, 408

The Great War and the Search for a Modern Order, 277

The Great War, 1914–1918, 407

Great Women of the Press, 568

The Greater City, 330

The Greater Roman Historians, 240

The Greatest Quotations, 21

The Greatest Transformation, 144

Greece, Gods, and Art, 622

Greece in the Bronze Age, 240

Greed, 588

Greek-American Folk Beliefs and Narratives, 596

The Greek and Macedonian Art of War, 244

Greek and Roman Technology, 243

The Greek City from Alexander to Justinian, 240

Greek-English Lexicon, 42

The Greek Historians, 240

Greek Historical Documents (Bagnall and Derow), 241

Greek Historical Documents (Lewis), 242

Greek Historical Documents (Wickersham and Verbrugghe), 242

Greek Homosexuality, 243

The Greek Islands, 621

Greek Medicine, 243

Greek Papyri, 242

Greek Political Oratory, 240

Greek Sculpture, 529

The Greek State, 239

The Greek Stones Speak, 242

The Greeks, 239

The Greeks Overseas, 242

The Green Flag, 369

Gregarious Saints, 270

Grey of Fallodon, 399

Groping for Ethics in Journalism, 566
Groucho and Me, 587
Group Dynamics, 172
Groups at Work, 172
Growing Up, 51
The Growth of an American Village in the Early Industrial Revolution, 289
The Growth of Federal Power in American History, 300
The Growth of Philosophic Radicalism, 392
Growth of Political Stability in England, 1675–1725, 396
The Growth of Southern Civilization, 1790–1860, 268
The Growth of the American Republic, 263, 329
The Growth of the American Revolution, 1766–1775, 266
Guests of the Sheik, 623
A Guide for Collectors of Oral Traditions and Folk Cultural Material in Pennsylvania, 600
A Guide for Field Workers in Folklore, 592
Guide to American Foreign Relations since 1700, 259
Guide to Atlases, 17
Guide to Congress, 255
A Guide to Historical Method, 403
A Guide to Keynes, 136
Guide to League of Nations Publications, 403
Guide to Reference Books, 10
Guide to the Diplomatic History of the United States, 1775–1921, 311
Guide to the Literature of Art History, 527
A Guide to the Study of Medieval History, 405
A Guide to the Study of the United States of America, 256
Guide to the U.S. Supreme Court, 255
Guide to U.S. Elections, 255

The Guinness Book of World Records, 14
The Gulag Archipelago, 425
The Gulf and Inland Waters, 471
The Gunpowder Empires and Modern Times, 446
The Guns of August, 409, 481
Gypsies, 195

Habits of the Heart, 102
The Halls of Ravenswood, 621
Hamlyn French Dictionary, 40
Hamlyn German Dictionary, 41
Hamlyn Italian Dictionary, 43
Hamlyn Spanish Dictionary, 46
Hammond Ambassador World Atlas, 18
Hammond-Jeans Dictionary: French-English, English-French, 40
Hammond-Jeans Dictionary: German-English, English-German, 41
Hammond-Jeans Dictionary: Spanish-English/English-Spanish, 46
Hammond Medallion World Atlas, 18
The Handbook of Aging and the Social Sciences, 189
Handbook of American English Spelling, 35
Handbook of American Folklore, 592
Handbook of British Chronology, 370
Handbook of English, 31
Handbook of English-Arabic for Professionals, 38
A Handbook of English-German Idioms and Useful Expressions, 41
Handbook of Latin American Studies, 352
Handbook of Middle American Indians, 352
Handbook of New Nations, 405

Handbook of Organizations, 197
Handbook of Perception, 174
The Handbook of Political Science, 149
Handbook of Small Group Research, 172
The Handbook of Social Psychology, 170
Handbook of Socialization Theory and Research, 202
Handbook of the Indians of California, 115
The Handbook of the Psychology of Aging, 189
Hands and Hearts, 293
Hannibal's Legacy, 479
Hanoi, 455
Hanoverian London, 1714–1808, 379
Harbrace College Handbook, 22
Harbrace Guide to the Library and the Research Paper, 23
Hard Rock Epic, 275
Hard Times, 280
The Harder We Run, 288
Harper Dictionary of Contemporary Usage, 31
Harriet, 58
Harry S. Truman and the Modern American Presidency, 281
Harry Warren and the Hollywood Musical, 577
Harvard College in the Seventeenth Century, 329
Harvard Concise Dictionary of Music, 490
Harvard Dictionary of Music, 487
Harvard Encyclopedia of American Ethnic Groups, 100, 195
Harvard Guide to American History, 256
The Harvest and the Reapers, 601
Hear Me Talkin' to Ya, 494
Hear That Lonesome Whistle Blow, 275
Heart of Oak, 379
The Heart of the Dragon, 447
The Heart of the Hunter, 648

Hearth and Home, 565

The Heavenly City of the Eighteenth-Century Philosophers, 310

The Heavenly City Revisited, 310

Heavens to Betsy and Other Curious Sayings, 36

Hell in a Very Small Place, 454

The Hellenica, 246

The Hellenist World, 240

The Hellenistic World from Alexander to the Roman Conquest, 241

Henry Adams, 308

Henry Cabot Lodge and the Search for an American Foreign Policy, 305

Henry VIII, 375

Henry VIII: The Mask of Royalty, 375

Henry Fielding, 58

Henry II, 372

Here the Country Lies, 285

The Heritage of America, 314

A Heritage of Her Own, 290

A Hero for Our Time, 72, 283

Heroes of the Dark Continent, 646

Heroes, Villains, and Ghosts, 603

Heroic Epic and Saga, 597

The Herring Gull's World, 186

Hey Traveller! Wanna Ride?, 617

The Heyday of American Communism, 278

The Hidden-Hand Presidency, 282

The Hidden Hinge, 234

The Hidden Order of Art, 527

High in the Thin Cold Air, 637

High Level, 621

The High Middle Ages in England, 1154–1377, 369

High School, 224

High Tide at Gettysburg, 274

The High Walls of Jerusalem, 430

Higher Civil Servants in American Society, 150

The Higher Learning in America (Hutchins), 232

The Higher Learning in America (Veblen), 220

Hindoo Holiday, 623

Hinduism, 453

His Day Is Marching On, 319

His First Life, 1838–1862, 306

His Was the Voice, 319

Hispanic Folk Music of New Mexico and the Southwest, 603

The Historian and the City, 322

Historians and the American West, 254

An Historian's Approach to Religion, 479

Historian's Fallacies, 402

The Historian's Handbook, 257

Historic Architecture Sourcebook, 532

Historic Preservation, 532

Historical Americana, 261

Historical Atlas of Britain, 369

An Historical Atlas of the Indian Peninsula, 404

The Historical Atlas of United States Congressional Districts, 1789–1983, 156

Historical Dictionary of Fascist Italy, 417

An Historical Essay on Modern Spain, 418

Historical Geography of the United States, 17

Historical Geography of the United States and Canada, 259

Historical Introduction to Modern Psychology, 169, 177

Historical Introduction to the Rolls Series, 398

Historical Introduction to the Study of Roman Law, 244

Historical Materialism and the Economics of Karl Marx, 462

Historical Periodicals Directory, 403

Historical Review of the Constitution and Government of Pennsylvania, from Its Origin, 64

Historical Sets: Collected Editions, and Monuments of Music, 489

Historical Sketch of the Native States of India, 453

Historical Sociology, 188

History and American Society, 334

History and Historians, 403

History and Historians in the 19th Century, 402, 465

History and Will, 76, 449

History as Art and as Science, 403

History as Literature and Other Essays, 336

History as the Story of Liberty, 462

History, Civilization and Culture, 216

History: Its Theory and Practice, 462

The History of Africa, 442

The History of Africa in Maps, 404, 442

A History of Alberta, 347

The History of American Electoral Behavior, 301

A History of American Foreign Policy, 303

History of American Life Series, 338

The History of American Political Theories, 166

The History of American Presidential Elections, 340

The History of American Sculpture, 531

A History of American Wars from 1745 to 1918, 305

History of Andersonville Prison, 273

History of Architecture, 531

History of Art, 528

A History of Asia, 445

A History of Brazil, 361

A History of British Trade Unionism, 370

A History of Canada, 347

The History of Canada: An Annotated Bibliography, 347

History of China, 464

History of Christian Missions in China, 468

A History of Christianity, 469

The History of Christianity in West Africa, 443

A History of Civilization, 405, 459, 460

History of Civilization in England, 387

A History of Dance, 518

History of Early Relations between the United States and China, 1784–1844, 468

A History of East Asian Civilization, 464

History of Economic Analysis, 124, 134, 142

History of Education in Antiquity, 245

History of England from the Accession of Edward Sixth to the Death of Elizabeth, 396

History of England from the Accession of James II, 394

History of England from the Fall of Wolsey to the Defeat of the Spanish Armada, 390

History of England in the Eighteenth Century, 394

History of England, 1603–1656, 391

The History of Europe in the Nineteenth Century, 462

History of European Morals from Augustus to Charlemagne, 394

A History of Experimental Psychology, 169, 177

A History of Exploration from the Earliest Times to the Present Day, 618

A History of Far Eastern Art, 530

A History of Florence, 474

The History of Folklore in Europe, 596

History of France, 414

History of Freedom, and Other Essays, 384

History of Friedrich II of Prussia, Called Frederick the Great, 461

History of Greek Art, 530

History of Greek Culture, 460

A History of Historical Writing (Barnes), 402

A History of Historical Writing (Thompson), 403

History of Impressionism, 530

History of Indian and Indonesian Art, 529

History of Ireland in the Eighteenth Century, 394

A History of Israel, 435

A History of Italy, 1871–1915, 462

A History of Japan (Latourette), 468

A History of Japan (Mason and Caiger), 451

A History of Japan, 1334–1615, 451

A History of Japan, 1615–1867, 451

A History of Japan to 1334, 451

History of Korea, 454

History of Labour in the United States, 133

A History of Latin America, 352

A History of Medieval Spain, 419

History of Modern Architecture, 532

A History of Modern France, 414

A History of Modern Germany, 416

A History of Modern Indonesia, 455

A History of Modern Norway, 1814–1972, 419

A History of Modern Thailand, 455

History of Mosaics, 534

A History of Musical Style, 485

A History of My Times, 246

The History of Nationalism in the East, 467

A History of Nazi Germany, 415

A History of Negro Education in the South, 290

The History of New England, 307

A History of Ornament. Ancient and Medieval, 534

A History of Painting in Italy, Umbria, Florence, and Siena from the Second to the Sixteenth Century, 529

A History of Persia, 438

A History of Persia under Quajar Rule, 437

A History of Philosophy in America, 285

A History of Political Parties in the Province of New York, 1760–1776, 310

History of Portugal, 418

A History of Postwar Britain, 1945–74, 382

A History of Postwar Japan, 450

The History of Postwar Southeast Asia, 445

A History of Psychology in Autobiography, 169, 176, 181

History of Renaissance Art, 530

A History of Russia (Kliuchevskii), 423

A History of Russia (Riasanovsky), 425

A History of Russia (Vernadsky), 426, 482, 483

A History of Scandinavia, 419

The History of Science and Technology, 405

A History of Sexuality, 411

A History of Socialist Thought, 157

A History of South Africa to 1870, 445

A History of South Asia, 452

A History of South East Asia, 446

A History of Soviet Russia (Carr), 420

A History of Soviet Russia (Dziewanowski), 421

A History of Soviet Russia (Rauch), 424

A History of Spain and
  Portugal, 419
A History of Spain Founded
  on the Historia de España
  y de la Civilización
  Española of Rafael
  Altamira, 418
A History of Sweden, 419
A History of the African
  People, 443
A History of the American
  People, 263
A History of the Ancient
  World, 239
History of the Arabs, 438
The History of the Balkan
  Peninsula, 474
History of the Bank of New
  York and Trust Company,
  1784–1934, 330
The History of the British
  Film, 1918–1929, 577
History of the Conquest of
  Mexico, 334
History of the Conquest of
  Peru, 334
History of the English
  People in the Nineteenth
  Century, 392
A History of the English-
  Speaking Peoples, 388
A History of the Expansion
  of Christianity, 468
History of the First World
  War, 408
A History of the Habsburg
  Empire, 1526–1918, 412
The History of the
  Illustrated Book, 534
History of the Inca Empire,
  353
A History of the Indians of
  the United States, 290
A History of the Jewish
  People, 427
The History of the Kingdom
  of Naples, 462
The History of the Kings of
  Britain, 392
A History of the Modern
  World, 406
The History of the Negro
  Race in America from
  1619 to 1880, 263
History of the Norman
  Conquest of England, 390

History of the Ottoman
  Empire and Modern
  Turkey, 439
History of the Reign of
  Ferdinand and Isabella the
  Catholic, 334
History of the Second World
  War, 408
History of the Southern
  Confederacy, 268
The History of the United
  States, 322
History of the United States
  Army, 409
History of the United States
  during the
  Administrations of
  Jefferson and Madison,
  306
History of the United States
  from the Compromise of
  1850 to the McKinley-
  Bryan Campaign of 1896,
  263
History of the United States
  Naval Operations in World
  War II, 1939–1945, 329
History of the United States
  of America: A Guide to
  Information Sources, 259
A History of the Weimar
  Republic, 416
History of the Westward
  Movement, 263
A History of the World, 406
The History of the Yorubas,
  443
History of U.S. Political
  Parties, 301, 340
History of Violin Playing,
  from Its Origins to 1761
  and Its Relationship to the
  Violin and Violin Music,
  495
A History of Western Art,
  528
History of Western
  Civilization, 472
A History of Western
  Education, 224
The History of Western
  Instruments, 496
A History of Western Music,
  485
A History of World Societies,
  406

A History of Zionism, 429
History of Zionism, 1600–
  1918, 431
History Remembered,
  Recovered, Invented, 403
Hitler, 415
Hitler's Europe, 479
Hitler's Social Revolution,
  417
Hitler's War, 408, 416
The Hittites, 239
Hog on Ice and Other
  Curious Expressions, 36
Hogs in the Bottoms, 601
Holidays and Anniversaries
  of the World, 14
Hollow Earth, 631
Hollywood Dynasties, 576
Hollywood Films of the
  Seventies, 576
Hollywood Genres, 575
Hollywood Scapegoat, 588
Hollywood: The First 100
  Years, 577
The Holocaust: Ideology,
  Bureaucracy and
  Genocide, 428
A Holocaust Reader, 428
The Holocaust: The
  Destruction of European
  Jewry, 1933–1945, 429
The Holy Roman Empire,
  159
Home Book of Quotations,
  21
Home Style, 299
The Homefront, 278
Homo Ludens, 105
Homonyms, "Sound-Alikes,"
  34
Honkers and Shouters, 492
Honorable Profession, 73
Hoosier Folk Legends, 601
Hopitutuwutsi-Hopi Tales,
  604
Horace's Compromise, 228
The Horizon Book of the Age
  of Napoleon, 57
Horror Film Stars, 575
Horsefeathers and Other
  Curious Words, 36
Hour, 316
The Hour of Decision, 475
The House of Saud, 438
Houses, Villas and Palaces in
  the Roman World, 242

How Children Learn, 226
How Communist China Negotiates, 448
How Congress Works, 298
How Democratic Is the Constitution?, 151
How I Found Livingstone, 646
How New Will the Better World Be?, 310
How Russia Is Ruled, 422
How the Conservatives Rule Japan, 452
How the North Won, 273
How the Reformation Happened, 386
How the Soviet Union Is Governed, 422
How to Do a Literature Search in Psychology, 170
How to Eat Like a Child, 610
How to Go around the World Overland, 617
How to Look at Dance, 518
How to Study History, 402
How to Survive on Fifty Thousand to One Hundred Fifty Thousand Dollars a Year, 609
How to Take Great Trips with Your Kids, 617
How We Live, 102
How We Think, 231
The Huddled Masses, 292
Human Action, 146
Human Associative Memory, 171
Human Behavior, 99
Human Capital, 126
The Human Condition (Arendt), 456
The Human Condition (McNeill), 473
The Human Dimension in International Relations, 181
Human Ecology, 192
The Human Factor in Changing Africa, 115
The Human Figure, 540
The Human Group, 172
Human Learning, 236
Human Nature and Biocultural Evolution, 107
Human Nature and Collective Behavior, 190

Human Nature and Conduct, 231
Human Nature and the Social Order, 205
Human Nature in American Thought, 285
Human Nature under Fire, 456
Human Nonverbal Behavior, 562
The Human Rights Reader, 151
Human Types, 113
Human Words, 36
Humanistic Education and Western Civilization, 232
Humanistic Radio Production, 571
The Humanities: A Selective Guide to Information Sources, 405
Humanities Index, 2, 8
Humanities through the Black Experience, 605
The Hummingbird and the Hawk, 356
Humor of a Country Lawyer, 610
Humor of the Old Southwest, 609
A Hundred Years of Music, 485
Hundred Years War, 373
Hungarian-English, English-Hungarian Concise Dictionary, 42
Hungarian Folk Beliefs, 596
The Hungarian Folk Song, 593
Hunters of the Great North, 648
Hunting Trips of a Ranchman, 335
Hush Child, Can't You Hear the Music, 606
The Hussey-Cumberland Mission and American Independence, 311

I Hear America Talking, 36
I Was There: Selected Dance Reviews and Articles, 1936–1976, 518
IMS Directory of Publications, 8

The IQ Controversy, 173
Iacocca, 52
Iberia, 622
Iceland, 648
The Idea of a Party System, 323
The Idea of Freedom, 150
The Idea of History, 462
The Idea of National Interest, 309
The Idea of Nationalism, 467, 468
The Idea of Social Structure, 201, 211
Idea of the Jewish State, 428
Ideas and Issues in Public Administration, 150
Ideas and Men, 460
Ideas of Jewish History, 430
Ideas of the Great Economists, 124
Ideas of the Great Psychologists, 170
Identifying American Architecture, 532
Identity and Anxiety, 103
Identity and the Life Cycle, 172, 178
The Ideological Origins of the American Revolution, 265
Ideology and Discontent, 154
Ideology and Experience, 431
Ideology and Organization in Communist China, 448
Ideology and Utopia, 154, 208, 209
Idioms and Phrases Index, 33
Ikiru, 586
The Illogic of American Nuclear Strategy, 157
Illustrated Dictionary of Ceramics, 534
An Illustrated Dictionary of Ornament, 535
Illustrated History of Black Americans, 320
Image, 312
The Image Decade, 571
The Image of Peter the Great in Russian Fiction, 422
Images of Society, 342
Images of Women in Antiquity, 243

Immediate Experience, 612
Immigration and American
  History, 314
Immigration as a Factor in
  American History, 322
Immoral Memories, 582
The Impact of Hitler: British
  Politics and British Policy,
  1933–1940, 382
The Impact of Intervention,
  362
Impact of Labour, Nineteen
  Twenty to Nineteen
  Twenty Four: The
  Beginning of Modern
  British Politics, 382
Impeachment, 298
Impending Crisis, 1848–
  1861, 334
An Imperfect Union, 270
Imperial Democracy, 304
Imperial Germany, 415
The Imperial Presidency, 340
The Imperial Republic, 280,
  457
Imperial Spain, 1469–1716,
  418
Imperialism, 470
The Impossible Dream, 282
The Improvement of
  Mankind, 142
In a Hundred Graves, 622
In Battle for Peace, 318
In Command of France, 415
In Defense of Decadent
  Europe, 458
In Defense of Liberal
  Democracy, 152
In Defense of the Indians,
  355
In Ethiopia with a Mule, 624
In Its Own Image, 572
In Praise of Sailors, 618
In Retrospect, 338
In Search of Identity, 436
In Search of Peace, 407
In Search of Southeast Asia,
  446
In Search of the Common
  Good, 203
In the Course of Human
  Events, 266
In the Margin of History,
  395
In the Nature of Materials,
  559

In the Public Interest—III,
  1979–1983, 566
In the Shadow of FDR, 300
In the Steps of the Master,
  642
In the Wake of the Tourist,
  614
In Their Own Words, 293
Incidents of Travel in
  Central America, Chiapas
  and Yucatan, 354
Income, Saving and the
  Theory of Consumer
  Behavior, 128
The Incompleat Folksinger,
  595
The Incorporation of
  America, 287
Indelible Shadows, 576
Independence and After, 473
The Independence
  Movement in Quebec,
  1945–1980, 349
The Independent Arab, 439
Independent Ireland, 382
The Indestructible Jews, 428
Index to Biographies of
  Contemporary Composers,
  488
Index to Business
  Periodicals, 1
Index to Characters in the
  Performing Arts, 519
Index to Legal Periodicals, 2
Index to United States
  Government Periodicals,
  13
Indexing and Abstracting, 11
India, 453
India after Nehru, 453
India and Pakistan in the
  Twentieth Century, 453
India and the West, 483
The Indian Fairy Book, 603
Indian Film, 576
The Indian in America, 261
The Indian Journals, 1859–
  1862, 120
Indian Legends from the
  Northern Rockies, 603
Indian Legends of the Pacific
  Northwest, 603
Indian Tales of C. C.
  Trowbridge, 604
Indian Tales of North
  America, 603

Indiana Folklore, 601
Indianized States of
  Southeast Asia, 445
Indians before Columbus,
  293
Indians of North America,
  110, 290
Indians of the Plains, 111
Indians of the United States,
  294
India's Quest, 473
Indicators of Social Change,
  200
The Individual and His
  Society, 106
Individual Delinquent, 193
Individualism Reconsidered,
  215
Indonesia: The Making of a
  Nation, 455
Industrial Concentration,
  127
Industrial Democracy, 148
Industrial Policies for
  Growth and
  Competitiveness, 128
Industrial Research
  Laboratories in the United
  States, 8
Industrial Revolution
  (Ashton), 385
Industrial Revolution
  (Beard), 309
The Industrial Revolution
  (Toynbee), 479
The Industrial Revolution
  and British Overseas
  Trade, 378
The Industrial Revolution
  and Economic Growth,
  378
Industrialization and the
  American Labor
  Movement, 1850–1900,
  289
The Industrialization of
  Egypt, 1939–1973, 436
The Industrialization of Iraq,
  437
Industry and Empire, 393
Inequality: A Reassessment
  of the Effect of Family and
  Schooling in America, 201
Inequality and
  Heterogeneity, 201
Infamy, 280

Inflation: Causes and Effects, 130, 131
Inflation, Exchange Rates, and the World Economy, 130
The Influence of Freud on American Psychology, 175
The Influence of Islam upon Africa, 434, 444
The Influence of Sea Power upon History, 1660–1783, 470, 471
The Influence of Sea Power upon the French Revolution and Empire, 1793–1812, 470, 471
Information and the Crisis Economy, 565
Information and the Transformation of Society, 565
The Information Empire, 567
Information Please Almanac, 16
Information Process, 565
The Information Sources of Political Science, 149
The Informed Heart, 427
Initiation Ceremonies, 110
Innocents Abroad, 613, 618
The Innocents at Cedro, 220
Input-Output Economics, 125
An Inquiry into the Nature and Causes of the Wealth of Nations, 125, 126, 145, 146
An Inquiry into the Principles of the Good Society, 325
The Inquisition in Hollywood, 285
Inside ABC, 572
Inside Africa, 634
Inside American Ballet Theatre, 520
Inside Australia, 634
Inside Europe Today, 634
Inside Russia Today, 634
Inside South America, 634
Inside Soviet Schools, 226
Inside the Third Reich, 417
Inside the Wall Street Journal, 566
Inside U.S.A., 634

An Insider's Guide to the Travel Game, 617
Institutional Economics (Commons), 133
Institutional Economics (Dorfman), 133
The Institutions of France under the Absolute Monarchy, 1598–1789, 415
The Intellectual between Tradition and Modernity, 190
Intellectual Life in America, 286
The Intellectual Life of Colonial New England, 329
Intellectual Origins of the English Revolution, 393
The Intellectuals and the Powers, 190, 200, 215
Intellectuals in Labor Unions, 198
Intelligence and Affectivity in Early Childhood, 184
Intelligence: Genetic and Environmental Influences, 173
The Intelligence of Democracy, 156
Interaction Process Analysis, 172, 188
Interaction Ritual, 207
Intercultural Attitudes in the Making, 233
Interest and Prices, 148
Interest Group Politics, 298
The Interest of America in Sea Power, 471
Inter/Media, 564
Intermediate Greek-English Lexicon, 42
International and Intercultural Communication, 563
International Directory of the Literature of Art, 529
The International Economy, 130
International Encyclopedia of Population, 100, 198
International Encyclopedia of Quotations, 21
International Encyclopedia of Statistics, 100

International Encyclopedia of the Social Sciences, 8, 100, 404
International Encyclopedia of Women Composers, 488
International Film Guide, 574
International Folk Dance at a Glance, 594
International Law, 155
International Maps and Atlases in Print, 17
International Politics in East Asia since World War Two, 446
International Politics of Energy Interdependence, 432
International Relations between the Two World Wars, 1919–1939, 407
International Studies and the Social Sciences, 155
The International Telecommunication Union, 563
The International Thesaurus of Quotations, 21
International Trade, 130
International Travel and Tourism, 614
The International Traveler's Security Handbook, 616
International Who's Who in Music, 489
Interpersonal Communication, 563
Interpersonal Communication: The Social Exchange Approach, 565
Interplay of East and West, 446, 483
The Interplay of Influence, 564
The Interpretation of Cultures, 105, 114
An Interpretation of Universal History, 479
Interpretations of American History, 262
Interpretations of Fascism, 411
Interpretations of Life, 463
Interpreting Folklore, 592

Intervention and Revolution,
   302
Interviewing, 101
Into the Dark, 456
Introduction to Ancient
   History, 238
An Introduction to Anglo-
   Saxon England, 371
An Introduction to Chinese
   Civilization, 448
An Introduction to Classical
   Ballet, 519
An Introduction to
   Contemporary History,
   410
An Introduction to
   Democratic Theory, 152
Introduction to English
   Historians, 308
Introduction to Japanese
   History and Culture,
   450
Introduction to Money and
   Banking, 131
An Introduction to
   Motivation, 173
Introduction to Roman Law,
   244
An Introduction to the
   Administrative History of
   Mediaeval England, 373
Introduction to the Dance,
   518
An Introduction to the
   History of Central Africa,
   445
An Introduction to the
   History of South East
   Asia, 446
Introduction to the Modern
   Economic History of the
   Middle East, 432
Introduction to the
   Philosophy of History, 402,
   457
An Introduction to the
   Principles of Morals and
   Legislation, 158
An Introduction to the
   Science of Comparative
   Mythology and Folklore,
   591
Introduction to the
   Sociology of Music, 485
An Introduction to the Study
   of Language, 112

Introduction to the Study of
   the Law of the
   Constitution, 151
Introduction to United
   States Public Documents,
   13, 256
Introduction to World Peace
   through World Law, 155
Introductory
   Macroeconomics, 1981–
   1982, 125
The Invasion from Mars,
   190, 589
The Invasion of Canada, 349
The Invasion of the Crimea,
   637
Invented Lives, 53
Inventing America, 297
The Invention of Tradition,
   393, 608
Invisible Colleges, 199
Invitation to Struggle, 303
The Ionian Islands to
   Rhodes, 621
Iran, 437
The Iran-Iraq War, 438
Iran Past and Present, 438
Iran's Foreign Policy, 1941–
   1973, 438
Iraq and Iran, 437
Iraq: Economics, Oil and
   Politics, 438
Iraq, 1900–1950, 437
Ireland: From Colony to
   Nation State, 370, 381
Ireland in the Twentieth
   Century, 383
Ireland since the Famine,
   370
Ireland: The Union and Its
   Aftermath, 381
Ireland's English Question,
   370
The Irish Countryman, 110
Irish Unionism, 380
Iron and Steel in the
   Industrial Revolution, 385
The Iron Cage, 221
Irregular Serials and
   Annuals, 8
Is Conscience a Crime?, 341
Isaac Asimov's Treasury of
   Humor, 609
Islam: A Way of Life, 434
Islam and Capitalism, 434
Islam and Modernity, 434

Islam and Muslim Art, 530
Islam and Revolution, 434
Islam and the West, 432
Islam: Beliefs and
   Observances, 434
Islam in Asia, 434
Islam in East Africa, 434
Islam in Egypt Today, 433
Islam in Foreign Policy, 434
Islam in Modern History,
   434
Islam in the Political
   Process, 434
Islam in Tropical Africa, 434
Islam Observed, 114, 434
Islam: Politics and Religion
   in the Muslim World, 433
The Islamic Concept of
   Religion and Its Revival,
   434
Islamic Culture and Socio-
   Economic Change, 434
Islamic Middle East, 700–
   1900, 434
Islamic Resurgence in the
   Arab World, 434
Islamic Revolution, 438
The Islamic Tradition, 434
The Islamic World since the
   Peace Settlement, 479
Islands and Empires, 445
The Islands of Boston
   Harbor, 645
Israel: A Colonial Settler
   State, 430
Israel after Begin, 435
Israel between East and
   West, 430
Israel in Folklore, 597
Israel in the Begin Era, 435
Israel: Years of Challenge,
   427
The Israelis, 428
Israel's Lebanon War, 435
It Seemed Like Nothing
   Happened, 281
Italian Bilingual Dictionary,
   43
Italian Fascism, 417
Italian Painters of the
   Renaissance, 529
Italy: A Modern History, 417
Italy and the Approach of
   the First World War, 417
Italy from Liberalism to
   Fascism, 1870–1925, 418

Italy in the Twentieth
Century, 417
Italy since 1945, 418
Italy: The Places in Between,
622
It's Good to Tell You, 602
Ivalu, the Eskimo Wife, 634
Ivan the Terrible, 582

Jack Nicholson, 578
Jack Tales, 600
Jack: The Struggles of John
F. Kennedy, 283
The Jacobins, 459
The Jacobite Army in
England, 1745, 379
Jacques Cousteau's Calypso,
625
James Madison and the
Search for Nationhood,
269
James the Second (Belloc),
386
James II (Miller), 376
James Truslow Adams, 330
Japan, 450
Japan: A Short Cultural
History, 451
Japan and the Decline of the
West in Asia, 452
Japan at War, 407
Japan before Tokugawa, 450
Japan-China, 623
Japan Emerges, 452
Japan Examined, 452
Japan: Its History and
Culture, 451
The Japan Reader, 451
Japan: The Fragile
Superpower, 450
Japan: The Story of a
Nation, 451
The Japanese Colonial
Empire, 1895–1945, 451
Japanese Economic Growth,
451
Japanese Folk Literature,
596
Japanese History, Politics,
and Society, 450
Japanese Inn, 451
Japanese Lantern, 624
The Japanese Seizure of
Korea, 1868–1910, 454
Japanese Society Today, 450

Japanese Words and Their
Uses, 44
Japan's Economy in World
Perspective, 450
Japan's Foreign Relations,
451
Japan's Modernization,
451
Japan's New Middle Class,
452
Japan's New Order in East
Asia, 450
Japan's Quest for
Comprehensive Security,
450
Jay's Treaty, 311
Jazz: America's Classical
Music, 494
Jazz Bibliography, 494
Jazz Dance, 520
The Jazz Heritage, 494
Jazz: Its Evolution and
Essence, 494
Jazz Masters in Transition,
1957–1969, 494
Jazz Reference and Research
Materials, 494
Jazz Style in Kansas City
and the Southwest, 494
Jazz Styles, 494
The Jazz Tradition, 494
Jazz Voices, 494
Jean-Jacques Rousseau, 58
Jefferson and His Time,
53
Jefferson, Nationalism, and
the Enlightenment, 315
Jerusalem: A History of
Forty Centuries, 435
Jerusalem: A Study in Urban
Geography, 435
Jesuit Relations and Allied
Documents, 348
The Jesuits in North
America, 332
The Jet Lag Book, 617
Jewish Ceremonial Art and
Religious Observance, 530
The Jewish Community in
America, 431
The Jewish Encyclopedia,
429
Jewish Historical Treasures,
428
Jewish Nobles and Geniuses
in Modern Hungary, 429

Jewish Origins of the
Psychoanalytic Movement,
429
The Jewish People, 426
The Jewish Religion in the
Soviet Union, 430
The Jewish War, 247
The Jews, 428
Jews, God and History, 428
The Jews in Russia, 428, 430
The Jews in Soviet Russia
since 1917, 429
The Jews in the Modern
World, 430
Jews in the Roman World,
428
The Jews in Their Land, 427,
435
The Jews in Weimar
Germany, 430
The Jews of East Central
Europe between the World
Wars, 430
The Jews of Georgian
England, 1714–1830, 378
The Jews of Ireland from
Earliest Times to the Year
1910, 429
The Jews of Poland, 431
Jews of Silence, 431
Jews of the Latin American
Republics, 358
Jews of the Middle East
(1860–1972), 427
The Jews of the United
States, 428
Jiddah, 438
The Jivaro, 619
John Bright, 382
John Brown, 318
John D. Rockefeller, 330
John Dewey's Challenge to
Education, 321, 322
John Foster Dulles: The
Road to Power, 283
John Marshall, 269
John Muir and His Legacy,
291
John Paul Jones, 328, 329
John Quincy Adams, 311
John Randolph of Roanoke,
306
John Wesley, 377
Johnny, We Hardly Knew
Ye, 72
Jokes, 609

Jonathan Draws the Long
    Bow, 599
Jonathan Edwards, 326
Jonathan Sewall, 265
Josiah Gregg and His Vision
    of the Early West, 324
Journal and Proceedings of
    the President, 1793–97, 94
Journal of a Cruise to the
    Pacific Ocean, 1842–1844,
    625
Journal of a Mission to the
    Interior of Africa, 643
Journal of H.M.S. En-
    deavour, 1768–1771, 632
Journal of Researches into
    the Natural History and
    Geology of the Countries
    Visited during the Voyage
    of the H.M.S. Beagle, 626
Journal of the Discovery of
    the Source of the Nile, 628
Journal of the Federal
    Convention, 90
Journal of the First Voyage
    to America, 631
Journalists Biographies
    Master Index, 567
The Journals of Lewis and
    Clark, 317
The Journals of Zebulon
    Montgomery Pike, 627
Journey into China, 624
Journey through Russia and
    Siberia, 1787–1788, 626
Journey to the Jade Sea, 623
Journeys, 627
The Journey's Echo, 647
Joys of Italian Humor and
    Folklore, 611
Judgment and Reasoning in
    the Child, 235
The Judiciary, 297
The Jugurthine War, 250
Jules and Jim, 587
Julian the Apostate, 240
Jurisprudence, 155
Justice without Trial, 155
The Justices of the United
    States Supreme Court,
    1789–1978, 256

KGB Today, 420
Kafka and the Yiddish
    Theatre, 427

Keeping Your Eye on
    Television, 570
Kentucky Country, 595
Kenya, 441
Key Monuments of the
    History of Art, 528
Keyboard Music, 496
Khrushchev, 421
Khrushchev and Brezhnev as
    Leaders, 420
Khrushchev and the Arts,
    423
Khrushchev Remembers,
    423
Kibbutz, 435
Kievan Russia, 482
Kind Words, 31
Kindergarten Chats and
    Other Writings, 554
King and People in
    Provincial Massachusetts,
    264
King George III, 378
King James VI and I, 377
King John, 372
King Leopold's Congo, 444
King Solomon's Ring, 171,
    182
The Kingdom and the
    Power, 567
The Kingdom by the Sea,
    622
Kingdoms of the Savanna,
    444
Kings and Queens of Early
    Britain, 371
Kings, Commoners,
    Concessionaires, 441
The King's English, 30, 32
The King's Parliament of
    England, 397
King's Peace, 377
Kino, 577
Kinship and Marriage
    among the Nuer, 108
Kinship in Bali, 114
Kister's Atlas Buying Guide,
    17
Kit Carson's Long Walk and
    Other True Tales of Old
    San Diego, 603
Knole and the Sackvilles,
    77
Knowledge for What?, 208
Kon-Tiki, 636
Korea, 454

Korean Politics in
    Transition, 455
The Korean War, 409
The Kosciusko Foundation
    English-Polish, Polish-
    English Dictionary, 44
Kronstadt, 1921, 420
The Kurdish Question in
    Iraq, 437
The Kuwait Fund and the
    Political Economy of Arab
    Regional Development,
    440

The L-Shaped Party, 351
The Labelling of Deviance,
    194
Labor Economics and Labor
    Relations, 131
Labor, Management, and
    Social Policy, 133
The Labour Governments,
    1945–1951, 382
Labyrinth of Solitude, the
    Other Mexico, and Return
    to the Labyrinth of
    Solitude, Mexico and the
    U.S., and the
    Philanthropic Ogre, 364
Ladies on the Loose, 616
The Lake Region of Central
    Africa, 629
Lamy of Sante-Fe, 324
Land and Politics in the
    England of Henry VIII,
    375
Land and Revolution in
    Iran, 1960–1980, 437
The Land before Her, 264,
    292
Land Behind Baghdad, 437
A Land of Our Own, 429
Land of the Firebird,
    423
Land or Death, 365
Landlord and Tenant in
    Nineteenth Century
    Ireland, 380
Landlords and Tenants in
    Imperial Rome, 244
Landmarks in French
    Literature, 60
Landscapes of Learning,
    226
Lanfranc of Bec, 372

Langenscheidt's Comprehensive English-German Dictionary, 41
Langenscheidt's Condensed Muret-Sanders German Dictionary, 41
Langenscheidt's Condensed Muret-Sanders German Dictionary: German-English, 41
Langenscheidt's New College German Dictionary, 41
Language (Bloomfield), 108, 112
Language (Sapir), 123
Language and Learning, 185
Language and Poverty, 109
Language and Social Identity, 108
The Language and Thought of the Child, 173, 184, 235
Language, Culture and Personality, 123
Language in Culture, 123
Language in Culture and Society, 108
The Language of Politics, 163
The Language of Social Research, 188, 208
The Language of Twentieth-Century Music, 489
Language, Thought, and Reality, 123
Languages and Lore of the Long Island Indians, 600
La Salle and the Discovery of the Great West, 332
The Last Days of Hitler, 400
The Last Half-Century, 282
The Last Hero, 641
The Last Lords of Palenque, 354
The Last One Hundred Days, 409
Last Palmerston Government, 381
The Last Prima Donnas, 497
The Last Trek, 444
The Later Middle Ages, 373
Later Middle Ages in England, 374
Latin America, 352
The Latin American Policy of the United States, 311

Latin American Scholarship since World War II, 352
Latin Journey, 195
Latin Literature, 241
Laugh after Laugh, 611
Laughing, 610
Lavengro, 628
La Vida, 117
Law and Life of Rome, 244
Law and Science in Collaboration, 129
Law and the Social Sciences, 155
The Law in Classical Athens, 244
Law, Legislation and Liberty, 137
Lawrence of Arabia: A Biographical Enquiry, 638, 639
The Laws, 167
The Laws of Imitation, 174
Le Petit Soldat, 584
Leader and Vanguard in Mass Society, 360
Leader at Large, 341
Leaders of Public Opinion in Ireland, 394
Leadership in Crisis, 336
The League of Nations, 409
The League of the Ho-de-no-sau-nee, or Iroquois, 120
The League of the Iroquois, 111
The Leaning Ivory Tower, 224
Learning How to Behave, 338
The Learning Society, 232
Lectures on Conditioned Reflexes, 183
Lectures on Early English History, 398
Lectures on Education, 233
Lectures on Human and Animal Psychology, 187
Lectures on Modern History, 384
Lectures on the Council of Trent, 390
Lectures on the Early History of Institutions, 118
Lectures on the French Revolution, 384
Lectures on the Relation between Law and Public

Opinion in England, during the Nineteenth Century, 156
Lee's Lieutenants, 57
The Left against Zion, 431
The Legacy of the Bolshevik Revolution, 425
Legal Foundations of Capitalism, 126
The Legal Mind in America, 327
Legend of Sleepy Hollow, Rip Van Winkle, President Van Buren and Brom, 600
Legends and Folk Beliefs in a Swedish American Community, 597
Legends and Popular Tales of the Basque People, 597
Legends of New York State, 599
Legends of Our Time, 431
Legends of Texas, 602
Legends of the World, 596
The Legislative System, 156
Leisure in the Industrial Revolution, 1780–1880, 378
Lenin, 425
Lenin on the Jewish Question, 429
Lenin: Red Dictator, 482
Leningrad's Ballet, 520
Lenin's Government, 425
Lenin's Last Struggle, 423
Lenin's Legacy, 426
The Leo Frank Case, 428
Les Brown's Encyclopedia of Television, 570
Less Than Glory, 266
The Lessons of History, 463
Lessons of Monetary Experience, 134
Lessons of the War with Spain, 471
Lester Ward and the Welfare State, 314
Let History Judge: The Origins and Consequences of Stalinism, 424
Let My Children Work, 234
Let the Trumpet Sound, 53, 283
Letter to Rafael Sanchez, 631

A Letter to the Sheriffs of
  Bristol, 387
Letter to Washington, 331
Letters and Notes on the
  Manners, Customs and
  Conditions of the North
  American Indian, 290
Letters and People of the
  Spanish Indies, 357
Letters from a Traveller, 628
Letters Home, 79
Letters of Grover Cleveland,
  1850–1908, 330
Letters, Speeches and Tracts
  on Irish Affairs, 387
Letters to a Niece and
  Prayer to the Virgin of
  Chartres, 306
Letters to Atticus, 249
Letters to Paula, 427
Leviathan, 153, 160
The Levittowners, 191
Li Ta-Chao and the Origins
  of Chinese Marxism, 448
Liber Studiorum, 555
The Liberal Mind in a
  Conservative Age, 102, 286
Liberal Politics in the Age of
  Gladstone and Roseberry,
  380
Liberalism and the Social
  Problem, 388
Liberals, Radicals and
  Social Politics, 1892–1914,
  380
Liberation and Its Limits,
  175, 178
The Liberation of the Jew,
  430
Liberia, 441
Liberty, 150
Liberty and Property, 378
Liberty in the Modern State,
  162
Library Literature, 2
Life and Confessions of a
  Psychologist, 179
The Life and Death of the
  Press Barons, 567
The Life and Labour of the
  People in London, 1890–
  1900, 191, 204
The Life and Letters of
  Erasmus and the
  Unknown Historical
  Significance of the

Protestant Reformation,
  390
The Life and Times of
  Cotton Mather, 54
The Life and Times of
  Edward I, 372
The Life and Times of Los
  Angeles, 567
The Life and Times of
  Richard II, 374
A Life Apart: The English
  Working Class, 1890–1914,
  383
Life Course Dynamics, 172,
  189
Life in a Haitian Valley, 115
Life in a Mexican Village,
  117, 122, 192
Life in Egypt under Roman
  Rule, 240, 243
Life in the English Country
  House, 369
The Life of George Cabot
  Lodge, 306
The Life of Herbert Hoover,
  277
Life of John Bright, 399
The Life of Lorena Hickok,
  78
The Life of Nelson, 471
The Life of the Mind in
  America, 327
Life on Daytime Television,
  570
Life-Span Developmental
  Psychology, 172
The Life That He Led, 510
Life with Two Languages,
  226
Life with Uncle, 350
The Lighthouses of New
  England, 1716-1973, 645
The Lights of Broadway and
  Other Essays, 625
Limericks Historical and
  Hysterical, 609
Limited War in the Nuclear
  Age, 157
The Limits and Possibilities
  of Schooling, 226
The Limits of Legitimacy,
  127
The Limits of Organization,
  132
The Limits to Capital, 141
The Limits to Growth, 194

Lincoln and Black Freedom,
  272
Lincoln and His Party in the
  Secession Crisis, 333
Lincoln Collector, 60
The Lincoln Image, 273
Lincoln's Quest for Union,
  274
Linguadex, 45
Lion Among Roses, 621
The Lion and the Throne,
  55
Listen, 486
Listener's Guide to Folk
  Music, 594
Listening to Jazz, 493
Literacy and the Social
  Order, 374
Literary Fallacy, 316
Literary Market Place 1986,
  23
Literary Memoranda, 334
Literature and Revolution,
  480
Literature and Revolution in
  Soviet Russia, 1917–1962,
  422
Literature and the Image of
  Man, 189
Little America, 630
The Little Community, 106,
  122
The Little Magazine in
  America, 561
A Little Revenge, 65
Lives and Letters, 49
The Lives of Talleyrand, 460
Lives of the Later Caesars,
  250
Lives of the Most Eminent
  Painters, Sculptors and
  Architects, 531
Lives of the Painters, 531
Living City, 559
Living in a World
  Revolution, 467, 468
Living the Revolution, 117
The Living U.S.
  Constitution, 296
Local Knowledge, 104, 105,
  115
The Log Cabin Myth, 301
The Logic and Limits of
  Trust, 196
Logic of Leviathan, 160
The Logic of Perception, 175

Logic: The Theory of Inquiry, 230, 231
The Logical Structure of Linguistic Theory, 108
Logistics and the Failure of the British Army in America, 1775–1783, 266
Lombard Street, 385
London Perceived, 622
The Loneliest Campaign, 80
The Lonely Crowd, 102, 214, 215
A Long Journey, 216
The Long March, 1935, 449
The Long March of the French Left, 414
Long Memory, 289
The Long Revolution, 448
Long Steel Rail, 593
Long Time Gone, 284
The Longest Voyage, 618
The Longhorns, 602
Longman Atlas of Modern British History, 368
Longman Dictionary of Contemporary English, 26
Longman Dictionary of the Mass Media and Communication, 562
Look-Alike, Sound-Alike, Not-Alike Words, 34
The Look of the West, 1860, 629
Looking at Art, 528
Looking Forward, 91
Looking Outward, 93
The Lopsided World, 483
Lord Burghley and Queen Elizabeth, 375
Lord Grey of the Reform Bill, 399
Lord Liverpool's Administration, 378
Lord North, 379
Lord Shaftesbury, 392
Losing Ground, 102
The Loss of El Dorado, 366
A Loss of Mastery, 253
Lost City of the Incas, 353
The Lost Peace: International Relations in Europe, 1918–1939, 406
The Lost Soul of American Politics, 285
The Lost World of the Kalahari, 648

The Lost World of Thomas Jefferson, 312
Louis D. Brandeis and the Progressive Tradition, 276
Louis D. Brandeis, Felix Frankfurter, and the New Deal, 278
Louis Napoleon and the Second Empire, 415
Louis the XV, 465
Louis the Fourteenth and the Greatness of France, 414
Love Canal, 194
The Love You Make, 492
Lumbering Songs from the Northern Woods, 594
The Lure of the Land, 290
Lust for Life, 556
The Lying Valet, 65
Lyndon: An Oral Biography, 283
Lyndon Johnson and the American Dream, 283

M A S H, 572
MLA Handbook for Writers of Research Papers, 22
Macao, 588
Machina Ex Dea, 203
Machine Politics in Transition, 153
Macmillan Dictionary, 26
The Macmillan Dictionary of Historical Slang, 33
Macmillan Encyclopedia of Architects, 533
The Macmillan Film Bibliography, 575
Macroeconomics and Micropolitics, 153
Madness and Civilization, 169, 411
Magazines for Libraries, 8
Magic, Myth and Medicine, 607
The Magic Orange Tree, 598
Magic, Science and Religion and Other Essays, 109, 118
Magical Medicine, 608
Magill Survey of Cinema, 575
Magill's Quotations in Context, 21
Magna Carta and the Idea of Liberty, 372

Mahatma Gandhi, 473
Main Currents in American Thought, 254
Main Currents in Sociological Thought, 205, 457
Main Currents of Indian History, 453
Main Problems in American History, 263
Main Trends of Research in the Social and Human Sciences, 100
The Mainstream of Civilization, 406
Major Documents in American Economic History, 321
Major Film Theories, 574
Major Operations of the Navies in the War of American Independence, 471
Major Peace Treaties of Modern History, 1648–1967, 404
Major Trends in Jewish Mysticism, 431
Major Writers of America, 327
Majority Rule and Minority Rights, 314
The Makers of Rome, 248
The Making and Using of Index Numbers, 143
Making It in Cable TV, 562
The Making of a Nation: A History of the Union of South Africa, 443
The Making of Elizabethan Foreign Policy, 1558–1603, 375
Making of Modern Ireland, 1603–1923, 369
The Making of Modern Japan, 451
The Making of Modern Russia, 420, 423
The Making of Post Christian Britain, 382
The Making of Southeast Asia, 445
The Making of the American Constitution, 296
Making of the English Working Class, 399

The Making of the Modern
    French Mind, 468
The Making of the New
    Deal, 278
The Making of the New Poor
    Laws, 380
The Making of the Roman
    Catholic Church in
    Ireland, 1850–1860, 381
The Making of the Wizard of
    Oz, 578
Making of Victorian
    England, 380
Making the News, 566
Malay Fishermen, 113
Male and Female, 119
Male Female Comedy Teams
    in American Vaudeville,
    1865–1932, 612
The Malthusian Controversy,
    140
Man and Aggression, 171,
    183
Man and Beast in American
    Comic Legend, 609
Man and Culture, 105, 113,
    119
Man and His Works
    (Herskovits), 115
Man and His Works
    (Thorndike), 236
Man, Economy and State,
    146
The Man from Monticello, 88
Man Makes Himself, 107
Man of Independence, 79
The Man-of-Words in the
    West Indies, 595
Man on His Past, 402
The Man Who Presumed,
    646
A Man with a Camera, 578
Management and the
    Worker, 172, 204
Mandarin Road to Old Hue,
    454
Manifest Destiny Denied,
    364
Mankind and Mother Earth,
    479
Mankind Evolving, 107
The Manor and the Borough,
    148
Man's Responsibility for
    Nature, 194
Manscapes, 619

Manual for Reading
    Japanese, 43
A Manual for Writers of
    Term Papers, Theses, and
    Dissertations, 23
Many Mexicos, 364
Mao and China, 448
Mao and the Chinese
    Revolution, 447
Mao Zedong, 448
Mao's Way, 448
A Map History of the
    Modern World, 404
Maps and Charts of the
    American Revolution, 255
Maps and Dreams, 349
Maps of the Mind, 170
Maps on File, 18
The March of Folly, 481
The March to Zion, 435
Maria Theresa and Other
    Studies, 465
Marienthal, 130, 207
Marine Mysteries and
    Dramatic Disasters of New
    England, 645
The Maritime History of
    Massachusetts, 329
Mark Twain at Work, 316
Mark Twain's America, 317
Markings, 67, 68
Marks and Monograms on
    European and Oriental
    Pottery and Porcelain, 534
The Marquis: A Study of
    Lord Rockingham, 379
Marquis de Custine and His
    Russia in 1839, 467
Marriage and Family in a
    Changing Society, 196
Marriage and the Family,
    196
Marriage, Divorce,
    Remarriage, 195
Martí, 359
The Martial Spirit, 328
Marxism: An Historical and
    Critical Study, 141
Marxism and the
    Existentialists, 457
Marxism and the Problems
    of Linguistics, 476
Marxism in Latin America,
    357
Marxism in Modern France,
    414

Marxism in Our Time, 480
Marxist Ideology and Soviet
    Criminal Law, 423
Marxist Inquiries, 126
Mary Chesnut's Civil War,
    51, 272, 345
Mary Second, 56
Maryland Folk Legends and
    Folk Songs, 600
The Mask of State, 300
Mass Communications Law,
    Cases and Comment, 561
Mass Media and American
    Politics, 299
Mass Media and Social
    Change, 564
The Mass Media and Social
    Problems, 564
Mass Media Policies in
    Changing Cultures, 564
Mass Media: Systems and
    Effects, 563
Masses and Man, 412
The Master Architect,
    559
The Master Builders, 543
Master Mariner, 632
Masterpieces of Humor, 611
Masters and Journeymen,
    378
The Masters and the Slaves,
    196
Masters of Social
    Psychology, 182, 210
Masters of Sociological
    Thought, 188, 211
Mathematico-Deductive
    Theory of Rote Learning,
    180
Matrilineal Kinship, 108
Max Weber on Methodology
    of the Social Sciences, 101
Maxima and Minima, 125
Maximilian's Triumphal
    Arch, 539
The Maya, 353
McGraw-Hill Dictionary of
    Art, 528
The McGraw-Hill Style
    Manual, 23
McKay's Modern
    Norwegian-English and
    English-Norwegian
    Dictionary, 44
McKay's Modern
    Portuguese-English and

English-Portuguese
Dictionary, 44
The Meaning of Death, 195
The Meaning of Human
History, 402
The Meaning of
Independence, 88
Measurement and
Prediction, 218
Measuring Business Cycles,
143
Media and the American
Mind, 563
Media Industries, 565
The Media Monopoly, 562
Media: The Second God, 565
Media Unbound, 568
Mediaspeak, 570
The Medici, 474
The Medieval Economy and
Society, 373
Medieval England, 369
The Medieval English
Economy, 1150–1500, 372
The Medieval Foundations of
England, 397
The Medieval Mind, 478
Medieval Music: The Sixth
Liberal Art, 489
The Medieval Near East, 432
Medieval Religious Houses
in England and Wales, 370
Medieval Russian Laws, 483
Medieval Slavdom and the
Rise of Russia, 424
The Mediterranean and the
Mediterranean World in
the Age of Philip Second,
459
Mediterranean Valleys, 433
Meeting at Potsdam, 279
Megalopolis, 202
Megatrends, 102
The Meiji Restoration, 449
Mein Kampf, 416
Melbourne, 382
Memories and
Commentaries, 514
Memories of Men and
Women, American and
British, 397
Memories of My Father, 338
Memories of the Future, 324
Memory: A Contribution to
Experimental Psychology,
177

Men and Centuries, 396
The Men and Machines of
American Journalism, 566,
568
Men and the Matterhorn,
617
Men in Dark Times, 456
The Men of Cajamarca, 355
Men of Destiny, 325
Men of Ideas, 189, 198
Men of the Supreme Court,
298
Men, Women and Pianos,
496
Men, Women, Messages and
Media, 565
The Menomini Language,
112
The Mensheviks, 422
Mental Illness and American
Society, 1875–1940, 291
Mere Literature and Other
Essays, 96
Mere Marie of the Ursulines,
348
The Merriam-Webster
Dictionary, 26
The Merriam-Webster
Thesaurus, 34
Merrily We Sing, 594
The Metamorphosis of
Greece since World War II,
473
Method and Appraisal in
Economics, 125
Method and Perspective in
Anthropology, 104
Method in Social
Anthropology, 104, 121
Method, Process, and
Austrian Economics, 146
The Methodist Revolution,
379
Methodology of Economics
and Other Social Sciences,
125
Methods of Social Research,
100
The Mexican Caribbean, 620
Mexican Folktales from the
Borderland, 595
Mexican Folkways, 598
A Mexican Ulysses, 364
Mexico (Coe), 354
Mexico (Simon), 620
Mexico Bay, 324

Michigan, 313
Microcomputers in
Elementary Education,
229
The Microeconomic
Foundations of
Employment and Inflation
Theory, 131
The Mid-Tudor Crisis, 1539–
1563, 374
The Middle Colonies and the
Coming of the American
Revolution, 267
Middle East, 433
The Middle East: A
Geographical Study, 432
The Middle East: A Political
and Economic Survey, 433
Middle East and Islam, 434
Middle East and North
Africa, 16, 433, 444
Middle East in the World
Economy, 1800–1914, 433
The Middle East in World
Affairs, 433
The Middle East, Oil, and
the Great Powers, 433
Middle East Oil Money and
Its Future Expenditure,
432
The Middle East since Camp
David, 432
Middle East: U.S. Policy,
Israel, Oil and the Arabs,
432
Middletown, 192, 208
Middletown Families, 208
Middletown in Transition,
192, 208
The Midwest and Its
Children, 191
Milestones in Mass
Communication Research,
561
The Militant South, 319, 320
The Military and Society in
Latin America, 358
Military Bibliography of the
Civil War, 259
The Military Coup d'Etat as
a Political Process, 362
The Military Half, 455
The Military in America,
304
Military Regimes in Africa,
442

Millenarianism and Peasant
  Politics in Vietnam, 454
Milton, 386
Mimekor Yisrael, 596
Minaret of Djam, 647
Mind and Media, 564
The Mind and Society, 143
The Mind of Germany, 468
The Mind of Modern Russia,
  468
The Mind of Napoleon, 57
The Mind of Primitive Man,
  112
The Mind of the Negro, 287
Mind, Self, and Society, 196,
  209
Mindstorms: Children,
  Computers, and Powerful
  Ideas, 227
Ministers of God, Ministers
  of the People, 364
Ministers of Reform, 276
Minnesota Folklife, 602
Minorities in the Arab
  World, 438
Minority Education and
  Caste, 227
Minority Report, 316
The Mint, 638
Miracle at Midway, 279
Miracle at Philadelphia, 55,
  151
The Mismeasurement of
  Man, 173
The Missionary Enterprise in
  China and America, 464
Missionary Travels and
  Researches in South
  Africa, 642
Mister Lincoln's Army, 313
Mr. Secretary Cecil and
  Queen Elizabeth, 375
Mister Socialism, 341
Mrs. Byrne's Dictionary of
  Unusual, Obscure, and
  Preposterous Words,
  Gathered from Numerous
  and Diverse Authoritative
  Sources, 32
Mistress to an Age, 57
Mobilizing Women for War,
  413
Models of Doom, 194
Models of Learning, Memory
  and Choice, 174
Modern Africa, 442

Modern American Usage, 30
Modern Arab Thought, 438
Modern Ballet, 520
Modern British Politics, 382
Modern China, 464
The Modern Corporation,
  128
The Modern Corporation and
  Private Property, 127
Modern Democracies, 102,
  152, 153, 159
The Modern Democratic
  State, 152
A Modern Dictionary of
  Sociology, 188
Modern England
  (Havighurst), 368
Modern England (Webb),
  370
Modern European Social
  History, 410
Modern European Thought,
  410
Modern Folk Ballads, 593
Modern French-English
  Dictionary, 39
Modern Historians and the
  Study of History, 397
Modern History of China
  and Japan, 451
The Modern History of Iraq,
  438
The Modern History of
  Japan, 449
Modern India, 452
Modern Italy, 1871–1982,
  417
Modern Jewish History, 427
Modern Latin America, 359
Modern Latin American
  Arts, 529
Modern Learning Theory,
  180
The Modern Middle East
  and Northern Africa, 440
The Modern Researcher, 402
The Modern Russian
  Dictionary for English
  Speakers, 45
Modern Russian
  Historiography, 424
The Modern School
  Movement, 224
Modern Scotland, 370
Modern Thai Politics from
  Village to Nation, 455

The Modern Theme, 189
The Modern-World System,
  129
Modern Yemen, 1918–1966,
  440
The Modernisation of Irish
  Society, 1848–1914, 381
The Modernity of Tradition:
  Political Development in
  India, 453
The Modernization of Turkey
  from Ataturk to the
  Present Day, 439
The Modulor and Modulor 2,
  543
Monastic Order in England,
  370
Moncada, 362
Monetary Equilibrium,
  148
Monetary History of the
  United States, 1867–1960,
  135
Monetary Theory and Fiscal
  Policy, 136
Monetary Theory and the
  Trade Cycle, 136
Monetary Trends in the
  United States and the
  United Kingdom, 131
Monetary versus Fiscal
  Policy, 131
Money and Banking in
  Islam, 433
Money, Banking and
  Economic Analysis, 131
Money, Credit and
  Commerce, 140
The Money Lords, 59
The Mongols and Russia,
  482
Monkey Business and Duck
  Soup, 587
Mont-Saint-Michel and
  Chartres, 306
Montcalm and Wolfe, 332
Montessori System
  Examined, 233
Monthly Catalog of U.S.
  Government Publications,
  12, 13
The Moors, 433
The Moral Judgment of the
  Child, 173, 184
Moral Principles in
  Education, 231

Morals and Manners among Negro Americans, 318
Moravians in Two Worlds, 199
A More Perfect Union, 260
More Roman Than Rome, 381
More Than News, 568
More Travels in a Donkey Trap, 621
Mori Arinori, 450
Mornings on Horseback, 337
Morris Dictionary of Word and Phrase Origins, 36
The Morrow Book of New Words, 26
Moscow Diary, 424
The Most Dangerous Man in America, 56, 64
Mother and Daughter, 78
Motherhood, 609
Motif Index for Lost Mines and Treasures, Applied to Redaction of Arizona Legends, and to Lost Mines and Treasure Legends Exterior to Arizona, 608
The Motion Picture Guide, 575
Motion Pictures from the Library of Congress Paper Print Collection, 575
Motion Pictures: The Development of an Art from Silent Films to the Age of Television, 576
Mottoes, 21
The Mountain of My Fear, 627
Mountain Standard Time, 324
Mountain Storm, Pine Breeze, 594
The Mountains at the Bottom of the World, 624
Mountbatten, 54
The Movie Business, 575
Movies: A Psychological Study, 190, 191
Movies and Money, 577
Movies as Mass Communication, 576
Movies as Social Criticism, 576

The Movies Grow Up, 1940–1980, 574
The Movies in Our Midst, 575
Moving Frontiers, 343
Mozambique, 443
Mozart, 52
Muir's Historical Atlas, 404
Mules and Men, 605
Multinational Oil, 432
Multinationals in Latin America, 359
Munich: The Price of Peace, 413
The Murder of Chile, 361
The Murder Trials, 249
The Murderers among Us: The Simon Wiesenthal Memoirs, 431
A Muse for the Masses, 611
Music and Imagination, 503
Music Criticism: An Annotated Guide to the Literature, 488
Music Cultures of the Pacific, the Near East and Asia, 492
The Music Guide to Austria and Germany, 487
The Music Guide to Belgium, Luxembourg, Holland and Switzerland, 488
The Music Guide to Great Britain, 488
The Music Guide to Italy, 488
Music in a New Found Land, 486
Music in India, 495
Music in the Baroque Era, 485
Music in the Classic Period, 486
Music in the Middle Ages, 486
Music in the New World, 485
Music in the Renaissance, 486
Music in the Romantic Era, 485
Music in the 20th Century, from Debussy through Stravinsky, 485

Music in the United States, 485
Music in the Western World, 487
Music in Western Civilization, 486
Music Industry Directory, 490
Music Is My Mistress, 504
The Music of Africa, 495
The Music of Ancient Greece, 490
The Music of Black Americans, 487
Music of the Americas, 492
Music of the Whole Earth, 493
Music of Three Seasons, 1974–1977, 486
Music of Three More Seasons, 1977–1980, 486
Music Reference and Research Materials, 488
Music since 1900, 491
Musical Instruments: A Comprehensive Dictionary, 496
Musical Instruments of the World, 490
Musical Instruments Through the Ages, 495
Musical References in the Chinese Classics, 495
A Musical Season, 486
The Musical Woman, 491
Musicalalia, 488
Musician's Guide to Copyright, 489
Musics of Many Cultures, 493
The Muslim Discovery of Europe, 434
Mussolini, 417
Mussolini and the Jews, 430
The Mute Stones Speak, 242
Mutual Aid, 150
My Apprenticeship, 148
My Bondage and My Freedom, 85, 273
My Country, 428
My Kalulu, Prince, King, and Slave, 646
My Lai Four, 454
My Life (Meir), 430
My Life (Trotsky), 480

My Past and Thoughts: The
   Memoirs of Alexander
   Herzen, 422
My Philosophy and Other
   Essays on the Moral and
   Political Problems of Our
   Time, 462
My Theatre Life, 522
The Mysterious Science of
   the Law, 312
The Myth of the Jewish
   Race, 430
The Myth of the Negro Past,
   115, 291
Myth, Symbol and Culture,
   114
Myths and Folktales of the
   Russians, Western Slavs,
   and Magyars, 596
Myths and Legends of the
   Great Dismal Swamp, 601
Myths and Legends of the
   Mackinacs and the Lake
   Region, 601
Myths and Legends of the
   Pacific Northwest, 603

Namibia, 444
Napoleon from 18 Brumaire
   to Tilsit, 1799–1807, 414
Napoleon from Tilsit to
   Waterloo, 1807–1815, 414
Napoleon I, 466
Napoleon III, 466
Narrative of a Journey to the
   Shores of the Polar Sea,
   320
Narrative of a Second
   Expedition to the Shores
   of the Polar Sea, 320
Narrative of a Voyage to the
   West Indies and Mexico in
   the Years 1599–1602, 619
Narrative of an Expedition
   to the Zambesi and Its
   Tributaries, 642
The Narrow Ground, 370
Nasser and His Generation,
   436
Nasser's New Egypt,
   437
Nat Turner's Slave
   Rebellion, 260
Nation at Risk, 229
The Nation at War, 305

The Nation Comes of Age,
   272
The Nation in Crisis, 1861–
   1877, 259
A Nation of Immigrants, 71
The National Archives and
   Foreign Relations
   Research, 256
The National Atlas of the
   United States of America,
   19
National Directory of Free
   Vacation and Travel
   Information, 615
The National Experience,
   262
National Geographic Atlas of
   the World, 18, 404
National Newspaper Index,
   8
The National Parks (Frome),
   619
The National Parks (Tilden),
   620
National Party Platforms,
   1840–1976, 261
National Tourism Policy
   Study Final Report, 615
National Union Catalog, 1
Nationalism, 468
Nationalism and Ideology,
   483
Nationalism and
   Imperialism in the Hither
   East, 467
Nationalism and Realism,
   468
Nationalism and Revolution
   in Egypt, 436
Nationalism and Social
   Communication, 155, 190
Nationalism in the Soviet
   Union, 468
The Nationalist Movement,
   452
Nationality and Population
   Change in Russia and the
   USSR, 423
The Nationalization of the
   Masses, 416
Nations in Conflict, 155
The Nations Within, 195
Native American Folklore,
   1879–1979, 603
Native Americans, 195
Native Son, 294

Natural and Political
   Observations Made upon
   the Bills of Mortality, 198
The Natural House, 559
The Nature and Study of
   History, 314
The Nature of Capital and
   Income, 134
The Nature of Culture, 105,
   115
The Nature of Human
   Intelligence, 173
The Nature of Prejudice,
   174, 175, 196
The Nature of the Social
   Sciences, 309
Nature's Nation, 326, 327
Naval Power and Naval
   War, 472
Naval Strategy, 471
The Naval War of 1812, 335
Naven, 105
Near East, 433
Nearest the Pole, 643
Nebraska Folklore, 602
Nebraska Symposium on
   Motivation, 173
Necessary Lessons, 228
The Necessities of War, 245
Negara, 115
The Negev, 435
The Negro, 318
The Negro Almanac, 16
Negro American Family, 318
The Negro and His Folklore
   in Nineteenth Century
   Periodicals, 605
The Negro Artisan, 318
Negro Cowboys, 290
The Negro Family in the
   United States, 287
Negro Folk Music, U.S.A.,
   605
Negro Folk Rhymes, Wise
   and Otherwise, 606
The Negro in America, 260
Negro in Business, 318
The Negro in the American
   Revolution, 267
The Negro in the Civil War,
   274
The Negro in the South, 237
The Negro in Twentieth
   Century America, 320
Negro Intelligence and
   Selective Migration, 181

The Negro on the American Frontier, 271
Negro Thought in America, 1880–1915, 237
The Negro's Civil War, 273
Neighborhoods That Work, 202
Nemesis, 281
The Nerves of Government, 153, 190
Never Call Retreat, 313
Never Done, 288
A New Age Now Begins, 268
New America, 93
The New American Roget's College Thesaurus in Dictionary Form, 34
New Architecture and the Bauhaus, 542
The New Book of Knowledge, 3
The New Book of World Rankings, 15
New Cambridge Modern History, 412
The New Century Dictionary of the English Language, 26
New Complete Walker, 626
New Contemporary French/English, English/French Dictionary, 40
The New Country, 289
The New Deal and the West, 279
The New Deal in Action, 339
The New Deal to the Carter Administration, 281
New Dictionary of Modern Sculpture, 530
A New Dictionary of Quotations on Historical Principles from Ancient and Modern Sources, 21
A New Dictionary of the Social Sciences, 100
New Directions in American Intellectual History, 286
The New Economics of Growth, 129
The New Empire, 275
The New Encyclopaedia Britannica, 3
New England Bean Pot, 599
New England Frontier, 265

New England in the Republic, 307
The New England Mind, 326
New England's Strange Sea Sagas, 599
The New English-French Dictionary of Slang and Colloquialisms, 40
The New Era and the New Deal, 1920–1940, 258
The New Federalism, 152
The New Functional Hebrew-English, English-Hebrew Dictionary, 42
The New Grove Dictionary of Music and Musicians, 490
A New Guide to Better Writing, 22
A New Historical Geography of England after 1600, 369
A New Historical Geography of England before 1600, 369
A New History of India, 454
A New History of Korea, 454
New History of Portugal, 418
New Iberian World, 356
The New Indians, 294
The New Industrial State, 135
New Information Technology in Education, 226
New International Atlas, 18
The New Jerusalem, 435
The New Jewish Encyclopedia, 427
The New Liberalism, 380
New Lives for Old, 119
New Masters, 274
The New Men of Power, 212
The New Metropolis in the Arab World, 438
The New Nationalism, 336
New Nationalisms of the Developed West, 154
New Orleans Jazz, 494
The New Oxford Companion to Music, 487
The New Oxford History of Music, 486
New Perspectives in Non-Verbal Communication, 565

A New Pictorial History of the Talkies, 576
A New Pronouncing Dictionary of the Spanish and English Languages, 46
The New Religions of Africa, 109, 199
New Rhyming Dictionary and Poets' Handbook, 35
The New Roget's Thesaurus of the English Language in Dictionary Form, 34
The New Schoffler-Weis German and English Dictionary, 41
The New Senate, 282
New Serial Titles 1950–1970, 8
The New Sociology, 212
The New Television Technologies, 561
New Towns in Israel, 435
The New Turks, 439
A New U.S. Policy toward China, 458
New Viewpoints in American History, 338
The New Woman and the Old Academe, 224
The New York Philharmonic Guide to the Symphony, 491
New York Times Atlas of the World, 18
New York Times Book Review 1896–1981, 8
New York Times Film Reviews, 1913–1968, 575
Newcomers, 322
News Dictionary, 404
News from the White House, 276
The News Media in National and International Conflict, 562
The News Media: What Makes Them Tick?, 568
News People, 567
Newspaper Indexes, 566
The Newspaper Industry in the 80's, 565
Newspaperman: S. I. Newhouse and the Business of News, 568
Newspapers and Democracy, 567

Newspapers and New
    Politics, 566
Newspapers in Microfilm:
    United States, 1948–1972,
    11
Newswatch, 569
The Newtonians and the
    English Revolution, 1689–
    1720, 376
Next Week, Swan Lake, 518
Nicaragua, 364
The Nicaragua Reader, 364
Nicholas and Alexandra,
    423
Nicholas Bacon, 375
Nicholas I, 423
Nigeria, 441
Night Creatures: A Journal
    of Jazz, 1975–80, 493
Night Riders in Black Folk
    History, 271
A Night with the Hants and
    Other Alabama
    Experiences, 600
Nightly Horrors, 568
The Nightmare of Reason,
    53
Nile Basin, 629
Nine American Film Critics,
    577, 578
The 900 Days: The Siege of
    Leningrad, 425
9,000 Words, 27
1900, 276
1939, 278
Nineteenth and Twentieth
    Century Art: Painting,
    Sculpture, Architecture,
    530
The Nineteenth Century, 623
The Nineteenth Century,
    1814–1880, 380
Nineteenth-Century Readers'
    Guide to Periodical
    Literature, 8
No Friendly Voice, 232
No Laughing Matter: An
    Analysis of Sexual Humor,
    610
No Laughing Matter:
    Rationale of the Dirty
    Joke, 610
Noa Noa, 541
Noah Webster's American
    Spelling Book, 314
Nomads of South Persia, 437

Nonconformity in Modern
    British Politics, 383
The Non-Jewish Jew and
    Other Essays, 428
The Nonsexist
    Communicator, 565
Nonviolence in Peace and
    War, 1942, 453
Non-Voting, 166
Normal Accidents, 200
The Norman Conquest, 372
The Norman Conquest and
    Its Effects on the
    Economy, 372
North American Indians, 292
The North Pole, 643
Northern Ireland since
    Nineteen Twenty, 383
Northumberland, 374
Northward over the Great
    Ice, 643
Northwest to Fortune, 647,
    648
Norwegian Folk Music, 593
Norwegian Folk Tales, 596
Not by Arms Alone, 468
Not-for-Profit, 128
Notable American Women,
    1607–1950, 50
Notable American Women:
    The Modern Period, 50
Notable Names in American
    History, 257
Notes from China, 481
Notes from the Century
    Before, 349
Notes of a Film Director, 582
Notes on Child Study, 236
Notes on Social
    Measurement, 100
Notes on the State of
    Virginia, 87
Nothing but Freedom, 273
Nothing Stands Still, 339
Nothing to Fear, 91
Nothing Venture, Nothing
    Win, 637
Novanglus, and
    Massachusettensis, 82
Novels, Mont-Saint-Michel,
    the Education, 306
Nubians in Egypt, 623
Nuclear America, 303
Nuclear Arms, 410
The Nuclear Crisis Reader,
    409

The Nuclear Delusion, 467
Nuclear Proliferation,
    409
The Nuclear Question, 408
The Nuer, 110, 113
Nuer Religion, 113
Nursery Rhymes and Tales,
    591
Nusantara, 455

O Canada, 332, 351
Obedience to Authority, 174
Objectivity and the News,
    286
Observations of Deviance,
    194
The Obsession, 63
The Occupation of Japan,
    450
The Ocean in English
    History, 623
Ocean to Ocean, 626
Oceana, 390
October and the World, 421
October 1917, 422
Odd Destiny, 86
Oedipus in the Trobriands,
    119
Of America East and West,
    324
Off the Record, 79
The Official Museum
    Directory, 9, 528
Old European Order, 1660–
    1800, 411
The Old Farmer and His
    Almanack, 599
The Old Farmer's Almanac,
    16
The Old Farmer's Almanac
    Book of Old Fashioned
    Puzzles, 599
Old Jewish Folk Music, 595
The Old Patagonian Express,
    620
Old Regime and the French
    Revolution, 342
The Old Revolutionaries, 266
The Old Social Classes and
    the Revolutionary
    Movements of Iraq, 437
The Old Time Fiddler's
    Repertory, 593
Oliver Cromwell, 391
The Olmec World, 353

-Ologies & -Isms: A
Thematic Dictionary, 33
Oman and Its Renaissance,
440
On Adolescence, 172
On Aggression, 171, 182
On Dealing with the
Communist World, 466
On Democracy, 87
On Double Consciousness,
176
On Heroes, Hero-Worship
and the Heroic in History,
461
On History (Braudel), 459
On History (Rowse), 397
On Ice and Snow and Rock,
617
On Jews and Judaism in
Crisis, 431
On Knowing, 174
On Liberty, 154
On Man in His Environment,
194
On Method, 170
On Our Way, 91
On Revolution, 456
On the American Revolution,
388
On the History and Method
of Economics, 139
On the Penitentiary System
in the United States, 341
On the Shoulders of Giants,
210
On Thermonuclear War, 157
On Understanding Women,
308
On Violence, 456
On War, 457
On What the Constitution
Means, 295
On Your Own in Europe,
622
One and Inseparable, 95
The One Best System, 229
One Boy's Boston, 328, 329
One Hundred and One More
Uses for a Dead Cat, 609
One Hundred Million
Japanese, 450
One Hundred Years of
Anthropology, 103
One Hundred Years of Negro
Freedom, 289
One Kind of Freedom, 288

One Man Alone across the
Atlantic in a Nine-foot
Boat, 626
One Potato, Two Potato, 608
One Thousand Journeys to
the Rivers, Lands and
Seas of Seven Continents,
618
One Writer's Beginnings, 54
Online Bibliographic
Databases, 7
Only a Miner, 594
Only One Earth, 483
Ontogeny and Phylogeny,
107
Ooty Preserved, 624
The Open Door at Home,
309
An Open Elite?, 398
The Open Hand, 543
Open Horizons, 620
The Open Society and Its
Enemies, 168
Open Veins of Latin
America, 358
Opera as Drama, 495
The Opera Companion, 495
Operetta: A Theatrical
History, 495
Opium of the Intellectuals,
457
Opportunity and Change,
201
Optimum Quantity of Money
and Other Essays, 135
Options for Tax Reform, 131
Orbit of China, 448
Ordeal by Fire, 273
The Ordeal of Civility, 427
The Ordeal of Power, 62
The Ordeal of the
Constitution, 296
The Ordeal of the Union, 330
The Ordeal of Thomas
Hutchinson, 265
The Ordeal of Total War,
1939–1945, 410
Order and Conflict in
Contemporary Capitalism,
127
Ordinary People and
Everyday Life, 253
The Oregon Trail, 332
Oregon's Ghosts and
Monsters, 603

The Organization of
American Culture, 1700–
1900, 285
Organizations, 197
Organizing the Executive
Branch, 301
Oriental Despotism, 157
Orientalism, 433
The Origin of the Family,
120, 134
The Original Lists of Persons
of Quality, 256
Origins: A Short
Etymological Dictionary of
Modern English, 37
Origins and Development of
Congress, 298
The Origins and
Development of Labor
Economics, 131
The Origins and Growth of
Communication, 563
The Origins of American
Politics, 298
The Origins of America's
Civil War, 272
Origins of English
Feudalism, 371
The Origins of Intelligence
in Children, 235
Origins of Rhodesia, 444
The Origins of Russia, 426
Origins of Scientific
Sociology, 188
The Origins of the Cold War
and Contemporary
Europe, 412
The Origins of the Federal
Republic, 267
The Origins of the First
World War, 408
Origins of the Israeli Polity,
435
The Origins of the Marshall
Plan, 408
The Origins of the Modern
Jew, 430
The Origins of the New
South, 1877–1913, 345
The Origins of the Second
World War (Offner), 279
The Origins of the Second
World War (Remak), 409
The Origins of the Second
World War (Taylor), 477,
478

The Origins of
    Totalitarianism, 455, 456
The Oscar Directors, 578
The Other American
    Revolution, 291
The Other Bostonians, 288
Other Cultures, 103
The Other Government, 299
Other People's Money, 193
The Other Side, 194
The Ottoman Centuries,
    439
The Ottoman Empire, 439
The Ottoman Empire and Its
    Successors, 433
The Ottoman Empire and Its
    Successors, 1801–1927,
    439
Our America, 359
Our Business Civilization,
    308
Our Primitive
    Contemporaries, 121
Our Selves/Our Past, 253
Ours Once More, 608
Out of the Ghetto: The
    Social Background of
    Jewish Emancipation, 429
Out of the Whirlwind, 428
Out to Work, 288
The Outbreak of the English
    Civil War, 376
Outbreaks, 190
Outdoor Pastimes of an
    American Hunter, 336
Outgrowing Democracy, 262
The Outlaws of Medieval
    Legend, 373
Outline of Cultural
    Materials, 104, 121
Outline of European
    Architecture, 533
An Outline of Indian History
    and Culture, 453
Outline of the Science of
    Political Economy, 145
Outline of World Cultures,
    121
Outlines of Psychology, 187
Outlines of South Indian
    History, 453
Outsiders: Studies in the
    Sociology of Deviance, 194
Outstanding International
    Press Reporting, 566
Over Here, 277

Over the Wire and on T.V.,
    569
Overdrive, 51
Overlord: Normandy, 1944,
    408
Overnight to Many Distant
    Cities, 615
An Ownership Theory of the
    Trade Union, 131
Oxford American Dictionary,
    27
The Oxford Book of
    Aphorisms, 22
Oxford Classical Dictionary,
    241
The Oxford Companion to
    American History, 262
Oxford Companion to Art,
    528
The Oxford Companion to
    Canadian History and
    Literature, 348
The Oxford Companion to
    Classical Literature,
    239
The Oxford Companion to
    the Decorative Arts, 534
The Oxford Companion to
    Twentieth-Century Art,
    530
Oxford Dictionary of Current
    Idiomatic English, 32
The Oxford Dictionary of
    English Etymology, 37
The Oxford Dictionary of
    English Proverbs, 22
The Oxford Dictionary of
    Modern Greek, 42
The Oxford Dictionary of
    Quotations, 21
The Oxford-Duden Pictorial
    English Dictionary, 27
The Oxford-Duden Pictorial
    English-Japanese
    Dictionary, 44
The Oxford-Duden Pictorial
    French-English Dictionary,
    40
The Oxford-Duden Pictorial
    German-English
    Dictionary, 41
The Oxford English-Arabic
    Dictionary of Current
    Usage, 38
The Oxford English
    Dictionary, 24, 27

The Oxford-Harrap Standard
    German-English
    Dictionary, Volume III, L–
    R, 41
Oxford History of England,
    370
The Oxford History of India,
    453
Oxford History of Modern
    Europe, 412
The Oxford History of
    Modern India, 1740–1975,
    453
The Oxford History of South
    Africa: South Africa, 1870–
    1966, 445
The Oxford History of the
    American People, 263, 328
Oxford History of the United
    States, 1783–1917, 328
Oxford Latin Dictionary, 44
Oxford Picture Dictionary of
    American English, 46
Oxford Regional Economic
    Atlas, 433
Ozark Baptizings, Hangings,
    and Other Diversions, 601
Ozark Folksongs, 601

The Pacific War, 278
Pacifist's Progress, 341
Paganism in the Roman
    Empire, 244
The Paideia Proposal, 223
Painting in the Twentieth
    Century, 530
Painting of the High
    Renaissance in Rome and
    Florence, 529
Pakistan (Wilber), 453
Pakistan (Wilcox), 453
Palestine and Israel in the
    Nineteenth and Twentieth
    Centuries, 435
The Palestine Campaigns,
    431
Palestine Jewry and the
    Arab Question, 1917–1925,
    427
Palestine, Retreat from the
    Mandate, 427
Pamphlets of the American
    Revolution, 1750–1776,
    260
Pan-Africanism, 443

Pan-Slavism, 468
The Panama Canal and Sea
  Power in the Pacific, 471
Panditji, 474
Panslavonic Folklore, 598
Paperbound Books in Print,
  9
The Parade's Gone By, 576
Paraguay, 365
Paraguay under Stroessner,
  365
Parallel Lives of Greeks and
  Romans, 247
The Paranoid Style in
  American Politics and
  Other Essays, 323
Parent-Child Interaction, 196
Paris and Oxford
  Universities in the 13th
  and 14th Centuries, 373
The Parliament of 1621, 377
Parliament Parties and
  Society in France, 414
Parliament, Policy and
  Politics in the Reign of
  William III, 376
Parliamentary History of
  England from the Norman
  Conquest in 1066 to the
  Year 1803, 389
Partial Justice, 193
Participation in America,
  153
Particulars of My Life, 185
Partition and Independence
  of India, 453
The Partition of Africa, 443
Party and Constituency, 153
Party and Political
  Opposition in
  Revolutionary America,
  266
Party Coalitions, 279
Party Politics, 300
Party Politics in Canada, 351
The Passage of Dominion,
  392
Passage through El Dorado,
  358
Passage through the Garden,
  640
The Passing of Traditional
  Society, 200, 433
Passing the Time in
  Ballymenone, 597
The Passionate People, 429

Passionate Pilgrims, 617
Passport to Anywhere, 627
Past and Future, 472
The Past and the Present,
  398
The Past before Us, 254
Patents, Invention, and
  Economic Change, 129
Paternalism in Early
  Victorian England, 382
The Path between the Seas,
  276, 365
The Path to European
  Union, 413
The Path to Power, 70
Paths of American Thought,
  339
Paths to the Present, 338
Pattern: A Study of
  Ornament in Western
  Europe from 1180 to 1900,
  534
Pattern in the Material Folk
  Culture of the Eastern
  United States, 608
Patterns in Comparative
  Religion, 109
Patterns in Criminal
  Homicide, 194
Patterns of Culture, 105, 106,
  111
Patterns of Learning, 226
Patterns of Realism, 575
Patterns of Renewal, 648
The Patton Papers, 407
Peace and War: A Theory of
  International Relations,
  457
The Peace Reform in
  American History, 285
Peaceful Conquest: The
  Industrialization of
  Europe, 1760–1970, 413
The Peacemakers, 267
Peacemaking 1919, 409
Pearl Harbor as History, 449
Peasant Life in China, 110
Peasant Society and Culture,
  122
Peasants and Government in
  the Russian Revolution,
  422
Peasants in History, 393
The Peasants' Revolt of
  Thirteen Eighty One, 373
Peckinpah, 578

The Peculiar Institution, 272
Pedagogical Anthropology,
  234
Pedagogy of the Oppressed,
  225
Pedro Martínez, 117
The Peelites and the Party
  System, 1846–52, 380
Pelican History of Art, 527,
  528
Pelican History of Canada,
  347
The Peloponnesian War, 245
The Penguin Dictionary of
  Art and Artists, 528
The Penguin Dictionary of
  Modern History, 1789–
  1945, 405
The Penguin Dictionary of
  Modern Quotations, 20
Pennsylvania Dutch
  American Folk Art, 600
Pennsylvania German
  Secular Folk Songs, 593
Penny Capitalism, 107, 126
People and Places in
  Colonial Venezuela, 366
The People and the King,
  357
The People Look at Radio,
  191
The People Look at
  Television, 191
The People of Great Russia,
  110
People of Plenty, 333
The People of Roman
  Britain, 371
People of the Twilight, 350
The People of the United
  States in the Twentieth
  Century, 218
The People's Champion,
  1902–1911, 383
The People's Choice (Agar),
  308
The People's Choice
  (Lazarsfeld), 153, 207
The People's Emperor, 76
A People's History of the
  United States, 263
The Pergamon Dictionary of
  Perfect Spelling, 36
The Perils of Democracy, 308
Periodical Title
  Abbreviations, 9

The Permanent Revolution, 157
Peron, 360
The Persian Expedition, 246
The Persian Gulf, 438
The Persian Letters, 166, 167
Persian Oil, 437
The Persian Wars, 245
The Persistent Problems in Psychology, 169
Persona and Shame, 579
Personal Character and Cultural Milieu, 106
Personal Equation, 465
Personal Influence, 191, 208
Personal Narrative of a Pilgrimage to Al Madinah and Meccah, 629
The Personal President, 154
Personalities and Powers, 395
Personality: A Psychological Interpretation, 175
Personality and Social Encounter, 175
Personality Theory, Moral Development, and Criminal Behavior, 175
Perspectives in American Indian Culture Change, 105
Perspectives in Economics, 124
The Perspectives of the World, 459
Perspectives on American Folk Art, 592
Perspectives on Education, 224
Peru: A Cultural History, 365
Peru: A Short History, 365
Peter Hurd, 324
Peter the Great (Kliuchevskii), 423
Peter the Great (Massie), 53
Phaidon Encyclopedia of Art and Artists, 529
Phaidon Guide to Glass, 534
The Philadelphia Negro, 318
A Philosophical Enquiry into the Origin of Our Idea of the Sublime and the Beautiful, 387
Philosophy and Civilization, 231

A Philosophy of Adult Education, 224
Philosophy of Giambattista Vico, 462
The Philosophy of History, 462
The Philosophy of History in Our Times, 403
The Philosophy of Politics, 462
The Philosophy of Teaching, 228
The Philosophy of Wealth, 132
Philosophy, Poetry, History, 462
The Photographic History of the Civil War, 314
Physics and Politics, 385
The Piano in Concert, 496
A Pictorial Encyclopedia of the Oriental Arts, 530
A Pictorial History of Chinese Architecture, 532
A Pictorial History of Immigration, 322
A Pictorial History of Sex in Films, 577
A Pictorial History of the Silent Screen, 576
Picturesque Expressions, 21
Pidginization and Creolization of Languages, 108
Pierrot LeFou, 584
The Pilgrimage to Santiago, 622
The Pillars of the Post, 567
Pinckney's Treaty, 311
Pineapples of Finest Flavour, 65
The Pinyin Chinese-English Dictionary, 39
Pioneers of France in the New World, 332
Pirates, Shipwrecks, and Historic Chronicles, 645
Pissing in the Snow and Other Ozark Folktales, 601
Pitt and Popularity, 379
A Place in Time, 265
Place-Name Changes since Nineteen Hundred, 19
The Place of Franklin D. Roosevelt in History, 330

Plague, Population and the English Economy, 1348–1530, 373
Plagues and People, 473
Plain Folk, 292
Plain Speaking, 80
The Plains Across, 272
Plainville USA, 110
The Planned Economies of Eastern Europe, 420
Planning a Tragedy, 280
Planning and Productivity under Soviet Socialism, 156
Play and Development, 178
Play, Dreams and Imitation in Childhood, 174, 184, 235
Pleasures of Music, 491
The Pleasures of Philosophy, 463
Plunder of the Arts in the Seventeenth Century, 400
Pocket History of the United States, 314, 330
The Pocket Oxford English-Russian Dictionary, 45
The Pocket Oxford Russian-English Dictionary, 45
Poetics of Music in the Form of Six Lessons, 514
The Poetry of Byron, 77
Policy and Police, 389
Policy Indicators, 156
The Policy Process in the Modern Capitalist State, 156
The Policy Sciences, 156, 163
Polish-American Folktales, 595
The Polish Peasant in Europe and America, 204, 218, 219
Political and Social Change in Modern Egypt, 436
The Political and Social Doctrine of Fascism, 417
Political and Social Thought in the Contemporary Middle East, 433
The Political Awakening of Africa, 442
Political Communication and Public Opinion in America, 564

Political Development and
Social Change in Libya,
440
The Political Economy of
Modern Iran, 437
The Political Economy of
Nigeria, 445
The Political Economy of
Slavery, 287
A Political Economy of
Uruguay since 1870, 366
Political Handbook of the
World, 404
Political History, 402
Political History of England
from the Ascension of
Henry 3rd to the Death of
Edward 3rd, 399
A Political History of Post-
War Italy, 417
Political Ideas of the English
Romanticists, 459
Political Ideologies of the
Twentieth Century, 468
Political Ideology, 154
Political Innovation in
America, 156
Political Man, 154
Political Mobilization of
Peasants, 436
Political Parties, 153, 211
Political Parties in Turkey,
439
Political Power, 166
Political Socialization, 202
The Political System, 149
The Political Systems of
Highland Burma, 111
Political Theory, 149
Political Tolerance and
American Democracy, 152
Political Violence in Ireland,
382
The Politician, 71, 281
The Politicos, 58
The Politics, 246
Politics among Nations, 305
Politics and Administration,
150
Politics and Cinema, 577
Politics and Constitution in
the History of the United
States, 295
Politics and History, 458
Politics and Ideology in the
Age of the Civil War, 273

Politics and Markets, 130
Politics and Modernization
in South and Southeast
Asia, 446
Politics and Society in De
Gaulle's Republic, 415
Politics and Society in
Israel, 435
Politics and Society in the
U.S.S.R., 423
Politics and the Military in
Jordan, 440
Politics and the Nation,
1450–1660, 375
Politics and Vision, 149
Politics as Communications,
564
Politics in Africa, 440
Politics in Rhodesia, 441
Politics in the Age of Peel,
391
Politics in the Ancient
World, 239
The Politics of
Accommodation, 419
The Politics of Assimilation,
429
The Politics of Broadcast
Regulation, 571
Politics of Compromise, 419
The Politics of Congress,
302
The Politics of Cultural
Despair, 417
The Politics of Deference,
381
The Politics of Domesticity,
290
The Politics of
Eurocommunism, 410
The Politics of Faction,
418
The Politics of Hope, 339
The Politics of Latin
American Development,
360
The Politics of Mass Society,
152, 190
The Politics of Moderation,
168
The Politics of Palestinian
Nationalism, 440
The Politics of Park Design,
290
The Politics of Recovery, 279
The Politics of Rescue, 92

Politics of Social Change in
the Middle East and North
Africa, 432
The Politics of Soviet
Agriculture, 422
The Politics of the Budgetary
Process, 150
Politics of the Prussian
Army, 1640–1945, 416
Politics, Parties and Pressure
Groups, 153, 161, 162
Politics, Personality and
Social Science in the
Twentieth Century, 163
Politics: Who Gets What,
When, and How, 154, 163
Polls and the Awareness of
Public Opinion, 156
Poole's Index to Periodical
Literature, 9
The Poor Pay More, 128
Poor Pearl, Poor Girl, 593
Poor People's Movements,
201
Poor Richard's Almanack, 63
Poor Robin's Almanac, 63
Poore's Descriptive
Catalogue of the
Government Publications
of the United States, Sept.
5, 1774–March 4, 1881, 14
The Popish Plot, 376
Popular Culture and
Libraries, 612
Popular Culture in Early
Modern Europe, 410
A Popular Guide to
Government Publications,
13, 256
Popular Justice, 294
The Popular Mood of Pre-
Civil War America, 272
Popular Names of U.S.
Government Reports, 14
Popular Periodical Index, 9
Popular Politics and Society
in Late Victorian Britain,
381
The Popular Sources of
Political Authority, 321,
322
Population, Economy, and
Society in Pre-Industrial
England, 374, 378
The Population History of
England, 1541–1871, 370

The Population of Japan, 218
The Population of the United
    States, 197
Populations of the Middle
    East and North Africa, 432
The Portable Age of Reason
    Reader, 460
Portrait of a Diplomatist, 76
Portrait of a Marriage, 77
Portrait of Canada, 347
Portrait of Mr. B, 521
Portrait of the Artist as an
    American, 59
Portraits from the
    Americans, 312
Portraits in Miniature and
    Other Essays, 60
Portugal, 418
A Portuguese-English
    Dictionary, 44
Portuguese-English, English-
    Portuguese Dictionary, 44
Portuguese in India, 452
Portuguese Voyagers to
    America in the Fifteenth
    Century, 329
Positive Images, 571
The Positive Philosophy, 205
Post War Britain, 384
The Pottery and Porcelain of
    the United States and
    Marks of American
    Potters, 534
Poverty and Plenty on the
    Turkish Farm, 439
Poverty of Abundance, 70
The Poverty of Progress, 358
Power and Order, 307
Power and Personality, 175
Power and Policy in China,
    447
Power and Protest in
    American Life, 289
The Power Elite, 211, 212
Power in the Kremlin, 425
The Power of the Modern
    Presidency, 299
Power, Politics, and People,
    212
The Powerful Consumer, 128
Powers of Congress, 298
Powers of the Press, 567
Practical Spanish Dictionary
    and Phrasebook, 46
Practicing History, 481
Pragmatic Illusions, 72

The Pragmatic Revolt in
    American History, 310,
    311
Pragmatism, 180
Prairie School Architecture,
    559
Prayers for Dark People,
    318
Pre-Columbian Art, 353
A Preface to Democratic
    Theory, 151, 152
A Preface to Morals, 164
A Preface to Politics, 164,
    325
The Prehistory of the
    Mediterranean, 239
Preindustrial City, 202
Prejudice, 197
Prelude to Greatness, 89
Prelude to Independence,
    338
Prelude to Revolution, 446
Prentice-Hall Handbook for
    Writers, 23
Prentice-Hall's Great
    International Atlas, 18
The Prerequisites for Peace,
    341
The Presentation of Self in
    Everyday Life, 206, 207
The Presidency: A Research
    Guide, 13, 256
Presidency and the Mass
    Media in the Age of
    Television, 568
The Presidency and the
    Political System, 300
The Presidency of Lyndon B.
    Johnson, 280
Presidency on Trial, 73
The President and Protest,
    70
The President Makers, 58
The President: Office and
    Powers, 153, 299
President Roosevelt and the
    Coming of the War, 1941,
    309
Presidential Anecdotes, 298
The Presidential Campaign,
    299
Presidential Campaigns, 298
Presidential Elections, 301
Presidential Elections and
    American Politics, 152, 297
The Presidential Game, 300

Presidential Influence in
    Congress, 299
The Presidential Quest, 268
Presidential Saints and
    Sinners, 297
The Presidents: A Reference
    History, 256
Presidents above Party, 300
Presidents, Politics, and
    Policy, 299
Press and America, 566
The Press and Public, 190
The Press and the American
    Revolution, 265
Press Control around the
    World, 565
Press, Party, and Presidency,
    301
Press Watch, 567
Presumed Guilty, 72
The Pretend Indians, 577
Pretend the World Is Funny
    and Forever, 610
The Price of Independence,
    267
The Price of Power, 308
The Price of Union, 308
The Price System and
    Resource Allocation, 127
Price Theory, 135
Prices and Production, 136
Pride's Purge, 377
Primary Elections, 166
Prime Movers, 520
Prime-Time America, 572
Prime-Time Television, 570
A Primer of Freudian
    Psychology, 175, 179
A Primer of Statistics for
    Political Scientists, 162
Primitive Art, 112
Primitive Classification, 206
Primitive Culture, 106, 114,
    123
Primitive Polynesian
    Economy, 107, 113
Primitive Rebels, 393
The Primitive World and Its
    Transformations, 105, 106,
    122
The Prince, 165
A Prince of Our Disorder:
    The Life of T. E.
    Lawrence, 53, 438
The Princeton Encyclopedia
    of Classical Sites, 241

Principall Navigations, Voyages, Traffiques and Discoveries of the English Nation, 635

Principles of Art History, 529

Principles of Behavior, 180

The Principles of Classical Dance, 519

The Principles of Economic Planning, 130

Principles of Economics (Marshall), 125, 140

Principles of Economics (Menger), 142

Principles of Economics and Sociology, 142

Principles of Gestalt Psychology, 174

Principles of Physiological Psychology, 187

Principles of Political Economy (Malthus), 139

Principles of Political Economy (Mill), 142

Principles of Political Economy and Taxation, 144

The Principles of Psychology (James and Miller), 180

The Principles of Psychology (Spencer), 217

The Principles of Science, 138

Principles of Topological Psychology, 182

Printing and Society in Early America, 562

Printmaking, 529

Prints and People, 534

Prisoner without a Name, Cell without a Number, 360

Private Wants and Public Needs, 132

Privileged Communication and the Press, 569

Privileged Persons, 56

Problem of Asia, 471

The Problem of Monopoly, 132

The Problem of Slavery in an Age of Revolution, 1770–1823, 268

Problems in Continuing Education, 224

Problems of Contemporary French Politics, 415

Problems of Lasting Peace, 69

Process and Effects of Mass Communications, 191

The Process of Political Domination in Ecuador, 362

Procession, 634

The Production and Distribution of Knowledge in the United States, 126

Production and Distribution Theories, 124, 126, 142

The Professional Soldier, 198

The Professional Thief, 193

Profiles in Courage, 71, 300

Programs in Aid of the Poor, 130

Progress and Poverty, 131

Progress and Power, 310

Progress, Coexistence and Intellectual Freedom, 425

The Progressive Era and the Great War, 1896–1920, 259

The Progressive Historians, 254, 310, 323, 344

The Progressive Movement, 1900–1915, 323

The Progressive Presidents, 275

Progressivism, 276

Projective Techniques and Cross Cultural Research, 104

Prominent Personalities in the U.S.S.R., 422

Promise of Eden, 350

The Promised Land, 426

Pronouncing Dictionary of American English, 31

Pronouncing Dictionary of English Place Names, 19

Propaganda Technique in the World War, 163

Property, Kin and Community on Truk, 107

The Prophet Armed, 421, 481

The Prophet Outcast, 421, 481

The Prophet Unarmed, 421, 481

Prophets and People, 468

Prophets of Prosperity, 287

Prophets of Regulation, 129

Prophets, Poets and Philosophers of the Ancient World, 478

Prose Quotations from Socrates to Macauley, 20

Proshauer, 321

The Prospective City, 202

Protest in Tokyo, 451

Protestant, Catholic, Jew, 199

The Protestant Ethic and the Spirit of Capitalism, 199, 220

Protestant versus Catholic in Mid-Victorian England, 379

Protracted Game, 75

The Proud Tower, 481

Proverbial Comparisons and Related Expressions in Spanish, 45

The Province and Function of Law, 118

Provincial Society, 308

Pseudonyms and Nicknames Dictionary, 9

Psychological Analysis of Economic Behavior, 128

Psychology: A Biosocial Study of Behavior, 171

Psychology: An Elementary Text Book, 177

Psychology: An Introduction, 170

Psychology from the Standpoint of a Behaviorist, 186

The Psychology of Intelligence, 235

The Psychology of Interpersonal Behavior, 172

The Psychology of Learning and Motivation, 174

The Psychology of Myth, Folklore and Religion, 608

The Psychology of Reasoning, 173, 176

The Psychology of Rumor, 174, 175, 190

Psychology of the Child, 184

The Psychology of Wants, Interests and Attitudes, 236

Psychology: The Science of
Mental Life, 169
Psychopathology and
Politics, 163
The Public Commission of
the University, 229
Public Finance in Theory
and Practice, 132
The Public Good, 272
Public Investment, the Rate
of Return, and Optimum
Fiscal Policy, 132
Public Library Catalog, 9
Public Opinion, 156, 163,
164, 325
Public Opinion and
American Democracy, 152,
154, 156, 162
Public Opinion and Popular
Government, 156
Public Papers of the
Secretaries-General of the
United Nations, 68
Public Persons, 325
The Public Philosophy, 325
Public Policies toward
Business, 127
Public School Law, 227
The Public's Use of
Television, 571
Publishers Directory, 9
Publishers' Trade List
Annual, 9
The Puerto Rican Journey,
211, 212
Puerto Rico: A Colonial
Experiment, 365
Puerto Rico: A Political and
Cultural History, 365
The Pugnacious Presidents,
297
Punjabi Century, 1857–1947,
453
The Purchasing Power of
Money, 134
The Pure Theory of Capital,
126, 137
The Puritan Moment, 376
The Puritans: A Sourcebook
of Their Writings, 261, 327
Puritans and Adventurers,
264
The Purpose of American
Politics, 300
The Pursuit of Happiness,
269

The Pursuit of Loneliness,
103
The Pursuit of Power, 473
Putnam's Contemporary
Dictionaries: English-
German, Deutsch-
Englisch, 40
Putnam's Contemporary
Dictionaries: Italian-
English, Inglese-Italiano,
43
Putnam's Contemporary
Dictionaries: Spanish-
English, Inglés-Español, 46
Putnam's Contemporary
French Dictionary, 40
Puttin' on Ole Massa, 606
The Pyramids of Egypt, 239

Qualitative Analysis, 208
Qualitative and Quantitative
Social Research, 189, 208
The Quality of American
Life, 102
Quantification, 101
Quantitative International
Politics, 155
Quarrels That Have Shaped
the Constitution, 295
Quebec, 349
Queen Anne, 376
Queen Charlotte, 378
Queen Elizabeth I, 395
Queen Victoria, 60
The Quest for Mind, 116, 185
The Quest for Peace, 68
Quest of the Silver Fleece,
318
The Question of Palestine,
440
The Question of Separation,
350
Quetzacoatl and Guadalupe,
357
Quiet Revolution, 284
The Quotable Woman, 1800–
1981, 21
Quotations from Chairman
Mao Tse-tung, 448
Quotations in History, 21

R. Buckminster Fuller on
Education, 225
R. E. Lee, 56, 57

RKO: The Biggest Little
Major of Them All, 577
Rx Television, 572
The Ra Expeditions, 636
Race and Colour in Islam,
434
Race and Nationality in
American Life, 322
Race Differences, 173, 181
Race Differences in
Intelligence, 173
Race: Science and Politics,
111
Racial Equality in America,
320
The Radiant City, 543
The Radical Left and
American Foreign Policy,
305
The Radical Politics of
Thomas Jefferson, 269
Radical Tories, 351
Radicals, Secularists and
Republicans, 382
Radio and Television: A
Selected Annotated
Bibliography, 562, 572
Radio and Television
Broadcasting in Eastern
Europe, 572
Radio and the Printed Page,
191
Radio Comedy, 573
Radio in the Television Age,
571
Radio Listening in America,
191
Radio Research, 1941,
207
Radio's Golden Years, 573
A Rain of Darts, 353
The Raj, the Indian Mutiny,
and the Kingdom of Oudh,
1801–1859, 453
The Rajput Rebellion
against Aurangzeb, 453
Ranch Life and the Hunting
Trail, 336
Rand McNally Cosmopolitan
World Atlas, 18
Rand McNally Road Atlas,
19
The Random House Basic
Dictionary, French-
English, English-French,
40

The Random House Basic Dictionary: German-English, English-German, 41

The Random House Basic Dictionary: Italian-English, English-Italian, 43

The Random House Encyclopedia, 4

The Random House Handbook, 22

The Random House Speller/Divider, 36

A Random Walk Down Wall Street, 131

The Rationale of Judicial Evidence, Specially Applied to English Practice, 158

The Raven and the Whale, 326

The Raw and the Cooked, 116

Reaching Judgment at Nuremberg, 417

Reaction and Reconstruction in English Politics, 1832 to 1852, 391

Reaction to Conquest, 104

A Reader in Bureaucracy, 197, 210

Reader in Comparative Religion, 109

Reader in Public Opinion and Mass Communication, 190

Reader's Digest Almanac and Yearbook, 1985, 16

A Reader's Guide to Canadian History, 347

Reader's Guide to Great Britain, 369

Readers' Guide to Periodical Literature, 2, 9

A Reader's Guide to the Social Sciences, 100

Reading and Writing Chinese, 39

Reading, Writing and Reconstruction, 227

Readings in American Nationalism, 468

Readings in Art History, 529

Readings in Ethnomusicology, 493

Readings in Jewish History, 428

Readings in Labor Economics and Labor Relations, 131

The Realities behind Diplomacy, 383

The Realities of American Foreign Policy, 466

Reality and Dream, 106

Reapportionment, 300

Reappraisals in History, 374

Reason and Revolution, 141

Rebellion and Democracy in Meiji Japan, 450

Rebellion in the Backlands, 361

Recent Social Trends in the United States, 166, 213

Recent Views on British History, 370

The Reckoning, 61

Recognizable Ideals, 336

Recommended Reference Books for Small and Medium-Sized Libraries and Media Centers, 11

Reconsiderations on the Russian Revolution, 421

Reconstructing American Law, 155

Reconstructing Europe after the Great War, 413

Reconstruction after the Civil War, 320

The Reconstruction of American Political Ideology, 1865–1917, 275

Reconstruction: The Negro and the New South, 273

The Records of the Federal Convention of 1787, 295

Recycling the Past, 254

Red China Today, 448

The Red Executive, 422

Red Guard, 446

Red October, 421

Red Star Over China, 449

Reference Guide to the Literature of Travel, 616

Reference Sources in Library and Information Services, 9

Reflections of Social Life in the Navaho Origin Myth, 604

Reflections on History (Force and Freedom), 460

Reflections on Modern History, 468

Reflections on Revolution in France, 388

Reflections on the Civil War, 314

Reflections on the Constitution, 162

Reflections on the French Revolution, 331

Reflections on the Revolution of Our Time, 162

Reflections on Violence, 150

Reform and Renewal, 389

Reform and Revolution in China, 447

The Reformation in England, 374

Reformatory Education, 230

Regarding Television, 571

Regicide and Revolution, 377

Regional Government and Political Integration in Southwest China, 1949–1954, 449

Regulating Safety, 129

Regulating the Professions, 129

Regulation and Its Alternatives, 288

Regulatory Bureaucracy, 127

Rehearsal for Reconstruction, 274

Reichswehr and Politics, 415

Reign of Henry Seventh from Contemporary Sources, 396

The Reign of Henry VI, 373

The Reign of Mary Tudor (Froude), 390

The Reign of Mary Tudor (Loades), 375

Reign of William Rufus and the Accession of Henry the First, 390

The Relationship of Verbal and Non-Verbal Communication, 564

The Relevance of Education, 224

Religion: An Anthropological View, 109

Religion and Freedom of
    Thought, 326
Religion and Politics in Iran,
    437
Religion and Politics in
    Israel, 435
Religion and Politics in
    Latin America, 366
Religion and Politics in
    Muslim Society, 452
Religion and Respectability,
    381
Religion and Ritual in
    Chinese Society, 199
Religion and Society in
    Industrial England, 380
Religion and the Decline of
    Magic, 375
Religion and the Rise of
    Capitalism, 398
Religion in Film, 577
The Religion of China, 199,
    220
The Religion of India, 199,
    220
The Religion of Java, 109,
    114, 199
The Religions of the Roman
    Empire, 244
Religious Broadcasting,
    1920–83, 568
The Religious Orders in
    England, 370
Religious Publishing and
    Communications, 563
Religious Television, 564
The Reluctant Patron, 286
Reluctant Regulators, 563
Renaissance, 463
Renaissance Diplomacy, 472
The Renaissance in Italy,
    476, 477
The Renaissance of Islam,
    434
The Renaissance Sense of
    the Past, 402
Rendezvous with Destiny, 91
Report from a Chinese
    Village, 448
Report of the Exploring
    Expedition to the Rocky
    Mountains in the Year
    1842, 626
Reporting for Television, 569
The Republic (Beard), 309
The Republic (Plato), 167

The Republic in Peril, 1812,
    268
Republican Germany, 416
Research Centers Directory,
    9
Research on Human
    Subjects, 199
Research Practices in the
    Study of Kinship, 104
Researches into the Early
    History of Mankind and
    the Development of
    Civilization, 123
Reshaping America, 281
Reshaping the International
    Order, 130
Resistance in Vichy France,
    414
The Resolution of Conflict,
    192
Resolving Social Conflicts,
    174, 182, 193
Resource Book for
    International
    Communications, 561
Resources and Needs of
    American Diplomacy, 305
Resources of American
    Musical History, 490
Responses of the Presidents
    to Charges of Misconduct,
    302
Responses to
    Industrialisation, 382
The Responsible Electorate,
    162
A Restless People, 322
The Restoration, 377
Rethinking Anthropology,
    104
Rethinking Sociology, 188
Rethinking the Soviet
    Experience, 421
Retrospect and Prospect, 471
The Return to Camelot, 369
Reunion and Reaction, 345
Reverse Dictionary of the
    Spanish Language, 47
Review of Child
    Development Research,
    172
A Revision of Demand
    Theory, 137
Revolt in the Desert, 638
The Revolt of the Masses,
    190

The Revolt of the
    Netherlands, 1555–1609,
    419
Revolution and
    Regeneration, 268
Revolution at Work: Mass
    Campaigns in China, 447
The Revolution Disarmed,
    361
Revolution in El Salvador,
    363
Revolution in Iran, 437
Revolution in the
    Revolution? Armed
    Struggle and Political
    Struggle in Latin America,
    358
Revolution in the Wasteland,
    570
The Revolution of 1688 in
    England, 376
The Revolution of the
    Saints, 377
Revolution, Reform, and the
    Politics of American
    Taxation, 1763–1783, 287
The Revolution
    Remembered, 266
Revolutionaries, 150, 393
The Revolutionary Age of
    Andrew Jackson, 272
Revolutionary America,
    1763–1789, 259
The Revolutionary Histories,
    266
Revolutionary Immortality,
    75, 448
Revolutionary Jews from
    Marx to Trotsky, 431
Revolutionary New England,
    307
Revolutionary New England,
    1691–1776, 307
Revolutionary Personality,
    481
Revolutionary Politics in the
    Long Parliament, 376
Revolutions and
    Dictatorships, 468
Revolutions and Military
    Rule in the Middle East,
    432
Revolutions in Americans'
    Lives, 294
The Rhymer and Other
    Helps for Poets, 35

Rhythm-a-ning, 493
Rhythm and Tempo, 487
Ricardian Economics,
145
The Rich Nations and the
Poor Nations, 483
Richard III, 374
Richard III: The Great
Debate, 373
Richard Nixon, 51
Riding the Storm, 75
The Rights of Man, 331
The Ring of the Nibelungen,
516
Riotous Victorians,
381
The Rise and Decline of
Nations, 129
The Rise and Fall of
American Communism,
278
The Rise and Fall of Athens,
248
The Rise and Fall of
Economic Growth, 128
The Rise and Fall of
Keynesian Economics, 138
The Rise and Fall of the
Confederate Government,
315
The Rise and Fall of the
Political Press in Britain,
381
The Rise of American
Civilization, 308
The Rise of German
Industrial Power, 1834–
1914, 416
The Rise of Industrial
America, 269
The Rise of Modern Europe,
412
The Rise of Modern
Industry, 392
The Rise of Modern Japan,
450
The Rise of Music in the
Ancient World, 487
The Rise of Party in
England, 379
The Rise of the American
Film, 576
The Rise of the Anglo-
German Antagonism, 383
The Rise of the Great
Powers, 412

The Rise of the Marginal
Utility School, 1870–1889,
142
The Rise of the New Model
Army, 376
The Rise of the New West,
1819–1829, 343
The Rise of the Roman
Empire, 248
The Rise of the Romanovs,
423
The Rise of the Soviet
Consumer, 424
The Rise of the West, 406,
472
Rise to Globalism: 1938–
1970, 302
The Rising in Western Upper
Canada, 1837–38, 350
Rising Sun: The Decline and
Fall of the Japanese
Empire: 1936–1945, 409,
452
Risk and Culture, 102
Risk, Uncertainty and Profit,
125, 139
The Risorgimento and the
Unification of Italy, 417
The Rites of Passage
(Gennep), 109
Rites of Passage (Kett), 292
Ritual, Myth and Magic in
Early Modern Europe, 597
The Ritual Process, 109
Road to Appomattox, 316
Road to Pearl Harbor, 407
The Road to Serfdom, 136,
137, 146, 150
The Road to the White
House, 302
The Road to War, 328
The Road to Yalta, 422
Roanoke Island, 265
The Robber Barons, 1861–
1901, 58
Robert J. Flaherty, 578
Robert Kennedy and His
Times, 54, 284, 340
Rock Encyclopedia, 490
The Rockefellers, 287
Roger of Salisbury, 372
Roget's International
Thesaurus, 33
Roget's II, 34
Roget's University
Thesaurus, 34

The Role of the Chinese
Army, 447
Roll, Jordan, Roll, 287
Roman Architecture, 242
Roman Britain, 371
Roman Canon Law in the
Church of England, 394
Roman Civilization, 242
Roman Coins, 242
The Roman Empire, 241
The Roman Empire and Its
Neighbors, 240
Roman Farming, 243
Roman History, 249
Roman Law, 244
Roman Law and Common
Law, 244
Roman Medicine, 243
The Roman Revolution, 241
Roman Sculpture from
Augustus to Constantine,
530
Roman Social Relations, 50
B.C. to A.D. 284, 243
The Roman Soldier, 244
The Romanovs, 423
Romans on the Rhine, 242
The Romantic Exiles, 150
Romantic Music: A History
of Musical Style in
Nineteenth-Century
Europe, 486
Romanticism and Revolt,
1815–1848, 413
The Romany Rye, 628
Rome and Italy, 250
Rome and the
Mediterranean, 250
Rome on the Euphrates, 647
Rommel Papers, 409
Room's Dictionary of
Confusibles, 35
Room's Dictionary of
Distinguishables and
Confusibles, 35
Roosevelt and the
Isolationists, 1932–1945,
278
Roots (Davies), 36
Roots (Haley), 52
The Roots of American
Bureaucracy, 1830–1900,
275
The Roots of American
Psychology, 169
Roots of Black Music, 605

Roots of Revolution, 437
The Roots of Rural Poverty
  in Central and Southern
  Africa, 444
Roots of the Bill of Rights,
  296
The Roots of War, 303
A Rope of Sand, 266
The Ropemakers of
  Plymouth, 329
Rosa Luxemburg, 416
Rough Riders, 336
Roumanian-English
  Dictionary, 45
Roumanian Folktales Retold
  from the Original, 598
Roumeli, 621
Round about Midnight, 503
Rousseau and Revolution,
  463
The Royal Ballet, 520
Royal Charles, 52, 376
Royal Commentaries of the
  Incas and a General
  History of Peru, 354
The Royal Road to
  Romance, 616
Rugged Individualism
  Reconsidered, 106
Rulers and the Ruled,
  191
The Rules of Sociological
  Method, 188, 206
The Ruling Class, 157
The Ruling Race, 271
The Rump Parliament,
  1648–1653, 377
Run, River, Run, 620
Run School Run, 224
Runaway Star, 307
Rural Education, 227
Rural Life in Victorian
  England, 381
Rural Russia under the Old
  Regime, 425
Russia, 424
Russia and the West under
  Lenin and Stalin, 466
Russia at the Dawn of the
  Modern Age, 482
Russia at War, 410
Russia in the Age of
  Catherine the Great, 423
Russia Leaves the War, 467
Russia 1917: The February
  Revolution, 423

Russia 1917: The Kornilov
  Affair, Kerensky and the
  Breakup of the Russian
  Army, 423
Russia, the Atom and the
  West, 466
Russia under Catherine the
  Great, 421
Russia under the Old
  Regime, 424
Russian Empire, 1801–1917,
  425
Russian English Dictionary,
  45
Russian English Dictionary
  of Abbreviations and
  Initialisms, 45
Russian-English Idiom
  Dictionary, 45
Russian Expansion on the
  Pacific, 1641–1850, 422
Russian Imperialism, 422
The Russian Jewry Reader,
  427
Russian Peasants and Soviet
  Power, 423
The Russian Revolution
  (Chamberlin), 420
The Russian Revolution
  (Fitzpatrick), 422
The Russian Revolution
  (Keep), 423
The Russian Revolution
  (Trotsky), 480
The Russian Revolution and
  the Baltic Fleet, 424
The Russian Revolution and
  the Soviet State, 1917–
  1921, 424
The Russian Revolution
  from Lenin to Stalin,
  1917–1929, 420
The Russian School of
  Painting, 420
Russia's Iron Age, 420
Russia's Road from Peace to
  War, 422
Ruth Benedict, 120

The Sacred in a Secular Age,
  199
Safeguarding Civil Liberty
  Today, 310
Sailing Alone Around the
  World, 645

Sailor Historian, 329
Saint and Sufi in Modern
  Egypt, 436
St. Martin's Dictionary of
  Twentieth-Century
  Composers, 1910–1971,
  491
Saint Thomas and the World
  State, 232
The Saintmaker's Christmas
  Eve, 324
Saints and Revolutionaries,
  264
Salazar and Modern
  Portugal, 418
Samuel De Champlain, 329
Samuel Johnson, 51
The Samurai, 452
Sandino, 364
The Sane Positivist, 236
Satchmo, 497
The Savage Mind, 109, 116
A Savage War of Peace:
  Algeria, 1954–1962, 414
The Saving Remnant, 308
Say It with Figures, 101
Sayings and Riddles in New
  Mexico, 602
The Sayings of Poor
  Richard, 64
Scandinavia: Denmark,
  Norway, Sweden, 1319–
  1974, 419
Scandinavian Countries,
  1720–1865, 419
The Scandinavians, 621
Scarcity and Growth
  Reconsidered, 129
The Scaremongers, 409
Scholars, Saints and Sufis,
  434
The School and Society, 230,
  231
School Effectiveness, 227
School Finance, 225
Schooled to Order, 227
Schooling and Achievement
  in American Society, 201
Schools, Scholars and
  Society, 225
The Schools We Deserve,
  228
Science and Civilization in
  China, 448
Science and Social
  Structure, 199, 211

Science and the Social Order, 199
Science as Intellectual Property, 200
The Science of Culture, 106
The Science of the Mind, 170
Science, Technology and Society, 200
Science, Technology and Society in Seventeenth Century England, 210
Sciences of the Artificial, 173
Scientific Elites, 200
A Scientific Theory of Culture and Other Essays, 106, 119
Scientists in American Society, 198
Scientists in Industry, 198
The Scientist's Role in Society, 198, 199
Scope and Method of Political Economy, 125
The Scope of Total Architecture, 542
Scotland and Nationalism, 369
Scotland from the Earliest Times to 1603, 369
Scotland: The Making of the Kingdom, 369
The Scottish Reformation, 374
Scottish Tradition, 596
The Scramble for Africa, 441
Screen and Society, 570
Screen World, 575
The Screenplay from the Jazz Singer to Dr. Strangelove, 575
Scribes and Scholars, 241
The Scribner-Bantam English Dictionary, 27
A Scroll of Agony: The Warsaw Diary of Chaim A. Kaplan, 429
Sculpture and Sculptors of the Greeks, 530
The Sea Change: The Migration of Social Thought, 1930–1965, 412
The Sea Chest, 617
Sea Power in Its Relations to the War of 1812, 471

The Sealed Train: Lenin's Eight-Month Journey from Exile to Power, 424, 470
The Search for a New Order, 450
Search for Consensus, 299
Searching for the Invisible Man, 363
A Season of Youth, 266
Seatramps, 627
The Second Barnhart Dictionary of New English, 27
The Second British Empire, 380
Second Chance, 303
The Second Coming: Popular Millenarianism, 1780–1850, 380
Second Speech on Conciliation with America, 159
The Second World War, 388
The Second World War: A Military History, 407
The Second World War and the Atomic Age, 1940–1973, 259
The Secret History of the American Revolution, 268
The Secret of Childhood, 234
The Secret War in Mexico, 363
See No Evil, 570
A Select Bibliography of the Negro American, 318
A Select Bibliography of Traditional and Modern Africa, 404
A Select Bibliography on Russian History, 1801–1917, 405
Selected Antitrust Cases, 127
Selected Guide to Travel Books, 614
Selected Highland Folktales, 598
Selected Studies in Marriage and the Family, 196
Selected Writings from a Connectionist's Psychology, 236
Selected Writings of Edward Sapir in Language, Culture, and Personality, 106, 108

Selections from the History of the Rebellion and the Civil Wars, and the Life by Himself, 389
Self-Directed Learning, 226
Semper Fidelis, 304
Senescence, 179
Senior High School Library Catalog, 9
The Senses Considered as Perceptual Systems, 174
Sensory Processes, 175
Sentiment and Romance in the Poetry by Shakespeare, 462
Separate Spheres, 383
The Servile State, 386
Seven Days of Freedom, 419
Seven Interpretive Essays on Peruvian Reality, 365
The Seven Lamps of Architecture, 533
The Seven Pillars of Wisdom, 638
Seven Samurai, 586
Seven Years in Tibet, 635
Seven Years War, 332
Seventeenth-Century New England, 264
The Seventh Hero, 461
The Seventh Seal, 579
Sex and Repression in Savage Society, 108, 118
Sex and Temperament in Three Primitive Societies, 119
Sex, Culture, and Myth, 118
Sex-Role Stereotyping in the Mass Media, 561
The Sexual Life of Savages in Northwestern Melanesia, 118
Sexual Politics, Sexual Communities, 201
Sexuality in the Movies, 575
Sexuality in World Cinema, 577
Shaker Music, 593
Shanghai Express and Morocco, 588
The Shape of European History, 473
The Shaping of America, 269
Shaping of Modern Thought, 460
The Shaping of Peace, 350

The Shaping of South African Society, 442

The Shaping of the American Tradition, 321

The Shaping of the Elizabethan Regime, 375

The Share Economy, 131

Shattered Dream, 70

Shattered Peace, 305

The Shepherd of the Ocean, 625

Shepherd's Historical Atlas, 405

The Shi'ite Religion, 434

Shingle Style and the Stick Style, 533, 552

Shingling the Fog and Other Plains Lies, 602

Shining Brow, 559

Ships and Seamanship in the Ancient World, 243

Shiva's Pigeons, 623

The Shogun's Reluctant Ambassadors, 451

A Short Dictionary of Furniture, 534

Short History of Chinese Communism, 447

Short History of North Africa, 443

A Short History of Opera, 495

Short History of Russia, 421

A Short History of Socialism, 412

A Short History of Sociological Thought, 188

Short History of the American Labor Movement, 309

A Short History of the American Nation, 262

A Short History of the Arab People, 438

A Short History of the Chinese People, 447

A Short History of the Egyptian People, 436

A Short History of the European Working Class, 410

A Short History of the Far East, 469

A Short History of the Labour Party, 383

A Short History of the Liberal Party, 1900–1975, 380

A Short History of the Near East, 432

A Short History of the New Deal, 321

A Short History of the Renaissance in Italy, 477

A Short History of the United States, 263, 314

Short History of World War Two, 1939–1945, 410

A Short Walk in the Hindu Kush, 624

Shorter Encyclopedia of Islam, 434

The Shorter Oxford English Dictionary on Historical Principles, 28, 37

Shuckin' and Jivin', 605

The Siberians, 623

Sidewalks of America, 607

The Siege of Quebec and the Campaigns in North America, 1757–1860, 348

Siena, 474

Sigmund Freud and the Jewish Mystical Tradition, 427

The Significance of Sections in American History, 343

The Significance of the Frontier in American History, 343

Silence, 502

The Silence of God, 579

The Silent River, 624

The Silent Traveller in Japan, 623

Silks, Spices and Empire, 623

The Simon and Schuster Book of the Ballet, 519

Simon and Schuster's International Dictionary, 47

Simple and Direct, 22

The Simple Life, 103, 286

Simulation in Social and Administrative Science, 101

Since Socrates, 228

Sindh and the Races That Inhabit the Valley of the Indus, 629

Sinful Tunes and Spirituals, 605

Singlehanded Sailing, 626

Sino-Soviet Relations since Mao, 447

Sir Robert Peel, 391

Sir Robert Walpole, 396

Sir Walter Raleigh (Greenblatt), 374

Sir Walter Raleigh (Rowse), 397

Sisters: The Story of Olivia de Havilland and Joan Fontaine, 578

Six Armies in Normandy, 408

Six Criminal Women, 58

Six Historians, 474

Six Journeys: A Canadian Pattern, 620

Six Lectures on Economic Growth, 129

Six Men, 93

1676: The End of American Independence, 265

The Sixties, without Apology, 102

Sixty Minutes, 568

A Sketch of English Legal History, 394

The Skilled Labourer, 1760–1832, 392

The Sky Is My Tipi, 603

Skyscrapers, and Other Essays, 395

Skywalking, 578

Skyward, 630

Slang and Its Analogues, Past and Present, 32

Slanted News, 93

Slave and Citizen, 85

The Slave Community, 270

Slavery and Freedom, 274

Slavery, Colonialism, and Racism, 293

Slavery: Letters and Speeches, 233

Slavery, Race and the American Revolution, 266

Slaves without Masters, 270

Slogans, 21

Small Escapes under the Sun, 618

Small Groups and Political Rituals in China, 449

Small Town America, 292

Small Town in Mass Society, 192
Small Voices and Great Trumpets, 572
So Proudly We Hail, 291
The Soap Opera, 570
Soaring on the Wind, 627
Social Accounting Systems, 188, 200
Social and Cultural Dynamics, 200, 216
Social and Cultural History of India: Kerala, 453
The Social and Economic History of the Hellenistic World, 240
The Social and Economic History of the Roman Empire, 240
The Social and Political Thought of Leon Trotsky, 423
Social and Psychological Factors Affecting Fertility, 198
A Social and Religious History of the Jews, 427
The Social Animal, 171
Social Anthropology, 113
The Social Anthropology of North American Tribes, 110
Social Behavior, 172
Social Behavior and Personality, 219
Social Behavior in Animals, 186
Social Change in Modern India, 453
Social Change in the Twentieth Century, 200
Social Change in Tikopia, 104, 113
Social Change: With Respect to Culture and Original Nature, 200, 213
Social Characteristics of Urban and Rural Communities, 202
Social Choice and Individual Values, 124, 132
Social Cognition and Communication, 171
The Social Construction of Communities, 192
The Social Contract, 168

Social Darwinism in American Thought, 323
Social Dimensions of Law and Justice, 155
Social Experimentation, 101
Social History and Literature, 398
The Social History of Art, 189, 528
A Social History of England, 1851–1975, 382
Social History of the United States: A Guide to Information Sources, 260
Social Impact Assessment Methods, 188
The Social Laws of the Qoran, 434
Social Learning and Imitation, 174, 177
Social Learning and Personality Development, 173
The Social Life of a Modern Community, 110
Social Mobility in Industrial Society, 201
Social Movements and Protest in France, 414
Social Movements of the Sixties and Seventies, 201
Social Networks, 201
Social Organization (Cooley), 205
Social Organization (Freedman), 114
The Social Organization of Australian Tribes, 121
Social Organization of the Western Pueblos, 110
Social Origins of Dictatorship and Democracy, 412
The Social Prelude to Stalinism, 424
Social Problems as Social Movements, 201
Social Process, 205
Social Psychology, 170
Social Research Ethics, 101
Social Research in the Judicial Process, 155
Social Research to Test Ideas, 218
The Social Role of the Man of Knowledge, 190, 198

Social Science Research Council, 100
Social Science Research Handbook, 404
Social Sciences Citation Index, 10
Social Sciences Index, 2, 10
Social Security, 135
Social Sources of Delinquency, 193
The Social Sources of Denominationalism, 199
Social Status and Psychological Disorder, 200
Social Stratification in Science, 199
Social Structure (Fortes), 122
Social Structure (Murdock), 108, 109, 121
Social Structure and Personality, 106
The Social Structure of Islam, 434
The Social System, 201, 214
The Social Teaching of the Christian Churches, 199
Social Theory and Social Structure, 201, 209, 210
Social Thought from Lore to Science, 187
The Social Transformation of American Medicine, 198, 293
Socialism, 146
Socialism and Communism in India, 453
Socialism, Politics and Equality, 421
Socialism Re-examined, 341
Socialism: Utopian and Scientific, 134
Socialist's Faith, 341
Socialization after Childhood, 202
Socialization and the Life Cycle, 202
Socialization as Cultural Communication, 120
Socialization to Old Age, 202
Society and Economy in Colonial Connecticut, 264
Society and Literature in America, 326
Sociobiology, 171, 174

Sociocultural Theory,
   Values, and Sociocultural
   Change, 217
Socioeconomic Background
   and Achievement, 200
Sociolinguistic Patterns,
   108
Sociological Ambivalence
   and Other Essays, 201
Sociological Approaches to
   Law, 155
The Sociological
   Imagination, 211, 212
Sociological Methodology,
   189
Sociological Theory and
   Modern Society, 214
Sociological Theory and
   Social Research, 205
Sociological Traditions from
   Generation to Generation,
   188
Sociology: A Text with
   Adapted Readings, 188
Sociology and History, 323
Sociology and Socialism,
   157
The Sociology of Journalism
   and the Press, 567
The Sociology of Literature,
   189
The Sociology of Race
   Relations, 197
The Sociology of Religion,
   199, 220
The Sociology of Science,
   200, 210
The Sociology of Science in
   Europe, 200, 210
The Sociology of Small
   Groups, 172
Sociology of the Absurd, 312
Sociology Today, 210
The Sod-House Frontier,
   1854–1890, 275
The Software Encyclopedia
   1985/86, 10
The Sokoto Caliphate, 453
Soldier and State in Africa,
   445
The Soldier and the State,
   198
Solzhenitsyn, 54
Some Considerations on the
   Keeping of Negroes, 81
Some Day Been Dey, 598

Some Intellectual
   Consequences of the
   English Revolution, 393
Some Notes on Negro Crime
   Particularly in Georgia,
   318
Some People, 76, 77
Some Problems of Greek
   History, 479
Somoza and the Legacy of
   U.S. Involvement in
   Central America, 364
Son of Tecun Uman, 363
Son of the Morning Star, 51
Son of the Revolution, 447
Sonata Forms, 486
Songs after Lincoln, 324
Songs and Ballads of the
   Maine Lumberjacks, 599
Songs of the American West,
   603
Songs of the Cowboys, 603
Songs of the Theater, 490
The Songwriter's Rhyming
   Dictionary, 35
Sons of the Shaking Earth,
   353
The Sophisticated Traveler,
   617
The Sorcerers of Dobu, 110
The Soul of Mbira, 494
The Souls of Black Folk, 317,
   318
Soundtrack: The Music of
   the Movies, 493
Source Readings in Music
   History from Classical
   Antiquity throughout the
   Romantic Era, 487
Sources and Documents
   Illustrating the American
   Revolution, 1764–
   1788 . . . , 328
Sources and Documents of
   U.S. Constitutions, 297
Sources and Methods of
   Historical Demography,
   198
Sources of Art Nouveau, 530
Sources of Culture in the
   Middle West, 344
Sources of Information in
   the Social Sciences, 405
Sources of Modern
   Architecture, 533
South Africa, 441

South Africa in Southern
   Africa, 441
The South African Economy
   (Houghton), 442
The South African Economy
   (Nattrass), 443
The South and the
   Concurrent Majority, 333
The South and the Sectional
   Conflict, 333
South Asian History, 1750–
   1950, 445
South East Asia, 445
South Seas Odyssey, 626
South-West Africa, 442
Southeast Asia, 405
Southeast Asia: Problems of
   United States Policy, 446
Southeast Asia's Political
   Systems, 446
Southern Africa, 442
Southern Africa since 1800,
   442
The Southern Appalachians,
   620
Southern Businessmen and
   Desegregation, 288
The Southern Common
   People, 293
The Southern Enigma, 601
The Southern Gates of
   Arabia, 647
A Southern Odyssey—
   Travelers in the
   Antebellum North, 320
Southern Politics in State
   and Nation, 162
The Southern Sudan, 440
Southerners, 291
The Southwest Pacific to
   1900, 445
Soviet Achievement, 424
Soviet-American Relations,
   1917–1920, 466
Soviet and Chinese Aid to
   African Nations, 444
Soviet Bloc, 420
The Soviet Design for a
   World State, 157
The Soviet Economic
   System, 424
The Soviet Empire, 422
Soviet Foreign Policy, 1917–
   1941, 466
Soviet Foreign Propaganda,
   420

Soviet Foreign Relations and
  World Communism, 422
The Soviet Image of Utopia,
  422
Soviet-Indian Relations, 453
Soviet Influence in Eastern
  Europe, 419
The Soviet Intelligentsia,
  421
Soviet Man, 425
Soviet Nationality Policies
  and Practices, 420
Soviet Policy toward the
  Middle East since 1970,
  432
Soviet Potentials, 421
Soviet Society and the
  Communist Party, 425
Soviet Trade Unions and
  Labor Relations, 420
Soviet Union, 425
The Soviet Union and Black
  Africa, 444
The Soviet Union and the
  Arms Race, 408
The Soviet Union since 1917,
  424
The Soviet Union since
  Stalin, 421
Soviet World Atlas in
  English, 19
Space, Earth and
  Communication, 564
Space, Time and
  Architecture, 532
Spaceship Earth, 483
Spain, 418
Spain and the Loss of
  America, 358
Spain: Dictatorship to
  Democracy, 418
Spain, 1808–1974, 418
Spain under the Habsburgs,
  418
The Spaniards, 418
Spanish-American Folk-
  Songs, 594
The Spanish Armada, 390
Spanish Bilingual
  Dictionary, 46
Spanish Central America,
  357
The Spanish Civil War
  (Mitchell), 418
Spanish Civil War (Thomas),
  419

The Spanish Empire in
  America, 357
Spanish Peru, 1532–1560,
  357
Spanish Republic and the
  Civil War, 1931–1939, 418
Spanish Revolution, 419
The Spanish War, 276
Spare Chancellor, 385
The Spartans, 240
The Special Relationship
  between West Germany
  and Israel, 435
Speech and Law in a Free
  Society, 150
The Sphinx and the
  Commissar, 436
The Spiral of Silence, 156
The Spirit and the Future of
  Islam, 433
The Spirit of Chinese
  Politics, 448
The Spirit of Democratic
  Capitalism, 127, 152
The Spirit of Place, 616
The Spirit of St. Louis, 640,
  641
The Spirit of '76
  (Bridenbaugh), 266
The Spirit of '76 (Commager
  and Morris), 314
The Spirit of '76 and Other
  Essays, 310
The Spirit of the Age, 142
The Spirit of the Laws, 166,
  167
Spirit World, 606
Spirits, Heroes and Hunters
  from North American
  Indian Mythology, 604
The Spiritual Conquest of
  Mexico, 356
The Spoiled System, 302
Sport and American
  Mentality, 1880–1910, 293
Sport in Greece and Rome,
  243
The Spot: The Rise of
  Political Advertising on
  Television, 568
Spreading the American
  Dream, 288
Stability and Change in
  Congress, 299
Stability and Strife, 379
Stalin, 421

Stalin and His Generals, 420
Stalin as Revolutionary,
  1879–1929, 425
Stalin Embattled, 424
The Stalin School of
  Falsification, 480
Stalinism, 426
Stalinism and After, 424
Stalinist Planning for
  Economic Growth, 1933–
  1952, 426
Standard English-Korean
  Dictionary for Foreigners,
  44
The Standard of Living in
  Britain in the Industrial
  Revolution, 379
The Standard Periodical
  Directory, 10
Stars, 578
The Starship and the Canoe,
  618
State and Local Finance in
  the National Economy,
  136
The State and Revolution,
  470
The State and Social
  Revolution in Iran, 438
The State Department Policy
  Planning Staff Papers, 467
The State of Music 1939, 515
The State of Nutrition in the
  Arab Middle East, 438
The State of Sociology, 188
State of the World, 194
The State Parks, 620
The State Universities and
  Democracy, 330
States and Social
  Revolutions, 201, 413
Statesman and Saint:
  Wolsey and More, 375
Statesman's Yearbook, 16
The Statesman's Yearbook
  World Gazetteer, 149
Statistical Abstract of the
  United States, 17, 257
A Statistical History of the
  American Presidential
  Elections, 301
Statistical Yearbook, 17
Statistics of Deadly
  Quarrels, 157
Statistics on Film and
  Cinema, 1955–1977, 575

Statistics Sources, 10
Stay Tuned (Levinson and Link), 571
Stay Tuned (Sterling and Kittross), 569
Stendhal, or The Pursuit of Happiness, 58
Stephen Langton, 372, 396
Steppin' Out, 285
Stigma, 194, 207
Still a Dream, 283
A Stillness at Appomattox, 67, 313
Stilwell and the American Experience in China, 1911–1945, 449, 481
Stone Age Economics, 107
The Stones of Florence, 622
Stories on a String, 598
The Story of Art, 528
Story of Civilization, 462, 463
The Story of Mt. Desert Island, Maine, 329
Story of the War in South Africa, 1899–1900, 471
The Strange Career of Jim Crow, 344, 345
Strange Ways and Sweet Dreams, 606
Strategies for Managing Nuclear Proliferation, 194
Strategies of Containment, 303
Strategy and Compromise, 329
The Strategy of Conflict, 155, 157
The Strategy of Economic Development, 129
The Strategy of Peace, 71
Street Corner Society, 172, 192
Strenuous Life, 336
The Stress of My Life, 171
Strictly Personal and Confidential, 79
Striking a Balance, 520
Structural Anthropology, 106, 116
Structural Equation Models in the Social Sciences, 101
Structure and Function in Primitive Society, 109, 121
The Structure of American History, 323

The Structure of Jewish History and Other Essays, 428
Structure of Politics at the Accession of George III, 395
The Structure of Science, 101
The Structure of Scientific Revolutions, 199
The Structure of Social Action, 140, 144, 201, 206, 214, 221
The Structure of the Ottoman Dynasty, 439
Structures of American Social History, 293
The Struggle for Black Equality, 1954–1980, 284
Struggle for Greece, 1941–1949, 420
The Struggle for Mastery in Europe, 1848–1918, 477, 478
The Struggle for Power in Syria, 440
The Struggle for Racial Equality, 314
The Struggle in Afghanistan, 440
Stuart England, 376
The Student-Physician, 198, 210
A Student's Guide to History, 402
Studies in Classical and Ottoman Islam (7th–16th Centuries), 439
Studies in East European Folk Narrative, 596
Studies in Folklore, 592
Studies in German History, 465
Studies in History and Jurisprudence, 159
Studies in Jewish Folklore, 597
Studies in Modern History, 465
Studies in Social Anthropology, 113
Studies in Social History, 396
Studies in the Economic History of the Middle East, 432

Studies in the Institutional History of Early Modern Japan, 450
Studies in the Quantity Theory of Money, 131, 135
Studies in the Social History of China and South-East Asia, 447
Studies on Hysteria, 178
The Study and Teaching of History, 315
A Study in the Theory of Investment, 126
The Study of Deviance, 194
The Study of Folklore, 105, 592
A Study of History, 403, 474, 478, 479
The Study of Instinct, 171, 186
The Study of Lives, 183
The Study of Sociology, 217
A Study of War, 158
Studying History, 402
Studying the Presidency, 299
Style and Idea, 512
Style in History, 402
Subject Collections, 10
Subject Guide to Books in Print 1984–1985, 10
Subject Guide to Humor, 610
The Subjection of Women, 142
The Subjection of Women and Enfranchisement of Women, 203
Subjects and Sovereigns, 377
Submarines, Diving, and the Underwater World, 625
Sub-Saharan Africa, 440
The Subtle Revolution, 204
Suez, 1956, 436
Suffixes and Other Word-Final Elements of English, 31
Suicide, 194, 206
Suicide or Murder, 640
Summerhill, 227
Sun Yat-Sen and the Origins of the Chinese Revolution, 448
Sunbelt Cities, 280
Super Chief, 301
Supermadre, 358

Supernatural Mysteries and Other Tales, 645
Superpower Games, 147
A Supplement to the Oxford English Dictionary, 28
Supply and Demand, 128
The Suppression of the African Slave Trade, 318
The Supreme Court and Constitutional Democracy, 151, 294
The Supreme Court and the Constitution, 309
The Supreme Court and the Idea of Progress, 298
The Supreme Court in the Federal Judicial System, 302
The Supreme Court: Justice and the Law, 298
The Supreme Court's Impact on Public Education, 228
Survey of Objective Studies of Psychoanalytic Concepts, 179
Survey of Organizations, 189
Survey Research in the Social Sciences, 101
A Survival Manual for the Independent Woman Traveler, 617
Survival of a Counterculture, 203
Survival or Hegemony?, 435
Susanna, Jeanie and the Old Folks at Home, 505
Suye Mura, 110
Swazi, 110
Swedish Legends and Folktales, 597
Sweet and Lowdown, 488
Sweet and Sour, 610
Sweet Man, 504
Sweet Promised Land, 622
Swinburne, 77
Swing That Music, 497
The Sword and the Scepter, 416
Symbol and Politics in Communal Ideology, 203
Symbol Sourcebook, 527
Symbolic Interactionism, 196
Symbolists and Symbolism, 529
Symlog, 172

The Symphony, 486
Syndicated Columnists, 568
The Synonym Finder, 34
Syntactic Structures, 108
Syria and Lebanon under French Mandate, 440
Syrian Pageant, 440
System of Positive Polity, 205
The Systematization of Russian Government, 426
A Systems Analysis of Political Life, 153

TV Facts, 573
TV, Family and Society, 571
TV Guide Index 1978–80, 573
TV Guide: The First 25 Years, 571
TV Guide Twenty-Five Year Index, 573
The TV Ritual, 571
TVA and the Grass Roots, 197
Tahiti, 306
Take 22, 578
Taking It All In, 576
Tales and Songs of Southern Illinois, 602
Tales from Africa, 597
Tales from China, 596
Tales from Hispanic Lands, 597
Tales from Thailand, 598
Tales from the First Americans, 604
Tales from the Japanese Storytellers as Collected in the Ho Dan Zo, 598
Tales from the United States, 597
Tales of Old-Time Texas, 602
Tales of the North American Indians, 604
Tales of the South Carolina Low Country, 601
Talking Minds, 171
Tall Tales of the Southwest, 611
Tanzania under Colonial Rule, 443
Tar Heel Ghosts, 601
Tavern Lamps Are Burning, 618

Teaching as a Conserving Activity, 228
Teaching Humanities in the Microelectronic Age, 223
The Teaching of Ethnic Dance, 594
Teaching: The Imperiled Profession, 225
The Technique of Special Effects Cinematography, 576
Technological Society, 199
Technology and Society, 312
Telecommunications America, 564
Telecommunications in Crisis, 563
Telematics in the Year 2000, 565
Television and Aggression, 171, 191, 573
Television and Cable Factbook 1984, 562
Television and the News, 573
Television and the Presidential Elections, 572
Television and Youth, 572
Television Drama Series Programming, 571
Television Experience, 573
Television in America, 570
Television in the Lives of Our Children, 191
Television in Transition, 571
Television, 1970–1980, 573
Television: The American Medium in Crisis, 572
Television: The Critical View, 572
Television: The Medium and Its Manners, 570
Television Today, 570
Television's Transformation, 571
Telling Lives, 50
The Temper of Western Europe, 460
The Ten Books on Architecture, 533
Ten Days That Shook the World, 424
Ten Great Economists, 142
Ten Keys to Latin America, 352

Ten Major Issues in
American Politics, 323
Ten Sixty Six, 372
The Ten Thousand Day War,
283
The Tenacity of Prejudice,
197
Tenement Songs, 608
Tennessee Folk Culture,
601
Tennyson, 77
The Tenors, 496
Tensions Affecting
International
Understanding, 181
Tepoztlán, a Mexican
Village, 122, 192
The Territory of the
Historian, 403
Terror Out of Zion, 435
Test Case: Italy, Ethiopia
and the League of Nations,
407
The Test of Freedom, 341
A Testament, 559
Testament of a Liberal, 465
Testimony, 513
A Texas-Mexican
Cancionero, 603
A Text-Book of Roman Law
from Augustus to
Justinian, 244
Texts and Studies in Jewish
History and Literature,
429
Thailand: A Short History,
455
Thames and Hudson
Dictionary of Art and
Artists, 529
"The Good War," 280
The Theatre: Stage to Screen
to Television, 574
Theft, Law and Society, 193
Thematic Catalogs in Music,
488
Themes and Conclusions,
514
Themes of Work and Love in
Adulthood, 178
Theodor Herzl, 427
Theodore Parker, 314
Theoretical Criminology, 194
Theories in Social
Psychology, 170
Theories of Learning, 173

Theories of Learning and
Instruction, 180
Theories of Mass
Communication, 190, 563
Theories of Personality, 175
Theories of Value and
Distribution since Adam
Smith, 124
Theory and History of
Folklore, 592
Theory and Practice of
Modern Government, 153
Theory Construction, 100,
188
The Theory of Business
Enterprise, 128
A Theory of Cognitive
Dissonance, 171
Theory of Collective
Behavior, 190, 201
The Theory of Committees
and Elections, 153
Theory of Culture Change,
106, 107
The Theory of Economic
Development, 129
A Theory of Economic
History, 137
Theory of Film, 189
The Theory of Games and
Economic Behavior, 125,
147
The Theory of Games and
Markets, 147
The Theory of Interest, 131,
134
The Theory of Money and
Credit, 146
The Theory of Moral
Sentiments, 146
The Theory of Political
Coalitions, 155
The Theory of Political
Economy, 138
The Theory of Social and
Economic Organization,
197, 220
The Theory of Social
Structure, 109
Theory of the Consumption
Function, 135
The Theory of the Leisure
Class, 128, 220
There Ain't No Such Animal
and Other East Texas
Tales, 602

There Are Alligators in Our
Sewers and Other
American Credos, 607
There Is a River, 291
Thereby Hangs a Tale, 36
They All Played Ragtime,
492
They Fought for Their
Country, 475
The Thin Mountain Air, 324
Thinkers of the Twentieth
Century, 10
Thinking Goes to School,
235
The Third French Republic,
1870–1940, 414
The Third International after
Lenin, 480
The Third Portuguese
Empire, 418
Thirteen Days, 73
Thirteenth Century, 1216–
1307, 397
Thirty Indian Legends of
Canada, 603
Thirty-Six Children, 227
The Thirty Years' War,
391
This Business of Music,
491
This Hallowed Ground, 313
This Honorable Court, 301
This I Remember, 78
This Is Pearl!, 327, 328
This Was America, 322
This Was Harlem, 285
Thomas Becket, 372
Thomas Carlyle: A History of
His Life in London, 1834–
1881, 390
Thomas Carlyle: A History of
the First Forty Years of
His Life, 390
Thomas Cranmer, 375
Thomas Cranmer and the
English Reformation,
1489–1556, 396
Thomas Hart Benton, 336
Those Radio Commentators,
569
Those Tremendous
Mountains, 640
Thou Improper, Thou
Uncommon Noun, 33
Thought and Expression in
the Sixteenth Century, 478

Thought Reform and the Psychology of Totalism, 448

Thoughts on African Colonization, 291

Thousand Days, 72, 339

Threats of Revolution in Britain, 1789–1848, 382

Three Apples from Heaven, 598

Three Centuries of Harvard, 1636–1936, 329

The Three Edwards, 373

Three Essays: On Liberty, Representative Government, the Subjection of Women, 142

Three Essays on the State of Economic Science, 125

Three Essays on the Theory of Sexuality, 178

Three Eyes on the Past, 600

The Three Kentucky Presidents, 316

Three Negro Classics, 320

Three Who Made a Revolution, 481

Three Years on the Ocean, 616

Through Paphlagonia with a Donkey, 625

Through the Dark Continent, 646

Tibet Is My Country, 635

Tibetan Foothold, 624

Tikopia Ritual and Belief, 113

Time and Social Structure and Other Essays, 109

Time on the Cross, 287

A Time to Dance, 518

Times Atlas of the World, 19

Times of Feast, Times of Famine, 412

Times of Passion, 283

The Timetables of American History, 257

To Become Somebody, 228

To Cuba and Back, 633

To Dwell among Friends, 196

To Irrigate a Wasteland, 572

To Make Democracy Safe for America, 276

To Peking and Beyond, 448

To Purge This Land with Blood, 271

To Seek a Newer World, 73

To Stand at the Pole, 643

To the Ends of the Earth, 625

To the Maginot Line, 414

Tokugawa Religion, 198

The Toll of Independence, 267

Tom Watson, 345

Too Serious a Business, 409

Total Institutions, 206

The Total Traveler by Ship, 615

Total War: The Story of World War II, 407

Totemism, 116

Touched with Fire, 69

Tourism Planning, 614

Tourism Policy and International Tourism in OECD Member Countries, 1981, 615

Tourism: Principles, Practices and Philosophies, 615

The Tourism System, 615

Tourism: The Good, the Bad, and the Ugly, 615

The Tourist: A New Theory of the Leisure Class, 617

The Tourist Business, 614

The Tourist: Travel in Twentieth Century North America, 616

Tourists, Travellers, and Pilgrims, 616

Toward a Metric of Science, 210

Toward a Steady-State Economy, 128

Toward a Structural Theory of Action, 201

Toward the Final Solution, 430

Toward the Year 2000, 204

Towards a New Architecture, 532, 543

Towards an American Army, 410

The Town Labourer, 1760–1832, 392

Toys and Reasons, 178

Trade and Diplomacy on the China Coast, 464

Trade and Market in the Early Empires, 107, 144

Trade, Plunder and Settlement, 374

Tradition, 215

Traditional American Folk Songs from the Anne and Frank Warner Collection, 595

Traditional Societies and Technological Change, 104

Traditions of American Education, 222, 225

The Tragedy of American Diplomacy, 305

The Tragedy of Paraguay, 365

Transcendentalism as a Social Movement, 1830–1850, 286

Transcendentalists, 326

The Transfer Agreement, 427

The Transformation of Political Culture, 268

The Transformation of the Roman World, 67

Transforming Traditional Agriculture, 126

Transition in Spain from Franco to Democracy, 418

Transitions, 172

Translated Documents of Greece and Rome, 241

Travel and Discovery in the Renaissance, 1420–1620, 617

The Travel Book, 614

A Travel Guide for the Disabled, 623

Travel in Asia, 623

Travel in England in the Seventeenth Century, 622

Travel in the Ancient World, 615

Travel in the United States, 614

Travel Industry, 614

Travel Industry World Yearbook, 615

Travel Literature and the Evolution of the Novel, 615

Travel Sense, 617

Travel Trends in the United States and Canada, 614

Travelers, 620

Travelers and Travel Liars, 1600–1800, 615
A Traveler's Guide to El Dorado and the Inca Empire, 619
Traveler's Reading Guide, 614
A Traveler's Tale, 623
A Traveller in Rome, 642
A Traveller in Southern Italy, 642
Traveller's Dictionary of Quotations, 618
Traveller's Health Guide, 618
Travels in Alaska, 619
Travels in Hawaii, 620
Travels in the Interior Districts of Africa, 643
Travels in West Africa, 626
Travels of Charlie, 617
Travels with Charley in Search of America, 628
Travels with Myself and Another, 616
A Treasury of African Folklore, 605
Treasury of American Folklore, 596
A Treasury of Jewish Folksong, 595
A Treasury of Nebraska Pioneer Folklore, 602
A Treatise on Money, 138
Treatise on Painting, 544
A Treatise on the Family, 195
Treatises on Goldsmithing and Sculpture, 537
The Treaty of Portsmouth, 338
Treblinka, 431
The Tree Where Man Was Born, 443
Trial, 589
Trial and Error: The Autobiography of Chaim Weizmann, 431
Trial by Fire, 274
Trial of Faith, 342
The Trials and Tribulations of Little Red Riding Hood, 608
Trials and Triumphs, 267
Tribe, Caste and Nation, 105
Tristana, 580

Tristes Tropiques, 116
The Triumph of American Capitalism, 321
Trotsky, 426
The Troubled Crusade, 228, 293
Troubled Journey, 284
The Trucial States, 440
The Truman White House, 282
Truman's Crises, 282
The Trumpet Shall Sound, 105
Truth in History, 322
Truth to Life, 49
The Tsardom of Moscow, 1547–1682, 483
The Tudor Constitution, 389
Tudor Dynastic Problems, 1462–1571, 375
Tudor England, 374
The Tudor Revolution in Government, 389
Tudor Studies, 396
Tumultuous Years, 281
Tune in Yesterday, 571
The Turbulent Era, 270
The Turkey of Ataturk, 439
Turkey, the Straits, and U.S. Foreign Policy, 439
Turn Left at the Pub, 622
Turn Right at the Fountain, 622
Turner and Beard, 253
Turning Points of the Civil War, 274
The Twelve Caesars, 251
Twelve Million Black Voices, 294
The Twentieth Century: A Brief Global History, 406
Twentieth-Century American Historians, 253
Twentieth Century American Nicknames, 15
Twentieth-Century China, 447
The Twentieth Century, 1880–1939, 383
Twentieth Century Europe (Vaughn), 413
Twentieth-Century Europe (Weber), 413
Twentieth-Century Germany, 417

Twentieth-Century Indonesia, 455
Twentieth-Century Iran, 437
Twentieth-Century Music (Peyser), 486
Twentieth-Century Music (Stuckenschmidt), 487
Twentieth-Century Pilgrimage, 326
Twentieth-Century Popular Culture in Museums and Libraries, 612
Twentieth-Century Russia, 425
Twentieth-Century Sociology, 188
Twenty Letters to a Friend, 475, 476
Twenty Thousand Quips and Quotes, 610
Twenty Thousand Words, 36
Twilight of Progressivism, 276
The Twilight of the Gods: The Music of the Beatles, 492
The Twisted Road to Auschwitz, 430
Two against Cape Horn, 627
Two Centuries of American Medicine, 1776–1976, 289
Two Hundred and Fifty Years of Afro-American Art, 530
Two Hundred Years of the Republic in Retrospect, 295
Two Innocents in Red China, 447
Two Interviews with Rossana Dalmonte and Balint Andras Varga, 499
The Two Koreas in World Politics, 454
Two Nations, Two Cultures, 349
The Two-Ocean War, 329, 409
Two on a Big Ocean, 627
Two Roads to Sumter, 89, 313, 315
Two Speeches on Conciliation with America and Two Letters on Irish Questions, 387

2001 Italian and English Idioms, 43
2001 Modismos en Inglés, 47
Two Thousand Years of Textiles, 535
Two Treatises of Government, 154, 164
Two Trips to Gorilla Land and the Cataracts of the Congo, 629
Two Tudor Portraits, 56
The Two Viet-Nams, 454
Two Worlds of Liberalism, 142
Two Years before the Mast, 633
Type and Motif Index of the Folktales of England and North America, 592
Types of Naval Officers, 471
The Tyranny and Fall of Edward II, 1321–1326, 373

UNESCO Dictionary of the Social Sciences, 404
U.S. Grant and the American Military Tradition, 313
Ulrich's International Periodicals Directory, 10
The Unadjusted Girl, with Cases and Standpoints for Behavior Analysis, 219
The Unanswered Question, 500
Unbound Prometheus, 412
An Uncertain Friendship, 337
Uncertain Glory, 607
Uncertain Passage: China's Transition to the Post Mao Era, 458
Uncivil Wars, 383
An Uncommon Man, 70
The Unconscious in Culture, 116, 117
Under Six Reigns, 465
The Underground Dictionary, 32
Understanding Laughter, 610
Understanding Media, 191
Understanding New Media, 190, 563
Understanding News, 566

Understanding Television, 569
The Uneasy Chair, 317
The Uneasy State, 102, 277
Unemployment versus Inflation, 130, 135
Unfinished Revolution, 421
The Unfinished War, 281
The Unheralded Triumph, 275
Union Democracy, 211
Union List of Film Periodicals, 574
Union List of Serials in Libraries of the United States and Canada, 10
The Union of Burma, 455
The Union of England and Scotland, 377
Union Pamphlets of the Civil War, 1861–1865, 273
The United Arab Emirates, 438
United Artists, 575
United Nations List of National Parks and Equivalent Reserves, 1980, 616
The United States: A History of a Republic, 263
U.S.: A Statistical Portrait of the American People, 256
United States and Britain, 460
The United States and China (Barnett), 458
The United States and China (Fairbank), 464
The United States and India, Pakistan, Bangladesh, 452
United States and Israel, 435
The United States and the Origins of the Cold War, 1941–1947, 278, 408
The United States and World War Two, 407
U.S. Arms Sales, 459
The United States Congress, 156, 259
United States Congress: People, Place and Policy, 300
U.S. Constitution: A Guide to Information Sources, 260

U.S. Cultural History: A Guide to Information Sources, 260
The United States, 1830–1850, 343
U.S. Foreign Policy: Shield of the Republic, 325
U.S. Government Manual, 257
United States Government Publications, 12
The United States in a Chaotic World, 330
The United States in 1800, 306
U.S.-Korean Relations, 1882–1982, 454
U.S. Occupation in Europe after World War II, 413
The United States Occupation of Haiti, 1915–1934, 363
U.S. Politics and Elections, 259
The United States, 1789–1890, 262
The United States since 1865, 321
U.S.-Soviet Relations in the Era of Détente, 409
The United States: The History of a Republic, 323
Unity in Diversity: Italian Communism and the Communist World, 417
Universals of Human Language, 108
The University and the Public Interest, 225
The University of Chicago Spanish Dictionary, 46
The University of Utopia, 232
Unknown Greece, 622
Unobtrusive Measures, 101
The Unraveling of America, 283
Unrecognized Patriots, 267
The Unredeemed: Anti-Semitism in the Soviet Union, 425
Unsolved Mysteries of the Arctic, 648
The Unwanted Symbol, 281
Up from Liberalism, 298
Up from Slavery, 237

Up from the Footnote, 568
Up the Tube, 573
Up to the Mountains and Down to the Villages, 447
Upheaval and Continuity: A Century of German History, 416
The Uprooted, 321, 322
Uprooted Americans, 323
Urban Decline and the Future of American Cities, 202
Urban Growth and City-Systems in the United States, 1840-1860, 272
The Urban Nation, 1920–1980, 277
The Urban Predicament, 202
The Urban Villagers, 202
Urbane Travelers, 1591–1635, 617
Urbanization in the Middle East, 432
Urbanization in the World Economy, 203
The Urbanization of the Suburbs, 202
Urge to the Sea, 423
Uruguay's Tupamaros, 366
The Use of History, 403
Use of Personal Documents in History, Anthropology, and Sociology, 101, 104
The Use of Personal Documents in Psychological Science, 170, 175
Uses of Disorder, 202
The Uses of the University, 226
Using Folk Tales in Multicultural Education, 608
Using Historical Sources in Anthropology and Sociology, 104
Utah Folk Art, 602

V Was for Victory, 278
The Valley of the Assassins, 647
Value and Capital, 124, 137
Value, Capital, and Growth, 137
Value, Capital and Rent, 148

Vanguards of the Frontier, 275
Vanished Supremacies, 395
The Vanishing Hitchhiker, 607
The Vantage Point, 70
A Vaquero of the Brush Country, 602
Variant Spellings in Modern American Dictionaries, 36
The Varieties of Religious Experience, 180
Velvet on Iron, 337
Venice, 473
Venice Observed, 622
Venture to the Interior, 648
Verb Synonyms and Related Words, 34
Verbal Behavior, 185
Vermont Folksongs and Ballads, 599
Vertical File Index, 11
Very Much a Lady, 51
A Very Private Eye, 53
Vichy France, 415
Vichy France and the Jews, 429
Victims, 274
Victor Hugo, 58
The Victorian Constitution, 381
Victorian England, 1837–1901, 368
Victorian Ladies at Work, 381
Victorian Lady Travellers, 622
Victorian People and Ideas, 379
The Video Encyclopedia, 562
Videotex and the Press, 569
Videotex Journalism, 569
Videotext, 565
The Viet Cong, 455
Vietnam, 455
Vietnam Reconsidered, 305
Vietnam: The Unforgettable Tragedy, 454
Vietnam: The Valor and the Sorrow, 454
The Vietnam Trauma in American Foreign Policy, 1945–75, 282
The Vietnam War, 454
The View from Afar, 116
View from New Delhi, 452

The View from the Top of the Temple, 354
A View of All the Russias, 648
The Vikings in Britain, 371
Village and Family in Contemporary China, 448
Village Communities in the East and West, 118
Village India, 105, 192
The Village Labourer, 1760–1832, 392
Village Life in Northern India, 117
The Village of Ben Suc, 455
A Village That Chose Progress, 122
A Vindication of Natural Society, 387
The Vineyard of Liberty, 262
Vineyard Tales, 599
The Vinland Map and the Tartar Relation, 622
The Virginia Report of 1799–1800, Touching the Alien and Sedition Laws, 90
Virtuoso, the Instrumentalist as Superstar, 490
Vision in Motion, 530
Visions of War, 577
Vistas of History, 329
The Visual Arts: A History, 528
The Visual Display of Quantitative Information, 101
Vital Center, 339
Vocabulary of Modern Spoken Greek (English-Greek and Greek-English), 42
Voice of Protest, 278
The Voice of the Folk, 607
Voices in Exile, 420
Voices of a People, 595
Voices of the Past, 566
Volkskapitalisme, 444
Voluntary Associations, 197
The Volunteers, 197
Voodoo Tales, as Told among the Negroes of the Southwest, 606
Voting: A Study of Opinion Formation in a

Presidential Campaign, 152, 207
Voting in Revolutionary America, 266
The Voyage of the Discovery, 645
The Voyage of the Komagata Maru, 350
The Voyage of the Liberdade, 645
Voyages and Discoveries, 635
Voyages and Documents, 635
The Voyages and Explorations of Samuel De Champlain, 1604–1616, 625
Voyages of Discovery, 632
The Voyages of St. Brendan, 621
Voyaging under Sail, 626

Wagnerism in European Culture and Politics, 517
Waiting for the Morning Train, 313
The Waiting Land, 624
The Wake of the Great Sealers, 624
Walden Two, 185
Wales in British Politics, 383
Walford's Guide to Reference Materials, 11
A Walk across America, 616
A Walk through Britain, 621
The Walk West, 616
Walker's Rhyming Dictionary of the English Language, 35
Walking in America, 620
Walpole and the Whig Supremacy, 378
Walter Lippmann and the American Century, 54
The Walton War and Tales of the Great Smoky Mountains, 600
Wanderings in West Africa from Liverpool to Fernando Po, 629
War and American Thought, 269
War and Imperialism in Republican Rome, 327–70 B.C., 244

War and Industrial Society, 157, 457
War and Society in Africa, 444
War and Warfare, 276
War Diaries, 75
War, Economy and Society, 1939–1945, 408
The War Everyone Lost— and Won, 304
War Lords of Washington, 313
The War of Atonement, October 1973, 435
The War of Conquest, 356
War of Illusions: German Policies from 1911 to 1914, 407
The War of the American Revolution, 258
The War on Land: The British Army in World War II, 408
War, Politics and Finance under Edward I, 373
The War with Hannibal, 250
The War without a Name, 415
Warfare in England, 386
The Warmup, 611
The Warrior and the Priest, 336
The Wars of America, 304
The Wars of the Roses, 373
Washington Information Directory, 11
The Washington Lobby, 299
The Washington Post, 568
The Washington Reporters, 567
Watching TV, 570
Watchmen in the Night, 302
The Way of the Fox, 267
Ways of Medieval Life and Thought, 397
We, 640, 641
We Americans, 312
We Eat the Mines and the Mines Eat Us, 360
We the People, 152, 296
We, the Tikopia, 108, 110, 113
We Were There, 289
Weakness and Deceit, 362
Wealth of Gentry, 1540– 1660, 375

Weather Almanac, 17
Weather Atlas of the United States, 19
The Web of Victory, 67
Webster's Collegiate Thesaurus, 35
Webster's French & English Dictionary, 40
Webster's Illustrated Contemporary Dictionary, 28
Webster's Instant Word Guide, 36
Webster's New Dictionary of Synonyms, 35
Webster's New Geographical Dictionary, 19
Webster's New World Dictionary of the American Language, 28
Webster's New World Dictionary of the American Language, College Edition, 28
Webster's New World Misspeller's Dictionary, 36
Webster's New World Quick Reference Dictionary, 28
Webster's New World Thesaurus, 34
Webster's Ninth New Collegiate Dictionary, 28
Webster's Third New International Dictionary of the English Language Unabridged, 29
Webster's Williams Spanish and English Dictionary, 47
Weekend and Wind from the East, 584
Weimar: A Cultural History, 416
Weimar Culture, 416
The Weimar Republic, 417
Welfare, Planning, and Employment, 130
Welfare: The Political Economy of Welfare Reform in the United States, 129
The Wellesley Index to Victorian Periodicals, 1824–1900, 11
The Wellsprings of Music, 493

West African Kingdoms in the Nineteenth Century, 442
West African Resistance, 441
The West and Reconstruction, 274
West Virginia Folk Music, 601
Western Attitudes toward Death from the Middle Ages to the Present, 410
Western Civilization in the Near East, 468
The Western Question in Greece and Turkey, 479
Westward Expansion, 289
Westward to Vinland, 621
What a Bunch of Characters!, 574
What I Think, 93
What Is a Jew?, 429
What Is Cinema?, 576
What Is Dance, 519
What Is History?, 402
What Is Living and What Is Dead in the Philosophy of Hegel, 462
What Is Property?, 150
What Is the Good of History?, 310
What Is to Be Done? Burning Questions of Our Movement, 469
What Schools Are For, 225
What Style Is It?, 533
What the Gunpowder Plot Was, 391
What They Said in 1981, 21
What to Listen for in Music, 503
What's Fair, 154
What's News, 562
What's the Difference? A British–American Dictionary, 30, 32
Wheels to Adventure, 627
When Harlem Was in Vogue, 286
When Men and Mountains Meet, 626
When Prophecy Fails, 197
When Rock Was Young, 492
When the Cheering Stopped, 97
When the Going Was Good!, 282

Where Have All the Voters Gone?, 300
Where Nights Are Longest, 623
Where the Chill Came From, 604
Where's the Melody, 494
Which Road to the Past?, 253
Whigs and Hunters, 399
While England Slept, 388
While Messiah Tarried, 429
Whitaker's Almanac 1986, 17
White and the Gold, 348
White Attitudes toward Black People, 196
White Collar Crime, 193
White Collar: The American Middle Classes, 102, 212
The White House Years (Eisenhower), 62
The White House Years (Kissinger), 283, 408
The White Man's Burden, 292
White Over Black, 292
The White Tribe of Africa, 442
Whitewater, 324
Whitfield's University Rhyming Dictionary, 35
Whither Mankind, 309
Who Governs, 153, 191
Who Owns America?, 308
Who Owns the Media?, 563
Who Paid the Taxes, 1966–85?, 131
Who Runs Congress?, 299
Who Spoke Up?, 284
Who Was When?, 14
Who Was Who in the Roman World, 241
Who Was Who in the U.S.S.R., 422
Who Was Who on Screen, 578
Who's Who in American Film Now, 575
Who's Who in American Music: Classical, 491
Who's Who in American Politics, 257
Who's Who in Architecture, 533
Who's Who in Rock, 487

Who's Who in Television and Video, 573
Who's Who of Jazz, 493
Whose News?, 566
Why England Slept, 71
Why Ireland Starved, 381
The Widening Gap, 483
The Wild Ass of the Ozarks, 315
Wild Strawberries, 579
Wilderness Days, 620
Wilderness Economics and Policy, 129
The Wilderness Hunter, 336
Wilderness USA, 619
The Wilhelmstrasse, 417
The Will to Believe, 180
William Fitzhugh and His Chesapeake World, 1676–1701, 264
William Pitt, Earl of Chatham, 378
William the Conqueror, 386
The Williams Spanish and English Dictionary, 47
Willing's Press Guide, 11
Willy Brandt, 416
The Winding Passage, 204
Winds of Change, 1914–1939, 74
The Winged Gospel, 287
Winners, 15
The Winning of the Midwest, 275
The Winning of the West, 336
Winslow: The Story of Jazz, 494
The Winter War: The Russo Finnish Conflict, 1939–1940, 421
Winthrop Papers, 328
Wisconsin Lore, 601
Wit and Wisdom from West Africa, 629
Witchcraft in Old and New England, 599
Witchcraft, Oracles, and Magic among the Azande, 113
Witches, Ghosts and Signs, 601
With a Daughter's Eye, 51, 120
With Malice Toward None, 53, 90

With Shield and Sword, 304
Within the Sound of These Waves, 619
Without Precedent, 78
The Wolf and the Lamb, 414
The Wolf by the Ears, 88
Wolsey (Belloc), 386
Wolsey (Pollard), 396
The Woman's Guide to Business Travel, 617
Woman's "True" Profession, 226
Women: A Feminist Perspective, 411
Women and Film, 577
Women and the Mass Media, 563
Women Artists (Bachmann and Piland), 531
Women Artists (Harris and Nochlin), 531
Women as a Force in History, 308
Women at War with America, 278
Women, Culture, and Society, 203
Women in American Architecture, 534
Women in American Music: A Bibliography of Music and Literature, 487
Women in Modern America, 289
Women in Motion, 574
Women in Muslim Family Law, 434
Women in Popular Culture, 611
Women in Television News, 569
The Women of England from Anglo-Saxon Times to the Present, 368, 369
Women of Mr. Wesley's Methodism, 378
Women of the Republic, 286
Women of the West, 292
Women Physicians, 198
Women Studies Abstracts, 11
The Women Who Made the West, 294
Women, Work and Wages, 203
Women's America, 292

Women's Film and Female Experience, 577
Women's Life in Greece and Rome, 244
Women's Pictures, 578
Women's Rights Movement in Iran, 438
The Wonder That Was India, 452
Woodrow Wilson and a Revolutionary World, 1913–1921, 276
Woodrow Wilson and World Politics, 277
Word for Word, 37
The Word Remains, 363
Word Watcher's Handbook, 31
Words into Type, 23
Work and Its Discontents, 204
Work and Personality, 201, 204
Work and Retirement, 131
Work Hard and You Shall Be Rewarded, 607
The Work of the Gods in Tikopia, 113
Work, Society, and Politics, 381
Work, Study, Travel Abroad, 1984–1985, 616
Worker Cooperatives in America, 203
Workers at Risk, 204
A Working Friendship, 513
Working Press of the Nation 1985, 11
The World after the Peace Conference, 479
World Almanac and Book of Facts, 17
The World and Africa, 318
World Architecture, 531
The World as I See It, 428
The World Book Encyclopedia, 4
World Chronology of Music History, 488
World Civilizations, 405
World Communications, 562
World Communications: A Handbook, 561
A World Destroyed, 409
World Folktales, 591

The World from Brown's Lounge, 605
World Furniture, 534
World Guide to Abbreviations of Organizations, 11
World Handbook of Political and Social Indicators, 149, 163
A World History (McNeill), 472, 473
World History (Spengler), 475
World History in the Twentieth Century, 405
World History of the Dance, 518
World Measurement Guide, 11
The World of Andrew Carnegie, 1865–1901, 321
The World of Daniel O'Connell, 381
World of Islam, 434
The World of Late Antiquity, 240
World of Learning 1986, 17
The World of Musical Comedy, 489
The World of Odysseus, 240
World of Our Fathers, 291, 429
A World of Strangers, 202
The World of Swing, 493
The World of the American Indian, 293
The World of the Ancient Maya, 354
World Politics and Personal Insecurity, 163
World Politics and the Arab-Israeli Conflict, 435
World Power or Decline, 407
World Press Encyclopedia, 566
World Radio TV Handbook, 573
World Revolution and Family Patterns, 196
The World Rushed In, 271
World-Systems Analysis, 101
The World Turned Upside Down, 393
World War I, 407

World War I and the Origin
of Civil Liberties in the
United States, 277
World War Two German
Military Studies, 416
The World We Have Lost,
376
A World without War, 328
The World's Discoverers,
626
The World's Great Dailies,
566
Worlds of Music, 493
The Wound Within, 454
The Writer in Extremis, 431
Writer's Market, 23
Writing American History,
253
The Writing and Selling of
Fiction, 23
Writing Lives, 49
Writing the News, 566
Writings and Buildings,
558
Writings from the Original
Manuscript Sources, 1754–
1799, 93
Writings on American
History, 253

Written History as an Act of
Faith, 309
The Wycliffe Historical
Geography of the Bible
Lands, 433

Yamagata Aritomo in the
Rise of Modern Japan,
1838–1922, 450
Yankee from Olympus, 55
The Year of Decision, 316
Yearbook of International
Organizations, 11
The Yearbook of the United
Nations, 17
Yearbook of World Affairs,
17
The Years of Lyndon
Johnson, 281
Years of Poverty, Years of
Plenty, 130
Yesterday and Today, 258
Yom Kippur and After, 432
The Yom Kippur War, 428
Yorkist Age, 373
You Learn by Living, 78
Young Children's Thinking,
235

The Young Lloyd George,
383
Young Man Luther, 178
Youth and History, 411
The Yugoslav Experiment,
1948–1974, 420
Yukon Wild, 619

The Zambesi Expedition,
1858–1863, 642
Zande Themes, 113
Zanzibar, 629
Zapata, 364
Zimbabwe's Inheritance,
444
The Zimmerman Telegram,
481
Zionism in Germany, 1897–
1933, 430
Zionism in Poland, 430
The Zionist Idea, 429
Zodiac Arch, 647
Zola and His Time, 58
The Zulu People as They
Were before the White
Man Came, 441
Zuni Folk Tales, 604
Zuñi Mythology, 111

Subject Index

This index provides detailed, multiple-approach access to the subject content of the volume, employing the subject headings as entry terms. Arrangement is alphabetical. Collective terms for authors are included, e.g., *Anthropologists, Artists, Economists, Educators,* but the reader is reminded to use the Name Index to locate individual writers.

Acculturation, in anthropology, 104–5
Administration, in political science, 150
Africa
 travel and exploration, 623–24
 in world history, 440–45
Afro-American folklore, 604–6
Age and aging, in sociology, 89
Aggression, in psychology, 170–71
Agriculture
 in ancient history, 243
 economics of, 126
Almanacs, general, 15–17
American Indians, folklore, 603–4
Americas (the), travel and exploration, 618–20
Anarchism, in political science, 150
Ancient history, 238–51
 agriculture, 243
 archaeology, 242
 diplomacy, 244
 documents, 241–42
 economy, 243
 Egypt, 239
 family, 243–44
 Greece, 239–40

historians
 Greek, 245–48
 Roman, 249–51
intellectual history, 244–45
law, 244
material culture, 243
Near East, 239
orators, 246–48
peace, 244
philosophy, 244–45
reference works, 238–39, 241
religion, 244–45
Rome, 240–41
science, 243
sex, 243–44
society, 243
source materials, 241
technology, 243
trade, 243
war, 244
women, 243–44
Angevin England, 371–72
Anglo-Saxon language dictionaries, 37–38
Anthropologists, 111–23
Anthropology, 103–23
 acculturation, 104–5
 caste, 105
 culture, 105–6
 economy, 107
 evolution, 107
 history of, 103

kinship, 108
language, 108–9
modern societies, 110
religion, 109
research methodology, 104
social structure, 109–10
surveys of, 103–4
tribal societies, 110–11
Antiquity, reference works, 241
Antitrust legislation, 127
Antonym dictionaries, English language, 33–35
Arabic language dictionaries, 38
Arabs, in world history, 438–39
Archaeology, 242
Architects, 535–59
Architecture, 526–27, 531–34
 biographical directories, 533–34
 reference works, 531–33
Arctic and Antarctica (the), travel and exploration, 624–25
Argentina, 360
Art, 526–31
 biographical directories, 531
 decorative arts, 534–35
 reference works, 527–31
 in sociology, 189–90

Artificial intelligence, in psychology, 173
Artists, 535–59
    film, 578
    mass media, 578–89
    radio and television, 573
Asia
    travel and exploration, 623–24
    in world history, 445–55
        reference works, 445–46
        separate states and areas, 446–54
Atlases, general, 17–19
Attitudes, in psychology, 174
Autobiographers, 61–81
Autobiography
    documentary collections, 81–97
    general, 48–97
    recent, 51–54
    reference works, 50
    writing of, 49–50

Ballet, 519–20
Behavior
    biological bases of, 171
    collective, 190
    deviant, 194
Belief(s)
    in political science, 154
    in psychology, 174
Bibliographic tools, general, 4–11
Bibliographies
    Canada, 347–48
    education, 223–29
    history
        Great Britain, 368–69
        U.S., 258–60
    Latin America, 352–53
Biographers, 54–60
Biography. See also under specific field, e.g., Artists; Economists
    architects, 533–34
    artists, 531
    general, 48–97
    published papers, 81–97
    recent, 51–54
    reference works, 50
    writing of, 49–50
Biology, in behavior, 171
Bolivia, 360
Brazil, 361

British-English language dictionaries, 30
British history. See Great Britain, history
Broadcast journalism, 568–69
Broadcast journalists, 569

Canada, 346–51
    bibliographies, 347–48
    early, 348
    history of Confederation, Dominion, and modern, 349–51
    reference works, 347–48
    surveys, 347–48
Capitalism, 126–27
Caste, in anthropology, 105
Chile, 361
China, in world history, 446–49
Chinese language dictionaries, 38–39
Choreographers, 521–25
Civil liberties, 150–51
Civil War(s), U.S., 272–74
Cognition, in psychology, 171
Collective behavior, 190
Colloquial English dictionaries, 31–33
Colombia, 361
Colonialism
    Latin America, 356–57
    U.S., 264–65
Communes, in sociology, 203
Communications
    in mass media, 561–65
        reference works, 561–65
    in sociology, 190–91
Communism, in political science, 156–57
Community, in sociology, 191–92
Competition, in economics, 127
Conductors (music), 495
Confederation
    Canada, 349–51
    U.S., 265–68
Conflict, in sociology, 192–93
Constitution, U.S., 294–97
Constitutions, in political science, 151–52

Corporations, in economics, 127–28
Costa Rica, 361
Courts (the), in political science, 155
Crime, in sociology, 193–94
Criticism
    broadcast journalism, 568–69
    dance, 518
    film, 575–77
    journalism, 565–67
    music, 485–87
    radio and television, 569–73
Cuba, 361–62
Culture
    in ancient history, 243
    in anthropology, 105–6
    and personality, 106
    popular, 611–12
    pre-Columbian, 353–55
    in U.S. history, 285–87

Dance, 484, 518–25
    American, 520
    ballet, 519–20
    choreographers, 521–25
    ethnic, 520
    folk, 593–95
    history and criticism, 518
    reference works, 518–19
Dance companies, 520
Dancers, 521–25
Danish language dictionaries, 39
Declaration of Independence (U.S.), 294–97
Decorative arts, 534–35
Democracy, in political science, 152
Deviant behavior (sociology), 194
Dictionaries, 24–47
    Anglo-Saxon, 37–38
    antonym (English), 33–35
    Arabic language, 38
    British-English, 30
    Chinese language, 38–39
    current English-usage, 30–31
    Danish language, 39
    Dutch language, 39
    English language, 25–29, 31–35

etymological, English language, 36–37
foreign-English, 37–47
French language, 39–40
German language, 40–42
Greek language, 42
Hebrew language, 42
history, U.S., 257–58
homonym (English), 33–35
Hungarian language, 42
Italian language, 42–43
Japanese language, 43–44
Korean language, 44
Latin language, 44
Norwegian language, 44
Polish language, 44
Portuguese language, 44–45
proverbs, 22
Rumanian language, 45
Russian language, 45
Serbo-Croatian language, 45
slang and colloquial, English language, 31–33
Spanish language, 45–47
synonym (English), 33–35
Diplomacy
in ancient history, 244
in U.S. history, 302–5
Documents
in ancient history, 241–42
U.S. history, 260–61, 294–97
Dominican Republic, 362
Dominion (Canada), 349–51
Dutch language dictionaries, 39

Eastern Europe, in world history, 419–20
Economics, 124–48
agriculture, 126
antitrust legislation, 127
capitalism, 126–27
competition, 127
corporation, 127–28
economic growth, 128–29
government regulation, 129
history of, 124
U.S., 287–89
income, 129–30
inflation, 129–30
international, 130
labor, 130–31

money, 131
monopoly, 127
poverty, 129–30
public choice, 132
public finance, 132
public goods, 132
research methodology, 125
surveys of, 124–25
unemployment, 130–31
work, 130–31
Economists, 132–48
Economy (the)
in ancient history, 243
in anthropology, 107
Ecuador, 362
Education, 222–37
bibliography, 223–29
Educators, 229–37
Egypt
ancient, 239
in world history, 436–37
El Salvador, 362–63
Elections, in political science, 152–53
Encyclopedias
general, 2–4
history, U.S., 257–58
sociology, 194–95
England. See Great Britain, history
English language, dictionaries, 25–29
foreign-English, 37–47
slang and colloquial, 31–33
English usage dictionaries, 30–31
Environment, in sociology, 194–95
Ethnic dance, 520
Ethnic folklore, U.S., 598–606
Ethnic groups, in sociology, 195
Ethnic music, 492–93
Etymological dictionaries, English language, 36–37
Europe
travel and exploration, 621–23
world history
general surveys, 410–13
separate states, 413–20
Evolution, in anthropology, 107

Exploration, 613–49
Africa, 623–24
Americas (the), 618–20
Antarctica, 624–25
Arctic, 624–25
Asia, 623–24
Europe, 621–23
individual exploits, 625–28
Oceania, 623–24
reference works
general, 615–18
scholarly, 614–15
Explorers, 623–49

Family
in ancient history, 243–44
in sociology, 195–96
Federalism, in political science, 151–52
Federalist Papers, 294–97
Film, 573–78
history and criticism, 575–77
reference works, 574–75
in sociology, 189–90
Film artists, 578
Film music, 493
Finance, public, 132
Folk dance, 593–95
Folk songs, 593–95
Folklore, 590–612
Afro-American, 604–6
American Indian, 603–4
as applied to other disciplines, 606–9
folk song and dance, 593–95
folktale, legend, myth, 595–98
general works, 591–92
Mid-Atlantic states (U.S.), 599–600
Midwest (U.S.), 601–2
New England, 599
reference works, 592
regional and ethnic, 598–606
southern U.S., 600–601
western U.S., 602–3
Folktales, 595–98
Foreign language dictionaries, 37–47
Foreign relations, in U.S. history, 302–5

France, in world history,
    413–15
French language dictionar-
    ies, 39–40

Gazetteers, general, 17–18,
    19
General works
    architecture, 531–32
    art, 527–29
    communications, 562–65
    exploration, 615–18
    folklore, 591–92
    history
        ancient, 238–39
        Great Britain, 369–70
        U.S., 284–97
        Latin America, 357–60
        travel, 615–18
        world history, 405–6
            Asia, 445–46
            Europe, 410–13
            Middle East, 432–33
German language dictionar-
    ies, 40–42
Germany, in world history,
    415–17
Government
    in political science, 153–
        54
    regulation of economics,
        129
Government publications,
    U.S., 12–14
Great Britain, history, 367–
    400
    bibliographies, 368–69
    general, 369–70
    Hanoverians, 377–79
    historians, 384–400
    later Middle Ages, 372–74
    Norman and Angevin En-
        gland, 371–72
    pre-Norman Conquest, 371
    reference works, 368–70
    Stuart England, 376–77
    Tudor England, 374–76
    twentieth-century, 382–84
    Victorian Age, 379–82
Greece, ancient history, 239–
    40
Greek language dictionaries,
    42
Groups
    ethnic, 195

in psychology, 172
Guatemala, 363

Haiti, 363
Hanoverians (Great Britain),
    377–79
Hebrew language dictionar-
    ies, 42
Historians
    British, 384–400
    Greek, ancient history,
        245–48
    Roman, ancient history,
        249–51
    U.S., 305–45
    world history, 455–
        83
History. See also Ancient his-
    tory; Great Britain,
    history; U.S. history;
    World history
    anthropology, 103
    broadcast journalism,
        568–69
    Canada, 348–51
    dance, 518
    economics, 124
    film, 575–77
    Greece, ancient, 239–
        40
    Jewish, 426–31
    journalism, 565–67
    Latin America, 351–66
    music, 485–87
    philosophy of, 401–3
    political science, 149
    psychology, 169–70
    radio and television, 569–
        73
    reference works
        Great Britain, 368–70
        U.S., 255–61
        world history, 403–5
    Rome, ancient, 240–
        41
    sociology, 187–88
    writing of
        U.S., 253–55
        world, 401–3
Homonym dictionaries, En-
    glish language, 33–35
Humor, folk and popular,
    609–10
Hungarian language dictio-
    naries, 42

Ideology, in political science,
    154
Imperialism, in U.S. history,
    275–76
Income (economics), 129–30
Indian subcontinent, in
    world history, 452–54
Individual development, in
    psychology, 172–73
Industrialism, U.S., 274–
    75
Inflation, in economics, 129–
    30
Intellectuals, in sociology,
    189–90
Intelligence, in psychology,
    173
Intergroup relations, in soci-
    ology, 196–97
International relations, in po-
    litical science, 155
Iran, in world history, 437–
    38
Iraq, in world history, 437–
    38
Islam, as idea and religion,
    433–34
Israel, in world history, 435.
    See also Jews, history
    of
Italian language dictionar-
    ies, 42–43
Italy, in world history, 417–
    18

Jacksonian era (U.S. his-
    tory), 270–72
Jamaica, 363
Japan, in world history,
    449–52
Japanese language dictionar-
    ies, 43–44
Jazz, 493–94
Jews, history of, 426–31
Journalism, 565–68. See also
    Broadcast journalism
Journalists, 567–68. See also
    Broadcast journalists

Kinship, in anthropology,
    108
Korean language dictionar-
    ies, 44

Labor, in economics, 130–31
Language, in anthropology,
 108–9
Latin America, 351–66
 bibliographies, 352–53
 colonial history, 356–57
 discovery and conquest,
  355–56
 modern, 357–66
  general works, 357–60
  individual countries,
   360–66
 pre-Columbian cultures,
  353–55
 reference works, 352–53
 surveys, 352–53
Latin language dictionaries,
 44
Law
 in ancient history, 244
 antitrust, 127
 in political science, 155
Learning, in psychology,
 173–74
Legend(s), 595–98
Legislation
 antitrust, 127
 in political science (U.S.),
  156
Low Countries, in world history, 419

Marriage, in sociology, 195–
 96
Mass media, 560–89
 artists, 578–89
 broadcast journalism,
  568–69
 communications, 561–65
 film, 573–78
 journalism, 565–68
 radio and television, 569–
  73
Material culture, in ancient
 history, 243
Media. See Mass media
Mexico, 363–64
Mid-Atlantic States (U.S.),
 folklore, 599–600
Middle Ages, Great Britain,
 372–74
Middle East, in world history, 432–40
 general works, 432–33
 Islam, 433–34

separate states, 435–40
Midwest (U.S.), folklore,
 601–2
Money, in economics, 131
Monopoly, in economics, 127
Motivation, in psychology,
 173–74
Music, 484, 485–518
 conductors, 495
 folk songs, 593–95
 history and criticism, 485–
  87
 non-Western, 494–95
 reference works, 487–91
 singers, 496–97
 types of, 492–95
  contemporary, 492
  ethnic, 492–93
  film, 493
  jazz, 493–94
  opera, 495
Music appreciation, 491–92
Musical instruments, 495–96
Musicians, 497–518
Mythology, 595–98

Nationalism, in U.S. history,
 268–70
Native Americans. See Ameri-
 can Indians, folklore
Natural resources, in sociol-
 ogy, 194–95
Near East, ancient, 239
New Deal (U.S.), 277–80
New England, folklore, 599
New France (Canada), 348
Nicaragua, 364
Norman England, 371–72
North America, travel and
 exploration, 618–20.
 See also United States
Norwegian language dictio-
 naries, 44

Oceania, travel and exploration, 623–24
Opera, 495
Opinions, in psychology,
 174. See also Public
 opinion, in political
 science
Organizations, in sociology,
 197

Panama, 365
Paraguay, 365
Peace
 in ancient history, 244
 in political science, 157–
  58
 in world history, 406–10
Perception, in psychology,
 174–75
Personality
 culture and, 106
 in psychology, 175
Peru, 365
Philosophy
 in ancient history, 244–
  45
 of history, 401–3
Policy making, in political
 science, 156
Polish language, dictionaries, 44
Political parties, 152–53
Political science, 148–69
 administration, 150
 anarchism, 150
 civil liberties and civil
  rights, 150–51
 communism, 156–57
 constitutions, 151–52
 courts, 155
 democracy, 152
 elections, 152–53
 federalism, 151–52
 government, 153–54
 history of, 149
 ideology and belief, 154
 international relations,
  155
 law, 155
 legislation, 156
 peace, 157–58
 policy making, 156
 political parties, 152–53
 public opinion, 156
 reference works, 149
 socialism, 156–57
 surveys of, 149
 totalitarianism, 157
 U.S. Congress, 156
 voting behavior, 152–53
 war, 157–58
Political scientists, 158–69
Politics, structure of U.S.,
 297–302
Population, in sociology,
 197–98

Portugal, in world history, 418–19
Portuguese language dictionaries, 44–45
Poverty, in economics, 129–30
Pre-Columbian cultures, Latin America, 353–55
Professions
  in social sciences, 101–2
  in sociology, 198
Progressivism, in U.S. history, 275–76
Proverbs, reference works, 22
Psychologists, 175–87
Psychology, 169–87
  aggression, 170–71
  artificial intelligence, 173
  attitudes, 174
  beliefs, 174
  biological bases of behavior, 171
  cognition, 171
  groups, 172
  history of, 169–70
  individual development, 172–73
  intelligence, 173
  learning, 173–74
  motivation, 173–74
  opinions, 174
  perception, 174–75
  personality, 175
  reference works, 170
  research methodology, 170
  surveys of, 170
Public choice (economics), 132
Public finance, 132
Public goods (economics), 132
Public opinion, in political science, 156
Published papers, personal, 81–97
Puerto Rico, 365–66

Quotation books, general, 19–21

Radio, 569–73
  artists, 573

history and criticism, 569–73
Reconstruction, in U.S. history, 272–74
Reference works. See also Dictionaries; Encyclopedias
  almanacs, general, 15–17
  antiquity, 241
  atlases, general, 17–19
  bibliography, general, 4–11
  biography and autobiography, 50
  communications, 561–62
  dance, 518–19
  dates and facts, 14–15
  exploration
    general, 615–18
    scholarly, 614–15
  film, 574–75
  folklore, 591–92
  gazetteers, general, 17–18, 19
  general, 1–23
  government publications, U.S., 12–14
  history
    Canada, 347–48
    Great Britain, 368–70
    Latin America, 352–53
    U.S., 255–61
    world, 403–5
  music, 487–91
  political science, 149
  proverbs and maxims, 22
  psychology, 170
  quotation books, 19–21
  research guides, U.S. history, 255–57
  social sciences, 99–100
  travel, 614–18
    general, 615–18
    scholarly, 614–15
  writing guides, 22–23
  yearbooks, general, 15–17
Religion
  in ancient history, 244–45
  in anthropology, 109
  Islamic, 433-34
  in sociology, 198–99
Research guides, U.S. history, 255–57
Research methodology
  anthropology, 104
  economics, 125

psychology, 170
social sciences, 100–101
sociology, 188–89
Revolution(s), U.S., 265–68
Rome, ancient history, 240–41
Rumanian language dictionaries, 45
Russia, in world history, 420–26
Russian language dictionaries, 45

Saudi Arabia, in world history, 438–39
Scandinavia, in world history, 419
Science
  in ancient history, 243
  in sociology, 199–200
Serbo-Croatian language dictionaries, 45
Sex, in ancient history, 243–44
Singers, 496–97
Slang dictionaries, English language, 31–33
Social change, in sociology, 200
Social class, in sociology, 200–201
Social history, U.S., 289–94
Social interaction, in sociology, 196
Social movements, in sociology, 201
Social relations, intergroup, 196–97
Social sciences, 98–221
  anthropology, 103–23
  economics, 124–48
  political science, 148–69
  professional aspects, 101–2
  psychology, 169–87
  reference books, 99–100
  research methodology, 100–101
  social scientists
    anthropologists, 111–23
    economists, 132–48
    political scientists, 158–69
    psychologists, 175–87
    sociologists, 204–21

society of modern America, 102–3
sociology, 187–221
Social structure
in anthropology, 109–10
in sociology, 201
Socialism, in political science, 156–57
Socialization, in sociology, 202
Society
in ancient history, 243
modern, in anthropology, 110
tribal, in anthropology, 110–11
U.S., 102–3
Sociologists, 204–21
Sociology, 187–221
age and aging, 189
art, 189–90
collective behavior, 190
communes, 203
communications, 190–91
community, 191–92
conflict, 192–93
crime, 193–94
deviant behavior, 194
energy, 194–95
environment, 194–95
ethnic groups, 195
family, 195–96
film, 189–90
history of, 187–88
intellectuals, 189–90
intergroup relations, 196–97
literature, 189–90
marriage, 195–96
natural resources, 194–95
organizations, 197
population, 197–98
professions, 198
religion, 198–99
research methodology, 188–89
science, 199–200
social change, 200
social class, 200–201
social interaction, 196
social movements, 201
social structure, 201
socialization, 202
surveys of, 188
technology, 199–200
urban life, 202–3

utopianism, 203
women, 203
work, 203–4
South (U.S.), folklore, 600–601
South America, travel and exploration, 618–20
Soviet Union, in world history, 420–26
Spain, in world history, 418–19
Spanish language dictionaries, 45–47
Stuart England, 376–77
Surveys
anthropology, 103–4, 124–5
Canada, 347–48
history, U.S., 261–63
Latin America, 352–53
political science, 149
psychology, 170
sociology, 188
Synonym dictionaries, English language, 33–35

Technology
in ancient history, 243
in sociology, 199–200
Television, 569–73
artists, 573
history and criticism, 569–73
Totalitarianism, in political science, 157
Trade, in ancient history, 243
Travel, 613–49
Africa, 623–24
Americas (the), 618–20
Antarctica, 624–25
Arctic, 624–25
Asia, 623–24
Europe, 621–23
individual exploits, 625–28
Oceania, 623–24
reference books
general, 615–18
scholarly, 614–15
Tribal societies, in anthropology, 110–11
Trinidad, 366
Tudor England, 374–76
Turkey, in world history, 439

Unemployment, in economics, 130–31
United States. See also U.S. history
folklore, 598–606
Afro-American, 604–6
Indian, 603–4
government publications, 12–14
society, modern, 102–3
U.S. Congress, 156
U.S. history, 252–345
bibliographies, 258–60
Civil War, 272–74
colonial period, 264–65
cultural and intellectual, 285–87
dictionaries, 257–58
diplomacy, 302–5
documentary histories, 260–61
documents, 294–97
early national period, 268–70
economic, 287–89
encyclopedias, 257–58
foreign relations, 302–5
Gilded Age, 274–75
imperialism to progressivism (1896–1917), 275–76
industrialism, 274–75
Jacksonian era, 270–72
New Deal through World War II, 277–80
post-World War II, 280–84
Reconstruction, 272–74
reference books, 255–61
research guides, 255–57
research monographs, 284–97
revolution and confederation, 265–68
social, 289–94
structure of politics, 297–302
surveys, 261–63
World War I to FDR, 276–77
writing of, 253–55
Urban life, in sociology, 202–3
Uruguay, 366
Utopianism, in sociology, 203

Venezuela, 366
Victorian Age, Great Britain
    in, 379–82
Voting (political science),
    152

War
    in ancient history, 244
    in political science, 157–
        58
    in world history, 406–10
West (U.S.), folklore, 602–3
Western hemisphere, 346–66
Women
    in ancient history, 243–44
    in sociology, 203
Work
    in economics, 130–31
    in sociology, 203–4
World history, 401–83
    Africa, 440–45
    Arabs, 438–39
    Asia, 445–55
        general works, 445–46

    separate states, 446–54
    China in, 446–49
    Eastern Europe, 419–20
    Egypt, 436–37
    Europe, 410–13
        separate states, 413–20
    France, 413–15
    general works, 405–6
    Germany, 415–17
    historians, 455–83
    Indian subcontinent, 452–
        54
    Iran, 437–38
    Iraq, 437–38
    Israel, 435
    Italy, 417–18
    Japan, 449–52
    Jewish, 426–31
    Low Countries, 419
    Middle East, 432–40
        general, 432–33
        Islam, 433–34
        separate states, 435–40
    modern, 406–10
    peace, 406–10

    philosophy of, 401–3
    Portugal, 418–19
    reference works, 403–5
    Russia, 420–26
    Saudi Arabia, 438–39
    Scandinavia, 419
    Spain, 418–19
    Turkey, 439
    war, 406–10
    writing of, 401–3
World War I, in U.S. history,
    276–77
World War II, in U.S. his-
    tory, 277–80
Writing
    of biography and autobiog-
        raphy, 49–50
    of history
        U.S., 253–55
        world, 401–3
Writing guides, 22–23

Yearbooks, general, 15–
    17